The Computer Music Tutorial

D1375823

po 42

Curtis Roads

with John Strawn, Curtis Abbott, John Gordon, and Philip Greenspun

The Computer Music Tutorial

The MIT Press
Cambridge, Massachusetts
London, England

This book was set in Times Roman by Asco Trade Typesetting Ltd., Hong Kong and was printed and bound in the United States of America.

Library of Congress Cataloging-in-Publication Data

Roads, Curtis.
   The computer music tutorial / Curtis Roads . . . [et al.].
      p.   cm.
   Includes bibliographical references and index.
   ISBN 978-0-262-18158-7 (hc. : alk. paper)—978-0-262-68082-0 (pbk. : alk. paper)
   1. Computer music—Instruction and study.   2. Computer composition.   I. Title.
MT56.R6   1995
780'.285—dc20   94-19027
                                                                          CIP
                                                                          MN

A list of corrections for this book can be found at http://mitpress.mit.edu/catalog/item/default.asp?ttype=2&tid=8218.

20   19   18   17   16   15   14

Contents

Foreword: New Music and Science

With the use of computers and digital devices, the processes of music composition and its production have become intertwined with the scientific and technical resources of society to a greater extent than ever before. Through extensive application of computers in the generation and processing of sound and the composition of music from levels of the microformal to the macroformal, composers, from creative necessity, have provoked a robust interdependence between domains of scientific and musical thought. Not only have science and technology enriched contemporary music, but the converse is also true: problems of particular musical importance in some cases suggest or pose directly problems of scientific and technological importance, as well. Each having their own motivations, music and science depend on one another and in so doing define a unique relationship to their mutual benefit.

The use of technology in music is not new; however, it has reached a new level of pertinence with the rapid development of computer systems. Modern computer systems encompass concepts that extend far beyond those that are intrinsic to the physical machines themselves. One of the distinctive attributes of computing is programmability and hence programming languages. High-level programming languages, representing centuries of thought about thinking, are the means by which computers become accessible to diverse disciplines.

Programming involves mental processes and rigorous attention to detail not unlike those involved in composition. Thus, it is not surprising that composers were the first artists to make substantive use of computers. There were compelling reasons to integrate some essential scientific knowledge and concepts into the musical consciousness and to gain competence in areas which are seemingly foreign to music. Two reasons were (and are) particularly compelling: (1) the generality of sound synthesis by computer, and (2) the power of programming in relation to the musical structure and the process of composition.

Sound Synthesis

Although the traditional musical instruments constitute a rich sound space indeed, it has been many decades since composers' imaginations have conjured up sounds based on the interpolation and extrapolation of those found in nature but which are not realizable with acoustical or analog electronic instruments. A loudspeaker controlled by a computer is the most general synthesis medium in existence. Any sound, from the simplest to the most complex, that can be produced through a loudspeaker can be synthesized with this medium. This generality of computer synthesis implies an extraordinarily larger sound space, which has an obvious attraction to composers. This is because computer sound synthesis is the bridge between that which can be imagined and that which can be heard.

With the elimination of constraints imposed by the medium on sound production, there nonetheless remains an enormous barrier which the composer must overcome in order to make use of this potential. That barrier is one of lack of knowledge—knowledge that is required for the composer to be able to effectively instruct the computer in the synthesis process. To some extent this technical knowledge relates to computers; this is rather easily acquired. But it mostly has to do with the physical description and perceptual correlates of sound. Curiously, the knowledge required does not exist, for the most part, in those areas of scientific inquiry where one would most expect to find it, that is, physical acoustics and psychobiology, for these disciplines often provide either inexact or no data at those levels of detail with which a composer is ultimately most concerned. In the past, scientific data and conclusions were used to try to replicate natural sounds as a way of gaining information about sound in general. Musicians and musician-scientists were quick to point out that most of the conclusions and data were insufficient. The synthesis of sounds which approach in aural complexity the simplest natural sound demands detailed knowledge about the temporal evolution of the various components of the sound.

Physics, psychology, computer science, and mathematics have, however, provided powerful tools and concepts. When these concepts are integrated with musical knowledge and aural sensitivity, they allow musicians, scientists, and technicians, working together, to carve out new concepts and physical and psychophysical descriptions of sound at levels of detail that are of use to the composer in meeting the exacting requirements of the ear and imagination.

As this book shows, some results have emerged: There is a much deeper understanding of timbre, and composers have a much richer sound palette with which to work; new efficient synthesis techniques have been discovered and developed that are based upon modeling the perceptual attributes of sound rather than the physical attributes; powerful programs have been developed for the purposes of editing and mixing synthesized and/or digitally recorded sound; experiments in perceptual fusion have led to novel and musically useful research in sound source identification and auditory images; finally, special purpose computer-synthesizers are being designed and built. These real-time performance systems incorporate many advances in knowledge and technique.

Programming and Composition

Because one of the fundamental assumptions in designing a computer programming language is generality, the range of practical applications of any given high-level language is enormous and obviously includes music. Programs have been written in a variety of programming languages for various musical purposes. Those that have been most useful and with which composers have gained the most experience are programs for the synthesis and processing of sound and programs that translate musical specifications of a piece of music into physical specifications required by the synthesis program.

The gaining of some competence at programming can be rewarding to a composer as it is the key to a general understanding of computer systems. Although systems are composed of programs of great complexity and written using techniques not easily learned by nonspecialists, programming ability enables the composer to understand the overall workings of a system to the extent required for its effective use. Programming ability also gives the composer a certain independence at those levels of computing where independence is most desirable—synthesis. Similar to the case in traditional orchestration, the choices made in the synthesis of tones, having to do with timbre and microarticulation, are often highly subjective. The process is greatly enhanced by the ability of the composer to alter synthesis algorithms freely.

The programming of musical structure is another opportunity which programming competence can provide. To the extent that compositional processes can be formulated in a more or less precise manner they may be implemented in the form of a program. A musical structure that is based upon some iterative process, for example, might be appropriately realized by means of programming.

But there is a less tangible effect of programming competence which results from the contact of the composer with the concepts of a programming language. While the function a program is to perform can influence the choice of language in which the program is written, it is also true that a programming language can influence the conception of a program's function. In a more general sense, programming concepts can suggest functions that might not occur to one outside of the context of programming. This is of signal importance in music composition, since the integration of programming concepts into the musical imagination can extend the boundaries of the imagination itself. That is, the language is not simply a tool with which some preconceived task or function can be accomplished; it is an extensive basis of structure with which the imagination can interact, as well.

Although computer synthesis of sound involves physical and psychophysical concepts derived from the analysis of natural sounds, when joined with higher-level programming of musical structure the implications extend far beyond timbre. Unlike the condition that exists in composition for traditional instruments where the relation of vibrational modes of an instrument is largely beyond compositional influence, computer synthesis allows for the composition of music's microstructure.

In the context of computing, then, the microstructure of music is not necessarily of predetermined form—associated with a specific articulation of a particular instrument. Rather, it can be subjected to the same thought processes and be as freely determined in the imagination of the composer as every other aspect of the work.

John Chowning

Preface

Music changes: new forms appear in infinite variety, and reinterpretations infuse freshness into old genres. Waves of musical cultures overlap, diffusing new stylistic resonances. Techniques for playing and composing music meander with these waves. Bound with the incessant redevelopment in music-making is an ongoing evolution in music technology. For every music there is a family of instruments, so that today we have hundreds of instruments to choose from, even if we restrict ourselves to the acoustic ones.

In the twentieth century, electronics turned the stream of instrument design into a boiling rapids. Electrification transformed the guitar, bass, piano, organ, and drum (machine) into the folk instruments of industrial society. Analog synthesizers expanded the musical sound palette and launched a round of experimentation with sound materials. But analog synthesizers were limited by a lack of programmability, precision, memory, and intelligence. By virtue of these capabilities, the digital computer provides an expanded set of brushes and implements for manipulating sound color. It can listen, analyze, and respond to musical gestures in sophisticated ways. It lets musicians edit music or compose according to logical rules and print the results in music notation. It can teach interactively and demonstrate all aspects of music with sound and images. New musical applications continue to spin out of computer music research.

In the wake of ongoing change, musicians confront the challenge of understanding the possibilities of the medium and keeping up with new developments. *The Computer Music Tutorial* addresses the need for a standard and comprehensive text of basic information on the theory and practice of computer music. As a complement to the reference volumes *Foundations of Computer Music* (MIT Press, 1985) and *The Music Machine* (MIT Press, 1989), this book provides the essential background necessary for advanced exploration of the computer music field. While *Foundations of Computer Music* and *The Music Machine* are anthologies, this textbook contains all new material directed toward teaching purposes.

Intended Audience

The intended audience for this book is not only music students but also engineers and scientists seeking an orientation to computer music. Many sections of this volume open technical "black boxes," revealing the inner workings of software and hardware mechanisms. Why is technical information relevant to the musician? Our goal is not to turn musicians into engineers but to make them better informed and more skillful users of music technology. Technically naive musicians sometimes have unduly narrow concepts of the possibilities of this rapidly evolving medium; they may import conceptual limitations of bygone epochs into a domain where such restrictions no longer apply. For want of basic information, they may waste time dabbling, not knowing how to translate intuitions into practical results. Thus one aim of this book is to impart a sense of independence to the many musicians who will eventually set up and manage a home or institutional computer music studio.

For some musicians, the descriptions herein will serve as an introduction to specialized technical study. A few will push the field forward with new technical advances. This should not surprise anyone who has followed the evolution of this field. History shows time and again that some of the most significant advances in music technology have been conceived by technically informed musicians.

Interdisciplinary Spirit

The knowledge base of computer music draws from composition, acoustics, psychoacoustics, physics, signal processing, synthesis, composition, performance, computer science, and electrical engineering. Thus, a well-rounded pedagogy in computer music must reflect an interdisciplinary spirit. In this book, musical applications motivate the presentation of technical concepts, and the discussion of technical procedures is interspersed with commentary on their musical significance.

Heritage

One goal of our work has been to convey an awareness of the heritage of computer music. Overview and background sections place the current picture into historical context. Myriad references to the literature point to sources for further study and also highlight the pioneers behind the concepts.

Concepts and Terms

Every music device and software package uses a different set of protocols—terminology, notation system, command syntax, button layout, and so on. These differing protocols are built on the fundamental concepts explained in this volume. Given the myriad incompatibilities and the constantly changing technical environment, it seems more appropriate for a book to teach fundamental concepts than to spell out the idiosyncracies of a specific language, software application, or synthesizer. Hence, this volume is not intended to teach the reader how to operate a specific device or software package—that is the goal of the documentation supplied with each system. But it will make this kind of learning much easier.

Use of This Book in Teaching

The Computer Music Tutorial has been written as a general textbook, aimed at presenting a balanced view of the international scene. It is designed to serve as a core text and should be easily adaptable to a variety of teaching situations. In the ideal, this book should be assigned as a reader in conjunction with a studio environment where students have ample time to try out the various ideas within. Every studio favors particular tools (computers, software, synthesizers, etc.), so the manuals for those tools, along with studio-based practical instruction, can round out the educational equation.

Roadmap

The Computer Music Tutorial is apportioned into seven parts, each of which contains several chapters. Part I, Fundamental Concepts, serves as an introduction to digital audio and computer technology. Familiarity with the material in these chapters will be helpful in understanding the rest of this volume.

The second part focuses on digital sound synthesis. Chapters 3 through 8 cover the major synthesis methods, including both experimental and commercially available methods.

Part III, Mixing and Signal Processing, contains four chapters that demystify these sometimes arcane subjects, including sound mixing, filtering, delay effects, reverberation, and spatial manipulation.

Analysis of sound, the subject of part IV, is on the ascendency, being key to many musical applications such as sound transformation, interactive performance, and music transcription. Chapters 12 and 13 cover the analysis of pitch, rhythm, and spectrum by computer.

Part V addresses the important subject of the musician's interface for computer music systems. The physical devices manipulated by a performer are the subject of chapter 14, while chapter 15 deals with the software that interprets a performer's gestures. Chapter 16 is a survey of music editing systems. Music languages are the subject of chapter 17. The last two chapters in part V introduce the universe of algorithmic composition methods and representations.

Part VI opens the lid of computer music systems, beginning with an examination of the internals of digital signal processors in chapter 20. Chapter 21 discusses the popular MIDI interface protocol, while chapter 22 looks at interconnections between computers, input devices, and digital signal processing hardware.

The seventh part contains a single chapter on psychoacoustics by John Gordon, which deals with the instrument of listening—human perception. Knowledge of the basic concepts in psychoacoustics can help in several aspects of computer music, including sound design, mixing, and interpreting the output of signal analysis programs.

The final part of the book is a technical appendix introducing readers to the history, mathematics, and overall design of Fourier analysis, in particular the fast Fourier transform—a ubiquitous tool in computer music systems.

Composition

Notwithstanding the broad scope of this book, it was impossible to compress the art of composition into a single part. Instead, readers will find many citations to composers and musical practices interwoven with technical discussions. Chapters 18 and 19 present the technical principles behind algorithmic composition, but this is only one facet of a vast—indeed open-ended—discipline, and is not necessarily meant to typify computer music composition as a whole.

We have surveyed composition practices in other publications. *Composers and the Computer* focuses on several musicians (Roads1985a). During my tenure as editor of *Computer Music Journal*, we published many reviews of compositions, interviews with, and articles by composers. These include a "Symposium on Composition," with fourteen composers partipating (Roads 1986a), and a special issue on composition, *Computer Music Journal* 5(4) 1981. Some of these articles were reprinted in a widely available text, *The Music Machine* (MIT Press 1989). Issue 11(1) 1987 featured microtonality in computer music composition. Many other periodicals and books contain informative articles on compositional issues in electronic and computer music.

References and Index

In a tutorial volume that covers many topics, it is essential to supply pointers for further study. This book contains extensive citations and a reference list of more than 1300 entries compiled at the back of the volume. As a further service to readers, we have invested much time to ensure that both the name and subject indexes are comprehensive.

Mathematics and Coding Style

Since this *Tutorial* is addressed primarily to a musical audience, we chose to present technical ideas in an informal style. The book uses as little mathematical notation as possible. It keeps code examples brief. When mathematical notation is needed, it is presented with operators, precedence relations, and groupings specified explicitly for readability. This is important because the idioms of traditional mathematical notation are sometimes cryptic at first glance, or incomplete as algorithmic descriptions. For the same reasons, the book usually uses long variable names instead of the single-character variables favored in proofs. With the exception of a few simple Lisp examples, code examples are presented in a Pascal-like pseudocode for readibility.

Appendix A presents advanced material and denser mathematical formulas. For this reason we fall back on traditional mathematical notation therein.

Corrections and Comments Invited

In the first edition of a large book covering a new field, there will inevitably be errors. We welcome corrections and comments, and we are always seeking further historical information. Please address your comments to the author in care of The MIT Press, 55 Hayward Street, Cambridge, Massachusetts 02142.

Acknowledgments

This book was written over a period of many years. I wrote the first draft from 1980 to 1986, while serving as Research Associate in computer music at the Massachusetts Institute of Technology and Editor of *Computer Music Journal* for The MIT Press. I am grateful to many friends for their assistance during the period of revisions that followed.

Major sections of part III (Mixing and Signal Processing) and part IV (Sound Analysis) were added during a 1988 stay as Visiting Professor in the Department of Physics at the Università di Napoli Federico II, thanks to an invitation by Professor Aldo Piccialli. I am deeply grateful to Professor Piccialli for his detailed comments on chapter 13 (Spectrum Analysis) and appendix A (Fourier Analysis), and for his generous counsel on the theory of signal processing.

Valuable feedback on part II (Sound Synthesis) came from composition students in the Department of Music at Harvard University, where I taught in 1989, thanks to Professor Ivan Tcherepnin. I thank Professors Conrad Cummings and Gary Nelson for the opportunity to teach at the Oberlin Conservatory of Music in 1990, where I presented much of the book in lecture form, leading to clarifications in the writing.

During spare moments I worked on part V (The Musician's Interface) in Tokyo at the Center for Computer Music and Music Technology, Kunitachi College of Music, in 1991, thanks to the center's director Cornelia Colyer, Kunitachi chairman Bin Ebisawa, and a commission for a composition from the Japan Ministry of Culture. I presented the first courses based on the completed text in 1993 and 1994 at Les Ateliers UPIC, thanks to Gerard Pape and Iannis Xenakis, and the Music Department of the University of Paris VIII, thanks to Professor Horacio Vaggione.

John Strawn, formerly my editorial colleague at *Computer Music Journal*, contributed substantially to this project for several years. In between his duties as a doctoral student at Stanford University, he wrote parts of chapters 1 and 3. Later, he reviewed drafts of most chapters with characteristic thoroughness. Throughout this marathon effort, John was consulted on myriad details via electronic mail. I am grateful to him for sharing his wide musical and technical knowledge and sharp wit.

Curtis Abbott and John Gordon kindly contributed two fine chapters that I am very pleased to include in the book. I would also like to thank Phillip Greenspun of the MIT Department of Electrical Engineering and Computer Science. Philip wrote a six-page text that served as the skeleton for the central part of appendix A and carefully reviewed the draft.

Many kind individuals helped by supplying information, documentation, photographs, or by reading chapter drafts. I am profoundly indebted to these generous people for their numerous suggestions, criticisms, and contributions to this book: Jean-Marie Adrien, Jim Aiken, Clarence Barlow, François Bayle, James Beauchamp, Paul Berg, Nicola Bernardini, Peter Beyls, Jack Biswell, Thom Blum, Richard Boulanger, David Bristow, William Buxton, Wendy Carlos, René Caussé, Xavier Chabot, John Chowning, Cornelia Colyer, K. Conklin, Conrad Cummings, James Dashow, Philippe Depalle, Mark Dolson, Giovanni De Poli, Gerhard Eckel, William Eldridge, Gianpaolo Evangelista, Ayshe Farman-Farmaian, Adrian Freed, Christopher Fry, Guy Garnett, John W. Gordon, Kurt Hebel, Henkjan Honing, Gottfried Michael Koenig, Paul Lansky, Otto Laske, David Lewin, D. Gareth Loy, Max V. Mathews, Stephen McAdams, Dennis Miller, Diego Minciacchi, Bernard Mont-Reynaud, Robert Moog, F. R. Moore, James A. Moorer, Peter Nye, Robert J. Owens, Alan Peevers, Aldo Piccialli, Stephen Pope, Edward L. Poulin, Miller Puckette, François Reveillon, Thomas Rhea, Jean-Claude Risset, Craig Roads, Xavier Rodet, Joseph Rothstein, William Schottstaedt, Marie-Hélène Serra, John Snell, John Stautner, Morton Subotnick, Martha Swetzoff, Stan Tempelaars, Daniel Teruggi, Irène Thanos, Barry Truax, Alvise Vidolin, Dean Wallraff, David Waxman, Erling Wold, and Iannis Xenakis.

I would also like to express my thanks to the staff of The MIT Press Journals—Janet Fisher, manager—publishers of *Computer Music Journal*. This work would have been nigh impossible without their backing over the past fourteen years.

I will always be grateful to Frank Urbanowski, Director of The MIT Press, and Executive Editor Terry Ehling for their extraordinarily patient and kind support of this project. I am also indebted to David Anderson, Sandra Minkkinen, Deborah Cantor-Adams, and Chris Malloy for their fine editing and production labors.

This book is dedicated to my mother, Marjorie Roads.

I Fundamental Concepts

Overview to Part I

Once upon a time—not too long ago—digital audio recording, synthesis, processing, and playback were the privilege of laboratory specialists. Today they are nearly as commonplace as television; virtually all computers are equipped for digital audio. Digital audio, the subject of chapter 1, is central to computer music. The *sample*—nothing more than a number—is the atom of sound. Theory says that we can construct any sound emitted by a loudspeaker by means of a series of samples that trace the pattern of a sound waveform over time. But theory becomes reality only when strict technical conditions concerning sampling rate and sample width are met. If the sampling rate is too low, the result is a sound that is either muffled or polluted by distortion. *Sample width* refers to the size of the digital word used to represent a sample; if it is too small, the sound is literally chopped by noise.

Chapter 2 introduces the art of programming. Knowing how to program is the key to doing something really new in computer music. Thus a familiarity with programming concepts is an essential topic for the student.

Organization of Part I

Part I introduces basic concepts in digital audio and programming that are developed throughout the rest of the book. Chapters 1 and 2 cover a great deal of material in summary form. Their goal is to convey a sense of the scope of these fields as they have evolved, and to prepare readers for the many chapters to follow.

The first chapter, by John Strawn and Curtis Roads, covers such basic topics as the history of digital recording, the sampling theorem, aliasing, phase correction, quantization, dither, audio converters, oversampling, and digital audio formats. Portions of chapter 1 were originally published in *Keyboard* magazine but have been extensively revised for this book.

Chapter 2, "Music Systems Programming" by Curtis Abbott, is an introduction to the art of programming from a master practitioner. The author traces the development of programming languages and the elements of programming style. He summarizes the basic concepts of programming languages, their control and data structures, and describes the fundamentals of object-oriented programming.

1 *Digital Audio Concepts*

with John Strawn

Background: History of Digital Audio Recording
      Experimental Digital Recording
      Digital Sound for the Public
      Digital Sound for Musicians
      Digital Multitrack Recording

Basics of Sound Signals
      Frequency and Amplitude
      Time-domain Representation
      Frequency-domain Representation
      Phase
      Importance of Phase

Analog Representations of Sound

Digital Representations of Sound
      Analog-to-digital Conversion
      Binary Numbers
      Digital-to-analog Conversion
      Digital Audio Recording versus MIDI Recording
      Sampling
      Reconstruction of the Analog Signal
      Aliasing (Foldover)
      The Sampling Theorem
      Ideal Sampling Frequency

The merger of digital audio recording with computer music technology creates a supple and powerful artistic medium. This chapter introduces the history and technology of digital audio recording and playback. After studying this introduction, you should be familiar with the basic vocabulary and concepts of digital audio. In the interest of brevity we condense topics that are large specialities unto themselves; for more literature sources see D. Davis (1988, 1992).

Background: History of Digital Audio Recording

Sound recording has a rich history, beginning with Thomas Edison and Emile Berliner's experiments in the 1870s, and marked by V. Poulsen's Telegraphone magnetic wire recorder of 1898 (Read and Welch 1976). Early audio recording was a mechanical process (figure 1.1).

Although the invention of the triode vacuum tube in 1906 launched the era of electronics, electronically produced records did not become practical until 1924 (Keller 1981). Figure 1.2 depicts one of the horn-loaded loudspeakers typical in the 1920s.

Optical sound recording on film was first demonstrated in 1922 (Ristow 1993). Sound recording on tape coated with powdered magnetized material was developed in the 1930s in Germany (figure 1.3), but did not reach the rest of the world until after World War 2. The German Magnetophon tape

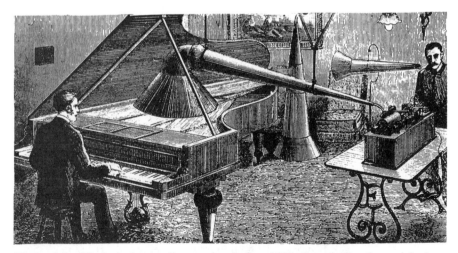

Figure 1.1 Mechnical recording session before 1900. Sound vibrations picked up by the large cone over the piano were transduced into vibrations of a cutting stylus piercing a rotating wax cylinder.

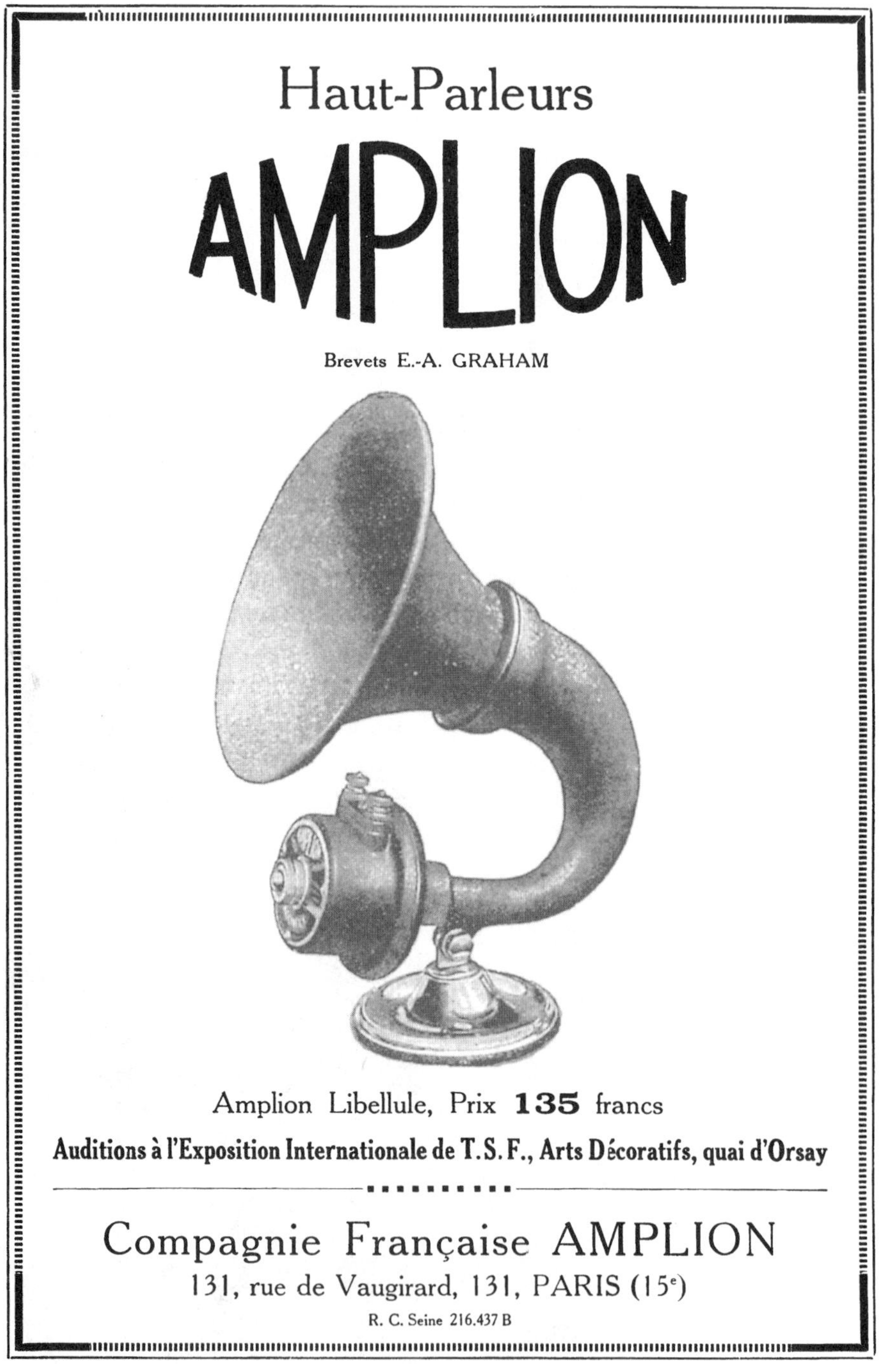

Figure 1.2 Amplion loudspeaker, as advertised in 1925.

Figure 1.3 Prototype of a portable *Magnetophon* tape recorder from 1935, made by AEG. (Photograph courtesy of BASF Aktiengesellschaft.)

recorders were a great advance over previous wire and steel band recorders, which required soldering or welding to make a splice. The Magnetophons and their descendants were *analog* recorders. The term "analog" refers to the fact that the waveform encoded on tape is a close analogy to the original sound waveform picked up by a microphone. Analog recording continues to be refined, but faces fundamental physical limits. These limits are most apparent when making copies from one analog medium to another—additional noise is inescapable.

For more on the history of analog recording, with particular reference to multitrack machines, see chapter 9.

Experimental Digital Recording

The core concept in digital audio recording is *sampling*, that is, converting continuous analog signals (such as those coming from a microphone) into discrete *time-sampled* signals. The theoretical underpinning of sampling is the *sampling theorem*, which specifies the relation between the sampling rate and the audio bandwidth (see the section on the sampling theorem later in this chapter). This theorem is also called the *Nyquist theorem* after the work of Harold Nyquist of Bell Telephone Laboratories (Nyquist 1928), but another form of this theorem was first stated in 1841 by the French mathematician Augustin Louis Cauchy (1789–1857). The British researcher A. Reeves developed the first patented *pulse-code-modulation* (PCM) system for transmission of messages in "amplitude-dichotomized, time-quantized" (digital) form (Reeves 1938; Licklider 1950; Black 1953). Even today, digital recording is sometimes called "PCM recording." The development of *information theory* contributed to the understanding of digital audio transmission (Shannon 1948). Solving the difficult problems of converting between analog signals and digital signals took decades, and is still being improved. (We describe the conversion processes later.)

In the late 1950s, Max Mathews and his group at Bell Telephone Laboratories generated the first synthetic sounds from a digital computer. The samples were written by the computer to expensive and bulky reel-to-reel computer tape storage drives. The production of sound from the numbers was a separate process of playing back the tape through a custom-built 12-bit vacuum tube "digital-to-sound converter" developed by the Epsco Corporation (Roads 1980; see also chapter 3).

Hamming, Huffman, and Gilbert originated the theory of *digital error correction* in the 1950s and 1960s. Later, Sato, Blesser, Stockham, and Doi made contributions to error correction that resulted in the first practical systems for digital audio recording. The first dedicated one-channel digital audio recorder (based on a videotape mechanism), was demonstrated by the NHK, the Japan broadcasting company (Nakajima et al. 1983). Soon thereafter, Denon developed an improved version (figure 1.4), and the race began to bring digital audio recorders to market (Iwamura et al. 1973).

By 1977 the first commercial recording system came to market, the Sony PCM-1 processor, designed to encode 13-bit digital audio signals onto Sony Beta format videocassette recorders. Within a year this was displaced by 16-bit PCM encoders such as the Sony PCM-1600 (Nakajima et al. 1978). At this point product development split along two lines: professional and "consumer" units, although a real mass market for this type of digital recording never materialized. The professional Sony PCM-1610 and 1630 became the standards for compact disc (CD) mastering, while Sony PCM-F1-compatible systems (also called EIAJ systems, for Electronics Industry Association of Japan) became a de facto standard for low-cost digital audio recording on videocassette. These standards continued throughout the 1980s.

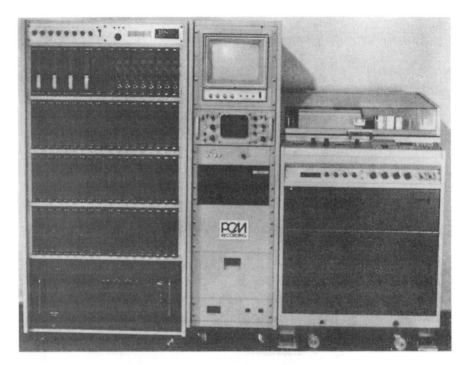

Figure 1.4   Nippon Columbia (Denon) digital audio recorder made in 1973 based on a 1-inch videotape recorder (on the right).

The Audio Engineering Society established two standard sampling frequencies in 1985: 44.1 and 48 KHz. They revised their specification in 1992 (Audio Engineering Society 1992a, 1992b). (A 32 KHz sampling frequency for broadcast purposes also exists.) Meanwhile, a few companies developed higher-resolution digital recorders capable of encoding more than sixteen bits at higher sampling rates. For example, a version of Mitsubishi's X-86 reel-to-reel digital tape recorder encoded 20 bits at a 96 KHz sampling frequency (Mitsubishi 1986). A variety of high-resolution recorders are now available.

Digital Sound for the Public

Digital sound first reached the general public in 1982 by means of the compact disc (CD) format, a 12-cm optical disc read by a laser (figure 1.5). The CD format was developed jointly by the Philips and Sony corporations after years of development. It was a tremendous commercial success, selling over 1.35 million players and tens of millions of discs within two years (Pohlman 1989). Since then a variety of products have been derived from

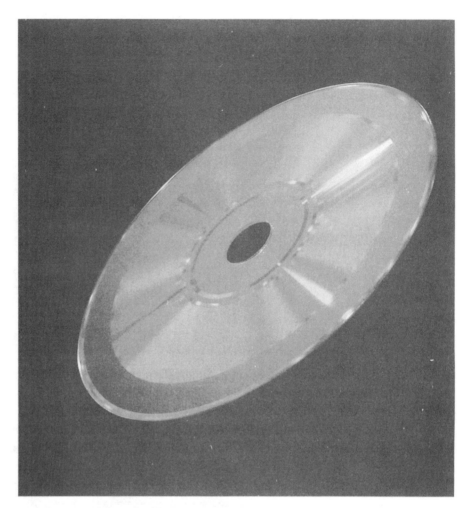

Figure 1.5   The Sony-Philips compact disc.

CD technology, including CD-ROM (Read Only Memory), CD-I (Interactive), and other formats that mix audio data, texts, and images.

By the early 1990s, manufacturers targeted the need for recordable digital media. Various stereo media appeared, including Digital Audio Tape (DAT), Digital Compact Cassettes (DCC), the Mini-Disc (MD), and recordable CDs (CD-R). (See the section on digital audio media below.)

Digital Sound for Musicians

Although CD players had inexpensive 16-bit DACs, good-quality converters attached to computers were not common before 1988. Prior to this time, a few institutional computer music centers developed custom-made ADCs and DACs, but owners of the new personal computer systems had to wait. They could buy digital synthesizers and control them from their computer using the MIDI protocol (see chapter 21), but they could not directly synthesize or record sound with the computer.

Only in the late 1980s did low-cost, good-quality converters become available for personal computers. This development heralded a new era for computer music. In a short period, sound synthesis, recording, and processing by computer became widespread. Dozens of different *audio workstations* reached the musical marketplace. These systems let musicians record music onto the hard disk connected to a personal computer. This music could be precisely edited on the screen of the computer, with playback from the hard disk.

Digital Multitrack Recording

In contrast to stereo recorders that record both left and right channels at the same time, *multitrack* recorders have several discrete channels or *tracks* that can be recorded at different times. Each track can record a separate instrument, for example, allowing flexibility when the tracks are later mixed. Another advantage of multitrack machines is that they let musicians build recordings in several layers; each new layer is an accompaniment to previously recorded layers.

The British Broadcasting Company (BBC) developed an experimental ten-channel digital tape recorder in 1976. Two years later, the 3M company, working with the BBC, introduced the first commercial 32-track digital recorder (figure 1.6) as well as a rudimentary digital tape editor (Duffy 1982). The first computer disk-based random-access sound editor and mixer was developed by the Soundstream company in Salt Lake City, Utah (see figure 16.38). Their system allowed mixing of up to eight tracks or *sound files* stored on computer disk at a time (Ingebretsen and Stockham 1984).

By the mid-1980s, both 3M and Soundstream had withdrawn from the digital multitrack tape recorder market, which was then dominated by the Sony and Mitsubishi conglomerates, later joined by the Studer company. For a number of years, digital multitrack recording was a very expensive enterprise (figure 1.7). The situation entered a new phase in the early 1990s with the introduction of low-cost multitrack tape recorders by Alesis and Tascam, and inexpensive multitrack disk recorders by a variety of concerns. (Chapter 9 recounts the history of analog multitrack recording.)

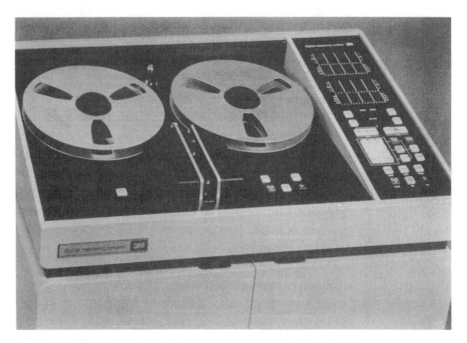

Figure 1.6   3M 32-track digital tape recorder, introduced in 1978.

Basics of Sound Signals

This section introduces the basic concepts and terminology for describing sound signals, including frequency, amplitude, and phase.

Frequency and Amplitude

Sound reaches listeners' ears after being transmitted through air from a source. Listeners hear sound because the air pressure is changing slightly in their ears. If the pressure varies according to a repeating pattern we say the sound has a *periodic waveform*. If there is no discernible pattern it is called *noise*. In between these two extremes is a vast domain of quasi-periodic and quasi-noisy sounds.

One repetition of a periodic waveform is called a *cycle*, and the *fundamental frequency* of the waveform is the number of cycles that occur per second. As the length of the cycle—called the *wavelength* or *period*—increases, the frequency in cycles per second decreases, and vice versa. In the rest of this book we substitute Hz for "cycles per second" in accordance with standard acoustical terminology. (Hz is an abbreviation for Hertz, named after the German acoustician Heinrich Hertz.)

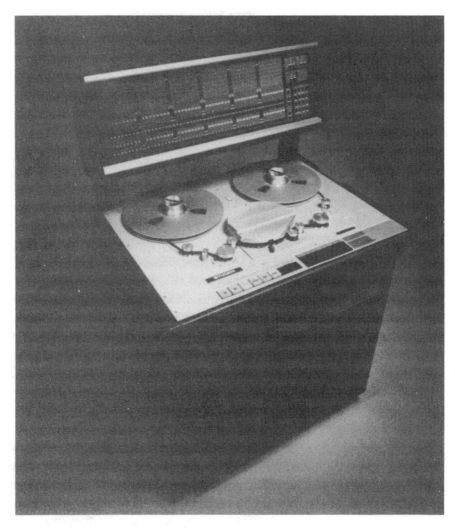

Figure 1.7 Studer D820-48 DASH digital multitrack recorder introduced in 1991 with a retail price of about $270,000.

Time-domain Representation

A simple method of depicting sound waveforms is to draw them in the form of a graph of air pressure versus time (figure 1.8). This is called a *time-domain* representation. When the curved line is near the bottom of the graph, then the air pressure is lower, and when the curve is near the top of the graph, the air pressure has increased. The *amplitude* of the waveform is the amount of air pressure change; we can measure amplitude as the vertical distance from the zero pressure point to the highest (or lowest) points of a given waveform segment.

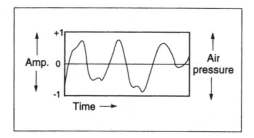

Figure 1.8 Time-domain representation of a signal. The vertical dimension shows the air pressure. When the curved line is near the top of the graph, the air pressure is greater. Below the solid horizontal line, the air pressure is reduced. Atmospheric pressure variations heard as sound can occur quickly; for musical sounds, this entire graph might last no more than one-thousandth of a second (1 ms).

An acoustic instrument creates sound by emitting vibrations that change the air pressure around the instrument. A loudspeaker creates sound by moving back and forth according to voltage changes in an electronic signal. When the loudspeaker moves "in" from its position at rest, then the air pressure decreases. As the loudspeaker moves "out," the air pressure near the loudspeaker is raised. To create an audible sound these in/out vibrations must occur at a frequency in the range of about 20 to 20,000 Hz.

Frequency-domain Representation

Besides the fundamental frequency, there can be many frequencies present in a waveform. A *frequency-domain* or *spectrum* representation shows the frequency content of a sound. The individual frequency components of the spectrum can be referred to as *harmonics* or *partials*. Harmonic frequencies are simple integer multiples of the fundamental frequency. Assuming a

Figure 1.9 Time-domain and frequency-representations of four signals. (*a*) Time-domain view of one cycle of a sine wave. (*b*) Spectrum of the one frequency component in a sine wave. (*c*) Time-domain view of one cycle of a sawtooth waveform. (*d*) Spectrum showing the exponentially decreasing frequency content of a sawtooth wave. (*e*) Time-domain view of one cycle of a complex waveform. Although the waveform looks complex, when it is repeated over and over its sound is actually simple—like a thin reed organ sound. (*f*) The spectrum of waveform (*e*) shows that it is dominated by a few frequencies. (*g*) A random noise waveform. (*h*) If the waveform is constantly changing (each cycle is different from the last cycle) then we hear noise. The frequency content of noise is very complex. In this case the analysis extracted 252 frequencies. This snapshot does not reveal how their amplitudes are constantly changing over time.

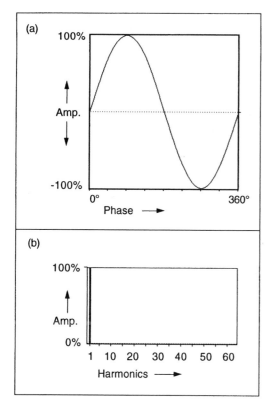

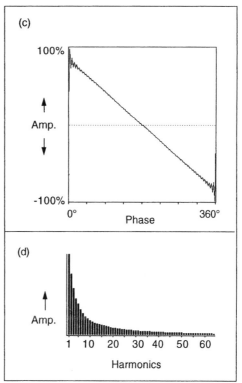

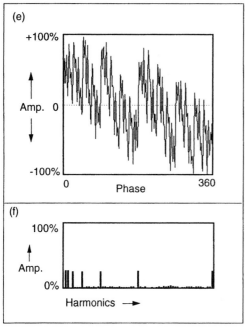

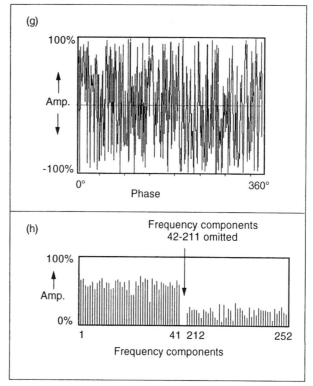

fundamental or *first harmonic* of 440 Hz, its second harmonic is 880 Hz, its third harmonic is 1760 Hz, and so on. More generally, any frequency component can be called a partial, whether or not it is an integer multiple of a fundamental. Indeed, many sounds have no particular fundamental frequency.

The frequency content of a waveform can be displayed in many ways. A standard way is to plot each partial as a line along an *x*-axis. The height of each line indicates the strength (or amplitude) of each frequency component. The purest signal is a *sine* waveform, so named because it can be calculated using trigonometric formulae for the sine of an angle. (Appendix A explains this derivation.) A pure sine wave represents just one frequency component, or one line in a spectrum. Figure 1.9 depicts the time-domain and frequency-domain representations of several waveforms. Notice that the spectrum plots are labeled "Harmonics" on their horizontal axis, since the analysis algorithm assumes that its input is exactly one period of the fundamental of a periodic waveform. In the case of the noise signal in figure 1.9g, this assumption is not valid, so we relabel the partials as "frequency components."

Phase

The starting point of a periodic waveform on the *y* or amplitude axis is its *initial phase*. For example, a typical sine wave starts at the amplitude point 0 and completes its cycle at 0. If we displace the starting point by 2π on the horizontal axis (or 90 degrees) then the sinusoidal wave starts and ends at 1 on the amplitude axis. By convention this is called a cosine wave. In effect, a cosine is equivalent to a sine wave that is *phase shifted* by 90 degrees (figure 1.10).

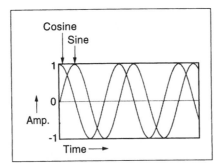

Figure 1.10   A sine waveform is equivalent to a cosine waveform that has been delayed or phase shifted slightly.

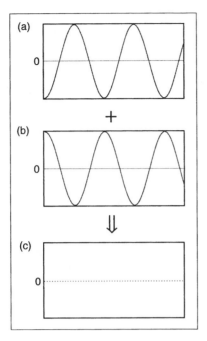

Figure 1.11   The effects of phase inversion. (*b*) is a phase-inverted copy of (*a*). If the two waveforms are added together, they sum to zero (*c*).

When two signals start at the same point they are said to be *in phase* or *phase aligned*. This contrasts to a signal that is slightly delayed with respect to another signal, in which the two signals are *out of phase*. When a signal *A* is the exact opposite phase of another signal *B* (i.e., it is 180 degrees out of phase, so that for every positive value in signal *A* there is a corresponding negative value for signal *B*), we say that *B* has *reversed polarity* with respect to *A*. We could also say that *B* is a *phase-inverted* copy of *A*. Figure 1.11 portrays the effect when two signals in inverse phase relationship sum.

Importance of Phase

It is sometimes said that phase is insignificant to the human ear, because two signals that are exactly the same except for their initial phase are difficult to distinguish. Actually, research indicates that 180-degree differences in absolute phase or *polarity* can be distinguished by some people under laboratory conditions (Greiner and Melton 1991). But even apart from this special case, phase is an important concept for several reasons. Every filter uses phase shifts to alter signals. A filter phase shifts a signal (by delaying its input for a short time) and then combines the phase-shifted version with the original signal to create *frequency-dependent phase cancellation* effects that alter the spectrum of the original. By "frequency-dependent" we mean that not all frequency components are affected equally. When the phase shifting is time-varying, the affected frequency bands also vary, creating the sweeping sound effect called *phasing* or *flanging* (see chapter 10).

Phase is also important in systems that resynthesize sound on the basis of an analysis of an existing sound. In particular, these systems need to know the starting phase of each frequency component in order to put together the different components in the right order (see chapter 13 and Appendix A.) Phase data are particularly critical in reproducing short, rapidly changing *transient* sounds, such as the onset of an instrumental tone.

Finally, much attention has been invested in recent years to audio components that phase shift their input signals as little as possible, because frequency-dependent phase shifts distort musical signals audibly and interfere with loudspeaker *imaging*. (Imaging is the ability of a set of loudspeakers to create a stable "audio picture" where each audio source is localized to a specific place within the picture.) Unwanted phase shifting is called *phase distortion*. To make a visual analogy, a phase-distorted signal is "out of focus."

Now that we have introduced the basic properties of audio signals, we take a comparative look at two representations for them: analog and digital.

Analog Representations of Sound

Just as air pressure varies according to sound waves, so can the electrical quantity called *voltage* in a wire connecting an amplifier with a loudspeaker. We do not need to define voltage here. For the purposes of this chapter, we can simply assume that it is possible to modify an electrical property associated with the wire in a fashion that closely matches the changes in air pressure.

An important characteristic of the time-varying quantities we have introduced (air pressure and voltage) is that each of them is more or less exactly analogous to the other. A graph of the air pressure variations picked up by a microphone looks very similar to a graph of the variations in the loudspeaker position when that sound is played back. The term "analog" serves as a reminder of how these quantities are related.

Figure 1.12 shows an analog audio chain. The curve of an audio signal can be inscribed along the groove of a traditional phonograph record, as shown in figure 1.12. The walls of the grooves on a phonograph record

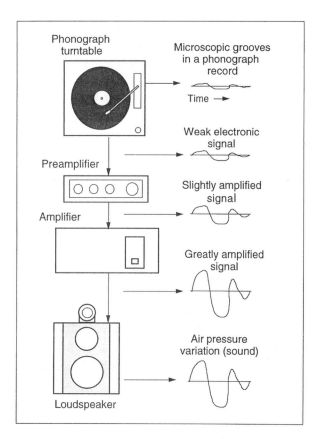

Figure 1.12 The analog audio chain, starting from an analog waveform transduced from the grooves of a phonograph record to a voltage sent to a preamplifier, amplifier, loudspeaker, and projected into the air.

contain a *continuous-time* representation of the sound stored in the record. As the needle glides through the groove, the needle moves back and forth in lateral motion. This lateral motion is then changed into voltage, which is amplified and eventually reaches the loudspeaker.

Analog reproduction of sound has been taken to a high level in recent years, but there are fundamental limitations associated with analog recording. When you copy an analog recording onto another analog recorder, the copy is never as good as the original. This is because the analog recording process always adds noise. For a *first-generation* or original recording, this noise may not be objectionable. But as we continue with three or four generations, making copies of copies, more of the original recording is lost to noise. In contrast, digital technology can create any number of generations of perfect (noise-free) clones of an original recording, as we show later.

In essence, generating or reproducing digital sound involves converting a string of numbers into one of the time-varying changes that we have been discussing. If these numbers can be turned into voltages, then the voltages can be amplified and fed to a loudspeaker to produce the sound.

Digital Representations of Sound

This section introduces the most basic concepts associated with digital signals, including the conversion of signals into binary numbers, comparison of audio data with MIDI data, sampling, aliasing, quantization, and dither.

Analog-to-digital Conversion

Let us look at the process of digitally recording sound and then playing it back. Rather than the continuous-time signals of the analog world, a digital recorder handles *discrete-time* signals. Figure 1.13 diagrams the digital audio recording and playback process. In this figure, a microphone transduces air pressure variations into electrical voltages, and the voltages are passed through a wire to the *analog-to-digital converter*, commonly abbreviated ADC (pronounced "A D C"). This device converts the voltages into a string of *binary numbers* at each period of the sample clock. The binary numbers are stored in a digital recording medium—a type of memory.

Binary Numbers

In contrast to decimal (or *base ten*) numbers, which use the ten digits 0–9, binary (or *base two*) numbers use only two digits, 0 and 1. The term *bit* is an abbreviation of *binary digit*. Table 1.1 lists some binary numbers and their decimal equivalents. There are various ways of indicating negative numbers in binary. In many computers the leftmost bit is interpreted as a sign indicator, with a 1 indicating a positive number, and a 0 indicating a negative number. (Real decimal or *floating-point* numbers can also be represented in binary. See chapter 20 for more on floating-point numbers in digital audio signal processing.)

The way a bit is physically encoded in a recording medium depends on the properties of that medium. On a digital audio tape recorder, for example, a 1 might be represented by a positive magnetic charge, while a 0 is indicated by the absence of such a charge. This is different from an analog

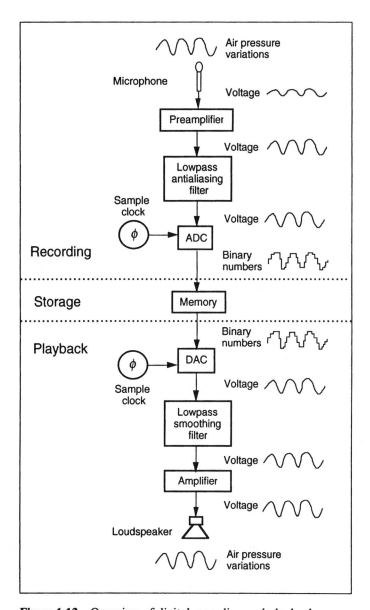

Figure 1.13 Overview of digital recording and playback.

Table 1.1   Binary numbers and their decimal equivalents

Binary	Decimal
0	0
1	1
10	2
11	3
100	4
1000	8
10000	16
100000	32
1111111111111111	65535

tape recording, in which the signal is represented as a continuously varying charge. On an optical medium, binary data might be encoded as variations in the reflectance at a particular location.

Digital-to-analog Conversion

Figure 1.14 depicts the result of converting an audio signal (a) into a digital signal (b). When the listener wants to hear the sound again, the numbers are read one-by-one from the digital storage and passed through a *digital-to-analog converter*, abbreviated DAC (pronounced "dack"). This device, driven by a sample clock, changes the stream of numbers into a series of voltage levels. From here the process is the same as shown in figure 1.13; that is, the series of voltage levels are lowpass filtered into a continuous-time waveform (figure 1.14c), amplified, and routed to a loudspeaker, whose vibration causes the air pressure to change. Voilà, the signal sounds again.

In summary, we can change a sound in the air into a string of binary numbers that can be stored digitally. The central component in this conversion process is the ADC. When we want to hear the sound again, a DAC can change those numbers back into sound.

Digital Audio Recording versus MIDI Recording

This final point may clear up any confusion: the string of numbers generated by the ADC are not related to MIDI data. (MIDI is the Musical Instrument Digital Interface specification—a widely used protocol for control of digital music systems; see chapter 21.) Both digital audio recorders and MIDI sequencers are digital and can record multiple "tracks," but they differ in the amount and type of information that each one handles.

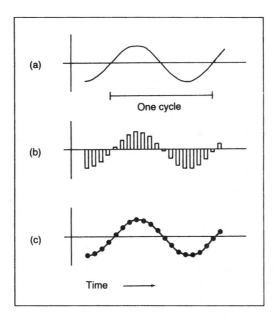

Figure 1.14 Analog and digital representations of a signal. (*a*) Analog sine waveform. The horizontal bar below the wave indicates one period or cycle. (*b*) Sampled version of the sine waveform in (*a*), as it might appear at the output of an ADC. Each vertical bar represents one sample. Each sample is stored in memory as a number that represents the height of the vertical bar. One period is represented by fifteen samples. (*c*) Reconstruction of the sampled version of the waveform in (*b*). Roughly speaking, the tops of the samples are connected by the lowpass smoothing filter to form the waveform that eventually reaches the listener's ear.

When a MIDI sequencer records a human performance on a keyboard, only a relatively small amount of *control information* is actually transmitted from the keyboard to the sequencer. MIDI does not transmit the sampled waveform of the sound. For each note, the sequencer records only the start time and ending time, its pitch, and the amplitude at the beginning of the note. If this information is transmitted back to the synthesizer on which it was originally played, this causes the synthesizer to play the sound as it did before, like a piano roll recording. If the musician plays four quarter notes at a tempo of 60 beats per minute on a MIDI synthesizer, just sixteen pieces of information capture this 4-second sound (four starts, ends, pitches, and amplitudes).

By contrast, if we record the same sound with a microphone connected to a digital audio tape recorder set to a sampling frequency of 44.1 KHz, 352,800 pieces of information (in the form of audio samples) are recorded for the same sound (44,100 × 2 channels × 4 seconds). The storage requirements of digital audio recording are large. Using 16-bit samples, it takes over 700,000 bytes to store a 4-second sound. This is 44,100 times more data than is stored by MIDI.

Because of the tiny amount of data it handles, an advantage of MIDI sequence recording is low cost. For example, a 48-track MIDI sequence recorder program running on a small computer might cost less than $100 and handle 4000 bytes/second. In contrast, a 48-track digital tape recorder costs tens of thousands of dollars and handles more than 4.6 Mbytes of audio information per second—over a thousand times the data rate of MIDI.

The advantage of a digital audio recording is that it can capture any sound that can be recorded by a microphone, including the human voice. MIDI sequence recording is limited to recording control signals that indicate the start, end, pitch, and amplitude of a series of note events. If you plug the MIDI cable from the sequencer into a synthesizer that is not the same as the synthesizer on which the original sequence was played, the resulting sound may change radically.

Sampling

The digital signal shown in figure 1.14b is significantly different from the original analog signal shown in figure 1.14a. First, the digital signal is defined only at certain points in time. This happens because the signal has been *sampled* at certain times. Each vertical bar in figure 1.14b represents one *sample* of the original signal. The samples are stored as binary numbers; the higher the bar in figure 1.14b, the larger the number.

The number of bits used to represent each sample determines both the noise level and the amplitude range that can be handled by the system. A compact disc uses a 16-bit number to represent a sample, but more or fewer bits can be used. We return to this subject later in the section on "quantization."

The rate at which samples are taken—the *sampling frequency*—is expressed in terms of samples per second. This is an important specification of digital audio systems. It is often called the *sampling rate* and is expressed in terms of Hertz. A thousand Hz is abbreviated 1 KHz, so we say: "The sampling rate of a compact disc recording is 44.1 KHz," where the "K" is derived from the metric term "kilo" meaning thousand.

Reconstruction of the Analog Signal

Sampling frequencies around 50 KHz are common in digital audio systems, although both lower and higher frequencies can also be found. In any case,

50,000 numbers per second is a rapid stream of numbers; it means there are 6,000,000 samples for one minute of stereo sound.

The digital signal in figure 1.13b does not show the value between the bars. The duration of a bar is extremely narrow, perhaps lasting only 0.00002 second (two hundred-thousandths of a second). This means that if the original signal changes "between" bars, the change is not reflected in the height of a bar, at least until the next sample is taken. In technical terms, we say that the signal in figure 1.13b is defined at *discrete* times, each such time represented by one sample (vertical bar).

Part of the magic of digitized sound is that if the signal is bandlimited, the DAC and associated hardware can exactly reconstruct the original signal from these samples! This means that, given certain conditions, the missing part of the signal "between the samples" can be restored. This happens when the numbers are passed through the DAC and smoothing filter. The smoothing filter "connects the dots" between the discrete samples (see the dotted line in figure 1.13c). Thus, a signal sent to the loudspeaker looks and sounds like the original signal.

Aliasing (Foldover)

The process of sampling is not quite as straightforward as it might seem. Just as an audio amplifier or a loudspeaker can introduce distortion, sampling can play tricks with sound. Figure 1.15 gives an example. Using the input waveform shown in figure 1.15a, suppose that a sample of this waveform is taken at each point in time shown by the vertical bars in figure 1.15b (each vertical bar creates one sample). As before, the resulting samples of figure 1.15c are stored as numbers in digital memory. But when we attempt to reconstruct the original waveform, as shown in figure 1.15d, the result is something completely different.

In order to understand better the problems that can occur with sampling, we look at what happens when we change the *wavelength* (the length of one cycle) of the original signal without changing the length of time between samples. Figure 1.16a shows a signal with a cycle eight samples long, figure 1.16d shows a cycle two samples long, and figure 1.16g shows a waveform with eleven cycles per ten samples. This means that one cycle takes longer than the interval between samples. This relationship could also be expressed as 11/10 cycles per sample.

Again, as each of the sets of samples is passed through the DAC and associated hardware, a signal is reconstructed (figures 1.16c, f, and i) and sent to the loudspeaker. The signal shown by the dotted line in figure 1.16c

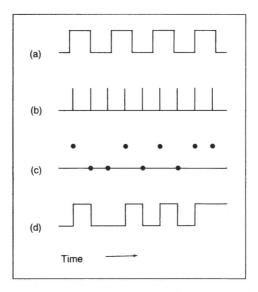

Figure 1.15   Problems in sampling. (*a*) Waveform to be recorded. (*b*) The sampling pulses; whenever a sampling pulse occurs, one sample is taken. (*c*) The waveform as sampled and stored in memory. (*d*) When the waveform from (*c*) is sent to the the DAC, the output might appear as shown here (after Mathews 1969).

is reconstructed more or less accurately. The results of the sampling in figure 1.16f are potentially a little less satisfactory; one possible reconstruction is shown there. But in figure 1.16i, the resynthesized waveform is completely different from the original in one important respect. Namely, the wavelength (length of the cycle) of the resynthesized waveform is different from that of the original. In the real world, this means that the reconstructed signal sounds at a pitch different from that of the original signal. This kind of distortion is called *aliasing* or *foldover*.

The frequencies at which this aliasing occurs can be predicted. Suppose, just to keep the numbers simple, that we take 1000 samples per second. Then the signal in figure 1.16a has a frequency of 125 cycles per second (since there are eight samples per cycle, and 1000/8 = 125). In figure 1.16d, the signal has a frequency of 500 cycles per second (because 1000/2 = 500).

The frequency of the input signal in figure 1.16g is 1100 cycles per second. But the frequency of the output signal is different. In figure 1.16i you can count ten samples per cycle of the output waveform. In actuality, the output waveform occurs at a frequency of 1000/10 = 100 cycles per second. Thus the frequency of the original signal in figure 1.16g has been changed by the *sample rate conversion* process. This represents an unacceptable change to a musical signal, which must be avoided if possible.

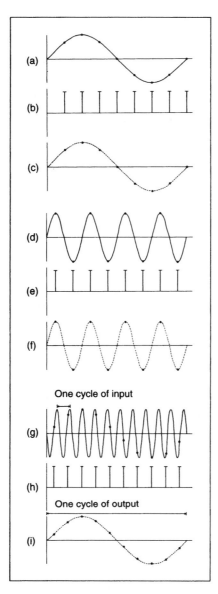

Figure 1.16 Foldover effects. At the bottom of each set of three graphs, the thick black dots represent samples, and the dotted line shows the signal as reconstructed by the DAC. Every cycle of the sine waveform (*a*) is sampled eight times in (*b*). Using the same sampling frequency, each cycle of (*d*) is sampled only twice in (*e*). If the sampling pulses in (*e*) were moved to the right, the output waveform in (*f*) might be phase-shifted, although the frequency of the output would still be the same. In (*h*), there are ten samples for the eleven cycles in (*g*). When the DAC tries to reconstruct a signal, as shown by the dashed lines in (*i*), a sine waveform results, but the frequency has been completely changed due to the foldover effect. Notice the horizontal double arrow above (*g*), indicating one cycle of the input waveform, and the arrow above (*i*), indicating one cycle of the output waveform.

The Sampling Theorem

We can generalize from figure 1.16 to say that as long as there are at least two samples per period of the original waveform, we can assume that the resynthesized waveform will have the same frequency. But when there are fewer than two samples per period, the frequency (and perhaps the timbre) of the original signal is lost. In this case, the new frequency can be found by the following formula. If the original frequency is higher than half the sampling frequency, then:

new frequency = sampling frequency − original frequency

This formula is not mathematically complete, but it is sufficient for our discussion here. It means the following. Suppose we have chosen a fixed sampling frequency. We start with a signal at a low frequency, sample it, and resynthesize the signal after sampling. As we raise the pitch of the input signal (but still keep the sampling frequency constant), the pitch of the resynthesized signal is the same as the pitch of the input signal until we reach a pitch that corresponds to one-half of the sampling frequency. As we raise the pitch of the input signal even higher, the pitch of the output signal goes down to the lowest frequencies! When the input signal reaches the sampling frequency, the entire process repeats itself.

To give a concrete example, suppose we introduce an analog signal at 26 KHz into an analog-to-digital converter operating at 50 KHz. The converter reads it as a tone at 24 KHz, since 50 − 26 = 24 KHz.

The *sampling theorem* describes the relationship between the sampling rate and the bandwidth of the signal being transmitted. It was expressed by Harold Nyquist (1928) as follows:

For any given deformation of the received signal, the transmitted frequency range must be increased in direct proportion to the signalling speed.... The conclusion is that the frequency band is directly proportional to the speed.

The essential point of the sampling theorem can be stated precisely as follows:

In order to be able to reconstruct a signal, the sampling frequency must be at least twice the frequency of the signal being sampled.

In honor of his contributions to sampling theory, the highest frequency that can be produced in a digital audio system (i.e., half the sampling rate) is called the *Nyquist frequency*. In musical applications, the Nyquist frequency is usually in the upper range of human hearing, above 20 KHz. Then the

sampling frequency can be specified as being at least twice as much, or above 40 KHz.

In some systems the sampling frequency is set somewhat greater than twice this highest frequency, because the converters and associated hardware cannot perfectly reconstruct a signal near half the sampling frequency (an idealized reconstruction of such a case is shown in figure 1.16f).

Ideal Sampling Frequency

The question of what sampling frequency is ideal for high-quality music recording and reproduction is an ongoing debate. Part of the reason is that mathematical theory and engineering practice often conflict: converter clocks are not stable, converter voltages are not linear, filters introduce phase distortion, and so on. (See the sections on phase correction and oversampling later.)

Another reason is that many people hear information (referred to as "air") in the region around the 20 KHz "limit" on human hearing (Neve 1992). Indeed, Rudolf Koenig, whose precise measurements set international standards for acoustics, observed at age 41 that his own hearing extended to 23 KHz (Koenig 1899). It seems strange that a new digital compact disc should have less bandwidth than a phonograph record made in the 1960s, or a new digital audio recorder should have less bandwidth than a twenty-year old analog tape recorder. Many analog systems can reproduce frequencies beyond 25 KHz. Scientific experiments confirm the effects of sounds above 22 KHz from both physiological and subjective viewpoints (Oohashi et al. 1991; Oohashi et al. 1993).

In sound synthesis applications, the lack of "frequency headroom" in standard sampling rates of 44.1 and 48 KHz causes serious problems. It requires that synthesis algorithms generate nothing other than sine waves above 11 KHz (44.1 KHz sampling rate) or 12 KHz (48 KHz sampling rate), or foldover will occur. This is because any high-frequency component with partials beyond the fundamental has a frequency that exceeds the Nyquist rate. The third harmonic of a tone at 12.5 KHz, for example, is 37.5 KHz, which in a system running at 44.1 KHz sampling rate will reflect down to an audible 6600 Hz tone. In sampling and pitch-shifting applications, the lack of frequency headroom requires that samples be lowpass filtered before they are pitch-shifted upward. The trouble these limits impose is inconvenient.

It is clear that high-sampling rate recordings are preferable from an artistic standpoint, although they pose practical problems of additional storage and the need for high-quality audio playback systems to make the effort worthwhile.

Antialiasing and Anti-imaging Filters

In order to make sure that a digital sound system works properly, two important filters are included. One filter is placed before the ADC, to make sure that nothing (or as little as possible) in the input signal occurs at a frequency higher than half of the sampling frequency. As long as this filter does the proper work, aliasing should not occur during the recording process. Logically enough, such a filter is called an *antialiasing filter*.

The other filter is placed after the DAC. Its main function is to change the samples stored digitally into a smooth, continuous representation of the signal. In effect, this lowpass *anti-imaging* or *smoothing filter* creates the dotted line in figure 1.14c by connecting the solid black dots in the figure.

Phase Correction

The issue of *phase correction* came rushing to the fore following the introduction of the first generation of digital audio recorders and players. Many complained about the harsh sound of digital recordings, a problem that could be traced to the the *brickwall* antialiasing filters before the ADCs (Woszczyk and Toole 1983; Preis and Bloom 1983). They are called brickwall filters because of their steep frequency rejection curve (over 90 dB/ octave at the Nyquist frequency, typically). These steep filters can cause significant time-delays (phase distortion) in midrange and high audio frequencies (figure 1.17). A smaller frequency-dependent delay is contributed by the smoothing filter at the output of a DAC.

No analog filter can be both extremely steep and *phase linear* around the cutoff point. (Phase linear means that there is little or no frequency-dependent delay introduced by the filter.) Hence, the effect of a steep filter "spills over" into the audio range. For compact disc recordings at a 44.1 KHz sampling rate, the Nyquist frequency is 22.05 KHz, and a steep antialiasing filter can introduce phase distortion that extends well below 10 KHz (Meyer 1984). This type of phase distortion lends an unnaturally harsh sound to high frequencies.

There are various ways to tackle this problem. The simplest is to trade off the antialiasing properties of the filter in favor of less phase distortion. A less steep antialiasing filter (40–60 dB/octave, for example) introduces less phase distortion, but at the risk of foldover for very high frequency sounds. Another solution is to apply a *time correction filter* before the ADC to

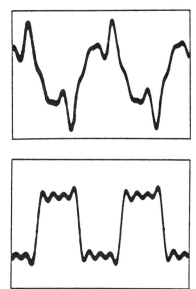

Figure 1.17   Phase distortion caused by an antialiasing filter. (*a*) 2.5 KHz square wave distorted by a brickwall antialiasing filter. (*b*) Phase-corrected square wave.

skew the phase relationships in the incoming signal so as to preserve the original phase relationships in the recording (Blesser 1984; Greenspun 1984; Meyer 1984). At present, however, the high-technology solution to phase correct conversion is to use *oversampling* techniques at both the input and output stages of the system. We discuss oversampling later.

Quantization

Sampling at discrete time intervals, discussed in the previous sections, constitutes one of the major differences between digital and analog signals. Another difference is *quantization*, or discrete amplitude resolution. The values of the sampled signal cannot take on any conceivable value. This is because digital numbers can only be represented within a certain range and with a certain accuracy, which varies with the hardware being used. The implications of this are an important factor in digital audio quality.

Quantization Noise

Samples are usually represented as integers. If the input signal has a voltage corresponding to a value between 53 and 54, for example, then the converter might round it off and assign a value of 53. In general, for each sample taken, the value of the sample usually differs slightly from the value

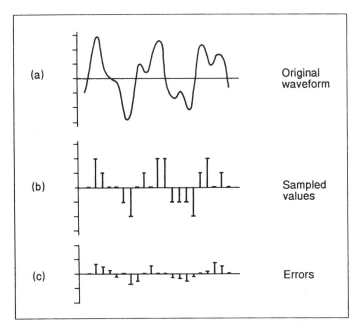

Figure 1.18   Effects of quantization. (*a*) Analog waveform. (*b*) Sampled version of the waveform in (*a*). Each sample can be assigned only certain values, which are indicated by the short horizontal dashes at the left. The difference between each sample and the original signal is shown in (*c*), where the height of each bar represents the quantization error.

of the original signal. This problem in digital signals is known as *quantization error* or *quantization noise* (Blesser 1978; Maher 1992; Lipshitz et al. 1992; Pohlmann 1989a).

Figure 1.18 shows the kinds of quantization errors that can occur. When the input signal is something complicated like a symphony, and we listen to just the errors, shown at the bottom of figure 1.18, it sounds like noise. If the errors are large, then one might notice something similar to analog tape hiss at the output of a system.

The quantization noise is dependent on two factors: the signal itself, and the accuracy with which the signal is represented in digital form. We can explain the sensitivity to the signal by noting that on an analog tape recorder, the tape imposes a soft halo of noise that continues even through periods of silence on the tape. But in a digital system there can be no quantization noise when nothing (or silence) is recorded. In other words, if the input signal is silence, then the signal is represented by a series of samples, each of which is exactly zero. The small differences shown in figure 1.18c disappear for such a signal, which means that the quantization noise disappears. If, on the other hand, the input signal is a pure sinusoid, then

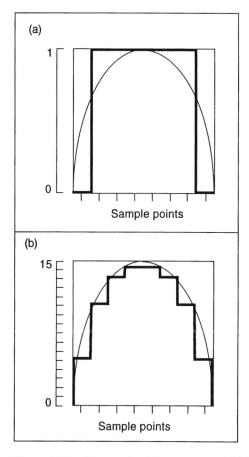

Figure 1.19 Comparing the accuracy of 4-bit quantization with that of 1-bit quantization. The thin rounded curve is the input waveform. (*a*) 1-bit quantization provides two levels of amplitude resolution, while (*b*) 4-bit quantization provides sixteen different levels of amplitude resolution.

the quantization error is not a random function but a deterministic truncation effect (Maher 1992). This gritty sound, called *granulation noise*, can be heard when very low level sinusoids decay to silence. When the input signal is complicated, the granulation becomes randomized into white noise.

The second factor in quantization noise is the accuracy of the digital representation. In a PCM system that represents each sample value by an integer (a *linear PCM* system), quantization noise is directly tied to the number of bits that are used to represent a sample. This specification is the *sample width* or *quantization level* of a system. Figure 1.19 illustrates the effects of different quantization levels, comparing the resolution of 1-bit versus 4-bit quantization. In a linear PCM system generally, the more bits used to represent a sample, the less the quantization noise. Figure 1.20

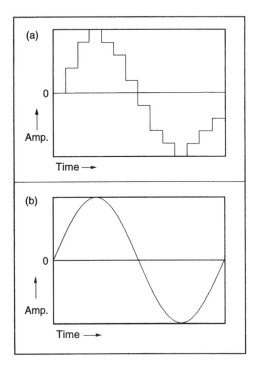

Figure 1.20   Effect of quantization on sine wave smoothness. (*a*) "Sine" wave with ten levels of quantization, corresponding to a moderately loud tone emitted by a 4-bit system. (*b*) Smoother sinusoid emitted by an 8-bit system.

shows the dramatic improvement in sine wave accuracy achieved by adding more bits of resolution.

The quantization measure is confused by *oversampling* systems, which use a high-speed "1-bit" converter. The quantization of a system that uses a "1-bit" converter is actually much greater than 1 bit. See the section on oversampling later.

Low-level Quantization Noise and Dither

Although a digital system exhibits no noise when there is no input signal, at very low (but nonzero) signal levels, quantization noise takes a pernicious form. A very low level signal triggers variations only in the lowest bit. These 1-bit variations look like a square wave, which is rich in odd harmonics. Consider the decay of a piano tone, which smoothly attenuates with high partials rolling off—right until the lowest level when it changes character and becomes a harsh-sounding square wave. The harmonics of the square wave may even extend beyond the Nyquist frequency, causing aliasing and introducing new frequency components that were not in the

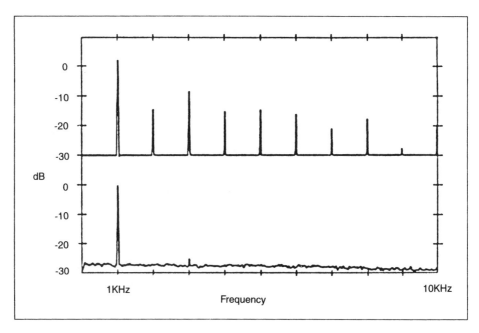

Figure 1.21 Dither reduces harmonic distortion in a digital system. The top part of the figure shows the spectrum of 1 KHz sine wave with an amplitude of 1/2 bit. Note the harmonics produced by the action of the ADC. The lower part shows the spectrum of the same signal after dithering of about 1 bit in amplitude is applied before conversion. Only a small amount of third harmonic noise remains, along with wideband noise. The ear can resolve the sine wave below the noise floor.

original signal. These artifacts may be possible to ignore if the signal is kept at a low monitoring level, but if the signal is heard at a high level or if it is digitally remixed to a higher level, it becomes more obvious. Hence it is important that the signal be quantized as accurately as possible at the input stage.

To confront low-level quantization problems, some digital recording systems take what seems at first to be a strange action. They introduce a small amount of analog noise—called *dither*—to the signal prior to analog-to-digital conversion (Vanderkooy and Lipshitz 1984; Lipshitz et al. 1992). This causes the ADC to make random variations around the low-level signal, which smooths out the pernicious effects of square wave harmonics (figure 1.21). With dither, the quantization error, which is usually signal-dependent, is turned into a wide-band noise that is uncorrelated with the signal. For decrescendos like the piano tone mentioned previously, the effect is that of a "soft landing" as the tone fades smoothly into a bed of low-level random noise. The amount of added noise is usually on the order of 3 dB, but the ear can reconstruct musical tones whose amplitudes fall below that of the dither signal. See Blesser (1978, 1983), Rabiner and Gold (1975), Pohlmann (1989a), and Maher (1992) for more details on quantization noise and methods for minimizing it. Lipshitz, Wannamaker, and Vanderkooy (1992) present a mathematical analysis of quantization and dither. See Hauser (1991) for a discussion of dither in oversampling converters.

Dither may not be necessary with an accurate 20-bit converter, since the low bit represents an extremely soft signal in excess of 108 dB below the loudest signal. But when converting signals from a 20-bit to a 16-bit format, for example, dithering is necessary to preserve signal fidelity.

Converter Linearity

Converters can cause a variety of distortions (Blesser 1978; McGill 1985; Talambiras 1985). One that is pertinent here is that an *n*-bit converter is not necessarily accurate to the full dynamic range implied by its *n*-bit input or output. While the *resolution* of an *n*-bit converter is one part in 2^n, a converter's *linearity* is the degree to which the analog and digital input and output signals match in terms of their magnitudes. That is, some converters use 2^n steps, but these steps are not linear, which causes distortion. Hence it is possible to see an "18-bit converter," for example, that is "16-bit linear." Such a converter may be better than a plain 16-bit converter, which may not be 16-bit linear. (See Polhmann 1989a for a discussion of these problems.)

Dynamic Range of Digital Audio Systems

The specifications for digital sound equipment typically specify the accuracy or *resolution* of the system. This can be expressed as the number of bits that the system uses to store each sample. The number of bits per sample is important in calculating the maximum *dynamic range* of a digital sound system. In general, the dynamic range is the difference between the loudest and softest sounds that the system can produce and is measured in units of *decibels* (dB).

Decibels

The decibel is a unit of measurement for relationships of voltage levels, intensity, or power, particularly in audio systems. In acoustic measurements, the decibel scale indicates the ratio of one level to a *reference level*, according to the relation

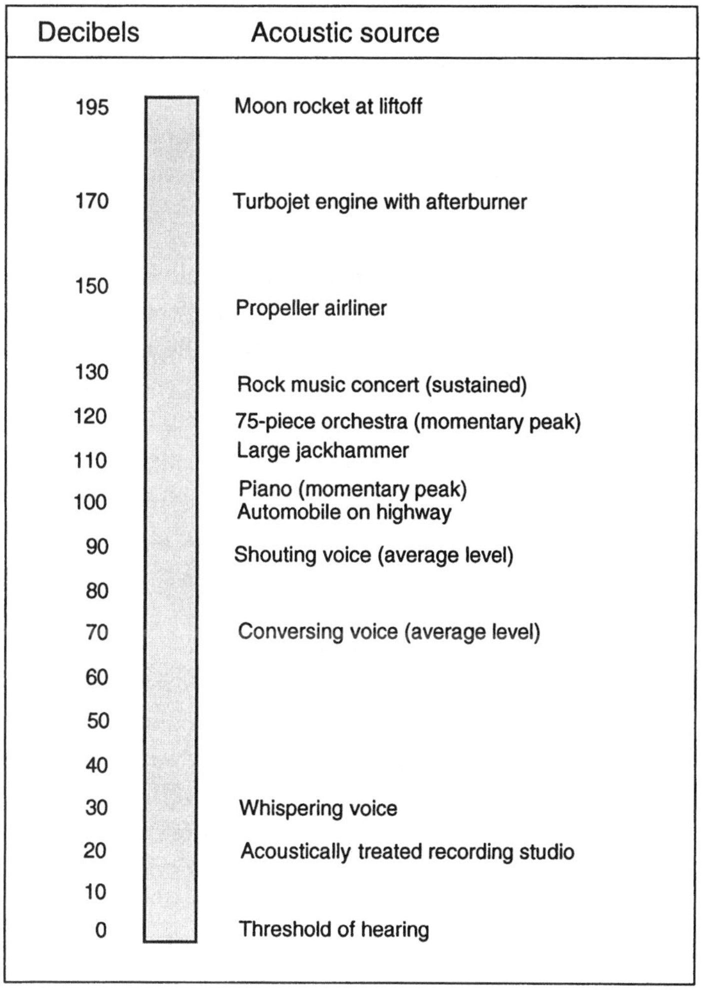

Decibels	Acoustic source
195	Moon rocket at liftoff
170	Turbojet engine with afterburner
150	
	Propeller airliner
130	Rock music concert (sustained)
120	75-piece orchestra (momentary peak)
110	Large jackhammer
100	Piano (momentary peak) Automobile on highway
90	Shouting voice (average level)
80	
70	Conversing voice (average level)
60	
50	
40	
30	Whispering voice
20	Acoustically treated recording studio
10	
0	Threshold of hearing

Figure 1.22 Typical acoustic power levels for various acoustic sources. All figures are relative to 0 dB = 10^{-12} watts per square meter.

number of decibels $= 10 \times \log_{10}(\textit{level/reference level})$

where the *reference level* is usually the threshold of hearing (10^{-12} watts per square meter). The logarithmic basis of decibels means that if two notes sound together, and each note is 60 dB, the increase in level is just 3 dB. A millionfold increase in intensity results in a 60 dB boost. (See chapter 23, Backus 1977, or Pohlmann 1989 for more on decibels.)

Figure 1.22 shows the decibel scale and some estimated acoustic power levels relative to 0 dB. Two important facts describe the dynamic range requirements of a digital audio system:

1. The range of human hearing extends from approximately 0 dB, roughly the level at which the softest sound can be heard, to something around 125 dB, which is roughly the threshold of pain for sustained sounds.

2. A difference of somewhat less than one dB between the amplitude levels of two sounds corresponds to the smallest difference in amplitude that can be heard.

These figures vary with age, training, pitch, and the individual.

In recording music, it is important to capture the widest possible dynamic range if we want to reproduce the full expressive power of the music. In a live orchestra concert, for example, the dynamic range can vary from "silence," to an instrumental solo at 60 dB, to a tutti section by the full orchestra exceeding 110 dB. The dynamic range of analog tape equipment is dictated by the physics of the analog recording process. It stands somewhere around 80 dB for a 1 KHz tone using professional reel-to-reel tape recorders without noise-reduction devices. (Noise reduction devices can increase the dynamic range at the price of various distortions. See chapter 10 for more on noise reduction.)

When a recording is produced for distribution on a medium that does not have a wide dynamic range (a mass-produced analog cassette, for example), the soft passages are made a little bit louder by the transfer engineer, and the loud passages are made a little bit softer. If this were not done, then the loudest passages would produce distortion in recording, and the softest passages would be masked by hiss and other noise.

Dynamic Range of a Digital System

To calculate the maximum dynamic range of a digital system, we can use the following simple formula:

maximum dynamic range in decibels = number of bits × 6.11.

The number 6.11 here is a close approximation to the theoretical maximum (van de Plaasche 1983; Hauser 1991); in practice, 6 is a more realistic figure. A derivation of this formula is given in Mathews (1969) and Blesser (1978).

Thus, if we record sound with an 8-bit system, then the upper limit on the dynamic range is approximately 48 dB—worse than the dynamic range of analog tape recorders. But if we record 16 bits per sample, the dynamic range increases to a maximum of 96 dB—a significant improvement. A 20-bit converter offers a potential dynamic range of 120 dB, which corresponds roughly to the range of the human ear. And since quantization noise is directly related to the number of bits, even softer passages that do not use the full dynamic range of the system should sound cleaner.

This discussion assumes that we are using a linear PCM scheme that stores each sample as an integer representing the value of each sample. Blesser (1978), Moorer (1979b), and Pohlmann (1989a) review the implications of other encoding schemes, which convert sound into decimal numbers, fractions, differences between successive samples, and so on. Other encoding schemes usually have the goal of reducing the total number of bits that the system must store. For some applications, like compact disc media that mix images with audio data (CD-ROM, CD-I, etc.), it may be necessary to compromise dynamic range by storing fewer bits in order to fit all needed information on the disk. Another way to save space is, of course, to reduce the sampling rate.

Oversampling

So far we have mainly discussed linear PCM converters. A linear PCM DAC transforms a sample into an analog voltage in essentially one straightforward step. In contrast to linear PCM converters, oversampling converters use more samples in the conversion stage than are actually stored in the recording medium. The theory of oversampling is an advanced topic, however, and for our purposes here it is sufficient to present the basic ideas, leaving ample references for those who wish to investigate the topic further.

Oversampling is not one technique but a family of methods for increasing the accuracy of converters. We distinguish between two different types of oversampling:

1. Multiple-bit oversampling DACs developed for compact disc players in the early 1980s by engineers at the Philips company (van de Plassche 1983; van de Plassche and Dijkmans 1984)

2. 1-bit oversampling with *sigma-delta modulation* or a related method as used in more recent ADCs and DACs (Adams 1990; Hauser 1991)

The first method converts a number of bits (e.g., 16) at each tick of the sampling clock, while the second method converts just one bit at a time, but at a very high sampling frequency. The distinction between multibit and 1-bit systems is not always clear, since some converters use a combination of these two approaches. That is, they perform multibit oversampling first, and then turn this into a 1-bit stream that is again oversampled.

Multiple-bit Oversampling Converters

In the mid-1980s many CD manufacturers used a DAC chip set designed by Philips that introduced the benefits of oversampling technology to home listeners. These converters take advantage of the fact that digital filters can provide a much more linear phase response than the steep brickwall analog filters used in regular DACs. (ADCs based on this concept have also been made, but we restrict the discussion here to the DAC side.) In a CD player, 44,100 16-bit samples are stored for each second per channel, but on playback they may be *upsampled* four times (to 176.4 KHz) or eight times (to 352.8 KHz), depending on the system. The is accomplished by interpolating three (or seven) new 16-bit samples in between every two original samples. At the same time all of the samples are filtered by a linear phase digital filter, instead of a phase-distorting brickwall analog filter. (This digital filter is a *finite-impulse-response* filter; see chapter 10.)

Besides phase linearity, a main benefit of oversampling is a reduction in quantization noise—and an increase in signal-to-noise ratio—over the audio bandwidth. This derives from a basic principle of converters stating that the total quantization noise power corresponds to the resolution of the converter, independent of its sampling rate. This noise is, in theory, spread evenly across the entire bandwidth of the system. A higher sampling rate spreads a constant amount of quantization noise over a wider range of frequencies. Subsequent lowpass filtering eliminates the quantization noise power above the audio frequency band. As a result, a four-times over-sampled recording has 6 dB less quantization noise (equivalent to adding another bit of resolution), and an eight-times oversampled recording has 12 dB less noise. The final stage of the systems is a gently sloping analog lowpass filter that removes all components above, say, 30 KHz, with insignificant audio band phase shift.

1-bit Oversampling Converters

Although the theory of 1-bit oversampling converters goes back to the 1950s (Cutler 1960), it took many years for this technology to become incorporated into digital audio systems. The 1-bit oversampling converters constitute a family of different techniques that are variously called *sigma-delta, delta-sigma, noise-shaping, bitstream,* or *MASH* converters, depending on the manufacturer. They have the common thread that they sample one bit at a time, but at high sampling frequencies. Rather than trying to represent the entire waveform in a single sample, these converters measure the differences between successive samples.

1-bit converters take advantage of a fundamental law of information theory (Shannon and Weaver 1949), which says that one can trade off sample width for sample rate and still convert at the same resolution. That is, a 1-bit converter that "oversamples" at 16 times the stored sample rate is equivalent to a 16-bit converter with no oversampling. They both process the same number of bits. The benefits of oversampling accrue when the number of bits being processed is greater than the number of input bits.

From the standpoint of a user, the rate of oversampling in a 1-bit converter can be a confusing specification, since it does not necessarily indicate how many bits are being processed or stored. One way to try to decipher oversampling specifications is to determine the total number of bits being processed, according to the relation:

oversampling factor × *width of converter.*

For example, a "128-times oversampling" system that uses a 1-bit converter is processing 128 × 1 bits each sample period. This compares to a traditional 16-bit linear converter that handles 1 × 16 bits, or 8 times less data. In theory, the 1-bit converter should be much cleaner sounding. In practice, however, making this kind of determination is sometimes confounded by converters that use several stages of oversampling and varying internal bit widths.

In any case, all the benefits of oversampling accrue to 1-bit converters, including increased resolution and phase linearity due to digital filtering. High sampling rates that are difficult to achieve with the technology of multibit converters are much easier to implement with 1-bit converters. Oversampling rates in the MHz range permit 20-bit quantization per sample.

Another technique used in 1-bit oversampling converters is *noise shaping*, which can take many forms (Hauser 1991). The basic idea is that the "requantization" error that occurs in the oversampling process is shifted into a high-frequency range—out of the audio bandwidth—by a highpass filter in a feedback loop with the input signal. This *noise-shaping loop* sends only the requantization error through the highpass filter, not the audio signal.

The final stage of any oversampling converter is a decimator/filter that reduces the sampling rate of the signal to that required for storage (for an ADC) or playback (for a DAC) and also lowpass filters the signal. In the case of a noise shaping converter this decimator/filter also removes the requantization noise, resulting in dramatic improvements in signal-to-noise ratio. With *second-order noise shaping* (so called because of the second-order highpass filter used in the feedback loop), the maximum signal-to-noise level of a 1-bit converter is approximately equivalent to 15 dB (2.5

bits) per octave of oversampling, minus a fixed 12.9 dB penalty (Hauser 1991). Thus an oversampling factor of 29 increases the signal-to-noise ratio of a 16-bit converter by the equivalent of 10 bits or 60 dB.

For more details on the internals of oversampling noise-shaping converters, see Adams (1986, 1990), Adams et al. (1991), and Fourré, Schwarzenbach, and Powers (1990). Hauser (1991) has written a survey paper that explains the history, theory, and practice of oversampling techniques in tutorial form and contains many additional references.

Digital Audio Media

Audio samples can be stored on any digital medium: tape, disk, or integrated circuit, using any digital recording technology, for example, electromagnetic, magneto-optical, or optical. Using a given medium, data can be written in a variety of *formats*. A format is a kind of *data structure* (see chapter 2). For example, some manufacturers of digital audio workstations implement a proprietary format for storing samples on a hard disk. For both technological and marketing reasons, new media and formats appear regularly. Table 1.2 lists some media and their distinguishing features.

Some media are capable of handling more bits per second and so have the potential for higher-quality recording. For example, certain digital tape recorders can encode 20-bits per sample with appropriate converters (Angus and Faulkner 1990). A hard disk can handle 20-bit samples at rates in excess of 100 KHz (for a certain number of channels at a time), while for semiconductor media (memory chips) the potential sample width and sampling rate are much greater.

Another characteristic of media is lifespan. Archival-quality optical disks made of etched tempered glass and plated with gold will last decades and can be played many thousands of times (Digipress 1991). Magnetic media like DAT and floppy disks are inexpensive and portable, but not nearly as robust.

An outstanding advantage of digital storage media is that one can transfer the bits from one medium to another with no loss. (This assumes compatibility between machines and absence of copy-protection circuits, of course.) One can clone a recording any number of times—from the original or from any of the copies. It also means that one can transfer a recording from an inexpensive serial medium (such as DAT) to a random-access medium (such as disk) that is more suited to editing and processing. After one is done editing, one can transfer the samples back to DAT. These transfers

Table 1.2   Digital audio media

Medium	Serial or random access	Notes
Stationary head (magnetic tape)	Serial	Typically used for professional multitrack (24, 32, 48 track) recording; several formats coexist; limited editing.
Rotary head videotape (magnetic tape)	Serial	Professional and consumer formats; consumer videocassettes are inexpensive; two machines needed for assembly editing (see Chapter 16); several tape formats (U-matic, Beta, VHS, 8 mm, etc.) and three incompatible international video encoding formats (NTSC, PAL, SECAM)
Rotary head audiotape (magnetic tape)	Serial	Professional Nagra-D format for four-channel location recording.
Digital Audio Tape (DAT) (magnetic tape)	Serial	Small portable cassettes and recorders; compatible worldwide; some machines handle SMPTE timecode (see Chapter 21)
Digital Compact Cassette (DCC) (magnetic tape)	Serial	A digitat format that can also be used in traditional analog cassette recorders. Uses data compression. Inferior sound quality as compared to CD format.
Hard disks (magnetic and optical)	Random	Nonremovable hard disks are faster (several milliseconds access time); removable hard disks are convenient for backup and transporting of sound samples. Note: a removable optical hard disk attached to a computer is usually not the same format as an audio CD, though they may look similar.
Floppy diskettes (magnetic)	Random	Floppy disks are small, inexpensive and convenient, but they are slow and can store only short sound files. Not reliable for long-term storage.
Sony Mini Disc (MD) (magnetic)	Random	A floppy disk format for sound that employs data compression. Inferior sound quality with respect to CD format.
Compact disc (optical)	Random	Small thin disc storing maximum of 782 Mbytes for a 74-minute disc; archive-quality disks last decades; can playback images as well as audio. Various levels of audio quality, depending on the application, from speech grade (CD-ROM) to very high

Table 1.2 (cont.)

Medium	Serial or random access	Notes
		fidelity (20-bit format). Slow access and transfer rate compared to other random-access media (Pohlmann 1989b, d)
Semiconductor memory (electronic)	Random	Very fast access time (less than 80 nanoseconds typically); excellent for temporary storage (for editing) but too expensive for large databases.

are accomplished through *digital input/output connectors* (hardware jacks on the playback and recording systems) and *standard digital audio transmission formats* (software protocols for sending audio data between devices; see chapter 22).

Synthesis and Signal Processing

As we have seen, sampling transforms acoustical signals into binary numbers, making possible digital audio recording. For musical purposes, the applications of sampling go beyond recording, to *synthesis* and *signal processing*. Synthesis is the process of generating streams of samples by algorithmic means. The six chapters in part II enumerate the many possible paths to synthesis.

Signal processing transforms streams of samples. In music we use signal processing tools to sculpt sound waves into aesthetic forms. Typical audio applications of signal processing include the following:

- Dynamic range (amplitude) manipulations—reshaping the amplitude profile of a sound

- Mixing—combining multiple tracks of audio, including crossfading

- Filters and equalizers—changing the frequency spectrum of the sound

- Time-delay effects—echoes, chorus effect, flanging, phasing

- Convolution—simultaneous time-domain and frequency-domain transformations

- Spatial projection, including reverberation

- Noise reduction—cleaning up bad recordings

- Sample rate conversion—with or without pitch shift
- Sound analysis, transformation, and resynthesis
- Time compression/expansion—changing duration without affecting pitch, or vice versa

Although it is a relatively new field, *digital signal processing* (DSP) has blossomed into a vast theoretical science and applied art. Parts III and IV explain essential concepts of DSP as they pertain to music.

Conclusion

This chapter has introduced fundamental concepts of digital audio recording and playback. This technology continues to evolve. In the realms of AD and DA conversion, signal processing, and storage technology—where there is always room for improvement—we can look forward to new developments for many years to come.

While recording technology marches on, the aesthetics of recording take this technology in two opposing directions. The first is the "naturalist" or "purist" school of recording, which attempts to recreate the ideal concert hall experience with as little artifice as possible. Listening to these recordings, it is as if we are suspended in air (where the microphones are) in the ideal listening location, eavesdropping on a virtuoso performance. The opposite approach, no less valid, is often employed in pop, electronic, and computer music: the creation of an artificial sound stage in which sources can move and we are presented with illusions such as sounds emanating from different spaces simultaneously. These illusions are created by the signal processing operations described in part III.

2   *Music Systems Programming*

Curtis Abbott

Programming is Problem-solving

Basic Elements of Programming Languages
Executing Programs
Flow Graphs and Structured Programming
Procedures
Assignment

Control Structures
Alternation
Repetition

Data Structures
Data Types
Type Declaration
Type-building Operations
Arrays
Records
Pointers and Their Discontents
Somewhat Abstract Data Types
Object-oriented Programming
Inheritance
Highly Abstract Data Types

Programming Language Themes

Functional Programming
Logic Programming
An Example in Lisp and Prolog
Constraint Programming

Conclusion

Programming is necessary in order to do anything really new in computer music. The issues raised by programming not only have practical significance in computer music but are of deep intellectual interest in their own right. Hence this chapter attempts to impart some perspective on programming—not only what it is, but why it is interesting. A single chapter on this vast topic is by necessity condensed, and all we can hope to do is to provide a glimpse of a large endeavor.

We begin by introducing the basic elements of mainstream programming languages, including control and data structures. Then we survey selected advanced themes, including functional programming, logic programming, and constraint programming—all with a view toward music systems programming.

Programming is Problem Solving

Fundamentally, programming is problem solving. Although many qualities of a program can be assessed, including practical aspects like speed and aesthetic concerns such as elegance, the most important test of a program is *correctness*—whether it solves the problem it was designed to solve. This criterion is not as simple as it may first appear. As the problems to which computers are applied become larger and more intertwined with our daily lives, it becomes increasingly difficult to state problems precisely and unambiguously. Without a precise and unambiguous statement of the problem, one cannot readily determine whether a program is correct. Also, when programs are very large or closely coupled to an unpredictable world, it becomes impossible to test them exhaustively.

Thus, programming is a problem-solving process in which the problems are often difficult to define exactly and completely. Indeed, the activities that dominate a creative programming task are often different than either nonprogrammers or programming theorists imagine—thinking about how to make vague problem statements more precise, exploring the consequences of different ways of doing this, discussing the best approach with others (such as potential users, although this happens all too rarely), and so on.

Music systems programming can have all the technical and intellectual challenges of programming generally. Composition problems are notoriously difficult to define precisely and completely, so satisfying one composer's needs may not lead to a universal solution. Sometimes it is better to provide a flexible toolkit that the user can play with than it is to attempt to solve all aspects of a musical problem once and for all. Many musical tasks call for interactions with unpredictable components external to the computer system (such as transducers, synthesizers, or musicians), typically in real time. The demands of real-time performance put special pressure on the software to handle all situations in a timely manner.

Basic Elements of Programming Languages

The earliest attempts to program computers resembled the analog synthesizer studio of yore: users set switches and interconnected the computational units of the computer by means of patch cords (figure 2.1). Today, programs are written in programming languages. Many programming languages exist, and new ones are constantly being developed. Generally, a programming language is designed around a particular way of looking at programming. In this chapter we pay the most attention to the higher-level programming languages that are widely accepted. We do not deal with low-level, machine-oriented code such as assembly languages. Also, we limit ourselves for the most part to *sequential programming*. This means programming for computers that do only one thing at a time. *Parallel programs*, which run on computers that can perform many operations concurrently, are becoming increasingly important, but it is easiest to become familiar with programming by thinking about the sequential case.

We can divide the subject of programming into two broad areas. *Control* has to do with the actions performed by the computer and the order in which they occur, while *data* has to do with objects in the computer's memory on which these actions are performed. In structuring the discussion this way, we are acquiescing to the implicit assumption that computers consist of an active part called a *central processing unit* (often called *CPU* or *processor*) wherein control resides, and a passive part called a *memory* wherein data reside. This is a good assumption for today's computers, but as computers evolve, it may become less good.

Executing Programs

A computer obeys precise and detailed *machine instructions*. A single machine instruction accomplishes little, but when we string together hundreds or thousands of machine instructions we can accomplish useful work. In contrast to machine instructions, programs are written documents, usually

Figure 2.1 Corporal Irwin Goldstein programming the Eniac computer by setting function switches. The Eniac was operational in December 1945. This historic computer contained 18,000 vacuum tubes, 70,000 resistors, 10,000 capacitors, and 6,000 switches. It was 30 meters long, 3 meters high, and 1 meter deep. It is currently in the collection of the Smithsonian Museum, Washington. (Photograph courtesy of the Moore School of Electrical Engineering, University of Pennsylvania.)

written in high-level languages that are easier for human beings to read. Graphical programming languages, such as Max (Puckette and Zicarelli 1990), make the visual aspect even more explicit. Although the examples in this chapter are all textual, virtually every point we make could also apply to graphical languages. Before diving into the details of programming languages, we would do well to understand how high-level language programs are turned into thousands of machine instructions.

A common way to prepare a program for execution is to use a *translator*—a program that translates the program you edit into *executable form* or *object code* (an ordered group of machine instructions). This translator is called a *compiler*. Historically, another approach has been important—this is to use a program called an *interpreter*. An interpreter reads each statement in the program, performs a quick translation of the statement into machine instructions, and then hands the instructions to the computer to execute directly, before moving on to the next program statement. Such an interpreter is acting, in a way, as a different kind of computer, one that executes a much more sophisticated program than any real, hardware computer. One important argument in favor of this approach has been that the translation process carried out by a compiler is relatively slow, since a compiler looks at the program more globally and performs many optimizations based on what it finds. When developing programs, it is important to minimize the time spent waiting to test changes. However, now that powerful computers are cheaper, this argument is less compelling, especially since programs executed by interpreters run much more slowly. (For some programming languages, there are still good arguments in favor of interpreters, but we do not have space to go into them here.)

Flow Graphs and Structured Programming

The executable form of a program is imperative: it contains the machine instructions that tell the processor what to do. However, not every instruction is executed each time the program is run because computers have *conditional instructions* that run a test to determine which instruction to execute next. *Conditional execution* of instructions is a key to the flexibility of computers.

Because instructions may or may not be executed when a program is run, it becomes important to have ways of thinking about patterns of conditional execution. Mathematicians have a convenient structure that they call *graphs*, which computer scientists have adapted as *control flow graphs*. They are drawn with boxes for the groups of instructions that are executed indivisibly, and arrows representing possible paths between them. These drawings are also called *flow charts*, and we will give some examples shortly. The pattern of instruction execution that these graphs represent is called the *flow of control* (or *control flow*) of a program. In this tutorial we introduce programming constructs that provide what is called *structured flow of control*.

The notion of structured flow of control is part of a more general area of *structured programming* (Dahl, Dijkstra, and Hoare 1972), which is an evolving set of rules and ideas for good programming style. Next we highlight various facets of structured programming and show how structured programming ideas apply to data as well as control.

Procedures

The most basic way of structuring a program is to divide it into a collection of *procedures* (also known as *functions*, *subroutines*, or sometimes *methods*). Procedures are ubiquitous in programming. A procedure is a program unit

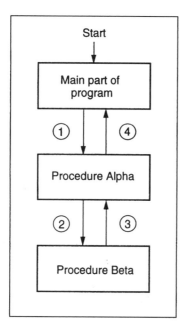

Figure 2.2 Program control flow in a nested procedure call. The main part of the program calls procedure *Alpha*, which in turn calls *Beta*. When *Beta* is done it returns control to *Alpha*, and when *Alpha* is done it returns control to the main program.

that can be *called* or *invoked*, like a mathematical function such as addition or multiplication. Procedures can be *nested*, meaning that one procedure calls another procedure before returning control to the original caller (figure 2.2).

A procedure can have *arguments* (again, like a mathematical function) that allow it to be a unit of activity with flexibility in different circumstances. This is because the arguments to a procedure are specified by the program part that calls it. Often a procedure also returns a *value*—a number or more complex data structure that the calling part can use. This is also analogous to mathematical functions—addition and multiplication generate values from their arguments.

Programming languages typically predefine a number of procedures that are the building blocks of larger programs. Some of these procedures reflect the underlying capabilities of the computer hardware, such as addition and multiplication of numbers. Others provide access to frequently used input/output facilities, such as the ability to store and retrieve files from disks or to display characters on a display. Procedures defined by programmers extend these basic capabilities.

Assignment

Another basic capability provided by most programming languages is *assignment*. Assignment is an operation that changes the value associated with a *variable*. In programs, variables are names for places in memory that hold values. These values can be interpreted in many different ways—as numbers, alphabetic characters, machine instructions, addresses of other memory locations, and so on. Hence, assignment changes the contents of the memory location corresponding to a variable.

In the C language, assignment is written with an equals sign as in

```
a=b;
```

This means the value in the memory location associated with *b* is copied to the memory location associated with *a*. This is very different from what the equals sign means to a mathematician. Some programming languages try to avoid this confusion by writing assignment with a variation of the equals sign. A common convention is to write

```
a:=b;
```

This is the syntax used in the Pascal language, for example. The control constructs in a language operate mostly on assignments and procedure calls, so we discuss them next.

Control Structures

Besides procedures and assignment, programming languages have operations that deal with flow of control. The simplest way that control can flow through a program is sequentially: each program statement is executed in order.

Alternation

Some control structures allow a program to define two or more *alternative* execution paths. When control reaches such a structure, one path is selected, based on a test, and control passes to the selected path.

Control structures based an alternation can be diagrammed in a flow graph as a structure that branches out and then comes back together again. Figure 2.3 shows several of these structures, using circles to denote tests

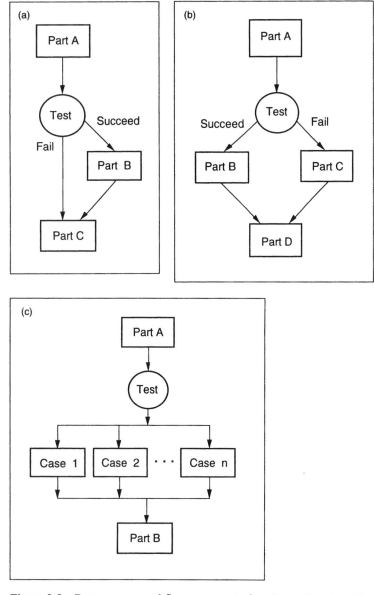

Figure 2.3 Program control flow constructs for alternation. (*a*) **if-then**. (*b*) **if-then-else**. (*c*) **case**.

(parts of the program that decide on the alternative to be executed) and
square boxes to denote the possible alternatives.

The simplest case of alternation is when there is one section of a program
that we may not want to execute. This is expressed with an **if-then** construct.
Here is the format of this construct:

```
if <test> then <program part>
```

The ⟨*test*⟩ corresponds to the circle in figure 2.3a, which decides whether or
not the ⟨*program part*⟩ is going to be executed.

A slightly more complicated instance of alternation is when one of two
different program parts should be selected. This is shown in figure 2.3b. It is
expressed in programming languages by extending **if-then** with **else**. The
format of this expression is

```
if <test> then <part 1> else <part 2>
```

The general case for selecting one of several alternatives is handled in a
variety of ways in existing programming languages. One way is by cas-
cading **if-then-else** constructs as in the following schematic example:

```
if <first test> then <part 1>
else if <second test> then <part 2>
...
else if <last test> then <part n>
```

An interesting generalization of this is the *guarded command list* proposed
by Dijkstra (1976). This is a list of tests and consequents that generalizes the
cascaded **if-then-else** by specifying that if more than one of the tests succeeds, any one of the associated consequents can be executed. This is potentially useful because it may allow us to express our thinking about the
underlying situation more clearly, without having to specify the order in
which the tests are performed. Despite its elegance, the guarded command
list has not become widely used.

Another commonly available construct is **case**. It is useful when a set of
alternatives depends on the value of a single expression. The format of this
construct is something like this:

```
case <expression>
    <first value>⇒<part 1>
    <second value>⇒<part 2>
...
    <last value>⇒<part n>
```

where the symbol ⇒ indicates that control is passed to the corresponding program part. This is essentially equivalent to the following **if-then-else** cascade:

```
if <expression>=<first value> then <part 1>
else if <expression>=<second value> then <part 2>
...
else if <expression>=<last value> then <part n>
```

The **case** construct is better not only because it makes the control structure clearer to the human reader but because the selection of the appropriate program part can often be made much faster by the computer.

Repetition

Another important pattern of control flow is the repetition of a program section over and over again, which is often called *looping*. Here it is necessary to specify how many times the repetition occurs and how the repetition terminates. A typical construct for repetition is the **while** construct, for which the format is

```
while <test> do <program part>
```

The effect of this is to evaluate the ⟨*test*⟩ before each execution of the ⟨*program part*⟩. Repetition terminates when the ⟨*test*⟩ fails. Figure 2.4 shows the flow graph of a **while** construct.

Programming languages have many constructs for repetition. Some constructs put the test after the program part (which guarantees that the program part is executed at least once), and some invert the sense of the test (which causes repetition until the test succeeds).

A more important variation on this theme are constructs that support the use of *auxiliary variables* associated with the repetition. Auxiliary variables are useful for enumerating the elements of collections of data, whether these collections are organized as matrices, lists, sets, or anything else. Here the possibilities for variation are enormous, and programming languages exhibit considerable diversity in the constructs that they provide for this kind of repetition. A canonical example is the **for** statement in Pascal (Jensen and Wirth 1974). The format of the **for** construct is as follows:

```
for <auxiliary variable> :=<initial value> to
  <final value> do <program part>
```

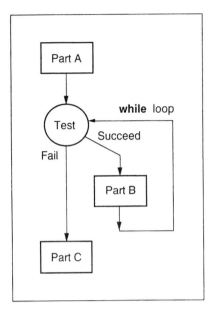

Figure 2.4 Flow graph of a **while** construct. The repetition of *Part B* continues while the tested condition is true. Otherwise the program goes on to *Part C*.

Here ⟨*auxiliary variable*⟩ is an integer that is newly created to go with the **for** statement. Its ⟨*initial value*⟩ is incremented after every repetition. Repetition continues until the variable attains the ⟨*final value*⟩.

The Pascal **for** construct has special restrictions that provide a good example of the constraints facing language designers. The restrictions are as follows:

1. The ⟨*auxiliary variable*⟩ cannot be changed except in the way shown— by incrementing before every repetition.

2. The ⟨*final value*⟩ is only evaluated once, before the repetition starts.

These two rules ensure that when a Pascal **for** loop begins, the number of repetitions is known. The advantage of this is that the **for** loop always terminates and can never run wild. The disadvantage is that, in some situations, it is inconvenient or impossible to determine in advance how many times the loop should be executed. (In this case, one must use the **while** construct in Pascal.)

It is interesting to compare the Pascal **for** construct with the analogous construct in C (Kernighan and Ritchie 1978). The format of the C **for** statement is as follows:

```
for (<initialize>; <test>; <increment>)
 <program part>
```

The use of this construct is similar to that of the **for** statement in Pascal. However, it is easier to understand the C **for** statement as a set of instructions for rewriting the components of the construct, because there are no restrictions as there are in Pascal. In particular, the ⟨*initialize part*⟩ is executed, then if the ⟨*test*⟩ succeeds, the ⟨*program part*⟩ is executed followed by the ⟨*increment part*⟩ and then back to the ⟨*test*⟩ again. This **for** loop can be viewed as a convenience, allowing programmers to write loops in a clear, concise way. By contrast, the Pascal **for** loop, by introducing restrictions and an auxiliary variable, is less general, but at the same time, it is better adapted to the situations it applies to.

These examples hardly exhaust the possibilities for repetitive constructs. Knuth (1974) contains a fascinating and accessible discussion of iterative constructs.

Data Structures

Inside any computer, data are represented in terms of *bits* (binary digits) of memory, which can take the values 1 or 0. These bits are organized into *bytes* and *words*. Bytes are (almost universally) 8-bit quantities that can represent many characters in Western alphabets. Hence, bytes are often used to represent alphanumeric characters.

Words are the "natural units" of operation on data in a computer, so the number of bits in a word varies from computer to computer. Today the most common computers use 32- or 64-bit words, but this was not true in the past and may not be true in the future.

It is important to understand the versatility of computer words. To illustrate, consider figure 2.5, which shows a 16-bit word and several interpretations of it. For our purposes, the specific interpretations are unimportant. Rather, we wish to illustrate that the interpretation of a bit pattern must be known if it is to have any meaning. This leads to our next concept, *data types*.

Data Types

The *type* of a data object (one or more computer words) refers how it is interpreted. Thus we say that the type of a data object x is integer, floating-point number, character, and so on.

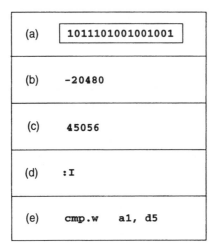

Figure 2.5 A 16-bit computer word and some possible interpretations of it. (*a*) Binary representation. (*b*) Two's complement integer. (*c*) Unsigned integer. (*d*) ASCII characters. (*e*) Machine instruction.

At the hardware level of "raw" computer memory and the machine operations that act on it, only a few types are available. Thus, if we were to stop a program and randomly look at a word in memory, it would be difficult to know for sure what that word represents. It could be an sample value, a small number of characters, a reference to another data object, a machine instruction, or any number of other things. One of the important jobs of a programming language is to present the programmer with an appropriate notion of type for the kind of problems the language is designed to solve. Usually this notion is somewhat different from that found at the machine level and is, as we say, "higher level." Thus, one of the jobs of the programming language *implementation* (that is, the compiler or other program that makes programs in a higher-level language execute on the machine) is to translate between the different notions of type provided by the two levels.

The question of just what notion of type is appropriate has always been controversial, and remains so. We have hinted that it depends on the kinds of problems the programming language is designed to be used for. This is generally acknowledged as a matter of principle, but it muddies the waters enough to make precise, technical discussions difficult. As we shall see, some of the most successful programming languages use a notion of type that is quite close to that provided by the vast majority of computers. On the other hand, much of the academic work that drives advances in programming language design has focused on more abstract notions of type.

Type Declaration

To make an already confusing subject a good deal more confusing still, there is controversy not only about what notion of type should be embodied in programming languages but also about whether these types should be visible in the written form of the program. In languages that make types visible, we say that variables and procedures are *declared*, along with their types. A declaration, in this context, is just a statement that a particular thing (variable, procedure, etc.) has a specific type. For example, we might say

```
integer v1;
```

to declare that the variable *v1* has type **integer**. There are two main arguments for explicit type declarations. One is that the translators can use the information in the declarations to catch programming errors and make the program execute more efficiently. The other argument is that declarations make programs easier for people to understand.

When the types of variables and procedures are not declared in a programming language, it is conventional to say that the language is *untyped*. This is extremely misleading! Any programming language embodies some notion of type, and its translator must deal with computer hardware that embodies a different notion. What is different about a language without required declarations is that the translator takes full responsibility for ensuring that the correct interpretation is given to all data according to its implicit notion of type. A common argument for "untyped" languages is that declaring types is too much work. This argument becomes less persuasive as programs become larger, longer-lived, and harder to understand.

The programming languages that are most commonly used in industry have type declarations. Several of the languages discussed in the last part of this chapter (Lisp, Smalltalk, Prolog) have no declarations, or optional declarations.

To summarize what we have said so far, words of computer memory represent data objects. These objects are characterized by their type, which determines how the computer interprets the data object. A programming language also provides a notion of type, which is sometimes quite different from the notion provided at the machine level. Controversy surrounds the issue of what notion of type is appropriate in programming languages, and to some extent, the answer depends on what applications the language is intended for. There is also some controversy about whether types should be declared, or whether such declarations should be optional.

Let us now consider some common properties of types in more detail. The simplest types are *atomic,* that is, not divisible into simpler types. Examples of atomic types are integers, floating-point numbers, and characters. In general, atomic types are directly supported at the machine level of the computer system, in the sense that the computer has hardware for operations on integers, floating-point numbers, and characters.

Type-building Operations

Programming languages generally provide ways of building up more complex types out of primitive ones. In examining these type-building operations, we will see some good examples of both abstract and concrete approaches to types.

Arrays

As a first example consider the *array,* which is a collection of items that can be selected by looking it up with an *index.* All the items in the array have the same type. If *A* is an array of type *X*, then we select an *X* by indexing *A*. The indexing operation is usually written $A[i]$, where *i* is the index. The indexed value can also be assigned to, thus the statement

```
A[i]=1023.99;
```

sets the *i*th element of the floating-point number array *A* to 1023.99. Arrays are usually implemented directly as blocks of memory in the underlying computer. The indexes provide a convenient way to access different parts of these memory blocks. As a result of the directness of the implementation, the type of the index value is restricted in most languages. In some languages, indexes are integers from 0 to some maximum, which is fixed when the array is initially declared. In other languages, one or another of these restrictions is removed, with corresponding extra complexity in the implementation.

The form of array declarations depends to some extent on what restrictions are in force in a given language. For example, in a language with integer indexes starting at 0 and a fixed size, only the size and the item type is required, so a statement like the following:

```
array[12] of pitch;
```

might declare an array of twelve items of type *pitch*, indexed by the integers from to 0 to 11. If we can specify both the lower and upper bound, the declaration looks like this:

```
array[19,108] of MIDI-pitch;
```

might declare an array of 88 equal-tempered pitches indexed by the integers from 19 to 108 according to the norms of the MIDI protocol. (See chapter 21 for more on MIDI.)

Arrays can also be *multidimensional*. This means that two or more indexes are required to identify an element of the array. A two-dimensional array can represent a *matrix*, which mathematically is a linear operator on a *vector space*. Since matrices and vector spaces are tremendously important in the scientific use of mathematics, arrays have always been important in scientific computation.

Arrays are common in computer music programs, since a one-dimensional array can represent the amplitude values of an audio waveform or envelope, while a two-dimensional array can represent the probabilities in a Markov chain for composition (see chapter 19) or the pitches of a *magic square* (showing a twelve-tone row in all its transpositions).

Records

Arrays provide one way of organizing a collection of similar kinds of data objects. Another type-building operation handles *records*, which allow programmers to organize heterogenous types of data objects. Each distinct kind of information within a record is called a *component* of the record. Sometimes components are called *slots* or *members* of the record.

Records are useful because they allow programmers to express logical associations, bringing together things that belong together. Properly used, they make programs easier to understand. For example, one might use a record to collect information about several aspects of a note: its pitch, register, duration, and so on. Records are declared as a list of names and types for the components:

```
record
     pitch : character-string;
     register : integer;
     duration : integer;
     ...
end
```

A collection of such records forms a *database*. Indeed, the notion of records was first made available in the Cobol programming language, which was designed for databases and related business applications. But records are much more widely useful, as we will see.

Pointers and Their Discontents

Array and record types are fundamental ways of organizing data, since they bring together collections of data objects into a single, more manageable object. Another fundamental notion is different. A *pointer* type represents a reference to a data object, where the reference is viewed as an object itself. Thus, if X is a type, the type **pointer to** X is the type of data objects that refer to Xs. Pointers have a *dereferencing* operation associated with them. Dereferencing a **pointer to** X gives an X, namely the one the pointer points to. The dereferencing operation is often written with an asterisk, so **ptr* dereferences the pointer *ptr* to produce the value it points to. Given a pointer to something, one can generally change its value with an assignment statement that uses the dereferencing operation. So pointers are like array elements in this way, and also a bit like variables.

When we say that a pointer *refers* to something else, we mean something quite simple—much simpler than reference in natural languages. Determining the reference in an English expression like "the one with the click" can be difficult to decide. In contrast, the notion of reference for pointers is simple. A pointer is implemented as a memory word whose contents are interpreted as the address of another memory word (namely the address where the pointed-to object resides). So the pointer refers to whatever is at the memory address that is the pointer's value.

Although the basic notion is simple, its ramifications are not. The idea of systematically interpreting a computer memory word as the address of another memory word is a fundamental programming technique. It is absolutely essential for doing anything useful or interesting with computers. The justification is a little subtle. Computer memories are addressed in a strictly linear fashion. (That is, there is a memory word whose address is 0, then a word whose address is 1, and so on.) Most problems do not fit into this linear straightjacket. The pointer technique (that is, the technique of interpreting memory words as addresses of other memory words) can be used to make a linearly addressed memory mimic any kind of structure conceivable. Learning in detail how to do this is one of the important aspects of learning how to program.

In order to see how pervasive this notion of interpreting values as addresses can be, let us go back to the array for a moment and think about it. Suppose we have an array A of integers (that is, of memory words), indexed by integers from 0 to 3999. This is like a memory array of 4000 words. Since it both contains and is indexed by integers, we can do the same trick with it as pointers do with the underlying computer memory. An expression like $A[A[12]]$ means to interpret the integer at $A[12]$ as an index (address) and

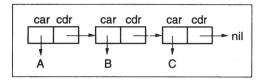

Figure 2.6 A Lisp list **(A B C)** represented as three cons cells. Each cons cell has two pointers. The car of the cons points to the value, while the cdr points to the next cons cell in the list. The final cdr points to **nil**; that is, the cdr contains zero. This indicates the end of the list.

return the value of the array at that index. Indeed, this trick with arrays is widespread in languages that do not have explicit pointer types.

The Lisp programming language does something a good deal more interesting. In so doing it provides a strong piece of evidence for the claim made previously that pointers can be used to map a linearly addressed array into any kind of structure at all. (Note: the following description is not strictly true of modern dialects of Lisp, but accurately reflects their general flavor.) Memory structures in the Lisp world are made up of *conses*—little objects that point to two other objects, which can be other conses or more basic things like numbers (figure 2.6). With conses, you can build lists and a myriad of other strange and wonderful structures. The Lisp world of conses is implemented in the underlying linear array of computer memory hardware.

Pointers are extremely powerful and useful, but with their power and utility come certain dangers. To see why, let us go back to that array again. Earlier we wrote $A[A[12]]$ to interpret the value of $A[12]$ as an index. But suppose the value of $A[12]$ is not a valid index (i.e., an integer between 0 and 3999)? Also, we are now intepreting elements of A in at least two ways, as numbers and as indexes. $A[12]$, at least, is an index, and the item it indexes is a number. There are many ways to make mistakes, many possible confusions.

Because of this danger, the explicit provision of pointers in programming languages has always been a controversial matter. As with other things, the right answer depends on what the programming language is for. The C language is among those in which pointers are provided in an unabashed way, but this is in keeping with its design as a *systems programming language*—one that hews fairly close to the underlying computer. The Lisp language does not have pointers at all, although they are ubiquitous in its implementation, partly because its design goals are so different.

An example of the use of pointers should help make this discussion more concrete. A canonical example is creating *linked lists*. A linked list is a

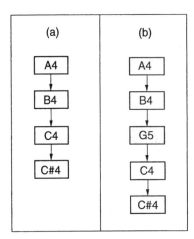

Figure 2.7 A linked list data structure of a melody, containing quoted strings representing pitch names. The last pointer value, to **nil**, is omitted in this figure. (*a*) Original melody. (*b*) New melody made by changing the pointer from "B4" and adding a new element "G5."

collection of records, each of the same type, where each component of each record is a pointer to the succeeding element in the linked list. Figure 2.6 showed a simple linked list as it is represented implicitly in Lisp. The following code is an explicit programming example:

```
linked_list_node record
     pitch : string;
     next_node : pointer to linked_list_node;
end
```

This record has two parts: a part called *pitch* that contains a quoted string, and a pointer called *next_node* that points to another *linked_list_node* record. Linked lists are often drawn as a simple box and arrow diagram, as in figure 2.7.

A more sophisticated example is a linked list record with two pointers. This models a common data structure called a *binary tree*. In a binary tree (figure 2.8), each node can have two branches:

```
linked_list_node record
          starting_time : integer;
          left_node : pointer to linked_list_node;
          right_node: pointer to linked_list_node;

end
```

A binary tree is a good representation to use when editing the performance schedule of a multiple-voice composition. Information organized as

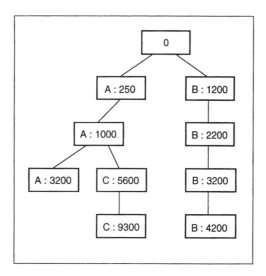

Figure 2.8   A linked list of nodes drawn as a binary tree graph, in which each node can have two subnodes. The characters in each node represent a performance schedule for three musical voices. The numbers in each node indicate the starting time in milliseconds of each event.

a binary tree can also be searched efficiently, so this data structure is a common one in computer science (Knuth 1973b).

These linked list examples bring up a number of issues. One of these is the way linked lists are used. Typically, linked lists are *traversed* by a program that follows the pointer in the subnode components until it reaches a special value that indicates that the end of the list has been reached. One of the things that makes linked lists useful is that it is easy to add or delete elements at any point in the list, by manipulating the value of the pointer components. This stands in contrast to arrays, where inserting a value in the middle of the array means that every value to the right of a new element must be shifted by one index value to the right to make room for the new element. Growing and shrinking arrays is time-consuming, whereas adding and deleting elements to a linked list is efficient.

Many programming environments provide standard procedures such as *insert_node* and *delete_node* for manipulating linked list data types. This idea of associating procedures with data types has been important in programming language research and has been adopted in different ways by two research communities, working respectively on *abstract data types* and *object-oriented programming*. We have more to say about both later.

Another issue raised by our linked list examples is the following. Suppose that, having defined the binary tree linked list, we now need another tree in which *starting_time* is not an integer, but a floating-point number. In most programming languages, this can only be done by defining a new data type and giving it a different name. This is bad, for at least two reasons. For the human reader, it tends to obfuscate the common pattern of use of all these record types (namely, as linked lists). From a technical point of view, many of the procedures associated with these data types (such as the ones for adding and deleting elements, and counting the number of elements by traversing the list) are exactly the same across all linked list data types.

One experimental approach to clearing up this difficulty is with *polymorphic* data types. Roughly, a polymorphic type takes an argument which is itself a type. A list is a good candidate: we can have lists of integers, of floating-point numbers, and of infinitely many other types of things.

Somewhat Abstract Data Types

Early work in programming language design concentrated on control issues, for example, what sorts of alternation and looping constructs to provide. Since then it has become clear that the issues surrounding data are much more difficult but also more important. This is because data structures in a program model parts of a world (real or imagined). In view of the importance of data structuring, it should not be surprising that there are a number of different research strands concerned with it.

One basic insight is that a data type is defined both by data structure (records, arrays, pointers, and so on) and by the *operations* it permits. Usually it is only these privileged operations that have access to the data—others must obtain access via the operations. We say that the operations *encapsulate* the data, and this is an important theme with many benefits.

At least two distinct sets of researchers have developed languages with data types designed around procedures that encapsulate their data. One group started from otherwise traditional languages and added constructs for these so-called *abstract data types*. Examples of this work include CLU (Liskov et al. 1979) and Alphard (Wulf, London, and Shaw 1976).The most visible success (and perhaps the culmination) of this work is the language Ada, supported by the United States Government (Department of Defense 1980).

Object-oriented Programming

Another, more diverse group proposed to put even more emphasis on the data and developed an approach called *object-oriented programming*. They also developed new ways of talking about their approach to emphasize its radicalness. In particular, data elements are called *objects*. Data types are called *classes* (at least, most of them are, although more traditional data types can also be present in object-oriented languages). The operations associated with a class are usually called *methods*. Calling a procedure is called *sending a message*. This difference is more than cosmetic. Whereas in traditional programming, all the arguments to a procedure have equal status, in object-oriented programming there is a privileged argument, which is the *receiver* of the message (the object to which it is sent).

Object-oriented programming was pioneered in the language Simula (Dahl and Nygaard 1966; Dahl, Dijkstra, and Hoare 1972), which was designed for programming discrete event simulations, in which time acts on a collection of simulated real-world objects. Although Simula was the first object-oriented programming language, Smalltalk (Goldberg and Robson 1983a,b) has probably been the most influential. Developed over a long period of time at the Xerox Palo Alto Research Center (PARC) and ParcPlace Systems, it has several essential properties that are synonymous with object-oriented programming. Smalltalk is *dynamically typed*, in the sense that variables can hold objects of any class, so that the appropriateness of a message must be checked when it is sent. In other words, Smalltalk is one of those languages sometimes misleadingly referred to as "untyped." Also, Smalltalk-80, the current version of Smalltalk, includes a superb programming environment and provides excellent support for developing graphical user interfaces for music (Krasner 1980; Pope 1991a,b; Scaletti 1989a,b; Scaletti and Hebel 1991).

Inheritance

One of the important contributions of object-oriented programming to data structuring is the idea of *class inheritance*. This means defining new types as variants of existing types (classes), rather than starting from scratch. Inheritance is especially appropriate when one class *specializes* another.

For example, suppose in a performance program we have a class that manages musical keyboards. We call this a **Keyboard** class. It has operations (methods) for translating a key number into a pitch, and for starting a note when a key is struck. Now suppose we need to hook up a *velocity-sensitive keyboard* (i.e., a keyboard that plays louder if you hit the keys harder and therefore faster). Since there are velocity data to be conveyed, we need to rewrite the note-starting operation, but the key-to-pitch translation operation need not change. We can use inheritance to make a **Velocity-Sensitive-Keyboard** class that inherits all the data parts of the **Keyboard** class, possibly adding new ones to deal with velocity information, and that inherits the translation operation while redefining the note-starting operation.

A less commonly available technique in object-oriented programming is *multiple inheritance*. This means that a class can inherit behavior (and data parts) from several other classes. This is an especially useful technique for "mixing in" functionality—adding a new feature to an existing class. For example, we might write a note-recording *mixin* that could be added to any class that has a note instantiation operation, and that would redefine the operation automatically so that its parameters are remembered in an auxiliary array of records each time it is called.

As typical programs grow larger and more complicated, it becomes more important to have facilities for organizing them, incrementally changing them, and so on. Such facilities are a large part of what object-oriented programming is about, and so as the complexity and size of problems increases, object-oriented programming has become increasingly visible and influential in the computing world. Earlier languages (especially Smalltalk) have been somewhat handicapped by slow execution speed, as well as the difficulty of learning them. Consequently, several languages have been developed that add object-oriented facilities to existing mainstream programming languages such as C or Pascal. An example of this trend is the C++ language (Soustrop 1991).

Highly Abstract Data Types

None of the approaches to abstract data types described so far is highly abstract. For example, if you define a class of sets, you must define exactly one implementation (i.e., collection of operations) for it. All sets use that implementation. However, there are a half dozen good ways to implement sets, each appropriate for sets of different sizes and domains. No programming language to date adequately addresses this problem. However, there is another research strand in which the implementation of a data type is given in a very abstract form, which can be viewed as leaving open the possibility for the underlying automatic system to decide how best to implement it. In such approaches, one merely specifies what properties the operations of the data type must satisfy, rather than saying exactly how to execute them. Most commonly, the specification is done with equations. The standard example, which appears hundreds of times in the research literature in this area, describes a *stack*. A stack is a data structure with three operations, **push**, **pop**, and **top.** The **push** operation stores an object on the stack; **pop** removes the most recently stored value, and **top** retrieves the most recently stored value.

These simple rules can be translated into equations as follows. Suppose S is a stack and x is a value. Just two equations define the stack's behavior, given some background assumptions:

pop(**push**(S, x))=S
pop(**push**(S, x))=x

The first equation says that **pop** undoes **push**. The second says that **push** has to remember the pushed value so that **top** can retrieve it.

The key idea behind this abstraction of abstract data types is to interpret the equational definitions as instructions that can effectively carry out the operations so defined. Thus, the equations, which make no reference to computer words and are not instructions in any obvious way, nevertheless become operationally effective. Indeed, we say this is an *operational interpretation* of the equations. From a programming point of view, what is important about this is that we have described the behavior of a stack in a very abstract way, with equations, rather than giving instructions for obtaining that behavior. This is an example of what is called *declarative programming,* discussed later in this chapter.

A good deal of mathematical theory stands behind operational interpretations of equations. The usual first step is to give a *preferred orientation* to the equations, so that they become *rewrite rules,* or in other words, *simplication rules* for expressions involving the given terms (**push**, **pop**, and **top** in our example). Note that in the example, the right-hand sides of both equations are much simpler than the left-hand sides. Thus, the preferred orientation is left to right. Often an orientation can be assigned, sometimes it can even be done automatically. Sometimes, however, it cannot be done at all, much less automatically. For example, a common algebraic law is commutativity. For the addition operator ($+$), it is written as the following equation:

$$x + y = y + x.$$

The intuitive interpretation is that the order of the arguments to the addition operator does not matter. This equation cannot be given a preferred orientation; the intuitive reason is that neither side is simpler than the other.

The automatic interpretation of very abstract specifications is a desirable goal, but one which is fraught with difficulties. These include many theoretical results showing that various problems are strictly unsolvable, in the sense defined by Gödel, Turing, and other mathematical pioneers. One of these is the problem of determining whether a preferred orientation can be automatically assigned to equations.

Besides this, the equational level of abstraction does not address the practical problem raised at the beginning of this section concerning abstract data types, such as sets, for which different implementations are appropriate according to the circumstances. For this, a more down-to-earth approach is needed. So far, no one has done a convincing job of it.

Programming Language Themes

Up until now we have explored programming by looking at control and data aspects. We conclude with a brief survey of three of the most important themes in programming research: functional programming, logic programming, and constraint programming.

Functional Programming

Functional programming is an approach that says the most important tool we can bring to bear in our problem-solving efforts is the *mathematical function*. A mathematical function defines a certain kind of relationship between a collection of inputs (called *arguments*) and a single output (called the *result*), namely, that for each distinct set of arguments, there is a unique output that is always the same. This is obviously an appropriate point of view when we are concerned with arithmetic operations on numbers. It can be extended in a natural way to many other situations, and it is, indeed, a way of thinking that is often useful. At the beginning of this chapter we stated that procedures are the single most important organizational device for programs, and procedures most closely mimic mathematical functions.

Functional programming is distinguished by its insistence that its "procedures" should depend not at all on context, but should always return the same result given the same inputs. This becomes problematical with operations that receive input from the outside world (as all interactive computer music programs do) or that affect the outside world in some way (and any program that does not is useless). Naturally, functional programming advocates have answers to this objection and others.

Rather than delve any further into controversies about the universality of the functional approach, we wish to point out some of the inarguably valuable work that has been done under its auspices. Functional programming arises historically from mathematical work by Church, who invented the *lambda calculus* (Church 1941) in order to study functions. The lambda calculus inspired the Lisp programming language, which was originally a functional language.

Much important knowledge that is now considered basic to computing came out of research that resulted from the juxtaposition of computers and the lambda calculus. For example, this research clarified the notion of the *recursive procedure* and affected programming practice by showing how in many cases such procedures can be extremely useful. (A recursive procedure is one that can be viewed operationally as calling itself, or more abstractly, as being defined partly in terms of itself. It is also possible to have *mutual recursion*, in which a collection of procedures are all defined in a mutually referential way.) Another valuable strand of work identified a set of ordering strategies for evaluation of functions and their arguments, demonstrating that the most obvious and cheapest implementation strategy may lead to a nonterminating computation in cases where a more expensive strategy would not.

Historically, functional programming surfaced early, in the form of Lisp. As Lisp developed, it became more pragmatic and lost its functional purity. The most widely used modern form of Lisp is Common Lisp, a large programming environment that brings together several Lisp dialects (Steele 1984). Scheme, a dialect of Lisp that has itself spawned other dialects, attempts to restore the benefits of compactness and purity (Abelson and Sussman 1985).

For a time functional programming was viewed as inefficient and therefore impractical. But functional programming has resurfaced, and an important motive is its potential use on parallel computers. There are a couple of reasons for this. First, if functions really are "pure" (in the sense of always returning the same result for the same arguments), then all the arguments to a function can be evaluated in parallel, and all of their arguments, and so on. Second, functional programming appears to be well suited to problems where large, uniform data sets (such as vectors, matrices, etc.) are acted on by functional operators; this leads to many opportunities for so-called "data parallelism" (Hillis 1987).

Logic Programming

The lambda calculus is one important mathematical development in this century. The *predicate calculus* is an even more important development, although one that began in the last century. A predicate can be thought of as a function that returns either true or false, and predicate calculus is the foundation of mathematical logic.

As functional programming is inspired by the lambda calculus, so *logic programming* is inspired by the predicate calculus. The predicate calculus can be viewed as a language with which to talk about mathematical theorems. An operational interpretation of the predicate calculus would be a theorem prover. Indeed, this is the correct abstract point of view to take with logic programming.

Earlier we described the equational approach to data types as a very abstract one, and pointed out that many problems within that area are strictly unsolvable. This is also true of the predicate calculus. Thus, the game in logic programming is to find restricted forms of the predicate calculus or restricted theorem-proving strategies that make things computationally tractable while still retaining whatever advantage there might be to stating things in an abstract form similar to mathematical theorems.

By far the most popular logic programming language is Prolog (Clocksin and Mellish 1987), and the source of its popularity is a set of clever ideas that allow Prolog programs to be executed quite efficiently. A Prolog program can be viewed as a set of declarations in a restricted form of the predicate calculus called *Horn clauses*. By stating relations among predicates, these declarations in effect define the predicates. The idea is similar to the equational definitions we saw earlier, except that the relationship between left and right sides is not one of equality but of *implication*. That is, the left-hand side is true if the right-hand side is true. One important difference between this approach and functional programming is that the predicates can represent arbitrary *relations* as easily as functions. Relations are less restrictive than functions, which makes them more flexible representational vehicles in some cases.

A Prolog program attempts to solve a problem involving a predicate defined by the program, some of whose arguments are *variables*. The program's job is to find one or more solutions for the variables. It does this in a predetermined way, searching the declarations (known as *clauses*) one after the other. When the left-hand side of a clause matches the problem, the Prolog interpreter attempts to solve the right-hand side, in just the same way it goes about solving the original problem. If it reaches an impasse (no clause matches), it *backtracks*, going back to the last clause that matched, giving up on it, and trying to find another matching rule.

The backtracking behavior built into Prolog is very powerful, and convenient for problems involving searches, but also somewhat unpredictable and difficult to control. In practice, many predicates do not require backtracking, and various mechanisms have been introduced to restrict it.

An Example in Lisp and Prolog

In order to convey a more concrete image of both Lisp and Prolog, we present definitions of a simple function in the two languages. This is the function that concatenates two lists, known as **append**. In Lisp, **append** takes two lists as arguments and produces the concatenated list as a result. In Prolog, everything is a predicate, and all the interest is in the arguments, so **append** has three arguments, the third being for the "answer." The Lisp definition is in figure 2.9a; the Prolog definition in figure 2.9b.

(a)

```
(defun append (list1 list2)
      (cond ((null list1) list2)
            ((null list2) list1)
            (t (cons (car list1) (append (cdr list1) list2)))))
```

(b)

```
append([.], X, X).
append(X, [], X).
append([X1 | X2], Y, [X1 | Z]) :- append(X2, Y, Z).
```

Figure 2.9 Definition of the **append** operation. (*a*) Lisp definition. (*b*) Prolog definition.

Let us first explain these definitions. In both Lisp and Prolog, lists are a fundamental data type. In Lisp, expressions are surrounded by parentheses. The first line introduces the definition of a function (**defun**), giving its name and arguments. The definition consists of a single expression whose first word is **cond**. This is a conditional expression, which tests the first part of each subexpression in turn, executing and returning the rest of the first such expression that evaluates to true. Thus, it says in essence: if *list1* is **null** (empty), return *list2*; if *list2* is **null**, return *list1*; otherwise ("t" stands for "true"), return this:

(cons (car *list1*) (append (cdr *list1*) *list2*))

This complicated expression glues together the first element of *list1* with the result of appending the rest of *list1* to *list2*. In other words, this is a recursive definition.

In Prolog, predicate arguments are in parentheses after the name, which is a more traditional mathematical notation. Names starting with a capital letter are variables. Usually clauses have many variables, and **append** is no exception. The first rule in figure 2.9b says that if the initial argument is the empty list (written "[]"), then the second and third arguments are equal. (Remember that the third argument is the "result.") The second rule makes a similar statement about first and third arguments. The third rule, which applies only if neither list is empty (because the first two rules are checked first by a Prolog interpreter), says essentially the same thing as the complicated expression in the Lisp program, in a slightly different way. The right-hand side of the rule is equivalent to Lisp's recursive call to **append**.

No three-line program can tell you very much about a programming language, and this simple example is only intended to give a flavor. Modern Lisp and Prolog compilers execute these programs very quickly.

Constraint Programming

Constraint programming is related to logic programming, although the relationship is obscured by history. Whereas research in logic programming has always been dominated by people well versed in mathematical logic, constraint programming originated in a more intuitive and less rigorous fashion. Most work in this area has been concentrated in certain areas of interest: the solving of geometric constraints (such as keeping lines parallel or perpendicular, etc.), graphics systems (Sutherland 1963; Borning 1979), or constraints imposed by Ohm's law in electrical circuits (Sussman and Steele 1981). More recently, researchers trained in mathematics have explored seriously the relationships between logic programming and constraints (Jaffar and Lassez 1987; Saraswat 1992).

A major attraction of constraint programming is that it allows a programmer to state rules with a higher degree of complexity than Prolog's Horn clauses, or similar logic programming formalisms, and have them solved by more powerful, but also more specialized, interpreters. Ultimately, constraint programming could give programmers very flexible access to a large variety of specialized, mathematical algorithms, which currently require a great deal of expertise to choose and use.

In a slightly different vein, constraints are a potentially useful way of formulating problems that require *incremental* solutions: a given state of the system is represented as a particular solution of a constraint system, and any perturbation causes a new solution to be arrived at, one which typically changes relatively few of the components of the previous solution. Incremental algorithms have become increasingly important in recent years as applications have become more interactive and graphical.

Conclusion

We have tried to convey a sense of what programming is—the issues it involves and the breadth of approaches that can be taken to it. At the outset, we observed that programming is fundamentally a problem-solving activity and discussed why the basic criterion of correctness may sometimes be difficult to apply. Many people enjoy problem-solving for its own sake. But surely one of the reasons programming is interesting is due to the nature of computer applications rather than in programming itself. Computers work according to simple rules that can be characterized in mathematical terms, and many programming formalisms and languages are derived from, or at least inspired by, mathematics, as has been amply discussed in this chapter. On the other hand, computers are physical objects and can be connected to the real world in interesting ways. When a computer controls a synthesizer, the result is a sound whose properties are much richer than any mathematical formalism (at least to the ear). The programmability of computers allows this abstract, mathematical simplicity to be juxtaposed with real activity and effect. The pleasure of coaxing a prototype music system to work is a pleasure of musical engineering. Programming is unlike earlier varieties of engineering in the ethereal nature of its materials, but it remains an engineering discipline in the way work is rewarded with tangible results.

Another aspect of the excitement is the interdisciplinary nature of computing. This is a point that we need not belabor to those interested in computer music. Computer science itself has borrowed ideas from many areas of mathematics and engineering, and has returned a number of favors as well. As computers become more deeply embedded in our society, the need to marry knowledge of computing with knowledge in other domains becomes more common.

Although computers have only been around for a few years, hundreds of programming languages and variants have been implemented, and thousands more proposed. With all these languages, people unfamiliar with the subject might think the territory has been thoroughly explored. Nothing could be farther from the truth. Programming is evolving continuously and quickly, entrenched languages like Cobol and Fortran notwithstanding. Thus, while many of the ideas and techniques described in this chapter will remain valid in a decade or two, some may not. Almost certainly, the traditional approach to programming, to which the bulk of our attention was devoted, will become relatively less important. As things evolve, some of the techniques described here that remain valid and useful will nevertheless come to be seen in a different light, and used in different ways.

Probably the most important realization to come out of the accumulated experience with programming so far is that it is a problem of organizing and managing complexity—to a far greater extent than was initially realized.

The structured programming movement, which has played an important role for more than 20 years now, can be viewed as a reaction to this. The languages it engendered now dominate programming practice and form the basis of this chapter. Object-oriented programming has the potential to carry these gains a few steps farther since many of its key contributions have to do with managing complexity. Constraint programming, and perhaps some forms of logic programming, may well come to play a more important role as well.

II   Sound Synthesis

Overview to Part II

On the 26th of September, 1906, the doors of "Telharmonic Hall" opened at 39th Street and Broadway in New York. An audience of nine hundred listeners entered to hear a concert by a new instrument, the massive Telharmonium of Thaddeus Cahill, the first and largest sound synthesizer ever developed (Cahill 1897; Rhea 1984; Weidenaar 1991). Powered by electricity, but without the benefit of electronic amplification, the smoothly rotating tone generators of the Telharmonium emitted synthetic tones purer than nature—sinusoidal waves in the precise integer ratios of just intonation. Moved by the spectacle of this demonstration, the elderly American author Mark Twain (1835–1910) wrote: "Every time I see or hear a new wonder like this I have to postpone my death right off. I couldn't possibly leave this world until I have heard it again and again!" (Rhea 1972).

At about the same time, the imagination of an Italian mystic named Luigi Russolo gravitated toward another sound world—the impurity of industrial noises and the destructive sounds of warfare, as outlined in his emotional manifesto *The Art of Noises* (Russolo 1916). Russolo constructed a battery of acoustical noise instruments and performed with them in a series of highly publicized concerts in the 1920s. These dramatic opening acts set the stage for more systematic exploration of electronic sound synthesis—a development that has profoundly affected the theory and the practice of music in the twentieth century.

Prior to digital techniques, electronic methods of sound production fell into two broad categories: (1) oscillating vacuum or gas tubes or oscillating transistor circuits, and (2) rotating or vibrating systems using a mechanical, electrostatic, or photoelectric driving source.

The invention of the stored program electronic digital computer in the 1940s opened the way for the present era of sound synthesis. Since the first experiments of Max V. Mathews in 1957, dozens of sound synthesis techniques have been invented. Modern sound synthesis is a grab bag of techniques. As in the field of computer graphics, it is difficult to say at any time which techniques will flourish and which will fade over time. This situation is fueled by competitive pressures in the music industry, making it inevitable that synthesis methods fall in and out of fashion, sometimes repeatedly. The catalog of synthesis techniques is bound to grow, since no one method can satisfy the needs of all musicians. Tastes and preferences vary, and the quest for new musical sensations and experiences continues.

Organization of Part II

Part II explains the basic principles of contemporary synthesis methods. The demands of teaching drive these tutorials. We present an intuitive description of how synthesis techniques work, without cluttering the presentation with details of a particular manufacturer's implementations. Given the constantly-changing technical environment, this seems the most prudent course. In a teaching environment, this text should be supplemented with practical work using available tools, be they synthesizers, interactive synthesis applications, or synthesis languages.

The material here builds on an understanding of basic terms such as frequency, amplitude, and spectrum, and assumes a grounding in the fundamental principles of digital audio as presented in chapter 1.

We have grouped different techniques into eleven categories within five chapters of similar length. In some cases the grouping within a chapter is arbitrary; for example, chapter 5 presents three techniques that are not closely related. The order of the chapters is not entirely arbitrary, however. Chapter 3 is a prerequisite to the rest of the part, and the discussion proceeds roughly from basic to more exotic approaches. Note that chapter 20 describes two additional methods of synthesis that are mainly of historical/novelty interest: *radio wave demodulation* and *pulse tone synthesis*.

One pitfall for composers of electronic and computer music is overreliance on a single synthesis approach. Any technique employed to the exclusion of others can result in overuse and cliché—unless it is guided in an unusually virtuosic manner. Synthesis techniques by themselves do not solve all problems of orchestration in computer music composition. One of the most promising extensions of synthesis is a counterpoint of different techniques—forming *compound sound objects* through mixing and signal processing (Roads 1985f). Part III explores these topics.

3 *Introduction to Digital Sound Synthesis*

with John Strawn

Background: History of Digital Sound Synthesis
>> **Music I and Music II**
>> **The Unit Generator Concept**

Fixed-waveform Table-lookup Synthesis
>> **Changing the Frequency**
>> **Algorithm for a Digital Oscillator**

Table-lookup Noise and Interpolating Oscillators

Time-varying Waveform Synthesis
>> **Envelopes, Unit Generators, and Patches**
>> *Graphic Notation for Synthesis Instruments*
>> *Using Envelopes in Patches*

Software Synthesis
>> **Instrument Editors and Synthesis Languages**
>> **Computational Demands of Synthesis**
>> **Non-real-time Synthesis**
>> **Sound Files**

Real-time Digital Synthesis

Comparing Non-real-time Synthesis with Real-time Synthesis

Specifying Musical Sounds

Sound Objects
Example of the Specification Problem for Additive Synthesis
The Musician's Interface
Musical Input Devices
Performance Software
Editors
Languages
Algorithmic Composition Programs

Conclusion

This chapter outlines the fundamental methods of digital sound production. Following a brief historical overview, we present the theory of table-lookup synthesis—the core of most synthesis algorithms. We next present strategies for synthesizing sounds that vary over time. This is followed by a practical comparison between "software synthesis" and "hardware synthesis," that is, between computer programs and dedicated synthesizers. Finally, we survey the various means of specifying musical sounds to a computer or synthesizer. The only prerequisite to this chapter is a knowledge of basic concepts of digital audio as explained in chapter 1.

Background: History of Digital Sound Synthesis

The first experiments in synthesis of sound by computer began in 1957 by researchers at Bell Telephone Laboratories in Murray Hill, New Jersey (David, Mathews, and McDonald 1958; Roads 1980; Wood 1991). In the earliest experiments, Max V. Mathews (figure 3.1) and his colleagues proved that a computer could synthesize sounds according to any pitch scale or waveform, including time-varying frequency and amplitude envelopes.

Their first programs were written directly in terms of machine instructions for a giant IBM 704 computer fabricated with vacuum tube circuits (figure 3.2). The 704 was a powerful machine for its day, with a 36-bit wordlength and a built-in floating-point unit for fast numerical operations. It could be loaded with up to 32 Kwords of magnetic core memory. Computers were so rare at that time that the synthesis calculations had to be carried out at IBM World Headquarters in New York City, because Bell Telephone Laboratories did not have a suitable machine. After traveling to Manhattan to compute a sound, Mathews and his associates would return to Bell Telephone Laboratories with a digital magnetic tape. There, a less powerful computer with an attached 12-bit vacuum tube "digital-to-sound converter" transformed the samples on the tape into audible form. This converter, designed by Bernard Gordon, was at that time the only one in the world capable of sound production (Roads 1980).

Music I and Music II

The Music I program developed by Mathews generated a single waveform: an equilateral triangle. A patient user could specify notes only in terms of pitch, waveform, and duration (Roads 1980). The psychologist Newman Guttman made one composition with Music I, a monophonic etude called

Figure 3.1 Max V. Mathews, 1981. (Photograph courtesy of AT&T Bell Laboratories.)

Figure 3.2 IBM 704 computer, 1957. (Photograph courtesy International Business Machines.)

In a Silver Scale written on 17 May 1957 (Guttman 1980). This was the first composition synthesized by the process of digital-to-analog conversion. Even in this first piece, the potential of the computer to generate any frequency precisely was recognized. Guttman was interested in psychoacoustics and used the piece as a test of the contrast between an "equal-beating chromatic scale" described by Silver (1957) and just intonation.

Max Mathews completed Music II in 1958; it was written in assembly language for the IBM 7094 computer, a transistorized and improved computer along the lines of the IBM 704. The 7094 ran several times faster than the older vacuum tube machines. It was thus possible to implement more ambitious synthesis algorithms. Four independent voices of sound were available, with a choice of sixteen waveforms stored in memory. Music II was used by several researchers at Bell Telephone Laboratories, including Max Mathews, John Pierce, and Newman Guttman.

A concert of the new "computer music" was organized in 1958 in New York City, followed by a discussion panel moderated by John Cage. Later that year Guttman played his computer-synthesized composition *Pitch Variations* at Hermann Scherchen's villa in Gravesano, Switzerland, where Iannis Xenakis was in the audience (Guttman 1980).

The Unit Generator Concept

One of the most significant developments in the design of digital sound synthesis languages was the concept of *unit generators* (UGs). UGs are signal processing modules like oscillators, filters, and amplifiers, which can be interconnected to form synthesis *instruments* or *patches* that generate sound signals. (Later in this chapter we discuss UGs in more detail.) The first synthesis language to make use of the unit generator concept was Music III, programmed by Mathews and his colleague Joan Miller in 1960. Music III let users design their own synthesis networks out of UGs. By passing the sound signal through a series of such unit generators, a large variety of synthesis algorithms could be implemented relatively easily.

Music N Languages

Since the time of Music III, a family of software synthesis systems—all based on the unit generator concept—have been developed by various researchers. Music IV was a recoding of Music III in a new macro assembly language developed at Bell Laboratories called BEFAP (Tenney 1963, 1969). Music V, developed in 1968, was the culmination of Max Mathews's efforts in software synthesis (Mathews 1969). Written almost exclusively in

Fortran IV—a standard computer language—Music V was exported to several dozen universities and laboratories around the world in the early 1970s. For many musicians, including the author of this book, it served as an introduction to the art of digital sound synthesis.

Taking Music IV or Music V as a model, others have developed synthesis programs such as Music 4BF, Music 360, Music 7, Music 11, Csound, MUS10, Cmusic, Common Lisp Music, and so on. As a general category these programs are often referred to under the rubric of "Music N" languages (see chapter 17).

Fixed-Waveform Table-lookup Synthesis

As chapter 1 explains, digital synthesis generates a stream of numbers representing the samples of an audio waveform. We can hear these synthetic sounds only by sending the samples through a *digital-to-analog converter* (DAC), which converts the numbers to a continuously varying voltage that can be amplified and sent to a loudspeaker.

One way of viewing this process is to imagine a computer program that calculates the sample values of a waveform according to a mathematical formula, and sends those samples, one after the other, to the DAC. This process works fine, but it is not the most efficient basis for digital synthesis.

In general, musical sound waves are extremely repetitive, a fact that is reflected in the notions of frequency and pitch. Hence a more efficient technique is to have the hardware calculate the numbers for just one cycle of the waveform and store these numbers in a list stored in memory, as shown in figure 3.3. Such a list is called a *wavetable*. To generate a periodic sound, the computer simply reads through the wavetable again and again, sending the samples it reads to the DAC for conversion to sound.

This process of repeatedly scanning a wavetable in memory is called *table-lookup synthesis*. Since it typically takes only a few nanoseconds for a computer to read a value from memory, table-lookup synthesis is much quicker than calculating the value for each sample from scratch. Table-lookup synthesis is the core operation of a *digital oscillator*—a fundamental sound generator in synthesizers.

Let us now walk through the valley of table lookup. Suppose that the value of the first sample is given by the first number in the wavetable (location 1 in figure 3.3). For each new sample to be produced by this simple synthesizer, take the next sample from the wavetable. At the end of the wavetable, simply go back to the beginning and start reading out the sam-

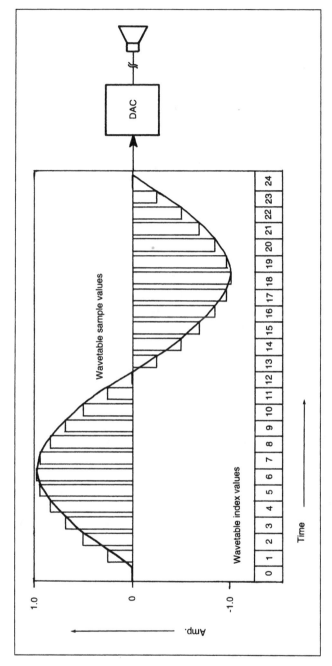

Figure 3.3 Graphical depiction of wavetable-lookup synthesis. The list 0–24 in the lower portion are numbered locations or "table index values." An audio sample value is stored in memory for each index point. The samples are depicted as the rectangles outlining a sine wave in the top portion. For example, Wavetable[0] = 0, and Wavetable[6] = 1. To synthesize the sine wave the computer looks up the sample values stored in successive index locations and sends them to a DAC, looping through the table repetitively.

ples again. The process is also called *fixed-waveform synthesis* because the waveform does not change over the course of a sound event.

For example, let us assume the table contains 1000 entries, each of which is a 16-bit number. The entries are indexed from 0 to 999. We call the current location in the table the *phase_index* value, with reference to the phase of the waveform. To read through the table the oscillator starts at the first entry in the table (*phase_index* = 0) and moves by an *increment* to the end of the table (*phase_index* = 999). At this point the phase index "wraps around" the ending point to the beginning of the wavetable and starts again.

Changing the Frequency

What is the frequency of the sound produced by table-lookup synthesis? It depends on the length of the wavetable and the sampling frequency. If the sampling frequency is 1000 samples per second, and there are 1000 numbers in the table, the result is 1000/1000 : 1 Hz. If the sampling frequency is 100,000 Hz, and the table contains 1000 entries, then the output frequency is 100 Hz, since 100,000/1000 = 100.

How is it possible to change the frequency of the output signal? As we have just seen, one simple way is to change the sampling frequency. But this strategy is limited, particularly when one wants to process or mix signals with different sampling rates. A better solution is to scan the wavetable at different rates, skipping some of the samples in it. This, in effect, shrinks the size of the wavetable in order to generate different frequencies.

For example, if we take only the even-numbered samples, then we go through the table twice as fast. This raises the pitch of the output signal by an octave. If we skip two samples, then the pitch is raised further (by an octave and a fifth, to be exact). In the table-lookup algorithm, the increment determines the number of samples to be skipped. The increment is added to the current phase location in order to find the next location for reading the value of the sample. In the simplest example, where we read every sample from the table, the increment is 1. If we read only the odd- or even-numbered samples in the table, then the increment is 2.

Algorithm for a Digital Oscillator

We could say that the oscillator *resamples* the wavetable in order to generate different frequencies. That is, it skips values in the table by an increment added to the current phase location in the wavetable. Thus the most basic oscillator algorithm can be explained as a two-step program:

1. *phase_index* = mod_L(*previous_phase* + *increment*)

2. *output* = *amplitude* × *wavetable*[*phase_index*]

Step (1) of the algorithm contains an add and a modulo operation (denoted mod_L). The modulo operation divides the sum by the table length *L* and keeps only the remainder, which is always less than or equal to *L*. Step (2) contains a table lookup and a multiply. This is relatively little computation, but it assumes that the wavetables are already filled with waveform values.

If the table length and the sampling frequency are fixed—as is usually the case—then the frequency of the sound emitted by the oscillator depends on the value of the increment. The relationship between a given frequency and an increment is given by the following equation, which is the most important equation in table-lookup synthesis:

$$increment = \frac{L \times frequency}{sampling Frequency}. \tag{1}$$

For example, if tablelength *L* is 1000 and sampling frequency is 40,000, while the specified *frequency* of the oscillator is 2000 Hz, then the *increment* is 50.

This implies the following equation for frequency:

$$frequency = \frac{increment \times sampling Frequency}{L}. \tag{2}$$

So much for the mathematical theory of digital oscillators. Now we confront the computational realities.

Table-lookup Noise and Interpolating Oscillators

All the variables in the previous example were multiples of 1000, which led to a neat integer result for the value of the phase index increment. However, for most values of the table length, frequency, and sampling frequency in equation 1, the resulting increment is not an integer, but rather a real number with a fractional part after the decimal point. However, the way we look up a value in the wavetable is to locate it by its index, which is an integer. Thus we need to somehow derive an integer value from the real-valued increment.

The real value can be *truncated* to yield an integer value for the table index. This means to delete the part of the number to the right of the decimal point, so a number like 6.99 becomes 6 when it is truncated.

Table 3.1   Phase index values in an oscillator wavetable, calculated and truncated

Phase index

Calculated	Truncated
1.000	1
2.125	2
3.250	3
4.375	4
5.500	5
6.625	6
7.750	7
8.875	8
10.000	10
11.125	11
12.250	12
13.375	13
14.500	14
15.625	15
16.750	16
17.875	17
19.000	19

Suppose that we use an increment of 1.125. Table 3.1 compares the calculated versus the truncated increments. The imprecision caused by the truncation means that we obtain a waveform value near to, but not precisely the same as, the one we actually need. As a result, small amounts of waveform distortion are introduced, called *table-lookup noise* (Moore 1977; Snell 1977b). Various remedies can reduce this noise. A larger wavetable is one prescription, since a fine-grain table reduces lookup error. Another way is to *round* the value of increment up or down to the nearest integer instead of simply truncating it, in this case, an increment of 6.99 becomes 7, which is more accurate than 6. But the best performance is achieved by an *interpolating oscillator*. This is more costly from a computational standpoint, but it generates very clean signals.

An interpolating oscillator calculates what the value of the wavetable would have been, if it were possible to reference the wavetable at the exact phase specified by the increment. In other words, it interpolates between the entries in the wavetable to find the one that exactly corresponds to the specified phase index increment (figure 3.4).

With interpolating oscillators, smaller wavetables can yield the same audio quality as a larger noninterpolating oscillator. Consider that for a 1024-entry wavetable used by an interpolating oscillator, the signal-to-noise ratio for a sine wave is an excellent 109 dB (worst-case), as compared with the

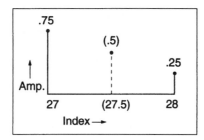

Figure 3.4 Action of an interpolating oscillator. The graph shows two *x*-points in a wavetable, at positions 27 and 28. The oscillator phase increment indicates that the value should be read from location 27.5, for which there is no entry, so the interpolating oscillator calculates a *y*-value in between the values for 27 and 28.

abysmal 48 dB for a noninterpolating oscillator using the same size wavetable (Moore 1977). These figures pertain to the case of linear interpolation; even better results are possible with more elaborate interpolation schemes (Chamberlin 1985; Crochiere and Rabiner 1983; Moore 1977; Snell 1977b).

This concludes our introduction to fixed-waveform table-lookup synthesis. The next section shows how aspects of synthesis can be varied over time.

Time-varying Waveform Synthesis

So far we have seen how to produce a sine wave at a fixed frequency: well and good. Since the maximum value of the sine wave does not change in time, the signal has a constant loudness. This is not terribly useful for musical purposes, since one can only control pitch and duration, leaving no control over other sound parameters. Even if the oscillator reads from other wavetables, they repeat ad infinitum. The key to more interesting sounds is *time-varying* waveforms, achieved by changing one or more synthesis parameters over the duration of a sound event.

Envelopes, Unit Generators, and Patches

To create a time-varying waveform, we need a synthesis *instrument* that can be controlled by *envelopes*—functions of time. For example, if the amplitude of the sound changes over its duration, the curve that the amplitude follows is called the *amplitude envelope*. A general way of designing a synthesis instrument is to imagine it as a *modular system*, containing a number of specialized signal-processing units that together create a time-varying sound.

The unit generator is a fundamental concept in digital synthesis. A UG is either a signal generator or a signal modifier. A signal generator (such as an oscillator) synthesizes signals such as musical waveforms and envelopes. A signal modifier, such as a filter, takes a signal as its input, and it transforms that input signal in some way.

To construct an instrument for sound synthesis, the composer connects together UGs into a *patch*. The term "patch" derives from the old modular analog synthesizers in which sound modules were connected via *patch cords*. Of course, when a program is making music, the connections are all done by the software; no physical wires or cables are connected. But if a UG produces a number at its output, that number can become the input to another UG.

Graphic Notation for Synthesis Instruments

Now we introduce the graphic notation that is often used in publications on digital sound synthesis to illustrate patches. This notation was invented to explain the operation of the first modular languages for digital sound synthesis, such as Music 4BF (Howe 1975) and Music V (Mathews 1969), and is still useful today.

The symbol for each unit generator has a unique shape. Figure 3.5 shows the graphic notation for a *table-lookup oscillator* called **osc**, a basic signal generator. It accepts three inputs (amplitude, frequency, waveform) and produces one output (a signal). The oscillator reads from a single wavetable that remains unchanged as long as the oscillator plays. (More complicated oscillators can read through several wavetables over the course of an event; see chapter 5 on *multiple wavetable synthesis*.)

In figure 3.5 the top right input to the oscillator is frequency. The top left input determines the peak amplitude of the signal generated by the oscillator. The box to the left is the wavetable *f1* containing a sine wave. (Note: In

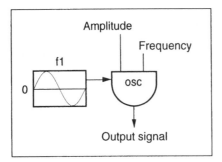

Figure 3.5 Graphical notation for an oscillator. See the text for explanation.

some implementations, instead of frequency, the value fed directly to the oscillator is a raw phase increment. Since phase increment is not a musically intuitive parameter, we assume here that the system automatically takes care of conversions from frequency to phase increment according to equation 1.)

Using Envelopes in Patches

If we supply a constant number (say, 1.0) to the amplitude input of an oscillator, then the overall amplitude of the output waveform is constant over the duration of each event. By contrast, most interesting sounds have an amplitude envelope that varies as a function of time. Typically, a note starts with an amplitude of 0, works its way up to some maximum value (usually *normalized* to be no greater than 1.0), and dies down again more or less slowly to 0. (A normalized wave is one that has been scaled to fall within standard boundaries such as 0 to 1 for amplitude envelopes, or −1 to +1 for other waves.) The beginning part of the envelope is called the *attack* portion, while the end of the envelope is called the *release*.

Commercial analog synthesizers used to define amplitude envelopes in four stages: *attack*, (initial) *decay, sustain* (a period that depends, for example, on how long a key on a keyboard is depressed), and *release*. The usual acronym for such a four-stage envelope is ADSR (figure 3.6). The ADSR concept is useful for describing verbally the overall shape of an envelope, for example, "Make the attack sharper." But for specifying a musical envelope, a four-stage limit is anachronistic. Amplitude shaping is a delicate operation, so more flexible envelope editors allow musicians to trace arbitrary curves (see chapter 16).

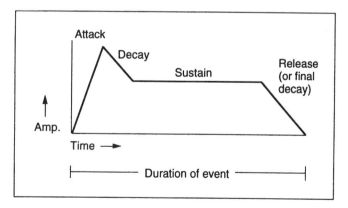

Figure 3.6 Graph of a simple ADSR amplitude envelope, showing the way the amplitude of a note changes over its duration.

The instrument of figure 3.5 can be easily adapted to generate a time-varying amplitude by hooking up an envelope to the amplitude input of the oscillator. We are now closer to controlling the oscillator in musical terms. If we set the duration and the curve of the envelope, then the envelope controls the amplitude of each note.

To design manually an envelope for each and every event in a composition is too tedious. What we seek is a simple procedure for generating an envelope that can scale itself to the duration of diverse events. One solution is to take another table-lookup oscillator (labeled **env_osc** in figure 3.7, but this time fill its wavetable *f1* with values of the amplitude envelope between 0 and 1 instead of a sine wave. Rather than finding the increment from the frequency, the *envelope oscillator* derives the increment from the duration of the note. If the duration of the note is 2 seconds, for example, the "frequency" of envelope oscillator is 1 cycle per 2 seconds, or 0.5 Hz. Thus, the **env_osc** reads through the amplitude table just once over this period. For each sample, **env_osc** produces at its output a value derived from the stored envelope *f1*. This value becomes the left-hand (amplitude) input for the sine wave oscillator, **osc**. After **osc** has looked up a sample in its wavetable *f2*, the value of the sample is scaled inside **osc** by whatever appears at its amplitude input, which in this case comes from **env_osc**.

Figure 3.7a is a typical instrument as defined in a synthesis language of the type described in chapter 17. Figure 3.7b shows another way to characterize the same structure, which is perhaps more common in synthesizers. This figure replaces the envelope oscillator with the simple *envelope generator* **env_gen**. The **env_gen** takes in a duration, peak amplitude, and a wavetable; it reads through the wavetable over the specifed duration, scaling it by the specified peak amplitude.

As the reader might guess, we could also attach an envelope generator to the frequency input of **osc** to obtain a pitch change such as vibrato or glissando. Indeed, we can interconnect oscillators and other unit generators in a wide variety of ways in order to make different sounds. Interconnected oscillators are the basis of many of the synthesis techniques described in chapters 4 through 8.

Software Synthesis

So far we have discussed digital synthesis in abstract terms. The next sections describe synthesis systems in more practical terms. The most precise and flexible approach to digital sound generation is a *software synthesis*

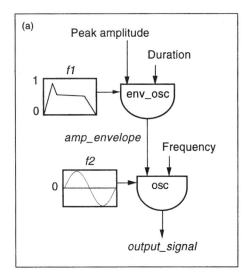

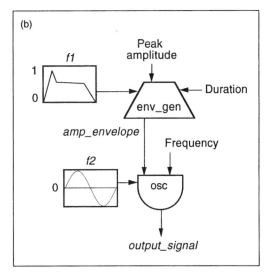

Figure 3.7   Time-varying amplitude control of oscillator. (*a*) Oscillator as envelope generator. The upper oscillator **env_osc** is employed as an envelope generator to control the amplitude of the sine wave generated by the lower oscillator **osc. env_ osc** assumes that it will complete one cycle. This structure is found in synthesis languages. (*b*) An equivalent structure to (*a*) using a simple envelope generator unit **env_gen**. This unit takes in duration, peak amplitude, and waveform. This structure is more typical of synthesizers.

program running on a general-purpose computer. Software synthesis means that all of the calculations involved in computing a stream of samples are carried out by a program that can be changed in arbitrary ways by the user. A canonical example of software synthesis is the Music V language (Mathews 1969) or its many Music *N* variants.

Software synthesis stands in contrast to *hardware synthesis,* which carries out synthesis calculations using special circuitry. Hardware synthesis has the advantage of high-speed real-time operation, but the flexibility and size of the synthesis algorithm are limited by the fixed design of the hardware. A typical example is a fixed-function commercial keyboard synthesizer. Its internal circuits cannot necessarily be reconfigured to perform a technique developed by a rival manufacturer, for example.

The distinction between software and hardware synthesis blurs in some cases. Consider the case of a system built around a programmable *digital signal processor* (DSP) with a large memory. It may be possible for such a system to run the same type of synthesis software as a general-purpose computer. (See chapter 20 for more on the architecture of DSPs.)

In any case, all of the pioneering work in computer music was carried out via software synthesis. Today a variety of synthesis programs run on inexpensive personal computers. Good-quality ADCs and DACs are either built in or readily available as accessories. A great advantage of software synthesis is that a small computer can realize any synthesis method—even the most computationally intensive—provided that the musician has the patience to wait for results. Thus, with little else needed but musical will, computers are primed and ready for high-quality music synthesis.

Instrument Editors and Synthesis Languages

Contemporary software synthesis programs can be divided into two categories: (1) *graphical instrument editors* and (2) *synthesis languages.* With a graphical instrument editor, the musician interconnects icons on the display screen of a computer, making *patches.* Each icon stands for a UG. (Chapter 16 presents this subject and gives examples.)

With a language, the musician specifies sounds by writing a text that is interpreted by a synthesis program. Figure 3.8a shows a textual representation of the same instrument shown in figure 3.7a. The example uses a simple hypothetical synthesis language that we call Music 0. The symbol ← means "is assigned to the value of." For example, the output of **env_osc** is assigned (routed) to the signal variable *amp_envelope.* Then the value of *amp_envelope,* at each sample period, is fed into the amplitude input of the **osc** module.

(a)

```
Instrument 1
     /* env_osc arguments are wavetable, duration, amplitude */
     amp_envelope ← env_osc   f1   p3   1.0;
     /* osc arguments are wavetable, frequency, amplitude */
     output_signal ← osc   f2   p4   amp_envelope;
     out output_signal;
EndInstrument 1;
```

(b)

```
/*  Score line for Instrument 1     */
/*  p1        p2      p3       p4   */
    i1         0      1.0      440
```

Figure 3.8 Textual representation of the instrument and score. (*a*) Instrument corresponding to figure 3.7. The remarks between the characters "/*" and "*/" are comments. The *parameter fields* (beginning with "p") indicate values that will be derived from an alphanumeric score, as in (*b*). p3 specifies duration, and p4 is frequency. Notice that the third argument to the second oscillator (the amplitude) is supplied by the *amp_envelope* signal generated by the first oscillator. (*b*) Score for instrument in (*a*). The first field is the instrument number. The second parameter field indicates the start time, the third duration, and the fourth frequency.

Figure 3.8b presents a simple score that supplies parameters to this instrument. (Chapter 17 explains the basic syntax and features of synthesis languages.)

Computational Demands of Synthesis

Every step in a synthesis algorithm takes a certain amount of time to execute. For a complicated synthesis algorithm, a computer cannot always complete the calculations necessary for a sample in the interval of a sample period.

To make this point more concrete, see the steps below that are necessary for calculating one sample of sound by the table-lookup method.

1. Add increment to current wavetable lookup location to obtain new location.

2. If the new location is past the end of the wavetable, subtract the wavetable length. (In other words, perform a modulo operation.)

3. Store the new location for use in calculating the next sample. (See step 1.)

4. Look up the value in the wavetable at the new location.

5. Multiply that value by the amplitude input.

6. Send the product to the output.

The important point here is that each step takes some amount of time to perform. For example, it might take a computer one microsecond to perform the calculations above. But if we are using a sampling rate of 50,000 samples per second, the time available per sample is only 1/50,000th of a second, or 20 microseconds (20,000 nanoseconds). This means that it is difficult for the computer to complete the calculations necessary for more than a few simple oscillators in *real time*. If the process is made more complicated, by adding filters, delays, more table lookups, random functions, or the time needed to interact with a musician, even one instrument may become impossible to realize in real time. What do we mean by real time? In this context, real time means that we can complete the calculations for a sample within the duration of one sample period.

Non-Real-time Synthesis

Certain synthesis and signal-processing techniques are costly from a computational standpoint and are therefore inherently difficult to realize in real time. This means there is a delay of at least a few seconds between the time we start computing a sound and the time that we can listen to it. A system with such a delay is called a *non-real-time* system.

Non-real-time synthesis was the only option in the early days of computer music. For example, a two-minute portion of J. K. Randall's *Lyric Variations for Violin and Computer*, realized between 1965 and 1968 at Princeton University (Cardinal Records VCS 10057), took nine hours to compute. Of course, if a small mistake was made, the entire process would have to be repeated. Even though this was a laborious process, a handful of dedicated composers with access to the proper facilities were able to create lengthy computer-synthesized works of music (see also Tenney 1969; Von Foerster and Beauchamp 1969; Dodge 1985; Risset 1985a).

Sound Files

Because it may longer than one sample period to compute each sample, software synthesis programs generate a *sound file* as their output. A sound file is simply a data file stored on a disk or tape. After all the samples for a composition are calculated, then the sound file can be played through the DAC to be heard.

A sound file contains a *header text* and numbers representing sound samples. The header contains the name of the file and relevant information about the samples in the file (sampling rate, number of bits per sample, number of channels, etc.). The samples are usually organized in data structures called *frames;* if there are N channels, each frame contains N samples. Thus, the sampling rate really indicates the number of frames per second.

As in other computer applications, different file formats coexist. The need to convert between formats is a practical fact of life in computer music studios.

Real-time Digital Synthesis

Just as computers have become faster, smaller, and cheaper, digital synthesis technology has also become more efficient. As early as the mid-1970s it was practical to build digital synthesizers (albeit bulky ones) that were fast enough to do all of the calculations necessary for a sample within the duration of one sample period. With advances in circuit technology, the bulky synthesizers of the past have been replaced by tiny *integrated circuits* (ICs or *chips*) that can realize multivoice synthesis algorithms in real time.

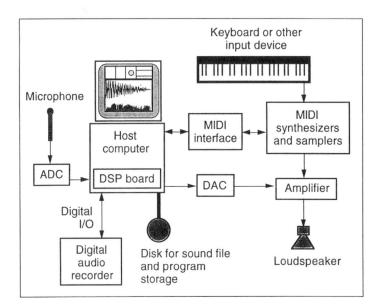

Figure 3.9   Simplified overview of a typical digital recording and synthesis facility. Musicians communicate with the synthesizers using keyboards or other input devices, or through programs running on the host computers. Sound can be recorded via the ADC and stored on disk for later playback through the DACs. In a computer equipped for multimedia production, all of the components except the MIDI keyboard may be built into the computer.

Figure 3.9 shows an overview of a real-time computer music synthesis system. This system actually has three ways of generating digital sound: (1) non-real-time software synthesis calculated on the computer, with sound from the DAC, (2) real-time synthesis calculated on the digital signal processing (DSP) board, with sound from the DAC, and (3) real-time synthesis using a synthesizer controlled via the Musical Instrument Digital Interface (MIDI; see chapter 21).

An obvious advantage of a real-time synthesizer is that *musical input devices* (also called *performance controllers*) such as musical keyboards, footpedals, joysticks, buttons, and knobs can be attached to it, so that the sound can be modified by the musician as it is being produced. *Sequencers* and *score editors* make it possible to record and edit these performances, and *patch editors* running on the computer can change the synthesis and signal-processing patches at any time.

Real-time systems are discussed in more detail throughout this book. In particular, part V discusses the internals of digital synthesizers and the MIDI protocol, and chapters 14 and 15 deal with performance controllers and performance software (see also Alles 1977a; Buxton et al. 1978; Strawn 1985c; Roads and Strawn 1985; Roads 1989).

Comparing Non-real-time Synthesis with Real-time Synthesis

Non-real-time software synthesis was the original method of digital sound generation, and it still has a place in the studio. As we have stressed before, the advantage of software synthesis using a patchable music language is programmability and therefore musical flexibility. Whereas commercial real-time synthesizers often set factory-supplied limits, software synthesis is open-ended, letting users create personalized instruments or arbitrarily complex synthesis algorithms. Many new and experimental synthesis and signal-processing methods are available only in the form of non-real-time software.

Another strong advantage of software synthesis is the flexibility of a programmed score. Even with a simple synthesis instrument, control via a *score language* (discussed later) can be extremely detailed or complicated, exceeding the range of human performers or the transmission rates of MIDI equipment.

Nonetheless, the disadvantages of non-real-time software synthesis are obvious. Time is wasted waiting for samples to be computed. Sound is disconnected from real-time human gestures—we cannot shape sound as we hear it being generated. The stilted quality of some computer music derives from this predicament. The advantage of programmability becomes a disadvantage when we have to encode simple musical phrases with the same overhead as more complicated ones. Even a trivial envelope may require us to precalculate and type in dozens of numbers. Non-real-time software synthesis is "the hard way" to make music.

Fortunately, dramatic speedups in hardware are pushing more and more synthesis methods into the arena of real-time operation. Commercial synthesizers based on DSP microprocessors circuits allow flexibility in programming synthesis algorithms. Only the most esoteric and complex methods, like some forms of *parameter estimation* and *analysis-resynthesis* (chapters 7 and 13), remain outside the limits of low-cost real-time hardware. So today we can choose between real-time and non-real-time synthesis, depending on the musical application. Besides the time savings, real-time synthesizers have the great advantage that they can be played—animated by a musician's gestures as sound is heard.

Specifying Musical Sounds

Now we turn to the different ways to specify a piece of music to a synthesis system. The traditional way of making a piece of music is to select various instruments and write a paper score that directs the performers to play specified musical events, allowing room for interpretation depending on the performers and the instruments they happen to play. But the possibilities of digital synthesis extend far beyond the ink of traditional scores.

Sound Objects

In traditional music theory, the note is a static, homogenous, unitary event. Modern synthesis techniques suggest a generalization of the concept of musical event called a *sound object* (Schaeffer 1977; Chion and Reibel 1976; Roads 1985f). The notion of sound object is often useful, since it can encompass sounds that are longer than one ordinarily considers a note to be, or more complicated. A sound object may contain hundreds of short subevents (as in vector and granular synthesis). Or it may be controlled by a dozen or more time-varying parameters, causing it to undergo mutations of identity from one pitch/timbre to another.

The burden of controlling the complicated parameter evolutions for sound object synthesis falls to the composer. This begs the question: how can we specify all these time-varying quantities? In the next section we show how much data a common synthesis technique may require. Then the section on the musician's interface presents five strategies for supplying it.

Example of the Specification Problem for Additive Synthesis

Additive synthesis is a venerable method of sound synthesis. Faithful to its name, it sums the output of several sine wave oscillators to form a composite sound waveform.

Figure 3.10 presents a digital synthesis instrument for additive synthesis. The instrument includes a frequency envelope as well as an amplitude envelope for each oscillator. The frequency envelope is a time-varying function with a range $[-1.0, +1.0]$. This envelope scales the *peak deviation* value specified as one input to **env_osc**. If the peak deviation is 100, for example, and the frequency envelope at its lowest point is -0.1, the value coming out of the frequency envelope at that point is -10. The adder $(+)$ sums this with the center frequency of the lower oscillator, causing the frequency to droop from its nominal center point. If the center frequency had been

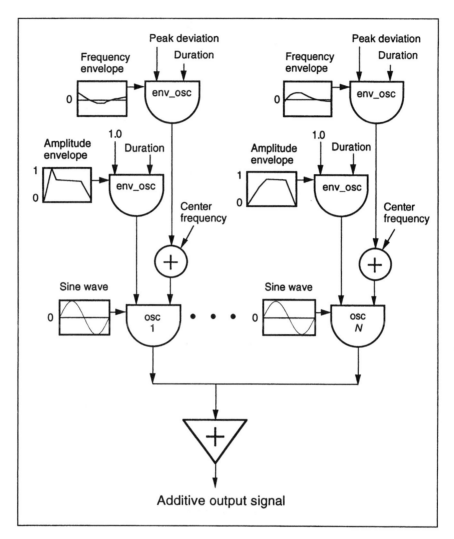

Figure 3.10 The patch shown in figure 3.7 expanded to form a simplified instrument for additive synthesis. Each sine oscillator is modified by an amplitude and frequency envelope. The outputs of many sine oscillators are added together to make one sample. More three-oscillator units might be added to this patch to make more complicated sounds.

specified as 440 Hz, the frequency envelope would cause it to go down to 430 Hz at some point.

Notice how each vertical slice of this instrument includes two envelope generators and an audio oscillator. We will call this unit a *voice*. Only two voices are shown, but the ellipses indicate that other voices are hidden. Such an instrument can generate an extremely wide range of sounds—provided that we can specify the data.

Now we turn to the problem of specifying the parameters for the instrument in figure 3.10. For each voice and each event, the instrument requires the following parameters:

1. Center frequency of audio oscillator **osc**

2. Peak amplitude (set as 1.0 in the figure)

3. Amplitude envelope

4. Begin time of amplitude envelope

5. Duration of amplitude envelope

6. Frequency envelope

7. Begin time of frequency envelope

8. Duration of frequency envelope

If the instrument has fifteen voices, and each voice requires these eight data values, that means 120 data values must be specified for just one event!

Thus no matter how powerful synthesis hardware becomes, the problem of specifying the *control data* remains. In chapter 4 we look in more detail at the data requirements of additive synthesis. The next section presents six general strategies that apply to all synthesis techniques.

The Musician's Interface

The different ways of supplying synthesis data to a computer and synthesizer fall into six categories:

1. Musical input devices

2. Performance software

3. Editors

4. Score languages

5. Algorithmic composition programs

6. Sound analysis programs

Figure 3.11 schematizes these categories. The first five categories correspond to the *musician's interfaces* explored in part V of this book. The last category is covered in part IV. The next six sections explain briefly each category.

Musical Input Devices

Musical input devices are the physical instruments manipulated by musicians (see chapter 14). The instrument directly links the musician's gestures to the production of sound. Electronic input devices decouple the manipulation of sound from the need to power it physically. Hence they are potentially more flexible than traditional instruments. For example, with electronic instruments, a single wind controller can create low bass sounds as easily as high soprano sounds. Indeed, electronic input devices are so easy that one research direction seeks to reinfuse the physical difficulty, to recreate the sense of effort that leads to expressive performances.

The benefits of real-time musical input devices are clear, although the technical problems associated with connecting them to a computer can be formidable. Traditional acoustical instruments developed over hundreds of years, whereas their digital counterparts have just begun their evolution. Musical input devices are best suited for fine control of a few musical parameters. For example, the keys on a keyboard can indicate pitch, while the velocity of key depression determines the amplitude of the higher-frequency oscillators. Most MIDI keyboards have one or more *continuous controllers* (such as footpedals, modulation wheels, or joysticks). These controllers can be assigned to any manipulable parameter, so we might set the foot pedal to control overall amplitude, and a modulation wheel to bend the shape of the fundamental pitch.

Performance Software

The use of real-time *performance software* is expanding due to the proliferation of MIDI-based systems (see chapter 15). Performance software includes such utilities as *sequencers* that can remember and play back keyboard performances. Sequencers record pure control data (such as the onset time of key depressions on a keyboard, signaling the beginnings of notes) rather than samples of audio waveforms. Computer music also provides the opportunity to go beyond traditional solo performance, for example, to provide control at the level of a conductor of an ensemble.

Fitted with eyes (a camera or another type of sensor) and ears (microphones and sound analysis software), computer-based instruments can

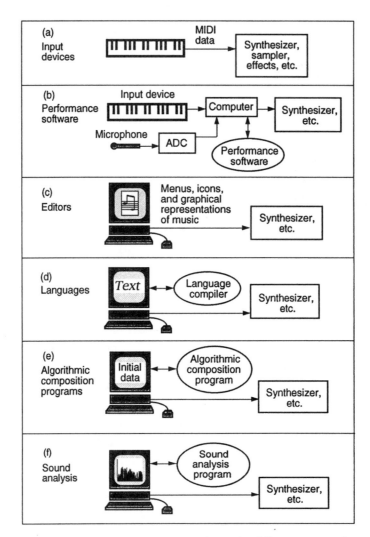

Figure 3.11   The musician's interface: six different ways of specifying synthesis data to a computer or synthesizer. (*a*) An input device can transmit the necessary data directly to a synthesizer, with or without a computer in between. (*b*) Performance software interprets the performer's gestures and may even be able to improvise. (*c*) Editors let the user build up a specification through interactive graphics techniques. (*d*) Languages encode the specification as a precise text. (*e*) Algorithmic composition programs typically require a small amount of initial parameter data from the composer before they generate music. (*f*) Sound analysis automatically derives data for modification and resynthesis from sounds fed into it.

respond to a human gesture in arbitrarily complex ways, through the use of procedures embedded in the performance software. It is increasingly common to see concerts in which a synthesizer controlled by a computer improvises with a human performer. Another application of such a system is a more flexible rendition of a prepared score, replacing the fixed tape recorder mode of performance.

As a simple example of performance software, one might set up a situation whereby a certain passage played on a keyboard triggers the start of a prerecorded score section, while a single high C key stops the sequence. A modulation wheel might determine the tempo of the prerecorded sequence.

Editors

An *editor* program lets a musician create and change a text, sound, or image (see chapter 16). Many interactive editors employ graphics techniques to provide an efficient environment for the musician. The material being edited can be quickly cut, pasted, or changed with simple gestures.

Graphical editors facilitate rapid prototyping of ideas, and hence they are most often found in the individual studio, where there is time for research. Musical ideas can be built up incrementally in an editor, and often the musician can hear the result as the change is being made.

Since music exists on many different levels and perspectives, it makes sense that there should be many types of editors for music. To set up a performance for an additive synthesizer, one uses score, instrument, and function editors. We enter the parameters for each sound object into a text editor, or manipulate a graphic image (such as common music notation or piano-roll notation). The instrument editor editor configures the additive synthesizer from unit generators such as oscillators and envelope generators. At the end of an editing session we tell the program to write the patch to the synthesizer. A function editor provides several ways of defining functions of time (waveforms and envelopes), including graphical methods and mathematical formulas. We apply the function editor to the task of creating the amplitude and frequency envelopes for the various oscillators.

Languages

Perhaps the most precise method of specifying music involves preparing *note lists* or *play lists* that are part of a *score language* (see chapter 17). The score language defines a syntax for the parameters of the instrument, listed in individual *parameter fields* (abbreviated *pfields*).

;	p1	p2	p3	p4	p5	p6
;	Ins	Start	Dur.	Freq.(Hz)	Amp.(dB)	Waveform
	i1	**0**	**1.0**	**440**	**70**	**3**
	i2	**1.0**	**.5**	**660**	**80**	**4**

Figure 3.12 Numerical score example. Three lines of comments followed by a two-line score. The first line specifies a note for synthesis instrument 1 (**i1**), while the second specifies a note for **i2**.

Our first example of a score language was the simple score line in figure 3.8b. Traditionally the first parameter after the name of the instrument gives the start time, and the second parameter gives the duration for the event. Subsequent parameters have different meanings, depending on the nature of the instrument. For example, the first line of the score file shown in figure 3.12 says that the event uses instrument 1, starts at 0, plays for 1.0 seconds, has a frequency of 440 Hz, an amplitude of 70 dB, and uses waveform number 3. (The two bottom lines in bold are the score; the other lines are comments.)

Score languages also contain *function table definitions*—the envelope and waveform definitions used by the instruments (see chapter 17).

Traditional score languages are basically numeric: instruments, pitches, and amplitudes are expressed as numbers. Alternative score languages support more "natural" specifications of music, allowing equal-tempered pitch names, for example. (For a discussion of score languages, see Smith 1973; Schottstaedt 1983, 1989a; Jaffe 1989; also Loy 1989a and chapter 17.)

The principal advantage of score languages is also their disadvantage: precision and detail. With a language, musicians are required to enter the score as an alphanumeric text. Not all composers care to specify their music in such minute detail at all times. In the additive synthesis example given above, the musician would be required to type 120 values for each sound object. On the other hand, a score language lets the musician precisely specify a score that is so detailed that it could never be played accurately by a human performer.

Algorithmic Composition Programs

Some of the earliest work in computer music involved *algorithmic composition:* the creation of a music score according to a procedure specified by the composer/programmer (Hiller and Isaacson 1959; Xenakis 1971; Barbaud

1966; Zaripov 1969). For example, the computer can calculate the parameters of sound according to a probability distribution or another type of procedure (see chapters 18 and 19).

For example, suppose that we feed a set of initial data to an algorithmic composition program, and then let it generate a complete score including all parameters needed for additive synthesis. Chapter 19 shows that there are many possible strategies that an algorithmic composition program might take. Hence it is understandable that the nature of the initial data varies from program to program. For a program that computes a score on the basis of probabilities, the composer might specify these general attributes of the score:

1. Number of sections

2. Average duration of sections

3. Minimum and maximum density of notes in a section

4. Grouping of frequency and amplitude envelopes into *timbre classes*

5. Probability for each instrument in a timbre class to play

6. Longest and shortest duration playable by each instrument

In this case, the control is global and statistical in nature. The composer can determine the overall attributes of the score, but all the details are calculated by the program. In other programs, the data might be more detailed and the stylistic constraints more specific.

Sound Analysis

Like music, sound can be dissected in innumerable ways. The established categories of sound analysis target three aspects: pitch, rhythm, and spectrum. We can use the output of these analyzers to drive synthesis, as in a convolver that maps the rhythm of one sound onto the timbre of another (Roads 1993a; chapter 10), a pitch detector tracking a human voice that drives the accompaniment pitch of a digital oscillator (chapter 12), or a spectrum analyzer that extracts the time-varying frequency and amplitude curves for additive resynthesis (chapter 13).

Conclusion

Developments in physical and electronic acoustics have opened the way for numerous experiments in musical tone production. Creations in this category represent the most

avant-garde developments in music today. The new sounds, added to new rhythmic, harmonic, and tonal concepts, make the music extremely difficult to evaluate in terms of normal musico-aesthetic standards.
—H. Miller (1960)

The musical potential of digital sound synthesis has begun to be explored, but much remains poorly understood. For now, digital technology allows precise and repeatable sound generation. With the proper hardware, software, and audio playback system, we can generate musical signals of very high audio quality. Perhaps even more important than precision is programmability, which translates into musical flexibility. Given enough memory and computation time, a computer can realize any synthesis algorithm, no matter how complicated.

While hardware continues to increase in speed, there is a continuing problem of finding the proper control data to drive the synthesis engine. One of the challenges of synthesis is how to imagine and convey to the machine the parameters of the sounds we want to produce. The point of specification is the musician's interface, discussed in the six chapters comprising part V, and sound analysis, presented in part IV.

Music theory lags a half century behind the actual practice of computer music. Synthesis techniques of leading composers are exploring the space of possibilities, leaving behind charts of musical sound geography for future generations to scan. The history of music in times of experimentation like these indicates that the current period is leading to an era of consolidation—when much of the experimentation of today will seem mundane, when the resources that at present seem radical will appear commonplace. Music composition will then enter a new era of refinement, and questions of orchestration can again be addressed within a systemic framework, as they were in the age of the symphony orchestra.

4 *Sampling and Additive Synthesis*

Sampling Synthesis

Additive Synthesis

Additive Analysis/Resynthesis

Line-segment Approximation
Principal Components Analysis
Spectral Interpolation Synthesis
Spectral Modeling Synthesis
Walsh Function Synthesis

Conclusion

This chapter introduces the method of sound sampling and several forms of additive synthesis. These techniques are fundamental to computer music and should be understood by every musician interested in synthesized sound.

Sampling Synthesis

In popular parlance, *sampling* means making a digital recording of a relatively short sound. The term "sampling" derives from established notions of digital *samples* and *sampling rate*. Sampling instruments, with or without musical keyboards, are widely available. All sampling instruments are designed around the basic notion of playing back prerecorded sounds, shifted to the desired pitch.

Sampling synthesis is different from the classical technique of fixed-waveform synthesis explained in chapter 1. Instead of scanning a small fixed wavetable containing one cycle of a waveform, a sampling system scans a large wavetable that contains thousands of individual cycles—several seconds of prerecorded sound. Since the sampled waveform changes over the attack, sustain, and decay portion of the event, the result is a rich and time-varying sound. The length of the sampling wavetable can be arbitrarily long, limited only by the memory capacity of the sampler. Most samplers provide an interface to an optical or magnetic disk drive so that groups of samples can be loaded into the sampler relatively quickly.

Musique Concrète and Sampling: Background

Composed manipulation of recorded sounds dates back at least as early as the 1920s, when composers such as Darius Milhaud, Paul Hindemith, and Ernst Toch experimented with variable-speed phonographs in concert (Ernst 1977). Magnetic tape recording, originally developed in Germany in the 1930s, permitted cutting and splicing, and therefore flexible editing and rearrangement of sequences of recorded sounds. Tape recorders were not available to musicians until the post–World War 2 period.

After experiments with variable-speed phonographs in the late 1940s, Pierre Schaeffer founded the Studio de Musique Concrète at Paris in 1950 (see figure 4.1). He and Pierre Henry began to use tape recorders to record and manipulate *concrète* sounds. *Musique concrète* refers to the use of microphone-recorded sounds, rather than synthetically generated tones as in pure electronic music. But it also refers to the manner of working with

Figure 4.1   Pierre Schaeffer's studio for musique concrète at rue de l'Université, Paris, 1960. The studio features three tape recorders on the left, along with a disk turntable. On the right is another tape recorder and the multiple-head Phonogène device (see figure 4.2). (Photograph courtesy of the Groupe de Recherches Musicales, Paris.)

Figure 4.2   Pierre Schaeffer with the Phonogène, a tape-based transposer and time-stretcher, 1953, Paris. (Photograph by Lido, supplied by the courtesy of the Groupe de Recherches Musicales.)

such sounds. Composers of musique concrète work directly with sound objects (Schaeffer 1977; Chion 1982). Their compositions demand new forms of graphic notation, outside the boundaries of traditional scores for orchestra (Bayle 1993).

Modern sampling instruments are based on a principle used in photo-electric and tape-loop devices such as the Edwin Welte's Light-tone Organ (Berlin, 1930s), Sammis's Singing Keyboard (Hollywood, 1936), Pierre Schaeffer's Phonogène (figure 4.2, Paris, early 1950s), Hugh LeCaine's Special Purpose Tape Recorder (Ottawa, 1955), the Chamberlain (Los Angeles, late 1960s), and the Mellotron (London, early 1970s). These devices played either optical disks (encoded with photographic images of waveforms), or magnetic tape loops of sound. Depending on the disk or tape selected and the key pressed on the musical keyboard, a playback head inside these instruments would play the sound on the disk or tape running at a rate that matched the pitch specified by the depressed key.

The designer of the Singing Keyboard, Frederick Sammis, described the potential of such an instrument in 1936:

Let us suppose that we are to use this machine as a special-purpose instrument for making "talkie" cartoons. At once it will be evident that we have a machine with which the composer may try out various combinations of words and music and learn at once just how they will sound in the finished work. The instrument will probably have ten or more sound tracks recorded side by side on a strip of film and featuring such words as "quack" for a duck, "meow" for a cat, "moo" for a cow.... It could as well be the bark of a dog or the hum of a human voice at the proper pitch. (Frederick Sammis, quoted in Rhea [1977].)

Perhaps the most famous predigital "sampler" was the Mellotron—an expensive instrument containing a number of rotating tape loops. The Mellotron enjoyed popular success with rock groups in the 1970s. They used the instrument to create "orchestral" or "choral" backings on popular songs. But the complicated electromechanical design of the Mellotron made it a temperamental instrument. The tape loops wore out due to head abrasion, and there were failures in the moving parts used in selecting and running multiple tape loops. Despite their problems, Mellotrons piqued interest in the prospect of playing recorded natural sounds on stage.

Several years later, the rise of digital electronics made it feasible to record and store sound in digital memory chips. In the 1970s, however, memory chips were still expensive, so the first "sampling" devices were simple delay units for the recording studio, designed to enrich a sound by mixing it with a sampled version of itself delayed by several milliseconds. (See chapter 10 for a discussion of delay effects.) As memory became cheaper it became possible to store several seconds of sounds for playback on a musical keyboard–based digital sampling instrument. The Fairlight Computer Music Instrument (CMI) was the first commercial keyboard sampler (1979, Australia). The CMI had a resolution of 8 bits per sample and cost over $25,000. Taking advantage of declining costs for digital hardware, the E-mu Emulator (figure 4.3), introduced in 1981, lowered the cost of 8-bit monophonic sampling (Vail 1993). For about $9000, the Emulator offered a total of 128 Kbytes of sample memory.

In order to create a commercial sampling instrument, three basic issues must be addressed: looping, pitch-shifting, and data reduction, which we discuss in the next three sections.

Figure 4.3   The E-mu Emulator sampling keyboard instrument (1981).

Looping

Looping extends the duration of sampled sounds played by a musical keyboard. If the musician holds down a key, the sampler should scan "seamlessly" through the note until the musician releases the key. This is accomplished by specifying beginning and ending *loop points* in the sampled sound. After the attack of the note is finished, the sampler reads repeatedly through the looped part of the wavetable until the key is released; then it plays the note's final portion of the wavetable.

Factory-supplied samples are often "prelooped." But for newly sampled sounds, the responsibility of specifying the begin and end loop points is usually left to the musician who sampled them. Creating a seamless but "natural" loop out of a traditional instrument tone requires care. The loop should begin after the attack of the note and should end before the decay (figure 4.4).

Some samplers provide automatic methods for finding prospective loop points. One method is to perform *pitch detection* on the sampled sound (Massie 1986). (See chapter 12 for a discussion of pitch detection methods.) The pitch detection algorithm searches for repeating patterns in the wavetable that indicate a fundamental *pitch period*. The pitch period is the time

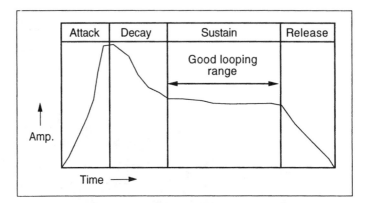

Figure 4.4   Sound with a characteristic ADSR amplitude envelope. The best area for a smooth loop is the sustained portion.

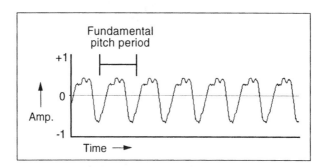

Figure 4.5   The fundamental pitch period is equal to one cycle of a periodic waveform, in this case, a waveform emitted by an alto saxophone.

interval that spans one cycle of a periodic waveform (figure 4.5). Once the pitch has been estimated, the sampler suggests a pair of loop points that match some number of pitch periods in the waveform. This kind of looping algorithm tends to generate smooth loops that are constant in pitch. If the body of the loop is too short, however, the result is similar to the sterile tones of fixed-waveform synthesis. For example, a loop encompassing one or two pitch periods of a violin note negates the time-varying qualities of a bowed string, yielding an artificial tone that has lost its identity.

The beginning and ending points of a loop can either be *spliced* together at a common sample point or *crossfaded*. A splice is a cut from one sound to the next. Splicing waveforms results in a click, pop, or thump at the splice point, unless the beginning and ending points are well matched. Crossfading means that the end part of each looped event gradually fades out while the beginning part slowly fades in again; the crossfade looping process repeats

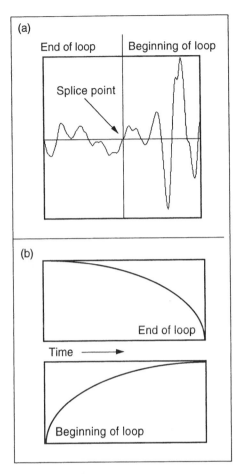

Figure 4.6 Splicing versus crossfading loops. (*a*) A vertical splice of two parts of a waveform at a common zero point. The ending point of the loop splices to the beginning of the same wavetable loop. (*b*) Crossfade looping can be viewed as a fade out of the end of the loop overlapped by a fade in of the beginning of the loop.

over and over as the note is sustained (figure 4.6). Typical crossfade times range from 1 to 100 ms, but crossfades can be extended as long as is desired.

When none of these techniques create a smooth loop, due to vibrato or other variations in the signal, more complicated methods can be brought to bear, such as *bidirectional looping*. A bidirectional loop alternates between forwards and backwards playback (figure 4.7a). Forwards and backwards loops can be layered on top of one another to mask discontinuities in either direction (figure 4.7b). Even more elaborate looping techniques based on spectrum analysis are available. For example, one can analyze the sound, randomize the phase of each spectral component in the loop, and resynthesize (Collins 1993).

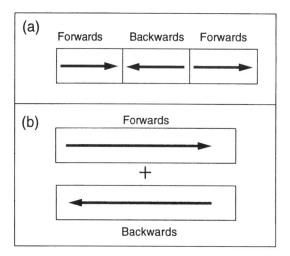

Figure 4.7   Looping methods for smoothing out variations. (*a*) Three cycles of a bidirectional loop. (*b*) In a layered forwards and backwards loop the two versions are added together.

Pitch-shifting

In an inexpensive sampler it may not be possible to store every note played by an acoustic instrument. These samplers store only every third or fourth semitone and obtain intermediate notes by shifting the pitch of a nearby stored note. If you record a sound into a sampler memory and play it back by pressing different keys, the sampler carries out the same pitch-shifting technique. A side effect of simple pitch shifting is that the sound's duration increases or decreases, depending on the key pressed. Chapter 10 describes methods of pitch shifting that preserve the original duration of the sound. Here we stay with simple pitch shifting.

Two methods of simple pitch shifting exist.

Method 1. Varying the clock frequency of the output DAC changes the playback sampling rate; this shifts the pitch up or down and changes the duration.

Method 2. Sample-rate conversion (*resampling* the signal in the digital domain) shifts the pitch inside the sampler and allows playback at a constant sampling rate for all pitches.

Some samplers employ the first method, others use the second method. Both of these methods are called *time-domain* techniques, since they operate directly on the time-domain waveform. This is different from the *frequency-*

domain pitch-shifting techniques discussed in chapter 10. Next we compare these two time-domain methods.

Since method 1 changes the playback sampling rate, it requires a separate DAC for each note that can be played simultaneously on the musical keyboard (typically up to 10 DACs). Each DAC must permit a variable clock rate and have a variable-frequency smoothing filter associated with it. For full transposibility, the DAC and the filter must work over extremely wide operating ranges. For example, if a tone with a pitch of 250 Hz sampled at 44.1 KHz is shifted up six octaves to 16 KHz, the clock frequency of the output DAC must shift up six octaves to 2.82 MHz.

Because of these ranges, either expensive parts must be used or (more typically) the audio performance of the system must be compromised in some ways. For example, one sampler that employs this pitch-shifting method allows only a single semitone of transposition (less than a 6% change of clock frequency) for sounds recorded at its highest sampling rate of 41.67 KHz. In this case the DAC and the filter are never forced to work at a sampling rate higher than 44.1 KHz. Other samplers do not permit any transposition above an arbitrary frequency.

Pitch-shifting method 2 performs sample-rate conversion. Sample-rate conversion, in effect, resamples the signal in the digital domain. This is essentially the same pitch variation technique as used in wavetable-lookup synthesis described in chapter 3. The output DAC's sampling frequency remains constant. Speeding up a sound and increasing its pitch is achieved by resampling at a lower sampling rate. This is analogous to time-lapse photography in which the frame rate is slowed down to achieve a speedup on playback. In a digital audio system samples are skipped in resampling. The number of samples that are skipped is proportional to the amount of pitch shifting that is desired (just as in wavetable-lookup synthesis). The process of skipping samples in resampling is called *decimation* (figure 4.8a). Resampling with decimation is also called *downsampling*. For example, to shift the pitch upwards by three octaves, the signal is downsampled by reading every third sample in playback.

To lower the pitch of a sound and slow it down, the sound is resampled at a higher frequency to stretch it out. This is analogous to the operation of a slow-motion camera that speeds up the frame rate to achieve a slowdown upon playback. In a digital audio system, new intermediate samples are inserted between existing samples by means of *interpolation* (figure 4.8b). Resampling with interpolation is also called *upsampling*.

The relationship between the various resampling rates and pitch-shifting can be confusing at first, because pitch-shifting method 1 and method 2 seem to go in opposite directions to achieve the same aim. Method 1 raises

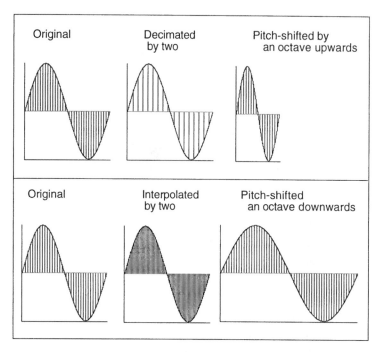

Figure 4.8 Pitch-shifting by sample-rate conversion with a constant playback sampling frequency. (Top) If every other sample is skipped on playback, the signal is decimated and the pitch is shifted up an octave. (Bottom) If twice the number of samples are used by means of interpolation on playback, the signal is shifted down an octave.

pitch by increasing the sampling rate on playback. Method 2, however, raises pitch by decreasing the resampling rate with decimation (downsampling), even though the playback sampling frequency is constant.

So far we have seen how to shift pitch by octave intervals. To shift pitch by any integer ratio, a combination of interpolation and decimation are used (Schafer and Rabiner 1973a; Moorer 1977; Rabiner 1983; Lagadec 1983; Crochiere and Rabiner 1983; Hutchins 1986a; Duncan and Rossum 1988). In particular, to pitch shift by a ratio N/M, we first interpolate by M and then decimate by N. For example, to shift a sound down by an interval of 3/4 (a perfect fourth) we upsample and interpolate by a factor of 4 and then downsample and decimate by a factor of 3. To shift up by a factor of 4/3 we first interpolate by 3 and then decimate by 4.

Sample-rate Conversion without Pitch-shifting

Many digital audio recorders operate at the standard sampling rates of 48 or 44.1 KHz. How can we resample a recording at one of these frequencies so as to play it back at the other frequency with no pitch shift? In this case the resampling rate is the same as the new output DAC sampling rate.

To convert a signal between the standard sampling rates of 44.1 and 48 KHz without a pitch change, a rather elaborate conversion process is required. First the rates are factored:

$$\frac{48000 = 2^5 \times 5}{44100 = 3 \times 7^2} = (4/3 \times 4/7 \times 10/7).$$

These ratios can be implemented as six stages of interpolations and decimations by factors of 2, 3, 5, and 7.

1. Interpolate by 4 from 44,100 to 176,400 Hz

2. Decimate by 3 from 176,400 to 58,800 Hz

3. Interpolate by 4 from 58,800 to 235,200 Hz

4. Decimate by 7 from 235,200 to 33,600 Hz

5. Interpolate by 10 from 33,600 to 336,000 Hz

6. Decimate by 7 from 336,000 to 48,000 Hz

The signal can then be played back at a sampling rate of 48 KHz with no change of pitch.

As long as the input and output sampling rates can be written as a simple fraction, then the conversion process is straightforward. If the rates do not have an integer ratio or they are constantly changing, then more sophisticated mathematical techniques must be used, which we will not venture into here (see Crochiere and Rabiner 1983; Rabiner 1984; Lagadec 1984). This is the case with *flanging effects* (see chapter 10) and audio *scrubbing* (simulating the manual back-and-forth motion of a magnetic tape rocking across a playback head to locate a splice point).

Problems in Resampling

The audio fidelity of resampling is limited by the precision of the hardware used in the conversion. When there are many intermediate resampling stages, a slight loss in fidelity in the form of added noise is to be expected. Aliasing (see chapter 1) can also be a problem. This is because resampling, like the original sampling process, can generate unwanted spectral artifacts due to aliasing. When a sampler skips samples in decimation, for example, it is throwing away intermediate samples. These intermediate samples may have smoothed the waveform's transition between two disjoint points. Thus

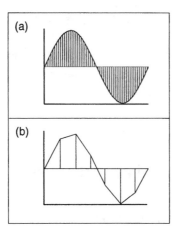

Figure 4.9   With enough decimation, even a sine wave can be turned into a jagged waveform. (*a*) Original sinusoidal waveform. (*b*) Decimation of (*a*) by a factor of eight.

a decimated signal is often full of jagged discontinuities (figure 4.9). At the same time, all frequencies are shifted up, meaning that aliasing can occur on playback. This problem can be reduced to a minimal effect by lowpass filtering the signal after decimation. Filtering smooths the jagged edges of the decimated waveform.

Filtering is also needed in interpolation because simple linear interpolation creates aliased components. Rather than devising a more complicated interpolation scheme, the usual approach in sample-rate conversion is to combine linear interpolation with filtering to shift the frequency content and also minimize aliasing.

Data Reduction and Data Compression in Samplers

The price of semiconductor memory has declined dramatically since it was introduced in the early 1970s. It is still not practical, however, to store a large library of sounds in semiconductor memory. To fit even a subset of such a library into their limited memories, many samplers use *data reduction* or *data compression* strategies to reduce the storage burden. The two are quite different. Data reduction throws away what it considers to be "nonessential" data, while data compression merely makes use of redundancies in the data to code it in a more memory-efficient form. Data compression can reconstitute the original data, while data reduction involves a loss of the original data. Both methods are sometimes grouped under the rubric of *coding* or *encoding* schemes in the audio literature.

Data Reduction

Most samplers do not have facilities for sound analysis and "intelligent" data reduction. In order to reduce the amount of memory needed for storage of audio samples, manufacturers have sometimes taken crude measures that directly affect audio quality. For example, an obvious way to reduce the data stored in a sampler is to limit the sample resolution or quantization (see chapter 1). Some inexpensive sample players use 12 bits or fewer to represent a sample. A variation on this is a *floating-point* encoding scheme that stores the samples in a low-resolution form along with several bits that indicate the original amplitude of the sound (Pohlmann 1989a). Despite shifts in apparent dynamic range, however, the signal-to-noise ratio of the low-resolution samples remains low. Another method is lowering the sampling rate. This diminishes the number of samples stored per unit of time, at the cost of shrinking the audio bandwidth. A third way is to store only every third or fourth note in the range of an instrument and then pitch-shift those samples to play in between pitches. This has the side effect of shifting the spectrum, which is not ideal. If the sound contains any variation like tremolo or vibrato, the rate of these variations is also affected noticeably by pitch-shifting. As the cost of memory declines, there is less and less justification for methods that uniformly compromise audio quality.

A more sophisticated approach to data reduction starts from an analysis stage, which stores sounds in a data-reduced form along with *control functions* that approximately reconstitute it. There are many possible approaches to this analysis and resynthesis. For example, the analysis may take into account *masking phenomena* and throw away those parts of a sound that are supposedly masked by louder parts. (For an introduction to masking, see chapter 23; for further details see Buser and Imbert 1991.) Later in this chapter we look at four experimental data reduction methods based on an additive synthesis model. Several commercial data reduction schemes are built into consumer audio products. This is not the place to enter into a broader discussion of the completeness of the perceptual models on which data reduction schemes are based. Suffice it to say that in any data reduction scheme there is a loss of data leading to a reduction in audio quality. These losses are especially apparent in musical material that exploits the full range of a fine audio system.

Data Compression

To conserve memory space, some systems use data compression techniques to limit the amount of space taken up by a stream of samples. This is done through the elimination of data redundancies and should not involve any sacrifice in audio quality. One common compression method is *run-length encoding*. The basic idea of run-length encoding is that every sample value is not stored. Rather, each sample that is different from the previous sample is stored, together with a value that indicates how many subsequent samples repeat that value. (For more on audio data compression see Moorer 1979b.)

Sample Libraries

Since a sampler is a type of recording system, the quality of the samples depends on the quality of the recording techniques. Making high-quality samples requires good players with fine instruments, excellent microphones, and favorable recording environments. Arranging all these elements for a large library of sounds takes a great deal of effort. Thus most users of samplers prefer to supplement their collection of samples with libraries prepared by professionals and distributed on magnetic or optical disks.

An Assessment of Samplers

Despite advances in sampling technology, samplers retain a "mechanistic" sound quality that makes them distinguishable from the animated sounds produced by good human performers. Most percussionists, for example, would not mistake the frozen sound of a sampled drum solo from that of a human drummer. In a live performance on acoustic drums, each drum stroke is unique, and there are major differences in the sound depending on the musical context in which the stroke is played. This is not to say that robotic performance is invalid. The commercial success of drum machines proves that lock-step rhythms and unvarying percussion sounds have a major audience.

In any case, it is understandable that the "naturalness" or "realism" of a sampler should be held up as a criterion for judging between different brands. It is well known that a given instrument tone may sound much more realistic on one sampler than it does on another.

Certain instruments, like organs, can be modeled more or less realistically by most samplers. That is, they all can generate a high-quality recording of a pipe or electronic organ. Other instruments like voices, violins, saxophones, electric guitars, and sitars are intrinsically more difficult to capture with existing sampling technology. Individual notes can be captured reasonably well, but when we put the notes together into phrases, melodies, and chords, it is apparent that major chunks of acoustic and performance information have been left out.

Factory-supplied samples model the generic singer, the generic saxophone played by the generic saxophonist, the generic orchestra played in the generic concert hall, and so on. Yet most knowledgeable listeners can tell the difference between two vocalists, saxophonists, and conductors with orchestras. It would be difficult to mistake a MIDI sequencer/sampler rendition of a saxophone solo for the signature style of the John Coltrane original. This points out a fundamental limitation in existing samplers. Beyond a certain point, it is impossible to increase the realism of present samplers without major advances in technology and in understanding of the relationship between sound structure and musical performance. One obvious evolutionary path for samplers is analysis/resynthesis (see chapter 13), which permits flexible, context-sensitive transformations of musical sounds.

In expressive instruments like voices, saxophones, sitars, guitars, and others, each note is created in a musical context. Within a phrase, a note is reached from another note (or from silence) and leads into the successive note (or leads to silence). In addition to these contextual cues, transitional sounds like breathing, tonguing, key clicks, and sliding fingers along strings punctuate the phrasing. Constraints of style and taste determine when context-sensitive effects such as rubato, portamento, vibrato, crescendi and diminuendi, and other nuances are applied.

These problems can be broken into two parts: (1) How can we model the sound microstructure of note-to-note transitions? (2) How can we interpret (analyze) scores to render a context-sensitive performance according to style-specific rules? These questions are the subject of the next two brief sections.

Modeling Note-to-note Transitions

The problem of what happens in note-to-note transitions was the subject of the doctoral research of John Strawn at Stanford University (1985b). He analyzed the transitions in nine nonpercussive orchestral instruments. The time- and frequency-domain plots that emerged from this research graphically depicted the context-sensitive nature of tone successions.

In wind instruments, one of the ways to articulate a transition is by *tonguing*—a momentary interruption of the windstream by an action of the tongue, as if the player were pronouncing the letter *t* or *k*. Figure 4.10 shows a time-domain plot of transitions of a trumpet played tongued (a) and untongued (b). The contrast between the two types of transitions is clear.

Figure 4.11 plots the spectrum of this transition. Strawn's research demonstrated that some transitions are very smooth, with a dip of as little as

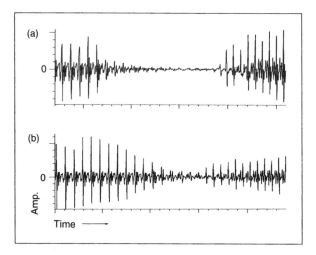

Figure 4.10   Time-domain plot of note-to-note transition of an ascending major third interval for a trumpet played tongued (*a*) and untongued (*b*). The time span for the plots is about 120 ms. (Courtesy of John Strawn.)

10 dB of amplitude between notes. Other transitions are laden with strong transitional cues in amplitude and spectrum changes that articulate the attack of the second note.

Modeling the microstructure of note-to-note transitions appears to be a tractable problem, since its solution depends on an expectable advance in technology. The problem could be solved by an increase in sampler memory capacities (storing all two-note transitions), fast signal processing, or some combination of the two. The diphone method, for example, stores transition data in a form that allows them to be stretched or compressed (Rodet, Depalle, and Poirot 1988). Holloway and Haken (1992) model transitions as overlapping tracks in a tracking phase vocoder (see chapter 13).

If transitions are to be calculated automatically—as a musician plays on a keyboard, for example, the instrument must be able to make a very quick determination of context. (Chapter 15 discusses the related issue of machine interpretation of musical scores.)

Figure 4.11   Spectrum plots of the transitions shown in figure 4.10. The plots show 50 harmonics plotted over a time span of 300 ms, with lower harmonics at the back. (*a*) Tongued. (*b*) Untongued. Notice how the "hole" in the middle of (*a*) is filled in when the note transition is untongued (more continuous). (Courtesy of John Strawn.)

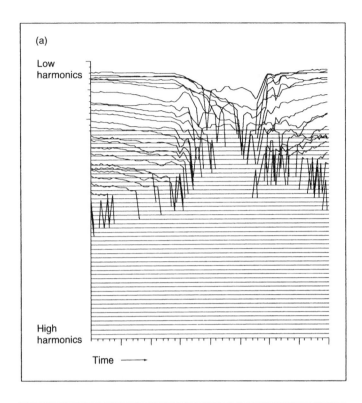

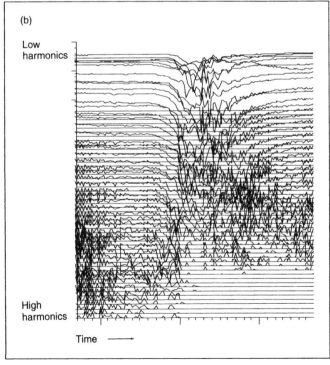

Additive Synthesis

Additive synthesis is a class of sound synthesis techniques based on the summation of elementary waveforms to create a more complex waveform. Additive synthesis is one of the oldest and most heavily researched synthesis techniques. This section starts with a brief history of additive synthesis and explains its fixed-waveform and time-varying manifestations. The next section is devoted to the process of analysis/resynthesis—linking an analysis of a sound to a resynthesis stage based on additive synthesis.

Additive Synthesis: Background

The concept of additive synthesis is centuries old, first being applied in pipe organs by means of their multiple *register-stops.* By pulling on a register-stop, air could be routed to a set of pipes. The air was actually released into the pipe—creating sound—by pressing a key on the organ keyboard. By pulling several register-stops in various proportions one could add together the sound of several pipes for each key pressed on the organ musical keyboard. According to one scholar, "The Middle Ages particularly favored the 'mixtures' in which every note was accompanied by several fifths and octaves based upon it" (Geiringer 1945). This idea of frequency "mixtures" is the essence of additive synthesis.

Additive synthesis has been used since the earliest days of electrical and electronic music (Cahill 1897; Douglas 1968; *die Reihe* 1955; Stockhausen 1964). The massive Telharmonium synthesizer unveiled in 1906 summed the sound of dozens of electrical tone generators to create additive tone complexes (figure 4.12).

Incorporating a miniature version of the Telharmonium's rotating tone generators, the famous Hammond organs were pure additive synthesis instruments (figure 4.13). The power of additive synthesis derives from the fact that it is theoretically possible to closely approximate any complex waveform as a sum of elementary waveforms. Methods exist for analyzing a sound such as a violin tone and resynthesizing it using time-varying combinations of sine waves of various frequencies, phases, and amplitudes. Due to intrinsic limitations in the resolution of the analysis, however, this reconstructed version is never a sample-for-sample replication of the original signal (see chapter 13).

Any method that adds several elementary waveforms to create a new one could be classified as a form of additive synthesis. For example, some forms of granular synthesis discussed in chapter 5 could be called additive synthe-

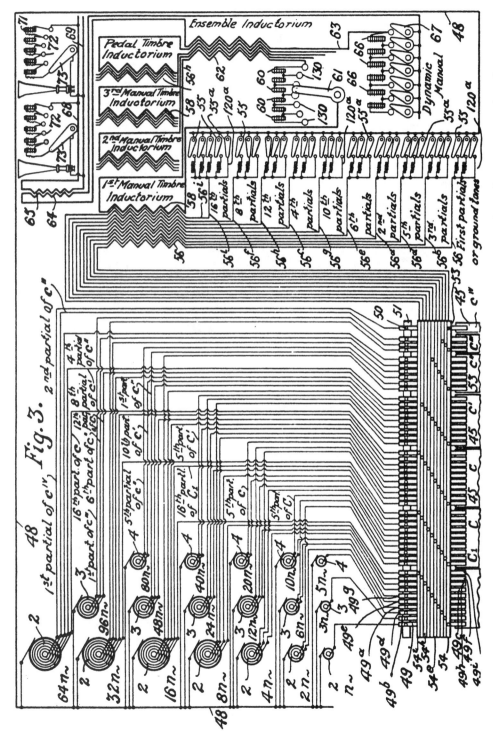

Figure 4.12 Additive synthesis of a complex tone in the Telharmonium. Sine wave harmonics from the tone-generating alternator are fed to bus bars (54). Pressing a key (C in this case) connects each harmonic to a multicoil transformer (56 "inductorium") where they mix. Each harmonic is attenuated to the desired level by the inductors in series with each winding (56a, b, etc.). The tap-switch inductors (60) regulate the amplitude of the mixing transformer output, as do the inductors near the loudspeakers (72, 73) at the listener's end of the transmission line. (Cahill patent drawing, reproduced in Johnson et al. 1970.)

Figure 4.13 Hammond B3 organ, an additive synthesis instrument based on electromechanical tone-wheels. Different mixtures of the various harmonics can be adjusted by pulling "drawbars" above the musical keys. (Photograph courtesy of the Institute of Organology, Kunitachi College of Music, Tokyo.)

sis techniques (Risset and Wessel 1982). However, we have separated these techniques from additive synthesis in this chapter in order to clarify the distinctions between the classical method of sine wave additive synthesis and those methods.

Fixed-waveform Additive Synthesis

Some software packages and synthesizers let the musician create waveforms by *harmonic addition.* In order to make a waveform with a given spectrum the user adjusts the relative strengths of a set of *harmonics* of a given fundamental. (The term "harmonic" as an integer multiple of a fundamental frequency was first used by Sauveur [1653–1716] in 1701.) For example, 400 Hz is the second harmonic of 200 Hz, since 2 times 200 equals 400. The harmonics can be displayed as a *bar graph* or *histogram,* with the height of each bar representing the relative strength of a given harmonic. Figure 4.14 shows a harmonic spectrum and the corresponding waveform.

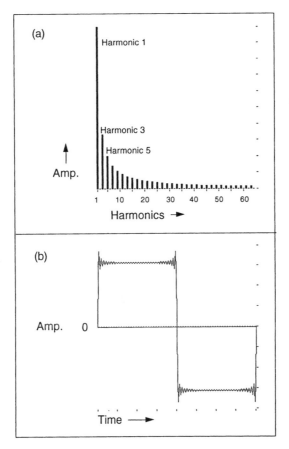

Figure 4.14 Waveform synthesis by harmonic addition. (*a*) Histogram showing the relative strength of the harmonics on a linear scale. In this case, the histogram has energy only in the odd harmonics. The amplitude of the third harmonic is one-third that of the fundamental, the amplitude of the fifth harmonic is one-fifth that of the fundamental, and so on. (*b*) Approximation to a square wave synthesized by harmonic addition using the histogram in (*a*).

Once a desirable spectrum is tuned, the software calculates a waveform that reproduces the spectrum when it is played by a digital oscillator. This spectrum template aligns to different frequencies when one changes the pitch of the oscillator. Figure 4.15 shows successive stages of waveform addition used to create a quasi-square wave.

The Phase Factor

Phase is a trickster. Depending on the context, it may or may not be a significant factor in additive synthesis. For example, if one changes the starting phases of the frequency components of a fixed waveform and resynthesizes the tone, this makes no difference to the listener. And yet such a

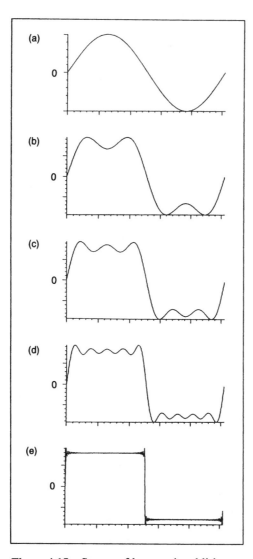

Figure 4.15   Stages of harmonic addition as seen in a series of time-domain waveforms. (*a*) Fundamental only. (*b*) First and third harmonics. (*c*) Sum of odd harmonics through the fifth. (*d*) Sum of odd harmonics through the ninth. (*e*) Quasi-square wave created by summing odd harmonics up to the 101st.

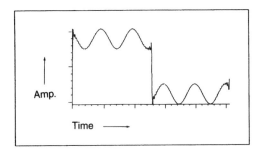

Figure 4.16   Effect of phase in additive synthesis. This waveform is the result of the same mixture of sine waves as in figure 4.15e except that the starting phase of the fifth harmonic is 90 degrees instead of 0 degrees.

change may have a significant effect on the visual appearance of the waveform, as shown in figure 4.16.

Phase relationships become apparent in the perception of the brilliant but short life of attacks, grains, and transients. The ear is also sensitive to phase relationships in complex sounds where the phases of certain components are shifting over time. As we see later in the section on sound analysis and resynthesis, proper phase data help reassemble short-lived components in their correct order, and are therefore essential in reconstructing an analyzed sound.

Addition of Partials

We can generalize from addition of harmonics to addition of *partials*. In acoustics, a *partial* refers to an arbitrary frequency component in a spectrum (Benade 1990). The partial may or may not be a harmonic (integer multiple) of a fundamental frequency *f*. Figure 4.17a shows a spectrum containing four partials: two harmonic and two *inharmonic*. An inharmonic partial is not in an integer ratio to the fundamental frequency. Figure 4.17b is the waveform that results from the sum of the four partials.

Addition of partials is limited in that it succeeds only in creating a more interesting fixed-waveform sound. Since the spectrum in fixed-waveform synthesis is constant over the course of a note, partial addition can never reproduce accurately the sound of an acoustic instrument. It approximates only the *steady-state* portion of an instrumental tone. Research has shown that the *attack* portion of a tone, where the frequency mixture is changing on a millisecond-by-millisecond timescale, is by more useful for identifying traditional instrument tones than the steady-state portion. In any case, a time-varying timbre is usually more tantalizing to the ear than a constant spectrum (Grey 1975).

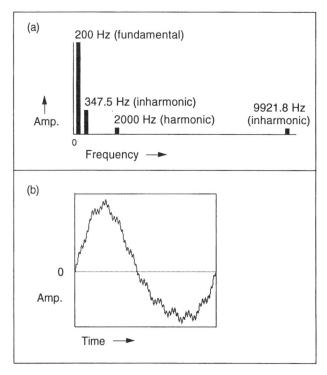

Figure 4.17   Partial addition with four components. The percentage contribution of each component is 73, 18, 5, and 4 percent, respectively. (*a*) Frequency-domain view. (*b*) Time-domain waveform.

Time-varying Additive Synthesis

By changing the mixture of sine waves over time, one obtains more interesting synthetic timbres and more realistic instrumental tones. In the trumpet note in figure 4.18, it takes twelve sine waves to reproduce the initial attack portion of the event. After 300 ms, only three or four sine waves are needed.

We can view the process of partial addition graphically in several ways. Figure 4.19a shows additive synthesis in the analog domain, as it was practiced in the 1950s (Stockhausen 1964). The figure shows several oscillator hardware modules, each with a manually controlled frequency knob. The outputs of the oscillators are routed to a mixer. The composer adjusted the balance of the oscillators in real time to determine the time-varying spectrum. With this setup, manual control was the only option. To precisely realize a time-varying mixture took several people working together (Morawska-Büngler 1988).

Figure 4.19b shows digital additive synthesis. An audio oscillator is represented as a quasi half-circle with a pair of inputs—one for amplitude and

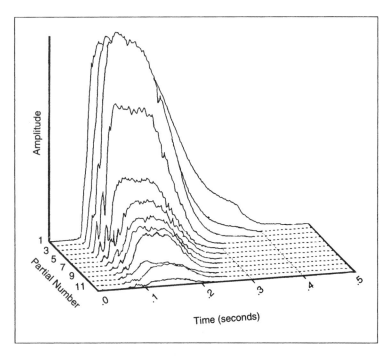

Figure 4.18 Time-varying spectrum plot of twelve partials of a trumpet tone, with the highest partials in the foreground. Time goes from left to right. Notice that the fundamental (at the back) is not the highest amplitude, but it lasts the longest.

one for frequency. To generate a time-varying spectrum, each frequency and amplitude input to the oscillators is not a constant but a time-varying envelope function read over the duration of the event. The sine wave audio oscillators feed into a module that sums the signals. The sum module then passes the additive result to a DAC for conversion to sound.

Demands of Additive Synthesis

Time-varying additive synthesis makes heavy demands on a digital music system. First, it requires large numbers of oscillators. If we make the musically reasonable assumptions that each sound event in a piece may have up to 24 partials (each generated by a separate sine wave oscillator), and that up to sixteen events can be playing simultaneously, we need up to 384 oscillators at any given time. If the system is running at a sampling rate of 48 KHz, it must be capable of generating 48,000 × 384 or 18,432,000 samples/second. Since each sample requires about 768 operations (multiply-adds), the total computational load is over 1.4 billion operations per second, without counting table-lookup operations. Table 20.1 in chapter 20

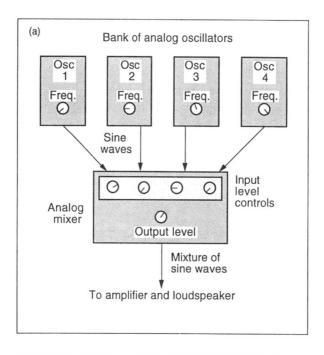

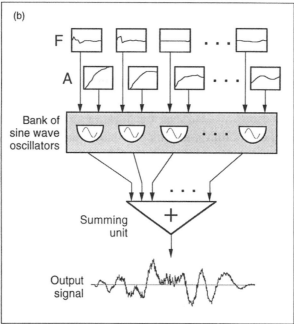

Figure 4.19 Two views of additive synthesis. (*a*) In the analog domain, oscillators feed a mixer. (*b*) Digital additive synthesis. Time-varying additive synthesis with separate frequency (F) and amplitude (A) envelopes. Figure 3.10 shows a more detailed instrument diagram for additive synthesis.

estimates the per-sample requirements for additive synthesis. Such computational demands, although formidable, are not outside the limits of current hardware. For example, one synthesizer specialized for additive synthesis offers the potential of several thousand sine waves in real time (Jansen 1991).

Yet computational power is only one requirement of additive synthesis. The method also has a voracious appetite for control data. If a piece contains 10,000 events (such as a typical orchestral score), each with up to 24 partials, one needs to have 240,000 frequency envelopes and 240,000 amplitude envelopes on hand. Even if the same envelope is used in more than one event, where do the control data come from? This is the subject of the next section.

Sources of Control Data for Additive Synthesis

Effective use of any digital synthesis technique—including additive synthesis—depends on having good control data for the synthesis instrument. To create animated sounds with a rich internal development, one drives the synthesizer with control data; hence, the control data are also referred to as the *driving functions* of the synthesis instrument. Control data can be obtained from several sources:

1. Imported from another domain and mapped into the range of synthesis parameters. For example, some composers have traced the shape of mountains or urban skylines and used these curves as control functions. This is the approach used in the early computer music piece *Earth's Magnetic Field* (1970) by Charles Dodge and in pieces derived purely from geometric, stochastic, or other mathematical or physical models.

2. Generated by a composition program that embodies composer-specified constraints on musical microstructure. An example is John Chowning's *Stria* (1977), realized with additive synthesis of inharmonic spectra.

3. Generated by an interactive composition system that translates high-level musical concepts such as *phrases* (in the Formes language of Rodet and Cointe 1984), *tendency masks* (as in the POD system of Truax 1977, 1985), *sound objects* (as in the SSSP system of Buxton et al. 1978), or *clouds* (as in asynchronous granular synthesis of Roads 1978c, 1991) into synthesis parameters.

4. Entered manually by the composer, using combinations of the previously mentioned sources or the composer's intuitive, theoretical, or empirical knowledge of psychoacoustics. An example of this method is Jean-Claude Risset's piece *Inharmonique* (1970).

5. Supplied from an analysis subsystem that mulches a natural sound and spews out the control data needed to resynthesize it. The data can also be edited in order to create transformations of the original sounds. Trevor Wishart (1988) used sound analysis as an intermediate stage in transforming vocal sounds for his piece *Vox-5* (see also Murail 1991).

Since methods 1 to 4 are based on compositional aesthetics, we do not discuss them further in this chapter. The fifth method requires a subsystem for sound analysis; this is the subject of the next section.

Additive Analysis/Resynthesis

Analysis/resynthesis encompasses different techniques that have a three-step process in common (figure 4.20):

1. A recorded sound is analyzed

2. The musician modifies the analysis data

3. The modified data are used in resynthesizing the altered sound

The concept of analysis/resynthesis is not predicated solely on additive synthesis. It can also be based on subtractive resynthesis (see chapter 5),

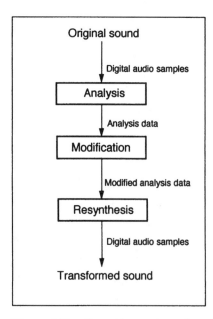

Figure 4.20 General overview of analysis/resynthesis. The modification stage may involve manual edits to the analysis data or modifications via *cross-synthesis* where the analysis data of one sound scale the analysis data from another sound.

combinations of additive and subtractive resynthesis (Serra 1989; Serra and Smith 1990), or other methods (see chapter 13).

Early experiments in additive analysis/resynthesis were carried out by H. Fletcher (of the famous Fletcher-Munson loudness curves) and his associates (Fletcher, Blackham, and Stratton 1962; Fletcher, Blackham, and Christensen 1963). They used entirely analog equipment. When digital additive methods are used for resynthesis, the entire system looks like figure 4.21. The analysis is carried out successively on short segments of the input signal. The process of segmenting the input signal is called *windowing* (discussed in chapter 13 and appendix A). We can think of each windowed segment as being sent through a bank of narrow bandpass filters, where every filter is tuned to a specific center frequency. In practice, a *fast Fourier*

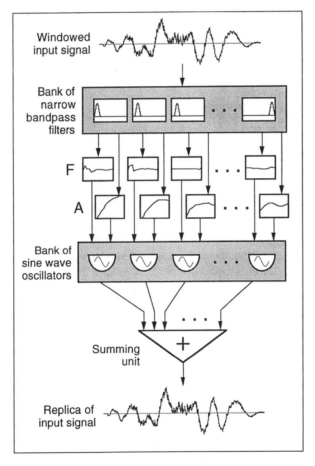

Figure 4.21 Additive analysis/synthesis. A windowed input signal is analyzed by a filter bank into a set of frequency (F) and amplitude (A) envelopes or *control functions* that drive a set of oscillators. If the analysis data are not changed, the output signal should be almost the same as the input signal.

transform (FFT) usually replaces the filter bank and performs essentially the same task in this application, that is, measuring the energy in each frequency band (again, see chapter 13 and appendix A).

The amplitude of the signal coming out of each filter is measured, and this time-varying value becomes the *amplitude control function* for that frequency range. At the same time, the system calculates control functions corresponding to small frequency deviations by looking at the output of adjacent filters (or *analysis bins,* in the case of the FFT).

The frequency and amplitude control functions drive a bank of oscillators in the resynthesis stage. In other words, we are using the information gleaned from the analysis of an existing sound to create the set of control functions needed to resynthesize that sound additively with sine waves. If the input sound is well modeled as a sum of sine waves, the summed signal generated by the oscillators should be much the same as the original input signal.

Of course, straightforward analysis/resynthesis of a sound is not interesting from a musical standpoint. In order to create musically interesting effects, we must modify the data generated by the analysis. This is the subject of the next section.

Musical Applications of Additive Analysis/Resynthesis

After the analysis has been performed, musicians can edit the control functions to create variations of the original input signal. Many different effects are possible with this technique, as listed in table 4.1. Three compositions produced in the 1980s stand as good examples of compositional manipulation of analysis data: *Mortuos Plango, Vivos Voco* (1981) by Jonathan Harvey, *Désintegrations* (1983, Salabert Trajectoires) by Tristan Murail, and *Digital Moonscapes* (1985, CBS/Sony) by Wendy Carlos.

In the Harvey piece, the composer analyzed the sound of a large bell. For each sinusoidal component in the resynthesis, the composer substituted the sound of a sampled boy's voice at the appropriate frequency. The voice samples followed the analyzed frequency and amplitude control functions of the chiming bells, creating an eerie effect of a boy/bell chorus. In the composition by Murail, the composer analyzed traditional instrument tones and created synthetic complements to these tones that blend seamlessly with the sounding instruments yet weave out dramatically when the instruments stop. *Désintegrations* is a classic example of *spectral composition* techniques where the harmonic structure of the work is based on an analysis of instrumental tones (Murail 1991). In *Digital Moonscapes,* Carlos used analysis data as the inspiration for creating an ad hoc synthetic orchestra of per-

Table 4.1 Musical transformations using additive analysis/resynthesis

Musical effect	Technique
Variations of recorded sounds	Change selected frequency or amplitude envelopes by editing or multiplications by arbitrary functions.
Spectrum scaling (without time scaling)	Multiply the frequency of all the partials (possibly excepting the fundamental) by a factor n or by arbitrary functions. Since multiplication does not preserve formant structures, vocal and instrumental sounds may lose their characteristic identity.
Spectrum shifting (without time scaling)	Add a factor n or an arbitrary function to all partials (possibly excepting the fundamental). For small values this preserves formant structures.
Spectrum inversion	Reversing the order of the frequency components before resynthesis, so that the amplitude of the first partial is assigned to the last partial, and vice versa, followed by exchange of the amplitudes of the second and next-to-last components, etc.
Hybrid timbres	Replace some envelopes from one sound with selected envelopes from another sound.
Time expansion and compression without pitch shifting	Extend the duration of the frequency and amplitude envelopes, or change the *hop size* on playback (see chapter 13).
Stretch a percussive timbre into a prolonged synthetic passage	Delay the onset time of each partial and smooth their envelopes.
Timbral interpolation from one instrumental tone to another	Interpolate over time between the envelopes of two instrument tones.
Mutating synthetic sounds	Interpolate between the envelopes of arbitrary synthetic sounds.
Enhance the resonance regions of recorded sounds	Increase the amplitude of selected frequency partials.
Cross-synthesis	Method 1: Use the amplitude envelopes for the partials of one sound to scale the amplitude envelopes of another sound (see *fast convolution* in chapter 10).
	Method 2: Apply the amplitude envelopes from one sound to the frequency (or phase) functions of another sound.
	Method 3: Apply the noise residual from one sound to the quasi-harmonic part of another sound (see, for example, the description of spectral modeling synthesis and the comb wavelet transform in chapter 13).

cussion-, string-, woodwind-, and brasslike timbres, used in an idiomatic orchestral style.

The next section briefly discusses current techniques of sound analysis with additive resynthesis with an emphasis on the data reduction problem. It serves as a prelude to the more detailed treatment in chapter 13 and appendix A.

Methods of Sound Analysis for Additive Synthesis

Many spectrum analysis methods, including *pitch-synchronous* analysis (Risset and Mathews 1969), the *phase vocoder* (Dolson 1983, 1986, 1989b), and *constant-Q* analysis (Petersen 1980; Schwede 1983; Stautner 1983), among others, are variations on the basic technique of Fourier analysis of component frequencies. The practical form of Fourier analysis is the *short-time Fourier transform* (STFT). This method can be thought of as analyzing a sampled sound by extracting successive short-duration overlapping segments (shaped by a window function) and applying a bank of filters to the selected segment. The output of each filter is measured, indicating the amplitude and the phase of the spectrum at that particular frequency. A series of these short-time analyses (akin to the frames of a film) constitute a time-varying spectrum. At the core of the STFT is the FFT, a computationally efficient implementation of Fourier analysis (Cooley and Tukey 1965; Singleton 1967; Moore 1978a, 1978b; Rabiner and Gold 1975).

The phase vocoder (PV) (Flanagan and Golden 1966; Portnoff 1978; Holtzman 1980; Moorer 1978; Dolson 1983; Gordon and Strawn 1985; Strawn 1985b) deserves special mention here, as it is a popular method of sound analysis/resynthesis that has been distributed with several music software packages. The PV converts a sampled input signal into a time-varying spectral format. In particular, it generates a set of time-varying frequency and amplitude curves. Many interesting sound transformations can be achieved by editing and resynthesizing PV data. For example, the phase vocoder can be used for *time compression* or *time expansion* without pitch change. In this effect a sound is made longer or shorter without significantly affecting its pitch or timbre. (See chapter 10 for a discussion of various approaches to time compression/expansion.)

Contrary to the expectations of the researchers who invented them (who were searching for efficient coding techniques), sound analysis techniques may generate an "information explosion" (Risset and Wessel 1982). That is, the analysis data (the control functions) can take up many times more memory space than the original input signal. The amount of data depends partly on the complexity of the input sound, that is, how many sine wave functions are needed to resynthesize it, and partly on the internal data representation used in the analysis program. Using the tracking phase vocoder, for example, a short sound file that takes up 2 Mbytes may generate tens of Mbytes of analysis data. Such storage requirements make it difficult to build libraries of analyzed sounds, and the volume of data becomes onerous to edit. This situation mandates some form of data reduction of the control data, the subject of the next section.

Data Reduction in Analysis/Resynthesis

Data reduction is important to efficient analysis/resynthesis. Data reduction takes two steps. First, the data—a set of amplitude and frequency control functions—are analyzed. Second, an algorithm transforms the original data into a more compact representation. An important goal of data reduction is to compact data without eliminating perceptually salient features of the input signal. Another important goal in computer music work is that the analysis data must be left in a form that can be edited by a composer. The goal is not simply to save bits; rather, one wants to make it easy to manipulate the data-reduced material (Moorer 1977).

A large body of research work on data reduction of digital audio samples is recorded in the literature, including studies by Risset (1966), Freedman (1967), Beauchamp (1969, 1975), Grey (1975), Grey and Gordon (1978), Charbonneau (1981), Strawn (1980, 1985a, 1985b), Stautner (1983), Kleczkowski (1989), Serra (1989), Serra and Smith (1990), Holloway and Haken (1992), and Horner, Beauchamp, and Haken (1993). Since real-time work is so important to musicians, one goal of analysis/resynthesis research is to speed up data reduction processing and facilitate real-time synthesis from reduced data. Papers by Sasaki and Smith (1980) and Schindler (1984) explain hardware designs for high-speed digital synthesis from reduced data.

Many volumes of engineering literature explore data reduction methods. Here we glance at four techniques that have been applied in computer music: line-segment approximation, principal components analysis, spectral interpolation synthesis, and spectral modeling synthesis. (See also Goldberg 1989 for a description of the genetic algorithm approach, which has recently been applied to synthesis data reduction [Horner, Beauchamp, and Haken 1993].)

Line-segment Approximation

Line-segment approximation of the amplitude and frequency control functions eliminates the need to store a distinct value for every sample analyzed.

Instead, the analysis system stores only a set of *breakpoint pairs,* which are time (*x*-axis) and amplitude (*y*-axis) points where the waveform changes significantly. Line-segment approximation represents the overall outline of a waveform by storing only the points of maximum inflection (change). In the resynthesis stage the system "connects the dots," usually by means of straight lines interpolated between the breakpoint pairs.

Initial work with line-segment approximation was done by hand, using an interactive graphics editor to construct functions with four to eight segments each (Grey 1975). A data reduction of a hundredfold was achieved. This manual editing work can also be partially automated, as demonstrated by Strawn (1985a, 1985b). Figure 4.22a shows a perspective plot of the sixteen harmonics of a violin tone, sampled at 25 KHz. Figure 4.22b plots an approximation to (a) using just three line segments.

Going beyond the storage of line-segment approximations, Beauchamp (1975) developed a heuristic technique for inferring the approximate amplitude curve of all harmonics of a tone from the curve of the first harmonic. For simple periodic tones, Charbonneau (1981) found that even more radical data reduction could be achieved. He used simple variations of a single envelope for all amplitude functions of a given tone. (See also Kleczkowski 1989 and Eaglestone and Oates 1990 for refinements of these proposals.)

Principal Components Analysis

The technique of *principle components analysis* (PCA) has been applied in several analysis/resynthesis systems (Stautner 1983; Sandell and Martens 1992; Horner, Beauchamp, and Hakken 1993). PCA breaks down a waveform using the mathematical technique of *covariance matrix* calculation. This results in a set of basic waveforms (the principal components) and a set of weighting coefficients for these basic waveforms. When the components are summed according to their weights, the result is a close approximation of the original waveform.

The advantage of PCA is its potential for data reduction. PCA analysis summarizes the underlying relationships between samples so the fewest number of components account for the maximum possible variance in the signal. The process of determining the principal components and their weighting coefficients is implemented as an iterative approximation that tries to minimize the squared numerical error (difference between the original and the approximation). The first principal component is a fit of a single waveform to the entire data set. The second principal component is a fit to the *residual* (sometimes called *residue*), or difference between the original and first approximation. The third component is a fit to the residual of the

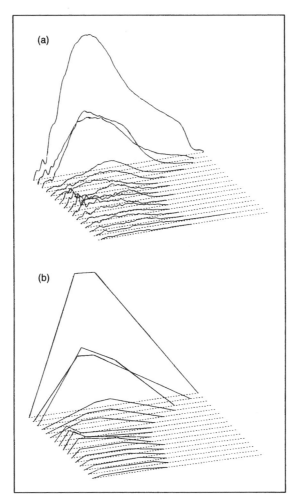

Figure 4.22 Drastic data reduction of analysis data for additive synthesis. Amplitude is plotted vertically, frequency goes from back to front, and time goes left to right. (*a*) Original frequency-vrs-time-vrs-amplitude curve of a violin tone. (*b*) The same violin tone as in (*a*), approximated with only three line segments per partial.

second component, and so on. For further details on PCA see Glaser and Ruchkin (1976).

Spectral Interpolation Synthesis

Spectral interpolation synthesis (SIS) (Serra, Rubine, and Dannenberg 1990) is an experimental technique that generates time-varying sounds by interpolating between analyzed spectra. Rather than crossfading between sampled sounds in the time domain (as in multiple wavetable synthesis discussed in chapter 5), SIS starts from analyses of recorded sounds and uses additive synthesis to crossfade between the analyses of successive spectra in the frequency domain. An automatic data reduction algorithm is necessary to compress the analysis data into a small set of common spectral paths between two successive sounds and a set of ramp functions that describe the transition from one spectrum to the next. The main difficulty with the procedure appears to be its handling of the attack portion of sounds.

Spectral Modeling Synthesis

Spectral modeling synthesis (SMS) (Serra 1989; Serra and Smith 1990) reduces the analysis data into a *deterministic* component (narrowband components of the original sound) and a *stochastic* component. The deterministic component is a data-reduced version of the analysis that models the most prominent frequencies in the spectrum. These frequencies are isolated by a process of *peak detection* in each frame of the analysis, and *peak continuation,* which tracks each peak across successive frames. SMS resynthesizes these tracked frequencies with sine waves. This is the same method as used in tracking phase vocoders described in chapter 13.

SMS goes beyond this representation, however, by also analyzing the residual or the difference between the deterministic component and the original signal. This is the called the "stochastic" component of the signal. The stochastic component takes the form of a series of envelopes that control a bank of frequency-shaping filters through which white noise is being passed. Thus a composer can transform the deterministic (sine) envelopes and the stochastic (filtered noise) components separately, if desired (figure 4.23). Noisy components remain noisy, even after transformations (such as filtering) are applied to them. This stands in contrast with a pure sine wave model, in which transformations (such as time compression/expansion) on noisy components often turn them into orderly sine wave clusters, denaturing their noisy texture.

Efficient algorithms for generation of *pseudorandom noise* are well known (Knuth 1973a; Keele 1973; Rabiner and Gold 1975). Thus the use of filtered noise results in a tremendous data reduction. In purely sinusoidal resynthesis without this kind of data reduction, noisy components must be approximated with hundreds of sine waves. The control functions for these sine waves take up a great deal of storage space, and the sine wave resynthesis is costly from a computational standpoint.

A problem of accuracy left open by SMS is that the filtered pseudorandom noise it uses to reconstruct the stochastic component is not necessarily the same quality of noise as the original source. In many sounds, "noise" is the result of complicated turbulences that have an audible char-

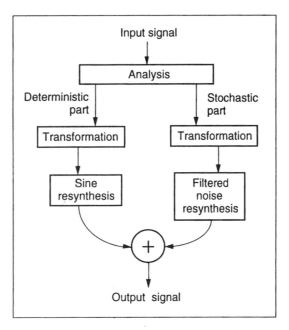

Figure 4.23 Overview of spectrum modeling synthesis. The input signal is divided into a deterministic part and a stochastic part. Each part can be modified separately before resynthesis. (See figure 13.16 for a more detailed view of the analysis stage.)

acter and identity. For some sounds, the approximation by uniform noise leaves room for improvement.

Walsh Function Synthesis

So far we have discussed analysis/resynthesis as a process based mainly on Fourier analysis with resynthesis based on sine wave summation. The Fourier sine wave approach has a long tradition of research and application stemming from the original theorem that states that for periodic signals, a combination of sine waves of various frequencies can be created that approximate arbitrarily closely the original signal. Mathematical research has shown that other groups of waveforms besides sine waves can be used to approximate signals. A family of square waves called the *Walsh functions* can be used to approximate a signal after it has been analyzed by means of the *Walsh-Hadamard transform*. Walsh functions, being rectangular waves, are a kind of "digital domain series," since they take on only two values $+1$ and -1 (Walsh 1923).

Figure 4.24 presents the first eight Walsh functions. Just as with the Fourier series and its sine waves, an arbitrary periodic waveform can be approximated as an additive sum of a finite series of Walsh functions. While

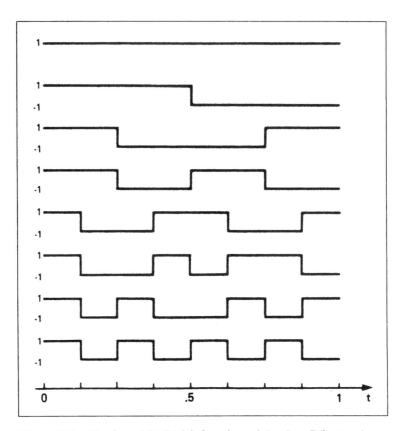

Figure 4.24   The first eight Walsh functions, 0 (top) to 7 (bottom).

the Fourier series builds up waveforms out of component frequencies, Walsh synthesis builds up waveforms using functions of different *sequencies*. Sequency is defined as one-half the average number of zero crossings per second (zps) (Hutchins 1973). Figure 4.25 shows a composite waveform derived by summing several Walsh functions. It suggests how sine wave additive synthesis and Walsh function synthesis are conceptual opposites. That is, the hardest waveform to synthesize in Walsh function synthesis is a pure sine wave. The Walsh approximation to a sine will stay jagged until a very high number of sequency terms are used. Any jaggedness gives an "unsinusoidal" and generally objectionable quality. By contrast, in sine wave synthesis, the hardest waveform to synthesize is one with a rectangular corner, such as a square wave! Figure 4.15, for example, depicts a quasi-square wave constructed by summing 101 sine waves.

The main advantage of Walsh functions in digital sound synthesis is their rectangular shape, a shape that can be computed at high speed by inexpensive digital circuits. A disadvantage of Walsh function synthesis as against

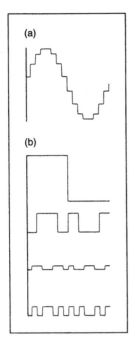

Figure 4.25 Demonstration of Walsh function summation. (*a*) A simple sine wave approximation built by adding the Walsh functions shown in (*b*). (After Tempelaars 1977.)

sine wave synthesis is that individual Walsh functions are not associated with specific harmonics, as they are in sine wave additive synthesis. It is, however, possible to pass mathematically from the Fourier (frequency) domain to the Walsh domain (Tadokoro and Higishi 1978). Thus, one can specify a sound in terms of the addition of various frequency components (partials), and then transform this specification into a set of parameter values for a Walsh function synthesizer. Moreover, natural sounds can be sampled and transformed into the Walsh domain using the Walsh-Hadamard transform and resynthesized using the fast Walsh transform (FWT) (Hutchins 1973, 1975).

A number of music synthesis operations have been redesigned for Walsh signal processing circuits. For example, Hutchins (1973) designed an envelope generator using Walsh function circuits. Rozenberg (1979) and Hutchins (1975) showed how to realize amplitude modulation, subtractive synthesis, frequency modulation, frequency shifting, and reverberation—all in the Walsh domain.

Despite the potential of Walsh function synthesis, only a few experimental devices based on this technique have been built (Hutchins 1973, 1975; Insam 1974). None are commercially available. This is probably due to the fact that the cost of circuits for sine wave additive synthesis has continued to decline (including memory chips and multipliers), so the economic advantage of Walsh function circuits has diminished. The weight of accumulated research in Fourier/sine wave methods and the more intuitive relationship between frequencies and perception have also contributed to the popularity of sine wave summation in contemporary synthesizer designs.

Conclusion

This chapter has discussed two widely used synthesis techniques: sampling and additive synthesis. The sampler is the mockingbird of musical instruments. Its creative synthesis capabilities may be weak, but it can copy any source through its ability to memorize and playback sound. Because it can also mimic the rich sounds of acoustic instruments, a sampler is among the most popular electronic instruments available.

Additive techniques have been studied in detail for decades. When coupled to an analysis stage, additive synthesis is a powerful means of simulating natural sounds and cloning variations of them. As we have seen, the main drawback of additive techniques is that they achieve a quasi generality by sacrificing computational efficiency. In order to simulate a given sound, a thorough analysis must be performed. This analysis can generate an explosion of data that must go through a data reduction stage before it becomes editable. Sound analysis tools require serious computing power, so in the past they were available only on expensive institutional-grade computing hardware. This situation is changing, with sophisticated sound analysis and editing tools available on even portable computers.

The next chapter discusses two synthesis techniques with links to sampling and additive synthesis, namely multiple wavetable synthesis and granular synthesis. The other technique discussed in chapter 5 is subtractive synthesis, the conceptual opposite of additive synthesis.

5   *Multiple Wavetable, Wave Terrain, Granular, and Subtractive Synthesis*

Multiple Wavetable Synthesis

        Wavetable Crossfading

        Wavestacking

Wave Terrain Synthesis

        Terrains and Orbits

        Generating Predictable Waveforms from Wave Terrains

        Periodic Orbits

        Time-varying Orbits

Granular Synthesis

        Granular Synthesis: Background

        Sonic Grains

        Grain Generator Instrument

        High-level Granular Organizations

        Fourier/Wavelet Grids and Screens

        Pitch Synchronous Granular Synthesis

        Quasi-synchronous Granular Synthesis

        Asynchronous Granular Synthesis

        Time Granulation of Sampled Sound

        Assessment of Granular Synthesis

Subtractive Synthesis

        Introduction to Filters

        Filter Types and Response Curves

Filter Q and Gain
Filter Banks and Equalizers
Comb and Allpass Filters
Time-varying Subtractive Synthesis

Subtractive Analysis/Synthesis

The Vocoder

Linear Predictive Coding

What Is Linear Prediction?
LPC Analysis
Filter Estimation
Pitch and Amplitude Analysis
Voiced/Unvoiced Decision
Analysis Frames
LPC Synthesis
Editing LPC Frame Data
Musical Extensions of Standard LPC
Assessment of LPC
Diphone Analysis/Resynthesis

Conclusion

This chapter encompasses a broad range of synthesis techniques, beginning with the *multiple wavetable* methods employed in commercial samplers and synthesizers. This is followed by an explanation of *wave terrain synthesis* and the family of *granular synthesis* methods. The rest of the chapter deals with *subtractive synthesis,* a powerful class of techniques that use filters to shape sound signals.

Multiple Wavetable Synthesis

By *multiple wavetable synthesis,* we refer to two simple yet sonically effective methods: *wavetable crossfading* and *wavestacking*. These are not the only synthesis methods that can use multiple wavetables; indeed most methods can be configured to do so. We distinguish the techniques discussed here by the fact that they are dependent on the existence of multiple wavetables. Both are common in commercial samplers and sample players.

Horner, Beauchamp, and Hakken (1993) have developed another technique they call "multiple wavetable synthesis." It is perhaps best classified as a variant of additive analysis/resynthesis (presented in chapter 4). But it also can be viewed as an instance of the wavestacking method presented here, where the wavetables are sums of sinusoids derived from an analysis and data reduction stage.

Wavetable Crossfading

As chapter 1 explains, in fixed-waveform synthesis, a digital oscillator scans repeatedly through a wavetable that has been previously filled with a single waveform. This creates a static timbre, since the waveform repeats without variance over time. By contrast, wavetable crossfading is direct way to generate time-varying timbres. Instead of scanning a single wavetable repeatedly, the oscillator *crossfades* between two or more wavetables over the course of an event. That is, the event begins with waveform 1, and as 1 begins to fade away, waveform 2 fades in, and so on. Figure 5.1 portrays the crossfading process. Wavetable crossfading is the core of what has been called variously *compound synthesis* (Roads 1985f), *vector synthesis* (by the Sequential Circuits, Korg, and Yamaha companies), and *L/A* or *Linear Arithmetic* synthesis (Roland).

Wavetable crossfading creates sounds that mutate from one source to another over time. For example, a common crossfading technique is to graft the rich attack of an acoustic instrument such as a guitar, piano, or percus-

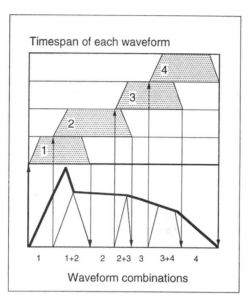

Figure 5.1   Wavetable crossfading. The bold outline traces the amplitude of a note event. Four waveforms crossfade over the span of the event. The numbers at the bottom indicate the sequence of waveforms alone and in combination. Each region indicated at the bottom represents a separate timbre; thus the event crossfades through seven timbres.

sion instrument onto the sustain part of a synthetic waveform. Figure 5.2 depicts an instrument for wavetable crossfading.

The first commercial synthesizer to implement wavetable crossfading was the Sequential Circuits Incorporated Prophet VS, introduced in 1985 (figure 5.3), which could crossfade between four waveforms. Newer synthesizers let users specify an arbitrary number of waveforms to crossfade during a single event (figure 5.4). The crossfading can be automatic (triggered by a note event) or it can be manually controlled by a rotating a joystick, as in the vector synthesis implementations designed by David Smith and manufactured in Korg and Yamaha synthesizers.

Wavestacking

Wavetable stacking or *wavestacking* is a simple and effective variation on additive synthesis. In this method, each sound event results from the addition of several waveforms (typically four to eight on commercial synthesizers). This is done in a different way than in classical additive synthesis. Classical additive synthesis sums sine waves, whereas in wavestacking each waveform can be a complicated signal, such as a sampled sound (figure 5.5).

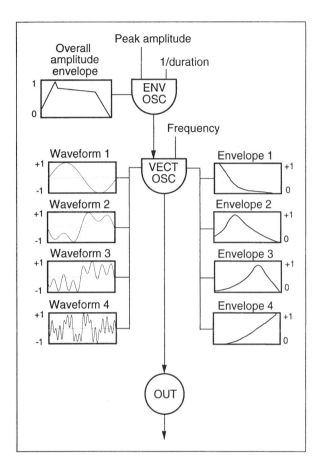

Figure 5.2   Wavetable crossfading (vector synthesis) instrument using four wavetables. Each envelope on the right applies to a wavetable on the left.

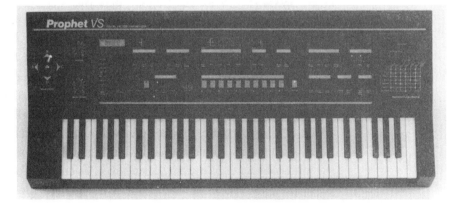

Figure 5.3   Prophet VS digital synthesizer made by Sequential Circuits Incorporated (1985).

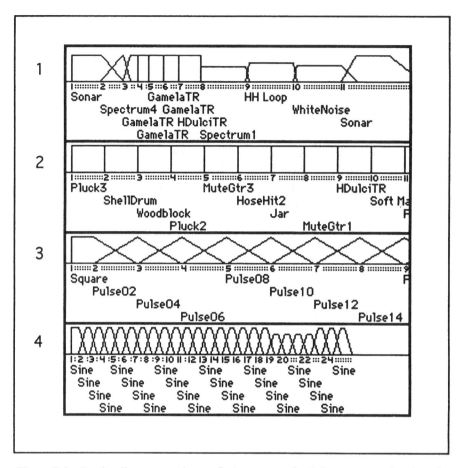

Figure 5.4   Patch editor screen image for vector synthesis instrument, showing the wavetable sequences for four voices. Notice that voice 4 fades through 24 wavetables. Although each is labeled "sine," these sines may be at different amplitudes and contain a different number of cycles, causing momentary variations.

By layering several sampled sounds, one can create hybrid timbres like saxophone/flutes or violin/clarinets. Each waveform in the stack has its own amplitude envelope, so sounds fade in and out of the stack of the course of a sound event. When four to eight complex waveforms can be stacked, deep and rich hybrid textures can be created for each sound event.

Wavestacking is implemented by storing a library of waveforms and using table-lookup oscillators to scan them. Each waveform's envelope must be scaled by a factor of $1/n$, where n is equal to the number of stacked waveforms, to avoid numerical overflow. (That is, the sum of all the waveforms should be within the quantization range of the synthesizer.) Wavestacking has been implemented on many commercial synthesizers.

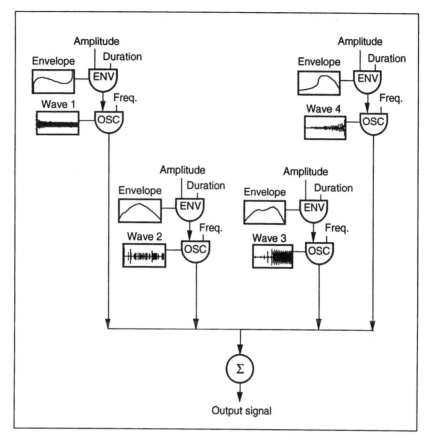

Figure 5.5 Wavetable stacking. The signals from four oscillators added together. Notice that the wavetables contain not simple periodic functions but long sampled sounds.

Sometimes it is combined with multiple wavetable crossfading to create sounds with turgid internal motion and spectral development.

Wave Terrain Synthesis

Many synthesis techniques start from the fundamental principle of wavetable lookup as explained in chapter 1: a wavetable is scanned by means of an index that is incremented at each sample period. It is possible to extend the principle of wavetable lookup to the scanning of three-dimensional "wave surfaces." We call such a surface a *wave terrain* (WT), after R. Gold's use of the term (Bischoff, Gold, and Horton 1978). Several computer music researchers, including Gold in consultation with Leonard Cottrell (Bischoff,

Gold, and Horton 1978), Mitsuhashi (1982c), and Borgonovo and Haus (1984, 1986), have explored the possibilities of techniques that scan a wave terrain using two indexes. (The article by Borgonovo and Haus 1986 contains code listings for realizing the technique.)

Terrains and Orbits

A traditional wavetable can be plotted in two dimensions as a function $wave(x)$ indexed by x. A two-index wave terrain can be plotted as a function $wave(x, y)$ etched on a three-dimensional surface (figure 5.6). In this case, the z-point or height of the surface at each point represents a waveform value for a given pair (x, y). The waveform stored in such a table is a *function of two variables*, and thus the technique has also been called *two-variable function* synthesis (Borgonono and Haus 1986).

A scan over the terrain is called an *orbit*. Although the astronomical term "orbit" connotes an elliptical function, the orbit can consist of any sequence of points on the wave terrain. We discuss orbits more in a moment; first we confront the problem of generating predictable waveforms with WT synthesis.

Generating Predictable Waveforms from Wave Terrains

For musical purposes, any three-dimensional surface can serve as a wave terrain—from a tightly-constrained mathematical function to an arbitrary topographical projection, such as a relief map of a geophysical region. It is not surprising, however, that systematic investigations of the technique have focused on wave terrains generated by relatively simple mathematical functions. As in techniques like frequency modulation and waveshaping (chapter 6), the advantage of using simple mathematical functions is that it is possible to predict exactly the output waveform and spectrum generated by a given wave terrain. Mitsuhashi (1982c) and Borgonovo and Haus (1986) devised smooth mathematical wave terrain functions in the range $[-1 \leq x \leq 1, -1 \leq y \leq 1]$. The following conditions must be met in order to predict the output waveform:

1. Both the x and y functions and their first-order partial derivatives are continuous (in the mathematical sense) over the terrain.

2. Both the x and y functions are zero on the boundaries of the terrain.

The second property ensures that the functions and their derivatives are continuous when the orbit skips from one edge of the wave terrain to

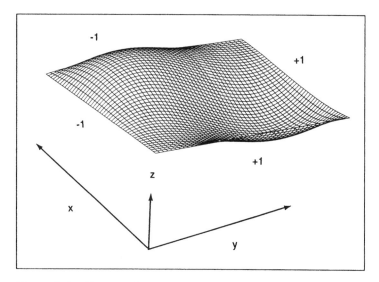

Figure 5.6 The waveform terrain is a three-dimensional surface. The height (*z*-axis) of the terrain represents the waveform value.

another edge. Such a skip is analogous to the right-to-left wraparound that occurs in one-index wavetable scanning.

The wave terrain depicted in figure 5.6 satisfies the above conditions and is defined by the following equation:

$$wave(x, y) = (x - y) \times (x - 1) \times (x + 1) \times (y - 1) \times (y + 1). \tag{1}$$

We will see how this function generates various waveforms depending on the scanning orbit. See Mitshuhashi (1982c) and Borgonovo and Haus (1986) for definitions of similar functions.

Periodic Orbits

The output signal generated by WT depends on both the wave terrain and the trajectory of the orbit. The orbit can be a straight or curved line across the surface, a random walk, a sinusoidal function, or an elliptical function generated by sinusoidal terms in both the *x* and *y* dimensions. If the orbit repeats itself (i.e., is periodic), so will the output signal. The top of figure 5.7 shows a periodic elliptical orbit defined by the functions

$x = 0.5 \times \sin(8\pi t + \pi/5)$
$y = \sin(8\pi t).$

The bottom of figure 5.7 displays the periodic waveform that results from using the elliptical orbit on the wave terrain of equation 1.

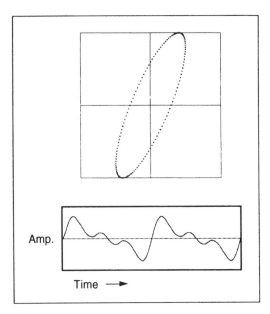

Figure 5.7 Elliptical orbit and resulting signal. (top) Plot of the orbit. Both the *x* and *y* dimensions vary from −1 to +1. (After Borgonovo and Haus 1986.) (bottom) Waveform generated by the elliptical orbit over the wave terrain defined in equation 1. (Note: This waveform is an approximation redrawn from Borgonovo and Haus 1986.)

Figure 5.8 shows an example of another periodic orbit that loops around the terrain, defined by the functions

$$x = 0.23 \times \sin(24\pi t)$$
$$y = (16 \times t) + 0.46 \times \sin(24\pi t + \pi/2).$$

Time-varying Orbits

When the orbit is fixed, the resulting sound is a fixed waveform characterized by a static spectrum. A way to generate time-varying waveforms is to change the orbit over time (figure 5.9). Orbits in the form of spirals, for example, have been shown to produce interesting results.

One can also imagine an extension where the orbit is fixed but the wave terrain is time-varying. In this case the wave-scanning process is equivalent to tracing the curves of an undulating surface, like wave motions on the surface of the sea.

WT synthesis has proven itself as an efficient experimental technique for generating synthetic sounds. However, in order to approximate familiar sounds like speech or the timbres of acoustic musical instruments, more research is needed to tune the parameters of the technique.

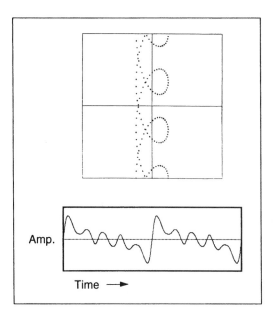

Figure 5.8   Looping orbit and resulting signal. (top) Plot of the orbit. Both the *x* and *y* dimensions vary from -1 to $+1$. (After Borgonovo and Haus 1986.) (bottom) Waveform generated by the elliptical orbit over the wave terrain defined in equation 1. (Note: This waveform is an approximation redrawn from Borgonovo and Haus 1986.)

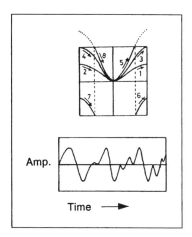

Figure 5.9   Aperiodic orbit and resulting signal. (top) Plot of orbit trajectories in eight passes through the wave terrain. (bottom) Notice the time-varying waveform. (After Mitsuhashi 1982c.)

Granular Synthesis

Just as light energy can be viewed both in terms of wavelike properties and in terms of particulate properties (photons), so can sound. *Granular synthesis* builds up acoustic events from thousands of sound *grains*. A sound grain lasts a brief moment (typically 1 to 100 ms), which approaches the minimum perceivable event time for duration, frequency, and amplitude discrimination.

Granular representations are a useful way of viewing complex sound phenomena—as constellations of elementary units of energy, with each unit bounded in time and frequency. Such representations are common inside synthesis and signal-processing algorithms, although there are many different terms for similar phenomena. The "quantum" (Gabor 1946, 1947), "Gaussian elementary signal" (Helstrom 1966; Bastiaans 1980), "short-time segment" (Schroeder and Atal 1962), "short-time weighting function" (Flanagan 1972), "window" (Arfib 1991; Harris 1978; Nuttall 1981), "sliding window" (Bastiaans 1985), "window function pulse" (Bass and Goeddel 1981), "wavelet" (Kronland-Martinet and Grossmann 1991), "formant-wave-function" or "FOF" (Rodet 1980), "VOSIM pulse" (Kaegi and Tempelaars 1978), "wave packet" (Crawford 1968), "toneburst" (Blauert 1983; Pierce 1990), "tone pulse" (Whitfield 1978), and even the "tone pip" (Buser and Imbert 1992) can all be described as granular representations of musical signals.

The grain is an apt representation for sound because it combines time-domain information (starting time, duration, envelope shape, waveform shape) with frequency-domain information (the period of the waveform inside the grain, spectrum of the waveform). This stands in opposition to representations at the sample level that do not capture frequency-domain information, and abstract Fourier methods that presume that sounds are summations of infinitely long sinusoids.

Granular Synthesis: Background

Atomistic views of sound as "particles" can be traced to the origins of the scientific revolution. The Dutch scholar Isaac Beekman (1588–1637) proposed in 1616 a "corpuscular" theory of sound (Beekman 1604–1634; Cohen 1984). Beekman believed that any vibrating object, like a string, cuts the surrounding air into spherical corpuscles of air that are projected in all directions by the vibration. When these corpuscles impinge on the eardrum, Beekman theorized, we perceive sound. While this theory is not strictly true in a scientific sense, it paints a colorful metaphor for the perception of granular synthesis.

Centuries later, the notion of a *granular* or *quantum* approach to sound was proposed by the British physicist Dennis Gabor in a pair of brilliant papers that combined theoretical insights from quantum physics with practical experiments (1946, 1947). According to Gabor's theory, a granular representation could describe any sound. This hypothesis was verified mathematically by Bastiaans (1980, 1985). In the 1940s Gabor actually constructed a sound granulator based on a sprocketed optical recording system adapted from a film projector. He used this to make experiments in *time compression/expansion* with *pitch shifting*—changing the pitch of a sound without changing its duration, and vice versa. (See chapter 10 for a discussion of time compression and expansion with pitch-shifting.)

A granular representation is implicit in the *windowing* technique applied in the *short-time Fourier transform,* developed in the 1960s (Schroeder and Atal 1962; see chapter 13 and appendix A). The MIT cybernetician Norbert Wiener (1964) and the information theorist Abraham Moles (1968) also proposed granular representations for sound.

The composer Iannis Xenakis (1960) was the first to explicate a compositional theory for grains of sound. He began by adopting the following lemma: "All sound, even continuous musical variation, is conceived as an assemblage of a large number of elementary sounds adequately disposed in time. In the attack, body, and decline of a complex sound, thousands of pure sounds appear in a more or less short interval of time Δt." Xenakis created granular sounds using analog tone generators and tape splicing. These appear in the composition *Analogique A-B* for string orchestra and tape (1959). The composition is described in Xenakis (1992). (The score and tape are available from Editions Salabert.)

The author of this book developed the first computer-based implementations of granular synthesis in 1974 at the University of California, San Diego (Roads 1978c) and in 1981 at the Massachusetts Institute of Technology (Roads 1985g). The technique appears in several compositions, including *nscor* (1980, Wergo compact disc 2010-50), *Field* (1981, MIT Media Laboratory compact disc), and *Clang-tint* (Roads 1993b). Granular synthesis has been implemented in different ways, notably by the Canadian composer Barry Truax (1987, 1988, 1990a, b), as we discuss in more detail later.

Sonic Grains

An amplitude envelope shapes each grain. This envelope can vary in different implementations from a Gaussian bell-shaped curve to a simple

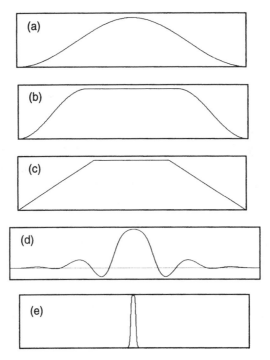

Figure 5.10   Grain envelopes. (*a*) Gaussian. (*b*) Quasi-Gaussian. (*c*) Three-stage linear. (*d*) Pulse. (*e*) Narrow impulse; this could be seen as equivalent to (*a*), but over a narrower timescale.

three-stage line-segment attack/sustain/decay (figure 5.10). The following equation defines a Gaussian curve $P(x)$:

$$P(x) = \frac{1}{\sigma\sqrt{2\pi}} e^{-(x-\mu)^2/2\sigma^2}$$

where σ is the standard deviation (spread of the bell) and μ is the *mean* or center peak.

Figure 5.10b shows a *quasi-Gaussian* curve or *Tukey window* (Harris 1978), where the peak is extended over 30 to 50 percent of the duration of the grain. This shape has proved sonically effective (Roads 1985g).

Complicated envelopes like a band-limited pulse (figure 5.10d) create resonant grains that sound like woodblock taps in sparse textures when the grain duration is less than 100 ms. Narrow envelopes like figure 5.10e create crackling and popping textures when the total grain duration is less than 20 ms. As one would expect, sharp angles in the envelope cause strong side effects in the spectrum. These side effects are due to the convolution of the envelope's spectrum with that of the grain waveform. (See chapter 10 for an explanation of convolution.)

The grain duration can be constant, random, or it can vary in a frequency-dependent way. This means, for example, that we can assign shorter durations to high-frequency grains. A correspondence between grain frequency and grain duration is characteristic of the *wavelet* analysis/resynthesis, discussed later in this chapter and in chapter 13.

The waveform within the grain can be of two types: synthetic or sampled. Synthetic waveforms are typically sums of sinusoids scanned at a specified frequency. For sampled grains, one typically reads the waveform from a stipulated location in a stored sound file, with or without pitch-shifting.

Several parameters can be varied on a grain-by-grain basis, including the duration, envelope, frequency, location in sound file (for sampled grains), spatial location, and waveform (a wavetable for synthetic grains, or a file name or input channel for sampled grains). It is this grain-by-grain level of control that leads to the unique effects made possible by this method.

Grain Generator Instrument

Granular synthesis can be implemented with a simple synthesis instrument: a sine wave oscillator controlled by an envelope generator (figure 5.11). One could easily extend this instrument to allow a choice between several wavetable functions.

Despite the simplicity of the instrument, to generate even a plain, uncomplicated sound requires a massive amount of control data—up to thousands of parameters per second of sound. These parameters describe each grain: starting time, amplitude, etc. Since one does not want to have to specify each grain's parameters manually, a higher-level unit of organization is necessary. This unit of organization should automatically generate the thousands of individual grain specifications.

High-level Granular Organizations

The complexity of the sound generated by granular synthesis derives from the amount of control data fed to it. If n is the number of parameters for each grain, and d is the average grain density per second of sound, it takes $d \times n$ parameter values to specify one second. Since d typically varies between a few dozen and several thousand, it is clear that for the purposes of compositional control, a higher-level unit of organization for the grains is needed. The purpose of such a unit is to let composers stipulate large quantities of grains using just a few global parameters.

Existing granular synthesis methods can be classified into five types, according to the organization of the grains:

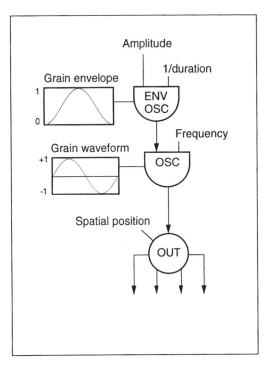

Figure 5.11   A simple granular synthesis instrument built from an envelope generator and an oscillator with multichannel output.

1. Fourier and wavelet grids

2. Pitch-synchronous overlapping streams

3. Quasi-synchronous streams

4. Asynchronous clouds

5. Time-granulated or sampled-sound streams, with overlapped, quasi-synchronous, or asynchronous playback

In the next sections we examine briefly each approach.

Fourier/Wavelet Grids and Screens

Two related spectrum analysis techniques, the short-time Fourier transform (STFT) and the *wavelet transform,* take in a time-domain sound signal and measure its frequency content versus time. (Chapter 13 presents both techniques.) In effect, these methods associate each point in the analysis grid with a unit of time-frequency energy—a grain or wavelet (figure 5.12).

The STFT is well known and can be computed using the fast Fourier transform (Rabiner and Gold 1975). The "grain" in this case is a set of

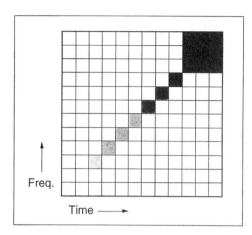

Figure 5.12 Fourier grid dividing the time domain and the frequency domain into bounded units. Each row represents a frequency channel, and each column indicates a period of time. The darkness in each square indicates the intensity in that time-frequency region. This example shows a sound that ascends in frequency and grows more intense. In the STFT the frequency grid is linear; in the wavelet transform it is typically logarithmic.

overlapping analysis windows within each of the N channels of the Fourier analyzer (the horizontal rows of figure 5.12). We can view the grains as if they were aligned on a two-dimensional time/frequency grid, where the intervals between the grid are equal. Arfib (1991) describes applications of the STFT in terms of granular operations.

The wavelet transform (Kronland-Martinet and Grossmann 1991) performs a similar operation, but the spacing of the analysis channels and the duration of the window (called the *analyzing wavelet*) is different from the STFT. In the STFT, the spacing between the channels on the frequency axis is linear, while in the wavelet transform it is logarithmic. That is, in the wavelet transform, the channel frequency interval (bandwidth) $\Delta f/f$ is constant. Also, in the STFT, the window duration is fixed, while in the wavelet transform it varies as a function of frequency. (See chapter 13 for more on wavelets.)

Both techniques permit analysis, transformation, and resynthesis, which make them potentially powerful musical tools for the manipulation of sampled sounds. The most obvious transformations using Fourier/wavelet grids involve stretching or shrinking the grid to effect time compression and expansion with pitch-shifting, that is, shifting pitch while keeping the duration the same, or vice versa.

Another grid-oriented conception, but not related to Fourier or wavelet analysis, is Xenakis's (1960, 1992) concept of *screens*. A screen is an amplitude-frequency grid on which grains are scattered. A synchronous sequence of screens (called a *book*) constitutes the evolution of a complex sound. Rather than starting from an analyzed sound, as in Fourier/wavelet grids, proposals for screen-based synthesis use generative algorithms to fill the screen with grains. Xenakis (1971, 1992) proposed scattering grains randomly into screens, then constructing new screens from set-theory operations—intersections, unions, complements, differences, among other operations:

Using all sorts of manipulations with these grain clusters, we can hope to produce not only the sounds of classical instruments and elastic bodies, and those sounds preferred in concrète music, but also sonic perturbations with evolutions unparalleled and un-imaginable until now.

Another screen-oriented proposal suggested that grain parameters could be derived from the interaction of cellular automata (Bowcott 1989).

Pitch Synchronous Granular Synthesis

Pitch synchronous granular synthesis (PSGS) is a technique designed for the generation of tones with one or more formant regions in their spectra (De Poli and Piccialli 1991). PSGS is a multistaged operation involving pitch detection, spectrum analysis and resynthesis, and impulse response-based filtering, technical processes that are described in later chapters; thus the description here is brief. (See De Poli and Piccialli 1991 for details.)

The first stage of the analysis is *pitch detection* (see chapter 12). Each pitch period is treated as a separate unit or grain. Spectrum analysis is performed on each grain. The system derives the *impulse response* of the spectrum and uses it to set the parameters for a resynthesis filter. (Chapter 10 discusses impulse response measurements.)

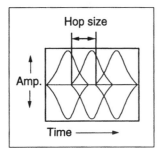

Figure 5.13 Stream of overlapped grains. The *hop size* is the delay between successive grains.

In resynthesis, a pulse train at the detected pitch period drives a bank of *finite impulse response* (FIR) filters. (FIR filters are discussed in chapter 10.) The output signal results from the excitation of the pulse train on the weighted sum of the impulse responses of all the filters. At each time frame, the system emits a grain that is overlapped and added with the previous grain to create a smoothly varying signal (figure 5.13). The implementation of PSGS by De Poli and Piccialli features several transformations that can create variations of the original sound. Later extensions allow separation of the quasi-harmonic part of the sound from the residual inharmonic part (Piccialli et al. 1992).

Quasi-synchronous Granular Synthesis

Quasi-synchronous granular synthesis (QSGS) generates one or more *streams* of grains, one grain following another, with a variable delay period between the grains. The stream concept has the advantage of being straightforward and intuitive. Orton, Hunt, and Kirk (1991) developed a graphical interface for drawing stream trajectories as curved lines on a display screen.

Figure 5.14 shows a stream of five grains, each with a quasi-Gaussian envelope and a variable delay before the next grain. We say "quasi-synchronous" because the grains follow each other at more-or-less equal intervals. When the interval between successive grains is equal, the overall envelope of a stream of grains forms a periodic function. Since the envelope is periodic, the signal generated by QSGS can be analyzed as a case of *amplitude modulation* (AM). AM occurs when the shape of one signal (the *modulator*) determines the amplitude of another signal (the *carrier*). (See chapter 6 for more on modulation.) In this case the carrier is the waveform within the grain, and the modulator is the grain envelope.

From a signal-processing standpoint, we observe that for each sinusoidal component in the carrier, the periodic envelope function contributes a series of *sidebands* to the final spectrum. (Sidebands are additional frequency components above and below the frequency of the carrier.) The sidebands are separated from the carrier by a distance corresponding to the inverse of the period of the envelope function. For a stream of 20 ms grains following one after the other, the sidebands in the output spectrum are spaced at 50 Hz intervals. The shape of the grain envelope determines the precise amplitude of these sidebands.

The result created by the modulation effect of a periodic envelope is that of a *formant* surrounding the carrier frequency. That is, instead of a single line in the spectrum (denoting a single frequency), the spectrum looks like a sloping hill (denoting a group of frequencies around the carrier). QSGS

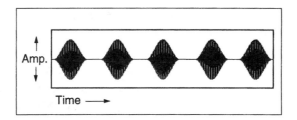

Figure 5.14   A stream of five 40 ms grains at 1.06 KHz with a Hanning envelope. In this case the delay period between the grains varies slightly.

is, in this sense, similar to the formant synthesis methods *VOSIM* (Kaegi and Tempelaars 1978) and *formant-wave-function* or FOF synthesis (Rodet 1980; Rodet, Potard, and Barrière 1984). (See chapter 7 for more on VOSIM and FOF synthesis.)

By combining several streams of quasi-synchronous grains in parallel (each stream creating its own formant around a separate frequency), the signal can simulate the resonances of the singing voice and acoustic instruments.

When the interval between the grains is irregular, as in figure 5.15, this leads to a controllable thickening of the sound texture through a "blurring" of the formant structure (Truax 1987, 1988). In its simplest form, the variable-delay method is similar to amplitude modulation (AM) using low-frequency colored noise as a modulator. (See chapter 6 for more on modulation.) In itself, this is not particularly interesting. The granular representation, however, lets us take this technique far beyond simple noise-modulated AM. In particular, we can simultaneously vary several other parameters on a grain-by-grain basis, such as grain waveform, amplitude, duration, and spatial location. On a more global level, we can also dynamically vary the density of grains per second to create a variety of striking effects.

Asynchronous Granular Synthesis

Asynchronous granular synthesis (AGS) gives the composer a precision spray jet for sound, where each dot in the spray is a sonic grain (Roads 1991). AGS scatters grains in a statistical manner over a specified duration within regions inscribed on the frequency-versus-time plane. These regions are called *clouds*—the units with which a composer works.

The composer specifies a cloud in terms of the following parameters, shown in figure 5.16.

1. Start time and duration of the cloud.

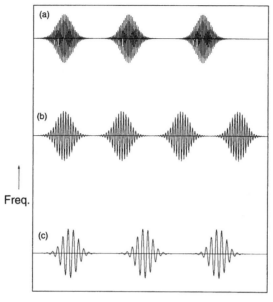

Figure 5.15 Schematic depiction of three streams in quasi-synchronous granular synthesis. The placement of a stream on the vertical axis indicates the grain frequency (i.e., the frequency of the waveform). The onset time between the grains is randomized.

2. Grain duration (usually from 1 to 100 ms, but it can also vary above and below these bounds). The grain duration can be set to a constant, random within limits, derived from a curve, or it can vary as function of the frequency of the grain, where high-frequency grains have shorter envelopes.

3. Density of grains per second; for example, if the grain density is low, then only a few grains are scattered at random points within the cloud. If the grain density is high, grains overlap to create complex spectra. The density can vary over the duration of the cloud.

4. Bandwidth of the cloud, usually specified by two curves that form high- and low-frequency boundaries within which grains are scattered (*cumulus* clouds); alternatively, the frequency of the grains in a cloud can be restricted to a specific set of pitches (as in the *stratus* clouds).

5. Amplitude envelope of the cloud.

6. Waveform(s) within the grains; this is one of the most powerful cloud parameters. For example, each grain in a cloud can have a different waveform; waveforms can be synthetic or sampled.

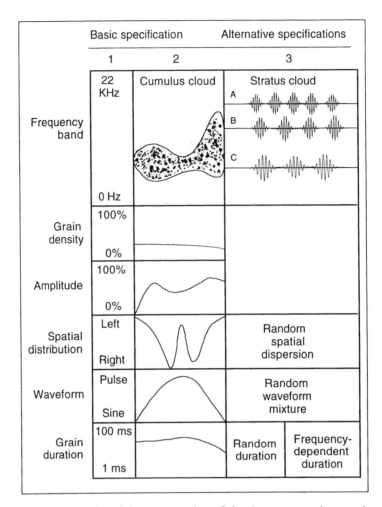

Figure 5.16   Pictorial representation of cloud parameters in asynchronous granular synthesis. The column labeled 1 shows the typical parameter ranges. Column 2 shows basic specifications for standard clouds. Column 3 shows alternative specifications for the frequency band, spatial distribution, waveform, and grain duration parameters.

7. Spatial dispersion of the grains in the cloud, where the number of output channels is specific to a given implementation.

By varying these seven parameters of AGS one can realize a wide range of effects. The rest of this section summarizes, in capsule form, the duration, waveform, frequency band, density, and spatial effects. The waveform and bandwidth parameters apply only to synthetic and not sampled grains. For a more detailed analysis of parametric effects in AGS, see Roads (1991).

As 5.16 shows, grain durations can be either constant (a straight line), variable, random between two limits, or frequency-dependent.

Grain duration changes the sonic texture of a cloud. Short durations lead to crackling, explosive sonorities, while longer durations create a much smoother impression. A profound law of signal processing comes into play in setting the grain duration: the shorter the duration of an event, the greater its bandwidth. Figure 5.17 demonstrates this law for three elementary signals.

Figure 5.18 shows the spectral effects of lowering the grain duration. Notice how the bandwidth expands dramatically as the grain duration shrinks.

Since the waveform can vary on a grain-by-grain basis, we can fill clouds with grains of a single waveform or multiple waveforms. A *monochrome* cloud uses a single waveform, for example, while a *polychrome* cloud contains a random mixture of several waveforms. A *transchrome* cloud mutates statistically from one waveform to another over the duration of the cloud.

For a cumulus cloud (figure 5.19a; see also figure 5.11, column 2), the generator scatters grains randomly within the upper and lower frequency bands. By narrowing these bands to a small interval we can generate pitched sounds. Various types of glissandi are easily achieved (figure 5.19b). An alternative specification is the stratus cloud (figure 5.19c; see also figure 5.11, column 3), where the grains are constrained to fall on a single pitch or specific pitches to create chords and pitch clusters.

The grain density combines with the bandwidth parameter to create various effects. Sparse densities, regardless of bandwidth, create pointillistic textures. At high grain densities, narrow frequency bands create pitched streams with formant spectra, while wide bands (an octave or more) generate massive blocks of sound.

Finally, in AGS as in all forms of granular synthesis, multichannel spatial distribution enhances granular texture. The spatial algorithm of a cloud can involve random scattering or panning effects over the duration of the cloud event.

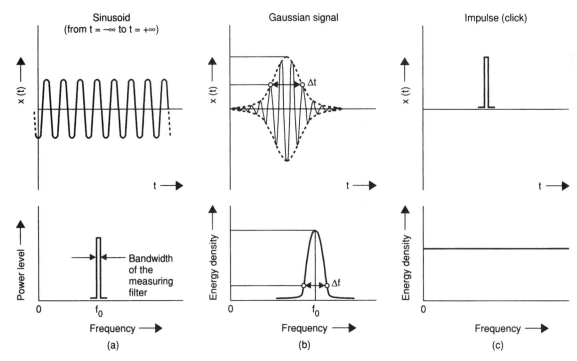

Figure 5.17   Time-domain functions (*top*) and spectra (*bottom*) of three elementary signals, after Blauert (1983). (*a*) Sine wave of infinite duration corresponds to a single line in the spectrum. (*b*) Gaussian grain and corresponding formant spectrum. (*c*) Brief impulse and corresponding infinite spectrum.

Time Granulation of Sampled Sounds

The *time granulation* of recorded (sampled) sounds feeds acoustic material into a kind of logical thrashing machine—delivering grains in a new ordering with a new microrhythm. That is, the *granulator* reads in a small part of a sampled sound (from a sound file or directly from an analog-to-digital converter) and applies an envelope to the portion read in. The order in which this grain is emitted (i.e., its delay) depends on the settings selected by the composer.

Time granulation takes three paths:

1. Granulation of a stored sound file, like a musical note, an animal sound, or a spoken text

2. Continuous real-time granulation of a given input sound or *time scrambling* (Truax 1987, 1988, 1990a, b)

3. Continuous real-time granulation of a given input sound with playback at variable time rate (Truax 1987, 1988, 1990a, b)

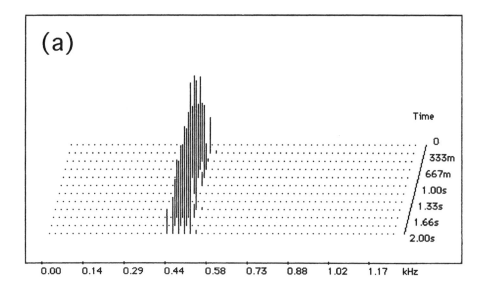

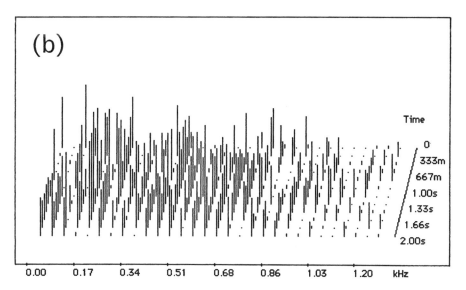

Figure 5.18 Spectral effect of the grain duration. (*a*) Spectrum of a cloud at a constant frequency of 500 Hz with 100 ms grains. Notice the formant region centered at 500 Hz. Time is plotted from back to front. (*b*) Spectrum of a cloud at a constant frequency of 500 Hz but with 1 ms grains. Notice the width of the spectrum.

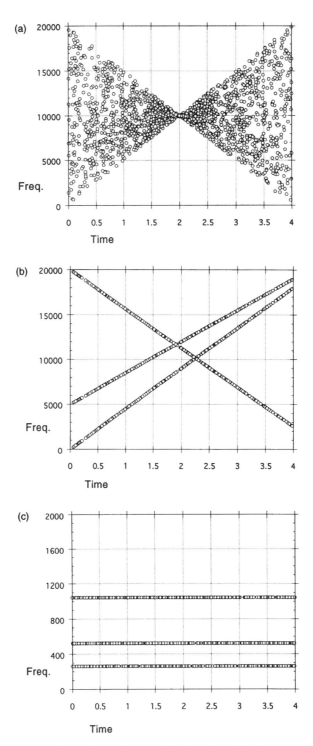

Figure 5.19   Cloud forms. (*a*) Cumulus. (*b*) Glissandi. (*c*) Stratus.

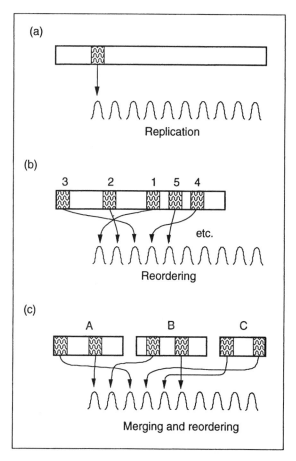

Figure 5.20   Three approaches to time granulation from stored sound files. (*a*) One grain is extracted and turned into a "roll." (*b*) Grains are randomly extracted from a sound file and recordered. (*c*) Grains are randomly chosen from different sound files and reordered. The grains need not be strictly sequential and may overlap.

The first case is the most flexible since one can extract grains from the file in any order. For example, one can extract a single large grain from a snare drum and clone a periodic sequence of hundreds of grains to create a snare drum roll (figure 5.20a). Alternatively the grain generator can sample randomly grains from longer file, such as speech or several notes, thus reordering them (figure 5.20b). An extension of this technique is to randomly sample several sound files and interweave their grains to create multicolored textures (figure 5.20c). These interwoven sound fabrics vary widely depending on the pitch and timbre of the individual grains used within them.

Case (2) above involves real-time granulation of continuous sound with the computer acting as a *delay line* or *window* that can be tapped to furnish the various grains. (See the description of delay lines and taps in chapter

10.) In this case the spectral side effects of the granulation distort and enrich the sound in a controllable way.

Case (3) resembles case (2) except that the playback rate can be varied by a parameter that controls the speed at which synthesis advances through the samples. The playback can vary from normal speed to a slowed-down rate in which a single sample is repeated over and over again. Hence this method can be thought of as an interpolation between case (1) and case (2).

Assessment of Granular Synthesis

Granular synthesis constitutes a diverse body of techniques that share only the concept of sonic grains. The granular representation is purely internal in Fourier and wavelet analysis, hidden from users. Indeed, a technical goal of these methods is creating the illusion of continuous, analog-like signal processing. A granular sonority appears only in pathological distortions such as too large a hop size in overlap-add resynthesis (see chapter 13). The pitch-synchronous analysis/resynthesis of A. Piccialli and his colleagues makes the granular representation more explicit. Techniques like quasi-synchronous granular synthesis (as developed by B. Truax) have been implemented on a variety of platforms.

Asynchronous granular synthesis (AGS) has proven valuable in modeling sounds that would be difficult to describe using earlier techniques. AGS sprays sonic grains into cloudlike formations across the audio spectrum. The result is often a particulated sound complex that can act as a foil to smoother, more sterile sounds emitted by digital oscillators. Time-varying combinations of clouds lead to dramatic effects such as evaporation, coalescence, and mutations created by crossfading overlapping clouds. A striking analogy exists between these processes and those created in the visual domain by *particle synthesis* (Reeves 1983). Particle synthesis has been used to create fire, water, clouds, fog, and grasslike textures, which are analogous to some of the audio effects possible with AGS (crackling fire, water gurgling, windy gusts, explosions). Finally, in combination with time granulation and convolution (Roads 1993a), granular methods are evolving from pure synthesis techniques to sound transformation applications.

Subtractive Synthesis

Subtractive synthesis implies the use of *filters* to shape the spectrum of a source sound. As the source signal passes through a filter, the filter boosts or attenuates selected regions of the frequency spectrum. If the original source is spectrally rich and the filter is flexible, subtractive synthesis can sculpt close approximations of many natural sounds (such as voices and traditional instruments) as well as a wide variety of new and unclassified timbres.

The rest of this section introduces the main tool of subtractive synthesis—filters—and leads to the section dealing with subtractive analysis/resynthesis techniques. In chapter 10 we go into more detail about the internal operation of filters. Here we are content to describe their effects.

Introduction to Filters

A filter can be literally any operation on a signal (Rabiner et al. 1972)! But the most common use of the term describes devices that boost or attenuate regions of a sound spectrum, which is the usage we take up here. Such filters work by using one or both of these methods:

- Delaying a copy of an *input signal* slightly (by one or several sample periods) and combining the delayed input signal with the new input signal (figure 5.21a)

- Delaying a copy of the *output signal* and combining it with the input signal (figure 5.21b)

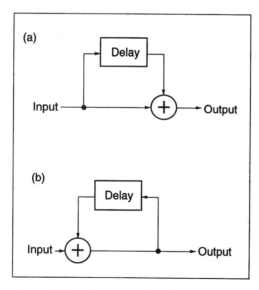

Figure 5.21   Two basic digital filters. (*a*) Delay the input and add it (FIR) (feedforward). (*b*) Delay the output and add it (IIR) (feedback).

Although figure 5.21 shows combination by summation ($+$), the combination can also be by subtraction ($-$). In either case, the combination of original and delayed signals creates a new waveform with a different spectrum. By inserting more delays or mixing sums and differences in various combinations, one can construct a wide range of filter types.

Next we discuss the properties of various filters. Since our main goal is to explain musical applications of subtractive synthesis, we do not dwell on how digital filters are implemented, or on the mathematics of filter theory. Chapter 10 contains a basic introduction to that vast universe. (See also Moorer 1977 and Moore 1978a, b.) Those with an engineering background could study texts such as Moore (1990), Smith (1985a, 1985b), Oppenheim and Willsky (1983), Rabiner and Gold (1975), and Oppenheim and Schafer (1975), among many others.

Filter Types and Response Curves

One of the main ways to characterize the various types of filters is to plot their *amplitude-versus-frequency response curve*. The specifications of audio equipment usually include a figure for "frequency response." This term is a shorter form of amplitude-versus-frequency response. The most accurate frequency response is a straight line which indicates a *linear* or *flat* amplitude across the frequency spectrum. This means that any frequency within the range of the audio device is passed without any boost or attentuation. Figure 15.22a shows a nearly flat frequency response, typical of a high-quality audio system. Here we show an arbitrary upper limit of 25 KHz. For high-quality analog audio components such as preamplifiers and amplifiers, the frequency response may extend up to 100 KHz. As chapter 1 explained, the frequency limits of digital audio systems depends on their sampling rate.

Practical devices are less than perfectly flat. Figure 5.22b shows the frequency response of a nonlinear system such as a small loudspeaker. We could describe the frequency response of this loudspeaker as follows: $+3$, -2.5 dB from 100 Hz to 16 KHz. This means that the loudspeaker boosts some frequencies by as much as 3 dB and attenuates other frequencies by as much as 2.5 dB over the specified range. Below 100 Hz and above 16 KHz the response falls off sharply. Since it alters the spectrum of a signal fed into it, the loudspeaker acts as a kind of filter.

Each type of filter has its own characteristic frequency response curve. Typical frequency response curves for four basic types of filters are shown in figure 5.23: *lowpass, highpass, bandpass,* and *bandreject* or *notch.*

Shelving filters, shown in figure 5.24, boost or cut all frequencies above or below a given threshold. Their names can be confusing, because a *high*

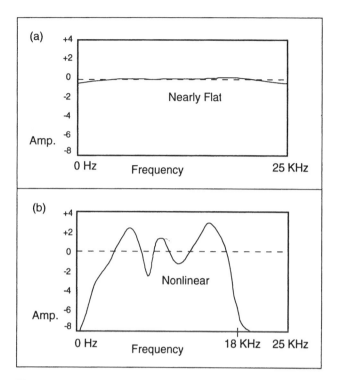

Figure 5.22 Amplitude-versus-frequency response, colloquially called "frequency response." The vertical axis is amplitude in decibels, and the horizontal axis is frequency. (*a*) Nearly flat response. (*b*) Nonlinear response.

shelving filter acts like a lowpass filter when it is adjusted to cut high frequencies, and a *low shelving filter* acts like a highpass filter when it is adjusted to cut low frequencies.

An important property of a filter is its *cutoff frequency*. Figures 5.23 and 5.24 show the cutoff frequency of the lowpass and highpass filters. By convention, this is the point in the frequency range at which the filter reduces the signal to 0.707 of its maximum value. Why 0.707? The *power* of the signal at the cutoff frequency is proportional to the amplitude of the signal squared, since $0.707^2 = 0.5$. Thus, the cutoff frequency is also called the *half-power point*. Yet another term for the cutoff frequency is the *3 dB point* (Tempelaars 1977). This is because 0.707 relative to 1.0 is close to −3 dB.

Spectral components that are attenuated below the half-power point of a filter are said to be in the *stopband* of a filter. Those above the half-power point are said to be in the *passband* of the filter. The difference between the higher and lower cutoff frequencies in a bandpass filter is the *bandwidth* of the filter. The center frequency of a bandpass filter is the maximum point of

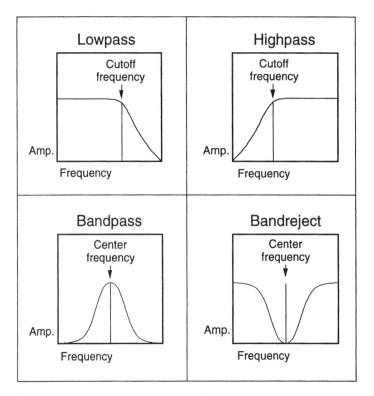

Figure 5.23   Four common types of filters.

amplitude; the center frequency of a bandreject filter is the minimum point of amplitude.

In an ideally sharp filter, the cutoff frequency is a kind of brick wall: anything outside it is maximally attenuated, dividing the frequency response neatly into a passband and a stopband (figure 5.25a). In actual filters, the slope of the filter is not linear leading up to the cutoff frequency (there is a *ripple* in the frequency response), and the area between the passband and the stopband is called the *transition band* (figure 5.25b).

The steepness of a filter's slope is usually specified in terms of decibels of attenuation or boost per octave, abbreviated "dB/octave." For example, a 6 dB/octave slope on a lowpass filter makes a smooth attenuation (or *rolloff*), while a 90 dB/octave slope makes a sharp cutoff (figure 5.26).

The use of a smooth or sharp slope depends on the musical situation. For example, a sharp notch filter might be needed to eliminate a tone centered on a particular frequency, while a gentle lowpass filter could be the most unobtrusive way of attenuating background noise in the high-frequency range.

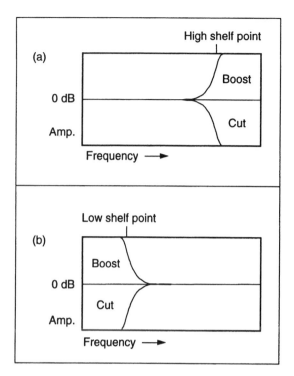

Figure 5.24 Shelving filters. (*a*) High shelving filter. Above the shelf point, the signal can be either boosted or cut. If the signal is cut, the effect of a high shelf filter is equivalent to a lowpass filter. (*b*) Low shelving filter. Below the shelf point, the signal can be either boosted or cut.

Filter Q and Gain

Many bandpass filters have a control knob (either in software or hardware) for Q. An intuitive definition of Q is that it represents the degree of "resonance" within a bandpass filter. Figure 5.27 shows a filter adjusted to various values of Q. When the Q is high, as in the narrowest inner curve, the frequency response is sharply focused around a peak (resonant) frequency. If a high-Q filter is excited by a signal near its center frequency, the filter *rings* at the resonant frequency, that is, it goes into oscillation, for some time after the signal has passed.

Q can be defined precisely for a bandpass filter as the ratio of the center frequency to the spread of its -3 dB point (cutoff point) bandwidth:

$$Q = \frac{f_{center}}{f_{highcutoff} - f_{lowcutoff}}$$

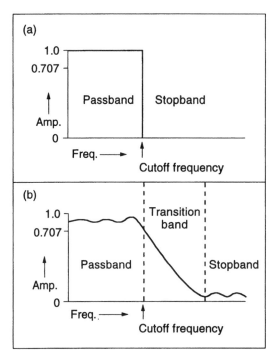

Figure 5.25 Ideal versus nonideal filters. (*a*) In an ideal filter, the frequencies affected by the filter can be neatly divided into a passband and a stopband, and the cutoff is rectangular. (*b*) In a nonideal (actual) filter, the response curve shows ripple, and there is a more or less steep transition band between the passband and the stopband.

where f_{center} is the filter's center frequency, $f_{highcutoff}$ is the upper 3 dB point, and $f_{lowcutoff}$ is the lower 3 dB point. Notice that when the center frequency is constant, adjusting the Q is the same as adjusting the bandwidth. Here is an example of a calculation of the Q of a filter. We define a bandpass filter with a center frequency of 2000 Hz and 3 dB points of 1800 and 2200 Hz. This filter has a Q of $2000/(2200 - 1800) = 5$. High Q resonant filters like this are useful in generating percussive sounds. Tuned drums like tablas, wood blocks, claves, and marimba effects can be simulated by exciting a high Q resonant filter with a pulsetrain.

Another property of a bandpass or bandreject filter is its *gain*. This is the amount of boost or cut of a frequency band. It shows up as the height (or depth) of the band in a response curve (figure 5.28). When passing a signal through a high Q filter, care must be taken to ensure that the gain at the resonant frequency (the height at the peak) does not overload the system, causing distortion. Many systems have *gain-compensation* circuits in their filters that prevent this kind of overload.

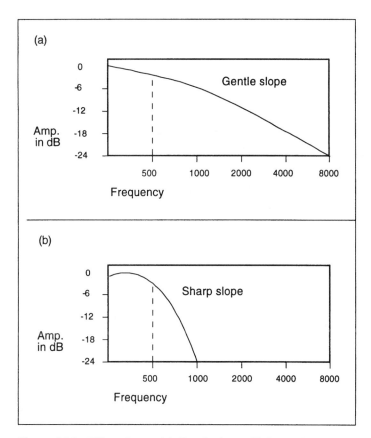

Figure 5.26   Filter slopes. (*a*) Gentle slope. (*b*) Steep slope.

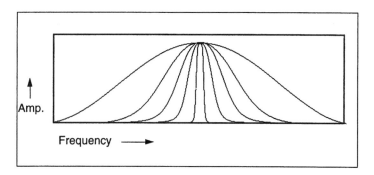

Figure 5.27   A filter set at various values for *Q*. A high *Q* corresponds to a narrow response. The *gain* (height of the peak) is constant.

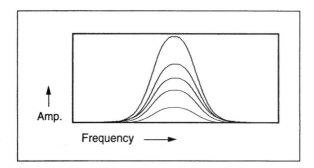

Figure 5.28 Different gain factors applied to the same filter. The bandwidth and Q remain constant.

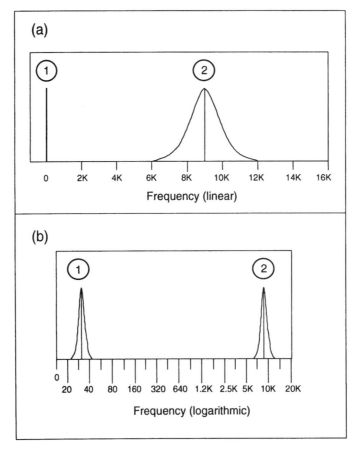

Figure 5.29 The same constant Q filters plotted on linear and logarithmic frequency ranges. Filter 1 has a center frequency of 30 Hz and extends from 20 to 40 Hz in bandwidth. Filter 2 has a center frequency of 9 KHz and extends from 6 to 12 KHz. (*a*) Linear. (*b*) Logarithmic.

A special type of bandpass filter is called a *constant Q filter*. To maintain a fixed Q, a constant Q filter must vary its bandwidth as a function of the center frequency. For example, when the center frequency is 30 Hz and the Q is 1.5 (or 3/2), the bandwidth is 20 Hz, because $30/20 = 1.5$. But if we tune the filter to 9 KHz and keep the Q constant at 1.5, then the bandwidth must be equal to 2/3 of the center frequency, or 6000 Hz. Figure 5.29 shows the curve of two constant Q filters plotted on linear and logarithmic frequency ranges. On a linear scale (figure 5.29a), the filter centered at 30 Hz appears as a very narrow band, while the filter centered at 9 KHz appears to have a much broader curve. On a logarithmic scale, the filters have the same shape (figure 5.29b).

A constant Q filter has the musical quality that the frequency interval it spans does not change as the center frequency changes. For example, a constant Q filter centered at A440 Hz with a Q of 1.222 spans the same musical interval as a filter with a Q of 1.222 centered at A880 Hz (C260 to D620, as compared with C520 to D1240, respectively).

Filter Banks and Equalizers

A *filter bank* is a group of filters that are fed the same signal in parallel (figure 5.30). Each filter is typically a narrow bandpass filter set at a specific frequency. The filtered signals are often combined to form the output sound. When each filter has its own level control the filter bank is called a

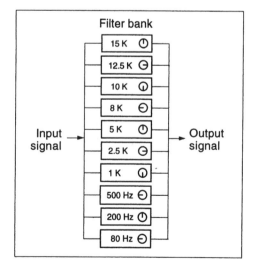

Figure 5.30   A ten-stage spectrum shaper with a control knob (boost or attenuate) associated with each frequency band.

spectrum shaper because the individual controls can radically modify the spectrum of the input signal. A spectrum shaper can be used to boost certain frequency regions or virtually eliminate others.

Another term for a spectrum shaper is an *equalizer*. The filtering it performs is called *equalization*. The term "equalization" derives from one of its original applications, namely, to compensate for irregularities in the frequency response of telephone channels and public address systems (Fagen 1975). For example, if a hall has a resonant boom at 150 Hz, an electronic equalizer can deemphasize that frequency and therefore compensate for the hall's exaggeration of it.

A *graphic equalizer* has controls that mirror the shape of the filter's frequency response curve (figure 5.31a). Each filter has a fixed center frequency, a fixed bandwidth (typically one-third of an octave), and a fixed Q. (Some units can switch between several Q settings.) The response of each filter can be varied by means of a linear fader to cut or boost specific frequency bands. The potential frequency response of such a filter is shown in figure 5.31b.

A *parametric equalizer* involves a fewer number of filters, but the control of each filter is more flexible. A typical arrangement is to have three or four filters in parallel. Users can adjust independently the center frequency, the Q, and the amount of cut or boost of each filter. A *semiparametric equalizer* has a fixed Q.

Comb and Allpass Filters

Two more filter types merit mention here before they are discussed in chapters 10 and 11. A filter that has several regular sharp curves in its frequency response is called a *comb filter*. Figure 5.32 shows the frequency response curves of two types of comb filters. One has deep notches in its response, while the other has steep peaks. The derivation of the term "comb" should be clear from these curves. Chapter 10 contains a more complete description of comb filters and their musical applications.

The final filter to mention is an *allpass filter*. For a steady-state (unchanging) sound fed into it, an allpass filter passes all frequencies equally well with unity gain—hence its name. The purpose of an allpass filter is to introduce a frequency-dependent phase shift. All filters introduce some phase shift while attenuating or boosting certain frequencies, but the main effect of an allpass filter is to shift phase. If the input signal is not steady-state, the allpass colors the signal, due to the frequency-dependent phase-shifting effects. This coloration is particularly evident on transient sounds where phase relations are so important to sound quality.

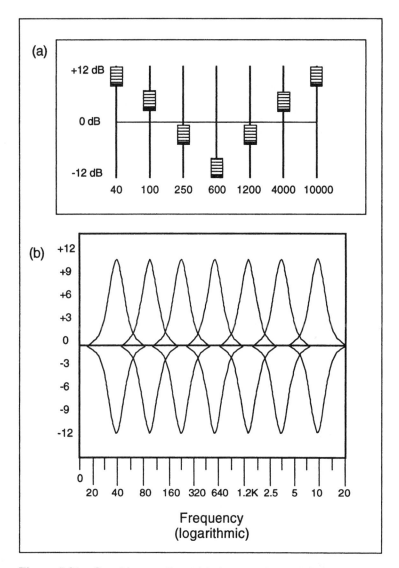

Figure 5.31 Graphic equalizer. (*a*) A seven-band graphic equalizer with linear potentiometers set to arbitrary levels. (*b*) The potential frequency response curve of a seven-band graphic equalizer.

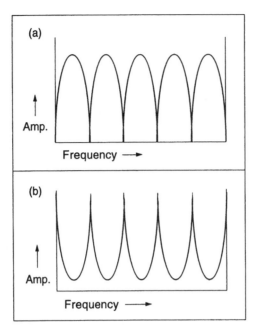

Figure 5.32   Comb filter frequency response curves. (*a*) FIR comb. (*b*) IIR comb. (See chapter 10 for an explanation of FIR and IIR.)

One application of an allpass filter is to correct for the unwanted phase shift of another filter. Allpass filters can also be used in musical sound processing. Here an allpass filter can imposes a time-varying, frequency-dependent phase shift on the input signal, which can lend richness to sounds. Allpass filters are one of the building blocks of digital reverberators. Chapters 10 and 11 discuss applications of allpass filters.

Time-varying Subtractive Synthesis

Filters can be *fixed* or *time-variant*. In a fixed filter, all the properties of the filter are predefined and do not change over time. This situation is typical of conventional music recording where the sound engineer sets the equalization for each channel at the beginning of the piece.

Time-variant filters have many musical applications, particularly in electronic and computer music where the goal is to surpass the limits of traditional instruments. A bandpass filter whose *Q*, center frequency, and attenuation change over time can impose a enormous variety of sound colorations, particularly if the signal being filtered is also time-varying. An example of a time-varying filter is a parametric equalizer section in a mixing console. The mixing engineer can change the *Q*, center frequency, and amount of cut or boost at any time during the mixing process, or these parameters can be programmed to change automatically.

A prime example of a system for time-varying subtractive synthesis is the SYTER—a digital signal processor developed in the late 1970s at the Groupe de Recherches Musicale (GRM) studio in Paris by Jean-François Allouis and associates (Allouis 1979; Allouis and Bernier 1982). Much of the SYTER software has since been ported to run on a signal-processing card for a personal computer (INA/GRM 1993).

SYTER was used as an engine for time-varying subtractive synthesis by composers such as Jean-Claude Risset in his composition *Sud* realized in 1985 (Wergo recording 2013-50). Running software written by B. Maillard, SYTER realized several dozen high Q bandpass filters in real time with dynamic parameter changes. The filters could also be driven by data generated from Fourier analysis of a sound (see the next section on subtractive analysis/resynthesis). When full-bandwidth sounds such as water and wind were processed through the system, the resonant filters "rang" in musical chords and clusters. Rich comb filter and phasing effects could also be created (see chapter 10).

Subtractive Analysis/Resynthesis

As with additive synthesis, the power of subtractive synthesis is enhanced by coupling an analysis stage to it. Analysis/resynthesis systems based on subtractive filters rather than on additive oscillators are capable of approximating any sound. In practice, most of the analysis and data reduction techniques employed in subtractive analysis/resynthesis are geared toward speech synthesis, since this is where most of research has been concentrated (Flanagan et al. 1970; Flanagan 1972).

Music research in subtractive analysis/resynthesis has focused on extending speech-oriented tools (such as linear predictive coding, discussed later in this chapter), to the domain of wide-bandwidth musical sound.

The Vocoder

The original subtractive analysis/synthesis system is the *vocoder,* demonstrated by a talking robot at the 1936 World's Fair in New York City (Dudley 1936, 1939a, 1939b, 1955; Dudley and Watkins 1939; Schroeder 1966; Flanagan 1972). The classic analog vocoder consists of two stages. The first stage is a group of fixed-frequency bandpass filters distributed over

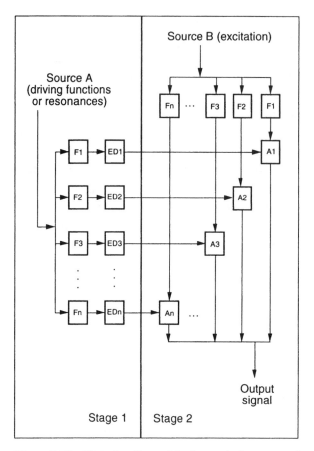

Figure 5.33   Vocoder. Stage 1 is the analysis part, and stage 2 is the synthesis. "F" stands for filter, "ED" stands for envelope detector, and "A" stands for voltage-controlled amplifier—an amplifier whose gain is determined by a control voltage fed into it from the envelope detector. The same structure can also be realized in digital form.

the audio bandwidth. The output of each filter is connected to an *envelope detector* that generates a voltage proportional to the amount of energy at the frequency tracked by the filter (figure 5.33).

The second stage of the vocoder is a bank of bandpass filters, identical to the first stage. All filters are sent the same input signal, and the output of each filter is sent to its own voltage-controlled amplifier (VCA). The outputs of all the VCAs combine into an output signal. The filters and detectors in the first stage generate control signals (also called *driving functions*) that determine the amplitude of the audio signal coming from the filters in the second stage of the vocoder.

Referring to figure 5.33, source A is the signal from which the formant spectrum is derived, such as a singing voice. If we were to trace an outline

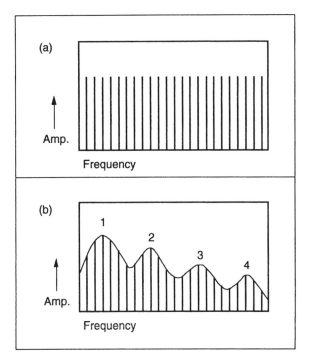

Figure 5.34 The effect of formant filters on an excitation function. (*a*) Simplified view of an excitation function like the spectrum produced by the open vocal cords; a buzz sound with a number of equal-strength harmonics. (*b*) Simplified view of the spectrum of a vowel showing four formant peaks labeled 1, 2, 3, and 4.

of this spectrum it would form the *spectral envelope* or *resonance curve*. Source B is the *excitation function*. The excitation function is usually a wide-bandwidth signal such as white noise or a pulsetrain. The output of this vocoder consists of the excitation function of source B with the time-varying spectral envelope of the singing voice of source A. Figure 5.34 depicts graphically the process of formant filtering applied to an excitation function.

The original mandate of vocoder research was data reduction for synthetic speech. The data rate and channel requirements of the slow-moving driving functions are indeed much less than those of the original signal.

In musical applications the separation of the driving functions (or resonance) from the excitation function means that rhythm, pitch, and timbre are independently controllable. For example, a composer can change the pitch of a singing voice (by changing the frequency of the excitation function), but retain the original spectral articulation of the voice. By stretching or shrinking the driving functions over time, a piece of spoken text can be slowed down or sped up without shifting the pitch or affecting the formant structure.

Linear Predictive Coding

Linear predictive coding (LPC) or *linear prediction* is a subtractive analysis/resynthesis method that has been extensively used in speech and music applications (Atal and Hanauer 1971; Flanagan 1972; Makhoul 1975; Markel and Gray 1976; Cann 1978, 1979, 1980; Moorer 1979a; Dodge 1985; Lansky 1987; Lansky and Steiglitz 1981; Hutchins 1986a; Lansky 1989; Dodge 1989; Depalle 1991). LPC takes in a sound, such as a speaking voice, analyzes it into a data-reduced form, and resynthesizes an approximation of it. LPC speech is quite efficient in the sense that it requires much less data than sampled speech; an inexpensive integrated circuit for LPC speech was developed in the early 1980s and was built into inexpensive speaking toys (Brightman and Crook 1982).

From the standpoint of the composer, the power of the LPC technique derives from the fact that one can edit the analysis data and resynthesize variations on the original input signal. LPC implements a type of vocoder. That is, it separates the excitation signal from the resonance, making it possible to manipulate rhythm, pitch, and timbre independently and permitting a form of *cross-synthesis* (explained later).

In speech, the vocal cords generate a buzzy excitation function and the rest of the vocal tract filters the sound to create resonances. The frequency of the excitation pulse determines the pitch of the output sound. Since LPC lets users manipulate the excitation independently, one can vary the excitation pitch to transform a talking voice into a singing voice, for example.

What Is Linear Prediction?

Linear prediction derives its obscure name from the fact that in the spectrum analysis part of the system, output samples are "predicted" by a linear combination of filter parameters (*coefficients*) and previous samples. A *prediction algorithm* tries to find samples at positions outside a region where one already has samples. That is, any extrapolation of a set of samples is prediction. Inherent in prediction is the possibility of being wrong; thus prediction algorithms always include an error estimation.

A simple predictor simply continues the slope of difference between the last sample and the sample before it (figure 5.35). This type of predictor can be made more sophisticated by taking more samples into account. It can also take into account the error or difference between the sample it predicts and the actual value of the signal, if this is known (and it is known in LPC).

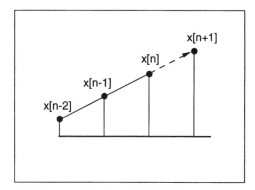

Figure 5.35   Linear prediction extrapolates a set of points.

Since the predictor is looking at sums and differences of time-delayed samples, it can be viewed as a filter—a filter that describes the waveform it is currently processing. (See chapter 10 for more on digital filters.)

If we take regular snapshots of these filter coefficients over time, invert them, and then drive the resulting filter with a rich, wide-bandwidth sound, we should have a good approximation of the time-varying spectrum of the original input signal. Thus a "side effect" of the prediction is to estimate the spectrum of the input signal: this is the important point. But spectrum estimation is only one stage of LPC analysis, the others being applied to pitch, amplitude, and the voiced/unvoiced decision. These are briefly described in the following section.

LPC Analysis

Figure 5.36 shows an overview of LPC analysis. LPC analysis branches into four directions: (1) spectrum analysis in terms of formants, (2) pitch analysis, (3) amplitude analysis, and (4) the decision as to whether the sound was voiced (pitched) or unvoiced (characteristic of noisy sounds). Each stage of analysis is carried out on a frame-by-frame basis, where a frame is like a snapshot of the signal. Frame rates of between 50 and 200 frames per second are typical in LPC analysis.

Filter Estimation

The next several paragraphs describe the operation of LPC analysis in general terms, but let us begin with a point about filter terminology used in LPC analysis. Engineers describe bandpass and bandreject filters in terms of the position of their *poles* and *zeros* (Rabiner and Gold 1975). Without

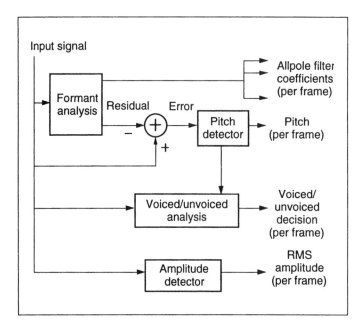

Figure 5.36 Four stages of LPC analysis. Spectrum (formant) analysis, pitch detection, voiced/unvoiced analysis, and amplitude detection.

going into the details of *pole-zero diagrams* (see any text on signal processing) let us just say that a filter pole is a point of resonance—a peak or formant region in a spectrum plot. In contrast, a zero is a null point or notch in the spectrum.

When a filter has several smooth peaks it is called an *allpole filter*. This type of filter is characteristic of LPC, which models spectra in terms of a few formant peaks. Such a model is a reasonable approximation to many sounds uttered by the human voice and certain musical instruments.

As mentioned earlier, linear prediction—or *autoregressive* analysis (see chapter 13)—takes in several input samples at a time, using the most recent sample as a reference. It tries to predict this sample from a weighted sum of filter coefficients and past samples. As a side effect of this prediction, the algorithm fits an inverse filter to the spectrum of the input signal. The inverse of an allpole filter is an *allzero filter* that creates a number of notches in the spectrum of signals sent through it.

The LPC analyzer approximates the inverse of the filter that one ultimately wants for synthesis. If the approximation is good, the result of linear prediction should be just the excitation signal (figure 5.37). In other words, the inverse filter cancels out the effect of the spectral envelope of the sound. The approximation is never perfect, so there is always a signal called the

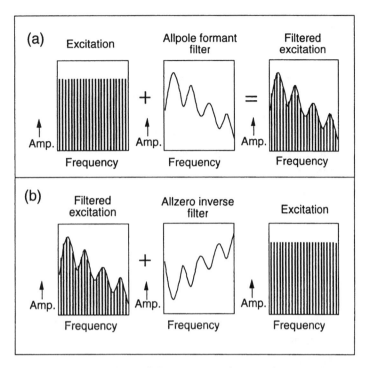

Figure 5.37 Relation of formant and inverse formant filters in the ideal case. (*a*) Result of formant filter. (*b*) Result of inverse formant filter.

residual that is the excitation function (a series of impulses) plus noise. The goal of LPC spectrum analysis is to minimize the residual.

Once a good fit to the inverse filter has been found, the inverse filter is itself inverted to create a resynthesis filter. Filter inversion is mathematically straightforward (Rabiner and Gold 1975); the sign of all the filter coefficients is reversed, and they are applied to past outputs instead of to past inputs. The filter is thus converted from a FIR filter to an IIR filter (see chapter 10). Chapter 13 discusses more of the internals of LPC filter analysis. For an engineering description see (Markel 1972; Makhoul 1975; Moore 1990).

The reader may wonder: how does LPC know what is the excitation function of an arbitrary sound put into it? The answer is: it doesn't, really. It assumes that the excitation is either a pitched pulsetrain or white noise. This assumption works reasonably well in approximating speech and some instruments, but it is not a universal model for all sounds. Thus the LPC method usually leaves traces of artificiality in the resynthesized sounds. Some improved methods of LPC analysis impose a *multipulse cluster* instead of a single pulse at each pitch period, where the form of the cluster (i.e., amplitude and spacing between pulses) derives from analysis data

(Atal and Remde 1982). This helps reduce the artificial quality of LPC resynthesis.

Pitch and Amplitude Analysis

The pitch detection technique used in LPC can be any of the methods described in chapter 12. The particular method used varies in different implementations. Figure 5.36 shows a scheme that tries to estimate the pitch from the residual signal.

Several techniques exist for characterizing the amplitude of each frame. A typical way is to calculate it on a frame-by-frame basis as an average value for the input waveform described by the frame.

Voiced/Unvoiced Decision

After pitch detection has been carried out, LPC analysis tries to make the voiced/unvoiced decision for each frame. This decision is important since it determines whether the sound will be pitched or not in resynthesis. A *voiced* sound has a pitch, like the vowels *a, e, i, o, u* created by the buzzing of the vocal cords. An *unvoiced* sound is like the sibilance of *s* and *z*, the explosive *t* and *p*, or the fricative *f* consonants. Besides voiced or unvoiced, a third category of excitation is "mixed voice," combining a pitched tone and noise, like the |z| of "azure."

In analyzing a wind instrument tone the voiced/unvoiced data usually indicate the amount of breathiness, and for a violin-like sound they can indicate bow-scraping noise. In resynthesis, voiced sounds are modeled by a pitched pulsetrain, while unvoiced sounds are modeled by white noise. Both are filtered, of course.

The voiced/unvoiced decision is hard to fully automate (Hermes 1992). In LPC systems that have been adapted for music, the analysis makes a first pass at the decision, but the composer is expected to make corrections to particular frames (Moorer 1979). The first-pass decision uses various heuristics. Figure 5.36 shows the result of pitch detection feeding into the voiced/unvoiced decision. For example, if the analysis cannot identify a pitch in the input signal, then it generates a large pitch estimation error. When this error—normalized to fall between 0 and 1.0—is greater than a certain value (around 0.2), it is likely that the sound at that moment is a noisy unvoiced sound like a consonant. The average amplitude of the residual is another clue. If the amplitude of the residual is low in comparison to the amplitude of the original input signal, then the signal is probably voiced.

Analysis Frames

The result of the analysis stage is a series of frames, representing a greatly data-reduced version of the input signal. Each frame is described by a list of parameters, including the following:

Average amplitude of the residual sound

Average amplitude of the original sound

Ratio of the two amplitudes (helps determine whether the frame is voiced or unvoiced)

Estimated pitch

Frame duration

Coefficients for the allpole filter (each pole creates a formant peak in the spectrum)

Figure 5.38 shows an example of the frame data for the word "sit" (Dodge 1985). The filter coefficients are omitted for clarity.

The ERR column is a strong clue as to whether the frame is voiced or not. A large value for ERR (greater than 0.2) usually indicates an unvoiced frame. But this indicator should be checked, since the voiced/unvoiced decision is difficult to automate perfectly. Notice how the ERR values change significantly at the boundary of "S" and "I". The RMS1 and RMS2 values are a better indicator of change at the boundary of "I" and "T."

LPC Synthesis

Figure 5.39 depicts the synthesis stage of LPC. The first parameter is the frame duration, which determines the number of output samples generated from a given set of parameters. The next parameter determines whether the frame is voiced or unvoiced. For standard voiced frames, the synthesizer uses the pitch parameter to simulate the excitation function (the glottal wave) of the human voice. This is a "buzzy" sound (typically a band-limited pulsetrain) used for vowels and dipthongs (sequences of vowels such as the "oy" on "toy"). For unvoiced frames, the synthesizer uses a noise generator to simulate turbulence in the vocal tract.

The output of the appropriate generator, shaped by the amplitude parameter, serves as input to the allpole filter. For speech and singing work, the allpole filter simulates the resonances of the vocal tract. Up to twelve poles in the allpole filter are used in speech synthesis, and as many as 55 or more poles have been used in music synthesis (Moorer 1979a).

Phoneme	Frame	RMS2	RMS1	ERR	PITCH	DUR
S	197	813.27	1618.21	0.252	937.50	0.010
	198	1189.36	2090.14	0.323	937.50	0.010
	199	553.71	838.38	0.436	937.50	0.010
	200	742.59	1183.17	0.393	937.50	0.010
	201	1041.95	1918.33	0.295	123.95	0.010
	202	1449.16	2677.06	0.293	123.95	0.010
	203	1454.84	2920.50	0.248	937.50	0.010
	204	1430.03	2496.88	0.348	937.50	0.010
	205	1570.88	2981.21	0.277	142.84	0.010
	206	1443.27	2665.22	0.293	142.84	0.010
	207	1172.67	2150.50	0.297	150.00	0.010
	208	1200.73	2080.20	0.333	150.00	0.010
	209	1095.51	2055.25	0.284	116.26	0.010
	210	1260.36	2408.14	0.273	116.26	0.010
	211	1105.17	2293.05	0.232	937.50	0.010
	212	809.10	1659.80	0.237	937.50	0.010
	213	428.20	784.93	0.297	250.00	0.010
I	214	419.45	3886.15	0.011	250.00	0.010
	215	925.86	6366.20	0.021	208.32	0.010
	216	746.28	8046.81	0.008	208.32	0.010
	217	829.82	8277.42	0.010	192.29	0.010
	218	754.64	8049.50	0.008	192.29	0.010
	219	771.84	8001.70	0.009	197.35	0.010
	220	726.81	7955.17	0.008	202.69	0.010
	221	807.63	7835.20	0.010	202.69	0.010
	222	874.27	7732.59	0.012	205.42	0.010
	223	776.87	7491.86	0.010	205.42	0.010
	224	684.64	7317.04	0.008	205.42	0.010
	225	560.87	6297.36	0.007	102.03	0.010
	226	175.63	1842.81	0.009	102.03	0.010
	227	46.53	1329.09	0.001	197.85	0.010
T	228	38.25	793.00	0.002	197.85	0.010
	229	39.26	316.92	0.032	202.69	0.010

Figure 5.38   A sequence of LPC frames as they might be displayed for editing purposes, after Dodge (1985). The Phoneme column is added for clarity in this figure. The RMS2 column indicates the residual amplitude, RMS1 is the original signal amplitude. ERR is an approximation to the ratio between the two and indicates an unvoiced signal if the ratio is high. PITCH is the estimated pitch in Hz, DUR is the frame duration in seconds.

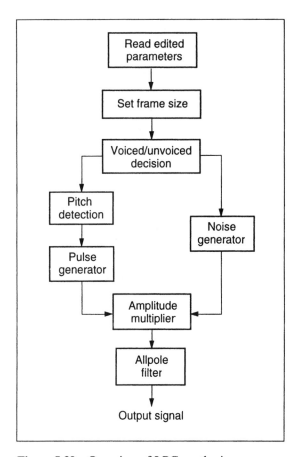

Figure 5.39 Overview of LPC synthesis.

Editing LPC Frame Data

The LPC technique can be adapted from pure speech work to musical purposes by means of an associated editing and mixing subsystem. In an article on composing with LPC, Dodge (1985) describes an editing command language that performs the operations shown in table 5.1 on LPC parameter frames. One of the main applications of these operations on LPC frames is to transform a plain spoken utterance into singing. Using LPC, a word can be expanded in time, and the original spoken pitch curve can be replaced with a flowing melody. Words and phrases can be repeated or rearranged at will. Sentences can also be compressed in time without affecting their original pitch.

Composers such as Charles Dodge and Paul Lansky have used LPC to achieve all these effects, in pieces such as Dodge's *Speech Songs* (1975) and

Table 5.1   Operations on LPC frames

Stretch or shrink the duration of the frame

Dilate the duration of frames between frame A and frame B

Change specific parameter values in a group of frames

Interpolate values between a group of frames (or create a pitch glissando, for example)

Move frames from point *A* to point *B*

Boost the amplitude of a frame

Crescendo over a group of frames

Set the pitch of a frame

Trill on every other frame

Lansky's *Six Fantasies on a Poem by Thomas Campion* (1979), and *Idle Chatter* (1985, Wergo compact disc 2010-50).

Musical Extensions of Standard LPC

LPC can implement a form of cross-synthesis (Mathews, Miller, and David 1961; Petersen 1975; Moorer 1979a). Cross-synthesis means different things depending on the system being used (LPC, convolution, phase vocoder, wavelets, etc.). In general, it refers to techniques that start from an analysis of two sounds and use the characteristics of one sound to modify the characteristics of another sound, often involving a spectrum transformation. LPC cross-synthesis takes the excitation from one source sound (pitch and event timing) to drive the time-varying spectral envelope derived from another source. For example, one can replace the simple pulsetrain signal used to create voiced speech by a complex waveform, such as the sound of an orchestra. The resulting effect is that of a "talking orchestra." Figure 5.40 is essentially the same as the vocoder in figure 5.33, except that the simple excitation function normally used in a vocoder is replaced by a wideband musical source (source B), and the internal method of analysis/resynthesis uses the LPC method.

When the desired effect is to make source B "talk," the intelligibility of the speech can be enhanced by using wide-bandwidth sources such as a full orchestra and chorus—as opposed to a narrow-bandwidth source such as a solo violin. If necessary, the excitation funtion can also be *whitened* to bring all spectral components up to a uniform level (Moorer 1979).

Another extension of LPC synthesis extrapolates the filter response of a single instrument into a family of like instruments. For example, starting with an analysis of a violin, one can clone a viola, cello, and double bass to

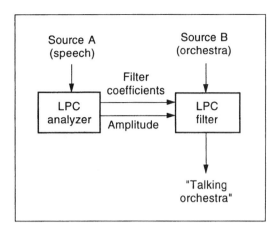

Figure 5.40 LPC cross-synthesis takes the spectral envelope from one sound and maps it onto another sound.

make up a string quartet (Lansky and Steiglitz 1981; Moorer 1981b, 1983a). These filter transformations can, in theory, be extended to emulate any instrument's resonances. In Paul Lansky's music, this method called *warped linear prediction* has been used to synthesize electronic versions of strings, saxophones, and harmonicas (New Albion Records NA 030CD 1990).

Assessment of LPC

LPC speech is intelligible, and it is easy to recognize the origins of traditional instruments simulated with the technique. However, LPC does not produce speech or music of extremely high audio quality. That is, the synthetic replica remains distinguishable from the original. Although this does not prevent it from being musically useful, an improvement in quality would be desirable in compositional applications. Moorer (1977, 1979a) experimented with high-order allpole filters and more complex excitation functions to try to improve LPC quality. His conclusion is that the critical increment of sound quality is "not readily forthcoming." He attributes this to a lack of effective tools for modeling the excitation function. See Depalle (1991) for a study of alternatives to LPC spectrum modeling.

If the audio quality of the LPC model could be improved further, subtractive synthesis would have several advantages over sine wave additive synthesis. For example, manipulations in the pitch, spectrum, and temporal domains can be made independently in subtractive synthesis. In additive synthesis, spectrum is usually linked to fundamental pitch. This means that if the pitch changes, the harmonics change frequency. Moreover, the LPC model is not sensitive to the frequency of the excitation function; it can generate filters for inharmonic as well as harmonic spectra on top of the fundamental (Moorer 1977).

Diphone Analysis/Resynthesis

The concept of *diphone synthesis* was established decades ago in the context of speech research (Peterson and Barney 1952; Peterson, Wang, and Silvertsen 1958; Olive 1977; Schwartz et al 1979). The basic idea is that most speech sounds consist of a series of stable sounds separated by transition sounds. Although this method managed to create intelligible speech, for example, there were distortions at points of concatenation. The diphone concept was first tested in the context of a subtractive analysis/resynthesis strategy, which is why we present it in this chapter. It has since been extended to other types of resynthesis.

By generalizing this concept from speech to the realm of musical sounds, one can build up dictionaries of stable and transition sounds to cover a particular class of sounds, such as traditional instrument tones, for example. Each diphone is coded as a pitch at a particular loudness. To alleviate the problem of distortions at diphone boundaries, recent work has centered on developing a dictionary of transition rules for each instrument that smooth the concatenation of adjacent diphones (Rodet, Depalle, and Poirot 1988; see also Depalle 1991). Hence this research is related to the problem of creating convincing transitions between notes (Strawn 1985a, 1987a). But

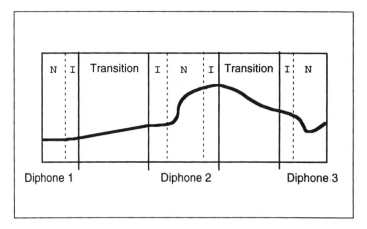

Figure 5.41   Transition over three diphones. The bold line indicates the trajectory of a synthesis parameter for a sound that has been stretched in time. The stretching projects from interpolation zones (I) defined in each diphone and extends over a transition zone. The zones of noninterpolation (N) are not stretched, preserving the central part of the diphone.

it also offers the possiblity of creating hybrid sounds that link diphones from different instruments. One can also create synthetic diphones.

Individual tones are analyzed to create a dictionary; here we assume that the analysis method is LPC, running at about 200 frames per second of input sound. If the data are stretched or compressed for musical effect, discontinuities may occur in rapidly changing signals such as attacks and the transition between two notes. Thus the diphone method recasts the analysis data for a rapid transition in a form that ensures continuous transitions, even when the data are subjected to articulation and phrasing transformations. For example, the rule for stretching or compressing a diphone may vary, depending on what diphone it is coming from and what diphone it is going toward (Depalle 1991). Within each diphone is a *zone of noninterpolation* that is preserved intact regardless of the transition (figure 5.41).

Conclusion

This chapter presented multiple wavetable, wave terrain, granular, and subtractive synthesis techniques. Multiple wavetable synthesis is the central technique in many popular synthesizers. It enriches sampled sounds by creating crossfaded and stacked hybrids. If desired, these blends can be combined with synthetic spectra to create exotic, quasi-realistic sounds.

Wave terrain synthesis is computationally efficient and seems promising, but requires additional musical development. Can it be adapted to scan sampled wavetables, for example, in musically effective ways?

Granular synthesis is a family of techniques based on the production of masses of short-duration sound particles. Synchronous and quasi-synchronous granular synthesis generate pitched formant spectra, while asynchronous methods can create more "particulated" sound effects, such as clouds of evolving sound spectra. We can also granulate sampled sounds and create mélanges of grains from different samples for especially rich textures.

Subtractive synthesis constitutes an established science with a long history. Yet digital filter design is still young, so we can expect refinements in the years to come. Increasing computational power is rapidly bringing applications like real-time filter banks and subtractive analysis/resynthesis into a favorable position.

Partly as a reaction to the complexity of additive and subtractive analysis/resynthesis, a variety of efficient and specialized techniques have appeared. These techniques have other advantages besides computational efficiency; they usually require less control information to be specified by the musician. They can be implemented inexpensively in hardware as well as fabricated into tiny mass-produced integrated circuits. In many cases the musical sounds produced by these techniques would be difficult to simulate and control using "general" analysis/synthesis methods. Hence, they add to the palette of available sounds, which stands as a justification for their use in and of itself. Chapters 6 and 7 survey these methods.

6 *Modulation Synthesis*

Multiple-Carrier FM

Musical Applications of MC FM

Multiple-Modulator FM

Parallel MM FM
Series MM FM
Musical Applications of MM FM

Feedback FM

Background: Feedback Oscillators
One-oscillator Feedback
Two-oscillator Feedback
Three-oscillator Indirect Feedback

Phase Distortion

Waveshaping Synthesis

Simple Waveshaping Instrument
Example Shaping Functions
Amplitude Sensitivity of Waveshaping Spectrum
Chebychev Shaping Functions
Amplitude Normalization
Variations on Waveshaping
Movable Waveshaping
Fractional Waveshaping
Postprocessing and Parameter Estimation

General Modulations

Conclusion

"Modulation" in electronic and computer music means that some aspect of one signal (the *carrier*) varies according to an aspect of a second signal (the *modulator*). The familiar effects of *tremolo* (slow amplitude variation) and *vibrato* (slow frequency variation) in traditional instruments and voices exemplify acoustic modulation. The carrier in these cases is a pitched tone, and the modulator is a relatively slow-varying function (less than 20 Hz). At the right moment and at the right speed, tremolo and vibrato charge both electronic and acoustic tones with expressivity.

When the frequency of modulation rises into the audio bandwidth (above 20 Hz or so), audible *modulation products* or *sidebands* begin to appear. These are new frequencies added to the spectrum of the carrier (typically on either side of the carrier).

To achieve the same complexity of spectrum, modulation synthesis is more efficient in terms of parameter data, memory requirements, and computation time than additive and subtractive synthesis. Modulation uses a small number of oscillators (typically two to six), whereas additive and subtractive techniques need several times this amount of computational power. Modulation is realized by a few table-lookup, multiplication, and addition operations, depending on the type of modulation desired. Because there are fewer parameters than in additive or subtractive techniques, musicians often find modulation techniques easier to manipulate.

By changing parameter values over time, modulation techniques easily produce time-varying spectra. Carefully regulated modulations generate rich dynamic sounds that come close to natural instrumental tones. It is also possible to use modulations in a nonimitative way to venture into the domain of unclassified synthetic sounds.

In this presentation of modulation, we use a minimum of mathematics combined with a liberal dose of instrument diagrams or "patches." These diagrams depict synthesis instruments as a configuration of elementary signal-processing *unit generators*. (See chapter 1 for an introduction to unit generators.)

The modulating signal can vary from a pure sinusoid at a fixed frequency to pure white noise containing all frequencies. See chapter 8 for details on noise modulations.

Bipolar and Unipolar Signals

Two closely related synthesis methods are *ring modulation* and *amplitude modulation* (RM and AM, respectively). In order to comprehend the difference between them, it is important to understand two types of signals that

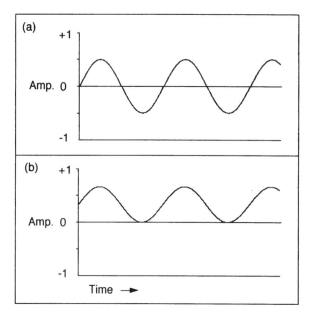

Figure 6.1 Bipolar versus unipolar sine waves. (*a*) Bipolar sine varies between −1 and 1. (*b*) Unipolar sine varies between 0 and 1.

they process: *bipolar* and *unipolar*. A bipolar signal is typical of most audio waveforms, in that it has both a negative and a positive excursion around zero when we look at it in the time domain (figure 6.1a). By contrast, the excursions of a unipolar signal remain within one-half of the full range of the system (figure 6.1b). One way to think of a unipolar signal is that it is a bipolar signal to which a constant has been added. This constant shifts all the sample values to the range above zero. Another term for such a constant is *direct current* (DC) *offset*—a signal varying at a frequency of 0 Hz (i.e., not varying).

This distinction is important because the fundamental difference between RM and AM is that RM modulates two bipolar signals, while AM modulates a bipolar signal with a unipolar signal. The next two sections cover both methods in more detail.

Ring Modulation

We start our discussion with RM. In theory, ring modulation is a form of amplitude modulation (Black 1953). In digital systems, RM is simply the multiplication of two bipolar audio signals by one another. That is, a carrier signal C is multiplied by a modulator signal M. The basic signals C and M are generated from stored waveforms, and one of them is usually a sine wave. The formula for determining the value of a simple ring-modulated signal *RingMod* at time *t* is a straightforward multiplication:

$$RingMod_t = C_t \times M_t.$$

Figure 6.2 portrays two equivalent implementations of at RM instrument. In figure 6.2a it is assumed that the carrier oscillator multiplies the value it reads from the wavetable lookup by the value it takes in from its amplitude input. In figure 6.2b this multiplication is made more explicit. In both cases, the modulator and the carrier vary between -1 and $+1$, hence they are bipolar.

When the frequency of the modulator M is below 20 Hz or so, the effect of ring modulation is that the amplitude of C varies at the frequency of M—a tremolo effect. But when the frequency of M is in the audible range, the timbre of C changes. For each sinusoidal component in the carrier, the modulator contributes a pair of *sidebands* to the final spectrum. Given two sine waves as input, RM generates a spectrum that contains two sidebands. These sidebands are the sum and the difference of the frequencies C and M. Curiously, the carrier frequency itself disappears. Furthermore, if C and M are in an integer ratio to one another, then the sidebands generated by RM are harmonic; otherwise they are inharmonic.

The sidebands in signal multiplication derive from a standard trigonometric identity:

$$\cos(C) \times \cos(M) = 0.5 \times [\cos(C - M) + \cos(C + M)].$$

Yet another way to understand ring modulation is to consider it as a case of *convolution*, as explained in chapter 10.

To give an example of RM, assume that C is a 1000 Hz sine wave and M is a 400 Hz sine wave. As figure 6.3 shows, their RM spectrum contains a components at 1400 Hz (the sum of C and M) and 600 Hz (the difference between C and M).

The phases of the output signal components are also the sum and difference of the phases of the two inputs. If C and M are more complex signals than sine waves, or if their frequency changes in time, the resulting output spectrum contains many sum and difference frequencies. A spectral plot would show many lines, indicating a complicated spectrum.

Negative Frequencies

As figure 6.3b shows, when the modulating frequency is higher than the carrier frequency, *negative frequencies* occur, as in the case of $C = 100$ Hz and $M = 400$ Hz, since $C + M = 500$, while $C - M = -300$. In spectral

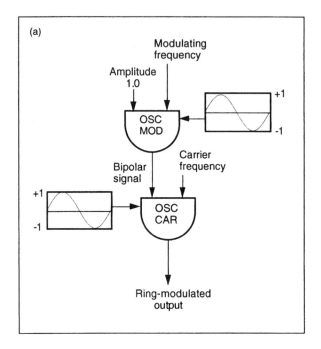

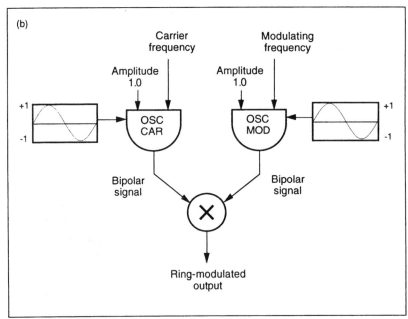

Figure 6.2   Two equivalent implementations of ring modulation or bipolar signal multiplication. The box to the left of each oscillator is its waveform. The top left input of each oscillator is the amplitude, and the top-right input is the frequency. (*a*) RM by implicit multiplication within the carrier oscillator. (*b*) RM by explicit multiplication of the carrier and the modulator signals.

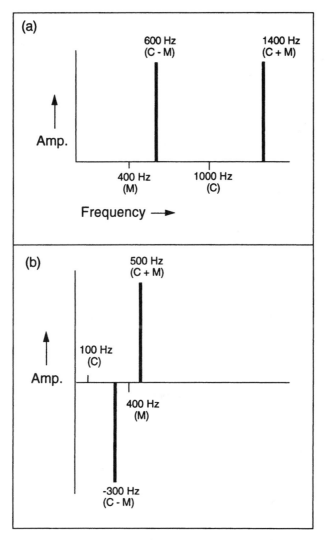

Figure 6.3 Ring modulation spectra. (*a*) For a carrier of 1000 Hz and a modulator of 400 Hz, the sum and difference frequencies are 1400 and 600 Hz, respectively. (*b*) For a carrier of 100 Hz and a modulator of 400 Hz, the sum and difference frequencies are 500 and − 300 Hz, respectively.

plots, a negative frequency can be shown as a line extending down from the *x*-axis. The change in sign merely changes the sign of the phase of the signal. (When the sign changes, the waveform flips over the zero or *x*-axis.) Phase becomes important when summing components of identical frequencies, since out-of-phase components can attenuate or cancel in-phase components.

Applications of RM

Typical musical use of RM involves the modification of sampled carrier signals (i.e., the human voice, piano, etc.) by sine wave modulators. Another strategy is to create pure synthetic sounds starting from sine waves in either harmonic or inharmonic ratios. This is the approach taken by composer James Dashow in his pieces such as *Sequence Symbols* (Dashow 1987).

Analog Ring Modulation and Frequency Shifting

Digital ring modulation relies on signal multiplication. In general, digital RM should always sound the same. In contrast, various analog RM circuits have a different "character," depending on the exact circuit and components used. This is because implementations of analog RM approximate pure multiplication with a four-diode circuit arranged in a "ring" configuration. Depending on the type of diodes (silicon or germanium) these circuits introduce extraneous frequencies (Bode 1967, 1984; Stockhausen 1968; Duesenberry 1990; Strange 1983; Wells 1981). For example, in an analog ring modulator based on silicon diodes, the diodes in the circuit clip the carrier (turning it into a quasi-square wave) when it reaches the momentary level of the modulator. This creates the effect of several sums and differences on odd harmonics of the carrier, of the form

$$C + M, C - M, 3C + M, 3C - M, 5C + M, 5C - M, \ldots .$$

Figure 6.4 compares the signals emitted by multiplying RM and diode-clipping RM. Analog ring modulation was used extensively in the electronic music studios of the 1950s, 1960s, and 1970s. The German composer Karlheinz Stockhausen was especially fond of ring modulation; he used it in a number of pieces composed in the 1960s, including *Kontakte, Mikrophonie I* and *II, Telemusik, Hymnen, Prozession,* and *Kurzwellen* (Stockhausen 1968, 1971b).

A pioneer of musical ring modulation, the inventor Harald Bode also developed a variation on RM called *frequency shifting* (Bode 1967, 1984;

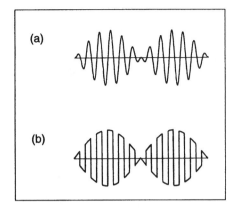

Figure 6.4 Two forms of ring modulation. (*a*) Multiplication RM. (*b*) Diode-clipping or "chopper" RM.

Bode and Moog 1972). A frequency shifter or *Klangumwandler* has separate outputs for the sum and difference frequencies. Another term for this method is *single-sideband modulation* (Oppenheim and Willsky 1983).

Amplitude Modulation

Amplitude modulation is one of the oldest modulation techniques (Black 1953) and has been used extensively in analog electronic music. As in RM, the amplitude of a carrier wave varies in accordance with a modulator wave. The difference between the two techniques is that in AM the modulator is unipolar (the entire waveform is above zero).

Perhaps the most mundane example of infraaudio AM occurs when superposing an envelope onto a sine wave. The envelope, which is unipolar since it varies between 0 and 1, acts as a modulator. The sine wave, which is bipolar since it varies between -1 and $+1$, acts as a carrier. To apply an envelope to a signal is to multiply the two waveforms C and M:

$$AmpMod_t = C_t \times M_t$$

where $AmpMod_t$ the value of an amplitude-modulated signal at time t. Figure 6.5 depicts the result.

Like RM, AM generates a pair of sidebands for every sinusoidal component in the carrier and the modulator. The sidebands are separated from the carrier by a distance corresponding to the inverse of the period of the modulator. The sonic difference between RM and AM is that the AM spectrum contains the carrier frequency as well (figure 6.6). The amplitude of the two

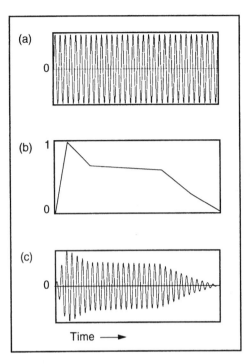

Figure 6.5   Applying an envelope to a signal is a simple case of infra-audio AM. The sine wave signal in (*a*) is multiplied by the envelope signal in (*b*) to produce the enveloped signal in (*c*).

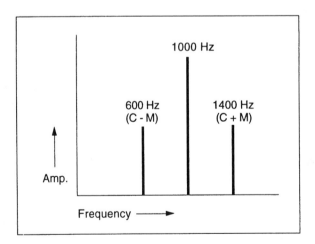

Figure 6.6   Spectrum produced by AM of a 1KHz sine wave by a 400 Hz sine wave. The two sidebands are at sum and difference frequencies around the carrier frequency. The amplitude of the each of the sidebands is *index*/2.

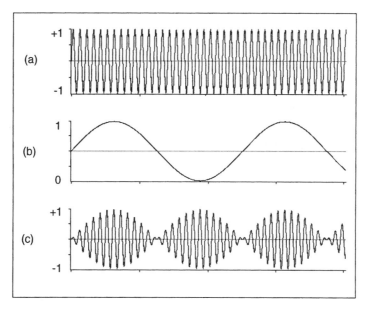

Figure 6.7   Time-domain view of audio frequency AM. The 1 KHz sine wave signal in (*a*) is modulated by the 40 Hz sine wave signal in (*b*) to produced the amplitude modulated signal in (*c*).

sidebands increases in proportion to the amount of modulation, but never exceeds half the level of the carrier.

Figure 6.7 shows a time-domain view of AM created by the modulation of two sine wave signals in the audio band.

AM Instruments

To implement classic AM one restricts the modulator to a unipolar signal—the positive range between 0 and 1. Figure 6.8a shows a simple instrument for AM where the modulator is a unipolar signal.

Modulation Index

A slightly more complicated instrument is needed to control the amount of modulation and the overall amplitude envelope. Figure 6.8b depicts an AM instrument that controls the amount of modulation with an envelope (top left of figure). This envelope functions as a *modulation index*, in the parlance of modulation theory (more on this later). The instrument scales a bipolar modulation signal into a unipolar signal varying between 0 and 1, and then adds this to an overall amplitude envelope over the duration of a sound event. The following equation describes the resulting AM waveform:

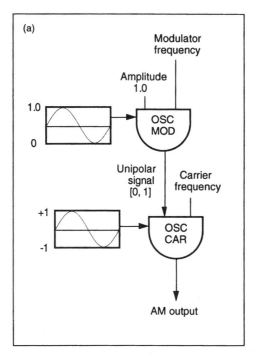

Figure 6.8 Two implementations of AM. (*a*) A simple instrument for AM where the modulating signal is assumed to be unipolar. (*b*) A more complicated instrument for AM with controls for the amount of modulation and the overall amplitude over the duration of the note event. The box to the left of each oscillator is its waveform. In the case of the envelope oscillators (denoted by ENV OSC), the frequency period is 1/*note_duration*. This means that they read through their wavetable once over the duration of a note event. The Positive scaler module ensures that the modulation input to the adder varies between 0 and 0.5.

$$AmpMod = A_c \times \cos(C) + (I \times A_c)/2 \times \cos(C + M)$$
$$+ (I \times A_c)/2 \times \cos(C - M)$$

where *AmpMod* is the amplitude-modulated signal, A_c is the amplitude of the carrier, I is the modulation index, C is the carrier frequency, and M is the modulator frequency.

Frequency Modulation

Frequency modulation (FM) is a very well known digital synthesis method, due to its adoption by the Yamaha corporation. However, FM is not one technique, but a family of methods that share the common property of wavetable lookup according to a nonlinear oscillating function.

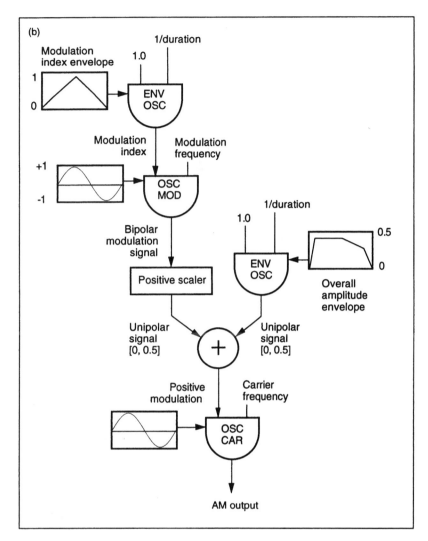

Figure 6.8 (b)

Background: Frequency Modulation

Applications of FM in communications systems date back to the nineteenth century. The theory behind FM of radioband frequencies (in the MHz range) was established early in the twentieth century (Carson 1922; van der Pol 1930; Black 1953). These studies are worth reading today, particularly Black's book, which walks the reader through a well-planned tour of the hills and dales of waveform modulation.

John Chowning at Stanford University was the first to explore systematically the musical potential of digital FM synthesis (Chowning 1973). Prior to this, most digital sound had been produced by fixed-waveform, fixed-spectrum techniques. Time-varying additive and subtractive synthesis were rare and costly from a computational standpoint. Since most digital synthesis work had to be done on multiple-user computers, there was a strong incentive to develop more efficient techniques, with the emphasis on time-varying spectra. This motivation was explained by Chowning as follows:

In natural sounds the frequency components of the spectrum are dynamic, or time variant. The energy of the components often evolves in complicated ways; in particular during the attack and decay portions of the sound. (Chowning 1973)

Hence, Chowning sought a way to generate synthetic sounds that had the animated spectra characteristic of natural sounds. The breakthrough came when he was experimenting with extreme vibrato techniques, where the vibrato becomes so fast it effects the timbre of the signal:

I found that with two simple sinusoids I could generate a whole range of complex sounds which done by other means demanded much more powerful and extensive tools. If you want to have a sound that has, say 50 harmonics, you have to have 50 oscillators. And I was using two oscillators to get something that was very similar. (Chowning 1987)

After careful experiments to explore the potential of the technique, Chowning developed a patent on an implementation of FM. In 1975 the Japanese firm Nippon Gakki (Yamaha) obtained a license to apply this patent in their products. After several years of development and extensions to the basic technique (described later), Yahama introduced the expensive GS1 digital synthesizer ($16,000, housed in a wooden pianolike case) in 1980. But it was the introduction of the highly successful DX7 synthesizer ($2000) in the fall of 1983 that made FM synonymous with digital synthesis to hundreds of thousands of musicians.

Frequency Modulation and Phase Modulation

FM and the closely related technique called *phase modulation* (PM) represent two virtually identical cases of the same type of *angle modulation* (Black 1953, pp. 28–30). The amplitudes of the partials generated by the two methods exhibit slight differences, but in musical practice there is no great distinction between PM and FM, particularly in the case of time-varying spectra. Hence we will not discuss PM further in this book. (A variation called *phase distortion* is discussed later in this chapter, however.) For details on the distinction between PM and FM, see Bate (1990), Holm (1992), and Beauchamp (1992).

Simple FM

In the basic frequency modulation technique (referred to as *simple FM* or *Chowning FM*), a carrier oscillator is modulated in frequency by a modulator oscillator (Chowning 1973, 1975). Figure 6.9 diagrams a simple FM instrument. (A slight discrepancy exists between the amplitudes of the spectrum components emitted by the instrument shown in figure 6.9 and the spectra described by the classic FM formula, presented in a moment. Overall these differences are minor. For a summary see Holm 1992 and Beauchamp 1992.)

Looking at the spectrum shown in figure 6.10 we can immediately see the difference between FM and the RM and AM methods presented earlier. Instead of just one sum and one difference sideband, FM of two sinusoids generates an series of sidebands around a carrier frequency C. Each sideband spreads out at a distance equal to a multiple of the modulating frequency M. Later we investigate the number of sidebands; suffice it to say

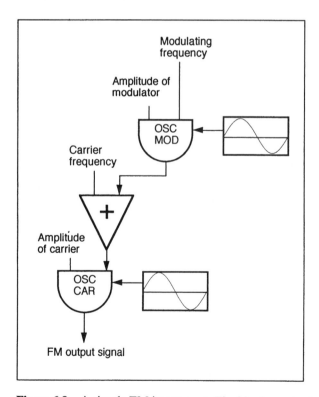

Figure 6.9 A simple FM instrument. The bipolar output of the modulating oscillator is added to the fundamental carrier frequency, causing it to vary up and down. The amplitude of the modulator determines the amount of modulation, or the frequency deviation from the fundamental carrier frequency.

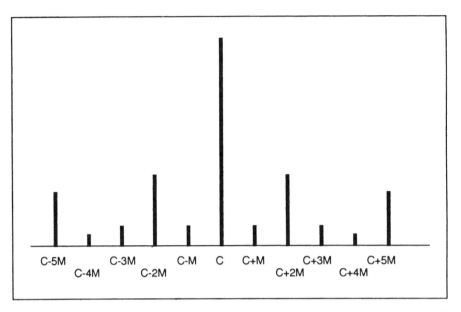

Figure 6.10   FM spectrum showing sidebands equally spaced around the carrier C at multiples of the modulator M.

now that the number of sidebands generated depends on the amount of modulation applied to the carrier.

$C:M$ Ratio

The position of the frequency components generated by FM depends on the ratio of the carrier frequency to the modulating frequency. This is called the $C:M$ *ratio*. When $C:M$ is a simple integer ratio, such as 4:1 (as in the case of two signals at 800 and 200 Hz), FM generates harmonic spectra, that is, sidebands that are integer multiples of the carrier and modulating frequencies:

$C = 800$ Hz   (carrier)

$C + M = 1000$ Hz   (sum)

$C + (2 \times M) = 1200$ Hz   (sum)

$C + (3 \times M) = 1400$ Hz, etc.   (sum)

$C - M = 600$ Hz   (difference)

$C - (2 \times M) = 400$ Hz   (difference)

$C - (3 \times M) = 200$ Hz, etc.   (difference)

When $C:M$ is not a simple integer ratio, such as $8:2.1$ (as in the case of two signals at 800 and 210 Hz), FM generates inharmonic spectra (noninteger multiples of the carrier and modulator):

$C = 800$ Hz   (carrier)

$C + M = 1010$ Hz   (sum)

$C + (2 \times M) = 1120$ Hz   (sum)

$C + (3 \times M) = 1230$ Hz, etc.   (sum)

$C - M = 590$ Hz   (difference)

$C - (2 \times M) = 380$ Hz   (difference)

$C - (3 \times M) = 170$ Hz, etc.   (difference)

Modulation Index and Bandwidth

The bandwidth of the FM spectrum (the number of sidebands) is controlled by the *modulation index* or *index of modulation I*. *I* is defined mathematically according to the following relation:

$I = D/M$

where D is the amount of frequency deviation (in Hz) from the carrier frequency. Hence, D is a way of expressing the *depth* or amount of the modulation. So if D is 100 Hz and the modulator M is 100 Hz, then the index of modulation is 1.0.

Figure 6.11 plots the effects of increasing the modulation index. When $I = 0$ (figure 6.11a) the frequency deviation is zero so there is no modulation. When I is greater than zero, sideband frequencies occur above and below the carrier C at intervals of the modulator M. As I increases, so does the number of sidebands. Notice in that as I increases, energy is "stolen" from the carrier and distributed among the increasing number of sidebands.

As a rule of thumb, the number of significant sideband pairs (those that are more than 1/100th the amplitude of the carrier) is approximately $I + 1$ (De Poli 1983). The total bandwidth is approximately equal to twice the sum of the frequency deviation D and the modulating frequency M (Chowning 1973). In formal terms:

FM bandwidth $\sim 2 \times (D + M)$.

Because the bandwidth increases as the index of moduation increases, FM can simulate an important property of instrumental tones. Namely, as the

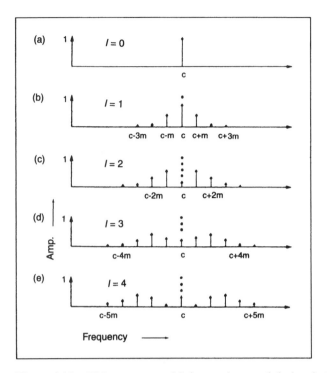

Figure 6.11 FM spectrum with increasing modulation index. (*a*) Carrier. (*b*)–(*e*) Carrier plus sidebands for $I = 0$ (see *a*) to 4 (see *e*). The sidebands are spaced at intervals of the modulating frequency M and are symmetrical about the carrier C. (After Chowning 1973.)

amplitude increases, so does the bandwidth. This is typical of many instruments, such as strings, horns, and drums, and is realized in FM by using similar envelope shapes for both the carrier amplitude and index of modulation.

Reflected Sidebands

For certain values of the carrier and modulator frequencies and I, extreme sidebands reflect out of the upper and lower ends of the spectrum, causing audible side effects. An upper partial that is beyond the Nyquist frequency (half the sampling rate) "folds over" (aliases) and reflects back into the lower portion of the spectrum. (Chapter 1 describes foldover in more detail.)

When the lower sidebands extend below 0 Hz, they reflect back into the spectrum in 180-degree *phase-inverted form*. By "phase inverted" we mean that the waveform flips over the *x*-axis, so that the positive part of a sine wave becomes negative and the negative part becomes positive. Phase-

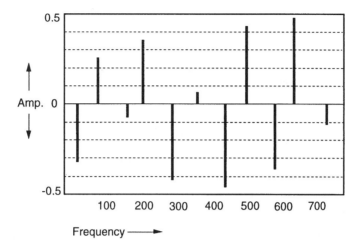

Figure 6.12 Spectral plot showing the effects of reflected low-frequency sidebands. The $C:M$ ratio is $1\sqrt{2}$, and the modulation index is 5. The downward lines indicate phase-inverted reflected components. (After Chowning 1973.)

inverted partials are drawn as lines extending downward, as in figure 6.12. In general, negative frequency components add richness to the lower-frequency portion of the spectrum, but if negative components overlap exactly with positive components, they can cancel out each other.

The FM Formula

When the carrier and the modulator are both sine waves, the formula for a frequency modulated signal *FM* at time t is as follows:

$$FM_t = A \times \sin(C_t + [I \times \sin(M_t)])$$

where A is the peak amplitude of the carrier, $C_t = 2\pi \times C$, $M_t = 2\pi \times M$, and I is the index of modulation. As this formula shows, simple FM is quite efficient, requiring just two multiplies, an add, and two table lookups. The table lookups reference sine waves stored in memory.

Bessel Functions

The amplitudes of the individual sideband components vary according to a class of mathematical functions called *Bessel functions of the first kind and the nth order $J_n(I)$*, where the argument to the function is the modulation index I. The FM equation just given can be reexpressed in an equivalent representation (adapted from De Poli 1983) that incorporates the Bessel function terms directly:

$$FM_t = \sum_{n=-\infty}^{\infty} J_n(I) \times \sin(2\pi \times [f_c \pm \{n \times f_m\}])t.$$

Each n is an individual partial. So to calculate the amplitude of, say, the third partial, we multiply the third Bessel function at point I, that is, $J_3(I)$, times two sine waves on either side of the carrier frequency. Odd-order lower-side frequency components are phase inverted.

Figure 6.13 depicts the Bessel functions in a three-dimensional representation for $n = 1$ to 15, with a modulation index range of 0 to 20. The vertical plane (an undulating surface) shows how the amplitudes of the sidebands vary as the modulation index changes. The figure shows that when the number of sidebands is low (at the "back" of the display) the amplitude variation is quite striking. As the number of sidebands increases (shown toward the "front" of the display), the amplitude variations in them (ripples) are small.

From a musical standpoint, the important property is that each Bessel function undulates like a kind of damped sinusoid—wide variations for low I and less variation for high I. Simple FM is audibly marked by this indulation as one sweeps the modulation index. Notice also that the $J_n(I)$ for different values of n cross zero at different values of I. So as the modulation index I sweeps, sidebands drop in and out in a quasi-random fashion.

A convenient feature of FM is that the maximum amplitude and signal power do not have to vary with I. This means that as I increases or decreases, the overall amplitude of the tone does not vary wildly. Musically, this means that one can manipulate the amplitude and the index independently by using separate envelopes without worrying about how the value of I will affect the overall amplitude. As we see later in this chapter, this is not the case with some other synthesis techniques, notably waveshaping and the discrete summation formulas. These techniques require *amplitude normalization* since the modulation can drastically affect the output amplitude.

Digital Implementation of FM

Figure 6.9 showed a simple FM instrument in which the depth of modulation is controlled by a constant frequency deviation. But since the bandwidth is directly related to the modulation index and only indirectly to the frequency deviation, it is usually more convenient to specify an FM sound directly in terms of a modulation index. In this case, the instrument needs to be modified to carry out additional calculation according to the following relation:

$$D = I \times M.$$

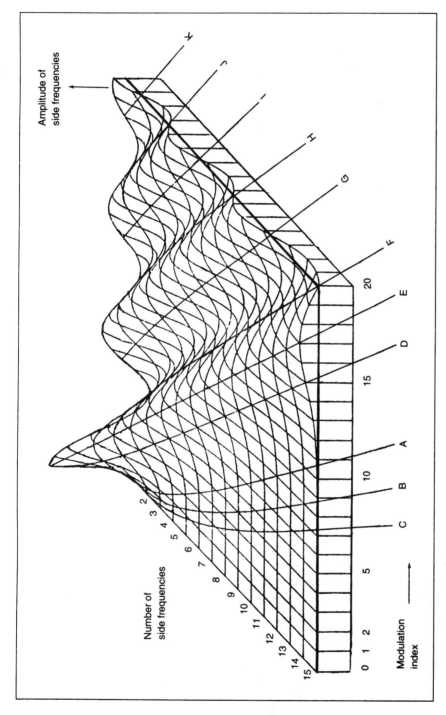

Figure 6.13 Three-dimensional graph of the Bessel functions 1 to 15 plotted (plotted back to front) as a function of modulation index *I* (plotted from left to right) showing the number of sidebands generated (after Chowning 1973). Lines A, B, and C show the points at which the amplitude falls off by −40, −60, and −80 dB, respectively. Line D indicates the cutoff point for "perceptually significant" sidebands. E is the maximum amplitude for each order. Lines F through K show the zero crossings of the functions and, therefore, values of the index that produce a null or zero amplitude for various side frequencies.

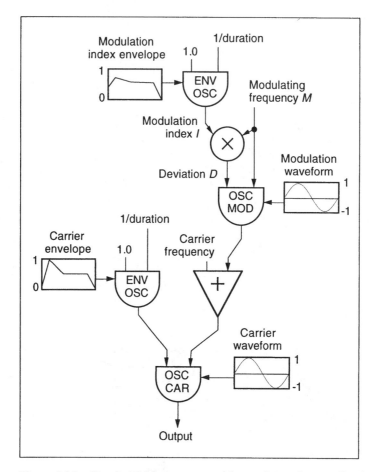

Figure 6.14   Simple FM instrument with envelopes for amplitude and frequency. This instrument also translates a user-specified modulation index envelope into a frequency deviation parameter.

A musician usually wants dynamic control of the overall amplitude as well as the modulation index. Figure 6.14 provides these envelopes. In Chowning's original paper (1973) he described a variation of this instrument with a modulation index that varies between two values *I1* and *I2* according to an envelope. (See Maillard 1976 for another implementation.)

Applications of Simple FM

A straightforward application of simple FM is generating brasslike tones. This family of sounds have a sharp attack on both the amplitude and index envelopes, and maintain a $C:M$ ratio of 1. The modulation index should vary between 0 and 7.

When the $C\!:\!M$ ratio is $1\!:\!2$, odd harmonics are generated, making possible a crude clarinet simulation. An irrational $C\!:\!M$ ratio like

$$C\!:\!\sqrt{2C}$$

yields an inharmonic complex that can simulate percussive and bell-like sounds (Moorer 1977).

Besides simulations of instrumental tones, another way to compose with FM is to take advantage of its "unnatural" properties and the uniquely synthetic spectra it generates. This is the approach taken by composers James Dashow and Barry Truax. Dashow uses FM to "harmonize" (in an extended sense of the word "harmony") pitch dyads (Dashow 1980, 1987; Roads 1985c). Truax systematically mapped out the spectral "families" made possible by various $C\!:\!M$ ratios (Truax 1977). For example, certain $C\!:\!M$ ratios generate harmonic spectra, while others generate combinations of harmonic and inharmonic spectra. Each $C\!:\!M$ ratio is a member of a family of ratios that produce the same spectrum and which vary only in the position of the carrier around which spectral energy is centered. By carefully choosing carrier and modulating frequencies a composer can generate a progression of related timbres with the same set of sidebands.

Another approach to composition with FM is to set a constant C or M and generate a set of related timbres with different $C\!:\!M$ ratios.

Exponential FM

In the usual digital implementation of FM, the sidebands are equally spaced around the carrier frequency. We call this *linear FM*. In FM on some analog synthesizers, however, the spacing of sidebands is asymmetrical around the carrier, creating a different type of sound altogether. We call this *exponential FM*. This section explains the difference between these two implementations of FM.

Most analog synthesizers let a voltage-controlled oscillator (VCO) be frequency modulated by another oscillator. However, in order to allow equal-tempered keyboard control of the VCO, the VCO responds to a given voltage in a frequency-dependent way. In particular, a typical VCO responds to a one-volt-per-octave protocol, corresponding to the voltage/octave protocol of analog keyboards. In such a system, for example, the pitch A880 Hz is obtained by applying one more volt to the control input of the VCO than that needed to obtain A440.

In the case of FM, a modulating signal that varies between -1 volt and $+1$ volt causes a carrier oscillator set to A440 to vary between A220 and

A880. This means that it modulates 220 Hz downward but 440 Hz upward—an asymmetrical modulation. The average center frequency of the carrier changes, which usually means that the perceived center pitch is detuned by a significant interval. This detuning is caused by the modulation index, which means that the bandwidth and the center frequency are linked. From a musical standpoint, this linkage is not ideal. We want to be able to increase the modulation index without shifting the center frequency. See Hutchins (1975) for an analysis of exponential FM.

In digital modulation the sidebands are spaced equally around the carrier; hence the term *linear FM*. As the modulation index increases, the center frequency remains the same. All digital FM is linear, and at least one manufacturer, Serge Modular, makes a linear FM analog oscillator module.

Analysis and FM

Since FM techniques can create many different families of spectra, it might be useful to have an analysis/resynthesis procedure linked to FM, similar to those used with additive and subtractive techniques. Such a procedure could take an existing sound and translate it into parameter values for an FM instrument. By plugging those values into the instrument, we could hear an approximation of that sound via FM synthesis. The general name for this type of procedure is *parameter estimation* (see chapter 13). Various attempts have been made to try to approximate a given steady-state spectrum automatically using FM (Justice 1979; Risberg 1982). The problem of estimating the FM parameters for complex evolving sounds is difficult (Kronland-Martinet and Grossmann 1991; Horner, Beauchamp, and Haken 1992).

As the power of digital hardware has increased, some of the motivation for estimating FM parameters has diminished. FM synthesis was originally proposed as a computationally efficient method, but now more powerful synthesis methods (such as additive synthesis) are no longer so difficult. Only a certain class of sounds are well modeled as modulations. Additive synthesis and physical models (see chapter 7) may be more appropriate models of traditional instruments.

Multiple-Carrier FM

By *multiple-carrier frequency modulation* (MC FM), we mean an FM instrument in which one oscillator simultaneously modulates two or more carrier oscillators. The output of the carriers sum to a composite waveform that

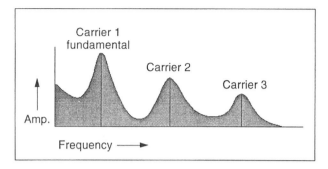

Figure 6.15 A spectrum with three formant regions created with a three-carrier FM instrument.

superposes the modulated spectra. Multiple carriers can create *formant regions* (peaks) in the spectrum, as shown in figure 6.15. The presence of formant regions is characteristic of the spectrum of the human voice and most traditional instruments. Another justification for separate carrier systems is to set different decay times for each formant region. This is useful in simulating brasslike tones where the upper partials decay more rapidly than the lower partials.

Figure 6.16 shows a triple-carrier FM instrument. In order to indicate clearly the multiple-carrier structure, the figure omits envelope controls and waveform tables. The amplitudes of the carriers are independent. When the *Carrier 2* and *Carrier 3* amplitudes are some fraction of *Carrier 1*, the instrument generates formant regions around the frequencies of the second and third carriers.

The equation for a multiple-carrier FM waveform at time t is simply the addition of n simple FM equations:

$$MCFM_t = A^{w1} \times \sin(C1_t + [I1 \times \sin(M)]) \ldots$$

$$+ A^{wn} \times \sin(Cn_t + [In \times \sin(M)])$$

where A is an amplitude constant, $0 < A \leq 1.0$,

$w1$ is the weighting of *Carrier 1*,

wn is the weighting of *Carrier n*,

$C1$ is the fundamental pitch = $2\pi \times$ carrier frequency 1 (in Hz),

Cn is the formant frequency = $2\pi \times$ carrier frequency n (in Hz), where Cn is an integer multiple of $C1$,

M is modulating frequency, usually set to be equal to $C1$ (Chowning 1989),

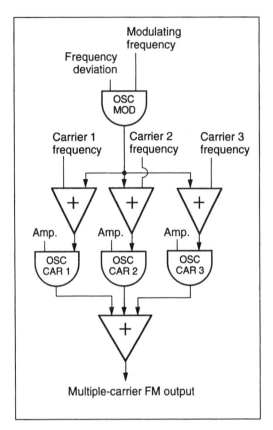

Figure 6.16   Triple-carrier FM instrument driven by a single modulating oscillator (OSC MOD).

I1 is the modulation index of *C1*

In is the modulation index of *Cn*

The exponents *w1* and *wn* determine how the relative contribution of the carriers vary with the overall amplitude *A*.

Musical Applications of MC FM

Documented applications of MC FM strive to simulate the sounds of traditional instrument tones. With MC FM—or any synthesis technique, for that matter—the secret of realistic simulation is attention to detail in all aspects of the sound—amplitude, frequency, spectral envelopes, vibrato, and musical context.

A straightforward application of MC FM is in the synthesis of trumpet-like tones. Risset and Mathews's (1969) analysis of trumpet-like tones showed a nearly harmonic spectrum, a 20–25 ms rise time of the amplitude envelope (with high partials building up more slowly), a small quasi-random frequency fluctuation, and a formant peak in the region of 1500 Hz. Morrill (1977) developed both single-carrier and double-carrier FM instruments for brass tone synthesis based on these data. A double-carrier instrument sounds more realistic, since each carrier produces frequencies for different parts of the spectrum. In particular, *C1* generates the fundamental and the first five to seven partials, while *C2* is set at 1500 Hz, the main formant region of the trumpet. Each carrier has its own amplitude envelope for adjusting the balance between the two carrier systems in the composite spectrum. For example, in loud trumpet tones, the upper partials standout.

Chowning (1980, 1989) applied the MC FM technique to the synthesis of vowel sounds sung by a soprano and by a low bass voice. He determined that a combination of periodic and random vibrato must be applied to all frequency parameters for realistic simulation of the vocal tones. "Without vibrato the synthesized tones are unnatural sounding" (Chowning 1989, p. 62). A quasi-periodic vibrato makes the frequencies "fuse" into a vocal-like tone. In Chowning's simulations, the *vibrato percent deviation V* is defined by the relation

$$V = 0.2 \times \log(\text{pitch}).$$

Hence for a pitch of 440 Hz, *V* is about 1.2 percent or 5.3 Hz in depth. The frequency of the vibrato ranges from 5.0 to 6.5 Hz according to the fundamental frequency range of the pitches F3 to F6.

Multiple-Modulator FM

In multiple-modulator frequency modulation (MM FM) more than one oscillator modulates a single carrier oscillator. Two basic configurations are possible: *parallel* and *series* (figure 6.17). MM FM is easiest to understand when the number of modulators is limited to two and their waveforms are sinusoidal.

Parallel MM FM

In parallel MM FM, two sine waves simultaneously modulate a single carrier sine wave. The modulation generates sidebands at frequencies of the form:

$$C \pm (i \times M1) \pm (k \times M2)$$

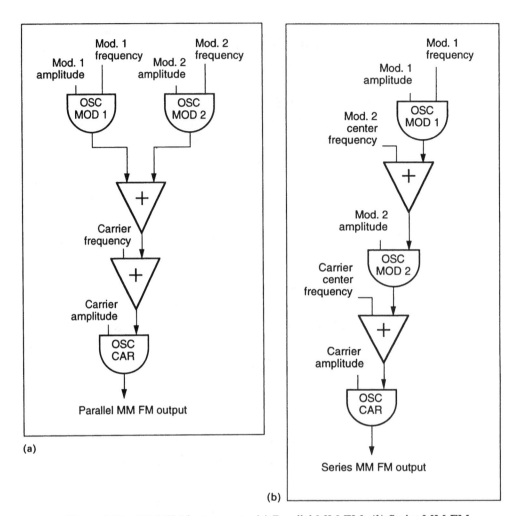

Figure 6.17   MM FM instruments. (*a*) Parallel MM FM. (*b*) Series MM FM.

where *i* and *k* are integers and *M1* and *M2* are the modulating frequencies. In parallel MM FM, it is as though each of the sidebands produced by one of the modulators is modulated as a carrier by the other modulator. The explosion in the number of partials is clear in figure 6.18, which lists both the primary and secondary modulation products.

The wave equation of the parallel double-modulator FM signal at time *t* is as follows:

$$PMMFM_t = A \times \sin\{C_t + [I1 \times \sin(M1_t)] + [I2 \times \sin(M2_t)]\}.$$

For mathematical descriptions of the spectra produced by this class of techniques, see Schottstaedt (1977) and LeBrun (1977).

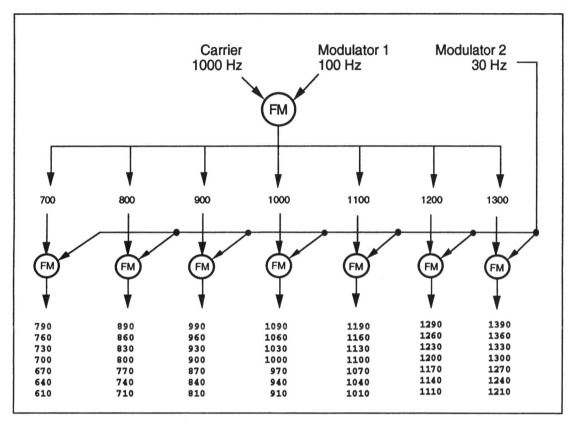

Figure 6.18   This diagram depicts the explosion in the number of partials produced by parallel MM FM. Each of the components emitted by the modulation of the *Carrier* by *Modulator 1* is then modulated by *Modulator 2*, producing the list of spectral components shown at the bottom.

Series MM FM

In series MM FM the modulating sine wave *M1* is itself modulated by *M2*. This creates a complicated modulating wave with a potentially immense number of sinusoidal sideband components, depending on the index of modulation. The instantaneous amplitude of series double-modulator FM is given in the following equation, adapted from Schottstaedt (1977):

$$SMMFM_t = A \times \sin\{C_t + [I1 \times \sin(M1_t + [I2 \times \sin(M2_t)])]\}.$$

The differences between the parallel and serial equations reflects the configuration of the oscillators. In practice, *I2* determines the number of significant sidebands in the modulating signal and *I1* determines the number of sidebands in the output signal. Even small values of *I1* and *I2* create complex waveforms. The ratio *M1*: *C* determines the placement of the carrier's sidebands, each of which has sidebands of its own at intervals determined by $M2:M1$. Hence, each sideband is modulated and is also a modulator.

Musical Applications of MM FM

Schottstaedt (1977) used double-modulator FM to simulate certain characteristics of piano tones. He set the first modulator to approximately the carrier frequency, and the second modulator to approximately four times the carrier frequency. According to Schottstaedt, if the carrier and the first modulator are exactly equal, the purely harmonic result sounds artificial, like the sound of an electric (amplified tuning bar) piano. This need for inharmonicity in piano tones agrees with the findings of acousticians (Blackham 1965; Backus 1977).

Schottstaedt made the amplitudes of the modulating indexes frequency-dependent. That is, as the carrier frequency increases, the modulation index decreases. The result is a spectrum that is rich in the lower register but becomes steadily simpler as the pitch rises. Since the length of decay of a piano tone also varies with pitch (low tones decay longer), he used a pitch-dependent decay time.

Chowning and Schottstaedt also worked on the simulation of stringlike tones using triple-modulator FM, where the $C:M1:M2$ ratio was $1:3:4$, and the modulation indexes were frequency dependent (Schottstaedt 1977). Chowning also developed a deep bass voice using a combination MC FM and MM FM instrument. See Chowning (1980,1989) for more details on this instrument.

Feedback FM

Feedback FM is a widely used synthesis technique, due to Yamaha's patented application of the method in its digital synthesizers (Tomisawa 1981). In this section we describe three types of feedback FM: *one-oscillator feedback*, *two-oscillator feedback*, and *three-oscillator indirect feedback*.

Feedback FM solves certain problems associated with simple (nonfeedback) FM methods. When the modulation index increases in simple FM, the amplitude of the partials vary unevenly, moving up and down according to the Bessel functions (figure 6.19). This undulation in the amplitude of the partials lends an unnatural "electronic sound" characteristic to the simple FM spectrum; it makes simulations of traditional instruments more difficult.

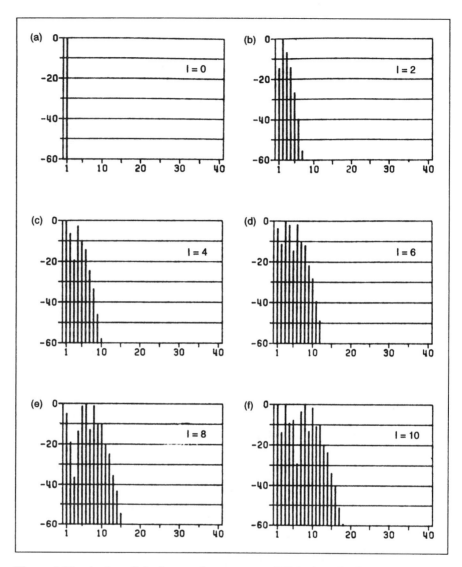

Figure 6.19   A plot of the harmonic spectrum of FM when the frequency of *C* is equal to that of *M*, for values of *I* ranging from 0 to 22 (after Mitsuhashi 1982b). Read the graphs starting from the top left, then top right, then go down a row to the left, then right, etc. Note how uneven the spectrum is, with partials going up and then down as the modulation index changes.

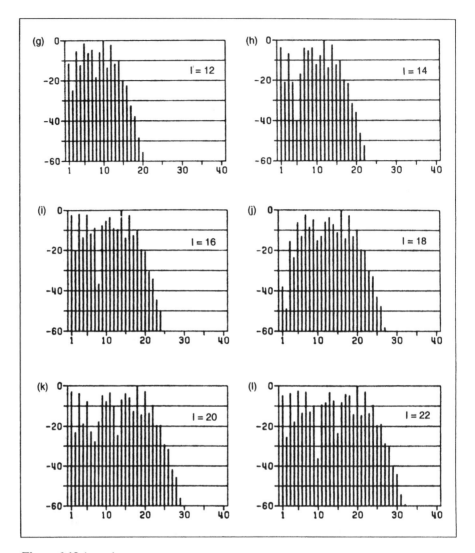

Figure 6.19 (cont.)

Feedback FM makes the spectrum more linear in its evolution. Generally, in feedback FM, as the modulation index increases, the number of partials and their amplitude increases relatively linearly.

Background: Feedback Oscillators

A feedback oscillator instrument first appeared in Jean-Claude Risset's *Introductory Catalog of Computer Generated Sounds* in 1969. Since this catalog was not publicly distributed, the technique first appeared in public in an obscure paper with the cryptic title "Some idiosyncratic aspects of computer synthesized sound" (Layzer 1971). In it, Arthur Layzer described work at Bell Telephone Laboratories in developing a self-modulating oscillator whose output is fed back to its input. This work was a collaboration with Risset, Max Mathews, and F. R. Moore. Moore implemented a feedback oscillator as a unit generator in the Music V language. (Music V is described in Mathews et al. 1969.)

The essential difference between the feedback oscillators developed at Bell Laboratories and the Yamaha feedback FM technique is that the former fed the signal back into the amplitude input, while the latter feeds the signal back into the frequency or phase increment input. Hence the early feedback oscillators were implementing a form of "feedback AM" rather than feedback FM.

One-oscillator Feedback

The basic idea of one-oscillator feedback FM is easy to describe. Figure 6.20 shows an oscillator that feeds its output back into its frequency input through a multiplier and an adder. The adder computes the phase index

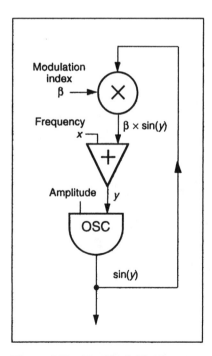

Figure 6.20 Feedback FM instrument. *x* is a phase increment to a sine wave lookup table. *x* is added with a signal fed back from the output, multiplied a feedback factor β.

for the sine table-lookup operation within the oscillator. At each sample period, a value x (the frequency increment) is added to the existing phase. The value in the sine table at this new phase is the output signal $\sin(y)$. In a synthesizer, x is usually obtained by pressing a key on a musical keyboard. This keystroke translates into a large phase increment value for a high-pitched note or a small phase increment value for a low-pitched note.

In feedback FM, the output signal $\sin(y)$ routes back to the adder after being multiplied by the *feedback factor* β. The factor β acts as a kind of scaling function or "modulation index" for the feedback. With the feedback loop the address of the next sample is $x + [\beta \times \sin(y)]$.

Figure 6.21 plots the spectrum of a one-oscillator feedback FM instrument as β increases. Notice the increase in the number of partials, and the regular, incremental differences in amplitude between the partials, all contributing to a quasi-linear spectral buildup. With increasing modulation, the signal evolves from a sine wave to a sawtooth wave in a continuous manner.

The equation for one-oscillator feedback FM can be characterized by reference to the Bessel functions (Tomisawa 1981):

$$FFM_t = \sum_{n-1}^{\infty} \frac{2}{n \times \beta} \times J_n(n \times \beta) \times \sin(n \times x)t$$

where $J_n(n)$ is a Bessel function of order n and $n \times \beta$ is the modulation index. The Bessel functions act in different ways in feedback FM as opposed to simple FM. In simple FM, the modulation index I is common for each Bessel component $J_n(I)$. This means that each Bessel function value $J_n(n)$ is represented by a height at a position where the common modulation index crosses. Accordingly, as the modulation index in regular FM increases, the spectral envelope assumes an undulating character. In feedback FM, the order n of the Bessel function $J_n(n \times \beta)$ is included in the modulation index, and the factor $2/(n \times \beta)$ is multiplied as a coefficient to the Bessel equation (Mitsuhashi 1982a).

In feedback FM, the modulation index $n \times \beta$ differs for each order n and increases approximately in the manner of a monotone function (i.e., the increase is by a constant factor). The scaling coefficient $2/n \times \beta$ ensures that as the order n of partials increases, their amplitude decreases.

Two-oscillator Feedback

Another feedback FM patch takes the output of a feedback oscillator and uses it to modulate another oscillator (figure 6.22). The multiplier M in the figure functions as the index of modulation control between the two oscillators.

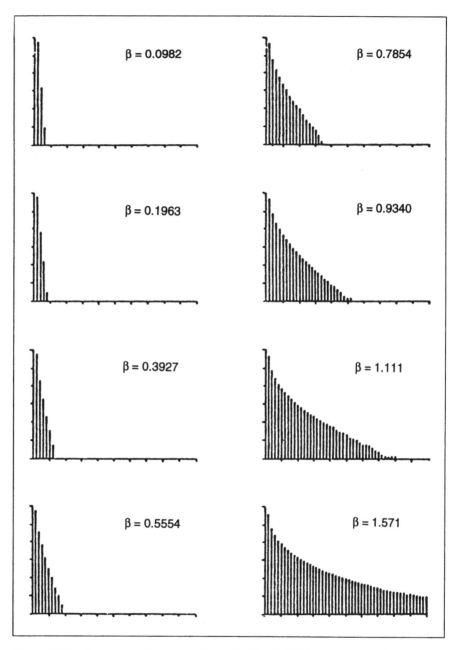

Figure 6.21   Spectrum of a one-oscillator feedback FM instrument as the feedback factor β increases, with the phase increment x set at 200 Hz. The horizontal axis shows frequency plotted from 0 to 10 KHz. The vertical axis shows amplitude on a scale from 0 to 60 dB.

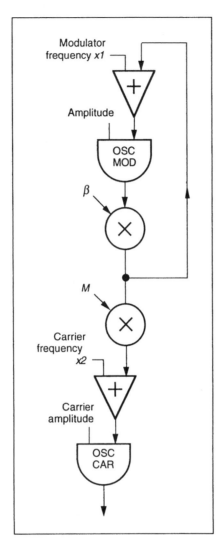

Figure 6.22   Two-oscillator feedback FM instrument. The output of a feedback FM oscillator modulates a second, nonfeedback oscillator.

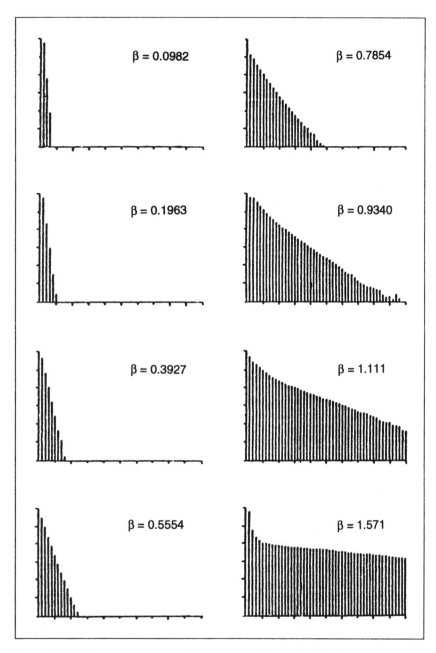

Figure 6.23 Spectrum generated by a two-oscillator feedback FM instrument as the feedback factor β increases from 0.0982 to 1.571. The frequency values for *x1* and *x2* are both set at 200 Hz, and the modulation index *M* is set to the constant value 2. The horizontal axis shows frequency plotted from 0 to 10 KHz. The vertical axis shows amplitude on a scale from 0 to 60 dB.

When M is in the range of 0.5 to 2, the spectrum has a monotonically decreasing tendency in which the amplitude of the partials decreases as the number of partials increases (figure 6.23). When the feedback parameter β is greater than 1, the overall amplitude of the high-order partials increases. This creates the effect of a variable filter. It thus has a more strident and shrill sound. However, when M is set to 1 and $x1$ and $x2$ are equal, this instrument generates the same spectrum as the single-oscillator feedback FM instrument shown in figure 6.20.

When the ratio between $x2$ (the carrier) and $x1$ (the modulator) is 2:1, the modulation index M is 1, and β varies between 0.09 and 1.571, the result is a continuous variation between a quasi-sine wave and a quasi-square wave.

Three-oscillator Indirect Feedback

Another variation on feedback FM in a three-oscillator technique with *indirect feedback*, shown in figure 6.24. The feedback parameter is $\beta1$. Indirect feedback produces a complex form of modulation. When the frequencies $x1$, $x2$, and $x3$ are noninteger multiples, nonpitched sounds are created. A beating chorus effect is produced when these frequencies are very close to being in an integer relationship. According to sound designer David Bristow (personal communication 1986) this instrument generates a rich spectrum, and when the feedback is increased the energy tends to focus at the high end of the spectrum.

Phase Distortion

Phase distortion (PD) synthesis is a term invented by the Casio corporation to describe a simple modulation technique developed for several of its digital synthesizers. PD synthesis uses a sine wave table-lookup oscillator in which the rate of scanning through the oscillator varies over the cycle. The scanning interval speeds up from 0 to π and then slows down from π to 2π. The overall frequency is constant, according to the pitch of the note, but the output waveform is no longer a sine. Figure 6.25 illustrates the effect of the bent (sped up and then slowed down) scanning function on the output waveform.

As the amount of speeding up and slowing down increases (bending the scanning function progressively), the original sinusoidal waveform turns into a kind of triangle wave, and finally into a quasi-sawtooth waveform that is rich in harmonics.

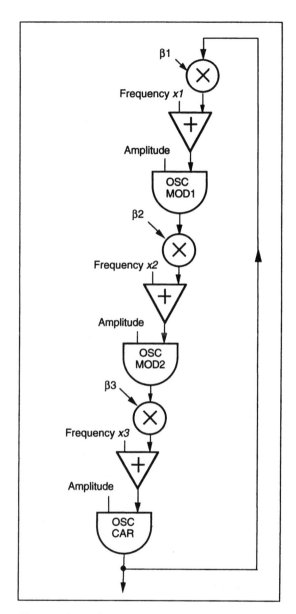

Figure 6.24   Three-oscillator indirect feedback FM instrument. A series of three oscillators modulate each other. Three modulation index factors *β1, β2,* and *β3* determine the amount of modulation. The global output is fed back into the first modulating oscillator.

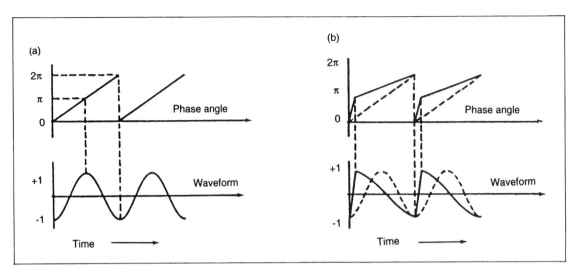

Figure 6.25   Waveforms in Casio phase distortion synthesis. The audio waveform changes by varying the rate at which a sine lookup table is read out. (*a*) A constant rate of readout generates a sine wave. (*b*) A readout whose rate changes twice per cycle, distorting the sine wave into a quasi-sawtooth waveform.

Waveshaping Synthesis

Jean-Claude Risset, working at the Bell Telephone Laboratories in New Jersey, carried out the first experiments with the method now known as waveshaping synthesis (Risset 1969). Daniel Arfib (1979) and Marc LeBrun (1979) independently developed theoretical and empirical elaborations of the basic method. Waveshaping is musically interesting because, as in FM synthesis, it gives us a simple handle on the time-varying bandwidth and spectrum of a tone in a computationally efficient way.

The fundamental idea behind waveshaping (also known as *nonlinear distortion*) is to pass a sound signal x through a "distortion box." In digital form, the distortion box is a function in a stored table (or array) in computer memory. The function w maps any input value x in the range $[-1, +1]$ to an output value $w(x)$ in the same range.

In the simplest case, x a sinusoidal wave generated by an oscillator. However, x can be any signal, not just a sinusoid. For each output sample to be computed we use the value of x to index table w. Table w contains the *shaping function* (also called the *transfer function*). We then simply take the value in w indexed by x as our output value $w(x)$.

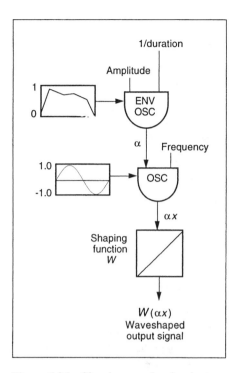

Figure 6.26 Simple waveshaping instrument. A sinusoidal oscillator, whose amplitude is controlled by the amplitude envelope signal α, indexes a value in the shaping function table *w*. As in other example instruments, the input *1/duration* that is fed into the frequency input of the envelope oscillator indicates that it goes through one cycle over the duration of the note.

Simple Waveshaping Instrument

An instrument for simple waveshaping synthesis is shown in figure 6.26. Here an envelope oscillator controls the amplitude of a sinusoidal oscillator that is fed into a shaping function table. The amplitude envelope α is important because it has the effect of scaling the input signal, making it reference different regions of the shaping function *w*. We look at the implications of this next.

Example Shaping Functions

As figure 6.27 shows, if the shaping function in table *w* is a straight diagonal line from -1 to $+1$, the output of *w* is an exact replica of its input *x*. This is because the table maps an input of -1 (shown at the bottom of the function) to -1 in the output (shown at the right of the function), 0 maps

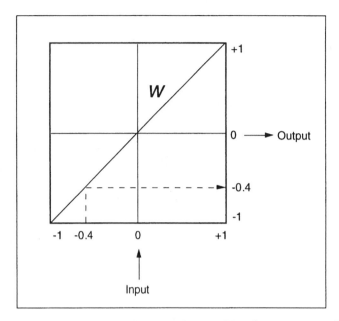

Figure 6.27 Shaping function shown with a linear response. The function maps an input signal scaled over the range shown at the bottom to an output function whose scale is shown at the right. To see how the function maps an input to an output value, read vertically from the bottom and then look to the right to see the corresponding output value. Thus an input value of −0.4 on the bottom maps to an output value of −0.4 on the right. This equivalence between the input and the output is only true for a linear shaping function.

to 0, 1 maps to 1, and so on. Because this simple relationship between the input and the output occurs only when the shaping function is a straight line, we say that in this case the output is a *linear function* of its input.

If the shaping table contains anything other than a straight diagonal line from −1 to +1, *x* is *distorted* by the shaping function in *w*. Figure 6.28 shows the effects of several shaping functions on an input sinusoid. Figure 6.28a shows an inverting shaping function. For every positive value of the input amplitude the waveshaper emits a correspond negative value and vice versa. Figure 6.28b is a straight line but with a narrower angle than the curve in figure 6.27. It maps to a narrower range on the right-hand (output) side of the shaping function, meaning that it attenuates the input signal. Figure 6.28c expands low-level signals and sends high-level signals into clipping distortion. The amplitude-sensitive nature of waveshaping in demonstrated well in figure 6.28d. The shaping function is a straight line around zero, which is the low-amplitude portion of the grid. Such a function passes a low-amplitude input signal with no distortion. When the amplitude of the

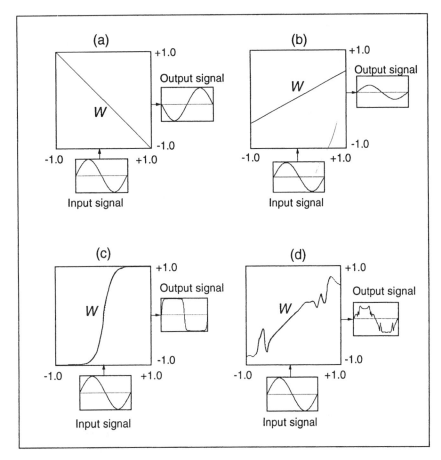

Figure 6.28   Four shaping functions. (*a*) Inversion of the input signal. (*b*) Attenuation. (*c*) Amplification of low-level signals (expansion) and clipping of high-level signals. (*d*) Complicated amplitude-sensitive distortion.

input signal increases, the extreme ends of the shaping function subject the input signal to a complicated form of distortion.

Amplitude Sensitivity of Waveshaping Spectrum

It is easy to see that the amplitude sensitivity of waveshaping can model a characteristic of acoustic instruments. That is, when one plays an acoustic instrument "harder," for example, by strumming a guitar forcefully, blowing a saxophone stridently, or striking a drum intensely, this enriches the spectrum. In waveshaping we can emulate this effect by passing a signal whose overall amplitude varies with time through the shaping function. As the amplitude of the input signal varies, one obtains a correspondingly time-varied spectrum at the output. Put another way, a variation in the time domain at the input is manifest as a variation in the frequency domain at the output. This is an important feature. Given a single shaping function (precomputed and stored in memory), a variety of output waveforms can be obtained simply by varying the amplitude or offset of the input signal in order to apply various regions of the shaping function. Hence waveshaping is an especially efficient synthesis technique. Arfib (1979) gives practical examples of the waveshaping technique in specific musical applications.

Chebychev Shaping Functions

Research by LeBrun (1979) and Arfib (1979) demonstrated that it is possible to predict exactly the output spectrum of the waveshaping technique under mathematically controlled conditions. By restricting the signal x to an unvarying cosine wave and using a family of smooth polynomials called *Chebychev functions*, which take values in the range $[-1, +1]$ to construct the shaping function w, one can produce easily any desired combination of harmonics in a steady-state spectrum. This derives from the following identity:

$$T_k \times (\cos[\theta]) = \cos(k \times \theta)$$

where T_k is the kth Chebychev function. In other words, by applying the kth Chebychev polynomial to an input sine wave, we obtain a cosine wave at the kth harmonic. This means that each separate Chebychev polynomial, when used as the shaping function, produces a particular harmonic of x. By summing a weighted combination of Chebychev polynomials and putting the result in the shaping table, a corresponding harmonic mixture is obtained as the output of the waveshaping technique. For example, to obtain a steady-state waveform with a first harmonic (fundamental), a second harmonic that is 0.3 the amplitude of the first harmonic, and a third harmonic that is 0.17 of the first harmonic, we add the equations

$$T_0 + (0.3 \times T_2) + (0.17 \times T_3),$$

and we put the result into the transfer function wavetable. If a cosine wave is passed through this table, then the output spectrum contains the desired harmonic ratios.

An advantage of using the Chebychev functions is that we can guarantee that the output of the waveshaper is bandlimited. That is, it does not contain frequencies above the Nyquist rate, and therefore it is free of foldover distortion. Table 6.1 lists the equations for T_0 through T_8 where $x = \cos(q)$.

Table 6.1 Chebychev functions T_0 through T_8

$T_0 = 1$

$T_1 = x$

$T_2 = 2x^2 - 1$

$T_3 = 4x^3 - 3x$

$T_4 = 8x^4 - 8x^2 + 1$

$T_5 = 16x^5 - 20x^3 + 5x$

$T_6 = 32x^6 - 48x^4 + 18x^2 - 1$

$T_7 = 64x^7 - 112x^5 + 56x^3 - 7x$

$T_8 = 128x^8 - 256x^6 + 160x^4 - 32x^2 + 1$

Amplitude Normalization

The main drawback of waveshaping synthesis is that the output amplitude of the simple waveshaping instrument shown in figure 6.28 varies considerably, even using only one shaping function. This variance is the result of different parts of the shaping function being applied. That is, it depends on the amplitude of the input signal to the shaping function.

In waveshaping the amplitude of x is actually used to control timbre, not the overall loudness of the sound. If we want full independence between timbre and the output amplitude, some form of amplitude normalization is required. At least three kinds of normalization are possible: loudness normalization, power normalization, and peak normalization.

For musical purposes, our ideal would be loudness normalization, in which the perceived loudness of the instrument is constant for all values of α. However, this involves complicated psychoacoustic interactions and context-dependencies, so it is too difficult and computationally expensive for most implementations. Power normalization is based on division by the *root mean square* (RMS) of the harmonic amplitudes generated by a particular shaping function. LeBrun (1979) gives details on this technique. Peak normalization is probably the least complicated and most practical of the three. It is accomplished by scaling the output in relation to the maximum value. Peak normalization ensures that the output amplitude of different tones will at least have the same peak value, and will therefore not overload the digital-to-analog converters with a value out of their range.

Figure 6.29 shows a waveshaping instrument with a peak normalization. The easiest way to do this is to prepare a table containing normalization factors for all values of α, since the envelope a determines the amplitude of x. For example, if the value of α input to the normalization table is 0.7, we

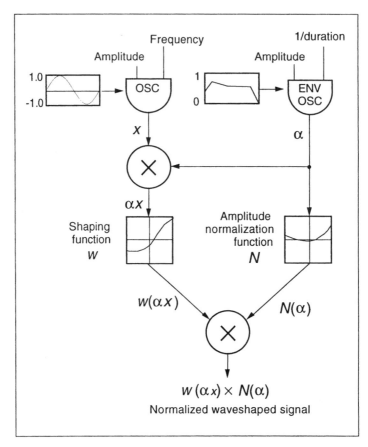

Figure 6.29   Waveshaping instrument with a normalization section. The value of α indexes a value in the normalization table that scales the output of the waveshaper.

multiply the output by the entry in the normalization table corresponding to α.

Variations on Waveshaping

The classic waveshaping technique—sending a cosine wave through a Chebychev polynomial shaping function—produces a range of harmonic spectra. We can extend this class of waveshaping spectra by changing the input or the shaping function. Another possibility is modifying the signal coming out of the waveshaping instrument by another signal-processing device, such as a filter.

As mentioned previously, the input x to the waveshaper can be any signal, not just a cosine wave. Reinhard (1981), for example, details what happens when x is the sum of two cosine waves at different frequencies.

Another variation is to use a frequency-modulated signal for the input x. The benefit of this is that one can obtain inharmonic combinations of partials and formant structures (Arfib 1979).

The signal x can also be a sampled or concrète sound. When the shaping function w is a simple and smooth polynomial, the effect is not unlike phasing, since the harmonics of the input undulate in a time-varying way. Hence a waveshaping instrument can generate an interesting hybrid of natural and electronic sound. If w contains any straight horizontal or vertical lines the effect is a strong distortion, like the distortion of transistorized electric guitar amplifiers turned to maximum.

Neither does w have to be a Chebychev polynomial. The main benefit of using Chebychev polynomials as shaping functions is that the output is bandlimited and is therefore not subject to foldover distortion. But if this benefit is not paramount, w can be constructed out of other kinds of equations. It can also be drawn by hand (Buxton et al. 1982). See chapter 8 for an account of waveshaping with a noise-modulated shaping function.

Movable Waveshaping

Another variation is called *movable waveshaping*, invented by Xin Chong at the Beijing Central Music Conservatory (Xin 1987). In this technique the shaping function itself varies with time. This can be accomplished by storing a longer shaping function and moving an index to scan various parts of it at different times. Starting from simple input signals and simple time-varying shaping functions, a multiplicity of results can be obtained.

Fractional Waveshaping

De Poli (1984) analyzed a configuration in which the shaping function is a fraction, specifically, a ratio between two polynomials. He calls this *fractional waveshaping*. Fractional waveshaping can generate such effects as exponential spectra and spectra whose shapes resemble a damped cosine wave. The multiple bumps of the damped cosine wave spectrum are heard as formants. Dynamically varying spectra are achieved as in regular waveshaping by varying the amplitude and offset of the input cosine signal.

Postprocessing and Parameter Estimation

The waveshaped signal can be passed through another signal processing device, what we could call *postprocessing* the waveshaped signal. This device could be, for example, an AM oscillator, a FM oscillator, or a filter. AM and FM can enrich the waveshaping spectrum by adding, for example, in-harmonic partials to a harmonic spectrum (Arfib 1979; Le Brun 1979; De Poli 1984).

De Poli (1984) and Volonnino (1984) developed an experimental filtering method called *frequency-dependent waveshaping*. This was aimed at provid-ing independent control of the phase and amplitude of each harmonic gen-erated by the waveshaping process. See the cited literature for more details on these techniques.

Beauchamp (1979) inserted a highpass filter on the output of his wave-shaping model of brass tones in order to mimic the damping effects of brass pipes. More recently, Beauchamp and Horner (1992) have simulated instru-mental tones by a multiple waveshaper + filter model. They first perform a parameter estimation of an instrumental tone and approximate its spectrum with a single waveshaper + filter model. They subtract this approximation from the original sound to obtain a difference or *residual* signal. They then approximate the residual with another waveshaper + filter model. Using two or even three waveshaping models in this way results in much closer simulations than a single model.

General Modulations

Many synthesis techniques can be turned into modulation techniques by substituting a time-varying function for a constant term in the equation of the original technique. If the time-varying function is periodic, the tech-nique is one of a family of synthesis techniques known under the rubric of *waveshape parameter modulation*. For example, amplitude modulation and frequency modulation can be classified as waveshape parameter modulation techniques. For more on this classification scheme see Mitsuhashi (1980).

James A. Moorer (1976) showed that the equation for single FM is one instance of a general class of equations called *discrete summation formulas* (DSFs). DSFs refers to a set of formulas that are the *closed form* solution of the sums of finite and infinite trigonometric series. By "closed form" is meant a more compact and efficient representation of a longer summation formula. These formulas are relevant to sound synthesis if we assume that they describe waveforms that are sums of sinusoidal waves. For example, the right-hand side of the following equation is the closed-form solution to the summation shown in the left-hand side:

$$\sum_{k=1}^{n} \sin(k\theta) = \sin[1/2(n+1)\theta] \sin[(n\theta)/2] \csc(\theta/2).$$

This equation shows that we can represent the sum of n sine waves with just five multiplications, three divides, and three table-lookup operations. As closed form equations, DSFs have only a few parameters to manipulate and can be realized economically in digital form. Moorer's paper describes four DSFs that show promise for sound synthesis. A much broader class of DSFs exists (Hansen 1975), but most of them are probably not useful in music synthesis.

Some DSFs can generate time-varying tones that sound-similar to FM spectra. Moorer also described DSFs that can generate spectra that are impossible with simple FM, such as *one-sided spectra* whose partials extend in just one direction from the carrier frequency. Another family of spectra possible with DSFs are those with partials whose amplitudes increase monotonically (i.e., by a constant factor).

A disadvantage of DSFs as against a technique like FM is the lack of amplitude normalization. Hence it is necessary to apply some kind of scaling or normalization to the output of a DSF synthesis algorithm. (See the discussion of amplitude normalization in the section on waveshaping.) Technically inclined readers with an interest in exploring DSF methods should refer to Moorer (1976, 1977) or Moore (1990).

Conclusion

Signal modulation is a rich source of musical effects and sonorities. AM and RM have a long history due to their applications in radioband communications. In the audio band, they generate classic "radiosonic" sounds. They are, however, more limited than FM, partly because they do not generate as many sidebands, and partly due to the flexibility of the FM panameters. In the case of FM, years of patient research by dozens of engineers in the USA and Japan paid off in numerous refinements. Musicians invested countless hours tuning the parameters of FM instruments to create a range of interesting "voices" or timbres.

One drawback of basic modulation techniques is inherent in the modulation formulas. The spectra of sounds generated by modulation techniques are constrained by mathematical law to fixed kinds of behavior. In practice, this means that each type of simple modulation has a characteristic sound "signature" that can be discerned after some exposure to the technique.

Depending on the skill of the composer, this signature can either be an annoying cliché, or an attractive musical force. In the latter category, Louis and Bebe Barron's electronic music soundtrack to the science-fiction film *Forbidden Planet* (1956) stands as an outstanding example of musical use of modulation. In the future, more elaborate synthesis techniques will be developed, but there will remain something deeply evocative about artfully deployed modulation.

7   *Physical Modeling and Formant Synthesis*

Karplus-Strong (Plucked String and Drum) Synthesis

Plucked Strings
Drumlike Timbres
Stretching Out the Decay Time
Extensions to KS

Formant Synthesis

Formant Wave-function Synthesis and CHANT
Fundamentals of FOF Synthesis
Anatomy of a FOF
FOF Parameters
The CHANT Program
FOF Analysis/Resynthesis
Models of Resonance
MOR Transformations
Matching the Spectrum Envelope with FOFs
VOSIM
VOSIM Waveform
Window Function Synthesis

Conclusion

Never, it is believed, since the very first sound of the human voice emanated from the earliest created of mankind, causing the oral mystery of sounded syllables to float upon the balmy airs of Paradise, until now, has aught been perfected which could approximate in any real degree to the Divinely bestowed "music of speech." Many and varied have been the efforts made, from time to time, to accomplish this apparently impossible purpose, but all have proved alike worse than futile. It has been reserved for Mr. Giacopo Saguish, of Constantinople, to become the wonderful and fortunate inventor of the Automaton Head, which (miraculous to relate) he has so contrived, by means of the nicest and most exquisitely constructed mechanism, that it can rival Nature herself in its vocal and elocutionary powers. (Description of the Anthropoglossos or Mechanical Vocalist, London ca. 1835, reprinted in Ord-Hume 1973.)

This chapter treats three overlapping categories of synthesis methods, all of which strive to emulate acoustical methods of sound production. *Physical modeling synthesis* models the acoustics of traditional instruments, such as a jet of air through a mouthpiece into a resonating column. A simple variant of physical modeling, *Karplus-Strong synthesis* simulates the sound of plucked-string instruments such as guitars, mandolins, and harpsichords; drumlike sounds and other effects can also be generated. *Formant synthesis* circumscribes a body of techniques designed to generate peaks in a frequency spectrum. Such techniques can simulate the resonances of the human vocal tract, as well as those of traditional and synthetic instruments. We examine each category in turn, beginning with physical modeling synthesis.

Physical Modeling Synthesis

Physical modeling (PhM) *synthesis* starts from mathematical models of the physical acoustics of instrumental sound production. That is, the equations of PhM describe the mechanical and acoustic behavior of an instrument being played. This approach has also been called *synthesis by rule* (Ferretti 1965, 1966, 1975), *synthesis from first principles* (Weinreich 1983), or more recently, *virtual acoustics* (Yamaha 1993).

The goals of physical modeling synthesis are twofold: one scientific, and one artistic. First, PhM investigates the extent to which mathematical equations and algorithmic logic can simulate the sound-producing mechanisms of existing instruments. This approach is based on the premise that the closer the simulation, the better understood the system is. In this sense, a physical model embodies the Newtonian ideal of a precise mathematical model of a complicated mechanico-acoustic process. (For a concise introduction to the physics of waves in mechanical and acoustic systems, see Pierce 1974, Crawford 1968, or Olson 1991.)

The second goal of PhM is more artistic. Simulation by physical models can create sounds of fanciful instruments that would otherwise be impossible to build. In this category we include phantasmagorical instruments whose characteristics and geometry can change over time—such as an elastic cello that "expands" and "shrinks" over the course of a phrase, or impossible drums whose heads cannot be broken no matter how intensely they are hit. PhM techniques are often scalable, so that from a description of one gong we can fabricate an ensemble of a dozen gongs, say, ranging in diameter from 30 centimeters to 30 meters. Extrapolating from a specification of a single string, a musician can construct a virtual guitar whose strings are as long and thick as bridge suspension cables. To the delight of musical alchemists, changing the materials of construction—from silver to brass, to exotic woods, to plastic—may be as simple as typing a few constants.

PhM excels at simulating transitions between notes and timbres. By dynamically changing the size of certain parts of a virtual instrument (such as elongating a resonating tube), believable sonic transitions often result. Another characteristic of PhMs is that they capture the accidents that occur in performance, such as squeaks, mode locking, and multiphonics. These sounds are uncontrollable when a novice performer attempts to play, but when used in a controlled manner they inject a dose of realism into the simulation. In PhM synthesis these sounds occur naturally, as a side effect of certain parameter settings. Compare this with the case of additive synthesis, where detailed specifications must be given for every aspect of sound.

PhM synthesis methods do not attempt to create a "complete" physical model of an instrument. Rather than accounting for all possible conditions of the instrument's existence, they need only to account for the physics of an instrument in the highly constrained situation of performance. In performance, the performer usually makes only a small number of idiomatic gestures with the instrument. This relatively low-bandwidth control information can usually be represented concisely in software.

Efficiency of Physical Modeling Synthesis

PhM synthesis circumscribes a family of techniques developed by various researchers over more than three decades. Because of the mathematical nature of many of these techniques and the heavy computational burden they can impose, PhM synthesis has emerged slowly from laboratory environments to musician's studios.

Only in recent years have relatively efficient implementations been developed for certain types of physical modeling synthesis (McIntyre,

Schumacher, and Woodhouse 1983; Smith 1986, 1987a, b, 1992; Keefe 1992; Adrien 1991; Woodhouse 1992; Cook 1991a, b, 1992, 1993; Borin, De Poli, and Sarti 1992). These efficient algorithms (such as waveguides) are based on common digital signal-processing structures such as delay lines, filters, and table-lookup operations. In general, however, their efficiency comes at the expense of drastic simplifications. This means that they often generate "instrument-like" tones without necessarily achieving striking realism. This is not to say that such simulations are uninteresting. From a compositional viewpoint, flexible instrument-like tones can be quite useful. Woodhouse (1992) confronts some shortcomings of contemporary models.

This chapter describes both the "classical" or computationally intensive approach as well as more efficient strategies such as modal synthesis, McIntyre, Schumacher, and Woodhouse synthesis, and waveguide methods. We also present a very efficient method called Karplus-Strong synthesis later in the chapter.

Background: Physical Modeling

The concepts, terminology, and some of the formulas used in physical modeling synthesis can be traced to nineteenth-century scientific treatises on the nature of sound, such as Lord Rayleigh's extraordinary volume *The Theory of Sound* (1894/1945). Rayleigh detailed the principles of vibrating systems such as membranes, plates, bars, and shells, and described the mathematical physics of vibrations in the open air, in tubes, and in boxes. Other nineteenth-century pioneers built mechanical models to simulate the physics of musical instruments (Helmholtz 1863; Poynting and Thomson 1900; Tyndall 1875; Mayer 1878). Following the invention of the vacuum tube, analog electronic models were built (Steward 1922; Miller 1935; Stevens and Fant 1953). See Olson (1967) for analog circuit physical models of percussion, lip-reed instruments, air-reed instruments, struck string instruments, and the voice. But progress was generally slow until the computer era.

John Kelly and Carol Lochbaum at Bell Telephone Laboratories were pioneers in adapting a physical model of the human vocal tract to a digital computer (Kelly and Lochbaum 1962). Their rendition of *Bicycle Built for Two,* which appeared on the Bell Telephone Laboratories disk *Music from Mathematics* produced by Max V. Mathews in 1960, became a world-famous symbol of the increasing capabilities of digital computers. (The Stanley Kubrick film *2001: A Space Odyssey* makes reference to this achievement when the once-powerful computer HAL regresses to its earlier days and sings this song. The version in the film is sung by a human actor, however.)

Lejaren Hiller, James Beauchamp, and Pierre Ruiz at the University of Illinois were the first to adapt physical models to the synthesis of instruments (Hiller and Beauchamp 1967; Ruiz 1970; Hiller and Ruiz 1971). Their work focused on synthesizing the sound of vibrating objects such as strings, bars, plates, and membranes set into motion by plucking and striking. Another pioneer of physical modeling synthesis is Ercolino Ferretti, who directed work by students at MIT, Harvard University, and the University of Utah in the 1960s and 1970s (Ferretti 1965, 1966, 1975).

Interest in applying waveguides to synthesis was provoked by the discovery of the Karplus-Strong plucked-string algorithm (described later in this chapter). This computationally efficient method came about more as an accident than as an intentional attempt at physical modeling (Karplus and Strong 1983; Jaffe and Smith 1983). Keefe (1992) summarizes other developments since 1963 (see also Fletcher and Rossing 1991). In 1993 the Yamaha company announced commercial synthesizers based on waveguides, the VL1 and VP1.

Excitation and Resonance

Question: The resonant modes of a wind instrument are not perfect harmonics, but the tone may be perfectly harmonic. On the other hand, a percussion instrument has non-harmonic resonances and produces a non-harmonic sound. What is the difference?

Answer: The key here is to consider not just to consider the resonant modes and how they are placed, but how the instrument is excited. If you pick up a trumpet and hit it with a hammer, the sound is percussive. If you take a snare drum and excite it with a [vibrator] the sound is harmonic. (B. Hutchins 1984)

A fundamental principle of physical modeling synthesis is the interaction between an *exciter* and a *resonator*. An *excitation* is an action that causes vibration, such as the stroke of a bow, the hit of a stick, or a blow of air. A *resonance* is the response of the body of an instrument to the excitation vibration. From a signal-processing point of view, the body acts as a time-varying filter applied to the excitation signal.

In general, the exciter has a *nonlinear* behavior, and the resonator has a *linear* behavior. We have already touched on this subject in chapter 5. As an intuitive explanation of a "linear" acoustical system, we mean one that responds proportionally to the amount of energy applied to it. If we put two signals into the system, we expect that output to be their sum. By "non-linear" we mean a system that has built-in thresholds that, if exceeded, cause the system to respond in a new way, as if a switch had been thrown.

Exciter/resonator interactions fall into two basic classes: *decoupled (*or *feedforward)*, and *coupled (*or *feedback)*. In subtractive synthesis techniques like linear predictive coding (see chapter 5), a source or excitation signal is injected into a resonant filter. There is no other interaction between the source and the excitation than this transfer of energy from the exciter to the resonator.

In contrast, the mechanism of tone production in a saxophone is an example of coupled excitation. By coupled we mean that the vibration of the resonanting part feeds back to the excitation part. For example, the frequency of the vibrating reed is strongly influenced by acoustic feedback from the resonanting bore (tube) of the instrument, after being excited initially by a blast of air from the mouth.

This interaction between the excitation and the resonance creates the variety and subtlety of sound we hear in performances by instrumental virtuosos. Because PhM techniques can model this interaction, they tend to communicate a sense of the gesture behind the emission of sound (Florens and Cadoz 1991; Adrien 1991). This stands in contrast to abstract synthesis methods that are controlled by mathematical formulas not directly related to gestural control.

In some implementations of PhM synthesis, the excitation comes from an input device (or performance controller) played by a performer (Cadoz, Florens, and Luciani 1984; Cook 1992). See the section on input devices for PhM synthesis later. (See chapter 14 for more on musical input devices in general.)

Classical Physical Modeling Methodology

The "classical" approach to physical modeling is represented by the early work of Hiller and Ruiz (1971) and many researchers thereafter. The classical methodology is as follows.

First, one specifies the physical dimensions and constants of vibrating objects such as their mass and elasticity. This is done because in acoustic instruments, sound is produced by vibrating objects such as strings, reeds, membranes, or flows of air within a tube or body of an instrument.

Next, the *boundary conditions* to which the vibrating object is constrained are stipulated. These are the limiting values of the variables that cannot be exceeded. The boundary conditions also allow for the possibility that the system has not fully "come to rest" or settled following a previous input.

The *initial state* is specified, for example, the starting position of a string at rest.

Next, the excitation is described algorithmically as a force impinging on the vibrating object in some way. Typical sources of excitation in acoustic instruments include percussive sources such as drumsticks, mallets, and piano actions, wind sources such as the flow of air between reeds, and bows of stringed instruments. Coupling between exciter and resonator can be specified in this algorithm.

Impedence effects must be accounted for. Impedence is a resistance to a driving force; in a medium with high impendence, a large force is required to generate a small amplitude. As waves pass from one part of an instrument to another, the impedence of the different parts alters the wave propagation. For example, consider two joined strings, where one is much heavier than the other. If we strike the light string, the wave will hit the heavier string, and nearly all the energy will be reflected back to the lighter string. Whereas if the two strings are of equal impedence, there will be no reflections. Researchers have measured the impedences of various instrument components, and the appropriate equations can be inserted into the physical model (Campbell and Greated 1987).

Finally, the filtering due to factors such as friction and sound radiation patterns are specified as a further restriction on the conditions of vibration.

At this point one has a rather complicated system of equations that represent a physical model of the instrument. The corresponding *wave equation,* which combines all these factors, is subjected to the initial conditions and the excitation (Morse 1936). The wave equation is then solved by an iterative successive approximation procedure that tries to find reasonable values for many interdependent variables simultaneously. This equation generates a discrete sample value representing a sound pressure wave at a given instant of time.

Underneath the classical methodology are a set of *difference equations* based on the *mass-spring paradigm*—a model of vibrating structures that we describe in the next sections.

Difference Equations

In the classical approach to physical modeling synthesis, sound samples result from the evaluation of *difference equations* that describe the vibrational behavior of physical objects. A difference equation involves differences and derivatives of functions. These equations are usually invoked when describing how a signal changes over time. Coincidentally, the first application of difference equations, by Joseph Bernoulli in 1732, was the simulation of a vibrating string of finite length—a central technique of physical modeling synthesis. Difference equations also describe the operation of *digital filters*. All of the FIR and IIR filter equations in chapter 10 are examples of difference equations. (For more on difference equations see Rabiner and Gold 1975 or any other digital signal-processing textbook.)

Physicists use difference equations to describe the laws of change of physical quantities. In modeling a phenomenon this way, the first step is to find the smallest number of variables that can accurately describe the state of the modeled phenomenon. The next step sets up the simplest difference equations that are precise descriptions of the laws governing the changes in these variables. Certain classes of difference equations have general algebraic solutions, while others can only be solved by time-consuming *successive approximation* methods (Press et al. 1988). In these methods a solution is determined by first guessing at a solution and then successively improving the solution, iteratively.

The Mass-spring Paradigm for Vibrating Strings

The study of vibrating strings in musical instruments has fascinated scientists and musicians for centuries. So it is not surprising that Hiller and Ruiz (1971) took the vibrating string as a point of departure in their pioneering research. They solved difference equations for strings plucked and stroked at the center, near the ends, and at the endpoint. The velocity of a bow, the applied pressure, and a friction coefficient were supplied as part of the initial conditions. They also took other factors into account, including air friction, string thickness, movement of the bridge, transmission of energy by the bridge to a resonator, and the radiation of energy from a resonating box.

In this work, as in some recent simulations, strings are modeled in the classical way as a series of discrete *masses* connected by *springs*. The *mass-spring* model has long been used by physicists and acousticians to describe vibrating objects and the waves they emit (Crawford 1968; Benade 1990; Cadoz, Luciani, and Florens 1984; Weinreich 1983; Smith 1982, 1983; Hutchins 1978; Adrien and Rodet 1985; Boutillon 1984; Chafe 1985). The mass-spring paradigm captures two essential qualities of vibrating media. First, vibrating media have a *density,* which is the mass per unit amount of the medium. For a string, the density can be measured as its weight. Second, vibrating media are *elastic;* if any part of the medium is displaced from its position of equilibrium, a restoring force immediately appears that tries to push it back. If we create a disturbance in one part of the string by plucking it, the displaced parts of the medium exert forces on adjacent parts, causing them to move away from their equilibrium position. This in turn causes the next portions to move, and so on, in a process called *wave propagation.* Because of the mass of the medium, the parts do not move instantly away from their equilibrium positions, but instead require a short time. As a result, the pluck impulse propagates through the medium at a specific speed.

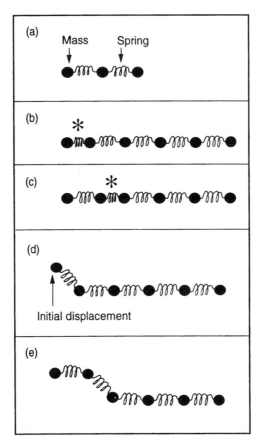

Figure 7.1   Mass-spring model of vibrating strings. (*a*) The springs model the elasticity of the string. (*b*) In a longitudinal wave, the disturbance is in the same direction as the wave propagation. The initial displacement (compression of the spring) is marked by an asterisk. (*c*) Following state. (*d*) In a transverse wave, the initial disturbance is perpendicular to the direction of wave propagation. (*e*) Following state.

Figure 7.1a depicts a string as a number of identical masses connected together by light springs. If the first mass is displaced to the right, the first spring compresses, exerting a force on the second mass (figure 7.1b). The second mass will then move to the right, compressing the second spring, and so on, as in figure 7.1c. Since the displacements of the successive masses are in the direction that the disturbance is traveling (that is, horizontally), this is called a *longitudinal wave*.

Figures 7.1d and 7.1e show *transverse wave* propagation that occurs when the initial displacement is perpendicular to the direction that the wave propagates. This is the main type of wave vibration occurring in musical strings that are plucked, hammered, or bowed. Another type of vibration is *rotational,* but this is not usually modeled in sound synthesis.

Separating the string into a set of discrete masses has the computational advantage that the effect of excitation on a given point of the string can be modeled as the application of a force to a single mass that transmits this force to the other masses via the springs. After a string has been struck, the shape of the string at a particular point in time is determined by solving a set of difference equations.

The Mass-spring Paradigm for Vibrating Surfaces and Volumes

The mass-spring representation can be extended to vibrating surfaces and volumes. Surfaces can be modeled as a fabric of masses connected to by more than one spring (figure 7.2a), or arranged in a circular pattern to model the skin of a drum (figure 7.2b). Volumes take the shape of a lattice (figure 7.2c), with the masses interconnected up to six ways.

The Mass-spring Paradigm for Excitation

So far we have described systems of masses and linear springs as models for resonators. If the springs are defined to have a nonlinear behavior, they become good models for excitation. The nonlinear oscillators that are often used as exciters in PhM methods can be viewed in terms of the mass and nonlinear spring model (Rodet 1992). The masses represent the inertial behavior, while nonlinear springs account for elastic properties of the body of the exciter. A nonlinear friction component accounts for the contact condition between the exciter and the resonator. Such a representation has been applied to a model of the hammer of a piano, for example (Suzuki 1987).

Modal Synthesis

The motion of a complicated system having many moving parts may always be regarded as compounded from simpler motions, called modes, all going on at once. No matter how complicated the system, we will find that each one of its modes has properties very similar to those of a simple harmonic oscillator. (F. Crawford 1968)

Modal synthesis (Calvet, Laurens, and Adrien 1990; Adrien 1991) is an alternative to the mass-spring paradigm. It starts from the premise that a sound-producing object can be represented as a collection of vibrating substructures. The number of substructures is usually very small in comparison with those in the mass-spring approach. Typical substructures include violin

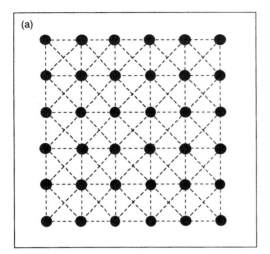

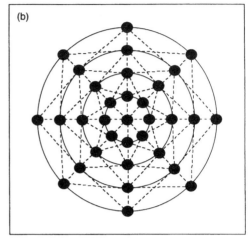

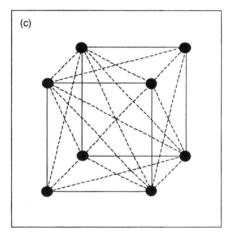

Figure 7.2   Models of vibrating surfaces and volumes as masses connected by springs. The black dots are the masses, and the lines represent springs. (*a*) Model of a vibrating surface. (*b*) Model of a drum head as a circular arrangement of springs and masses. (*c*) A vibrating volume can be modeled as a lattice of masses connected by springs on six sides.

bridges, violin bodies, acoustic tubes, bells, drum heads, and so on. As in the mass-spring paradigm, the substructures respond to an externally applied excitation (forces, air flows, pressures, or movements). When they are excited, each substructure has a set of natural *modes of vibration*. These modes are specific to a particular structure and depend on many physical factors that we will not go into here (see Benade 1990, for example). A factor in favor of modal synthesis is that a well-defined methodology for analysis of modes of vibration already exists, due to its many industrial applications (Hurty and Rubinstein 1964; Hou 1969); this methodology can be adapted to sound synthesis. See Bork (1992) for a brief description of modal analysis of musical instruments, with additional references.

Modal synthesis characterizes each substructure as a set of modal data, consisting of (1) the frequencies and damping coefficients of the substructure's resonanting modes, and (2) a set of coordinates representing the vibrating mode's shape. Hence, the general instantaneous vibration of an instrument can be expressed as the sum of the contributions of its modes.

In Adrien's implementation, the instantaneous vibration is described by a vector of *N* coordinates associated with *N* chosen points over the structure. These coordinates are bound together in such a way that the geometrical and mechanical features are close to the instrument's characteristics. The set of *N* points is equivalent to the corresponding *N* sets of modal data. A given vibration mode can be described by the relative displacements of the *N* points.

For simple vibrating substructures such as an undamped string, the modal data are available in the mechanical engineering literature in the form of equations. For complex vibrating structures the modal data can be obtained through experimentation with actual instruments. Tools for this type of mechanical engineering analysis—such as transducers and analysis software—are available to researchers, since they are used in industrial applications such as aircraft design.

The modal approach has an advantage of flexibility over the mass-spring paradigm. This derives from the modularity of the modal substructures. Modal synthesis partitions sound-producing mechanisms into vibrating substructures. It is possible to add or subtract substructures to create time-varying synthesis effects, such as "expanding" or "shrinking" the size of an instrument. The method also permits timbral interpolations from one instrument to another by combining substructures in an unnatural manner.

MOSAIC: A Practical Implementation of Modal Synthesis

The MOSAIC system, developed by Jean-Marie Adrien and Joseph Morrison, is a particularly clear realization of modal synthesis, as a modular software toolkit (Morrison and Waxman 1991; Morrison and Adrien 1991). For this pedagogical reason, we present a full example here.

In the world of MOSAIC, you sit before a virtual workbench with a collection of *objects* that you assemble into instruments. The objects include strings, air columns, metal plates, membranes, and violin and cello bridges. Other objects excite the instrument, such as bows, hammers, and plectrums. Interactions between objects are called *connections*. Connections can be thought of as black boxes that go between objects and specify a relationship between them. For example, two objects can be connected by means of gluing, bowing, plucking, striking, and pushing. On each connection are *controllers*—knobs that stipulate the parameters of the control. A bow connection, for example, has controllers for speed of bowing, amount of rosin, and so on. Finally, a physical location on an object is called an *access*. To connect two objects, for example, we need to specify their accesses.

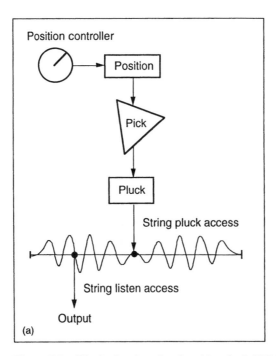

Figure 7.3   Plucked string simulated by the MOSAIC program. (*a*) Graphical representation. (*b*) MOSAIC code corresponding to (*a*). Lines beginning with a semicolon are comments. See the text for an explanation of the code.

```
(b)
;;; MOSAIC plucked string example, written in Scheme

;;; Make string and plectrum objects

(define my-string (make-object 'monostring))
(define my-plectrum (make-object 'bi-two-mass))

;;; Make pluck connection between plectrum and string

(define my-string-pluck
      (make-access my-string (const .6) 'trans0))
(define my-plectrum-pluck
      (make-access my-plectrum (const 1) 'trans0))

(make-connection 'pluck my-string-pluck
      my-plectrum-pluck 0 .1 (const 50))

;;; Make position connection to push plectrum

(define my-plectrum-move
      (make-access my-plectrum (const 0) 'trans0))

;;; Move plectrum from .1 meter to -.5 meter in .5 secs

(make-connection 'position my-plectrum-move
      (make-controller 'envelope 1
                       (list (list 0.00  .1)
                             (list 0.50 -.5)))))

;;; Make listening point on string

(define my-string-out
      (make-access my-string (const .3) 'trans0))

(make-point-output my-string-out)

;;; Run the synthesis and play the sound

(run 2) ; Make 2 seconds of sound
(play)
```

Figure 7.3 (cont.)

Figure 7.3a is an example of the use of the concepts of objects, connections, controllers, and accesses. The example is represented in the diagram shown in figure 7.3b.

The example is written in Scheme (Abelson and Sussman 1985), a dialect of the Lisp programming language. The Scheme language follows a general syntax of the form:

```
(function arguments)
```

This means that the "verb" or operation is specified first, followed by the specific arguments to that operation. When parenthetical expressions are nested, the inner ones are executed before the outer ones. For example, the command

```
(define my-string (make-object 'mono-string))
```

creates a string object named **my-string** and places it on the virtual workbench. When MOSAIC carries out this command it performs a full modal analysis. The name **my-string** points to the data generated by this analysis. Besides a string we need a plectrum:

```
(define my-plectrum (make-object 'bi-two-mass))
```

We want to tell MOSAIC to use the plectrum to pluck the string, but MOSAIC requires that we stipulate specific access points. These are given by the lines:

```
(define my-string-pluck
        (make-access my-string (const .6) 'trans0))
(define my-plectrum-pluck
        (make-access my-plectrum (const 1) 'trans0))
```

The names **my-string-pluck** and **my-plectrum-pluck** are just names for the points where the two objects touch. The next line makes the plucking connection:

```
(make-connection 'pluck my-string-pluck
        my-plectrum-pluck 0 .1 (const 50))
```

The first argument after the **'pluck** are the access points for the *object plucked* and the *plucker*. The following two arguments say that the position of the object plucked is 0 and the plucker is 0.1 meter from that point. The third argument directs a controller decides when to release the string. The number 50 is the force in newtons. (A newton is a unit of force. A force of

1 newton pushes 1 kilogram to accelerate 1 meter per second.) When the plucker is pushing harder than 50 newtons, the pluck connection disengages. The next lines make a second access on the plectrum so that it can be moved by an envelope controller.

```
(define my-plectrum-move
       (make-access my-plectrum (const 0) 'trans0))
(make-connection 'position my-plectrum-move
       (make-controller 'envelope 1
                        (list (list 0.00  .1)
                              (list 0.50 -.5)))))
```

The envelope values are specified in terms of pairs of the form (*time value*). The **list** functions create a list of two lists out of these pairs. The last statements (**define my-string-out** ... etc.) make an access for listening to the string and command the instrument to play.

McIntyre, Schumacher, and Woodhouse Synthesis

Another approach to physical modeling is the McIntyre, Schumacher, and Woodhouse (1983) model. They described an elegant, though highly simplified model of the mechanics of instrumental sound production. Starting from the premise that oscillations (self-sustaining back-and-forth vibrations) generate tones in woodwinds, bowed strings, and organ pipes, MSW focused in detail on the time-domain behavior of tones. That is, they studied the birth and evolution of waveforms and the physical mechanisms behind these phenomena. Prior to MSW's research, previous work (such as Benade's) stressed the importance of the resonant frequencies in determining the sound of instruments. But this did not account for important details in the instrument's waveform, such as the attack transient. The MSW time-domain approach gives insight into the physical reasons for waveform variations in a range of instruments and accounts for such phenomena as pitch flattening in bowed strings, subharmonics, and the duration of the attack transient.

After studying several instruments, MSW described an efficient synthesis method, which we call *MSW synthesis*. MSW synthesis has the advantage that the control parameters are related to those exploited by musical performers.

The next section discusses the theory behind the MSW approach. This is followed by a sketch of the MSW synthesis technique.

Nonlinear Excitation and Linear Resonance

In MSW synthesis, tone production can be divided into two main parts: a *nonlinear excitation* and a *linear resonance* (figure 7.4). In the MSW model of a clarinet, the nonlinear excitation is caused by blowing into the clarinet mouthpiece, where the reed acts as a kind of switch, alternately opening and closing to allow the flow of air into the resonating tube (clarinet bore) (Benade 1960, 1990). The switching action is caused by pressure variations in the mouthpiece. The reed is half-open at the start, but the flow of air into the mouthpiece creates pressure in the mouthpiece that closes the reed. This in turn gives the air a chance to escape from the mouthpiece into the bore and out the open end of the clarinet, which opens the mouthpiece again. Hence the reed converts a steady flow of air into a series of puffs. The frequency of the puffs is determined by the effective length of the bore, which is varied by opening and closing keyholes. That is, the waves in the bore resonate at the pitches playable by the clarinet. The mass and stiffness

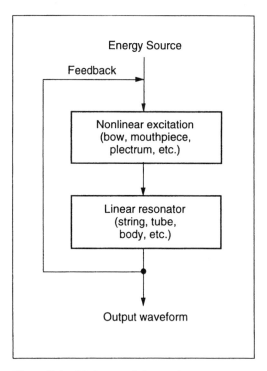

Figure 7.4 McIntyre, Schumacher, and Woodhouse (1983) model of instrumental oscillation. Wave reflections from the linear resonator influence the nonlinear exciter, constituting a feedback path.

of the bore give it almost complete domination over the reed in determining pitch. This interaction constitutes a kind of feedback from the resonator to the exciter, as shown in figure 7.4. Thus the MSW model accounts for exciter/resonator coupling.

In the MSW model of bowed strings, nonlinear switching occurs when the friction of the bow "captures" the string for a brief interval until the string slips and is "released" by the bow. Then friction builds again, and the string is again "captured," and so on. In a flute or an organ pipe, the nonlinear excitation is caused by air pressure buildups in the short end of the tube. When the pressure buildup is high, the force of its release overcomes the incoming airjet and causes a brief interruption in the air flow into the tube.

In all three of these cases (woodwinds, bowed strings, and pipes), the excitation is a nonlinear switching mechanism that sends a sharp impulse wave into the linear part of the instrument. The linear part acts like a filter to round the waveform into the characteristic timbre of the instrument.

Sketch of MSW Synthesis

For a given instrument, MSW synthesis models the objects and actions as a compact set of equations. The most complicated and instrument-specific equations describe the excitation. The main variables are the *energy source* (flow of air in a clarinet, flute, organ pipe, or the friction force of a bow in a stringed instrument), the fluctuating *energy of the nonlinear element*, and a *reflection function* that describes the waveform filtering effect played by the linear part of the system. The equations for the nonlinear and the linear parts are evaluated simultaneously. For details on these equations we refer the reader to McIntyre, Schumacher, and Woodhouse (1983). Smith (1986) and Keefe (1992) describe efficient implementations of the MSW model. Their implementations substitute table lookups and multiplications in place of the more costly simultaneous solution of equations for each sample point.

The sound produced by the pure MSW model is not terribly realistic, due to its many simplifications. Considerable refinement is required to make convincing models of real instrument tones. For example, Keefe (1992) describes an extension of MSW synthesis to brass instruments. He implemented a detailed subprogram for specification of air columns (such as those of brass instruments, flutes, and organ pipes) in order to test various designs for sonic accuracy.

Waveguide Synthesis

Waveguides are an efficient implementation of PhM synthesis that serve as the engine of synthesizers introduced by Yamaha and Korg in 1993 and 1994 (Smith 1982, 1983, 1986, 1987a, b; 1991b, 1992; Garnett 1987; Garnett and Mont-Reynaud 1988; Cook 1991a, b, 1992, 1993; Hirschman 1991; Hirschman, Cook, and Smith 1991; Paladin and Rocchesso 1992; Van Duyne and Smith 1993). A waveguide (or *waveguide filter*) is a computational model of a medium along which waves travel. In musical applications this medium is usually a tube or a string. Waveguides have long been used by physicists to describe the behavior of waves in resonant spaces (Crawford 1968).

A basic waveguide building block is a pair of *digital delay lines* (see chapter 10). Each delay line is injected with an excitation wave propagating in the opposite direction and reflecting back to the center when it reaches the end of the line. A delay line is a good model of this process because wavefronts take a finite amount of time to travel the length of a resonating medium. Traveling waves running up and down the waveguide cause resonances and interferences at frequencies related to its dimensions. When the waveguide network is symmetric in all directions, the sound it produces when excited tends to be harmonic. If the waveguide twists, changes size, or intersects another waveguide, this changes its resonant pattern. As we will see, the voice and instruments such as brass, woodwinds, and strings can be simulated by means of oscillators driving a waveguide network. Garnett (1987) built a simplified model of a piano out of waveguides. Chapter 11 describes applications of waveguides to reverberation.

An attractive feature of waveguides is that they are largely compatible with the Music *N* synthesis language paradigm. This means that the building blocks of waveguide networks can be merged with standard unit generators (Link 1992).

The next four sections describe a waveguide model of plucked strings, a generic waveguide instrument that can simulate either stringed or wind instruments, and more specific models of a clarinet and a horn.

Waveguide Model of Plucked Strings

The simplest waveguide model is perhaps a monochord or single-string instrument. This model can be understood as a picture of what happens when a string is struck at a particular point: two waves travel in opposite directions from the impact point (figure 7.5). When they reach the bridges, some of their energy is absorbed, and some is reflected back in the opposite

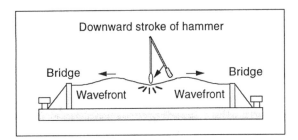

Figure 7.5 A string struck at the center generates two waves moving in opposite directions. This behavior is the basis of the delay line paradigm of string vibration.

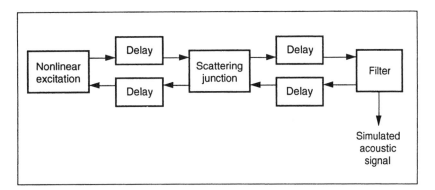

Figure 7.6 Generic waveguide instrument model capable of simulating stringed or wind instruments (after Cook 1992). A nonlinear excitation injected into the upper delay line travels until it hits the scattering junction, which models the losses and dispersion of energy that occur at junctions in acoustical systems. Some energy returns to the oscillator junction, and some passes on to the output junction, modeled by a filter.

direction—toward the point of impact and beyond where the two waves interact, causing resonances and interferences. In the parlance of waveguide theory, the bridges act as *scattering junctions* since they disperse energy to all connected waveguides. The pitch of the vibrating string is directly related to the length of the two waveguides.

Generic Waveguide Instrument Model

Figure 7.6 shows a generic model of a simple waveguide instrument capable of modeling stringed or wind instruments (Cook 1992). A sharp nonlinear excitation wave is injected into a delay line until it hits a scattering junction that passes some energy on and bounces some energy back. The scattering junction is a linear or nonlinear filter that models the effect of a finger or

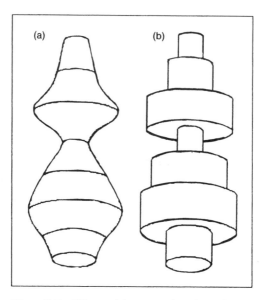

Figure 7.7   Waveguide approximation of noncylindrical tubes. (*a*) Smooth acoustic tube, such as an exotic horn or a portion of the vocal tract. (*b*) Approximation by partitioning the tube into sections, in effect, sampling in space.

bow pressing on a string, or a tonehole on a wind instrument. The filter at the end models the effect of the bridge, body, or bell of the instrument.

In order to approximate a noncylindrical tube such as a horn or the vocal tract, the tube is divided into equal-length sections, each of which is represented by a waveguide filter. This is called *sampling in space,* directly corresponding to *sampling in time,* since it takes a finite amount of time for a wavefront to travel a certain distance in space. The parameters of the scattering junction at the boundary of adjacent waveguides derive from physical dimensions of the tube at that point.

Figure 7.7 shows how a smooth acoustic tube is partitioned into a series of discrete sections, each modeled by a waveguide. Similar approximations can be fitted to two-dimensional surfaces and three-dimensional spaces (for reverberation simulation) (Smith 1991b; Cook 1992).

In brass and woodwind simulations, a waveguide simulates each section of tube of the instrument. The reed or mouthpiece, which serves as the excitation, is modeled either by a simple table-lookup oscillator or by a more complicated nonlinear oscillator driving the waveguide network. The nonlinear oscillator is modeled as a mass-spring-damper mechanism, as described earlier. This same scheme (nonlinear oscillator driving waveguide network) can also be applied to string synthesis, where the nonlinear oscillator models the interaction between the bow and the string (Chafe 1985).

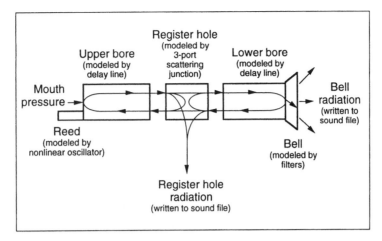

Figure 7.8 Clarinet modeled as a five-part structure using waveguide techniques. Only a single hole is needed since the size of the upper and lower bores changes according to the pitch being played.

By adjoining different waveguides via scattering junctions, adding filters at strategic points, and inserting nonlinear junctions that excite the waveguide network, researchers have constructed models of whole families of musical instruments. The next two sections give specific examples of waveguide instrument models.

Waveguide Clarinet

Figure 7.8 shows a waveguide model of a clarinet, after Hirschman, Cook, and Smith (1991) and Hirschman (1991). The clarinet model has five parts:

1. Reed
2. Upper bore
3. Register hole
4. Lower bore
5. Bell

Only a single hole is needed because the size of the upper and lower bores change according to the pitch being played. This type of model produces a clarinet-like tone with several realistic features, including the generation of harmonics according to input amplitude, and instrument squeaking—given appropriate inputs.

Waveguide Horn

Figure 7.9 shows a screen image from TBone, a brass instrument simulation using waveguides controlled by a graphic interface (Cook 1991b). The display divides into three windows: French Trumbuba Controller, Performer Controller, and Time-varying Event Controller.

The French Trumbuba Controller, at bottom, provides graphical controls for modifying the instrument. Sliders control the position of the trombone slide, the flare of the bell, and individual sections of the mouthpiece. Text fields let users specify the length of the bell, the slide, and each section of tubing associated with the four valves. Clicking the valve buttons causes them to toggle between the up and down positions, and causes the appropriate piece of tubing to be placed in or removed from the acoustic circuit. The spectrum display shows the magnitude Fourier transform of the impulse response of the current horn configuration. This is often called the *transfer function* and describes the gain each frequency would experience in a trip through the horn system.

The Performer Controller window at upper right provides controls for modifying the model of the brass player's lip. Simple controls of mass, spring constant, and damping are enough to specify the natural frequency of the lip oscillator. The transfer function of the lip is shown in a spectrum display. When the "Toot" button is pressed, the instrument synthesizes and plays a short note. The "Play" button causes the same sound file to be played again.

The Time-varying Event Controller at the upper left has controls for time-varying sound synthesis. Sweeps of the lip and slide and valve trills can be specified by begin and end times.

Input Devices for Physical Modeling Synthesis

Graphical interfaces provide a good visual picture of a PhM instrument, but it is difficult to play the instrument in a realistic manner with only a mouse and an alphanumeric keyboard, due to the need to control many parameters simultaneously. Some work can be done to group parameters, but for effective performance the ideal controller is a musical input device with several degrees of freedom. When the model can be realized in real time, as is the case for many waveguide models, PhM techniques come almost full circle: from an actual instrument to a virtual instrument played using an input device. Figure 14.5 in chapter 14 shows two examples of input devices for PhM synthesis. The ACROE keyboard (figure 14.5g) contains motors

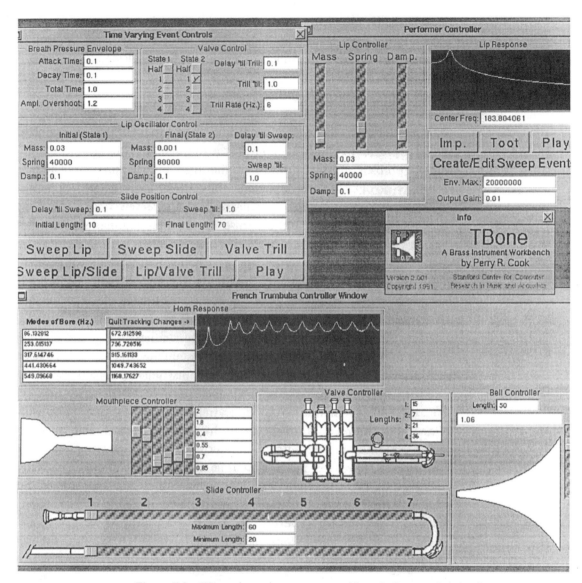

Figure 7.9   TBone brass instrument workbench. See text for details.

that model the physical action of various types of mechanical keyboards. The HIRN (figure 14.5i) combines several different types of controllers (mouth interface, buttons, sliders, different blowing angles) into one device.

Assessment of Physical Modeling Synthesis

PhM synthesis has made great progress in recent years. Some have gone so far as to predict that PhM toolkits are the future of digital synthesis. A conceptual problem remains, however, in that there is a vast domain of sounds for which no one has yet built a model. Building an accurate physical model of an instrument is a serious scientific project. Only a few laboratories have the necessary equipment and expertise for this undertaking. The pages of acoustics journals are rife with details that scientists have gleaned from years of patient experimentation and measurement. Thousands of different types of acoustical instruments exist in the world, yet only a few PhM models have been attempted. Once a model is constructed, the issue remains of determining the proper settings for dozens of parameters for each sound.

One of the fundamental problems of PhM synthesis is the fact that an instrument alone is not a complete system of sound production; instruments need players. Initial attempts to play PhM instruments sometimes sound like the painful practice sessions of a novice. For each instrument one creates, much effort remains in order to learn how to play the instrument well. When the instrument is driven purely by software (rather than an input device), one must, in effect, define a physical model of a player as well as the instrument. This player model should be able to realize idiomatic gestures and good playing technique—in whatever ways these goals are defined for a particular instrument. Initial steps toward player models have been taken, but much work remains (Garton 1992).

Given a model of a traditional instrument, the task of developing a player model could be aided by an analysis system that extracted parameter settings from performances. The next section surveys the first steps toward developing an analysis stage for PhM synthesis.

Source and Parameter Analysis for Physical Modeling

All sound analysis can be seen as a form of *parameter estimation*. That is, analysis tries to characterize an incoming sound in terms of the parameter settings that would be needed to approximate that sound with a given re-synthesis method (Tenney 1965; Justice 1979; Mian and Tisato 1984).

Given a physical model of an existing instrument, the usual method of determining the proper performance parameters is to carry out laborious trial-and-error experiments on individual tones, transitions, and gestures, in collaboration with accomplished players. This detail work could be greatly speeded up by an analysis stage that could listen to a performance of a virtuoso and estimate the characteristic parameters automatically.

Another motivation for an analysis stage in physical modeling is *automatic instrument construction.* Existing physical models correspond to only a tiny corner of the universe of sound. What about sounds that are not currently realizable with existing models? One can dream of an automatic compiler that would create a virtual instrument for any input sound—even a synthetically generated one. The automatically constructed physical model would give the musician gestural, "instrumental" control over this sound and a family of similar sounds. Such an idea may seem far-fetched, but keep in mind that Fourier analysis already acts as a similar sort of compiler, realizing an additive synthesis instrument corresponding to any sound fed into it.

Parameter Estimation Experiments

Initial experiments with parameter estimation for PhM synthesis show both the difficulties and the potential of this direction (Szilas and Cadoz 1993). Here we report on three projects.

Source Separation

Wold (1987) is an important study in parameter estimation based on a physical model approach to resynthesis. His ultimate goal was not synthesis per se, but separation of polyphonic sources. That is, the system was fed a mixed signal of two different instruments. It then tried to estimate what the resynthesis parameters would be for each instrument, with reference to a physical model synthesizer, rather than an additive synthesizer, for example.

He began by designing approximate physical models of acoustic instruments such as voices, marimbas, and clarinets. The form of these models was a set of parameterized state equations. For any given input sound, the goal was to compare the input sound with the state-equation model and try to identify a combination of parameter settings that would result in the same sound.

Figure 7.10 diagrams Wold's parameter estimation system. The first part of the system addressed the problem facing all estimators—making an edu-

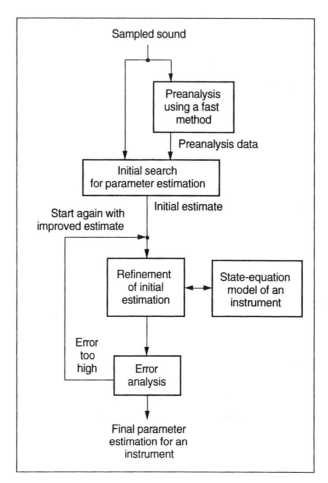

Figure 7.10   Parameter estimation sound analyzer implemented by Wold (1987). The goal was to estimate parameters for a physical model-based synthesizer, with a view toward separation of two mixed signals. If a given estimate was too far from the approximate state-equation model, the system tried another iteration of estimation.

cated guess as to where to start. His system used spectrum analysis and pitch detection to make a "first pass" estimate. Based on the initial estimate, the system refined its analysis using iterative techniques and checked its results against a state-equation model for resynthesis. The part dealing with refinement of an initial estimate was based on a *Kalman filter* approach. A time-varying Kalman filter provides, by technique comparable to least-squares approximation, an error estimate of a sampled signal based on noisy observations. Its essential feature is that it is based on statistical criteria. (Kalman filter theory is an advanced topic; for more, see Rabiner et al. 1972.)

The computational burden of this type of procedure—Kalman filter estimation of physical model synthesis parameters—is extremely heavy. High-fidelity parameter estimation based on percussion, voice, and clarinet models requires billions of floating-point operations per second of analyzed sound (Wold 1987). It is significant that Wold concluded his thesis with a discourse on the new type of computer architectures that would be required to realize these methods in real time.

P. Cook's Singer is a waveguide filter physical model of the human vocal tract (Cook (1991a, 1993). Distinguishing this PhM for vocal sounds from approaches like linear predictive coding (chapter 5) or the formant methods discussed later in this chapter, Singer contains models of the lips, vocal tract, and nasal tract, allowing it to capture articulatory details more realistically.

The complexity of the synthesis model is evident from the patch in figure 7.11. Dozens of parameters must be carefully tuned for each utterance. Such a model begs the question: Where can one obtain the proper data in order for it to make realistic speaking and singing? Based on the Singer model, Cook employed parameter estimation on speech in an effort to match the parameters of the model to the speech signal.

A notable aspect of this research was the effort to model the *glottal waveform*—the speech excitation signal emitted by the vocal cords. Cook used deconvolution to derive the glottal waveform and estimated pitch using a comb filter method. Vocal tract noise was modeled using a fluid dynamics approach. (See Blake 1986 for more on fluid dynamics models of sound and vibration.) D. Matignon has also pursued the Kalman filter analysis strategy, starting from a state-equation model and employing the waveguide resynthesis model (Matignon 1991; Matignon, DePalle, and Rodet 1992).

Higher-order Spectrum Analysis

Another strategy to mention in passing is a family of new techniques called *higher order spectrum* (HOS) analysis. HOS methods are an advanced technical topic. The goal of HOS analysis is to characterize nonlinear systems. The advantage of HOS analysis is that it shows the relationships between components. This is especially important in nonlinear systems, because they always contain intermodulation effects. HOS can show where a component derives from other components through a nonlinear process. Since, as we have seen, many sounds start from a nonlinear excitation, HOS methods appear to be a good tool for analyzing this source (Wold 1992; Nikias and Raghuveer 1987).

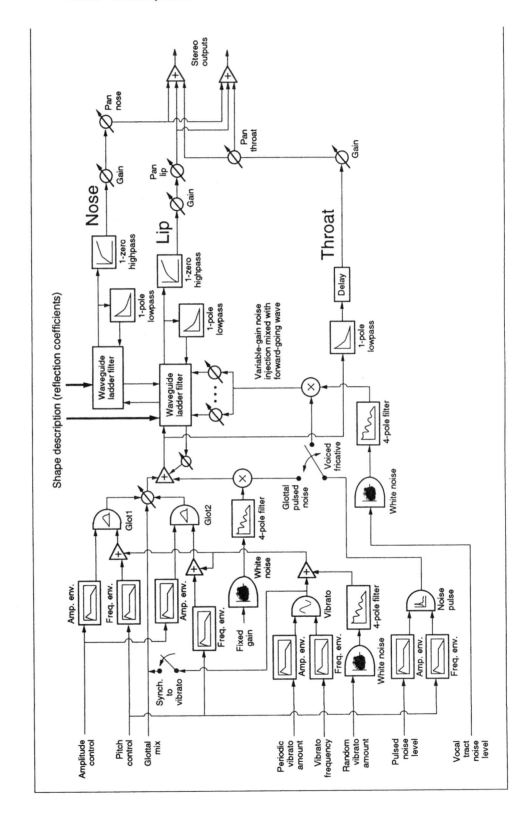

Karplus-Strong (Plucked String and Drum) Synthesis

The Karplus-Strong (KS) algorithm for plucked string and drum synthesis is an efficient technique based on the principle of a delay line or *recirculating wavetable* (Karplus and Strong 1983; Jaffe and Smith 1983). In its implementation, KS related to the MSW and waveguide synthesis techniques described in the previous sections. The computational resources needed for basic KS synthesis are modest (no multiplications necessary). So it is not surprising that the technique has been implemented on hardware ranging from a slow 8-bit microprocessor to a large digital synthesizer to a custom integrated circuit called the Digitar chip (Karplus and Strong 1983).

Plucked Strings

The basic KS algorithm starts with a wavetable of length p filled with random values. As values are read out of the wavetable from the right (figure 7.12), they are modified in some way, and the result is reinserted at the left of the wavetable. The simplest modification is an averaging of the current sample with the previous sample—the core operation of a simple lowpass filter. (See chapter 10 for an explanation of averaging lowpass filters.) At each sample interval, the wavetable read and write pointers are incremented. When the pointers reach the end of the wavetable they wrap around and start at the beginning again. The audible result of this simple algorithm is a pitched sound that sounds "bright" at the outset, but as it

Figure 7.11 Block diagram of Singer, a physical model synthesizer for vocal sounds. The left side of the figure depicts the excitation sources. The middle part depicts the waveguide resonators. The right side depicts the output stage. Two glottal wavetable oscillators (Glot 1 and Glot2) allow slow, vibrato-synchronous variations in the excitation signal. The glottal noise source consists of filtered white noise, multiplied by an arbitrary time-domain waveshape synchronized to the glottal oscillators. This model permits pulsed noise to be mixed in with the periodic source. A sine wave oscillator simulates vibrato, where the frequency of the vibrato is randomized by noise. Filtered white noise is injected into the forward-moving glottal wave. The noise can be inserted into any number of waveguide sections, each with independent level controls. The mixed glottal source feeds into the vocal tract filter. Glottal reflections are modeled by a simple reflection coefficient, and a lowpass filter simulates lip and nostril effects. A lowpass filter and delay line model the radiation from the skin in the Throat output path.

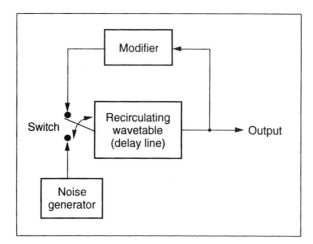

Figure 7.12   Core of the Karplus-Strong recirculating wavetable. The input to the recirculating wavetable switches to the noise source at the beginning of each event, then switches back to the modifier loop for the rest of the event. The modifier averages successive samples, simulating a damping effect.

decays the timbre rapidly darkens to a single sine tone—much like the sound of a plucked string.

If the wavetable is initially filled with random values, the reader may wonder why the result does not sound like noise—at least at the outset of the tone. The reason it sounds pitched is because the wavetable is being repeated (with a slight modification) at each pass through the wavetable. Since these repetitions occur hundreds of times per second, what was initially a random waveform becomes in an instant a quasi-periodic waveform. Without the decay part of the algorithm (the lowpass filter) the waveform has (in theory) equal harmonic content up to one-half the sampling frequency, with a reed-organ-like timbre (Karplus and Strong 1983).

In practice, it is a good idea to reload the wavetable with a new set of random values for each note. This gives each note a slightly different harmonic structure. A *pseudorandom number generator* routine (such as feedback shift-register random-bit generator; Knuth 1981, p. 29) can supply the random values.

Drumlike Timbres

KS generates drumlike timbres by using a slightly more complicated modifier to the fedback sample. The timbre is controlled by setting the value of a probability parameter b called the *blend factor*, where $0 \leq b \leq 1$. Then the modifier algorithm is as follows:

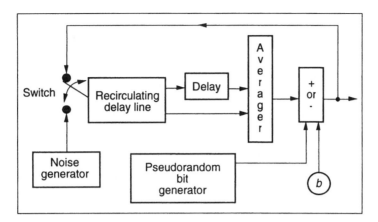

Figure 7.13   The Karplus-Strong drum synthesis algorithm. The quantity *b* is the blend factor (see text).

$$Signal_t = \begin{cases} +1/2\ (Signal_{t-p} + Signal_{t-[p-1]}),\ \text{with probability } b \\ -1/2\ (Signal_{t-p} + Signal_{t-[p-1]}),\ \text{with probability } 1-b \end{cases}$$

where *t* is the current sample index, and *p* is the length of the wavetable.

When *b* is 1, the modifier is a lowpass filter as before, and the sound is like that of a plucked string. When *b* is 0.5, the sound is no longer stringlike. It loses its pitch and sounds more like a drum. When *b* is set to 0, the signal is negated every *p* + 0.5 samples. This cuts the perceived frequency in half and leaves only odd harmonics in the spectrum, creating a harplike sound in the low registers.

Figure 7.13 depicts a KS instrument for drum synthesis. Notice how samples from the recirculating wavetable are averaged with previous samples and given a positive or negative sign based on the blend factor *b*. When *b* is close to 0.5, the wavetable length no longer controls pitch, since the waveform is no longer periodic. Rather, the length *p* determines the decay time of the noise burst at the beginning of the drum tone. When *p* is relatively large (over 200) the instrument sounds like a noisy snare drum. When *p* is small, (less than 25) the effect is that of a brushed tom-tom. To make a resonant drum, the wavetable is preloaded with a constant value instead of random values.

Stretching Out the Decay Time

Since the decay time of the sound produced by KS is proportional to the length *p* of the wavetable, this means that notes using a short wavetable decay very rapidly. Ideally, we want to decouple the decay time from the wavetable length. This is done by a technique known as *decay stretching*. The algorithm for decay stretching is as follows:

$$Signal_t = \begin{cases} Signal_{t-p}, \text{ with probability } 1 - (1/s) \\ 1/2(Signal_{t-p} + Signal_{t-[p-1]}), \text{ with probability } 1/s \end{cases}$$

where s is the *stretch factor*. With s set to 1, the usual averaging algorithm is applied, and the decay time is not stretched. When s is close to zero, the tone is not averaged so it stretches out its decay time.

Extensions to KS

Karplus and Strong's colleagues, Jaffe and Smith, developed a number of extensions to the KS technique (Jaffe and Smith 1983). By adding filters to the basic KS circuit, they obtained the following kinds of effects:

- Eliminating the initial "plucked" sound
- Varying the loudness of the tone in relation to its bandwidth
- Glissandi and slurs
- Mimicking the effects of sympathetic string vibrations
- Simulating the sound of a pick that moves in relation to its distance from the bridge
- Simulating up and down picking

These techniques are specialized, and their description has been reprinted in Roads (1989); hence, we refer the reader to that exposition. Another set of extensions aim at simulating the sounds of electric guitars. The particular focus is on timbres with distortion and feedback characteristic of amplified guitars with high-gain preamplification circuits. See Sullivan (1990) for details. Karjalainen et al. (1991) apply the KS model to flutelike tones.

Formant Synthesis

A *formant* is a peak of energy in a spectrum (figure 7.14), which can include both harmonic and inharmonic partials as well as noise. Formant peaks are characteristic of the vowels spoken by the human voice and the tones radiated by many musical instruments.

As shown in figure 7.15, within the range of 0 to 5000 Hz, the vocal tract is usually characterized as having five formant regions (including the fundamental). See Bennett and Rodet (1989) for charts of the formants of

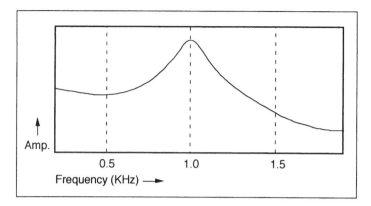

Figure 7.14 A formant region appears as a peak in the spectrum. Here a formant centers at 1 KHz.

soprano, alto, countertenor, tenor, and baritone singers for different phonemes.

Formant regions serve as a kind of "spectral signature" or timbral cue to the source of many sounds. (See Grey 1975 and Slawson 1985 for an introduction and further references to studies of timbre.) But this is not to say that the formants of a voice or an instrument are fixed. Rather, they change relative to the frequency of the fundamental (Luce 1963; Bennett and Rodet 1989). In any case, formants are only one clue the ear uses to identify the source of a tone.

Understanding the formant nature of human speech has long been a scientific research goal. Ingenious methods for synthesizing the formants of vowel-like tones have been developed through the ages, including "singing flames," "singing water jets," and mechanical contraptions designed to emulate the formants of dogs and men (Tyndall 1875). Taking the physical modeling approach literally, Dr. Marage in Paris made a vocal tone emulator wherein each vowel was voiced by a pair of rubber lips attached to an artificial mouth. The air flow for the speech was supplied by a pair of electromechanical lungs: bellows powered by an electric motor (Miller 1916). Other experimental devices used special combinations of organ pipes to create vowel-like sounds.

Thus it is not surprising that speech research has served as a wellspring of ideas for musical formant synthesis. The rest of this section discusses three synthesis techniques that generate formants: formant wave-function or FOF synthesis, VOSIM, and window-function (WF) synthesis. FOF and VOSIM evolved directly out of attempts to simulate human speech sounds, whereas WF was developed to emulate the formants of traditional musical instruments.

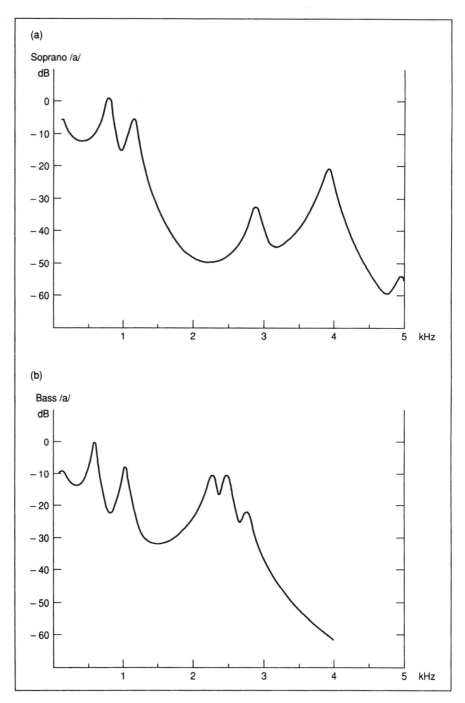

Figure 7.15   Vocal formant regions over the range 0 Hz to 5 KHz. (*a*) Soprano singing the vowel [a]. (*b*) Baritone singing the vowel [a]. (After Bennett and Rodet 1989.)

To be sure, many techniques besides the ones presented in this chapter can generate formants. These include additive synthesis (chapter 4), subtractive synthesis (chapter 5), granular synthesis (chapter 5), frequency modulation (chapter 6), and physical modeling (chapter 7), to name a few. We distinguish FOF, VOSIM, and WF here for two reasons: first, because they do not fit neatly into any of the aforementioned synthesis categories, and second, because they were designed primarily for formant synthesis.

Formant Wave-Function Synthesis and CHANT

Formant wave-function synthesis (abbreviated according to the French translation *fonction d'onde formantique* or FOF) is the basis of the CHANT sound synthesis system. ("Chant" means "singing" or "song" in French.) Over the decades since it was first conceived (Rodet and Santamarina 1975; Rodet and Delatre 1979; Rodet and Bennett 1980; Bennett 1981; Rodet, Potard, and Barrière 1984), CHANT has been reimplemented on a variety of platforms, ranging from large synthesizers like the 4X (Asta et al. 1980) to personal computers (Lemouton 1993). FOF generators have also been implemented in the Csound synthesis language (Clarke 1990).

CHANT was designed to model a large class of natural mechanisms that resonate when excited, but that are eventually damped by physical forces such as friction. Bells resonate for a long time, for example, but a woodblock is a damped resonance that cuts off almost immediately. One can excite a resonance of the cheek by tapping on it with one's finger. This single impulse produces a pop. The vocal cords generate a series of fast impulses to continuously excite resonances in the vocal tract, creating a pitched sound. These systems are all analogies for the way that FOF generators operate.

The basic sound production model embedded in CHANT is the voice. However, users can tune the many parameters of CHANT to take it beyond vocal synthesis—toward emulations of instruments and synthetic effects. Xavier Rodet and his colleagues have used CHANT to develop models of male and female singers, traditional stringed instruments, woodwinds, horns, and percussion. As we will see, CHANT can also be used as a filter bank processor for sampled sound, a mode favored by some composers.

Fundamentals of FOF Synthesis

FOF, the core of CHANT, departs from formant synthesis methods based on a traditional subtractive approach such as linear prediction (see chapter

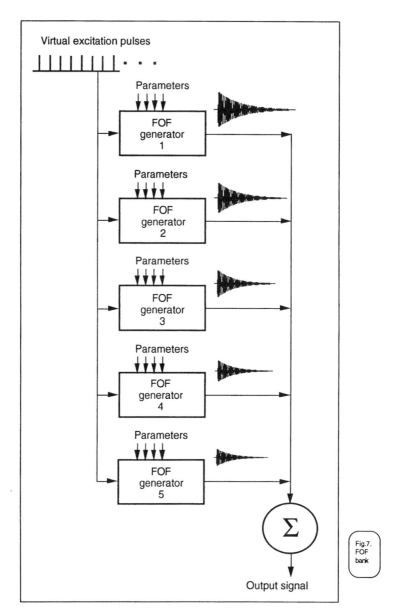

Figure 7.16   A bank of FOF generators driven by input pulses that trigger a FOF "grain" at each pitch period. The output of all FOF generators is summed to generate a composite output signal.

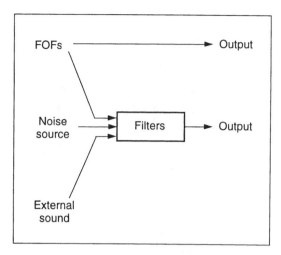

Figure 7.17   FOF synthesis and processing configuration. The output can be either sine waves, filtered noise, filtered sampled sounds, or a combination thereof.

5). In a traditional subtractive approach, a source signal with a broad spectrum—such as a pulsetrain or a noise signal—passes through a complicated filter. The filter carves out most frequencies, leaving only a few resonant peak frequencies or formants in the spectrum.

Rodet showed that the complicated filters used in subtractive synthesis can be broken down to an equivalent set of parallel bandpass filters excited by pulses. (The filters are *second-order sections,* as described in chapter 10.) A FOF realizes one of these parallel bandpass filters; several FOFs in parallel can model a complicated *spectrum envelope* with several formant peaks. The spectrum envelope is a smooth outline that traces the peaks of a spectrum (Depalle 1991), akin to the curve produced by linear predictive coding analysis.

FOFs have a dual nature, however. An alternative implementation of FOFs replaces the filters with a bank of damped sine wave generators. The signal and spectra of these generators are equivalent to those generated by a pulse-driven filter (figure 7.16). According to Rodet, the advantages of replacing the filters with sine generators are several. The sine generators are efficient and require less numerical precision than their filter counterparts. Also, one or more of the formants can be continuously changed to a sinusoid with controllable amplitude and frequency, making a continuous transition between formant synthesis and additive synthesis (Rodet 1986).

Both the filter and the damped sine wave generator methods can be combined to make a single sound, as depicted in figure 7.17.

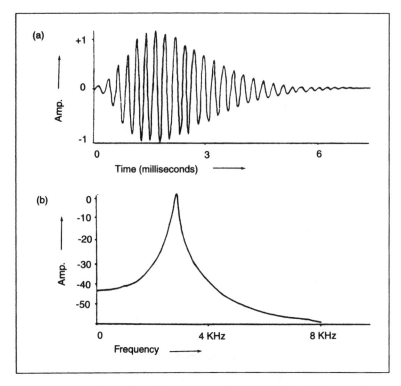

Figure 7.18 FOF grain and spectrum. (*a*) A single "grain" or tonebrust emitted by a FOF generator. (*b*) Spectrum of the grain in (*a*), plotted on a logarithmic amplitude scale. (After d'Allessandro and Rodet 1989.)

Anatomy of a FOF

For synthesis, a FOF generator produces a grain of sound at each pitch period. Thus a single musical note contains a number of grains. To distinguish these grains from those discussed in chapter 5, we call them *FOF grains*. A FOF grain is a damped sine wave with either a steep or smooth attack and a quasi-exponential decay (figure 7.18a). The envelope of a FOF grain is called the *local envelope,* as opposed to the global envelope of the note.

The local envelope is formally defined as follows. For $0 \leq t \leq tex$:

$$env_t = 1/2 \times [1 - \cos(\pi_t/tex)] \times \exp(-atten_t).$$

For $t \geq tex$,

$$env_t = \exp(-atten_t)$$

where π is the initial phase of the FOF signal, *tex* is the attack time of the local envelope, and *atten* is the decay time (D'Allessandro and Rodet 1989).

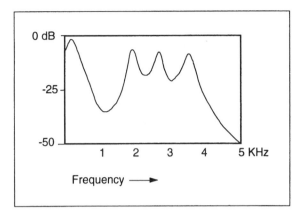

Figure 7.19 Formant spectrum of a vocal tone produced by several FOF generators in parallel.

Since the duration of each FOF grain lasts just a few milliseconds, the envelope of the FOF grain contributes audible sidebands around the sine wave, creating a formant. (This is caused by the convolution of the envelope with the sinusoid; see chapter 10 for an explanation of convolution.) The spectrum of the damped sine generator is equivalent to the frequency response curve of one of the bandpass filters (figure 7.18b).

The result of summing several FOF generators is a spectrum with several formant peaks (figure 7.19).

FOF Parameters

Each FOF generator is controlled by a number of parameters, including fundamental frequency and amplitude. Figure 7.20 shows the four formant parameters, which we call *p1* through *p4*:

p1 is the center frequency of the formant.

p2 is the formant bandwidth, defined as the width between the points that are −6 dB from the peak of the formant.

p3 is the peak amplitude of the formant.

p4 is the width of the *formant skirt*. The formant skirt is the lower part of the formant peak, about −40 dB below the peak, akin to the foothills of a mountain. The skirt parameter is independent of the formant bandwidth, which specifies the breadth at the peak of the mountain.

The inherent link between time-domain and frequency-domain operations is exemplified in the way FOF parameters are specified. Although it is counterintuitive for the musician not versed in signal-processing theory, two

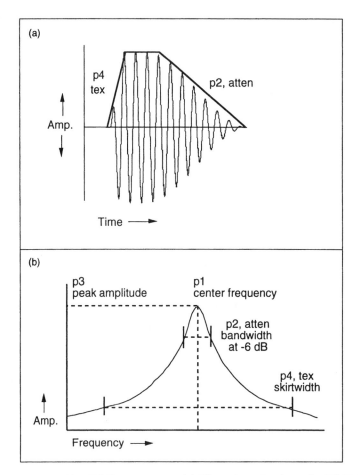

Figure 7.20 FOF parameters. (*a*) Time-domain view of a FOF. Parameter *p4* represents the attack time (called *tex* in most implementations), while *p2* represents the decay (called *atten*). (*b*) Frequency-domain view of the four formant parameters. Parameter *p1* is the center frequency of the formant, while *p2* is the formant bandwidth. Parameter *p3* is the peak amplitude of the formant, while *p4* is the width of the formant skirt.

of the main formant (frequency-domain) parameters are specified in the time domain—as properties of the envelope of the FOF grain. First, the duration of the FOF attack controls parameter *p4*, the width of the formant skirt (around −40 dB). That is, as the duration of the attack lengthens, the skirtwidth narrows. Figure 7.21 depicts this relationship.

Second, the duration of the FOF decay determines *p2*, the formant bandwidth at the −6 dB point. Hence a long decay length translates into a sharp resonance peak, while a short decay widens the bandwidth of the signal. (This link between the duration of a sound and its bandwidth also shows up in granular synthesis, as discussed in more detail in chapter 5.)

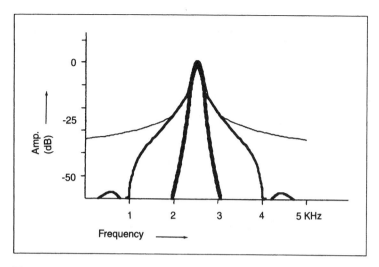

Figure 7.21   Effect of varying the attack time on the formant skirt bandwidth. Thin line, wide formant: *p4* = 100 μs. Medium line, medium formant: *p4* = 1 ms. Thick line, narrow formant: *p4* = 10 ms.

Typical applications of FOF synthesis configure several FOF generators in parallel. Beyond the six main parameters per FOF generator, implementations of CHANT offer supplementary parameters for more global control. Table 7.1 lists the main parameters. Some implementations have over 60 parameters. The numerous parameters mandate a database structured into rules for controlling the synthesis engine. This is particularly necessary for the emulation of vocal and instrumental sounds, where parameter settings are critical. Part of the job of CHANT and associated high-level languages like FORMES (Rodet and Cointe 1984; see also chapter 16) and PatchWork (Barrière, Iovino, and Laurson 1991) is to provide a rule database.

The CHANT Program

The CHANT synthesis program (Baisnée 1985) offers three modes of interaction to users. In the first and simplest mode, the user supplies values for a preset list of variables for singing synthesis. These variables translate into the parameters *p1* to *p4* for the individual FOF generators, described previously. The variables can be grouped into the following categories:

- Loudness
- Fundamental frequency
- Vibrato and random variation of the fundamental frequency

Table 7.1   Main FOF parameters

For each FOF generator

Amplitude
Fundamental frequency
Octaviation–attentuation of alternate grains
Center frequency of the formant (p1)
Formant bandwidth at −6 dB from the peak of the formant (p2)
Peak amplitude of the formant (p3)
Width of the formant skirt (p4)
Grain overlap
Function tables (usually sine)
Initial phase
Spectrum correction for vocal synthesis

Filter Parameters

Center frequency of formant
Amplitude of formant
Bandwidth of formant

- Spectrum shape and formant amplitude

- Local envelope of the formant waveforms

- Overall amplitude curves

In the second mode, FOFs serve as time-varying filters applied to sampled sounds. This mode has been used by composers as a sound transformation technique.

In the third mode of interaction, users write rules—algorithms that describe transitions and interpolations between timbres. Composition assistant environments like PatchWork also support this strategy (Iovino 1993; Barrière, Iovino, and Laurson 1991; Malt 1993).

FOF Analysis/Resynthesis

With its formants and sine waves, FOF synthesis represents a potentially general method. Here we briefly describe efforts to develop analysis systems that generate parameters for FOF resynthesis.

Models of Resonance

Models of resonance (MOR) refers to a methodology for capturing the timbre of traditional acoustic instrument tones; the resynthesis uses FOFs

(Barrière, Potard, and Baisnée 1985; Potard, Baisnée, and Barrière 1986, 1991). The premise of MOR is the classic excitation-resonance model. That is, sound-producing mechanisms are divided into an excitation stage and a resonance stage. MOR assumes that the excitation is an impulse like a pluck of a plectrum or a tap of a drumstick. The resonance is the acoustical response of the instrument body to the excitation.

In MOR, each resonance is simulated as a sine wave at a particular frequency with an exponential decay over time. (This corresponds to the impulse response of a narrow bandpass filter, a topic discussed in chapter 10.) When an impulse (such as the strike of a piano hammer) excites the resonances, each of them sounds at its characteristic amplitude and frequency. Since MOR emulates the instrument body, the sound of the instrument depends not only on the current notes played but on the state of previously played notes.

MOR analysis captures only the resonance portion. As such, it is not a complete physical or spectral model of an instrument. Nor was it designed to replicate its input signal exactly. Its goal, rather, was to extract features that could be used "for elaboration and control of timbral structures" (Barrière, Potard, and Baisnée 1985).

According to the developers, the analysis methodology of MOR is a somewhat arduous and imperfect process (Potard, Baisnée, and Barrière 1986; Baisnée 1988; Potard, Baisnée, and Barrière 1991). Basically, it involves taking a single fast Fourier transform (FFT) of a segment of a tone. (The FFT is explained in chapter 13 and appendix A.) A peak extraction algorithm isolates the most important resonances in this spectrum, eliminating other components. Then another analysis is tried with a larger time window, and the spectrum peaks are merged in a common file. Resynthesis from these peaks can be tried to see how closely it matches the original. This user repeats the analysis with successively larger windows until a satisfactory resynthesis can be obtained. For complex tones, the analysis can be divided into several segments starting at different times, and the iterative procedure applied to each segment separately. Best results have been obtained for pitched percussive tones such as marimba, vibraphone, and tubular bells (Baisnée 1988).

MOR resynthesis uses up to several hundred standard FOF generators, either sine wave oscillators with exponential decay, or bandpass filters excited by pulses of noise. One implementation employed special hardware allowing real-time control via the MIDI protocol (Wessel et al. 1989). (MIDI is presented in chapter 21.)

MOR Transformations

One of the goals of MOR was to act as a bridge between natural and synthetic sounds. The separation between the excitation and resonance parts of a tone provides a fertile area for experiments in transforming analyzed sounds. To create cross-synthesis effects, for example, it is possible to replace the usual excitation (pulses of white noise) with a sampled instrumental sound.

The developers implemented a library of analyzed models and another library of rules for transforming one MOR into another. These rules can stretch MORs in frequency or time or create hybrids by adding resonance models together. Other rules interpolate over time between the resonances of one instrument and the resonances of another instrument.

The MOR approach is efficient when the excitation is a single impulse or a noise burst, but it may be poorly adapted to cases where the excitation depends on coupling phenomena between resonant and exciting structures. In these cases there is significant interaction between the excitation and the resonance, as with a bow on a string of a violin. Accounting for coupling phenomena is the strong suit of the physical modeling synthesis techniques described earlier.

Matching the Spectrum Envelope with FOFs

D'Allessandro and Rodet (1989) reported on an experiment with FOF analysis/resynthesis that starts from *linear predictive coding* (LPC) spectrum analysis (see chapter 5). After tracing the outline of the spectrum envelope on a frame-by-frame basis, the process extracted formants corresponding to a bank of FOF generators. The results were not an identity reconstruction (the authors cite problems in the first two or three harmonics) but were said to be similar to the original. Depalle (1991) is largely given over to FOF analysis/resynthesis, using techniques to approximate the time-varying spectrum envelope of the analyzed sound. Most of his research concentrated on autoregressive (AR) spectrum analysis methods, as discussed in chapters 5 and 13.

VOSIM

The VOSIM synthesis technique was developed by Werner Kaegi and Stan Tempelaars at the Institute of Sonology in Utrecht during the early 1970s (Kaegi 1973, 1974; Tempelaars 1976; Kaegi and Tempelaars 1978). The core idea is the generation of a repeating tone-burst signal, producing a strong formant component. In this sense, the technique has links to the FOF technique described earlier. Like FOF, VOSIM was originally used to model vowel sounds. Later, it was extended to model vocal fricatives—consonants like [sh]—and quasi-instrumental tones (Kaegi and Tempelaars 1978).

VOSIM Waveform

The VOSIM waveform was derived by roughly approximating the signal generated by the human voice. This approximation takes the form of a series of pulsetrains, where each pulse in the train is the square of a sine function. The amplitude of the highest pulse is set by parameter A. Each of the pulsetrains contains $N \sin^2$ pulses in series that decrease in amplitude by a decay factor b (figure 7.22). The width (duration) of each pulse T determines the position of the formant spectrum. A variable-length delay M follows each pulsetrain, which contributes to the overall period of one pulsetrain, and thus helps to determine the fundamental frequency period. We can calculate the period as $(N \times T) + M$, so for seven pulses of 200 μsec duration and a delay equal to 900 μsec, the total period is 3 ms so the fundamental frequency is 333.33 Hz. The formant centers at 5000 Hz.

Two strong percepts emerge from the usual VOSIM signal: a fundamental corresponding to the repetition frequency of the entire signal, and a formant peak in the spectrum corresponding to the pulsewidth of the $\sin^2$ pulses (figure 7.23). One formant is produced by each VOSIM oscillator. In order to create a sound with several formants, it is necessary to mix the outputs of several VOSIM oscillators (as with FOF generators).

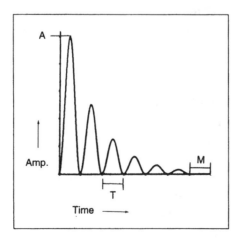

Figure 7.22 A VOSIM pulsetrain. The parameters are explained in the text.

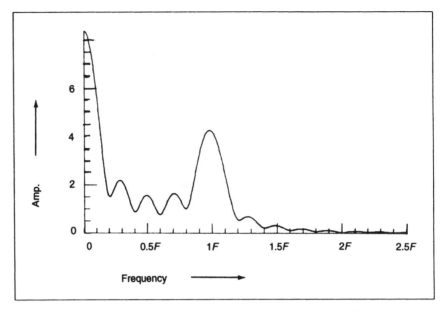

Figure 7.23 Spectrum produced by a VOSIM oscillator with five pulses and an attentuation constant of 0.8. (After De Poli 1983.)

A VOSIM oscillator is controlled by varying a set of parameters that affect the generated sound (table 7.2). T, M, N, A, and b are the primary parameters. In order to obtain vibrato, frequency modulation, and noise sounds, one modulates the delay period M. This constraint led Kaegi and Tempelaars to introduce three new variables: S, D, and NM, corresponding to the type of modulation (sine or random), the maximum frequency deviation, and the modulation rate, respectively. They also wanted to be able to provide for "transitional" sounds, which led to the introduction of the variables NP, δT, δM, and δA. These are the positive and negative increments of T, M, and A, respectively, within the number of periods NP.

By changing the value of the pulsewidth T, the formant can be made to change in time. The effect is that of *formant shifting*, which has a different sound than the kind of progressive spectral enrichment that occurs in frequency modulation synthesis, for example (see chapter 6).

The unadulterated VOSIM signal is not bandlimited. This can cause aliasing problems in systems with a low sampling rate (see chapter 1). Above twice the formant frequency, the amplitudes of the spectral components are at least 30 dB down from the fundamental. Above six times the formant frequency, components are at least 60 dB down (Tempelaars 1976).

J. Scherpenisse at the Institute of Sonology (Utrecht) designed and built a number of VOSIM oscillators controllable by a minicomputer (Tempelaars

Table 7.2 VOSIM parameters

Name	Description
T	Pulsewidth
δT	Increment or decrement of T
M	Delay following a series of pulses
δM	Increment or decrement of M
D	Maximum deviation of M
A	Amplitude of the first pulse
δA	Increment or decrement of A
b	Attentuation constant for the series of pulses
N	Number of pulses per period
S	Type of modulation (sine or random)
NM	Modulation rate
NP	Number of periods

1976; Roads 1978a). VOSIM oscillators were also built into the hardware of the SSSP digital synthesizer at the University of Toronto (Buxton et al. 1978b).

Window Function Synthesis

Window function (WF) synthesis is a multistage technique for formant synthesis using purely harmonic partials (Bass and Goeddel 1981; Goeddel and Bass 1984). The technique begins with the creation of a broadband harmonic signal. Then a weighting stage emphasizes or attenuates different harmonics in this signal to create time-varying formant regions that emulate the spectra of traditional instruments.

The building block of the broadband signal used in the initial stage of WF synthesis is a *window function pulse* (figure 7.24a). Window functions are special waveshapes used in a variety of signal-processing tasks, such as filter design and sound analysis. See chapter 13 and appendix A for more on window functions.

A variety of window functions have been devised. (See the discussion in appendix A, as well as Harris 1978; Nuttall 1981.) Plots of window spectra always exhibit a characteristic *center lobe* and *side lobes*. The center lobe is typically much higher in amplitude than the side lobes, meaning that the signal is, in effect, bandlimited. In the Blackman-Harris window function chosen by Bass and Goeddel, the frequencies in the side lobes are attenuated by at least 60 dB (figure 7.24b). Since the audible harmonics are within the center lobe, this ensures that aliasing is not a problem. (See chapter 1 for a discussion of aliasing.)

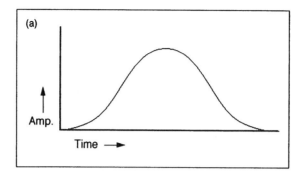

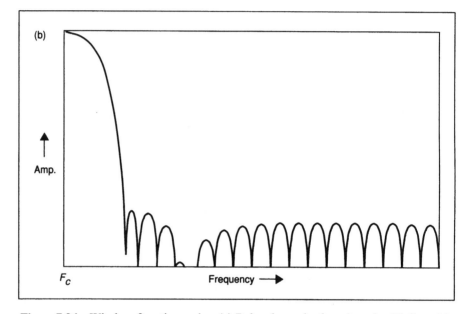

Figure 7.24   Window function pulse. (*a*) Pulse shown in time domain. (*b*) One side of the frequency spectrum. The left edge of the figure corresponds to the center frequency of the pulse, and the lobes represent sidebands, all of which are more than 70 dB down from the center frequency peak. (After Nuttall 1981.)

The broadband signal is created by linking together a periodic series of WF pulses separated by a period of zero amplitude called *deadtime*. For different fundamental frequencies, the duration of the WF pulse stays the same; only the interpulse deadtime varies. Figure 7.25 shows two signals an octave apart, with the only difference between them being the deadtime interval. In this use of a pulse followed by a period of deadtime, the WF technique is not unlike VOSIM and the FOF methods explained earlier. As explained in more detail later, WF synthesis, like VOSIM and FOF, adds the output of several generators to create complex, time-varying spectra. In other respects, however, the techniques are not similar.

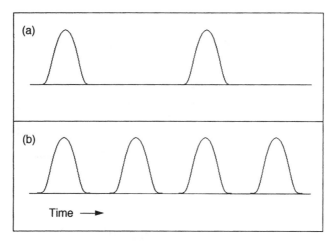

Figure 7.25 Time domain view of two WF signals an octave apart. (*a*) Low-frequency signal. (*b*) Higher-frequency signal.

In WF synthesis, the number of harmonics increases as the fundamental frequency decreases. This is because the higher harmonics fall outside the center lobe of the WF pulse's spectrum. Thus low tones are timbrally rich, while high tones are less so. This is characteristic of some traditional instruments such as pipe organs and pianos, which Bass and Goeddel wanted to simulate. Note that some other instruments, such as harpsichords, do not exhibit this behavior. In addition, some instruments do not have a purely harmonic spectrum and thus are not good models for the WF technique.

So far we have discussed a scheme in which fixed tones are generated. These tones vary from broadband (at a low fundamental frequency) to narrowband (at a high fundamental frequency). In order to create formant regions in the spectrum, further processing called *slot weighting* is required.

A *time slot* is defined as the duration of a single WF pulse plus a portion of its deadtime. By weighting the slots (i.e., multiplying a slot by a value) with a periodic sequence of *N slot weights*, the timbre of the output signal can be manipulated. This weighting is accomplished by feeding a stream of WF pulses as an input signal to a multiplier along with a periodic stream of slot weights. The multiplier computes the product of each input pulse with a specific weight. The result is an output stream containing WF pulses at different amplitudes (figure 7.26). The spectrum of such a stream exhibits peaks and valleys at various frequencies. For time-varying timbres, each slot weight can be specified as a time-varying function.

WF synthesis requires an amplitude compensation scheme, because low frequencies contain few pulses and much zero-amplitude deadtime, while high frequencies contain many pulses and almost no deadtime. A nearly

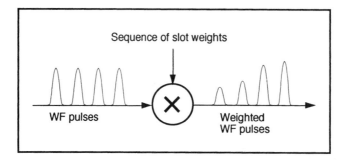

Figure 7.26 A stream of WF pulses multiplied by a periodic sequence of slot weights to obtain a series of weighted WF pulses.

linear scaling function can be applied for scaling amplitude inversely proportional to frequency. That is, low tones are emphasized and high tones are attentuated for equal balance throughout the frequency range.

Like the Karplus-Strong plucked-string and drum algorithm, the basic WF algorithm can be augmented by various tricks that increase its flexibility while preserving computational efficiency. For more details, see Bass and Goeddel (1981) and Goeddel and Bass (1984). In a practical implementation, with eight WF oscillators, 256 slots per period (maximum), a sampling rate of 40 KHz, a WF pulse width of 150 μsec, and 28 piecewise linear segments used to model each slot weight as a function of time, reasonable emulations of traditional instrument tones were reported by Bass and Goeddel.

Figure 7.27 shows two plots of an alto saxophone tone. (In general, alto saxophone is a difficult test for a synthesis method.) Figure 7.27a is the original tone, and 7.27b is a synthetic tone generated by the WF technique.

Conclusion

This chapter has explored a broad range of synthesis techniques, including physical modeling, the Karplus-Strong algorithm, and various approaches to formant synthesis. Not all of these techniques have been exploited in commercial systems, leaving many opportunities for experimentation.

Physical modeling represents a vast potential resource for sound synthesis, one that is only beginning to be exploited in music compositions. Physical models capture many expressive aspects and are a welcome addition to the catalog of the computer musician.

Formant synthesis gives musicians a direct handle on one of the most important sound signatures—the spacing and amplitude of spectrum peaks.

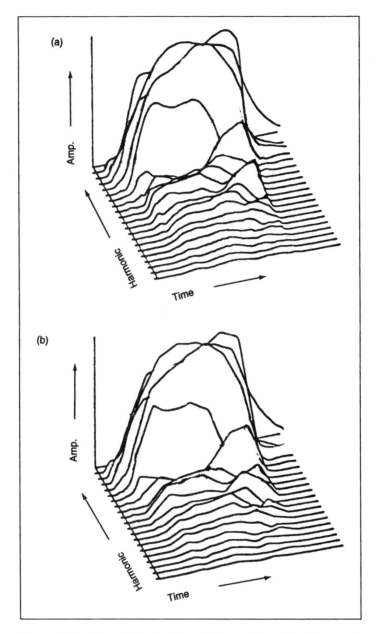

Figure 7.27   Plots of the first twenty harmonics of the time-varying spectrum of an alto saxophone tone. Low harmonics are toward the back of the plot. (*a*) Original played on alto saxophone. (*b*) Synthetic tone created with WF synthesis. (After Goeddel and Bass 1984.)

8 Waveform Segment, Graphic, and Stochastic Synthesis

Waveform Segment Techniques

    Waveform Interpolation
    Linear Interpolation Equation
    Interpolation in Oscillators and Envelope Generators
    Interpolation in GEN Functions
    Interpolation Synthesis
    SAWDUST
    SSP
    Instruction Synthesis

Graphic Sound Synthesis

    Graphics in Sound Synthesis: Background
    Interaction with UPIC
    The First UPIC
    Real-time UPIC
    Graphic Synthesis with MIDI
    Assessment of Graphic Sound Synthesis

Noise Modulation

    Discourse On Noise
    Noise-modulated AM and FM
    Waveshaping with a Random Shaping Function

Stochastic Waveform Synthesis

Dynamic Stochastic Synthesis
GENDY

Conclusion

This chapter explores four "nonstandard" synthesis methods. They are nonstandard in the sense that were conceived for the production of new electronic sounds, rather than starting from simulations of traditional instrument tones. They are motivated by compositional aesthetics, by the desire of creative imagination for fresh musical resources.

The techniques studied here include the following:

Waveform segment techniques are idiomatic to the computer. They begin with the specification of individual amplitude points and commands to construct simple waveforms segments by connecting the points. The commands link segments into more complex waveforms. One version of this technique creates waveforms automatically, as the side effect of the operation of a "virtual machine," programmed by the composer.

Graphic synthesis follows a visual and sculptural strategy for sound specification. The composer creates sound images by drawing on a tablet or screen; these drawings are translated into sound. In addition, images of sampled sounds can be transformed using graphic tools.

Noise modulations are ideal for generating sounds that range from aperiodic vibrato and tremolo effects to band regions of colored noise.

Stochastic synthesis techniques compute sound waveforms by referencing probabilistic formulas that are subjected to time-varying constraints.

A common feature among these techniques is that they can easily generate rich, wide-bandwidth, and noisy sounds that may be difficult to achieve with other methods. As such, they form an important pole in the orchestration continuum.

Waveform Segment Techniques

All differences in acoustic perception can be traced to the differences in the temporal structure of sound waves.... If all of the experiential properties of sound could be traced to a single principle of ordering—such as temporally composed successions of pulses—compositional thought would have to be radically reoriented.... One would not proceed from sound properties that had already been experienced and then allow these to determine temporal variations; instead one would compose the temporal arrangements of pulses themselves, and discover their resultant properties experimentally. (Karlheinz Stockhausen 1963)

Waveform segment techniques constitute a collection of methods for building up sounds from individual samples and wave fragments that are linked together to create larger waveforms, sections, and entire pieces. In effect, digital sounds are created out of their atomic constituents: samples. Waveform segment techniques represent a time-domain approach to synthesis since they construct the sound out of individual amplitude points. Concepts such as "frequency" and "spectrum" may not be explicitly represented in the synthesis parameters, but arise as a by-product of compositional manipulations.

This section describes four waveform segment techniques:

- Waveform interpolation
- SAWDUST
- SSP
- Instruction synthesis

Waveform interpolation can be directly related to the frequency domain, since interpolation methods have predictable effects on the spectrum of a signal, as we see later. In two of the techniques described here, SAWDUST and SSP, the composer works directly with sample points. Time-varying spectra result from the composer's operations on waveforms. Instruction synthesis is an abstract approach to synthesis, since the composer specifies sounds in terms of logical instructions that have no direct connection to acoustical parameters.

Waveform Interpolation

Interpolation is a mathematical technique for generating a line between two *endpoints* or *breakpoints*, where each breakpoint is a pair (point-on-*x*-axis, point-on-*y*-axis). Many interpolation algorithms exist, including *constant, linear, exponential, logarithmic, half-cosine,* and *polynomial,* among others. Each generates a different family of curves between the breakpoints. As figure 8.1 shows, constant interpolation draws a straight line parallel to the abscissa between the two breakpoints. Linear interpolation draws a straight line connecting the breakpoints.

The two points of inflection (curvature) in half-cosine interpolation ensure a smooth curve between the breakpoints. Figure 8.2a shows half-cosine interpolation between two points, while figure 8.2b shows half-cosine interpolation connecting several points. Polynomial interpolation techniques (including cubic splines and Chebychev polynomials) fill the space between two points with arbitrarily smooth or wildly varying curves, depending on the polynomial used.

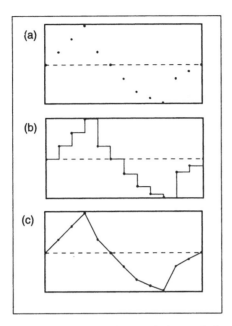

Figure 8.1 Simple interpolation techniques. (*a*) Original breakpoints. (*b*) Constant. (*c*) Linear.

Linear Interpolation Equation

Linear interpolation is simple and ubiquitous. It tries to find an intermediate point *i* between two known endpoints. An equation to achieve this is as follows:

$$f(i) = f(start) + \{([i - \text{start}]/[end - start]) \times [f(end) - f(start)]\}$$

where $f(start)$ and $f(end)$ are the starting and ending breakpoints, respectively, and *i* is an intermediate point on the abscissa between *start* and *end*. In effect, linear interpolation figures out how far along *i* is between *start* and *end*, multiplies that ratio times the difference between $f(end)$ and $f(start)$, and adds that to $f(start)$.

Interpolation in Oscillators and Envelope Generators

Computer music systems often use interpolation. We find it inside oscillators (Moore 1977) and envelope generators, for example. Chapter 3 explains how an interpolating oscillator generates a waveform with a dramatically improved signal-to-noise ratio when compared to a noninterpolating oscillator. In envelope generators, interpolation connects breakpoint pairs (*x-y* coordinates) that describe the outline of an envelope. This

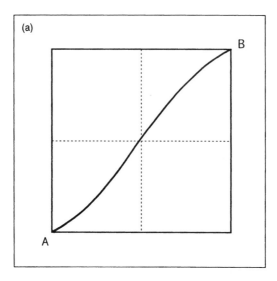

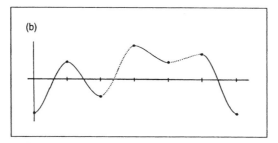

Figure 8.2   Half-cosine interpolation. (*a*) Half-cosine drawn between two points *A* and *B*. Notice the two points of inflection (bending points). (*b*) Half-cosine interolation between several points. (After Mitsuhashi 1982b.)

technique is much more memory-efficient than storing every point of the envelope, but requires more computation.

Interpolation can also be used to generate new waveforms from existing waveforms. Some implementations of Music *N* languages, for example, include unit generators for waveform interpolation (Leibig 1974). These units take two signals as their input and generate a signal that is a weighted interpolation between the two (figure 8.3). By varying the weight over time we obtain a time-varying cross between the two input waveforms.

Interpolation in GEN Functions

Several of the table generation (GEN) functions of the Music *N* languages, described in chapters 3 and 17, interpolate between composer-specified breakpoints. These GEN functions create envelopes and waveforms that

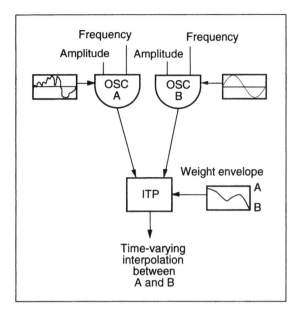

Figure 8.3 Instrument for waveform interpolation using the ITP unit generator found in some Music *N* software synthesis languages. The weight envelope specifies which waveform will predominate. When the weight envelope is 1, the left oscillator waveform is heard. When it is 0, the right oscillator plays. When it is 0.5, the waveform is the point-by-point average of the two waveforms.

are used in Music *N* instruments. Typical interpolating GEN functions in Music *N* languages include line-segment (linear interpolation), exponential, cubic spline (polynomial), and Chebychev (polynomial).

Interpolation Synthesis

Bernstein and Cooper (1976) proposed a method of waveform synthesis based exclusively on linear interpolation. In this method, one period of a waveform is assumed to contain *n* breakpoints spaced at equal intervals of time. The main drawback to linear interpolation for waveform synthesis is that the sharp angles in the waveforms it generates create harsh-sounding uncontrollable high-frequency partials. Mitsuhashi (1982b) presented several alternatives to the linear interpolation approach, including *constant, half-cosine,* and *polynomial interpolation.* He demonstrated that constant interpolation is similar to Walsh function synthesis (see chapter 4) in terms of the waveforms it generates (all right angles) and the number of parameters needed to create the waveforms. In contrast to Walsh function synthesis, constant interpolation does away with the additions needed to sum the weighted coefficients in Walsh synthesis. Thus, it has the potential of being more efficient. Unfortunately, like linear interpolation, constant interpolation also suffers from the problem of generating uncontrollable higher partials.

Half-cosine interpolation does not suffer from this problem. By using half-cosine interpolation functions, Mitsuhashi could determine the mixture of harmonics in the waveform, producing results equivalent to those produced by additive synthesis. The advantage is that half-cosine interpolation uses fewer computational resources than an additive synthesis system.

Mitsuhashi also analyzed the case of interpolation by arbitrary polynomial functions. When uniformly spaced breakpoint intervals are used, the polynomial can be evaluated very efficiently using the method of *forward differences*. The mathematical details of polynomial interpolation by the method of forward differences are beyond the scope of this book. For more information see Mitsuhashi (1982a, 1982b), and Cerruti and Rodeghiero (1983).

The spectrum of the signal generated by interpolation is a result of two terms: the ordinates of the breakpoints $f(i)$ and the interpolation function chosen. When synthesizing a periodic waveform whose one period incorporates n breakpoints, the amplitude of $n/2$ harmonics can be controlled by varying the height (ordinates) of the breakpoints (Mitsuhashi 1982b). Thus, if the number of breakpoints is 20, the zeroth through the tenth harmonics can be controlled.

It follows that time-varying spectra can be generated by changing the ordinates of the breakpoints at each period. Conveniently, linear changes in the ordinates of the breakpoints cause linear changes in the amplitudes of the harmonics.

Up to this point we have considered the case of uniformly spaced breakpoint intervals. Nonuniform breakpoint intervals can also be employed. When they are chosen carefully, nonuniform breakpoint intervals can provide a much better approximation to a given waveform than uniform breakpoints. This results in lower distortion. Figure 8.4 indicates how uniformly spaced breakpoints provide a poor approximation to a waveform, while nonuniformly-spaced breakpoints, positioned at points of greatest change, provide a much better approximation. Bernstein and Cooper (1976) give the Fourier coefficients determining the spectra of waveforms approximated by nonuniformly spaced breakpoint intervals. Further study is needed to determine all the benefits and liabilities of this approach.

SAWDUST

The SAWDUST system, designed by Herbert Brün and implemented by a team of programmers at the University of Illinois (Blum 1979), represents

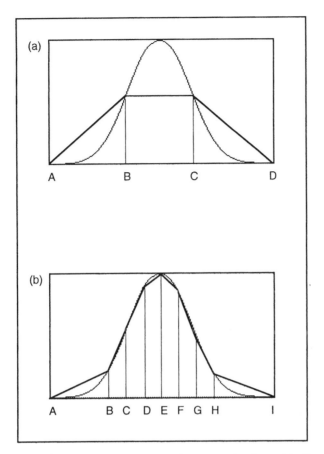

Figure 8.4 Effect of nonuniform breakpoints. (*a*) Curve drawn with uniform breakpoints. (*b*) Curve drawn with nonuniform breakpoints, yielding a better fit to the curve.

an original approach to sound synthesis. (See Grossman 1987 for commentary on SAWDUST from the standpoint of implementation.)

The term "sawdust" concatenates two words: "saw"—a tool, and "dust"—tiny particles, by-products of a process. In Brün's conception, the "saw" is a computer and the "dust" is the data, consisting of miniscule amplitude points (samples). The SAWDUST system is an interactive environment for manipulating amplitude points (which Brün calls *elements*) and combining them hierarchically into pieces of waveforms, sections, and, ultimately, complete compositions. As with other waveform segment techniques, the signals produced by the SAWDUST system often exhibit a raw, jagged-edged quality.

The basic operations in SAWDUST include concatenation of elements, cycling (looping), mixing, and varying. The operations are carried out by the subprograms LINK, MINGLE, MERGE, and VARY. LINK is an ordering function that transforms a collection of unordered elements *A* into a set of ordered elements called a *link*. Formally speaking, LINK(*A*) → *L*, where *A* is a list of elements or links.

MINGLE is a cycling operation that takes a collection of ordered links and forms a new set in which the original collection is repeated *n* times. This is one mechanism for creating periodic waveforms in SAWDUST. For example, MINGLE(*2, L3, L4*) = {*L3, L4, L3, L4*}.

MERGE is an ordering operation that alternatively selects successive elements from two links to form a new link. For example, given two links L_j and L_k, with $L_j = \{e1, e2, \ldots e10\}$ and $L_k = \{e21, e22, \ldots e30\}$, then MERGE($L_j, L_k$) = L_m = {*e1, e21, e2, e22, ... e10, e30*}.

VARY transforms one link into another. The composer specifies an initial link, a duration, and a final link. In addition, the composer stipulates the degree of a polynomial. In the resulting operation of VARY, each point in the initial link varies according to a computer-generated polynomial of the degree specified by the composer, until it winds up at its corresponding endpoint in the destination link.

SSP

SSP is a waveform segment synthesis system designed by the German-Dutch composer G. M. Koenig and implemented by Paul Berg at the Institute of Sonology (Utrecht) in the late 1970s (Berg 1978b). Like Brün's SAWDUST, SSP is an interactive system for manipulating individual elements into waveforms and large-scale compositional structures.

SSP was designed by a composer with a serial and postserial background. As a result, the system owes more to the post–World War II era of composition theory than it does to signal-processing theory. In particular, SSP's library of operations can be traced directly to serial and postserial *selection principles* used in Koenig's composition programs Project 1 (Koenig 1970a) and Project 2 (Koenig 1970b). These operations act on *elements* and *segments*. Elements in SSP are time and amplitude points, that is, samples. The SSP system connects sample points in between the elements specified by the composer by linear interpolation. Segments are waveforms constructed from operations on elements.

In working with SSP, the composer prepares a database of time points and a database of amplitude points. By associating a set of time points and amplitude points, the composer can specify such familiar waveform patterns as sine, square, sawtooth, and triangle waveforms, as well as more idiosyncratic patterns, possibly derived from probabilistic procedures. SSP selection principles create or extract parts of the element database and com-

Table 8.1 Selection principles in SSP

Selection principle	Arguments	Explanation
Alea	A, Z, N	N random numbers are chosen between A and Z.
Series	A, Z, N	N random values are chosen between A and Z. When a value is selected it is removed from the pool of available values. The pool is refilled when it is empty.
Ratio	*Factors,* A, Z, N	N random values are chosen between A and Z. The probability of occurrence of values between A and Z is specified by a list of probability weightings called *Factors.*
Tendency	$N, M, A1, A2,$ $Z1, Z2 \ldots$	N random values are chosen for each of M tendency masks. The N values occur between the initial boundaries $A1$ and $A2$ and the final boundaries $Z1$ and $Z2$.
Sequence	*Count, Chunks*	Directly specify a sequence of elements. *Count* is the number of elements specified; *Chunks* is a list of their values.
Group	A, Z, LA, LZ	A random value between A and Z is chosen. This happens one or more times, forming a group. The size of the group is randomly chosen between LA and LZ.

bine these into waveform segments. The composer determines the time order of the segments by using another round of selection principles. Table 8.1 lists the six selection principles in SSP.

Both Brün's SAWDUST and Koenig's SSP are well matched for direct synthesis with a digital-to-analog converter attached to a small computer. The sound material generated by both methods tends toward raw, spectrally rich waveforms that are not derived from any standard acoustical or signal-processing model.

Instruction Synthesis

Instruction synthesis (also called "non-standard synthesis" by G. M. Koenig, see Roads 1978a) uses sequences of computer instructions (e.g., binary addition, subtraction, AND, OR, loop, delay, branch) to generate and manipulate binary data. This data is considered to be a sequence of sound samples to be sent to a digital-to-analog converter. All synthesis methods, of course, use computer instructions at the lowest level of software. The point of instruction synthesis is that the sound is specified exclusively in terms of logical instructions, rather than in terms of traditional acoustical or signal-processing concepts.

"Synthesis by instruction" is a conceptual opposite to synthesis by rule or physical modeling synthesis, discussed in chapter 7. Physical modeling starts from a mathematical description of an acoustical mechanism. This model can be complex, requiring a great deal of computation. In contrast, instruction synthesis starts from the idiomatic use of computer instructions, with no acoustic model. The technique is efficient and can be run in real time on the most inexpensive microcomputers.

The sounds produced by instruction synthesis are different in character than those produced by rule-based synthesis. In many cases, it would be difficult to produce these sounds using "standard" digital or analog synthesis techniques, much less mechanical-acoustic means.

Most work in instruction synthesis has been carried out by associates of the Institute of Sonology, first in Utrecht and then in The Hague. One category of instruction synthesis system is an *assembler* for a *virtual machine* (Berg 1975; Berg 1978a, 1979). An assembler is a low-level programming language, where each statement corresponds to a hardware instruction. A virtual machine is a program that simulates the operation of an abstract computer with its own instruction set, data types, and so on. These systems require the composer to write fairly long programs that generate the individual samples. The program is the specification for a composition, and so it is also the score.

Paul Berg's PILE language (Berg 1978a, 1979) is a canonical example of instruction synthesis. The motivation for the PILE language springs from an aesthetic belief that "computers produce and manipulate numbers and other symbolic data very quickly. This could be considered the idiom of the computer" (Berg 1979). To implement his idea, Berg designed a virtual machine for numeric and symbolic operations, emulated by a program written for a small computer. The PILE language is the instruction set of the virtual machine. The execution of these programs by the virtual machine causes samples to be generated and sent to a digital-to-analog converter (DAC).

The instruction set of PILE consists of operations such as RANDOM (create a random number), INCR (add one to a number), SELECT (assign a random value to a variable), and CONVERT (send a sample to the digital-to-analog converter). Other operations change bit masks and manipulate program control flow by performing various random operations and inserting delays. Although tight control of pitch, duration, and timbre selection is possible in PILE (Berg realized a popular song to prove this point), the language is biased toward interactive experimentation with sound and trial-and-error improvisation. Due to the presence of random variables, the sonic results of a particular set of PILE instructions cannot always be predicted in advance. This is in keeping with the exploratory aesthetic of the language's inventor.

Holtzman's system (1979) was an attempt at controlling instruction synthesis from a higher level. He developed a program generator that produced short sound synthesis programs. Using a high-level notation, the composer could specify the order in which these programs were executed.

It is in the nature of instruction synthesis that the acoustic qualities of the sounds produced may not always be predictable. Accepting this, the composer who relies on instruction synthesis works in a trial-and-error mode. Since it is easy to produce a wide variety of sounds quickly with these techniques, many possibilities can be tried out in a single studio session. The composer then selects the most useful sounds.

Graphic Sound Synthesis

Graphic sound synthesis characterizes efforts that start from a visual approach to sound specification. These systems translate images into sound. This section examines the history of this approach and then focuses on recent work based on this principle.

Graphics in Sound Synthesis: Background

Free Music demands a non-human performance. Like most true music, it is an emotional, not cerebral, product, and should pass directly from the imagination of the composer to the ear of the listener by way of delicately controlled musical machines. (Percy Grainger 1938, quoted in Bird 1982)

Graphical techniques for generating sound have an illustrious history. In 1925 R. Michel patented a process for photographic notation of musical tones, similar to the technique used in making optical film soundtracks (Rhea 1972). Four years later, A. Schmalz developed an electronic music instrument with *photoelectric* tone generators. By placing a new *phonogram* into the instrument (an image of a waveform etched on glass), the timbre played by the tone generator changed.

These early experiments were followed by commercial instruments based on rotating photoelectric tone generators, such as the Celluophone, the Superpiano, the Welte Organ, the Syntronic Organ, and the Photona. The latter two were developed by Ivan Eremeef, working at the WCAU broadcasting station in Philadelphia. A consultant and supporter of Eremeef's experiments was the noted conductor Leopold Stokowski (who also premiered many of Varèse's works in the 1920s.) This represented one of the rare collaborations between engineers and prominent musicians prior to the 1950s. See also Clark (1959) for a description of a photoelectric instrument.

Perhaps the most imaginative and elaborate use of optical techniques was by the Canadian filmmaker Norman McLaren. With painstaking effort, McLaren made films in which he drew sound waveforms directly onto a sprocketed optical soundtrack, one frame at a time (McLaren and Lewis 1948).

Optical techniques have also been used to control analog synthesis. In the Oramics Graphic System developed by Daphne Oram in the United Kingdom (Douglas 1973), the composer drew control functions for an analog synthesizer onto transparent film. These control functions determined pitch, vibrato, tremolo, filter setting, and the amplitude level of several voices. The sprocketed film ran by an optical scanning head; the head transformed the image into an electronic control voltage fed into various modules of a synthesizer.

Another group of instruments could scan graphical notation. L. Lavallée's *sonothèque* or "sound library" read music encoded graphically using conductive ink sensed by a series of electrically-charged brushes (Rhea 1972). The Cross-Grainger Free Music Machine (first version 1944) read a graphic notation inscribed on paper (Bird 1982), and synthesized sound with eight vacuum-tube oscillators.

The Coded Music Apparatus (1952) of Hugh LeCaine let composers control sound generation by means of five continuous curves: for pitch, amplitude, and three timbre controls (Young 1989). His analog Oscillator Bank (1959) was driven by an optical apparatus to scan a sonogram-like score (Young 1989). (See chapter 13 for more on sonograms.) The Composer-Tron, developed by O. Kendall in the late 1950s, scanned envelopes drawn by hand on the face of a cathode-ray tube (a display screen). It then used these envelopes to control analog synthesis equipment.

Graphic control of digital sound began with the experiments of Mathews and Rosler (1969). (See chapter 16 for more on graphic data entry.) Several graphically oriented synthesis systems have been implemented on personal computers in recent years (see Oppenheim 1987, for example). The UPIC system, described next, is the most highly developed.

Interaction with UPIC

The UPIC (Unité Polyagogique Informatique de CEMAMu) is a synthesis system conceived by Iannis Xenakis and engineered by researchers at the Centre d'Etudes de Mathématique et Automatique Musicales (CEMAMu) in Paris (Xenakis 1992). The UPIC system combines various synthesis methods with a flexible graphical user interface to create a unique approach to sound composition.

The First UPIC

An initial version of the UPIC system dates from 1977. In this implementation, interaction was mediated by a large, high-resolution graphics tablet, mounted vertically like a painter's easel (Lohner 1986). We describe some of the functions of this system, since many of them are present in later versions of the UPIC system.

At the level of creating sound microstructure, waveforms and event envelopes could be drawn directly on the tablet and displayed on a graphics terminal. Alternatively, composers could tap a set of points to be connected by the computer by means of interpolation. With a waveform and an envelope defined, their product could be auditioned.

Figure 8.5 A page from Iannis Xenakis's *Mycenae-Alpha* (1980), created on the UPIC system. The vertical axis is frequency, and the horizontal axis is time.

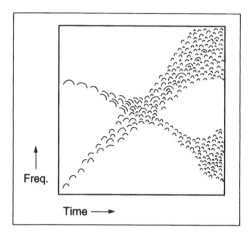

Figure 8.6 A page from *Message* (1987) by Curtis Roads. Each arc represents the pitch curve of an alto saxophone tone.

At a higher level of organization, composers could draw the frequency/time structure of a score *page.* As the composer moved a pointing device, lines—called *arcs,* in the UPIC terminology—appeared on the display screen. Individual arcs could be moved, stretched or shrunk, cut, copied, or pasted. Figure 8.5 is an example from Iannis Xenakis's *Mycenae-Alpha* (1980), created on the UPIC system.

Musicians also had the option of recording, editing, and scoring sampled sounds. The sampled signals could be used as either waveforms or as envelopes. When samples are used as envelopes, dense amplitude modulation effects occur. Graphic scores could be orchestrated with a combination of synthetic and sampled sounds, if desired.

As figure 8.6 demonstrates, gestural and graphical interaction lets composers create easily score structures that would be cumbersome to specify by any other means. At the level of a page, the UPIC captures both microstructural detail and macrostructural evolution.

Real-time UPIC

The first version of the UPIC system ran on a slow and bulky minicomputer. Although designing the graphics was an interactive process, the calculation of sound samples from the composer's graphical score involved a delay. A major breakthrough for the UPIC was the development of a real-time version, based on a 64-oscillator synthesis engine (Raczinski and Marino 1988). By 1991 this engine was coupled to a personal computer running the Windows operating system, permitting a sophisticated graphical interface

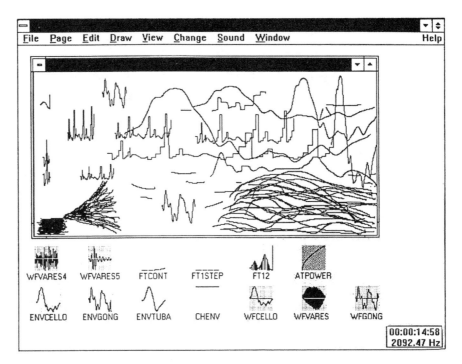

Figure 8.7 A page from a 1992 score by Gerard Pape, realized with a real-time UPIC system at Les Ateliers UPIC, Paris. The icons in the lower part of the screen represent a working set of waveforms and envelopes.

(Marino, Raczinski, and Serra 1990; Raczinski, Marino, and Serra 1991; Marino, Serra, and Raczinski 1992; Pape 1992).

Figure 8.7 is a page created with the real-time UPIC. A page can have 64 simultaneous arcs, with 4000 arcs per page. The duration of each page can last from 6 ms to more than 2 hours. Editing operations such as cut, copy, and paste rearrange the arcs, which can also be stretched or compressed in time and frequency. These operations can occur while a page is being played. Four different musical scales can be assigned to the same page. When played with a discrete scale, the arcs follow the frequency steps defined in a tuning table.

Real-time synthesis turns the UPIC into a performance instrument. Normally the synthesis unit performs the score from left to right, moving at a constant rate defined by the page duration set by the user. However, the rate and direction of score reading can also be controlled in real time by a mouse. This allows discontinuous jumps from one region of the score to another region, for example. The sequence of control motions can be recorded by the system as it is playing a score. Later the same performance can be played or edited.

Graphic Synthesis with MIDI

Following in the train of UPIC are a number of graphic composing environments with MIDI output (Yavelow 1992). Some have sophisticated features, such as a "multiple harmonics" mode where one line traced by a mouse is displayed as several lines spaced at harmonic intervals (Lesbros 1993).

A problem with this approach is mapping a possibly large amount of graphical control data into the limits of the MIDI protocol (see chapter 21 for more on MIDI). An image such as figure 8.8 may contain more than a hundred simultaneous events. Few MIDI synthesizers accept this volume of data, so considerable planning must go into configuring a MIDI setup that will handle it.

Assessment of Graphic Sound Synthesis

Graphic sound synthesis is a direct and intuitive approach to sound sculpture. At the level of events inscribed on the time-frequency plane, interaction with graphical synthesis can be either precise or imprecise, depending on how the user treats the process. A composer who plans each line and its mapping into sound can obtain exact results. The composer who improvises on-screen treats the medium as a sketchpad, where initial drawings are refined into a finished design.

Graphic control of pitch is natural for many composers, making it easy to create melodic shapes and phrases that would be difficult to achieve with other means. Obvious examples include microtonal phrases with multiple glissandi or with a detailed filigree of portamento and vibrato effects.

Graphic design of envelope shapes has proved effective in many systems. But the problem with hand-drawn acoustic waveforms remains that it is difficult to infer from a waveform image what it will sound like. (Chapters 1 and 16 discuss this problem.) Regardless of its shape, any waveform repeated without variation takes on a static quality. So in graphic synthesis systems, as in other approaches, waveform generation has shifted from individual fixed waveforms to evolving sources such as sampled sounds or groups of time-varying waveforms.

The UPIC system is an especially pliable musical tool since it integrates many levels of composition within a common user interface. Graphic functions created on-screen can be treated equally as envelopes, waveforms, pitch-time scores, tempo curves, or performance trajectories. In this uniform treatment of composition data at every level lies a generality that should be extended to more computer music systems.

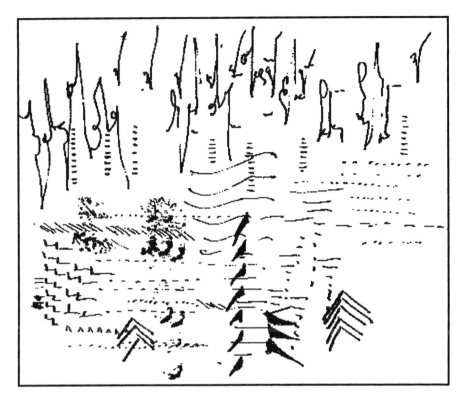

Figure 8.8   A page of the score *Poly5* created by Vincent Lesbros using his Phonogramme program developed in 1993. Notice the evidence of the use of the multiple harmonics drawing mode. In this mode, the user draws a single line, and multiple harmonics automatically appear above it.

Noise Modulation

I believe that the use of noise to make music will continue and increase until we reach a music produced through electrical instruments. . . . Whereas in the past, the point of disagreeement has been between dissonance and consonance, it will be, in the immediate future, between noise and so-called musical sounds. (John Cage 1937)

This section explores methods of generating noisy sounds. The primary idea is to use filtered noise to modulate other waveforms such as sine waves. This category of techniques includes noise-driven amplitude modulation, frequency modulation, and waveshaping.

Discourse on Noise

To implement noise modulation we need a digital source of noise. This takes the form of a series of randomly valued samples. But defining an algorithm for generating random numbers is very difficult mathematically (Chaiten 1975). Any computer-based method for random number generation ultimately rests on a finite, deterministic procedure. Hence we refer to an algorithm for generating "random" numbers as a *pseudorandom number generator,* since the sequence generated by such an algorithm repeats after several thousand or million iterations. Programming language environments provide pseudorandom number generators with different characteristics, such as the frequency range, and the length of the sequence. Hence we will not go into the details of creating such an algorithm here. Knuth (1973a) and Rabiner and Gold (1975) contain algorithms. Chapter 19 contains additional notes on this subject.

The pseudorandom noise, defined by statistical criteria, is just one family of noisy textures. Many synthesis techniques can also generate interesting chaotic noises, including sinusoidal modulations (chapters 6 and 8) and granular synthesis (chapter 5).

Indeed, the term "noise" serves as a linguistic substitute for a more precise description of a complicated, not well-understood signal, such as the nonharmonic and chaotic parts of wind and string tones, or the attack transients of percussion instruments. The processes that create these air pressure curves are complicated turbulences that science is just beginning to understand—not necessarily "random" behavior (whatever that means).

At present, a main challenge for musical acoustics is creating more sophisticated algorithmic models for noise. The global statistical criteria that define a pseudorandom numerical sequence, for example, are not optimum for describing many noisy sounds. As early drum machines taught us, white noise is a poor substitute for a cymbal crash. The paradigm of *nonlinear chaos*—deterministic algorithms that generate complex behavior—has replaced stochastic models of certain phenomena observed by scientists (Gleick 1988). Chapter 19 introduces this topic.

Noise-modulated AM and FM

The composer who disposes himself to aleatoric modulation will ... discover that this type of modulation leads directly into a world of phenomena previously described as "noises."
(Meyer-Eppler 1955)

Noise modulation techniques use a pseudorandom signal generator or *noise generator* to control the amplitude or frequency of an oscillator. (See chapter 5 for a discussion of AM and FM.) As figure 8.9 shows, when the noise is filtered down to the infrasonic frequency range (below about

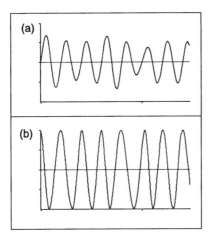

Figure 8.9 Waveforms generated by noise modulation. (*a*) Sine wave that is amplitude modulated 50 percent by lowpass filtered noise. This affects the vertical span of the individual pitch periods. (*b*) Sine wave that is frequency modulated 50 percent by lowpass filtered noise. Note that the width of each pitch period varies slighty.

20 Hz), the effect is a kind of aleatoric tremolo (in the case of AM) or vibrato (in the case of FM).

When the noise has a wider bandwidth, the result of modulation is a type of *colored noise,* that is, a noise band centered around the carrier frequency of the oscillator. Figure 8.10 shows the patch diagrams for noise-modulated AM and FM instruments. In both cases, it is a good idea to use a noise source that has been lowpass filtered such that the randomness introduced by the noise is itself near the carrier frequency. If the noise is not filtered, the effect may sound like a high-frequency noise component has been added to the carrier signal.

Waveshaping with a Random Shaping Function

Waveshaping, explained in chapter 6, makes possible another kind of noise modulation. In waveshaping, the instantaneous amplitude of a signal is remapped by a *shaping function.* A random shaping function distorts the periodic signal into a more broadband sound. Figure 8.11 depicts four progressively noisy shaping functions, while figure 8.12 shows the effects of the four shaping functions in figure 8.11 on a sine wave passed through a waveshaper.

A more subtle use of randomness in waveshaping employs a smooth waveshaping function at low amplitudes and introduces increasing randomness at higher amplitudes. Another possibility is to link the amount of

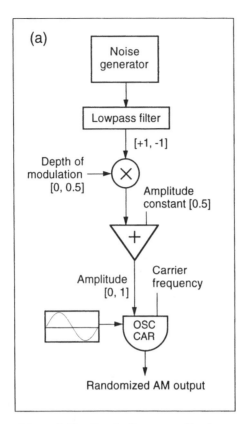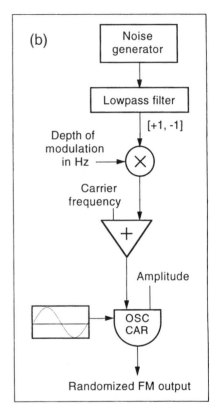

Figure 8.10 Patch diagrams of noise modulation instruments. (*a*) Noise-modulated AM. The output of the noise generator is filtered and scaled by a depth of modulation parameter. Then it is added to an amplitude constant to form the composite amplitude value fed to the oscillator. (*b*) Noise-modulated FM. The output of the noise generator is filtered and scaled by a depth of modulation parameter, which specifies the bandwidth on either side of the carrier frequency.

randomness in the waveshaping function to the duration of the tone or another parameter of the event.

Stochastic Waveform Synthesis

Musical sound is too limited in its variety of timbres. The most complicated orchestras can be reduced to four or five classes of instruments in different timbres of sound: bowed instruments, brass, woodwinds, and percussion. Modern music flounders within this tiny circle, vainly striving to create new varieties of timbre. We must break out of this limited circle of sounds and conquer the infinite variety of noise-sounds!
(Luigi Russolo 1916)

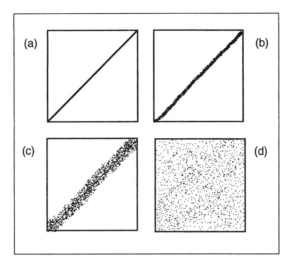

Figure 8.11 Four progressively random waveshaping functions. The shaping functions remap values on the input (read across the bottom) to values on the output (read along the side). See chapter 6 for more on waveshaping.

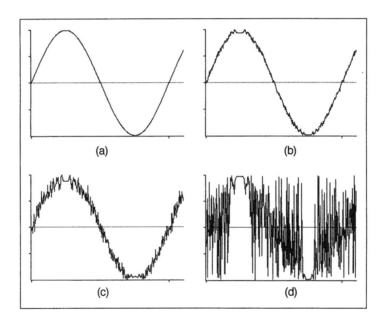

Figure 8.12 Sine wave subjected to the four shaping functions depicted in figure 8.11.

Stochastic waveform synthesis generates sound samples by comparing the value of a pseudorandom number against a *probability distribution*. A probability distribution is a curve (stored in an array in computer memory) that indicates the numerical probability of a range of possible outcomes. In the case of waveform synthesis, the "outcomes" are the amplitude values of samples. Chapter 19 describes a process of melody generation by probability table lookup. All that is needed to adapt such an algorithm to waveform generation is to substitute waveform values (e.g., between −1 and 1) for the pitch values.

Since algorithms for waveform generation must produce tens of thousands of sample values for each second of sound, small computational efficiencies may add up to large savings in calculation time. For example, one efficiency could be to preload a large table with pseudorandom values, rather than calling a pseudorandom number generator routine for each sample. Then all that is needed to obtain a pseudorandom number is a table lookup.

Devising an appropriate probability distribution for a particular compositional application is an art. Chapter 19 introduces this subject and presents a classification of probability distributions into categories. Many texts on probability theory are available; see Drake (1967) for example. An excellent reference article with musical examples and program code is Lorrain (1980); a revised, corrected version of this paper is accessible in a widely distributed anthology (Roads 1989). Other good references on stochastic techniques in composition include Xenakis (1992), Jones (1981), and Ames (1987a, 1989a). Related experiments in fractal waveform generation have been reported in Waschka and Kurepa (1989; see chapter 19 for more on fractals).

Waveform generation by simple probability table lookup without further constraints generates a fixed-spectrum noise. Thus it is important to impose constraints—additional rules that vary the probabilities in order to produce interesting time-varying sounds. This is the goal of dynamic stochastic synthesis, described next.

Dynamic Stochastic Synthesis

In *Formalized Music*, the composer Iannis Xenakis (1992) proposes an alternative to the usual method of sound synthesis. Instead of starting from simple periodic functions and trying to animate them by injecting "disorder" (i.e., various distortions and modulations), why not start with pseudorandom functions and tame them by adding "order" (i.e., weights, constraints, and barriers)? This proposal takes the form of eight strategies

Table 8.2   Xenakis's proposals for stochastic waveform generation

1. Direct use of probability distributions (such as Poisson, exponential, Gaussian, uniform, Cauchy, arcsine, and logistic) to create waveforms

2. Multiplications of probability functions with themselves

3. Combining probability functions into mixtures through addition, possibly over time

4. Using the random variables of amplitude and time as functions of elastic forces or other random variables

5. Using random variables that bounce back and forth between elastic boundaries

6. Using probability functions to generate the values of parameters of other probability functions (these latter functions used to produce sound waveforms)

7. Assigning probability curves into classes, and considering these classes as elements of higher-order sets and processes (i.e., introducing hierarchical control over waveform generation)

8. Injecting the choice of stochastic sound synthesis techniques into a stochastic composition program (an extension of item 7)

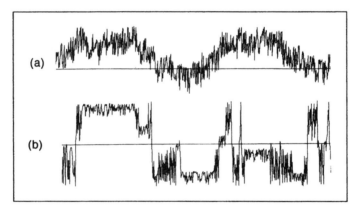

Figure 8.13   Two waveforms generated using stochastic methods. (*a*) The product of a hyperbolic cosine function with exponential densities using barriers and non-randomized time. (*b*) The same algorithm as (*a*) with randomized time intervals. (After Xenakis 1992.)

for exploring a *dynamic stochastic* approach to waveform synthesis, listed in table 8.2.

Figure 8.13 shows two waveforms generated using stochastic methods. Figure 8.13a shows the product of a hyperbolic cosine with exponential densities using barriers and nonrandomized time. Figure 8.13b shows the same algorithm with randomized time intervals.

GENDY

The GENDY (GENeration Dynamique) program is an implementation of stochastic dynamic synthesis, with conceptual links to the interpolation synthesis techniques described earlier in this chapter. This section describes, in particular, the GENDY3 program (Xenakis 1992; Serra 1992).

GENDY makes sound by repeating an initial waveform and then distorting that waveform in time and amplitude. Thus the synthesis algorithm computes each new waveform by applying stochastic variations to the previous waveform.

In the program, the waveform is represented as a polygon, bounded by sides on the time axis and sides on the amplitude axis. The segments of the polygon are defined by vertices on the time and amplitude axes (figure 8.14). The program interpolates straight line segments between these vertices.

GENDY synthesizes the vertex points according to various stochastic distributions. If the stochastic variations are not held within a finite interval, the signal tends quickly toward white noise. For this reason the program constrains time and amplitude variations to remain within the boundaries of a *mirror*. The mirror consists of an amplitude barrier and a time barrier. Points that fall outside the mirror are reflected back into the mirror (figure 8.15). In effect, the mirror filters the stochastic variations. By increasing or decreasing the amplitude barrier, the composer controls the amount of reflections. Reflections represent discontinuities in the waveform, so this is a timbral control. Since the time barrier sets the interval between time points, it has an influence on the perceived frequency of the sound.

The control parameters of the GENDY system are thus the number of time segments, the mirror boundaries, and the choice of stochastic distribution for time and for amplitude vertices. These are set on a per voice basis. Figure 8.16 shows the evolution of a waveform produced by GENDY. It is quasi-periodic, as determined by small mirror. By adding secondary mirrors, effects such as vibrato and tremolo can also be imposed on the varying waveform.

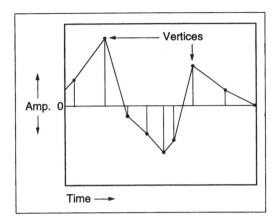

Figure 8.14 Waveform structure in GENDY. The waveform is a collection of polygons formed by drawing straight line segments between vertices on the time-frequency plane. Note the unequal time intervals between vertices.

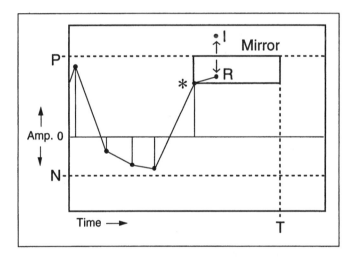

Figure 8.15 The time and amplitude barriers defining a mirror constrain the next vertex generated from the vertex marked by an asterisk. If the next vertex generated stochastically falls outside the barriers indicated by the box (the initial projection I), the barriers override this choice, reflecting the vertex back into the box (reflection R).

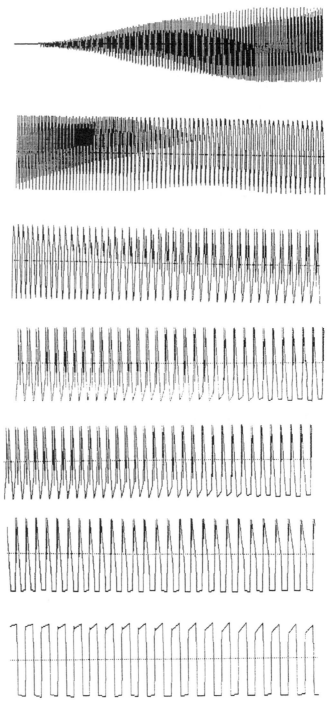

Figure 8.16   Waveform evolution generated by the GENDY program. The progession starts at the top and proceeds to the bottom, plotting time to the right on each line.

Conclusion

Writing in 1916, Luigi Russolo predicted a new world of music based on "the art of noises." The techniques explained in this chapter, waveform segment, graphical, noise modulation, and stochastic waveform synthesis, lead us into the uncharted galaxy of synthetic sound. Many of the signals we encounter there have spectral undercurrents that swell and break the crest of a fundamental pitch, scattering its energy along the frequency plane. We call this dispersed energy "noise," a term that has unpleasant associations. Yet noise elements always have been a fundamental ingredient of musical sound, from the sharp punctuation of percussion, to the gentle scraping of a bow across a string, and the sensual breathy effects of the wind instruments. The noisy sounds generated by the techniques explained in this chapter can serve as structural foils to the smooth and familiar textures generated by more standard methods. Their importance in orchestration, therefore, should not be overlooked.

III Mixing and Signal Processing

Overview to Part III

Sound is a supple medium. We can delicately blend sound waves into a smoothly flowing musical process, or juxtapose them sharply for articulation, contrast, or shock effect. The process of balancing the levels of several audio channels is *sound mixing*. As we mix, it is often useful to filter, delay, reverberate, localize, or layer other effects onto sounds. These operations fall within the domain of *signal processing*. This part of the book, comprising chapters 9 through 11, devotes itself to signal processing in mixing and sound transformation.

Another aspect of signal processing is sound analysis. Since this is a large subject in itself, we have allocated a separate part of the book to cover it.

Why Study Signal Processing?

For many musicians, initial experiences with signal processing take place in operating an effects processor, such as an equalizer, delay unit, or reverberator. Commercial devices reduce each algorithm to a descriptive name controlled by a few parameters. Is there any need to go further? Indeed, to the musician confronting a signal-processing text for the first time, the subject exudes a dry mathematical air, far removed from the musical experience. Why study signal processing?

There are many reasons. One is that in order to grasp the fundamental nature of musical materials, one must understand them as acoustic signals. The artificial division between "composition" on the one hand, and "orchestration" on the other, need not apply in computer music. To generate and process acoustical signals is to compose—more directly than inscribing ink on paper.

Certain topics in signal processing are not terribly profound from the standpoint of theory, but they are so ubiquitous that a basic knowledge of them is essential; mixing and dynamic range processing are cases in point.

Other topics stand out because they have both profound theoretical significance and direct practical applications. Into this category go the continuum of effects along the delay plane: from phase shifting, to comb filtering, spatial positioning, doubling, and echo. Here also goes convolution, with its myriad ramifications in filtering, temporal and spatial processing, and modulation.

Much of the energy that was invested into synthesis techniques in the formative years of computer music is now being channeled into signal processing. Any sound can be enhanced by effects and spatial processing, for example. And an increasing number of "synthesis" techniques are actually "analysis, transformation, and resynthesis" techniques that demand an understanding of sound analysis as presented in part IV.

Finally, by demystifying signal processing, we hope to foster increased self-reliance among musicians and reduce their dependence on technical assistants. Basic knowledge will lead student musicians out of a kind of dabbling, guessing phase to a more directed phase of command of their musical materials.

Organization of Part III

Chapter 9 outlines many approaches to mixing and multitrack recording. Composers and remix engineers have taken over many of the musical functions that were formerly assigned to conductors—among the most exalted of musical professions. As conductors have long known, by adjusting the balance of the various musical forces, individual sounds or lines can be spotlighted or shaded to enhance their musical role within a piece. The final part of chapter 9 introduces the issue of synchronization of several media, linking audio, video, lighting, or other effects together. Synchronization is an especially pertinent topic for aspiring sound engineers since professional studios deal with these challenges on a daily basis.

Chapters 10 and 11 introduce the vast art of sound transformation via signal processing. The chapters are aimed at musicians with no previous knowledge of the field, save for a basic understanding of digital audio principles as explained in chapter 1. Our main goal is to demystify topics that are either hidden by manufacturers or presented with a flood of arcane equations, devoid of motivation or interpretation. We want to teach readers how to operate the musical "handles" provided by signal-processing tools. Toward this end, chapters 10 and 11 define dozens of terms and explain interrelationships among fundamental concepts, while stressing the immense range of possible sound transformations.

Chapter 10 is divided into several sections. The first section examines basic concepts behind dynamic range processors like limiters and compressors. The following sections introduce the internals of simple digital filters and explain the musical significance of convolution. The final sections survey time delay effects (fixed and variable) and time/pitch changing algorithms.

Sound spatialization has been an important compositional parameter since the dawn of electronic music. Chapter 11 studies the fundamental concepts behind reverberation, localization, moving sound sources, and the modeling of sound spaces.

As a profession, digital signal processing requires a mastery of applied mathematics (calculus, linear systems theory, probability theory, linear algebra). In part III we take a less formal and more musical perspective on the field. Simple equations are given, but, wherever possible, we avoid mathematical notation. Dozens of citations to the engineering literature are sprinkled throughout the text for the technically inclined reader.

9 *Sound Mixing*

Mixing and Dynamic Range

Non-real-time Software Mixing

Mixing by Script
Object-oriented Mixing
Graphical Mixing
Assessment of Software Mixing

Mixing Consoles

Properties of Mixers
Input Section
Output Section
Auxiliary Return Section
Talkback Section
Monitor Section
Metering Section
Grouping Facilities

Hybrid Consoles

Playing Back the Mix

Features of Digital Mixing Consoles

Stand-alone Mixers versus Audio Workstations

Multitrack Recording and Remixing

Multitrack Recording: Background

Advantages of Multitrack Recording

Problems Posed by Multitrack Remixing

Audio Monitoring

Headphones

Loudspeaker Monitoring

Near-field Monitoring

Control Room Monitoring

Listening Room Monitoring

Mixing and Monitoring in Performance

Mix Automation

MIDI Control of Audio Mixers: Patching and Channel Muting

Synchronization of Audio Mixing and Video

Multiple-machine Synchronization

SMPTE Timecode

MIDI Timecode

Conclusion

Nature mixes sounds acoustically in the air—for example, in the "fused" orchestral sonority at a symphony concert, or the cacophony of a city street corner. Analog electronic circuits also mix sound signals, where each signal is represented as a time-varying voltage. A circuit sums many signals to a composite signal.

In the digital domain, audio signals mix according to the rules of simple addition. To help visualize this process, figures 9.1, 9.2, and 9.3 show mixing at three different timescales. In figure 9.1 a sample from source (a) at time t_1 with a value of 32,767 is added to another sample from source (b) at time t_1 of $-32,767$, and the resulting summed sample value is 0 (c). When two positive signals of 10,000 each are added at time t_2, the result is 20,000.

Figure 9.2 shows mixing at the level of waveform addition, combining a low-frequency wave with a high-frequency wave.

Finally, figure 9.3 shows the result of mixing two different sound files, each lasting about 2.5 seconds.

Mixing and Dynamic Range

The *dynamic range* (DR) is the span (expressed in decibels) between the softest and loudest sounds that can be handled by a system. For example, the DR of the human ear is about 120 dB. As chapter 1 explains, the DR of a digital audio system is proportional to the quantization of the system; with about 6 dB for every quantized bit. Hence, a 16-bit system's DR is limited to 96 dB, while an audio system that can handle 20-bit audio has about the same dynamic range as the human hearing mechanism.

Dynamic range limits pose special problems for digital mixing systems because mixers add many sample values to create a sum. If the sum exceeds the quantization range, the result is nonlinear or an error. When hundreds of samples hit the quantization limit, the audio result is a rough crackling from the digital-to-analog converters caused by "digital clipping" or over-load.

Most digital mixers provide 24 to 64 bits of quantization resolution at summing points in the signal path. This many bits are needed because it is common for a mixer to combine sixteen or more channels simultaneously. Adding sixteen 16-bit numbers of significant magnitude results in a 20-bit number. Another reason for high resolution within a mixer is that many digital filter operations require at least 24 bits (144 dB of dynamic range) to maintain high audio quality. Various roundoff methods can scale the samples down to fewer bits at the output of a mixer.

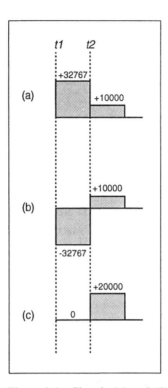

Figure 9.1   Signals (*a*) and (*b*) consisting of two samples at time points t_1 and t_2 mixed, showing the result as signal (*c*).

Inside the mixer (or mixing program) the use of integers for audio samples is characteristic of a *fixed-point* representation. Standing in contrast to this is a *floating-point* representation, where samples are represented in terms of two numbers: a *mantissa* and an *exponent*. The exponent acts a scale factor, allowing the representation of very small and very large numbers—increasing the dynamic range. Thus a floating-point representation is one way system designers can alleviate problems of dynamic range in digital systems. See chapter 20 for more on fixed-point versus floating-point systems.

Non-real-time Software Mixing

Digital audio mixing can be performed in either hardware or in software. Software-based mixers generally operate in two steps: the musician plans the mix in some way, and then the software carries out the mix. In general, we are referring to non-real-time mixing, or more specifically to mixing without real-time control.

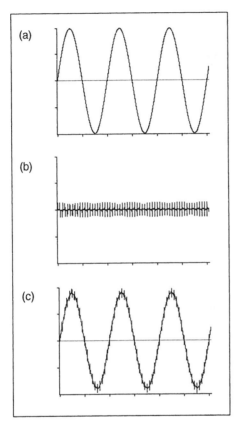

Figure 9.2 Waveform mixing. (*a*) Sine tone at 50 Hz. (*b*) Sine tone at 500 Hz. (*c*) Mix of (*a*) + (*b*).

Even without real-time control, software mixing programs have several advantages over other types of mixers. First, they can carry out precise and complicated mixes that would be impossible to realize by any other means. This includes mixes involving large numbers of sources that would exceed the capabilities of an automated mixing console. A well-designed software mixer, for example, should have no problem dealing with a hundred or more sound files over the course of a mix. If desired, signal processing can be applied with microscopic precision on a short timescale. Second, software mixers can be integrated with other tools in the software environment (e.g., a sound file may be transformed by one program even as it remains in the mix window of another program). Third, some software mixers are open systems that can be extended in arbitrary ways by programming.

Software mixers fit into three main categories: mixing by script, object-oriented mixing, and graphical mixing, the subjects of the next sections.

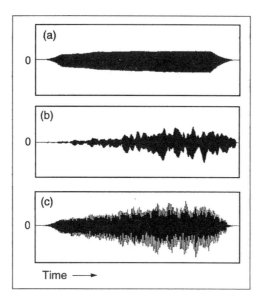

Figure 9.3   Sound file mixing. (*a*) Alto saxophone tone. (*b*) Granular synthesis texture. (*c*) Mix of (*a*) + (*b*).

Mixing by Script

The Music *N* languages for software synthesis, described in chapters 3 and 17, contain facilities for adding sound signals. Most implementations permit the sources to be sound files, which opens up the possibility of using these languages for precision mixing. The level of individual sound files can be scaled using envelopes, and all the signal-processing facilities of the language are available for additional transformations. The result of the mix is typically a sound file.

Examples of this approach include Paul Lansky's MIX and Cmix systems developed at Princeton University (Lansky 1982, 1990a, b, c). MIX was a flexible but non-real-time mixing system that combined up to 20 channels of 32-bit floating-point digital sound on tape into a two-channel disk file. This file could be written to another tape, converted to sound, or remixed at will.

Cmix is a later system that has been ported to UNIX-compatible computers. It is implemented as a library of signal-processing functions embedded in the C programming language. Users interact with Cmix by preparing a *mixing script*. At its most basic, the script tells the system when to start and stop mixing and what amplitude curves to use. Signal-processing functions in Cmix let users filter, reverberate, and spatially process sound files. Users can write their own sound file manipulation functions and intermingle them with predefined ones.

The programming approach embodied by Cmix allows the musician to compute the mix of individual notes, phrases, sections, or voices, and combine these *submixes* in a separate step. This approach can be likened to individual practice sessions, followed by sectional rehearsals, followed by a more efficient rehearsal of the whole ensemble.

Object-oriented Mixing

Another software approach to mixing is the Sound Kit written by Lee Boynton for NeXT computers. Sound Kit is a library of object-oriented routines, written in the Objective C programming language, designed for sound file manipulation. Sound Kit defines a set of messages that can be sent to sound file objects telling them to splice, cut, paste, delete, access individual samples, combine sound files, and play arbitrary parts of a sound file (Jaffe and Boynton 1989; Lansky 1990c).

Graphical Mixing

Many graphical mixing programs run on inexpensive personal computers. A classic example is the MacMix program, originally developed by Adrian Freed (Freed and Goldstein 1988) and later adapted to Apple Macintosh computers attached to Studer Dyaxis audio workstations.

MacMix displays individual tracks to be mixed as horizontal bars (figure 9.4). The user can select bars and move them horizontally along the time line—a useful operation that is impossible with serial media such as multitrack tape recorders. Each track can be faded in or out, with the envelope adjustable on-screen. The right column adjusts the gain.

Following the example of MacMix, many companies have developed multichannel mixing programs with similar graphical controls. For example, systems developed by the Digidesign and Opcode companies combine multichannel audio with MIDI sequence data (figure 9.5).

Assessment of Software Mixing

Software mixing running on a general-purpose computer has the advantages of flexibility and precision. The software approach involves a preparation stage that gives the engineer time to plan a precise mix. In a programmable mixing environment, the mix can be arbitrarily complex

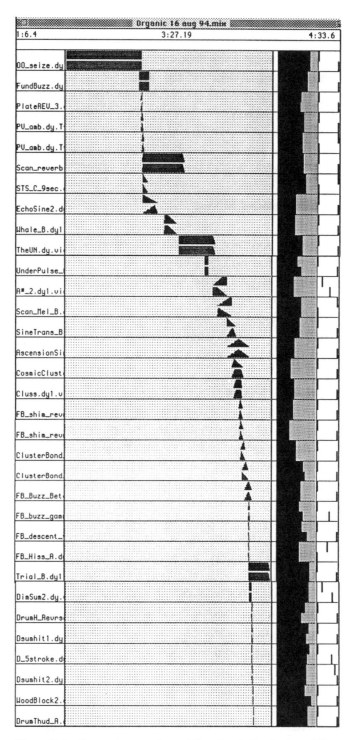

Figure 9.4 Screen image of a multitrack mix in the MacMix program. The shaded bars represent 33 tracks to be mixed. Each stereo track corresponds to a sound file stored on disk. The slopes at the beginning and end of the tracks indicate fades. The black horizontal bars indicate the relative amplitude level of each track, while the vertical lines in the right column indicate the spatial position of each track. From the author's composition *Clang-tint* (1994).

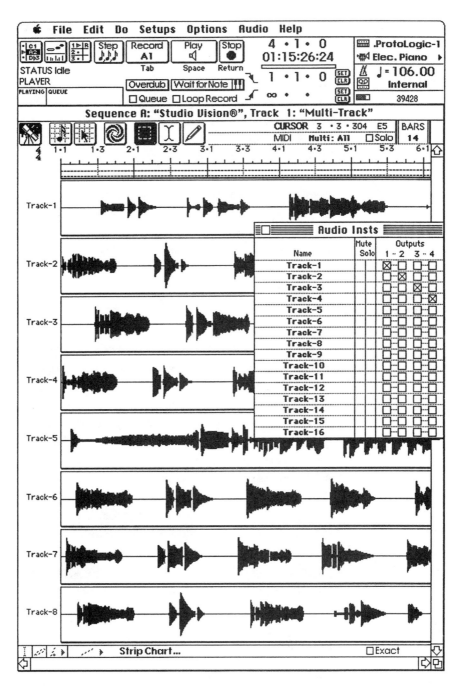

Figure 9.5   Screen image of the Studio Vision program by Opcode, showing audio tracks in the midst of a MIDI sequence editor. The MIDI sequence data are not shown, but their presence is indicated by the 4/4 measure and beat numbers above Track 1, and various sequencer controls.

in terms of number of channels and mixing operations, far exceeding the capabilities of human beings at a mixing console, even an automated one.

For all its flexibility and precision, software mixing has certain drawbacks. More-or-less elaborate planning is necessary even in the case of a simple mix. If the mixing takes place in non-real-time, it may take several rehearsals to adjust the timings and mix envelopes properly. A major drawback is the lack of "feel" in non-real-time software mixing. When there are no real-time faders to manipulate, it is impossible to respond intuitively as one listens. Some computer-based mixers use a mouse or alphanumeric keys to control the channel amplitudes, but these are not ideal controllers for this delicate task; a set of precision faders is preferable. Hence, a *mixing console* (analog or digital) that combines real-time mixing hardware with precision faders is a valuable complement to software mixing.

Mixing Consoles

A sound mixing console (also called a *mixing desk* or just a *mixer*) combines a number of input channels into some number of output channels in real time. Mixers also perform auxiliary operations such as filtering and signal routing. For many years, mixing consoles were built exclusively from analog circuits, sometimes to a very high sonic standard. Gradually, digital technology was added to analog consoles. *Hybrid consoles,* discussed later, combine analog audio circuits with digital control and automation circuits. All-digital mixers are increasingly used.

Often a mixer a more than just an audio signal summer. It is also the main "control panel" in a studio or live performance. Therefore it integrates specialized control and coordination features. The specific features available depend on the manufacturer of the mixer and options chosen by the purchaser. Since this chapter deals with general principles, we do not attempt to describe the range of exotic control options on some mixing consoles.

Properties of Mixers

Mixing consoles can be characterized by a ratio that represents the number of input channels they handle versus the number of mixed output channels they produce. For example, a mixer that can handle eight channels of input and mix it down to two channels of output is called an 8/2 ("eight-to-two") mixer. Many mixers have several *output busses* to which signals can be

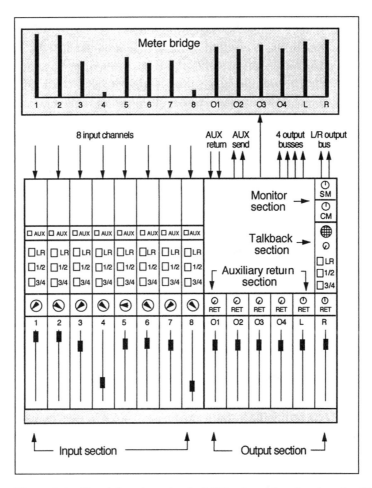

Figure 9.6 Signal flow in a simple 8/4/2 mixer, also showing the different sections of the mixer. The squares represent push-button switches, while the circles represent rotary knobs. 01 through 04 indicate output busses, as do L and R (left and right). The indicators CM and SM in the monitor section refer to controls for studio monitor and control room monitoring levels.

routed simultaneously. To give an example, a mixer with eight inputs, a four-output bus, and a two-output bus can be referred to as an 8/4/2 mixer. On such a mixer one could make simultaneous four-track and two-track recordings, via the four-output bus and the two-output bus, respectively.

A typical recording studio mixer consists of six main sections: an *input* section, an *output* section, an *auxiliary return* section, a *talkback* section, a *monitor* section, and a *metering* section. A simple 8/4/2 mixer is shown in figure 9.6. The eight channels of input are routed to one or more of the six output busses through a set of *output bus assignment buttons* (LR, 1/2, and 3/4) and *pan pots*. By pressing one of the output bus assignment buttons the signal is routed to two output busses; turning the pan pot left or right selects one of the two output busses. The input can also be routed to two *auxiliary send* (AUX) busses for outboard signal processing. The *auxiliary return* (RET) from the effects unit can be mixed into the output busses by a small rotary potentiometer above the output level fader. Alternatively, the output from the effects unit can be routed into one of the input channels for more control over the sound. The CM and SM potentiometers at the top right set the amplitude of the monitor loudspeakers in the control room (CM) and studio (SM), respectively. They take their input from the L/R busses. A *talkback microphone* (right) lets the mixing engineer communicate with musicians or label a recording. The *meter bridge* shows the amplitude levels of the eight input channels and the six output busses.

The next paragraphs discuss the sections of a mixer in more detail.

Input Section

The input section usually consists of a number of identical input modules (figure 9.7). Table 9.1 explains the parts of the input module.

Output Section

Operating the output section of a mixer is usually very simple. It consists of a fader to control the output level of a signal sent to an output bus, and a meter display.

Auxiliary Return Section

The auxiliary return section can also be called the *effects, cue,* or *foldback* section. All four terms are used by various sectors of the recording industry. The auxiliary returns allow the mixing engineer to blend sounds processed by effects units into the output signal. Alternatively, they allow the engineer to create special monitor submixes for individual musicians who are listening on headphones (in a recording studio) or through a loudspeaker (onstage).

Talkback Section

The talkback section lets the recording engineer communicate with musicians in the recording studio. Another use of talkback in the computer music studio is to *slate* or *log* a recording with comments for later reference.

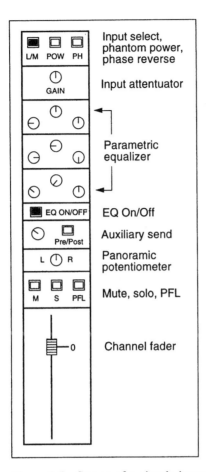

Figure 9.7 Stages of a simple input module on a mixer. Table 9.1 explains each stage.

Technically, the talkback section consists of a microphone, a level control, and various switches to determine where the engineer's voice is routed.

Monitor Section

This section takes its input from the left/right output bus and routes it to loudspeakers and headphones in the control room (where the mixer is) and the studio (where musicians are).

Metering Section

Meters indicate sound levels in the input channels and the output busses. *Peak meters* reflect the instantaneous peak amplitude of the signal. Their

Table 9.1   Functions of a mixer input module

Input select, phantom power, phase reverse switches	Selector switches. The input select chooses either microphone, line-level, or subgroup input. The phantom power switch sends a DC power signal to a condenser microphone. Phase reverse inverts the phase of the incoming signal (useful in multiple microphone setups).
Input attentuator/pad	Attenuates the level of the incoming signal so that the input channel is not overloaded by a high-level signal. For line-level signals, the input attenuator ensures that the mixer is aligned to the operating level of the external input device (e.g., tape recorder or instrument).
Parametric equalizer	Alters the spectrum of the sound by boosting certain bands of frequencies and attenuating others. Shown is a three-band parametric EQ. The three controls for each band adjust the bandwidth, the center frequency, and the amount of boost or cut for each band. A *semiparametric equalizer* omits the bandwidth control.
EQ On/Off	Switches the equalization section in or out of the circuit.
Auxiliary send	Routes the sound to an effects unit (e.g., a delay unit or reverberator) or a *cue* output. A cue output is usually routed to headphones worn by performers in a recording studio, or to a monitor loudspeaker onstage. Thus, the cue output constitutes a submix of the music that can be balanced so that each musician can hear their own instrument above the rest. The *send* knob controls the level of the sound sent to the effects unit or cue. The *return* knob controls the level of the sound coming back from the effects unit. (See the effects/ auxiliary return section.) When the sound is routed to the effects send after the input fader (postfader), if the fader is off, so is the send. Otherwise (prefader) the input sound is always sent to the effects send bus.
Pan pot (panoramic potentiometer)	Controls the spatial location of the sound between two or more channels
Mute, Solo, and PFL	The mute button shuts off a channel. The solo button allows an individual channel to be auditioned. All other channels mute when the solo button is pressed. PFL (*pre-fader listen*) is used when an input channel needs to be checked without opening a fader. For example, radio broadcast engineers push the PFL button to hear the beginning of a record through

Table 9.1 (cont.)

	headphones, but since the fader is down, the audience does not hear it. PFL provides a means to set levels and equalization at a time when a normal soundcheck might be impossible.
Channel assignment (*not shown*)	The channel assignment section is usually a set of buttons, with one button per output bus. The signal passing through the input channel is routed to all output channels selected.
Channel fader (*or potentiometer*)	A linear slider or rotary knob that controls the amplitude (or *gain*) of the sound.

rise time (the time it takes to reach 99 percent of final value) is a few milliseconds, while their *decay time* is over a second. (Different peak reading meters have different specifications.) *Volume unit* (VU) meters have a much slower rise time, on the order of 300 ms, so they tend to reflect the average amplitude (akin to loudness) of the signal over a brief time period. Some meters combine both peak and average characteristics of a signal.

Grouping Facilities

Some mixers have *subgrouping* facilities. These let the engineer to *assign* several input channels to a single fader, called the *submix* or *subgroup fader*. Subsequent movements of the subgroup fader control the level of all the channels assigned to the subgroup simultaneously.

Hybrid Consoles

Digital hardware technology came to mixers in the early 1970s. The first benefit of digital technology was *fader automation*—the ability to recall switch settings and fader positions to recreate a particular mix. (See the section on mix automation later.) Today some mixers are hybrids of digital and analog technology, combining the automation facilities of digital with the wide bandwidth of analog signal processing (figure 9.8). The frequency response of analog circuits often exceeds 100 KHz, which is well beyond the range of digital mixers that are designed to work with the standard 44.1 and 48 KHz sampling frequencies.

Automation systems in hybrid consoles allow the engineer to save mix control data and later recall the mix from memory to reproduce it. To write

Figure 9.8   A large hybrid mixing console (manufactured by Solid State Logic) with analog signal processing controlled by an onboard console computer. Automation is a necessity when operating such a large console. (Photograph courtesy of Capri Digital Studio, Capri.)

mix data, the fader positions (represented by analog voltages) are sampled by an analog-to-digital converter and stored in the console computer.

Playing Back the Mix

Two different schemes may be used to recall or "playback" the mix on the console. In one, the digital mix data for each channel are sent to a digital-to-analog converter, where, in analog form, it controls the level of a *voltage-controlled amplifier* (VCA) (figure 9.9).

Since VCAs may not achieve the audio quality of non-VCA circuits, some manufacturers implement automation by robotic means. That is, the DACs control motors that physically move the faders (and hence the channel level) according to previously recorded motions of a mixing engineer. Motorized faders can be constructed to high standards, performing top to bottom fades in less than 100 ms over 4096 steps of 0.1 dB. In this case, no VCAs are involved in the audio processing. Another advantage of moving faders is that the mixing engineer can see previously recorded mixing levels change over time by watching the fader motions. In order to modify a recorded mix, the engineer can press on a moving fader, overriding computer control and enabling the fader to be adjusted manually.

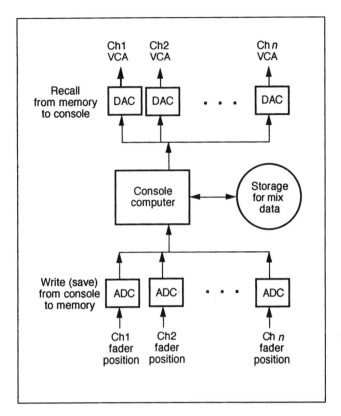

Figure 9.9 The general scheme for writing and recalling mix data in a hybrid (analog-digital) console based on voltage-controlled amplifiers.

Features of Digital Mixing Consoles

Digital mixing consoles have capabilities that are not possible with analog and hybrid consoles. Here are some of these features (not all are available in every digital mixer):

1. Signal processing operations occur in the digital domain, so the artifacts of multiple DAC and ADC conversions are avoided.

2. Control panels can be redesigned to use fewer control knobs. Instead of having one knob for each circuit (up to 4000 knobs, buttons, and sliders on large consoles), *assignable* control knobs manipulate different things at different times. A centralized control facility can be accessed by any channel (figure 9.10), or one fader can be assigned to control any number of input channels.

3. Control panels and mixing hardware can be separated, so a digital control panel takes up much less space than an analog mixer would.

4. Digital effects such as delay, reverberation, and dynamic range processing can be built into the mixer.

5. Other digital technologies like fader automation, automatic signal routing, graphics displays, hardcopy printing, network communications, and computer interfaces can be more easily integrated into the system since all devices "talk digital."

6. To the degree that the system is software-based (i.e., uses programs or microcode to control hardware), the software can be updated to provide improvements or new features.

7. If the mixing hardware is flexible, it can be reconfigured via software to realize different numbers of input and output channels, equalizers, etc., to meet the needs of different sessions. A studio may keep a dozen "patches" with different configurations for various types of studio sessions.

8. Diagnostic routines in software can spot and display error conditions and log instances of errors for later analysis by a technician.

Stand-alone Mixers versus Audio Workstations

In chapter 20 we make the distinction between *fixed-function* and *variable-function* hardware architectures. These internal differences are usually reflected in the external packaging and operation of digital mixing systems. Fixed-function systems are often designed as *stand-alone mixers* optimized for specific audio functions that they perform particularly efficiently (figure 9.11a).

Variable-function audio workstations operate under the guidance of a standard host computer (figure 9.11b). Hence they can run a much wider range of software packages and interface more easily with other computer peripherals. Instead of a stand-alone unit, the mixing hardware may consist of a circuit card or box that plugs into the computer together with faders for controlling audio parameters in real time. The advantage of having many software packages may be illusory, however, if they do not work well together.

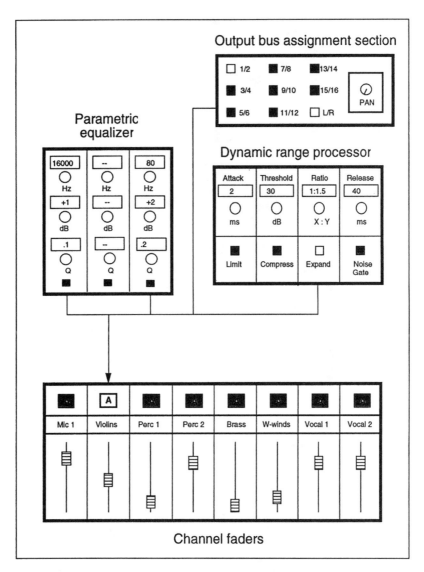

Figure 9.10 In an assignable console, each input channel has a fader, but the console has just one set of controls for equalization, dynamics, output bus assignment, etc. Access to a control on any channel is obtained by touching an *assign button* (marked A) above the relevant fader. This switches control to that channel. In this figure, channel 2 accesses two parametric equalization units, a dynamic range expander, and routes its output to several output busses. Endless turn rotary knobs are ideal assignable controls.

(a)

(b)

Multitrack Recording and Remixing

Early audio recording was *monophonic*—recorded on a single channel. Sound reproduction was correspondingly monophonic, usually through a single loudspeaker. *Stereophonic* (two-channel) recording was pioneered in the 1930s (Blumlein 1933; Keller 1981), and for years all sound recording was based on either one- or two-channel recording. Performances were recorded live, and the relative balance of the various sound sources was fixed at the time of the recording.

In contrast, *multitrack* recorders have several discrete channels or *tracks*, and each track can be recorded at a different time. In the rest of this section we look briefly at the history of multitrack recording, describe its advantages, and also consider the remixing problems it poses.

Multitrack Recording: Background

Working in collaboration with the Ampex Corporation in California, the electric guitarist Les Paul pioneered the concept of overdubbing using multitrack techniques in the 1950s (Bode 1984). Multitrack tape recorders were placed on the market in 1960. That year, Karlheinz Stockhausen used a Telefunken T9 four-track recorder at the West German Radio (WDR) studios to realize his electronic music opus *Kontakte* (Stockhausen 1968; Morawska-Büngeler 1988). By 1964, the Swiss-based Studer company produced its first four-track tape recorder, which was shipped to producer George Martin for the production of the famous *Sgt. Pepper* album by The Beatles.

Chapter 1 recounts the history of digital multitrack recording. Modern professional digital tape recorders can record 48 or more audio channels. If more channels are necessary, several machines can be synchronized. While

Figure 9.11 Standalone mixers versus general purpose workstations. (*a*) A standlone mixer, the Solid State Logic 01, designed for CD master tape production. The left side looks similar to an analog mixing console. (*b*) A multitrack audio workstation (Studer Dyaxis II) operates in conjunction with a standard personal computer (Apple Quadra at left) that can run a wide range of software packages. Other peripherals in the digital mixing studio include an eight-track digital tape recorder (just to the right of the screen). On top of this is a CD recorder. To the right are two professional DAT recorders. (Photograph courtesy of Cornelia Colyer, Center for Computer Music and Music Technology, Kunitachi College of Music, Tokyo.)

certain professional multitrack recorders are expensive, digital multitrack-ing for the small studio is possible using low-cost videotape-based recorders or hard disk-based workstations.

Advantages of Multitrack Recording

Multitrack recording media offer flexibility in several stages of recording practice. First, sound engineers can separate each sound source on its own track. Instead of trying to balance all the channels when the sound is rec-orded, they can postpone the level balancing to the *remix* stage.

For synthesized music, the multitrack approach to recording and the possibility of layering tracks is very attractive. Digital recording allows the possibility of *track-bouncing* (mixing several tracks to a single track on the same machine at the same time) and overdubbing without *generation loss* (i.e., noise buildup caused by copying—a serious constraint with analog media).

Some systems provide digital *sound-on-sound* capabilities. In a sound-on-sound recording, a new sound signal (for example, a two-channel signal) is simply added to an existing signal to make a new two-channel signal. By careful adjustment of the balance between the old and the new signal, com-plex textures can be built up, or an intricate filigree of sound threads can be created step by step.

Problems Posed by Multitrack Remixing

Although it makes recording more flexible, multitrack recording is not a universal panacea. In order to take advantage of the independence offered by multiple channels, sounds on one channel must be isolated from the sounds being recorded on other channels simultaneously. In order to ap-proach this ideal, recording engineers use isolation booths, baffles, direc-tional microphones, and close microphone ranges to achieve maximum isolation. The signals from electric and electronic instruments are fed directly to individual tracks without a microphone.

When these isolated sources are added together, the result is a highly unnatural sound perspective. Particularly when heard through headphones, each track sounds as if one's ear was within inches of each different instru-ment. For music in which the goal is to create a synthetic sound stage (such as much pop and electronic music), this situation is not necessarily a prob-lem. To fuse the individual tracks into a unified sound stage, engineers add global reverberation along with careful balancing and spatial assignment in the stereo plane. If we are not concerned about artificially "unifying" these diverse sources, we can create fantastic and otherworldly artificial spaces by applying spatial effects to individual tracks.

However, when the goal is to recreate the sound image that a listener would hear in a concert hall, the multitrack approach is not ideal. This is the case with much acoustic music (orchestras, ensembles, soloists, vocalists). As a reaction to multitrack practices, some recording engineers have returned to a "purist" approach to recording, using fewer microphones and fewer channels (Streicher and Dooley 1978). Success with the purist approach requires that the engineer properly position the musicians and the microphones in a good-sounding hall. This puts more pressure on the original recording technique since the mix is essentially determined at the time of recording.

Audio Monitoring

The audio monitoring or listening environment is important in recording and mixing. Various monitoring philosophies coexist. We can invoke rational arguments on behalf of each approach, but ultimately the choice is determined by taste and budget.

Headphones

For *location recording* (recording on site, away from the studio), where there is no separate room for listening, headphones are the only option. But headphones are not just for location recording. Listening through good headphones is like viewing a sound under a magnifying glass. Headphones are the best way to check a recording for subtle flaws such as splice points, clicks, noise, distortion, and phase problems. These may not be as obvious on loudspeakers at moderate volume.

Loudspeaker Monitoring

Loudspeakers and rooms work together. In this section we look at three types of loudspeaker monitoring environments: near-field, control room, and listening rooms. By distinguishing three environments we do not mean to suggest that these are the only three—many variations exist. In general, feelings about monitoring environments have evolved in line with the audio fashions of the day.

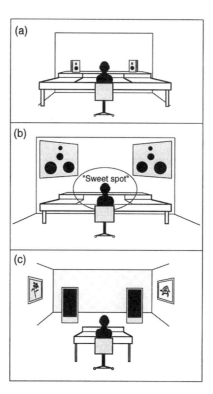

Figure 9.12   Three monitoring environments. (*a*) In a "near-field" monitoring environment, small loudspeakers are positioned within one to two meters of the listener. (*b*) In a control room environment, large wall-mounted loudspeakers about three to five meters from the listener point toward a "sweet spot" at the center of the console. (*c*) In a living room environment, large floor-standing loudspeakers are positioned two to five meters from the listener.

Near-field Monitoring

In small studios and apartments, *near-field* or *close-field* monitors are popular (figure 9.12a). Near-field monitors are also used in large studios when the sound engineer wants to hear what the music sounds like on loudspeakers that are similar to those in most home music systems. Mounted on top of or near the mixing console at ear level, these small dynamic loudspeakers should be less than two meters away from the mixing engineer. In this setup, the direct sound from the loudspeakers predominates over any room-induced indirect reflected sound. The smallness of the near-field monitor is important, since the listener is so close to the unit that the monitor should project a "fused" spatial image; this effect cannot be achieved in close proximity to a large multiple-driver loudspeaker where the *tweeter* (high-frequency driver) may be a meter or more away from the *woofer* (low-frequency driver).

A serious problem with near-field monitors is lack of bass frequency response due to their small size. Two or three octaves of sound may be missing or strongly attenuated in reproduction via near-field monitors.

Control Room Monitoring

Another approach to audio monitoring derives from the design of traditional recording studios, which are split into two parts: the *studio*—where the musicians perform, and the *control room*—where the recording engineering and the mixing console are. The *control room* approach to monitoring involves mounting the loudspeakers in the forward wall of an acoustically tuned environment (figure 9.12b). Each loudspeaker driver can be powered by a separate amplifier; this is referred to as *biamplification* or *triamplification,* depending on the number of drivers in the loudspeaker system. The entire system (including the room) is equalized for flat response at a "sweet spot" centered at the engineer's head. The control room approach supports monitoring at high sound pressure levels, which are typical of large pop music studios.

Listening Room Monitoring

The *listening room* approach places the monitor speakers on or just above the floor in a more informal environment as is typical of a living room (figure 9.12c). The room may be acoustically treated, but not as radically as the pop studio control rooms. The loudspeakers are large, full-range models with flat frequency response and accurate spatial imaging. Three-way *dynamic* loudspeakers (tweeter, midrange diaphragm, low-frequency woofer) or ultrathin *electrostatic* loudspeakers project the sound. The living room approach is preferred by many classical recording engineers and producers for monitoring at moderate levels. Figure 9.13 shows a variation on this approach in a compact disc mastering studio. The rectangle in the center of the front wall is a *diffuser panel* that scatters sound waves in an irregular pattern. This helps break up room resonances.

Mixing and Monitoring in Performance

From the standpoint of judging what the audience is hearing, the best position for mixing a performance of music projected over loudspeakers is in the

Figure 9.13   Example of a "listening room" environment in a compact disc mastering studio. (Photograph courtesy of John Newton at Soundmirror, Boston.)

middle of the hall, among the audience. The question of loudspeaker configuration is an open one, and is primarily an artistic decision. Another aesthetic question occurs in presenting acoustic instruments in combination with electronic sound. Should they be blended or should they be separated? See Morrill (1981b) for a discussion of these issues by a composer who has written many works for instruments and computer-generated sound. See chapter 11 for more on the projection of sound in space.

Mix Automation

Remixing a multitrack recording can be complicated, easily exceeding the physical capabilities of a single human being. Up until the development of *mix automation,* a complicated multitrack mix (such as a film soundtrack) could involve as many as four people working at a single console. The benefit of mix automation is that a lone engineer can perform a complicated mix in a number of simple steps. For example, the engineer may start by mixing two stereo programs, on tracks 1–2 and 3–4. The automation system built into the mixing console records the control information needed to replicate this mix in real time. Once the first step is complete, another stereo program (5–6) can be blended into the mix. At each stage of mixing, previously entered mix data are recalled as the mix is built up incrementally. Only in the final stage is the entire audio mix recorded.

The extent of automation in mixing consoles varies. "Automation" can refer to features as diverse as console reconfiguration at the touch of a button, to *fader automation* (recalling the movement of the channel faders in time), to memorizing all functions and settings entered into a large mixing console for an entire session.

Full-function automation systems continuously scan all settings on the console many times per second. During the scan, the current position of a fader or button is compared to the stored representation of the previous scan. If the position has changed, a burst of data is sent, identifying the control and the new position. On playback, the console computer updates the console controls from memory at the same rate. The engineer can, at any time, override the stored settings by adjusting the desired control knob manually.

MIDI Control of Audio Mixers: Patching and Channel Muting

Although not created for mixing console automation, the Musical Instrument Digital Interface (MIDI) 1.0 specification has had an impact on the design of mixers, particularly those for small studios. (See chapter 21 for more details on MIDI.) Console setup functions can easily be carried out under MIDI control. For example, MIDI *program change messages* can repatch the input/output routing of the mixer, or *mute* (switch off) certain channels at specified times. In these cases, an inexpensive microprocessor built into the mixer interprets the messages and modifies the internal switches of the mixer to accomplish the desired change.

Channel muting is an important production technique in popular music, where it is used in combination with multitrack tape recording. As an example, imagine a drum track recorded on three different channels, each with a different effect applied to the drum. By muting channels on a dynamic basis with a MIDI sequencer, we can switch in different drum effects at different points in the rhythm. Another common application of muting is to record several takes of a vocal performance on different tracks and use muting to select the best parts of each take.

But patching and muting are only two functions out of dozens that occur in a mix, including continuously varying the faders, equalization, spatial panning, and effects. The limited data rate of MIDI does not permit full-function dynamic automation of the type used in large professional consoles (Cooper 1989; Rogers 1987; McGee 1990). MIDI can handle the functions of a small console, but not too many of them at one time and not continuously. MIDI-controlled mixers require compromises in order to reduce the data rate to the range acceptable to MIDI.

Console automation is typically directed by a sequencer that is dedicated exclusively to this task. Since there is no standard for MIDI console automation, three basic schemes are in use, each of which employs a different category of MIDI messages: program change, note/velocity, and MIDI Timecode. (See chapter 21 for an explanation of MIDI messages.)

The use of MIDI's program change messages is exemplified in *MIDI-controlled attenuator* (MCA) systems (figure 9.14). MCAs represent an inexpensive solution to the problem of fader automation for a small studio. The system (usually eight to sixteen audio channels) connects to the inputs of a traditional analog mixer. A MIDI sequencer sends program change messages to the individual channels of the MCA, causing the amplitude of the

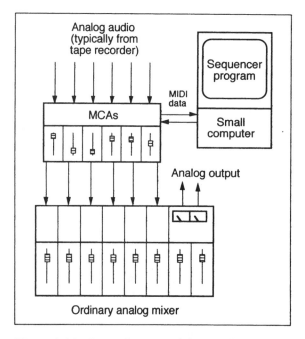

Figure 9.14 Setup for a remixing session with a MIDI-controlled attenuator (MCA) system for a 6/2 analog mixer. The levels on the analog mixer stay at unity, while the recording engineer manipulates the levels on the MCA mixer. As each channel's mix is perfected, the control data is recorded as a track in the MIDI sequencer, allowing a complicated mix to be built up a step at a time.

channels to change. Programming a mix is a matter of creating and saving static snapshots or "scenes" for each point in the music where changes in fader settings are to occur. In some systems you can specify a *crossfade time* during which the system automatically changes from the old to the new setting—simulating a form of quasi-continuous control.

Another approach is to assign each control knob and button on the mixing console to a MIDI note message. As the sound engineer changes a knob setting, the console sends note events indicating a change in that knob. Since each MIDI note event has a 7-bit "velocity" associated with it, this velocity value is interpreted as the new value of the knob. Seven bits means that 128 fader values can be represented, which may result in "stepped" fades since the fader resolution is low.

The third approach to MIDI console automation involves sending *cue messages* via MIDI Timecode (see chapter 21 and the section on MIDI Timecode later in this chapter). The cue messages are sent in advance of the action time. They might, for example, tell the mixer to begin a fade at a certain rate at a particular timecode point.

Synchronization of Audio Mixing and Video

This section discusses an increasingly important subject in mixing studios: multiple-machine *synchronization*. Synchronization in this case means that the operation of one or more devices is simultaneous and parallel. A typical application of synchronization occus in *video postproduction* (mixing the soundtrack to a video production). Here the goal is to synchronize an audio multitrack recorder (containing the dialog, sound effects, and music tracks on separate channels) with an edited video production. The audio machine must follow the video playback so that we watch and listen to the synchronized image and sound.

Later, in the section on MIDI Timecode, we present several other applications of synchronization, such as control of sequencers, effects, and sound file playback via MIDI. This section does not discuss another type of synchronization, namely *sample clock synchronization* for digital audio. Chapter 22 presents this type of synchronization, along with more on SMPTE and MIDI-based synchronization links.

Multiple-machine Synchronization

Multiple-machine synchronization links machines together via cables to a *synchronizer*—a standard device in audio/video postproduction suites and an increasingly common item in music studios. The synchronizer's job is to read *timecode* already recorded on both machines, and ensure that one machine follows the other. Timecode labels a special track on each machine with a unique identifying address called a *frame*. Each frame always retains its original identity, making operations such as editing and synchronization efficient and frame-accurate. (See the section on SMPTE timecode later.)

The synchronizer links the behavior of one machine, called the *master*, to the other machine(s), called the *slave*(s), by tracking the timecode locations on the master. In the case of tape recorders, the synchronizer does this by controlling the tape transport of the slave machines. When the master moves to a given timecode location, the slave machine follows.

In disk-based systems, the synchronizer accomplishes the same task by telling the disk controller of the slave to access specified addresses. For example, some disk recorders can be programmed to play back sound files when they read certain timecode addresses from a master machine.

Figure 9.15 shows a typical layout for audio/video postproduction—the process of layering on sound effects, dialogue, and music to a videotape. Both an audio multitrack audio recorder and a professional videotape recorder (VTR) are linked to a synchronizer. One track on the audio multi-

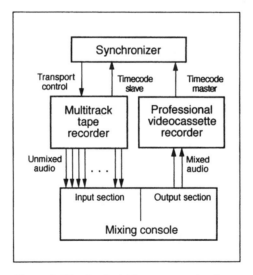

Figure 9.15   Audio/video postproduction configuration for remixing a soundtrack on a multitrack audio tape recorder to a professional videocassette recorder. The audio multitrack and the video machine are both connected to a synchronizer. The videocassette recorder is the master, and the audio multitrack is the slave, in this case. That is, a tape playing back on the video machine causes timecode to be sent to the synchronizer, which in turn controls the transport of the multitrack recorder.

track and a track on the VTR each contain timecode that was *striped* (written) onto each tape separately by a *timecode generator*. The sounds on the audio multitrack at a given point correspond to the images on the VTR.

When the recording engineer advances the videotape, the synchronizer reads the new timecode location and tells the audio multitrack recorder to follow it as closely as possible. To record audio on the videotape, the recording engineer presses a button on the VTR as the audio multitrack begins to play. The recording engineer mixes the tracks coming from the multitrack into a stereo version for the VTR. (This mix can also be automated in a separate phase of production.)

SMPTE Timecode

The standard timecode formats are all grouped under the rubric of *SMPTE timecode*. SMPTE stands for the Society of Motion Picture and Television Engineers. Two basic varieties of SMPTE timecode exist: *longitudinal timecode* (LTC) recorded horizontally on the side of a tape, and *vertical interval timecode* (VITC) recorded in a frame of a *helically scanned* videotape. (Helical scanning refers to the usual type of videotape recorder in which the playback and record heads spin vertically as the tape passes by horizontally. The recording heads write information in densely packed vertical strips.) Longitudinal timecode can be further subdivided into *24-frame/second* (film), *25-frame/second* (PAL), *30-frame/second* (black-and-white), and *drop-frame* (NTSC). SMPTE's data rate is 2400 bits/second.

The advantage of VITC is that it can be read from a tape in video still-frame mode. A disk-based system can use any SMPTE format, but in synchronization applications it is important to specify the correct frame rate, or else audible problems may occur due to dynamic changes in the time base.

All SMPTE formats represent time as an 80-bit number with fields for hours, minutes, seconds, and frames. For example, the SMPTE code "01:58:35:21" means 1 hour, 58 minutes, 35 seconds, and 21 frames. Since the timecode itself does not take up all 80 bits, there is room to encode other information along with the timecode, such as elapsed time, index numbers, or labels. When any event is marked by a SMPTE timecode, that timecode becomes a permanent address for that event. For more details on SMPTE timecode, see Hickman (1984).

As explained previously, in a typical setup, each device to be synchronized writes a form of SMPTE timecode on one track. Many recorders have a special track allocated specifically for recording SMPTE timecode. Slave machines follow the timecode being read from a master machine.

MIDI Timecode

MIDI can also be used for quasi-synchronous mixing. (Inherent MIDI transmission delays mean that synchronization to the millisecond is not possible.) Typical applications include the following:

1. One MIDI keyboard can control several synthesizers and samplers so that the sound of several MIDI-linked synthesizers can be mixed as a musician performs on the controlling keyboard.

2. A MIDI sequencer can store a series of notes whose playback is *triggered* at a certain point in a mix.

3. A sequencer can also store a previously encoded series of program changes for a MIDI-controllable effects unit. In this way, complex sequences of effects can be automatically applied to sounds being mixed. (A variation on this is MIDI-controlled channel muting, described in a previous section.)

4. Some computer-based sound file systems can play back a series of sound files in response to a trigger message sent via MIDI.

The main technical question in applications (2), (3), and (4) is: How do we trigger the start of MIDI sequences to achieve quasi-synchronous playback of a sequence with the rest of the audio signals? A direct method is manu-

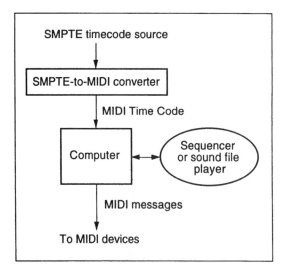

Figure 9.16 Logical flow of data in SMPTE-to-MIDI timecode conversion. A SMPTE timecode source, such as a video playback, sends timecode to the converter. The MIDI timecode is interpreted by a MIDI sequencer or a sound file playback program, which in turn controls other MIDI devices.

ally, by pressing a button on a computer keyboard to initiate a sequence. A more consistent method is via a connection between SMPTE timecode and MIDI Timecode (MTC).

In this scheme, a track of SMPTE timecode is striped onto an audio multichannel recorder, for example, and played back along with audio data on other tracks. The SMPTE timecode track is routed to a *SMPTE-to-MIDI converter* box. This box converts a SMPTE time into MTC, which can trigger the start of a MIDI sequence or the playback of a sound file (figure 9.16). Triggering points are called *cues* in the jargon of synchronization. Various sequencer programs provide support for this scheme.

Exotic musical synchronization schemes can be developed with interactive MIDI performance software. See chapters 15 and 21 for more information.

Conclusion

Sound mixing is just one stage in a production process that begins with recording, editing, and signal processing. But mixing is more than technical craft; it requires musical insight and judgement. In the studio and onstage, the mixing engineer plays a role analogous to the conductor in a concert hall, responsible for the overall balance of voices within a composition.

The critical choice of monitoring environment is largely a matter of taste and convention, whereas in console automation and synchronization there is a more linear relationship between price, quality, and features. Meanwhile, mixing technology continues to evolve. This is reflected in the wide range of approaches that characterize the scene, from analog and hybrid consoles, to a variety of software systems, stand-alone digital mixers, and audio workstations. We have tried to show that no single approach is ideal for all musical situations.

The increasing storage capacities of digital media make it possible to store thousands of sound files in a single system. Several hundred files may go into a single intricate mix. An unresolved issue is how to organize and access so many files efficiently, a likely problem for audio database management systems of the future (see chapter 16).

10 *Basic Concepts of Signal Processing*

Dynamic Range Processing

        Envelope Shapers
        Noise Gates
        Compressors
        Peak versus Average Detectors
        Compression Ratio
        Expanders
        Limiters
        Noise Reduction Units and Companders
        Dangers of Dynamic Range Processing

Digital Filters

        Presenting Filter Theory to Musicians
        Filters: Background
        Impulse, Frequency, and Phase Response of a Filter
        Filters as Equations
        Simple Lowpass Filter
        Simple Highpass Filter
        General Finite-impulse-response Filters
        Simple Infinite-impulse-response Filters
        General Infinite-impulse-response Filters
        FIR versus IIR Filters
        Filter Design from an Arbitrary Specification
        Building Blocks of Complicated Filters
        Comb Filters
        FIR Comb Filters
        IIR Comb Filters
        Allpass Filters

Convolution

The Operation of Convolution
Convolution by Scaled and Delayed Unit Impulses
Mathematical Definition of Convolution
Comparison of Convolution with Multiplication
The Law of Convolution
Relationship of Convolution to Filtering
Fast Convolution
Musical Signifance of Convolution
Filtering as Convolution
Temporal Effects of Convolution
Modulation as Convolution
Convolution with Grains
Linear versus Circular Convolution
Deconvolution

Fixed Time Delay Effects

Comparison of DDL with FIR Lowpass and Comb Filters
Implementation of a Delay Line
Fixed Delay Effects
Delays and Sound Localization

Variable Time Delay Effects

Flanging
Phasing
Chorus Effects

Time/Pitch Changing

Time/Pitch Changing by Time-granulation
Electromechanical Time-granulation
Digital Time-granulation
Time/Pitch Changing with a Harmonizer
Time/Pitch Changing with the Phase Vocoder
Overlap-add Transformations
Tracking Phase Vocoder Transformations

Conclusion

This chapter introduces the basic concepts behind the most important signal-processing operations available to musicians: dynamic range alterations, filters, convolution, time delay effects, and time/pitch changing. These operations directly transform sound. Chapters 12 and 13 present another class of signal-processing operations: sound analysis techniques such as pitch detection, rhythm recognition, and spectrum analysis.

Dynamic Range Processing

Dynamic range techniques transform the amplitude of signals. These serve as the foundation of devices such as *envelope shapers, noise gates, compressors, limiters, expanders, noise reduction units,* and *companders* (McNally 1984). The applications of dynamic range processing vary from practical tasks such as cleaning up noisy signals to creative tasks such as reshaping the envelope of an instrument or voice.

Envelope Shapers

Most sound-editing systems let musicians rescale the overall amplitude envelope of a sampled sound. This rescaling may involve a simple change in gain (i.e., some number of dB higher or lower in amplitude), or a redesign of the overall envelope of a sound. The reshaping can apply to an individual sound object or to an entire section of music.

Figure 10.1 shows how the sharp attack of a harpsichord tone has been rounded off by the envelope shown in 10.1b. The middle portion of the tone becomes a kind of sustained ringing before it fades out.

Noise Gates

A noise gate is one way to clean up music signals that are obscured by a constant noise, such as hiss or hum. In general, the noise is assumed to be below the level of the music signal. The noise gate functions as a switch that is open when higher-amplitude music signals pass through it, but switches off when the music stops, thus cutting off any residual system noise. In particular, when the peak amplitude of the input signal to a noise gate drops below a specific *threshold,* the noise gate maximally attenuates (switches off) the input signal. Figure 10.2 depicts this process. In figure 10.2a, a noisy signal fades until all that is heard is noise. In figure 10.2b, as soon as the signal drops below the threshold, the noise gate eliminates both the signal and the noise.

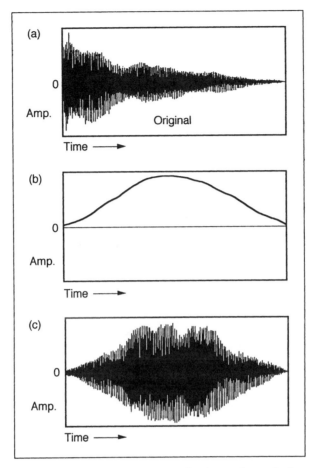

Figure 10.1 Reshaping the amplitude envelope of a harpsichord tone. (*a*) Original tone. (*b*) New envelope drawn by hand. (*c*) Reshaped harpsichord tone that follows the outline of the new envelope.

It should be obvious that a simple noise gate cannot eliminate noise when the music signal is playing, so this device works well only when the music signal masks the noise signal.

Compressors

A compressor is an amplifier whose gain (i.e., amount of amplification) is controlled by its input signal. One use of a compressor is to keep the output signal relatively constant. When the input signal rises above a specified upper bound, the compressor attenuates it.

A good way to characterize a compressor is by its *transfer function,* which shows how a given amplitude value sent into the device is mapped to a given

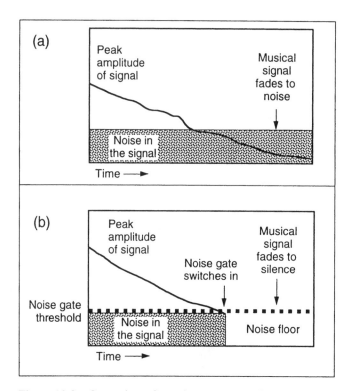

Figure 10.2   Operation of a noise gate. (*a*) Without a noise gate, a musical signal that contains low-level noise fades to noise. (*b*) With a noise gate, the fading signal crosses the noise gate threshold so the noise gate switches in. Hence the signal fades to silence instead of to a mixture of signal and noise.

amplitude value at the output. This representation of a transfer function is exactly the same as that used to explain waveshaping synthesis in chapter 6.

Figure 10.3 shows the transfer functions of several dynamic range processors. We can think of the input signal coming into the box from the bottom and exiting out to the right. Figure 10.3a shows a perfectly linear transfer function. A value of -1 on the bottom maps to a value of -1 on the right; a value of $+1$ on the bottom maps to $+1$ on the right, and so on.

Figure 10.3b shows the transfer function and processed waveform for a relatively "soft" compression effect. Note how peaks on the input map to lesser values on the output of the transfer function.

Peak versus Average Detectors

Inside the compressor, a *detector* circuit monitors the amplitude of the input signal. The detector circuits in compressors can respond to either *peak* or *average* amplitude of the input. A peak detector reacts to amplitude peaks

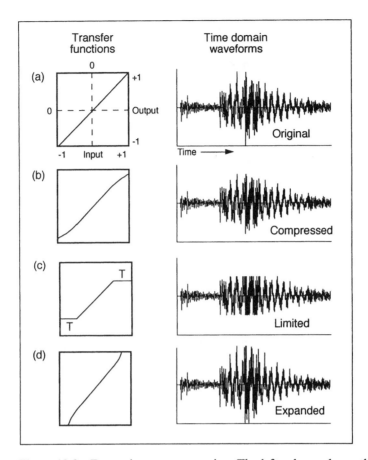

Figure 10.3 Dynamic range processing. The left column shows the transfer functions associated with the various processing methods. (*a*) Original signal—a cymbal crash with a linear transfer function. (*b*) Soft compression of peaks scales them down several dB. (*c*) Hard limiting flattens peaks to keep them within the threshold boundaries indicated by T. (*d*) Expansion exaggerates peaks, creating several new ones.

even if these occur for just an instant. The dynamic range processors shown in figure 10.3 are all peak-based. In contrast, an average detector responds more slowly to the overall amplitude of the signal, typically over a period of one or two seconds. Peak detectors react quickly, providing good insurance against amplitude overload. On the other hand, average detectors provide smoother response to input signal changes.

Compression Ratio

The *compression ratio* or *input/output ratio* is the ratio of change of the input signal versus the change in the output signal. An ordinary amplifier has a compression ratio of 1:1. A ratio of 4:1 means that a 4 dB change in the input signal causes only a 1 dB change in the output signal. Compression ratios greater than about 8:1 tend to "squash" the signal audibly, flattening transients and thereby introducing timbral changes.

High compression is a common cliché in the production of popular music. For example, ratios in the range of 10:1 make pop vocals sound "intimate" due to the exaggeration of tongue gesticulations, lip smacking, saliva dripping, and breathing noises when all vocalisms are scaled to the same amplitude range. With plucked string instruments like electric guitars, extreme compression creates sostenuto effects. That is, the compressor reduces the pluck transient while elevating the overall level by a large factor. When this compressed signal is highly amplified, as in electric guitars, it reinforces sustained oscillation of the string.

Expanders

An *expander* is the opposite of a compressor. It exaggerates small changes in its input signal into wide-ranging changes in its output signal. The *expansion ratio* determines the degree of expansion. For example, an expansion ratio of 1:5 means that a 1 dB change in the input signal is converted into a 5 dB change in the output signal. A main application is restoring old recordings. Noise reduction units often contain compressor-expander pairs, as we explain in a moment. Figure 10.3d shows a peak expansion effect applied to the input signal of figure 10.3a.

Limiters

Limiting is extreme compression—where the compression ratios are beyond 10:1. As figure 10.3c shows, the relationship between the input and the output is linear up to a certain level. This level is indicated by the positive and negative threshold bounds **T**. (Note: in practical systems, one specifies a single absolute value for the threshold, rather than separate upper and lower bounds.) Beyond the threshold the output remains constant regardless of the input level.

Limiters are used in live concert recording when it is imperative not to overload the absolute dynamic range of any component in the recording chain. For example, digital recorders have an absolute input level threshold beyond which harsh numerical clipping distortion occurs. A recording engineer might insert a limiter before the recorder inputs to ensure that the recorder's threshold is never exceeded.

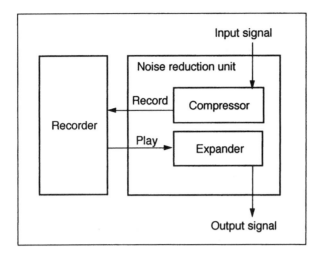

Figure 10.4   Noise reduction units compress on recording and expand on playback.

Noise Reduction Units and Companders

Noise reduction (NR) units usually employ a compressor on the input stage of a recorder and an expander on the output stage (figure 10.4). For this reason, they are sometimes called *companders* (a contraction of compressor and expander). The compressor stage reduces transients and boosts the rest of the input signal to an artificially high level. On playback, the expander stage restores the dynamic range of the original. Since the compressed recording contains little noise (it is all recorded at a moderately high level above the noise floor of the recorder), the result is a low-noise but wide dynamic range recording.

Figure 10.5 depicts the process of compansion. The dynamic range of the recording shrinks within the noisy channel (e.g., an analog cassette recorder or a low-bit-rate digital recorder). The recording signal remains at a high enough level to avoid some of the noise in the noisy channel, but is low enough to avoid clipping or overload distortion.

Certain noise reduction schemes, like those developed by Dolby Laboratories, carry out compression and expansion in a frequency-dependent way. That is, the input signal is filtered into several frequency bands, each of which is compressed and expanded separately—a process called *bandsplitting*. By segregating the compansion into individual frequency bands, each with their own compression and expansion curves, the side effects of compansion can be made less audible. Only certain bands, for example, may need to be companded; the rest can be left as they are.

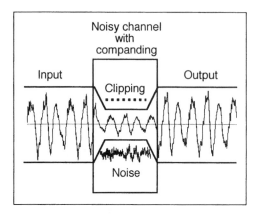

Figure 10.5 Companding noise reduction unit reduces the wide dynamic range going into the noisy channel. It tries to keep the signal above the noise level and below the clipping level. The final stage of the compander expands the dynamic range.

Sounds that cross frequency bands, like continuous glissandi, may still pose a problem for such systems, since audible artifacts can occur as each band's noise reduction circuits trigger into operation. Moreover, even small irregularities (<1 dB) in the amplitude-versus-frequency response of the bands can lead to audible colorations in the overall sound (Lagadec and Pelloni 1983). (See chapter 5 for a definition of amplitude-versus-frequency response.)

Dangers of Dynamic Range Processing

In general, it is difficult to alter the amplitude of a sound in a time-varying way without introducing distortions to waveform *transients*—the sharp edges of attacks and some decays that serve as a principal timbre cue. Transients can be smeared easily by dynamic range processing; thus, these techniques should be used with full knowledge of their side effects.

Dynamic range processors impose attack and decay envelopes on a global basis, affecting all sounds passed through them, regardless of musical context. They react to the amplitude of the signal passing through them. The reaction delay between the "cause" (an amplitude variation in the signal) and the "effect" (switching in the processing) is a well-known problem. Certain devices reduce this effect by delaying the input signal slightly and "looking ahead" to see if there are any waveforms that will trigger dynamic range processing. If so, they can switch in the effect more or less synchronously with these waveforms. Other processors employ no such lookahead. One can change the "trigger threshold" to cause it to react more quickly, but then the effect switches in and out too often, leading to a noticeable "pumping" sound.

No single setting of trigger threshold, envelope, and delay is optimal for any more than one sound. Thus, adjusting these parameters is usually a compromise between no processing on the one hand, and audible distortion on the other. In the case of compression, it is precisely this quality of distortion that many pop music producers seek. Ultimately, compression, like any effect, is easy to overuse.

Digital Filters

A committee of signal-processing engineers defined a filter as follows:

A digital filter is a computational process or algorithm by which a digital signal or sequence of numbers (acting as input) is transformed into a second sequence of numbers termed the output digital signal. (Rabiner et al. 1972)

Thus, any digital device with an input and an output is a filter! The most common use of the term describes devices that boost or attenuate regions of a sound spectrum. Reverberators and audio delay lines are also filters. This should hint at the fact that a filter can change not only the spectrum of an input signal, but also its temporal structure—either on a fine scale (delaying the certain frequency regions by a few microseconds), or on a large scale (delaying the entire signal for hundreds of milliseconds).

Presenting Filter Theory to Musicians

The theory of digital filtering is a rarefied specialty, couched in mathematics that are removed from human experience. The equation of a digital filter, for example, does not necessarily reveal its audio qualities. This is unfortunate, since perception and emotion are sharply attuned to the effects of filters. The profound subject of the aesthetics of filtering is seldomly addressed in the signal-processing literature (Gerzon 1990, Rossum 1992, and Massie and Stonick 1992 are exceptions), even though the impact of filters on musical sound can range from the sublime to the horrific. Musicians speak of filters as being "harsh" or "warm" or "musical" in an attempt to describe these different effects. Perhaps more precise terminology will evolve as this art matures.

Standing between our subjective experience of filters and their practical implementation is a forest of theory. Myriad representations explain the operation of filters. Electrical engineering texts inevitably describe filters by means of the *z transform*. The *z* transform maps the effects of sample delays into a two-dimensional image of the frequency domain called the *complex z plane*. *Poles* above this plane represent resonance peaks, while *zeros* represent points of null amplitude. A *two-pole filter*, for example, has two resonance peaks. The *z* transform is an essential concept for professional filter designers, since it provides a mathematical bridge between the desired characteristics of the filter and its implementation parameters. But the chain of reasoning required to explain the *z* transform and its applications is long and abstract, only indirectly related to parameters that have physical significance.

Thus our presentation of filter theory takes a simpler and more musical approach. We characterize the internals of filters in terms of delays and simple arithmetical operations on samples, which is how a filter is represented in software. We present images of signal flow, impulse response, and frequency response to complement the explanations. Taken with the explanation of basic filter concepts in chapter 5, this presentation covers the essential knowledge needed by musicians using filters in composition and performance.

Adventurous readers who trek the woods of filter theory will find hundreds of papers to wander through. The better musically motivated papers include Moore (1978b, 1990), Cann (1979–1980), Smith (1985a, b), and Moorer (1981b, 1983a). See also the fine tutorials on filter design by Hutchins (1982–1988), complete with code listings. Dozens of engineering textbooks are devoted to filters, either wholly or in part.

After a brief historical note, the rest of this section presents the fundamental notion of the impulse response of a filter, and explicates the implementation of simple lowpass and highpass filters. It contrasts the two basic filter structures, discusses filter design, and presents filter sections, comb filters, and allpass filters.

Filters: Background

Primordial electronic music devices used analog filters to shape the raw waveforms emitted by their tone generators, a process dubbed *subtractive tone forming* by Douglas (1968). Among the notable instruments that contained filters were the Mixtur-Trautonium, Solovox, Clavioline, Warbo Formant Organ, Hammond Novachord, RCA Synthesizer, and the Ondioline (Jenny 1958; Rhea 1972; Bode 1984).

Stand-alone analog filters like the Albis Tonfrequenz filter (figure 10.6) were standard components in electronic music facilities such as the West German Radio (WDR) studio in which K. Stockhausen, G. M. Koenig,

**ALBISWERK
ZURICH S.A.**

You may obtain any desired
frequency characteristic in
acoustical transmission

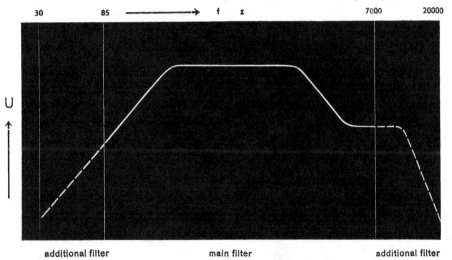

with the variable **ALBIS
voice-frequency filter.**

The variable ALBIS voice-frequency filter is used in many Radio-
and TV-Studios, in several research
laboratories, institutes and fac-
torys, as well as in clinics in
Switzerland and abroad.

Top : **main filter**
Bottom : **additional filter**

ALBISWERK ZURICH S.A.
ZURICH 9/47 SWITZERLAND

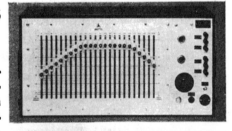

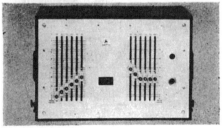

Figure 10.6 Albis "voice-frequency" (Tonfrequenz) filter, a graphic equalizer used
extensively in the electronic music studios of the West German Radio, Cologne.

J.-C. Eloy, and other composers worked in the 1950s and 1960s. Later, voltage-controlled filters typified the golden era of modular analog synthesizers (Chamberlin 1985; Rossum 1992).

Experiments with digital filter circuits began in the 1950s. The theory of digital filtering was pushed forward in the 1960s with the general adoption of the *z* transform calculus (Kaiser 1963; Rabiner and Gold 1975). Simple digital filters appeared in sound synthesis languages such as Music IV and Music 4B (Mathews and Miller 1963; Winham 1966). Large and expensive synthesizers like the Systems Concepts Digital Synthesizer (Samson 1980, 1985) and Giuseppe Di Giugno's 4X (Asta et al. 1980) could realize dozens of digital filters in real time. But it was not until the late 1980s that speedups in hardware made it possible to implement real-time digital filters in low-cost synthesizers, plug-in signal-processing cards, effects units, and digital sound mixers.

Impulse, Frequency, and Phase Response of a Filter

We can view the effects of a filter in either the time domain or the frequency domain. "Before" and "after" images of the signal show the effects of filtration (figure 10.7). Of course, some inputs reveal the filter's effects more clearly than others. Is there an ideal input signal that will clearly characterize the response of all filters? In order to thoroughly test the filter, we need a signal that contains all frequencies. White noise, which contains all frequencies, will tell us how the filter responds in the frequency domain. But an equally important measure of a filter is how it responds to transients. For this we need a measure of its response in the time domain.

As Fourier showed in the eighteenth century, an inverse relationship exists between the duration of a signal and its frequency content. A sine wave of infinite duration expresses a sole frequency. As we shrink the duration of the sine wave, its Fourier spectrum becomes more and more complicated. That is, we need to add together more and more sine waves, which finally cancel each other out, to create a short-duration signal. Thus, the shorter the signal, the wider its spectrum.

In a digital system, the briefest possible signal lasts just one sample. This signal contains energy at all frequencies that can be represented at the given sampling frequency. Hence, a general way of characterizing a filter is to view its response to a one-sample pulse, which is an approximation to the abstract and infinitely brief *unit impulse* or *Kronecker delta*. The output signal generated by a filter that is fed a unit impulse is called the *impulse response* (IR) of the filter. The IR corresponds exactly to the system's amplitude-versus-frequency response. (Chapter 5 explains this term, colloquially

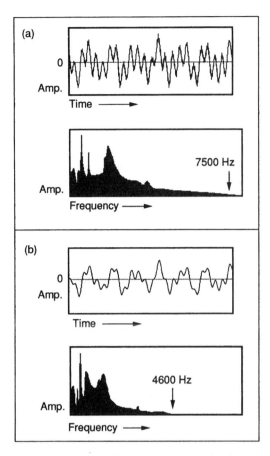

Figure 10.7   The effect of an attenuating lowpass filter, shown in both time-domain and frequency-domain views. (*a*) Segment of an original signal emitted by a Dulcitone (English keyboard instrument of the nineteenth century). (*b*) Same tone, lowpass filtered by −12 dB at 3000 Hz. Notice the bandwidth reduction.

called the "frequency response.") The IR and the frequency response contain the same information—the filter's response to the unit impulse—but plotted in different domains. That is, the IR is a time-domain representation, and the frequency response is a frequency-domain representation. The bridge between the two domains is convolution, explained later.

Figure 10.8a shows how a sharp boosting filter stretches the energy in an impulse. In general, a long IR corresponds to a narrow frequency response, since a sharp narrow filter causes an effect for a significant time after the original impulse. As we see in chapter 13, the long "lag time" of narrow filters becomes problematic in spectrum analysis. On the other hand, a short IR corresponds to a broad, smooth frequency response. Figure 10.8b displays the effect of a smoothing lowpass filter.

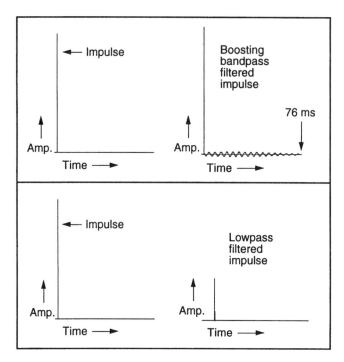

Figure 10.8   Effects of filters on impulses. (*a*) Boosting bandpass filter. At left is a line indicating an impulse. At right is the same impulse filtered by +24 dB at 200 Hz, with a narrow band filter (20 Hz bandwidth). Notice the low-level "ripple" extending the response out to 76 ms. (*b*) Lowpass filter. Cut of −15 dB at 1 KHz.

Another characteristic of filters is their effect on the phase of sinusoidal signals sent through them. The *phase response* of a filter plots the phase shift (in radians) experienced by each sinusoidal component of the input signal (Smith 1985a). Perhaps a more intuitive measurement is *phase delay*, which plots the phase shift as a time delay (in seconds) experienced by each sinusoidal component fed into the filter.

Filters as Equations

Besides looking at images of impulse responses, we can also describe a digital filter by an equation that relates an input signal to an output signal. The output of the equation is described as a result of sums, differences, and multiplications of current and past input samples. The technical term for this type of equation is *linear difference equation*. Linearity means that if the input to a filter is a sum of two scaled functions, the output is the same as the sum of each of these functions fed separately into the filter. See Rabiner and Gold (1975) or any signal-processing textbook for more on linear difference equations.

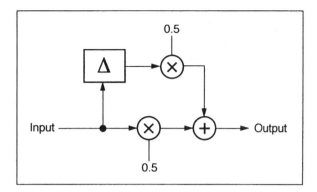

Figure 10.9 A simple averaging filter attenuates ("rolls off") high frequencies to up to half the sampling rate. See the text for an explanation of the notation used in this and subsequent figures.

In the signal-processing literature, the input signal fed into the filter is conventionally called *x*, and the output is *y*. The input and output samples are numbered or indexed (e.g., the sample at time *n*, the next sample at *n* + 1, etc.), and the sample number is often put in brackets. So *x*[0] is the zeroth sample of the input, *x*[1] is the next input sample, and so on.

Simple Lowpass Filter

A simple lowpass filter averages the values of the current and previous input samples. That is, it adds the current input sample with the previous input sample and divides by two. An averaging filter tends to smooth out jags in the input signal. Such jags are sudden changes and therefore represent high-frequency components. The equation for a simple averaging filter is as follows:

$$y[n] = (0.5 \times x[n]) + (0.5 \times x[n - 1]).$$

current	half of	half of
output	the current	the previous
	input	input

The scaling constants (0.5) in the expression are called the *filter coefficients*. Figure 10.9 shows a circuit that realizes this equation.

Note that in this and subsequent circuit figures, the following notation applies: arrows indicate signal flow, lines without arrows indicate coefficient inputs (to multipliers and adders), the small black dot indicates a branching point where a signal branches to two different destinations, the × sign

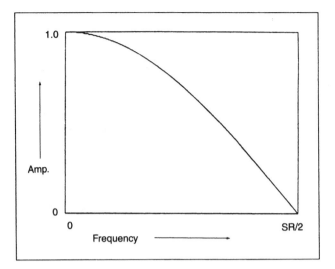

Figure 10.10   Frequency response of the simple averaging lowpass filter shown in figure 10.9.

indicates a multiplication, the + sign indicates an addition, and the Δ indicates a delay of one sample period.

Figure 10.10 depicts the frequency response of the filter, which looks like the first quadrant of a cosine wave. Averaging not just two samples, but three, four, or more samples enhances the high-frequency attenuation effect of the filter. This averaging over several samples is equivalent to connecting two or more like filters in series.

Simple Highpass Filter

Next we present a *highpass* filter that attenuates low frequencies. This filter subtracts samples instead of adding them. That is, it calculates the differences between successive pairs of samples:

$$y[n] = (0.5 \times x[n]) - (0.5 \times x[n-1]).$$

current   half of   half of
output   the current   the previous
          input   input

Now the output sample $y[n]$ is the current input sample minus the previous input sample, divided by two. A highpass filter suppresses low frequencies—where the differences between samples are small—and it exaggerates high frequencies because the differences between successive samples are

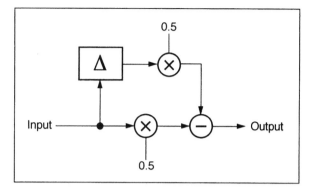

Figure 10.11   Circuit of a simple highpass filter that subtracts successive input samples.

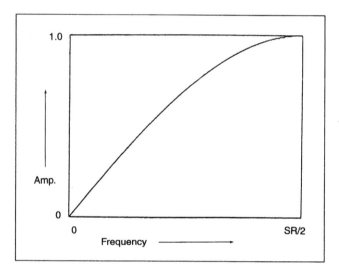

Figure 10.12   Frequency response of the simple highpass filter depicted in figure 10.11.

large. Figure 10.11 shows the circuit that realizes this equation. Figure 10.12 plots the filter's frequency response.

To make this filter (or the preceding lowpass filter) more flexible, we can transform the constant coefficients valued at 0.5 into variables a_0 and a_1 as in this equation:

$$y[n] = (a_0 \times x[n]) - (a_1 \times x[n-1]).$$

The coefficient with a subscript 0 indicates a nondelayed signal, while a subscript of 1 indicates a one-sample delay. By changing the value of the coefficients, one changes the frequency response of the filter.

General Finite-impulse-response Filters

The general equation for such a filter is as follows:

$$y[n] = (a_0 \times x[n]) \pm (a_1 \times x[n-1]) \pm \ldots (a_i \times x[n-i])$$

where a_i is the last coefficient and $x[i]$ is the last stored sample. The coefficients can be positive or negative, for lowpass or highpass applications, respectively.

A general filter of this type can be likened to a *delay line*—a recirculating memory unit that delays incoming signals by i samples. The memory of this delay line goes back only a finite distance in time—i samples—corresponding to the length of the delay line. Thus, the filter's response to a brief input signal (such as in impulse) dies away after a finite period of time. For this reason, such filters are called *finite-impulse-response* (FIR) filters.

Figure 10.13 shows the structure of such a filter, which is also called a *transversal filter*. In effect, the input signal enters a delay line n samples long. The filter multiplies the input and all its delayed versions by fractional coefficients and then sums them to obtain the output. By adjusting the

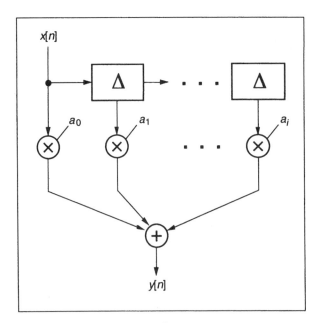

Figure 10.13   General FIR filter structure, consisting of a series of one-sample delays, such that by the last delay unit, the input signal has been delayed i samples. Each of these delayed signals is scaled by a corresponding coefficient a. The output is the sum of all these scaled and delayed samples.

coefficients, the filter response can be controlled down to a lower limiting frequency of approximately the sample rate divided by the number of stages of delay. For example, at a sampling rate of 44.1 KHz, a ten-stage FIR lowpass filter rolls off frequencies down to about 4400 Hz.

The greater the length of the filter, the narrower its transition band, and the sharper its cutoff. Not surprisingly, a longer filter requires more computation. In practice, there is a length above which little perceivable sharpness is gained, though the peaks on the side of the main lobe of the filter (i.e., the *ripple peaks*) become more numerous and crowd together (figure 10.14).

Simple Infinite-impulse-response Filters

If we route the filter's output back into its input, the filter blends more of the past history of the signal than a simple FIR filter can, and with fewer coefficients. Fewer coefficients means fewer multiplies, and therefore less computation. A filter that uses past output samples is said to operate by means of *feedback* or *recursion*. Because the length of this history is potentially infinite, such a filter is called an *infinite-impulse-response* (IIR) or *recursive* filter.

An example of a simple IIR filter is an *exponential time average* (ETA) filter. The ETA filter adds the current input $x[n]$ to its last output $y[n-1]$ and divides by two to generate the new output sample:

$$y[n] = (0.5 \times x[n]) + (0.5 \times y[n-1]).$$

Figure 10.15 presents a signal flow graph of the filter, showing the feedback path. Figure 10.16 plots the frequency response of the ETA filter. Analysis of this filter shows that it is equal to an "infinitely long" FIR filter:

$$y[n] = (1/2 \times x[n]) + [1/4 \times x[n-1]) + [1/8 \times x[n-2]) \ldots .$$

As with FIR filters, one can substitute variable coefficients in place of constants:

$$y[n] = (a \times x[n]) + (b \times y[n-1]).$$

Here we use the notational convention that b coefficients modify the feedback path. As b increases, the filter cutoff frequency moves lower. (The term cutoff frequency is defined in chapter 5.) The absolute value of coefficient b must always be less than 1.0 or the filter becomes *unstable*. In an unstable filter, the output values $y[n]$ grow larger and larger, resulting in numerical *overflow* (numbers bigger than the audio converters can handle) and a distorted sound.

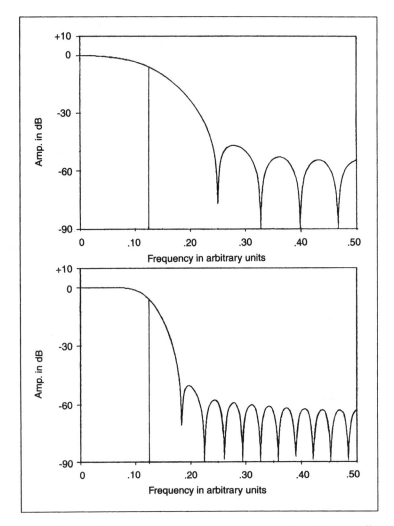

Figure 10.14   Frequency response plot comparing the filter cutoff slopes for FIR filters of different lengths. The frequency axis is measured in arbitrary units. (*a*) 15-stage filter. (*b*) 31-stage filter. Vertical line indicates the cutoff frequency (0.125). Adding more delay stages to a filter tightens its cutoff slope.

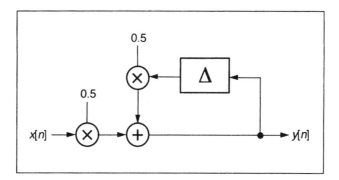

Figure 10.15   Signal flow graph for an ETA IIR filter; notice the feedback path.

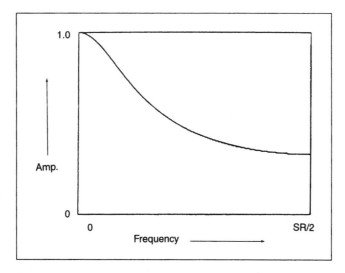

Figure 10.16   Plot of frequency response for the ETA IIR filter depicted in figure 10.15.

A simple *recursive highpass filter* subtracts the current input sample from the previous output sample, then divides by two. Figure 10.17 plots its frequency response. The filter's equation is as follows:

$$y[n] = (a \times x[n]) - (b \times y[n-1])$$

where $a = b = 0.5$. In this case, increasing b raises the highpass cutoff frequency, attenuating more and more low frequencies.

General Infinite-impulse-response Filters

More complicated IIR filters can be designed by including previous input samples (multiplied by nonzero coefficients) and feedback from previous output samples. The general form of an IIR filter is as follows:

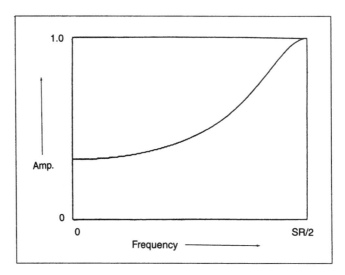

Figure 10.17   Plot of frequency response for an IIR highpass filter.

$$y[n] = (a_0 \times x[n]) + \ldots (a_M \times x[n - M]) - (b_1 \times y[n])$$
$$- \ldots (b_N \times y[n - N])$$

which can be written

$$y[n] = \sum_{i=0}^{M} a_i \times x[n - i] - \sum_{j=1}^{N} b_j \times y[n - j].$$

FIR versus IIR Filters

The existence of two basic types of filters (FIR and IIR) begs the question: Why use FIR filters in some applications and IIR filters in others? Each type has its advantages and disadvantages. In general it is easy to design an FIR filter with a *linear phase response*. This is usually thought to be better for audio signals because it prevents *phase distortion*—a degradation in sound quality caused by frequency-dependent delays that tend to smear transients and blur stereo images. Also, because FIR filters have no feedback, they are always stable and never go into oscillation. A disadvantage of FIR filters is that they require more arithmetic operations and memory than an IIR filter with similar frequency characteristics would. (Some FIR filters have thousands of delay stages, as the section on convolution makes clear later.) Hence a given FIR filter may be more costly in terms of hardware than an IIR filter that has a similar effect.

IIR filters can produce sharp, exponentially shaped cutoffs and boosts using much less computation than an FIR filter. This is because the IIR filter's feedback of past output eliminates many of the arithmetic steps and memory accesses that would be necessary to achieve the same effect in an FIR filter. IIR filters suffer, however, from phase distortion and *ringing* (Preis 1982). Ringing means that transients tend to excite the filter, causing it to oscillate (ring) for some time after the transient has passed through the system. In other words, IIR filters smear the transients over time, blurring the high frequencies and lending a harsh quality. Moreover, due to the recursive nature of the computation, IIR filters are more sensitive to the accumulation of roundoff errors in the filter arithmetic than are corresponding FIR filters. (See chapter 20 for more on this subject.)

Filter Design from an Arbitrary Specification

Up to this point we have presented examples of several basic filter types, each with its particular characteristics. The task taken up by filter design engineers goes in the other direction, however. They must design a realizable filter—including settings for its coefficients—starting from a set of desired characteristics. The characteristics might include audio specifications such as amplitude-versus-frequency response, phase-versus-frequency-response, impulse response, group delay, cutoff frequency, and so on, as well as practical constraints such as word length, computation speed, and compatibility with existing software and hardware, not to mention economic constraints.

In general, realizing a filter from an arbitrary set of specifications is a nontrivial task. Even when the desired specifications do not conflict with one another, a more-or-less complicated algebraic and numerical derivation must be carried out. The result is often an approximation of the desired specification, requiring choices that balance one characteristic against another.

As stated earlier, the theory of filter design is a vast discipline in its own right, with various and competing design strategies. Many engineering textbooks treat the theory of filter design in a rigorous and detailed manner that is out of place in a musical tutorial such as this; hence we recommend this literature to technically oriented readers. The text by Rabiner and Gold (1975), which we have cited numerous times, is a classic source.

Fortunately, the vexing detail of filter design has been coded into automatic filter design systems (McClellan, Parks, and Rabiner 1973). These are available as code libraries (Smith 1981) and as interactive programs running on popular computers (Hebel 1987, 1989; Zola Technologies 1991; Hyperception 1992). Interactive programs let users specify the design strategy and characteristics of a filter while hiding most of the algebraic and numerical manipulations required to implement it. Many of these systems let users test the simulated filter with audio signals.

Building Blocks of Complicated Filters

In any filter the maximum time span used in creating each output sample is called the *order* of the filter. A *first-order* filter, for example, has only one-sample delays, while a *second-order* filter contains two-sample delays. It is common practice to design complicated filters out of a network of first- and second-order filters, each of which is relatively stable and robust, rather than implementing a large and more delicate structure. See Rabiner and Gold (1975) for a discussion.

A *second-order section* is an IIR structure that is particularly popular in digital audio systems (Shpak 1992). As a second-order IIR filter, it looks back two samples, to the past of its output y. The term "section" means that this filter can be combined with other of like kind to form a more complicated filter. It realizes a bandpass frequency response, so it is often used as a building block for parametric and graphic equalizers. By setting some of its coefficients to zero, it can also realize lowpass and highpass filters, hence its wide application.

The literature presents several forms of second-order sections. Here we present "the most general" form, after Rabiner and Gold (1975, pp. 19–20). The equation is as follows:

$$y[n] = (a_0 \times x[n]) + (a_1 \times x[n-1]) + (a_2 \times x[n-2]) \\ - (b_1 \times y[n-1]) - (b_2 \times y[n-2]).$$

Here the a coefficients scale the feedforward paths, and the b coefficients scale the feedback paths. Feedback paths usually contribute peaks to the response, while the feedforward paths cause notches.

Another term for a second-order section is a *biquadratic* or *biquad* filter, referring to the two quadratic formulas in its equation (one for a and one for b). Figure 10.18 presents a circuit diagram corresponding to the equation just presented. Such a design is so common that the audio-processing power of a DSP system is sometimes expressed in terms of the number of second-order sections that it can realize in real time (Moorer 1983b).

Comb Filters

A comb filter creates a regular series of peaks and dips—equally spaced in frequency—in the spectrum of the input signal. It is so named because the

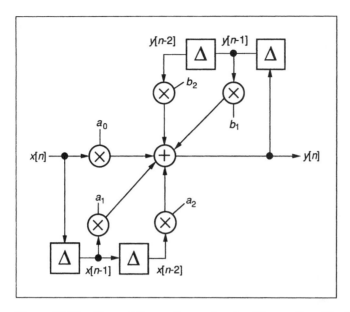

Figure 10.18 General form of second-order filter section. The feedforward path is below the center, controlled by the *a* coefficients. The feedback path is above the center, controlled by the *b* coefficients.

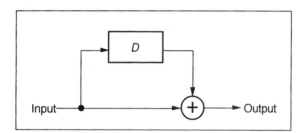

Figure 10.19 Simple feedforward comb filter circuit.

peaks and dips resemble the teeth of a comb. FIR comb filters process their past inputs, while IIR comb filters process their past outputs. We explain both types of comb filters in this section.

FIR Comb Filters

A simple FIR comb filter splits an incoming audio signal into two paths and inserts a multiple-sample time delay *D* into one of the paths, before summing them (figure 10.19). The equation for a simple FIR comb filter is as follows:

$$y[n] = x[n] + x[n - D].$$

The structure of an FIR comb filter is similar to that of an FIR lowpass filter. However, neither the original nor the delayed signal are scaled in this comb filter (although they can be); more important, the delay time D of a comb filter is longer. At a sampling rate of 48 KHz, a one-sample delay in the circuit creates a mild lowpass filter effect. This is because the delay is only 0.00002083ths of a second or about 0.02 ms. Only when the delay is greater than 0.1 ms does the filter begin to create multiple *null points* (points where the amplitude is zero) in the spectrum due to phase cancellation effects, resulting in a comb filter effect.

The comb effect results from phase cancellation and reinforcement between the delayed and undelayed signals. If the original and the delayed signals add together—as in the *positive summing comb filter*—the resultant filter has its first peak at a frequency of $f = 1/D \times f_s$, where D is the delay in samples and f_s is the sampling frequency. Successive peaks occur at $2f$, $3f$, $4f$, etc. Hence, this filter can be used for reinforcing a fundamental f and all its harmonics.

For example, if the sampling rate is 48 KHz, the delay is 12 samples (0.25 ms), and the original and delayed signals are positively summed, the first audible peak occurs at $1/12 \times 48,000 = 4$ KHz, with subsequent peaks at 8 KHz, 12 KHz, and so on, up to the Nyquist frequency (24 KHz). The same comb filter has nulls at 2 KHz, 6 KHz, and other 4 KHz intervals up to the Nyquist frequency (figure 10.20).

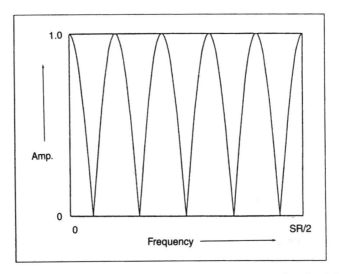

Figure 10.20   Plot of FIR comb filter spectrum for $f = 4$ KHz and a delay of 0.25 ms.

The phase cancellation and reinforcement effect can be explained as follows. At low frequencies the delay has virtually no effect on the phase of the signal, and the two signals (original plus delayed) add together, boosting the output signal. As the delays affect higher frequencies, they become closer and closer to a 180-degree phase shift. At 2 KHz, a 0.25-ms delay causes precisely a 180-degree phase shift. When this is added to the original signal, the two signals cancel at that frequency (figure 10.21). Beyond 180 degrees the signals add again until the phase shift delay reaches 0 or 360 degrees, which produces a reinforcement peak at 4 KHz. At 6 KHz they are again 180 degrees out of phase, producing a null, and so on.

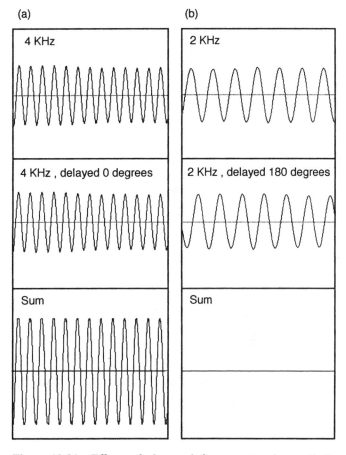

Figure 10.21 Effects of phase reinforcement and cancellation. (*a*) is left column and (*b*) is right column. (*a*) Top: 4 KHz tone. Middle: 4 KHz tone with no phase shift. Bottom: Sum of top and middle signals, resulting in a reinforcement. (*b*) Top: 2 KHz tone. Middle: 2 KHz tone 180 degrees out of phase. Bottom: Sum of top and middle signals, resulting in cancellation.

Table 10.1   FIR comb filter peaks

Delay time (in ms)	First peak and peak spacing
20	50 Hz
10	100 Hz
2	500 Hz
1	1 KHz
0.5	2 KHz
0.25	4 KHz
0.125	8 KHz
0.1	10 KHz

As table 10.1 indicates, longer delays create more closely spaced teeth in the comb. For example, when the delay is 50 ms, the first null appears at 10 Hz with subsequent nulls at 30, 50, 70 Hz, and so on. Short delays of less than 5 ms produce the richest comb filter effects, since the space between the peaks and nulls increases, so the teeth of the comb become broader in frequency and appear more striking to the ear.

What happens when the two signals (original and delayed) are subtracted rather than added together? This is the *negative summing* case, since the effect is the same as adding together the two signals with one of them 180 degrees out of phase. The equation for this simple subtracting FIR comb filter is

$$y[n] = x[n] - x[n - D]$$

where D is the delay in samples. If the two signals are subtracted rather than added, the first null appears at 0 Hz, with successive nulls at f, $2f$, $4f$, and so on. In this case the comb filter removes the fundamental and its harmonics. The signal is reinforced at $f/2$, $3f/2$, $5f/2$, and so on.

IIR Comb Filters

A *recursive* (IIR) *comb filter* feeds some of its output back into the input. The equation for a simple recursive comb filter is

$$y(n) = (a \times x[n]) + (b \times y[n - D]).$$

Coefficients a and b are scaling factors that range from 0 to 1. Figure 10.22 plots the frequency response of this filter. Depending on the value of the coefficient b in particular, this IIR comb filter has a more pronounced "resonance" effect on the signal than a corresponding FIR filter. Indeed, if b is set too high, the filter feeds back excessively, causing numerical overflow and subsequent distortion.

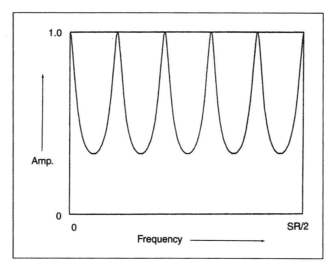

Figure 10.22   Plot of IIR comb spectrum.

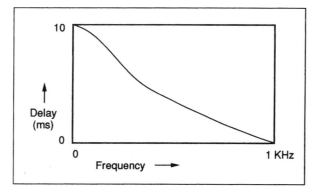

Figure 10.23   The delay-versus-frequency response of a dispersive allpass filter. (After Chamberlin 1985.)

Allpass Filters

An *allpass filter* is a peculiar signal processor. For steady-state tones fed into it, the allpass filter passes all frequencies equally well with no change in amplitude—hence its name. Thus, it is said that an allpass filter has a flat frequency response throughout the audio bandwidth. However, the allpass also imposes a frequency-dependent phase shift on the incoming signal. That is, it delays various frequency regions by different amounts. This type of frequency-dependent delay is also called *dispersion*.

Figure 10.23 displays a delay-versus-frequency curve for a allpass filter. Notice how low frequencies are delayed. The audible effects of an allpass filter show up in sharp attacks and decays, when it "colors" the signal through frequency-dependent phase shifting (Preis 1982; Deer, Bloom, and Preis 1985; Chamberlin 1985). Moorer described the allpass filter in this way:

We must remember that the all-pass nature is more a theoretical nature than a percep-tual one. We should not assume, simply because the frequency response is absolutely uniform, that the filter is perceptually transparent. In fact the phase response of an all-pass can be quite complex. The all-pass nature only implies that in the long run, with steady-state sounds, the spectral balance will not be changed. This implies nothing of the sort in the short-term, transient regions. In fact, both the comb and the all-pass have very definite and distinct "sounds" that are immediately recognizable to the experienced ear. (J. A. Moorer 1979)

The next equation describes a simple allpass filter with a flat long-term frequency response (from zero to half the sampling rate) that delays various frequencies by different amounts. When the delay in samples D is large, the allpass generates a series of decaying echoes, an effect used in *allpass rever-berators* (see chapter 11).

$$y[n] = (-g \times x[n]) + x[n - D] + (g \times y[n - D]).$$

Figure 10.24 shows the structure of such an allpass filter, equivalent to the one presented by Schroeder (1961, 1962; see also Moorer 1977). This allpass consists of an IIR comb filter with feedback (controlled by g) em-bedded in a circuit that also feeds forward a part of the direct input signal with gain $-g$. This subtraction cancels out the comb filter's spectral effect, while preserving the echo and delay characteristics.

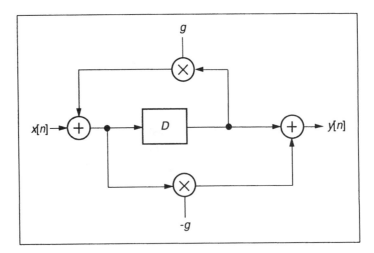

Figure 10.24   Structure of a simple allpass filter.

In general, the phase shift (in degrees) of an allpass filter is a logarithmic function of the delay. That is, a 100 msec delay is only a small fraction of a low-frequency cycle—only several degrees of phase shift. But at 10 KHz, the same 100 msec delay constitutes a full 360 degrees of phase shift relative to that frequency's period.

Two properties characterize allpass filters. The *turnover frequency* is the frequency at which the phase shift reaches 180 degrees. The *transition width* of an allpass filter is the sharpness of the transition from a 0 degree to a 360 degree phase shift. The transition width for an allpass filter is analogous to the Q (peakedness) of a bandpass filter (see chapter 5 for an explanation of Q).

Musical applications of allpass filters are manifold. In a mundane use, an allpass filter can help compensate for the phase shift introduced by another filter (Meyer 1984). For example, several audio companies marketed allpass filters as retrofits for early digital audio recorders to compensate for the phase distortion inherent in the unmodified recorders. Another application is found in some synthesizers. Here an allpass filter creates a time-varying, frequency-dependent phase shift, which can lend richness to otherwise static sounds. This is one means of creating a so-called *chorus effect*—a combination of delay and phase shifting. Perhaps the most important application of allpass filters is in reverberators, as discussed in chapter 11.

Convolution

Convolution is a fundamental operation in digital audio signal processing (Rabiner and Gold 1975; Dolson 1985; Oppenheim and Schafer 1975; Oppenheim and Willsky 1983). Everyone is familiar with its effects, even if they they have never heard of convolution. Any filter, for example, *convolves* its impulse response with the input signal to produce a filtered output signal. (Recall the definition of impulse response or IR given earlier.) Convolution is often disguised under more familiar terms such as filtering, modulation, reverberation, or cross-synthesis. But explicit use of convolution is becoming more common—hence this section.

Convolution of a given sound with an arbitrary IR can result in a huge variety of musical effects. For example, we can make a reverberator, which is a type of complicated filter, by obtaining the IR of a room, and then convolve that IR with an arbitrary input signal. When the convolved sound is mixed with the original sound, the result sounds like the input signal has been played in the room.

Beyond reverberation effects, the IR of any audio processor (microphone, loudspeaker, filter, distortion, effect, etc.) can be convolved with an audio signal to make that signal take on characteristics of the system.

This leads to a musically potent application of convolution: *cross-synthesis* by convolution of two arbitrary sounds. The offspring of cross-synthesis bear characteristics of the parent sounds but may resemble neither. If the input sounds are instrumental, the result may sound as if one instrument is "playing" the other (e.g., a chain of bells playing a gong). At the end of this section we assess the musical significance of convolution in more detail and give rules of thumb for using it.

The Operation of Convolution

To understand convolution let us look at the simplest case: convolution of a signal a with a unit impulse, which we call $unit[n]$. A unit impulse was introduced earlier as a digital sequence defined over n time points. At time $n = 0$, $unit[n] = 1$, but for all other values of n, $unit[n] = 0$. The convolution of $a[n]$ with $unit[n]$ can be denoted as follows:

$$output[n] = a[n] * unit[n] = a[n].$$

Here "$*$" signifies convolution. This results in a set of values for *output* that are the same as the original signal $a[n]$ (figure 10.25a). Thus, convolution with the unit impulse is said to be an *identity operation* with respect to convolution, because any function convolved with $unit[n]$ leaves that function unchanged.

Convolution by Scaled and Delayed Unit Impulses

Two other simple cases of convolution tell us enough to predict what will happen at the sample level with any convolution. If we scale $unit[n]$ by a constant c, the operation can be written as follows:

$$output[n] = a[n] * (c \times unit[n]).$$

The result is simply

$$output[n] = c \times a[n].$$

In other words, we obtain the identity of a, scaled by the constant c (figure 10.25b).

If we convolve signal a by a unit impulse that has been time-shifted by t samples, the impulse appears at sample $n\text{-}t$ instead of at $n = 0$. This can be expressed as:

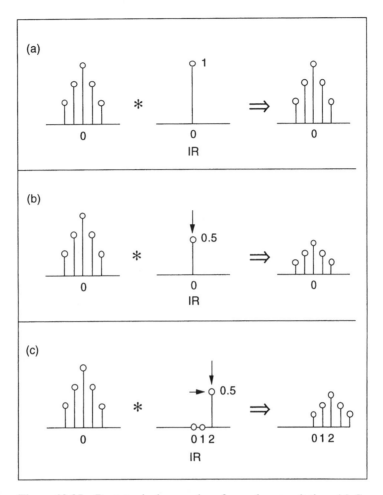

Figure 10.25 Prototypical examples of sample convolution. (*a*) Convolution of an input signal with the unit impulse is an identity operation. (*b*) Convolution with a scaled unit impulse of value 0.5 scales the input by 0.5. (*c*) Convolution with a delayed or time-shifted unit impulse time-shifts the input sequence correspondingly.

$$output[n] = a[n] * unit[n - t],$$

the result of which is

$$output[n] = a[n - t].$$

That is, *output* is identical to *a* except that it is time-shifted by the difference between n and t (figure 10.25c).

Putting together these two facts, one can view any sampled function as a sequence of scaled and delayed unit impulse functions. For example, the convolution of a signal *a* that contains two impulses spaced widely apart with any function *b* results in a two instances of *b*, scaled and delayed by the

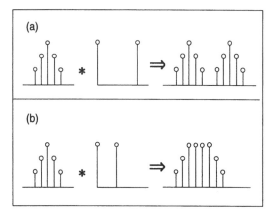

Figure 10.26 Time-domain effects of convolution. (*a*) Convolution with two impulses spaced widely apart produces an echo effect. (*b*) Convolution with two impulses close together produces a time-smearing effect.

impulses of *a* (figure 10.26a). Thus convolution can create echo effects. When the impulses in *a* are close together, the scaled repetitions of *b* overlap each other (figure 10.26b). This results in a *time-smearing* effect. When the time-smearing is dense (hundreds of impulses per second) and randomly distributed, it assumes the character of reverberation.

Thus, to convolve an input sequence *a*[*n*] with an arbitrary function *b*[*n*], place a copy of *b*[*n*] at each point of *a*[*n*], scaled by the value of *a*[*n*] at that point. The convolution of *a* and *b* is the sum of these scaled and delayed functions (figure 10.27).

Mathematical Definition of Convolution

A mathematical definition of the convolution of two finite sequences of samples is

$$a[n] * b[n] = output[k] = \sum_{n=0}^{N-1} a[n] \times b[k-n]$$

where *N* is the length of the sequence *a* in samples and *k* ranges over the entire length of *b*. Each sample of *a*[*n*] serves as a weighting function for a delayed copy of *b*[*n*]. These weighted and delayed copies are all added together. The conventional way to calculate this equation is to evaluate the sum for each value of *k*. This is called *direct convolution*. At the midpoint of the convolution, *n* copies are summed, so the result of this method of convolution is usually rescaled (normalized) afterward.

The length of the output sequence generated by direct convolution is

length(*output*) = **length**(*a*) + **length**(*b*) − 1.

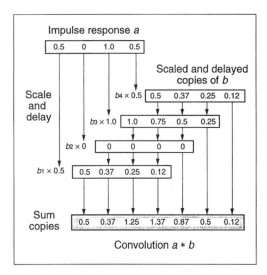

Figure 10.27   Direct convolution of two four-sample signals *a* and *b* means that each sample of *a* scales a delayed copy of *b*. The convolution sequence *c* is the sum of these scaled and delayed copies of *b*. The length of the resulting sequence is seven samples.

In the typical filtering case, *a* is an IR that is rather short compared to the length of the *b* signal. For example, for a broad smooth filter, the IR lasts less than a millisecond.

Comparison of Convolution with Multiplication

Convolution involves multiplication, but the convolution of two signals is different from multiplication of two signals. The multiplication of one signal *a* by another signal *b* means that each sample of *a* is multiplied by the corresponding sample in *b*. Thus:

$output[1] = a[1] \times b[1]$,

$output[2] = a[2] \times b[2]$,

etc.

Convolution, on the other hand, means that each sample of *a* is multiplied by every sample of *b*, creating an array of samples of length *b* for every sample of *a*. The convolution is the sum of these arrays. Compare convolution by the unit impulse (discussed previously) with multiplication by the unit impulse. In sharp contrast to convolution, the multiplication of $a[n]$ by the unit impulse $unit[n]$ results in all values of $output[n]$ being set to zero except for $output[0]$, where $unit[n]$ equals 1.

The Law of Convolution

A fundamental canon of signal processing is that the convolution of two waveforms is equal to the multiplication of their spectra. The inverse also holds. That is, the multiplication of two waveforms is equal to the convolution of their spectra. Another way of stating this is as follows:

Convolution in the time domain is equal to multiplication in the frequency domain and vice versa.

The law of convolution has profound implications. In particular, convolution of two audio signals is equivalent to filtering the spectrum of one sound by the spectrum of another sound. Inversely, multiplying two audio signals (i.e., performing *amplitude modulation* or *ring modulation;* see chapter 6) is equal to convolving their spectra. Convolution of spectra means that each point in the discrete frequency spectrum of input *a* is convolved with every point in the spectrum of *b*. Convolution does not distinguish whether its input sequences represent samples or spectra. To the convolution algorithm they are both just discrete sequences.

The law of convolution means that every time one reshapes the envelope of a sound, one is convolving the spectrum of the envelope with the spectrum of the reshaped sound. In other words, every time-domain transformation results in a corresponding frequency-domain transformation, and vice versa.

Relationship of Convolution to Filtering

Convolution is directly related to filtering. Recall the equation of a general FIR filter:

$$y[n] = (a \times x[n]) \pm (b \times x[n-1]) \pm \ldots (i \times x[n-j]).$$

We can think of the coefficients $a, b, \ldots i$ as elements in an array $h(i)$, where each element in $h(i)$ is multiplied times the corresponding element in array $x[j]$. With this in mind, the general equation of an FIR filter presented earlier can be restated as a convolution:

$$y[n] = \sum_{m=0}^{N-1} h[m] \times x[n-m]$$

where N is the length of the sequence h in samples and n ranges over the entire length of x. Notice that the coefficients h play the role of the impulse response in the convolution equation. And indeed, the impulse response of an FIR filter can be taken directly from the value of its coefficients. Thus any FIR filter can be expressed as a convolution, and vice versa.

Since an IIR filter also convolves, it is reasonable to ask whether there is also a direct relation between its coefficients and its impulse response. In a word, the answer is no. There exist, however, mathematical techniques that design an IIR filter that approximates a given impulse response. See Rabiner and Gold (1975, p. 265).

Fast Convolution

Direct convolution is notoriously intensive computationally, requiring on the order of N^2 operations, where N is the length of the longest input sequence. Thus direct convolution is rarely used to implement narrow band filters or reverberators (both of which have long impulse responses) when simpler methods suffice. (See the discussion of reverberation by convolution in chapter 11.)

Many practical applications of convolution use a method called *fast convolution* (Stockham 1969). Fast convolution for long sequences takes advantage of the fact that the product of two N-point *discrete Fourier transforms* (DFTs) is equal to the DFT of the convolution of two N-point sequences. Since the DFT can be computed very rapidly using the *fast Fourier transform* (FFT) algorithm, this leads to a tremendous speedup for convolution. (Chapter 13 and appendix A present the DFT and FFT.) Before the FFTs are taken, both sequences are lengthened by appending zeros until they are both equal to the convolution output length (as discussed previously). This process is called *zero-padding* and is also discussed in chapter 13 and appendix A. The results of the convolution can be resynthesized by applying the inverse FFT. Figure 10.28 depicts the overall scheme for fast convolution.

This means that we can replace direct convolution by FFTs, which are dramatically quicker for large values of N. In particular, fast convolution takes on the order of $N \times \log_2(N)$ operations. To cite an example, consider the direct convolution of two 2-second sounds sampled at 48 KHz. This requires on the order of $96,000^2$ or $9,216,000,000$ operations. Fast convolution with the same two sounds requires less than $1,500,000$ operations, a speedup by a factor of 6100. Put another way, a fast convolution that takes one second to calculate on a given microprocessor would require 101 minutes to calculate via direct convolution.

For real-time applications where more-or-less immediate output is needed, it is also possible to implement convolution in sections, that is, a few samples at a time. Sectioned and nonsectioned convolution generate equivalent

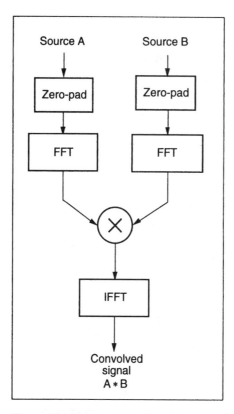

Figure 10.28   Fast convolution scheme.

results. See Rabiner and Gold (1975) and Kunt (1981) for an explanation of standard techniques for sectioned convolution. Rabiner and Gold also discuss the implementation of a real-time convolver.

Musical Significance of Convolution

Various sonic transformations can be explained as convolutions, including filtration, temporal effects, and modulation, discussed in the next three sections.

Filtering as Convolution

Filtering is a good example of the multiplication of spectra, since we can implement any filter by convolving an input signal with the impulse response of the desired filter. But convolution goes beyond simple filtering to cross-synthesis—filtering one sound by another. Let us call two sources *a* and *b* and their corresponding analyzed spectra *spectrum_a* and *spec-*

trum_b. If we multiply each point in *spectrum_a* with each corresponding point in *spectrum_b* and then resynthesize the resulting spectrum, we obtain a time-domain waveform that is the convolution of *a* with *b*. For example, the convolution of two saxophone tones, each with a smooth attack, mixes their pitches, sounding like the two tones are being played simultaneously. Unlike simple mixing, however, the filtering effect in convolution accentuates metallic resonances that are common in both tones. Another effect, which is subtle in this case but not in others, is time smearing, discussed next.

Temporal Effects of Convolution

Convolution also induces time-domain effects such as echo, time-smearing, and reverberation (Dolson and Boulanger 1985; Roads 1993a). These effects may be subtle or obvious, depending on the nature of the signals being convolved.

A unit impulse in one of the inputs to the convolution results in a copy of the other signal. Thus if we convolve any sound with an IR consisting of

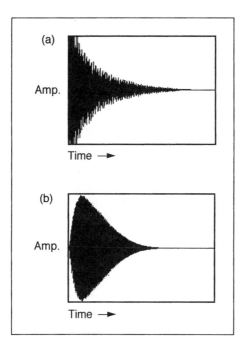

Figure 10.29 Example of time-smearing. (*a*) Original source, a cowbell strike with a sharp attack. (*b*) Result of convolution of the cowbell with itself. Notice the time-smearing in the attack.

two unit impulses spaced 500 ms apart, the result is a clear echo of the first signal.

The IR of a room may have many impulses, corresponding to reflections off various surfaces of the room—its echo pattern. When such an IR is convolved with an arbitrary sound, the result is as if that sound had been played in that room, because it has been mapped into the room's echo pattern.

If the peaks in the IR are closely spaced, however, the repetitions are time-smeared (refer back to figure 10.26b). Time-smearing smooths out sharp transients and blurs the precise onset time of events. Figure 10.29 shows how the convolution of a cowbell sound with itself results in a time-smeared version.

The combination of time-smearing and echo explains why noise signals, which contain thousands of sharp peaks, result in reverberation effects when convolved. If the amplitude envelope of a noise signal has a sharp attack and an exponential decay, the result of convolution will be a kind of naturalistic reverberation envelope. To color this reverberation, one can filter the noise before or after convolving it. If the noise has a logarithmic decay, however, the second sound will appear to be suspended in time before the decay.

Modulation as Convolution

Amplitude and ring modulation (see chapter 6) both call for multiplication of time-domain waveforms. The law of convolution states that multiplication of two waveforms convolves their spectra. Convolution accounts for the sidebands that result from these modulations. Consider the examples in figure 10.26, and imagine that instead of impulses in the time domain, the convolution is working on lines in the frequency domain. The same rules apply—with the important difference that the arithmetic of *complex numbers* applies. The FFT, for example, generates a complex number for each spectrum component. Appendix A presents this representation; here the main point is that this representation is symmetric about 0 Hz, with an exact replica of each spectral component (halved in amplitude) in the negative frequency domain. This negative spectrum is rarely plotted, since it only has significance inside the FFT.

Figure 10.30 is a graphical depiction of the spectrum convolution that occurs in ring modulation (see chapter 6). Figure 10.30a shows the spectrum emitted by an FFT for a single sinusoid at 100 Hz. Figure 10.30b shows a sinusoid at 1 KHz. Figure 10.30c depicts their convolution. The two

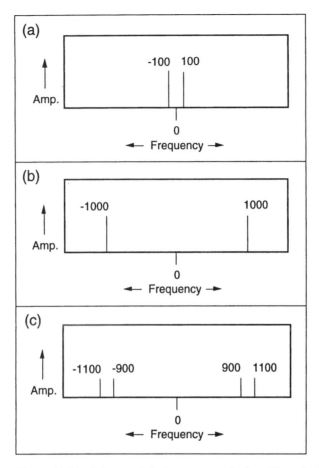

Figure 10.30 Ring modulation as convolution. These images show the representation of spectra inside the FFT, where a symmetrical representation applies. (*a*) Sinusoid at 100 Hz. (*b*) Sinusoid at 1 KHz. (*c*) Convolution of (*a*) and (*b*).

pulses at -100 and $+100$ are delayed and scaled to the region around 1 and -1 KHz. The frequencies of 900 and 1.1 KHz represent the sum and difference frequencies of the two input signals, which is typical of ring modulation.

Convolution with Grains and Pulsars

A unique class of sound transformations involves convolutions of sounds with *clouds* of sonic grains. (See the description of *asynchronous granular synthesis* presented in chapter 5.) In this application the grains are not heard on their own; rather, they can be thought of as the "virtual impulse response" of an unusual filter or synthetic space (Roads 1992b).

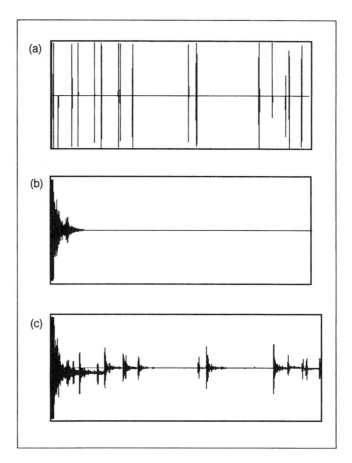

Figure 10.31   Convolution with grains. (*a*) Sparse cloud of brief grains lasting 0.5 ms each. (*b*) Tambourine hit. (*c*) Convolution of (*a*) and (*b*) results in multiple tambourine hits, corresponding to the temporal pattern of the cloud. Notice the momentary shift to negative energy caused by the second grain in (*a*).

The results of convolution with grains vary greatly, depending on the properties of the granular cloud and the input signal. For a sharp-attacked input signal, convolution with a sparse cloud containing a few dozen short grains contributes a statistical distribution of echoes of the input sound (figure 10.31). The denser the cloud, the more the echoes fuse into an irregular reverberation effect. Longer grains accentuate time-smearing and round off sharp attacks. When the input sound has a smooth attack—as in a legato saxophone tone—the result is like a time-varying filtering effect on the tone, which depends on the spectrum of the waveform within the grains. (See Roads 1993a for more details on this technique.)

Another class of synthesized sounds arises out of convolution between sampled sounds and trains of variable-waveform impulses called *pulsars*.

The pulsar trains fall into the continuum between the infra-audio and audio frequencies, leading to a range of rhythmic as well as timbral effects. See Roads (1994) for more details on this technique.

Linear versus Circular Convolution

Direct convolution is *linear convolution*. As mentioned earlier, direct convolution lengthens its inputs as follows:

length(*output*) = **length**(*a*) + **length**(*b*) − 1.

Given an input signal *a* that is 1024 samples long and an impulse response *b* that is 512 samples long, the length of the output of direct convolution is

length(*a*) + **length**(*b*) − 1 = 1535 samples.

This is because each and every sample of *a* convolves with each and every sample of *b*, including the 1024th element of *a*, which the impulse response extends by 511 samples.

Circular convolution is an anomaly that can occur when convolution is implemented with the FFT. Each FFT takes in N samples as its input (where N is the longer of the two input sequences). Fast convolution emits N samples as its output. What happened to the extension that occurs in linear convolution?

In fast convolution the extension points are additively "wrapped around" back into the beginning of the 1024-point series, as though it were a circular list with the end spliced back to the beginning. The result is that both the beginning and the end of the convolution contain invalid data. Fortunately, it is easy to avoid the distortion of circular convolution by specifying FFT *window sizes* that are equal to or greater than the length of the expected output sequence. (See chapter 13 for a discussion of window sizes.) This can be done by setting the FFT window size equal to the nearest power of two greater than the N samples of the longest input sequence. The additional sample points are *zero-padded*.

Deconvolution

Unfortunately, once two signals are convolved, there is no known way to separate or *deconvolve* them perfectly. Provided that one knows the spectrum of one of the signals, one can filter the convolved signal to remove that spectrum, but other artifacts of the convolution due to time-smearing (such as echoes and envelope reshaping) will remain.

Due to the particular nature of speech signals, however, two categories of deconvolution have achieved approximate separation of the excitation (glottal pulses) and the resonance (vocal tract formants) of vocal sounds. These are *autoregressive* and *homomorphic* deconvolution (Rabiner and Gold 1975). Chapter 13 introduces autoregressive analysis, which is closely related to the *linear predictive coding* presented in chapter 5. A method of homomorphic deconvolution is the *cepstrum* analysis technique described in chapter 12 (see also Galas and Rodet 1990).

Fixed Time Delay Effects

Time delay is a versatile musical signal-processing technique. A *digital delay unit* or *digital delay line* (DDL) takes in a stream of input samples and stores them in its memory for a brief period before sending them out again. Mixing a delayed sound with the original undelayed signal can cause a variety of musical effects, which we describe in a moment.

Comparison of DDL with FIR Lowpass and Comb Filters

Figure 10.32 depicts a simple *digital delay line* (DDL) circuit. Notice the similarity between this circuit, the simple FIR lowpass filter of figure 10.9, and the FIR comb filter of figure 10.19. The main difference between them is not the structure of the circuit, but the delay time involved. For a lowpass

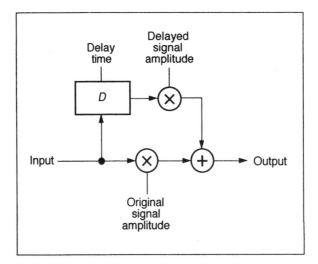

Figure 10.32 Circuit of a digital delay line. Notice the similarity between this structure and the structures in figures 10.9 and 10.19.

filter, the delay is one sample, so the circuit has the effect of averaging successive samples. For a comb filter the effective delay times are around 0.1 to 1 ms. For a DDL, the delays are greater than 1 ms.

Implementation of a Delay Line

Inside a signal processor, a data structure called a *circular queue* is an efficient means of implementing a delay line (figure 10.33). Such a queue is simply a list of sequential memory locations containing audio samples. At

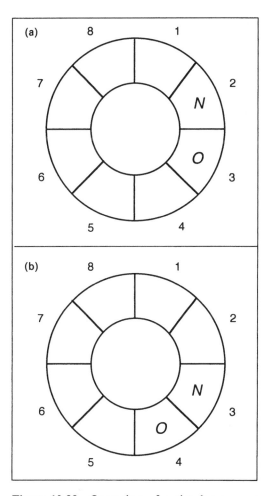

Figure 10.33 Operation of a circular queue to implement a delay line. *N* is the newest sample in the queue, while *O* is the oldest sample. (*a*) "Before." Pointers in a circular queue at time *t*. (*b*) "After." Pointers in the queue at time *t* + 1, indicating that the space held by the oldest sample at time *t* has been read out and replaced by a new incoming sample.

every sample period the delay program reads the oldest sample and replaces it by writing a new incoming sample at the same location. The read/write pointer then goes on to the next position in the queue, which now contains the oldest sample. (See chapter 2 for an explanation of lists and pointers.) When the pointer reaches the "end" of the queue it "wraps around" (skips) to the "first" location—hence the term circular.

So far we have described a delay with a fixed duration, proportional to the length of the queue. This delay has one read pointer—or *tap* in the parlance of signal processing, and the tap always precedes a write into the same location. By allowing the read pointer to tap any point in the queue, we can implement delays that are shorter than the length of the queue, including delays that change over time. These possibilities lead to the variable time delay effects described later.

Logically enough, a *multitap delay line* has more than one tap. Figure 10.34 depicts a multitap delay line implemented as a circular queue. At each sample period, a new sample is written into the queue at the position marked N. Simultaneously, two samples are read out from the positions marked Tap_1 (a one-sample delay) and Tap_2 (a three-sample delay). Then all the pointers increment to the next position to prepare for the next sample period.

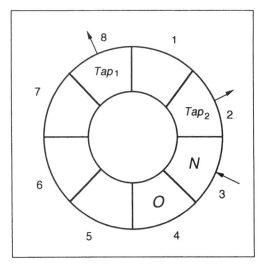

Figure 10.34 A two-tap delay line implemented as a circular queue. The two read taps, Tap_1 and Tap_2, circulate around the queue along with pointers O (old) and N (new). Incoming samples are written into the position occupied by N at each sample period.

Fixed Delay Effects

For simplicity, it is useful to distinguish between *fixed* and *variable* delay effects. In a fixed delay unit, the delay time does not change while sound is passed through it. In a variable delay unit, the delay time is constantly changing; this is implemented by varying the tap points at each sample period. Here we focus on the fixed delay case; the next section treats the variable delay case.

Fixed audio delays can be grouped into three time spans, corresponding to different perceptual effects they create:

- *Short* (less than about 10 ms)
- *Medium* (about 10 to 50 ms)
- *Long* (greater than about 50 ms)

Short delays are perceptible primarily in terms of the frequency-domain anomalies they introduce. For example, a delay of one to several samples, mixed with the original signal, is equivalent to an FIR lowpass filter. When the delay extends over the range [0.1 ms, 10 ms], comb filter effects appear.

Medium delays can enhance a "thin" signal. For example, medium delays are extensively used in popular music to bolster vocal, drum, and synthesizer tracks. A medium delay creates an "ambience" around the signal, giving an illusion of increased loudness without a corresponding increase in measured amplitude. (Note that "loudness" is a perceptual term and "amplitude" is a physical measurement.) A delay of between 10 and 50 ms "fuses" with the original sound to create a "doubling" effect. The doubling effect can be enhanced by applying subtle time-varying pitch shifts and delays to the signal before mixing it with the original.

Long delays (greater than about 50 ms) create discrete echoes—sounds heard as repetitions of the original sound. In nature, echoes occur when sound waves travel away from their source, bounce off a reflective surface, and hit listeners late enough that they hear it as a discrete repetition. Since sound travels at about 1100 feet (344 meters) per second in air at 20 degrees centigrade, a delay of 1 ms corresponds to a total sound path from the source to the listener of about 1 foot (0.3 meters). To create a discrete echo requires a time delay of at least 50 ms. This implies a distance of at least 25 feet (8 meters) from the reflective surface, or about 50 feet (16 meters) for the total distance from the source to the reflective surface to the listener (figure 10.35).

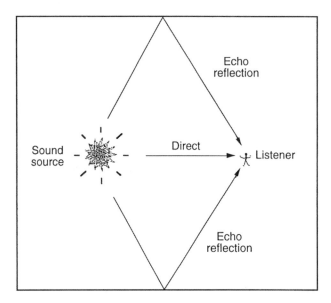

Figure 10.35   Echo effect caused by mixture of direct sound with reflected sound.

Delays and Sound Localization

Localization refers to the ability of the ear to detect the location from which a sound emanates. Delays are one type of localization cue in a multichannel sound system. To give an example, if a sound is sent at equal amplitude to two loudspeakers and the listener sits in the middle of the listening area, the "sound image" concentrates in the center of the listening stage. If a short (0.2 to 10 ms) time delay is applied to the sound emanating from the right loudspeaker, the apparent source of the sound shifts to the left speaker (Blauert 1983). This shows that our ears use delay as a cue to localization. Judiciously used, multiple echoes can conjur up the illusion of a sound emanating from a specific space. Chapter 11 covers the subject of localization in more detail.

Variable Time Delay Effects

Variable time delay effects result from delay lines whose delay times vary as signals pass through them. Two of the most well-known of these are *flanging* and *phasing* (or *phase shifting*), which first became common in popular music in the 1960s and 1970s. The techniques are similar, but offer different possible effects.

Flanging

The electronic flanging effect derives from a natural acoustic phenomenon that occurs whenever a wideband noise is heard in a mixture of direct and delayed sound. Bilsen and Ritsma (1969) give a history of the effect, beginning with its discovery by Christian Huygens in 1693. The guitarist and recording innovator Les Paul was the first to use flanging as a sound effect in the recording studio. His 1945 flanging system employed two disk recorders, one with a variable speed control (Bode 1984). In the 1960s, flanging was achieved in recording studios with two analog tape recorders and a mixing console. The tape recorders were fed an identical signal. The engineer monitored their combined tape output, while putting occasional pressure on the flange (rim) of one of the reels to slow it down (figure 10.36). The use of two recorders was necessary in order to synchronize the overall delay introduced by monitoring from the playback head of the flanging recorder. At a 38 cm/second tape speed, the distance between the record head and the playback head on a typical analog tape recorder introduces a fixed delay of about 35 ms. (The precise delay depends on the configuration of the record and playback heads.) Thus one could also substitute a fixed delay line for the left tape recorder in figure 10.36.

The general principle of flanging is clearly

flanging = signal + delayed signal

where the delay time is constantly varying.

Electronic flanging uses a continuously varying delay line to achieve the same effect (Factor and Katz 1972). In place of manual pressure on a tape reel, the delay time of an electronic flanger is varied by a low-frequency oscillator (usually emitting a sine or triangle wave) operating in the range of about 0.1 to 20 Hz.

Flanging could be called a *swept comb filter effect*. In flanging, several nulls sweep up and down the spectrum. Filter peaks are located at frequencies that are integral multiples of $1/D$, where D is the delay time. The depth of flanging is maximum if the amplitudes of the original signal and the delayed version are equal.

The structure described so far is a equivalent to a feedforward or FIR comb filter with a time-varying delay. In practice, most modern implementations of flanging use an IIR or recursive feedback comb structure with time-varying delay, as shown in figure 10.37. One can usually switch between positive and negative feedback to compare which is most effective for a particular sound to be flanged.

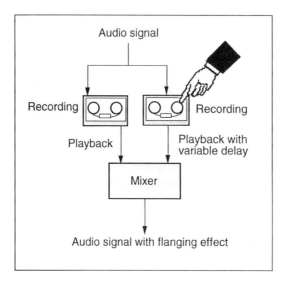

Figure 10.36 Tape flanging using two analog tape recorders. The playback speed of the second tape recorder varies as an operator applies finger pressure to the flange of the reel.

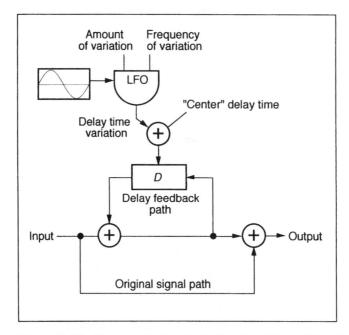

Figure 10.37 Flanger circuit with feedback, mixing a delayed signal with an original signal. A low-frequency oscillator (LFO) supplies the variation in the delay time around a "center" delay time. This circuit could be made more sophisticated by inserting multipliers on the delay feedback path and the original signal path, so that one could adjust the ratio between the two signals or invert the phase of the feedback.

Phasing

Phasing is similar in effect to flanging but the "churning" sound produced by the sweeping comb filter is usually not as pronounced. In phasing, a spectrally rich signal is typically sent through a series of allpass filters (Hartman 1978; Beigel 1979; Smith 1984). The allpass filters have a flat frequency response (i.e., they do not attentuate any frequencies) but they shift the phase of the original signal. A low-frequency oscillator can be used to sweep the amount of phase shift introduced by each allpass filter. The outputs of the filters are mixed at unity gain with the original signal. As in flanging, a kind of sweeping comb filter effect results.

What is the difference between flanging and phasing? Flanging results in complete peaks and nulls in the spectrum, and these are spaced at uniform intervals in frequency. By contrast, the number of peaks and notches in the response of the phase shifter corresponds to the number of filter stages in it. The spacing, depth, and width of the notches can be varied.

Phasing leads to a variety of sonic effects. Chamberlin (1985) gives an example of four allpass filters in series with the same turnover frequency and a broad transition width. A 1 KHz sine tone is fed into the filters. If the turnover frequency is swept from 10 to 100 Hz, the tone undergoes a constantly increasing phase shift. The effect of this is to lower momentarily the frequency of the sine wave. If the turnover sweep is reversed, the sine tone will momentarily shift up in frequency. If the sine wave is replaced by a signal with many harmonics, the temporary frequency shift causes an audible "ripple" through the harmonics as the turnover frequency changes.

Chorus Effects

The quest for *chorus* effects has long fascinated musicians and musical engineers. Given an instrument with one voice (which can be any electronic timbre), is there a way to process this signal so that it becomes as full as a chorus of like voices? Such an effect requires that there be small differences between the various voices of the simulated ensemble, including slight delays, alterations of fundamental frequency (resulting in beating effects), and asynchronous vibrato. There is no single algorithm for chorus effect; various implementations use different means to achieve it.

Efforts to build chorus effect generators date back at least as early as the 1940s, when Hanert constructed electromechanical delay lines for electronic music (Hanert 1944, 1945, 1946). These were manufactured in Hammond organs to achieve a *choral tone effect* (Bode 1984). By the 1950s W. C.

Wayne, Jr., had constructed a purely electronic *choral tone modulator* for the Baldwin electric organ (Wayne 1961).

In digital systems, one type of chorus effect can be realized by sending a sound through a multitap delay line, where the time delays are constantly varying over a narrow range. This variation causes detuning and time-varying doubling effects. This is equivalent to putting the signal through a bank of parallel flangers, although the delays in a flanger tend to be shorter than those used for a chorus effect.

These types of techniques can be enriched by using negative feedback (routing back a phase-reversed version of the delayed sound), as in flanging. This means phase reversing the feedback path of the flanger in figure 10.37. Negative, rather than positive, feedback minimizes the risk of resonances and system overload.

Another chorus effect technique splits the input signal into several octave-wide bands and applies a separate *spectrum* or *frequency shifter* to each band. The frequency shifter can be thought of as adding a constant to the frequency of every component in the spectrum. With a frequency shift of 10 Hz, 220 Hz becomes 230, 440 Hz becomes 450, 880 Hz becomes 890, and so on. Clearly, the frequency shifter destroys harmonic relationships among the components. The amount of frequency shifting varies randomly over a narrow range. Following the frequency shifter is a time-varying delay line. According to Chamberlin (1985), this type of design is best for simulating the effect of large ensembles.

Using several allpass filters in parallel, a type of chorus effect can be achieved by driving the filter turnover frequencies with low-frequency quasi-random signals (Chamberlin 1985).

Time/Pitch Changing

Some sound transformations are combinations of time- and frequency-domain manipulations. This includes a pair of related techniques called *time compression/expansion* and *pitch-shifting*. Since these techniques are usually used together, this section conjoins them under the term *time/pitch changing*. These techniques have two sides. On the one hand, the duration of a sound can be stretched or shrunk while the pitch remains constant. On the other hand, the pitch of the sound can be shifted up or down while the duration remains constant.

The most effective time/pitch changing happens when it is applied in a selective, context-sensitive manner. In order to preserve the identity of the original sound, it is important to preserve the fine structure of attacks and other transients while processing only the steady-state part of the signal. In stretching speech, for example, intelligibility and "naturalness" can be enhanced by stretching vowels more than consonants.

Time/pitch changing can be realized, with varying degrees of success, by several means: granular time-domain techniques, real-time harmonizers, the phase vocoder, wavelets, and linear predictive coding. The rest of this section synopsizes each one. To avoid redundancy with more detailed descriptions in other parts of the book, the presentation of each method here is necessarily brief.

Time/pitch Changing by Time-granulation

Time-granulation involves segmenting a stream of sound samples into short duration units called *grains*. This is equivalent to the process of *windowing* that occurs in many sound analysis algorithms (see chapter 13). The grains may simply be segments cut at regularly spaced successive intervals along the time line, or they may be extracted from overlapping intervals and enveloped so that their sum reconstitutes the original waveform. In time-granulation, the duration of each grain can vary from as short as 1 ms to as long as 200 ms or more. Chapter 5 describes granular representations in more detail.

Electromechanical Time-granulation

The British physicist Dennis Gabor (1946) built one of the earliest electromechanical time/pitch changers. A German company, Springer, made a similar device based on magnetic tape that was used in analog electronic music studios (Springer 1955; Morawaska-Büngler 1988). This device, called the Tempophon, processed speech sounds in Herbert Eimert's 1963 electronic music composition *Epitaph für Aikichi Kuboyama* (recorded on Wergo 60014). (See also Fairbanks, Everitt, and Jaeger 1954 for a description of a similar device.) The basic principle of these machines is time-granulation of recorded sounds. Contemporary digital methods can be explained by reference to the operation of these early tools.

In an electromechanical time/pitch changer, a rotating head (the sampling head) spins across a recording (on film or tape) of a sound. The sampling head spins in the same direction that the tape is moving. Because the head only comes in contact with the tape for a short period, the effect is that of "sampling" the sound on the tape at regular intervals. Each of these sampled segments is a grain of sound.

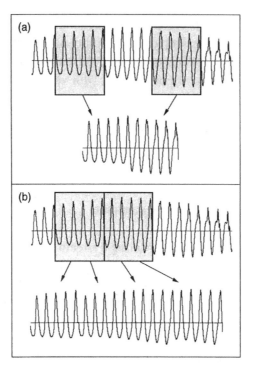

Fig.10.38   Time granulation. (*a*) Time shrinking by extracting separated grains. (*b*) Time expansion by cloning two copies of each grain. In both cases the local frequency content of the signal is preserved.

In Gabor's system, the grains were reassembled into a continuous stream on another recorder. When this second recording was played back, the result was a more-or-less continuous signal but with a different time base. For example, shrinking the duration of the original signal was achieved by slowing down the rotation speed of the sampling head. This meant that the resampled recording contained a sequence of grains that had formerly been separated (figure 10.38a). For time expansion, the rotating head spun quickly, sampling multiple copies (clones) of the original signal. When these samples were played back as a continuous signal, the effect of the multiple copies was to stretch out the duration of the resampled version (figure 10.38b). The local frequency content, in particular, the pitch, of the original signal is preserved in the resampled version.

To effect a change in pitch without changing the duration of a sound, one need only to change the playback rate of the original and use the timescale modification just described to adjust its duration. For example, to shift the pitch up an octave, play back the original at double speed and use time-granulation to double the duration of the resampled version. This, in effect, restores the duration to the original length.

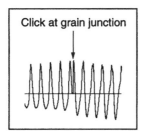

Figure 10.39 When two grains are arbitrarily spliced, the end of one grain may not match the beginning of the next grain. This can cause a transient (click) at the splice point.

Digital Time-granulation

Pioneering research at the University of Illinois Experimental Music Studio led to an early digital implementation of time-granulation at the University of Illinois (Otis, Grossman, and Cuomo 1968). This implementation simulated the effect of rotating-head sampling; it also pointed out the flaws of this method in its most basic form. The main problem is that the waveforms at the beginning and end of a sampled grain may not match in level with preceding and successive resampled grains. This creates a transient at the junction of the two grains, an effect shown in figure 10.39. Electromechanical time-granulators and some digital implementations exhibit a periodic clicking sound caused by these splicing transients.

Lee (1972) developed the Lexicon Varispeech system as a digital time compressor/expander interfaced with an analog cassette recorder. Lee's design featured an electronic circuit for level matching at splice points to reduce the clicking sound. More recent work by Jones and Parks (1988) showed how a more smooth reconstruction of the signal can be achieved by using smooth grain envelopes that overlap slightly, creating a seamless crossfade between grains.

Just as in the electromechanical time/pitch changer, doubling the duration of a sound means that each grain is cloned into two. To halve the duration, every other grain is deleted before playback. The local frequency content of the grains is preserved, while the timescale is altered by cloning (to stretch duration) or deleting (to shrink duration) grains.

To shift the pitch of a sampled signal up an octave but not change its duration, the playback sampling rate is doubled, and every grain is cloned to restore the duration to the original. To shift the pitch down an octave but not change the duration, the playback sampling rate is halved and every other grain is deleted to restore the duration to the original.

So far we have described operations that double or halve pitch or time, but these operations are not limited to products of two. The frequency and timescale can be altered by arbitrary ratios by sample rate changing with grain cloning or deleting in corresponding ratios.

Time/Pitch Changing with a Harmonizer

A *harmonizer* is a real-time transposing device that shifts the pitch of an incoming signal without altering its duration. Based purely on time-domain techniques, the Eventide H910 Harmonizer, released in the mid-1970s, was the first commercially available digital device of this type (Bode 1984). The following description describes the Publison, a sampling effects processor developed in France in the early 1980s, and is adapted from Bloom (1985).

The basic notion of a harmonizer is to load a random-access memory with an incoming signal sampled at a rate of SR_{in} and to read out the samples at a rate SR_{out}. The ratio SR_{in}/SR_{out} determines the pitch change.

To maintain a continuous output signal, samples must be repeated (for upward pitch shifts) or skipped (for downward pitch shifts). Because the output address pointer repeatedly overtakes the input address pointer (for pitch increases) or is overtaken by the recirculating input address pointer (for pitch decreases), the output address must occasionally jump to a new point in the memory. In order to make this "splice" inaudible, the precise jump is calculated based on an estimate of the periodicity (pitch) of the incoming signal. When the decision has been made to splice, a smoothing fade-out envelope ramps the amplitude of the presplice signal to zero and a corresponding fade-in envelope ramps to postsplice the signal to full amplitude.

To this basic scheme can be added refinements that improve its performance. One is a noise gate connected to the input to the system so that the pitch-shifting does not try to shift the ambient noise associated with the input signal.

The sound quality of a simple harmonizer is based on the nature of the input signal and on the ratio of pitch change it is asked to perform. Small pitch changes tend to generate less audible side effects. Some commercial devices produce undesirable side effects (such as buzzing at the frequency of the splicing) when used on critical material, such as vocal sounds.

Time/Pitch Changing with the Phase Vocoder

The phase vocoder (PV), explained in increasing levels of detail in chapters 5 and 13 and appendix A, applies *fast Fourier transforms* (FFTs) to short—

usually overlapping—segments of an incoming sound. The FFTs result in a series of spectrum frames that capture the frequency-domain evolution of the sound over time. Based on these data, the original sound can be resynthesized by additive synthesis; each sine wave oscillator's frequency corresponds to an analyzed frequency component. The output of the additive resynthesis is usually a simulacrum of the original.

Overlap-add Transformations

The compositional interest of the PV lies in transforming the analysis data prior to resynthesis, producing variations of the original sound. One of the most common transformations is time compression/expansion. This can be accomplished in two ways, depending on which version of the PV is used. In the version that uses *overlap-add resynthesis* (explained in chapter 13 and appendix A), time expansion is accomplished by moving the onset times of the overlapping frames farther apart in the resynthesis. Time compression moves the onset times closer together. As Dolson (1986) notes, the phase vocoder prefers integer transposition ratios, both for time and pitch changing. For smooth transpositions, the PV should multiply the phase values by the same constant used in the time base changing (Arfib 1991).

Pitch transposition is simply a matter of scaling the frequencies of the resynthesis components. For speech signals in particular, however, a constant scale factor changes not only the pitch but the formant frequencies. For upward shifts of an octave or more, this reduces the intelligibility of the speech. Thus Dolson (1986) suggests a correction to the frequency scaling that reimposes the original spectral envelope on the transposed frequency spectrum. If the original spectrum went only to 5 KHz, for example, the transposed version will also cutoff at this point, regardless of how stretched the component frequencies are within this overall envelope.

Tracking Phase Vocoder Transformations

Another way to alter the time base of analyzed sounds requires the *tracking phase vocoder* or TPV (see chapter 13). The TPV converts a series of spectrum frames into a set of amplitude and frequency envelope functions for each analyzed frequency component. These functions are typically represented as arrays in computer memory. By editing these amplitude and frequency functions one can shift the pitch or extend the duration of a sound independently of one another (Portnoff 1978; Holtzman 1980; Gordon and Strawn 1985). For example, to stretch the duration, points are interpolated between existing points in the amplitude and frequency arrays. To shrink

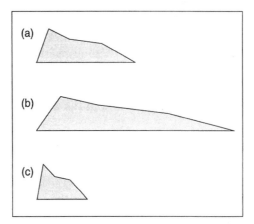

Figure 10.40   Timescale modification of tracking phase vocoder envelopes. All plots show amplitude on the vertical axis, and time on the horizontal axis. (*a*) Original. (*b*) Stretched in time. (*c*) Shrunk in time.

the duration by a factor of *n,* only every *n*th value is used in reading the amplitude and frequency arrays. In effect, this shifts the sampling rate (figure 10.40). Maher (1990) discusses some of the distortions these simple interpolations may entail and offers remedies for better "envelope warping."

To shift the pitch of a sound but not change its duration, one multiplies the frequency values assigned to each of the frequency functions by the desired factor. For example, to shift a sound up an interval of a major second, each frequency component is multiplied by 11.892 percent; a 1 KHz sine wave becomes 1118.92 Hz. One can also shift pitch selectively, altering only the fundamental frequency and leaving other partials the same.

Time/Pitch Changing with the Wavelet Transform

As in the phase vocoder, the first stage in the wavelet time/pitch changing is a type of spectrum analysis (Kronland-Martinet 1988; Kronland-Martinet and Grossmann 1991; Vetterli 1992). Chapter 13 explains the basic concept of wavelets. They are similar to the windowed segments used with the FFT, but the duration of each wavelet is dependent on its frequency content: the higher the frequency, the shorter the wavelet. This means that the temporal resolution of the wavelet transform (i.e., its ability to pinpoint the onset time of events) is greater at high frequencies.

As in Fourier transform methods, the wavelet transform splits a sampled sound into a collection of individual components, localized in time. These components are characterized by amplitude and phase values gleaned from the analysis. In order to modify the pitch or the time base, one must alter the analysis data before resynthesis.

To shift pitch by a constant factor, one multiplies the phase values of the analyzed wavelets by this factor (Kronland-Martinet and Grossmann 1991). To stretch or shrink the time base while keeping the pitch the same, one stretches or shrinks the point of overlap of the wavelets in resynthesis.

Time/Pitch Changing with Linear Predictive Coding

Chapter 5 introduces *linear predictive coding* (LPC)—a subtractive analysis/ resynthesis method that can generate speech, singing, instrument-like tim- bres, and resonant synthetic sounds (Cann 1979–1980; Moorer 1979a; Dodge and Jerse 1985; Dodge 1989; Lansky 1989; Lansky and Steiglitz 1981). LPC analysis models an input signal as an *excitation function* (such as produced by human vocal cords or the vibrations of a reed or bowed string) and a set of *time-varying resonances* (such as the human vocal tract or the body of a saxophone or violin). The resonances are implemented as a time-varying filter that simulates a response to the excitation. For more on LPC spectrum analysis, see chapter 13.

LPC is not a perfect analysis/synthesis method. It was originally designed to be an efficient coding for speech, permitting low-bandwidth communica- tion. It has been extended for musical purposes, but the resynthesized sound generally has an artificial character, due to details lost in the analysis (Moorer 1979a). If this limitation is accepted, however, LPC has been and will continue to be used in effective compositional applications.

LPC encodes the analysis results as a sequence of short-duration *frames,* with each frame capturing the filter coefficients, pitch, and voiced/unvoiced data for a given time slice of sound. See chapter 5 for an explanation of the frame data. For musical purposes, composers edit the frames, transforming the original sound. Figure 5.38 in chapter 5 shows a sequence of data in LPC frames.

To realize time/pitch changing, one edits the frames and then uses the edited frames to drive the resynthesis. LPC analysis frames are usually cal- culated at regular intervals, from 50 to 120 per second. By issuing an editing command the duration of frames can be changed, for example, to extend a single frame from 10 to 100 ms. The pitch column can be edited separately to change only the pitch of the resynthesized version. Thus duration and pitch can be independently transformed. In addition to time/pitch changing, the LPC data can be edited in other ways to create radical variations on the original analyzed sound. (See Cann 1979–1980 and Dodge 1985 for exam- ples of editing LPC data.) Musical applications of time/pitch changing via LPC can be found in compositions by Paul Lansky and Charles Dodge, for example.

Conclusion

Research in signal processing is incessant, and the literature has mushroomed in recent years. One way to keep up with developments is by reading periodicals such as the *IEEE Transactions on Signal Processing*, the *Journal of the Audio Engineering Society*, and *Computer Music Journal*.

Current signal-processing techniques are wedded to available technology. The continuing deployment of smaller, faster, and cheaper systems means that many methods that were formerly confined to large institutions can be released into personal studios and employed in live performance.

Most audio processing involves global operations that take little account of the nature of the sounds being treated. A contrasting trend, however, is the rise of *signal-responsive* algorithms. A typical example is a time-stretching algorithm that elongates steady-state signals but leaves transients untouched. Another is a compressor that delays its input and then looks ahead to anticipate wide amplitude swings. As analysis merges with signal processing, it is easy to imagine that sophisticated signal-responsive algorithms will grow more common.

11 *Sound Spatialization and Reverberation*

Sound Spatialization

Spatialization in Music: Background

Examples of Spatial Processing in Electronic Music

Enhancing Spatial Projection in Performance

Localization Cues

Simulating the Azimuth Cue

Linear Panning

Constant Power Panning

Reflections

Simulating Distance Cues

Local and Global Reverberation

The Velocity Cue or Doppler Shift

Simulating Altitude (Zenith) Cues

Problems with Vertical Sound Illusions

Binaural Sound

Sound Radiation

Rotating Loudspeakers

Rotating Loudspeakers: Background

Simulation of Rotating Loudspeakers

Reverberation

Properties of Reverberation

Impulse Response of a Room

The art of sound spatialization has assumed a similar position today as the art of orchestration had in the nineteenth century. To deploy space is to choreograph sound: positioning sources and animating movement. Immersing sound in reverberation, we bathe listeners in its lush ambience.

Sound spatialization has two aspects: the virtual and the physical. In the virtual reality of the studio, composers spatialize sounds by imposing delays, filters, panning, and reverberation—lending the illusion of sounds emerging from imaginary environments. Sometimes these virtual spaces take on characteristics that would be impossible to realize architecturally, such as a continuously changing echo pattern. In the physical world of concert halls, sounds can be projected over a multichannel sound system from a variety of positions: around, above, below, and within the audience.

Sound architecture or spatialization has evolved into an important aspect of composition. A trend toward "cinematic" use of space is seen in compositions that feature dramatic appositions between sounds that are closely miked and those that are distantly reverberated. Some composers use microphone techniques and spatial processing in a manner similar to the cinematic use of camera angle, lens perspective (width), and depth of field. Jean-Claude Risset's *Sud* (1985, Wergo 2013-50) comes to mind.

This chapter opens with a glimpse at the projection of sound in three-dimensional space. The second part describes the art of digital reverberation, an area of spatialization that will continue to be refined in years to come. The final section extends the discussion of the first two sections by surveying research that attempts to model specific spatial environments. A recommended prerequisite to this chapter is a familiarity with the concepts of filtering introduced in chapters 5 and 10.

Sound Spatialization

The movement of sound through space creates dramatic effects and can serve as an important structural element in composition. Composers can articulate the voices in a contrapuntal texture by giving each one a unique spatial location. The virtual and physical *sound stage* around the audience can be treated as a landscape, with its background and foreground, and fixed and moving sources. This sound stage can be fixed in playback, or controlled by gestures in concert (Harada et al. 1992).

Digital simulations of moving sound sources pose special problems. In many concerts the audience is surrounded by a number of loudspeakers. How does one create the illusion of a sound traveling about the hall, moving away from or toward the listener as it goes? In listening situations with only two loudspeakers or with headphones, the illusion of sounds moving freely in space is even more difficult.

The most popular spatial illusions are horizontal *panning*—lateral sound movement from speaker to speaker—and *reverberating*—adding a dense and diffuse pattern of echoes to a sound to situate it in a larger space. Vertical panning (up and down and overhead) can also create striking effects in electronic music. (See Gerzon 1973 for a discussion of "sound-with-height" recording and playback.)

Spatialization in Music: Background

Von welcher Seite, mit wievielen Lautspechern zugleich, ob mit Links- oder Rechts-drehung, teilweise starr und teilweise beweglich die Klänge und Klanggruppen in den Raum gestrahlt werden: das alles ist für das Verständnis dieses Werkes massgeblich. (From which side, with how many loudspeakers, whether with rotation to left or right, whether motionless or moving, how the sounds and sound groups should be projected into space: all this is decisive for the understanding of the work.) (Karlheinz Stockhausen 1958, describing his composition *Gesang der Jünglinge* [*Song of the Youths*])

Spatial techniques in music composition are not new. In the sixteenth century, composers associated with the Basilica San Marco in Venice (notably Adrian Willaert and his pupil Andrea Gabrieli) employed spatial antiphony in their compositions for two or more choirs. In these works, an initial verse was heard from one side of a hall, and a response verse came from another side. This arrangement was facilitated by two facing organs in the basilica. W. A. Mozart wrote compositions for two spatially separated orchestras (K. 239 and K. 286), and Hector Berlioz and Gustav Mahler wrote compositions for multiple orchestras and choruses, some of which were offstage. After these experiments, however, there is little documentation of spatial techniques in composition until the electronic era.

The invention of the loudspeaker could be compared to the invention of the light bulb. Suddenly it was possible to project sonic energy in spaces small and large, at any angle or intensity. But the use of loudspeakers—in movie theaters, stadiums, railroad stations, and home radios—remained for the most part plain and functional. Only with the dawn of the post–World War 2 era were the aesthetic possibilities of sound projection via loudspeakers exploited in electronic music.

Examples of Spatialization in Electronic Music

A number of famous examples of spatial projection in electronic and computer music deserve mention here.

- Karlheinz Stockhausen's *Gesang der Jünglinge* was projected in a 1956 concert over five groups of loudspeakers in the auditorium of the West German Radio (Stockhausen 1961). His opus *Kontakte,* realized in 1960, was the first electronic music composition performed from a four-channel tape, using the Telefunken T9 tape recorder (Stockhausen 1968).

- In 1958 Edgard Varèse's classic tape music composition *Poème Electronique* and Iannis Xenakis's *Concret PH* were projected over 425 loudspeakers through an eleven-channel sound system installed on the curved walls of the Philips pavillion, designed by Xenakis and Le Corbusier at the Brussels World's Fair.

- Stockhausen played his electronic music over loudspeakers distributed on the interior surface of the geodesic dome of the German pavilion at EXPO 70 in Osaka (Stockhausen 1971a).

- At the same exposition, Iannis Xenakis performed his twelve-channel electroacoustic composition *Hibiki Hana Ma* in the Japanese Steel Pavilion on a system of 800 loudspeakers distributed around the audience, over their heads, and under their seats (Matossian 1986). A twelve-channel sound projection system animated his sound-and-light spectacle *Polytope de Cluny* projected on the interior of the ancient Cluny Museum in Paris (Xenakis 1992).

- Composer Salvatore Martirano built a complex digital apparatus called the Sal-Mar Construction to control a custom analog synthesizer and distribute the sound to 250 thin loudspeakers suspended at various heights from the ceilings of concert halls (Martirano 1971).

- The idea of projecting sound over an orchestra of dozens of loudspeakers on stage was realized in the Gmebaphone, conceived by the Groupe de Musique Expérimentale de Bourges, and first heard in concert in 1973 (Clozier 1993).

- The first concert of the Acousmonium—an assemblage of dozens of "sound projectors" conceived by the Groupe de Recherches Musicales (figure 11.1)—took place at the Espace Cardin, Paris, in 1974 (Bayle 1989, 1993).

- The steel frame used in the mid-1980s performances of Pierre Boulez's *Répons* held loudspeakers suspended over the heads of the audience. Spatial control was implemented using Di Giugno's 4X synthesizer (Asta et al. 1980; Boulez and Gerzso 1988).

- In 1987 researchers at Luciano Berio's Tempo Reale studio in Florence developed a computer-based sound distribution system called Trails that

Figure 11.1 The Acousmonium—a multichannel spatializer designed by the Groupe de Recherches Musicales (GRM)—installed in Olivier Messiaen concert hall, Maison de Radio France, Paris, in 1980. Projecting sound over 80 loudspeakers played through a 48-channel mixer, the Acousmonium achieves a complexity of sound image rivaling that of an orchestra. It lets a composer "reorchestrate" an electronic composition for Acousmonium spatial performance. (Photograph by L. Ruszka and supplied courtesy of F. Bayle and the Groupe de Recherches Musicales.)

could distribute sound to up to 32 audio channels, combining preprogrammed and real-time spatial patterns (Bernardini and Otto 1989).

Many other sound spatialization systems have been developed, including Edward Kobrin's sixteen-channel HYBRID IV (Kobrin 1977) (figure 11.2), the SSSP sound distribution system (Federkow, Buxton, and Smith 1978), the AUDIUM installation (Loy 1985b), Hans Peter Haller's Halaphon used by P. Boulez and L. Nono (Haller 1980), the computer-controlled Sinfonie developed by the GRAME studio in Lyon, and the all-digital spatializer implemented by Marina Bosi (1990) at Stanford University.

Enhancing Spatial Projection in Performance

Even ad hoc concerts of electroacoustic music without elaborate sound projection systems can take steps to enhance the spatial qualities of the performance. Figure 11.3 illustrates a few standard configurations.

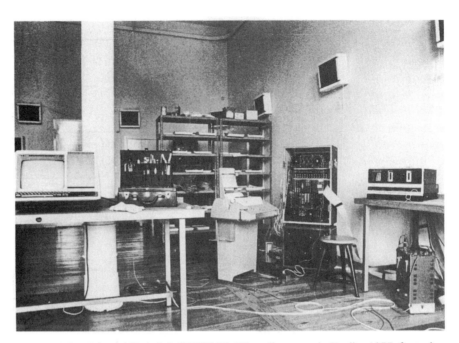

Figure 11.2 Edward Kobrin's HYBRID IV studio set up in Berlin, 1977, featuring a computer-controlled 16-channel spatialization system. The loudspeakers are mounted on the walls.

1. When possible, use at least a *quadraphonic* sound projection system (four channels of amplification with four loudspeaker systems), located around the audience (figure 11.3b).

2. When two-channel recordings are played on the quadraphonic system, route two channels to the front and two channels to the back with the left-right configuration in the back channels reversed. This way, when a sound pans from left to right in the front, it also pans from right to left in the back, increasing the sense of spatial animation.

3. To add even more spatial articulation, situate the loudspeakers at opposite corners in an elevated position. This is called *periphony* or "sound with height" playback (Gerzon 1973). In this scheme, when a sound pans from left to right, it also pans vertically (figure 11.3c).

4. When amplified instruments or vocalists are employed, give each performer their own amplifier and loudspeaker unit, along with effects (such as equalization) that articulate that particular instrument. To root each instrument on the sound stage and mitigate the "disembodied performer" syndrome, the loudspeaker should be near the performer (Morrill 1981b). In the disembodied performer syndrome, the sound of an instrument is

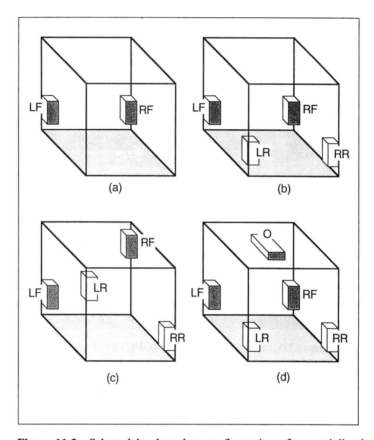

Figure 11.3 Selected loudspeaker configurations for spatialization of electronic and computer music. (*a*) Basic stereo, LF = left front, RF = right front. (*b*) Quadraphonic, RR = right rear, LR = left rear. (*c*) Quadraphonic periphony. The right front and left rear loudspeakers are mounted above ear level, so that when sound pans from horizontally it also pans vertically. (*d*) Five-speaker configuration with vertical loudspeaker projecting downward.

fed to a general sound reinforcement system that is far from the performer. Since listeners's image of the source of a sound in dominated by the first sound to reach their ears (this is the *precedence effect;* Durlach and Colburn 1978), any global amplification of a performer playing an acoustic instrument should be delayed by 5 to 40 ms to allow the local amplifier to make the first impression as to the source (Vidolin 1993). (Sometimes, of course, the composer wants to project the sound of an instrument around a hall, or to merge it with a prerecorded source; this is another case.)

5. A different approach is to assemble an "orchestra" of different loudspeakers onstage (the Gmebaphone/Acousmonium approach). This

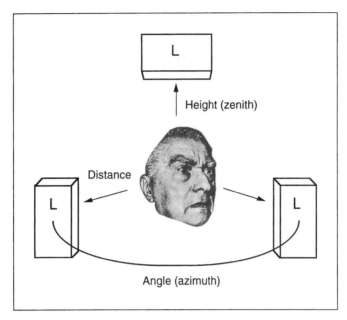

Figure 11.4 The attentive listener can localize a sound source from cues of its horizontal angle, height, and distance. L = loudspeaker.

creates a spatial source multiplicity and sonic diversity usually associated with an orchestra of acoustic instruments.

Precise control of spatial illusions requires knowledge of the *theory of localization*—how human beings perceive a sound's direction, the subject of the next section.

Localization Cues

Before delving into techniques of sound spatialization, it is important to understand basic principles of how listeners pinpoint the locale from which a sound emanates. This subject, an extensively mined area of psychoacoustics, is called *sound localization*. Localization is dependent on cues for three dimensions (figure 11.4; localization):

Azimuth or horizontal angle

Distance (for static sounds) or *velocity* (for moving sounds)

Zenith (altitude) or vertical angle

To determine the azimuth of a sound, listeners use three cues:

- The different arrival times of a sound to the two ears when the sound is coming from one side
- The difference in amplitude of high-frequency sounds heard by two ears, which results from the "shadow effect" of the head
- Spectral cues provided by asymmetrical reflections of sound off the outer ears (pinnae), shoulders, and upper torso

The cues for distance are threefold:

- The ratio of direct signal to reverberated signal, when the direct signal decreases in intensity according to the square of the distance
- The loss of high-frequency components with increasing distance
- The loss of detail (absence of softer sounds) with increasing distance

When the distance between the sound and the listener is changing, the cue to the velocity of the sound is a pitch change called the *Doppler shift effect* (explained later).

The main cue for zenith is a change in the spectrum caused by sound reflections off the pinnae and shoulders.

Simulating the Azimuth Cue

Listeners can easily localize an intense high-frequency sound coming from a particular direction at ear level. Logically enough, for a sound source to be positioned directly at a loudspeaker position, all of the signal should come from that loudspeaker. As the source pans from one loudspeaker to another, the amplitude in the direction of the target loudspeaker increases, and the amplitude in the direction of the original source loudspeaker decreases.

In performances where a number of loudspeakers are placed equidistantly in a circle around the audience, an algorithm for spatial position needs only to calculate the amplitudes of two adjacent loudspeakers at a time, regardless of the total number of loudspeakers. To position a sound source at a precise point P between the two loudspeakers A and B, first find the angle (θ) of the source measured from the middlepoint between A and B (figure 11.5).

Many different panning curves are possible, each of which lends a slightly different spatial impression of sound movement. We discuss two panning curves next: linear and constant power. For a symmetrical pan these curves assume that a listener sits in the exact center between the two loudspeakers.

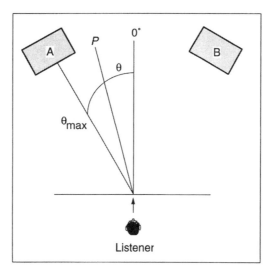

Figure 11.5. To position a sound source at a point *P* between the two loudspeakers A and B, ascertain the angle (θ) of the source measured from the middlepoint between A and B. In the middle θ equals 0 degrees. The angle θ_{max} is the maximum angle, typically plus or minus 45 degrees. Use the formulas given in the text to derive the amplitude of the signals sent to the two loudspeakers.

When the listener sits off center there is an azimuth offset in the sound image. For efficiency the curves can be computed in advance, requiring only a table-lookup operation using the index θ.

Linear Panning

The most simple formula for positioning is a simple linear relation:

$$A_{amp} = \theta/\theta_{max}$$

$$B_{amp} = 1 - (\theta - \theta_{max})$$

The problem with this type of pan is that it creates a "hole in the middle" effect since the ears tend to hear the signal as being stronger in the endpoints (the loudspeakers) than in the middle (figure 11.6). This is due to the *law of sound intensity*, which states that the perceived loudness of a sound is proportional to its intensity. The intensity of the sound can be given as follows:

$$I = \sqrt{A_{amp}^2 + B_{amp}^2}.$$

In the middle of the pan (i.e., where $\theta = 0$), $A_{amp} = B_{amp} = 0.5$), this becomes

$$\sqrt{0.5^2 + 0.5^2} = \sqrt{0.25 + 0.25} = \sqrt{0.5} = 0.707.$$

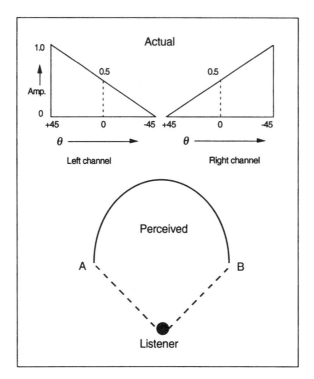

Figure 11.6   A linear panning curve is perceived as receding in the middle due to a diminution of intensity. The amplitude curves for each channel are shown at the top; the perceived trajectory is shown at the bottom.

Thus the intensity drops to 0.707 in the middle, from a starting point of 1 at the side. This is a difference of 3 dB. To the ear, whose sensitivity is more correlated to intensity than to amplitude, the sound appears to be fainter in the center, as if it has moved away from the listener.

Constant Power Panning

A constant power pan uses sinusoidal curves to control the amplitude emanating from the two loudspeakers (Reveillon 1994). This creates the impression of a pan with a more stable loudness:

$$A_{amp} = \frac{\sqrt{2}}{2} \times [\cos(\theta) + \sin(\theta)]$$

$$B_{amp} = \frac{\sqrt{2}}{2} \times [\cos(\theta) - \sin(\theta)].$$

In the middle of this pan, $A_{amp} = B_{amp} = 0.707$, thus:

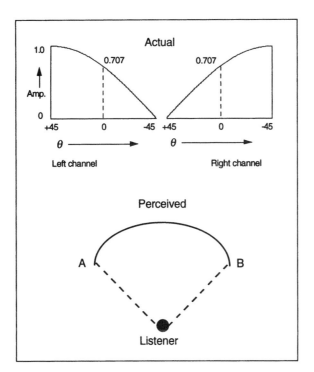

Figure 11.7 A constant-power panning curve maintains the perceived distance and intensity in the middle. The amplitude curves for each channel are shown at the top; the perceived trajectory is shown at the bottom.

$$I = \sqrt{0.707^2 + 0.707^2} = \sqrt{0.5 + 0.5} = \sqrt{1} = 1$$

and a constant intensity is preserved.

Figure 11.7 shows the constant intensity pan. The perceived pan is seen as rotating between the two loudspeakers at a constant distance from the listener.

Reflections

As sound pans from loudspeaker to loudspeaker in a concert hall, reflections in the hall provide more cues to source position. (At certain positions in some halls they may confuse the sense of directionality, but this is a degenerate case.) Thus to enhance the localization effect, the composer can add small delays to the signal coming from the "nondirect" channels (i.e., the channels from which the main source is not being projected). These delays simulate the reflections of a hall; they tell the ear that the source direction is elsewhere. In the ideal, the reflection pattern should change as the sound pans.

Table 11.1   Distance traveled by sound waves per unit of time

Time (in ms)	Total distance (in m)	Wavelength frequency (in Hz)
1.0	0.34	1000
3.4	1	340
6.8	2	168
34	10	34
68	20	16.8
100	34	10
340	100	3.4
680	200	1.68
1000	340	1

Note: The corresponding wavelength is also shown. To calculate the delay time of a reflection, use the total distance from the source to the reflecting surface to the listener. The speed of sound is assumed to be about 340 m/sec.

To impart an idea of the relationship between the delay time and the perceived distance of a sound, consider table 11.1. This shows the distance sound travels per unit time. The third column in table 11.1 is added for the sake of the curious, showing the wavelength corresponding to a given distance. As the third row down shows, for example, an acoustical tone at 166 Hz (about an E) takes shape in two meters of air.

Simulating Distance Cues

To make a sound recede into the distance, one can lower its amplitude, apply a lowpass filter, add echoes, or blend in reverberation. The first two

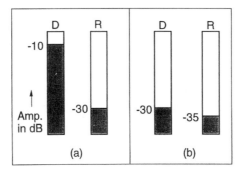

Figure 11.8   Level indicators for simulating a sound that moves away from the listener. D = direct, R = reverberated. (*a*) Close sound in which the direct sound is much higher in amplitude than the reverberated sound. (*b*) Distant sound. The overall amplitude is lower, and the ratio of the direct to the reverberated sound has narrowed.

cues model what happens outdoors in a large open field, where we sense the distance of a sound by its intensity and the filtering effect of air absorption on high frequencies.

Echo and reverberation cues model what happens in an enclosed space such as a concert hall. To simulate a specific distance within a room, the simplest method is to keep the level of reverberation constant and scale the direct signal to be inversely proportional to the desired distance (figure 11.8). An extension of this technique is to scale the reverberant signal as well, according to a function that decreases less rapidly than the direct signal. As the source moves away, the total sound emanating from the source diminishes.

Local and Global Reverberation

Another distance cue is the relationship of *local* reverberation to *global* reverberation, which can be demonstrated with a multiple loudspeaker system. Global reverberation is distributed equally among all loudspeakers, while local reverberation feeds into adjacent pairs of loudspeakers. Thus, a sound might have a short and weak global reverberation but have a long and strong local reverberation coming from one pair of loudspeakers in a multispeaker setup. This would simulate the case of an opening into a large space between the two loudspeakers.

A distinction between local and global reverberation helps overcome a masking effect that occurs at distances where the amplitudes of the direct and global reverberant signals are equal. This masking eliminates the azimuth cue. One way to negate this effect is to split the reverberation into local and global components and make local reverberation increase with distance according to the relation:

local_reverberation $\cong 1 - (1/distance)$.

As the distance increases, this relation tends toward 1. Thus, when the source is close to the listener, the reverberation is distributed equally well in all channels. As the source moves away, the reverberant signal concentrates in the direction of the source.

The Velocity Cue or Doppler Shift Effect

Basic localization cues for static sounds can be extended to the simulation of moving sound sources. This is accomplished through a cue to the velocity of the sound source, namely *Doppler shift*, first described by the astronomer

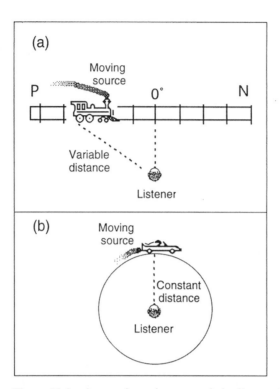

Figure 11.9   A sound moving toward the listener has positive (P) radial velocity. Sound moving away has negative (N) radial velocity. (*b*) Sound moving in a circle is always the same distance away from the listener and so has zero radial velocity.

C. Doppler (1842). The first simulations of Doppler shift to computer music were carried out by John Chowning (1971).

Doppler shift is a change in pitch that results when the source and the listener are moving relative to each other. A common example is heard when standing next to a train track as a train approaches at high speed and then passes. As the train moves closer, the wavefronts of the sound reach us more quickly, causing the pitch to be raised. When the train passes we hear the pitch shift downward.

A Doppler shift is a cue to the *radial velocity* of a source relative to a listener. Radial movement is motion with respect to a center—in this case, a listener (figure 11.9a). Radial velocity is different from *angular velocity*. For a sound to have angular velocity, it must move in a circle around a listener (figure 11.9b). In this case the distance from the source to the listener is constant (i.e., the radial velocity is zero), so there is no Doppler effect. If the position of the listener remains fixed, the Doppler shift effect can be expressed as follows:

new_pitch = original_pitch × [vsound/(vsound − vsource)]

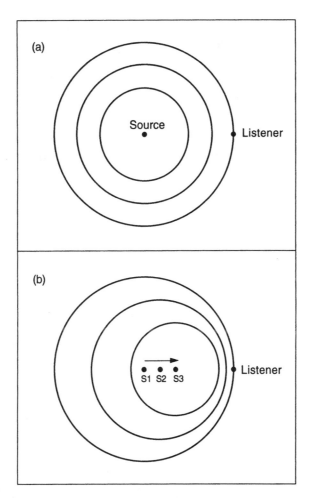

Figure 11.10   Doppler shift wavefront patterns. (*a*) Static sound, wavefronts arrive at constant intervals so there is no pitch change. (*b*) S1, S2, and S3 represent successive positions of a moving sound source. Upward pitch shift.

where *original_pitch* is the original pitch of the sound source, *vsound* is the velocity of sound (∼ 344 meters/second or 1100 feet/second), and *vsource* is the velocity of the source relative to the listener. If *vsource* is positive, the sound is moving closer to the listener, and the pitch shift is upward. If it is negative, the pitch shifts downward.

The pitch change that occurs in Doppler shifting can be explained as a shrinking of the interval between wavefronts as the source moves closer to the listener. Figure 11.10a depicts a static sound emitting wavefronts at a constant rate or pitch. Figure 11.10b depicts a sound source moving toward the listener. The dots S1, S2, and S3 represent successive positions of a moving sound source. As the sound approaches, the wavefronts become closer together, producing an upward pitch shift.

At a given instant the Doppler effect is shifting all frequencies by the same logarithmic interval. For example, an approaching sound moving at 20 meters/second (about 45 miles/hour) raises by about a minor second (6.15 percent). A shift of 6.15 percent for a component at 10 KHz is is 615 Hz, while a 6.15 percent shift for a 100 Hz component is only 6.15 Hz. Thus the Doppler effect preserves the logarithmically scaled interharmonic relations within a sound. This is opposed to a linear frequency shift that occurs in modulation. An example of linear frequency shift is the addition of 50 Hz to all components. Shifting a pitch from 100 to 150 Hz constitutes a major fifth interval, while at a range of 10 KHz, a 50 Hz shift is barely perceptible. Linear frequency shifting destroys existing interharmonic relationships in a sound. (See chapter 6.)

Simulating Altitude (Zenith) Cues

The effect of sound sources descending from on high can be dramatic. Since the 1970s it has been shown that vertical sound illusions can be achieved with a regular stereo sound system positioned at ear level. This research has inspired the development of commercially available vertical spatialization systems, the effects of which can be heard in numerous recordings.

In general, "3D sound" systems are based on research that shows that high-frequency sound (greater than about 6 KHz) reflecting off the outer ears (pinnae) and shoulders provides a critical cue to vertical localization. The surfaces of the pinnae and shoulders act as reflectors, creating short time delays that are manifested in the spectrum as a comb filter effect (Bloom 1977; Rodgers 1981; Kendall and Martens 1984; Kendall, Martens, and Decker 1989).

Zenith cues can be simulated electronically, giving the impression that a sound is emanating from high places. This is done by filtering the input signal, imposing the change in spectrum caused by reflections off the head and shoulders. The filters are set according to the position of the source that one is trying to simulate. This frequency response of this filtration is

---

Figure 11.11   HRTF spectra for sounds heard at 90 degrees (straight into left ear) at various altitudes. (Top) 15 degrees above ear level. (Middle) Ear level. (Bottom) Below ear level. (After Rodgers 1981; published courtesy of the Audio Engineering Society.)

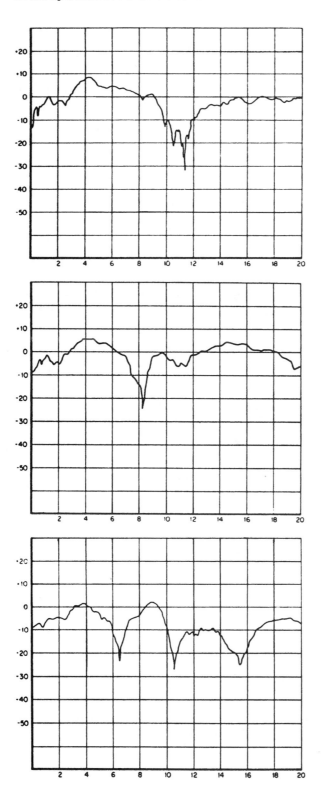

called the *head-related transfer function* (HRTF) (Begault 1991). Figure 11.11 plots typical HRTFs for sounds above, at, and below ear level.

In practice, vertical spatial effects are greatly enhanced if the sound is projected in an environment with both front and rear loudspeakers. By panning the sound from front to back or vice versa and applying the HRTF effect, the sound is heard is going over the head of the listener as it pans. Like all spatial effects, vertical panning works best on broadband impulsive sounds rather than low-frequency sounds with smooth envelopes.

Problems with Vertical Sound Illusions

As figure 11.12 shows, a problem with projecting sound in a simulated vertical plane is the variation in HRTFs for different people (Begault 1991; Kendall, Martens, and Decker 1989). When the wrong HRTF is used for a particular person, the vertical panning effect weakens. For a home listening situation, where the filtering is performed in real time on playback, one solution to this problem is to provide several different HRTFs and test signals so that individuals can tune their system to match the response of their ears beforehand.

The robustness of vertical illusions is dependent on the quality of the loudspeakers used and the proximity of the listener to the loudspeakers. Listening to small nearfield monitors, for example, one must remain within their direct sound path, or the vertical illusion falls apart. Thus in a concert

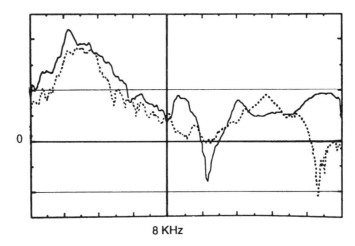

8 KHz

Figure 11.12   HRTF spectra for two different persons. Left ear, source at ear level. The frequency plot goes from 1 to 18 KHz. The vertical line indicates the 8 KHz mark. The differences between the two HRTFs above 8 KHz are striking. The horizontal lines indicate 20 dB differences.

situation it is more practical to suspend actual loudspeakers over the heads of the audience (see figure 11.3d) than to rely on the more fragile illusion of virtual sources.

Binaural Sound

In psychoacoustics research, *binaural* originally referred to a unique listening situation in which subjects are placed in an anechoic chamber with their heads held still by a mechanical restraint and probe tubes inserted into their ear canals. These conditions are designed to analyze a variety of auditory mechanisms in a controlled environment (Durlach and Colburn 1978; Colburn and Durlach 1978; Buser and Imbert 1992). Due to the difficulty of such experiments, many investigations employ headphones. In other experiments, a dummy head with microphones in its ears substitutes for the human subject.

An outgrowth of this research is a genre of *binaural recordings,* made with two microphones in a dummy head or a similar construction, that are meant to be heard through headphones. This genre has been particularly popular in radio productions and has led to the availability of binaural recording systems, including computer-based mixing consoles with horizontal and vertical panning controls.

One of the results of binaural research has been the realization that is possible to create an illusion of a sound source at a specific position in a binaural field through filtering alone. By "binaural field" we refer to the space perceived through headphones, including above and behind the head. These techniques employ the HRTFs discussed earlier. See Blauert (1983), Durlach and Colburn (1978), and Begault (1991) for details.

Sound Radiation

We conclude the discussion of localization with a note on sound radiation. Every sound-producing mechanism has a characteristic *radiation pattern.* This three-dimensional pattern describes the amplitude of sound projected by the device in all directions. In traditional acoustical instruments, the radiation pattern is frequency-dependent (Fletcher and Rossing 1991). That is, it changes depending on the frequency being radiated. Radiation pattern is one clue to the identity and locale of the source.

Loudspeaker systems exhibit their own radiation patterns, characterized by the technical specification called *dispersion pattern.* The dispersion pattern of a front-projecting loudspeaker indicates the width and height of the region in which the loudspeaker maintains a linear frequency response.

To the extent that listeners can detect the difference between a real violin and playback of a violin recording has been blamed on their different radiation patterns. Thus one line of acoustics research over the years has concentrated on modeling the radiation patterns of instruments, projecting them on spherical multiloudspeaker setups (Bloch et al. 1992). Such systems, under computer control, could also be used for compositional purposes, to give each voice in a piece its own radiation pattern, for example.

Rotating Loudspeakers

The radiation of sound emitted by a spinning loudspeaker creates a striking spatial effect. The physical rotation of a loudspeaker enlivens even dull, stable sounds, animating them with time-varying qualities.

Rotating Loudspeakers: Background

The original rotating loudspeaker mechanism was the Leslie Tone Cabinet, which routed an incoming signal into two separate rotating mechanisms: a spinning horn for high frequencies and a rotating baffle (blocking and unblocking a stationary woofer) for low frequencies. A remote control for motor speed let musicians adjust the speed of rotation. The resonant horn of the Leslie Tone Cabinet makes it immediately identifiable.

The Leslie Tone Cabinet was designed to enrich the static sound emitted by electric organs such as the famed Hammond B3, with which it was often coupled. But musicians and recording engineers discovered that any sound could be enriched this way, including voice and electric guitar.

In the 1950s, engineers working Hermann Scherchen's Experimental Studio Gravesano in Switzerland developed a spherical loudspeaker (figure 11.13) that rotated both horizontally and vertically (Loescher 1959, 1960). Their goal was to reduce the "directional soundbeam" characteristics of normal loudspeakers. According to one of the designers:

A double rotation in the horizontal and vertical plane results in inclined rotational planes of the single speakers and gives best results. The sound field becomes practically homogenous, reproduction takes on an astonishing fullness and smoothness, and the harshness of normal reproduction is completely gone. (Loescher 1959)

K. Stockhausen manually rotated a loudspeaker affixed to a turntable to create the spinning sounds in his compositions *Kontakte* (1960) and *Hymnen* (1967) (figure 11.14). Later, engineers at the West German Radio

Figure 11.13   Rotating spherical loudspeaker constructed in 1959 at the Experimental Studio Gravesano.

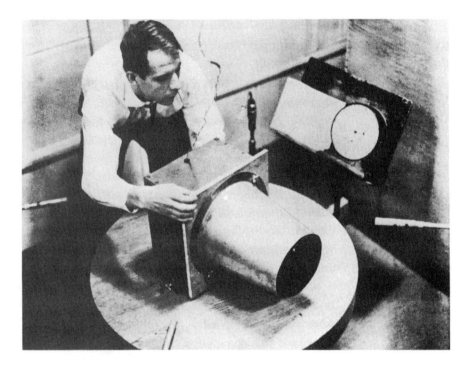

Figure 11.14   K. Stockhausen with rotating loudspeaker mechanism (1960). Four microphones are positioned around the loudspeaker turntable, which was manipulated by hand. A later version was controlled by a motorized mechanism. (Photograph copyright WDR, Cologne.)

(WDR) built a motorized sound rotation system for concert performance of Stockhausen's works (Morawska-Büngler 1988).

Simulation of Rotating Loudspeakers

The effects of rotation are manifold, involving Doppler shift vibrato, time-varying filtering, phase shifts, distortions caused by air turbulence, and echo reflections from adjacent surfaces—not to mention the transfer characteristics of the amplifiers and loudspeakers used. The Leslie Tone Cabinet, for example, employed vacuum tube electronics with "overdrive" distortion if desired. These complicated and interacting acoustical and electronic effects are difficult to simulate convincingly using digital signal processing. Nonetheless, a number of synthesizers and effects units offer programs that simulate rotating loudspeakers. Such programs should improve as more sophisticated algorithms are developed.

Reverberation

Reverberation is a naturally occurring acoustical effect. We hear it in large churches, concert halls, and other spaces with high ceilings and reflective surfaces. Sounds emitted in these spaces are reinforced by thousands of closely spaced echoes bouncing off the ceiling, walls, and floors. Many of these echoes arrive at our ears after reflecting off several surfaces, so we hear them after the original sound has reached our ears. The ear distinguishes between the *direct* (original) sound and the *reflected* sound because the reflected sound is usually lower in amplitude, slightly delayed, and lowpass filtered due to absorption of high frequencies by the air and reflecting surfaces (figure 11.15). The myriad echoes fuse in our ear into a lingering acoustical "halo" following the original sound.

A microphone recording of an instrument in a concert hall is surrounded by an envelope of reverberation from the hall. This is particularly the case when the microphone has an omnidirectional pattern. For recordings made in small studio spaces, it is often desirable to add reverberation, since without it a voice or ensemble sounds "dry," lacks "space" or "depth."

Certain synthesized sounds have little or no intrinsic spaciousness. These acoustically "dead" signals can be enhanced by spatial panning, echoes, and reverberation processing.

But space is not merely a cosmetic appliqué for sounds. Spatial depth can be used to isolate foreground and background elements in a compositional architecture. Further, reverberation is not a monolithic effect; there are

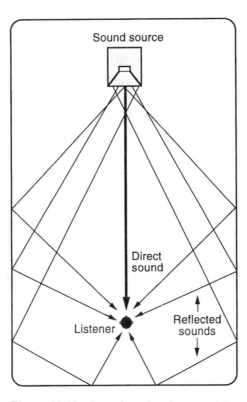

Figure 11.15 Reverberation is caused by reflections of sound off surfaces in a space. The dark line is the path of direct sound; all other lines represent sonic reflections that arrive later than the original due to their longer paths.

many colors and qualities of reverberation—as many as there are natural spaces and synthetic reverberators. No single type of reverberation (natural or synthetic) is ideal for all music. Most electronic reverberation units simulate several types of reverberation. Some attempt (often crudely) to simulate known concert halls, while others create bizarre spatial images that would be impossible to duplicate in a real hall.

Properties of Reverberation

Glorious-sounding salons and concert halls have been constructed since antiquity, but their basic acoustical properties were not well understood from a scientific standpoint until the late nineteenth century. The pioneering work on the analysis of reverberant spaces was carried out by Wallace Sabine (1868–1919), who advised in the construction (starting from an existing structure) of Boston's acclaimed Symphony Hall in 1900. Symphony Hall was the first performance space designed according to rigorous, scientifically derived principles of acoustics. Sabine observed that a room's reverberation is dependent on its volume, geometry, and the reflectivity of its surfaces (Sabine 1922). It is no surprise that large rooms with reflective surfaces have long reverberation times, and small rooms with absorptive surfaces have short reverberation times. Smooth, hard surfaces like glass, chrome, and marble tend to reflect all frequencies well, while absorptive surfaces like heavy curtains, foam, and thick carpeting tend to absorb high frequencies.

The geometry of the room surfaces determines the angle of sound reflections. Walls that are not parallel scatter the wavefronts in complicated dispersion patterns, and small irregularities such as plaster trimmings, indentations, columns, and statues tend to diffuse the reflections, creating a richer, denser reverberation effect.

Sabine also observed that humidity affects the reverberation time in large halls, since up to a point, humid air tends to absorb high frequencies.

Impulse Response of a Room

One way to measure the reverberation of a room is to trigger a very short burst (an *impulse*) and plot the room's response over time. This plot, when corrected for the spectrum of the burst, shows the *impulse response* of the room. As mentioned in chapter 10, circuits also exhibit an impulse response, making the impulse response measurement an often-used tool both in circuit design and concert hall design. Natural reverberation typically has an

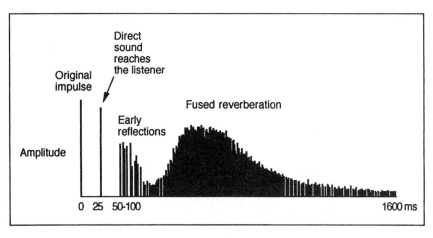

Figure 11.16   Impulse response envelope of a reverberant hall. The components of reverberation are shown as the *predelay* (shown as a 25-ms delay before the direct sound reaches the listener), the early reflections, and the fused reverberation.

impulse response envelope similar to that shown in figure 11.16. The build-up of reverberation follows a quasi-exponential curve that reaches a peak within a half-second and decays more or less slowly.

In general, an irregular time interval between peaks is desirable in a concert hall. Regularly spaced peaks indicate "ringing"—resonant frequencies in the hall—which can be annoying.

Reverberation Time

Another important measurement of reverberation is *reverberation time* or RT60. The term RT60 refers to the time it takes the reverberation to decay 60 dB from its peak amplitude (1/1000 of its peak energy). Typical RT60 times for concert halls are from 1.5 to 3 seconds. The RT60 point of the plot in figure 11.17 is 2.5 seconds.

Artificial Reverberation: Background

The earliest attempts at artificial reverberation of recordings transmitted the sound through an *acoustic echo chamber*, then mixed the reverberated signal with the original. Some large recording studios still allocate a separate room as an echo chamber. They place a loudspeaker at one end of a reflective room and put a high-quality microphone at the other end. The sound to be reverberated is played over the loudspeaker and picked up by the micro-phone (figure 11.18). An echo chambers offers a unique acoustical ambience created by a specific room, loudspeaker, and microphone. When all these conditions are sympathetic, the quality of reverberation may be excellent. A drawback to the echo chamber approach (besides the practicalities of

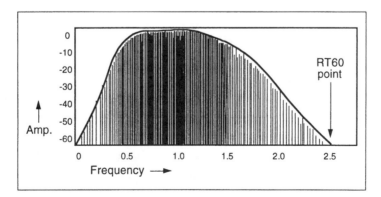

Figure 11.17 Reverberation time is measured as the point at which the reverberation decays to − 60 dB of its peak level.

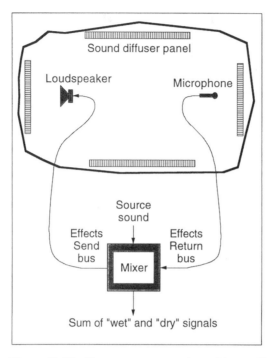

Figure 11.18   To create an acoustic ambience effect, sound can be fed into an echo chamber via a loudspeaker. The reflected, indirect sound is picked up by a microphone at the other end of the room. Ideally, the room is irregularly shaped. To maximize and randomize the reflections, the room should be fitted with *sound diffuser panels*. Sound diffuser panels contain many recesses spaced at different distances. As sound waves strike them they are reflected back at different delay times, depending on which recess they hit. This diffusion effect tends to eliminate *standing waves* (resonant frequencies in the room) caused by parallel walls.

constructing such a space) is that the reverberation cannot be varied tremendously.

The more usual way of adding reverberation is with a *reverberation unit* or *reverberator*. Before digital reverberators were introduced in the mid-1970s, reverberators were electromechanical contraptions containing two transducers (input and output) and a reverberating medium like a long metal spring or a metal plate. The sound to be reverberated was transmitted from the input transducer to the medium. The medium transmitted the sound to the output transducer mixed with myriad echoes caused by vibrations/reflections of the signal within the medium. The result was amplified and mixed with the original signal to create a rather "colored" artificial reverberation effect. The best plate reverberators produced relatively clean and diffuse reverberation, but they were limited to an RT60 of only a few seconds and a fixed reverberation pattern.

Digital Reverberation Algorithms

Digital reverberators use time delays, filters, and mixing to achieve the illusion of sound scattering within a room. From a signal-processing standpoint, a reverberator is a filter with an impulse response that resembles the impulse response of a room. Manfred Schroeder of the Bell Telephone Laboratories (1961, 1962, 1970) was the first to implement an artificial reverberation algorithm on a digital computer. His reverberation programs soaked up hours of computation time on the behemoth mainframe computers of the epoch. Modern reverberation units are compact and run in real time. Control knobs and buttons on their front panels let musicians dial up a variety of effects. Most reverberators can be controlled via MIDI (see chapter 21).

Parts of Reverberation

The effect of reverberation can be broken into three parts, shown earlier in figure 11.16.

- *Direct (unreflected) sound* travels in a straight path and is the first sound to arrive at the listener's ears
- *Discrete early reflections* hit the listener just after the direct sound
- *Fused reverberation* contains thousands of closely spaced echoes but takes some time to build up and then fade away

Commercial reverberation units usually provide controls that let one manipulate these parts more or less independently. On these units, the balance between the reverberated and direct sound is sometimes called the *wet/dry* ratio (the reverberated sound is said to be "wet"), and the delay just before the early reflections is called the *predelay*.

Effective simulation of natural reverberation requires high *echo density*. Some early digital reverberators produced as few as 30 echoes per second, while in actual concert halls, an echo density of more than 1000 echoes per second is typical. Many reverberators today provide a control that lets users adjust the echo density to suit the desired effect, from discrete echoes to a dense, fused reverberation pattern.

The discrete early reflections of a concert hall can be simulated by means of a *tapped delay line*. This is simply a delay unit that can be "tapped" at several points to put out several versions of the input signal, each delayed by a different amount. (See chapter 10 for an explanation of tapped delay lines.)

The lush sound of fused reverberation requires a greater echo density than a tapped delay line can efficiently provide. Many different algorithms for fused reverberation exist, but they all usually involve a variation on M. R. Schroeder's original algorithms, described next.

Unit Reverberators

Schroeder called the building blocks *unit reverberators,* of which there are two forms: *recursive comb filters* and *allpass filters,* both of which were introduced in chapter 10.

Recursive Comb Filters

As explained in chapter 10, a recursive or *infinite impulse response* (IIR) comb filter contains a feedback loop in which an input signal is delayed by D samples and multiplied by an amplitude or gain factor g, and then routed back to be added to the latest input signal (figure 11.19a).

When the delay D is small (i.e., less than about 10 ms) the comb filter's effect is primarily a spectral one. That is, it creates peaks and dips in the frequency response of the input signal. When D is larger than about 10 ms, it creates a series of decaying echoes, as shown in figure 11.19b. The echoes decay exponentially, so for the maximum number of echoes (the longest decay time), g is set to nearly 1.0. The time it takes for the output of the comb filter to decay by 60 dB is specified by the following formula (Moore 1990):

$$decay\_time = (60/-loopGain) \times loopDelay$$

where *loopGain* is the gain g expressed in decibels $= 20 \times \log_{10}(g)$, and *loopDelay* is the delay D expressed in seconds $= D/R$, where R is the sampling rate. Thus if $g = 0.7$, then *loopGain* $= -3$ dB.

Allpass Filters

Allpass filters transmit all frequencies of steady-state signals equally well (see chapter 10). But they "color" sharp transient signals by introducing frequency-dependent delays. When the delay time is long enough (between 5 and 100 ms), the allpass filter shown in figure 11.20a has an impulse response as shown in figure 11.20b: a series of exponentially decaying echo pulses, like a comb filter with a long delay. The uniform spacing between the pulses suggests that when a short, transient sound is applied, the filter rings with a period equal to the delay time of the filter. This explains why allpass

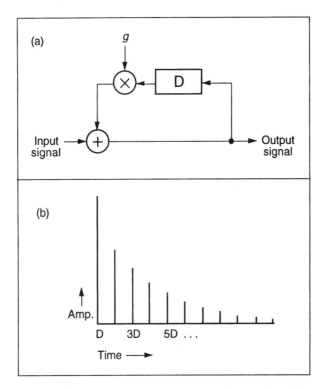

Figure 11.19 A recursive comb filter for reverberation. (*a*) Circuit of comb filter with coefficients D (number of samples to delay) and g (amount of feedback). (*b*) Impulse response, as a series of echoes.

filters are not "colorless" when they treat sounds with sharp attack and decay transients.

Reverberation Patches

We have established that both recursive comb and allpass filters can generate a series of decaying echoes. For lush reverberation, it is necessary to interconnect a number of unit reverberators to create sufficient echo density so that the echoes fuse. When unit reverberators are connected in parallel, their echoes add together. When they are connected in series, each echo generated by one unit triggers a series of echoes in the next unit, creating a much greater echo density. The number of echoes produced in series is the product of the number of echoes produced by each unit.

In Schroeder's designs, comb filters are interconnected in parallel to minimize spectral anomalies. For example, a frequency that passes through one comb filter might be attenuated by another. Allpass filters are usually connected in series. Because of the phase distortion they introduce, connecting

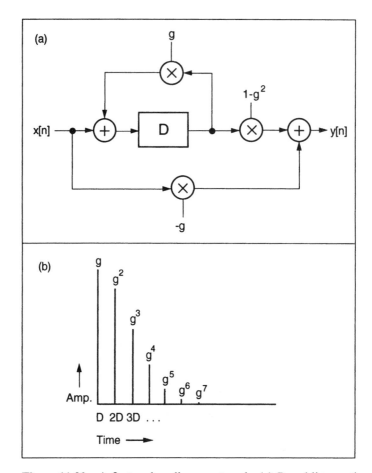

Figure 11.20   A first-order allpass network. (*a*) By adding -*g* times the input into the output of the delay, a comb filter is changed into an allpass filter. (*b*) The impulse response of an allpass filter is an exponentially decaying series of echo pulses. This makes the impulse filter useful as a building block of reverberators.

allpass filters in parallel can result in a nonuniform amplitude response due to phase cancellation effects.

Figure 11.21 shows two reverberators proposed by Schroeder. In figure 11.21a the parallel comb filters initiate a train of echoes that are summed and fed to two allpass filters in series. In figure 11.21b five allpass filters cause the echo density to be multiplied by each unit. If each allpass generates just four audible echoes, the end result is 1024 echoes at the output of allpass number 5.

The characteristic sound of a digital reverberation system of this type is dependent on the choice of the delay times D (these determine the spacing of the echoes) and amplitude factors g (these determine the decay or rever-

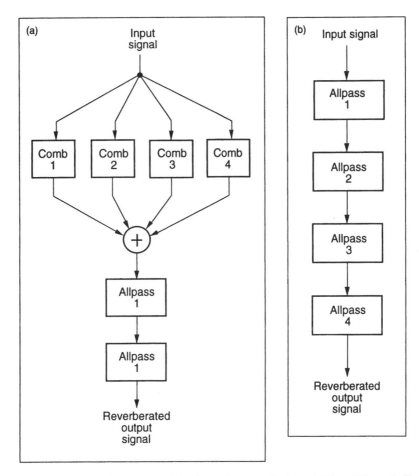

Figure 11.21 Schroeder's original reverberator designs. (*a*) Parallel comb filters fed into two allpass filter stages. (*b*) Five allpass filter stages in series.

beration time) for each of the unit reverberators inside it. The delay time is also called the *loop time*.

For natural-sounding reverberation it is important to choose delay times that are relatively prime to one another (i.e., that have no common divisor) (Moorer 1977, 1979c). Why is this? Consider two comb filters, where the delay time of the first is 10 ms and that of the second is 12.5 ms. The length of their delay lines are 800 samples and 1000 samples, respectively, at a sampling rate of 40 KHz. Because the lengths of both delay lines are divisible by 200, a reverberator built from these two units does not have a smooth decay. At multiples of 200 ms, the echoes coincide to increase the amplitude at that point, causing a sensation of discrete echoes or regular "bumps" in the decay. When the delay times are adjusted to 10.025 and 24.925 ms, the length of their delay lines are 799 and 997, respectively. Now the first coincidence of echoes does not occur until $(799 \times 997)/40$ KHz $= 19.91$ seconds. (See Moorer 1979c for a discussion of how to tune these parameters.)

As might be expected, shorter delay times correlate with the sound of smaller spaces. For a large concert hall, the reverberator in figure 11.21a uses comb filter delay times around 50 ms with a ratio of longest : shortest delay of 1.7 : 1. For a small tiled room effect the comb filter delay times can be set in the range of 10 ms. The allpass filters have relatively short loop times of 5 msec or less. The reverberation time of the allpass filters must be short (less than 100 msec) because their purpose is to increase the density of the overall reverberation, not its duration.

Simulation of Early Reflections

Schroeder's reverberation algorithms can be characterized as *tapped recirculating delay* (TRD) models. As explained earlier, the reverberator is usually partitioned into comb and allpass sections, which generate sufficient echo density to create a reasonable simulation of *global reverberation*. The TRD model is efficient, but it simulates only generic global reverberation, and not the detailed acoustic properties of an actual performance space.

In 1970 Schroeder extended his original reverberator algorithms to incorporate a *multitap delay line* to simulate the early reflections that are heard in a hall before the outset of the fused reverberant sound. (See chapter 10 for more on multitap delay lines.) This design, which has been adopted in most commercial reverberators, is shown in figure 11.22. Thus to simulate a particular concert hall, a straightforward way to improve the basic TRD model is to graft the measured early reflection response of the hall onto the generic global reverberator (Moorer 1979c). A further extension is to lowpass filter the global reverberation according to the measured sound absorptic char-acteristics of the hall.

Another important consideration in reverberation design is that the sounds presented in each ear should be *mutually incoherent*. That is, the reverberation algorithm should be slightly different (*decorrelated*) for each channel of processing.

Fictional Reverberation Effects

The goals of the electronic music composer extend beyond the simulation of natural reverberant spaces. A reverberator can conjur up many unusual "fictional" spatial effects that are not meant to be realistic. A common example is "gated" reverberation that explodes quickly in echo density,

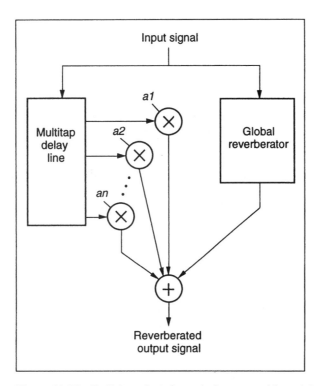

Figure 11.22   In Schroeder's later designs, a multitap delay line simulated the early reflections of sound in a concert hall.

Table 11.2   Typical parameters of reverberators

Parameter	Description
Type of reverberation	Choice between "Hall," "Chamber," "Plate," or "Gated"
Size	Sets the delay times within the unit reverberators
Predelay	Controls the onset time of the effect
Input delay	Causes the effect to precede the cause (the wet sound precedes the dry sound)
Reverberation time	Sets the decay time
Diffusion	Determines the echo density
Mix	Ratio of input sound to reverberated sound at the output of the device
Highpass filter	Reverberates only the upper octaves of the sound, creating a "sizzling" reverberation effect
Lowpass filter	Reverberates only the lower octaves of the sound, creating a "muffled" reverberation effect

then cuts off suddenly. Gated reverberation was used on snare drums in the 1980s and quickly became a pop music cliché. Other effects include a "sizzling" reverberation, obtained by applying a highpass filter to the reverberated sound, and its opposite, a muffled reverberation obtained by applying a steep lowpass filter. By manipulating the parameters of a reverberator, one can create weird combinations such as tiny rooms with long reverberation times. Table 11.2 lists the parameters provided on many commercial reverberators.

The section on reverberation by convolution, later in this chapter, presents another type of nonrealistic reverberation using the asynchronous granular synthesis technique covered in chapter 5.

Modeling Sound Spaces

The study of reverberation is ongoing. The algorithms described in the earlier section on reverberation are a starting point for the designs discussed here. This section explains several approaches to more realistic reverberation that have been developed in recent years. These include extensions to the basic Schroeder algorithms, geometric models, reverberation via convolution, waveguide reverberation, and multiple-stream reverberation.

Several of these techniques represent a *physical modeling* approach to reverberation. (See chapter 7 for an introduction to the theory of physical modeling in the context of sound synthesis.) These mathematically intensive methods model the diffusion of acoustical waves in actual spaces. Besides creating more realistic models, they offer the possibility of simulating imaginary spaces. In this category we include rooms whose characteristics and geometry can change over time—such as an elastic concert hall that "expands" and "shrinks" over the course of a phrase—or impossible spaces such as a closet with a long reverberation time. Thus the goal of these techniques is not always realistic reverberation, but rather a dramatic spatial transform.

Extensions to Schroeder Reverberation Algorithms

In the standard Schroeder reverberation algorithms, the allpass filters generate a series of echoes with an exponential decay. An extension to the Schroeder model is to substitute an *oscillatory allpass* filter for the regular allpass filter in the Schroeder design. In this case, the impulse response of the allpass filter is a pulse train with an amplitude of a damped sinusoid

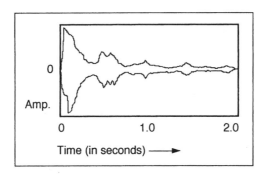

Figure 11.23   The impulse response of an oscillatory allpass unit reverberator.

(figure 11.23). This models the case of a "good sounding" room with a slightly undulating reverberation pattern (Chowning et al. 1974; Moorer 1979c).

Geometric Modeling of Sound Spaces

An alternative to the TRD approach is to build a physical model of a room's geometry using a computer-aided design (CAD) system. The loudspeakers that project the sound constitute an "acoustic window" into the simulated room surrounding them.

In F. R. Moore's design (1983), each sound source becomes a vector with an adjustable position, directionality, magnitude, and dispersion. Starting from the projection of a source vector into the room, the computer traces the path of sound reflections (Moore 1983). In a complete geometric model, the reverberation algorithm would model the reflection patterns of hundreds of simulated sound rays. Depending on the detail of the model, this approach can be computationally expensive. For efficiency's sake, Moore used a geometric approach to model only the early reflections of a simulated room. He used a standard Schroeder TDR model for global reverberation.

A problem of a too-simple geometrical approach to reverberation has been pointed out by Moorer (1979). Such an approach fails to take into account the *diffusion* (scattering) of sound rays that occurs in real halls. Diffusion occurs since no surface is 100 percent smooth and reflective, meaning that sound waves scatter and their energy is partially absorbed at each point of reflection. Thus a number of methods try to improve on the ray-tracing model by explicitly modeling sound diffusion. These may insert a stochastic scattering function at each point of reflection. The *waveguide network* reverberation, discussed later, is another attempt to model explicitly sound diffusion.

Reverberation via Convolution

An accurate but computationally intensive means of simulating the reverberation in a given space is to convolve the impulse response of the space with the signal to be reverberated. (See chapter 10 and Smith 1985a for more on convolution.) One can think of reverberation as a type of filter, where the length (in samples) of the impulse response corresponds to the reverberation time (in samples) of the simulated hall. The impulse response of a room is gathered by recording the room's response to a very brief explosive sound. This set of samples is then convolved with the signal to be reverberated.

Chapter 10 distinguishes between *direct* and *fast* convolution. Direct convolution is not practical for reverberation because of the enormous amount of computation it entails. For example, at a sampling rate of 48 KHz and an impulse response length of three seconds, each sample of each channel of the input signal must be multiplied and summed $48,000 \times 3$ times. For a second of input sound this translates into the following:

144,000	$\times$	48,000	=	6,912,000,000.
Multiply/adds per sample		Samples per second		Multiply/adds per second per channel

(impulse response)

Thus, to reverberate one second of stereo sound by convolution would require 13.824 billion multiply/adds. Calculating this in real time requires a level of performance that is currently associated with expensive supercomputers. On a signal-processing engine benchmarked at 100 million multiply/adds per second in a practical application, such as a plug-in board for a personal computer, this calculation would take about two minutes and eighteen seconds to compute, a factor of $138:1$ as compared to real time.

Thus the only practical reverberation by convolution uses fast convolution, taking advantage of speedups offered by the fast Fourier transform (FFT). See chapter 10 for details on fast convolution; Appendix A explains the FFT.

Granular Reverberation

The rolling of thunder has been attributed to echoes among the clouds; and if it is to be considered that a cloud is a collection of particles of water ... and therefore each capable of reflecting sound, there is no reason why very [loud] sounds should not be reverberated ... from a cloud. (Sir John Herschel, quoted in Tyndall 1875)

This section describes a reverberation effect that can be achieved by convolving an arbitrary input sound with a cloud of sonic grains.

It is well known that clouds in the atmosphere contribute a reverberation effect. The nineteenth-century French acoustical scientists Arago, Mathieu, and Prony, in their experiments on the velocity of sound, observed that under a perfectly clear sky the explosions of cannons were always singular and sharp. Whereas, when the sky was overcast or a large cloud filled part of the sky, cannon shots were frequently accompanied by a long continuous "roll," similar to thunder (Tyndall 1875). (See Uman 1984 for an analysis of the acoustics of thunder.)

Provided that one understands convolution, it is not a great surprise to learn that the convolution of a sound with a cloud of sound particles creates a scattershot "time-splattered" effect akin to atmospheric reverberation. Time-splattering begins with a more-or-less dense cloud of sound grains generated by the technique of *asynchronous granular synthesis* (AGS), described in chapter 5. AGS scatters grains statistically within a region defined on the time/frequency plane. In convolution, this mass of grains can be thought of as the impulse response of a cumulus cloud enclosure. The virtual "reflection" contributed by each grain splatters the input sound in time; that is, it adds multiple irregularly spaced delays. If each grain was a single-sample pulse, then the echoes would be faithful copies of the original input. Since each grain may contain hundreds of samples, however, each echo is locally time-smeared.

Time-splattering effects can be divided into two basic categories, which depend mainly on the attack of the input sound. If the input begins with a sharp attack, each grain generates an echo of that attack. If the cloud of grains is not continuous, these echoes are irregularly spaced in time. If the input has a smooth attack, however, the time-splattering itself is smoothed into a kind of strange colored reverberation (figure 11.24). The "color" of the reverberation and the echoes is determined by the spectrum of the grains, which is a factor of the duration, envelope, and waveform of each grain. See chapter 5 for more details on grain parameters.

Waveguide Reverberation

A *waveguide* is a computational model of a medium in which waves travel. Physicists have long used *waveguide networks* to describe the behavior of waves in resonant spaces (Crawford 1968). The waveguide network approach to reverberation is built out of a set of bidirectional delay lines (Smith 1985c, 1987a, b; Garnett and Mont-Reynaud 1988; chapter 7 presents more on waveguides in the context of sound synthesis). Each delay line

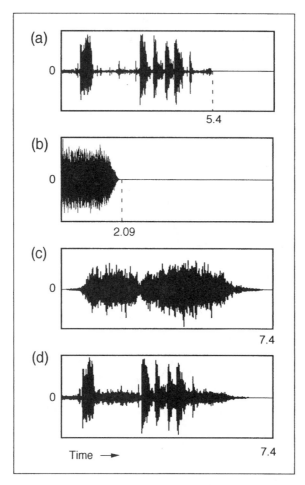

Figure 11.24 Reverberation by granular convolution. (*a*) Speech input: "Moi, Alpha Soixante." (*b*) Granular impulse response, consisting of 1000 9-ms sinusoidal grains centered at 14,000 Hz, with a bandwidth of 5000 Hz. (*c*) Convolution of (*a*) and (*b*). (*d*) Mixture of (*a*) and (*c*) in a proportion of 5:1, creating reverberation around the speech.

contains a wave propagating in the one direction and reflecting back to the center junction when it reaches the end of the line. By connecting a number of waveguides together into a network, one can build a model of acoustical media, such as the reflection pattern of a concert hall.

In waveguide reverberation, the lengths of the individual waveguide delay lines are different from one another to simulate the different echo times within a hall. At the junction of multiple waveguides the energy is scattered among them, causing a diffusion effect that is typical of fused reverberant sound (figure 11.25). In a *closed network,* once a signal is introduced it recirculates freely throughout the network without loss of energy. To obtain

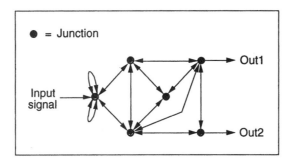

Figure 11.25 A three-port waveguide network with six nodes. This waveguide propagates energy out of the outputs, meaning that it is an open network that eventually loses energy, as a reverberant hall does.

a reverberation effect one must introduce small losses of amplitude energy within the network to achieve the desired reverberation time. Signal inputs and outputs can be chosen anywhere in the network.

Waveguide networks make efficient reverberation models. A network with N junctions requires N multiplies and $2N - 1$ additions to generate an output sample. The number of junctions N depends on the system being modeled. A model of a resonating box might require eight intersections, while a model of a complex room's reverberation response might take hundreds of junctions, since any place where a signal might scatter requires a junction.

The structure of a waveguide network ensures that there is never any numerical overflow or oscillation within the network. Moreover, the important property of diffusive scattering of sound rays (Moorer 1979), which is poorly handled by a simple geometric model, is simulated well by a waveguide network. A "moving walls" effect can be obtained by smoothly varying the delay line lengths.

Multiple-stream Reverberation

Multiple-stream reverberation can be viewed as a compromise between detailed but computationally intensive approaches to reverberation (such as geometrical modeling or reverberation via convolution) and the efficient but global TRD model. Multiple-stream reverberation splits the reverberated signal into several *streams,* each of which models the local reverberation emanating from a small spatial region of the virtual room. Each stream is implemented with a TRD network (comb and allpass filters) tuned for that region of the room.

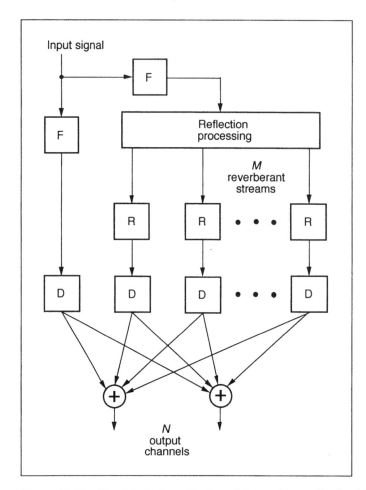

Figure 11.26   Simplified view of a "spatial reverberator" after Kendall, Martens, and Decker (1989). This system models a space by summing the contributions of *M* local reverberators, which ultimately generate *N* output channels. F is a prefilter that imposes spectrum changes caused by distance and air absorption. R is a local reverberant stream, modeling the reverberation in a subspace of the total room. D is a directionalizer that filters the sound according to its position in the virtual space. The implemented system has two independent reflection processors, and some cross-feeding in the reverberant streams.

The "spatial reverberator" system, developed at Northwestern University in the 1980s, takes the multiple-stream approach and combines it with two other processes: (1) a model of room reflections, and (2) localization cues caused by the reflection of sound off of the pinnae, shoulders, and upper torso (Kendall and Martens 1984; Kendall et al. 1986; Kendall, Martens, and Decker 1989). First- and second-order reflections determine the delay times of each independent reverberation stream. Then, after reverberating each stream separately, a "directionalizer" filters each stream to impose additional cues as to its position in a virtual three-dimensional space (figure 11.26).

The user of the system can specify the characteristics of a virtual space in acoustical terms such as room dimensions, sound location, listener location, sound absorption of the walls, and so on. To simulate a room's reverberation pattern, each of the main directions of reverberation is processed as a separate stream, with up to eighteen streams in one implementation (Kendall, Martens, and Decker 1989). As figure 11.26 shows, the number of reverberation streams is independent of the number of output channels used ultimately to project the sound.

The concept of separate reverberation streams was also present in quadraphonic reverberation research carried out at MIT in the early 1980s (Stautner and Puckette 1982). In this work the loudspeaker outputs were spatially responsive to the input channel of the source. For example, a direct sound emanating from a left front loudspeaker would be heard to reverberate from two adjacent loudspeakers and finally from the opposite right rear loudspeaker.

Conclusion

Sound spatialization by electronic means pervades musical production, through microphone techniques, signal processing, and sound projection via loudspeakers or headphones. As psychoacoustical knowledge about spatial perception has increased, systems for spatialization have grown more sophisticated. Many studios own several spatial effects processors. As always, there is a wide range in the audio quality reflected in the devices available at a given time.

Simulations of natural effects such as loudspeaker rotation and reverberation remain approximations to the real world. What happens to sound when a loudspeaker rotates is not entirely understood. The best concert halls have a lush and enveloping quality of reverberation that exceeds the best synthetic reverberation. Although this sensuous quality is best appreciated in the hall, the presence of fine natural reverberation transmits even on recordings played through loudspeakers.

A main advantage of synthetic spatial processors is flexibility—many different types of reverberation and spatial processing. They can also implement supernatural effects that would be impossible in the real world, as well as such features as the ability to switch from one spatial effect to another in synchrony with a musical line.

As a final word, a comment about stereo audio media is in order. Stereophonic recording and playback was a great advance when it was introduced in the 1930s. But the continued dominance of two-channel media for broadcast and sale make it difficult and impractical to realize more sophisticated spatial processing. A true multiple-channel audio medium distributed on a mass scale would greatly stimulate further advances in musical spatialization.

IV   Sound Analysis

Overview to Part IV

Sound analysis is profoundly important in computer music—the means by which a computer "listens," enabling it to recognize, understand, and respond musically to what it hears. It is the first stage in many musical applications, including the following:

- Analysis/resynthesis, in which sounds are analyzed, modified, and resynthesized after modifications by a musician.

- Making responsive instruments that "listen" via a microphone to a performer and respond in real time (Roads 1985b, 1986b).

- Creating sound databases in which sounds can be accessed according to their acoustic properties (Feiten and Ungvary 1990).

- Enhancing a performing or listening space, that is, tuning a sound reinforcement system according to an analysis of the space.

- Restoring old recordings for reissue (Borish 1984; Lagadec and Pelloni 1983; Moorer and Berger 1986). Restoration can be as mundane as identifying and eliminating clicks and hum or as exotic as removing an instrumental background from a vocal performance. A famous example of this is the restoration of the opera singer Enrico Caruso's singing, where a new high-fidelity orchestra was substituted for a poorly recorded orchestra while leaving the voice more or less intact (Miller 1973; Stockham, Cannon, and Ingebretson 1975).

- Data compression algorithms that reduce the storage requirements for digital audio samples (Stautner 1983; Moorer 1979b; Pohlmann 1989a).

- Transcribing sound into common music notation (Moorer 1975; Piszczalski and Galler 1977; Chafe et al. 1982; Foster et al. 1982; Haus 1983), or from sound to a spectrogram representation for musical analysis (Potter and Teaney 1980; Cogan 1984; Waters and Ungvary 1990; Lundén and Ungvary 1991).

■ Development of music theories based on the sound of musical performances and not just paper scores.

Several historical sections in part IV recount the saga of sound analysis over the centuries. Sound analysis was quite difficult prior to the computer era, requiring heroic effort. During the 1960s signal analysis came of age as a practical scientific tool. It was only in the late 1980s, however, when theoretical advances merged with inexpensive and yet powerful hardware, that analysis became common in music applications. Musicians can now can apply the armamentarium of physics, engineering, and artificial intelligence to the job of segmenting, analyzing, recognizing, understanding, and interpreting features of musical signals.

Organization of Part IV

Part IV divides sound analysis into three parts: pitch and rhythm—covered in chapter 12—and spectrum—covered in chapter 13. The chapters survey both time-domain and frequency-domain methods. The final part of chapter 13 examines systems that combine numerical signal-processing algorithms with sophisticated control structures and decision-making—the realm of intelligent signal processing.

Pitch, rhythm, and spectrum are merely the most established sound analysis categories. Emerging techniques dissect sounds into excitation and resonance components, or separate out different sources combined into one signal. Other methods spot formants, seek hidden modulations, or derive chaotic driving functions (Bernardi, Bugna, and De Poli 1992; Pressing, Scallan, and Dicker 1993); innumerable other possibilities can be imagined, making sound analysis an open field of exploration.

12 *Pitch and Rhythm Recognition*

Pitch, Rhythm, and Waveform Analysis: Background

> **Early Images of Sound**
> **Early Sound Recorders**

Pitch and Rhythm Recognition in MIDI Systems

The Pitch Detection Problem

> **Applications of Pitch Detection**
> **Difficulties in Pitch Detection**
> *Attack Transients*
> *Low Frequencies*
> *High Frequencies*
> *Myopic Pitch Tracking*
> *Acoustical Ambience*

Pitch Detection Methods

> **Time-domain Fundamental Period Pitch Detection**
> **Autocorrelation Pitch Detection**
> **Adaptive Filter Pitch Detectors**
> **Frequency-domain Pitch Detection**
> *Tracking Phase Vocoder Analysis*
> *Cepstrum Analysis*
> **PDs Based on Models of the Ear**
> **Polyphonic Pitch Detection**
> **Analysis of Musical Context**

Rhythm Recognition

Applications of Rhythm Recognition
Levels of Rhythm Recognition
Event Detection
Amplitude Thresholding
Separating Voices in Polyphonic Music
Transcription
Tempo Tracking
Note Duration Assignment
Grouping into Patterns
Estimating Meter and Measure Boundaries
Recovery

Conclusion

Sound analysis has emerged recently as one of the central forces behind the future development of computer music. It plays a pivotal role in such applications as interactive composition (responsive instruments), accompaniment systems, and new methods of sound transformation. Due to either a lack of knowledge about human hearing or a lack of computer power, contemporary methods for sound analysis tend to be a jumble of techniques chosen for their computational efficiency or intuitive appeal. Methods based on detailed models of human perception are surfacing, however.

This chapter and the next describe basic concepts behind the art of sound analysis. Chapter 12 focuses on machine analysis of pitch and rhythm—two young fields. No single standard approach to either domain stands out, and new methods continue to be developed. Thus we do not attempt to account for every possible approach in this chapter. For example, the application of neural networks to pitch and rhythm analysis appears promising, but is not covered in this chapter (D'Autilia and Guerra 1991; Desain and Honing 1989; Todd and Loy 1991). Our goal is here to present the basic issues, survey past strategies, and describe musical applications of these techniques. It is likely that future work will build on the foundations of the approaches presented here.

Before plunging directly into the current of pitch and rhythm analysis, we recommend a preliminary dip into the history of inquiry into the properties of sound: hence the following background section.

Pitch, Rhythm, and Waveform Analysis: Background

Efforts to describe and measure the properties of musical sound date back to antiquity. Ancient Vedantic (orthodox Hindu) texts on music acknowledge the notion of octave equivalence and divide the octave into 22 *shruti* intervals (Framjee 1958; Daniélou 1958). This *shruti* scale, which the Greeks called the *Enarmonikos,* was considered by the Hellenic peoples as the basis of all musical scales. Pythagoras (ca. 580–500 B.C.) documented a correspondence between musical pitches and divisions of a length of string, which led him to describe musical intervals and scales in terms of arithmetic ratios. The Greeks also developed a set of rhythmic patterns or "modes" that served as the rhythmic basis for much European medieval music. Although music notation evolved slowly thereafter, it was hardly a basis for accurate acoustic measurements.

Before the invention of electronic devices such as audio amplifiers, oscillators, and oscilloscopes, acoustic measurements were limited to the most basic properties of sound. In 1636, Galileo (1564–1642) and Mersenne

(1588–1648) experimentally ascribed pitch to the frequency of a waveform. Mersenne and Gassendi (1592–1655) made the first attempt to determine the speed at which sound waves travel. Around 1700 Sauver (1653–1716) invented a method to count acoustic vibrations. He coined the term *les harmoniques* to describe higher tones that accompany a fundamental tone.

The tuning fork, which vibrates at a constant pitch, was invented in 1711 by the Englishman John Shore, a trumpeter and lutenist. He humorously referred to the instrument as a "pitch fork." In 1830 Savart developed a pitch-measuring technique using rotating serrated wheels. Savart pressed a reed against different wheels to determine the precise frequencies of sounds based on the number of teeth and the speed of rotation (Beranek 1949). Working in a quiet laboratory on the Île Saint Louis in Paris, the German-born acoustician Rudolf Koenig (1842–1914) built a precision *tonometer*, covering the audible range, for measuring the pitch of sounds by resonant beating of 154 tuning forks (Miller 1916; Wood 1940).

The first precision instruments for measuring the intensity of sound waves were the *phonic wheel* of La Cour (1878) and the *Rayleigh disk* (1882), named after the great British acoustician Lord Rayleigh (1842–1919). The first electronic sound level meter did not appear until G. W. Pierce constructed one in 1908, two years after the invention of the triode vacuum tube by Lee DeForest (1873–1961).

Early Images of Sound

One problem that early acousticians faced in studying sound is that waveforms could be heard but not seen. They devised ingenious, though contrived, methods of viewing sound. One method involved modulating a bunsen burner with sound and observing the effect on the flame. Apparently the first documented attempts at analysis of sound flames was carried out by a Dr. Higgens in 1777 (Tyndall 1875). Rudolf Koenig built precision instruments for generating sound images that he called *manometric flames* (figure 12.1). (For details, see Mayer 1878; Poynting and Thomson 1900; Beranek 1949.)

By placing a resonant tube around a bunsen burner, John Tyndall (1820–1893) made flames "sing." He also described experiments with what he called *sensitive naked flames*—not surrounded by tubes. Tyndall analyzed sound flame patterns according to their "tails, wings," and " forks." Other media for representing sound waveforms included sound-modulated smoke and high-pressure water jets.

More direct images of sound waveforms appeared in the mid-nineteenth century. The Wheatstone Kaleidaphone (1827) projected vibrating motions

(a)

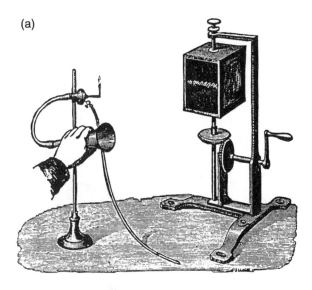

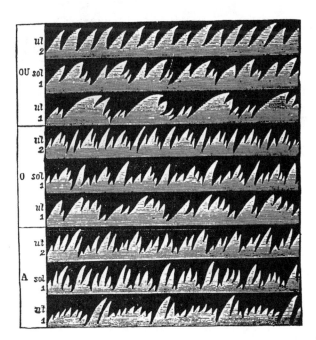

Figure 12.1 Manometric flames for waveform analysis. (*a*) Apparatus. Sounds picked up by the mouthpiece modulate the bunsen burner flame within the box. When the box is rotated, mirrors on the outside of the box project the flame as a continuous band with jagged edges or teeth corresponding to the pitch and spectrum of the input sound. (*b*) Flame pictures of the French vowel sounds [OU], [O], and [A] by R. Koenig, sung at the pitches C1 (bottom of each group), G1 (middle of each group), and C2 (top of each group). (After Tyndall 1875.)

(a)

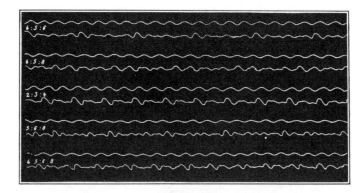

Figure 12.2   Rudolf Koenig's version of the Phonoautograph for recording images of sound waveforms. (*a*) Apparatus. (*b*) Recordings.

onto a screen. This led Lissajous (1857) to develop his Lissajous patterns, which indicate both the frequency interval and the difference of phase between two vibrating signals. The Scott-Koenig Phonautograph (1857) was a diaphragm at the end of an acoustic horn. Attached to the diagram was a stylus that traced its vibration on a smoked paper carried on a rotating cylinder (figure 12.2). The Phonodeik (1916) by D. C. Miller was a great advance in display of time-domain waveforms since it wrote on an optical film traveling at the speed of 13.3 meters/second.

Early Sound Recorders

The first sound recorders grew out of efforts to capture sound pictorially. Inspired by the Phonautograph, Thomas Alva Edison's Phonograph (1878) inscribed sound waveforms on tin foil cylinders that permitted subsequent playback of sounds. A year later Edison switched to wax cylinders. A number of researchers concocted methods for photographing the sound waveforms inscribed on phonograph cylinders (Miller 1916). Another recording device, Emile Berliner's Gramophone system (1887), used rotating lacquer disks, which eventually became the medium of choice. The Poulson Telegraphone (1900) was the first audio recording system to use magnetic signals. In the Telegraphone, a wire spun from one rotating spool to another spool while passing across a recording head. By 1924 Stille devised a recording system called the Magnetophon that used magnetic tape as its storage medium. The transition to magnetic media, of course, was central to the development of digital computer technology. And it is this ability to store acoustical data—even if only momentarily in random access memory—that has led to genuine progress in sound analysis.

Pitch and Rhythm Recognition in MIDI Systems

Pitch and rhythm recognition start from either of two points of departure: analysis of raw sound waveforms, or parsing streams of MIDI messages (chapter 21). Obviously, the latter is the easier approach. When a musician plays a MIDI input device such as a keyboard or horn controller, pitch and event detection are taken care of electromechanically by the input device itself. A microprocessor inside the input device is constantly monitoring the state of the keys, buttons, and other control surfaces of the instrument. As the musician plays, the state of these controls change, and the microprocessor detects these events. It generates a MIDI note message containing the start and end time of each event and the MIDI pitch that is associated with the control that was changed. These messages can be routed via a MIDI cable from the controller to analysis programs running on a computer. These programs have only to parse the MIDI messages to obtain the pitch and timing information. From there they can proceed directly to higher forms of analysis.

This said, there remain controllers for which the pitch detection problem remains nontrivial. Stringed instruments pose serious problems to pitch detectors, requiring a scheme that combines several strategies at once (a combination of acoustic and electromechanical sensors). And how does one derive a "pitch" from the signals emitted by a brain-wave transducer? Only a rather indirect scheme seems possible.

Analysis starting from sound waveforms is the focus of the section on pitch recognition in this chapter. MIDI systems only face this issue when the data stream derives from a *pitch-to-MIDI converter* (PMC). A PMC attempts to emit MIDI pitch values that correspond to the pitch of sounds fed into it (Fry 1992). The section on rhythm recognition also starts from analysis of sound waveforms, but then moves on to issues such as tempo tracking and score transcription that can equally be applied to MIDI systems.

The Pitch Detection Problem

In the width of perception the ear exceedingly transcends the eye; for while the former ranges over eleven octaves, but little more than a single octave is possible to the latter. (John Tyndall 1875)

We can define a *pitch detector* (PD) or *pitch estimator* as a software algorithm or hardware device that takes a sound signal as its input and attempts to determine the *fundamental pitch period* of that signal. That is, it attempts to find the frequency that a human listener would agree to be the same pitch as the input signal (assuming that there is one such pitch). Partly because the concept of pitch is ambiguous in many sounds, and because human pitch perception is not completely understood, PDs can be successful only on a limited corpus of sounds. It makes no sense to attempt to find "the pitch" of a noisy percussive sound such as a cymbal crash, brief impulses, low rumblings, or complex sound masses. Indeed, if we look closely at the frequency traces of traditional instrumental tones, we see that their pitch is never perfectly steady and is full of microvariations. In many musical applications, such as live performance, the job of a PD is to ignore these microvariations and locate a central pitch. So what we ask of a PD is inherently difficult. It should be accurate, but not too accurate, like a human listener.

Beyond pitch detection lies the vast universe of pitch interpretation within a musical context, or composition analysis. This level of analysis falls outside the scope of this chapter, but we briefly discuss certain issues later in the section on analysis of musical context.

Applications of Pitch Detection

Musical applications of pitch detection are myriad. An early application derived from ethnomusicologists' needs to capture the florid melodies of world music cultures, such as Indian singing. These elaborate microtonal melodies cannot be properly represented in common music notation. A one-of-a-kind device called the Seeger Melograph scanned the output of 100 third-octave bandpass filters every four milliseconds and searched for a

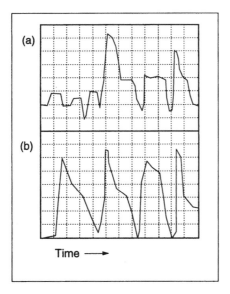

Figure 12.3 Melodic trace like that of a Melograph for two seconds of an Indian singer. Time moves horizontally. (*a*) Fundamental pitch trace. (*b*) Amplitude trace. (After Gjerdingen 1988.)

maximum. The first maximum is assumed to contain the fundamental. After some processing, the Melograph produced a two-tiered chart or *melogram* (figure 12.3) showing fundamental frequency and amplitude versus time (Seeger 1951; Moorer 1975). The technique of the Seeger Melograph continues to be updated using computer technology to provide different views of melodic motion (Gjerdingen 1988).

Another application of pitch estimation is in sound transformation. Sound-editing programs often include pitch estimation routines that are used as a guide for pitch-shifting and time-scaling operations. Another studio-based application is in transcribing a solo played on an acoustic instrument such as a saxophone, for example, into a music notation program. Advanced procedures like the separation of two simultaneous voices start from pitch detection (Maher 1990).

In concert, PDs can help a synthesizer follow the performance of an instrumentalist or a singer. As the instrumentalist plays into a microphone, the signal is sent to a pitch detector that generates MIDI note messages corresponding to the pitches being played. These messages can instruct the synthesizer to echo the pitches the instrumentalist is playing. More sophisticated performance scenarios are possible if we interpose a computer between the pitch detector and the synthesizer. In this case, software running on the computer could instruct the synthesizer to harmonize or create variations on the instrumentalist's pitches. The computer might instruct the synthesizer to remain silent except when triggered by specific cues played by the instrumentalist.

Difficulties in Pitch Detection

Human pitch perception is a complex phenomenon (Goldstein 1973; Moorer 1975; Hermes 1992). Our ears sense musical pitch even in the presence of noisy signals. We can follow several pitches simultaneously (otherwise harmony and counterpoint would be indecipherable) and also detect slight but expressive pitch deviations (vibrato, melisma, microtonal intervals). Nonetheless, the ear can be led into hearing pitches that are not there (e.g., fundamental frequencies implied by the presence of their harmonic series—an effect heard from any small loudspeaker), and illusory pitch trajectories (e.g., *Shepard tones*—sounds that appear to be continuously ascending or descending). Many sounds evoke no sense of pitch. The mechanisms by which we detect pitch are not fully understood, since they involve cognitive processing and subjective factors such as training and familiarity, as well as the mechanics of the inner ear.

Some PDs try to emulate a theoretical model of human pitch perception mechanisms, but the majority of practical devices involve simpler techniques chosen primarily for their computational efficiency. Efficiency is especially important in PDs that must work in real time to identify the pitch being played. In any case, no pitch detector is 100 percent accurate, although some computationally intense (often non-real-time) methods are reliable when the input signal is constrained in various ways.

Attack Transients

The first problem faced by PDs is sorting out the attack transient of a sound. Detailed analysis of the attack of many instruments reveals chaotic and instable waveforms. If a fundamental frequency is present in the attack, it is probably obscured by noise and inharmonic partials. Some instruments may take 100 ms or more for the instrument to settle into a stable pitch; this period of instability confuses PDs (Fry 1992).

Low Frequencies

Pitch detectors that start from spectrum analysis usually have difficulties with low tones, necessitating the use of time-domain PDs (Lyon and Dyer 1986). Any PD has problems identifying low pitches in real time. In order to determine the fundamental pitch period, at least three cycles of the steady-state waveform should be sampled before the analysis can begin. For a low-frequency pitch, for example, an A at 55 Hz, three cycles take 54 ms to sample. If one adds to this the duration of the attack transient and the pitch detection algorithm itself, then a perceivable delay is inevitable.

High Frequencies

High frequencies can also pose problems to some real-time PDs. As the frequency rises, one pitch period is represented by fewer samples. The resolution with which pitch can be determined in the time domain is directly affected by the length of the pitch period or the number of samples of delay used in comparing a signal with its past (Amuedo 1984).

Myopic Pitch Tracking

All PDs start with an analysis of a grain of time that lasts from about 20 to 50 ms; thus their analysis is based on a narrow time segment. In contrast, human pitch perception is not so time-localized. Expectations shape pitch perception; that is, we estimate pitch based on musical context. Since PDs work only from local details they may myopically track irrelevant details that were produced unintentionally, such as unsteadiness at the beginning of a note or excessive vibrato.

Acoustical Ambience

The acoustical ambience within which an instrument or voice is heard affects the accuracy of pitch detection. A closely miked and compressed studio recording may exaggerate incidental playing or singing noises, such as bow scraping, key clicking, or breathing sounds, cluttering the signal heard by the PD. By contrast, tones bathed in reverberation and echoes smear early notes over the start of new notes. Provided that the analysis is carried out in non-real time, an attempt at ambience removal may help the PD. (See Beachamp, Maher, and Brown 1993 and the description in the section on frequency-domain pitch detection.)

Pitch Detection Methods

The majority of PD algorithms grow out of speech recognition and speech synthesis research. The nontrivial nature of the problem is reflected by the number of complex methods that have been developed (Gold 1962; Noll

1967; Schafer and Rabiner 1970; Moorer 1973; Rabiner et al. 1976; Hess 1983; Amuedo 1984; Fry 1992; Hermes 1992; Hutchins and Ku 1982; Hutchins, Parola, and Ludwig 1982; Beauchamp, Maher, and Brown 1993). We can classify most methods for pitch detection into five general categories: *time-domain, autocorrelation, adaptive filter, frequency-domain*, and *models of the human ear*, discussed in the next sections.

Time-domain Fundamental Period Pitch Detection

Fundamental period methods look at the input signal as a fluctuating amplitude in the time domain (TD), like the signal that appears on the screen of an oscilloscope. They try to find repeating patterns in the waveform that give clues as to its periodicity. Perhaps a more apt term for these types of pitch detectors would be "periodicity detector" (Moorer 1975).

One type of pitch detector tries to find periodicities in the waveform by looking for repeating *zero-crossings*. A zero-crossing is a point where the waveform's amplitude goes from positive to negative or vice versa. For example, a sine wave crosses the zero amplitude threshold at the middle and end of its cycle. By measuring the interval between zero-crossings and comparing successive intervals, the PD infers a fundamental frequency (figure 12.4). A variation on zero-crossing detection is measuring the distances between peaks (Hermes 1992). In general, zero-crossing and peak PDs are relatively simple and inexpensive, but they are also less accurate than more elaborate methods (Voelkel 1985; Hutchins and Ku 1982). This is because other frequencies that are not the pitch frequency may also generate waveforms that cross the zero point or exhibit peaks. In figure 12.4b, for example, to track the visually obvious fundamental frequency, the PD must ignore the three or four rapid, low-amplitude zero-crossings caused by the high-frequency component at every major zero-crossing.

Preprocessing by filters may improve the accuracy of time domain PDs. Kuhn (1990) proposed an improvement to the basic zero-crossing method that passes the input signal through a bank of filters. Then the algorithm checks the amplitude of the filter outputs and performs zero-crossing detection only on the output of the lowest two filters that have significant amplitude after filtering.

Finally, for speech and singing signals only, an *electroglottograph* or *laryngograph* has been used with some success. These methods require a vocalist to wear a neckband that senses pulses emitted by the vocal cords. The method fails to sense unvoiced (whispered) speech and may generate errors in certain nasal vowels, however (Hermes 1992). It also has the same problems as any real-time PD in handling note attacks (Fry 1992).

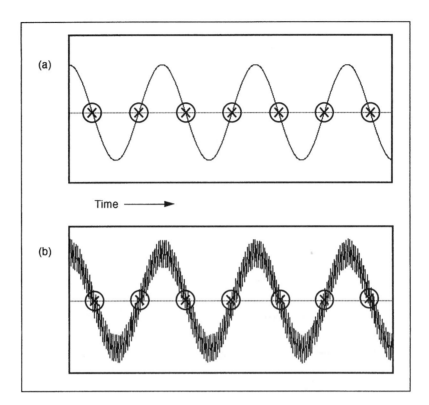

Figure 12.4 Zero-crossing pitch detector. (*a*) By measuring the interval between the zero crossings (marked ⊗), we obtain a clue as to the lowest periodicity of the signal. (*b*) For signals with a strong fundamental this works regardless of the presence of high-frequency components superposed on the signal, provided that the PD ignores the rapid low-amplitude zero-point variations caused by the high-frequency components.

Autocorrelation Pitch Detection

Correlation functions compare two signals. The goal of correlation routines is to find the "similarity" (in a precise mathematical sense) between the two signals. Correlation functions compare signals on a point-by-point basis; thus the output of a correlation function is itself a signal. If the correlation function is 1, the two signals are exactly correlated at that point. If it is 0, then the two signals are uncorrelated.

Autocorrelation methods compare a signal with versions of itself delayed by successive intervals, while *cross-correlation* methods compare two different signals over a range of time delays or *lags*. The point of comparing delayed versions of a signal is to find repeating patterns—indicators of periodicities in the signal. It is this periodicity detection that interests us here.

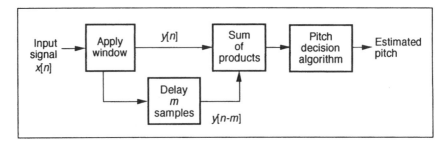

Figure 12.5 Autocorrelation scheme. The input signal is windowed, and the windowed segment is compared with versions of itself delayed by one sample, two samples, and so on up to *m* samples. The strongest correlation is estimated as the dominant or fundamental pitch.

Autocorrelation pitch detectors hold part of the input signal in a buffer (Moorer 1975; Rabiner 1977; Brown and Puckette 1987). As more of the same signal comes in, the detector tries to match a pattern in the incoming waveform with a part of the stored waveform. If the detector finds a match within a given error criterion, this indicates a periodicity, and the detector measures the time interval between the two patterns to estimate the periodicity. Figure 12.5 shows a scheme for an autocorrelation pitch detector.

Various autocorrelation algorithms exist (Moorer 1975). For a given delay or *lag time,* a typical autocorrelation function is as follows:

$$autocorrelation[lag] = \sum_{n=0}^{N} signal[n] \times signal[n + lag]$$

where *n* is the input sample index, and $0 < lag \leq N$. The degree to which the values of *signal* at different times *n* are the same as the values of the same *signal* delayed by *lag* samples determines the magnitude of *autocorrelation*[*lag*]. The output of an autocorrelation shows the magnitude for different lag times.

The autocorrelation of a sine wave illustrates the principle. In figure 12.6, case (a), the *lag* = 0, and the two functions are identical. Thus the autocorrelation function normalized by the power of the sine wave is 1. The autocorrelation function is plotted at the bottom of figure 12.6. Now suppose that the sine wave is delayed by one-quarter period. As case (b) shows, the sum of the products of *signal*[*n*] and *signal*[*n* + *lag*] over one period is 0. In case (c), the delay is one-half period, and the correlation is −1. In case (d) the delay is three-quarters of a period, and the correlation is 0. Finally, in case (e) the delay is one full period, so the correlation is 1. Thus we see that the autocorrelation of a sine wave is itself a sine wave with maxima at integral multiples of the period of the input sine.

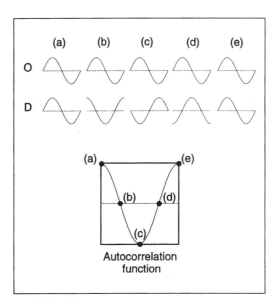

Figure 12.6 Autocorrelation of a sine wave is itself a sinusoidal wave. O indicates original signal, D indicates delayed signal. The text explains cases (*a*) through (*e*). The autocorrelation function is plotted at the bottom.

For more complex signals, PD routines search for recurrent peaks in the autocorrelation, indicating (possibly hidden) periodicities in the input waveform (figure 12.7).

Pitch detection by autocorrelation is most efficient at mid to low frequencies. Thus it has been popular in speech recognition applications where the pitch range is limited. In musical applications, where the pitch range is broader, direct calculation of the autocorrelation requires several million multiply-add operations per second of sound input. Another way to compute the autocorrelation of a signal is to segment it in a particular way and apply the fast Fourier transform to each segment; this can result in a significant speedup over direct calculation. See, for example, Rabiner and Gold (1975) for details on this algorithm.

Adaptive Filter Pitch Detectors

An adaptive filter operates, as its name implies, in a self-tuning manner, depending on the input signal. One pitch detection strategy based on an *adaptive filter* sends the input signal into a narrow bandpass filter. Both the unfiltered input signal and the filtered signal are routed to a *difference detector* circuit. The output of the difference detector circuit is fed back to control the bandpass filter center frequency (figure 12.8). This control forces the

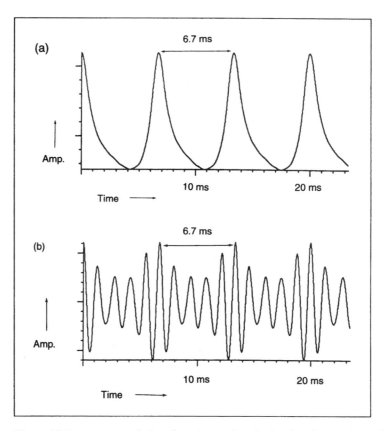

Figure 12.7   Autocorrelation functions of periodic signals are themselves periodic functions of time. (*a*) Autocorrelation of a signal with five harmonics, including the fundamental with a period of 6.7 ms or 149 Hz (close to D3). The autocorrelation is periodic, but its harmonic amplitudes are different from the input. Notice the peak corresponding to the fundamental. (*b*) Autocorrelation of a signal with only three harmonics, the fifth, sixth, and seventh. The autocorrelation is periodic with a period of 6.7 ms equal to the missing fundamental (implied pitch) of the waveform. (After Moorer 1975.)

bandpass filter to converge to the frequency of the input signal. The convergence test measures the difference between the filter output $y(n)$ and the filter input $x(n)$. When the difference is close to zero then the system makes a pitch decision.

Another adaptive filter technique is the *optimum comb method* (Moorer 1973). This method seeks to find a comb filter that minimizes its input signal. (Chapter 10 discusses comb filters.) In order to minimize the input signal, the notches of the comb filter must be tuned to the dominant frequency of the input. Thus, by finding the optimum comb filter, one has found the dominant pitch. This method is mainly applicable to sounds with a strong fundamental and regularly spaced harmonics.

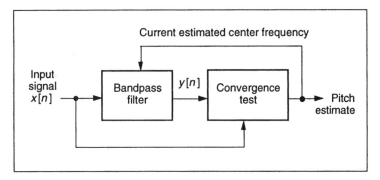

Figure 12.8 Pitch detector based on an adaptive filter scheme. Notice the feedback loop from the estimate back to the filter.

See Lane (1990), Hush et al. (1986), and Hutchins (1982–1988) for more on adaptive filter pitch detectors.

Frequency-domain Pitch Detectors

Frequency-domain (FD) pitch detection methods dissect the input signal into frequencies that make up the overall spectrum. The spectrum shows the strength of the various frequency components contained in the signal. The goal is to isolate the dominant frequency, or "pitch" out of the spectrum.

A typical FD approach analyzes successive segments of the input signal using the short-time Fourier transform (STFT). (See chapter 13 and appendix A for more on Fourier analysis.) FD pitch detectors seek peaks in the spectrum that correspond to prominent frequencies. After finding the peaks, the pitch detector must decide which frequencies are fundamentals (generally perceived as pitches) and which frequencies are merely harmonics or extraneous partials (Kay and Marple 1981). A quick real-time FD pitch detector might simply select the strongest frequency as the pitch. A more sophisticated detector might look for harmonic relationships that imply a fundamental frequency. This fundamental may not be the strongest component, but it may be the most prominent perceived pitch due to the "reinforcement" of multiple harmonics.

A problem with STFT-based pitch detectors is that the STFT divides the audio bandwidth into a set of equally spaced frequency *channels* or *bins* where each channel is *n* Hz apart from its neighbors. Since human pitch perception is basically logarithmic, this means that low pitches may be tracked less accurately than high pitches. For example, an analyzer with frequency resolution of 20 Hz can resolve microtones in the register between 10 and 20 KHz, but offers less than a semitone resolution below middle C.

Accurate pitch resolution at the low end of the spectrum demands a large number of analysis channels. As chapter 13 points out, the price paid for increasing the number of analysis channels is a loss of time resolution. Alternative methods may be better adapted for pitch tracking at low frequencies. (See chapter 13 for further discussion of these issues.)

Tracking Phase Vocoder Analysis

The *tracking phase vocoder* (TPV) stands in contrast to the fixed-frequency channels of the STFT by allowing the possibility of changing frequencies (McAulay and Quatieri 1986; see also chapter 13). The TPV starts from data generated by the STFT and then generates a set of *tracks,* with each track representing a prominent partial in a spectrum. The tracks can change frequency in time, interpolating across the fixed analysis bands. Implicit in the tracking process is a data reduction; since only the most prominent partials are tracked, the TPV generates a "sanitized" version of the input that attentuates extraneous noises and ambience.

Maher (1990) and Beauchamp, Maher, and Brown (1993) developed a FD pitch detector that starts from the output of a TPV. Their system scans the tracked frequencies and compares them in various ways to harmonic frequencies of a hypothetical fundamental. The hypothesis with the least difference overall becomes the estimated fundamental pitch.

Figure 12.9 depicts three plots generated by the system. In figure 12.9a, the system accurately tracks a computer-synthesized version of *Partita III* by J. S. Bach. Figure 12.9b shows how the performance degrades when confronted with a studio recording of a violin performance. Glitches between the notes indicate points where the system is confused by bow noises. Figure 12.9c shows a further degradation caused by a "chord effect" (in which previous notes continue to ring in the presence of new notes) when analyzing a violin recording made in a reverberant space.

As a step toward improving the performance of such a system, the authors applied the same algorithm to a version of the violin recordings that had been sanitized by the TPV. As part of its data reduction, the TPV removes some noise and grit from the recording, including bow scraping noise and reverberation. When the PD is run on resynthesized versions, its performance becomes more accurate.

Cepstrum Analysis

A common frequency-domain pitch detection method in speech research is the *cepstrum* technique, having first been used in analysis of speech (Noll

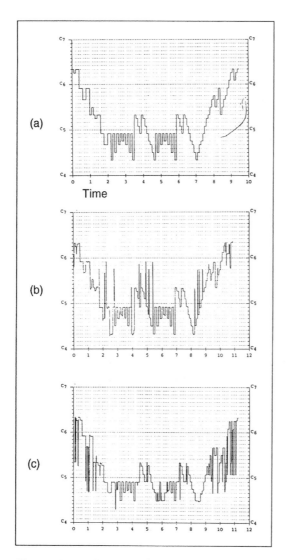

Figure 12.9 Plots generated by frequency-domain pitch tracking of the estimated pitch of the first eight measures of *Partita III* by J. S. Bach. The vertical axis is divided into semitones of the equal-tempered scale, from C4 to C7. The horizontal axis is time. (*a*) Computer-synthesized pitches. (*b*) Studio recording. (*c*) Reverberant recording. (After Beauchamp, Maher, and Brown 1993.)

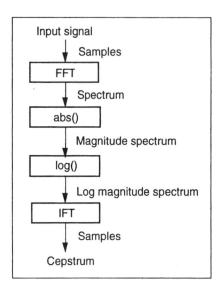

Figure 12.10   Scheme for cepstrum computation.

1967; Schafer and Rabiner 1970). Cepstrum analysis has often been applied in conjunction with the technique of *linear predictive coding* (LPC), described in chapter 5. The term "cepstrum" was formed by reversing the first four letters of "spectrum." A simple way of describing the cepstrum is to say that it tends to separate a strong pitched component from the rest of the spectrum. This is a reasonable model of many vocal and instrumental sounds whose spectrums can be considered as the sum of an *excitation* (the original vibrational impulses, typically at the pitch of the sound) and the *resonances* (the filtered part of a sound created by the body of an instrument or the vocal tract). (The section on physical modeling synthesis in chapter 7 explains the excitation/resonance concept.)

Technically, the cepstrum is the inverse Fourier transform of the *log-magnitude Fourier spectrum* (figure 12.10). This is the absolute value of the log (base 10) of the output of the *discrete Fourier transform*. (Appendix A explains the discrete Fourier transform and its inverse.)

The result of cepstrum computation is a time sequence, like the input signal itself. If the input signal has a strong fundamental pitch period, this shows up as a peak in the cepstrum. By measuring the time distance from time 0 to the time of the peak, one finds the fundamental period of this pitch (figure 12.11).

How does cepstrum analysis work for speech? The cepstrum serves to separate two superposed spectra: the glottal pulse (vocal cord) excitation, and the vocal tract resonance. The excitation can be viewed as a sequence of quasi-periodic pulses. The Fourier transform of these pulses is a line spec-

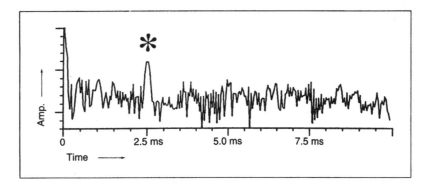

Figure 12.11 Cepstrum plot from a note of a trumpet solo recorded in a large reverberant hall. The note is 396 Hz. The peak marked by an asterisk indicates the period of the signal, about 2.52 ms, which corresponds to the detected pitch. Notice that the cepstrum peak appears clearly even in the presence of reverberation. (After Moorer 1975.)

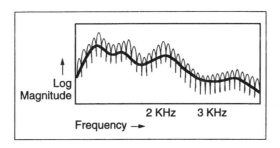

Figure 12.12 Cepstrum separation of vocal cord impulse response from the vocal tract impulse response. Applying the log function separates the thin wiggly lines (corresponding to the excitation) from the thick undulating broad spectrum (corresponding to the impulse response or resonance).

trum where the lines are spaced at harmonics of the original frequency (see the thin wiggly lines in figure 12.12). The process of taking the log magnitude does not affect the general form of this spectrum. The inverse Fourier transform yields another quasi-periodic waveform of pulses. By contrast, the spectrum of the response of the vocal tract (acting as a filter) is a slowly varying function of frequency, shown as the thick undulating line in figure 12.12. The process of applying the log magnitude and the inverse Fourier transform yields a waveform that has significant amplitude only for a few samples, generally less than the fundamental pitch period. It can be shown that the impulse response decays as a function of $1/n$, then its cepstrum decays as $1/n^2$. Thus the cepstrum clusters the impulse response into a short burst at the beginning of the cepstrum wave, and it clusters the pitch into a series of peaks at the period of the fundamental frequency (see figure 12.11).

Cepstrum computation has many applications because it tends to sort out the impulse response from the excitation. In other words, the cepstrum tends to *deconvolve* the two *convolved* spectra (Smith 1981). (See chapter 10 for an explanation of convolution.) We say "tends to" because, for musical signals, the deconvolution is rarely perfect. The log magnitude operations in the cepstrum procedure tend to cluster these two quasi-separate components of the spectrum. By advanced operations that we will not describe here, either of these features can be filtered out so that cepstrum contains spectrum information associated with either timbre or pitch. (For details see Noll 1967; Schafer and Rabiner 1970; Rabiner and Gold 1975; Rabiner et al. 1976.)

Another application of the cepstrum is found in speech analysis/resynthesis. If there is no peak in the cepstrum this is an indication that the sound being analyzed is *unvoiced*—that is, it is a breathy or consonant sound with no pitch, like "f" or "s," as opposed to a voiced vowel like "ah."

PDs Based on Models of the Ear

After decades of systematic study, hearing science is converging toward detailed understanding of the mechanisms of the human auditory system. A trend in sound analysis is to hitch this knowledge to the train of super-computer technology with the goal of achieving new insights into sound microstructure (Hermes 1992; Slaney and Lyon 1992). An application of these models is pitch detection. Recent PDs combine algorithms based on perception theories with models of known mechanisms of the human auditory system. Licklider's theories of pitch perception anticipated modern implementations of this approach (Licklider 1951, 1959).

Figure 12.13 shows the overall structure of such a PD, which divides into three submodels: outer and middle ear, cochlea, and central nervous system. The first step is a preprocessing stage of filtering based on the responses of the outer and middle ear. The next stage transforms the input signal into a frequency-domain representation by means of a bank of bandpass filters. Then follows a transduction stage in which the energy of the basilar membrane is transformed into a series of nerve firing probabilities and subsequently a train of spikes in the time domain (Meddis, Hewitt, and Schackleton 1990). Up to this point the process is based on well-established, if simplified, scientific data. The next stage is the most speculative part, modeling central nervous system processing of the incoming spikes. The goal is to measure the period between spikes and estimate their most frequency interval or pitch. These final stages are akin to the time-domain and autocorrelation PDs. The advantage of combining FD and TD methods in

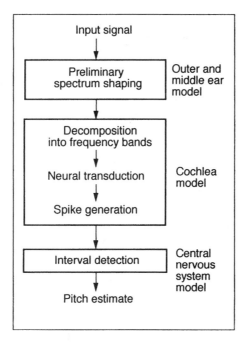

Figure 12.13 Schema of pitch detector based on a model of the human auditory system.

this way is that inharmonic "contamination" is filtered out when the channels of the frequency domain are converted to time-domain spikes.

Polyphonic Pitch Detection

All the difficulties of pitch detection magnify for a pitched sound in the presence of noise or several pitched sounds. This is the difficult task faced in *polyphonic transcription,* that is, generating a written score from an acoustic signal. Most theories of human pitch perception focus on hearing a single pitch. Much less is known about the mechanisms by which people listen to polyphony.

Attempts at polyphonic pitch detection usually apply frequency-domain analysis techniques within a search and decision mechanism. The main task is to sift out individual melodic lines from a spectrum containing many amplitude peaks, where the peaks may be either fundamental pitches or strong harmonics. In order to determine which peaks are probably fundamental pitches, the analysis must examine the data from several perspectives and weigh different factors in estimating from the results (Moorer 1975; Maher 1990). Techniques derived from artificial intelligence research are often employed, such as *expectation-driven search* through lists of prominent frequencies. Systems are said to be expectation driven when they use knowledge about the domain being analyzed to direct the search strategy (Moorer 1975; Terhardt 1982; Chafe et al. 1982, 1985; Foster et al. 1982; Strawn 1980, 1985a, b; Maher 1990). (See the section on signal-understanding systems in chapter 13.) Because of the extra data-gathering, searching, and complex decision-making algorithms, the computation time for polyphonic pitch detection is much greater than that required in the monophonic case.

Analysis of Musical Context

In many performance situations it is necessary to go beyond mere pitch detection to pitch analysis—the examination of melody and harmony in the broad sense. That is, having isolated the pitches that have occurred, what is their musical significance, what do they imply? Another name for this task is *analysis of musical context*. An example of analysis of musical context is the identification of the key and clef of a piece of tonal music (Chafe et al 1982; Holtzman 1977). Proceeding from this analysis, the further goal might be to assign the proper note name (e.g., F-sharp or G-flat) for the purposes of score transcription.

In interactive performance systems, the computer is expected to respond in an appropriate way to a human performer. Thus it must very quickly discern the musical context. Various algorithms for fast chord and melodic analysis have been developed. These are usually customized for the style requirements of the composers who use the system (Chabot, Dannenberg, and Bloch 1986; Roads 1985b; Rowe 1992a, b). Beyond such rapid algorithms lies the vast domain of computer-assisted musical style analysis, a topic in its own right that is outside the scope of this book.

Rhythm Recognition

One of the basic skills acquired in the music conservatory is playing rhythms written in common music notation. A related skill is learning to recognize played rhythms, transcribing them into notation. A long period of practice stands between the beginner and the master of these skills. Transcribing musical rhythms appears to be a mechanical counting task, something that would be easy to teach to the machine. As it turns out, the problem is far more difficult than it might seem at first glance. Furthermore, the skill of rhythmic dictation is already simplified, since it is based on recognition of metrically related rhythms. Many rhythms exist without a regular meter, and any type of rhythmical grouping (including those with no simple metrical relation) can occur within a metrical structure. Thus the general problem of rhythmic recognition is quite open. (A good introduction to the theory of musical rhythm is Yeston 1976, which cites earlier theorists, starting from ancient times.)

Machine recognition of rhythm from an acoustic signal turns input samples into a list of individual sonic events. It assigns these events to note duration values (half note, quarter note, etc.), then groups the notes into larger musical units: beamed groups, tuplets (triplets, etc.), measures, and perhaps phrases, while also determining the meter. These tasks are inherently problematic, partly because human performance of musical scores is not perfectly accurate, and music notation is ambiguous. That is, the same or very similar rhythms can be written in different ways. As in pitch detection, a rhythm recognizer must ignore "insignificant" variations in order to extract the "essential" rhythm. For example, it must realize that a slightly staccato whole note is not a tied half-quarter-eighth-sixteenth-thirty-second. This is related to the *quantization* problem in sequencers, but the problem is much harder when starting from an acoustic signal because it is up to the system to find the note list, and the tempo is not known at the outset.

Systems that try to segment the music by rhythmic phrases are hampered at the outset by the fact that the concept of "phrase" is context- and style-dependent. Moreover, expert musicians do not always agree about the phrase structure of a given piece of music.

The diversity of methods for rhythm recognition mirrors the situation in pitch detection, with an important difference. Pitch detection research is rooted in years of development in the larger speech and signal-processing world, while rhythm recognition research is specific to the music community. (A rare exception is the research by Selfridge and Neisser 1960 to parse Morse code by computer.) As a result there has been less research and standardization. Compounding this, various musical tasks and styles of music call for different approaches; there is not one rhythm recognition problem, but many.

Applications of Rhythm Recognition

Rhythm recognition from acoustic sources is valuable in applications including tempo tracking in live performance, estimation of meter, and as one component of automatic music transcription. It also has applications in musicology and in studies of musical performance.

Tempo-tracking algorithms try to "tap their foot" to the beat of the acoustic signal, which can vary as a function of rubato or abrupt tempo changes. This is useful in a concert situation when a computer accompaniment is trying to follow the performance of a human instrumentalist or vocalist.

Parsing the note list into hierarchical rhythmic units extends as far as needed by a particular musical application. An interactive improvisation system may only scan for a few rhythmic formulas or cues to trigger its response. Its memory is short-term, and when it does not find the pattern that it is looking for it moves on, throwing away its previous input. An accompanist program is continuously trying to match incoming rhythmic patterns with those of the score in its memory. It tries to anchor tightly to the beat in order to stay "with it." A system for transcription into a printed score must reconcile all its input data. It strives to find the meter, establish the boundaries of measures, and assign proper duration values to every note. Full automatic music transcription from an acoustic source to a printed score is a bona fide artificial intelligence problem, since the system must employ a battery of analysis methods and then select between multiple hypotheses at every stage. Not only must durations and rests be accurately represented, but special cases such as tuplets, ornaments, grace notes, and ties must be rendered in a natural notation style. Simultaneous pitch and amplitude analysis may help the rhythm analyzer make the proper note assignment. Many research problems remain in this field, particularly for transcription of polyphony.

Levels of Rhythm Recognition

Analysis of rhythm can take place on three levels:

- Low-level: *event detection*
- Middle-level: *transcription into notation*
- High-level: *style analysis*

In the low-level case, the input is a raw acoustic signal that must be converted to digital form and then segmented into a list of starting and ending times for discrete musical events. In the middle-level case, the input stream is already segmented and encoded, as is the case with MIDI data emanating from a keyboard. Here the task is to convert the note list into a meaningful musical score from the segmented data. Note assignment and note grouping are the main subtasks at this level. High-level rhythm analysis falls into the domain of composition theory or style analysis, depending on the application. Since music can be parsed into high-level structures in innumerable ways (Roads 1985d, e), we discuss only the first two levels here.

Event Detection

Low-level rhythm analysis centers on event detection—isolating individual events in a stream of audio samples and determining their durations.

Amplitude Thresholding

For simple monophonic music recorded in an nonreverberant room, event detection can be solved with time-domain techniques such as *amplitude thresholding* (Foster et al. 1982; Schloss 1985). In this method, the system scans the input waveform looking for the amplitude envelopes of events, in particular, for obvious attack and decay curves. If it sees an attack envelope that exceeds a given amplitude threshold, this indicates the start of an event. This method can be enhanced by preprocessing the sound with highpass filters to bring our *transients* (points where sharp onsets and decays occur).

However, amplitude plots can be misleading as a cue to event onset and duration. Some musical signals are inherently hard to segment by time-domain techniques alone. Examples include slurred bowed string attacks, new notes blurred by sustained notes or reverberation, or polyphonic signals such as chords. In these cases, a continuous amplitude envelope may encapsulate several events, even obscuring accented events that play a significant rhythmic role (Foster et al. 1982). For example, when a vibraphone is played with the sustain pedal down, the amplitude plot is not a clear guide to note attack times (figure 12.14). In such cases, pitch and spectrum changes are excellent clues to new events.

Hence a combination of time-domain and frequency-domain techniques may be most effective (Chafe et al. 1985; Piszczalski and Galler 1977; Piszczalski et al 1981; Foster et al. 1982). For example, a frequency-domain event segmenter based on an *autoregression* (AR) model fit of the input data succeeds where simple amplitude thresholding fails (Makhoul 1975; Foster et al. 1982). Autoregression detects changes in the periodicity of the signal, making it sensitive to changes in pitch. Repeated attacks of the same note are not recognized by the AR model, however. AR and amplitude thresholding work well together because AR is frequency-sensitive and thresholding is amplitude-sensitive. (See the explanation of AR techniques in chapter 13.)

Separating Voices in Polyphonic Music

Separating the onset times of individual sources or voices in polyphonic music is difficult. Beyond a certain level of complexity it is currently impos-

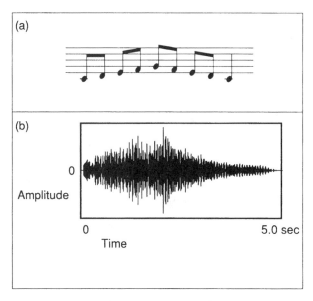

Figure 12.14 A problem case for time-domain event detection. (*a*) Sequence of notes. (*b*) Time-domain signal generated by a vibraphone playing these notes with the sustain pedal pushed down.

sible. No one has yet attempted to segment each note of each instrument in a tutti section played by a chamber ensemble. For a small number of distinct instruments, the problem is tractable, given enough processing power (Moorer 1975; Foster et al. 1982; Wold 1987). Besides the methods already mentioned, the following strategies have been employed for polyphonic source separation:

- Isolating instruments sounding in different registers (like a piccolo and a tuba) by filtering.

- Using spatial location as a clue, if the sources are widely separated in a multichannel recording.

- Comparing the input signal with *spectrum templates* (a known spectrum pattern of an instrument) to separate some tones out of others played; this template may be based on a physical model of the instrument (Wold 1987).

- Finding common vibrato and tremolo patterns (frequency and amplitude modulations) in a spectrum that indicate which partials were played by a particular instrument. These are called *source coherence criteria* in psychoacoustics research (Chafe and Jaffe 1986).

- Identifying the characteristic attack pattern of individual instruments, even at the start of a chord, since the instruments rarely start exactly synchronously.

For systems that employ can apply several strategies in event detection, the question becomes when to try a particular approach. When several techniques are used in combination, the system needs a means of weighing the results obtained by different methods and deciding on a specific answer. For more on this subject see the section on signal understanding systems in chapter 13.

Transcription

Any given sequence of note values is in principle infinitely ambiguous, but this ambiguity is seldom apparent to the listener. (H. C. Longuet-Higgins 1976)

Transcription—the middle level of rhythm recognition—begins once a list of discrete events is assembled. MIDI-based rhythm recognizers commence from this point. Transcription includes the subtasks of tempo tracking, rhythm value assignment, note grouping, determination of meter, setting measure boundaries, and possibly sorting out basic phrase structure. We treat each of these subtasks as separate here, but in practice they may well interact.

The ultimate goal of transcription is not always preparing a score for printing. It may be directed toward parsing data to feed to an interactive composition program, an accompaniment system, a musicological analysis program, or a model of musical listening. Since these goals differ, in each case the methods of parsing the score may be different.

Tempo Tracking

Tempo tracking tries to find the "beat"—a perceived pulse that marks off time intervals of equal duration. In a commercial music notation program, this problem is solved by having the musician play in the music along with a metronome sound generated by the program. Although this is an expedient data entry method, we consider here the more difficult problem of tempo tracking without a metronome reference, which corresponds to the task of tracking actual musical performances (Rowe 1975; Pressing and Lawrence 1993).

The first step in tempo tracking is measuring the time distances between events. This measurement can be used to set up a hierarchical *metrical grid*. The beat is usually a common denominator of the measured durations. This process sounds straightforward, but tempo variations warp the grid and make it difficult to estimate the basic pulse initially. Also, if there is any syncopation in the rhythmic pattern, the tempo tracker must somehow realize that the beat is not changing in the presence of off-beat accented notes.

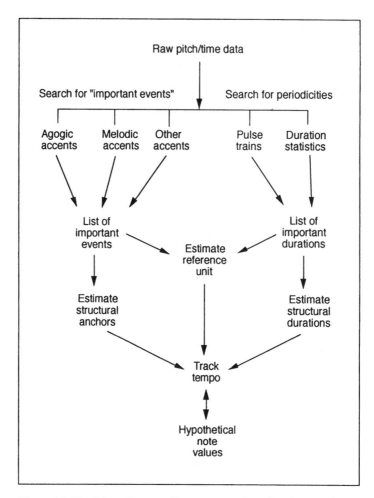

Figure 12.15   Mont-Reynaud's tempo tracker. See the text for an explanation.

One way to reduce the complexity of the task is to scan over a finite-duration window, say, five seconds at a time (Miller, Scarborough, and Jones 1992). A history mechanism with a decaying memory of past beats captures a similar idea (Dannenberg amd Mont-Reynaud 1987; Allen and Dannenberg 1990). A short memory ignores past events, allowing rapid tempo fluctuations, but tends to instability. A long memory steadies the tempo at the expense of ignoring fast tempo changes.

Figure 12.15 demonstrates a tempo tracker that pursues two strategies in parallel. The upper left part of figure 12.15 shows the procedures that extract the "important events." These events serve as structural anchors in the music. The heuristic applied here is that easily recognized rhythmic or melodic accents normally happen at structurally important points such as strong beats. Thus the duration from anchor to anchor is often a simple relationship. Since this is not always true, the upper right part of figure 12.15 shows the procedures that use an independent method of tracking tempo fluctuations. These procedures search for repeating patterns in successive durations and keep running statistics on the most common durations. Significant durations are usually in a simple relationship to one another and to the anchor-to-anchor durations. By combining these two approaches, tempo-tracking decisions select a reasonable hypothesis about the current tempo. The flexibility of the approach is demonstrated in the presence of syncopation—the anchors occur off beat, but the significant durations keep track of the tempo. Conversely, when anchors give strong hints, major tempo adjustments are accommodated.

Another family of approaches to tempo tracking are based on connectionist strategies (D'Autilia and Guerra 1991; Rowe 1992a, b). In these systems, a network of nodes representing the time span between events interact with one another. They alter their values so as to become simpler rational multiples of one another. In the ideal these values define a metrical grid.

Note Duration Assignment

Given a steady beat, each detected event can be assigned a metrically related duration. This would be simple if the performance were mechanically perfect, but expressive musical performances exhibit considerable variation in the durations of supposedly equal-duration notes (Chafe et al. 1982; Clarke 1987; Clynes and Nettheim 1982; Clynes and Walker 1982). Agogic accents, which stretch the duration of important notes, abound in performed music.

To make the task of deducing the metrically related duration easier, the analysis program may *quantize* the durations of notes, that is, round them off to a metrically related duration such as an eighth note or sixteenth note. Practical notation programs usually solicit hints from performers before the transcription, such as requiring them to stipulate the smallest note value to be played, which presets the quantization grid. Even so, as Desain and Honing (1992c) show in a comparative study, simple grid-based quantization strategies such as those employed in commercial music notation programs can lead to pathological transcriptions. Figure 12.16, from their paper, shows what happens when a program quantizes a triplet according to a sixty-fourth-note grid. One problem is that the note labeled *A* is played shorter than note *B,* even though they are notated the other way round. Alternative quantization strategies exist, including those based on connectionist models, but each seems to have its own limitations. (See also figure 16.10 in chapter 16.)

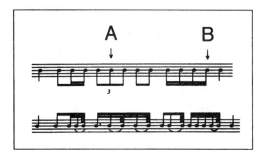

Figure 12.16   Deleterious effects of quantization. (*a*) Musical input written appropriately. (*b*) Transcription by a commercial music editing program using quantization according to a sixty-fourth-note grid.

Figure 12.17   A rhythmic grouping problem. (*a*) Sequence of notes as seen by a rhythmic parser. (*b*) Plausible interpretation of (*a*).

Grouping into Patterns

The next step in recognition is subdividing the list of notes into groups of notes or rhythm patterns. Figure 12.17a shows the starting point of the grouping process: a list of note durations with no indication as to measure boundaries or time signature. How does the program reckon that bar lines should be inserted after notes 1, 7, and 14, as in figure 12.17b? How does it determine that the most musical interpretation of the second, third, and fourth notes of the input is a triplet?

Various music application programs may group the notes according to different criteria. A notation system, for example, may look for groups of notes to beam, such as a series of eighth notes. A program that attempts to model human listening may attempt to build a hierarchy of phrases. Grouping notes by measure requires some hypothesis about the meter, so we discuss it in the next section.

Rhythm pattern recognition is dominated by search-and-compare techniques (Rowe 1975; Mont-Reynaud 1985b; Mont-Reynaud and Goldstein 1985). Quasi-grammatical theories of rhythm parsing, such as those in Lerdahl and Jackendoff (1983), Longuet-Higgins (1976, 1987), and Longuet-Higgins and Lee (1983), have served as guides for parsing algorithms. For example, Rosenthal (1988) cites five rules derived from Lerdahl and Jackendoff and presents a step-by-step walkthrough of these rules applied to simple musical rhythms. We list them here as an example of typical grouping rules.

1. Groups begin on accented notes.

2. Do not form groups of a single event.

3. Events of short duration tend to be grouped together with subsequent events of long duration.

4. A grouping boundary separates events of long duration from subsequent events of short duration.

5. Groups at the same hierarchical level should be as equal as possible in duration.

These theories, it should be stressed, derive from written and not necessarily performed music. Thus, in practice, such algorithms are usually embellished by empirical rules derived by experimentation. More complicated rules, for example, may take into account pitch and amplitude patterns in order to resolve two competing rhythmic hypotheses (Katayose and Inokuchi 1989; Katayose et al. 1989).

As an alternative to rule-based pattern classifiers, connectionist methods using neural network models have been used (Desain and Honing 1989, 1992b, 1992c; Linster 1992).

Estimating Meter and Measure Boundaries

Meter is a ratio between two time levels. One is the beat period (e.g., one quarter note equals one second), and the other is a larger period based on a fixed number of beats—the measure. Meter generally imposes an accent structure on beats, a structure that tends to articulate the measure. Determining meter can be divided into two problems. The first is finding the *perceived meter* based on recurring patterns that are divisible by an integer n (e.g., duple, triple, quadruple, quintuple). This is usually the goal of interactive composition programs and models of listening. The second problem is estimating the exact time signature of a piece (e.g., 2/4 and not 4/4), which is the problem faced in transcription to printed score.

Because of the ambiguities of rhythmic relations, the task of estimating the perceived meter and subdividing the music by measure is not straight-forward (Rosenthal 1992). Rosenthal's strategy was to deploy multiple specialized agents, each of which gathered statistics about note placement, note durations, accents, and characteristic pitch and rhythm patterns. Each agent proposed an hypothesis, and a manager program decided among the multiple hypotheses presented to it. It did this by noting that certain agents were more reliable than others (and so had more weight) and that when certain agents agreed on an hypothesis, it was likely to be the correct one. Miller, Scarborough, and Jones (1992) compare a rule-based versus a connectionist strategy in estimating meter. The rule-based method is somewhat rigid, and its strengths and weaknesses are predictable. The connectionist strategy, being more flexible, can handle situations that cause the rule-based method to fail, such as estimations in the presence of tempo variations. But sometimes the connectionist approach makes a wild estimate, pointing out the general difficulty of predicting and interpreting the output of connectionist analyzers.

Estimating the exact time signature is quite difficult, partly because many time signatures can sound the same. For example, a given melody can be played in 1/2, 2/2, 2/4, 4/4, 4/8, 8/8, etc., and sound identical, assuming the tempo is adjusted accordingly. Assigning a specific time signature to a given rhythm requires knowledge of the style in which the piece was composed. For example, a piece composed in eighteenth-century Vienna is likely to adhere to conventions that limit the choice of time signature. Generally, the best that current programs can do is make an educated guess, based on the style of the music. For contemporary music compositions with frequently changing time signature the problem is obviously harder. Once again, in commercial notation programs, the time signature can be prespecified by the musician, so the program may not face this problem.

Recovery

Many factors may confuse a rhythm recognizer: a wild performance, a rhythmic ambiguity, a low-amplitude passage where the note onsets are not clear, or simply a hole in the ability of the recognizer to parse a particular type of passage. Thus any practical rhythm recognizer must try to recover smoothly from a point of confusion, to pick up again as a human musician would. This subject is complicated, and the strategies for recovery depend on the task being performed, so we can only mention it as an issue here. As

Allen and Dannenberg (1990) stress, if the system maintains multiple interpretations of the performance, it is less likely to become completely confused in the first place.

Conclusion

The difficulties we face in teaching machines how to hear music reminds us of how sensitive and powerful the human perceptual systems are (Carterette and Friedman 1978; Buser and Imbert 1992). The human ability to pinpoint the source of an isolated sound (both in direction and timbre), to follow complex harmony, counterpoint, and polyrhythms, and to recall entire pieces of music from fragments of as few as two or three notes—more or less instantaneously—puts to shame the current generation of machine recognizers.

Machine methods for pitch and rhythm recognition continue to evolve, however. Speech pitch detectors that work in non-real time are "very reliable" (Hermes 1992), although reliable pitch detection in music is inherently harder, even if we exclude polyphony (i.e., almost all music!).

Rhythm value detection is practical when a metronome reference beat is provided to the machine and a quantization range is prespecified. But in the absence of these strong hints, rhythmic recognition does not always achieve reasonable results. Successful systems can account for only the most conventional rhythmic formulas. Even if we develop new parsing rules, for every rule in music there are exceptions. Thus numerous scores exceed the complexity that can be handled by machine rhythmic analyzers. Understanding more about human rhythm perception seems to be the key to progress in this domain.

13   *Spectrum Analysis*

Applications of Spectrum Analysis

Spectrum Plots

Static Spectrum Plots
Power Spectrum
Time-varying Spectrum Plots

Models behind Spectrum Analysis Methods

Spectrum and Timbre

Spectrum Analysis: Background

Mechanical Spectrum Analysis
Computer-based Spectrum Analysis
Heterodyne Filter Analysis
The Saga of the Phase Vocoder

The Short-time Fourier Spectrum

Windowing the Input Signal
Operation of the STFT
Overlap-add Resynthesis from Analysis Data
Limits of Overlap-add Resynthesis

Why Overlapping Windows?
Oscillator Bank Resynthesis
Analysis Frequencies
Time/Frequency Uncertainty
Periodicity Implies Infinitude
Time/Frequency Tradeoffs
Frequencies in between Analysis Bins
Significance of Clutter
Alternative Resynthesis Techniques

The Sonogram Representation

Sonogram Parameters

The Phase Vocoder

Phase Vocoder Parameters
Frame Size
Window Type
FFT Size and Zero-padding
Hop Size
Typical Parameter Values
Window Closing
Tracking Phase Vocoder
Operation of the TPV
Peak Tracking
Editing Analysis Envelopes
Cross-synthesis with the Phase Vocoder
Computational Cost of the Phase Vocoder
Accuracy of Resynthesis
Problem Sounds
Analysis of Inharmonic and Noisy Sounds
Deterministic plus Stochastic Techniques

Constant Q Filter Bank Analysis

Constant Q versus Traditional Fourier Analysis
Implementation of Constant Q Analysis

Analysis by Wavelets

Operation of Wavelet Analysis
Wavelet Display
Wavelet Resynthesis
Sound Transformation with Wavelets
Comb Wavelet Separation of Noise from Harmonic Spectrum
Comparison of Wavelet Analysis with Fourier Methods

Signal Analysis with the Wigner Distribution

Interpreting Wigner Distribution Plots
Limits of the Wigner Distribution

Non-Fourier Sound Analysis

Critiques of Fourier Spectrum Analysis
Autoregression Spectrum Analysis
Autoregressive Moving Average Analysis
Source and Parameter Analysis
Parameter Estimation
Analysis by Other Functions
Walsh Functions
Prony's Method

Auditory Models

Cochleagrams
Correlograms

Signal-understanding Systems

Pattern Recognition
Control Structure and Strategy
Examples of Signal-understanding Systems

Conclusion

Will not the creative musician be a more powerful master if he is also informed in regard to the pure science of the methods and materials of his art? Will he not be able to mix tone colors with greater skill if he understands the nature of the ingredients and the effects which they produce? (D. C. Miller 1916)

Just as an image can be described as a mixture of colors (frequencies in the visible part of the electromagnetic spectrum), a sound object can be described as a blend of elementary acoustic vibrations. One way of dissecting sound is to consider the contribution of various components, each corresponding to a certain rate of variation in air pressure. Gauging the balance among these components is called *spectrum analysis*.

A working definition of spectrum is "a measure of the distribution of signal energy as a function of frequency." Such a definition may seem straightforward, but no more general and precise definition of spectrum exists. This is because different analysis techniques measure properties that they each call "spectrum" with more-or-less diverging results. Except for isolated test cases, the practice of spectrum analysis is not an exact science (see Marple 1987 for a thorough discussion). The results are typically an approximation of the actual spectrum, so spectrum analysis is perhaps more precisely called *spectrum estimation*.

Spectrum analysis is evolving rapidly. The survey in this chapter, though broad, cannot account for every possible approach. Given the technical nature of the subject, our major concern in this chapter is to render sometimes abstruse concepts in terms of musical practice. Appendix A treats Fourier analysis in more detail and is a complement to this chapter.

Applications of Spectrum Analysis

Spectrum plots reveal the microstructure of vocal, instrumental, and synthetic sounds (Moorer, Grey, and Snell 1977; Moorer, Grey, and Strawn 1978; Piszczalski 1979a, b; Dolson 1983, 1986; Stautner 1983; Strawn 1985a, b). Thus they are essential tools for the acoustician and psychoacoustician (Risset and Wessel 1982).

Musicologists are increasingly turning to sonograms and other sound analysis techniques in order to study music performance and the structure of electronic music (Cogan 1984). This extends to automatic transcription of music—from sound to score—either in common music notation or a graphic form (Moorer 1975; Piszczalski and Galler 1977; Chafe et al. 1982; Foster et al. 1982; Haus 1983; Schloss 1985).

Real-time spectrum analysis is one type of "ear" for interactive music systems. Spectrum analysis reveals the characteristic frequency energy of instrumental and vocal tones, thus helping to identify timbres and separate multiple sources playing at once (Maher 1990). As chapter 12 shows, the results of spectrum analysis are often valuable in pitch and rhythm recognition.

But musicians want not only to analyze sounds; they want to modify the analysis data and resynthesize variants of the original sounds. More and more sound transformation techniques begin with an analysis stage, including time compression and expansion, frequency-shifting, convolution (filtering and reverberation effects), and many types of cross-synthesis—hybrids between two sounds. Techniques based on spectrum analysis allow continuous transformation between "natural" and "synthetic" tones in resynthesis of analyzed tones (Gordon and Grey 1977; Risset 1985a, b; Serra 1989). For more on analysis/resynthesis see chapters 4 and 5.

Spectrum Plots

Many strategies exist to measure and plot spectra. This section looks at strategies falling into two basic categories: *static* (like a snapshot of a spectrum), and *time-varying* (like a motion-picture film of a spectrum over time).

Static Spectrum Plots

Static plots capture a still image of sound. These sonic snapshots project a two-dimensional image of amplitude versus frequency. The analysis measures the average energy in each frequency region over the time period of the analyzed segment. This time period or window can vary from a brief instant to several seconds or longer. (Later we discuss the tradeoffs of various window lengths.)

One type of static plot is a *discrete* or *line spectrum*, where a vertical line represents each frequency component. For a mostly harmonic tone, the clearest analysis is *pitch-synchronous*. This type of analysis measures the amplitude of the harmonics of a tone whose pitch can be determined beforehand. Figure 13.1a shows the line spectrum of the steady state part of a trumpet tone, measured using a pitch-synchronous technique. Notice that at the instant this spectrum was measured, the third harmonic is higher in amplitude than the fundamental.

Figure 13.1b shows another trumpet spectrum plotted on a logarithmic (dB) amplitude scale. Such a scale compresses the plot into a narrower vertical band. By tracing the outline of the peaks one can see the overall formant shape.

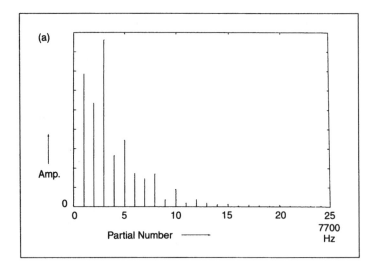

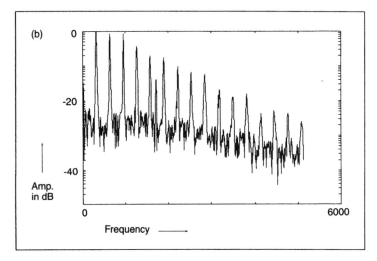

Figure 13.1   Static spectrum plots. (*a*) Line spectrum amplitude-versus-frequency plot of the sustained portion of a trumpet tone. Each line represents the strength of a harmonic of the fundamental frequency of 309 Hz. Linear amplitude scale. (*b*) Spectrum of trumpet tone in (*a*) plotted on a logarithmic (dB) scale, which compresses the plot into a narrower vertical band. (*c*) Spectrum plot in a continuous form, showing the outline of the formant peaks for a vocal sound "ah." Linear amplitude scale. (Plots courtesy of A. Piccialli, Department of Physics, University of Naples.)

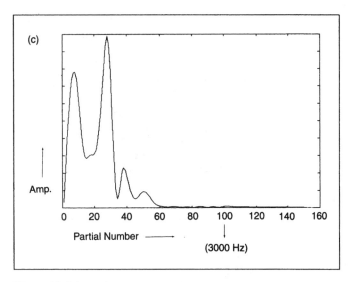

Figure 13.1 (cont.)

Figure 13.1c plots the spectrum of a vocal sound "ah" in a *continuous* form, where the discrete points measured by the analyzer have been filled in by graphical interpolation. Individual sinusoidal components are hidden, but the overall shape of the spectrum is clear.

Each type of static spectrum plot has its advantages, depending on the signal being analyzed and the goal of the analysis.

Power Spectrum

From the amplitude spectrum one can derive the *power spectrum*. Physicists define *power* as the square of the amplitude of a signal. Thus, power spectrum is the square of the amplitude spectrum. Displays of spectrum sometimes show power, rather than amplitude, because this correlates better with human perception. Yet another measure is the *power spectrum density* or PSD, which applies to continuous spectra like noise. A simple definition of the PSD is that it is the power spectrum within a specified bandwidth (Tempelaars 1977).

Time-varying Spectrum Plots

Details in the spectrum of even a single instrument tone are constantly changing, so static, timeless plots can represent only a portion of an evolving sound form. A time-varying spectrum depicts the changing blend

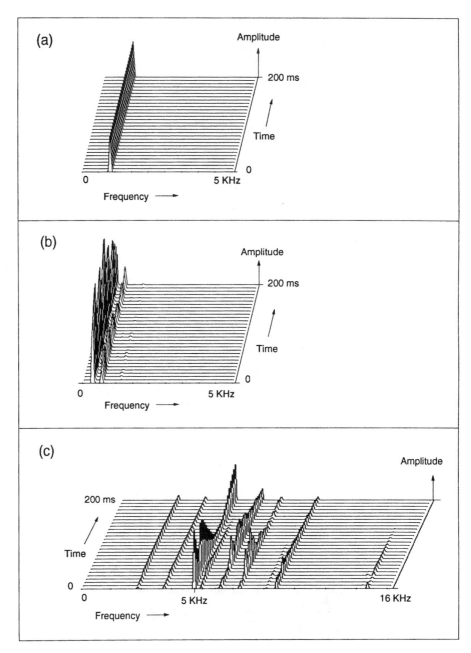

Figure 13.2   Time-varying spectra plotted on a linear amplitude scale. Time moves from front to back. (*a*) Sine wave at 1 KHz. (*b*) Flute playing fluttertongue at pitch E4. (*c*) Triangle, hit once.

of frequencies over the duration of an event. It can be plotted as a three-dimensional graph of spectrum versus time (figure 13.2). These plots essentially line up a series of static plots, one after the other.

Figure 13.3 shows two more display formats for time-varying spectrum analysis. Figure 13.3a is a still photograph from a *waterfall display*—a spectrum plot in which the time axis is moving in real time. The term waterfall display comes from the fact that this type of plot shows waves of rising and falling frequency energy in a fluidlike depiction. Figure 13.3b depicts a vocal melody.

Another way to display a time-varying spectrum is to plot a *sonogram* or *spectrogram*—a common tool in speech analysis, where it was originally called *visible speech* (Potter 1946). A sonogram shows the frequency versus time content of a signal, where frequency is plotted vertically, time is plotted horizontally, and the amplitudes of the frequencies in the spectrum are plotted in terms of the darkness of the trace. That is, intense frequency components are plotted darkly, while soft frequency components are plotted lightly (figure 13.4). We discuss the sonogram representation in more detail later.

Models Behind Spectrum Analysis Methods

There does not seem to be any general or optimal paradigm to either analyze or synthesize any type of sound. One has to scrutinize the sound—quasi-periodic, sum of inharmonic components, noisy, quickly or slowly evolving—and also investigate which features of the sound are relevant to the ear. (Jean-Claude Risset 1991)

No single method of spectrum estimation is ideal for all musical applications. Fourier analysis—the most prevalent approach—is actually a family of different techniques that are still evolving. A variety of non-Fourier methods continue to be developed, as we show later.

Every sound analysis technique should be viewed as fitting the input data to an assumed model. Methods based on Fourier analysis model the input sound as a sum of harmonically related sinusoids—which it may or may not be. Other techniques model the input signal as an excitation signal filtered by resonances, as a sum of exponentially damped sinusoids or square waves, as a combination of inharmonically related sinusoids, as a set of formant peaks with added noise, or as a set of equations that represent certain behavior of a traditional instrument. Innumerable other models are conceivable. As we see in detail later, variations in performance among the different methods can often be attributed to how well the assumed model

(a)

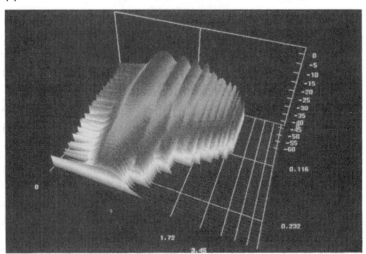

(b)

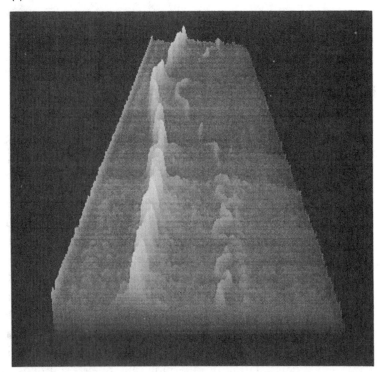

Figure 13.3 Still images from real-time waterfall displays. (*a*) Synthetic trumpet tone. Time comes from the back toward the front, with the most recent time at the front. The frequency scale is logarithmic, going from left to right. The fundamental frequency is approximately 1 KHz. Amplitude is plotted vertically on a logarithmic dB scale. (*b*) Vocal melody. Time is coming toward the reader, with the most recent time at the front. Low frequencies are at left. (Images courtesy of A. Peevers, Center for New Music and Art Technologies, University of California, Berkeley.)

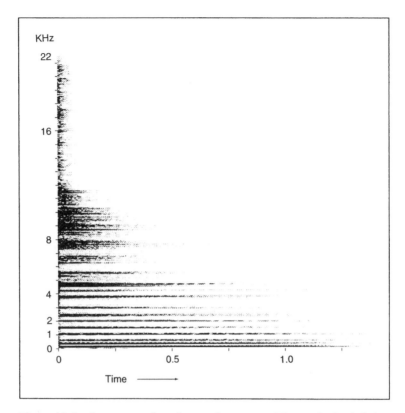

Figure 13.4 Sonogram plot of a struck tam-tam. The vertical axis is frequency, and the horizontal axis is time. This sonogram uses 1024 points of input data, and a Hamming window. The plot has a frequency resolution of 43 Hz and a time resolution of 1 ms. The analysis bandwidth of 0 to 22 KHz, and the measured dynamic range is −10 to −44.5 dB, plotted on a linear amplitude scale.

matches the process being analyzed. Hence it is important to choose the appropriate analysis method for a particular musical application.

Spectrum and Timbre

The term "timbre" is a catchall for a range of phenomena. Like the vague terms "sonority" and "Klangideal" (Apel 1972) it may some day be superseded by a more precise vocabulary of sound qualities. The classification of musical timbre is an ancient science. Early Chinese civilization developed sophisticated written descriptions of timbre, including a taxonomy of instrumental sources (metal, stone, clay, skin, silk threads, wood, gourd, and bamboo), and elaborate accounts of the different "touches" (attack forms, pulls, and vibratos) involved in playing the silk strings of the classical *chhin* instrument (Needham, Ling, and Girdwood-Robinson 1962). Indeed, a main playing technique of the *chhin* is the production of different timbres at the same pitch.

Spectrum and timbre are related concepts, but they are not equivalent. Spectrum is a physical property that can be characterized as a distribution of energy as a function of frequency. How to measure this energy precisely is another question! Psychoacoustics uses the term "timbre" to denote perceptual mechanisms that classify sound into families. By this definition, timbre is at least as concerned with perception as it is with sound signals. It is certainly easiest to discuss timbre in the realm of traditional instrument and vocal tones, where almost all past research has focused. Only a few attempts have been made to classify the universe of sound outside this category, the most heroic being the studies of Pierre Schaeffer (1977; see also Schaeffer, Reibel, and Ferreyra 1967).

A common timbre groups tones played by an instrument at different pitches, loudnesses, and durations. No matter what notes it plays, for example, we can always tell when a piano is playing. Human perception separates each instrument's tones from other instrument tones played with the same pitch, loudness, and duration. No one has much trouble separating a marimba from a violin tone of the same pitch, loudness, and duration. Of course a single instrument may also emit many timbres, as in the range of sonorities obtained from saxophones blowed at different intensities.

Numerous factors inform timbre perception. These include the amplitude envelope of a sound (especially the attack shape), undulations due to vibrato and tremolo, formant structures, perceived loudness, duration, and the *time-varying spectral envelope* (frequency content over time) (Schaeffer 1977; Risset 1991; McAdams and Bregman 1979; McAdams 1987; Gordon and Grey 1977; Grey 1975, 1978; Barrière 1991; see also chapter 23).

In identifying the timbre of an instrumental source, the attack portion of a tone is more important perceptually than the steady state (sustained) portion (Luce 1963; Grey 1975). Traditional instrument families such as reeds, brass, strings, and percussion each have characteristic attack "signatures" that are extremely important in recognizing tones made by them.

Amplitude and duration have an influence on the perception of timbre. For example, the proportions of the frequencies in the spectrum of a flute tone at 60 dB may be the equivalent to those in a tone amplified to 120 dB, but we hear the latter only as a loud blast. Similarly, a toneburst that lasts 30 ms may have the same periodic waveshape as a tone that lasts 30 seconds, but listeners may find it difficult to say whether they represent the same source.

The point is that spectrum is not the only clue to perceived timbre. By examining the time-domain waveform carefully, one can glean much about the timbre of a sound without subjecting it to a detailed spectrum analysis (Strawn 1985b).

Spectrum Analysis: Background

In the eighteenth century, scientists and musicians were well aware that many musical sounds were characterized by harmonic vibrations around a fundamental tone, but they had no technology for analyzing these harmonics in a systematic way. Sir Isaac Newton coined the term "spectrum" in 1781 to describe the bands of color showing the different frequencies passing through a glass prism.

In 1822 the French engineer Jean-Baptiste Joseph, Baron de Fourier (1768–1830) published his landmark thesis *Analytical Theory of Heat*. In this treatise he developed the theory that complicated vibrations could be analyzed as a sum of many simultaneous simple signals. In particular, Fourier proved that any periodic function could be represented as an infinite summation of sine and cosine terms. Due to the integer ratio relationship between the sinusoidal frequencies in Fourier analysis, this became known as *harmonic analysis*. (For a brief history of Fourier analysis, see appendix A.) In 1843, Georg Ohm (1789–1854) of the Polytechnic Institute of Nürnberg was the first to apply Fourier's theory to acoustical signals (Miller 1935). Later, the German scientist H. L. F. Helmholtz (1821–1894) surmised that instrumental timbre is largely determined by the harmonic Fourier series of the steady state portion of instrumental tones (Helmholtz 1863). Helmholtz developed a method of harmonic analysis based on mechanical-acoustic resonators.

Translating Helmholtz's term *Klangfarbe* ("sound color"), the British physicist John Tyndall coined the term *clang-tint* to describe timbre as "an admixture of two or more tones" and carried out imaginative experiments in order to visualize sound signals, such as "singing flames" and "singing water jets" (Tyndall 1875).

Mechanical Spectrum Analysis

Manually operated mechanical waveform analyzers were developed in the late nineteenth and early twentieth centuries (Miller 1916; see also appendix A). Backhaus (1932) developed an analysis system for a single harmonic at a time. This consisted of a carbon microphone connected to the input of a tunable bandpass filter. The output of the filter was routed to an amplifier, whose output was in turn connected to a pen and drum recorder. Backhaus tuned the filter to the frequency of the harmonic of interest and commanded an instrumentalist to play a note. As the musician played, Backhaus cranked a drum while a pen traced the output of the filter for that frequency on a roll of paper. The resulting trace was taken to represent the behavior of a single harmonic. Meyer and Buchmann (1931) developed a similar system.

Advances in the design of oscilloscopes in the 1940s generated a wave of new research. Scientists photographed waveforms from the oscilloscope screen and then manually traced their outline into mechanical Fourier analyzers.

A theoretical leap forward was described in Norbert Wiener's classic paper on *generalized harmonic analysis* (Wiener 1930), which shifted the emphasis of Fourier analysis from harmonic components to a continuous spectrum. Among other results, Wiener showed, by analogy to white light, that white noise was composed of all frequencies in equal amounts. Blackman and Tukey (1958) described a practical implementation of Wiener's approach using sampled data. After the advent of computers in the early 1950s, the Blackman-Tukey approach was the most popular spectrum analysis method until the introduction of the *fast Fourier transform* (FFT) in 1965, sometimes credited to Cooley and Tukey (1965). (See Singleton 1967, Rabiner and Gold 1975, and appendix A for more on the history of the FFT.)

Most precomputer analyses, such as those of Miller (1916) and Hall (1937) averaged out the time-varying characteristics of instrumental tone. As in the research of Helmholtz, these studies presumed that the steady state spectrum (sustained or "held" part of a note) played a dominant role in timbre perception. As mentioned earlier, it is now recognized that the first half-second of the attack portion of a tone is more important perceptually than the steady state portion to the identification of an instrumental note.

Dennis Gabor's pioneering contributions to sound analysis (1946, 1947) had a delayed impact, but are now viewed as seminal, particularly because he presented a method for analysis of time-varying signals. In Gabor's theories, sound can be analyzed simultaneously in the time and frequency domain into units he called *quanta*—now called *grains, wavelets,* or *windows,* depending on the analysis system being used. See chapter 5 for more on grains. Wavelet analysis and windows are discussed later in this chapter.

Figure 13.5   James Beauchamp performing sound analysis experiments at the University of Illinois, ca. 1966.

Computer-based Spectrum Analysis

Early experiments in computer analysis of musical instrument tones required heroic efforts. Analog-to-digital converters were rare, computers were scarce, theory was immature, and analysis programs had to be cobbled from scratch on punched paper cards (figure 13.5). Against these obstacles, computer-based analysis and synthesis developed in the 1960s yielded more detailed results than did analog models. At Bell Telephone Laboratories, Max Mathews and Jean-Claude Risset analyzed brass instruments using a *pitch-synchronous* analysis program (Mathews, Miller, and David 1961; Risset 1966; Risset and Mathews 1969). Pitch-synchronous analysis breaks the input waveform into *pseudoperiodic segments*. It estimates the pitch of each pseudoperiodic segment. The size of the *analysis segment* is adjusted relative to the estimated pitch period. The harmonic Fourier spectrum is then calculated on the analysis segment as though the sound were periodic; as though the pitch is quasi-constant throughout the analysis segment. This program generated time-varying amplitude functions for each harmonic of a given fundamental. Luce's (1963) doctoral research at the Massachusetts Institute of Technology implemented another pitch-synchronous approach to analysis/resynthesis of instrumental tones.

Several years later, Peter Zinovieff and his colleagues at EMS, London, developed a hybrid (analog-digital) real-time Fourier analyzer/resynthesizer for musical sound (Grogorno 1984).

Heterodyne Filter Analysis

The next step in computer analysis of musical tones involved *heterodyne filters* (Freedman 1965, 1967; Beauchamp 1969, 1975; Moorer 1973, 1975). The heterodyne filter approach is good for resolving harmonics (or quasi-harmonics) of a given fundamental frequency. This implies that the fundamental frequency is estimated in a prior stage of analysis. The heterodyne filter multiplies an input waveform by a sine and a cosine wave at harmonic frequencies and then sums the results over a short time period to obtain amplitude and phase data.

Figure 13.6a shows the operation of the heterodyne method. The input signal is multiplied by an analysis sine wave. In figure 13.6a, the frequency of the two signals exactly match, so the energy is completely positive, indicating strong energy at the analysis frequency. In 13.6b the two frequencies are not the same, so we obtain a waveform that is basically symmetrical

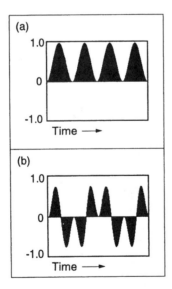

Figure 13.6   Heterodyne filter analysis. (*a*) Product of an input signal (a 100 Hz sine wave) with an analysis signal (a 100 Hz sine wave). The result is entirely positive, indicating strong energy at 100 Hz. (*b*) Product of an input signal (a 200 Hz sine wave) with an analysis signal (a 100 Hz sine wave). The result is scattered positive and negative energy, indicating no strong energy at 100 Hz in the input signal.

about the amplitude axis. When the heterodyne filter sums this waveform over a short time period it basically cancels itself out.

After a period of experimentation in the 1970s, the limits of the heterodyne method became well known. Moorer showed that the heterodyne filter approach is confused by fast attack times (less than 50 ms) and pitch changes (e.g., glissando, portamento, vibrato) greater than 2 percent (about a quarter tone). Although Beauchamp (1981) implemented a *tracking* version of the heterodyne filter that could follow changing frequency trajectories (similar in spirit to the tracking phase vocoder discussed later), the heterodyne approach has been supplanted by other methods.

The Saga of the Phase Vocoder

One of the most popular techniques for analysis/resynthesis of spectra is the *phase vocoder* (PV). Flanagan and Golden of Bell Telephone Laboratories developed the first PV program in 1966. It was originally intended to be a coding method for reducing the bandwidth of speech signals. Far from compressing audio data, however, the PV causes a data explosion! That is, the raw analysis data are much greater than the original signal data.

The PV is computationally intensive. Early implementations required so much computing time that the PV was not applied in practical applications for many years. Working at the Massachusetts Institute of Technology, Portnoff (1976, 1978) developed a relatively efficient PV, proving that it could be implemented using the FFT. He experimented with sound transformations of speech such as time compression and expansion. This led to Moorer's landmark paper on the application of the PV in computer music (Moorer 1978).

During the 1970s and 1980s, computer-based spectrum analysis yielded significant insights into the microstructure of instrumental and vocal tones (Moorer, Grey, and Snell 1977; Moorer, Grey, and Strawn 1978; Piszczalski 1979a, b; Dolson 1983; Stautner 1983; Strawn 1985b). In the 1990s spectrum analysis has evolved from an esoteric technical specialty to a familiar tool in the musician's studio—for analysis, transcription, and sound transformation. The next sections discuss various forms of spectrum analysis, including the short-time Fourier transform and the phase vocoder. Then we present extensions of Fourier analysis, including constant Q filter banks and the wavelet transform. Although Fourier methods dominate spectrum analysis, other methods have gained ground in recent years. So we also survey these "non-Fourier techniques" later in this chapter. (For a technical overview of spectrum analysis written in an anecdotal style, see Robinson 1982.)

The Short-time Fourier Spectrum

The *Fourier transform* (FT) is a mathematical procedure that maps any continuous-time (analog) waveform to a corresponding infinite Fourier series summation of elementary sinusoidal waves, each at a specific amplitude and phase. In other words, the FT converts its input signals into a corresponding spectrum representation. To adapt Fourier analysis to the practical world of sampled, finite-duration, time-varying signals, researchers molded the FT into the *short-time Fourier transform* or STFT (Schroeder and Atal 1962; Flanagan 1972; Allen and Rabiner 1977; Schafer and Rabiner 1973b).

Windowing the Input Signal

As a preparation for spectrum analysis, the STFT imposes a sequence of *time windows* upon the input signal (figure 13.7). That is, it breaks the input signal into "short-time" (i.e., brief) segments bounded in time by a window function. A window is nothing more than a specific type of envelope designed for spectrum analysis. The duration of the window is usually in the range of 1 ms to 1 second, and the segments sometimes overlap. By analyz-

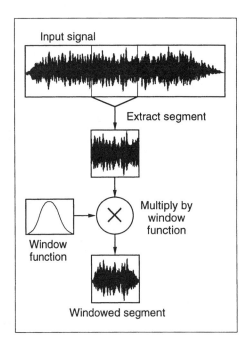

Figure 13.7   Windowing an input signal.

ing the spectrum of each windowed segment separately, one obtains a sequence of measurements that constitute a time-varying spectrum.

The windowing process is the source of the adjective "short-time" in "short-time Fourier transform." Unfortunately, windowing has the side effect of distorting the spectrum measurement. This is because the spectrum analyzer is measuring not purely the input signal, but rather, the product of the input signal and the window. The spectrum that results is the convolution of the spectra of the input and the window signals. We see the implications of this later. (Chapter 10 explains convolution. Appendix A discusses windowing in more detail.)

Operation of the STFT

After windowing, the STFT applies the *discrete Fourier transform* (DFT) to each windowed segment. Here all we need say about the DFT is that it is a type of Fourier transform algorithm that can handle discrete-time or sampled signals. Its output is a discrete-frequency spectrum, that is, a measure of energy at a set of specific equally spaced frequencies. (See appendix A for an introduction to the DFT.)

The fast Fourier transform or FFT, mentioned earlier in the historical section, is simply an efficient implementation of the DFT. Thus most practical implementations of the STFT apply the FFT algorithm to each windowed segment. Figure 13.8 diagrams the STFT.

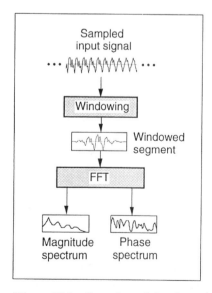

Figure 13.8   Overview of the short-time Fourier transform (STFT).

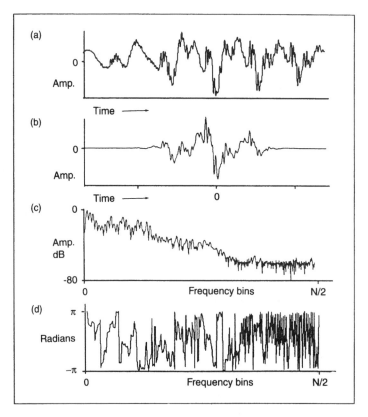

Figure 13.9   STFT signals. (*a*) Input waveform. (*b*) Windowed segment. (*c*) Magnitude spectrum plotted over the range 0 to −80 dB. (*d*) Phase spectrum plotted over the range −π to π. (After Serra 1989.)

Each block of data generated by the FFT is called a *frame*, by analogy to the successive frames of a film. Each frame contains two things: (1) a *magnitude spectrum* that depicts the amplitude of every analyzed frequency component, and (2) a *phase spectrum* that shows the initial phase value for every frequency component. All of the plots in figures 13.1–13.4 are magnitude spectrum plots.

We could visualize each of these two spectra as histograms with a vertical line for each frequency component along the abcissa. The vertical line represents amplitude in the case of the magnitude spectrum, and starting phase (between −π and π) in the case of the phase spectrum (figure 13.9). The magnitude spectrum is relatively easy to read. When the phase spectrum is "normalized" to the range of −π and π it is called the *wrapped phase* representation. For many signals, it appears to the eye like a random function. An *unwrapped phase* projection may be more meaningful visually. Appendix A explains the concepts of wrapped and unwrapped phase.

To summarize, the application of the STFT to a stream of input samples results in a series of frames that make up a time-varying spectrum.

Overlap-add Resynthesis from Analysis Data

To resynthesize the original time-domain signal, the STFT can reconstruct each windowed waveform segment from its spectrum components by applying the *inverse discrete Fourier transform* (IDFT) to each frame. The IDFT takes each magnitude and phase component and generates a corresponding time-domain signal with the same envelope as the analysis window.

Then by overlapping and adding these resynthesized windows, typically at their −3 dB points (see chapter 5 for an explanation of this term), one obtains a signal that is a close approximation of the original. Figure 13.10 depicts the overlap-add process in schematic form. (Appendix A explains both the IDFT and overlap-add resynthesis in more detail.)

We use the qualification "close approximation" as a way of comparing practical implementations of the STFT with mathematical theory. In theory, resynthesis from the STFT is an identity operation, replicating the input sample by sample (Portnoff 1976). If it were an identity operation in practice, we could copy signals through an STFT any number of times with no generation loss. However, even good implementations of the STFT lose a small amount of information. This loss may not be audible after one pass through the STFT.

Limits of Overlap-add Resynthesis

Resynthesis with the plain *overlap-add* (OA) method is of limited use from the standpoint of musical transformation. This is because the OA process is designed for the case where the windows sum perfectly to a constant. As Allen and Rabiner (1977) showed, any additive or multiplicative transformations that disturb the perfect summation criterion at the final stage of the OA cause side effects that will probably be audible. Time expansion by stretching the distance between windows, for example, may introduce comb filter or reverberation effects, depending on the number of frequency channels or *bins* used in the analysis. Using speech or singing as a source, many transformations result in robotic, ringing voices of limited use.

One way to lessen these unwanted artifacts is to stipulate a great deal of overlap among successive windows in the analysis stage, as explained in the next section. The method of "improved overlap-add" resynthesis is another

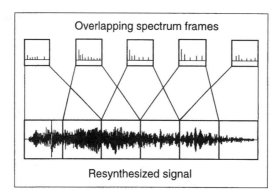

Figure 13.10   Overlap-add resynthesis. The gray areas indicate overlapping spectrum frames. Note: for visual clarity, we show only five frames. In practice it is typical to use more than 100 frames per second of analyzed sound.

strategy for overcoming these problems (George and Smith 1992; see also the description later in this chapter).

Why Overlapping Windows?

The motivation behind the overlapping analysis windows in the STFT can be confusing. After all, theory says that we can analyze a segment of any length and exactly resynthesize the segment from the analysis data. Evidently we can analyze in one pass Stravinsky's *Le sacre du printemps* using a 30-minute-long window, and reconstruct the entire piece from this analysis. This being the case, why bother to break the analysis into small, overlapping segments?

The reasons are several. The analysis of a monaural sound sampled at 44.1 KHz and lasting 30 minutes would result in a spectrum of over 79 million points. A visual inspection of this enormous spectrum would eventually tell us all the frequencies that occurred over a 30-minute duration, but would not tell us when precisely they occurred; this temporal information is embedded deep in the mathematical combination of the magnitude and phase spectra, hidden to the eye. Thus the first thing that windowing helps with is the visualization of the spectrum. By limiting the analysis to short segments (less than a tenth of a second, typically), each analysis plots fewer points, and we know more accurately when these frequencies occurred.

A second reason for using short-time envelopes is to conserve memory. Consider an analysis of a 30-minute chunk of sound swallowed in one gulp. Assuming 16-bit samples, one would need a computer with at least 79 million 16-bit words of random-access memory (RAM) just to hold the input while the computer calculates the FFT. By breaking the input into bite-sized segments it becomes easy to calculate the FFT on each small segment at a time.

A third reason for short-time windows is that one obtains results quicker. For *Le sacre du printemps* one would have to wait up to 30 minutes just to read in the input signal, plus however long it takes to calculate an FFT on a 79 million point input signal. Windowing the input lets one obtain initial results after a few milliseconds of the input has been read in, opening up applications for real-time spectrum analysis.

These three reasons explain the segmentation, but why overlap the windows? As explained earlier, smooth bell-shaped windows minimize the distortion that occurs in windowing. And of course, bell-shaped windows must overlap somewhat in order to capture the signal without gaps. But even greater overlap is often desirable, more than is dictated by the perfect summation criterion. Why is this? Increasing the overlap factor is equivalent to *oversampling the spectrum,* and this protects against the aliasing artifacts that can occur in transformations such as time-stretching and cross-synthesis. An overlap factor of eight or more is recommended when the goal is transforming the input signal.

Later we discuss basic criteria for selecting a window and setting its length. Appendix A goes into the subject of windowing in more detail. Next we present an alternative to the overlap-add resynthesis model.

Oscillator Bank Resynthesis

Sinusoidal additive resynthesis (SAR) (or *oscillator bank* resynthesis) differs from the overlap-add approach. Rather than summing the sine waves at each frame—as in the OA resynthesis model—SAR applies a bank of oscillators driven by amplitude and frequency envelopes that span across frame boundaries (figure 13.11). This implies that the analysis data must be converted beforehand into such envelopes. Fortunately, the conversion from analysis data (magnitude and phase) to synthesis data (amplitude and frequency) takes little calculation time.

The advantage of the SAR model is that envelopes are much more robust under musical transformation than the raw spectrum frames. Within broad limits, one can stretch, shrink, rescale, or shift the envelopes without worrying about artifacts in the resynthesis process; the perfect summation criterion of the OA model can be ignored. A disadvantage of SAR is that it is not as efficient computationally as OA methods.

A tracking phase vocoder can be seen as a SAR method since it also constructs frequency envelopes for additive sine wave synthesis. We discuss this approach in more detail in the section on the phase vocoder later.

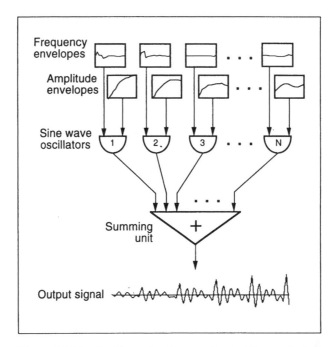

Figure 13.11   Oscillator bank resynthesis. The analysis data have been converted into a set of continuous amplitude and frequency envelopes. The number of oscillators needed for the resynthesis grows and shrinks depending on the complexity of the sound.

Analysis Frequencies

One can think of the STFT as applying a bank of filters at equally spaced frequency intervals to the windowed input signal. The frequencies are spaced at integer multiples (i.e., harmonics) of

$$\frac{sampling\ frequency}{N}$$

where N is the size of the analyzed segment. (As we will later see, the value of N is usually greater than the actual number of sound samples analyzed; for now we assume they are the same length.) Thus if the sampling frequency is 50 KHz and the window length is 1000 samples, the analysis frequencies are spaced at intervals 50,000/1000 = 50 Hz apart, starting at 0 Hz. The analyzer at 0 Hz measures the *direct current* or *DC offset* of the signal, a constant that can shift the entire signal above or below the center point of zero amplitude.

Audio signals are bandlimited to half the sampling rate (25 KHz in this case), and so we care about only half of the analysis bins. (As mentioned earlier, a bin is a frequency channel in the parlance of signal processing.) The effective frequency resolution of an STFT is thus $N/2$ bins spread equally across the audio bandwidth, starting at 0 Hz and ending at the Nyquist frequency. In our example, the number of usable audio frequency bins is 500, spaced 50 Hz apart.

Time/Frequency Uncertainty

All windowed spectrum analyses are hampered by a fundamental *uncertainty principle* between time and frequency resolution, first recognized by quantum physicists such as Werner Heisenberg in the early part of the twentieth century (Robinson 1982). This principle means that if we want high resolution in the time domain (i.e., we want to know precisely when an event occurs), we sacrifice frequency resolution. In other words, we can tell that an event occurred at a precise time but we cannot say exactly what frequencies it contained. Conversely, if we want high resolution in the frequency domain (i.e., we want to know the precise frequency of a component), we sacrifice time resolution. That is, we can pinpoint frequency content only over a long time interval. It is important to grasp this relationship in order to interpret the results of Fourier analysis.

Periodicity Implies Infinitude

Fourier analysis starts from the abstract premise that if a signal contains only one frequency, then that signal must be a sinusoid that is infinite in duration. Purity of frequency—absolute periodicity—implies infinitude. As soon as one limits the duration of this sine wave, the only way that Fourier analysis can account for this is to consider the signal as a sum of many infinite-length sinusoids that just happen to cancel each other out in such a way as to result in a limited-duration sine wave! While this characterization of frequency neatens the mathematics, it does not jibe with our most basic experiences with sound. As Gabor (1946) pointed out, if the concept of frequency is used only to refer to infinitely long signals, then the concept of changing frequency is impossible!

Still, we can understand one aspect of the abstract Fourier representation by a thought experiment. Using a sound editor, imagine that we zoom into the limit of the time domain of a digital system. In the shortest "instant" of time we see an individual sample point (the shaded rectangle marked **O** in figure 13.12a). We know exactly when this sample occurs, so we have high temporal resolution. But we cannot see what waveform it may be a part of; it could be a part of a wave at any frequency within the Nyquist range

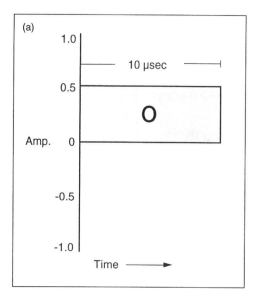

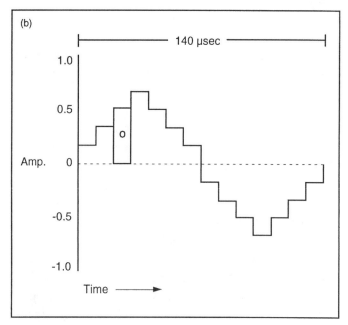

Figure 13.12 Frequency uncertainty at a small timescale. (*a*) The shaded box O represents a zoom into a precise sample period in a system with good time resolution (a 10 μsec sample period implies a sampling rate of 100 KHz). No frequency information is revealed at this time resolution; we lose any sense of what larger waveform this might be a part of. Thus a frequency estimation from one or a few samples is bound to be only a rough guess. (*b*) Zooming out to a timescale of 140 μsec gives a much better picture of the overall waveform and the local frequency period.

of the system. As we zoom out (figure 13.12b), we have more samples to analyze, and so the more sure we can be about what possible frequencies they might represent. But since Fourier analysis calculates the spectrum for the entire analyzed segment at a time, spectrum displays of long segments leave uncertainty as to when a particular frequency occurred. Once again, frequency precision comes at the expense of temporal imprecision.

Filter design provides more clues. Recall from chapter 10 that the number of delay stages influences the sharpness of a filter. In order to isolate a very narrow band, such as a single frequency component, we need extremely sharp edges in the filter response. This implies that one needs to look back into the distant past of the signal in order to extract a pure frequency. Another way of saying this is that such a filter has a long *impulse response*. (See chapter 10 for an explanation of impulse response.)

Time/Frequency Tradeoffs

The FFT divides up the audible frequency space into $N/2$ frequency bins, where N is the length in samples of the analysis window. Hence there is a tradeoff between the number of frequency bins and the length of the analysis window (figure 13.13). For example, if N is 512 samples, then the number of frequencies that can be analyzed is limited to 256. Assuming a sampling rate of 44.1 KHz, we obtain 256 bins equally spaced over the bandwidth 0 Hz to the Nyquist frequency 22.05 KHz. Increasing the sampling rate only widens the measurable bandwidth. It does not increase the frequency resolution of the analysis.

Table 13.1 demonstrates the balance between time and frequency resolution. If we want high time accuracy (say 1 ms or about 44 samples at a 44.1 KHz sampling rate), we must be satisfied with only 44/2 or 22 frequency bins. Dividing up the audio bandwidth from 0 to 22.05 KHz by 22 frequency bins, we obtain 22,050/22 or about 1000 Hz of frequency resolution. That is, if we want to know exactly when events occur on the scale of 1 ms, then our frequency resolution is limited to the gross scale of 1000-Hz-wide frequency bands. By sacrificing more time resolution, and widening the analysis interval to 30 ms, one can spot frequencies within a 33 Hz bandwidth. For high resolution in frequency (1 Hz), one must stretch the time interval to 1 second (44,100 samples)!

Because of this limitation in windowed STFT analysis, researchers are examining hybrids of time-domain and frequency domain analysis, *multiresolution analysis,* or non-Fourier methods to try to resolve both dimensions at high resolution. Later sections discuss these approaches.

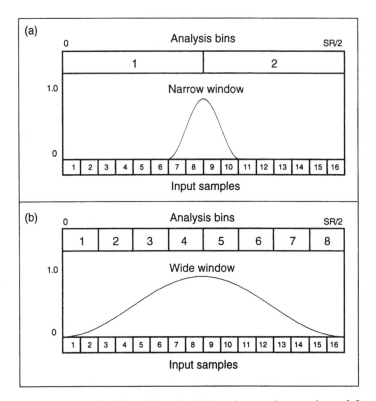

Figure 13.13 Relationship of window size to the number of frequency analysis bins. (*a*) A narrow window of four samples can resolve only two frequencies. (*b*) a wider window of sixteen samples divides the spectrum into eight bins.

Table 13.1   Time versus frequency resolution in windowed spectrum analysis

Length of time window (in ms)	Frequency resolution (analysis bandwidth) (in Hz)
1	1000
2	500
3	330
10	100
20	50
30	33
100	10
200	5
300	3
1000 (1 sec)	1
2000	0.5
3000	0.3

Frequencies in between Analysis Bins

The STFT knows only about a discrete set of frequencies spaced at equal intervals across the audio bandwidth. The spacing of these frequencies depends on the length of the analysis window. This length is effectively the "fundamental period" of the analysis. Such a model works well for sounds that are harmonic or quasi-harmonic where the harmonics align closely with the bins of the analysis. But what happens to frequencies that fall in between the equally spaced analysis bins of the STFT? This is the case for inharmonic sounds such as gongs or noisy sounds such as snare drums.

Let us call the frequency to analyzed f. When f coincides with the center of an analysis channel, all its energy is concentrated in that channel, and so it is accurately measured. When f is close to but not precisely coincident with the center, energy is scattered into all other analysis channels, but with a concentration remaining close to f. Figure 13.14 shows three snapshots of a frequency sweeping from 2 to 3 Hz, which can be generalized to other frequency ranges. The leakage spilling into all frequency bins from components in between bins is a well-known source of unreliability in the spectrum estimates produced by the STFT. When more than one component is in between bins, *beating effects* (periodic cancellation and reinforcement) may occur in both the frequency and amplitude traces. The result is that the analysis shows fluctuating energy in frequency components that are not physically present in the input signal.

Significance of Clutter

If the signal is resynthesized directly from the analysis data, the extra frequency components and beating effects pose no problem; they are benign artifacts of the STFT analysis that are resolved in resynthesis. Beating effects are merely the way that the STFT represents in the frequency domain a time-varying spectrum. In the resynthesis, some components add constructively and some add destructively (canceling each other out), so that the resynthesized result is a close approximation of the original. (Again, in theory it is an identity, but small errors creep into practical applications.)

Beating and other anomalies are harmless when the signal is directly resynthesized, but they obscure attempts to inspect the spectrum visually, or transform it. For this reason, the artifacts of analysis are called *clutter*. Dolson (1983) and Strawn (1985a) assay the significance of clutter in analysis of musical instrument tones. Gerzon (1991) presents a theory of "super-resolving" spectrum analyzers that offer to improve resolution in both time

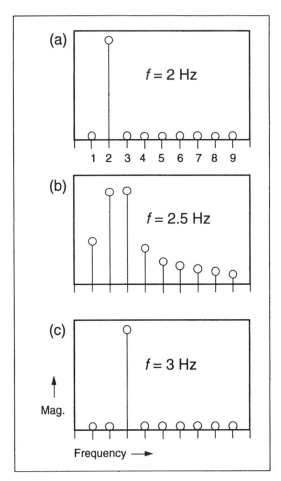

Figure 13.14 Three STFT "snapshots" of a sound changing frequency from 2 to 3 Hz. The STFT in this case has analysis bins spaced at 1 Hz intervals. When the input frequency is 2.5 Hz, it falls in between the equally spaced frequency bins of the analyzer, and the energy is spread across the entire spectrum. (After Hutchins 1984.)

and frequency, at the expense of increased clutter, which, Gerzon argues, has some perceptual significance.

Alternative Resynthesis Techniques

Two alternatives to the standard techniques of resynthesis merit a brief word here. The first is an adaptive method that offers improved resolution and more robust transformations; the second offers greatly increased resynthesis speed.

Analysis-by-synthesis/overlap-add (ABS/OLA) refines the STFT with overlap-add resynthesis by incorporating an error analysis procedure

(George and Smith 1992). This procedure compares the original signal with the resynthesized signal. When the error is above a given threshold, the procedure adjusts the amplitudes, frequencies, and phases in the analysis frame to approximate the original more closely. This adaptive process may occur repeatedly until the signal is more-or-less precisely reconstructed. As a result the ABS/OLA method can handle attack transients, inharmonic spectra, and effects such as vibrato with greater accuracy than the plain overlap-add method. It also permits more robust musical transformations. As we will see later, a method called the tracking phase vocoder has similar benefits.

The "FFT^{-1}" method is a special hybrid of overlap-add and oscillator bank resynthesis optimized for real-time operation. The method is so named because the resynthesis is carried out by the inverse FFT, which is sometimes abbreviated FFT^{-1}. It starts from previously calculated oscillator bank resynthesis data. It then converts these data by an efficient algorithm into an overlap-add model with data reduction and optimization steps that greatly speed up resynthesis. See Rodet and Depalle (1992) and French patent 900935 for details.

The Sonogram Representation

A *sonogram, sonograph,* or *spectrogram* is a well-known spectrum display technique in speech research, having been used for decades to analyze utterances. A sonogram shows an overview of the spectrum of several seconds of sound. This enables the viewer to see general features such as the onset of notes or phonemes, formant peaks, and major transitions. A trained viewer can read a speech sonogram. See Cogan (1984) for an example of using sonograms in the analysis of music. The sonogram representation has also been employed as an interface for spectrum editing (Eckel 1990; see chapter 16).

The original sonogram was Backhaus's (1932) system, described earlier in the background section on spectrum analysis; see also Koenig et al. (1946). In the 1950s the Kay Sonograph was a standard device for making sonograms. It consisted of a number of narrow bandpass analog filters and a recording system that printed dark bars on a roll of paper. The bars grew thicker in proportion to the energy output from each filter. Today sonograms are generally implemented with the STFT.

Figure 13.4 showed a sonogram, representing a sound signal as a two-dimensional display of time versus "frequency + amplitude". The vertical dimension depicts frequency (higher frequencies are higher up in the diagram) and shades of gray indicate the amplitude, with dark shades indicating greater intensity.

Sonogram Parameters

The parameters of the modern sonogram are the same as those of the STFT, except for certain display parameters. Adjustments to these parameters make a great difference in the output image:

1. Range of amplitudes and the type of scale used, whether linear or logarithmic.

2. Range of frequencies and the type of scale used, whether linear or logarithmic.

3. Time advance of the analysis window, also called *hop size* (in samples) or *window overlap factor*. This determines the time distance between successive columns in the output display. (We discuss this parameter in more detail in the section on the phase vocoder.)

4. Number of samples to analyze and the size of the FFT analysis window; the resolution of time and frequency depend on these parameters.

5. Number of frequency channels to display, which determines the number of rows in the graphical output and is related to the range and scale of the frequency domain; this cannot exceed the resolution imposed by the window size.

6. Window type—see the discussion in the section on the phase vocoder and in appendix A.

Parameter 4 includes two parameters; the FFT window size is usually greater than the actual number of sound samples analyzed, the difference being padded with zero-valued samples. (See the section on phase vocoder analysis parameters.) These parameters have the most dramatic effect on the display. A short window results in a vertically oriented display, indicating

---

Figure 13.15 Time-versus-frequency tradeoffs in sonogram analysis and display. All displays show speech sound sampled at 44.1 KHz. (*a*) Analysis window is 32 samples long, time resolution is 0.725 ms, and frequency resolution is 1378 Hz. (*b*) Analysis window is 1024 samples long, time resolution is 23.22 ms, frequency resolution is 43.07 Hz. (*c*) Analysis window is 8192 samples long, time resolution is 185.8 ms, frequency resolution is 5.383 Hz. (Sonograms provided by Gerhard Eckel using his SpecDraw program.)

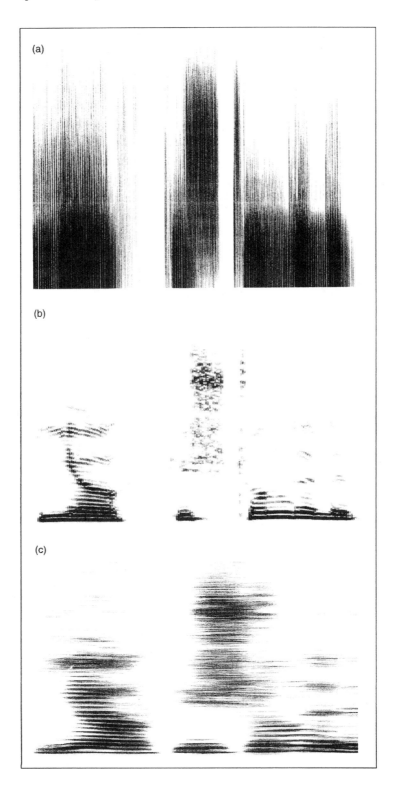

the precise onset time of events but blurring the frequency reading (figure 13.15a). A medium length window resolves both time and frequency features fairly well, indicating the presence of formant frequencies (figure 13.15b). A long window generates a horizontally oriented display, as individual frequency bands come into clear view, but their position in time is smeared along the horizontal axis (figure 13.15c).

The speech sonogram has to be modified to handle the more stringent demands of music. Musical sonograms tend to be longer than speech sonograms, including sections or entire pieces. The dynamic range of music is much wider than speech. Also, as Lundén and Ungvary (1991) point out, speech sonograms are oriented toward an accurate physical representation of the spectrum, whereas musicians are more interested in a perceptual view that is in accord with what we can hear. The cochleagram display, explained later, may be a more accurate perceptual picture. For a critical analysis of traditional sonograms from the standpoint of accuracy, see Loughlin, Atlas, and Pitton (1992).

The Phase Vocoder

The phase vocoder has emerged as an increasingly popular sound analysis tool, being packaged in several widely distributed software packages. (Gordon and Strawn 1985 and Moore 1990 contain annotated code for practical phase vocoders.) One can view the PV as passing a windowed input signal through a bank of parallel bandpass filters spread out at equal intervals across the audio bandwidth. These filters measure the amplitude and phase of a sinusoidal signal in each frequency band. Through a subsequent operation (explained in appendix A), these values can be converted into two envelopes: one for the amplitude of the sine, and one for the frequency of the sine. This corresponds to the case of oscillator bank resynthesis previously discussed. Various implementations of the PV offer tools for modifying these envelopes, allowing musical transformations of analyzed sounds.

In theory, analysis and resynthesis via the phase vocoder is a sample-by sample clone (Portnoff 1976). In practice, there is usually a slight loss of information, which may not be audible in one analysis/resynthesis pass. In any case, a musician's use of the PV inevitably involves modification of the analysis data before resynthesis. For what the composer seeks in the output is not a clone of the input, but a musical transformation that maintains a sense of the identity of the source. That is, if the input signal is a spoken voice, one usually wants it to sound like a spoken voice even after being transformed. One can also use the PV for radical distortions that destroy the identity of the input signal, but more efficient distortion algorithms are easily found, such as the modulations discussed in chapter 6.

See chapter 5 for a description of the first vocoder. For more on the PV, including descriptions of practical implementations, see Portnoff 1976, 1978, 1980; Holtzman 1978; Moorer 1978; Moore 1990; Dolson 1983, 1986; Gordon and Strawn 1985; Strawn 1985b; Strawn 1987; Serra 1989; Depalle and Poirot 1991; Erbe 1992; Walker and Fitz 1992; Beauchamp 1993.

Phase Vocoder Parameters

The quality of a given PV analysis depends on the parameter settings chosen by the user. These settings must be adjusted according to the nature of the sounds being analyzed and the type of results that are expected. The main parameters of the PV are the folllowing:

1. Frame size—number of input samples to be analyzed at a time

2. Window type—selection of a window shape from among the standard types (see the discussion later)

3. FFT size—the actual number of samples fed to the FFT algorithm; usually the nearest power of two that is double the frame size, where the unit of FFT size is referred to by *points,* as in a "1024-point FFT" (equivalent to "1024-sample FFT")

4. Hop size or overlap factor—time advance from one frame to the next

Now we discuss each parameter in turn. Then in the following section we give rules of thumb for setting these parameters.

Frame Size

The frame size (in samples) is important for two reasons. The first is that the frame size determines one aspect of the tradeoff in time/frequency resolution. The larger the frame size, the greater the number of frequency bins, but the lower the time resolution, and vice versa. If we are trying to analyze sounds in the lower octaves with great frequency accuracy, large frame sizes are unavoidable. Since the FFT computes the average spectrum content within a frame, the onset time of any spectrum changes within a frame is lost when the spectrum is plotted or transformed. (If the signal is simply resynthesized, the temporal information is restored.) For high-frequency sounds, small frames are adequate, which are also more accurate in time resolution.

The second reason frame size is important is that large FFTs are slower to calculate than small FFTs. Following the rule of thumb that the calculation time for an FFT is proportional to $N \times \log_2(N)$, where N is the length of the input signal (Rabiner and Gold 1975), it takes more than a thousand times as long to calculate a 32,768-point FFT, for example, than a 64-point FFT. The latency of a long FFT may be too onerous in a real-time system.

Window Type

Most PVs give the option of using one of a family of standard window types, including Hamming, Hanning (or Hann; see Marple 1987), truncated Gaussian, Blackman-Harris, and Kaiser (Harris 1978; Nuttall 1981; see also appendix A). All are quasi-bell-shaped, and all work reasonably well for general musical analysis/resynthesis. For analyses where precision is important (such as creating a systematic catalog of spectra for instrumental tones) the choice of analysis window may be more critical. This is because windowing introduces distortion, and each type of window "bends" the analysis plots in a slightly different way. For more on windows see appendix A.

FFT Size and Zero-padding

The choice of FFT size depends on the transformation one plans to apply to the input sound. A safe figure for cross-synthesis is the nearest power of two that is double the frame size. For example, a frame size of 128 samples would mandate an FFT size of 256. The other 128 samples in the FFT are set to zero—a process called *zero-padding* (see appendix A).

Hop Size

The hop size is the number of samples that the analyzer jumps along the input waveform each time it takes a new spectrum measurement (figure 13.16). The shorter the hop size, the more successive windows overlap. Thus some PVs specify this parameter as an overlap factor that describes how many analysis windows cover each other. Regardless of how it is specified, the hop size is usually a fraction of the frame size. A certain amount of overlap (e.g., eight times) is necessary to ensure an accurate resynthesis. Even more overlap may improve accuracy when the analysis data are going to be transformed, but the computational cost is proportionally greater.

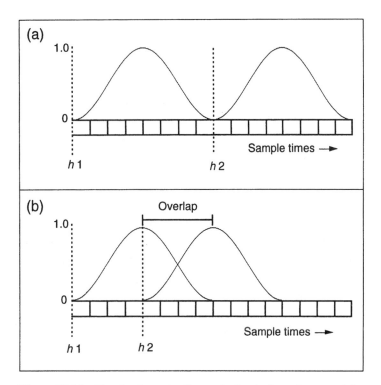

Figure 13.16 Varying hop size for analysis windows that are eight samples long. $h1$ and $h2$ are the starting times for each window. (*a*) Nonoverlapping windows when hop size = window size. (*b*) Overlapping windows when hop size is less than window size. In this case the hop size is four samples.

Typical Parameter Values

No parameter settings of the PV are ideal for all sounds. But when the parameters are set within a certain range, a variety of traditional instrumental sounds can be analyzed and resynthesized with reasonable fidelity. Here are some rules of thumb for PV parameter settings that may serve as a starting point for more "tuned" analyses:

1. Frame size—large enough to capture four periods of the lowest frequency of interest (Depalle and Poirot 1991). This is particularly important if the sound is time-stretched; too small a frame size means that individual pitch bursts are moved apart, changing the pitch, although formants are preserved.

2. Window type—any standard type except rectangular.

3. FFT size—double the frame size, in samples.

4. Hop size—if the analysis data are going to be time-distorted, the recommended hop size is an eighth of the frame size, in samples (i.e., eight times overlap). In general, the minimum technical criterion is that all windows add to a constant, that is, all data are equally weighted. This typically implies an overlap at the -3 dB point of the particular window type chosen, from which can be derived the hop size.

Window Closing

Once is not enough. (S. J. Marple 1987).

Any given setting of the window size results in an analysis biased toward harmonics of the period defined by that window size. Frequency components that fall outside the frequency bins associated with a given window size will be estimated incorrectly. Thus some spectrum analysis procedures run the same signal through the analyzer repeatedly with different settings for the window size. A procedure that starts from high time and low frequency resolution and works progressively to low time and high frequency resolution is called *window closing* (Marple 1987).

Some STFT analyzers try to estimate the pitch of the signal in order to determine the optimal window size. As mentioned earlier, pitch-synchronous analysis works well if the sound to be analyzed has a basically harmonic structure.

Tracking Phase Vocoder

Many current implementations of the PV are called tracking phase vocoders (TPVs) because they follow or track the most prominent peaks in the spectrum over time (Dolson 1983; McAulay and Quatieri 1986; Quatieri and McAulay 1986; Serra 1989; Maher and Beauchamp 1990; Walker and Fitz 1992). Unlike the ordinary phase vocoder, in which the resynthesis frequencies are limited to harmonics of the analysis window, the TPV follows changes in frequencies. The result of peak tracking is a set of amplitude and frequency envelopes that drive a bank of sinusoidal oscillators in the resynthesis stage.

The tracking process follows only the most prominent frequency components. For these components, the result is a more accurate analysis than that done with an equally spaced bank of filters (the traditional STFT implementation). The other benefit is that the tracking process creates frequency and amplitude envelopes for these components, which make them more robust under transformation than overlap-add frames. A disadvantage is that the quality of the analysis may depend more heavily on proper parameter settings than in the regular STFT.

Operation of the TPV

A TPV carries out the following steps:

1. Compute the STFT using the frame size, window type, FFT size, and hop size specified by the user

2. Derive the squared magnitude spectrum in dB

3. Find the bin numbers of the peaks in the spectrum

4. Calculate the magnitude and phase of each frequency peak

5. Assign each peak to a *frequency track* by matching the peaks of the previous frame with those of the current frame (see the description of peak tracking later)

6. Apply any desired modifications to the analysis parameters

7. If additive resynthesis is requested, generate a sine wave for each frequency track and sum all sine wave components to create an output signal; the instantaneous amplitude, phase, and frequency of each sinusoidal component is calculated by interpolating values from frame to frame (or use the alternative resynthesis methods described earlier)

Peak Tracking

The tracking phase vocoder follows the most prominent frequency trajectories in the spectrum. Like other aspects of sound analysis, the precise method of peak tracking should vary depending on the sound. The tracking algorithm works best when it is tuned to the type of sound being analyzed—speech, harmonic spectrum, smooth inharmonic spectrum, noisy, etc. This section briefly explains more about the tracking process as a guide to setting the analysis parameters.

The first stage in peak tracking is peak identification. A simple control that sets the *minimum peak height* focuses the identification process on the most significant landmarks in the spectrum (figure 13.17a). The rest of the algorithm tries to apply a set of *frequency guides* that advance in time (figure 13.17b). The guides are hypotheses only; later the algorithm will decide which guides are confirmed frequency tracks. The algorithm continues the guides by finding the peak closest in frequency to its current value. The alternatives are as follows:

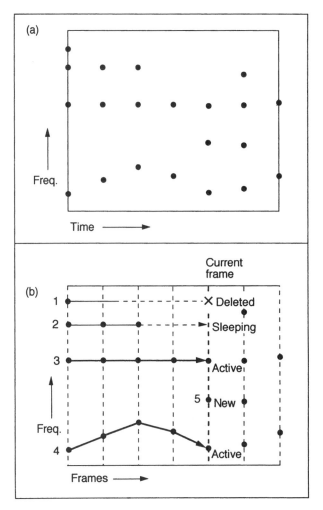

Figure 13.17 Peak identification and tracking. (*a*) Isolation of a set of spectrum peaks. (*b*) Fitting frequency guides to peaks. Guide 1 at the top did not wake up after three frames, so it is deleted. Guide 2 is still sleeping. Guides 3 and 4 are active. Guide 5 starts from a new peak.

- If it finds a match, the guide continues.

- If a guide cannot be continued during a frame it is considered to be "sleeping."

- If the guide does not wake up after a certain number of frames—which may be specified by the user—then it is deleted. It may be possible to switch on *guide hysteresis*, which continues tracking a guide that falls slightly below the specified *amplitude range*. Hysteresis alleviates the audible problem of "switching" guides that repeatedly fade slightly, are cut to zero by the peak tracker, and fade in again (Walker and Fitz 1992). With hysteresis the guide is synthesized at its actual value, which may be less than the amplitude range, instead of with zero amplitude.

- If there is a conflict between guides, the closest guide wins, and the "loser" looks for another peak within the *maximum peak deviation*, a frequency band specified by the user.

- If there are peaks that are not accounted for by current guides, then a new guide begins.

The process of windowing may compromise the accuracy of the tracking, particularly in rapidly moving waveforms such as attack transients. Processing sounds with a sharp attack in time-reversed order helps the tracking algorithm (Serra 1989). This gives the partial trackers a chance to lock onto their stable frequency trajectories before encountering the chaos of the attack, resulting in less distortion. The data can be reversed back to its normal order before resynthesis.

The next section discusses step 6, modification of the TPV analysis envelopes.

Editing Analysis Envelopes

Changing the parameters of the resynthesis creates transformations in the sound. By modifying the hop size in the playback, for example, one can implement time expansion and compression effects. Due to the underlying sinusoidal model, however, when a time expansion is performed on a complex attack or a noisy sound, individual sine waves emerge and the noisy quality is lost. The spectral modeling synthesis of Serra (1989), described later, addresses this problem.

To create sophisticated musical transformations one must edit the analysis data generated by the TPV—the frequency, amplitude, and phase curves (Moorer 1978; Dolson 1983; Gordon and Strawn 1985). This laborious process of transmutation is greatly aided by automatic data reduction procedures and graphical editor programs. (See chapter 4 for information on data reduction in additive synthesis, and see the section on spectrum editors in chapter 16.) Table 4.1 in chapter 4 lists some of the musical effects made possible by modification of PV spectrum data.

Cross-synthesis with the Phase Vocoder

Another possibility for sound transformation with less editing is *cross-synthesis*. Cross-synthesis is not one technique; it takes a number of forms. The most common form uses the magnitude functions from one spectrum to control the magnitude functions of another. That is, the strength of each frequency component in sound A scales the strength of the corresponding frequency component in sound B. This is implemented by mutiplying each point in spectrum A by each corresponding point in spectrum B. Another term for this type of cross-synthesis is *filtering by convolution* (see chapter 10 for more on convolution). Musically, cross-synthesis is most effective when one of the sounds being filtered has a broad bandwidth, like a noise source. By using a phase vocoder with two inputs, cross-synthesis is basically automatic (Depalle and Poirot 1991). Another type of cross-synthesis uses the magnitude functions from one sound with the phase functions of another sound to create a hybrid sound effect (Boyer and Kronland-Martinet 1989).

Musical guidelines for cross-synthesis with the PV are much the same as for cross-synthesis by fast convolution. See chapter 10 for more on these guidelines.

Computational Cost of the Phase Vocoder

The phase vocoder is one of the more computationally expensive operations available to musicians, particularly when tracking is carried out. The tracking phase vocoder soaks up large quantities of computer power even though the inner core is implemented using the efficient FFT algorithm. The PV also generates a large amount of analysis data; in some cases this is many times greater than the size of the sample data being analyzed. A panoply of techniques may be applied to reduce computation and conserve space. For example, the envelopes generated by the TPV may be computed at a lower sampling rate. This may not compromise the audio quality since these control functions tend to change more slowly than the audio sampling rate. Before resynthesis they can be restored to the original sampling rate by interpolation. Other *data reduction* methods can also be applied; see the discussion of data reduction in chapter 4.

Accuracy of Resynthesis

The accuracy of all Fourier-based resynthesis is limited by the resolution of the analysis procedures. Small distortions introduced by numerical round-off, windowing, peak-tracking, undersampling of envelope functions, and other aspects of the analysis introduce errors. In a well-implemented PV, when the analysis parameters are properly adjusted by a skilled engineer and no modifications are made to the analysis data, the error is negligible perceptually.

The tracking PV, on the other hand, interprets the raw analysis data in constructing its tracks. It discards all information that does not contribute to a track. This sifting may leave out significant portions of sound energy, particularly noisy, transient energy. This can be demonstrated by subtracting the resynthesized version from the original signal to yield a *residual signal* (Strawn 1987a; Gish 1978, 1992; Serra 1989). One can consider this residual or difference to be analysis/resynthesis error. It is common to refer to the resynthesized, quasi-harmonic portion as the "clean" part of the signal and the error or noise component as the "dirty" part of the signal. For many sounds (i.e., those with fast transients such as in cymbal crashes), the errors are quite audible. That is, the "clean" signal sounds unnaturally "sanitized" or sinusoidal, and the "dirty" signal, when heard separately, contains the missing grit. (See the section on analysis of inharmonic and noisy sounds in a moment.)

For efficiency, some PVs have the option of discarding phase information, saving only the amplitude and frequency data. This results in a data reduction and corresponding savings in computation time, but also degrades the accuracy of the resynthesis. Without proper phase data, a resynthesized waveform, for example, does not resemble the original, although it has the same basic frequency content (Serra 1989). In certain steady state sounds, a rearrangement of phases may not be audible. But for high-fidelity reproduction of transients and quasi-steady-state tones, phase data help reassemble short-lived and changing components in their proper order and are therefore valuable.

Problem Sounds

The PV handles harmonic, static, or smoothly changing tones best. Transformations such as timescale expansion and compression on these sounds result in natural sounding effects. Certain sounds, however, are inherently difficult to modify with PV techniques. These include noisy sounds such as raspy or breathy voices, motors, any sound that is rapidly changing on a timescale of a few milliseconds, and sounds that contain room noise. Transformations on these types of sounds may result in echoes, flutter, unwanted resonances, and undesirable colored reverberation effects. These are mainly due to phase distortions that occur when the analysis data is transformed.

Analysis of Inharmonic and Noisy Sounds

Demonstrations prove that tracking phase vocoders can analyze and resynthesize many inharmonic sounds, including bird songs (Serra and Smith

1990), and tuned percussion tones (gongs, marimba, xylophone, etc.). But since the TPV is based on Fourier analysis, it must translate noisy and inharmonic signals into combinations of periodic sinusoidal functions. Particularly for noisy signals, this can be a costly process from a storage and computational standpoint. To synthesize a simple noise band, for example, requires an ever-changing blend of dozens of sine waves. Storing the control functions for these sines fills up a great deal of space. In some TPVs this amounts to more than ten times as many bytes as the original sound samples. Resynthesizing the sines demands a tremendous amount of computation. Moreover, since the transformations allowed by the TPV are based on a sinusoidal model, operations on noisy sounds often result in clusters of sinusoids that have lost their noisy quality.

Deterministic Plus Stochastic Techniques

To handle such signals better, the TPV has been extended to make it more effective in musical applications. Serra (1989) added filtered noise to the inharmonic sinusoidal model in *spectral modeling synthesis* (SMS). (See also chapter 4 and Serra and Smith 1990.) As figure 13.18 shows, SMS reduces the analysis data into a *deterministic* component (prominent narrowband components of the original sound) and a *stochastic* component. The deterministic component tracks the most prominent frequencies in the spectrum. SMS resynthesizes these tracked frequencies with sine waves. The tracking follows only the most prominent frequency components, discarding other energy in the signal. Thus SMS also analyzes the *residue* (or *residual*), which is the difference between the deterministic component and the original spectrum. This is used to synthesize the stochastic component of the signal. The residual is analyzed and approximated by a collection of simplified spectrum envelopes. One can think of the resynthesis as passing white noise through filters controlled by these envelopes. In the implementation, however, SMS uses sine waves with random phase values, which is equivalent to the filtered noise interpretation.

The SMS representation, using spectrum envelopes and sine waves, rather than a filter bank, makes it easier to modify the stochastic part in order to transform the sound. Graphical operations on envelopes are intuitive to a musician, whereas changing filter coefficients leads to technical complications. A problem with SMS is that the perceptual link between the deterministic and stochastic parts is delicate; editing the two parts separately may lead to a loss of perceived fusion between them.

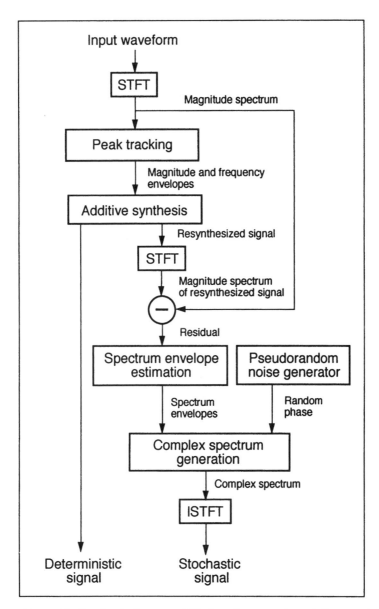

Figure 13.18 Analysis part of X. Serra's spectral modeling synthesis technique. The deterministic part follows a strictly sinusoidal additive synthesis approach. The stochastic part of the signal derives from the difference between the resynthesis of the deterministic (quasi-harmonic) part and the STFT of the input waveform. The system simplifies each residual component by fitting an envelope to it. The envelope representation makes the stochastic part easier to modify by musicians. The resynthesis of the stochastic part then uses these envelopes with a random phase component—equivalent to filtered white noise.

Constant *Q* Filter Bank Analysis

Various spectrum analysis methods can be grouped under the rubric of *constant Q* filter bank techniques—applied in audio research since the late 1970s (Petersen 1980; Petersen and Boll 1983; Schwede 1983; Musicus, Stautner, and Anderson 1984). Within this family are the so-called *auditory transform* (Stautner 1983) and the *bounded-Q frequency transform* (Mont-Reynaud 1985a; Chafe et al. 1985). The wavelet transform, discussed in the next section, could also be classified as a constant *Q* technique.

Recall from chapter 5 that *Q* can be defined for a bandpass filter as the ratio of its center frequency to its bandwidth. In a constant *Q* filter bank, each filter has a similar or the same *Q*. Thus the bandwidth of the high-frequency filters is much broader than those of the low-frequency filters, because, like musical intervals, constant *Q* analyzers work on a logarithmic frequency scale. For example, a one-third octave filter bank is a constant *Q* device.

Constant *Q* Versus Traditional Fourier Analysis

The constant *Q* filter bank's logarithmic frequency analysis is different from regular Fourier analyzers. Fourier analysis divides the spectrum into a set of equally spaced *frequency bins,* where there are half as many bins as there are samples taken as input (for real signals, negative frequency components duplicate the positive frequency components). In Fourier analysis, the width of a bin is a constant equal to the Nyquist rate divided by the number of bins. For example, for a 1024-point FFT at a sampling rate of 48 KHz, the width of a bin is 24,000/1024, or 23.43 Hz.

When the results of the FFT are translated to a logarithmic scale (such as musical octaves) it is clear that the resolution is worst in the lower octaves. To separate two low-frequency tones E1 (41.2 Hz) and F1 (43.65 Hz) that are a semitone apart requires a large time window (e.g., 2^{14} or 16,384 samples). But to use the same resolution at higher frequencies is a waste, since human beings have difficulty distinguishing between two tones that are 2.45 Hz apart in the octave between 10 and 20 KHz. Hence there is a mismatch between the logarithmic continuum of frequencies that we hear and the linear frequency scale of FFT analysis. This problem is addressed by methods like the constant *Q* transform, in which the bandwidth varies proportionally with frequency. That is, the analysis bands are thin for low frequencies and wide for high frequencies (figure 13.19). Thus in constant *Q* analysis the length of the analysis window varies according to the fre-

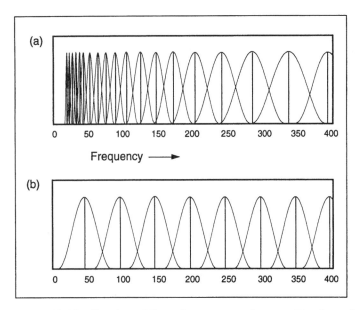

Figure 13.19   Spacing of filters for constant Q versus Fourier techniques. (*a*) Using only 43 filters (19 of which are shown), the constant Q method achieves 1/4-octave frequency resolution from 20 Hz to 21 KHz. (*b*) Fourier filter spacing, with a band every 46 Hz. Using almost 12 times as many filters (512, or which 8 are shown), Fourier methods still do not have the low-frequency resolution as constant Q methods. The Fourier method will have 46 Hz resolution throughout the audio bandwidth, even in the highest octave where the ear cannot accurately resolve these differences.

quency being analyzed. Long windows analyze low frequencies, and short windows analyze high frequencies.

Constant Q filter banks do not avoid the uncertainty relationship between time and frequency, discussed earlier, but temporal uncertainty is concentrated in the lower octaves, where the analysis bands are narrow, and therefore the windows and the filter impulse responses are long. Since sonic transients (attacks) tend to contain high-frequency components, a constant Q response has the advantage of time localization in high frequencies with frequency localization in low frequencies.

Another attractive feature of constant Q techniques is that the human ear has a frequency response that resembles constant Q response, particularly above 500 Hz (Scharf 1961, 1970). That is, the auditory system performs a type of filter bank analysis with a frequency dependent bandwidth. These measured auditory bandwidths are of such a fundamental nature that they are called *critical bands*. (See chapter 23 for more on critical bands.) Figure 13.20 plots center frequencies versus bandwidths for a bank of 23 bandpass filters used in the so-called auditory transform, which was based on an

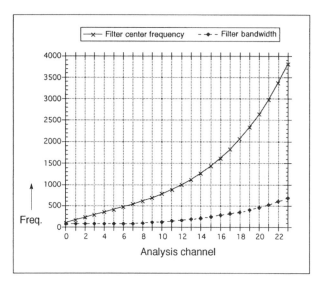

Figure 13.20   Plot of center frequency and bandwidth for the so-called auditory transform system developed by Stautner (1983). The plot shows the data for 23 analysis channels with center frequencies between 99 and 3806 Hz and bandwidths between 80 and 700 Hz, which resemble the critical band response of the human ear.

approximation of critical bandwidth data by Stautner (1983). For increased frequency resolution, Stautner also used a version with 42 filters between 79 and 3177 Hz.

Implementation of Constant Q Analysis

The direct method of implementing constant Q analysis uses a bank of filters where the bandwidth of a filter is proportional to its center frequency (Stautner 1983). By measuring the output of several dozen such filters we should be able to estimate the spectrum of the input signal fairly accurately. The main problem with the direct approach is that it does not take advantage of the efficiencies of the FFT for its computations. Thus a body of research has focused on constructing a constant Q analysis based on data generated by a traditional FFT analysis (Nawab, Quatieri and Lim 1983), or on methods such as "frequency warping" a fixed filter implemented with the FFT (Musicus 1984).

Constant Q algorithms may not be as efficient as those based on the fast Fourier transform, but the logarithmic spacing of the analysis channels means that the number of channels can be fewer for constant Q methods, while maintaining the same perceptual resolution as the STFT. The number of analysis channels in the STFT typically varies between several hundred and several thousand. The number of constant Q filter channels required to cover the same gamut is often less than 100.

Another issue with constant Q filter banks is invertibility. The existence of a constant Q filter bank does not necessarily imply a method for resynthesis. Some implementations provide this capability, while others do not.

Analysis by Wavelets

The *wavelet transform* (WT) was originally developed by scientists at the University of Marseille for applications in physics and acoustics (Dutilleux, Grossmann, and Kronland-Martinet 1988; Kronland-Martinet and Grossmann 1991; Evangelista 1991; Boyer and Kronland-Martinet 1989; Kronland-Martinet 1988; Strang 1989; Kussmaul 1991; Vetterli 1992). A wavelet is a signal that forms a sinusoid with a smooth attack and decay. The term "wavelet" and its French equivalent *ondelette* are not new, however, being used in early-twentieth-century physics to describe the packets of energy emitted by atomic processes (Crawford 1968; Robinson 1982).

From a musical perspective, the WT can be considered as a special case of the constant Q filter paradigm. Wavelets inject the notion of a "short-time" or "granular" representation into the constant Q filter model. The WT represents and manipulates sounds mapped onto a time-frequency *grid* or *plane*. Each rectangle in this grid represents its *uncertainty product*. The center of each grid is the mean time of occurrence and the spectral centroid. Such a grid is also implicit in constant Q methods, but it is rarely used explicitly. In music analysis with the WT, one sets up the grid according to the goals of the analysis and distorts the grid according to the goals of the resynthesis.

In the wavelet theory, every input signal can be expressed as a sum of wavelets having a precise starting time, duration, frequency, and initial phase. The prototypical wavelet for music has a Gaussian envelope (see chapter 5), but other types of wavelet envelopes can be defined. Thus the wavelet is similar to the grain discussed in chapter 5, and to the windowed segments of the short-time Fourier transform discussed earlier in this chapter. The peculiar aspect of the wavelet is that no matter what frequency it contains, it always encapsulates a constant number of cycles. This implies that the size (duration) of the wavelet window expands or compresses according to the frequency being analyzed (figure 13.21). This stretching and shrinking is referred to as *dilation* in the literature and is usually specified as a factor of 1/*frequency*.

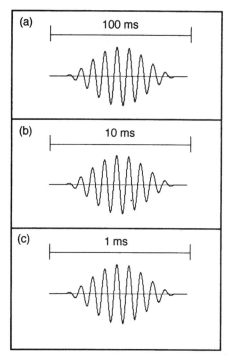

Figure 13.21   Dilation of elementary wavelets at different frequencies. The duration of the wavelet shrinks at higher frequencies so that the number of cycles of the waveform remains the same. (*a*) 100 Hz wavelet. (*b*) 1 KHz wavelet. (*c*) 10 KHz wavelet.

The implication of the dilating window size is that the WT trades frequency resolution for time resolution at high frequencies, and trades time resolution for frequency resolution at low frequencies. Thus the WT can simultaneously detect precise onset times signaled by high-frequency transients, and also resolve the low-frequency spectrum well.

Operation of Wavelet Analysis

The WT multiplies the input signal by a grid of *analyzing wavelets*, where the grid is bounded by frequency on one axis and by time dilation factor on the other (figure 13.22). The operation of this multiplication process is equivalent to a bank of filters. Indeed, a way to think of wavelets is that each one represents the impulse response of a bandpass filter.

Dilation of of this impulse response corresponds to an inverse frequency scaling. Thus, the duration of each wavelet corresponds to the center frequency of a filter; the longer the wavelet, the lower its center frequency.

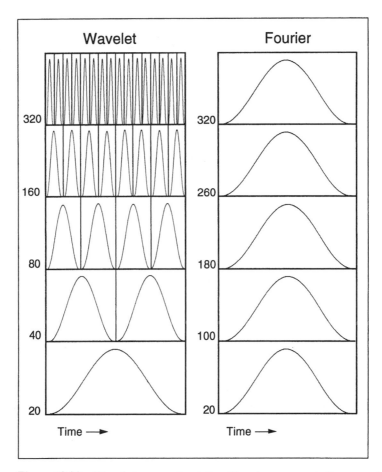

Figure 13.22   Wavelet versus short-time Fourier representation over the same time-versus-frequency area. The wavelet grid on the left has finer time resolution in the upper range of the spectrum, while the short-time Fourier's resolution is constant.

The WT simultaneously windows the input signal and measures the energy of the input signal at the frequency of each analyzing wavelet. The result is another grid where the energy at each cell (i.e., in each kernel) reflects the time-frequency energy of the original signal. The output of the WT is, as in short-time Fourier analysis, a two-part spectrum, with one part representing the magnitude at a given frequency and the other part representing phase.

The frequency scale of the analysis grid is typically logarithmic. This means that the frequency of each analyzing wavelet is related to the others by a logarithmic musical interval such as a fifth, third, or whatever, depending on the way the system is set up. The use of a logarithmic scale is not

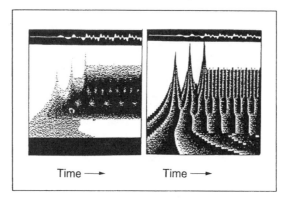

Figure 13.23   Three overlapping sinusoids shown in a wavelet display. The wavelet display has two parts: the modulus (or magnitude), shown at left, and the phase display. Both show time going from left to right. The vertical axis plots frequency on a logarithmic scale. At the top of both parts is a standard time-domain plot of the waveform for reference. (*a*) In the modulus, darkness indicates energy. Notice the high-frequency "pointers" showing the onset time of each sinusoid. (*b*) Phase diagram basically shows excursions of the waveform directly. The U-shaped "mountains" follow the peaks of the waveform. Any changes show up as chaotic surfaces, again with "pointers" to the instant of change. (After Arfib 1991.)

mandatory, however, since the WT can be aligned on any arbitrary frequency scale. Of course, the durations of the wavelets are scaled according to their frequency.

Direct computation of the wavelet transform is an onerous computational task, similar in load to direct compution of the discrete Fourier transform (see Appendix A). Various proposals have been advanced for cutting down on the labor required for wavelet transform calculations (Dutilleux, Grossmann, and Kronland-Martinet 1988; Mallat 1989; Evangelista 1991). See the literature for the details of these algorithms.

Wavelet Display

A by-product of research in wavelet analysis is a display method used by the Marseille group and shown in figure 13.23. This can be thought of as a traditional spectrum plot projected in time and flipped on its side. Another way to see it is as a kind of sonogram: plotting time horizontally, and frequency from the low frequencies on the bottom to the high frequencies on the top.

The difference between the sonogram plot and this wavelet plot is the pattern of time localization they project. Short wavelets detect brief transients, which are localized in time. These wavelets sit at the apex of a trian-

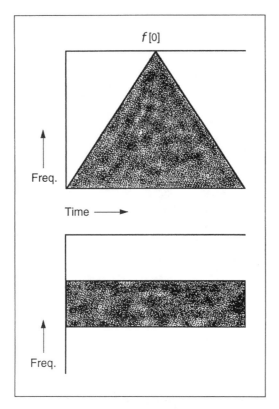

Figure 13.24   Wavelet domains of influence. (*a*) Time. (*b*) Frequency. See the text for an explanation.

gle on the frequency versus-time plane (figure 13.24a). Long wavelets detect low frequencies; they sit at the bottom of the triangle, spread out (blurred) over time. This triangle is the wavelet's *domain of influence in time*. The *domain of influence for frequencies* is a constant horizontal band, as in the spectrogram (figure 13.24b). The darker the band, the stronger the magnitude within that frequency range.

Of course, this technique of plotting is just one of many other ways of projecting the data generated by the WT. In the Marseille work, both modulus (magnitude) and phase images are plotted. The phase spectrum is sometimes referred to as the *scalagram*. Phase is plotted only above a given magnitude threshold to avoid unreliable estimation.

If the frequency grid is aligned to a musical interval, the display projects a strong dark indicator when the input signal contains that interval. This is shown in figure 13.25 for a WT configured for octave detection. The four instances of octaves show up as dark triangles. In this case, one could say

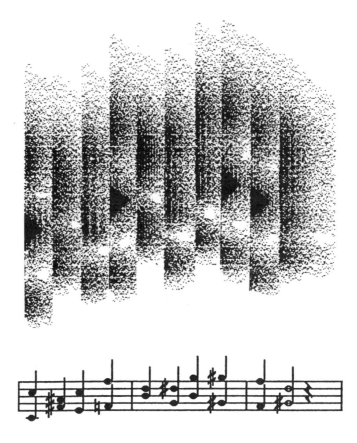

Figure 13.25   Modulus of the wavelet transform corresponding to the music notation written below. Dark triangles indicating maxima occur when octaves play. (After Kronland-Martinet and Grossman 1991.)

that the analyzing wavelet is the sum of two simpler wavelets an octave apart in frequency.

Wavelet Resynthesis

As in the STFT, wavelet resynthesis can be carried out in two ways: overlap-add and additive. Each method lends itself to certain types of transformations. In the case of the overlap-add method, we need as many oscillators as there are overlapping wavelets. In additive resynthesis, the number of oscillators is constant, since each frequency component is assigned its own oscillator.

Sound Transformation with Wavelets

Various musical transformations based on wavelet analysis/resynthesis have emerged (Boyer and Kronland-Martinet 1989). An obvious one is to perform a type of filtering by suppressing certain frequency channels in the resynthesis. The logarithmic spacing of the frequency channels makes it easier to extract certain musical chords from a sound. When this technique is applied to the speaking voice, for example, it gives the impression of a person talking "harmonically." Another effect is a form of cross-synthesis that uses the amplitude components from one sound and the phase components from another to create a hybrid sound.

Other types of transformations include changing the geometry of the frequency grid, such as adding or multiplying a scaling factor to all the frequencies in resynthesis. Time compression/expansion effects are also possible (warping the time grid). In both frequency and time warping, the phase components must be multiplied by the same scale factor as the pitch or time operation (whichever is being modified). (This is called *phase unwrapping;* see Arfib 1991 for a discussion of phase unwrapping in the wavelet transform; Appendix A describes the phase unwrapping process in the phase vocoder.) Kronland-Martinet (1988) describes a pitch-shifting method based on waveshaping the phase values in resynthesis.

Comb Wavelet Separation of Noise from Harmonic Spectrum

The *comb wavelet transform*, developed at the University of Naples, sorts out transients, nonpitched sounds, and pitch changes from quasi-periodic signals (Evangelista 1992; Piccialli et al. 1992). The comb WT starts from a windowed segment of sound. The fundamental pitch period is estimated, and a comb filter is fitted to the segment, with peaks aligned on the harmonics of the fundamental. The comb filter sifts out the energy in the harmonic spectrum. A wavelet analysis is then performed on this "clean" harmonic signal. When the inverse WT is subtracted from the original signal, the residual or "dirty" part of the signal remains (figure 13.26). The dirty part includes the attack transient and the details that give the sound its identity and character.

Once the clean and dirty part are separated, one can perform a kind of cross-synthesis by grafting the dirty part of one sound into the clean part of another. This type of separation is similar in concept—though not in implementation—to the technique used in the spectral modeling synthesis of Serra (1989), described earlier.

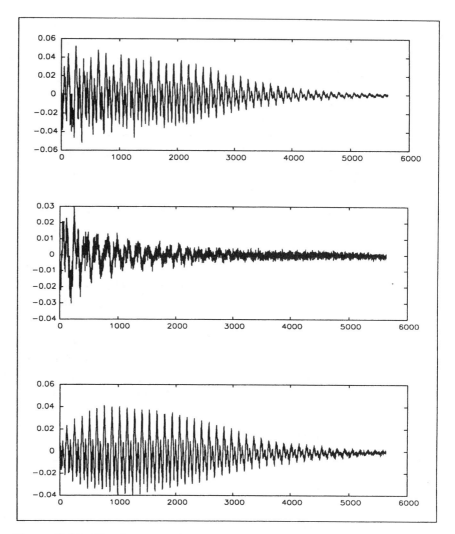

Figure 13.26   Wavelet separation of noise from harmonic spectrum. Amplitude (vertical) versus time (horizontal) plots. The top part is the original guitar tone. The middle part is the noisy residual from the comb wavelet transform, which includes the characteristic attack part of the note. The bottom figure shows the resynthesis from the quasi-harmonic part of the comb wavelet method. (Figure courtesy of Gianpaolo Evangelista, University of Naples.)

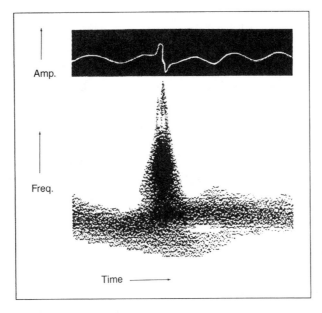

Figure 13.27 Transient detection by wavelets. The top graph shows a glitch in the time-domain signal. The bottom graph shows the wavelet representation. High-frequency wavelets point precisely to the time of the glitch. The glitch is invisible to the low-frequency wavelets (the horizontal band at the bottom). (After Kronland-Martinet 1988.)

Comparison of Wavelet Analysis with Fourier Methods

Traditional Fourier methods measure the average energy across a window whose duration remains constant, no matter what frequency component is being analyzed. This tends to *delocalize* the view of the onset time of high-frequency transients. In contrast, the WT offers a multiresolution view of a musical signal, since fine temporal analysis is done with short, high-frequency wavelets, and fine frequency analysis uses long, low-frequency wavelets. A cymbal crash remains invisible to a "slow" (low-frequency) wavelet, but will be detected by a burst of very "fast" wavelets. Thus the WT is well suited for the study of transients or onset times in musical signals. As figure 13.27 shows, the WT plot exhibits great time sensitivity at high frequencies.

In applications where computational efficiency is paramount, FFT-based methods have an advantage over wavelet and other constant Q methods of similar resolution. Optimizations for the WT have been developed for the case of strictly logarithmic frequency grids, however (Dutilleux, Grossmann, and Kronland-Martinet 1988). See also Shensa (1992) for more on fast wavelet techniques.

Signal Analysis with the Wigner Distribution

The *Wigner distribution* (WD) was first applied in the 1930s to problems in quantum physics (Wigner 1932). In acoustics applications, the goal of the WD is not sound analysis *per se,* but system analysis. In other words, the input to the WD is not necessarily a sound, but the response of a loudspeaker, transducer, or circuit to a sound. The WD then characterizes the time-versus-frequency distribution of this system. From a theoretical standpoint, the WD is a direct relative of other Fourier-based methods such as the sonogram. For details on the mathematics of the WD, see Janse and Kaizer (1983, 1984), Preis et al. (1987), and Gerzon (1991).

Interpreting Wigner Distribution Plots

The typical input to the WD is either the impulse response or the amplitude-versus-frequency response of the system being measured. (See chapter 5 for a definition of amplitude-versus-frequency response.) The output is a plot of frequency versus time. Engineering measurements such as group delay, instantaneous frequency and power, transient distortion, and spectrum can be derived from a WD plot, which can be displayed in two or three dimensions. For a two-dimensional plot, the area under a horizontal slice of a given frequency gives the value of the frequency response (magnitude squared) at that frequency (figure 13.28a). The *center of gravity* of that horizontal slice (the point at which all the area could be concentrated to produce the same "weight" on the vertical axis) gives the group delay time

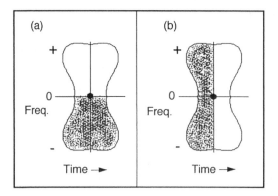

Figure 13.28 Interpreting Wigner distribution plots. See the text for an explanation.

for that frequency. This is shown as a black dot in figure 13.28a. Similarly, the area under a vertical slice at a given time yields the *instantaneous power* of the signal's envelope at that time (figure 13.28b), whereas the center of gravity of that slice equals the *instantaneous frequency* (black dot in figure 13.28b). In this case, the plots are symmetrical in both the *x*- and *y*-axes so the centers of gravity are at the center. In real signals they vary as the signal varies. When the instantaneous power and the instantaneous frequency are plotted over time, the effects of amplitude modulation and frequency modulation on the signal can be revealed.

Janse and Kaizer (1983, 1984) present three-dimensional plots and guidelines for interpreting the WD. In particular, they compare the plots of ideal systems (ideal filters, for example) with real-world devices like loudspeakers.

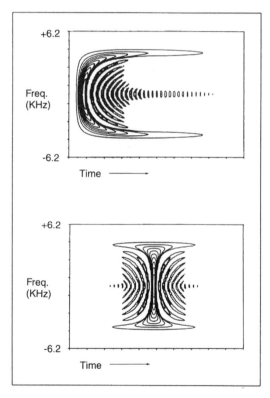

Figure 13.29 Comparison of Wigner distribution plots for two lowpass filters. The time span is 5 ms. (*a*) Phase-distorted filter. The stretching of frequencies along the time axis is a clear indication of the phase distortion. There is a strong audible difference between the two filters. (*b*) Linear phase (undistorted) filter. (After Preis et al. 1987.)

Limits of the Wigner Distribution

In practice, the WD is based on sampled and windowed data, and is sometimes called the *pseudo-Wigner distribution* (Janse and Kaizer 1983). Known
distortions are introduced by sampling and windowing, as in other analysis
techniques. These are relatively minor in effect.

A more major problem with the WD is that it is nonlinear. That is, the
WD of the sum of two signals is not the sum of their individual WDs. For
example, a single sinusoid at 100 Hz run through a WD shows up as an
individual frequency component, as does a single sinusoid at 300 Hz. But if
we run the sum of two sinusoids at 100 and 300 Hz through the WD, we see
a third component at 200 Hz—the difference between the two frequencies.
This clutter represents a frequency that is not present at the input. Clutter
makes visual inspection of WD plots difficult for musical signals.

The WD's relevance to the human perception of sound is limited. Its plot
graphically depicts perceptible phase distortion (see chapter 10). We can see
this in figure 13.29. The *x*-axis of figure 13.29 shows time from 0 to 5 ms.
The *y* axis shows a time-frequency distribution, ranging from -6.25 to
$+6.25$ KHz, where negative frequencies are phase-inverted images of positive frequencies. The stretching of certain frequencies along the *x*-axis
shows clearly the effects of frequency dependent group delay. For details on
how these plots were calculated see Janse and Kaizer (1984), and Preis et al.
(1987).

Non-Fourier Sound Analysis

This section looks at problems with traditional Fourier spectrum analysis
and examines briefly several alternative methods, including autoregressive
analysis, source/parameter analysis, and analysis in terms of other ortho-
gonal functions besides sine waves.

Critiques of Fourier Spectrum Analysis

Spectrum analysis based on the classic methods of the Baron de Fourier
have fundamental limitations for finite-length signals: first, limited frequency resolution (inability to distinguish two close frequencies), particularly
over a small number of samples, and second, "leakage" in the spectral
domain that occurs as a side effect of the windowing that is implicit in the
FFT (Gish 1978; Kay and Marple 1981). Fourier analysis is an inherently
inefficient way to analyze noisy sounds, since it assumes that these sounds

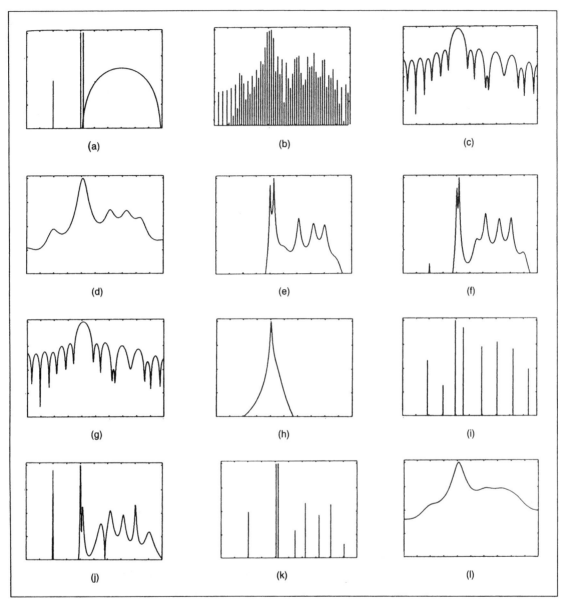

Figure 13.30 Different ways of measuring spectrum for a single input sound. In the descriptions, "PSD" means power spectrum density. The horizontal scale in all cases is frequency, from 0 up to half the sampling rate. The vertical scale is amplitude, from 0 dB at the top to -40 dB at the bottom, plotted linearly. (*a*) Input source, consisting of three sinusoids and a band of noise. (*b*) Periodogram with double-zero padding FFT. (*c*) Blackman-Tukey PSD (*d*) Autoregressive PSD via Yule-Walker approach. (*e*) Autoregressive PSD via Burg approach. (*f*) Autoregressive PSD via least-squares approach. (*g*) Moving average PSD. (*h*) ARMA PSD via extended Yule-Walker approach. (*i*) Pisarenko spectral line decomposition. (*j*) Prony PSD. (*k*) Special Prony via Hildebrand approach. (*l*) Capon or maximum likelihood.

are combinations of harmonically related sinusoids. The premise of periodicity inherent in Fourier methods can introduce errors when complicated transient phenomena are analyzed.

In an attempt to alleviate the limitations of the FFT approach, many alternative spectrum analysis methods have been proposed. Figure 13.30 portrays the multiplicity of methods and the diversity of results that can be obtained from an input of three sinusoids and a band of filtered noise, shown as (a). Fourier methods are shown in (b), (c), and (g). They cannot resolve the sinusoids or even separate the sinusoids from noise. A technique like (k) accurately measures the three sinusoids, but then depicts the noise band as a sum of five sinusoids! Evidently, there is no "best" spectrum measurement technique for all seasons; it depends on what we are looking for.

Autoregression Spectrum Analysis

The autoregression (AR), linear predictive coding (LPC), and maximum entropy methods (MEM) constitute a family of essentially equivalent techniques for designing a filter that corresponds to the spectrum of the input signal (Makhoul 1975; Burg 1967; Atal and Hanauer 1971; Flanagan 1972; Markel and Gray 1976; Cann 1978, 1979, 1980; Moorer 1979a; Dodge 1985; Lansky 1987; Lansky and Steiglitz 1981; Hutchins 1986a). Hence it is possible to apply them as methods of spectrum analysis. Here we treat all three methods under the rubric AR. (Chapter 5 describes a practical LPC music system with editing.)

An advantage of AR methods over Fourier methods is that they can estimate a spectrum from a small amount of input data; hence they have the potential for improved time/frequency resolution. But the form of spectrum analysis performed by AR is not directly comparable to Fourier analysis. The AR model assumes the spectrum is the result of an excitation signal (such as glottal pulses emitted by the vocal cords) applied to a resonator (like the rest of the vocal tract). The AR estimates the overall spectrum shape of the resonance rather than the energy at a number of isolated frequencies. Figure 13.30d shows this effect.

The AR method takes in several input samples and then uses the most recent sample as a reference. It tries to "predict" this sample from a sum of past samples weighted by filter coefficients. As a side effect of this prediction, the AR algorithm fits an inverse filter to the spectrum of the input signal. It is this side effect that is of musical interest. When the inverse filter is itself inverted—a trivial procedure—the resulting filter response is an estimate of the spectrum of the input signal.

The AR method predicts the tth value of a signal according to the equation:

$$signal[t] = \sum_{i-1}^{p} \{coeff[i] \times signal[t - i]\} - noise[t].$$

That is, the predicted value *signal*[t] is calculated by convolving the *p* number of prediction filter coefficients with the *p* known values of *signal*. (Convolution is described in chapter 10.) The choice of *p* is a complicated one. Too low a value for *p* produces an overly smoothed spectrum; too high a choice of *p* results introduces spurious peaks. So this parameter has to be adjusted depending on the application (Kay and Marple 1981). Interative methods for choosing *p* exist. The goodness of fit of the prediction can be measured as *p* increases from a small value. When there is no further improvement in the fit, the process stops.

Usually *noise*[t] is assumed to be a white-noise–driven signal that is filtered to yield a spectrum matching the input signal. Several algorithms employing *linear regression* methods can compute the filter coefficients from a block of data—hence the name "autoregression." This process is carried out by matrix operations that are described in the engineering literature (Burg 1967; Makhoul 1975; Markle 1972; Markel and Gray 1976; Bowen and Brown 1980). See Kay and Marple (1981) for a comparison of these methods.

Autoregressive Moving Average Analysis

The AR method is an efficient model for smooth, continuous spectra with sharp peaks but no deep nulls. Hence it does not model well sounds such as nasal vowels—where there are holes in the spectrum—or percussive impulses (snare drum, cymbals, etc.) where its prediction error is large. For these types of sounds a better choice may be a generalization of the AR method called the *autoregressive moving average* (ARMA) method. ARMA derives an output sample by a combination of both past input values and past output values. Hence an ARMA filter has both poles and zeros and is potentially more accurate than an AR approach. ARMA filters are much more costly from a computational standpoint than AR, however.

Source and Parameter Analysis

In some types of analysis, notably AR, cepstrum analysis (described in chapter 12), and the *physical model* approach described in chapter 7, the goal of the analysis is not simply to tally up the frequencies present in a signal, but rather to recover source information, such as the parameters of the excitation and the resonance needed to resynthesize that sound. This approach is useful for certain sounds that have great musical interest, such as snare drum hits and cymbal crashes. These types of sounds carry a great deal of information about their source, such as their size, mass, geometry, and the material from which they are made. Another application of source and parameter analysis is the separation of multiple sound sources. Indeed, the scientific motivation for these techniques has been their use in separating a signal from noise, or resolving several mixed signals (Kashino and Tanaka 1993).

Parameter Estimation

All sound analysis is a form of *parameter estimation* that tries to analyze the incoming sound in terms of the parameter settings that would be needed to approximate that sound with a given synthesis method (Tenney 1965; Justice 1979; Mian and Tisato 1984). For example, we can think of Fourier analysis as a kind of parameter estimation method for sine wave resynthesis because it computes all the frequencies, amplitudes, and phases needed to approximate the input sound.

In theory, parameter estimation can be applied to any synthesis technique. In practice, successful simulation of a given input sound by an arbitrary synthesis method is not guaranteed. Numerous attempts to develop parameter estimation analyses for frequency modulation synthesis, for example, resulted in gross approximations of the original input sound. There is no universal analysis/resynthesis technique. Certain techniques were not made to create specific types of sounds.

Certain types of parameter estimation employ *adaptive* signal-processing algorithms that try to minimize the error between the input signal and the simulation through adjusting the parameters of the simulation model. In a real-time system the measurements and adjustments must be made with the time period of a single sample, forcing compromises on mathematically ideal solutions.

Chapter 7 presents the subject of source analysis for physical model synthesis, so we refer the reader to that exposition.

Analysis by Other Functions

Fourier's method adds together sine waves to reproduce a given input signal. But sine waves are just one instance of a large class of functions that can be used to decompose and then replicate a given input function. *Walsh functions* (square waves) and *complex exponentials* (sinusoids with a decaying amplitude envelope) are just two of these basic units. Innumerable other functions can be conceived, but since these two have special properties and have already been applied to music, we discuss them next.

Walsh Functions

The main advantage of Walsh analysis is that its basic unit—the binary pulse or square wave—seems natural to implementation in digital systems, seemingly more natural than a sinusoidal wave, for example. A disadvantage of Walsh analysis is that it breaks down a signal into a combination of so-called *sequencies* that are not directly related to the frequency domain. Since chapter 4 explains Walsh functions in more detail, we refer the reader to that discussion.

Prony's Method

Damped sinusoids are the basic units in what is called *Prony's method* of analysis (Kay and Marple 1981; Marple 1987; LaRoche and Rodet 1989). By damped sinusoids we mean sinusoids that start with a sharp attack but are abruptly attenuated, typically by an exponential decay. The technique is named after Gaspard Riche, Baron de Prony, who originally developed a method for analyzing the expansion of various gases (Prony 1795). The modern version of the technique has evolved from Prony's original method, and is similar to the AR methods described previously.

Prony's method is now a family of related techniques that model an input signal as a combination of damped sinusoids plus noise (Kay and Marple 1981). Like AR techniques, Prony's method estimates a set of coefficients based on past input samples. But instead of driving a filter, as in AR methods, the coefficients in Prony's method drive the frequency, damping factor, amplitude, and phase of a set of damped sinusoids that approximate the input signal. Prony's method is turned into a spectrum analysis technique by taking the FFT of the output signal emitted by Prony's method. An advantage of Prony's method over AR techniques is that it yields phase information that makes for more accurate resynthesis. See Marple (1987) for an algorithmic description of the method.

In computer music, Prony's method has been applied in the analysis stage of the CHANT synthesis system (d'Alessandro and Rodet 1989; see chapter 7) and in an experimental analysis/resynthesis system by LaRoche (1989a, b). LaRoche used it to analyze and resynthesize damped percussive sounds, such as glockenspiel, vibraphone, marimba, low piano tones, and gong. According to LaRoche, the results were less promising with high piano tones and cymbals.

In comparing Prony's method to Fourier analysis, LaRoche (1989a) notes that in general, Prony's method is more "sensitive" than Fourier analysis. Users must meticulously adjust the analysis parameters, or else the resulting spectrum estimation may bear little resemblance to the actual spectrum (LaRoche 1989a). In contrast, the primary parameter in Fourier methods is the window. The results of Fourier analysis may be incomplete and imprecise, but they are never totally incoherent.

When the parameters of Prony's method are properly set, it has little problem accounting for inharmonic partials and can resolve multiple closely spaced sinusoids. By contrast, Fourier analysis arbitrarily divides up the spectrum into equally spaced harmonic partials and lumps closely spaced sinusoids into an overall formant-like peak in the spectrum. The Prony method is limited to analyzing up to about 50 partials at a time, since beyond this point the polynomials used to calculate it do not converge to a solution. And Prony's method is more intensive computationally than Fourier analysis. To summarize, in Prony's method we have an analysis method that is good at resolving accurately a certain class of signals, in particular percussive tones consisting of a few sinusoidal components, provided that it is carefully adjusted beforehand.

Auditory Models

We can cluster sound analysis methods around two poles: those that try to emulate the known behavior of the human hearing system, and those that do not. In the former category are *auditory models,* and in the latter category are mathematically inspired techniques like the Wigner distribution. Auditory models usually start from some form of spectrum analysis, but the output of this stage is merely the starting point for more-or-less elaborate postprocessing according to a computational model of hearing mechanisms (Mellinger 1991).

The goals of auditory modeling are twofold: (1) clearer views of musical signals that are more in accord with what we perceive, and (2) deeper understanding of human hearing mechanisms by using models in simulation experiments. Here we discuss briefly two auditory models, namely, the cochleagram and the correlogram.

Cochleagrams

The *cochlea* is the tiny snaillike organ in the inner ear that maps incoming vibrations into nerve impulses that are transmitted to the brain (see chapter 23). Each place along the length of the cochlea responds to vibrations broadly tuned around a center frequency specific to that place. Auditory scientists have measured the average firing rate of the neurons along the length of the cochlea and have determined that they are related to different frequencies perceived by the ear.

A software model of the cochlea's response to incoming signals is called a *cochleagram* (Slaney and Lyon 1992). Rather than mapping frequency to the vertical axis, like the spectrogram, the cochleagram maps *cochlear place* to the vertical axis. That is, it represents the response of different parts of the cochlea to incoming sound. When the cochleagram is plotted at a coarse resolution it looks something like a sonogram representation, but with an enhanced representation of onsets. A more important difference between the sonogram and the cochleagram can be seen in figure 13.31. This zoomed-in view on a high-resolution cochleagram image reveals the timing of the individual glottal pulses of a speech signal. Thus the cochleagram provides a way to study both low-level timing (onsets) and spectrum.

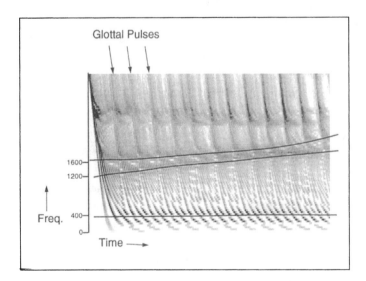

Figure 13.31 Expanded cochleagram of the American dipthong "ree." The horizontal lines indicate the first three formant tracks. The vertical lines indicate glottal pulses, which are tilted slightly due to the natural delay through the cochlea. (After Slaney and Lyon 1992.)

Correlograms

Correlograms were proposed in the early 1950s by Licklider (1951, 1959), but it is only in the 1990s that they became practical from a computational standpoint. The correlogram starts with a model of the cochlea and follows this with an autocorrelation of the signals emitted by each channel of the cochleagram (Slaney and Lyon 1992). This autocorrelation is done on a "frame-by frame" or windowed basis 30 to 120 times per second, depending on the application.

The resulting display is a three-dimensional function of frequency, time, and autocorrelation delay. The correlogram is an "in-time" moving picture image. Slaney's correlograms can be seen on video media or as digital movies running on personal computers (Slaney and Lyon 1991a,b).

The position along the cochlea is plotted on the vertical axis, with high frequencies corresponding to the upper portion of the image. The horizontal axis shows autocorrelation time delay. As in a conventional sonogram, dark areas represent areas of higher amplitude. Sounds with a strong sense of pitch and harmonic structure show up as vertical lines at autocorrelation lag times where a large number of cochlear cells are firing at the same period. (See Slaney and Lyon 1992 for an application of the correlogram to pitch detection.) When the pitch increases, the dominant vertical line moves to the left to a lag representing the shorter period. Horizontal bands represent large amounts of energy in a frequency band, such as a formant. Noisy, unpitched sounds show up only as horizontal bands, with no vertical pitch lines.

Recall from chapter 12 that the autocorrelation of a sine tone is itself a sine wave, with peaks spaced at subharmonic periods of the fundamental period f, that is, $f, f/2, f/3, \ldots$ Similarly, a single sine tone passed through a correlogram shows up as a series of vertical lines, corresponding to "virtual" subharmonics of the fundamental period, which is in the leftmost position. We do not necessarily hear these subharmonics; they are an artifact of the periodicity seeking nature of the autocorrelation function.

Figure 13.32 shows three frames of a correlogram movie, taken at 0 seconds, 600 ms, and 2 seconds, respectively. In this case we see the striking of a chime. At first there are many harmonics, and the sound is rich. Different overtones decay at various rates, as shown in the second frame. By the last frame there are only two components left.

The advantage of the correlogram is that it presents a time-sensitive simultaneous display of pitch and formant information. The horizontal or delay dimension represents pitch, and the vertical dimension represents spectrum. Calculating the correlogram is a computationally intensive oper-

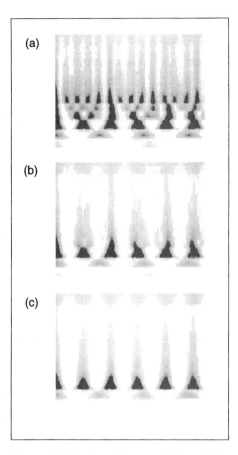

Figure 13.32 Correlogram of the striking of a chime. (*a*) Onset. (*b*) 600 ms. (*c*) 2.0 seconds.The U-shaped curve, particularly evident in (*a*), results from successive divisions of the grid in time—as if you were looking at the waveform peaks of a band of frequencies, with low frequencies (and therefore longer periods between peaks) at the bottom. (After Slaney and Lyon 1992.)

ation. Recently the correlogram has been used as a basis of resynthesis (Slaney, Naar, and Lyon 1994).

Signal-understanding Systems

It is becoming common in signal analysis to see applications that combine low-level signal-processing tools with software techniques drawn from research in artificial intelligence (Nii et al. 1982; Roads 1985d; Oppenheim and Nawab 1992). The goal of this line of inquiry is to move beyond raw signal analysis to a deeper *signal-understanding* (SU). We speak loosely, of course, since there are clearly many types and levels of "understanding."

But for practical purposes, we could say that a system understands a musical signal if it can recognize it as a musical unit or collection of units and relate its analysis with musical concepts above the acoustic level.

We can divide musical SU systems into two groups: those that try to simulate the listening skills of trained human listeners (including models of the human auditory system), and those that make no attempt to emulate a human skill. In the former category we include systems for expressive accompaniment in real time, instrumental timbre classification (source separation), and music transcription from polyphonic sources. In the latter category we include the tedious tasks of reduction of analysis data and extracting music from background noise. A system for understanding musical signals may encapsulate many levels of expertise. In this section we have space only to touch on global issues and cite typical examples.

Pattern Recognition

Unlike purely numerical signal-processing methods, which transform audio data from one representation to another via a global mathematical operation, SU systems apply *expectation-driven pattern recognition* to seek out and identify musical landmarks (Mont-Reynaud and Goldstein 1985; Chafe et al. 1982, 1985; Foster, et al. 1982; Strawn 1980, 1985a, b; Dannenberg and Mont-Reynaud 1987). We say they are "expectation-driven" because they they have been programmed to look for typical features. For example, in an automatic transcription system that starts from an acoustic source, the analysis first looks for musical notes. After segmenting the notes, it may try to identify their timbre from a list of spectrum templates of previously analyzed instruments, or try to group the notes into larger musical units such as tuplets and measures according to conventional rhythmic grouping rules.

Low-level pattern recognition processes often rely on clues derived from studies of human hearing and psychology. Using such clues, they may or may not try to emulate the entirety of human hearing mechanisms and musical cognition. High-level pattern recognition is more a matter of following conventional rules of style, which are much more culturally dependent. A pitch classification system developed for the rigid syntax of Viennese twelve-tone music would likely become lost when presented with the nuances of Indian classical singing.

Control Structure and Strategy

In ordinary signal processing, the strategy of the analysis is not subject to change. For example, every short-time Fourier analysis follows the same sequence of operations. By contrast, an SU system may have to plan an initial strategy that it periodically evaluates, possibly altering course and taking a different approach if necessary. Thus the control structure and strategy of the analysis system is a central problem in its design. This determines how the work is distributed among various analysis agents of the system, and how they intercommunicate. Sometimes a common memory area called a *blackboard* is used by the various agents to post the results of competing analysis strategies. This information can be used by other agents or by a decision-making manager procedure that picks from the various hypotheses provided to it (Mont-Reynaud 1985b).

Interaction between the different levels and components of an analysis system is a crucial factor in their performance (Minsky 1981; Rosenthal 1988). For example, if midlevel rhythm analysis can establish a metrical context from previously detected events, this knowledge can inform the low-level event detectors as to where subsequent events are likely to occur. As another example, knowledge of the spectrum of the instruments that are playing in a polyphonic texture can improve the performance of a system that is trying to pick out individual voice lines in the texture. On the other hand, Maher (1990) points out problems that occur in coordinating multiple strategies.

Besides clearly defined tasks like transcription or data reduction, an open area is the creation of high-level music analysis programs (Brinkman 1990; Castine 1993). Such systems can assist with or take over some of the menial tasks of musicologists and music theorists. Ultimately, these programs should be able to understand the structure of a composition well enough to explain it or create variations on it. If the musical knowledge required for such tasks is not preprogrammed, a substantial learning subsystem must be incorporated into the system.

Examples of Signal-understanding Systems

Signal-understanding systems started with J. A. Moorer's landmark research at Stanford University to create a "musical scribe" (Moorer 1975). Figure 13.33 outlines the strategy followed by Moorer. Figure 13.34 compares an original score with the score transcribed by his system. Moorer's automatic music transcription work was soon followed by that of Piszczalski and Galler (1977).

A more restricted example of SU is interpretation of the "information explosion" generated by systems such as the phase vocoder (see the discussion of the phase vocoder earlier). The raw analysis data (amplitude and frequency envelopes for each analysis channel) generated by the phase vocoder can take up many times more memory space than the original input

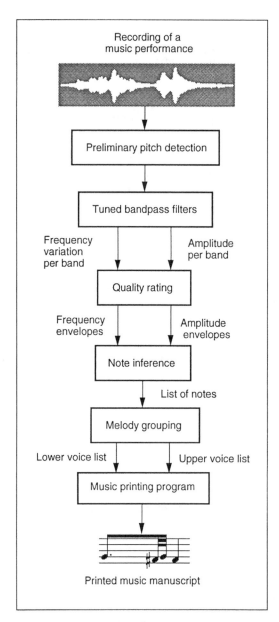

Figure 13.33 Strategy for an automatic music scribe developed by James A. Moorer.

Figure 13.34 Comparison of the original score with the transcription from acoustic performance accomplished by Moorer's system. The lengths of longer notes are underestimated, and a note is missing in the penultimate measure. The most conspicuous change, however, is due to the fact that the guitar was mistuned a half step high. The literal-minded computer faithfully reports the score mistuned a semitone high throughout.

signal. These data are tedious to edit and interpret manually. Data reduction algorithms using pattern recognition methods can be applied so that the data can be manipulated by a user in a simplified form, without significant loss of fidelity (Strawn 1980, 1985b). In order to accomplish this task, the system must understand which features of envelopes are important to human perception, and which are not.

In the 1980s, another automatic music transcription system was developed at Stanford University (Chowning et al. 1984; Chowning and Mont-Reynaud 1986). This system analyzed recorded performances of music (primarily melodies from eighteenth-century music) and attempted to perform

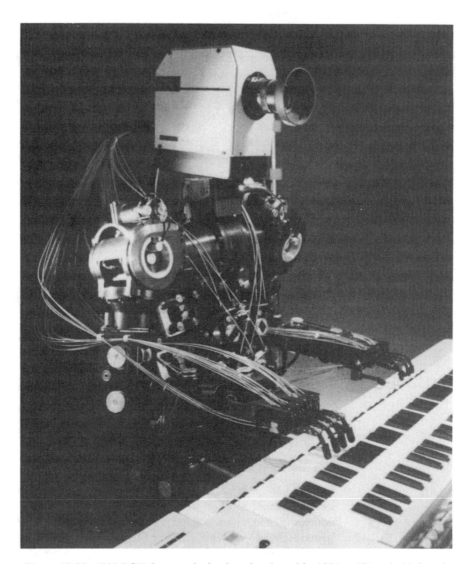

Figure 13.35 WABOT-2, a musical robot developed in 1985 at Waseda University in Japan, with further engineering by Sumitomo Corporation. The robot could understand spoken requests (in Japanese) and read music notation to accompany a singer on an organ. The robot followed the singer's performance (pitch and tempo) and adjusted its own playing to follow the singer.

automated transcription into music notation typical of that period. The performances deviated from the original score, yet the goal of the transcription system was to recover the original score, not what was actually played. This required both low-level analytic prowess and also a knowledge of the idioms of eighteenth-century notation. A combination of low-level and high-level operation is characteristic of SU systems.

A dramatic demonstration of SU was WABOT-2 (figure 13.35), a robot constructed by a large group of students and faculty at Waseda University (Tokyo) and later reimplemented by the Sumitomo Corporation in Japan (Matsushima et al. 1985; Roads 1986b). The robot was displayed to millions of visitors to the Tsukuba World Expo in 1985 and 1986. WABOT-2 understood speech signals, musical signals, and visual score notation. It could respond to song requests spoken in Japanese, and it could read music notation. While memorizing a score placed in front of its robot eye, WABOT-2 planned its performance. It could also accompany a human singer. If the singer strayed from the original intonation or rhythm, the robot made adjustments to the pitch of the organ and the rhythm of the accompaniment to try to match the singer (Roads 1986b).

Conclusion

The diversity of approaches presented in chapters 12 and 13 indicates that every sound analysis method has strengths and weaknesses. Table 13.2 is a suggestion list, matching analysis methods according to the musical goal sought.

The musical implications of sound analysis are now clearly appreciated. Sound analysis means two things to musicians. First, we have measuring instruments that let us examine the fine structure of sonic structure. This makes it possible to separate out the different components of interest (amplitude envelope, excitation and resonance signals, pitch, rhythm, and spectrum) and perform microsurgery that rearranges the components at will. Second, the music machine has ears. It can be programmed to respond to cues and patterns in performance, or to perform operations on sampled acoustic signals in musical terms.

Spectrum estimation is a rapidly evolving field; one could say that it is still growing out of a primitive period, since some analysis tools are finicky and can only be operated by experts. Each technique has musical limitations, yet few systems combine several techniques to adapt to the signal being measured or to measure the same signal from several perspectives.

Table 13.2   Applications of spectrum analysis

Feature sought	Possible analysis methods
Formant structure	Spectrogram with wide channel bandwidths (around 300 Hz), linear predictive coding
Overall time-varying musical spectrum	FFT spectrogram with a narrow bandwidth (< 50 Hz), projected in a three-dimensional "waterfall" display
Onset time of events (segmentation)	Amplitude thresholding, highpass filtering, autoregressive segmentation, wavelet phase display
Scratches, transients	Discontinuities in phase display projected by wavelet analysis
Separation of harmonic part from noisy part of signal	Comb wavelet transform, spectral modeling synthesis
Instances of specific pitch intervals	Wavelet analysis, with grid aligned to the intervals sought
Pitch detection	Fundamental period method, autocorrelation, adaptive filter method, frequency-domain methods, cepstrum method
Perceived spectrum	Constant Q analysis based on critical bandwidths; correlogram, cochleagram, other auditory models
Phase distortion	Wigner distribution

The standard techniques work reasonably well provided that their input parameters are set carefully by the operator. But many current techniques start from a blank slate. Unlike human listeners, they cannot apply knowledge gleaned in a previous analysis in a subsequent analysis. Future systems may be more intelligent in this respect.

Creating musically sensitive analysis tools will never be easy. For example, how does one tell a computer to remove "noise" in a bad recording of piano music while preserving a pianist's humming and breathing? In attacking the "denoising" problem we are immediately confronted by questions of taste. Some people prefer the vintage sound and authenticity of older recordings to the sterile quality of denoised, deconvolved, resynthesized, and artificially reverberated renditions. A "new and improved" simulacrum is not always a step forward on the path of aesthetics.

A theme throughout this chapter has been the diversity of approaches to spectrum analysis. Before choosing an analysis method, we must know what types of measurements we are looking for. In order to adjust the parameters of the analysis properly, it is best to know in advance about the types of sounds to be analyzed. Every analysis method is based on an underlying model of sound production. So in interpreting an analysis we must always take into account the limitations of this model.

V The Musician's Interface

Overview to Part V

Musicians interact with a computer music system through its *user interface*—a combination of hardware and software that determines how information is presented to and gathered from the user. Information can be conveyed to the musician through several senses:

Sight: via displays on graphics terminals, display panels, meters, and indicator lights, as well as switch and fader settings

Touch: via settings of knobs, switches, potentiometers, and the "play" and "feel" of the feedback from responsive input devices

Hearing: via sounds and silences generated by the system

In turn, the musician can specify musical information to a computer in a variety of ways: through an input device such as a musical keyboard, a graphical score editor, a music language, or an algorithmic composition program.

Composers should be able to prototype a musical idea in a short amount of time, listen to it, and modify, discard, or save it. In the past, with traditional scores, orchestras, and performance lags, this process could take years. Concert halls were the proving grounds for many untested and since unheard-from experiments. Today's interactive systems make it possible to speed up greatly the musical prototyping process (Pennycook 1985; Roads 1987, 1992a).

Background: Development of Musical Interfaces

Real-time interactive systems were envisaged from the earliest days of electronic computation (Eckert 1946), but it took decades before this dream became a practical reality. In the 1950s and 1960s, very few musicians were allowed direct access to the computers on which their programs ran. To create a sound, for example, composers typed instructions on a deck of punched cards. This labor was carried out on an *offline* card typewriter, that is, one not connected to the computer. They submitted the deck to a human "computer operator" who fed the cards into a card-reading machine connected to the computer. Returning the next day, the composer picked up a report of the job, including a bill for the cost of computation and memory usage. If there were no errors, there was also a large reel of magnetic tape containing sound samples. Conversion of the tape into sound was a separate and equally removed process, carried out on another computer at a different site.

Not until the mid-1970s did the advance of interactive time-sharing terminals and lower-cost minicomputers for digital synthesis improve the situation. Alphanumeric display terminals let musicians edit the input data *online* (connected to the computer). They could issue electronic commands to launch calculations. This was an improvement over the previous epoch, but typing command strings is hardly a rich form of musical interactivity.

In contrast, dozens of analog electronic instruments built between 1920 and 1970 allowed gestural control of music synthesis. The first digital systems to allow real-time gestural input were the *hybrid* music systems of the 1970s. Hybrid systems combined a digital computer with an analog sound synthesizer. For example, the Hybrid IV system developed at the University of California, San Diego (Kobrin 1977) used a music language consisting of short commands typed on an alphanumeric keyboard during performance. The meaning of the keystrokes was interpreted by a program running on a small computer. The program then generated control signals that were sent to an analog synthesizer.

By the late 1970s, commercial hybrid synthesizers incorporated microcomputers and organ-type keyboards. Programmers wrote *keyboard scanner* programs to capture keystroke information as it was played and relay it to the synthesizer (Knowlton 1971; Andersen 1978; Roberts 1979; Chamberlin 1985). The GROOVE (hybrid) system at Bell Telephone Laboratories allowed musicians to use joysticks and knobs as well as a computer terminal (Mathews and Moore 1970). A musician could draw curves on a graphic display screen that represented the frequency or amplitude envelopes of oscillators or filters. Higher levels of musical control were also possible. For example, the CONDUCT program for the GROOVE system was an attempt to allow overall control of amplitude, tempo, and instrument balance, analogous to the global controls exercised by a conductor.

We could extend this historical note to include interactive score editors, music languages, and systems for algorithmic composition, but these chronologies are presented in chapters 16, 17, and 18, respectively.

Improving Musical Interfaces

We conclude this introduction with a general observation. In the early years of computer music, the user interface was an afterthought—the last part of a system to be designed. Today the importance of good user interface design is well recognized. Synthesizers and software packages can succeed or fail on the basis of their interface, regardless of their functionality.

Programs become more agreeable when they are kept open and flexible, so that musicians can customize them to suit their needs. Even minor cosmetic improvements make a complicated program more tolerable to work with. For example, many programs let users customize the "desktop" layout on the display screen. The courtesy of providing user-adjustable preferences or options should be encouraged.

The best user interfaces are both easy to work with and, not coincidentally, incorporate deeper knowledge of musical structure and music-making strategies. What makes a system "deep"? One sign is strategic flexibility—whether it allows several ways of accomplishing a task. Another sign of depth is flexibility in grouping music information. These criteria imply a multiple-perspective representation of music. Another aspect of depth is the ability to infer concepts from partial descriptions—to "fill in the blanks" in the way that a trained practitioner would.

Here we reach a delicate balance. As systems—even input devices—become smarter, there is a temptation to let them impose their knowledge. Like any assistant, a system that thinks it knows what the user wants can be either helpful or annoying. One of the most difficult tasks faced by interface designers is choosing where and when to offer machine assistance.

Organization of Part V

Part V, comprising chapters 14 through 19, deals with all aspects of the musician's interface. This covers a great deal of territory, so we have broken the subject down according to four types of interaction between musicians and computer music systems:

Gestural—input devices and performance software, covered in chapters 14 and 15

Graphical editing—score, instrument, sound object, spectrum, and sample editors, covered in chapter 16

Formal linguistic—composition and synthesis languages, covered in chapter 17

Automated—algorithmic composition systems, covered in chapters 18 and 19

We separate these four categories for the purposes of explanation, but in practice they are often combined in one system, and the distinction between them is blurred. For example, a system like Max (Puckette 1988, 1991; Puckette and Zicarelli 1990) could be considered an "interactive performance program," a "graphical editor," or an "iconic programming language." Our description of Max fits most naturally into chapter 15 (performance software), but it could have also been worked into chapter 16 or 17.

One goal of this broad survey is to demonstrate the diversity of possible musical interfaces. No single interface is best for all musical styles and applications. Indeed, a composer may well use all four types of interaction to realize one piece.

14   *Musical Input Devices*

Advantages of Electronic Input Devices

Model of an Input Device

Background: History of Gestural Input to Computers
> **Voltage Control**
> **Digital Control**

Traditional versus Innovative Input Devices

Types of Input Devices

Mapping the Data from the Input Device

Ergonomics and Precision of Input Devices
> **Temporal Precision**

Musical Keyboards
> **State of the Keyboard**
> **Keyboard Scan Rate**

Remote Controllers

Responsive Input Devices

Conclusion

An instrument is the most traditional "musician's interface," mediating gesture and sound. Virtuoso musicians are capable of great subtlety and grace in the range of expressions that can be communicated through instruments by means of gestures of the mouth, hands, and feet. These inflections of the human body infuse music with signs of life: breath, body rhythm, a sense of effort, motion, and feeling. Listeners react instinctively to these performance qualities; instrumental virtuosity can lift even a mundane composition onto a higher plane of interest.

This chapter explores the instruments of real-time performance: *musical input devices* (also called *controllers*) played by musicians. If computers provided an ideal vehicle for formally oriented composers who wanted to distance themselves from habitual phrasing, this same built-in distance must now be overcome by composers and performers seeking more immediacy of expression (Ryan 1991). After a historical background section, we explore the ergonomics of input devices with particular focus on temporal precision—how fast an instrument can respond to a human gesture. The next section examines the most popular input devices: musical keyboards. Then follows a look at controllers with *remote control* capabilities, giving performers freedom to move around onstage without cumbersome cables. The final part of the chapter deals with *responsive input devices* that can be programmed to respond to a performer's gestures differently for each piece played on them. This chapter also includes two tables and a photographic collage that demonstrate the diversity of possible input devices.

To simplify the presentation we focus on control of synthesizers, but virtually everything in this chapter also applies to applications such as control of effects units, mixing systems, and lighting systems.

The input device is, of course, only one component of interactive, real-time performance. Other chapters cover performance software (chapter 15), pitch and rhythm recognition (chapter 12), and MIDI (chapter 21).

Advantages of Electronic Input Devices

A musician playing a traditional acoustic instrument must supply the energy for both controlling and producing the sound. Even a beautiful and cleverly designed instrument is constrained by inescapable mechanical limitations. Simply obtaining a good basic sonority on many instruments requires a long period of practice and expert counsel. Some instruments are more physically difficult to play than others. For example, the large instruments of the lower registers (bass and baritone saxophones, double bass, and tuba) require more strength to play and may necessitate stretching to achieve the proper note selection. Certain acoustic instruments are hard to play softly, while others are difficult to play loudly. Extremely high or low pitches may require extraordinary effort if they can be played at all. Retuning the instrument to a different scale may be arduous or impossible, and the timbre of the instrument is predetermined by its physical construction.

Electronics technology has sparked a new wave of instrument design (Snell 1983). Input devices transduce human motion into electrical form (either analog or digital signals). This transduction provides two main advantages. First, electronic input devices detach the control of sound from the need to power the sound; any one of dozens of input devices can control the same sound generator (figure 14.1). This translates into musical flexibility. With electronic instruments, a single wind controller can create the low bass sounds as easily as the high soprano sounds. Creating extremely soft or loud sounds requires minimum effort since the control is electronic. Obviously, the detachment of sound control from sound production has a negative side—a reduction of the "feel" associated with producing a certain kind of sound. The section on responsive instruments discusses this problem and its palliatives.

The second main advantage of electronic input devices is their tuning and timbral flexibility. Changing the scale on many electronic instruments is a matter of pressing a button; some allow users to create their own scales. Being able to add selective vibrato to a piano sound gives this familiar

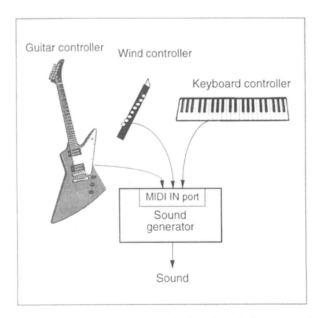

Figure 14.1   Electronic input devices detach the gesture from the sound production mechanism. Any one of a number of input devices can generate the same sound.

timbre a new expressiveness. The musical possibilities of instruments that can sound like a wood flute one minute and Balinese *jecogan* the next—or that can play both at the same time—are inviting from a compositional standpoint.

Model of an Input Device

A simple model of an input device is a *sensor* connected to an *electronic interface circuit* (figure 14.2). The sensor responds to a physical stimulus, such as the depression of a key, the pressure of air being blown, or movement within an ultrasonic field. This action is translated by the interface circuit into either a *discrete* or a *continuous* control signal. Discrete control refers to switching, on-off actions like pressing a key on a keyboard or pushing a button to select a new timbre. Continuous control refers to smoothly varying actions made by wheels, faders, and pedals.

The sensor is typically a mechanical/analog device; at some point the interface circuit translates its output into digital form—usually a MIDI message. In commercial input devices, the sensor and the interface are combined in one unit that directly emits MIDI messages. For the experimenter, a low-cost approach is to have the interface circuit translate the sensor's output into electrical current that can be fed into the pedal or breath input of an existing MIDI synthesizer. Then the synthesizer itself converts the current into *continuous controller* messages that can be tapped via the MIDI OUT port. (See chapter 21 for more on MIDI messages.)

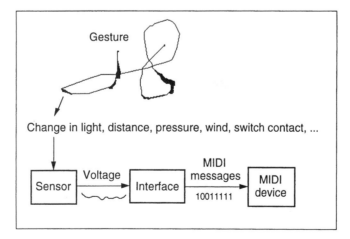

Figure 14.2   Model of an input device as a sensor connected to an electronic interface.

Background: History of Gestural Input to Computers

Decades of performance with analog electronic instruments preceded computer music experiments (Rhea 1972, 1984; Young 1989). Today's digital performance systems grew out of a strong tradition of live electronic music (with or without traditional instruments), as well as free jazz and improvisation (Mumma 1975; Battier 1981; Bernardini 1986; Roads 1985b; Valentino 1986). Expressive electronic instruments such as the Theremin (1928), Ondes Martenot (1928), Croix Sonore (1934), Ondioline (1941), Electronic Sackbut (1948), and the Mixtur-Trautonium (1949), among others, pioneered new performance techniques and electronic sounds years before manufacturers formulated MIDI (figure 14.3).

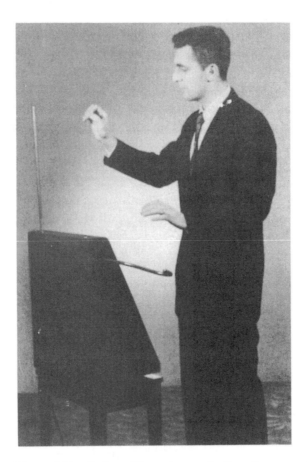

Figure 14.3 Robert Moog demonstrating the correct position for playing the Theremin, from *Operating Instructions for the Vanguard Theremin Model 505,* ca. 1960.

Voltage Control

The modular analog synthesizers of the 1970s offered flexible possibilities for external control since they operated by the principle of *voltage control*. In a voltage-controlled synthesizer, the pitch, amplitude, filter center frequency, and many other parameters can be varied by applying a changing voltage to the *control input* jack on a synthesis module. Modular analog synthesizers were flexible because the musician could repatch the interconnection between an input device and the modules it controlled. Electronic performances in the 1970s sometimes involved synthesizers controlled by exotic input devices such as capacitance keyboards or brain-wave transducers (Rosenboom 1976, 1990).

In analog systems, the synthesizer could, in a crude sense, "listen" to a performer's gestures by means of *triggers* (pulses emitted when a performer touched a key on a keyboard, for example) and *envelope followers* (devices that traced the amplitude envelope of an event). Digital technology, with its increased memory and more flexible processing capabilities, provides more sophisticated recognition of external gestures. (See chapters 12 and 13 for a discussion of pitch, rhythm, and spectrum analysis.) Computers can create elaborate and context-sensitive responses to the gestures they detect.

Digital Control

Pioneering work on the use of gestural input to computers was carried out in the 1960s by Mathews and Rosler (1969) at Bell Telephone Laboratories. Users could draw graphic scores quickly on a display screen with a light pen. Researchers at the National Research Council (Ottawa, Canada) developed a system for graphical interaction with a music notation editor via a mouse-like pointing device. The Dartmouth digital synthesizer (Alonso, Appleton, and Jones 1977) was the first digital synthesizer to incorporate real-time controllers such as a keyboard, an assignable knob, and a bank of buttons and switches. From that time on, virtually all hybrid (analog plus digital) and purely digital synthesizers have incorporated keyboards and other input devices. (See Metlay 1990 for a survey of MIDI input devices.)

Traditional versus Innovative Input Devices

A main question in designing an input device for a synthesizer is whether to model it after existing instruments. For example, synthesizer keyboards

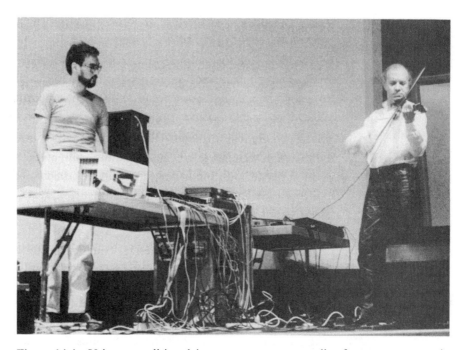

Figure 14.4   Using a traditional instrument as a controller for computer music (Negyesy and Ray 1989). Violinist Janos Negyesy playing a violin equipped with sensors to control electronic music hardware. Left: Lee Ray, system designer.

are modeled after keyboards built into traditional instruments in use since antiquity.

The advantages of using a traditional instrument as a model are several. First, musicians who are already familiar with a traditional instrument such as a violin can adapt more easily to a traditional controller attached to a synthesizer (figure 14.4). They can immediately apply highly developed performance skills built up over many years. Finding virtuosos on new input devices will be difficult, since music education is tradition-bound. From a commercial standpoint, an input device that looks like a familiar instrument probably stands a better chance in the music marketplace than a bizarre-looking strap-on appliance.

But the traditional instrument model has disadvantages. The full power of a synthesizer may be limited by a traditional instrument in control. To exploit the full sound palette of today's synthesizers, we also need special input devices tailored to their unique capabilities (Cadoz, Luciani, and Florens 1984; Florens and Cadoz 1991). The design of traditional instruments tends to reflect historical considerations that may not be relevant today. For example, the fingering scheme used to produce tones on the woodwind family is partly dictated by the acoustic properties of the instruments. With an electronic wind instrument, the fingerings can be made simpler and more intuitive (Yunik, Borys, and Swift 1985). Many instruments are designed around an equal-tempered pitch scheme. A musician who would like to explore other tunings might prefer a more flexible design.

The possibilities inherent in digital synthesis, processing, and playback call for new modes of control that require special input devices and interaction styles (Collins 1991a, b). Witness the various "conducting gloves" that have been developed (Waisvisz 1985).

In a studio situation, flexibility and management of complexity are prime concerns, rather than ease of spontaneous expression. The studio environment favors tools that aid the musician or sound engineer in building planned structures—complex, multilayered productions. Noninstrumental devices such as alphanumeric keyboards, mice, linear faders, rotary knobs, and lighted switches are suited for programming and fine control of audio workstations.

Types of Input Devices

Musical gestures can be expressed through a wide range of body movements. Dozens of input devices have been developed to capture these gestures. Table 14.1 summarizes the major types of input devices as well as several rare types. Figure 14.5 is a photocollage of electronic and computer music input devices.

Mapping the Data from the Input Device

The messages coming from digital input devices are streams of binary numbers. A microprocessor inside the receiving synthesizer must decode these streams before commanding the synthesis engine to emit sound. The separation of the input device from the sound production (figure 14.6) leaves the opportunity to *process* and *map* the information coming from the input device in a variety of ways.

Processing shapes the data, by inversion, compression and expansion, limiting, smoothing, or quantizing (thresholding). The data can be analyzed for rates of change, delayed, convolved, or distorted by linear or nonlinear transforms.

By means of mapping, one input device can control different parameters on a synthesizer at various times. A single message received from the input

Table 14.1   Input devices

Device	Description	Typical use, references
Switch	Multiposition switches	Most synthesizers, effects units and mixing consoles
Pushbuttons	On or off, in-out motion	Most synthesizers, effects units, and mixing consoles
Linear potentiometer or fader	Usually made of conductive plastic; up means increase, down means attentuate	Most sound mixing consoles and synthesizers
Rotary potentiometer or fader	Circular knob, either continuous rotation or limited to *n* degrees of rotation	Many synthesizers and effects units
Motorized faders	Linear faders that remember how they are moved and can reproduce that movement by means of motors attached to the faders	Sound mixing consoles by Neve, Amek, Yamaha, and others
Trackball	Ball housed such that the top half can be rotated, pushed forward, or pulled back in continuous motion	Some portable computers; Synclavier
Joystick	A hand-held stick that can be rotated, pushed, or pulled	Some mixing consoles set up for quadraphonic sound and some synthesizers
Game Paddles	Inexpensive, imprecise joystick	Early computer-controlled synthesis
Light pen	A light pen does not draw with light; rather, it senses light emanating from the display screen. Held up to screen by the user	Early research at Bell Laboratories and the National Research Council (Canada); Fairlight Computer Music Instrument (1979)
Alphanumeric keyboard	Regular computer keyboard	All computers
Music typewriters	Typewriter modified to write on several vertical levels as well as horizontally	(Dal Molin 1975, 1978; Hiller and Baker 1965)

Table 14.1 (cont.)

Device	Description	Typical use, references
Hand-held; movement of mouse	Personal computers on table-top causes cursor on display screen to move; buttons on the mouse select menu items and cause other actions	Mouse and workstations
Digitizer tablet	Hand-held puck is moved over a special surface; usually more precise than a mouse	Xenakis's UPIC system. Also, the NoteWriter music notation program supports a "scrawl" mode in which note symbols are hand-drawn first and converted to standard symbols later
Touch-sensitive pad; Elographics, KoalaPad, Big Briar pad; Chalkboard Power tablet	Detects finger position and pressure on a special pad	Spiral System Trazor Touch panel TASA Touch panel TASA tablet, (Lee et al. 1985), portable computers
Touch-sensitive display screen	Detects position and pressure of fingers on screen; acts as a kind of "see-through" touch-sensitive tablet	SoundStation by Digital Audio Research (1989)
Musical keyboard	Usually equal-tempered note layout; in its simplest form just an array of switches with white and black keys; more sophisticated keyboards have a responsive "action," and detect velocity and pressure	Many synthesizers
Three-dimensional keyboard	Keys move forward and backward as well as up and down, or in Moog's scheme, the keyboard senses where the finger is on the key	Notebender by KeyConcepts (Moog 1987; U.S. Patent 4,498,365; Moog and Rhea 1990)
"Thumb-" wheel	Used for pitch and vibrato control, typically with about 30 degrees of forward travel and 30 degrees of backward travel	Many synthesizers

Table 14.1 (cont.)

Device	Description	Typical use, references
Footpedal and foot switch	Can be either a "swell" pedal or just a pushbutton; used to control volume, sustain, and to switch in effects	Most synthesizers can support one or more footpedals and foot switches
Organ pedals	Keyboard so that feet can play bass lines; the keys are long so that both toes and heels can be used	Some digital and electronic organs
Drum pad and other percussion devices	Detects drum strokes and sends a signal to a drum synthesizer or computer; different areas of the pad can be programmed to respond. Robert Boie's Radio drum uses transmitters in the drum sticks and antennae in the drum pad. The Buchla Thunder controller has a capacitance surface that is played with bare hands	Many electronic percussion controllers; Max Mathews's Sequential Drum (Mathews and Abbott 1980) Daton (Mathews 1989), Radio Drum (Boie, Mathews, and Schloss 1989)
Ribbon controller or fingerstrip	Thin, long strip touched by fingers for continuous gestures	Moog and Buchla analog synthesizers; Zimmerworks Zeebar for digital synthesizers
Breath controller	Generates a time-varying control function depending on how hard one blows into a mouthpiece	Supported on Yamaha digital synthesizers
Lyricon wind controller	Blown and fingered like a clarinet; contains breath sensor, switches, and reed pressure sensor	Lyricon instrument
Flute controllers	Flute with electrical pickup connected to a pitch detector; may also have sensors to detect key depressions; also includes new flutelike instruments	IRCAM 4X flute, flute of Yunik, Borys, and Swift (1985)
Saxophone or saxlike wind controller	Blown and fingered like a saxophone, with extensions for MIDI performance	Yamaha WX, Casio DH, Softwind Instruments, Synthophone, MIDI Horn (Nelson 1991)
Guitar	Special guitar that generates digital data or special pickup and synthesis electronics	New England Digital Corporation SynthAxe (Aitken 1985);

Table 14.1 (cont.)

Device	Description	Typical use, references
		Yamaha, Zeta, Roland and other guitar controllers
Violin and cello controllers	Electrified string instrument connected to a pitch detector and other sound analysis software	Zivatar (Négyesy and Ray 1989), Zeta violins and cellos
Microphone (directed at a music source)	Transduces acoustic energy into continuously-varying analog voltage that can be converted to digital form and analyzed for pitch, time, amplitude, spectral information, etc.	Ubiquitous in recording and sound reinforcement; also used in interactive performance with software that recognizes musical cues.
Microphone (directed at a speaking voice)	Transduces acoustic energy into continuously-varying voltage that can be converted to digital form and analyzed for word content and meaning	Used in conjunction with speech recognition hardware and software to issue commands and give directions to music systems (*Computer Music Journal* 1990)
Sensor Frame VideoHarp	Optically-scanned controller that senses finger movements on both sides of a flat surface and converts them into MIDI messages	(Rubine and McAvinney 1990)
Polhemus Tracker	Position and orientation sensor based on miniature radio transmitter; transmitter can be held in hand or mounted on a baton, etc.	(Fry 1982)
Theremin	The "conductor" waves her hands in the vicinity of two radio antenna. The antenna generate voltages that vary with the positon of the hands; these are usually interpreted as amplitude and pitch controls; Theremins built by Robert Moog generate MIDI data as well as control voltages.	(Chadabe 1984) Moog's MIDI Theremin

Table 14.1 (cont.)

Device	Description	Typical use, references
Ultrasonic (sonar) ranger	The ultrasonic ranger can "see" the motion of a conductor's wand, or follow a dancer.	(Haflich and Burns 1983; Chabot 1990)
Camera and wand	Machine vision; tracks a conductor's hands or a baton	(Prerau 1971; Morita, Hashimoto, and Ohteru 1991; Distasi, Nappi, and Vitulano 1992; Bertini and Carossi 1991)
Camera and image processing software	Machine vision; maps observations of human movement into control of sound	(Collinge and Parkinson 1988; Morita, Hashimoto, and Ohteru 1991); Mandala system (*Computer Music Journal* 1989)
Camera and score reading software	Machine vision; computer reads a score for the purpose of music data entry	(Matsushima, et al. 1985; Fujinaga, et al. 1989, 1991)
Camera, robot, and keyboard	Robot reads music score and uses mechanical arms, fingers, and feet to play a digital organ	WABOT-2, Sumitomo robot at Tsukuba World Expo (Matsushima, et al. 1985; Roads 1986b)
Data Glove (VPL), The Hands (STEIM)	One or two hand-held controllers transmit button pressures, slider movements, orientation and distance between hands	(Waisvisz 1985)
Airdrums by Palmtree Instruments and MIDI baton.	Airdrums are short sticks fitted with accelerometers along three dimensions. Handheld or bound to feet, they generate MIDI data. The MIDI baton is used for tempo conducting and also contains an accelerometer.	(Chabot 1990; Keane, Smecca, and Wood 1990; Downes 1987)
Brain waves and other bioelectrical signals	Electrodes attached to the head send electrical signals that correspond to the brain waves being generated by the brain; electromyograms detect muscle tension; electrooculograms measure eye movements.	Eaton 1971; Rosenboom 1976, 1990) Biomuse (Knapp and Lustad 1990), BodySynth (Jacobs 1992)

Figure 14.5 Photocollage of electronic and computer music input devices.

(*a*) Yamaha Disklavier MIDI upright piano.

(*b*) Roland MIDI keyboard controller.

(*c*) Lync portable MIDI keyboard controller.

(*d*) Excelsior Digisyzer MIDI accordion.

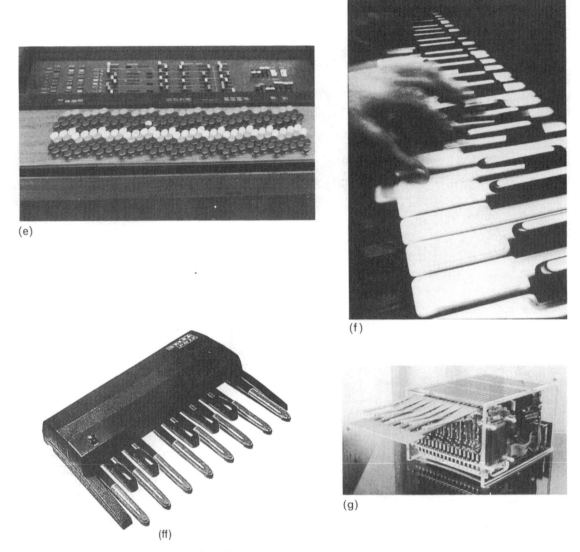

(e)

(f)

(ff)

(g)

Figure 14.5 (cont.)

(*e*)   George Secor's Generalized Keyboard for the Motorola Scalatron.

(*f*)   Notebender keyboard by Key Concepts.

(*ff*) Elka MIDI pedalboard (foot controller).

(*g*)   ACROE keyboard or "modular feedback controller" has motorized keys for a programmable action (Cadoz, Lisowski, and Florens 1990).

(*h*)   Edward Kobrin typing at an alphanumeric display terminal.

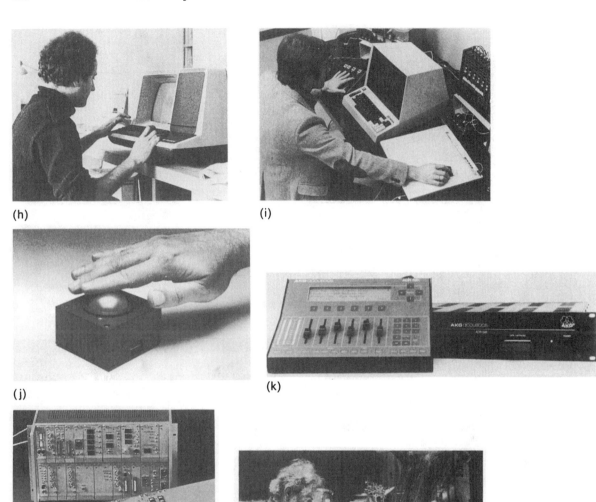

(h)   (i)

(j)   (k)

(l)      (m)

Figure 14.5 (cont.)

(*i*)   William Buxton at the console of the SSSP synthesizer in Toronto. At left, continuous potentiometers. In the middle, traditional alphanumeric terminal. At right, slider on tablet.

(*j*)   Trackball.

(*k*)   Sliders and buttons on the AKG ADR 68K reverberator remote controller.

(*l*)   Sliders and buttons on the controller of the Harmonia Mundi Acustica bw102 digital audio processor.

(*m*)   Salvatore Martirano at the all-button control panel of the Sal-Mar Construction.

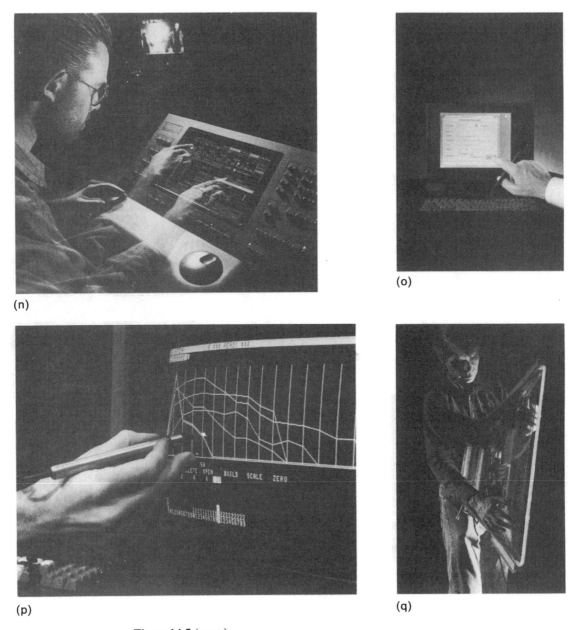

(n)

(o)

(p)

(q)

Figure 14.5 (cont.)

(n)   Touch display of the Digital Audio Research Sound Station.

(o)   MicroTouch Touch Pen and NEC computer for pen (handwritten) interaction.

(p)   Fairlight CMI light pen drawing envelopes for additive synthesis.

(q)   VideoHarp. The surface is divided into a number of different regions, each of which invokes a different timbre or other MIDI message.

(r)

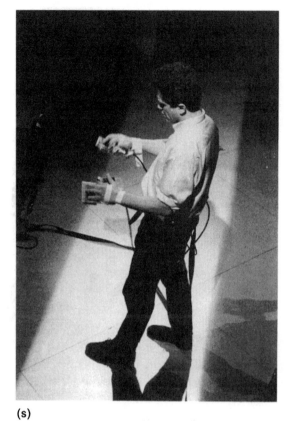

(s)

(t)

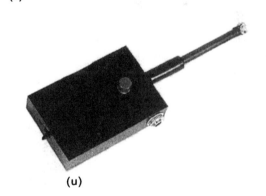

(u)

Figure 14.5 (cont.)

(*r*)   Ondes Martenot pitch-shifting ring.

(*s*)   Michel Waisvisz playing The Hands.

(*t*)   The Moog MIDI Theremin, with a cabinet similar to the one supplied with the original RCA Theremin in the 1930s.

(*u*)   Buchla Lightening infrared controller.

(v)

(w)

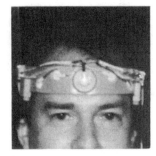

(x)

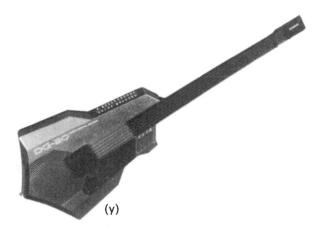

(y)

Figure 14.5 (cont.)

(*v*)   Xavier Chabot's hand in the path of an ultrasonic detector.

(*w*)   EMS Soundbeam ultrasonic controller box and secondary beamer.

(*x*)   Hugh Lusted wearing the Biomuse, a brain wave MIDI controller.

(*y*)   Casio digital guitar.

(z)

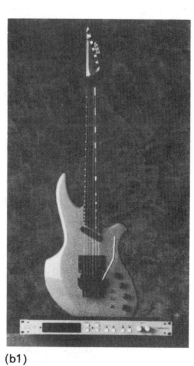

(a1)

(b1)

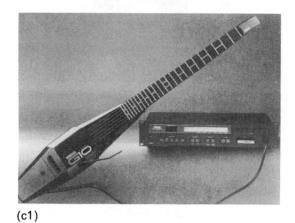

(c1)

Figure 14.5 (cont.)

(*z*)   Max Mathews playing one of his electronic violins. Photograph by Ivan Massar.

(*a1*)   Zeta electronic violin (foreground) and cello.

(*b1*)   Zeta MIDI guitar.

(*c1*)   Yamaha MIDI guitar controller.

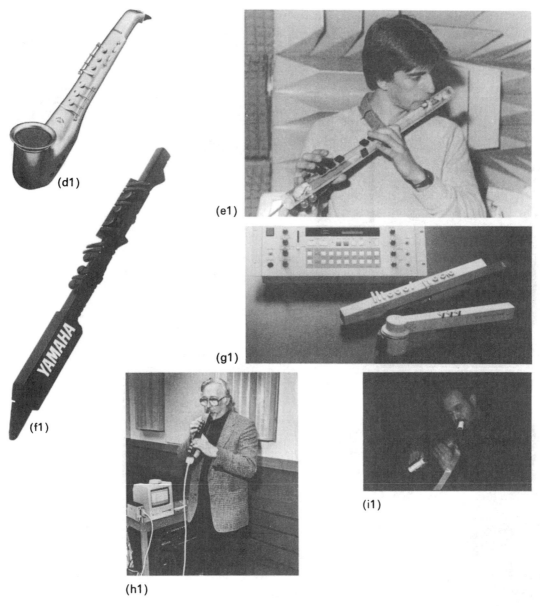

Figure 14.5 (cont.)

(*d1*) Casio DH-100 digital horn.

(*e1*) Yunik and Swift digital flute.

(*f1*) Yamaha WX7 MIDI wind controller.

(*g1*) Akai EV1000 and EW1000 wind controllers.

(*h1*) Gary Nelson playing the MIDI Horn designed in collaboration with John
Talbot. Photograph by John Corriveau.

(*i1*) Perry Cook with his HIRN MIDI controller for physical modeling synthesis.

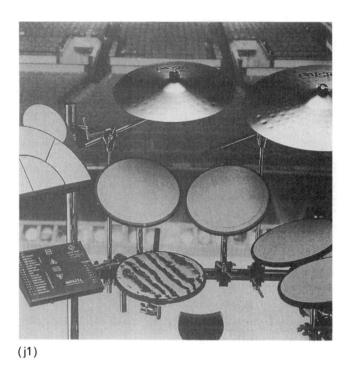

(j1)

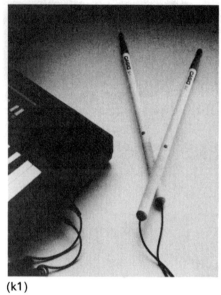

(k1)

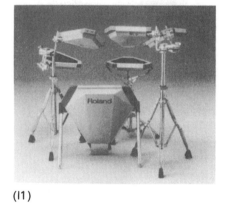

(l1)

(m1)

Figure 14.5 (cont.)

(*j1*) KAT MIDI percussion kit.

(*k1*) Casio SS-1 Sound Sticks.

(*l1*)   Roland electronic drum set.

(*m1*) Airdrum controller.

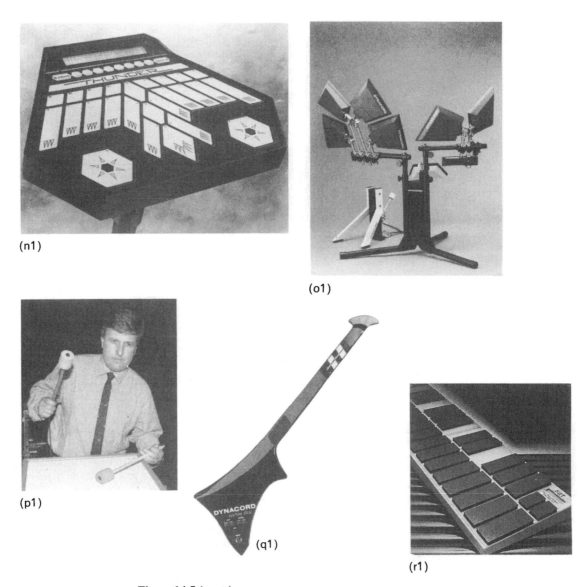

(n1)

(o1)

(p1)

(q1)

(r1)

Figure 14.5 (cont.)

(*n1*) Buchla Thunder controller. The user taps on the various surfaces of the pad.

(*o1*) Dynacord MIDI drums.

(*p1*) Richard Boulanger playing the Radio Drum (Boie, Mathews, and Schloss 1989).

(*q1*) Dynacord Rhythm Stick. Although this looks like an electronic guitar, it is actually a percussion controller.

(*r1*) KAT electronic marimba.

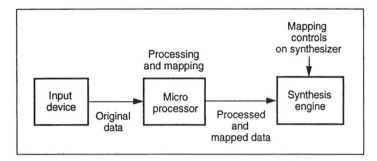

Figure 14.6 A microprocessor in between the input device and the synthesizer allows the possibility of interpreting and remapping the instrumentalist's gestures. This microprocessor may be inside the synthesizer or part of an external *MIDI mapper*. (See table 21.3 in chapter 21.)

device, such as key velocity (how fast a key is pressed on a keyboard), can be mapped to spatial movements, loudness, or other parameters.

Setting up the mapping between the input device and a synthesizer requires a coordination between the two. Mapping may be as simple as selecting the parameter the input device will control on the receiving synthesizer. For this, one can use MIDI's *channel* mechanism, which splits the incoming data stream into sixteen independent channels (see chapter 21). By entering the "global edit" mode on the synthesizer, the musician can assign incoming data associated with particular channels to specific synthesizer parameters:

incoming MIDI channel → synthesizer parameter

where the incoming MIDI channel is an integer from 1 to 16 and the synthesizer parameter is a controllable aspect of the sound like amplitude, pitch, modulation, or timbre selection (in MIDI this is called a *program change*). For analog input, one selects the pair

analog input port → synthesizer parameter

where the analog input port is named something like "Pedal 1," "Breath," or "Damper."

So much for the simple case. In practice, the mapping between the input device and the synthesizer can be arbitrarily complex, depending on the goals of the person setting up the mapping. This complexity derives from three sources:

1. Programmable input devices

2. Remapping devices or performance software

3. Programmable synthesizers

In case (1), many input devices can be programmed to emit different signals depending on the gesture. Keyboards and other devices can be split to emit different signals depending on key position or key velocity. As for case (2), a MIDI "black box" remapper interposed between the input device and the synthesizer may transform the data coming from the input device. For example, the remapper may compress it into a smaller range, limit the data to certain discrete values (*quantization*), or add information that was not in the original, such as accompanying a melody played on the keyboard with chords or a bass line. *Interactive performance software*, discussed in chapter 15, may treat the controller data more abstractly, triggering entire sequences or improvisations. Programmable synthesizers (3) let users set up correspondences between all the signals emitted by the input device and the myriad parameters of the synthesis engine.

Ergonomics and Precision of Input Devices

"Ergonomics" refers to the design of objects that are suited to human proportions and gestures. Good ergonomics ensures that we can exploit the effective precision of an input device. That is, if a device is easy to manipulate, it is easier to use it precisely. Conversely, if a device is hard to manipulate, whatever precision is built into the device is likely to be squandered in practice. For example, in a cheap guitar, the strings are often too high from the fretboard, making the instrument difficult to play. Precision and "feel" also go together. For example, if a potentiometer has mechanical resistance or "rough spots" it is difficult to make a precise fade with it.

Another factor in the design of an input device is size. A general rule of thumb is that the larger the device (but still within the scale of the human hand), the more precision we can obtain with it. This is why *long-throw linear faders* are favored by recording studio professionals on mixing consoles (figure 14.7). "Long-throw" refers to the 100 mm or longer faders, as opposed to shorter and inherently less precise faders. Large rotary faders have the same benefit. Since the dynamic range of a channel is mapped onto the travel of the fader, it is more precise when a slight nudge of the fader produces a small increment of change rather than a large change.

Beyond a certain point, however, size and ergonomics compete against each other. A double bass requires more physical effort to play than the smaller violin. Huge sound-mixing consoles are too awkward to be controlled by a single engineer.

For some highly evolved input devices, only one size is optimal, for it bears a uniquely efficient relationship to the human being manipulating it.

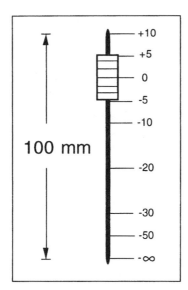

Figure 14.7 Long-throw linear faders such as found in mixing consoles.

For example, the keys of piano keyboards are just the right size for performers with long, thin fingers. If they were any smaller the fingers would be cramped, like on a toy piano. If they were larger, certain wide-spanning chords would be impossible to play.

Temporal Precision

High temporal precision is needed to capture the subtleties injected by musicians in performance. These expressive variations are not random, but are infused with musical meaning and structural significance (Sundberg et al. 1983; Gabrielsson 1986; Wessel, Bristow, and Settel 1987). This begs the question: how fast must a device track a human gesture in order to capture every nuance? A related question is: if a pianist performs on a keyboard, to how many decimal places must we compute the durations of the events played? The problem is more complicated than it appears at first glance, because there is more to a musical event than note-on and note-off. That is, one usually wants to measure more than simply the duration between the poles of key down and key up. To measure the *velocity* of key depression (a clue to the intended amplitude and envelope), one needs much more temporal precision. This is because one measures velocity by comparing the time it takes for the key to travel its downward path.

Some MIDI-based keyboard instruments lack precision. This partially accounts for the mechanical-sounding performances heard from some synthesizers. In the easiest case—one voice monophonic—the MIDI specification probably has enough resolution to handle any temporal subtleties played on a keyboard. However, in a five-to-six-voice texture the best-case resolution is reduced to several milliseconds—resulting in a "smearing" of chords. With sixteen voices—MIDI's channel limit—the congestion is obvious. Added to these inherent MIDI delays are delays caused by the microprocessor inside the instrument. For this reason, some musicians feel that temporal resolution in MIDI systems is lacking. (See chapter 21 for more on MIDI.)

It must be said that keyboards are a special case in comparison to other input devices. They require an especially high degree of precision because the performance techniques associated with keyboards are so complicated and subtle, involving ten fingers on the keys, not to mention two feet on pedals. The same complexity is not necessarily associated with simpler controls such as the rotary faders, switches, buttons, and sliders on a synthesizer. These devices may be sampled at much lower rates, on the order of 100 to 200 Hz (Mathews and Moore 1970; Alles 1980). Even so, a modern synthesizer or effects device can have numerous manual controls, so the total sample rate for all input devices can reach several thousand values per second. This amount of data is sometimes handled by a dedicated microprocessor whose main job is to filter or *data-reduce* it into a manageable form for the main microprocessor within the synthesizer. See Kaplan (1981) and the discussion of performance software in chapter 15 for more on this subject.

Figure 14.8 Digital synthesizer keyboard (Yamaha SY77, 1990) with 61 keys, three thumbwheels at the left for pitch bend and vibrato, amplitude sliders for the two output channels (above the D1 and E1 on the keyboard), a data entry slider (above G3). Also visible are a liquid-crystal display screen, 70 pushbutton switches, and memory cartridge slots for voice program storage. On the back of the unit are jacks for footpedal and breath controller inputs, audio outputs, and MIDI input and output.

Musical Keyboards

More instruments have been made with keyboards than with any other type of controller (figure 14.8). This trend shows no sign of changing; virtually all analog and digital synthesizers developed in the past two decades can be configured with a keyboard, and the widespread MIDI 1.0 specification (chapter 21) was designed with keyboard performance in mind.

In its simplest form, a keyboard is simply an array of on/off switches, with each key corresponding to a switch. The keyboards attached to early analog synthesizers were *monophonic*, meaning that only one key depression (i.e., one note) could be handled by the synthesizer. Today's digital synthesizer keyboards are *polyphonic,* meaning that several keys (several notes) can be processed at once. Unlike a piano, however, most digital synthesizers are not 88-note polyphonic, but are limited to 8, 10, 16, 32 or some other number of simultaneous notes. This is usually due to a shortage of oscillators in the synthesizer, but it can also be attributed to the slowness of the control microprocessor within the synthesizer.

State of the Keyboard

Within the memory of a keyboard microprocessor, the state of the keys can be represented as a sequence of bits, in which a 1 signifies that a key is currently depressed, and a 0 signifies that the key is not depressed. If the microprocessor scans the key switches a hundred or more times per second, this state information can amount to tens of thousands of bits per second. Clearly, some means of *data reduction* on all this key state information is desirable. The most straightforward approach is to capture only changes in key states.

In order to determine when a change takes place, the raw binary data are reduced via a logical *exclusive-or* operation, which takes just one instruction cycle. The exclusive-or operation compares the current keyboard state with the previous keyboard state: keys that change state take a value of 1; all others take a value of 0. For example, consider the following sequence of keyboard states:

Key number	*1 2 3 4 5 6 7 8 9*
Previous state	1 0 0 1 1 0 0 0 0
Current state	0 0 0 1 1 1 0 0 0
Changed keys	1 0 0 0 0 1 0 0 0

Here the system detected that keys 1 and 6 have changed. Thus the exclusive-or acts as a kind of filter that quickly reduces the entire keyboard state down to a handful of bits.

Keyboard Scan Rate

How fast should the keyboard be scanned for changes? An early investigator, Knowlton (1971), estimated that a scanning time of 20 times per second per key would suffice to capture complex keyboard activity. He drew this conclusion from an examination of mechanical player-piano rolls. For a simple on-off keyboard, this resolution may be adequate for perfunctory performances of some traditional music. If we intend to build an expressive keyboard, much more resolution is required, on the order of several hundred times per second per key (Alles 1980). The next section explains why this is so.

Sensitivity to Velocity, Aftertouch, and Pressure

A *velocity sensing* keyboard measures how hard the musician hits each key by gauging the speed (velocity) with which a key is depressed. If a key takes 5 ms to travel from resting position to the bottom of its travel range, we can deduce that the key was hit harder than a key that took 50 ms to travel the same downward distance. A computer and a synthesizer can make use of velocity information to alter the sound produced. Just as a piano key makes a special sound if we strike it hard (louder and brighter), so a synthesizer can be programmed to respond to key velocity with corresponding loudness and timbre changes.

Various means exist to measure the speed of key depressions. Some keyboards use an optical sensing technique (Dworak and Parker 1977; Andersen 1978; Moog and Rhea 1990) in which key depressions cause a photosensitive switch to trigger. *Capacitive coupled antennas* inside the keyboard are also possible (Alles 1977b). However, the most common way to measure key velocity is to use a switch in the form of a standard two bus-bar keyboard (Alles 1980; Chamberlin 1985). The contacts of the keyboard switch are arranged so that when the key is in the up position, the switch makes contact with the *up bus bar* common to all the key switches. When the key is down, it makes contact with the *down bus bar* (figure 14.9). When the key is going from up to down, there is a period of time during which the key switch makes no contact with either bus. This is called the *transition time* of a keystroke. The transition time is inversely proportional to the key velocity. That is, the greater the transition time, the less the key velocity is. In a

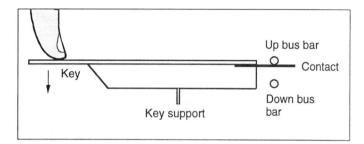

Figure 14.9 Horizontal cutaway view of bus bars in a keyboard. The contact plinth moves from the upper to the lower bus bar when the key is pressed.

scheme designed for a player-piano action, the Bösendorfer 290 SE recording piano measures the velocity of the hammer about to strike the string, not the velocity of the key (Moog and Rhea 1990).

Practical transition times fall between 5 and 35 ms. Longer transition times delay the start of the note, since the note does not start sounding until it hits the down bus bar. A skilled pianist can use about 30 different velocities in the range of 5–35 ms transition times. Many of these velocities are concentrated in the 5–15 ms range, so transition timing needs to be accurate to about 0.5 ms (Alles 1980).

In order to detect velocity information, the keyboard's microprocessor must scan the state of the keyboard much more rapidly than it would for a non-velocity-sensing keyboard. For example, one of the first commercial digital synthesizers, the Digital Keyboards Synergy (Alles 1980; Kaplan 1981) sampled the keyboard at 40 KHz. This speed is necessary because the microprocessor must sample each key at more than one point in the keystroke. As an example, a typical organ keyboard has 61 keys. If each key is examined every 500 μsec (0.5 ms), an examination of a key can only take 500/61 or about 8 μsec.

More expressiveness can be obtained by measuring the *release time*—how quickly or slowly the keys are let up by the performer.

Simple *aftertouch* information can be gleaned by adding another level or sensing to the keyboard (e.g., another bus bar or another optical switch). Hard playing on the keyboard causes the key to touch the third level of switches, and this information is sent to the synthesizer for a sonic response (such as vibrato). The cheaper keyboards have monophonic aftertouch, if they have aftertouch at all. Monophonic aftertouch means that if any key is pressed hard, a global effect is applied to all currently playing notes. Much better is polyphonic aftertouch, in which an effect, such as vibrato, is applied only to those keys held down hard.

Figure 14.10   Thumbwheels for pitch bend and vibrato next to a keyboard.

True *pressure-sensitive* keyboards can gauge the amount of pressure applied at the bottom of a keystroke, or more specifically, how hard the key is held down. Various means for measuring key pressure exist. Chamberlin (1985) recommends the substitution of a linear transducer instead of a contact switch at the bottom of the keyboard key's travel. One option is to use conductive rubber to detect key pressure (Moog 1987). As the key is pressed harder, more of the conductive rubber is engaged in the pressure-detection circuit.

Pressure information can be used in a number of ways. The most common is to have it determine loudness, timbre change, vibrato, or tremolo. Pressure pads beneath the key can also be used to bend pitch, but this application can cause problems. First, the pad gives no physical response corresponding to the amount of pitch bend. Second, the amount of arm weight required for a specific pitch bend varies depending on whether the player is seated or standing. Finally, holding a bent pitch this way can be difficult. Pitch bend wheels or *thumbwheels* (figure 14.10) or three-dimensional keyboards (see table 14.1) are better suited for pitch bending.

Keyboard Actions

The "feel" or "action" of a keyboard is important to performing musicians. Unweighted organ-type keyboards provide little feedback to the musician. Various ways exist to improve the feel of a keyboard. Since each key of an organ-type keyboard has a return spring that brings the key back to its

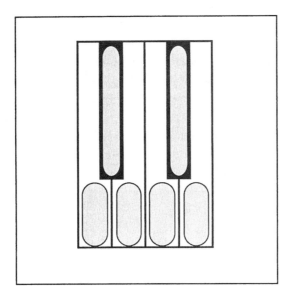

Figure 14.11 Six keys on a touch-sensitive keyboard, where the shaded areas are the touch-sensitive regions. By stroking the touch-sensitive region one can varying aspects of the performed sound, such as vibrato, pitch bend, spectral envelope, etc.

resting position, substituting a heavy spring can give the keyboard a more substantial feel.

Weighted wood keys with heavy springs are another approach. Introducing a rubber barrier at the bottom of a key's path gives the key a more mechanical feel. As mentioned previously, if the rubber is electrically conductive, pressure information can be gauged as well.

Another twist is installing a mechanical piano-type action (minus the strings and soundboard) inside an electronic keyboard, to add the feel of the true piano action.

Extended-action Keyboards

One of the possiblities inherent in attaching a keyboard to a computer and a synthesizer is the notion of extending the action of the keyboard. The Multiply-touch-sensitive keyboard designed by Robert Moog (Hybrid Management 1984; Moog 1987; Kramer, Moog, and Peevers 1989) uses conductive rubber to detect the position (left-right, front-back) of the performer's finger on the surface of the key (figure 14.11). This information can be conveyed to a digital synthesizer. For example, if the performer's finger is near the front of the key, this could be interpreted as a "smooth" timbre, while touches near the back of the key signify a more "rough" timbre.

Another possibility is mapping finger position to vibrato, pitch bend, or another musical parameter.

The Notebender keyboard developed by Key Concepts allowed in-and-out key motion as well the normal up-and-down motion (see figure 14.5). With the Notebender, a player can bend pitch with each finger independently and polyphonically. The range of pitch bend is adjustable in software, and the bending can be made continuous or quantized in steps for precise microtonal performances (*Computer Music Journal* 1984; Moog 1987, U.S. Patent 4,498,365).

Computer-controlled Pianos

For many pianists, a mechanical action of a piano keyboard represents the most expressive kind of keyboard feel possible. Thus many attempts have been made to link a piano action with a computer (Moog and Rhea 1990). The computer can record the player's gestures for playback. This playback may occur on the piano (outfitted with an automatic player mechanism) or on a synthesizer/sampler.

Automatic player-piano systems go back to the nineteenth century. (See the fascinating books by Ord-Hume 1973, 1984 for a historical and technical account.). In recent years the Marantz Pianocorder system (*Computer Music Journal* 1980) was one of the first to couple a piano action with microprocessor control, along with Helmers's experimental microcomputer-controlled pneumatic piano (Helmers 1979). At the present time, computer-controlled pianos are available from a number of piano manufacturers (figure 14.12). See Coenen and Schäfer (1992) for a survey and comparison of their performance and editing features.

Key Layout and Splitting

The design of the key layout on the keyboard is another area of experimentation with a long history. In inexpensive electronic music instruments and toys, keys can be as small as 1 cm wide by 3 cm long. This key size is suitable only for monophonic hunt-and-peck performances by amateurs. A normal piano key measures 2 cm wide by 14 cm long. This size seems optimal for the equal-tempered black-and-white key layout. Keyboard-based synthesizers aimed at professional musicians use keys of about this size.

The numbers of keys remains a variable. The traditional 88-key piano layout is available only on more expensive keyboard controllers and synthesizers (figure 14.13).

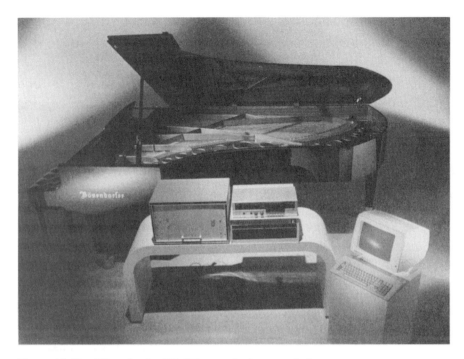

Figure 14.12 Bösendorfer 290 SE reproducing grand piano.

Many synthesizer keyboards offer a five-octave 61-note span. To some extent, this limitation in pitch range can be overcome in software by means of *keyboard splitting.* A split keyboard divides the span into two or more *regions* or *zones* divided at *split points,* with each region assigned to a particular synthesizer voice or patch (figure 14.14). For example, the lower half of the keyboard might be assigned to a low-register bass voice, while the top half of the keyboard is assigned to a high-register melodic voice. This is accomplished via the MIDI channel mechanism. assigning one region of the keyboard to MIDI channel *A,* which is routed to synthesizer voice *A,* assigning another region to MIDI channel *B* routed to synthesizer voice *B,* and so on.

With lightweight plastic keys and compact microelectronics, synthesizer keyboards can be packaged with a shoulder strap for live performance onstage (see figure 14.5). In this setup, the right hand plays the keyboard while the left hand controls functions like sustain, loudness, pitch bend, and vibrato.

Of course, the equal-tempered black-and-white key keyboard is not the only possible design; it is merely the most common. The demands of microtonal music call for different key arrangements. Numerous electronic instruments, from the Motorola Scalatron (Secor 1975, see also figure 14.5), to

Figure 14.13.   Yamaha KX88 MIDI master keyboard.

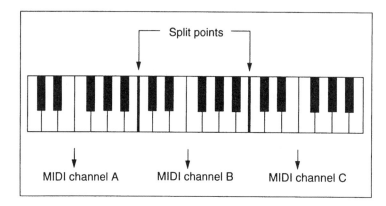

Figure 14.14   A split keyboard is divided into several regions, each of which transmits over a different MIDI channel.

the 31-tone organ (Fokker 1975), to the Egg digital synthesizer (Andersen 1978; Manthey 1978, 1979), incorporate innovative key layouts. (See Keislar 1987 for an illustrated history of microtonal keyboards.)

Remote Controllers

Certain musical situations call for remote control of electronic instruments and signal-processing devices. In recording studios, for example, the engineer would like to have all controllable devices within arm's length. If a device such as a digital reverberator is in a rack-mounted cabinet in the back of the studio, a small remote controller near the mixing console is a great convenience. Onstage, a musician might prefer the mobility of a small portable keyboard in concert as against a bulkier package in which the keyboard is integrated into the synthesizer electronics. Many musicians

Figure 14.15   Hector Berlioz. (Copyright Bibliothíque Nationale de France.)

using MIDI control an entire rack of synthesis and signal-processing devices from a single onstage keyboard.

Conducting Batons and Gloves

The original remote controller for music is the conductor's baton. Without touching an instrument, conductors can signal beginnings, endings, changes in tempo, balance, articulation, and expression—all through the baton and their spare hand. The first electromechanical remote controller was also wielded by a conductor. In his 1843 treatise "On Conducting," Hector Berlioz (figure 14.15) recounted his use of an electrified key (similar to a piano key) installed in a Brussels concert hall (Berlioz and Strauss 1948). This key flashed a light on and off, thereby signaling the musical tempo to an offstage chorus.

An updated version of the electric conductor's baton was developed at MIT (Haflich and Burns 1983). The conductor held a special wand that reflected ultrasonic signals back to a Polaroid ultrasonic rangefinder. A computer interpreted this information; under rigidly controlled conditions, the wand could transmit the performance tempo of a synthesized composition. Since this experiment, various electronic batons have been developed. Some are based on a hand-held *accelerometer*—a device that senses movement in one or more dimensions (Keane, Smecca, and Wood 1990). A microprocessor connected to the baton translates accelerometer movements into a standard code like MIDI messages that signify beats. The conducting system of Morita, Hashimoto, and Ohteru (1991) is simultaneously tracked by a camera (watching the baton in one hand) and an electronic glove (sensing the position of the fingers on the other hand).

The problem of decoding a conductor's gestures in real time seems to be well matched to a neural network pattern-matching system (Rumelhart and

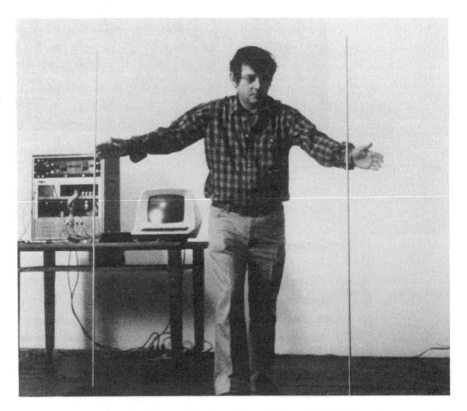

Figure 14.16   Joel Chadabe conducting a New England Digital Synclavier synthesizer using modified Theremin antennae designed and built by Robert Moog. Performance at The Kitchen performance space, New York City, 1979. (Photograph by Carlo Carnevali.)

McClelland 1986). Neural nets can be trained to recognize arbitrary gestures; their output can in turn be translated into control parameters for real-time synthesis (Lee, Garnett, and Wessel 1992).

Conductor-like control need not be linked to traditional conducting technique. This was proved in the late 1970s by composer/performer Joel Chadabe (figure 14.16), who used Theremin antennae to assume conductor-like control of a digital synthesizer (Chadabe 1984).

Transmission Media for Remote Control

Most remote controllers transmit information via one of four means: electrical cable, infrared light, radio-frequency broadcast, or fiber optic cables. For example, electrical cables connect most alphanumeric keyboards and mice to a computer, and most electric guitars and keyboards are also con-

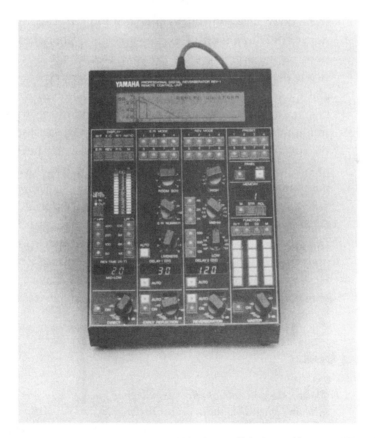

Figure 14.17 Remote controller for a digital reverberator (Yamaha), featuring buttons and rotary potentiometers. The signal-processing circuits are housed in a separate rackmount box (not shown) connected by a cable.

nected to sound processors and amplifiers via cables. Remote control units for multitrack tape recorders and sophisticated effects processors are also usually connected via cables (figure 14.17).

Infrared light is light at frequencies too low to be perceived by the human eye. Most modern hand-held remote controllers for compact disk players, DAT and videocassette recorders, televisions, and other stereo equipment are based on this technology. The infrared beam conveys digital information that must be decoded by the controlled device. It is also possible to detach the alphanumeric keyboard from a computer by using a keyboard with an infrared transmitter. One restriction on this type of device is that the controller must be pointed at the infrared "eye" on the device to be controlled, or toward a wall that reflects toward the infrared eye. Genevese et al. (1991) present a creative use of infrared technology—as a control tablet that detects a conductor's hand movements above it.

Some remote controllers are based on short-distance radio broadcast technology. The controller contains a radio transmitter, and the controlled device contains a receiver. Radio controllers are not as hampered by restrictions on the orientation of the controller or the existence of obstacles between the controller and the controlled device. The wireless microphone and the wireless electric guitar are now commonplace. Hence, it is easy to imagine a wireless controller for a computer music system. However, radio technology is not perfect. If the performer moves too much, anomalies in the signal can be heard. Also, the signal-to-noise ratio of a wireless microphone is never as good as a similar microphone connected via a high-quality microphone cable.

Fiber-optic cables, which transmit digital information as a sequence of rapid light pulses, could be a means for connecting a remote controller to a computer music system. Fiber-optic cables offer a wide bandwidth with a high signal-to-noise ratio. These thin, lightweight cables are immune to electrical and radio-frequency interference so they can span long distances. (See chapter 22 for more on fiber-optic interconnections.)

Responsive Input Devices

Though the principle of effortlessness may guide good word processor design, it may have no comparable utility in the design of a musical instrument.... Effort is closely related to expression in the playing of traditional instruments. It is the element of energy and desire, of attraction and repulsion in the movement of music.
(J. Ryan 1991)

Any mechanical instrument, such as a piano, trumpet, sitar, or glockenspiel, is a "naturally responsive input device" for music. That is, the physical construction of the device constrains the instrument to a particular action or "feel." This action varies, depending on the force and the shape of the gesture that the performer attempts to play on the instrument. On a trumpet, for example, high-pitched notes require more physical effort; the trumpet conveys this feedback to the performer. The strings of a sitar or a guitar require manual force to be bent. With any lessening of this force, they bend right back. The chimes of a glockenspiel move when they are struck, and if they are hit too hard they bump into one another. Many more examples from the world of mechanical-acoustical instruments could be cited.

By contrast, a typical electronic instrument involves little, if any, mechanical action to generate sound. Any pitch is as easy to play as any other; pitch bending and loudness controls are simply additional knobs or pedals that demand only a minor effort to manipulate. The input devices attached to many electronic instruments, such as organ keyboards, joysticks, and knobs, have little mechanical "feel" to orient the musician. And yet experience shows that virtuosic performance is greatly aided by mechanical feedback cues from the instrument. This is one reason that manufacturers of more costly synthesizers have attempted to improve the mechanical action of their keyboards and controls. (See the earlier section on keyboards.)

Computer control of mechanical devices offers another possibility: input devices with a *programmable response* to the touch. There have been several experiments to build input devices with a programmable response. By using digitally controlled electrical motors, researchers have designed keyboard keys and joysticks with a variable *force-feedback* response (Cadoz, Luciani, and Florens 1984; Cadoz, Lisowski, and Florens 1990; Florens and Cadoz 1990; Gillespie 1992). For example, a single keyboard can be made to react like piano, harpsichord, or organ. A key can be made to have a stiff or loose action. It can be programmed to have "steps" that can correspond to steps in amplitude, in timbre, or in both.

Responsive input devices require special electrical motors with a wide bandwidth and strong force (for simulating rigid objects). Cadoz, Lisowski, and Florens (1990) describe a keyboard in which there is one motor per key. The Atari force-feedback joystick, developed in the early 1980s, could be programmed to feel like a 360-degree audio panner, an automobile gear box, a spring-loaded joystick, or other mechanical systems. (See also Cadoz, Luciani, and Florens 1984 for a description of a similar device.) The benefits of an input device whose action can be "tuned" for a particular piece are clear. Table 14.2 lists responsive input devices.

Table 14.2   Responsive input devices

Device	Description	Typical use
Piano action	Mechanical action with "feel"	Pianos, and piano controllers
ACROE joystick	Programmable reaction to gestures; can be stiff, stepped, supple, etc.	ACROE Cordis system (Cadoz, Luciani, and Florens 1984; Florens and Cadoz 1990; Cadoz, Lisowski, and Florens 1990)
ACROE key and keyboard	Programmable action; can be stiff, stepped, supple.	ACROE Cordis system (see references in previous entry)
Atari joystick	Programmable motorized action; can simulate a gear box, a surface, a circular joystick, etc.	Experimental game research at Atari Cambridge Research Center (now defunct)

Conclusion

Diverse input devices can control a single music synthesizer. As a result, the number of different input devices has multiplied since the development of digital synthesizers. Refining innovative designs will continue for many years to come. In any case, instruments alone do not music make; players are needed. Conservatories lag behind instrument designers in recognizing the need for training in new performance techniques.

Meanwhile, the musical keyboard remains a most popular input device. For many keyboard players, the action of the concert grand piano is still the standard by which keyboards should be judged. Although it is possible to integrate a grand piano action into computer music systems, it will always be cheaper to provide a simpler organ-type keyboard with little response.

Perhaps *virtual reality* (VR) research will lead to more sophisticated musical controllers. One line of VR attempts to monitor the gestures of a person and transmit to that person synthetic sensations correlated to their gestures. In some VR setups, the user wears ear- and eye-phones. When looking up and turning the head, one hears sounds and sees images that follow one's gestures. While a great deal of research remains, it is not difficult to imagine the musical potential of such systems, wherein "exploring musical space" becomes a literal experience.

15 *Performance Software*

Sequencers

Sequencers: Background
Paper-tape Sequencers
Analog Electronic Sequencers
Digital Sequencers
Musical Robots
The Nature of MIDI Performance Data
Anatomy of a Note
Digital Audio Data
Using a Sequencer in Performance
Quantizing
Performance Setup and Orchestration
Performing with a Sequencer
Subsequences and Performance Logic
Inside a Sequencer

Software for Interpreting a Score

Rule-based Performance
Example of Performance Rules

Interactive Performance Software

Transmitting Cues
Conducting an Ensemble of Synthetic Instruments
Accompanying a Human Performer
Recognizing Musical Patterns
Shared Control of One Instrument
Computer Bands

Improvisation Systems Onstage and in Installations

Designing an Interactive Performance

Internals of Performance Software

Conclusion

This chapter examines *performance software*—the programs that interpret music scores and gestures and transmit them to sound synthesis equipment. Performance software is designed for the concert hall, the gallery, and the interactive media channel, as well as the studio. Hence it must be able to respond in *real time* to a musician's gestures. As we will see later, the "electronic brain" behind real-time operation is a scheduler program that can juggle several tasks and dynamically shift priorities to follow a changing musical context.

Our goal with this chapter is twofold: to introduce the main categories of performance software, and to describe in basic terms the internal operation of performance programs and schedulers. The first category discussed is sequencers. Chapter 16 also discusses sequencers, but with an emphasis on sequence editing. Here we stress their performance capabilities.

Sequencers

A sequencer is a type of recording and playback system with a programmable memory. Instead of recording the waveform of a sound, however, a sequencer records the only the *control* or *performance data* needed to regenerate a series of musical events. For example, when a musician performs on a synthesizer keyboard, the times of key up and key down events can be recorded by a sequencer program. Later, the sequencer can play back this sequence and send the control information to the synthesizer to recreate the musician's performance (figure 15.1).

A sequencer can be implemented in any of three forms:

1. A software package running on a general-purpose computer

2. A dedicated box with buttons and knobs for entering, editing, and playing back sequences.

3. A robot, more or less in the image of a human performer.

A software package is flexible and has a graphical display, but a dedicated box may be more portable and convenient. Some ancient music sequence players took the form of humanoid robots, a trend that has seen a resurgence in recent years.

The MIDI specification (IMA 1983) is the present standard protocol for communication between a sequencer and the devices it controls. This means that sequencers sold today receive and transmit MIDI messages, and the control data they store are MIDI data. (See chapter 21 for more on MIDI.)

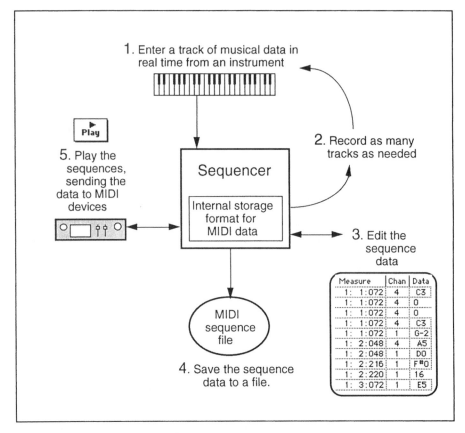

Figure 15.1   Overview of a sequencer, showing (clockwise) the operations of (1) music data entry, (2) multitracking, (3) editing, (4) saving edited data, (5) performing.

The next sections develop the history of sequencing technology and stress the performance features of sequencers. Later we discuss the internal operation of a sequencer.

Sequencers: Background

The first recorded attempt to describe the construction of an instrument that could play by itself is found in the manuscripts of the Banu Masa, a treatise on organ-making dating to 890 (Ord-Hume 1973). As early as the 1200s, Dutch instrument builders designed and constructed programmable mechanical carillons (chimes or bells). Inside the mechanism of the carillon was a revolving cylinder covered with holes (analogous to the binary digit 0). If a wooden peg (analogous to the binary digit 1) was inserted into a hole, it triggered a bell-ringing mechanism when the cylinder revolved. By

Figure 15.2 Programming a carillon in "step mode" at Bruges (from Buchner 1978).

placing pegs in various holes, a musician could program different melodies and chords (Buchner 1978). According to Leichtentritt (1934) some Flemish carillons had nine thousand memory locations (holes) for the insertion of note pegs (figure 15.2). Today we would call this type of programming the sequencer *step mode* recording. (See the discussion of step mode later in this chapter.)

The designs of Robert Fludd, alias de Fluctibus (1574–1637), which he published in his book *De Naturae Simia* (1618), inspired a wider appreciation of the possibilities of mechanical performance. Indeed, sequence control of musical mechanisms was implemented centuries before its industrial and mathematical applications. The first sequence-controlled loom, operating under the programmed control of a perforated paper roll, did not appear until 1725 (Usher 1954). James de Vaucanson (1709–1782), a developer of automatic looms, was also a celebrated designer of musical robots or *androides*—as he called them. Performing robots (including some frauds) were a popular attraction in the late 18th and 19th centuries, and can still be found at some amusement parks.

The first attempt to make a *sequence recorder*—able to register a series of key depressions played on a keyboard for later reproduction—was implemented in the eighteenth century (Leichtentritt 1934; Boalch 1956; Buchner 1978). The term *melography* was coined by J. Charpentier in 1880 to name this process. A *melograph* was a punched paper roll, which a skilled human reader translated into music notation (not to be confused with the Seeger Melograph discussed in chapter 12). Thus the recording process was only half automated.

In the mid-1800s, the French instrument builder Alexandre Debain built the first portable sequence players (Ord-Hume 1984). Debain's Antiphonel devices could be fitted on a normal keyboard instrument and operated by moving a lever up and down. The coding of music into an Antiphonel and all early sequence players was a tedious process carried out in a factory. It was not until the early 1900s that pneumatic paper-punching machines were developed to record keyboard performances (figure 15.3). These were the first fully automatic *real-time sequence recorders*, since the rolls they produced could be used to drive a player piano.

Paper-tape Sequencers

All of the mechanical music boxes, player pianos, and other musical automata constructed up through the early twentieth century were essentially sequence-controlled devices. Thus it was not a new idea when someone decided to control an electronic music instrument via sequences. The pioneering effort at electronic music automation was undertaken by the French engineers A. Givelet and E. E. Coupleux, who in 1930 designed and built a synthesizer consisting of four vacuum tube oscillators controlled by a punched paper-tape mechanism. Some years later, in 1945, J. Hanert built a programmable synthesizer employing a punched-card technology to control an oscillator bank (Ernst 1977, U.S. Patent 2,541,051). In the Inge-Schole Stiftung Studio für Elektronische Musik, Munich (which later became the Siemens studio), engineers built an analog synthesis system that was programmable via punched paper tape (Tjepkema 1981; Kaegi 1967).

The two RCA Synthesizers were the last grand effort at sequence automation by paper tape. Dubbed the Mark I (1955) and Mark II (1964), these room-sized vacuum tube machines were designed by Harry F. Olsen and Herbert Belar of the RCA Research Laboratories (Olson and Belar 1955; Olson 1967, 1991; Babbitt 1964). Milton Babbitt used the Mark II in a number of electronic music compositions (e.g., *Ensembles, Philomel, Vision*

Figure 15.3 Melograph sequence recording on a continuous roll of paper. Below the keys of the piano (or whatever keyboard instrument the Melograph is connected with) lies a brass strip connected to the positive terminal of a battery. If a key is depressed, a spring establishes contact with the corresponding wire of the key. The circuit is closed, and current passes through the paper where the corresponding tooth of a comb lies. A chemical reaction takes place and produces a colored line on the moving paper so long as the key is depressed. (Engraving reproduced from Ord-Hume 1973.)

Figure 15.4   RCA Mark II Synthesizer installed at the Columbia/Princeton Electronic Music Center in New York City. The typewriters punch holes in paper tape, which is fed into the control mechanism of the synthesizer.

and Prayer) composed at the Columbia/Princeton Electronic Music Center in New York City (figure 15.4).

Continuous graphical techniques stood as an alternative to the discrete note-oriented paper tape controllers. Chapter 8 describes several pioneering optoelectrical mechanisms for reading graphic notation.

The commercial introduction of *voltage-controlled synthesizers,* by companies such as Moog, Arp, and Buchla in the late 1960s brought new possibilities for musical expression to thousands of musicians worldwide. These transistorized systems contained a dozen or more modules that could be interconnected via patch cords. Voltage control meant that individual parameters of the sound could be controlled either by input devices such as keyboards, or automatically by signals from other modules—opening up a new field of sonic possibilities.

In 1967 the composer Emmanuel Ghent introduced the Coordinome, a device that allowed for programmable (via punched paper tape) control synthesizer modules (Ghent 1967a). Another class of sequence-control devices using relays and other electromechanical devices were built in the 1960s for controlling sound generators and audio equipment. These include Hugh Le Caine's elaborate Hamograph, in which six channels of voltage

Figure 15.5 Moog 960 analog sequencer module. The 24 steps of the sequencer are divided into three rows. A clock module is at the left. Lights above each column indicate active steps. (Photograph courtesy of Robert Moog.)

control information could be stored on a magnetically sensitive sprocketed foil tape (Young 1985, 1989).

Analog Electronic Sequencers

By the early 1970s, manufacturers of analog synthesizers offered *analog sequencers* as optional modules (figure 15.5). To use such a device, the musician tuned a series of knobs, each corresponding to a voltage that controlled a sonic parameter (such as oscillator pitch). At the push of a button, the sequencer then stepped through these voltages, sending each voltage in turn to the module connected to it by a patch cord (e.g., an oscillator). If desired, the sequence could be set up to loop, thus realizing, for example, a repeating melody. More generally, the voltage sequence could control any module, such as filter center frequency, the amplitude of an amplifier, etc. The rate at which the sequencer stepped was set by a clock knob or controlled from another voltage source.

One can see how the demands of *integral serial* composition techniques of the 1950s motivated the development of some early sequencers (for example, see Young 1989, pp. 140–146; Scherpenisse 1977). Integral serial composition organizes each musical parameter (pitch, duration, amplitude, etc.) as an independent series. (A classic exegesis of integral serialism is G. Ligeti's (1960) analysis of P. Boulez's composition *Structure 1a*.) Integral serial patterns can be realized using a sequencer that has several parallel "tracks"—one for each parameter—that can be programmed individually. As is often the case, however, the logic inherent in the technology suggested a new direction for music. The repeating patterns generated by looping analog sequencers also spawned the repetitive, minimalist music of the 1970s (Reich 1974).

A major technical limitation in analog sequencers was the number of different steps that they contained, corresponding to the size of their voltage memory. The Moog 960 sequencer module shown in figure 15.5 offered 24 steps, while the Arp 1027 module provided 30, and the Buchla 246 module had 48 steps. In these sequencers, when more than one parameter was controlled at each step, then the number of steps was reduced by that factor. For example, a 24-step Moog sequencer could control the pitch, duration, and amplitude of just eight notes (24 divided by three parameters). To add more notes, one needed another sequencer module. Moreover, each parameter at every step had to be tuned by hand with a control knob; it was not possible to program the sequencer by playing. For this, digital memory technology was needed.

Digital Sequencers

The GROOVE system engineered at Bell Telephone Laboratories in the late 1960s was a computer-controlled analog synthesizer (Mathews and Moore 1970). GROOVE stored performance information in its memory, in the form of functions of time for each synthesis parameter. These functions could be edited to change the original performance. By 1970 a research team at the University of Utah used a small computer to scan an organ keyboard and capture sequences of notes played on it. Their system also displayed a form of rudimentary music notation (Ashton 1971; Knowlton 1971, 1972).

Within a year, Peter Zinoviev and his associates at Electronic Music Studios (EMS), London, had developed a commercial digital sequencer. Unlike hand-tuned analog sequencers, the EMS sequencer could record and play up to 256 events, with each event having six parameters, for a total of 1536 stored values. This control information was stored in digital form and could be edited. By the end of the 1970s, digital sequencers were built into a number of commercial instruments such as the hybrid Sequential Circuits Prophet-5 (Darter 1979) and the Digital Keyboards Synergy (Kaplan 1981). But when the MIDI protocol was introduced, the concept of digital sequencing became widespread (Tobenfeld 1984). (See chapter 21 for more on MIDI.)

Digital sequencing suffuses popular music today. All modern synthesizers and samplers can be connected to an external sequencer via a MIDI cable.

Many synthesizers have built-in sequencers. Modern sequencer programs are *multitracking*. This means they can layer several simultaneous sequences into a single performance. Besides capturing notes and parameter settings, sequencers can transmit changes in orchestration by means of MIDI program change messages. These messages switch the "patch" (or "voice" or timbre) being played.

Musical Robots

[The Musical Lady] could play sixteen tunes and her music was played as by a human performer, by the depression of the piano keys by her fingers. As well as playing the instrument, she moved her head and her breast heaved in a lifelike impression of breathing. (Ord-Hume 1973)

The most theatrical form of sequence player has always been a robot—a motorized android with a mechanical or electronic brain. We have already cited part of this history; a rich literature awaits those wish to explore further. (See, for example, Leichtentritt 1934, Chapuis 1955, Bowers 1972, Buchner 1978, Prieberg 1975, Losano 1990, Ord-Hume 1973, 1984, and Weiss-Stauffacher 1976.)

Musical robots are a common attraction in amusement parks, but ongoing research is leading to a more sophisticated breed, able to accompany human performers, read music, and carry on limited conversations (Matsushima et al. 1985; Roads 1985b; Katayose, Inokuchi. 1989). Another interesting direction is the creation of robots for non-keyboard instruments, such as drums and bagpipe (Sekiguchi, Amemiya, and Kubota 1993; Ohta et al. 1993).

The Nature of MIDI Performance Data

The *lingua franca* of sequencers is the MIDI protocol. What aspects of performance are captured in MIDI data? Chapter 21 analyzes MIDI in detail; here it suffices to cite four basic types of MIDI data that are important in performance:

1. *Discrete note data* such as start and stop times, pitch, amplitude, and channel.

2. *Discrete MIDI program change* messages that select new patches on a synthesizer or signal processor. Program change messages can be entered into the sequencer in real time by pressing "program select" or "voice select" buttons on a MIDI device. Or they can be entered later through editing operations in the sequencer.

3. *Discrete system exclusive messages* supply parameters to selected synthesizer and effects programs. Consider the example of controlling an effects processor in performance. After a program change message selects the "Program 5: Concert Hall Reverberation" program, a system exclusive message might set the parameters of Program 5, such as the room size, reverberation time, filter cutoff, and so on.

4. *Continuous controller* data coming from pitch bend and vibrato wheels, volume pedals, and sliders.

MIDI can handle other types of data, such as audio samples and time-code, but these are not usually transmitted during live performance.

Notice the distinction between "discrete" and "continuous" in the above list. Discrete means that notes and program change messages occur when a button is pushed or released. (For our purposes, a key on a musical keyboard can be thought of as a button.) In contrast, continuous data come from analog controllers like wheels, pedals, and sliders. Since all MIDI transmits are discrete digital messages, the word "continuous" is a relative term. In practice a "continuous controller" continually transmits discrete messages whenever their position changes from a preset null position.

We have already mentioned that a note event captures the "velocity" and the "channel" of the note. If the reader is not familiar with the MIDI system, the meaning of these terms is not yet clear. Before going on, let us explain these terms, because they are ubiquitous in the sequencing world.

Anatomy of a Note

The MIDI system encodes a note in two separate messages: note-on and note-off. The difference in time between the on and the off is the duration of the note. Either type of note message has four main parameters:

1. *On or off*—Indicates whether to start or stop a note.

2. *Pitch*—Encoded as a number from 0 (C0) to 127 (G10).

3. *Key velocity*—On a keyboard, this is a measure of how fast a key moved in a vertical direction. Since a fast-moving key indicates that the note was played with more force, it is usually interpreted by a synthesizer as the initial amplitude of the note.

4. *Channel*—A number from 1 to 16; the channel mechanism is one of MIDI's ways of indicating timbre differences, since one can assign different synthesizer voices to different channels.

Digital Audio Data

The concept of sequencing has evolved to a point where many sequencers can simultaneously play back MIDI data and also trigger the playback of sound files stored on disk. The sound files are organized as individual audio sample tracks running alongside MIDI data tracks (see also chapter 16).

An issue that immediately appears in this configuration is synchronizing audio tracks with MIDI data, particularly if the tempo of the MIDI data changes. Some audio sequencers change the sample rate to conform to the new duration, but this may also change the pitch. To solve this problem, signal-processing tools that perform time compression and expansion without affecting the pitch are becoming ubiquitous (see chapter 10 for more on time/pitch changing). But these tools are not perfect, so there is a need for handcrafted editing if high quality is to be maintained.

Next we look at practical aspects of sequencers in performance.

Using a Sequencer in Performance

A sequencer is a strange *chien savant*—incapable of perfoming the simplest of tricks without a spoon-fed diet of musical data, yet once trained, it astonishes with its quickness and agility. This section examines the training phase and the practice of performance.

Quantizing

Preparation for performance—sequence entry, editing, quantizing, and set-up for playback—can be a major task. Chapter 16 presents methods of entering and editing sequencer data. Here we focus on the art of quantizing, while the next section deals with performance setup.

Many sequencers offer the option of *quantizing* or rounding off the durations of previously performed events to align them to an imaginary timing grid. For example, events might be quantized to sixteenth-note resolution and aligned to a steady metronome beat. Quantization can correct slight timing errors in performances that are played to a metronome accompaniment. It also makes the events easier to transcribe into a readable form of common music notation. Without quantized input data, a notation editor must fabricate weird configurations of tied notes—connected thirty-seconds, sixty-fourths, and one-hundred-twenty-eighths—in order to accurately reflect the duration of performed events that are slightly shorter or longer than sixteenth notes.

Another type of quantization is *chord quantization:* grouping all events that start within a brief time interval into chords. Chord quantization is important, because without it, when the sequence is slowed down, notes that are slightly staggered in the original performance are strung out into arpeggios (Kaplan 1981). MIDI already strings out chords due to its serial—one note at a time—protocol. For large chords, this serial communication protocol, combined with processing delays in the synthesizer, may introduce its own note onset delays, even if the specified starting time of a group of notes is the same (see chapter 21).

Besides the positive benefit of correcting errors, quantization also lessens the "feel" of a performed rhythm, so it should be used carefully. As an antidote to quantization, a "humanize" operation is sometimes available to add small timing variations and amplitude changes. Since these deformations may be random and without any sensitivity to rhythmic context, "humanizing" should perhaps be used even more carefully than quantizing.

Performance Setup and Orchestration

Performance setup means establishing a correspondence between sequencer tracks, MIDI channels, devices, and specific patches (figure 15.6). By and large, the setup process is equivalent to orchestration of the sequence. The MIDI protocol divides orchestration into several parts that must be coordinated in the setup phase:

1. Tracks in sequencer software

2. MIDI channels

3. Physical device interconnections

4. Program change messages

5. System exclusive messages

Apart from the General MIDI mode (chapter 21), which establishes a standard performance configuration, musicians must set up their own correspondences between these parts.

Tracks segregate compositional data into an arbitrary number of separate streams that start at arbitrary times in the sequence. As we point out in chapter 16, tracks are a convenience for organizing compositional structure and do not necessarily map neatly into MIDI output channels.

The MIDI protocol defines sixteen transmission channels. A *multiline MIDI interface* can support several independent sixteen-channel MIDI

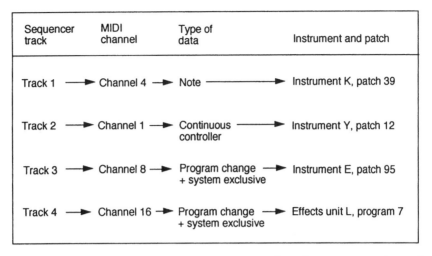

Figure 15.6 Sequencer performance setup. Mapping of sequencer tracks to channels, instruments, and patches.

lines. In the usual case, each channel carries the data for a single timbre or voice.

Connected to the sequencer via cables are the various MIDI devices themselves: synthesizers and effects units, primarily. Each device has a MIDI IN port and must be tuned to receive messages on one or more incoming channels.

Program change messages switch from one patch or timbre to another on the MIDI device.

System exclusive messages pass parameter data to the selected patch. That is, they "tune" or customize the patch with data prepared in advance (filter settings, oscillator tunings, effects parameters, etc.). Changes in orchestration are greatly aided by a sequencer that can record system exclusive messages. Without such data, the sequencer can switch the patch number in performance, but the patch plays with generic or preset parameters. An alternative is to store the parameter data in the synthesizer along with each patch.

Performing with a Sequencer

Performing with a sequencer means playback of prerecorded sequences in a planned or spontaneous manner, depending on the musical intent. Various characteristics of the playback can be controlled in real time by a musician, such as the tempo, panning, pitch, vibrato, and loop points, among others. Software sequencers provide real-time faders displayed on the screen of the

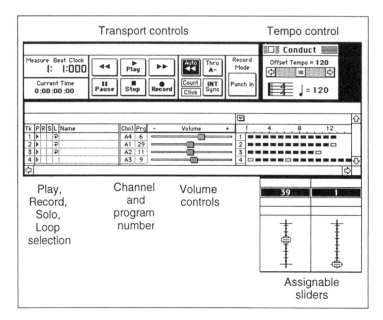

Figure 15.7   Performance controls of a sequencer screen.

computer that can be manipulated in performance. Figure 15.7 shows some performance controls of a sequencer screen.

Alphanumeric keyboard and mouse control are fine for editing, but performing musicians usually prefer more tactile input devices. A *MIDI fader unit*—a small box with several programmable potentiometers and switches —is a common external controller. Beyond this, any MIDI input device can (after a setup stage) be used as a sequence controller.

Subsequences and Performance Logic

Most sequencers let a musician record many individual sequences called *subsequences* that can be assigned as *macros* to the keys of an alphanumeric or MIDI keyboard. By pressing various keys, the musician starts various subsequences running in series or concurrently. One can also program a sequencer to trigger subsequences according to external events such as a switch on a footpedal or a hit on a drum pad.

Although this is usually more of a studio than a stage technique, professional sequencers can be "slaved" to audio or video media. In this case, the sequences are triggered by SMPTE timecode addresses received by the sequencer from the other medium. (See chapters 9, 21, and 22 for more on SMPTE timecode.)

Another possibility is to chain together sequences in performance according to a subroutine logic of conditional execution. That is, the start of sequence B may be dependent on the start of an event in sequence A. If an event in sequence B occurs before the musician starts sequence C, this may cause sequence D to start. In general, however, sequencers are "canned" programs that do not let users extend their functionality. For truly programmable control of sequence playback, one of the interactive performance toolkits described later may be a more suitable vehicle than a sequencer, per se.

Inside a Sequencer

How does a sequencer work? This section digs a level deeper into the mechanism of a sequencer.

Professional sequencers perform a dozen jobs, but their core task is to record a performance while simultaneously playing back previously recorded performances stored on multiple tracks. To accomplish this task, the sequencer must first determine which new notes have been started or finished. Second, it must find all notes in previously recorded tracks that should start playing soon. Finally, the sequencer must monitor its input controls, such as an alphanumeric keyboard used to issue commands, and update its displays.

Here is a simple scheme for accomplishing these tasks, adapted from the description in Mauchly (1982). It is not the only possible design, but it clearly illustrates the basic issues. First we look at the software needed for recording sequencer tracks. This software assumes that the note event information from a musical keyboard has been preprocessed into *event packets*. An event packet contains the following information:

- Key number
- Key status—whether the key is pressed or released
- Key velocity
- Time that the key status changed

Within a sequencer, time is typically measured as a count of *clock ticks* since the sequencer began recording a track. The sequencer program then assembles the event packets for a track into a *track event array*. A track event array has two parts: a value indicating the number of events packets in the array, and the track event packets themselves.

This sequential array representation has the advantages of simplicity and compactness. However, if the musician wants to edit the track, for example,

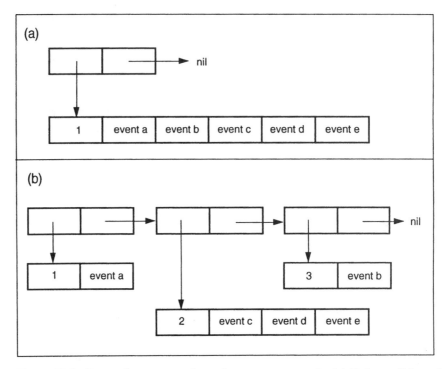

Figure 15.8   Internal representation of a sequencer track. (*a*) Before editing, the track can be represented as an array. (*b*) During and after editing the track becomes a linked list, intermingling individual events and subarrays. Here *event b* has been moved from the second element to the last element position. In general, inserting a sublist is more efficient than shifting all the elements in an array.

to insert a note event at point *t,* an array representation poses problems. In order to make a slot for the new event, all events after event *t* would have to be copied (shifted) one slot down. So a sequential array representation is not optimal for editing purposes. For editing purposes, the editor program might use a *linked-list* representation for the events. At each edit point, the editor creates a *link* data structure. A link contains of two *pointers* (or memory addresses): one pointer contains the address of a track event array, and the second pointer contains the memory address of the next link. (See chapter 2 for an introduction to data structures, including linked lists.)

Figure 15.8 presents a hybrid combining the sequential array representation with a linked-list representation. For the unedited note events the sequencer uses the array representation (figure 15.8a). Whenever an array is altered, the sequence editor creates a link to make room for new events or to fill in the gap between deleted events (figure 15.8b). The playback portion of the sequencer can read either type of representation.

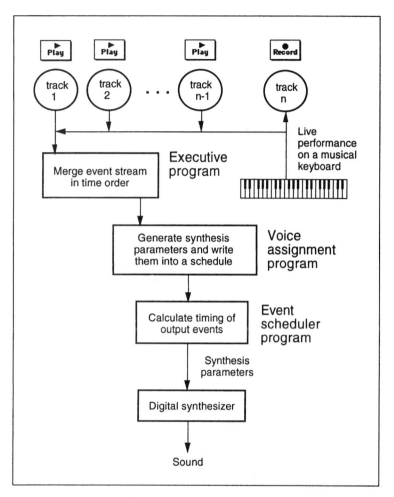

Figure 15.9 Operation of a sequencer program simultaneously recording and playing back. The sequencer merged existing tracks with input from a real-time performance.

When it is time to play back a stored sequence, the sequencer merges event data from several sequencer tracks into a single stream, sorting the events in time order (figure 15.9). It packages the events into MIDI messages and sends them out via a MIDI cable to one or more MIDI devices.

Software for Interpreting a Score

Music teaches us all that is beautiful in this world. Let us not hamper it with a machine that tells the story day by day, without variation, without soul, barren of the joy, the passion, the ardor, that is the inheritance of man alone. (John Phillip Sousa 1906)

One of the first proofs derived from computer music research was that machines could outperform their human counterparts with respect to speed and precision. A new genre of *machine music,* as in Arthur Roberts's *Sonatina for CDC 3600* (1966) echoed the spirit of mechanical music but took it to a higher degree of control (Dumour 1993). The sequencer is the present incarnation of the machine spirit. It renders a score with literal note values, resulting in performances that are technically perfect, and ice cold. "Perfect" performance is based on accuracy, while expressive performance requires context-sensitive transformation of the written score. Skilled performers take a score as a starting point for interpretation. They add rubato, subtle pitch bends, vibrato, slight changes in note duration, and dynamic nuances in order to articulate phrase structure and infuse expression into the score.

More expressive computer performances can be achieved in several ways:

- Playing the score into the computer using a gestural input device (e.g., keyboard) instead of typing in literal note values (see chapter 14)

- Varying the playback by an input device (see the section on interactive performance software later)

- Entering the score with a language or editor that has phrase-level constructs for expressive performance (Rodet and Cointe 1984; Anderson and Kuivila 1991; Collinge and Scheidt 1988; Oppenheim 1992; see also chapter 17)

In all three cases, the expressive performance information is entered manually by a musician. Can the machine be taught to play with more "expression" on its own?

Rule-based Performance

Here we present another possibility: *rule-based performance.* This involves score analysis software that applies transformation rules (akin to pronunciation rules for speech) to an encoded music score in order to make its performance more lively.

For a performer, the choice of when and where to vary the tempo and the articulation in a performance is a matter of training, knowledge, taste, and feeling. Although each musical performer interprets a score in a personal way, aspects of interpretation can be turned into formal rules that may improve machine performances.

Various attempts have been made to find rules for more expressive performance (Morrill 1981a; Sundberg, Askenfelt, and Frydén 1983; Clynes and Nettheim 1982; Clynes and Walker 1982; Gabrielsson 1986; Wessel, Bristow, and Settel 1987; Friberg et al. 1991; Friberg 1991; Johnson 1991; Baggi 1991; Bressin, De Poli, and Vidolin 1992; Bilmes 1993; Todd 1993; Noike et al. 1993). The goal of these studies is to find "pronunciation rules" for musical texts—akin to prosodic rules for speech—that correspond to the appropriate style. For example, Sundberg and his colleagues found a simple correlation between amplitude and pitch in performances on most acoustic instruments. They developed another rule by noticing that string instrument performers inserted pauses between wide melodic leaps. Such rules are based on scientific observations; textbooks on instrumental technique contain many other suggestions for more expressive performance based on aesthetic principles.

Experimental software has been developed to emulate expressive performance. Given a note list transcribed literally from a score, these programs analyze the score and apply style-specific rules to create expressive renditions. The term "style-specific" is important because there are many different ways to interpret a score. Recordings of music by J. S. Bach, for example, vary from "authentic" versions in the style of the Baroque era to versions for nineteenth-century large orchestra, as well as jazz and rock interpretations. The experiments of the Italian computer music pioneer Pietro Grossi show how far a score can be transmogrified by performance rules (Grossi 1987).

Example of Performance Rules

A simple example of a performance rule for classical era melodies is the following: "If a note terminates a melodic leap, increase the note's duration by 3% for tones terminating in a minor or major third, 6% for leaps wider than fifths, and 5% for intermediate intervals" (Sundberg, Askenfelt, and Frydén 1983). The researchers derived two types of rules for polyphonic music: *differentiation rules* and *grouping rules* (Friberg, Frydén, Bodin, and Sundberg 1991; Friberg 1991). Differentiation rules help listeners identify musical structure by enhancing the differences between duration and pitch categories. For example, one such rule takes notes of unequal durations and assigns different amplitudes to each of them. The grouping rules, on the other hand, help listeners hear related notes as a unit. Unity is made more obvious, for example, by moving grouped notes closer together in time, and by avoiding discontinuities in loudness and envelope.

Interactive Performance Software

Computer music offers the opportunity to go beyond traditional performance modalities, which are usually limited to supplying pitch and time information for a single instrument. This section describes some musical possibilities opened up by interactive performance software. We begin by looking at musical applications of this technology, and then glance at two opposite strategies for implementing interactive systems. The end of the section explains how a computer-based accompanist operates.

Transmitting Cues

The first category is perhaps the least interactive: transmitting visual or sonic cues. In effect, the computer tells the performer what to do and/or when to do it. One way is to transmit audible signals via headphones. Emmanuel Ghent (1967b) pioneered this technique, which has since been used by numerous composers. (See, for example, the description and photograph of performers of L. Austin's *Canadian Coastlines* in Strawn et al. 1982.) Another tack is the projection of visual cues. This can be organized as a signal-and-response system, where the visual cues (projected cinematically or merely displayed on a computer screen) indicate precise cues in a score. On the other hand, it may involve the projection of artistic images that performers are expected to respond to in an arbitrary manner.

Conducting an Ensemble of Synthetic Instruments

[The electrical conducting mechanism installed in the Verbrugghe theater in Brussels] *consists of copper wires attached to a voltaic pile* [battery] *placed beneath the the stage; these wires connect the conductor's desk with a movable baton attached by a pivot in front of a board which is placed at any desired distance from the conductor. The desk is furnished with a copper key similar to a piano key.* (Hector Berlioz 1843, in Berlioz and Strauss 1948)

Performance software offers the possibility to go beyond the kinds of control given to a traditional instrumentalist—such as control of a single voice—to control at the level of a conductor (Kobrin 1977; Dannenberg and Bookstein 1991; Mathews 1989; Keane, Smecca, and Wood 1990; see also the discussion of conducting in chapter 14). Such a system must be able to interpret a performer's gestures and translate these into the manipulation of *ensemble parameters*. Ensemble parameters include tempo, overall articulation, stress, balance of voices, and spatial projection.

The system designed by Morita, Hashimoto, and Ohteru (1991) controls performance by means of a human conductor's hand gestures. These gestures are simultaneously tracked by a camera (watching the baton in one hand) and an electronic glove (sensing the position of the fingers on the other hand). See also Chadabe (1984) for an example of control at the conductor level by means of input devices such as Theremin antennae (an image of a Theremin appears in chapter 14).

For "open" or aleatoric forms of music that allow for performer choice or improvisation, a related possibility is a system that watches for specific cues in a live performance. Once it recognizes a cue, it can react by transmitting visual signals to human performers or by playing a musical response on a synthesizer. (See the section on improvisation systems later.)

Accompanying a Human Performer

An *accompaniment system* plays along with a human musician, following the performance of a score by the human, and playing its own score simultaneously. The goal of an accompaniment system is a more time-flexible rendition of a prepared score, replacing the fixed-duration "tape recorder mode" of performance in which the instrumentalist plays along with a tape or disk.

The main technical problem in accompaniment is following the performance of the instrumentalist. This problem is many faceted, and there is a tendency for systems to solve one aspect of it, while ignoring others. Some try to follow the pitches played by the instrumentalist, some track only the tempo, some merely look for isolated cues without trying to follow every note. In the playback, some alter the tempo according to the instrumentalist's tempo, some try to match dynamics, some modify only the onset time of the accompaniment sequence. Even when the accompaniment system is performing flawlessly, it is possible for the human instrumentalist to make a mistake; thus it has been recommended to keep a backup musician on hand to initiate sequences manually in case synchronization is lost (Puckette and Lippe 1992).

Accompaniment systems developed by Dannenberg (1984), Dannenberg and Mukaino (1988), Dannenberg and Mont-Reynaud (1987), Chabot and Beauregard (1984), Vercoe (1984), Horiuchi and Tanaka (1993), and Inoue, Hashimoto, and Ohteru (1993) track a live performer and attempt to alter the playback tempo of a prepared score for synthesizer. Dannenberg's system performed real-time pitch detection on a trumpet performance, while the system developed by Beauregard and Vercoe tracked the key clicks

Figure 15.10   Morton Subotnick, live in concert at Lincoln Center, New York in 1983. The synthesizer is a computer-controlled Buchla analog system. The conductor is L. Newland. (Photograph by B. Bial.)

on an electronically modified flute to measure the tempo of the performance. Pennycook (1991) developed a similar system that tracks a modified clarinet.

Many works of composer Morton Subotnick involve interaction between one or more performers and a sequenced accompaniment (figure 15.10). To support this work, Subotnick and M. Coniglio developed the Interactor program, which tracks real-time performance of a precomposed score and triggers the playback of sequences (Coniglio 1992). By looking only for landmarks in the score—unique pitch and rhythmic configurations—the Interactor program allows a great deal of interpretive leeway on the part of the performer.

Recognizing Musical Patterns

Figure 15.11 shows a block diagram of an accompanist system. An input processing subprogram handles data from the soloist. Optimally, these input data are already encoded with timing information (like MIDI note-on

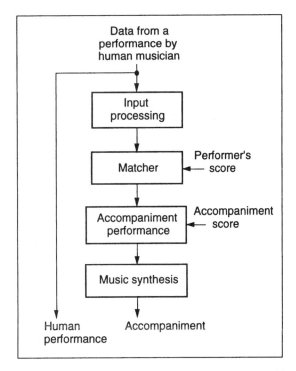

Figure 15.11 Overview of a computer accompaniment system. It listens to a human performer and generates an accompaniment that matches the direction and flow of the human performer. See the text for further description.

and note-off messages). If the data stream is raw audio samples, the input processor must be capable of converting this into symbolic score data—a major task (see chapter 12). The Matcher subprogram compares the actual performance of the soloist with the soloist's score. In doing so, it must be able to ignore extraneous notes played by the human performer, and track missing notes to find the best possible correspondence. The Matcher program tries to infer chords, for example, even when the notes are not played exactly simultaneously. For complicated polyphonic music, the program may maintain several hypotheses about the current location and discard an hypotheses when evidence points strongly to a single conclusion. The third subprogram is the Accompaniment performance, which controls the timing of the accompaniment. In the simplest case, timing is the only aspect of the accompaniment that varies from one performance to another.

See Buxton (1986), Dannenberg and Mont-Reynaud (1987), Rowe (1992a, b), Puckette and Lippe (1992) for a discussion of issues involved in accompaniment systems. Chapter 12 examines the specifics of pitch and rhythm recognition.

Shared Control of One Instrument

Part of the flexibility of digital instruments is that they can be controlled by a variety of input devices. We can plug a keyboard, wind, guitar, or exotic controller into the same sound generating instrument. For a complex sound-generating instrument, we can even have all of these devices connected simultaneously. Thus another performance situation is to have several musicians control one instrument—typically a large multivoice synthesizer. For example, at a performance at the 1982 International Computer Music Conference in Venice, the 4X synthesizer was controlled by three performers at the same time (Blum 1983).

Computer Bands

In addition to physical, acoustical, and visual channels, some responsive instruments accept messages in the form of *interrupt signals*. Interrupts are asynchronous signals that tell the computer to stop what it is doing momentarily to handle an external event that has just occurred. This event might be an urgent update sent from one computer to another, indicating a change in musical context. The hardware to coordinate communication between several closely linked computers can be custom-built or designed around standard network or MIDI interconnection boxes.

Networks of musical microprocessors can be formed to make up a computer band (Bischoff et al. 1978). The musicians may let their systems run autonomously, or they may interact with it and each other in a musical way. Depending on how the rules of interaction are defined, the results can vary from the extreme of free improvisation to tightly synchronized ensemble performance.

The musical potential of such a setup is profound—combining the power of multiple interacting computer improvisers with multiple human musicians. A prime example of this approach is the work of the composers emerging from Mills College and affiliated with the League of Automatic Music Composers and The Hub (figure 15.12) in the San Francisco area (The Hub 1989).

Improvisation Systems Onstage and in Installations

The flexibility inherent in software means that computer-based instruments can respond to a gesture in arbitrarily complex ways (Nelson 1989; Roads 1986c). For each gesture of the musician, a procedure might execute an

Figure 15.12 The Hub—a computer band—performing in concert at Mills College, Oakland, California. Each musician interacts with a computer that in turn interacts with other computers to create an ensemble performance. From left to right: T. Perkis, P. Stone, C. Brown, S. Gresham-Lancaster, M. Trayle, J. Bischoff. (Photograph copyright Jim Block.)

arpeggio or chord, or trigger an entire sequence. This interaction is not necessarily based on score following, since the human performer may be improvising. And the system's response is not necessarily predetermined, but rather improvised on the spot.

Improvisation Systems: Background

One of the first computer-based interactive improvisition system was demonstrated in 1968 at London's Institute for Contemporary Art. In the system developed at the Electronic Music Studios, Ltd., by Peter Zinoviev and his associates, gallery visitors whistled a few measures of melody into a microphone connected to a Digital Equipment Corporation PDP-8/s minicomputer. The computer then rearranged the melody and calculated variations, performing them on an attached analog synthesizer (Grogono 1984).

In the 1970s and early 1980s, composers such as Giuseppe Englert with the Groupe Art et Informatique Vincennes (GAIV), Peter Zinoviev, Salvatore Martirano, Edward Kobrin, Laurie Spiegel, Joel Chadabe, and David Behrman pioneered the use of real-time algorithmic composition in performance. Activity in this domain has expanded rapidly since the spread of MIDI systems, which simplify and standardize the technical aspects of real-time performance (Rowe 1992b).

The aesthetic aims of improvisation systems owe much to the confluence of algorithmic composition, live electronic music, free jazz, the improvisatory tradition, and the tradition of "sound sculpture" (Mumma 1975; Stockhausen 1971b, 1978; Battier 1981; Bernardini 1986; Roads 1985b; Valentino 1986). Besides the purely aesthetic aspect, a practical benefit of improvisation systems is that they allow a virtuoso soloist to a create a dialog onstage.

Autonomous Performance

Stand-alone performance systems are evolving into increasingly sophisticated droids. Their sharply focused intellects can recognize patterns in external events and respond according to programmed rules. They can respond in a quasi-random fashion (Bartlett 1979), or interpret gestures by altering the balance between several melodic lines (Chadabe 1984).

We find these systems onstage, improvising with soloists or ensembles, but also in art galleries, where interactive installations respond to environmental cues like light, temperature, sound, and proximity to sensors and capacitance fields (figure 15.13). Dance movements can drive music improvisation, by attaching electronic sensors to dancers, or by placing dancers within the sensory field of the computer. At least one composition system was programmable via touch-tone telephone. Over a period of several months more than ten thousand callers interacted with the system (Langston 1989).

Problems in Improvisation Systems

Real-time operation places great demands on software improvisers. Only the most efficient recognition algorithms work in the heat of performance, such as phrase parsing according to time gaps between notes (Wessel 1991). In systems that are expected to respond in an original manner—either to a human performer or to other intelligent instruments—the musical problem is to avoid mechanistic behavior. The computer must have an understanding of specific musical contexts, and it must interpret gestures within such contexts. The Neurswing system (Baggi 1991), for example, takes in a harmonic progression and is controlled by three context parameters: *hot/cool, dissonance/consonance, as-is-ness/free*. An increase in the hot context knob favors louder playing, more appogiaturas, more nervous drum patterns, and more cymbal crashes. An increase in the dissonance context knob favors the insertion of dissonant harmonic patterns, flattened fifths in dominant seventh chords, inverted piano chords, and half-step appogiaturas. An

Figure 15.13   Two interactive installations by Liz Phillips. (*a*) *Soundtable II*, 1992 installation at the Threadwaxing Space, New York City. The water in the table conducts and transmits a capacitance field. As viewer/listeners move near the table, a loudspeaker under it emits reverberated resonances. Sound formations respond to the gestures of those who approach the table. They can watch as waves of sound energy vibrate the surface of the water, creating a framed image in the pool. (Photograph by R. Winard.) (*b*) *Graphite Ground*, 1987 installation at the Capp Street Project, San Francisco. The computer and electronic music synthesis equipment is housed in the structure in the center. Large shards of raw copper ore rest in four "nodes" within the space. Four loudspeakers are set in the corners of the room. Phillips uses the ore elements as antennae, each radiating a differently shaped capacitance envelope. As visitors walk through the space on the wooden walkways, the relationship of their bodies' movements to the ore groupings generates voltages that are sensed by the computer and interpreted by improvisation software. This software in turn controls a number of Serge analog synthesizer modules configured for quadraphonic performance. (Photograph by E. Blackwell.)

increase in the free context knob causes the improvising program to deviate from the original harmonic progression.

George Lewis's system listens to his trombone playing through a microphone connected to the computer (Roads 1985b). The computer follows the pitch of the melodic line and responds according to rules of improvisation provided by Lewis. In concert, a synthesizer controlled by a computer improvises with the live performer. Since group improvisation involves listening as well as playing, the most successful concerts occur when the performer and the computer listen and play as equals, according to Lewis.

Designing an Interactive Performance

How does one set up an interactive performance? Three paths can be followed: canned applications, custom approaches, or designs using a standard toolkit. Canned applications include sequencers or packaged algorithmic composition systems. A custom system is personal to a specific composer-performer, with specialized software and input devices. The PODX, GSX, and GSAMX programs developed by Barry Truax (1985, 1988, 1990a,b) are an example. These programs represent various stages of a custom performance system. They strongly support one composer's way of making music. For a well-defined aesthetic and technical configuration, the custom approach is optimal.

In contrast, a toolkit is an extensible, quasi-general solution. We prefer the term "quasi-general" to "general" because every toolkit has biases and limits in terms of representation, functionality, and performance. The toolkit offers musicians a set of modules for creating interactive performance situations. Musicians can configure or "patch" the internal mechanisms of the setup to suit a particular musical idea. Most of the *environments* and *microworlds* cited in chapter 18 fall into this category of toolkits. The quasi-generality of toolkits makes a good foundation for experimentation and prototyping of new performance setups. But the toolkit approach requires engineering aptitude and a training period to learn how to program it for a specific application.

Example of a Performance Toolkit: Max

The Max program is a prime example of an iconic toolkit tailored for interactive music performance (Puckette 1985, 1988; Puckette and Zicarelli 1990). Some Max icons take in musical data from MIDI and audio sources.

Other icons, connected by *patch cords* on the display screen, decode and transform these data, possibly generating new data to merge into the output. The output can be MIDI data, audio signals, or messages sent to applications running alongside Max.

The Max program has been used by hundreds of composers around the world in applications ranging from patch editors, responsive instruments, interactive composition, and control of audio devices. In the rest of this section we present a condensed tutorial based on the Max implementation for NeXTStep-based computers, in which audio processing is integrated with MIDI message processing (Puckette 1991; Roads 1993c). A caveat may be appropriate before we begin. In explaining Max patches, the cliché "One picture is worth a thousand words" applies. Even a simple patch requires a lengthy textual description if it is assumed that the reader is a novice, as we do here. Thus we must limit the presentation here to a very basic example that illustrates general principles but does not expose the full power of the toolkit. Although simple, the patch has the advantage of showing how MIDI and audio processing can work together.

Basics of Max

The *patch* is a fundamental concept in Max: a graphical configuration of *objects* (boxes) connected by *patch cords*. When a patch becomes too complicated onscreen, Max lets users collapse an entire patch into a single object called a **patcher** object. This greatly simplifies a patch's appearance, modularizes its functions, and provides a mechanism for arbitrarily complex nested patches.

A patch onscreen is in either *edit mode* or *run mode*. In edit mode, all the interconnections can be changed, and new objects can put in the window by selecting from an *object palette*. In run mode, the object palette disappears, and the patch reacts to external events such as mouse clicks, keyboard tapping, MIDI messages, and sound input.

When objects receive a message or signal through their *inlet,* they can respond by sending a message or signal through their *outlet.* Depending on the type of data emitted by an object, it may be sent to another patch, through a MIDI OUT port on the computer, or to a digital-to-analog converter (DAC). The inlets and outlets appear as small dark rectangles at the top and bottom of the object box.

Messages passed between objects contain numbers, symbols (strings), lists, or the symbol *bang*. The *bang* symbol is special in Max; it indicates that a "significant event" has occurred, and it is often used as a semaphore to start and stop processes. Knowing the order in which messages are sent is important for Max programming, but the example here does not require an exposition of this topic (see Roads 1993c).

Message Boxes

Message boxes are ubiquitous in Max patches because they can send arbitrary messages to multiple destinations in a patch without patch cords. Thus a message box is a "wireless" message transmitter. Each message in a message box is separated by a semicolon. Look at the message boxes in the top left of figure 15.14, labeled "Start" and "Stop." A message box assumes that its first message is to be sent directly out its outlet—if it is connected to another box by a patch cord. Since these messages boxes are not connected directly to another box, the semicolon in the first line says "There is nothing to send out the outlet." The rest of the messages in the box are in the form

```
receive_object_name message;
```

The second line sends the message *start* to the **receive** object named *dac* (see the label 2), which passes it immediately to the **dac~** object. When the **dac~** object receives a *start* message, it causes the digital-to-analog converters to begin operating. The third line sends the message 0.1 100 to the **receive** object *amp* (see the label 3). We will explain the meaning of this message in a moment.

Max sends messages to their destinations every time either *bang* or a message starting with a number is sent to the message box. Mouse-clicking on a message box in run mode is like sending it a *bang*. Now that we have explained the operation of message boxes, we can go on to a complete description of the Max patch in figure 15.14.

Control Objects versus Signal-processing Objects

The IRCAM version of Max includes *signal-processing objects* that can generate and process *signals* in addition to the *control objects* that process *messages* (Puckette 1991; Roads 1993b). While messages are triggered by external events (mouse clicks, MIDI notes, etc.), signals flow at a regular sampling rate through a Max patch.

The names of signal-processing objects end with the symbol tilde (~), like **osc1~**, **sig~**, **line~**, **adc~**, and **dac~**. The **sig~** object acts as an interface between the control and signal-processing objects. That is, it converts numerical messages into signals that the signal-processing objects can understand. We present an example below.

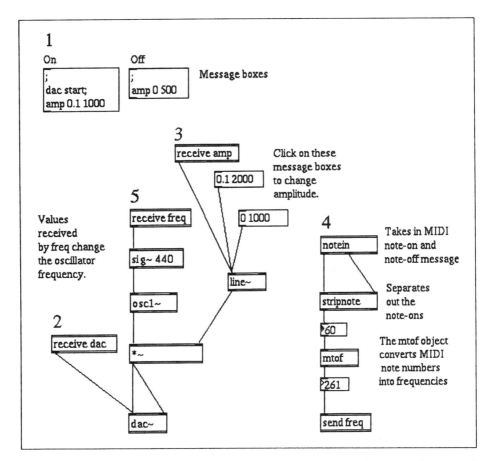

Figure 15.14 A Max patch that generates a cosine wave at a frequency determined by incoming MIDI note messages. See the text for an explanation.

A Waveform Generator Patch

Figure 15.14 depicts a simple signal-generating patch, which we explain following the labels 1 to 5 in the patch. Label 1 identifies the message boxes. As mentioned, the *start* message sent to the **receive** *dac* object at label 2 eventually causes the **dac ~** object to turn on the audio converters. At label 3, the **receive** object named *amp* picks up the arguments to be fed to a **line ~** object. The **line ~** object generates a straight line or ramp, which in this patch serves as a simple amplitude envelope for an oscillator **osc1 ~**. The arguments to **line ~** take the form

```
target_value duration
```

In the *duration* (in milliseconds) specified, **line ~** emits a ramp, starting at its current value and going to the specified *target_value*. When the patch begins, the initial value of **line~** is 0, so the first message it receives tells it to go from 0 to 0.1 in 1000 ms, or 1 second. (The signals passed through Max are floating-point values in the range of -1.0 to 1.0.) After 1 second, the **line~** object continues to emit a value of 0.1 until we send it a new message. The two other message boxes connected to the **line~** object can be clicked on in real time to change the amplitude of the oscillator. The box with the arguments 0 1000 causes the amplitude to drop to zero in 1 second. The other box causes it to go back up to 0.1 over a 2-second period.

Now let us look at the MIDI processing part of the patch, labeled 4. The **notein** object receives MIDI messages from the computer's MIDI IN port and filters out everything except note-on and note-off messages. No patch cord or message box needs to be connected to a **notein** object, since it is "hard-wired" to the MIDI IN port. A note-on message is MIDI's way of starting a note; the note-off ends it. (See chapter 21 for more on these messages.) The outlets of **notein** go to the **stripnote** object, which filters out the note-off messages, and passes only the note-on messages. The output of **stripnote** goes to a number box that displays the MIDI pitch value, which in figure 15.14 is 60 or MIDI middle C. From here the data pass to the **mtof** object, which converts a MIDI note number into a frequency value, shown in the number box below it as 261 Hz. The **send** object passes its input to the **receive** object named *freq*, labeled 5.

The frequency value coming out of the **receive** object is a control message. In order to be usable by a signal-processing object, it needs to be converted into a signal that is passed at the signal rate. The **sig~** object performs this conversion. Notice the default value of 440 in the **sig~** object. This is the frequency value that **osc1~** uses to generate a waveform before the patch receives a MIDI note-on message. As soon as the patch receives a note-on message from the external world, it ignores the initial 440 setting. Finally, the **osc1~** object generates a cosine wave by default, accepting the frequency in its left inlet. After the multiplier object ***~** scales the amplitude of the cosine, the signal splits into two, flowing out dual DAC channels.

Internals of Performance Software

The rest of this chapter peers inside real-time performance programs to observe how they work. We focus on two areas of software design, *representations of music* for real-time performance and *event processing*.

At the core of every performance program is a software representation of the music. The architecture of this representation has a profound effect on the flexibility and responsiveness of the system. It determines how music will be displayed, edited, transformed, performed, and communicated between devices. The next section serves as an overview of this important aspect of music software engineering. Later, we present an example of a simple object-oriented music representation for performance. Finally, we look at the real-time software inside a synthesizer or digital signal processor.

Music Representation for Performance

Music can be represented in innumerable ways. Various programs capture different aspects of music: the list of notes, the control envelopes, the music notation symbols, the sound-generating instrument, the audio waveform, the orchestration, the higher-level structure (measures, sections, pieces, sequences, tracks, channels, etc.). Here we are concerned with the representation of the control information supplied by musical gestures during a performance. The goal is to map raw sensor data coming from input devices into the control of meaningful musical parameters. Music has both discrete (e.g., pitched notes) and continuous elements (e.g., envelopes, crescendi), and performance representations have to support both aspects simultaneously.

Depending on the application, programmers must decide whether the software should try to immediately parse incoming data—to recognize preset cues, melodic patterns, chords, etc.—or simply read and store the data as fast as possible. Parsing the input immediately means that the information can be accessed more quickly later. A related question is how to organize incoming data into an efficient and logical structure. Myriad forms are possible: as a list, an array, a set of records in a disk file, an object-oriented representation, a rule, a semantic network, or another structure. (See chapter 2 for more on data structures.)

In all representations, a tradeoff exists between computation time and memory space. A compact encoding consumes minimal space but may require extra encoding and decoding time. Both memory and computation time constrain the performance of real-time systems. This is particularly the case for systems aimed at the individual musician's budget. Such systems must capture only necessary data. For example, it is much more efficient to store just the changes in the keyboard state than it is to store the entire state of the keyboard (i.e., each key's position) at every sampling interval. Tracking changes may require extra computation time, but this time is worth the effort in terms of memory space saved and search time when the data are processed later.

Performance with an Object-oriented Representation: An Example in MODE

One approach to music representation has gained increasing currency in recent years: *object-oriented* (OO) systems. Chapter 2 cites advantages of object-oriented systems (see also Pope 1991a, b; Garnett 1991; Lieberman 1982). This section develops an example of a real-time performance system organized around an OO representation.

Three features of OO systems are particularly important in music representation: *object encapsulation, message-passing,* and *inheritance.* Traditional programming languages define procedures and data separately; encapsulation means that OO systems bundle together state (data) and behavior (procedures) into entities called *objects.* Object encapsulation leads to neater representations that are less cluttered with implementation details, as we see in a moment.

In an OO system, only an object that is the "owner" of a piece of data has direct access to it. We label such an object A. All other objects communicate with object A by passing it relatively simple *messages* that request A to perform an action. The behavior of an object is defined by the messages to which it can respond. This behavioral view is independent of the internal implementation of the object. For example, we can set up an orchestra of synthesis instruments defined as objects. Each instrument accepts the simple message "trill," but internally each implements it in a different way, depending on the instrument it is (additive, subtractive, physical model, etc.). In a non-OO technique, each instrument would be passed a variable number of implementation-specific parameters to realize the trill. An OO representation hides implementation details and simplifies communication protocols. Every instrument knows how to trill; how it does it is its own business.

Every object is an *instance* of an abstract *class* of objects. Classes are related to each other in a "tree of behavioral refinement." This means that one class can be described as a refinement—a more specific case of—another class. Each subclass inherits data and procedures from a higher, more general class. A musical example of inheritance is a system in which complex chords can be defined as being refinements of simpler ones (Pope 1989).

The use of these features of OO systems for music description has been demonstrated by various music software developers (Scaletti and Hebel 1991; Garnett 1991; Pope 1991a; Anderson 1990; Taube 1991). The next section presents some examples of an OO representation for music performance derived from the Musical Object Development Environment, or MODE (Pope 1991a). MODE is written in the Smalltalk-80 language

(Goldberg and Robson 1983a, b) and is compatible with popular input/output formats such as MIDI, Cmusic note lists (Moore 1990), or Adagio scores (Dannenberg 1986).

Basic Event Classes

Performance with MODE is built on a basic class that describes all its musical structures. An **Event** is an object that has a duration and other properties. The start time of an event is always defined relative to some outer scope. Events understand messages that set or get the value of one of their properties, for example:

setDuration: *value*—set the duration of the event to a value such as seconds or beats

getDuration—return the duration value

Other messages set or get other properties associated with the event like pitch, timbre, envelope, amplitude, etc. So in general, messages of the form

setProperty: *value*

getProperty

set and get values of properties associated with the event.

NoteEvents

Only a small number of subclasses of **Event** exist, such as **NoteEvent** and **EventList**, described in the next section. **NoteEvent** objects are specialized **Events** that represent musical notes. They have the default parameters **pitch**, **amplitude**, and **voice** (or instrument). A **NoteEvent** understands messages for setting and accessing its pitch, amplitude, and voice. **NoteEvent** also understands creation messages such as

NoteEvent duration: *1.0* **pitch:** *'c#3'* **amplitude:** *'mf'*

This creates a new note event with the given arguments as its parameters. Such a message could be generated in a performance situation by an interactive improvisation system, for example.

EventLists

EventList objects are building blocks for larger forms—the middle layers of musical structure. In MODE there are no fixed notions of scores, parts, sections, tracks, measures, or voices. Rather, all are constructed as compositions of parallel or sequential event lists. **EventList** objects hold collections of events sorted by start time. An **EventList** is itself an **Event** and can therefore be hierarchically nested. That is, one event list can have another event list as one of its elements. For large compositions, event list hierarchies can grow broad and deep.

The primary messages to which event lists respond (in addition to the behavior they inherit by being events), are

add: *anEvent* **at:** *aTime*—add an event to the list at a specific time

play—play the event list

edit—open a graphical editor for the event list

Event lists also handle accessor messages such as

select: [*criterion*]—select events within the list that satisfy the specified criterion

Symbolic Links between Events and EventLists

Because an **Event**, and therefore its subclass **EventList**, can have arbitrary properties associated with it, one can set up *symbolic links* between events as a way of organizing musical structure in performance. These symbolic links are like threads that interconnect pieces of musical structure. A symbolic link is just another property whose name is a type of relationship and whose value is another event or event list, as in the following example, where the symbolic link indicates a variation relationship:

EventListB **isVariationOf:** *EventListA*

This link is "active," in that it can invoke a procedure that realizes the semantic intent of the link. In the above example, *EventListB* might be empty at first, but if it is seen in a score, it could fill itself with events by invoking the **isVariationOf** relationship, which would cause a procedure to create a variation of *EventListA*. In an interactive performance system, we could set up links between *cues*—events or event lists that we expect the system to watch for, and *responses* that the system should play when it recognizes a cue, for example:

CueD **HasResponseOf:** *EventListD*

Figure 15.15 shows chain of symbolic links connected with two real-time performance cues, *Cue 1* and *Cue 2*, played by a human performer. In this

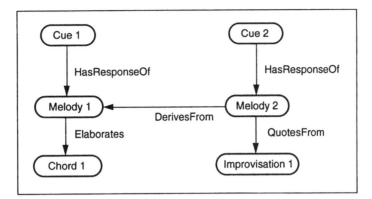

Figure 15.15 A network of symbolic links associated with two real-time performance events, *Cue 1* and *Cue 2*. The direction of the arrow, together with the name of the symbolic link, indicates the meaning of the relationship. For example, *Melody 1* is the response to *Cue 1*. This melody elaborates *Chord 1,* and the same melody is also heard in filtered form—juxtaposed with quotes from *Improvisation 1*—in *Melody 2*, which is triggered by *Cue 2.*

scheme, the arrows indicate the path of computation. When *Cue 1* is recognized by the system, it follows its **HasResponseOf** link to find *Melody 1*. But *Melody 1* has its own link and must generate itself according to the relation **Elaborates** *Chord 1*. Meanwhile, the system is recording *Improvisation 1,* played by a human performer. When the performer plays *Cue 2, Improvisation 1* and *Melody 1* are both used to generate *Melody 2.*

Event Generators and Modifiers

Two further classes provide a means of generating new events and modifying existing ones in performance: **EventGenerator** and **EventModifier**. An **EventGenerator** can either create a single event list, or it can behave like an ongoing musical process that we tell to start or stop playing. One benefit of the OO representation is that we can substitute an **EventGenerator** for an **EventList** at any point in the score. OO systems make no distinction between static data (like note lists) and active processes (like fugue generators). This allows a great deal of flexibility in music performance, because the score does not have to be completely fixed before the performance. Rather it can be generated dynamically by an **EventGenerator** that may be responding to a human performer (Pope 1989). This concludes our look at object-oriented representations.

Event-processing Software inside a Synthesizer

So far, our look at music representations has focused on the high level of
application programs like sequencers, accompanists, or improvisers. These
programs, running on a host computer, handle only part of the work of
musical performance. The other part is carried out "in the line of fire" by
the device that receives the performance instructions: a synthesizer or DSP
(Loy 1981). In a MIDI environment, for example, once a MIDI message has
been received by an instrument, a certain amount of *message decoding, voice
allocation, scheduling,* and *resource allocation* must be done inside the instrument before sound is emitted. We call this work *event processing,* and it
is the subject of this section.

Event-processing programs run on a microprocessor inside a synthesizer.
We assume here that this *control microprocessor* is mainly concerned with
managing the numerical calculations carried out by DSP chips, which perform the sample-level audio processing tasks. Another possible paradigm is
a fast microprocessor that handles both control and synthesis.

The control microprocessor in the synthesizer must respond to asynchronous events like button presses and knob twists in a matter of microseconds,
interrupting other tasks to handle these signals. Such asynchronous signals
are ubiquitous in real-time systems and scheduling programs. The next section presents a simplified model of event processing, with a focus on real-
time scheduling. The theory of musical scheduling continues to evolve. For
more on this subject, see Collinge (1980), Rodet and Cointe (1984), Jaffe
(1985), Anderson and Kuivila (1986, 1989), Loy (1987), Holm (1989),
Dannenberg (1989b), Honing (1991), Orlarey (1990), and Desain and
Honing (1992a).

The first task of event processing is message decoding. This is a mechanical task of parsing a message according to a predefined message grammar,
so we will not discuss it further here. (See any computer science textbook on
scanners and parsers.) The rest of event-processing software can be divided
into three subprograms: *voice assignment, event scheduling,* and *resource
allocation,* discussed in the next three sections.

Voice Assignment Subprogram

A voice assignment subprogram (VAS) converts the raw list of note events
into a finished product, that is, a list of parameters for a specific DSP device.
The VAS figures out which DSP voice is assigned to this event, and it
references memory tables in the DSP to find the frequency, amplitude, envelope, and waveform data (or other parameters) associated with this voice

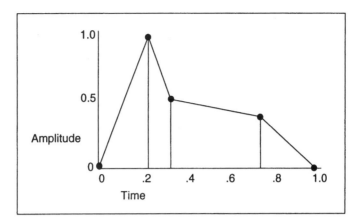

Figure 15.16 Envelope made from four ramps (line segments) defined by connecting five breakpoint pairs in the form (*time point, slope*).

played at this key number and velocity. The VAS writes each set of parameter data into a schedule that lists each action to be undertaken for the next *n* clock ticks.

Envelope data that change over time are written into the schedule each time a value changes. Many DSPs can compute *ramps* (line segments) so that the control microprocessor need only supply a list of *breakpoint pairs* to the DSP. A breakpoint pair is a time/amplitude representation consisting of a point on the *x*- or time axis and an amplitude argument, which can be either a specific point on the *y*-axis or a slope for the amplitude to go until the next breakpoint. An envelope with two breakpoint pairs could be translated into a statement such as: "After 100 clock ticks, use slope +90 until the next breakpoint; after 400 clock ticks, use slope 0 until the next breakpoint". In this case, only the changes at times 100 and 400 need be written into the schedule. The DSP automatically computes all the intermediate points between the breakpoints. Figure 15.16 shows an envelope constructed from five breakpoint pairs.

Event-scheduling Subprogram

The schedule of synthesis parameters to be sent to the DSP is managed by an event-scheduling subprogram (ESS) program running on the control microprocessor. The ESS sees to it that synthesis data are fed to the DSP chips at the right time. The ESS "wakes up" at every clock tick. It checks the schedule to see if there are any parameters to be shipped at that time. If so, it writes them to DSP; if not, it goes back to sleep.

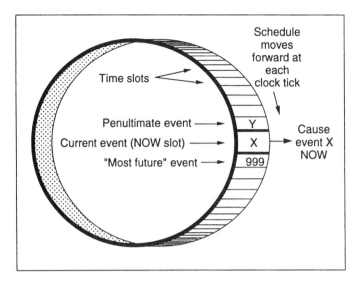

Figure 15.17   Schedule of events in the form of a continuously updated ring buffer. Each slot in the buffer represents a clock tick prior to "Now." The scheduler can write events anywhere into this buffer. At each clock tick, the event in the "Now" slot (if any) occurs, then the "Now" pointer moves up one location and clears the old "Now" location (which then stands at the end of the ring buffer).

The schedule typically operates as a *ring buffer*—a kind of recycling list. Each entry in the schedule represents one clock tick. Thus, if there are no notes to be played at a particular clock tick, the entry is left empty. A filled entry contains a pointer to the synthesis parameters. When the ESS sends out the data attached to position *i* in the schedule, position *i* is then freed to be used by the VAS for a later event (figure 15.17).

So far, we have described what happens when sequencer tracks are played back from memory. What happens when a key on the synthesizer is pressed? A microprocessor concerned with key presses sends an event packet directly to the VAS running on the control microprocesor. The VAS inserts a pointer to the synthesis parameters at the head of the event list attached to the next-to-be-played location in the schedule.

Resource Allocation Subprogram

All DSPs have performance limitations, such as the number of oscillators that can be realized in real time, number of sampled voices, number of simultaneous effects, and so on. Complications arise when combination of sequencer tracks and real-time keyboard input exceed the resources of the DSP (Kaplan 1981; Moorer 1981a). Even as DSPs become more powerful, this issue remains because of the trend toward more sophisticated signal-processing algorithms.

For example, if a 32-oscillator synthesizer allocates four oscillators per voice, then only eight notes can play simultaneously. For keyboard music, this usually suffices until nine or ten fingers press at once—then what happens? The problem can also arise with even more oscillators and voices if the performer uses a sustain pedal (unpressed notes still "ring") or if live performance is combined with multitrack sequencer playback. Some sequencers can support hundreds of tracks, which swamp the capabilities of almost any synthesizer.

When resources are limited, the performance software must be able to "gracefully degrade" the performance; that is, deteriorate gradually in the least noticeable ways. Sometimes notes have to be deleted to make room for new notes; various rationales for deleting notes can be formulated. For example, some synthesizers delete only the oldest notes in the middle registers of a complicated passage. The reasoning is that deleting older interior notes is not as noticeable as deleting newly pressed notes at the extremes of the passage. The performance software must also ensure that deleted notes are not cut off unnaturally, but rather are faded out quickly. Another solution is to implement an "overflow" mode. If the number of notes exceeds the capability of one synthesizer, remaining notes are passed on to another via MIDI. (See Kaplan 1981 for a down-to-earth discussion of these and other practical problems in synthesizer design.)

Conclusion

Musicians have only begun to explore the possibilities of computer-based interactive performance systems. A central challenge of these systems is combining the complexity and precision of automation with the gesture and feeling of human performance. Sequence playback is at the core of most performance software, although the concept of sequencing continues to evolve.

MIDI sequencers are merging with multimedia playback of graphics, animation, and video. The effects of multimedia sequencers are spilling into opera, dance, and theater performance. Accompaniment systems have potentially broad application in music education and in the concert halls of the future. By their nature, improvisation systems resist standardization and remain a wide open field.

16 *Music Editors*

Scope in Editing

Common Music Notation Editors

Unconventional Score Editors

MIDI Sequence Editing

Channel, Track, and Pattern Organization
Sharing Sequence Data between Programs
Representations for Editing
Event Lists
Piano Roll Notation
Common Music Notation
Metrical Grids
Controller Envelopes
Graphic Faders
Digital Audio Waveforms
Sequence-editing Operations
Time Editing
Pitch Editing
Amplitude Editing
Channel Editing
Program Change Editing
Continuous Controller Editing

Function Editors

Function Editors: Background
Filling Function Tables
Operations on Waveforms

Patch Editors

Patch Editors versus Instrument Editors
Graphical Patch Editors
Examples of Patch Editors

Instrument Editors

Instrument Editors: Background
Present Modular Instrument Editors
Front Ends versus Self-contained Synthesis Packages
Examples of Modular Instrument Editors: Music V Graphic Editor
   and Turbosynth

Sound Sample Editors

Spectrum Editors

Sound Database Editors

Media Editors

Toward Musically Intelligent Editors

Conclusion

An *editor* program lets one create and modify a text, image, or sound. Interactive editors speed up prototyping; ideas can be built up incrementally; often one can see and hear the result as the change is being made. Attention to proper syntax, which is all-important in languages, is much less of an issue in a graphical editor, since pushbuttons, menus, icons, fill-in-the-blank templates, and mouse gestures handle the details of most commands. The burden to remember the arbitrary details of a language ("Is it double-pound-sign or pound sign-asterisk that means double-sharp? What does this pointer refer to?") can be eliminated in a well-designed editor.

In any editor, flexibility in *scope*—the range over which an editing operation applies—is important to efficiency. Therefore we start with a discussion of this general issue. Since music exists on many different dimensions of representation, it is not surprising that there are numerous types of editors. This chapter examines score, instrument, function, patch, sound sample, spectrum, and media editors. We conclude with a look at databases and a discussion of musically intelligent editors.

Scope in Editing

Scope defines the sphere of action of an editing operation—the range of things that can be affected by it (Buxton et al. 1981). One way to judge an editor is to look at its flexibility in handling different scopes of operations. The more things that one can access in a single gesture, the more efficient one is in editing. Thus, scope determines how the editor groups things. Figure 16.1 shows one of the simplest scope rules; the darkened rectangle has been selected for an editing operation.

Musical events and their parameters can be grouped in an infinite number of ways, according to arbitrary criteria. Some of these same criteria can define rules of scope. A rule of scope can only access something that the system "understands" about the material it is editing. Many sound sample editors, for example, could not handle a request like "Delete the C4 played by the piano in measure 36" because their knowledge of musical signals is limited to time and amplitude points. Some MIDI sequence editors would have trouble with a request like "Add a minor seventh to the G Major chord in measure 97" because their knowledge of musical scope does not include groups based on harmonic relations. (See the section on musically intelligent editors for more on this subject.)

Practical considerations force software developers to limit the scope of operations to the most obvious ones. Table 16.1 summarizes the typical range of scope rules available in music editors of all kinds.

Figure 16.1 Scope definition in a score editor. The darkened rectangle has been selected by a mouse, defining the scope of a subsequent editing operation (reposition, delete, change pitch, etc.).

Table 16.1   Scope of operations in music editing

Scope rule   Explanation and example

Multiple selection   A group of things scattered about a file and selected one-at-a-time, but operated on as a group, for example, "delete note C in measure 1, note D in measure 3, and note F in measure 5"

Time   A group of things within a time interval, for example, "delete all notes in the third measure" or "copy the waveform from 1.0 to 2.0 seconds."

Screen space   A group of contiguous elements displayed on a screen that can be encircled by a mouse.

Local properties   A group of things with a common property, for example, "raise the amplitude of all notes below C3, " or "make all events in track 29 louder by 3 dB"

Contextual properties   A group of things that fall within a stated context, for example, "increase the amplitude of the topmost voice in all chords"

Labeled structural   A group of things that have been previously labeled, *groups* for example, "insert section RESPONSE after section INTRODUCTION."

Common Music Notation Editors

Common music notation (CMN) is the standard music notation system originating in Europe in the early seventeenth century. This section assumes familiarity with CMN.

The Complexity of Music Notation

CMN editors have many of the same commands as text editors, such as cut, copy, and paste, but they work on notes, measures, parts, and systems of staves, instead of characters, words, and paragraphs. Music notation is much more complicated than text or even mathematical notation. Roman alphabetic text (such as this) follows only a few syntactical rules; characters line up in a straight line; spaces or an occasional punctuation mark separate words. Mathematical notation is more complicated than unadorned text, but the simplicity of graphical mathematical notation editors proves that almost all mathematical expressions fall into one of several templates. Formulas typically fit on one line, and there is no need to precisely align several dozen lines, as one does in an orchestral score. Of course, the simplicity of mathematical notation derives from its powers of abstraction; one can always compress a long expression into a single character.

Notwithstanding the presence of "macro instructions" such as *accelerando* and *allegro ma non troppo,* common music notation is less susceptible to abstraction. In music, the separate parameters of a single event—pitch, rhythm, and amplitude—each divide into graduated scales with their own graphical symbols. When music symbols meet, they must change in a systematic way. In a single chord, numerous elements—note heads, note stems, augmentation dots, flags, accidentals, and expressive markings—must make room for one another to form a meaningful chord symbol. Arranging sequences of musical symbols properly involves many context-sensitive decisions. The spatial distance between successive notes varies with the duration of those notes. Stems, beams, and glissandi link notes; ties and slurs link phrases. The need to align vertically many staves in polyphonic music adds another level of constraints. And these are only the most basic considerations; we have not mentioned artful or aesthetic aspects of score layout. Volumes are devoted to instruction in the practice of music notation (Read 1969; Risatti 1975; Stone 1980).

These complexities put into perspective the task consigned to notation programs. They explain why it is difficult to create a truly "easy" CMN editor. The main way to cut down the complexity of an editor is to cut down the complexity of the music. This is precisely what some commercial editors do. Low-cost, "easy" music editors serve a useful purpose in introducing musicians to notation editing. But the range of the music they can handle is quite restricted. Thus a split exists between "easy" music editors and more professional programs.

Rule-based versus Graphics-based Editors

An important distinction between CMN editors is *rule-based* versus *graphics-based* (Yavelow 1992). Rule-based editors understand some of the rules of music notation. They keep track of the pitch and duration of notes, for example, enabling operations such as pitch transposition, rhythmic error detection, automatic positioning of notes and other symbols, and playback of score via the Musical Instrument Digital Interface (MIDI). (See chapter 21 for an introduction to MIDI.) The automatic decisions made by rule-based editors speed up the setting of conventional music.

Graphics-based music editors treat music notation as a collection of music symbols to be arranged as the user wishes. Figure 16.2 depicts some of the symbols possible in the graphics-based editor NoteWriter (Hamel 1987, 1989). Although the score is not necessarily linked to a MIDI representation, a graphical approach has many advantages for composers of new and experimental music. (See the section on unconventional score editors later.)

Probably the most useful category handles both types of editing: *rule-* and *graphics-based* (Diener 1989b; Roeder and Hamel 1989). These editors let users configure them, so that only the rules a user selects are applied. In addition, users can override automatic decisions. Nonstandard graphical notation can be inserted into the score.

This distinction between rule-based and graphics-based is not peculiar to music editors. Painting and drawing programs confront a similar "object" versus "bitmap" image dichotomy, and some programs provide separate tools for handling each domain.

Advantages of Computer-based Music Editing and Printing

All of the benefits of text editors over typewriters and handwriting accrue to users of CMN editors. The computer memorizes score fragments, which can be edited at will and freely combined. Many CMN editors take dictation from a MIDI instrument, an enormous time-savings when all goes well in the transcription. Optical reading of handwritten scores provides another alternative (Wolman et al. 1992). The output of a CMN editor, printed on an inexpensive laser printer, is usually neater and easier to read than a

Figure 16.2 Music symbols and examples of the graphics-based notation editor NoteWriter.

Figure 16.3   Notation editors permit easy extraction of parts from a full score. (*a*) Full score, *Symphony in G minor*, K. 550, W. A. Mozart (1788). (*b*) Extracted violin part.

handwritten manuscript. When plotted on a high-resolution printer, it rivals the quality of engraved scores.

Some CMN editors can format the same score in a variety of stave arrangements, such as full score, piano score, or as individual parts in a multipart score. The parts extracted by such a program can replace many hours of manual part-copying labor (figure 16.3).

When the score is prepared, many CMN editors can then perform the score on MIDI instruments. As well as providing immediate sonic realization of musical ideas, this gives composers the opportunity to check the accuracy of the notation. One may overlook a missing accidental on a page, for example, but its absence should be obvious when heard.

Goals of CMN Editors

Various CMN editors are designed for different goals. We have already pointed out a distinction between "professional" and "easy" editors aimed at two different classes of users. Some editors have been designed to serve the composer in a MIDI studio. They allow note input from a MIDI source, such as a musical keyboard or a sequencer file. Once the score is prepared, they can play it by transcribing it into MIDI codes sent to a synthesizer. In such an editor, the quality and accuracy of the printed score may be secondary to the goal of interactive response with aural and visual feedback.

Other music editors aim at latter-day "music engravers," who are not so interested in music creation as they are in notational quality. In such systems, the correctness and "prettiness" of the notation is paramount (Hamel 1987, 1989; Müller and Giuletti 1987). The complexity of the layout process means that computational delays sometimes occur before printing commences. Furthermore, there is not necessarily a possibility for music playback.

Still in the experimental stage are more advanced rule-based editors that incorporate deeper knowledge about musical structure (Böcker and Mahling 1988). These systems link the graphic representation displayed on the screen with underlying musical context (e.g., clef, key signature, harmony). Obviously such constraints make sense only for music that fits a well-known style, so these features should be implemented as "style context" options that can be switched in and out by the user.

Music Printing and Editing: Background

Music written before the fifteenth century was scribed by hand. The introduction of movable-type printing in 1450 had a tremendous impact on the intellectual world. The output of books in the first fifty years after its discovery was greater than in the previous thousand years (Derry and Williams 1960). But music publishing took a long time to adapt to new technology. The first known printed music notation appeared in 1473, but it took a full century after Gutenberg's invention for the first collection of polyphonic music notation using movable type to appear. These were the fifty nine volumes published by Ottaviano de Petrucci at Venice (Grout 1973). Around 1600, music notation evolved into the form known today as common music notation. The practice of music printing did not vary much for a period of about 360 years.

In 1961 Lejaren Hiller and Robert Baker undertook the first experiments in music-printing programs at the University of Illinois, Urbana-Champaign. They used a modified Musicwriter typewriter for both input and output of notation symbols (Hiller and Baker 1965).

One of the first CMN editors based on computer graphics techniques was developed at the National Research Council (NRC) laboratory in Ottawa, Canada in the late 1960s (Pulfer 1971). Musicians entered notes, rests, and other musical symbols using a clavier and a "positioning wheel," similar in function to a mouse (figure 16.4). The NRC system also included a waveform editor and a simple sound synthesizer. Another early CMN editor developed at Harvard University used several display terminals to edit two-voice scores. Musicians entered a score via a menu selection method and could play back the score with square-wave sound synthesis (Cantor 1971). These experiments tested the waters of music-editing technology, but it was only in the 1970s that practical systems emerged.

Mainframe-based Music Editors

Some music editors of the 1970s ran on the mainframe computers of the time. These giant and extremely expensive computers served dozens of users at a time under time-sharing operating systems.

To enter music into Leland Smith's music printing program MS (Smith 1973) developed at Stanford University, musicians typed command scripts. That is, each music symbol had a corresponding textual representation. Although it had a reputation of being not easy to use, MS was a powerful music printing system from the standpoint of notational flexibility. (See examples in Roads 1985a.) In particular, it allowed musicians to create new symbols and customize score layout. These features were later taken up in Smith's program Score, implemented on personal computers. Score is interactive: users can adjust the score directly on a display screen. The program

Figure 16.4   One of the earliest graphical music notation editors, developed at the National Research Council, Canada, in the late 1960s (described in Pulfer 1971). Notice that the operator is using positional controllers, rather than the alphanumeric keyboard to select and edit notes.

Figure 16.5 Dataland Scan-note system score printout on a large-format pen plotter (1978).

offers many features, such as horizontal and vertical justification, that have made it the choice of some publishers.

Donald Byrd's experimental SMUT (System for Music Translation), was a batch-oriented music printing program originally developed at Indiana University (Byrd 1974, 1977, 1984). SMUT accepted musical data encoded in the Mustran language. Its strong suit was device independence. That is, the program, written in the Fortran language, was portable to an extraordinarily wide range of computers and printers. (As a proof of its portability, Kimball Stickney once demonstrated a version of SMUT he had adapted to plot music notation on a tiny cash register printer interfaced to a large mainframe computer!)

Some of the first commercial music printing systems include Dal Molin's Musicomp (Dal Molin 1978), La Ma de Guido (Hand of Guido, Barcelona), and Dataland's Scan-Note system (*Computer Music Journal* 1979) developed by Mogens Kjaer in Aarhus, Denmark (figure 16.5). Using a combination of manual and automatic methods, these large systems produced output that rivaled hand-engraved quality in many respects. Music publishers starting using these services for score production in the late 1970s.

Minicomputer-based Music Editors

By the late 1970s, a handful of research groups had implemented experimental interactive editors for minicomputers running the UNIX operating system environment. These included Ludwig (Reeves et al. 1979) and Scriva (Buxton 1979; Buxton et al. 1981) developed at the University of Toronto, and MIT's prototype Nedit (Wallraff 1979b). A major topic of research at the time was to find the best way to enter notes and rests—whether from a musical keyboard, menus and mouse, an alphanumeric keyboard command, or symbols manually scribbled with a pointing device. No "best way" for all circumstances has emerged; one can find all four ways in current music editors.

Early editors suffered from severe limitations. They were all implemented on slow and extremely memory deficient minicomputers. The programs ran in a time-sharing environment (i.e., more than one user per machine) using *vector display* screens. Vector displays draw objects as a set of connected lines. Today virtually all displays are based on the principle of *bit-mapped raster display*. In a bit-mapped system, each dot (or *pixel*) on the screen maps to a word in a graphics memory. Bit-mapped systems are faster and more flexible than the vector displays they replaced.

Workstation-based Editors

A new generation of CMN editors appeared in the early 1980s. Designs based on *workstation* computers showed how to create more sophisticated editors. Workstation computers are single-user systems, typically connected to other computers via a *local area network* (see chapter 22). William Kornfeld's experimental MUZACS editor, implemented on a Lisp Machine at the MIT Artificial Intelligence Laboratory, demonstrated in 1980 the power of bit-mapped graphics in CMN editing.

The Mockingbird CMN editor, created at Xerox's Palo Alto Research Center (PARC), ran on an especially powerful workstation in its day, the Xerox Dorado. The program's speed and impressive graphical displays stunned musicians when it was demonstrated in 1981 (Maxwell and Ornstein 1983; Roads 1981b). Mockingbird was designed exclusively for piano notation (figure 16.6). In a typical session, the musician entered part of a piece by playing it on a musical keyboard. The score was displayed in a kind of piano-roll notation with staves. That is, each notehead was positioned on a stave without stems, flags, or other markings. The musician then edited the score using menu selection techniques to modify the displayed

Figure 16.6   Example of music printing using the Mockingbird score editor.

representation, adding measure lines, time signatures, key information, note stems, beams, and rests.

Mockingbird was never made available commercially. However, the Synclavier Music Engraving System, whose development began about the same time, offered high-quality music printing (figure 16.7) and could be purchased as an adjunct to the New England Digital Synclavier II synthesizer.

Score Editing and Printing on Personal Computers

After prototype CMN editors proved the viability of the concept, their features were incorporated into programs for low-cost personal computers. Development has been rapid since that time. The first generation of music editors appeared in 1985, with such programs as Professional Composer, Score, Personal Composer, and Deluxe Music Construction Set. By 1988, a second wave of editors appeared, including the programs Finale, Note-Writer, and HB-Engraver. These offered improved print quality, notational flexibility, and the ability to transcribe score data from a MIDI source.

Functionality of CMN Editors

The functionality of music notation editors can be divided into six classes of operations, explained in table 16.2: setup, raw note entry, editing music data, text data entry, printing, and playback.

Entering notes may be as simple as selecting a symbol from a menu (figure 16.8) or playing on a music keyboard. The distinction between "raw note entry" and "editing music data" in table 16.2, however, indicates that note data are just the starting point in preparing a finished score.

Music notation editors continue to evolve. See Yavelow (1992) for a comprehensive survey of available CMN editors, comparing them on a feature-by feature basis. Although focused on Apple Macintosh editors, much of his analysis is applicable to editors running on other platforms. Correira's (1991) survey of notation editors crosses many platforms. The annual reports by Hewlett and Selfridge-Field catalog ongoing progress in this domain.

Music Font Resolution

The print quality of notation programs improved greatly in 1986 with the introduction of the PostScript music font Sonata, designed by Cleo Huggins of Adobe Systems. By now, a number of other PostScript music fonts are available. These fonts are *scalable*. This means that only the outline of the

Choeur des Fileuses

FRANZ LISZT

Figure 16.7   Score printed by the Synclavier Music Engraving System.

Table 16.2   Functionality of common music notation editors

Setup

Set clef, time signature (possibly complex, such as 2 + 3/4), and key signature

Set score layout on page (number of staves, adjust margins, page size)

Specify system bracket style and clefs

Raw note entry

Music symbol entry from alphanumeric keyboard, menus, special command keys, optical score reader, MIDI input device, other MIDI source such as a sequencer file or algorithmic composition program

Editing music data

Cut, copy, paste of selected symbols, measures, and regions

Cut, copy, paste of selected items into a draw program for nonstandard scores

Edit note stems (up or down, no stems, stem between staves)

Edit beaming between notes, including tuplets

Edit ties , slurs, and phrase marks

Edit system breaks

Edit a voice or part alone and afterward remerge the voice with the full score

Number or label measures

Place chord symbols over staves

Adjust spacing (compress, expand, add or delete white space)

Edit the parameters of music symbols:

Note heads—head type, x and y offset, dots, accents

Note stems—offset and length

Note flags—width and style

Tremolo marks

Note beams—width, slope, offset

Ties—curvature, offsets, width

Slurs—slope, offset, line width

Transpose pitches by clef, chromatically, diatonically, enharmonically, or by mode

Design custom symbols for unconventional scores

Zoom into the the score to make fine adjustments on elements such as slurs; zoom out to adjust global layout

Text entry

Choose fonts

Enter title, lyrics, and expressive markings and annotations

Printing

Set characteristics of printing (reduction, printer type. etc.)

Print whole score

Table 16.2 (cont.)

Print selected pages or selected regions

Extract and print a part alone

Playback

Playback selected region or voice at specified tempo and amplitude via MIDI

Adjust tuning for playback

Map dynamic markings to specific decibel levels

Map selected region to a MIDI output channel (MIDI orchestration)

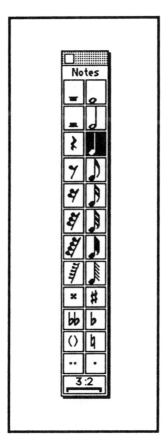

Figure 16.8   Palette of note and rest symbols from the Passport Designs Encore program.

font is stored in computer memory—as a set of mathematical curves that can be scaled to any size with minimum error. Thus the outline adjusts to whatever the size and *resolution* of the device on which the font appears.

Resolution is often expressed in terms of *dots* or *pixels per inch* (or centimeter). On an inexpensive display screen with a resolution less than 75 dots per inch, for example, certain symbols appear jagged. A difficult test case for printer resolution is long and slightly angled note beams (Stickney 1987). For normal size music printing, "high-resolution" without "jaggies" (jagged edges in supposedly smooth curved shapes) requires a printer capable of packing over 1000 dots into a line an inch long. Some phototypesetting machines can print over 2500 dots per inch.

Automatic Transcription

A potentially timesaving feature of many CMN editors is *automatic transcription* of performed music. In the usual case, a musician performs on a musical keyboard along with a metronome generated by the notation program. But the note data can also come from other sources, including any MIDI controller (see chapter 14), or files in the Standard MIDI File (SMF) format (see chapter 21). The possibility of reading SMF means that the output of virtually any program that generates MIDI data can be fed to a notation editor. This includes sequencers and algorithmic composition programs, among others.

Automatic Transcription of Keyboard Music: Background

Automatic transcription of performed music played on a clavier dates back centuries before electronic computers. A mechanism for recording the time of key depressions and their durations was developed by Père Marie Dominique Joseph Engramelle (1727–1781) and documented in his text *La Tonotechnie ou l'Art de Noter les Cylindres* (1775). Keystrokes were inscribed in real time on paper in a piano roll form of notation. This recording could be transcribed to common music notation by a musician (Leichtentritt 1934). By 1747 the Reverend Creed of London presented a paper to the British Royal Society demonstrating the possibility of automatic music transcription from keyboard improvisation. The German musical engineers J. F. Unger and J. Hohlfeld first implemented such a system—attached to a harpsichord—in 1752 (Boalch 1956; Buchner 1978).

Over two centuries later, a computerized keyboard transcription system at the University of Utah used a minicomputer to scan an organ manual, capture keystrokes, and display rudimentary music notation (Ashton 1971; Knowlton 1971, 1972; see also Ben Daniel 1983).

Practical Issues in Automatic Transcription

When a performer plays on a MIDI instrument, a microprocessor inside the instrument is transmitting control information such as "note C3 played at time 23:39:67 at velocity 20 on channel 1." The task of the transcription program is to segment these data into musical time units such as beats and measures and convert them into graphical commands for the display screen.

Human performance is not metrically perfect. Small deviations from constant note durations are typical. If the note data as performed are transcribed literally, the result is unreadable (figure 16.9). Thus the temporal *quantization factor* is an important setup parameter. The quantization factor sets the minimum note duration to be transcribed. This causes the program to ignore small variations in note and rest durations.

Given the current state of the art, a reference beat is a necessity for accurate automatic music transcription. To allow flexibility, some programs let users tap their own beat along with the music. Transcription without any metronome source is a difficult problem for a computer. In effect, the computer must "find the beat" and "tap its foot" to the rhythm while transcribing. For more on this research topic, see chapter 12 (see also Rowe 1975; Chafe et al. 1982; Foster et al. 1982; Piszczalski and Galler 1977; Piszczalski et al. 1981; Stautner 1983; Schloss 1985).

Even with a reference beat and a reasonable quantization factor, the result of automatic transcription inevitably requires manual editing (figure 16.10). Some programs transcribe only pitches and do not attempt to parse the rhythmic structure. Other typical problems include colliding symbols, errors in rhythmic parsing, lack of recognition of key signature and meter

Figure 16.9 When the quantization factor is a sixty-fourth note, a half note must last precisely as long as sixteen tied sixty-fourth notes or it is transcribed "incorrectly." This figure shows the transcription that results when the duration is only fifteen sixty-fourth notes long. If an entire performance is transcribed this way, the notation becomes unreadable.

Figure 16.10 Difference between transcribed and final score, F. Mendelssohn, *Six Songs Without Words,* Op. 19, no. 2. (*a*) Score as transcribed automatically by a notation program. (*b*) Final score as corrected.

changes, missing dynamic markings and slurs, and aesthetically poor justification (layout and spacing of measures, staves, and systems) (Yavelow 1992).

Custom Symbols and Integration with Graphics Programs

The notational flexibility of a CMN editor can be extended in several ways. Most editors let users import images from graphics (draw and paint) programs into the score; this could include custom symbols or unconventional score elements, such as symbols representing electronic sounds on tape. Some editors let users design libraries of custom music symbols for insertion into a score (figure 16.11).

When the notation program cannot handle the graphical demands of a score, sometimes the best strategy is to use the notation editor only to prepare fragments of notation. These fragments can be arranged in a graphics program. There are several ways to extract score fragments from CMN editors, but perhaps the best way is to save the fragments in a scalable graphics format, such as Encapsulated PostScript (EPS). In this case, the music can be scaled to fit whatever size is needed. At this point, we begin to exceed the boundaries of conventional notation. The next section presents the gamut of unconventional score editors.

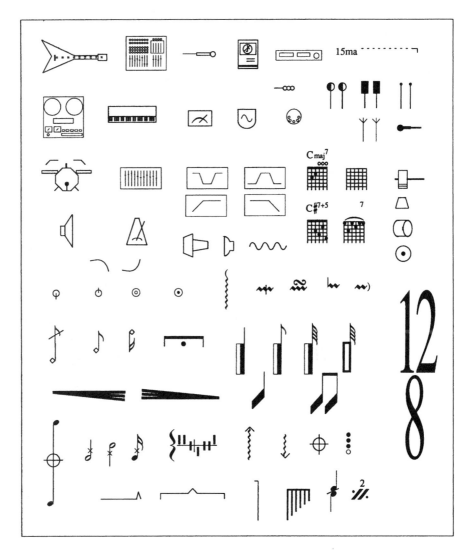

Figure 16.11   Symbols created for a notation editor library. From the NoteWriter II program.

Unconventional Score Editors

Common music notation describes almost all conventional Western music written between 1600 and 1900. As vast as this repertoire is, a considerable amount of notated music falls outside its scope. For occidental music written before 1600, such as medieval music notation, another kind of editor must be used (Crawford and Zeeff 1983; see also the description of the mensural notation program Subtilior Press in Yavelow 1992, pp. 959–960). Many non-European music systems (Indian, Chinese, Japanese, Indonesian, for example) require a different set of symbols and conventions from those used in CMN. Some music derives from an aural tradition (including certain forms of African and Native American music) and has never been completely codified.

At the same time, music notation used by composers continues to evolve. In the twentieth century, CMN has been extended in many directions. Musical imagination ranges far beyond the precepts of common music notation (figure 16.12). A catalog of scores that use unconventional notation could fill a library. John Cage's book *Notations* (1969), for example, contains score fragments by 269 composers, approximately one-third of whom do not use conventional staved notation. (See also Karkoschka 1966).

Criticisms of Common Music Notation

Plain CMN has been bypassed by many composers. The reasons are several:

CMN is biased toward pitch and duration of notes, to the detriment of other facets of music. Its pitch and time representations are limited to equal-tempered pitches (or offsets therefrom), fractional durations of a single geometric series (1/4, 1/8, 1/16, etc.), and pulsed rhythms (see the critique in Stone 1963).

CMN has few provisions for the representation of timbre and does not represent spatial trajectories. The note concept is a single-event abstraction and does not account for the mutating multievent sound complexes possible with computer music. Synthesis parameters, for example, are difficult to represent in CMN, such as multiple envelopes on sound parameters.

CMN addresses only one level of musical form; it was not designed to represent an overview of high-level musical structure; neither is it possible to look below the level of a note to examine the details of the evolving sound structure.

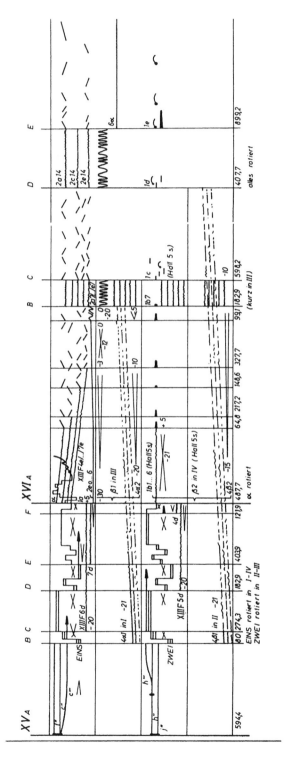

Figure 16.12 Example of unconventional music notation. Score excerpt from Karlheinz Stockhausen's *Kontakte* (1960) for electronic tape. (Copyright 1968 by Universal Edition (London) Ltd., London. Copyright renewed. All rights reserved. Used by permission of European American Music Distributors Corporation, sole U.S. and Canadian agent for Universal Edition London.)

Musicians who work with improvised music have little need of a strict notation system, except to document a recorded improvisation.

Sequencers and synthesis languages allow alphanumerical or gestural input; a CMN editor is not a necessity for editing music data.

These reasons all boil down to the truism that CMN evolved to match conventional European concert performance practices. CMN notation is a framework for an interpreter working within an established tradition. In today's studios, however, the composer often plays the role of the interpreter. The expanded palette of sound and the changing performance possibilities of computer music prompt a need for new notation schemes.

New Notation Editors

New notation schemes serve at least four functions:

1. To aid the composer in visualizing a work during its creation—notation as an expressive medium

2. To specify parameters for sound synthesis—notation as synthesis specification

3. To convey instructions to a musician in concert—notation as performance guide

4. To serve as documentation—notation as a reading score for study and teaching purposes

Several computer-based editors for unconventional music notation have been implemented. One of the first, Scriva (Buxton et al. 1978a; Buxton 1979; Buxton et al. 1981), was a remarkably advanced editor for its time. Scriva permitted several types of notation:

1. CMN mode with or without staves

2. Piano roll notation, with or without staves

3. Envelope notation, showing each event's amplitude envelope, with or without staves

4. Iconic notation, indicating the timbre of each event by icons

Scriva provided various means of specifying the scope of an editing operation. In the simplest technique, the user encircled the notes to be affected using a hand-held pointer, as shown in figure 16.13. A similar notion of selection was taken up later in other programs.

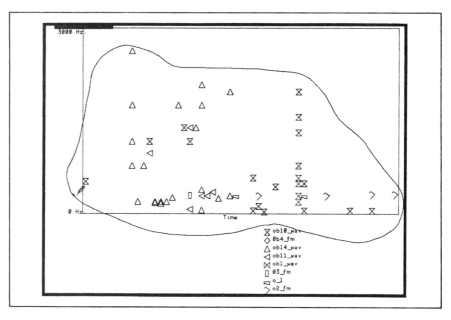

Figure 16.13   Iconic timbre representation in the Scriva editor, showing a fragment of the composition *nscor* (1980) by Curtis Roads.

Notation as Graphics

Chapter 8 discusses several graphics-based approaches to sound synthesis, where composers can literally draw sonic events on a display screen. Of these, the UPIC (Unité Polyagogique Informatique du CEMAMu) system developed at the Centre d'Etudes Mathematiques et Automatiques Musicales (CEMAMu) in Paris is the most advanced (Xenakis 1992; Lohner 1986; Marino, Raczinski, and Serra 1990; see the description of the system in chapter 8).

Graphics-based editors offer the ultimate in notational flexibility. For example, the NoteWriter program (Hamel 1987, 1989) treats the score page as a canvas to be decorated by the user with musical symbols provided by the program. Users can also draw new symbols or import an image in standard "paint program" format to incorporate into the score.

There is no reason why draw and paint programs cannot be used alone to create new styles of notation. Indeed, the integration of traditional notation, waveforms, spectrograms, new icons, and unusual graphics is probably best handled by a professional drawing or drafting program.

Notation from Sound

One trend in notation programs is transcription from sound. Chapters 12 and 13 present some of the difficult issues surrounding transcription into traditional notation. Computer-aided transcription into nontraditional notation may be more tractable, to the extent that stays close to the representations emitted by analysis tools.

Figure 16.14 depicts one of the Pierre Schaeffer's experiments with *notation concrète,* machine-aided transcription of electroacoustic music, starting from a trace of amplitude versus time (Schaeffer and Moles 1952).

Spectrum analysis—plotting the frequency domain—opens up another class of possibilities. Goffredo Haus's EMPS notation system (Haus 1983) started from a computer-based spectrum analysis. This system stands as one of the few attempts to transcribe the sound of computer-synthesized music into a reading score by means of sound analysis. Haus developed a graphic notation in which sounds in different registers appear as distinct symbols, and amplitudes are plotted as closely spaced histograms (figure 16.15). The technique is similar to that used in the transcription of Gyorgy Ligeti's electronic music composition *Artikulation* (Ligeti and Wehinger 1970).

The Acousmographe, developed at the Groupe de Recherches Musicales by Olivier Koechlin and Hughes Vinet (Bayle 1993), represents a more recent effort to transcribe electroacoustic music starting from a spectrogram representation (figure 16.16). A spectrogram projects the frequency versus-time output of a mathematical operation—the *short-time Fourier transform* (STFT, see chapter 13 and appendix A). The displays projected by the STFT are sensitive to setup parameters such as the analysis *window length* (see chapter 13) and in any case do not necessarily correspond to what the composer has specified or what listeners hear. The Acousmagraphe lets the user inscribe a library of color graphic symbols onto a spectrogram, condensing the display into a more readable and expressive form.

MIDI Sequence Editing

A sequencer is a type of recording system. Instead of recording the waveform of a sound, however, a sequencer records the control or performance data needed to regenerate a series of musical events on one or more synthesizers or other MIDI devices. The performance data include the time and velocity of key depressions, position changes in vibrato wheels, footpedals, knobs, buttons, and so on. Chapter 15 recounted the history of sequencers and described their features from the perspective of performance. This sec-

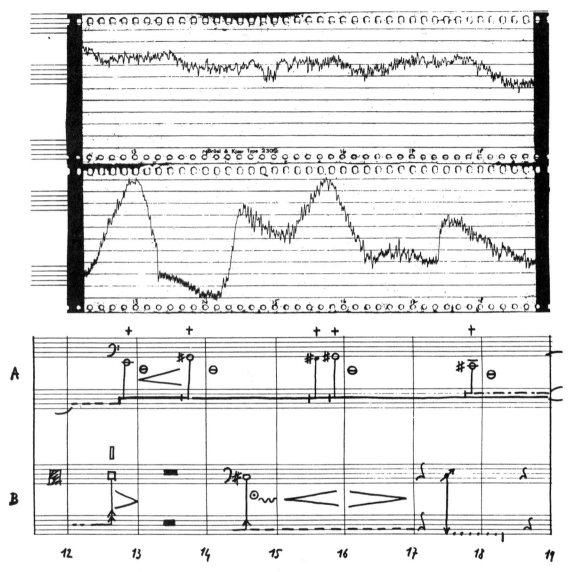

Figure 16.14 Extract of Pierre's Schaeffer's machine-aided transcription of an *étude* of musique concrète. The upper curve is a Bathygramme, an intensity versus-time trace. The lower portion shows Schaeffer's transcription into staved notation. (Courtesy of the Groupe de Recherches Musicales, Paris.)

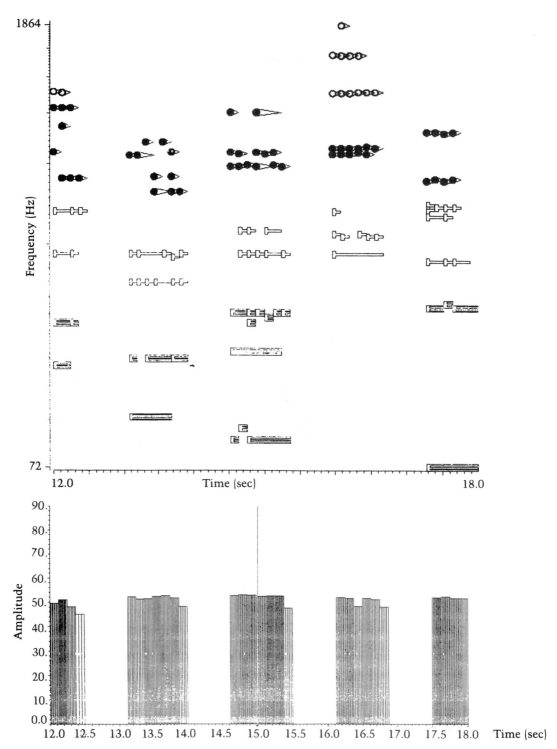

Figure 16.15 Graph of the melody/harmony (top) and the spectral density (bottom) of a 6-second excerpt of a sound example by James Dashow, with sound analysis and printing using the EMPS system (Haus 1983).

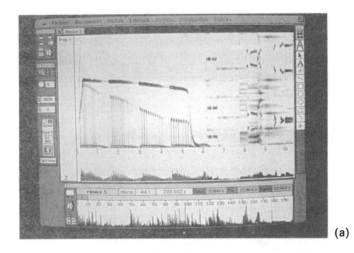

(a)

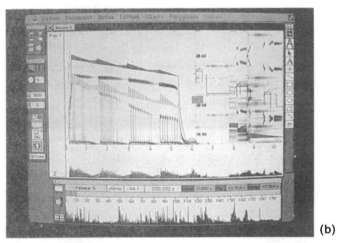

(b)

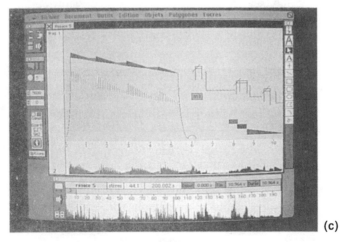

(c)

Figure 16.16 Acousmagraphic notation of *Rosace V* by François Bayle. Transcription realized by Dominique Besson. (*a*) Original sonogram of sound fragment. (*b*) Inscription of graphical symbols onto the sonogram, according to cues heard by the ear. (*c*) Final symbolic notation. (Courtesy of the Groupe de Recherches Musicales, Paris.)

tion focuses on their editing features. (See Yavelow 1992 for a feature-by feature comparison of eighteen sequence editors. For more on MIDI itself, see chapter 21.)

Channel, Track, and Pattern Organization

The MIDI specification provides for sixteen *channels*—addresses from which musical data can be received and to which they can be sent. With special hardware and software, many more channels are possible (see chapter 21). In addition to channels, MIDI sequencers use tracks and patterns (or *subsequences*) as organizing concepts.

Tracks are arbitrary units of musical organization in a sequencer; they typically refer to the separate recording takes or layers of a composition. In practice, the scope of a track varies depending on the musician and the sequencer. Some sequencers let musicians choose whether to record the channel data associated with incoming events. Without channel data, a track is an undifferentiated stream of MIDI events. This leaves room for the composer to assign the channels on playback, possibly mapping more than one channel to an event. Hence, a "track-oriented" sequencer prompts the composer to reorchestrate the material.

How do musicians use the track concept? Some use a track for each synthesizer voice, separate tracks for each controller message type—volume pedal, pitch bend, modulation wheel, etc.—and separate tracks for other MIDI-controlled equipment (such as effects units). MIDI drum programmers may segregate each voice of a percussion part to a separate track in order to customize each voice's rhythmic "feel" through quantization (see the discussion of quantization later). Another way to use tracks is to keep different versions (takes) of a musical line in separate tracks, with the idea of selecting one track for the final mix at a later stage of composition. In any case, it is common for a simple sequence to consume 50 or more tracks. Track-oriented editing operations in many sequencers apply to every event in a track (e.g., "transpose track 38 by a whole tone").

"Channel-oriented" sequencers record channel assignment data within a track. This is useful when recording an ensemble of devices transmitting on separate channels into one track. This data can be "unmerged" later, with each channel going to a separate track to separate out melodic lines, for example. The advantage of a channel-oriented approach is that one can record in a single pass what might take up to sixteen passes with a track-oriented approach. Many sequencers have operations that can be applied to every event assigned to a particular channel (e.g., "increase the amplitude of channel 7 by 6 dB").

Pattern orientation means that the data can be broken into subsequences within a sequence. A pattern can be looped, played back in combination with other patterns, or triggered to play from an external event. Patterns or subsequences are a unit of organization in many sequencers. This means that one can add, delete, insert, transpose, or operate in other ways on patterns the same as note events.

Sharing Sequence Data between Programs

Since each music program has special strengths, it is often useful to transfer sequences between two programs. This can be done in two ways: in non-real time via the Standard MIDI File (SMF) formats that most sequencers read, or real-time transfer from one program to another. Depending on the compatibilities of the programs this may be straightforward or difficult. For example, SMF comprises three formats, Type 0, 1, and 2, and not all sequencers support all three formats. Only Type 2 files preserve independent track, tempo, and time signature data. (See chapter 21 for more on SMF.) Real-time transfer requires a MIDI driver in the operating system that can accomodate two or more simultaneous MIDI programs. Real-time transfer opens up the possibility of transformation of the data as it is being transferred, using the MIDI-processing capabilities of the receiving program. For example, many of the interactive performance programs discussed in chapter 15 (such as Max) can take in a MIDI sequence and let users transform it in real time.

Representations for Editing

For editing purposes, MIDI information can be displayed in several representations, each of which highlights a particular view on the data. Typical representations include: *event list, piano roll* or "graphical," *common music notation, controller envelope*, and *digital audio waveforms,* discussed in the following sections.

Event Lists

An *event list* representation is an alphanumeric listing of the recorded MIDI data, sorted in time order (figure 16.17). The event list is the most detailed and complete representation so musicians often use it in fine-tuning a sequence. A typical event list will indicate the event type, channel, and data associated with the event, such as the pitches and velocities of note events.

Event	Measure	Chan	Data				
♪	1: 1:072	1	G-2	!80	i64	0: 0:030	
♪	1: 2:048	4	A5	!80	i64	0: 0:030	
♪	1: 2:048	1	D0	!80	i64	0: 0:030	
♪	1: 2:216	1	F#0	!80	i64	0: 0:030	
PC	1: 2:220	1	16				
♪	1: 3:072	1	E5	!80	i64	0: 0:030	
♪	1: 3:192	1	B0	!80	i64	0: 0:030	
♪	1: 4:072	1	G#3	!80	i64	0: 0:015	
♪	2: 1:000	1	A3	!80	i64	0: 0:015	
♪	2: 1:012	1	G3	!80	i64	0: 0:015	
PC	2: 1:048	1	9				
♪	2: 1:072	2	D5	!80	i64	0: 0:120	
♪	2: 1:084	1	A#3	!80	i64	0: 0:015	
♪	2: 1:120	1	E3	!80	i64	0: 0:015	
♪	2: 1:156	1	E3	!80	i64	0: 0:015	
♪	2: 1:168	1	F0	!80	i64	0: 1:000	
♪	2: 1:180	1	A3	!80	i64	0: 0:015	
♪	2: 2:000	1	E3	!80	i64	0: 0:015	
♪	2: 2:000	1	F#3	!80	i64	0: 0:015	
♪	2: 2:012	1	F#3	!80	i64	0: 0:015	
♪	2: 2:024	2	C#6	!80	i64	0: 0:120	
♪	2: 2:060	1	B3	!80	i64	0: 0:015	
♪	2: 2:072	1	D5	!80	i64	0: 1:000	
♪	2: 2:072	1	G#3	!80	i64	0: 0:015	
PC	2: 2:096	1	9				
♪	2: 2:096	1	G1	!80	i64	0: 0:015	
♪	2: 2:108	1	F3	!80	i64	0: 0:015	
♪	2: 2:132	1	E2	!80	i64	0: 0:015	
♪	2: 2:132	1	G#1	!80	i64	0: 0:015	
♪	2: 2:156	1	F#3	!80	i64	0: 0:015	

Toolbar: Goto... Filter Insert: ♪ PC ... ↓ ↓↓ T1

Figure 16.17   MIDI sequencer event list representation showing the type of event, where notes are indicated by the eighth note in the left column, and program change messages are indicated by the letters PC. Also shown is the measure number and exact starting time of the event, along with its channel and associated data. The number "9" highlighted within the program change event at 1:048 indicates "Change to patch 9." It is highlighted because it has been selected for editing. Notice the button for "Filter" at the top. This lets users filter out certain types of data, so that only certain messages appear, such as note messages. The "Insert" button at the top lets users add new events. The icons next to the "Insert" button stand for, from left to right, notes, program changes, pitch bends, controller changes, aftertouch, and key pressure. Screen image from the Passport Pro 4 sequencer.

Piano Rolls

Piano roll notation derives from the days of player pianos, when notes were encoded as punched holes in a roll of thick paper. Individual pitches are laid out vertically, while the start time and duration of events are encoded as a horizontal dot or line, depending on the duration (figure 16.18).

Common Music Notation

Some sequencers perform transcription of MIDI performance data into a more-or-less raw form of common music notation (figure 16.19). For much music, this representation is more direct and evocative than event lists or piano rolls.

Metrical Grids

Some sequencers and most drum machines use a metrical grid to display rhythmic patterns (figure 16.20). The horizontal axis represents time, divided depending on the rhythmic units being edited. That is, a 4/4 measure divided by quarter notes shows four divisions; the same measure divided on a sixteenth-note grid shows sixteen divisions. The vertical axis divides into rows according to the number of percussion instruments.

Some sequencers use a similar but coarser grid to display measures. Each measure is a box; if the box is shaded, it contains an event. This view allows an overview of a large piece. To edit a measure, one can click on its box with the mouse.

Controller Envelopes

Pitch and vibrato wheels, footpedals, and breath controllers, among other devices, generate continuous controller messages. These are essentially envelopes for differents aspects of the sound. Many sequencers display these envelopes graphically as a shape that can be easily edited by hand (figure 16.21).

Graphic Faders

Graphic faders allow control of synthesizer parameters like amplitude. If the sequencer records the fader movements, this allows for a simple form of automated mixing (figure 16.22).

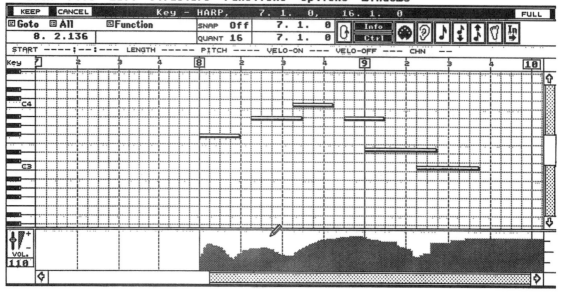

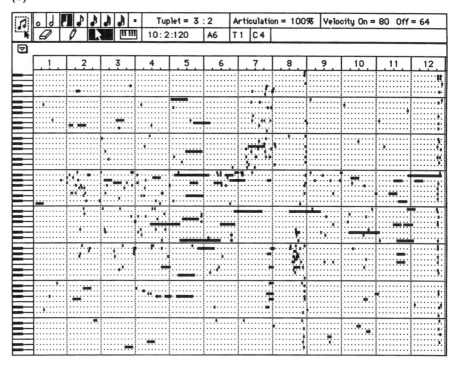

Figure 16.18 Screen image of a MIDI sequencer piano roll notation. Time plots from left to right. Pitch plots along the vertical axis. Notice the piano keyboard to the left, indicating the pitch. (*a*) Zoomed-in view. The envelope below the piano roll notation shows the overall volume and can be edited using a pencil tool. Screen image from Steinberg Cubase sequencer. (*b*) Zoomed-out view of another sequence using the Passport Pro 4 sequencer.

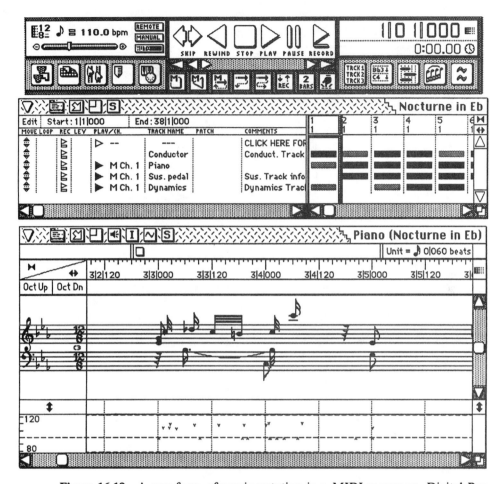

Figure 16.19 A raw form of music notation in a MIDI sequencer, Digital Performer by Mark of the Unicorn. The top window shows the sequencer transport controls (stop, start, record, pause, rewind, skip).

Digital Audio Waveforms

Time-domain images of prerecorded audio waveforms can be displayed alongside MIDI data in some sequencers (figure 16.23). These waveforms typically represent vocals or other microphone-recorded sounds. The waveforms can be moved around the time line and edited using the sound sample editing tools (see the section on sound sample editing later). The graphical representation is convenient for viewing the time correspondence between the pure MIDI data and digital audio waveforms.

(a)

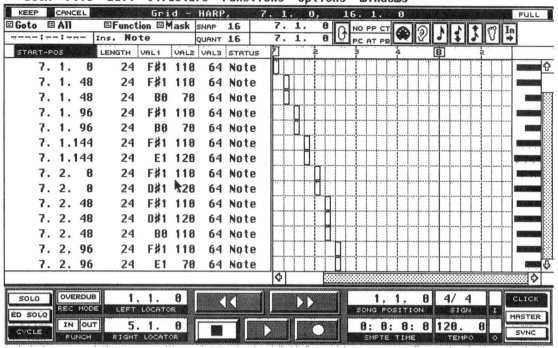

(b)

Tool palette   Instrument, tempo, time signature setting   Metrical grid, divided by 32nd notes

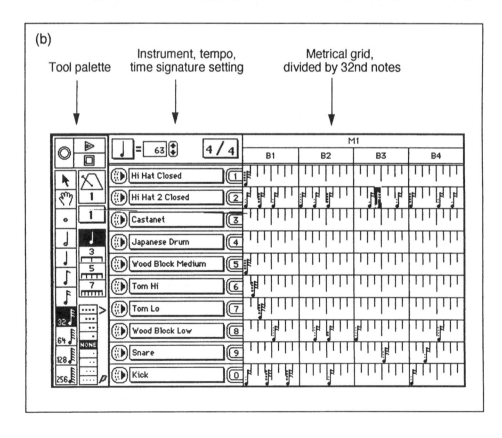

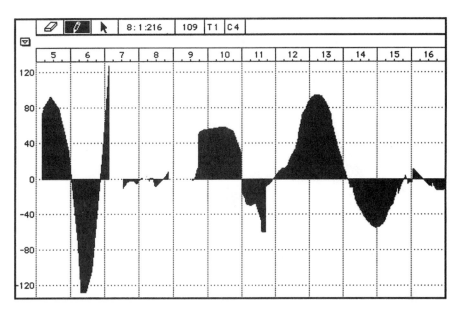

Figure 16.21   Pitch bend controller envelope editor in a MIDI sequencer. These data can be read in from a pitch bend controller, to be edited onscreen, or they can be drawn directly.

Sequence-editing Operations

MIDI sequence editors can operate on individual events or on groups of events defined by common properties such as track, channel, pattern, or other criteria. An important issue in sequence editing is how these edits are made, for example as *real-time replacement edits* (called "punch-in/punch-out" with reference to editing on analog tape recorders invoked by the Record button), or non-real-time *step mode* or *random-access* edits. In step mode editing, musicians step through a composition one event at a time, adding, deleting, or changing events as they go. In random-access editing, musicians can look at a representation of all or part of the sequence (e.g., an event list or a piano roll) and edit material at any point.

Figure 16.20   Metrical grid representations (*a*) The right half of this screen image shows the metrical grid in Steinberg Cubase sequencer. This type of representation, which divides each measure into an equal number of slots, is favored by drum machine programmers and pop music producers. The left half is an event list representation. (*b*) Metrical grid in the program Different Drummer. The example shows one measure divided into four beats divided into a thirty-second-note grid.

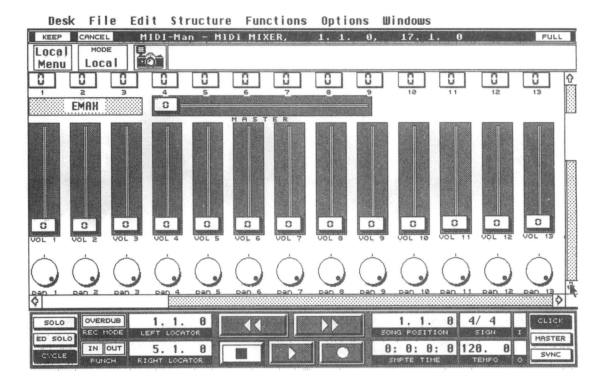

Figure 16.22   Graphical MIDI faders in Steinberg Cubase sequencer. Notice also the rotary pan pot controls.

Besides the usual insert, delete, and copy operations, typical sequence editing operations can be divided into several groups: time, pitch, amplitude, channel, program change, and continuous controller editing. (See chapter 21 for more on these categories of MIDI data.)

Time Editing

Time-editing operations include rhythmic *quantization* and *dequantization*. Quantization means "rounding off" rhythms to align them to a meter, while dequantization or "humanization" does the opposite. Abrupt tempo changes can be inserted at any point, or the music can be made to accelerate or decelerate over a specified duration. *Time offsets,* such as shifting a track by several milliseconds, may lend a different rhythmic feel to a track.

Pitch Editing

Pitch editing can include transposition, pitch bend, or vibrato applied to individual notes or selected regions in a track.

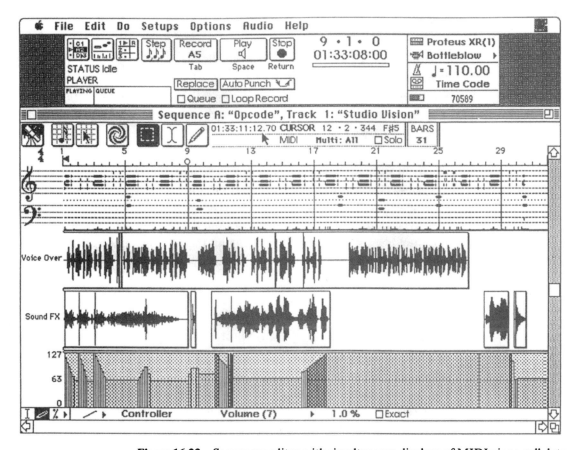

Figure 16.23 Sequencer editor with simultaneous displays of MIDI piano roll data and time-domain audio waveforms. Display created with the Studio Vision program by Opcode Systems.

Amplitude Editing

Following the keyboard bias of MIDI, amplitude editing is usually expressed in terms of *note velocity*—how fast a key was pressed, specified in the range of 0 to 127 MIDI velocity units. Besides note-by note changes, one can compress or expand the velocities in a track or in a selected region. This is similar to compression/expansion in signal processing (see chapter 10), but applied to MIDI velocities instead of samples. Another option is to apply crescendi and diminuendi via a continuous controller envelope from a foot pedal or MIDI fader.

Channel Editing

Channel editing means reassigning the channel data associated with a one or more notes or a track. Since each channel is usually assigned to a different voice or instrument, changing channels is akin to reorchestration.

Program Change Editing

Program change editing refers to the practice of inserting MIDI *program change messages* into a note event list. Program change messages are a way to orchestrate a sequence, since they select the voice or patch to be played on a synthesizer, just as one might do from the front panel. Another use for program change messages is in changing the settings on an effects device, such as a reverberator.

Continuous Controller Editing

We have already mentioned the application of continuous controller editing to pitch and amplitude. Continuous controller data can also be used to vary aspects of timbre in a synthesizer. For example, we might assign a filter setting on a synthesizer voice—such as center frequency—to a continuous controller. Then by editing the envelope for this controller we can vary the center frequency of the filter over time.

Function Editors

Function editors let musicians create and modify waveforms, envelopes, spatial paths, and other functions of time using interactive graphics techniques. Musicians can easily draw or generate the desired waveform interactively by defining a few points (figure 16.24). Function editors are built into many music applications, including sequencers, sound editors, synthesis systems, and patch editors.

Function editors are most useful for creating amplitude and frequency envelopes, since the relation between what is drawn and what is heard is clear. They are less effective in specifying waveforms for oscillators, since it is difficult to predict the spectral content of a given waveform from its visual appearance in the time domain. Two waveforms *A* and *B* can look dissimilar and yet sound exactly the same, because they are the same waveform seen in different phases (figure 16.25).

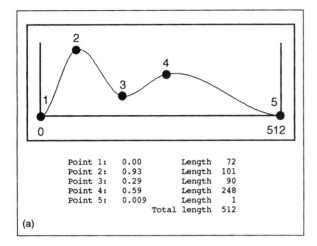

Point 1:   0.00   Length   72
Point 2:   0.93   Length   101
Point 3:   0.29   Length   90
Point 4:   0.59   Length   248
Point 5:   0.009   Length   1
                  Total length   512

(a)

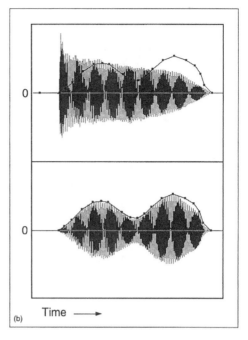

Time ⟶

(b)

Figure 16.24 Function editors. (*a*) Spliner by J. Bellsey lets users design waveforms and envelopes using cubic spline curves. The editor generates a textual description of the curve that is compatible with the GEN waveform functions used in the Csound synthesis language. These data are shown below the envelope. (*b*) Direct reenveloping in a sound editor. The original signal is at the top, shaded in gray. A new amplitude envelope is superposed on it. The lower image shows the newly reenveloped signal after a rescale operation has been performed using the new amplitude envelope.

Function Editors: Background

The first musical application of interactive computer graphics was the GRIN (Graphical Input) program developed at Bell Telephone Laboratories (Mathews and Rosler 1968, 1969). Images drawn on a display screen with a light pen were translated into envelope and waveform definitions for the Music IV sound synthesis language. Mathews and Rosler also used functions to control tempo, metric modulations, and counterpoint.

Another early application of a function editor was the specification of spatial paths in quadraphonic (four-channel) sound systems. Chowning (1971) pioneered this use, which was also pursued by Moore (1983) and Loy (1985a). Such programs let users mark a spatial trajectory; the software fits a smooth curve to the path (figure 16.26). Newer programs offer similar capabilities. (See chapter 11 for more on spatial manipulation of sounds.)

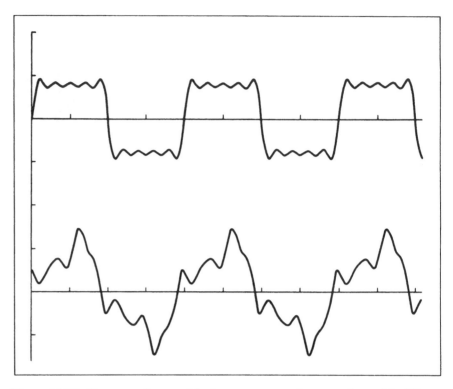

Figure 16.25   Two waveforms with the same spectral content but with different phase relationships among their partials. Two components of the bottom waveform are inverted in phase with respect to the top waveform. They sound identical. (After Plomp 1976.)

Filling Function Tables

Drawing functions by hand is not always an effective means of specifying oscillator waveforms, for the reasons already discussed. Hence it is useful to be able to generate waveform functions by means other than hand-drawing. Many systems have a method of specifying a waveform in the frequency domain via *harmonic addition*. In this technique, the user sees a bar graph where the height of each of the *n* bars represents the strength of each of the *n* harmonics (figure 16.27a). (See figure 1.7 in chapter 1 for more examples of frequency-domain representations.) By motioning up or down with a mouse, the user can change the relative amplitudes of the harmonics. Ideally, the sound changes as the user moves the mouse. Once the desired spectrum is defined, the software calculates the time-domain waveform that reproduces the desired spectrum (figure 16.27b).

Some programs offer similar interfaces for function table-filling based on Chebychev polynomial functions, frequency modulation, or band-limited pulse functions.

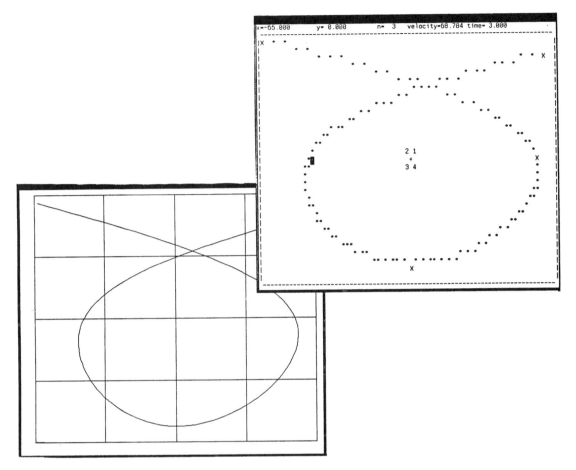

Figure 16.26 Screen images from the sndpth spatial path editor. Top right: points defined by a composer on a four-channel sound path, with speakers in the four corners. Lower left: smooth spatial path interpolated by the sndpth program by D. G. Loy.

A function table contains a line plotted in two dimensions that can be subjected to innumerable distortions. Table 16.3 lists operations available in some function editors. Finally, some editors incorporate a library of function segments that can be spliced into existing functions or concatenated to create new functions (Brandao and Nascimento 1991).

Operations on Waveforms

Many function editors go beyond simple waveform drawing to provide operations on waveforms. A "merge" command, for example, causes two waveform tables to be *crossfaded* (gradually mixed from one to the other); the resultant waveform gradually changes from waveform *A* to waveform

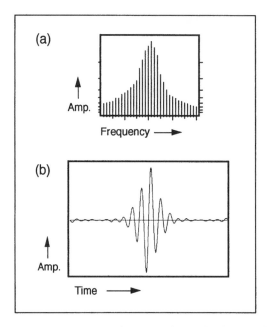

Figure 16.27 Creating waveforms by harmonic addition. (*a*) Histogram of harmonic partials. Each bar represents a harmonic, and the bar's height is the amplitude of the harmonic relative to the others. (*b*) Resultant time-domain waveform.

Table 16.3 Operations on functions

Reverse
Invert
Absolute value
Clip negative
Square
Cube
Shift down
Shift up
Compress
Stretch
Apply window function
Apply comb filter
Smooth table
Normalize

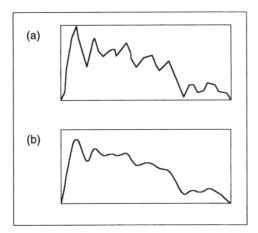

Figure 16.28   Effect of a smoothing operation on a waveform. (*a*) Before smoothing. (*b*) After smoothing.

B. Other common operations include splicing or adding (mixing) of two waveforms. A *smoothing/unsmoothing* function in an editor can also be useful. With a smoothing operation, a jagged envelope "melts" into a similar envelope with rounder curves (figure 16.28). The unsmoothing operation turns a continuous function into a jagged one.

Patch Editors

A *patch* or *voice editor* lets musicians adjust the parameters of a synthesis instrument, preferably while listening to the sound. The term "patch" originates from the modular analog synthesizers of the 1960s and 1970s, where a patch was a configuration of modules interconnected with *patch cords*. Instead of pulling out patch cords and repatching like a modular analog synthesizer, however, a patch editor simply tunes a patch that has been programmed already at the factory. This is a *preset patch,* or just a *preset.* The importance of patch editing today is underscored by the flood of commercial software that offers the same synthesizer voice settings used by popular artists on their hit records.

Patch Editors versus Instrument Editors

We draw a distinction between a patch editor and an *instrument editor* (discussed later). A patch editor allows variations of a preset patch, while an instrument editor lets users design new patches out of a collection of signal-processing modules.

A gray area between patch editors and instrument editors exists in synthesizers that allow a limited amount of repatching. Some patch editors let one reroute modulation signals, for example. Another patch editor offers a collection of patch templates; users select the modules used at each stage of the patch.

In general, patch editors work with *fixed-architecture* DSPs, while modular instrument editors work with programmable software synthesis and *variable-architecture* DSPs. (See chapter 20 for more on the distinction between fixed and variable DSP architecture.)

Graphical Patch Editors

Modular analog synthesizers gave the musician a "hands-on" approach to exploring the possibilities of a particular synthesis "patch." Although the hands-on approach offered immediate feedback, it also had drawbacks. In analog synthesizers, each sound parameter required a separate knob or switch, and each interconnection between sound-processing modules required a patch cord. For example, a Moog III or Arp 2500 synthesizer manufactured in the early 1970s had about 150 rotary knobs and 35 switches. A typical Buchla 200 system had almost 300 knobs and 100 switches. As many as 30 to 50 patch cords might be used for a single patch. Once a setting was changed, there was no way to store and recall it. Repatching and retuning could take hours, without guaranteeing reproducibility of the original sound.

In the digital domain, computer graphics, display panels, and multiplexed, multiple-function controls can greatly reduce the need for so many knobs and switches. A *multiplexed* knob can be switched under software control so that one knob can control any number of parameters, either one at a time or all at the same time. For example, a Yamaha DX7 synthesizer digital synthesizer has just two linear sliders and 40 switches. In one mode, the switches selected preset voices. In another mode, the same switches let musicians customize the amount of pitch bend, portamento, and determine the effects of the various input devices such as the footpedal and breath controller. Computer memories make it possible to save critically tuned settings for later recall at the touch of a switch.

Examples of Patch Editors

The Toronto Structured Sound Synthesis Project's (SSSP) Objed "sound object editor" program, operational between 1978 and 1983, was one of the first programs to use interactive graphics techniques for patch editing

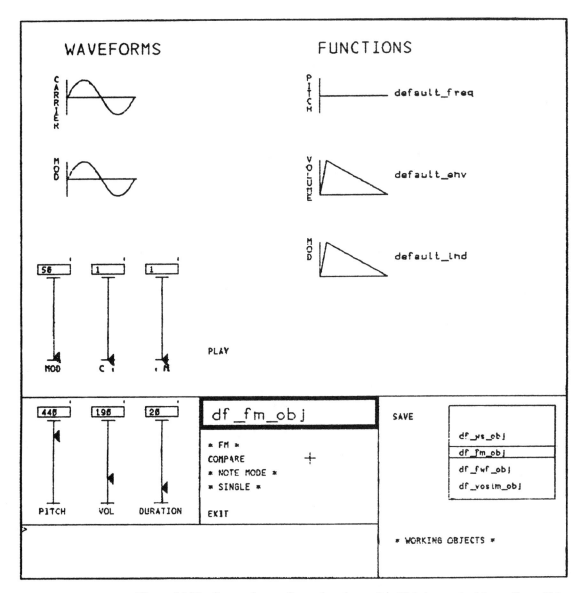

Figure 16.29   Screen image from the pioneering Objed sound object editor. This screen shows an editing panel for a simple frequency modulation voice. The carrier and modulator frequencies are shown in the upper left corner. Amplitude and modulation index envelopes are to the right of the waveforms. Other parameters are manipulated by linear faders on the screen. The name of the voice being edited is shown in the lower center, and the directory in which these voice settings are saved in shown at the lower right.

(Buxton et al. 1982). To edit a frequency modulation (FM) instrument, for example, the musician could graphically manipulate all the waveforms and envelopes associated with the patch (figure 16.29). (See chapter 6 for a description of FM.)

A command to edit a waveform opened a window to a function editor of the type described in the previous section. By moving a mouse a musician could change other parameters by means of graphic potentiometers on the display screen.

One of the premises behind Objed was that musical context is extremely important in tuning a sound. That is, we need to be able to hear a sound in the context in which it is to be used. Objed provided three playback contexts for tuning sounds: a *repeat mode* in which a sound is repeated from beginning to end until the user signals it to stop, a *steady state mode* in which a sound is held constant except for changes the user makes, and a s*core mode* in which a sound orchestrates a score provided by the user.

MIDI-based patch editors for commercial synthesizers are widely available. These systems work by manipulating *system exclusive data* (see chapter 21). In particular, they edit a representation of the synthesizer's internal

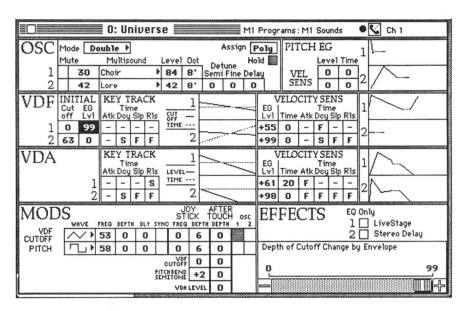

Figure 16.30 Screen image from a patch editor program for the Korg M1 sample player. The four main windows provide parameter and function editors for the oscillators (OSC), variable digital filters (VDF), amplitude envelope generators (variable digital amplifier or VDA), modulators (MODS), and effects. Subwindows for pitch envelope generator (EG), filter velocity sensitivity (SENS), and amplitude velocity sensitivity are also shown. All of the envelopes and numerical parameters are editable. At the bottom right is a graphical fader.

memory, in the form of *bulk patch data*—the parameter settings of all the voices in the synthesizer (figure 16.30). For example, all of the editing information for the 32-patch Yamaha DX7 synthesizer could be completely contained within its 4096-byte bulk patch data. All 158 parameters for each patch could be stored in a mere 128 bytes; some parameters took only a single bit to store, while others took up to a byte.

Instrument Editors

An instrument editor lets users design sound synthesis instruments by interconnecting signal-processing modules. The signal-processing modules are the equivalent of the *unit generators* discussed in chapter 1, including oscillators, filters, envelope generators, and so on. Although the result of the editing—the instrument—is sometimes called a patch, we have already defined a patch editor as a program used to tune the parameters of a predefined instrument.

Instrument Editors: Background

As explained in chapter 1, Max Mathews invented the unit generator concept for his music synthesis language Music III in 1963, and he extended it in successive programs leading to Music V (Mathews 1969). Parallel to this, Robert Moog and others were inventing new hardware modules for analog voltage-controlled synthesizers. These systems defined the basic concept of a modular instrument, as a specific configuration of interconnected modules—a synthesis patch.

A precursor of today's graphical instrument editors was the MITSYN system developed by William Henke, a speech scientist at the Massachusetts Institute of Technology (Henke 1970). The MITSYN program was designed for scientific applications, but it was also used in compositions. As seen in figure 16.31, a user could connect the output of a *pulsetrain generator* (which produces a buzzy sound like that of a human glottis) to a filter, in order to create a vocal-like sound.

Oedit, a demonstration program developed at the MIT in the mid-1970s, borrowed ideas from MITSYN and was intended for music sound synthesis. Although it was not general enough to be called an instrument editor, the Reved editor implemented at Stanford by Ken Shoemake was similar in its interaction style to MITSYN. Reved was designed for creating digital reverberators. The program let users patch together a collection of signal-processing modules, in particular, allpass and comb filters. Users could

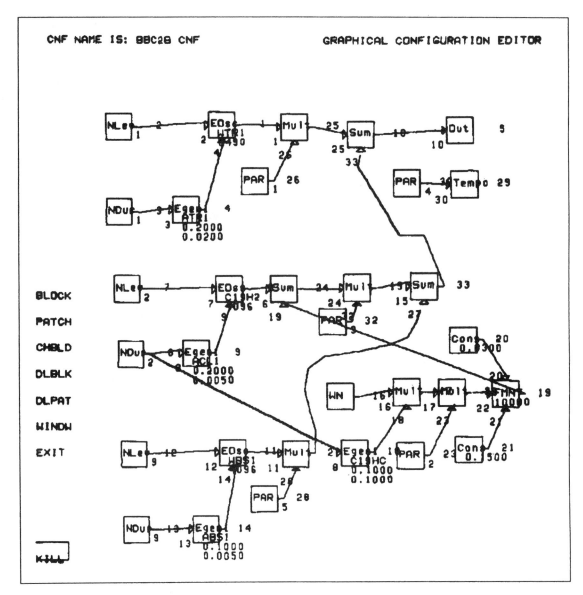

Figure 16.31 "Graphical Configuration Editor" of the MITSYN program for graphical interconnection of signal-processing modules (ca. 1978). The image is typical of vector display screens.

submit an impulse wave to their reverberator and view an analysis of its frequency response. Within Reved, a user could tune the delay times and filter coefficients to achieve the desired effect.

Present Modular Instrument Editors

Today we find modular instrument editors in both commercial and experimental systems (Sandel 1989; Wilkinson et al. 1989; Tarabella and Bertini 1989; Lent, Pinkston, and Silsbee 1989; Puckette 1991; Armani et al. 1992). The starting point for these editors is the modular patching found in the Music *N* model described in chapter 17. That is, musicians patch together modules to make a synthesis instrument. Some of the modules generate signals (e.g., oscillators and noise generators), while others process signals (e.g., filters and delay units). Depending on the system, the code defining the synthesis instrument may run in the host computer or be transferred to a high-speed signal processor. An example of the latter approach would be a DSP card plugged into the host computer.

Front Ends versus Self-contained Synthesis Packages

Some instrument editors serve as "front-end" programs, that is, graphical interfaces, to traditional Music *N* software. The front-end programs allow users to design a patch graphically. They then translate a graphical patch into an equivalent text code that conforms to the syntax of a Music *N* language. This code may or may not be run on the same computer that created the graphical patch.

Other instrument editors act as self-contained synthesis packages that can generate sound files and transfer them to samplers. The self-contained packages may add new features to the Music *N* model, such as analysis/resynthesis, sophisticated waveform editing, file transfer to and from samplers, and exotic signal processing modules.

Examples of Modular Instrument Editors: Music V Graphic Editor and Turbosynth

This section presents short examples of both the front-end and the self-contained types of modular instrument editors. The Music V Graphical Editor (Sandel 1989) provides a graphical front end for the venerable Music V language (Mathews 1969). Figure 16.32a shows a simple UG network created by the system, while figure 16.32b shows the Music V code that the graphical editor generates. Notice the way that pfields are depicted in figure

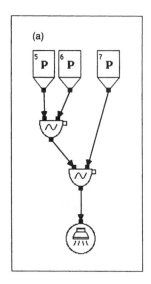

(a)

(b)

```
INS  0 1 ;

 OSC  P5  P6  B2  F6  P50 ;
 OSC  B2  P7  B2  F1  P49 ;
 OUT  B2  B1 ;


COM  GEN functions for the instrument ;

COM  Modulation envelope ;
 GEN 0 1 6 256 0 1 500 64 500 128 500 193 0 256 ;

COM  Pure sine wave of 4096 samples ;
 GEN 0 2 1 4096 1000 1000 1 ;


COM  Conversion routines for the pfields ;

COM  P5 Amplitude ;
COM Conversion 200: from dB to linear amplitude ;
 PLS 0 1 1 205 ;

COM  P6 Modulation frequency ;
COM Conversion 0: from Hertz to sample increment ;
 PLS 0 1 1 6 ;

COM  Carrier frequency ;
COM Conversion 0: from Hertz to sample increment ;
 PLS 0 1 1 7 ;
```

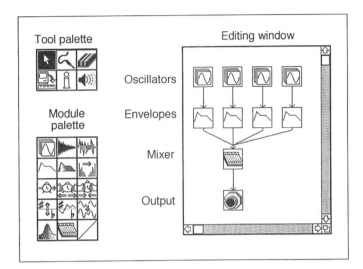

Figure 16.33   The Editing window contains an additive synthesis instrument created with the Turbosynth program. Four oscillators feed into four envelope generators. All of the signals are mixed in the mixer module before being passed to the output module. At the left are the Tool palette, containing (left to right, row by row): a selector arrow, patch cable, eraser, sample transfer button, information button, and play button. The Module palette contains (left to right, row by row): oscillator, sample file player, noise generator, envelope generator, lowpass filter, spectrum inverter, fixed delay, time stretcher, time compresser, fixed pitch shifter, variable pitch shifter, modulator, resonator, mixer, and waveshaper.

16.32a. Upon selecting a pfield, an editing window opens up so a user can enter a value and also specify the type of conversion routine to be used in interpreting that value. For example, a pitch value can be specified in frequency or in a symbolic *octave:pitch class* form. There are conversion routines for each type of specification. Upon selecting an oscillator module, the user can select which GEN function to use for the oscillator waveform. A GEN function editor can be invoked for creating new envelopes and waveforms. The front-end approach has the advantage of flexibility. Users can

Figure 16.32   The Graphical Music V modular instrument editor. (*a*) Graphical image of a simple instrument for amplitude modulation. Each score pfield is indicated by a "P" module. The left input to the oscillator is amplitude, while the right input is frequency. The white squares in the upper right part of the oscillator are optional inputs for initial phase (unused in this example). (*b*) Code generated by compiling the instrument diagrammed in 16.32(*a*) along with Music V GEN function definitions and pfield conversion routines specified in other editors within the system. Comment statements have been typed into the automatically generated code.

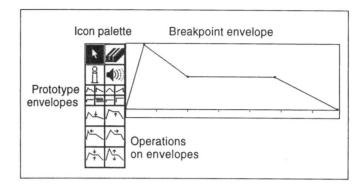

Figure 16.34 Selecting the envelope module in Turbosynth causes this function editor to appear on screen. The icons at the left include drawing and erasing tools, as well as prototype envelopes (to be edited to taste) and operations on envelopes.

edit the code generated by the editor (although this is not necessary), and the instrument can be driven in the usual Music *N* way by a note list score.

Turbosynth is a commercially available iconic editor program (Wilkinson et al. 1989). Figure 16.33 shows a four-oscillator additive synthesis instrument. Unlike the Music *N* model, the amplitude envelopes are below the oscillator. That is, the output of the oscillator feeds into the envelope generator, which scales the incoming signal according to the shape of the envelope. The output of the envelope generators feed into a mixer module, which combines the four signals. Finally, the mixer module sends the sum to an output module.

The instrument was created interactively by selecting the arrow tool and then dragging DSP icons into the editing window. One can then edit the parameter settings for each module by double-clicking on the module's icon. Figure 16.34 portrays the editing window that appears when the envelope generator icon is selected.

Turbosynth is easy to use, but the program is closed, so that it is not possible to add new modules, for example. Unlike Graphical Music V, the program lacks a score language. Users of Turbosynth are expected to create one sound at a time.

Sound Sample Editors

Using a *sound sample editor* (also called a *sound editor* or *digital audio editor*), musicians and recording engineers modify sampled sound waveforms. These editors work primarily in the time domain, operating directly on a stream of samples. Dozens of systems intertwine the operations of editing, mixing, and processing of sound; to simplify this discussion we focus on editing here. See chapters 9, 10, and 11 for more on sound mixing and signal processing.

Analog audio editing involves physically cutting segments of magnetic tape and splicing them back together using adhesive tape. As troublesome as this seems today, it was sometimes taken to a high art form. Digital audio editors use terms derived from the tape era. An editor *cuts* two segments apart and *splices* (joins) the segments together. To avoid clicks, most splices use *crossfading*—a central operation in sound editing. A crossfade imposes a gradual transition from one signal to the next. This makes the splice sound seamless. We discuss this important topic in more detail later.

Only digital audio editors allow *rehearsable* or *nondestructive editing*. With rehearsable editing, a musician can try out an edit before making the definitive version. This is possible because memory buffers in the editor store rehearsal edits along with the original version. Only when the user decides that the splice is right does the editor save the new sample sequence. Another face-saving feature of digital editors is an *undo facility*—allowing one to reverse the effect of a disastrous editing operation as if it had never occurred.

Two major types of interactive editors can be distinguished: those that use computer graphics techniques for displaying and editing waveforms, and those that do not. We begin with nongraphical editors, which includes a discussion of digital audio tape recorders. The final section explores interactive graphics editors.

Sample Editors Based on Tape Recorders

Editing techniques are closely linked with the medium on which the data reside. Most sound-editing systems that do not use graphics-based interaction rely on *serial media*—tape recorders—to store samples. In serial media, the *retrieval time* (the time it takes to fetch a set of samples) varies depending upon its location. When the tape is loaded, information at the beginning of the tape can be retrieved quickly, while information at the end of the tape may take minutes to retrieve by fast-forwarding the tape. Digital tape recorders fall into two categories: *stationary-head* and *rotating-head,* which we cover in separate sections below. First we present a note about the form of audio data on tape.

Interleaving Samples

Editing on an analog tape recorder is a matter of cutting the tape with a razor blade and splicing the two ends together with an adhesive tape. This is possible because the voltages representing sound waveforms appear in time order on the tape. Digital tape-editing tools give the illusion that the samples are written onto the tape one after the other in time order. Actually, more than one copy of the samples are *interleaved* (reordered) upon recording, and a single copy is restored to linear order on playback by a microprocessor within the recorder. The rationale for dispersing the samples this way is to minimize *tape dropouts*—caused by tiny irregularities in the tape —and *reading errors* caused by dust particles. These errors affect a topographically close group of samples.

Interleaving samples means that a contiguous group of samples represent different time points in the recorded material. Hence, a problem in one segment of the tape causes small (usually one-sample) errors scattered at different time points in the material. These errors can usually be corrected by using another copy of the samples scattered on a different segment of the same tape. The important point here is that tape-based digital editing systems must always decode and reassemble a linear order of samples from the interleaved stream. (See Pohlmann 1989a; Nakajima et al. 1983; and Doi 1984 for a description of error correction schemes.)

Editing with Stationary-head Tape Recorders

The tape transport of a stationary head digital recorder behaves like a traditional analog reel-to-reel transport. That is, the tape passes horizontally across the fixed erase, record, and playback heads. These systems may let the audio engineer splice the traditional way—with a razor blade (Lagadec and Takayama 1985; Watkinson 1985). Physical splicing depends on the user being able to rock the tape by hand back and forth over the head until the desired splice point is heard. Since the encoding scheme (interleaved samples) for digital information often depends on a more-or-less steady tape speed that cannot be rocked, an analog *cue track* is recorded alongside the digital information. When the tape is rocked, the user hears this cue track.

In digital tape splicing, the physical splice point is merely a marker. When the tape recorder detects the presence of a physical splice it performs a preset crossfade, regardless of the angle of the splice. Digital tape cutting is less and less common, since stationary head recorders also support electronic editing features, such as punch-in and punch-out replacement editing. This means that new material can be seamlessly inserted in place of old material. For more advanced editing needs, users of stationary head recorders can transfer tracks in the digital domain to a disk-based editing system where the material can be manipulated more freely.

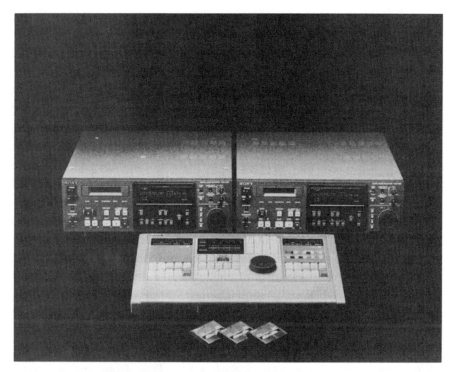

Figure 16.35 Editing DAT recorders. Sony PCM-7000 DAT recorders with SMPTE timecode-based editing controller.

Editing with Rotating-head Tape Recorders

Rotating-head tape recorders include digital audio tape (DAT) recorders (figure 16.35), as well as videocassette-based recorders introduced in the 1980s. Rotating-head tape recorders are based on *helical scanning* heads pioneered in videotape recorders. Helical scanning writes information vertically on the tape as it passes by the head block horizontally. Vertical scanning packs information more densely onto the tape than stationary heads can at a given tape speed. The disadvantages of helical scanning include the difficulty of physically cutting the tape, increased wear on the tape, heads, and transport motors, and more moving parts to service.

Early rotating-head digital audio recorders, like the Sony professional model PCM 1630 and its consumer nephew, the PCM 601, were packaged in two parts. One part was a *pulse code modulation* (PCM) processor, and the other part was a videocassette recorder (VCR). The PCM processor performs analog-to-digital and digital-to-analog conversion, and encodes the data as a *pseudovideo* signal that is recorded by the attached VCR. To be made into a pseudovideo signal, the sample data are grouped into *lines* (for example, eight samples per horizontal line in the standard Japanese format) and *frames* for every 1/30th of a second (Sony Corporation 1983). Digital audio editors for PCM/VCR recorders use frame-based video techniques for locating and synchronizing VCRs.

DAT editing equipment incorporates the transport and the PCM encoder in one compact housing. Both DAT timecode and SMPTE timecode can be used as a reference when editing. (See chapters 9 and 22 for more on SMPTE timecode.) SMPTE timecode is a sequential numbering scheme stored on a per-frame basis on the tape. SMPTE code has two main uses: to synchronize several devices (slave devices read and "track" the timecode of a master device), and to locate information stored at a particular time point or address. In conjunction with an *autolocator* unit, SMPTE timecode lets a user find information associated with a particular SMPTE frame on a tape or other medium: the autolocator simply reads the timecode written on a spare track of the tape and searches for the desired location.

Several companies have developed electronic editing systems for use with rotating-head tape recorders. The Sony Compact Disc Mastering System— a videotape-based medium—was for a long time the de facto standard for compact disc (CD) master tape editing. This system and later DAT editors are designed for *assembly editing* from one or more *player* machines to a *master recorder*. Assembly editing refers to the practice of splicing together disparate fragments of a composition to make the final product (figure 16.36). No mixing is involved, with the exception of short crossfades between the fragments. It is assumed that all of the fragments reside on the player machines, and the main task is simply assembling them in the proper order onto the master recorder.

A major drawback of editing on serial media is the time wasted in tape searching and setup. Before an edit can be attempted, the machines must search for the specified timecode and then position the tape. After one has spent several hours in an editing session, these delays become disconcerting. Finally, serial media editors are closed systems, designed around proprietary hardware and preset operations.

Sample Editing with Random-access Media

The term *random-access media* refers to disks (optical or magnetic) and semiconductor memory chips (Freed 1987). In random-access media, any piece of sample data can be retrieved as fast as any other piece, regardless of its location in the flow of music. The mechanical overhead of serial media, such as rewinding and tape-loading routines, are unnecessary with random-access media.

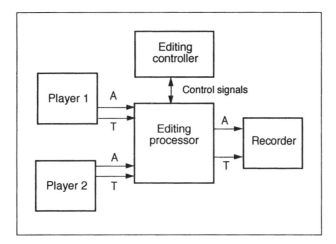

Figure 16.36 Assembly editing on serial media. One or more player machines transmit digital audio and timecode information to an editing processor linked to an editing controller. The editing controller contains the user interface to the system. Timecode synchronizes all the systems and is also used to locate material to be assembled onto the recorder. In an editing DAT recorder, everything except the player machines may be housed in a single unit.

Random-access media paired with editing software running on a general-purpose computer have proved to be a powerful and highly flexible combination (Griffiths and Bloom 1982; Abbott 1984b; McNally et al. 1985; Ingebretson and Stockham 1984). Through updates issued over a period of time, this software can grow in sophistication with little or no change in hardware configuration. The rest of this section surveys this editing software.

Graphical Sample Editors: Background

Graphical sample editors display sound signals as time-domain waveforms on a screen (figure 16.37). The Edsnd and S editors developed at Stanford in the 1970s were among the first editors of this type (Moorer 1977; Roads 1982).

The first commercial graphical sound editor was the Soundstream system, shown in figure 16.38, developed in Salt Lake City (Warnock 1976). In the Soundstream system, a digital tape recorder sampled the original signal. Then the data on the tape were transferred onto a disk attached to a 16-bit minicomputer—a Digital Equipment Corporation PDP-11. Up to 84 *track-minutes* minutes of music could be stored on the disk for editing. (A track-minute is a single track or channel of audio.) The 84 minutes on the disk

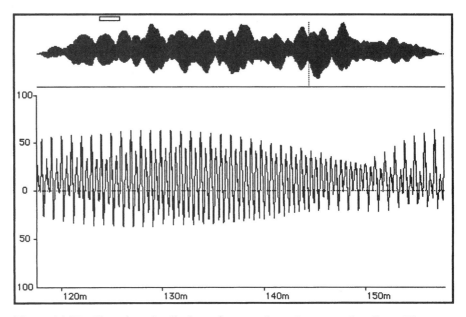

Figure 16.37   Time-domain display of a waveform in a sample editor. The top portion is an overview of the entire sound file. The small rectangle in the top left indicates the portion of the sound file that appears in the lower window. The vertical line in the overview (center right) indicates the current cursor position. Screen image from the Alchemy program by Passport.

Figure 16.38   The Soundstream editing system, ca. 1982. The console in the center was used to enter editing commands. The monitor at the left displayed time-domain waveform images.

could be divided into 42 minutes of stereo audio, or about 10 minutes of 8-track material.

During the late 1970s and early 1980s, several university based laboratories developed experimental graphical sound editors. These include DPYSND (W. Schottstaedt, Stanford), SE (S. Milne 1980, MIT), the New York Institute of Technology editor (Kowalski and Glassner 1982), and GCOMP (Banger and Pennycook 1983). Today dozens of graphical sound editors are available as commercial software packages. These systems exploit the freedom possible with the combination of random-access media, general-purpose computers, and software control.

Features of Graphical Sample Editors

A visual or graphical display of the time domain can be likened to a window on sound. The window's aperture can vary from microseconds to minutes; users can scroll forwards or backwards through the sound file. They select portions of the display with a mouse and then choose an operation to apply to the selected portion. Table 16.4 lists typical operations provided by graphical sound editors.

To edit, the user needs to be able to *zoom* in and out to examine waveforms at different levels of temporal resolution. To find a large silent gap, for example, requires an overview display that shows a minute of sound. But to find a click in a complex passage requires resolution at the level of individual samples.

Fading and Crossfading

One of the fundamental capabilities of an audio editor—analog or digital—is the ability to fade and crossfade sounds. Without it, sounds are merely juxtaposed, and artifacts such as clicks, pops, and thuds inevitably appear at the splice point (figure 16.39).

Figure 16.40 dissects a crossfade. Here (a) will be crossfaded into the end of (b). Figures (c) and (d) show the same sounds with their proper fade-in and fade-out envelopes. Figure (e) depicts the result of a smooth crossfade with overlap between them. A sound editor should make this operation quick and easy. See chapter 9 for a brief description and screen image of the MacMix program, an example of an intuitive interface for aligning and crossfading multiple sound files.

Recognizing the importance of smooth fades and splices, many editors offer several fade functions for different musical situations, including linear (straight line), quarter-sine, and logarithmic curves (figure 16.41). As figure

Table 16.4   Operations in graphical sound sample editors

Cuts—Delete audio flaws or other unwanted material

Splice two sample segments using crossfade functions drawn by hand or selected from a menu

Insert edit—Inject a new segment within an existing segment, thereby increasing the overall length; with or without crossfade

Replacement edit—Write over a previously recorded segment, like punchin and punchout on a tape recorder

Assembly edit—Link disparate passages by splicing

Move samples from point *A* to point *B* by graphical cut-and-paste methods

Mix numerous tracks into a smaller number of tracks

Synchronize tracks—adjust the timing of audio tracks relative to each other or to video or film

Compress or expand the playing time without pitch change

Shift pitch by a constant interval with or without changing the duration of the selected sound object

Equalize—emphasize or deemphasize certain frequency regions by filtration

Convert sample rate from a higher rate to a lower rate or vice versa

Transfer sounds to a keyboard sampler

Display samples in various time-domain formats, e.g., peak, average, data-reduced

Display multiple views of a single sound file in different windows—at different time scales, or in different parts of the file

Display multiple sound files simultaneously

Manipulate the *X* and *Y* axes of the display (horizontal and vertical zoom)

Find the maximum sample value in a region of a sound file

Trace the amplitude envelope of a signal (peak or RMS value)

Reshape amplitude—Rescale the amplitude of the samples according to a curve drawn by the user or extracted from another sound.

Reshape pitch—Perform a continuous pitch shift over a selected region according to a curve drawn by a user or extracted from another sound.

Play samples at full speed, half speed, double speed, or varispeed

Print a display of the samples on printer

Perform spectrum analysis on a sound file for graphical editing and resynthesis

Segment and label musical notes detected in the continuous stream of samples.

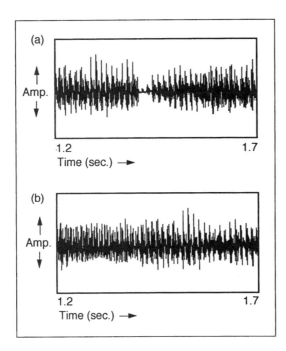

Figure 16.39 Splicing. (*a*) A simple paste command is equivalent to a hard cut. This juxtaposes the end of one sound against the beginning of another. (*b*) A crossfade smooths the transition between the two sounds. In this case, the crossfade time is 90 ms, during which the first sound fades down and the second sound fades up.

16.41 makes clear, logarithmic fades apply more effective energy than a linear fade or quarter-sine fade, so they are good for crossfades where the goal is to avoid the "hole in the middle" effect (a drop in energy in the middle of the crossfade).

Sound File Format Conversion

Sample editors operate on sound files. The format of the sound file defines the internal data structure of files containing audio samples. This format usually involves a *header* text and numbers representing sound samples. The header contains the name of the file and relevant information about the samples in the file (sampling rate, number of bits per sample, number of channels, etc.). The samples are usually organized in *frames;* if there are N channels, each frame contains N samples. Thus, the sampling rate really indicates the number of frames per second.

A profusion of sound file formats is a fact of life in digital audio editing (van Rossum 1992). Many computer manufacturers define an arbitrary format that is unique to their machines. In addition, many synthesis and edit-

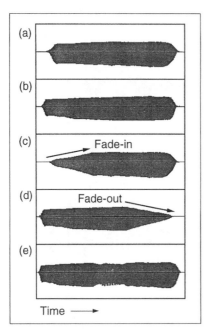

Figure 16.40   Crossfading two saxophone notes. (*a*) and (*b*) shows the amplitude envelope of the original two notes, a minor third apart in pitch. (*c*) and (*d*) are their faded versions. (*e*) is the result of crossfading (*c*) with (*d*).

ing programs use proprietary formats. There is some technical justification in proprietary formats for editing purposes. Editors may divide the editing data into several files, for example: sound samples, editing pointers (indicating cuts, for example), display files, and mix files. These formats are optimized for maximum speed and flexibility with a particular editor program. What is unfortunate is that some programs do not allow users to save data in a standard format. This necessitates format conversion routines in other editors.

Spectrum Editors

Sample editors operate on waveforms in the time domain, while *spectrum editors* operate on partials in the frequency domain. An acoustician might use a spectrum editor to understand the detailed nature of sound evolution or to explore data reduction techniques. A musician might want to edit spectral data in a creative way in order to modify an analyzed sound.

A spectrum editor presumes a prior analysis stage. Chapter 13 and appendix A explain spectrum analysis. Several chapters in part II describe analysis/resynthesis methods that start from spectrum analysis.

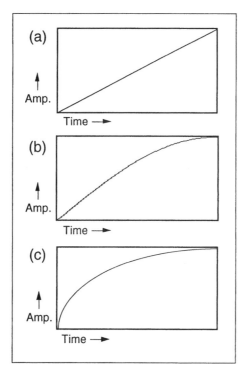

Figure 16.41   Fade functions in sound editors. (*a*) Linear. (*b*) Quarter-sine. (*c*) Logarithmic.

Two-dimensional Spectrum Displays

Spectrum displays fall into two main categories: *two-dimensional* (2D) and *three-dimensional* (3D). A 2D display shows a timeless frequency domain image that plots frequency versus amplitude (figure 16.42). To generate such a display, the user selects a short segment of sound in a sample editor; this sound is analyzed using *fast Fourier transform* (FFT) techniques (see appendix A). Why should the sound be a short segment? Because a 2D plot favors frequency resolution over time resolution. That is, it shows the overall frequency content of the segment but does not indicate at what instant in the segment each frequency component appeared. Resynthesizing the segment from the unmodified analysis reassembles all the components into a very close approximation of the time-varying waveform.

Spectrum modifications are quite context-sensitive. In a smooth sound with only a few harmonics, one must be careful to make only slight modifications if the resynthesized segment is going to be reinserted into the middle of the original. Otherwise the overall result may sound like a filter switched in suddenly—with an accompanying transient. In contrast, the complete

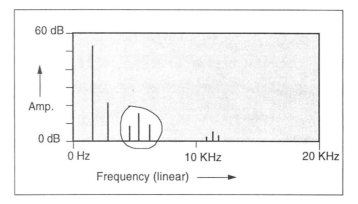

Figure 16.42 Schematic image of a two-dimensional spectrum editor. The region within the circle has been selected for an editing operation such as cut, move, scale amplitude, etc.

removal of several dozen frequency components in the midrange of a wide-bandwidth sound (such as a chord played by synthesized brass ensemble) has surprisingly little aural impact, even though its effect on the waveform is visually striking. This confirms how *masking effects* in human auditory perception can hide modifications in the physical spectrum (see chapter 23).

Three-dimensional Spectrum Displays

A 3D spectrum projects each frequency component over time. This usually takes three main forms:

- Perspective plots (waterfall or spectrum envelope displays)
- Control function plots
- Spectrogram-like plots

Perspective plots (figure 16.43) show a time-varying topology of energy on a frequency versus-amplitude terrain, where the amplitude is usually the vertical dimension. When these displays operate in real time, they are called *waterfall displays,* due their undulating wave motions.

Control function plots may separate the amplitude and frequency envelopes for each partial (figure 16.44). Figure 16.44 is an example from Strawn (1987b), created with his eMerge editor. The figure depicts a 3D representation of the first eight harmonics of part of a violin tone.

Figure 16.45 shows a spectrogram-like representation generated by the LemurEdit program (Holloway 1993). Notice the darkened region, which has been selected for editing. The analysis data displayed here were gener-

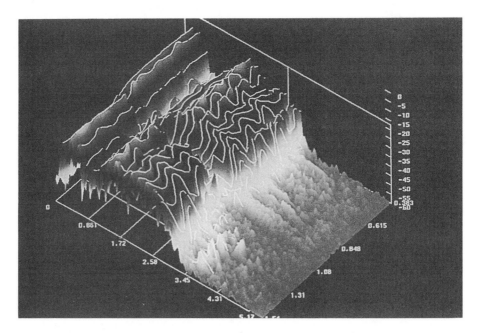

Figure 16.43   Perspective plot of an additive synthesis of a tenor voice singing two notes. The gap between the notes is visible. Frequency is plotted from left to right; time projects from the back to the front. Amplitude (plotted on a logarithmic scale) is on the vertical axis. One of the advantages of a 3D display is how it reveals both amplitude and frequency modulation in the tone. The white lines along the tops of the partials are the estimated amplitude envelopes, after an algorithm by X. Rodet. (Image courtesy of Alan Peevers, Center for New Music and Audio Technologies, University of California, Berkeley.)

ated by the Lemur program (Walker and Fitz 1992), an implementation of a *tracking phase vocoder* (see chapter 13).

Spectrum editors of all types let users adjust the amplitude of individual partials or groups of partials. The display software should label clearly the specific times, amplitudes, and frequencies being edited. Table 16.5 lists typical spectrum-editing commands.

Examples of Spectrum Editors

At Stanford University, John Strawn implemented an editor for time-varying spectra called eMerge, which stands for "edit merge file" (Strawn 1985a, 1987b). A *merge file* contains one or more time-varying control functions and is usually generated by a spectrum analysis program. For example, the *phase vocoder* (Portnoff 1978; Holtzman 1980; Dolson 1983; Gordon and Strawn 1985; also see chapter 13) can produce a time-varying

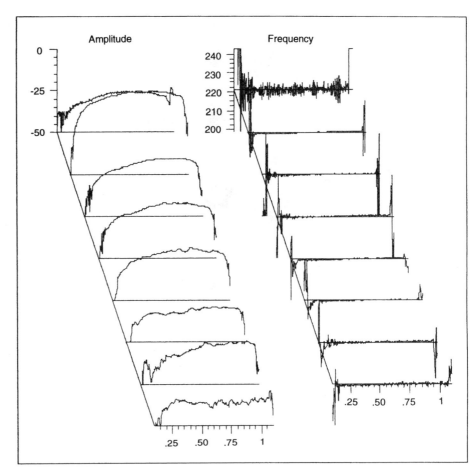

Figure 16.44 Separate plots for frequency and amplitude envelopes of the first eight harmonics of a violin tone. Lower harmonics at back. (After Strawn 1987b, p. 342.)

Table 16.5 Spectrum editor commands

Perform analysis and display with different parameter settings (window type, window size, etc.)

Zoom in and out to different time scales

Add, modify, or delete amplitude or frequency functions, cutting and pasting from one spectrum to another, if desired.

Show a three-dimensional perspective plot of frequency versus amplitude versus time

Simplify the data with automatic line-segment approximation or another data reduction technique

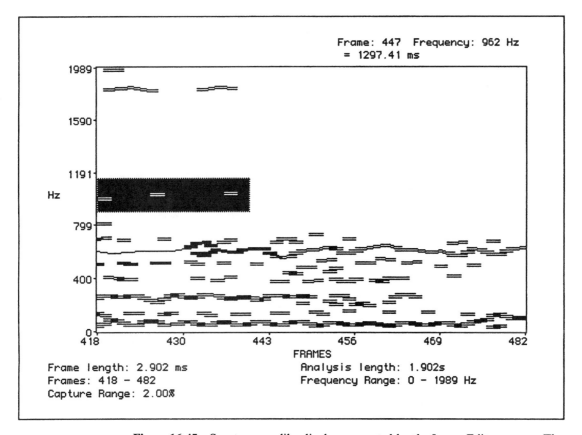

Figure 16.45 Spectrogram-like display generated by the LemurEdit program. The editor has been zoomed into a region between 0 and 1989 Hz, stretching over about 200 ms. Notice the darkened region, which has been selected for editing.

amplitude and frequency function for each channel of the analysis. This is a great deal of data. A musician might want to edit these data in order to change the analyzed sound before resynthesis or to reduce the burden of storing the raw, unedited data.

Figure 16.46 depicts plots of the amplitude of the first 24 harmonics of a violin tone. Notice how different they appear from the raw curves shown in 16.44. This is because these functions were derived by automatic line-segment approximation using the Pavlidis split/merge algorithm described in Strawn (1980). Most 3D plots of this kind show the amplitudes of the harmonics relative to the maximum of all of them; this plot shows each harmonic scaled to its own maximum, an option which makes it easier to see detail in the higher harmonics.

Using the editor, a musician can add, move, and delete breakpoints. In the example in figure 16.46b, the attacks of the harmonics were cleaned up

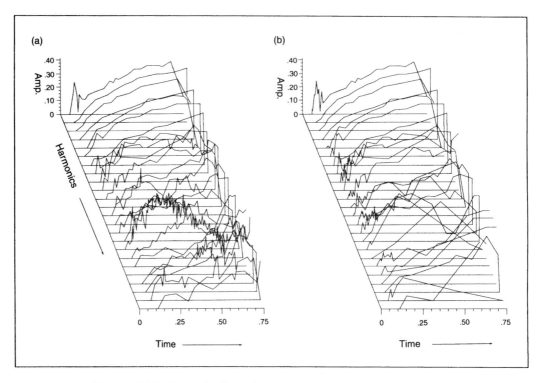

Figure 16.46   Examples from the eMerge spectrum envelope editor. (*a*) Before. 3D representation of amplitude traces for the first 24 harmonics of a violin tone at A 220 Hz. Time goes from left to right. The fundamental is at the back of the plot, with higher harmonics placed closer to the viewer. Notice the jagged envelopes above the fifteenth harmonic. (*b*) After. The same functions after being edited by hand using eMerge. Some attacks have been made more jagged, while the noisy traces in the higher harmonics are straightened.

by manual editing. This is especially easy to see in the fundamental. Also, some detail, especially in the upper harmonics, was removed. This extraneous detail resulted when the line-segment approximation algorithm "worked too hard" in a few cases. Such detail must be removed for more than cosmetic reasons: according to Strawn (1987b), audible artifacts called *breebles* occur if the amplitudes of the upper harmonics change too rapidly relative to each other. If appropriate frequency functions and the amplitude func-

Figure 16.47   Separation of voice from orchestra using SpecDraw. This sonogram representation shows frequency vertically and time horizontally. The wavy lines indicate a common vibrato pattern, characteristic of a vocal tone. By encircling these lines one can separate the vocal part from the orchestra part, resynthesizing either one without the other. (Figure courtesy Gerhard Eckel, IRCAM.)

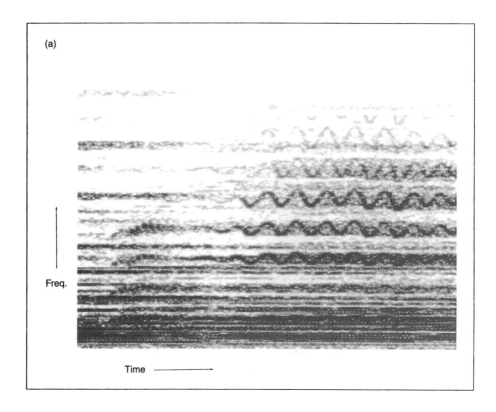

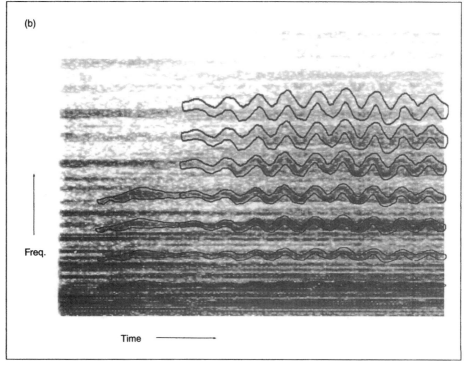

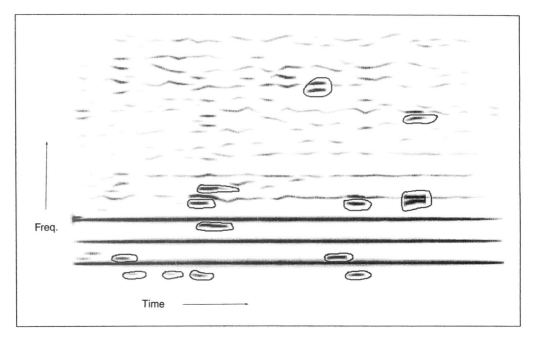

Figure 16.48   Removal of artifacts from flute resynthesis using SpecDraw. The circled areas represent the artifacts. They will be removed when the spectrum is resynthesized. (Figure courtesy Gerhard Eckel, IRCAM.)

tions in figure 16.46b are used in additive synthesis, the resulting tone sounds close to the original.

Figure 16.45 showed an example from the LemurEdit program, an editor for a sonogram-like representation developed at the University of Illinois. Figures 16.47 and 16.48 show examples of another sonogram-type editor, SpecDraw, a prototype developed by Gerhard Eckel at IRCAM. SpecDraw lets users directly edit and resynthesize sonograms using drawing tools. These figures make clear how musically intuitive this type of editing is.

Looking at the future of spectrum editing, it is clear that sound analysis is evolving at a rapid pace, so spectrum editors are becoming more widespread. Future editors should be able to compare spectra from a variety of analysis techniques. Ideally, users should be able to edit the topography of spectral surfaces at a macro level, meaning that a single gesture ramifies into numerous envelope changes.

Sound Database Editors

The early development of tape music and musique concrète already made clear the necessity to classify and organize the sound universe. Moles (1960) described a sound classification scheme based on sonogram analysis, where the sonograms are interpreted by a human reader typing pertinent characteristics onto punched cards. Far ahead of their time, Schaeffer, Reibel, and Ferreyra (1967) made a three-record set as a first solfège of sound objects. Their "Typology of Musical Objects" follows the classification scheme of Schaeffer's monumental *Traité des Objets Musicaux* (1966/1977).

As the capacity of storage media increases, it is becoming more common to work with large numbers of sound files. Commercially available sound collections on optical media, for example, offer hundreds of sound files on a single disk. When sounds are read in and out en masse from high-capacity media, working with sound-mixing and -editing programs can involve thousands of files. Keeping track of these files is a major task, so database programs have become available, some of which are specialized to music (Jaslowitz, D'Silva, and Zwaneveld 1988; Feiten and Ungvary 1990).

A *database management system* (DBMS) or *database editor* lets a user access a sound file by a set of *keywords* that have previously been assigned to the file. In a traditional database, the keywords are usually kept in separate *index file* for efficiency. That way the database editor can access the index file for a given keyword to obtain the location of all sound files with that keyword. For example, all sound files containing piano tones might have the keyword "piano" associated with them. When we ask the system to list all sound files with the keyword "piano," it lists the contents of the "piano" keyword index file.

Since a large database might have hundreds of piano tones, it is important that each sound file be indexed with several keywords so that one can locate it more directly. One might index piano sound files by keywords like "complete composition" (to denote a file containing a complete performance of a piano score), "composition fragment" (to denote a partial performance), "phrase," "note," "trill," "arpeggio," etc. Further keywords identify subgroups within each of these categories. Each file might have additional keywords to indicate its pitch content, amplitude, duration, the type of piano and microphones used, the performer's name, and so on. Then later when we try to retrieve a sound file from the database, the more specific our specification is, the fewer candidates the DBMS will have to find for our audition.

Automatic Sound Classification

Entering keywords for a database is tedious. Automatic analysis of sound files according to perceptual and acoustical properties may spare much of the labor involved in indexing (Feiten and Ungvary 1990; Feiten, Frank, and Ungvary 1991; de Koning and Oates 1991; Eaglestone and Vershoor 1991). Existing technology permits automatic labeling of sound files according to such criteria as general spectral weight (grave versus acute), spectral bandwidth, density of events, overall amplitude, steadiness versus wavering quality, attack type, sustain type, decay type, and so on. One can imagine systems that would perform transcription and apply music analysis routines to a sound file, identify the presence of instruments or human voices (perhaps even determining the performer), as well as recognize lyrics.

Media Editors

The poet Stephane Mallarmé thought "the world exists to end in a book." We are now in a position to go beyond that and transfer the entire show to the memory of a computer. (Marshall McLuhan 1964)

Multimedia means many things. Opera is multimedia, so is an electronic game. Perhaps the simplest definition is the integration of two or more media types: audio, video, still images, animation, text, and interactivity. The problem of combining these elements in electronic form is confronted in the *postproduction* stage of video or filmmaking, and in the *authoring* stage of interactive multimedia development. Computers can control videocassette recorders, audio tape recorders, and disk drives that store images, text, and sound. *Media editors* help coordinate all the elements into a finished product.

The final result of multimedia production may be an object like a tape to be broadcast, or a disc to be viewed at home. Or it may be a performance, such as an animated accompaniment to a lecture/demonstration, or a light and sound spectacle for the theater.

The advent of *digital videotape recorders* (DVTRs) and other digital vidio media provides more incentive for coordinating audio and video media. Digital video media record digital color (*chroma*) and brightness (*luminance*) samples with several channels of digital audio, in addition to timecode and cue tracks (Lagadec and Takayama 1985).

After a brief look at the background of media editors, this section focuses on media editors for personal computers, the focal point of much interest in recent years.

Media Editors: Background

Primitive graphical and sound editors developed along separate paths until the early 1980s. The EditDroid and SoundDroid systems developed at

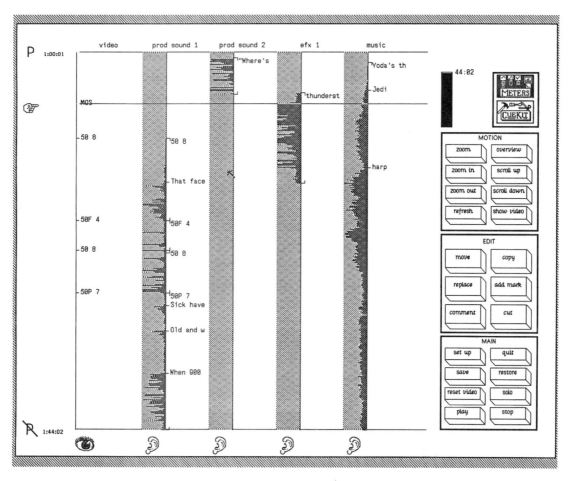

Figure 16.49 Prototype of the SoundDroid sound editor "cuesheet" screen. Each shaded vertical stripe represents a track of sound, with time going from the top to the bottom of the screen. The amplitude envelope in each track is shown by the solid black outline. Text annotations (partially obscured here) show the incipits of spoken text fragments, among other things. (Image provided by Peter Nye.)

Lucasfilm in California showed how random-access media, interactive graphics, and automated mixing can be combined into a picture-and-sound editing system. Figure 16.49 shows a prototype four-channel sound editor dating from around 1983 with picture cues indicated beside the audio tracks.

Audiovisual editing can be quite complicated, since the two domains can be interlinked in complex ways. For example, when a video editor changes a scene, many channels of sound must be redone to fit the new sequence of images. Dialogue, effects, and musical soundtracks are all affected by changes in the visual domain. The visual information is often recorded on many tracks, each one corresponding to a particular camera angle or special effects overlay. To manage the complexity of this information, the usual approach taken is to prepare the raw material as a database of audio and visual data (Hawthorne 1985). The first step is to transfer the material to be edited to a random-access medium such as magnetic or optical disk. The author or director annotates the material with pertinent facts about a particular segment, for example, the scene, the take, and other data.

This kind of audiovisual editing is nondestructive; nothing is physically cut or deleted. Edits can be rehearsed and adjusted ad infinitum. Each edit causes the system to write a description of the edit in an *electronic logbook*. Since the audio and visual editors share a common logbook, any decisions made in picture editing are reflected in the corresponding soundtracks. At the end of an editing session, the result is a list of entries in the logbook that can be used to reconstruct the desired sound and image combination. If the ultimate medium is, for example, a 70-mm film with 6-channel soundtrack, the logbook shows which segments of film and sound must be spliced and mixed to create the finished product.

Media Editors on Personal Computers

Until the 1990s, a high-quality media editing suite reflected an investment of hundreds of thousands of dollars. Dramatic advances in video technology, DSP hardware, and editing software have brought the cost of media editors to within reach of many more users. In general, these are divided into two classes: professional workstations for editing of film or video productions (figure 16.50), and authoring systems for presentations or interactive media (Flurry 1989).

Authoring programs running on personal computers allow one to coordinate still images, text, animated graphics, and video with sound tracks. But how to make such a presentation interactive? Authoring systems let developers integrate user interface elements into the presentation, such as buttons, menus, movable objects, or "hot" click areas that cause new events to occur. The insertion of "waiting points" into the dialogue forces users to respond in order to continue the presentation.

Toward Musically Intelligent Editors

In the early years of interactive computing, communication with the machine required the typing of cryptic codes. Today, editors based on graphic windows and menus are common. But providing a graphical "front end" to a music system does not necessarily make it more musically intelligent. As

Figure 16.50 Avid Media Composer. This professional system lets a user edit a digitized version of a film or video production, including many tracks of both sound and picture. The result of the work is usually an edit decision list referenced to timecode that is used as a guide in assembling the original medium (film or videotape).

we discussed at the beginning of this chapter, the scope of operations depends on internal representations, and not how fancy the graphics are; the machine can only access and manipulate what it understands. To move beyond the cosmetic stage we need to deepen musical interfaces (Roads 1984, 1985d). The goal of this line of research should be to bring the machine more up to the level of a human musical assistant, rather than forcing the musician to descend to the machine's level.

Designing an "intelligent" editor is an elusive task, since people's expectations of intelligent behavior vary widely. Text editors, for example, "know" about the structure of documents in the sense that they know how to recognize and skip over word, line, and paragraph boundaries. Some can also check spelling and aspects of grammar. Editors for programming languages know the syntactic structure of the language and can detect syntactic errors in code; some check the semantics (Lieberman 1981; Waters 1982). A few computer music editors are developing similar capabilities. For example, music notation editors are becoming increasingly sophisticated in their knowledge of score notation and in their ability to transcribe from MIDI keyboard performance. Many patch editors can generate a synthesizer voice based on an acoustic description. But sample and spectrum editors have much further to go in developing an understanding of musical signals. An intelligent sample editor would allow a musician to issue a command like "Go to measure 23 and delete the first G played by the trumpet." Before this capability can be implemented, the core problem to be solved is reliable transcription from sound to score (Moorer 1975; Piszczalski and Galler 1977; Piszczalski et al. 1981; Chafe et al. 1982; Foster et al. 1982; Katayose and Inokuchi 1989; 1990). Chapters 12 and 13, dealing with sound analysis, explore these issues further.

Conclusion

The first generation of computer-based editors of all types were musically limited. By now, however, the flexibility offered by software editors tends to outweigh their remaining limitations. The power of software editors is not without cost, however. Some editors (in particular, notation editors) require a substantial time commitment in order to learn how to use them skillfully.

Editors are primary tools of the studio-based musician, music engineer, and producer. Because music can be represented in so many different ways, it is not surprising that new types of editors continue to be developed. Indeed, it would be hard to imagine a "universal" editor for all aspects of music. A diversity of editors is potentially a healthy situation, since musicians can select the editors that suit their particular approach to music making.

17   *Music Languages*

Assessing Languages

Software Synthesis Languages

Advantages and Disadvantages of Software Synthesis
Unit Generator Languages
Scores and Orchestras
Score Language
Orchestra Language
Interconnections between Unit Generators
Instrument Definition Example
Score Definition Example
Function Table Definition
Note List
Alternative Score Representations
Example of an Alternative Score Format: Scorefile
Non-note-list Score Representations
Soundfile Processing
Implementations of Music N
Portability
Extensibility
Graphical Tools
Block versus Sample Computation

Languages for Controlling Real-time Synthesis

Fixed-function versus Variable-function Hardware
Control of Real-time Synthesis: Background
MIDI Languages for Fixed-function DSPs

This chapter surveys music languages for sound synthesis, control of real-time synthesizers, and composition. For the purposes of this presentation, we define languages as formal text—strings of alphanumeric characters—in contrast to the "visual programming languages" based on graphical icons and treated in chapter 16. Another type of linguistic interaction is natural language input to a music system, like spoken or written English or Japanese. Although there has been progress in speech recognition, it is not yet widespread, so we refer readers to the research literature (Schmidt 1987; Roads 1986b; *Computer Music Journal* 1990).

Assessing Languages

Formal languages lend precision and flexibility to music specification because they require that musical ideas be turned into abstract symbols and stipulated explicitly. Herein lies both the advantage and disadvantage of linguistic interaction with a computer music system. The advantage is that formalized and explicit instructions can yield a high degree of control. To create an imagined effect, composers need only specify it precisely. They can easily stipulate music that would be difficult or impossible to perform by human beings.

In some cases, a linguistic specification is much more efficient than gestural input would be. This is the case when a single command applies to a massive group of events, or when a short list of commands replaces dozens of pointing and selecting gestures. The *shell scripts* of Unix operating systems are a typical example of command lists (Thompson and Ritchie 1974).

These advantages turn into a disadvantage when simple things must be coded in the same detail and with the same syntactic overhead as complicated things. For example, with an alphanumeric language, envelope shapes that could be drawn on a screen in two seconds must be plotted out on paper by hand and transcribed into a list of numerical data to be typed by the composer. For many tasks, graphical editors and visual programming systems, in which the user selects and interconnects graphical objects, are more effective and easier to use than their textual counterparts (see chapter 16).

Some languages are interactive; one can type individual statements and each of them is interpreted in turn. This can occur in a concert situation, but the slow information rate of typing—not to mention the mundane stage presence of a typist—precludes this approach in fast-paced real-time music-making. Gestural control through a musical input device is more efficient and natural. Hence, languages for music, although important, do not answer all musical needs. In the ideal, music languages should be available alongside other kinds of musical interaction tools.

The rest of this chapter surveys three types of languages: languages for software synthesis of sound, languages for controlling a real-time digital signal processor (DSP), and languages for composition (including music data entry and algorithmic composition).

Software Synthesis Languages

We can partition sound synthesis languages into two broad categories. *Software synthesis languages* compute samples in non-real time on a general-purpose computer. *Languages for controlling real-time synthesis hardware* (discussed later) generate instructions that are sent to a real-time digital synthesizer. The rest of this section presents the former category.

Advantages and Disadvantages of Software Synthesis

Software synthesis is one of the most ancient technologies of computer music. It evokes an image of the Paleolithic composer chipping away at punched paper cards to be fed to a dinosaur mainframe computer, waiting days to hear a primitive sound emission. Since that bygone epoch, interactive graphical methods and synthesizers have displaced languages from many situations where their awkwardness could not be disguised. But software synthesis retains three undeniable strong points:

1. An open toolkit approach to synthesis, where each user can configure the kit for their own needs. The curious can experiment with new synthesis algorithms.

2. Arbitrarily complicated synthesis algorithms played by an arbitrary number of voices.

3. Precision: a composer can specify sonic events in extraordinarily fine numerical detail.

For each of these advantages there is a corresponding disadvantage.

1. Toolkits imply a learning curve and obligate the musician to take up software engineering—program debugging, maintenance, and documentation.

2. Complicated synthesis algorithms imply non-real-time performance and lack of gestural control.

3. Precision implies that the musician must specify and keep track of masses of minutiae, possibly involving hundreds of values for each second of sound.

Despite these disadvantages, there are times when software synthesis is the only way to realize a musical idea—therefore it is an essential utility in the well-equipped computer music studio.

Chapter 3 introduced the basic principles of synthesis languages and is a prerequisite to the discussion that follows. Here we enter into a more detailed exposition, using a generic language as a model. See Pope (1993) for a detailed comparison of the features and performance of three available synthesis languages.

Unit Generator Languages

Most synthesis languages are designed around the notion that the composer creates a synthesis *orchestra* and a *score* that references the orchestra (figure 17.1). The *instruments* in the orchestra are patches in the form of text. These texts specify interconnections between *unit generators* and also stipulate their input parameters. Each unit generator is a software module that emits audio or control signals (envelopes) or modifies these signals. The synthesis program or compiler reads both the orchestra and score files, constructs a machine-level representation of the patches, and feeds them the data from the score file. The final audio signal is written to a *soundfile* for later playback.

The unit generator (UG) concept allows great flexibility, since the output of a UG can be connected (or *patched*) to the input of virtually any other UG. The most basic UGs are either signal generators (oscillators, noise generators, impulse generators, etc.) or signal modifiers (filters, delays, reverberators, spatializers, etc.). Other types of UGs include routines to handle soundfile input/output, and data coming from an input device.

Later in this chapter we present simple examples of instruments made out of UGs, using a model language called Music 0 created for this book. Music 0 is compact and simple, which suits our purposes well. It should be easy to translate Music 0 code into other Music *N* languages.

The original unit generator language was the Music III language developed in 1960 by Max V. Mathews and his colleagues at Bell Telephone Laboratories in New Jersey. Since then, there have been numerous recodings of this model, including Music IV, Music 4BF, Music V, Music 7, Music 11, MUS10, and so on. Table 17.1 lists Music *N* languages developed up to 1991. Although newer languages add features and refinements, many

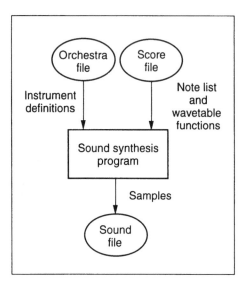

Figure 17.1   A software synthesis program takes in score and orchestra files and generates a sound sample file.

aspects of the basic organization and functionality of the Music *N* model have not changed significantly.

For historical reasons, one should cite the Music 4F language developed by Arthur Roberts (1966, 1969; Dumour 1993). Although it emulated the functionality of the Music IV program, it does not appear in table 17.1 because instead of the interconnectable unit generators of the Music IV model, Music 4F was a single large instrument controlled by many parameters.

Scores and Orchestras

UG languages encapsulate two sublanguages: a *score language* and an *orchestra language*. A specific score and orchestra are stored in a score file and an orchestra file, respectively.

Score Language

The score language typically serves two purposes:

1. It specifies the *note list:* the instrument names, start times, durations, and parameters of sonic events to be synthesized by the orchestra.

2. It defines the *function tables:* functions of time that are used as waveforms and envelopes by the instruments of the orchestra.

A typical line in a score file defines the parameters for one *note event.* Each note event enumerates the name of the instrument (where the instru-

Table 17.1 Unit-generator-based software synthesis languages

Program	Date introduced	Author(s)	Original host computer	Language	Location
Music III	1960	M. Mathews	IBM 7090	Assembler	Bell Laboratories, Murray Hill
Music IV	1963	M. Mathews J. Miller	IBM 7094	Macro assembler	Bell Laboratories, Murray Hill
Music IVB	1965	G. Winham H. Howe	IBM 7094	Macro assembler	Princeton University Princeton
Music V	1966	M. Mathews J. Miller	GE 645	Fortran IV	Bell Laboratories, Murray Hill
MUS10	1966	J. Chowning D. Poole L. Smith	DEC PDP-10	PDP-10 assembler	Stanford University, Stanford
MUSIGOL (Music-Algol)	1966	D. MacInnes W. Wulf P. Davis	Burroughs 5500	Burroughs Algol	University of Virginia, Richmond
Music 4BF	1967	H. Howe G. Winham	IBM 360	Fortran II and BAL assembler	Princeton University, Princeton
Music 360	1969	B. Vercoe	IBM 360	BAL assembler	Princeton University, Princeton
Music 7	1969	H. Howe	Xerox XDS Sigma 7	Assembler	Queens College CUNY, Flushing
TEMPO	1970	J. Clough	IBM 360	BAL assembler	Oberlin Conservatory, Oberlin
B6700 Music V	1973	B. Leibig	Burroughs B6700	Fortran and Algol	University of California at San Diego (UCSD), La Jolla
Music 11	1973	B. Vercoe S. Haflich R. Hale C. Howe	DEC PDP-11	Macro-11 assembler	MIT, Cambridge
MUSCMP	1978	Tovar	Foonly 2 (DEC PDP-10 clone)	FAIL assembler	Stanford University, Stanford
Cmusic	1980	F. R. Moore D. G. Loy	DEC VAX-11	C	UCSD, La Jolla
MIX	1982	P. Lansky	IBM 370	IBM 360 assembler	Princeton University, Princeton

Table 17.1 (cont.)

Program	Date introduced	Author(s)	Original host computer	Language	Location
Cmix	1984	P. Lansky	DEC PDP-11	C	Princeton University, Princeton
Music 4C	1985	S. Aurenz J. Beauchamp R. Maher C. Goudeseune	DEC VAX-11 (later ported other UNIX computers)	C	University of Illinois to at Urbana-Champaign
Csound	1986	B. Vercoe R. Karstens	DEC VAX-11 (later ported to IBM PC, Apple Macintosh, etc.)	C	MIT, Cambridge
Music 4C	1988	G. Gerrard	Apple Macintosh	C	University of Melbourne, Parkville
Common Lisp Music	1991	W. Schottstaedt	NeXT	Common Lisp	Stanford University, Stanford

ment is defined in the orchestra file), starting time, duration, and other parameters that are specific to the instrument. Since the number and type of parameters are specific to each instrument, some note events may have more parameters than other events.

The score may also include composition procedures (see the section on procedural composition languages), but in the simplest case it is simply a list of note events.

Orchestra Language

The orchestra language is a toolkit for constructing instruments by interconnecting UGs. For example, one might specify that the output of an oscillator should be connected to the input of a filter. This is done by assigning the output of the oscillator to a *signal variable,* and then using that signal variable in the input argument list of the filter. In the following example in the Music 0 language, the lines beginning with "/*" and ending with "*/" are comments. The symbol "←" means "is assigned the value of."

```
/*                wave    freq    amp.   */
signal1 ← osc     f1      440.0   1000;
/*                        input   cutoff dB */
signal2 ← low_filter signal1     880     6;
```

Table 17.2   Syntax of Music 0 unit generators

Output	UG name	Argument 1	Argument 2	Argument 3
output_signal ←	**envelope**	*waveform number*	*duration*	*amplitude*
output_signal ←	**osc**	*waveform number*	*frequency*	*amplitude*
output_signal ←	**low_filter**	*input signal*	*cutoff frequency*	*cutoff slope in dB*
(Output is *input signal* written to a sound file named in a dialog with the user)	**out**	*input signal*		

The first line (after a comment line) specifies that the output of an oscillator **osc** is assigned (routed) to the signal variable *signal1*. On the second line (after a comment line) the value of *signal1*, at each sample period, flows to the input of the **low_filter** module.

Table 17.2 explains the syntax of Music 0 unit generators.

Interconnections between Unit Generators

It is not difficult to understand how interconnections between UGs are implemented in software. The synthesis language contains data areas that can be shared by (accessible to) more than one UG procedure. For two connected UGs **osc** and **low_filter**, the output of **osc** spills into an array called *signal1* that is common to both UGs. The **low_filter** UG reads the output value of **osc** from the array, thus making the connection (figure 17.2).

After the musician defines the score and orchestra and saves them in their respective files, the synthesis compiler reads both files, generating samples that go to the output sound file. If the synthesis algorithm is simple enough and the computer on which it runs is fast enough, it is possible to generate sound directly through converters, rather than writing a file first.

The next two sections explain simple orchestra and score files in more detail.

Instrument Definition Example

This section presents a complete example of a simple instrument definition. Figure 17.3a depicts a graphical representation of an instrument that uses

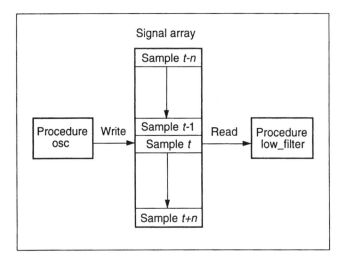

Figure 17.2   Connecting unit generators in software through shared data arrays in memory. The output of an **osc** UG is read as the input to a **low_filter** UG.

an envelope generator to control the amplitude of an oscillator. The output of the oscillator is lowpass filtered and then written to a soundfile through the **out** UG. Figure 17.3b presents an orchestra file (text) description of the same network, conforming to the Music 0 syntax.

In the text of figure 17.3b the unit generator **env_gen** emits the control signal *env_signal*. The parameters of the unit generators can appear to their right either as numbers, variable names (like the functions *f1* and *f2*), or names of *parameter fields* (*pfields* or columns in the score). Pfields begin with the letter *p*, as in *p3, p4,* etc. Function table *f1* holds the waveform for the envelope, and *f2* contains the oscillator waveform.

Score Definition Example

This section presents a simple score file that drives the instrument just defined. The score file contains two parts: function table definitions and the note list. Function tables contain waveforms that are fed to envelope generators and oscillators, as we saw in figure 17.3. The note list defines the start time, duration, and parameters of the notes.

Function Table Definition

Figure 17.4 shows a score file. The upper part consists of two function table definitions. Notice that the fourth arguments (**line_segment** and **fourier**) are *function generator types.* A *function generator* is a predefined algorithm that

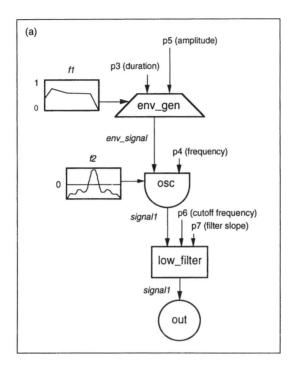

(b)

```
Instrument 1
      /* Define envelope signal */
      env_signal ← env_gen f1 p3 p5;
      /* Generate audio signal using the env_signal to control amplitude */
      signal1 ← osc  f2 p4 env_signal;
      /* Send signal1 to filter. p6 is cutoff freq., p7 is filter slope */
      signal1 ← low_filter signal1 p6 p7;
      out signal1;    /* Send signal to soundfile */
EndInstrument 1
```

Figure 17.3   Orchestra language example. Definition of an instrument with an envelope for amplitude, an oscillator, and a lowpass filter. (*a*) Graphical representation. (*b*) Textual representation. The remarks surrounded by slash-asterisk ("/*" and "*/") are comments.

```
/*
Function definitions in the form:
Fname, start time, table size, function generator type, arguments
————————————————————————————————————————————————————————— */
f1 0  1024  line_segment  (0 0) (256 1) (512 .5) (768 .5) (1024 0);
f2 0  1024  fourier  11   (1 .4) (2 .3) (3 .05) (4 .06)  (5 .04)
                          (6 .04) (7 .03) (8 .04) (9 .02) (10 .03)
                          (11 .01);


/* Instr.  Start  Dur.   Freq.   Amp.    Filt.cutoff  Filter
      ID    time                          frequency   slope
   p1       p2     p3     p4      p5       p6          p7
   ——————————————————————————————————————————————————————————— */
   i1        0    1.0    440.0   2000     4100         6;
   i1       1.0   1.0    560.0   2000     3000         5;
   i1       1.0   2.0    440.0   2000     2050         4;
   i1       2.0   2.0    880.0  10000     9000;        3;
```

Figure 17.4 Score language example. A score corresponding to the instrument shown in figure 17.3. The score consists of two parts: the two function definitions at the top, followed by the note list at the bottom.

produces waveform functions. Music *N* languages typically provide a range of function generators. Some create waveforms by adding together sine waves in various combinations, while others create waveforms out of line segments, exponentials, or polynomial functions.

Figure 17.5 explains the syntax of the **line_segment** and **fourier** function table definitions in figure 17.4.

Note List

The lower part of figure 17.4 presents a typical *note list* score format defining four notes for the instrument described in figure 17.3. Each note has several pfields, indicated in the score. The pfield layouts per note are as follows:

p1   Instrument number

p2   Start time in beats

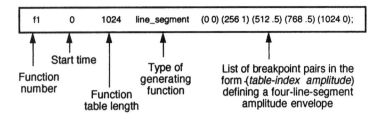

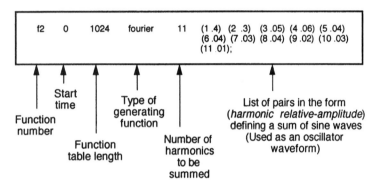

Figure 17.5 Syntax of the function table definitions of figure 17.4.

p3   Duration in beats

p4   Fundamental frequency of oscillator

p5   Peak amplitude

p6   Filter cutoff frequency

p7   Filter slope in dB per octave

The lowpass filter attentuates spectral components above the cutoff frequency. The steepness of the attenuation is set by p7.

Alternative Score Representations

In Music N languages, the score is a flat (nonhierarchical) list of notes, mostly encoded as numbers. The note list is a precise means of specifying sound events, but the weaknesses of numerical and note-oriented score languages have been known for some time. (See Haynes 1980 for a good survey.) The main issues are the numerical orientation, rigid syntax, and a lack of higher-level structures (such as phrases and voices).

In a complicated instrument with many parameters, the note list is unreadable as music. Since the position of each number in the list determines the parameter to which the number applies, all parameters must be supplied for every note, or else a special character must be inserted into that position to indicate a repeating or null value.

Some of the music input and composition languages described later in this chapter attempt to provide a more intuitive syntax. They may allow the use of traditional musical terminology or a more flexible syntax. Instead of typing pitch in terms of frequency in Hertz, for example, the composer can use a pitch-class and octave code, like "C4." *Score preprocessors* interpret these more intuitive specifications and convert them to a numerical note list before synthesis (Smith 1972; Fry 1980; Ames 1989b; De Poli and Vidolin 1984; Tochetti 1984; Jaffe 1989).

Another valuable feature in a score language is *expression evaluation*— allowing computation within the score itself. In the simplest case we might want to specify that one parameter is a function of another parameter, as in the following: p8 ← p7/2.

Some languages permit expression evaluation in the orchestra only, but for maximum flexibility it should also be possible in the score. This capability means that composers set a few global variables at the head of a large score and let the language compiler calculate specific parameters based on these settings. Composers can quickly try out variations of a score with such a facility. Music languages embedded in a general-purpose programming language make this easier.

Note lists represent only the lowest level of musical structure. The middle levels of structure, including phrases and voice interaction, are not addressed at all by note lists. To effect a crescendo over a phrase, for example, it is necessary to specify the amplitudes of each of the individual notes in the phrase in relation to their point in the crescendo; note lists offer no phrase-level controls. Compositional languages like Formes (Rodet and Cointe 1984) and Pla (Schottstaedt 1983, 1989a) were developed to alleviate some of the problems of the note list representation. They provide explicit constructs for phrases and voices. These programs can act as "front ends" to a Music *N* program, since their output can be a note list that can be fed to a Music *N* compiler.

Example of an Alternative Score Format: Scorefile

This section presents a brief introduction to Scorefile for NeXTStep-compatible computers. We present it because it exemplifies a more flexible score format than the traditional note list, although its roots remain within the classical note list structure (Jaffe 1989; Jaffe and Boynton 1989). Scorefile supports real-time synthesis, non-real-time synthesis, and MIDI. It draws some features from the Pla language. For example, instead of using ordered pfields, each parameter is specified as a pair *keyword: value*. For example, the parameter list for a note might look like the following:

```
violin (2) freq:C4 amp:0.5 pan:-45
```

Unlike Music *N* scores, parameters for the same note could also be specified in another order, for example:

```
violin (2) pan:-45 amp:0.5 freq:c4
```

Duration is always indicated by a value in parentheses. Here the frequency parameter is set to pitch-class C, octave 4, the amplitude parameter is set to 0.5 (the maximum is 1.0), and the panning parameter is set at -45 degrees (the left loudspeaker). Only the parameters that differ from the defaults need to be specified for a given note.

The use of keywords makes reorchestration easier. One score can be performed on different instruments, since parameters that are unrecognized by an instrument are ignored. In the object-oriented programming sense (see chapter 2), parameters can be thought of as messages whose precise meaning depends on the instrument that responds to them.

Another feature that aids reorchestration is a *part* construct—a way of grouping notes that are realized by the same software instrument. The traditional Music *N* note list names the instrument associated with each note, for example, i1, i2, etc. In contrast, Scorefile groups notes into parts, where the mapping from part to software instrument can be declared in the header of the score. Depending on the type of synthesis application that reads the score, this specification can refer to a software instrument or a MIDI channel.

We can see other features of Scorefile in figure 17.6. Notice that the onset time of each note appears in a separate time (**t**) statement preceding the note. This makes chords more readable. Note starting time is specified absolutely (**t 0**) or relative to the start of the previous note (**t +1**). Relative time makes cut-and-splice score editing easier.

Unlike traditional languages, Scorefile also supports events whose duration is determined by a performer in real time, similar to MIDI's note-on and note-off events, as in the following:

```
violin (noteOn, 4) freq: c4;
violin (noteOff, 4);
```

The **noteOn** occurs when a performer triggers the designated key; the **noteOff** occurs when the performer releases the key. The number 4 following the note type is a *note-tag* that matches note-on and note-off events.

```
info tempo 84;
part soprano;


soprano synthPatch:"Fm1vi"  midiChan: 3;


waveTable wave1 = [{1,1} {3, .1}];
waveTable wave2 = [{"onePeriodOfASoprano.snd"}];


BEGIN


t 0; /* Time is in beats */
soprano (2)  freq:c4  amp: -30 dB  waveform:wave1
t 1;
soprano (2)  freq: d4;
t + 1;
soprano (2)  freq: e4  waveform:wave2;


print "Score is finished.";


END;
```

Figure 17.6 Scorefile example. The **synthPatch** declaration indicates that if the score is played on the NeXT internal digital signal processor, the instrument to be used is **Fm1vi**—one of the standard instruments. The **midiChan** declaration indicates that if the score is played over MIDI it is to be transmitted over MIDI channel 3. Both frequency-domain and time-domain envelope declarations are shown. **wave1** is a sum of sines in the form (*harmonic number, relative amplitude*). **wave2** takes its values from the sampled waveform in the named file in quotation marks.

Note-tags can also represent phrase structure, by grouping notes of a given phrase with the same tag. The Music Kit interprets several **noteOn**s within the same note-tag as legato rearticulations within a single melody with no overlap between notes. A single **noteOff** disables all **noteOn**s, unlike the MIDI protocol. Time-scalable envelopes support the variable-length notes. Parameter updates to playing notes or phrases can be sent via the **noteUpdate** statement. A **noteUpdate** is similar to a **noteOn**, in that it conveys parameter values to an instrument, but unlike a **noteOn** it does not trigger envelopes.

Non-note-list Score Representations

For some synthesis methods, the traditional note-list representation is inadequate. For example, Chafe (1985) indicates that the note list may be inappropriate for the control of synthesis involving *physical modeling* of traditional instruments. (See chapter 7 for more on physical modeling.) Note lists consist of separate isolated event calls. On the other hand, physical models simulate the cause-and-effect chain of mechanical-acoustical events within a single instrument. This requires multiple parallel processes whose synchronization varies in different musical situations. For example, violin slurs (sliding from one note to the next) involve asynchrony between the two hands of a violinist. Only certain languages, like Scorefile, with its **noteUpdate** construct, can handle these complicated situations.

The note concept is not relevant in systems that scatter hundreds of sound events within the bounds of a composer-defined spectral region (i.e., a region inscribed on a plane where the *x*-axis is time and the *y*-axis is frequency). This includes systems like POD and PODX (Truax 1977, 1985; chapter 18), and *asynchronous granular synthesis* (Roads 1991; chapter 5).

Soundfile Processing

One of the most musically important applications of modern Music *N* languages is soundfile processing. Most languages provide a unit generator for reading in a soundfile, like the **soundin** UG of Csound. This means that arbitrary signal processing operations can be applied to soundfiles, such as filtering, reenveloping, reverberation, or spatialization.

Soundfile reading is triggered just like an oscillator, that is, by a note statement. By lining up a dozen overlapping note statements we can crossfade a dozen soundfiles in a precise manner. Logically extrapolating from this point leads to complex, algorithmically controlled sound-mixing processes, where the note list is generated by a separate composition program. These capabilities have been exploited by composers such as Horacio Vaggione (1984) and Paul Lansky (1990c).

Implementations of Music *N*

So far we have treated the basic structure of orchestras and scores in the Music *N* languages. This section discusses the compilers for these languages and mentions some of the differences between the implementations.

Once we have defined an instrument we submit it, along with an associated score, to a Music *N* compiler. Most Music *N* compilers break synthesis into three stages, called *Pass 1, Pass 2,* and *Pass 3.* Pass 1 reads the score specified by the composer, calling composition subroutines and sometimes performing transformations that make the score more digestible to the computer. Pass 2 sorts the score and function definitions in time order. Pass 3 reads the transformed score and calls the user's instruments to generate sound samples. Output routines in Pass 3 write the samples to a soundfile, usually played later. If the score and orchestra are simple enough, the music program may be able to generate sound output in real time.

Pass 3 is by far the most computationally intensive stage of the synthesis, since for each second of sound it must carry out hundreds of thousands of floating-point calculations. In order to make Pass 3 as efficient as possible, some dialects of Music *N* have been optimized for a specific computer architecture. These optimizations usually involve writing the unit generator code in assembly language. For example, MUS10 (Tovar and Smith 1977) ran efficiently on a Digital Equipment Corporation PDP-10 computer, and Music 7 (Howe 1975) ran efficiently on a Xerox Sigma 7 computer.

Portability

Some implementations have attempted to make the program as portable as possible by rendering the code in a widely available language such as Fortran, C, or Lisp. Examples of this approach include the following:

Music 4BF and Music V	(Fortran)
Cmusic, Csound, Music 4C	(C)
Common Lisp Music, Nyquist (Dannenberg and Mercer 1992)	(Common Lisp)

Simply because a program is written in a widely available language does not mean it will work on any computer, however. Some languages depend strongly on the underlying operating system for protocols such as installation, user interaction, input and output, and soundfile format. Thus while 90 percent of the code is portable, the remaining 10 percent prevents its use on any other system except the one it was written on.

Another type of configuration is seen in languages that can run either on a host computer or on an attached DSP subsystem, as is the case with Common Lisp Music (Schottstaedt 1991). The DSP microprocessor may not be as flexible as the host microprocessor, but it may offer a speedup for simple orchestras, enabling real-time synthesis.

Extensibility

One distinction between the various dialects of Music *N* is their degree of openess to user-written extensions. For example, Common Lisp Music is embedded in Lisp so all the data structures and control flow constructs of that language can be used in designing an instrument. By contrast, Music 11 was a closed system; it provided a limited set of data types and control constructs that could not be extended, and the source code was not distributed. Most other languages stand somewhere between these poles. For example, Music V is a closed system, but it provides hooks in Pass 1 and Pass 2 for user-written subroutines. MUS10 was implemented starting from an existing Algol compiler, so it provided the data structure and control facilities of an actual programming language.

Graphical Tools

Several synthesis systems provide a graphical tools for instrument design and envelope specification that augment or replace the textual language. Instead of specifying an instrument as a text, as in figure 17.3b, users interconnect icons on a display screen, similar to the graphical notation shown in figure 17.3a (Sandel 1989; Wilkinson et al. 1989). Graphical aids for envelope design can be enormously helpful, since textual specification is both error-prone and tedious. Chapter 16 describes the features of graphical instrument editors.

Block versus Sample Computation

In order to understand the internal operation of music languages (and many synthesizers) it is essential to realize that they can be characterized as either *block-* or *sample-oriented*. A block-oriented compiler computes sound samples a *block* at a time, where a block is an arbitrary number of samples greater than one. Block computation is efficient since computer registers are loaded with synthesis parameter values just once for each block. Sample-oriented compilers are more flexible, since every aspect of the computation can change for any sample, but they are less efficient since the setup time for each sample (such as loading registers with parameter values) adds up over time.

Among the languages of the Music *N* family, Music IV and its derivatives (including Music 4C) are sample-oriented, whereas Music V and Cmusic are block-oriented. The Csound language is also block-oriented, since it updates synthesis parameters at a *control rate* set by users. The control rate determines the block size. In some implementations it is possible to set the control rate to be equal to the sampling rate, in which case Csound operates in an essentially sample-oriented manner. Cmusic lets users specify the block size, which allows similar flexibility.

Several dialects of Music *N* let users set variables on larger blocks, namely at the beginning of each note. These variables are called *note initialization variables* (or *i*-variables), and they provide control from note to note. One application is to allow slurs and glissandi across separate note statements in the score, by storing the pitch where the previous note left off, for example. But they can be used for any compositional purpose. Languages like Music 4BF and Music 4C use a different mechanism to achieve the same end. They have the concept of initialization variables built into their user-written **setup** routine, which is part of the orchestra and is called once per note (Howe 1975; Beauchamp and Aurenz 1985; Gerrard 1989; Beauchamp 1992b).

Languages for Controlling Real-time Synthesis

This section looks at the many issues surrounding control of real-time synthesis hardware by means of a synthesis language. In general, by "synthesis hardware" we imply digital signal processors (DSPs), including both synthesizers and devices that sample and transform sounds. At the same time, the increasing speed of microprocessors means that more and more synthesis algorithms can be run in real-time on standard computers without additional hardware.

Fixed-function versus Variable-function Hardware

Two global factors shape the design of real-time synthesis software: the architecture of the synthesis hardware (*fixed-function* or *variable-function*) and the number and type of input and output devices. Chapter 20 presents distinction between fixed- and variable-function architecture, so here we keep the description brief. Fixed-function DSPs are made up of dedicated components such as oscillators, filters, and envelope generators. These components are interconnected in a standard configuration in order to realize a well-defined set of signal-processing tasks. Many commercial MIDI products are based on the fixed-function concept. For example, a frequency modulation synthesizer can be manufactured inexpensively with a fixed-function circuit designed for FM. The software for a fixed-function DSP is much simpler than that needed for variable-function signal processing.

By contrast, a variable-function DSP contains a more flexible collection of functional units. The functional units consist of multiple memories and special processors. Interconnecting the functional units via software is often called *patching* the DSP, by analogy to the patch cords connecting the modules of analog synthesizers. This flexibility allows the DSP to realize different synthesis and signal-processing tasks, although its adds to the complexity of the internal software and the musician's interface.

Earlier we mentioned a third possible category of architecture—a standard general-purpose microprocessor without any specialized DSP functionality. Since the language issues are largely the same in both DSPs and general-purpose microprocessors (i.e., both can be easily reprogrammed), we lump the two together in the rest of this chapter.

Control of Real-time Synthesis: Background

Control of real-time synthesis hardware is not a trivial task. Slow computers, small memories, and limited synthesis and sound-processing engines all constrained the music software of the 1970s. The landmark software system MUSYS (Grogorno 1973) developed at Electronic Music Studios (EMS), London, ran on a slow 12-bit computer with a total of 8 Kwords of random-access memory (RAM).

By the time digital synthesizers were introduced in the late 1970s, little was known about how to write usable software for them, despite years of experience with software synthesis programs such as Music V (Mathews 1969). Early commercial synthesizers, like the New England Digital Synclavier, coped by imposing a fixed-function architecture, thus eliminating many difficult issues and reducing the control problem to that of sequencing. Martin Bartlett shoehorned his music control program for a KIM-1 microprocessor into a grand total of 1152 bytes of RAM by using an analog synthesizer for sound output (Bartlett 1979).

The problems of managing interactive control of a variable-function real-time synthesizer remained unresolved for some time. Attempts to control DSPs such as the 4A and 4B synthesizers at IRCAM ended with little more than a "learning experience" to show for it (Rolnick 1978). Part of the blame could be laid on an inadequate understanding of the communication demands between the host computer and the DSP. Such difficulties resulted, for example, in the *parameter update problem*, in which some part of the music system has trouble keeping up with the rate of parameter changes in the music. This arises because musical data have a tendency to change in bursts—for example, at the beginning and ending of notes, chords, and sections. The problem can occur in either the computer (which cannot handle the incoming information fast enough or send it out fast enough), the communication channel (such as a MIDI cable, which may not have enough bandwidth), or the DSP. In commercial synthesizers, the parameter update problem sometimes exists, but its effects are minimized in many cases by limiting the musical functionality of the system through safe, preset modes of behavior. See Kaplan (1981) for an enlightening discussion of the issues involved in programming a commercial synthesizer.

In the rest of this section we look at two approaches to control of DSPs: languages for MIDI control of fixed-function DSPs, and languages for variable-function DSPs.

MIDI Languages for Fixed-function DSPs

Within every commercial fixed-function synthesizer is a microprocessor. This microprocessor runs an operating system that manages user interaction, input/output, memory allocation, and audio processing. The operating system is usually resident in read-only memory (ROM) and is visible to users only via the front panel of the synthesizer. The job of the synthesizer's internal software is mainly to translate front panel settings (buttons and sliders) and musical gestures played on attached input devices into commands for the synthesizer.

Another way to manipulate the synthesizer is via external MIDI messages sent to it through one of its MIDI IN ports. (See chapter 21 for more on MIDI.) MIDI messages contain control information transmitted between musical instruments and computers. The messages say, in effect, "play a C4 note at amplitude 50 on channel 6," "start playing a sequence," "increase the vibrato depth," and so on.

Besides the usual closed commercial packages for score editing, sequencing, patch editing, and so on, a variety of programming languages provide explicit support for MIDI constructs by means of libraries of MIDI functions that can be called from within a program. These languages let users write their own programs to manipulate MIDI devices. Special versions of APL, Basic, C, Pascal, Hypertalk, Forth, and Lisp have MIDI extensions. MIDI languages enable more-or-less complete programmable control of a MIDI device. A program can—in effect—push buttons and sliders on the front panel of the device, play note sequences on its keyboard, or load new instrument patches into the device. This means we have three ways of controlling a MIDI device: via its front panel, with a MIDI input device, or with a program that generates MIDI messages (figure 17.7).

The usual type of data handled by a MIDI synthesizer is of three types:

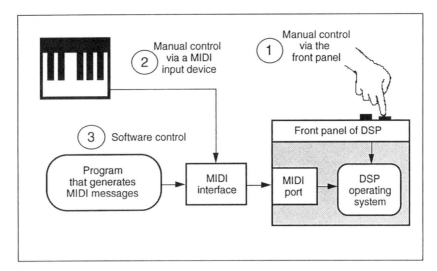

Figure 17.7   Three ways to control a MIDI device: via its front panel, with a MIDI input device, or with a program that generates MIDI messages.

1. Discrete note data (start time, stop time, channel number, etc.)

2. Continuous controller messages (equivalent to volume pedal changes, vibrato wheel, etc.)

3. Discrete program change messages (e.g., switch the timbre from *Voice 1: Piano* to *Voice 39: Choir*, etc.)

Another possibility is transmitting a fourth category of data in the form of *system-exclusive* messages that set up the internal synthesis parameters particular to a specific synthesizer (see chapter 21). But since detailed timbral manipulation is rarely the goal of MIDI programming, the control problem typically boils down to supplying the score, along with occasional program change messages that alter the orchestration. See the section on composition languages later.

MIDI programming languages also make it possible to create interactive performance programs, for example, a computer accompanist or an interactive improviser. See chapter 15 for more on these applications.

Languages for Variable-function DSPs

In a variable-function DSP, software can "repatch" the internal hardware to implement different synthesis and signal-processing techniques. This poses a more difficult programming task than that required for a fixed-function architecture (Abbott 1979, 1985; Loy and Abbott 1985). A signal-processing microprogram must interconnect the different processing modules of the DSP (memories, multiplier, adder, etc.) and manage the flow of audio and control data through them. These tasks become critical when the repatching occurs in the midst of a performance.

Real-time Unit Generators: 4CED and Max

A "great leap forward" in software control of real-time DSPs was the application of the unit generator concept that had already proven successful in software synthesis languages (table 17.3). Software synthesis languages such as Music IV and Music V had a strong influence on the pioneering real-time synthesis package 4CED (Abbott 1981) developed at IRCAM. 4CED was a package of three languages: an orchestra language for patching together unit generators, a score language with a special envelope definition facility, and an interactive command language for controlling real-time effects. The command language allowed the programmer to couple the orchestra and score to real-time input devices such as potentiometers and buttons.

The result of interpreting programs written in these languages was a collection of microprograms and data that controlled the 4C synthesizer designed by Giuseppe Di Giugno (Moorer et al. 1979; Moorer 1981a).

In 4CED each score acted as an independent process that could accept input data and trigger events that caused other scores to start playing. This "score as active process" capability goes far beyond the passive data model of a note list embodied in many languages. In particular, it encourages interactive performance, as discussed in chapter 15.

The chronological successor to languages of the 4CED type was the visual programming language Max, developed by Miller Puckette at IRCAM (Puckette 1985, 1988, 1991; Puckette and Zicarelli 1990). The later implementations of Max include unit generators for audio signal processing. See chapter 15 for more on Max.

A Simple DSP Program Example

A simple example of the unit generator concept in a DSP language is the Music 1000 language for the Digital Music Systems DMX-1000 signal processing computer (Wallraff 1979a). Although the hardware technology of the DMX-1000 is antiquated, Music 1000 is an easily understood language, so we use it to demonstrate basic techniques of programming a variable-function DSP.

Figure 17.8 presents an example of an orchestra definition that produces a sine wave (specified in the table **fnctn**) whose frequency and amplitude are

Table 17.3   Unit-generator-based languages for control of real-time DSPs

Program	Date Introduced	Author(s)	Host computer	Language	Target DSP	Location
4B control program	1978	D. Bayer	DEC LSI-11	Macro-11 assembler	IRCAM 4B	Bell Laboratories Murray Hill
SYN4B	1978	P. Prevot N. Rolnick	DEC LSI-11	Macro-11 assembler	IRCAM 4B	IRCAM, Paris
4PLAY	1978	C. Abbott	DEC PDP-11	Pascal and Macro-11 assembler	IRCAM 4C	IRCAM, Paris
Musbox	1979	G. Loy W. Schottstaedt	DEC PDP-10	Sail	Systems Concepts Digital Synthesizer ("Samson Box")	Stanford University, Stanford
4CED	1980	C. Abbott	DEC PDP-11	C	IRCAM 4C	IRCAM, Paris
Music 1000	1980	D. Wallraff	DEC LSI-11	Macro-11 assembler	DMX-1000	Digital Music Systems, Boston
4X control program	1981	J. Kott	DEC PDP-11	Macro-11 assembler	IRCAM 4X	IRCAM, Paris
FMX and Cleo	1982	C. Abbott	DEC VAX-11	C	Lucasfilm ASP	Lucasfilm, San Rafael
Music 400	1982	M. Puckette	DEC PDP-11	C	Analogic AP-400 array processor	MIT, Cambridge
Cleo	1983	C. Abbott	Sun	C	Lucasfilm ASP	Lucasfilm, San Rafael
Music 320	1983	T. Hegg	MC68000-based microprocessor	68000 assembler	Texas Inst. TMS 32010	MIT, Cambridge
Music 500	1984	M. Puckette	DEC VAX-11	C	Analogic AP-500 array processor	MIT, Cambridge
4XY	1986	R. Rowe O. Koechlin	DEC VAX-11	C	IRCAM 4X	IRCAM, Paris

Table 17.3 (cont.)

Program	Date Introduced	Author(s)	Host computer	Language	Target DSP	Location
Csound	1989	N. Bailey A. Purvis I. Bowler P. Manning	Inmos Transputer	Occam	Inmos Transputer	University of Durham, U.K.
Music 56000	1989	K. Lent R. Pinkston P. Silsbee	IBM PS/2 and Apple Macintosh	56000 assembler	Motorola DSP56001	University of Texas, Austin
NeXT Music and Sound Kits	1989	D. Jaffe L. Boynton J. Smith	NeXT	Objective C	Motorola DSP56001	NeXT, Redwood City
Digital Signal Patcher	1990	A. Pellecchia	IBM PC	C	Texas Instruments TMS320C30	Centro Richerche Musicali, Rome
MUSIC30	1991	J. Dashow	IBM PC with Spirit-30 DSP board	Prolog	Texas Instruments TMS320C30	Studio Sciadoni, Castello Poggio San Lorenzo
IRCAM Max	1991	M. Puckette	NeXT	C	Intel i860	IRCAM, Paris
IRIS Edit20	1992	P. Andenacci E. Favreau N. Larosa A. Prestigiacomo C. Rosati S. Sapir	Atari SM1000	C	MARS	IRIS, Paliano
Unison	1992	J. Bate	Apple Macintosh	C	Motorola DSP56001	University of Manitoba, Winnipeg

```
orch

; func1 is a sine wave
fnctn    func1, 512, fourier, normal, 1, 1000

instr         1                          ; Begin instrument 1
     kscale   amp, knob1, 0, 10000       ; Knob1 controls amplitude
     kscale   freq, knob2, 20, 2000      ; Knob2 controls frequency
     oscil    x8, #func1, amp, freq      ; oscil uses waveform 1
     out      x8                         ; End instrument 1
endin
```

Figure 17.8 Music 1000 instrument for fixed-waveform synthesis with real-time control from two knobs. The table length is always a power of two. The keyword **fourier** indicates that the function is to be built using sine wave summation. The **normal** (normalize) keyword means that the largest amplitude of the sine wave will be 1.0. The number of sine waves components (1) is next, followed by an obligatory amplitude value, which is redundant in this case because the function is normalized. (It would not be redundant if there were more sine wave components to be summed, since then we would be compelled to type a list of numbers, each one indicating the relative strength of a partial.)

set by the score. There are minor syntactic differences between Music 1000 and the Music *N* language previously described. Whereas Music *N* gives the signal to the left of the ← sign, Music 1000 has no assignment sign, and the signal variable is shown immediately to the right of the unit generator name. The syntax of the **fnctn** statement is similar to the function table definition **f** statement explained in figure 17.5; the main difference is that in Music 1000 function definitions are part of the orchestra and not the score. See the caption of figure 17.8 for more details.

In figure 17.8, the Music 1000 UG **oscil** puts its output to the signal variable **x8**. The UG **oscil** uses the waveform stored in the function table **func1**, defined previously. **oscil** gets its frequency value from **knob1** and its amplitude value from **knob2**. The knobs produce signals that vary between 0 and 1. Their output can be scaled using the **kscale** unit generator, whose syntax is shown in figure 17.9. The last unit generator is **out**, which sends the audio signal to the DAC. It takes one argument, the name of the signal to be output, here **x8**.

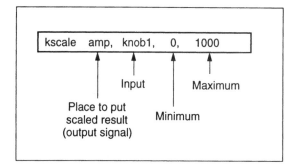

Figure 17.9 Syntax of a Music 1000 **kscale** input control function declaration.

MIDI Control of Variable-function DSPs

Past digital synthesizers were closed, fixed-function systems that could not be reprogrammed to realize different synthesis techniques. Today an increasing number of synthesizers use a variable-function DSP architecture, meaning that they can be programmed to realize a variety of synthesis and signal-processing operations. In many cases, system exclusive messages—defined by the manufacturer—can repatch the hardware to realize different functions. (See chapter 21 for more on MIDI system exclusive messages.) Thus any MIDI language could ostensibly manipulate the internal workings of the DSP hardware.

Merging Multiple Control Streams

The Music 1000 example just shown takes input data from two control knobs—a simple setup. It is not difficult to imagine a more complicated performance situation with multiple input devices and sequences. Before MIDI became popular, only a few general languages were developed for confronting the problem of merging data from multiple input devices, including FMX (Abbott 1982a, 1982b) and Cleo (Abbott 1983, 1986) developed at Lucasfilm. Today, MIDI standardizes the protocols for data coming from musical input devices. The MIDI protocol assigns incoming data to *channels,* and the channel number can be easily parsed from the data. The MIDI solution is independent of whether the DSP is fixed- or variable-function. As a result, many systems today can handle control data coming from multiple sources. These include some of the languages discussed in the section of fixed-function DSPs, the procedural composition languages cited in table 17.4, as well as the graphical editors and environments mentioned in chapters 16 and 18.

Composition Languages

Let us distinguish two basic types of composition languages: *score input* or *encoding* languages, and *procedural* languages. Score input languages are slanted toward the entry of musical scores that have already been composed. Procedural languages take a generative or algorithmic approach. That is, they generate musical events by stipulated procedures or rules. We discuss each type in turn in the next two sections.

Score Input Languages

Score input languages exist for the purpose of *data entry*. They permit a score written in common music notation (CMN) to be transcribed into an alphanumeric code for entry into a computer. Many dozen music input languages have been implemented, aimed at different musical contingents. Languages like DARMS (Erickson 1975) and MUSTRAN (Wenker 1972) were developed for musicological purposes. Their goal was faithful transcription of the graphic symbols found in music scores into a computer, usually for the purpose of archiving or score analysis. The Standard Music Description Language (SMDL) is a more recent effort along these lines (Newcomb and Goldfarb 1989).

The encryption of a traditional score into character strings can result in codes of baffling complexity. In 1965 Milton Babbitt suggested that the need for such input languages might disappear with the advent of optical scanners connected to computers. After early attempts to coax a computer to read music notation visually (Entwistle 1973; Prerau 1970, 1971; Pruslin 1966), the most spectacular success in recent years was WABOT-2, the Tsukuba musical robot. WABOT-2 read a single sheet of simple notation in about ten seconds while simultaneously planning all the motions needed to play it (Matsushima et al. 1985; Roads 1986b). Research in optical recognition of music is ongoing, and we expect further progress to be made (Fujinaga, Alphonce, and Pennycook 1989; Fujinaga et al. 1991). But for the present, the majority of composers must be content to enter their scores into a computer by other means.

A myriad of music-encoding languages have been implemented for score transcription as a preparation for synthesis or printing. Some of these include SCORE (Smith 1972), Musica (De Poli 1978), SCRIPT (New England Digital 1981), Scriptu (Brown 1977), ASHTON (Ames 1985), Note-pro (Beauchamp, Code and Chen 1990), and YAMIL (Yet Another Music

Figure 17.10   Fragment of H. Birtwistle's *Verses* (top) coded in the Musica score input language.

Input Language, Fry 1980), among others. A main feature of these languages is their direct correspondence with the structures of CMN. They support such constructs as measures, metrical rhythms, equal-tempered pitches and accidentals, slurs, ties, and simultaneous parts. In some cases they allow the user to specify synthesis-related information, such as envelopes and microtonal pitches (Ames 1985).

Figure 17.10 is a one-part score fragment and its encoding in the Musica language developed at the Centro di Sonologia Computazionale in Padua, Italy (De Poli 1978). Musica is interfaced to the Music V synthesis system, so all note values are translated into Music V note statements by the Musica interpreter. In figure 17.10 the first number, 4, indicates a quarter-note duration, and the 'A indicates A440. (An octave higher would be encoded "A.) Since the subsequent three notes in the measure (GAG) are also quarter notes, there is no need to respecify the duration for them. The slash "/" indicates a measure boundary, and the period after the 4 indicates a dotted quarter note. The 8 before the G indicates an eighth-note duration, and the 2 before the E indicates a half note.

This is probably the simplest example we can give of a score transcription language. A more complicated multipart example would require a great deal of explanation, since the encoding is less readable than the score, at least to a novice. After some training, however, one can learn to read multipart score encodings, with the qualification that some input languages are clearer than others.

Impact of MIDI on Score Input Languages

With MIDI-based sequencers and music printing packages the need for score input languages has decreased, since a great deal of music can be entered part by part either by playing into a sequencer or by graphical editing with note lists, piano roll notation, or CMN (see chapter 16). This is not to say that score input languages have been entirely replaced by MIDI, since the MIDI protocol imposes many limits on musical expression. For example, MIDI is not capable of expressing the many parameters and multiple envelopes used in software synthesis. Nor is there any standard for expressing score symbols via MIDI. It is likely that languages for archival score entry will prevail at least until reliable scanners for music notation are common.

Encoded Scores and the Performance Problem

An unresolved issue concerning input languages is that a score is an incomplete description of a musical performance. If we try to synthesize a score directly from the encoding, it will tend to exhibit a wooden, machine-like quality. A satisfactory realization of an encoded work can be achieved through interpretation by trained performers, but this interpretive information is not usually encoded in software along with the score. There have been attempts to formalize performance rules for improved machine realizations (notably Sundberg, Askenfelt, and Frydén 1983; Clynes and Nettheim 1982; Clynes and Walker 1982; Friberg et al. 1991; Johnson 1991), but such rules are dependent on the style of music being performed. (See chapter 15 for more on rule-based software for expressive performance.)

Literal-minded score input languages are designed to encode faithfully all the text markings of the score, but they do not necessarily capture other layers and dimensions of music representation that are important in music understanding and performance. Phrasing, which is essential in performance, requires an explicit representation of phrase structure in the language. Several of the composition languages discussed in the next section handle phrasing directly.

Procedural Composition Languages

Procedural composition languages go beyond the representation of traditional scores to support the unique possibilities of computer music. These possibilities include alternative tunings, multiple envelopes for control of timbres and spatial paths, voice interplay, performer interaction, and compositional procedures. These languages let composers specify music algorithmically. They represent the flow of music as a collection of interacting processes.

Two advantages of representing a compositional process as a program stand out. First, the compositional logic is made explicit, creating a system with a degree of formal consistency. Abstract formal unity in a composition is prized by many music theorists and composers. Second, rather than

abdicating decision-making to the computer, composers can use procedures
to extend control over many more processes than they could manage with
manual techniques. Here are a few examples of how algorithms can expand
the scope of compositional decisions:

Controlling the microfrequency variations among the partials of a given
tone

Sifting through massive amounts of data to select a specified sound or
sound combination

Sending sounds on precise spatial paths computed according to composer-
specified rules

Generating numerous variations quickly to provide the composer with
many alternatives of a given sound or series of sounds

Realizing complex polyphonic textures that would otherwise be impossible
to perform

Generating algorithmic music accompaniment in real time based on a performer's input

No "standard" language for procedural composition dominates the field.
This is not surprising, since there are so many diverse approaches to composition. Table 17.4 lists examples of procedural composition languages.
Much of this software is organized as a collection of routines that are called
from a traditional programming language, or are embedded within a special
musical dialect of that language. The boundary is blurry between some of
the procedural composition languages cited here and the composition
"microworlds," "toolkits," "environments," and "libraries" mentioned in
chapter 18.

Music Languages Embedded in Programming Languages

Extensible languages support the notion of a specialized *embedded language*
or *microworld* written in terms of the original language. The advantage of
this implementation is that the facilities of the general language are always
available to the sublanguage. A music composition language, for example,
can always count on the general language for routines to handle floating-
point arithmetic, files, input/output, window management, and other utili-
tarian tasks.

The power of embedding a composition language in a general-purpose
programming language is also reflected in languages like MPL (Nelson
1977, 1980) embedded in APL, and Pla (Schottstaedt 1983, 1989a) em-

Table 17.4 Examples of procedural composition languages

Language	References	Comments
MUSICOMP	Baker 1963, Hiller and Leal 1966	First composition language, included stochastic routines
GROOVE	Mathews and Moore 1970	Oriented toward functions of time; integrated with an analog synthesizer
TEMPO	Clough 1970	Combined synthesis and composition algorithms
SCORE	Smith 1972	Preprocessor for Music V and MUS10, included motivic transformations
PLAY	Chadabe and Meyers 1978	Interactive process-oriented; music is represented by sequences, functions of time, and countdown timers
Tree and Cotree	Roads 1978b	Grammar-oriented (see chapter 19)
GGDL	Holtzman 1981	Grammar-oriented (see chapter 19)
MPL	Nelson 1977, 1980	Array-oriented, updated for MIDI
Pla	Schottstaedt 1983, 1989a	Flexible syntax for control of sound synthesis; voices can interact
SAWDUST	Blum 1979 Hamlin and Roads 1985	Herbert Brün's waveform segment composition command language
PILE	Berg 1979	Designed for real-time instruction synthesis (see chapter 8)
Flavors Band	Fry 1984	Based on phrase-processing networks
FORMES	Rodet and Cointe 1984	Scheduling and manipulation of phrase envelopes
Formula	Andersen and Kuivila 1986, 1991	Forth-based process-scheduling orientation for real-time algorithmic performance
MIDI-LISP	Boynton et al. 1986	Large environment with many built-in MIDI functions

Table 17.4 (cont.)

Language	References	Comments
HMSL	Polansky, Rosenboom, and Burk 1987 Polansky et al. 1988	Forth-based with MIDI support and functions for stochastic music composition
Personal Composer Lisp	Miller 1985	Integrated within a score editor and MIDI sequencer
Player	Loy 1986	Experimental language for interacting musical processes
LOCO	Desain and Honing 1988	Logo-based algorithmic composition environment
COMPOSE	Ames 1989b	Modular; user links score-processing procedures into networks
Canon	Dannenberg 1989a	Lisp-based score language that can adapt transformation procedures to the context in which they appear
Hyperscore	Pope 1986a, b	Object-oriented, extensible
MODE	Pope 1991a	Multileveled object-oriented view of music, with many graphical features
Music Kit	Jaffe and Boynton 1989	Advanced score language and instrument library
Lisp Kernel	Rahn 1990	Portable, with flexible output formats
Keynote	Thompson 1990	MIDI-oriented, inspired by the UNIX shells, also supports graphical interaction
Arctic	Dannenberg, McAvinney, and Rubine 1986	Functional language for processing synthesizer parameter functions of time
Esquisse	Baisnée et al. 1988	Designed for "precompositional" calculations using a toolbox of data structures
Moxc	Dannenberg 1989b	Scheduling language for interactive performance
Common Music	Taube 1991	Schedule-based runtime environment for generating score files plus a pattern-oriented composition language

Table 17.4 (cont.)

Language	References	Comments
PatchWork	Laurson and Duthen 1989 Malt 1993	Graphical patching of Lisp functions, with specialized music editors and libraries
Symbolic Composer	Tonality Systems 1993	Lisp-based language with many function libraries (chaos, fractals, neural nets, etc.) and MIDI output

bedded in Sail (Pla version 1) and Lisp (Pla version 2). An intrinsically open language like Lisp encourages embedded languages. For example, the composition languages MIDI-LISP (Boynton et al. 1986), FORMES (Rodet and Cointe 1984), Esquisse (Baisnée et al. 1988), PatchWork (Laurson and Duthen 1989; Barrière, Iovino, and Laurson 1991), Canon (Dannenberg 1989a), Flavors Band (Fry 1984), Symbolic Composer (Tonality Systems 1993), Lisp Kernel (Rahn 1990), and Common Music (Taube 1991) are all embedded in Lisp.

A number of software synthesis languages can be instructed to call user-written compositional procedures coded in general programming languages. Examples include Music V, through user-written Fortran PLF subroutines (Mathews 1969), the Cscore part of Cmusic (Moore 1982; 1990), and the Music 4C language (Beauchamp and Aurenz 1985; Gerrard 1989; Beauchamp 1992b). Since Cscore and Music 4C are embedded in the C programming language, composers are free to use the resources of that language and its operating system environment in specifying a composition. The Music Kit (Jaffe 1989) can be used as a composition language for those versed in the Objective C programming language.

Conclusion

Textual languages are a precise and flexible means of controlling a computer music system. In synthesis, score entry, and composition, they can liberate the potential of a music system from the closed world of canned software and preset hardware.

In the mid-1980s it looked as if the Music *N* synthesis language dynasty might languish, due to the spread of inexpensive synthesizers. But synthesizers have never quite matched the flexibility of the Music *N* model. Modern implementations of Music *N*—embedded in powerful programming languages and running on fast hardware—have infused new life into this most traditional approach to computer music.

The note list of the Music *N* languages exists in dozens of forms. In MIDI systems, however, the use of a score language is less common, since most music can be entered by other means (such as a music keyboard, notation program, or scanner). For musicological applications that involve score analysis, however, a text-based score representation may be optimum.

New textual languages for procedural composition continue to be developed, but there is a strong parallel trend toward interactive programs with graphical interfaces. Instead of typing text, one patches together icons, draws envelopes, and fills in templates. The textual language representation supporting the graphics is hidden from the user.

Early programming languages for music tended to favor machine efficiency over ease of use. The present trend in programming has shifted from squeezing the last drop of efficiency out of a system to helping the user manage the complexity of layer upon layer of software and hardware. The most common solution to this problem is *object-oriented programming* (see chapter 2), and compositional applications are no exception to this trend (Pope 1991b).

18 *Algorithmic Composition Systems*

Background: Algorithmic Composition
> **Brief History of Formal Processes in Music**
> **Automated Composition Machinery Prior to Computers**
> *Sequence Control of Composition*
> **Lejaren Hiller: Pioneer of Computer Music**
> **Other Pioneers of Algorithmic Music**

Aesthetic Motivations behind Algorithmic Music

Deterministic versus Stochastic Processes

Three Pioneering Composition Programs
> **Stochastic Music Program**
> **Project 1**
> **The POD Programs**

Transcription and Interpretation

Total Automation versus Interactive Composition
> **Batch Mode Interaction**
> **Automation with Interaction**

Musical Assistants

Environments and Microworlds

Conclusion: Assessment of Algorithmic Composition

Models of process are natural to musical thinking. As we listen, part of us drinks in the sensual experience of sound, while another part is constantly setting up expectations, and in so doing, constructing hypotheses of musical process. Composers have known for centuries that many musical processes can be *formalized* into a symbolic representation. A *formal composition algorithm* is an engine for music creation; thus a computer can serve as a vehicle for musical ideas.

We find compositional algorithms in assorted forms:

- Self-contained automated composition programs

- Command languages for generation and transformation of musical data and control of musical processes

- Extensions to traditional programming languages

- Graphical or textual environments designed for music (including music programming languages)

This chapter looks at process models of composition found in algorithmic composition programs and environments. Chapters 15 and 17 contain more discussion of composition algorithms in the context of performance systems and languages, respectively. Chapter 19 explains common strategies used within algorithmic composition systems.

In order to focus the discussion on original composition, we exclude systems that compose music according to the norms of a historical style. This includes, for example, programs that realize chorales in the style of J. S. Bach (for example, Ebcioglu 1988 and Baroni et al. 1984) or that generate species counterpoint (Schottstaedt 1989b). Although they may be of great interest, these programs have different aims (usually musicological or scientific) and must be assessed according to those criteria. At the same time, one should note the rise of increasingly sophisticated systems for *style template* composition. The program shown in figure 18.1, for example, generates a multiple-part accompaniment from a user-supplied list of chords according to a preset style template selected by the user. Although such programs tend to serve primarily as amusement, they exemplify the broad trend toward formalization of compositional processes.

Background: Algorithmic Composition

The operating mechanism [of the Analytical Engine] ... might act upon other things besides number, were objects found whose mutual fundamental relations could be expressed by those of the abstract science of operations, and which should be also suscep-

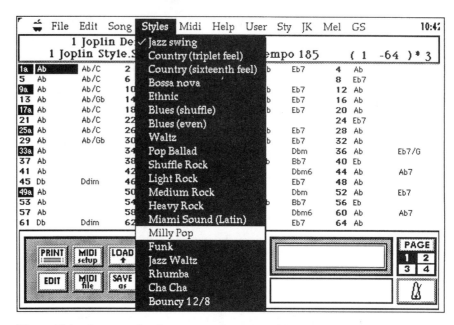

Figure 18.1   An example of a program for composition and performance according to style templates. Given a list of chords, this program (Band-in-a-Box, by PG Music, Incorporated) generates automatic accompaniment for bass, drums, piano, guitar, and strings according to rules formalized in a style template. See the open menu in the center for a listing of some of the available styles. It is also possible create a personal style and play any song in this style. The user can record melodies or solos to complete the arrangement.

tible of adaptations to the action of the operating notation and mechanism of the Engine. Supposing, for instance, that the fundamental relations of pitched sounds in the science of harmony and of musical composition were susceptible of such expression and adaptations, the Engine might compose and elaborate scientific pieces of music of any degree of complexity or extent. (Ada Augusta, Countess of Lovelace, referring to C. Babbage's mechanical computer, the Analytical Engine 1842)

Behind modern efforts in algorithmic composition is a long tradition of viewing music procedurally. A definitive history of this tradition has yet to be written. As an orientation to the subject, this section quickly scans developments in formal processes (software) and machinery (hardware) employed in algorithmic composition. This sets the historical context for the discussion of aesthetics that follows.

Brief History of Formal Processes in Music

Procedures for composition date back to ancient times. Around 1026, Guido d'Arezzo developed a formal technique for composing a melody to

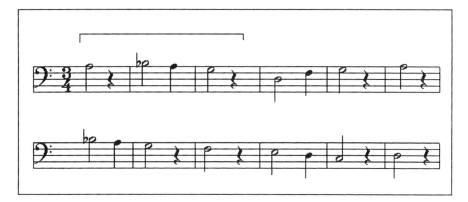

Figure 18.2   An example of the process of isorhythm in one voice.

accompany a text (Kirchmeyer 1968). His scheme assigned a pitch to each vowel, so the melody varied according to the vowel content of the text. (See Loy 1989a for more on this method.)

Compositional procedures based on number ratios abound. An early exponent of this approach was Guillaume Dufay (1400–1474), who derived tempi for one of his motets from the proportions of a Florentine cathedral and used the ratio known as the *golden section* (1 : 1.618 . . .) in other works. Dufay also applied systematic procedures like *inversion* (make all positive intervals negative, and vice versa) and *retrograde* (reverse the order) to tone sequences centuries before they were expropriated by composers of serial music (Sandresky 1981).

The use of recurring rhythmic sequences as a formal technique shows up in the *isorhythmic* motets composed by G. Machaut and others in the period 1300–1450. The isorhythmic technique inserts a recurring rhythmic pattern into different melodic layers of a composition (figure 18.2).

The rounds, hockets, canons, fugues, and variations of traditional music are all examples of formalizable musical processes. Perhaps the most famous historical example of algorithmic composition is W. A. Mozart's *Musikalisches Würfelspiel*—a dice game for assembling minuets out of a set of prewritten measures of music (figure 18.3). The sequence of measures was determined by a set of dice throws. Hence this program incorporated an element of chance—a feature of many algorithmic programs to this day.

American businessmen marketed what could be called the first commercial music software. In 1822, Boston newspapers carried an advertisement for the Kaleidacousticon system—a deck of playing cards with instructions indicating how up to 214 million waltzes might be composed with the cards (Scholes 1975). A similar venture, dubbed the Quadrille Melodist, sold by Professor J. Clinton of the Royal Conservatory of Music, London, in 1865,

Zahlentafel

1. Walzerteil

	I	II	III	IV	V	VI	VII	VIII
2	93	22	141	41	105	122	11	30
3	32	6	128	63	146	46	134	81
4	69	95	158	13	153	55	110	24
5	40	17	113	85	161	2	159	100
6	148	74	163	45	80	97	36	107
7	104	157	27	167	154	68	118	91
8	152	60	171	53	99	133	21	127
9	119	84	114	50	140	86	169	94
10	98	142	42	156	75	129	62	123
11	3	87	165	61	135	47	147	33
12	54	130	10	103	28	37	106	5

2. Walzerteil

	I	II	III	IV	V	VI	VII	VIII
2	70	121	26	9	112	49	109	14
3	117	39	126	56	174	18	116	83
4	66	139	15	132	73	58	145	79
5	90	176	7	34	67	160	52	170
6	25	143	64	125	76	136	1	93
7	138	71	150	29	101	162	23	151
8	16	155	57	175	43	168	89	172
9	120	88	48	166	51	115	72	111
10	65	77	19	82	137	38	149	8
11	102	4	31	164	144	59	173	78
12	35	20	108	92	12	124	44	131

Figure 18.3   Numeric tables from *Musikalisches Würfelspiel* (*Musical Dice Game*) by W. A. Mozart. (Edition by B. Schott's Söhne, Mainz.) The Roman numerals over the eight columns of the refer to the eight parts of the waltz, while the arabic numerals in the rows to the left indicate the possible values of two dice when thrown. The numbers in the matrix refer to measure numbers of four pages of musical fragments.

was marketed as a practical aid to composition. This set of cards, presumably notated with fragments of music notation, "enabled a pianist at a quadrille party (an early square dance) to keep the evening's pleasure going by means of a modest provision of 428 million quadrilles" (Scholes 1970).

In the twentieth century, the spread of scientific thinking led to the introduction of mathematical procedures for composition. These include serial and stochastic strategies, in which musical elements are manipulated according to set theory operations or probabilistic processes (Hiller and Isaacson 1959; Babbitt 1960, 1961; Gill 1963; Barbaud 1966, 1968; Zaripov 1960, 1969; Xenakis 1971, 1992; Austin 1992). As chapter 19 demonstrates, virtually any mathematical formula can be turned into a music data generator (Schillinger 1946; Clarke and Voss 1978).

The current proliferation of approaches to algorithmic composition is directly related to the spread of electronic computers. The next section is a capsule survey of earlier engines for musical ideas.

Automated Composition Machinery Prior to Computers

Automation implies machinery. Machinery for automated performance of music, such as mechanical carillons, goes back many centuries (Ord-Hume 1973; Buchner 1978). Machines for composition were less numerous than those for performance, but they did exist. Composition machinery reflects available technology of the time. Gusts of wind powered the Aeolian harp and wind chimes—ancient devices for aleatoric, ambient composition. In 1660, Athanasius Kirchner designed his Arca Musirithmica, a kind of composition game in a box, to be manipulated by hand (Prieberg 1975). Another composing machine was powered by hand-pumping a lever-and-gear mechanism. Dietrich Winkel's room-sized Componium, a mechanical contraption completed in 1821, produced variations on themes programmed into it (Lyr 1955; Buchner 1978). Years later, a large-scale mechanical machine similar to the Componium was devised by a Baron Giulani and exhibited in Vienna (Scholes 1970).

With the rise of electronics in the twentieth century came new possibilities for musical automation. H. Olson and H. Belar, inventors of the RCA synthesizers and pioneers of analog sequencing, also built an electromechanical composing machine around 1951 (Olson and Belar 1961; Hiller 1970). The primary innovation in the Olson and Belar machine was the automation of a probabilistic system of composition. Their machine used a pair of asynchronous bistable multivibrators (square wave generators) to generate random digits for a probabilistic rhythm and pitch generator.

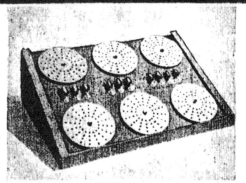
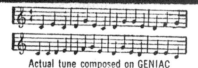

Figure 18.4   The GENIAC Electric Brain as advertised in a popular magazine in 1958.

The appearance of "electronic brains," as computers were called in the 1950s, caught the public imagination. The promise of machine composition was the selling point of the battery powered GENIAC, shown in figure 18.4 (Sowa 1956). Advertisements touted the box as "A genuine brain machine —not a toy."

Sequence Control of Composition

The possibility for automated playback of musical sequences contributed to the drive toward algorithmic composition. A sequence-controlled device reads a sequence of input data that tells it when and what to play (pitches, amplitudes, etc.). The MIDI specification, for example, described in chapter 21, is a protocol for sequence control. The coupling of hardware logic for composition with sequence-controlled performance led to several one-of-a-kind systems. Some were developed after computers had already been invented, but during a period when computers were still bulky, very expensive, and difficult to interface with other equipment.

Sequence-controlled electronic music devices started to appear after the principle was demonstrated in the Coupleux-Givelet synthesizer prototype shown in 1929 (Prieberg 1963; Rhea 1972, 1984, U.S. Patent 1,957,392). The RCA Mark I and Mark II synthesizers used by Milton Babbitt were another sequence-controlled synthesizer (Olson and Belar 1955; Olson 1967, 1991; Babbitt 1964; see also chapter 15).

The Barr and Stroud Solidac composing computer (figure 18.5), installed in a retrofitted desk at the University of Glasgow in 1959, served both as an algorithmic composition engine and a digital sound generator (using a frequency divider circuit, as described in chapter 3). Operating at a clock rate of 30 KHz (present computers operate at over 1000 times this speed), the paper-tape–reading Solidac ran a "Dice-Music Master Programme" that, according to its developers, could generate almost a billion Haydn-like trios.

An entirely different sort of beast, the Electronium (early 1960s, Los Angeles) was a large-scale composing machine programmed by knobs and switches. (It is not to be confused with the Elektronium, a keyboard instrument invented by the Hohner company in 1950 and used by composers such as Stockhausen.) A composer would ask the Electronium to suggest a motive, which was then auditioned on a loudspeaker. When the composer heard a suitable motive, he actuated a switch that set the electrical relays and the drum memory of the Electronium in motion. The musical output of the system could be modified by the composer by means of knobs and switches, but not in a direct manner, since the response of the Electronium

Figure 18.5 Desk converted into the Barr and Stroud Solidac composing computer (1959). Notice the large clockface on the left, and the rotary dial mechanism (from a telephone) on the center panel. The circuit boards were installed in the file drawers.

to these input controls was not entirely predictable. According to the inventor and composer, Raymond Scott, "The Electronium is not played; it is guided" (Rhea 1984; Freff 1989).

In contrast to the custom-built Electronium, the Coordinated Electronic Music Studio (CEMS) at the State University of New York at Albany, set up by composer Joel Chadabe (1967), was assembled out of standard sequencer and synthesis components made by the R. A. Moog Company. While the CEMS system was studio-based, the Sal-Mar Construction (figure 18.6) developed by composer Salvatore Martirano and engineer Sergio Franco was designed to be performed live in concert (Martirano 1971). Although the Sal-Mar composition logic was digital, the machine did not contain a general-purpose computer. Like the Electronium, the Sal-Mar Construction was guided through an improvisation, rather than played in the virtuoso sense.

Figure 18.6   The Sal-Mar Construction (1971) set up for a concert.

Figure 18.7   Lejaren Hiller lecturing in 1978. (Photograph by J. V. III.)

Lejaren Hiller: Pioneer of Computer Music

Lejaren Hiller (figure 18.7) laid much of the groundwork of modern computer music. Bored with the life of an industrial chemist—in which he received his doctorate and established an early career—Hiller turned his intellect to the muses in 1955, never looking back. Many "firsts" surround his name: he was first (or one of the first) to apply computers to algorithmic composition (Hiller and Isaacson 1959), music printing (Hiller and Baker 1965), and physical modeling synthesis (Hiller and Ruiz 1970; see chapter 7), among other achievements. Acutely aware of the cultural significance of his era, he served as the earliest historian of computer music, contributing a seminal survey on "Music Composed with Computers" in 1970.

Hiller's core interest remained algorithmic composition. In the mid-1950s, the newly developed digital computer provided the ideal vehicle for his compositional visions (Hiller 1970, 1979, 1981). Computers were rare at the time he began his experiments; it was typical for a major research university to design its own computer hardware. Thus his early trials used an Illiac computer constructed by engineers at the University of Illinois, Urbana-Champaign (Hiller and Isaacson 1959). Coding in binary machine language (sequences of ones and zeros accepted directly by the computer), Hiller and his collaborator Isaacson created in 1956 the first computer-composed composition: *The Illiac Suite for String Quartet*—a landmark in the history of music. The *Computer Cantata* (Hiller and Baker 1964) and *HPSCHD*, a collaboration with John Cage (Hiller and Cage 1968; Austin 1992), followed. Outside the Illinois campus, the concepts behind Hiller's "experimental music" echoed throughout the world of music (Hiller 1964).

Other Pioneers of Algorithmic Music

A handful of brave composers followed in the immediate wake of Hiller. These include Herbert Brün and John Myhill (Urbana-Champaign), James Tenney (Murray Hill), Pierre Barbaud, Michel Phillipot, Iannis Xenakis (Paris), and G. M. Koenig (Utrecht). While their computerized efforts came slightly later than Hiller's, in some cases they had already been composing according to formal procedures for some time. Xenakis's *Metastasis* for orchestra, for example, a piece composed according to stochastic formulas worked out by hand, was premiered in 1955—the same year Hiller began his computer experiments.

In Los Angeles the orientation was commercial: *Push-Button Bertha* (1956), a pop song featuring lyrics by Hollywood tunesmith M. Klein and a melody excreted by a Burroughs Datatron computer (programmed by D. Bolitho), failed to storm the hit parade. This was the trio's only foray into the computer arts. Several years later, Rudolf Zaripov, working in Moscow, analyzed and then recomposed folk music using URAL computers made in the Soviet Union (Zaripov 1960, 1969; Hiller 1970).

Early British experiments in computer composition were realized outside of established musical institutions, by D. Champernowne and S. Gill, an economist and a mathematician, respectively (Hiller 1970). While Italian composers such as Luciano Berio and Luigi Nono were leaders in analog electronic music, computer music per se took time to establish roots in Italian soil. By 1970 Pietro Grossi and his colleagues in Pisa developed a hybrid computer system for composing original pieces and adulterating existing ones (Baruzzi, Grossi, and Milani 1975; Camilleri, Carreras, and Mayr 1987). Development throughout Italy was particularly rapid after 1980.

Programs written in the primordial epoch of algorithmic composition faced severe constraints. For example, the room-sized Illiac computer on which Lejaren Hiller's programs ran contained a total of 1024 words of memory (figure 18.8). (History repeated itself in the 1970s when the first microcomputers appeared with similar memory limitations. See, for example, Bartlett 1979.)

In the late 1960s, the first computer graphics terminals opened up the possibility of coupling algorithms to graphical interaction. Scientists such

Figure 18.8 Lejaren Hiller and the ILLIAC computer as portrayed in *Scientific American* 1959. (Printed with permission of W. H. Freeman and Company.)

as Max Mathews at Bell Telephone Laboratories explored radical new possibilities offered by graphical control of composition and synthesis. These included experiments in which curves drawn on a computer screen controlled the degree of pitch and rhythm interpolation between two songs, as shown in figure 18.9 (Mathews and Rosler 1969). Mathematically speaking, interpolation is a process of filling in an intermediate point between two points on a curve. The term is also used loosely to denote a blending or averaging of two functions, starting from one function and passing in time to the other function. In figure 18.9, the two functions determine the relative influence of two songs on an algorithmic composition process that chooses its pitch and rhythm by averaging the two songs according to the scaling functions.

Here we must end our brief look at the technical history of algorithmic music composition. For more detailed studies, good starting points for in-

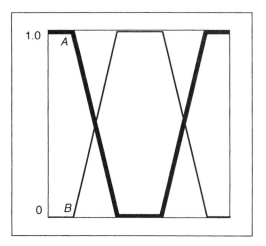

Figure 18.9 Graphical functions used to control compositional processes (after Mathews and Rosler 1969). The thick line is a scaling function for voice A; the thin line scales the influence of voice B. Notice that A dominates at first, then B enters, and then A returns to influence.

vestigation are Hiller (1970), Barbaud (1966, 1968), Ames (1987a), and Xenakis (1992).

Aesthetic Motivations behind Algorithmic Music

It would be remiss to portray algorithmic composition purely from a technical standpoint. Aesthetic trends emerging from the musical world—as well as rapidly developing technical possibilities—inspired early research in algorithmic composition. This section discusses some of these developments.

The rupture of the Second World War led to an acceleration of the trend toward formalized and systematic methods of composition in the early 1950s. The tone-row method of composition—promulgated 30 years earlier by Arnold Schoenberg—had been generalized from pitch to other musical parameters (note durations, dynamic markings, etc.) by Anton Webern, Olivier Messiaen, and others. Ever-more-elaborate rationales dominated journals devoted to music. As the complexity of these procedures increased, so did the "precompositional" burden on composers. Herbert Brün observed this about his work from this period:

I started writing a score for orchestra in which I used the method of having a table and precompositional material ready on the walls and on the table and on the floor—to an absurd state of completeness. I got, as could be predicted, totally stuck—confused. It was not really an unhappy affair, but it was a puzzling situation (Hamlin and Roads 1985).

In an attempt to break out of the extreme determinism of serial composition, European and American composers such as Karlheinz Stockhausen, Pierre Boulez, John Cage, and Earle Brown experimented with *aleatoric* methods of composition. By aleatoric is meant that certain details of the piece were left open to the interpreter (in the case of instrumental music) or else they were composed according to a random technique like throwing dice. Figure 18.10 gives an example of an aleatoric score. Taking a more systematic path, Iannis Xenakis in the mid-1950s was composing music according to *stochastic* formulas, which formalize weightings across a range of probabilities.

Hiller's celebrated experiments with automated composition proved that the computer could model any formal procedure: from the canons of traditional harmony to the tenets of serial technique; both deterministic and stochastic methods could be coded (Hiller and Isaccson 1959). Programs sped up the time-consuming labor associated with systematic composition. Hence, software appeared as a logical extension of the aesthetic of formalized composition.

Deterministic versus Stochastic Algorithms

The programs of Hiller and other pioneers of algorithmic composition contrasted two approaches: *deterministic* versus *stochastic* (or *probabilistic*) procedures. Deterministic procedures generate musical notes by carrying out a fixed but possibly complicated compositional task that does not involve random selection. The variables supplied to a deterministic procedure are called the *seed data*. These may be a set of pitches, a musical phrase, or some constraints that the procedures must satisfy.

An example of a deterministic procedure would be a program to harmonize a chorale melody in the style of J. S. Bach. In this case, the seed is the melody. The rules of harmonization and voice-leading, derived from a textbook, ensure that only certain chord sequences are legal. In more recent music, deterministic algorithms include C. Barlow's formulas for determining the dynamics of an attack at a given point in a given meter (Barlow 1980), and C. Ames's "constrained search" routines that generate counterpoint by applying a battery of tests on a set of alternative solutions—selecting one that best fits the specified constraints (Ames 1983).

Figure 18.10 An example of aleatoric music. Karlheinz Stockhausen's *Klavier-stücke XI* (1957/1963). The composer instructs the performer to look at random at the sheet of music and begin with any group at any tempo, dynamic level, and type of note attack. At the end of a group, look at the tempo, dynamic, and attack markings and look at random at any other group, playing it according to the markings at the end of the previous group. (Copyright 1957 by Universal Edition (London) Ltd., London. Copyright renewed. All rights reserved. Used by permission of European American Music Distributors Corporation, sole U.S. and Canadian agent for Universal Edition London.)

Stochastic procedures, on the other hand, integrate random choice into the decision-making process. They generate musical events according to probability tables that weight the occurrence of certain events over others. These tables guarantee an overall trend, but the filigree of local events remains unpredictable. A basic stochastic generator produces a random number and compares it to values stored in a probability table. If the random number falls within a certain range of values in the probability table, the algorithm generates the event associated with that range. Chapter 19 presents stochastic generation in more detail.

Certain algorithms exhibit such mechanistic behavior that we can identify them by listening. Apart from these simple cases, however, it is not possible to ascertain by listening whether a given fragment of music was generated by a stochastic or deterministic process. Hence, the choice of algorithm is a matter of compositional philosophy and taste. Many types of algorithms can be mixed in one system and applied to various dimensions of the composition process.

Three Pioneering Composition Programs

Many algorithmic composition programs have been written, but only a few have been used by more than one composer. Here we take a brief look at three of the most well-known programs that have been used by others besides the original author: Iannis Xenakis's Stochastic Music Program (SMP), G. M. Koenig's Project 1, and Barry Truax's POD programs. These programs represent the first generation of automated composition programs—all written by composer-programmers. SMP and Project 1 were written in the 1960s, and the first version of POD was written in the early 1970s.

SMP and Project 1 generate a list of notes (represented alphanumerically) as their output. Originally, the note lists were meant to be transcribed into common music notation and played by traditional instruments. However, both programs have been connected to digital sound synthesis systems at several studios. The POD programs were designed to be connected to a digital sound synthesis system, so the results can be heard more or less immediately.

Stochastic Music Program

With the aid of electronic computers, the composer becomes a sort of pilot: pressing buttons, introducing coordinates, and supervising the controls of a cosmic vessel sailing

Figure 18.11   Iannis Xenakis in the late 1960s.

in the space of sound, across sonic constellations and galaxies that could formerly be glimpsed only in a distant dream. (Iannis Xenakis 1971)

The author of SMP, the Paris-based composer Iannis Xenakis (figure 18.11), is a pioneer of automated composition. His work in this domain is, however, only one of his many innovative achievements. An early version of the SMP program is published in his book (Xenakis 1971, 1992) as the Free Stochastic Music program. The stochastic formulas in SMP were originally developed by scientists to describe the behavior of particles in gasses. In Xenakis's view, a composition was thus represented as a sequence of *clouds of sound,* with the particles corresponding to individual notes. (See Xenakis 1960, 1971, 1992 for a full discussion of the aesthetic ideas behind the program.)

SMP models a composition as a sequence of sections, each characterized by a duration and the density of notes within it. Figure 18.12 depicts the overall logic of the SMP program. The composer interacts with SMP by stipulating global attributes of the score and then executing the program. The global attributes include

1. Average duration of sections

2. Minimum and maximum density of notes in a section

3. Classification of instruments into *timbre classes*

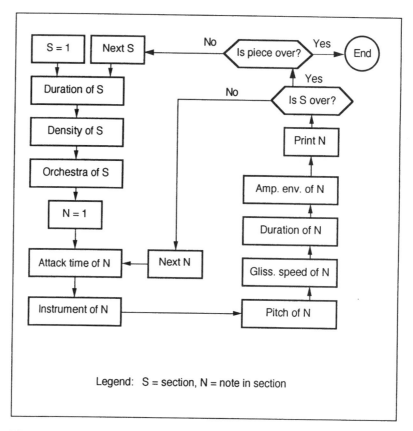

Figure 18.12   Overall logic of Xenakis's Stochastic Music Program.

4. Distribution of timbre classes as a function of density

5. Probability for each instrument in a timbre class to play

6. Longest duration playable by each instrument

The SMP program helped create a number of important works in Xenakis's oeuvre, including *Eonta* (1964, Editions Salabert), for piano and brass, premiered by Yuji Takahashi on piano (Vanguard Records). Later, the program was improved by the mathematician-composer John Myhill (1979) and has since been recoded for personal computers.

Project 1

Only very few composers may be inclined to schematize their work. But when out of sheer curiosity they try to compose with the aid of a computer, they are forced to do so ... precisely because of the regulated combination of musical processes with results that cannot always be foreseen. These contacts between the composer and the musical

Figure 18.13　G. M. Koenig at the teletype of the Digital Equipment Corporation PDP-15 computer, Institute of Sonology, Utrecht, the Netherlands, 1971.

material forcibly lead to reflection on the craft of composing and to the formulation of new musical theories. (G. M. Koenig)

Gottfried Michael Koenig (figure 18.13) created the Project 1 program at the Institute of Sonology, Utrecht, in 1970. Project 1 composes by applying seven *selection principles* to a database of five musical event *parameters:* instrument, rhythm, harmony, register, and dynamics.

In Project 1 the selection principles range from completely random (nonrepetitive) to completely deterministic (repetitive). The most random selection principle chooses freely from a set of elements (such as a set of pitch classes or amplitudes). In a "serial" selection principle that combines randomness and determinicity, the algorithm chooses at random from a set of elements without replacement of that element back into the set. Subsequent choices draw from a smaller set of elements until none are left to choose from. Then the cycle of choices can begin again. In the most deterministic selection principle, the range of available choices is very limited, causing a great deal of repetition.

In using Project 1, the composer provides the following data to the program:

1. A set of weightings for different sizes of chords

2. The total number of events to be generated

3. A set of tempi

4. A random number that serves as a seed to stochastic procedures

The program then generates seven sections or "structures." Within a structure, each of the five parameters parameter runs through the seven selection principles in a random order (figure 18.14). The results are printed out in the form of a note list. This list can be transcribed into music notation for performance by instrumentalists. One version of Project 1 at the Institute of Sonology was connected to a real-time synthesis system. A more recent implementation has been adapted for MIDI data output.

Project 1 produces variants of a given compositional structure embodied in the program. As Koenig states: "I regard serial compositional technique as a special case of aleatoric compositional technique" (Koenig 1978a). Hence, the score generated by Project 1 obeys a logic of what Koenig has called "Serial music, Cologne style," with reference to the mixture of deterministic and aleatoric composition techniques explored by Koenig and other German composers in the 1950s and 1960s (Koenig 1978b). The results of Project 1 can be heard in a number of Koenig's pieces including *Output* (1979, recorded on the compact disc BV/HAAST 9001/2, Amsterdam).

Koenig has developed another program called Project 2 that adds more flexibility. In Project 2 the user can specify the selection principle to be used in generating values for a particular parameter in the output score (Koenig 1970b).

Koenig never considered Project 1 and Project 2 to be complete composing systems. He acknowledged the creative opportunities in transcribing and interpreting the numerical lists generated by his programs into scores for electronic and instrumental performance (Koenig 1979). (See the section on transcription and interpretation later.)

The POD Programs

Modern technology has given us unprecedented powers of control over the design of new sound experiences, but not inherently, over the language with which to ensure communication. A compositional language based on a thorough knowledge of the behavior of sound and on the principle of balance between variety and structural coherence seems to provide a means of realizing the potential of contemporary music. (Barry Truax)

While the SMP and Project 1 programs generate scores for traditional instruments, Barry Truax's POD (POisson Distribution) programs were designed expressly for direct digital synthesis of sound (Truax 1975, 1977, 1985). The POD system replaces the traditional *note concept* used in SMP

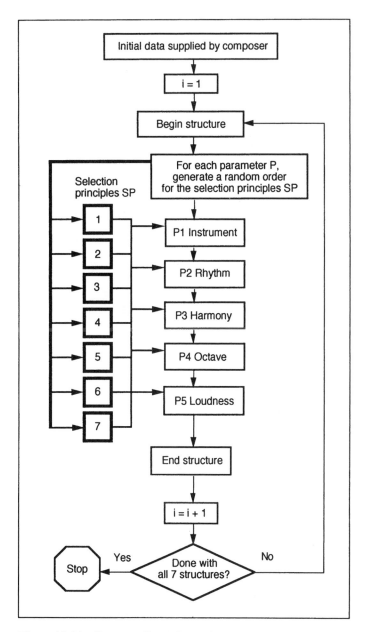

Figure 18.14   Program flow of Koenig's Project 1 program. The program generates seven structures, each of which applies the seven selection principles (SP) to each of the five parameters in a random order.

Figure 18.15   Barry Truax lecturing, 1978. (Photograph by J. V. III.)

and Project 1 with the more general concept of *digital sound objects*. Truax (figure 18.15) began development of the first POD system at the Institute of Sonology at Utrecht in 1972. Over a period of several years he wrote new versions for different computer systems.

Figure 18.16 shows the overall scheme of the POD programs, involving a mixture of human and machine decisions.

POD generates events within the bounds of *tendency masks*—frequency versus-time regions shown in figure 18.17. The distribution of events in time and frequency follows the Poisson distribution—a standard probability function. (For more on probability distributions in music, see chapter 19, Xenakis 1992, Lorrain 1980.) The composer specifies the number of events within the tendency mask by adjusting the *event density* parameter.

In addition to sound objects, tendency masks, and densities, composers also stipulate the selection principles (similar to those in Project 1) to be employed in choosing sound objects to be placed in the mask. Once a synthesis score is generated, users can vary the performance of the score in a variety of ways, by changing the tempo, direction, degree of event overlap, envelope, and various synthesis variables.

Selection principles and tendency masks allow composers to work on a higher level of musical architecture than that of individual notes. "The composer is not only concerned with the nature of the individual sound event, but also with ... larger groups of events, including entire compositional sections" (Truax 1975, p. ii).

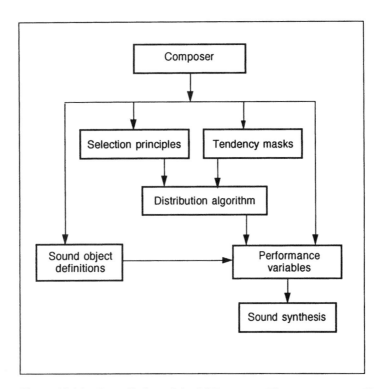

Figure 18.16 Overall plan of the POD system. The composer specifies the selection principles, tendency masks, performance variables, and sound object definitions. The distribution algorithm scatters sounds in time within the constraints specified by the composer. The result is synthesized by computer.

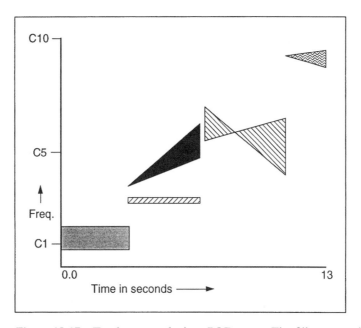

Figure 18.17 Tendency masks in a POD score. The fill patterns indicate different timbral settings.

Although POD's synthesis flexibility was limited, this can be partially explained by the fact that it was implemented on small computers that could not have supported a more general-purpose synthesis system. An early implementation of POD generated sound in batch mode from prepared digital tapes. A later version of the program, PODX, allowed quick interaction, since the sound synthesis task was directed to a real-time digital synthesizer. This system was used to create works such as *Arras* (1980, Cambridge Street Records CSR-CD 9101, Burnaby) and *Wave Edge* (1983, Wergo 2017-50, Mainz).

Transcription and Interpretation

Programs such as SMP and Project 1 were designed to generate alphanumeric note lists. These printouts were to be transcribed by the composers into scores for traditional instruments. Today the data generated by composing programs can be transmitted to sound synthesis equipment, displayed on a computer terminal, or printed out. The printouts can be numerical (lists of parameter values), traditional notation, or in the form of a graphic score.

An early integrator of music programs was Donald Byrd (currently known for his Nightingale music notation program). Working at Indiana University, Byrd interfaced SMP and his own MUSC composing program to his music printing system SMUT (1977). As a result, the scores generated by the programs could be given immediately to musicians for performance.

The Project 1 program has no music notation option; it generates an alphanumeric printout. Koenig has always seen the process of transcribing the printout into a musical score as an important interpretive task for the composer. For example, the same printout could be used to make a score for piano or chamber ensemble. The task of orchestrating the printout leaves considerable leeway to the composer (Koenig 1979; Laske 1979). In a program with synthesis capability like POD, different orchestration schemes can be tried out directly.

Total Automation versus Interactive Composition

An early fear of automated composition was that it would replace human composers, just as recordings have replaced performing musicians in many venues. Four decades after Hiller's highly publicized experiments, this has not occurred. Even so, the use of composition programs remains controversial. For a composer who is not a programmer, totally automated composition programs demand little in the way of creativity. The composer's interaction is limited to supplying a small amount of seed data prior to execution of the program. The compositional strategy is fixed in the program, and the user merely reaps the harvest of notes when it is done. In its most extreme form, automated composition resembles a form of "found art"; the composer selects the output and, in effect, signs and frames the work with a title and a performance medium. Even in this case, however, some composers find it fascinating to initiate an intricate set of musical processes.

One way to bypass the fixed strategy is to modify the program logic. In this case, a composer who is also a programmer retains overall responsibility.

Another departure from a fixed strategy is to revise the program's output. Some proponents of automated composition, notably Hiller and Barbaud, adhered to the doctrine that the output score generated by a composition program should not be edited by hand; rather, the program logic should be changed and run again. This doctrine stems from an aesthetic that values music that is formally consistent. Other composers feel there is nothing sacrilegious about modifying the output score of a composing program. Xenakis, in particular, has rearranged and refined the raw data emitted by the SMP program. His oeuvre contains numerous examples of selection and rearrangement of program output (Roads 1973).

Batch Mode Interaction

Perhaps the most fundamental limitation of fully automated composition programs is the *batch* mode of interaction they impose on the composer. The term "batch" refers to the earliest computer systems that ran one program at a time; there was no interaction with the machine besides submitting a deck of punched paper cards for execution and picking up the printed output. No online editing could occur; all decisions had to be predetermined and encoded in the program and its input data.

In the batch mode of composition, the composer follows these steps:

1. Prepare and enter the input data

2. Execute the program

3. Wait while the program runs

4. Accept or reject the output (usually an entire composition)

If we follow the batch doctrine and a single note or phrase is not to our taste, we must modify the program logic, recompile it, and generate another score. However, if the program includes any stochastic routines, the second output will differ from the first one. We cannot simply correct the offending events without generating an entirely new score. This is because in a batch approach to automated composition, the unit of composition and interaction is an entire score.

Proponents of batch composition argue that the rules of the program ensure logical consistency and originality in the generated output. But it could also be argued that the rules embodied in such programs are shallow and formalistic. Simply because certain parameters of a piece follow a twelve-tone series or conform to an arbitrary set of axioms is no guarantee that the listener will hear consistency or originality in the final product. Musical consistency and originality are cognitive categories for which little theory yet exists.

Automation with Interaction

By enriching an automated system with more interaction, we add the flexibility that is missing from a batch approach. In so doing, we gain access to the different layers of compositional structure and process. We can edit on a small scale (a single parameter, an envelope, a note), on a medium scale (a phrase, a voice, a procedure), or on a large scale (all notes, the entire compositional strategy).

We distinguish two degrees of interaction: (1) relatively light interaction experienced in a studio-based "composing environment," where there is time to edit and backtrack if necessary; (2) intense real-time interaction experienced in working with a performance system onstage, where the emphasis is on controlling an ongoing music process and there is no time for editing. The rest of this chapter focuses on the first case. Chapter 15 describes software that supports the second case.

Musical Assistants

The trade of musical assistant is not officially taught in music schools, but it is a well-established profession. Many prominent composers increase the quantity of their musical output by employing musical assistants.

A commercial film music composer may hire dozens of subcontracting composers to realize a soundtrack. Some subcontractors develop a basic theme supplied by the composer, or orchestrate a piano score created by another subcontractor. Since the maestro may have no competence in music technology, musical assistants are required to operate the tools of the computer music studio, touching up plain musical landscapes with dabs of exotic sound effects.

Since one stage of composition involves experimentation and trial-and-error procedures, the managing composer can increase efficiency by assigning the same task to several assistants to see how each one solves the task. The managing composer can then select a favorite rendition from these examples. The maestro's role is analogous to that of a master chef who designs the menu and tastes the work of subordinates (making suggestions if things are not right), but who is not involved in the hands-on preparation of materials.

The composer who is not wealthy or institutionally powerful can also benefit from assistance if it is provided in the form of a suite of programs running on a personal computer (Roads 1981a). Today's musical environments (or *microworlds*) give composers the tools to build specialized assistants. These tasks may involve generating musical data according to an algorithmic procedure, selecting materials from a database, calculating variations on a given structure, or any number of more special tasks. The next section discusses these systems.

Environments and Microworlds

A machine set up for the production of electric light bulbs represents a combination of processes that were previously managed by several machines. With a single attendant, it can run as continuously as a tree with its intake and output. But, unlike a tree, it has a built-in system of jigs and fixtures that can be shifted to cause the machine to turn out a whole range of products from radio tubes and glass tumblers to Christmas tree ornaments. (M. McLuhan, "Automation" 1964)

An algorithmic composition environment is a toolkit: a collection of "jigs and fixtures" assembled in combinations chosen by the user. The flexibility of the toolkit lets composers design custom strategies for composition.

Chapter 17 presented the topic of procedural composition languages. Speaking generally, there is no sharp distinction between "environments" and "procedural composition languages." Some of the environments cited in a moment are oriented toward interactive graphics or command strings, as opposed to the programming languages discussed in chapter 17. But other composition environments are embedded in programming languages, making the distinction moot.

In general, environments are extensible. This means that it is easy to add new functionality, in contrast to a closed or "canned" application program. We interact with closed applications through different facets or editors. We can select menu items or fill in templates, but cannot change the program logic or extend it significantly. In contrast, many environments do nothing until the user assembles them into a custom system.

Perhaps the original music software environment was the MUSICOMP library of assembly language subroutines developed by Robert Baker and Lejaren Hiller at the University of Illinois (Baker 1963; Hiller and Leal 1966; Hiller 1969). The MUSICOMP library included tools for selecting items from a list according to a probability distribution, randomly shuffling items in a list, tone row manipulation, enforcing melodic rules, and coordination of rhythmic lines. As Baker put it:

MUSICOMP is a 'facilitator' program. It presents no specific compositional logic itself, but is capable of being used with nearly any logic supplied by the user (Baker 1963, p. i).

The output of MUSICOMP routines could be printed or formatted for input to sound synthesis programs. Hiller used the MUSICOMP routines to create a number of works for both traditional instruments and computer-generated sound, including his *Algorithms I* (1969).

A more recent example of an algorithmic composition environment is MIDIDESK, created by Clarence Barlow. This interactive program manipulates MIDI data previously entered by the composer. Table 18.1 lists typical commands. Barlow has used the system to help him compose solo piano works as well as large-scale orchestral compositions.

Composer-programmers have developed numerous other environments and composition languages in recent years (Pope 1986a, 1991a; Lentczner 1984, 1985; Boynton et al. 1986; Blevis, Jenkins, and Glasgow 1988; Cope 1987, 1989, 1990; McAdams, Gladkoff, and Keller 1984; Dannenberg 1989a; Desain and Honing 1988; Camilleri, Carreras, and Mayr 1987; Baisnée et al. 1988; Collinge 1980; Collinge and Scheidt 1988; Greenberg 1987; Hamel et al. 1987; Polansky, Rosenboom, and Burk 1987; Polansky et al. 1988; Laurson and Duthen 1989; Barrière, Iovino, and Laurson 1991; Scaletti 1989a, b; Jaffe and Boynton 1989; Flurry 1989; Diener 1989a; Ames 1989b, 1992; Rahn 1988; Camurri et al. 1991; see also the discussion of composition languages in chapter 17).

These environments strive toward different aesthetic aims, but they share the goal of providing a toolkit that can be assembled into particular configurations by individual composers. Many environments provide score and sound editors, algorithmic generators, and real-time performance features. The most flexible environments are modular, meaning that composers need use only those functions that interest them, combining them in the manner that suits their needs. Figure 18.18 presents an image created using

Table 18.1 A partial list of commands available in the MIDIDESK system (Barlow 1989)

Command	Action
HEAR	Records new note data in real time from a MIDI input stream, such as a MIDI keyboard.
READ	Enter new note data step by step with an alphanumeric keyboard or a musical keyboard.
GRID	Quantizes the durations of notes to multiples of an arbitrary duration.
JOIN	Concatenates two note sequences.
PLAY	Plays a specified sequence (64 tracks allocated to 16 MIDI channels).
PLAN	Displays the sequence in a piano-roll notation that shows each note's track assignment.
VIEW	Displays a piano-roll notation of a sequence that shows each note's pitch.
NOTE	Displays a sequence in proportional duration notehead notation.
SWAP	Exchanges one set of tracks for another.
FUSE	Merges several tracks to form one sequence.
VARY	Changes pitch, amplitude, track assignment, or duration of notes in a sequence in *shift, spread,* or *slide* modes. Shift mode transposes a sequence according to a fixed interval. Spread mode expands the range of the sequence. Slide mode applies a continuous change between the values in the sequence.
RIDE	Substitutes many notes for one note according to a fixed algorithm; provides a graphical display allowing the composer to focus the expansion on different instruments at a time.
PART	Splits a sequence in two according to various criteria, such as the type of a MIDI event (note on, note off, etc.)
TIDY	Eliminates redundancies, and deficiencies of a sequence caused by other operations.
EDIT	Direct graphic alteration of a element in a sequence.
FADE	Interpolates between two sequences; the result begins like one sequence and ends like another sequence.
MOCK	Imitates a sequence using a Markov chain based on a statistical analysis of the sequence.

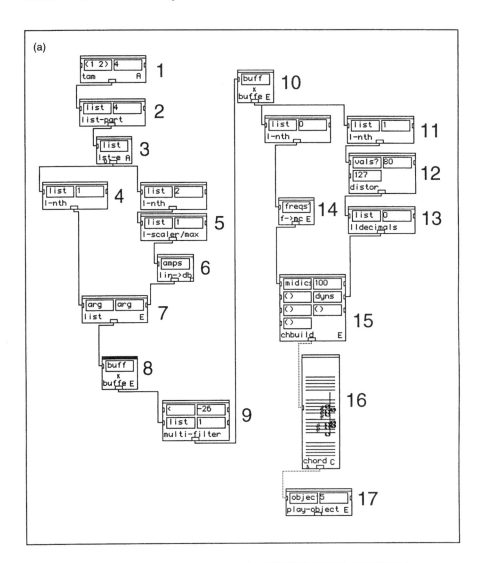

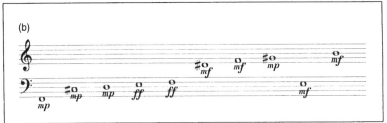

the PatchWork environment, developed by M. Laurson, C. Rueda, and colleagues.

Conclusion: Assessment of Algorithmic Composition

This chapter has portrayed a variety of approaches taken by the creators of algorithmic composition systems, and we hope to have revealed some of the aesthetic motivation behind their efforts.

Composition programs can handle more detail in a shorter amount of time than would be possible by a human composer working alone. They let composers shift their attention from the tiniest details of composition (which are handled by the program, according to instructions specified or at least endorsed by the composer) to concentrate on a higher level of abstraction. At this level, the composer manages the creation of the piece in terms of its large-scale gestures, formal architecture, and process model.

A danger of composition programs is that they can serve as a substitute for the creativity of the user who invokes them. The batch composition programs of the past were particularly susceptible to this kind of abuse. Interactive programs and performance systems demand more of the composer, since they balance preprogrammed automation with spontaneous decisions (intervention).

Long ago, human beings learned that machines can easily outdo their human counterparts in certain tasks. If composition was merely a puzzle or

Figure 18.18 A PatchWork program created by linking together boxes on the screen. Each box represents a Lisp function. This patch uses the data from a spectrum analysis of a struck tam-tam to generate harmonies for traditional instrumental composition. This is a typical procedure in the "spectral composition" technique represented by T. Murail and G. Grisey in Paris, who sometimes use spectrum models to generate their instrumental parts. (*a*) Description of each box. 1. Read analysis data from tamtam. 2. Separate data by columns. 3. Format data into structured list. 4. Separate the frequency and amplitude lists. 5. Normalize amplitude data to between 0 and 1. 6. Convert amplitudes to dB. 7. Rejoin frequency and amplitude lists. 8. Store results temporarily. 9. Filter out all low-amplitude components. 10. Store results temporarily. 11. Separate the frequency and amplitude lists. 12. Scale amplitudes into the MIDI range between *mp* and *ff*. 13. Round amplitude data to integer values. 14. Convert frequencies to microtonal MIDI note values. 15. Construct chords with the frequencies and dynamics. 16. Display and edit chord. 17. Play chord via MIDI for testing purposes. (*b*) Notes, in quarter-tone approximation, generated by the program in (*a*). (Example by J. Fineberg.)

parlor game, then the technical virtuosity of the machine would already have relegated human efforts to a sideshow. The machine can execute formal composition rules that are far more intricate than any human being could possibly keep track of. It can effortlessly spin a web of n-part microtonal counterpoint and fugue from any germ series subject to an arbitrarily complicated system of constraints. Like a sequencer that races through performances with superhuman speed and precision, the complex ratiocinations of machine composition inspire awe—up to a point. Excessive complexity, like excessive precision or virtuosity for its own sake, is a vapid and tiresome musical diet. The talent of composers who use algorithmic composition methods is reflected in their skill in managing the excesses of their occasionally self-indulgent software prodigies.

19 *Representations and Strategies for Algorithmic Composition*

Music Representations

Systems Theory: Linked Automata

       Deterministic versus Stochastic Automata

       Links between Automata

Cellular Automata

       Behavior of Cellular Automata

       Musical Applications of Cellular Automata

Models of Musical Control Structure

Stochastic Processes

       Probability Table Lookup

       Uniform Random Distribution

       Pseudorandom Numbers

       Deterministic Distribution

       Naive Selection Algorithm

       Cumulative Distributions

       Extending Probability Table Lookup

       The Choice of Probability Distribution

       From Equations to Code

       Markov Chains

Advanced Markov Techniques for Music
Hierarchical Markov Chains

Fractals

1/f Noise
Self-similarity
A Fractal Algorithm
Extensions of 1/f

Chaos Generators

Linear versus Nonlinear Systems
A Chaos Algorithm

Grammars

Musical Applications of Grammars
Notation of Formal Grammars
Musical Grammar Example
Assessment of Grammars

Generate-and-test

Extensions to Generate-and-test

Pattern Matching and Search Techniques

Examples of Pattern-directed Search in Composition

Constraints

Musical Examples of Constraints
Solving Constraint Networks

Expert Systems

Expert System Shells
Assessment of Expert Systems

Neural Networks

Analysis and Composition

Examples of Analysis in Composition Programs

Conclusion

Music is inescapably sensual, subjective, and emotional in its appeal, yet logical and symbolic manipulations have long been associated with its composition. Chapter 18 introduced the history and concepts of algorithmic composition. This chapter examines common representations and strategies within them. The specific strategies studied here include automata, stochastic processes, fractals, chaos generators, grammars, search procedures, constraints, expert systems, neural networks, and analysis procedures.

New algorithms are constantly being incorporated into musical systems, many imported from the world of science. Thus any list of compositional algorithms could be extended indefinitely as time goes on. Indeed, one goal of this chapter is to convey a sense of the multiplicity of possible approaches. For pedagogical reasons, we treat each strategy as a separate topic, but clearly, one could also combine different stategies. Tutti-frutti assortments of algorithms have been rolled into interactive environments for generation and transformation of musical data; see chapters 15 and 16 for more on this subject.

Each strategy presented here is the subject of entire volumes of literature. By necessity, the descriptions here are quite condensed. Our task is a delicate one—to convey the flavor of each stategy without entangling the reader in a web of technical minutiae. We strongly recommend the cited references to readers for details on a particular technique. Books such as Xenakis (1992), Winsor (1987, 1990, 1991), Barbaud (1966, 1968), and Hiller and Isaacson (1959) survey various strategies and present example programs. Articles by Ames (1987b), Langston (1989), and Lorrain (1980) also summarize many techniques.

Music Representations

The *representation issue* underlies all strategies for algorithmic composition. This issue involves four questions, which each strategy answers in a different way:

1. How is music displayed to the musician?

2. How is music represented within the computer?

3. What controls does the representation offer the musician?

4. How is music transmitted between different programs and devices?

The debate over flexible and extensible representations for music is a continuing one (see De Poli, Piccialli, and Roads 1991 and *Computer Music Journal* 1993a, b, for example). Years ago, the composer Herbert Brün

(1969) observed that computer music systems are not neutral. Every system constrains musicians to a restricted set of operations; every view on a piece is a filter that biases the viewer's attention to a particular perspective. Indeed, the holy grail of a "universal" representation is antipodal to creative music. Music is constantly evolving, so perhaps one should not pray for a definitive solution to questions of music representation.

Practical work pushes toward standard representations for display, internal data structures, controls, and transmission protocols. In a chaotic world, standards are welcome, particularly for the exchange of output data treated by various application programs. Yet the representations associated with an algorithmic strategy tend to be particular to that algorithm. Thus the rest of this chapter studies each strategy and its corresponding representation together.

Systems Theory: Linked Automata

An *automaton* (sometimes called a *state machine*) is a procedure whose output depends on its internal state and its input (Starke 1972; Bobrow and Arbib 1974; von Neumann 1951). Any computable function can be represented in terms of an automaton, so this formalism is common in mathematics and computer science. Automata representations include *deterministic* and *stochastic automata, cellular automata,* and *neural networks.* Petri nets, discussed later in this chapter, are also a form of automaton. The automaton representation has been used to represent many kinds of musical processes, including harmonization and counterpoint generation (Pope 1986b; Chemillier 1992a, b).

In a *mathematical systems theory* approach to composition, the basic elements of a musical score are partitioned into a number of parameters (e.g., pitch, amplitude, etc.). An automaton models the behavior of each parameter. This division of labor can be taken farther, so that several automata work on different aspects of pitch (register, pitch class, deviation, vibrato, glissando/portamento, etc.).

An example of a simple automaton is a procedure that harmonizes an input note alternately by a perfect fourth or fifth interval, as shown in figure 19.1. Two properties make it an automaton: (1) it maintains an internal state (remembering the interval it used the last time), and (2) it calculates the output pitch depending on its input.

A more formal definition of an automaton is as follows. An automaton is specified by a quintuple:

```
procedure harmonize(input_note, output_note);

    integer input_note, output_note;

    static boolean harmony_state;

    if harmony_state = true then

    begin

        (* Harmonize by a fifth (7 semitones) *)

        output_note := input_note + 7;

        harmony_state:= false;

    end

    else

    begin

        (* Harmonize by a perfect fourth (5 semitones) *)

        output_note := input_note + 5;

        harmony_state := true;

    end

end procedure;
```

Figure 19.1 Simple automaton that harmonizes an input note (coded as a number) alternatively by a perfect fourth or a fifth. The Boolean variable *harmony_state* stores the internal state of the automaton. (A static variable retains its values between calls to the procedure.)

$A = (States, Inputs, Outputs, \textbf{Next\_state}, \textbf{Current\_output})$

where *States*, *Inputs*, and *Outputs* are sets, and

Next_state(*Inputs, Outputs*) → *States*
Current_output(*States, Inputs*) → *Outputs*

are functions. The right arrow (→) indicates the output. The automaton is finite if *States*, *Inputs*, and *Outputs* are finite.

To each finite automaton we can associate a labeled directed graph called the *state diagram* or *state graph* that has one *node* for each state and one *arc* for each state-input signal pair. Figure 19.2a represents an automaton (rectangular box) called *Alpha* with *Inputs*, *Outputs*, and the state diagram that defines *Alpha*. We can label each arc with a symbol **Current_output** (*state, input*) that represents both the input and output signals associated with the transition represented by the arc. Figure 19.2b shows the function definitions for **Next_state** and **Current_output** below the graph. Note that a

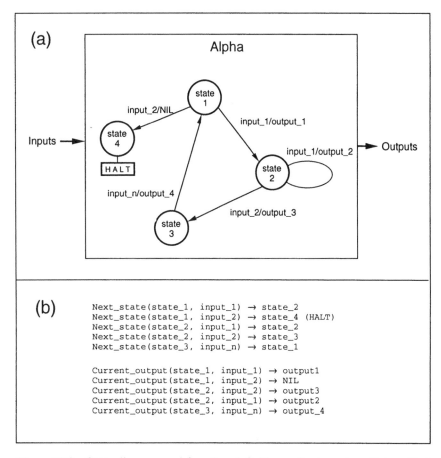

Figure 19.2 State diagram and function definitions of automaton *Alpha* with four internal states. (*a*) State diagram. The input signals to the automaton enter through the left side, and the output signals exit through the right. Each link is labeled with an *input/output* pair that indicates the signals associated with the state transition of the link. (*b*) Rule definitions for the functions **Next_state** and **Current_output**.

transition from *state_1* to *state_4* invokes a HALT instruction that generates no output signal.

Figure 19.3 shows a more musical example in the form of a melody generator. This automaton generates a repeating melodic pattern consisting of the first, fourth, fifth, and major second degrees of a scale, and then halts on the tonic on the third time through the melody. The rules for **Next_state** and **Current_output** determine the logic of all melodies generated by this automaton. We can start the automaton by providing it an initial *pitch* value. The value for *count* is used by the automaton as an index to the number of times the melody has repeated. This is the seed data of this

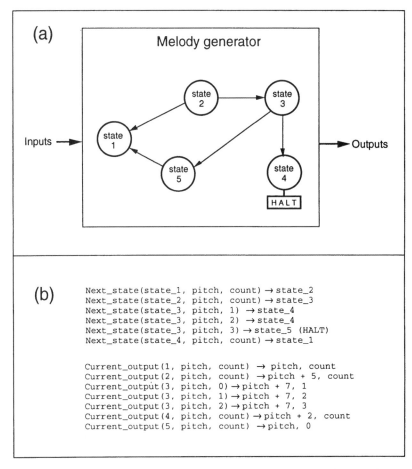

Figure 19.3   Melody generator automaton. To avoid cluttering up the graph, the input and output signals are not labeled in the state diagram (*a*), but are stated in the rules in (*b*).

algorithm. From the seed data, the automaton generates a series of output values until it reaches a HALT state.

Deterministic versus Stochastic Automata

The simple automata we have sketched so far are *deterministic*. This means that if we know their initial state and input data, we can predict their output with complete certainty. Another class of automata are *stochastic;* some aspect of their behavior is determined by a random or probabilistic procedure. To impose stochastic behavior one can introduce random decisions in either the **Next-state** or the **Current-output** functions. In other words, one can make either the *state-transition rules* or the *output generator* probabilistic.

For example, if the state-transition rules are stochastic functions, the automaton's internal behavior becomes more unpredictable; it may jump from state to state, perhaps even cycling through a temporary loop, before it arrives at a terminating state. If, on the other hand, the output generator function is stochastic, the internal behavior of the automaton is predictable, but not its output value. The choice of whether to "stochastify" the state-transition rules or the output generator depends on several factors. If making the automaton's internal behavior more complicated has the side effect of accomplishing a musical task, then this may be desirable. For example, one could design an automaton that accepted as input a musical phrase, and at each internal state made a stochastic decision whether or not to apply a variation. But if the logic of the state-transition rules is very simple, it may be more efficient just to randomize the output.

Later in this chapter we present a long section on stochastic processes, so we leave the subject here and return to issues specific to automata.

Links between Automata

Automata can be *linked* with one another in a network, constituting a *system*. At each step of a clock, the links transmit the previous output of one or more automata to the input of other automata. The algorithm inside an automaton uses these input data to alter its behavior at each step.

Linkages can be *direct* (causing causing a direct influence of one automaton on another) or *inverse* (causing an inverse influence). Figure 19.4 shows the two types of linkages, where the black dots indicate an inverse link. The strength or *weight* of the links can be changed by scaling the values transmitted between the automata. In this way, the input of certain automata can be weighted more heavily than the input of others. One might, for example, set the weights so that all the automata concerned with calculating a parameter like pitch are strongly linked.

Once the initial system of automata and links has been set up, the system can run autonomously, with its evolution determined by internal analysis routines that change the sources, destinations, and weights of the links in the system (Roads 1976, 1984, 1987, 1992a). Changing the linkages affects the musical behavior generated by the system. Given the appropriate interfaces, such a program can also be guided by interaction with a performer (Chadabe and Meyers 1978).

It is hard to generalize about the musical behavior of automata systems, since this depends strongly on the way that a given system has been defined

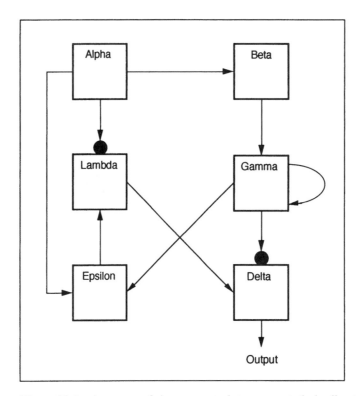

Figure 19.4   A system of six automata interconnected via direct and inverse links. The inverse links are indicated by the black circles. The output of the system might be taken from a single automaton, as is shown here with *Delta,* or it might be taken as a sum from more than one automaton.

and the type of input data it receives. The chief variables of an automata system are the individual automata definitions, their linkages, the rules for reconnecting the system, and the input or initialization data. Once these are specified, the automata run—as their name implies—autonomously. This means that the musician has mainly global control over their behavior. (See also Baffioni, Guerra, and Lalli 1984; Ozzola, Melzi, and Corghi 1984. For an introduction to a form of systems theory for music analysis, see Hiller and Levy 1984.)

Cellular Automata

Systems of cellular automata (CA) are like linked automata systems. They have two additional constraints, however: (1) the behavior of every automaton or *cell,* as defined by its state diagram, is the same, and (2) the interconnection network between the automata is a regular symmetrical structure, such as an array or lattice that does not change over time as it may with ordinary linked automata. All CA in a network execute a single rule synchronously.

For a given cell $A[i, t]$ at position i and time t, its next value is a function of three factors:

1. Its previous value or state

2. The value of cells in its immediate *neighborhood r*

3. The *transition rule* for all the cells

We can express this formally as follows:

$$A[i, t] \leftarrow \mathbf{rule}\{A[i - r, t - 1], A[i - (r - 1), t - 1] \ldots$$
$$A[i, t - 1], \ldots A[i + r, t - 1]\}$$

Here the index r spans the entire neighborhood of the cell.

In a one-dimensional array of automata, r is typically two, corresponding to the left and right neighbors (figure 19.5a). A simple transition rule for note manipulation using a CA array could take this form, where i is the location of the automaton being computed:

```
if A[i-1, t-1] = 1 and
   A[j, t-1] = 0 and
   A[i+1, t-1] = 1 then
       {
       A[i, t] ← 1;
       Pitch_class ← A;
       Duration ← 8;
       Amplitude ← ff;
       }
```

The left arrow symbol ($\leftarrow$) indicates assignment.

Another common automaton is the five-cell Life automaton, with a neighborhood r of two, but in two dimensions (figure 19.5b).

Behavior of Cellular Automata

Some CA systems are initialized by putting a different random number in each cell. Although each cell executes the same rule, the random number within each cell allows a chance for individualistic behavior. Complex behavior emerges as many simple automata interact locally and assemble themselves into hierarchies.

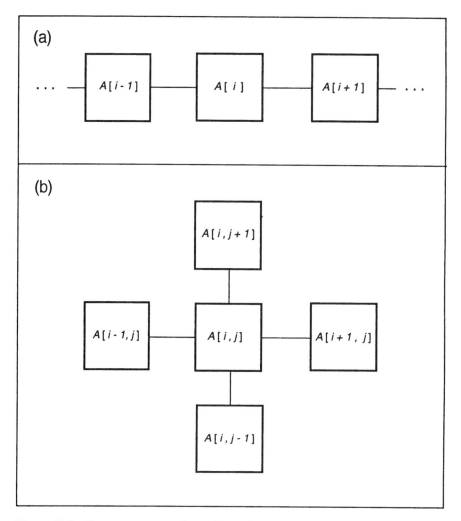

Figure 19.5 Two common configurations of cellular automata with neighborhood of two. (*a*) One-dimensional array. (*b*) Two-dimensional lattice.

Simple cellular automata can be extended in many ways, for example, by incorporating feedback from the past, or through multilevel organization, wherein different rules apply at each level. It is also possible to combine CA with other types of algorithms. In this case the CA often function as "transducers" (processing input or output signals) for nonautomata procedures.

In any case, the behavior of a CA system generally falls into one of four classes:

1. The system "disappears" or "dies" after a small number of steps; the initial random structure is "eaten up" by the interacting cells.

2. Evolution leads to fixed or pulsating periodic behavior.

3. Evolution leads to chaotic patterns that appear to contain special instances of organized behavior, such as repetitions with variations. Fluctuations increase at a regular pace.

4. *Strange attractors* (irregular cyclic patterns) appear. Behavior propagates irregularly; contraction and expansion is unpredictable. (See the section on chaos later.)

Musical Applications of Cellular Automata

In scientific studies, CA have been used as models of evolution, growth, and wave propagation (Wolfram 1984, 1986), processes that have analogies in different types of musical development. Composers have applied CA as pitch, duration, and timbre selectors in MIDI-based composition systems (Beyls 1989; Millen 1990). The composer prepares a table that maps each result generated by a CA state to a particular pitch, duration, or timbre.

CA have also been applied to the synthesis of sound. Bowcott used CA to generate parameters for the *screen-based* approach to granular synthesis of sound (Bowcott 1989; see chapter 5 for more on granular synthesis), to generate self-modifying waveforms (Chareyron 1990), and to create amplitude envelopes for an additive synthesis engine (Beyls 1991). Figure 19.6 shows an example of this last application. Here the automaton can take a value for amplitude between 0 and 255. The partials of a sound act as "neighbors" engaged in a process of communication. During the first 255 generations an *attack rule* applies; for the second part of the sound, a *decay rule* applies. The composer can also supply additional rules for *harmonic masks* (weights) to favor activity in certain harmonic regions.

Models of Musical Control Structure

Many programming languages have explicit constructs for specifying *control flow,* that is, the sequence of execution of code segments and the rules governing transfer of control between procedures. These constructs include the standard conditional tests (**if** *true* **then** *action*), iteration forms (loops), procedure calls, and **go to** expressions. Grouping constructs such as **begin, end** pairs define the syntactic units being sequenced.

We can also design representations for expressing *musical control structure,* that is, the sequencing of musical events and the rules governing musical transitions. Representations of control structure are natural to music, being embodied in score directives such as *Da Capo* and *Del Segno,* and the

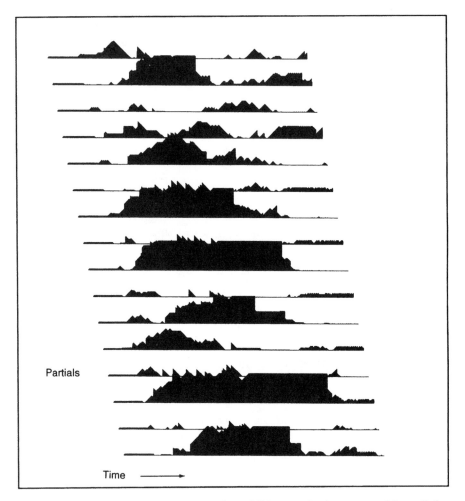

Figure 19.6 A set of envelopes used for additive synthesis generated by cellular automata. The lower partials are shown at the front, with higher partials in the back. This image shows 512 time slices of the sound (attack plus decay). (After Beyls 1991.)

various repetition constructs of common music notation. Aleatoric scores such as *Klavierstücke XI* by Karlheinz Stockhausen (described in chapter 18) supply instructions for score navigation.

Section markings and explicit "go to" statements like these are only the most obvious structural indicators. Most musical control structure is implicit. A variation, for example, could be defined as a procedure call to "decorate the pitch motive" or "double the note durations" of the syntactic unit prior to it. Thus a representation of the control structure of a piece requires that it be parsed into syntactic units and operations on these units. Hence, it constitutes a kind of analysis of a composition.

```
harmonize
voice1 {
      do 2 times {(C 4), (D 4), (E 4), (C 4); }
      do 2 times {(E 4), (F 4), (G 2); }
      do 2 times {(G 8), (A 8), (G 8), (F 8), (E 4), (C 4); }
      do 2 times {(C 4), (G 4), (C 2); }
      }

piece {
      do 3 times {play(voice1); wait(2 measures);}
      }
```

Figure 19.7 A representation of the control structure of the children's round *Frère Jacques*. The piece consists of three voices that each enter after waiting two measures. Within a voice, notes are represented by a pair: (*pitch duration*). In the *voice1* part, each measure is on a separate line.

To the extent that a piece exhibits redundancies and regularities, a logical model of its control structure is usually more compact than an enumeration of the entire list of events in a piece. To give a simple example, consider the children's round *Frère Jacques*. If we list the notes for one voice, the list is 32 notes long. To enumerate one cycle of the round for three voices takes 96 notes. But if we represent the redundancies using control flow directives, the result is a concise procedural description (figure 19.7).

To represent musical control flow requires that we handle time relations in a flexible way. For example, we should be able to stretch and shrink event durations (for staccato and legato articulation) and perform arbitrary distortions of tempo without affecting the order of events (see Garnett 1991; Dannenberg, McAvinney, and Rubine 1986; Dannenberg 1989a, b; Anderson and Kuivila 1986; Desain and Honing 1992a).

One of the main applications of control flow algorithms is interactive music performance systems. Through conditional tests, a music-generating algorithm can be made to respond to external musical events and alter the sequence of events that it plays. (See chapter 15 for more on interactive performance software.)

One of the first systems for programmed specification of musical control structure was Euterpe (Smoliar 1967a, b, 1971), which represented a piece of music as a set of sequential and parallel *voice processes*. Since then a number of other languages for explicit handling of musical control flow have been developed. These include PLAY (Chadabe and Meyers 1978), MOXIE (Collinge 1980; Collinge and Scheidt 1988), Pla (Schottstaedt 1983, 1989a), Flavors Band (Fry 1984), 4CED (Abbott 1981), FORMES (Rodet and Cointe 1984), HMSL (Polansky et al. 1988), Arctic (Dannenberg 1986), and Canon (Dannenberg 1989a, b). (See chapter 17 for more on music languages.)

A general formalism for representing the control structure of interacting processes is *Petri nets*. Like automata, Petri nets have internal states and transitions. However, Petri nets denote internal states as objects that are selected based on their internal behavior or the values of their variables. Transitions are represented as separate entities whose "firing" (transition) is based on the condition of a state variable or an arbitrary control factor.

Petri nets make explicit the conditions that must be met for certain sequences of behavior to occur. Thus, they provide a model of process control structure. For example, Petri nets can model interactions between several voices in a polyphonic setting. The most basic net modules for process description are sequence, alternative branching, conjunction, and forking. Figure 19.8 shows three basic Petri net structures.

The clarity of the graphical representation of process structure is one of the strengths of Petri nets. However, like all "patch" displays, beyond a certain threshold of complexity, the tangle of interconnections take on a spaghetti-like appearance. One solution is a hierarchy of Petri net representations, where high-level networks hide details of lower-level networks. See Haus (1984) and Pope (1986b) for more details on Petri nets and applications to music.

Stochastic Processes

Stochastic composition processes are algorithms in which decisions are taken according to the values of random numbers. From a historical viewpoint, stochastic processes represent one of the most important classes of compositional algorithms (Hiller and Isaacson 1959; Xenakis 1992). It is safe to say that most composers employing algorithmic composition techniques have used stochastic processes in some form. Stochastic processes efficiently organize large amounts of data, such as the parameters of sound masses. But one can also apply carefully regulated stochastic processes to sparser textures.

This section presents the basic stochastic algorithms for composition, including probability table lookup and Markov chains.

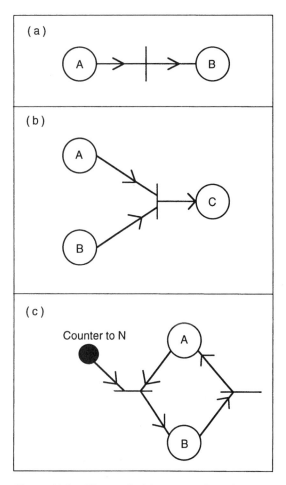

Figure 19.8 Three primitive types of Petri nets that can be used to build up process representations of musical processes. (*a*) Sequence indicates that *A* follows *B*. (*b*) Fusion indicates that *A* and *B* must occur for *C* to start. (*c*) Loop shows that *A* follows *B* follows *A* as long as the counter (black circle) is less than *N*. The counter is one of several *control object* types that can be used in a Petri net.

Probability Table Lookup

A stochastic strategy implies the use of *probability distributions*. A probability distribution is a table that shows the likelihood of occurrence of one or more events, where the probability of the occurrence of a given event is expressed as a value between 0 and 1.0. A probability of zero implies that the event never occurs, and a probability of 1.0 implies that the event always occurs. Thus one could say that a probability of 0.5 implies a 50 percent chance of occurrence.

Uniform Random Distribution

The simplest and purest probability distribution is the *uniform random* distribution, an instance of which is plotted as in figure 19.9a. Each line on the vertical axis represents the probability of a corresponding value on the horizontal axis. In this case, the horizontal axis represents the pitches of a chromatic scale. Every pitch has the same probability, 0.8. This equiprobable outcome is the characteristic of a uniform random distribution. The uniform random distribution is important because it captures extreme randomness and can be used when the composer wants a texture that is utterly aleatoric.

Pseudorandom Numbers

In the final analysis, randomness, like beauty, is in the eye of the beholder. (R. W. Hamming 1973)

It is easy to fill a small probability table with equal values, as in figure 19.9a, but how does one define a numerical recipe to generate a series of random numbers, where the probability of any specific number is $1/N$, where N is the number of possible outcomes? Here we open up a profound subject (if not a can of worms), since there exists no truly random number generator in the mathematical sense, the formal concept of randomness being difficult to define (Chaitin 1975). Any practical "random" number generator is ultimately a deterministic procedure that repeats itself after a large number of trials. Such routines are more properly referred to as *pseudorandom number generators.*

The most popular pseudorandom number generator is the *linear congruential* method, which derives the next number in a pseudorandom sequence by performing arithmetic operations on the previous number, with the initial number being the *seed.* (Moore 1990 gives an algorithm.) But since every reasonable programming system provides pseudorandom generators, there would seem to be little need for music programmers to cook up their own functions from scratch. The engineering literature offers a wealth of detail on pseudorandom numbers (Knuth 1973a; Rabiner and Gold 1975; Hamming 1973). (See also the discourse on noise in chapter 8.)

As a practical tip, it is useful to realize that one can (and should) "randomize" a pseudorandom number generator by supplying it with ever-changing seed value, like a numerically encoded date and time, or indeed, another pseudorandomly generated number.

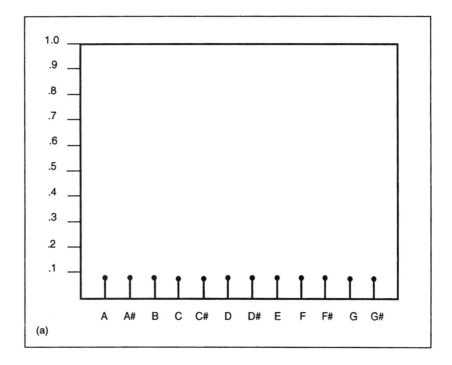

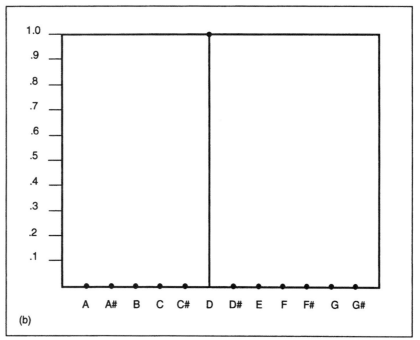

Figure 19.9 Plot of values in a probability table associated with the set of pitches in the chromatic scale. (*a*) Since all pitches are equiprobable, this is a uniform random distribution. (*b*) Pitch D has a probability of 1.0, making this a deterministic distribution.

Deterministic Distribution

Figure 19.9b plots the conceptual opposite of uniform randomness: a deterministic distribution where the pitch D always occurs because it has a probability of 1.0.

What about something in between these two extreme cases? Figure 19.10 shows an arbitrary probability distribution. All the values in the table are less than 1.0 (the largest value is 0.3, a 30 percent probability of occurrence). The table is *normalized,* which means that all the values add up to 1.0. (This was the case for the tables in figure 19.9 also.) This should imply that some event always occurs, but as we see in a moment, this condition can only be met by the proper stochastic generator or *selection algorithm.*

Naive Selection Algorithm

One can generate a melody with this table by comparing random numbers (between zero and one) to successive values in the table, starting at the left and moving to the right. A naive algorithm is

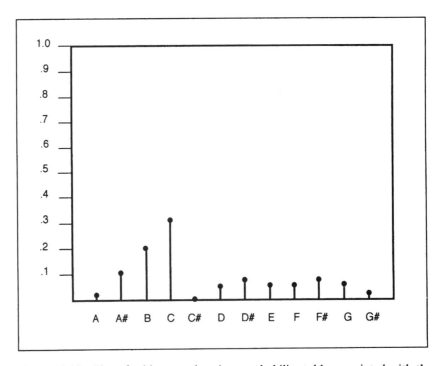

Figure 19.10 Plot of arbitrary values in a probability table associated with the set of pitches in the chromatic scale.

IF the random number is less than a given value in the table,

THEN play the pitch associated with that value.

This algorithm is inefficient and inaccurate, however. Referring to figure 19.10, any random number over 0.3 produces nothing; we could make many comparisons and still no pitch would have been generated. Furthermore, since the algorithm always starts comparing from the left, any random number less than 0.3 selects a pitch between A and C-sharp only; pitches higher than C-sharp are never tested.

Cumulative Distributions

Efficiency and accuracy demand a slightly more sophisticated selection algorithm. The first step is to convert the probability table into a *cumulative distribution* before the testing. The cumulative distribution sums the values successively (figure 19.11). That is, the second probability value in the cumulative distribution is the sum of the first and second probabilities in the original table, the third is the sum of the first three, and so on. Thus each value in the probability table is converted into a proportion or interval of the total of 1.0. This ensures that any random number tested against the table results in a match. A drawback of cumulative distributions is that they are more difficult to read at a glance, so for visualization, the "raw" distributions, rather than their cumulative counterparts, are often preferred.

As an example of using the cumulative distribution in figure 19.11, imagine that a random number of 0.5 is generated, which selects B from the table. (One of the efficiencies of the summing is to delete elements of zero probability like the note C in figure 19.10; C is not present in figure 19.11.) To use this table in a melody generating algorithm, employ the following procedure. Let *ptable* be the name of the probability table, indexed by a value i in the set of chromatic pitches. So for example, if $i = A$, *ptable* $(i) = 0.02$. To generate a melody of ten pitches, run through the following loop ten times:

```
for i=A to G# do
begin
  if random(seed) is less than ptable(i) then
  play(i);
end
```

The call to **random**(*seed*), where *seed* is an arbitrary integer, generates a pseudorandom value less than 1.0. One can easily extend this table-lookup

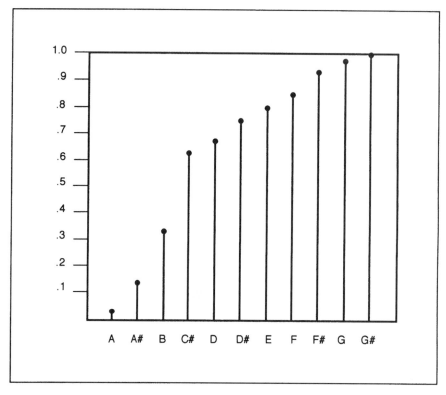

Figure 19.11   Same as figure 19.10 but plotted as a cumulative distribution. The pitch C has been deleted because it had zero probability.

process to other musical parameters, such as register, duration, dynamic intensity, instrument, articulation type, etc.

Extending Probability Table Lookup

A probability table lookup test is the core of most stochastic composition algorithms. Of course, a plain algorithm such as this can be dressed up in many ways. One of the most straightforward ways is to allow the possibility of changing probabilities, so that a section of a piece obeys one distribution at the beginning, and quite another at the end. This can be accomplished efficiently by interpolating between the two probability tables over the course of the section.

The computer music literature is replete with creative strategies based on probability table lookup in composition; see Ames (1987a, b, 1990, 1992), Lorrain (1980), Jones (1981), and Bolognesi (1983), for example. (Several of these are reproduced in Roads 1989.) Historically significant composition programs that employ probabilities include Pierre Barbaud's Algom 7

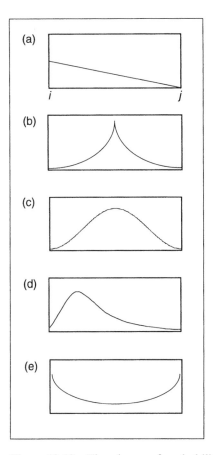

Figure 19.12 Five classes of probability distributions. The vertical axis is the probability, going from 0 to 1. The horizontal axis is the range of values covered by the distribution, i.e., the possible outcomes. (*a*) Linear distribution between two points i and j. (*b*) Exponential with peak at point c. (*c*) Bell-shaped with peak at point c. (*d*) Asymmetrical. (*e*) U-shaped.

(Barbaud 1966, 1968; Lachartre 1969), Project 1 and Project 2 (Koenig 1970a, b; chapter 18), and the Stochastic Music Program (Xenakis 1971, 1992; Myhill 1979; chapter 18). All these programs mix deterministic logic with stochastic procedures.

The Choice of Probability Distribution

The choice of probability distribution for a musical application is a delicate one. A variety of well-known probability distributions provide starting points for the design of stochastic music processes (Lorrain 1980; Xenakis 1992). These distributions can be classed by shape into several categories, listed next and shown schematically in figure 19.12:

1. Linear distributions—A line of fixed, increasing, or decreasing probability between two specified limits; includes the uniform random distribution

2. Exponential distributions—An exponential concave slope from a specified peak or *mean* (the two-sided exponential shown in figure 19.12b is called the *bilateral exponential*)

3. Bell-shaped distributions—*Gaussian* and *quasi-Gaussian, Cauchy, Poisson* (under certain conditions), *hyperbolic cosine,* and *logistic* distributions, centered around a mean

4. Asymmetrical distributions—Peak skewed around a mean, including the *gamma* distribution (under certain conditions), and Poisson distribution (under certain conditions)

5. U-shaped distributions—Peaks at the extremes, including *arcsine* and *beta distribution* (under certain conditions)

Table 19.1 proffers an equation for each category of distribution. Numerous other equations in each category could be listed. Lorrain (1980), Xenakis (1992), and textbooks on probability theory compare the various alternatives.

From Equations to Code

To turn an abstract equation into a working piece of software requires several steps. The raw probability distribution must be rendered into a cumulative distribution, normalized over the domain of probabilities 0 to 1.0. The range of outcomes over which the equation is defined (e.g., $0 \leq x \leq 1$) must be mapped to the (often discrete) range of the musical parameter being controlled. Consider, for example, the calculation of probabilities for a set of eight dynamic markings *ppp, pp, p, mp, mf, f, ff, fff*). This entails substituting a discrete array index $P[i]$ for the continuous differential dx (see Lorrain 1980), and mapping the effective range of the probability equation (e.g., from -10 to $+10$) into eight regions, one associated with each dynamic marking. One assigns probabilities for just eight outcomes *i:* $0 = ppp, 1 = pp, 2 = p, 3 = mp, 4 = mf, 5 = f, 6 = ff, 7 = fff$.

The rigorous implementation of the classic equations of probability theory demands great attention to mathematical detail. Composers, however, are usually more interested in the quality of the results generated by a distribution—which depends on its overall shape—than they are in passing the muster of mathematical inspection. Just as a musician tunes the timbre of a synthesizer by listening and adjusting, so probability tables can be

Table 19.1　Formulas for five categories of probability distributions

---

Linear distribution

Any linear interpolation algorithm can calculate a straight line from one value in a probability table to another (see chapter 8). Xenakis (1992) and Lorrain (1980) give an alternative formulation—an algebraic description of half of a triangle.

Exponential distribution

This distribution is symmetric around a center point of 0, so is more properly called a *bilateral exponential* distribution:

$$P(x) = \frac{1}{2\tau}e^{-|x|/\tau}\,dx$$

where τ is the spread or dispersion, and $-\infty \leq x \leq \infty$.

Bell-shaped Gaussian

A classic symmetric bell-shaped curve:

$$P(x) = \frac{1}{\sigma\sqrt{2\pi}}e^{-(x-\mu)^2/2\sigma^2}$$

where σ is the *standard deviation* or spread of the bell and μ is the mean (center peak) of the bell.

Asymmetrical Gamma

The gamma function is asymmetric for small values of its mean v:

$$P(x) = \frac{1}{\Gamma(v)}e^{-x}x^{v-1}\,dx$$

for $x \geq 0$, where $\Gamma(v)$ is the *Eulerian gamma function* defined as follows:

$$\Gamma(v) = \int_0^\infty e^{-x}x^{v-1}\,dx.$$

The highest probabilities of $P(x)$ are around $v - 1$, while the mean is v. As v increases past 10, the curve loses its asymmetry and approaches a Gaussian bell shape.

U-shaped Arcsine

The curve has a concave shape, with peaks at the extremes of 0 and 1:

$$P(x) = \frac{1}{\pi\sqrt{x(1-x)}}\,dx$$

for $0 \leq x \leq 1$.

---

tuned to meet specific compositional needs. Ultimately, graphical function editors—rather than equations—may be the most effective interface for tuning musical probability tables.

An important subclass of stochastic algorithms are the family of Markov chain techniques, studied next.

Markov Chains

The Markov chain is one of the earliest and most popular strategies for algorithmic composition of music (Pinkerton 1956; Brooks, et al. 1957; Hiller and Isaacson 1959; Xenakis 1960; 1971; Meyer 1967; Olson 1967). First formulated in 1906 by the Russian mathematician A. A. Markov (1856–1922), a Markov chain is a probability system in which the likelihood of a future event is determined by the state of one or more events in the immediate past.

The probabilities in a Markov chain can be laid out in a *state-transition matrix*. The state-transition matrix in figure 19.13 is a Markov chain for a simple melody composition, using the notes of a pentatonic scale: G, A, C, D, and E. The cells show the probability of a next pitch, given a current pitch shown at the left of the row. For example, if the starting pitch is G, we look to the first row of the matrix to see the probabilities for the next pitch. We see there is a 50 percent chance that another G will be played, and a 50 percent probability that a C will be played. Notice that a zero probability for A, D, and E means that only another G or a C will follow a G.

Figure 19.14 shows a possible sequence of pitches generated by this matrix. On a local scale, that is, in the two-note successions, the character of the chain is clear. On a more global scale, however, this type of Markov chain exhibits a kind of aimless meandering; there is no sense of phrase structure—of beginning, middle, or end—in the melodies it generates. Part of the reason for this meandering behavior is that the chain looks back only one state, to the previous pitch. One can increase the sophistication of this method by increasing the *order* of the chain. The order of a Markov chain indicates the number of prior states that are taken into consideration. Events in a *zeroth-order* chain (equivalent to a regular probability table with no looking back at previous states) are independent of one another. Events in a *first-order* chain have one predecessor (such as the example in figure 19.13). Events in a *second-order* chain look back two states, and so on.

Higher-order chains extend the window of local coherence over several events. Moorer (1972) noticed how eighth-order chains produced sequences of juxtaposed phrases. In the hymn composition studies by Brooks et al. (1957), low-order chains generated meandering, random melodies, while

	Destination states				
	G	A	C	D	E
G	.5	0	.5	0	0
A	0	.25	.25	.25	.25
C	.25	.25	.25	.25	0
D	.5	0	.5	0	0
E	.33	0	0	.33	.33

Source states

Figure 19.13 A Markov chain for melody composition. The rows represent the probabilities of a next pitch, given a current pitch (indicated at the left of the row).

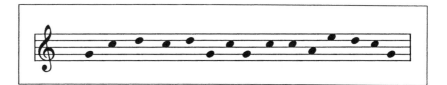

Figure 19.14 Melody generated by the Markov state-transition matrix shown in figure 19.13.

high-order chains consist of parts of the original hymns spliced together, such as the first half of one hymn crudely spliced onto the second half of another hymn. This can be explained as a strong probabilistic tendency toward coherence over several notes that is broken suddenly by a more unlikely event, at which point a new coherent melody starts. Results such as these prove that interesting music has several layers of structure, and a composition system that only addresses one layer (such as making locally coherent phrases) will exhibit deficiencies in another layer, such as transitions between phrases, or higher-level sectional organization.

Advanced Markov Techniques for Music

Various techniques exist for coaxing more complex musical behavior from a Markov chain (Jones 1981). A common thread in these techniques is to extend the concept of state from a single unit—like a pitch—to multiple-valued units like the note set: {pitch, duration, amplitude, instrument}. To account for all possible note variations requires a large state-transition matrix.

Another way to extend the concept of state is to treat a grouping like chords, phrases, or measures as a single state. Then instead of composing sequences of individual notes, the chain composes sequences of chords, phrases, or measures. This is the method that W. A. Mozart used in his famous *Musikalisches Würfelspiel* (cited above).

An interesting extension involves turning the Markov chain into an interactive composition and performance game. Playing with the control parameters in real time, musicians can change the state of the Markovian process on a moment-to-moment basis, as music is generated (Chadabe 1984, 1992; Zicarelli 1987).

Hierarchical Markov Chains

In order to handle different layers of musical organization, it is also possible to arrange Markov chains in a hierarchy. One chain that generates high-level structure could select one of a number of types of sections, for example, a fast movement, a slow movement, a movement in a particular key, or a movement that relied on a particular pitch row. Within a section intermediate-level chains might select the sequence of phrases contained in the section. The details of each phrase type might be filled in by a low-level chain. The music language HMSL (Hierarchical Music Specification Language) supports this kind of construction (Polansky, Rosenboom, and Burk 1987; Polansky et al. 1987). For more on Markov chains in music, see Ames (1989a).

Fractals

As we have seen, a primary characteristic of Markov chains is that previous results influence future results. Another way of saying this is that Markov chains maintain a context for decisions. *Fractals* represent another class of probabilistic systems that maintain a context. The theory of fractals entails many fascinating ideas, including the powerful concept of *fractal dimension* (Mandelbrot 1977; Gleick 1988). In order to contain the discussion in this chapter, however, we limit the presentation to a few key aspects that have already been tested in the domain of music.

1/*f* Noise

Fractals are also referred to as 1/*f noise.* This is because *fractional noises* have a spectrum that diminishes as 1/f^g, where *f* represents frequency, and $0 \leq g \leq 2$. For example, pure *white noise,* which contains all frequencies, is uncorrelated with frequency, so its spectrum is 1/f^0. The most intriguing class of fractional noises is pure 1/f^1. In pure 1/*f* noise, the probability of a given frequency occurring diminishes as the frequency increases.

Sequences generated by a pure 1/*f* noise algorithm possess interesting mathematical properties. For example, they correlate logarithmically with the past. Thus the averaged activity of the last ten events has as much influence on the current value as the last hundred events, and the last thousand (using logarithms of ten). Thus 1/*f* processes have a relatively long-term memory. This makes them attractive as models of musical processes that refer to events in the past, such as tonal melodies that wander off but ultimately return to a tonic context (Bartlett 1979). Scientists who have studied fractals have observed that the pitch and loudness patterns of some traditional music sometimes have the same overall shape as a 1/*f* pattern (Clarke and Voss 1978).

But what musical parameter does *f* refer to in these cases? In the studies cited, *f* does not directly represent the frequency of the waveform of the music. Rather, *f* represents the "frequency" or ambitus of change. For example, a melody that could use 36 different equal-tempered pitches but only uses three closely spaced intervals could be plotted as in figure 19.15a. This is a "low-frequency" curve since the intervals never span more than a minor third. A melody with larger melodic leaps is plotted in figure 19.15b. Such a melody has more differences or "high-frequency" content, with analogy to waveforms with sharp high-frequency transients. Of course, fractal algorithms can be applied to any musical parameter, not just pitch selection. For example, McNabb (1981, 1986) used fractal algorithms to generate vibrato effects, and Waschka and Kurepa (1989) applied fractals to the control of timbre in granular synthesis.

Self-similarity

An important property of 1/*f* noise is *self-similarity.* In a self-similar sequence, the pattern of the small details matches the pattern of the larger forms, but on a different scale (figure 19.16). This concept is also found in hierarchical musical compositions based on the "germ cell" approach, in which a large-scale musical form is generated by elaborating a tiny germ of an idea such as a pitch row or a set of ratios. (For a presentation of this

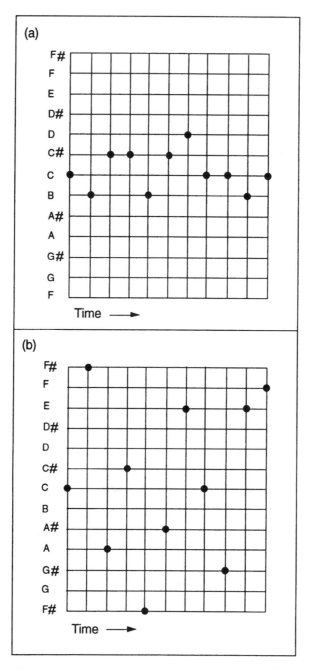

Figure 19.15 Plots of fractal melodies. (*a*) Low-frequency melody. (*b*) High-frequency melody.

Figure 19.16   Triadic Koch island showing self-similarity in that the details mirror the large-scale form.

notion in the context of electronic music, see Stockhausen 1959, 1963.) A way to apply the self-similar concept in polyphonic music is to generate a motive of a few intervals and durations, which serves as the slowest moving musical line. To this is added a faster repetition of the same motive that starts on each of the notes of the first line (Dodge 1988; Thomas 1991).

A Fractal Algorithm

An essential part of a $1/f$ algorithm is a memory that stores the previous context. Figure 19.17 shows such an algorithm for generating a $1/f$ se-

```
procedure one_over_f (N);
    {* N determines the number of random generators and length of sequence *}
    integer N;
    begin {* procedure one_over_f *}
        integer seq_length, i, N, seq_index, previous_seq_index;
        real output_value, random_max;
        real array values[N];
        outputfile outfile;
        {* Compute length of output sequence *}
        seq_length := 2**N;
        {* Set scale factor for random generators *}
        random_max := 1.0/N;
        {* Initialize the previous index value *}
        previous_seq_index := seq_length - 1;
        {* Generate the 1/f seq *}
        seq_index := 0;
        while seq_index < seq_length do
            begin {* Generate output loop *}
                output_value := 0;
                i = 0;
                while i < N do
                    begin {* Bit check loop *}
                {* Compare bit i of seq_index with that of previous_seq_index.
                    If they are not the same, generate new random number *}
                        if bit_compare(i, seq_index) not_equal
                            bit_compare(i, previous_seq_index) then
                            values[i] := random(0, random_max);
                        output_value := output_value + values[i]);
                        i := i + 1;
                    end; {* Bit check loop *}
                previous_seq_index := seq_index;
                seq_index := seq_index + 1;
                {* Write output value *}
                write(outfile, output_value);
            end; {* Output loop *}
    end; {* procedure *}
```

Figure 19.17 $1/f$ algorithm that generates 2^N output values. See text for explanation.

quence, derived from Voss's algorithm in Gardner (1978). This method uses *N* random number generators labeled from 0 to *N*. Their output is stored in an array called *values*. The *values* array maintains the context of past decisions, since any new output value that we generate is a composite of old and new random numbers stored in the *values* array.

For efficiency, this code uses selection logic based on a binary number representation, but a binary number representation is not essential to the logic of the algorithm. The first thing the program does is compute the length of the output sequence, which is 2^N. The next line of code scales the output of the generators so their sum is always between 0 and 1.0. Then the code initializes the *previous_seq_index* to the final value of a complete sequence, as if when we start we are looking back to a previous cycle of the sequence that has just completed. Then begins the body of the 1/*f* algorithm, which is a loop that generates a composite random number for every step of the sequence.

At each step in the loop an inner loop checks the binary representation of the *seq_index* to see if any bits changed in the transition from *previous_seq_index*. The *bit_compare* procedure interprets its first argument as a bit index and its second argument as the bit pattern to be tested. The procedure returns a value of true if the tested bit has a value of 1. When one of the bits changes from 0 to 1 or 1 to 0, the corresponding generator produces a new random number into the *values* array. Each entry in the *values* array corresponds to a bit in the binary representation of *N*.

Table 19.2 shows the bit pattern for $N = 4$. Bit 0 changes at every step, so generator *N* is selected every time and there is a high probability that the sequence produced by the sum of the four generators is different at each step. Bit 1 changes half as often, so generator 3's contribution has a lower frequency than that of generator 4. Bit 3 (generator 4) has the lowest frequency.

The output value is a composite of all of the random numbers (new and old) in the *values* array. Notice from table 19.1 that only at the beginning and middle of the sequence are all the generators changing, resulting in an output value that is independent of the previous value. The resulting sequence is a close approximation of 1/*f* noise.

Extensions of 1/*f*

For flexibility in shaping musical phrases, Bolognesi (1983) made two extensions to the basic 1/*f* algorithm. First, he made the generator selection logic stochastic rather than deterministic. This means that at each step a variable number of generators may fire, according to a stochastic formula rather

Table 19.2   The fractal algorithm in figure 19.17 generates a random number every time the bit pattern changes in the sequence index. The sum of old and new random numbers for each bit is the output value.

Bit					Generator			
3	2	1	0		1	2	3	4
1	1	1	1		(See note)			
0	0	0	0		•	•	•	•
0	0	0	1					•
0	0	1	0				•	•
0	0	1	1					•
0	1	0	0			•	•	•
0	1	0	1					•
0	1	1	0				•	•
0	1	1	1					•
1	0	0	0		•	•	•	•
1	0	0	1					•
1	0	1	0				•	•
1	0	1	1					•
1	1	0	0			•	•	•
1	1	0	1					•
1	1	1	0				•	•
1	1	1	1					•

Note: Initial value of **previous_seq_length**

than the binary scheme of the algorithm in figure 19.17. This allows phrases to be divided into any number of subphrases, not just binary subdivisions. Another modification is to give certain generators more weight, that is, to scale the output of the individual generators. By adjusting these weights over the course of a piece, the composer can regulate the amount and type of change in the output.

Lévy flight is a related stochastic process that is statistically self-similar. A single parameter determines the degree of hierarchical "clustering" of a random variable. See Bolognesi (1983) and Mandelbrot (1977) for details.

See Moore (1990) for a method that uses the discrete Fourier transform to generate random sequences of arbitrary lengths that approximate the spectrum of $1/f^g$ for an arbitrary value of g greater than or equal to zero.

Chaos Generators

The shapes of classical geometry are lines and planes, circles and spheres, triangles and cones. They inspired a powerful philosophy of Platonic harmony.... [But] clouds are not spheres.... Mountains are not cones. Lightning does not travel in a straight line. The new geometry models a universe that is rough, not rounded, scabrous, not smooth. It is the geometry of the pitted, pocked, and broken up, the twisted, tangled, and intertwined. . . . The pits and tangles are more than blemishes distorting the classical shapes of Euclidean geometry. They are often the keys to the essence of the thing. (J. Gleick 1988)

Like the related theory of fractals, chaos theory is a body of abstract thought that offers profound insights into natural phenomena. Both fractals and chaos theory are *en vogue;* but we hope the intellectual fad phenomenon does not put off the reader, for their content is well worth looking into (Gleick 1988; Holden 1986). The modern study of chaos began with the realization in the 1960s that very simple mathematical equations could model systems every bit as turbulent as a waterfall. These equations were extremely *sensitive* to changes in their input parameters; tiny differences in the input ramified into tremendous differences in output.

The term "chaos" conjures up images of randomness, but chaotic algorithms are strictly deterministic. Thus, when their output is examined under the analytical microscopes of chaos theory, it can be shown that there is a hidden order, a shadowed organization in the behavior of these systems.

At the core of chaotic formulas is a kind of push-versus-pull relationship—a driving tendency and a damping tendency coexisting. First one, then the other dominates, and in turbulence they fight violently until the inputs change, perhaps causing a return to fragile balance and stability.

Linear versus Nonlinear Systems

A basic grasp of the distinction between linear and nonlinear systems is important to understanding chaos theory. Linear relationships can be plotted in straight lines on a graph. Even complicated linear systems can be divided into modular parts. That is, they can be taken apart and put back together again unchanged. They are solvable, meaning that they can be reduced to a tidy closed-form algebraic solution. A example of a linear system is a series of digital bandpass filters. The effect of these filters accumulates in proportion to their characteristics. For example, the effect of two bandpass filters in series with a boost of $+3$ dB each is equivalent to a single bandpass filter with a boost of $+6$ dB.

By contrast, nonlinear systems are not strictly proportional. One can think of them as having internal thresholds; when these thresholds are crossed, they switch into another mode of behavior. As mentioned, nonlinear algorithms are quite sensitive to their input values. Nonlinear equations often cannot be solved in a neat algebraic way; instead a solution must be approximated using an iterative algorithm.

A classic example of a nonlinear system is an algorithm like frequency modulation. The result of frequency modulating two sine waves at 1000 and 100 Hz is not the sum of these two signals, but rather a complicated transmutation, possibily containing dozens of sidebands (see chapter 6 for more on the theory of FM). For certain (relatively high) values of the modulation index, small changes may result in explosive changes in the output signal. Waveshaping, also presented in chapter 6, is another example of a nonlinear system.

A Chaos Algorithm

A classic chaotic generator, the *logistic* function, was first unearthed by R. May (1976). This function can be defined quite simply:

$$x_{n+1} = \lambda \times x_n \times (1 - x_n)$$

where $0 < \lambda \leq 4$. That is, for every new value of x, one recycles the old value of x multiplied by some scaling factors. It behaves as follows:

For $0 \leq \lambda \leq 1$, all iterations converge on the fixed point 0.

For $1 < \lambda < 3$, a fixed limit value of $1 - 1\lambda$ attracts all initial values of x.

For $\lambda \geq 3$, the fixed point continues at first but becomes unstable so that x points in its neighborhood are not attracted but are rather repelled. This same range sees the birth of a two-member *limit cycle* (i.e., an alternation between values).

At $\lambda = 3.449499$, the 2-cycle bifurcates into a 4-cycle.

From $\lambda = 3.54409$ to 3.569946, the 4-cycle splits into an 8-cycle, and so on indefinitely, creating a harmonic cascade; this corresponds to physical phenomena such as the onset of turbulence in fluids.

Between 3.8 and 3.86 a region of stability appears, with only a few alternating values, only to be destabilized again into even more turgid chaos.

Figure 19.18, made famous in many reprints, plots the behavior of this function over the critical range of 2.9 to 3.9. It clearly displays many of the properties deemed interesting in chaotic functions: the coexistence of fixed points (no variations), attractors (slow variations that pull in other values toward them), period doublings or bifurcations (splits into alternating values), and turbulence—disorder at all scales, small eddies within larger ones.

The logistic function is just one of innumerable chaotic functions (Gleick 1988; Holden 1986). But the challenge in algorithmic composition goes be-

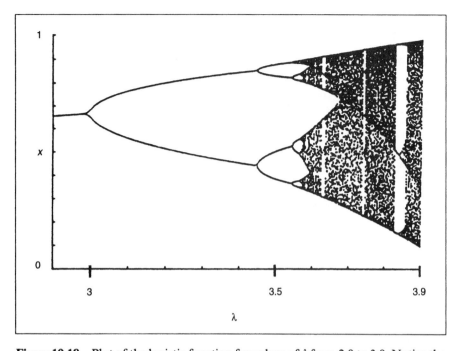

Figure 19.18 Plot of the logistic function for values of λ from 2.9 to 3.9. Notice the bifurcations at around 3.0 and 3.45. In the chaotic region the function takes quasi-random values, but then for certain values stablizes again, only to break into chaos. What this diagram does not show, but which can be seen in Gleick (1988) in the figure entitled "Windows of order inside chaos," is that the stable region between 3.8 and 3.9 bifurcates on a microscale in the same way as the overall diagram in figure 19.18. And within this microscale is a stable region that itself bifurcates on a nanoscale in the same way as figure 19.18, and so on.

yond choosing the "right" chaos; it involves setting up an interesting mapping between chaotic behavior and musical parameters on some plane (waveform, notes, high-level structure, etc.). See Pressing (1988), Bidlack (1992), Ames (1992), Di Scipio (1990), Gogins (1991), and Degazio (1986) for initial explorations of these issues.

Grammars

It has long been observed that much music exhibits a hierarchical structure. Notes or sound objects are subsumed into phrases, which can be encapsulated by measures, periods, subsections, sections, movements, and ultimately an entire piece. In the discussion of Markov chains, we saw how important it is for an algorithmic composition system to handle different levels of musical structure. A system that generates only one level of musical structure suffers from a kind of myopia. It may be clever at a task like generating melodies or chord sequences, but it has no concept of the larger context into which these are embedded. Such a system will probably generate music that suffers from macrostructural deficiencies, the main symptoms of which are endless variations on one level, weak development, clumsy transitions, and unconvincing overall form.

A *formal grammar* is a way of representing hierarchical relationships. The grammar is called "formal" because hierarchical relationships are formalized using a special mathematical notation of alphanumeric characters and strings. (See Roads 1985e for a survey of grammars in music.)

Shorthand descriptions of musical syntax are not new. We refer to "measure 21," "section B," "the third movement," "the countersubject"—all of which characterize groupings of contiguous musical events. Formal grammars, however, are relatively new. These abstract forms for describing syntactic relationships were first axiomatized in the late 1950s as a way of characterizing structures in natural languages like French (Chomsky 1957, 1965).

Musical Applications of Grammars

The literature of musical applications of grammars is substantial (Molino 1975; Nattiez 1975; Ruwet 1972, 1975; Bernstein 1976; Lerdahl and Jackendoff 1983; Lidov and Gabura 1973; Baroni et al. 1984; Roads 1978b, 1985e, Holtzman 1981; Jones 1981; Winograd 1968; Laske 1975; Bel 1992; Bel and Kippen 1992). These applications can be broken into two major categories:

1. *Synthesis of syntactic structures:* Starting from a specification of large-scale syntactic structure, fill in the details for each of these structures. This could be an approach to composition, given a composer-specified grammar. It has also been used by music theorists as a method of proving a theory of composition, that is, as a way of verifying an analysis of a musical style.

2. *Analysis of syntactic structures:* Parse (recognize and classify) a stream of low-level musical events (like individual notes) into larger syntactic categories. The most immediate application is the analysis of music. However, this analysis could be put to work in an interactive performance system that listens and responds to a human performer.

In the case of a composition application, the composer defines a grammar. The grammar is a set of substitution rules for converting symbols representing high-level compositional structure (for example, "section A" or "movement C") into all the surface details of an actual piece (the start time for every note in the piece, for example). It is important to realize that the grammar rules define a class of compositions, not necessarily a single composition.

The grammar rules are fed into a computer. The composer can then use a compact shorthand notation to specify the macrostructure of a composition. When sentences of this shorthand notation are fed into a generator program, the computer expands the shorthand according to the rules of the grammar. The automatic expansion provided by the grammar and the generator program allows composers to test out different orderings of large-scale structure—more variations than they could work out themselves by hand. This is because each high-level symbol can represent an entire section of a composition. It is not necessary always to work at the highest level; the composer can intermingle large-scale and small-scale structure in a specification. See Bel (1992) and Bel and Kippen (1992) for a description of a practical grammar-based system, integrated with MIDI, that runs on a personal computer.

Notation of Formal Grammars

The notation of abstract grammars is a collection of alphanumeric characters, for example, $a, b, \ldots A, B \ldots, 0, 1, \ldots$ Other symbols (such as Greek letters) can also be added to this basic set. Out of one or more characters are composed individual *tokens*, for example, *aa, ZZ, motive_X, measure21*. The collection of tokens together with the null token $\varnothing$ make up the vocabulary of tokens V. V is divided into two classes: *nonterminal tokens* and *terminal tokens*. The nonterminals represent macrostructure—groupings of musical events. The terminals represent the lowest-level tokens that make up the surface structure of a piece. For example, the terminals might represent the individual notes of a composition.

A *generative grammar* consists of a set of nonterminals, an alphabet of terminals, a *root token*, and a collection of *rewrite rules*. The following expression:

$$\alpha \rightarrow \beta$$

is a *rewrite rule*. The right side of the rule is a replacement for the left side. This basic rule constitutes the algorithm for generating *sentences* using the grammar. A *derivation* is a complete sequence of rewrite rules leading from the root token to a terminal. For example, the sequence of rules

$$\Sigma \rightarrow \alpha$$
$$\alpha \rightarrow \beta$$

$$\beta \to \chi$$

$$\chi \to \tau$$

is a derivation from the root Σ to the nonterminal levels α, β, and χ to the terminal τ.

Different types of formal grammars can be classified according to the form of their rewrite rules. Some rules generate only a single token at a time, while others can generate a mixture of nonterminal and terminal tokens. Another type of rule provides a form of *context-sensitivity*. That is, instead of following the same rule for every instance of α in the general rewrite rule $\alpha \to \beta$, the content of the rule can be altered depending on the context in which α is found. Here is an example of two context-sensitive rules that expand α into ρ or σ, depending on the context in which α appears:

$$A\alpha B \to A\rho B$$

$$B\alpha C \to B\sigma C$$

The basic types of grammars can be extended by means of *transformations* attached to the rewrite rules. Transformations are, in effect, procedures that add (possibly more) context-sensitivity to the rules and simplify the form of the rules themselves. (For a more detailed examination of the different grammar types, see Chomsky 1957 and Roads 1985e.)

Musical Grammar Example

Unlike a grammar for speech, a musical grammar must be able to handle a parallelism, since music contains chords and multiple parts that play simultaneously. Figure 19.19 shows three rules in both textual and graphical form that one might find in a musical grammar (Roads 1978b). Figure 19.19a is a sequential rule, while 19.19b is a parallel rule, meaning that all subtokens start at the same time. Figure 19.19c is an "or" rule, meaning that Z produces I or J, depending on what **procedure p** decides in its current context.

An example of a simple grammar built up from these three types of rules is shown in figure 19.20. In this case the terminals are soundfile objects. When we process a statement such as the following through the grammar:

SECTION_1, E, SECTION_2

a parser references the grammar to expand each nonterminal into its corresponding terminals. Figure 19.21 depicts the expanded result.

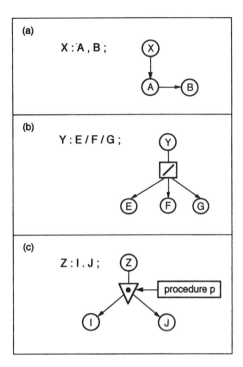

Figure 19.19 Textual and graphic forms of three rules in a musical grammar coded in the TREE grammar specification language (Roads 1978b). (Note that in TREE the colon replaces the arrow shown in previous rewrite rules.) (*a*) A comma indicates a sequential rule: *A* is followed by *B*. (*b*) Slashes indicate a parallel rule: *E, F,* and *G* start at the same time. (*c*) The period signifies an "or" rule. *I* or *J* is produced depending on what **procedure p** decides.

Assessment of Grammars

The major conundrum with formal grammar representations is the separation between "syntax" and "semantics" that they imply. Rewrite rules and the notion of context-sensitivity are usually based on hierarchical syntactic categories, whereas in music there are innumerable nonhierarchical ways of parsing music that are difficult to represent as part of a grammar. (For a discussion of these issues, see Minsky 1965, 1981 and Roads 1985e.)

Generate-and-test

One of the earliest methods used in algorithmic composition experiments is the *generate-and-test* (GAT) approach. In 1956 Klein and Bolitho used it to compose the melody of their tune *Push Button Bertha,* and Lejaren Hiller

```
tree begin

    {* Nonterminal rewrite rules *}
    nonterminal begin
       {* Top-level structures *}
       SECTION_1 : A , B;
       SECTION_2 : C / D;
       SECTION_3 : E , F;
    end

    {* Nonterminal-to-terminal rewrite rules *}
    terminal begin
       {* Control procedure for or-rule *}
       globalcontrol = decider_1;

       {* Silences are indicated by s(time-units) *}
       A : obj1 . s(500) / obj2;
       B : obj32 / obj4 , s(1000);
       C : obj99 , s(750);
       D : obj9 . obj11;
       E : obj21 , obj78;
       F : obj97 / obj54 / obj1;
    end

end tree
```

Figure 19.20 Example of a grammar for music coded in the TREE language. The definition is in two blocks: a nonterminal (high-level) block and a terminal (low-level) block.

used it in a number of compositions beginning about the same time (Hiller 1970, 1981; Ames 1987a). The basic concept is a simple three-step procedure (figure 19.22):

1. Generate a parameter value at random from a repertoire of possible values.

2. Subject the random value to a series of tests that determine the valid values at that step of the process.

3. If the value passes all the tests, write the value as the output, otherwise generate a new random value.

Depending on the nature of the tests, the GAT method can realize a wide variety of composition processes, including rules for melodic construction, harmony, and counterpoint. For flexibility, the rules encoded in the tests can vary in terms of their strictness. That is, some rules may be absolute strictures, while others are guidelines that allow a wide range of possible values, or rate the "degree of success" of a value without failing any value. The "degree of success" value might be used in a later stage of testing.

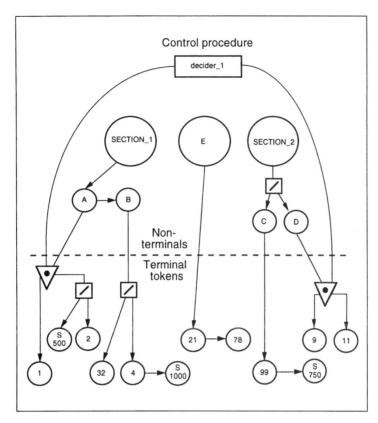

Figure 19.21 Graphical realization of a statement interpreted by the grammar shown in figure 19.20 (see the text).

(See Schottstaedt 1989b for an example of rules for species counterpoint that vary in their strictness.)

The GAT method can be inefficient, however, if the range of possible values is large relative to the range of acceptable values at a given stage. In this case the system spends a great deal of time generating and testing values that are ultimately rejected. Hence, a number of extensions to GAT have been developed.

Extensions to Generate-and-test

One way to make GAT methods more efficient is to add a planning component that prunes the range of random values to be tested. *Constrained selection* sets the priority of the values to be tested and organizes them into a schedule at each stage (Ames 1983, 1987a). This method is also called *plan-generate-test* in the literature of artificial intelligence research (Rich 1983).

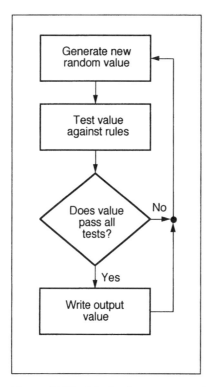

Figure 19.22   The basic generate-and-test algorithm.

GAT methods can be seen as a kind of *depth-first search* operation (Winston 1984). But instead of starting from a known pattern to be matched in a database (the usual search paradigm; see the next section), GAT starts the search from a random value and narrows the scope of the search at each test point. The searchlike structure of a GAT is made clearer if we add *backtracking* to a GAT to increase its efficiency. Backtracking is a search control mechanism for terminating a dead-end search when a test fails and returning to an earlier starting point. GATs with backtracking have been developed for musical purposes (Gill 1963; Ames 1987a).

Early artificial intelligence research used a kind of self-modifying GAT approach (Miller, Galanter, and Pribram 1960; Newell and Simon 1972; Laske 1975). After generating a value, a battery of tests measure the differences between the generated value and the desired value, a process called *means-ends analysis* (figure 19.23). Then the system applies appropriate transformations to reduce the difference. Like many other problem-solving techniques, means-ends analysis relies on a set of rules that can transform one problem state into another. However, these rules are not represented as complete state descriptions. Instead they are represented as *production rules*. The left side of a production rule describes the conditions that must

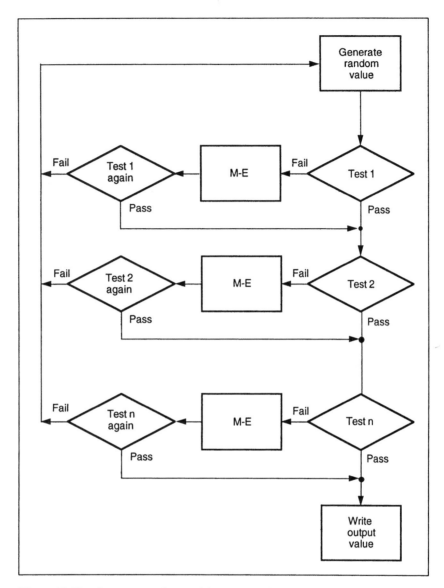

Figure 19.23   Generate-and-test with means-ends analysis. The box labeled "M-E" performs means-ends analysis and transformation.

be met for the rule to be applicable (the *preconditions*). The right side describes the aspects of the problem state that are changed by the application of the rule (Rich 1983).

An example of such a system would be a program that generates progressions of simple harmonic triads, working from left to right without lookahead. The program first generates a random triad of pitches from the chromatic scale. Suppose the program generates a triad that is not a good successor to the previous triad; that is, it fails a test. Means-ends analysis determines if two out of the three pitches are part of a good successor triad. If this precondition is met, then a transformation is applied to the remaining pitch to form a good successor chord. (See Mathews and Miller 1965 for comparable procedures.)

Backtracking is usually part of this method if a path becomes unpromising, for example, if minimizing one difference introduces a new one that was harder to eliminate. This method was used as early as 1960 to compose fugal processes (Reitman 1960; Hiller 1970).

Pattern Matching and Search Techniques

By pattern matching and search we refer to a family of techniques that scan a database of musical material looking for specific configurations of symbols. A composition program based on this method searches for instances of symbols in the database that match a general pattern specified by a composer. The database can be supplied by the composer, or it can be a more general database of material. A pattern-matching approach combines the intuition of the composer in specifying patterns and selecting results with the logical rigor of search algorithms.

Many systems that support pattern-directed search operations (such as the Prolog programming language) have automatic backtracking. Backtracking can greatly reduce the time spent searching the database. A variety of approaches to searching with backtracking exist. Winston (1984), for example, lists fourteen different algorithms.

Examples of Pattern-directed Search in Composition

The Rome-based composer James Dashow has developed a "precompositional" method that relies on pattern-directed search techniques built into the Prolog programming language (Dashow 1989). A foundation of Dashow's compositional approach is the concept of a *generating dyad*—a pair of pitches that are embedded in every sound the composer creates by digital synthesis (Dashow 1980; 1987). An interactive program helps the composer select the dyadic material for a given piece. Taking a set of three dyads at a time, the program creates a database of dyads based on two principles:

1. Keep the pitch collection constant while changing the dyadic pairs, that is, articulate the same pitches in combination with different intervals.

2. Keep the interval content constant while changing the pitch material that makes up the dyads, that is, articulate the same intervals with different pitch collections.

When these principles are applied together with transpositions, each set of three dyads yields several hundred variations stored in the database.

Next, to compose with this system, Dashow's program asks him to specify three dyads and the number of common tones between them. The program then searches through the previously generated database to find instances that satisfy the conditions specified by the composer. The program displays each variation and allows the composer to print it or save it to a file. By having the program generate and store these variations, the composer saves hours of manual labor in each interactive session. These pitch collections serve as the raw material of a piece, the rest of which is composed intuitively. Dashow has used this program in such pieces as *Archimedes* and *Oro, Argento, and Legno.*

Another composer who has used pattern-matching and search techniques in composition programs is Charles Ames, a former student of Lejaren Hiller. To generate Ames's composition *Protocol,* for example, a program ran through a series of algorithmic tests; then it searched for the alternative that best satisfied various criteria. For details, see Ames (1982, 1987b).

Constraints

Constraints are a promising representation for music. A constraint is an intrinsically multiple-viewpoint representation. A simple constraint can be viewed as a network of devices connected by wires (Sussman and Steele 1981). Data values can flow along the wires, and computation is performed by the devices. As a simple example, a device might check whether a pitch value sent to it was equivalent to another pitch value sent to it. A device computes only locally available information and places newly derived values on other locally attached wires. Computed values propagate in this way.

In a constraint network some of the values of the variables in the devices are dependent on the values of the variables in other devices. The notion of *dependent variables* is familiar; it is the same as in an algebraic equation like the following:

$$(a \times b) + c = 3.$$

This constraint is no more about how to compute *a* given *b* and *c* than it is about how to compute *c* given *a* and *b*. We can easily derive the value of the dependent variable by knowing the value of the other two.

Constraints are not limited to modeling quantitative relationships. They can also represent qualitative semantic dependencies. Just as "story problems" can be decomposed into elementary algebra, the essentials of other kinds of relationships—such as logical interrelations among musical objects —can be expressed with constraints. Because variables are defined in several ways simultaneously (i.e., with respect to several different relationships among variables), constraints provide multiple viewpoints on the entities they represent.

Musical Examples of Constraints

As a simple example of a constraint definition of a musical object, let us consider a six-note chord in equal temperament consisting entirely of intervals of two semitones (a chord constructed out of the whole tone scale). For example, starting with the pitch C, the other notes are D, E, F-sharp, G-sharp, and A-sharp. Using the constraint representation we want to be able to manipulate this chord in several ways. First we would like to be able to transpose the chord by any interval. This is trivial since the computer simply adds that interval to all the notes. In a slightly more complicated example, we want to be able to tell the computer to play the chord in all its inversions. One way to do this is to choose a new root and compute all the notes of the chord from that root. Finally, we want to be able to reconstruct the entire chord given any one of its pitches and its position in the chord. Since the notes are defined by their intervallic relationship to their neighbors, this is easily accomplished from the constraints. The ability of a constraint representation to "fill in the blanks" from a partial description of an object is one of its main features. Starting from this simple example, it is not difficult to imagine constraint representations for musical entities such as scales, modes, chord sequences, and rhythmic progressions.

A good example of constraints applied to music is Levitt's jazz improvisation system that embodied a constraint model of tonal consonance (Levitt 1981, 1983, 1984). In his model (simplified for the purpose of explanation),

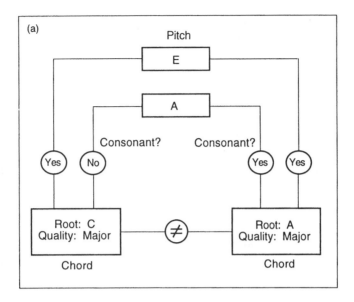

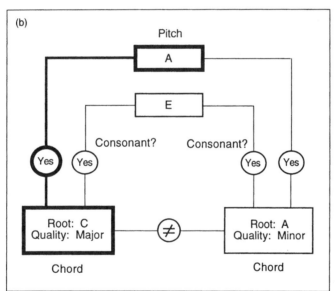

Figure 19.24 Graphic representation of constraints. (*a*) Constraint relation between two pitches and two chords. (*b*) Overconstrained network; the bold outline indicates a contradiction. (See the text for further explanation.)

a pitch is consonant with a chord only if the pitch is contained in that chord. A further simplification is that the chords are of two types only: major and minor triads. Thus the pitch E is consonant with the chord C-major because E is a member of the set {C E G}, while the pitch B is dissonant with respect to the C-major triad. In figure 19.24a the two pitches at the top are related to the two chords at the bottom via **Consonant?** constraints depicted by circles. A Not-equal constraint exists between the chords. In figure 19.24a the network answers the questions: "Is the pitch E consonant with the chord C-major? Is the pitch A consonant with the C-major triad? Is the pitch E consonant with the A-minor triad? Is the pitch A consonant with the A-minor triad?" The answers are shown in the circles representing the constraint rules. In figure 19.21b the network is overconstrained. The parts outlined in bold indicate sources of inconsistency. In particular, the pitch A is not consonant with the C-major triad, even though A is constrained to be consonant by the network.

See Courtot (1992) and Ebcioglu (1992) for additional examples of constraint representations for music composition.

Solving Constraint Networks

A general method for solving a constraint network is to employ a back-tracking search. This procedure sets the value of the variables in a constraint network until a constraint is not met, then tries another value for the last variable, backing up to a previous variable if necessary. This process can be speeded up if the range of possible values is pruned before the search begins. In most present systems, each constraint is implemented as a more or less complicated program module. Progress in constraint representations is dependent on the development of programming systems that explicitly support the constraint paradigm.

Expert Systems

An expert system is a computer program that uses knowledge and inference procedures to solve problems that are difficult enough to require significant expertise. The "expertise" in an expert system must be gathered and codified in terms of *facts, rules,* and *heuristics,* which are collectively called the *knowledge base* (Barr, Cohen, and Feigenbaum 1981).

A fact is a direct statement about the state of something, as in "The tempo is 60 MM." A rule is a conditional "IF-THEN" expression, such as

"IF this is Section 1 AND the last four quarter-note pitches of voice 3 are A C E F-sharp AND the tempo is approximately 90 THEN play sequence 89." A heuristic is an educated guess that is taken in the absence of a firm rule. A simple example might be, "IF the last seven pitches were C D E F G A B THEN the mostly likely next pitch is C."

An example of an expert system for composition is D. Cope's Experiments in Musical Intelligence (EMI) system, which acts as a "friendly protagonist" to the composer (Cope 1987). EMI is particularly expert at developing pitch motives into elaborate linear and contrapuntal structures. A feature of EMI is that it can be loaded with any style dictionary. Hence, the system has generated music in the style of Bach, Beethoven, Brahms, and Mozart, as well as Cope. Other examples of expert systems include B. Garton's Elthar program for interactive signal processing (Garton 1989), and P. Beyls's Oscar, designed for an interactive composing environment (Beyls 1988).

Expert System Shells

The first expert systems were one-of-a-kind programs (Winston 1984), but since then a variety of *expert system shells* have become available. An expert system shell is a packaged programming environment with tools that assist the user in creating a knowledge base. Programming an expert system shell is not a trivial task, although some shells provide rule templates and can infer rules from examples given by the user.

In general, the shell provides a rule interpreter, inference engine, explanation facility, and an interface toolkit. The rule interpreter builds a knowledge base from facts and rules stipulated by the user. The inference engine turns rules into chains of reasoning and adds new facts based on inferences that it makes. The explanation facility allows the user to interrogate the system by asking "Why did you arrive at this result?" The interface toolkit provides mechanisms for opening files, interacting with the user, and printing reports.

Assessment of Expert Systems

Expert systems emulate the logical inferences made by technical experts. The power of an expert system is directly related to the quality of the rules in its knowledge base. Certain types of formal knowledge about music, such as rules of counterpoint, common-practice harmony, or Mozart sonata form, can be realized convincingly with this approach (Ebcioglu 1980, 1988;

Schwanauer 1988; Schottstaedt 1989b; Cope 1989). However, the expert system approach demands a codified body of acknowledged facts, accepted rules, and known heuristics, and so may not be well suited to less formalized or unorthodox new musical styles.

Another barrier to the spread of expert systems in music is the problem of *knowledge acquisition*—how to codify the facts, rules, and heuristics of a style. This labor, which requires a fresh and systematic look at musical processes, stands in the way of many applications. An expert system that can make inferences from partial descriptions meets the musician halfway. It has been suggested that expert systems will flourish only when the technology of machine learning is better understood (Michalski, Carbonell, and Mitchell 1983). Some work in musical learning by example has already been carried out (Levitt 1981, 1983). Another direction is using *parallel distributed processing* (of which neural networks are one example) that can be trained by examples presented to them.

Neural Networks

Neural networks (NNs; also called *connectionist* models or *parallel distributed processors*) were first conceived as models of biological computation (McCulloch 1965). The late 1980s saw a great resurgence in the idea (Rumelhart and McClelland 1986; Loy 1989b, c; Todd and Loy 1991). Like the linked automata models discussed earlier in this chapter, the NN paradigm consists of a large number of identical, interconnected processing elements. Each element receives a set of input activations in the form of a numerical vector.

Knowledge in an NN is represented by the *connection strengths* between elements and the mutual *reinforcement* or *inhibition* of elements by other elements. The output of an element is determined by a rule, typically a nonlinear function of the sum of the inputs. Nonlinearity is essential for endowing the network with "decision-making power." That is, quantitative changes in the input can produce qualitative changes in the output, rather than simply moving in direct proportion to the input.

Another important property of modern NN models is their *multilayer* organization (figure 19.25). A typical network might have an *input layer* that accepts input data from the external world, a *hidden layer* that combines information gathered from the input layer, and an *output layer* whose output is the result of the network as a whole (Dolson 1989a). These layers

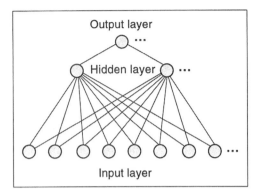

Figure 19.25 A three-layer feedforward neural network. Data flow in from the bottom and percolates to the top.

give the network the capability to generalize, that is, to gather information from many low-level elements and feed their cumulative decision to higher-level elements.

Part of the popularity of multilayer NNs derives from the existence of *training algorithms* for them. Networks can be trained to adjust their connection strengths automatically until a desired mapping between a set of inputs and a set of outputs is achieved. A simple example of a training sequence for a melodic composition system would be a set of desirable and undesirable melodies together with the trainers's rating expressed as a 1 or a 0. For some complex computations, it is easier to train an NN to generate the desired result than it is to decompose the problem into a sequence of steps for a traditional programming language or expert system.

Musical applications of NNs include rhythmic analysis, pitch perception, performance planning, and tonality and polyphony simulations. Dolson (1989a) has suggested that timbre analysis and synthesis may also be fruitful areas for this approach. Todd (1989) outlined a connectionist approach to melodic composition in which a sequential network with feedback is trained by a set of melodies. The feedback (from the output layer to the input layer) gives the network a memory of its past output. Training forces the network to construct an abstract melody space in which each melody is represented by a point in the space. Melodic interpolation and extrapolation can be generated by presenting the network with melodic structures that are outside the training set. This interpolation is of a different character than the weighted average interpolation used in the function editors of Mathews and Rosler (1968) described in chapter 16. See Todd (1989) and Lewis (1989) for more on this subject.

Analysis and Composition

A product composed by a machine, realized and edited by another, should perhaps be judged by a third. (Peter Zinoviev 1968)

Analysis is a neglected issue in algorithmic composition, even though critical listening and analysis are central to the ongoing training of composers. The feedback that occurs when composers hear their work performed for the first time often prompts a revision. The output of composition programs is sometimes unpredictable, particularly when many procedures interact, no one of which is responsible for the overall result. Thus it is odd that few composition programs have facilities for analysis or feedback.

An analysis component can act as a system of checks and balances to interacting generative algorithms (figure 19.26). When an algorithm falls into overly predictable behavior, analysis can act as a critic, saying "Enough of this, let's try something different" and relay feedback parameters that change the generative logic. Another use of analysis is as a "post-processing" phase that transforms the data produced by the generative stage.

The rise of interactive music systems that listen and respond to human gestures puts analysis in the forefront. But the machine must also be taught to listen to itself.

Examples of Analysis in Composition Programs

Examples of analysis in composition programs are found in the programs PROCESS/ING (Roads 1976) and IOS (Roads 1983). The PROCESS/ING program generated output as the product of a number of interacting automata. At each time step, the program analyzed this output. Depending on the analysis results, it altered the interconnection structure of the automata to ensure that the musical logic did not remain static or fall into repetitious behavior. With three levels of analysis and control, the system could not only change its behavior, it could change the way that it changed the behavior. The output score exhibited patterns and correlations between variables that shifted asynchronously over the course of events.

IOS demonstrated how a *composer's assistant* program could help a composer test various orchestrations of a score. The system analyzed a score in order to find features that are important in orchestration. These include extremal notes, lines, phrases, and chords. A composer could assign different instruments to the features recognized automatically by the analysis

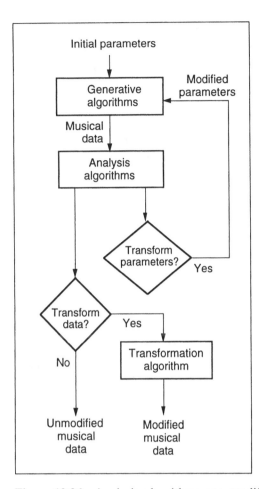

Figure 19.26 Analysis algorithms can modify the output of a generative composition algorithm or send parameters back to the generative logic to change its behavior.

component and hear the results simulated on synthetic instruments. In this way, a number of orchestrations could be tested quickly.

Conclusion

Two unresolved issues envelop algorithmic composition. The first can be stated as follows. Since there are so many different algorithmic strategies, how can we choose the best one for a particular musical application? This issue is complicated, since many algorithms are *formally equivalent,* meaning that they compute exactly the same results, but in a different manner. For example, Chomsky and Schuetzenberger (1963) used abstract algebra to describe the formal properties of grammars, while Wolfram used grammars to describe the properties of cellular automata (Wolfram 1984). Meanwhile, composers have applied algebras, grammars, and cellular automata to music, possibly unaware that these different "engines" can produce equivalent results.

Computer scientists evaluate algorithms on the basis of their efficiency—how much memory space and computation time they consume. In music, efficiency is only a concern if the calculations must be carried out in real time, such as in a performance. Much more important to musicians is the quality of interaction they have with the algorithm. Each algorithm—even those that are formally equivalent—represents musical processes in a different way, giving the composer unique "handles" to manipulate. For example, Markov chains offer global statistical control, while deterministic grammars let composers test different combinations of predefined sequences.

A related question we can ask about the appropriateness of a particular algorithm is: to what level of musical structure is it to be applied? A fractal algorithm, for example, can be used at a high level to select between different phrases, at an intermediate level to select individual pitches, or at a low level to determine the microvariations of a waveform. Academic consistency aside, is there a musical benefit to be gained by using the same algorithm at every level? Or is it better to assign different algorithms to various levels of structure, giving musicians the most appropriate controls at each stratum?

The second unresolved issue in algorithmic composition is the importance of rationalism. Music and formalistic thought have a long history, and music education often attempts to show how the masterpieces of great composers can be explained as a product of systematic, rational thought processes. There is a strong tendency in academia to equate musical structure with a formal logic.

Many pieces are indeed inspired by formal ideas, such as "all permutations of a pitch-class series," or "the fives sides of a pentagon translated into parameters for frequency modulation synthesis," or "durations corresponding to Fibonacci series," and so on. Such rationalistic designs prompt several questions. Is formal consistency perceived as such? And if it is, is there something intrinsically fascinating about the sound of an arbitrary mathematical engine? For this approach to succeed, a great deal hinges on the composer's talent in choosing the right engine and in interpreting its output into sound.

Some composers who use formal methods feel that what the listener hears is secondary. They take professional satisfaction in knowing that their structures are logically generated, whether or not they are perceived as such.

For another group, the algorithm is merely a starting point for composition. They use formalized procedures to generate initial material, and then they select and shape this material intuitively.

A scientist may be justified in building a rule system (or *style template*) for a compositional style based purely on the logical relations in the scores of a style period. The surface of any music can be encoded into such rules. But no one would mistake the logic of a style template as anything resembling the actual process of human composition. More sophisticated scientific models of human composition must capture the intuitive and emotional aspects that inform it. Emotional involvement is inseparable from musical behavior of all kinds, yet there have been only a few attempts to consider affect as part of a model of compositional thought (Minsky 1981; Roads 1985d; Duisberg 1984; Katayose and Inokuchi 1989, 1990; Imberty 1976, 1979; Meyer 1956; Coker 1972). Cognitive psychology research points to the fundamental role played by the emotions in motivation, attitude, attention span, memory, and interest—factors that drive music-making and listening (Mandler 1975). A model that relates musical structure to its emotional significance, however crude, may lessen the disparity that exists between our experience of music and the rationalizations we use to specify it.

VI Internals and Interconnections

Overview to Part VI

As more musicians set up computer music studios, it is important to consider the internal design of music devices and their interconnections. This design can either suggest new expressive possibilities, or obstruct musical expression. It shapes the way the musician must conceive of and realize a musical idea, and therefore it cannot be neglected.

Organization of Part VI

Part VI includes three chapters. Chapter 20 looks at the internal design of *digital signal processors* (DSPs). A DSP is a general term encompassing all devices that synthesize and process digital sound. The chapter examines the tasks that DSPs are expected to perform and explains the design tradeoffs encountered in them. A multiplicity of approaches to DSP architecture exist; chapter 20 points out their significance in music systems.

The Musical Instrument Digital Interface (MIDI) protocol, the subject of chapter 21, is a hardware and software specification for communication of control information between instruments and computers (IMA 1983). The music industry has embraced MIDI wholeheartedly, so that today nearly every electronic music product is compatible with MIDI. Through the grammar of MIDI *messages,* MIDI constitutes a language for communication about musical events. For example, when a musician improvises on a synthesizer keyboard attached to a sequence recorder, the keyboard sends out MIDI messages—one for each note played by the improviser. This code, stored as a series of messages, can be sent back to the synthesizer to reproduce the performance. In addition, the musician can edit the MIDI data to create variations of the original performance. This same data can recreate the performance on another MIDI-equipped instrument.

In addition to explaining the grammar of MIDI, chapter 21 surveys its main musical applications. The chapter explores both the potential and the limitations of MIDI as a representation of musical events. It also suggests ways in which MIDI could be improved or extended.

MIDI cables are just one way to interconnect devices. The modular analog synthesizer of the 1970s provided an all-in-one package for musical control, synthesis, and sound processing. In these relatively simple systems, patch cords connected one module to another. In today's complex digital music systems, the various components of the system may require a dozen or more different types of interconnections, due to the diverse nature of the signals being routed. Chapter 22 surveys the different types of interconnections needed to set up a modern computer music studio. These range from AC lines and analog cables to computer interfaces, network connections, and specialized digital audio links.

20 *Internals of Digital Signal Processors*

Background: Musical Synthesis Hardware

Levels of Design

Fundamentals of Digital Synthesis Hardware
> **Pulse Tone Synthesis**
> **Sample Generation**
> **Pulse Tone Synthesis versus Sample Generation**

Criteria for Digital Sound Quality
> **Sampling Rate**
> **Input/Output Sample Width**
> **Internal Coding Resolution**
> **Floating-point versus Fixed-point Systems**
> **Wavetable Size**
> **Frequency Resolution and Tuning**

Computational Demands of Digital Synthesis
> **Time-division Multiplexing**
> **DSP Performance Factors**
> *Data Memory and Program Memory*
> *I/O Bandwidth*

Architecture of Digital Signal Processors

Fixed- versus Variable-function DSP Architectures
Differences between General-purpose Microprocessors and DSPs
RISC Microprocessors for DSP
Fractional Addressing
Operation of a DSP
Example of DSP Architecture
The Question of Branching
Parallelism and Pipelining within a Single DSP
The Parameter Update Problem
Method 1: Provide an Update Period
Method 2: Provide a DSP Controller
MIDI Black Boxes
Discussion of the Parameter Update Problem

Programming and Microprogramming a DSP

Microprograms
Horizontal Microcoding
Advantages and Disadvantages of Microprogramming

VLSI and DSP

Benefits of VLSI
The Trend to Miniaturization: Background
Low Power Consumption: Background

Array Processors

Operation of an Array Processor

Multiprocessor Architectures

Fixed-function versus General Processing Element
Data Flow
Connectionist Architectures

Conclusion

Speed and synthesis are the characteristics of our era.
—Edgard Varèse (1920)

This chapter sets forth the musical tasks *digital signal processors* (DSPs) are expected to perform and explains the tradeoffs encountered in actual systems. Throughout the chapter, the term "DSP" includes devices that synthesize sound as well as those that transform acoustic sounds. This broad category can include synthesizers, samplers, musical workstations, effects units, and digital audio mixers. We can group all these devices together because their underlying hardware is much the same. What sets them apart from each other is the way they have been programmed for a specific application.

In order to make the chapter accessible to nontechnical readers, we assume only a basic knowledge of digital circuit technology. The chapter steers away from implementation details such as instruction sets, chip selection, and wiring diagrams. This kind of information, which is dependent on shifting trends in the marketplace, can be obtained from the data sheets and technical memoranda offered by manufacturers. In any case, the goal of this chapter is not to turn readers into hardware designers, but rather to foster better-informed users and purchasers of DSPs. First we begin with a bit of history.

Background: Musical Synthesis Hardware

When digital sound synthesis was first tested in 1957 at Bell Telephone Laboratories, the computer that calculated the sound samples was slow and extremely expensive. A short sound might take hours to compute. The transistor had yet to be introduced, meaning that the size and power consumption of the vacuum tube computers in use at the time was enormous, not to mention the cost of maintaining them. It took many years for hardware technology to evolve to a state that made it cost-effective to construct a real-time digital music synthesizer.

The first instrument based on a digital table-lookup oscillator with programmable waveforms was the Allen Computer Organ, developed in conjunction with North American Rockwell and demonstrated to the press in May 1971 (Markowitz 1989). Soon afterward, the Dartmouth Digital Synthesizer was constructed by Sydney Alonso and his colleagues at Dartmouth College (Alonso 1973). Alonso later formed New England Digital Corporation to market digital synthesis to recording studios. The company's first product, the Synclavier, introduced in 1977, was a keyboard instrument with a built-in sequencer that generated 8-bit sound samples (Alonso,

Figure 20.1   Peter Samson standing next to the Systems Concepts Digital Synthesizer.

Appleton, and Jones 1977). The company introduced the highly successful Synclavier II in 1979, which eventually added a sampling option.

In 1974 Peter Samson, one of the pioneer experimenters in digital tone generation synthesis during his early career at the Massachusetts Institute of Technology's Project MAC, began research to develop a large-scale digital sound synthesizer capable of producing 256 independent sound sources in real-time. The Systems Concepts Digital Synthesizer (or "Samson Box") was delivered to the Center for Computer Research in Music and Acoustics at Stanford University in 1977 (figure 20.1). The Samson Box, controlled by a mainframe computer, served as the central synthesis and sound processing facility at Stanford throughout the 1980s (Samson 1980, 1985).

The Institut de Recherche et Coordination Acoustique/Musique (IRCAM) in Paris was founded in 1976. One of the first researchers there, invited by Luciano Berio, was a physicist from the University of Naples named Giuseppe Di Giugno (figure 20.2). Di Giugno created a family of increasingly powerful synthesizers starting from the 4A (1976) and including the 4B, 4C, and the culmination, the 4X (1980). The 4X filled eight densely packed rackmounted circuit boards with hundreds of chips and could exe-

Figure 20.2 Giuseppe Di Giugno at the controls of the 4X synthesizer preparing for a performance in Venice.

cute up to 200 million instructions per second. The machine was used by several composers, generally in modes where it promoted the IRCAM aesthetic as an effects processor for traditional instrumental performers.

The technology of sampling synthesis requires a large memory in which are stored relatively long wavetables, typically recordings of acoustic instrument tones. By 1979 the declining cost of semiconductor memory made it possible to market a digital sampling instrument. The Fairlight Computer Music Instrument (CMI), developed in Australia, was the first commercial instrument to offer 8-bit sampling with pitch shifting on playback (figure 20.3). (See chapter 4 for more on sampling). But the cost of the Fairlight CMI and its market counterpart, the Synclavier II with sampling option, was substantial. The E-mu Emulator, introduced in the pre-MIDI era of 1981, was the first instrument to bring the cost of 8-bit monophonic sampling under $10,000. The Digital Music Systems DMX-1000 created by Dean Wallraff of Boston, fit into the same price range but was aimed at a smaller market, since it required users to program their sounds with a synthesis language (Wallraff 1979a). Unlike other commercial synthesizers, the

Figure 20.3   The Fairlight Computer Music Instrument, model I, ca. 1979. Notice the lightpen attached to the terminal for graphical input.

DMX-1000 was a true programmable *digital signal processor* (DSP), capable of processing sounds from external sources as well as synthesizing sounds.

In 1980 Yamaha unveiled an expensive digital keyboard synthesizer called the GS1, housed in a wooden case with a pianolike shape. It was not a commercial success. A major breakthrough occurred in 1983, shortly after the ratification of the MIDI protocol, when Yamaha introduced a family of low-cost digital synthesis instruments, including the DX7—a major commercial success. A keyboard synthesizer, the DX7 offered 32 preset synthesis voices based on the technique of frequency modulation explained in chapter 6. The front panel of the DX7 and its successor, the DX7II

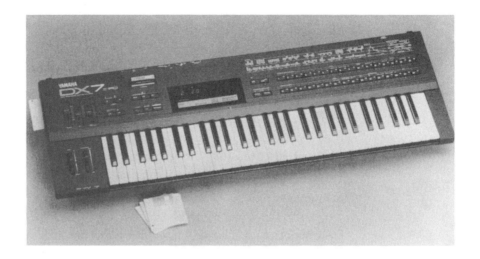

Figure 20.5   The Kurzweil K250 sampling synthesizer, with a weighted 88-key keyboard.

(figure 20.4) set a standard for the design of many synthesizers to follow: liquid crystal display, multifunction buttons, sliders for data entry, and rotary modulation and pitch wheels at the side of the keyboard.

Wide press coverage surrounding the 1984 launch of the Kurzweil K250 keyboard sampler (figure 20.5) made more people aware of the potential of sampling technology. But with a selling price of about $10,000 (excluding options), the cost of sampling instruments remained rather high.

Throughout the 1980s, synthesizers were split into two groups: (1) those designed to make the most of small wavetables and reliance on a single synthesis technique, like frequency modulation or phase distortion (exemplified by the Yamaha DX7 and the Casio CZ1000), and (2) expensive instruments with relatively large memories designed around sample playback (exemplified by the NED Synclavier and the Fairlight CMI). By 1990 advances in technology began to resolve these limitations. Declining costs brought large sampling memories into the budget of most musicians, and new DSP chips—on plug-in cards for popular computers (Lowe and Currie 1989)—brought the benefits of programmable signal processing to the home studio environment.

Levels of Design

Figure 20.6 depicts a typical computer music system. It can analyze and process acoustic sounds as well as synthesize sound and control MIDI equipment. It accepts performance information from a keyboard or other input device and plays back an edited version of this performance. It can display and print music notation, sound waveforms, spectra, and other representations of musical signals.

The hardware and software design of this system has many layers, shown in figure 20.7. The starting point for music creation is a human gesture, translated by the musician's interface. This interface can consist of a graphics display, a pointing device, an alphanumeric keyboard, other input devices, and appropriate software. At the lowest level is the flow of electrons through the circuit components in the DSP hardware. Where should we begin to describe the "internals" of this many layered system? In order to focus the discussion, we concentrate on the four middle levels in this chapter:

1. Interconnection between the host computer and the DSP

2. Microprograms on the DSP

3. Overall architecture of the DSP engine

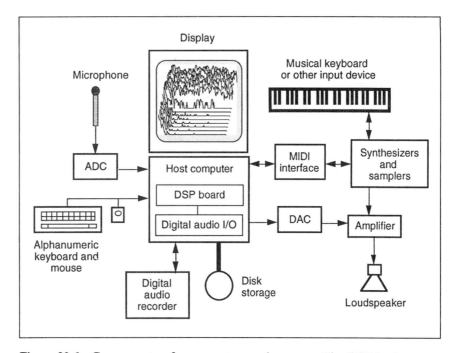

Figure 20.6 Components of a computer music system. The DSP is shown as a circuit board that plugs into the computer. It can also take the form of several circuit boards in their own box along with appropriate converters and digital interfaces. The system is also linked to external synthesizers, samplers, and effects units via MIDI.

4. The level of functional units within the DSP engine: low-level digital circuit components that perform such operations as add, multiply, and compare—core operations of DSP algorithms

At the end of the chapter we also look at multiprocessor DSP architectures.

Fundamentals of Digital Synthesis Hardware

A digital circuit can generate sound signals at least three ways:

1. *Radio wave demodulation*—Radio-frequency waves emitted by a computer running a looping program can be received by a radio closeby. The loops can be heard as tones and modulation noises through the radio.

2. *Pulse tone synthesis*—This category includes any technique that emits a serial stream of binary ones and zeros from the output of a digital circuit. When these are filtered and amplified they can create pitched tones.

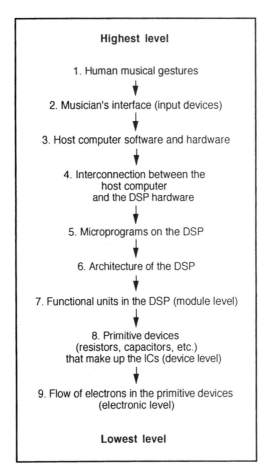

Figure 20.7 Levels of organization of a DSP system in a computer music environment.

3. *Sample generation*—Creating waveforms out of streams of multiple-bit binary numbers, where each number represents a time slice of the waveform.

Methods 1 and 2 were used in the early days of computer music, with method 1 mostly a novelty. The next section compares methods 2 and 3.

Pulse Tone Synthesis

Pulse tone synthesis came about in the early days of computer music, as an inexpensive alternative to sample-based techniques. The basic programming task is to generate alternating patterns of ones and zeros at audio rates.

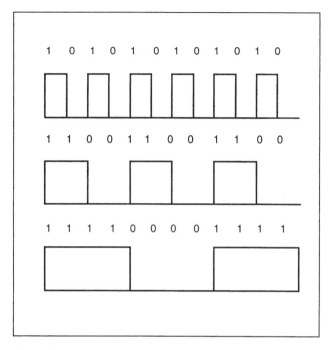

Figure 20.8 Pulse tone synthesis. Examples of three frequencies generated by different sequences of ones and zeros.

Pulse tone synthesis emits a *pulsetrain* (figure 20.8), where each pulse in the train is a single bit. A stream of pulses interspersed with variable-length silences creates a characteristic sonority: a hard-edged square wave sound at a fixed amplitude. These raw output can be reenveloped and filtered, usually in the analog domain. Chamberlin (1985, pp. 590–600) describes hardware for realizing several pulse tone generation techniques.

One variation on pulse tone synthesis is frequency divider (FD) or *divide-down* tone synthesis, whose history antedates computer technology. FD synthesis generates a waveform by counting the pulses emitted by a fast clock, and sending out a pulse when the chosen divisor—the *counter limit*—is reached. The counter is then reset to zero and begins again. This method generates a periodic pulsetrain at the frequency: *clock frequency/counter limit*. For example, if the clock frequency is 1,000,000 Hz and the counter limit is 1000, the FD technique generates a pulsetrain at 1000 Hz.

Divide-down counters of different sizes spawn other frequencies. For example, to obtain a pulsetrain at 100 Hz, another 10-pulse divide-down counter is applied to the 1 KHz signal (figure 20.9).

The first implementations of FD synthesis used analog circuits, beginning in 1930 with the Vierling organ designed in Germany (Kühnelt 1980).

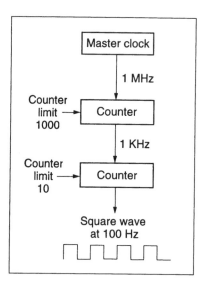

Figure 20.9   Divide-down synthesis. Generating a tone at 100 Hz from a master clock frequency of 1 MHz.

Douglas (1968) describes vacuum and neon tube implementations of the FD tone synthesis in instruments such as the Hammond Novachord (figure 20.10)—seen by thousands in the "Novachord orchestra" at the 1939 World's Fair—and built into electronic organs made by the Wurlitzer, Baldwin, and Lowrey companies.

At present the FD method is mainly of historical interest, but it is pertinent here since the earliest efforts at real-time synthesis with digital hardware used a divide-down technique (Divilbiss 1964; Hiller et al. 1966; Cotton 1972; Small 1973; Franssen 1973; Sneider 1979; O'Beirne 1968). In 1959 Peter Samson programmed the MIT TX-0 computer to generate a single voice of square wave sounds in real time. In the winter of 1960 he built a crude digital tone generator at the level of flip-flop circuits and latches using discrete transistors. By programming these circuits appropriately, he was able to generate three-part polyphony under real-time control of the TX-0 computer—a signal achievement.

Another such synthesizer, the CSX-1 Music Machine, took pulsetrains emitted by the CSX-1 computer and fed them into analog envelope shapers and formant filters. Designed by J. L. Divilbiss of the University of Illinois, the system was used by composers such as Lejaren Hiller, Herbert Brün, R. A. Baker, and John Myhill (Divilbiss 1964; Hiller et al. 1966). Pulse tone techniques were revived in the 1970s by avant-garde composers such as David Behrman, a pioneer in the use of microcomputers in live performance.

Figure 20.10   The Hammond Novachord (1939), a polyphonic keyboard instrument with synthesis based on the frequency divider method. (From Douglas 1968.)

Pulse tone synthesis does not permit much timbral or dynamical variety. The square waves it generates can be smoothed into a rounder tone by a lowpass filter. Or the pulses may trigger a formant filter. But apart from these basic modifications the sound is that of a fixed waveform at a preset amplitude.

Sample Generation

Expressive and flexible synthesis and processing mandates the production of a stream of sound samples, where each sample is an n-bit binary number. Chapter 1 introduced this method. For high-quality sound, the sample width must be around 16 bits, and 40,000 to 50,000 samples per second must be generated per audio channel. Each sample of the waveform is computed directly by the synthesizer hardware or is read from a memory table containing recorded (sampled) waveforms. Arbitrarily elaborate numerical operations can go into generating each sample; these are the synthesis and signal-processing techniques discussed in parts II and III of this book.

The samples are ultimately routed to a digital-to-analog converter (DAC). The DAC transforms the stream of digital numbers into an analog signal. This analog signal is lowpass filtered to smooth it and then amplified and sent to a loudspeaker to produce acoustical waves.

Signal transformations on samples can be reduced to numerical operations. Thus:

- Mixing is simply a sample-by sample addition of several streams of numbers.

- Amplitude envelopes are implemented by multiplying each sample in the signal by a corresponding value in an array containing the envelope. Multiplication by 1.0 is a unity gain operation (i.e., no change in amplitude), while multiplication by 0.5 creates a 6 dB reduction in amplitude. One can invert the phase of the signal by specifying a negative multiplicand.

- Time delay effects are accomplished by storing samples in memory, waiting for a delay period before reading them out, and then adding them to the original signal.

- Filters, which alter the spectrum of a signal, involve multiplications and sums of signals with the same signal delayed by one or more samples.

- Digital reverberation, one of the more complicated DSP operations, combines multiple time delays, several kinds of filters, and mixing.

Chapter 10 explicates the logic behind other signal-processing effects. The correspondence between signal transformations and numerical operations on samples means that any microprocessor can realize the full range of audio effects.

Pulse Tone Synthesis versus Sample Generation

Pulse tone synthesis has the advantages of low cost and simplicity, and it has been used in inexpensive electronic games, organs, and portable keyboard synthesizers. No DAC is associated with this method. This was a cost advantage years ago when DACs were more expensive than they are at present. But fundamental limitations plague pulse tone synthesis, including the following:

- Static, limited timbres
- Lack of extensibility in the synthesis algorithm (techniques like FM, waveshaping, etc., are not realizable)
- Poor audio quality (low signal-to-noise ratio)
- No facilities for processing of acoustical sounds
- No mechanism for digital storage (no samples are produced)

For these musical reasons, pulse tone techniques are not a good method on which to base the design of a digital synthesizer.

Sample generation resolves all of the above-listed problems. It is more general, since it can produce any sound that the pulse tone techniques can, and much more. Hence, the rest of this chapter focuses on sample-based processors.

Criteria for Digital Sound Quality

In any DSP, the most important audio criteria are the *sampling rate, sample width, internal coding resolution,* and, for machines that synthesize tones, the *wavetable length* and the *frequency resolution.* All these criteria translate into perceivable audio specifications.

Sampling Rate

The sampling rate is important, since it is directly related to the *audio bandwidth* or *frequency range* of the system. As chapter 1 explains, in order to reproduce accurately frequency components up to 20,000 Hz, the synthesizer must, according to the *sampling theorem,* use a sampling rate of at least double that frequency, or 40,000 Hz (Nyquist 1928). Using a sampling rate less than twice the highest frequency to be reproduced results in *foldover* or *aliasing* distortion when the high frequencies are played. In practice, the sampling rate is usually set at least slightly higher than twice the highest audio frequency, to allow for the transition bands of the antialiasing (input) and anti-imaging (output) filters (see chapter 1).

Current audio industry standards set the sampling rate at 48 KHz for professional audio equipment, and 44.1 KHz for equipment that is compatible with compact disc players. The 44.1 KHz consumer product sampling frequency was originally fixed because of its relationship to the National Television System Committee (NTSC) video scanning rate, established in 1953 (Nakajima et al. 1983; Doi, Tsuchiya, and Iga 1978; Freeman 1984).

Systems offering lower and higher sampling frequencies are also available. But it is important to distinguish between *oversampling systems* (described in chapter 1) that convert at high frequencies but store at low frequencies, and true high-sampling rate systems that store more samples per second.

Input/Output Sample Width

If we look at a time-domain image of a sampled signal, that is, a representation of amplitude versus time, the sampling rate is indicated by the number of slices on the time (x) axis. The number of slices on the amplitude (y) axis corresponds to the sample width. The *input/output (I/O) sample width* is the size (in bits) of the word used to represent each sample going into or coming out of a digital audio system. (Another term for this specification could be *I/O quantization*.)

When the sample width is too small, there are not enough bits in the word to describe accurately the variations in the desired waveform, resulting in quantization error. Suppose we try to represent a sine wave with a 1-bit sample width. When the sine wave is positive, the sample bit is set to 1; when it is on the negative half of its cycle, the sample bit is set to 0. The resulting square wave is a crude simulacrum of the original sine. By adding more bits to the sample width, we obtain finer and finer resolution in the digitized waveform. Specifically, we reduce the quantization noise and increase the dynamic range (see chapter 1).

Some digital audio systems employ a 16-bit sample width (65,536 levels of resolution) at the input and output (I/O) stages. Others can handle 20 bits (over one million levels) or more. As mentioned in chapter 1, a rule of thumb is to assume that for each added bit of resolution, we gain about 6 dB of dynamic range. Thus a 16-bit linear digital audio system can have a theoretical maximum dynamic range of 96 dB. A 20-bit converter handles 120 dB of dynamic range, which is close to the human ear's resolution. Craven (1993) presents arguments for 24-bit conversion. (For more on dynamic range and noise in digital audio systems, see Blesser and Kates 1978, Talambiras 1985, and Pohlmann 1989a.)

Internal Coding Resolution

The sample width represents the resolution of the audio signal only at the I/O stages of a DSP. One of the most important specifications of digital audio quality is the *internal coding resolution*—the sample width of the buses and the functional units of the DSP (figure 20.11). (A bus is a high-

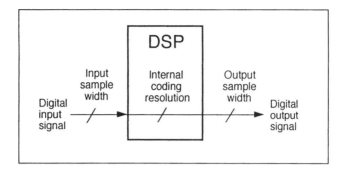

Figure 20.11 Internal coding resolution is measured inside the DSP, whereas the sample width is measured at the I/O ports of the DSP.

speed data "highway.") High-quality audio processing requires more than 20 bits of resolution for operations such as mixing, filtering, and reverberating. Suppose, for example, that we are trying to mix down 24 channels of 16-bit digital audio into one channel. If all 24 channels peak at their full 16-bit range for an instant, we need an *accumulator* (a memory register to hold the sum) to contain the value $24 \times 2^{16} = 1{,}572{,}792$. It takes 21 bits to hold this number. Alternatively, we can scale each input to the mixer so that the 24-channel sum never exceeds a 16-bit word. Each channel's scaling is done by a multiplication of the form

fader level $\times$ input signal = scaled signal.

Even in this case one needs high internal coding resolution because the product of two n-bit integers requires a maximum of $2n - 1$ output bits to hold the result (Pohlmann 1989a). Hence a 16-bit integer system needs 31 bits of dynamic range to avoid *numerical overflow* (one or more numbers that exceed the resolution of the system, causing a pop or harsh noise), and *truncation errors* (deleting the low-order bits of a number, which is a form of distortion).

Another place where high resolution is required is inside digital filters. Since recursive or IIR digital filters use the results of previous calculations, numerical inaccuracies caused by roundoff error can compound quickly into gross audio distortions (Rabiner and Gold 1975). (See chapter 10 for an explanation of IIR filters.) Another source of inaccuracies in digital filter response can be traced to too small a coding resolution for *filter coefficients*. (Coefficients are multiplication factors inside the filter that determine the the filter's characteristics, such as its cutoff frequency and bandwidth.)

The question of just how many bits of resolution are needed inside a DSP is subject to debate. Although inexpensive 24-bit DSP chips have been employed in many audio systems, a 24-bit word length is not adequate for certain high-fidelity filtering operations. For example, when filter peaks and dips are close to one another, small numerical errors can drive the filter into oscillation. One programming solution is to drop into a double-precision mode, using two 24-bit words to represent each sample, but this also halves the processing speed. Alternatively, many systems implement a 32- or 64-bit *floating-point* format in hardware, as discussed in the next section.

Floating-point versus Fixed-point Systems

In a *fixed-point* processor, all computation is performed on integers. For audio applications these integers are usually 16-, 24-, or 32-bit quantities. Some DSPs, however, implement a *floating-point* representation for numbers. Floating-point is the machine equivalent of "scientific notation" for numbers, and it is used because it can represent very large and very small numbers in a compact form. Floating-point quantities are represented as two numbers in the following relationship:

$$mantissa^{exponent}.$$

For example, a floating-point format translates large and small numbers as follows:

$$6,170,000,000 \Rightarrow 6.17 \times 10^{10}$$
$$0.000000000617 \Rightarrow 6.17 \times 10^{-10}.$$

In *full floating-point* systems, each number involved in a calculation is represented by such an exponential expression. Adding two floating-point numbers with different radix (magnitude) exponents requires that hardware causes the decimal point of the smaller number to "float" to the right until the exponent equals that of the larger expression.

Neither an n-bit fixed-point representation nor an n-bit floating-point representation is more precise than the other. An n-bit number representation, fixed or floating, can only represent 2^n different quantities. The advantage of floating-point computation is its wide dynamic range. For example, the dynamic range of a 32-bit floating-point system is 1670 dB. This is possible because the exponent can scale the mantissa from tiny to extremely large magnitudes.

To cite an example, a 16-bit system (fixed or floating) can represent 65,535 different quantities. If a fixed-point integer representation is used, this can represent numbers over the range $[0, 65535]$ or $[-32767, +32767]$, if we want to halve the positive range to allow for negative numbers, which is usually the case. By contrast, a 16-bit system with a 12-bit mantissa and a 4-bit exponent can represent values up to

$(2^{12})2^4 = 4096^{16} \sim 6.27 \times 10^{57}$.

To allow allow for equal representation of negative numbers we can use an 11-bit mantissa and allocate one bit to represent the sign; this divides the dynamic range in half. This is called a *sign-magnitude* representation. For small numbers less than 1.0, there is a vast disparity in the ranges handled by fixed-point and floating-point representations. For example, the smallest number in a 16-bit integer system is 1/65,535, while the smallest number in the 12/4 16-bit floating-point system is $1/(6.27 \times 10^{57})$.

This wide numerical range makes a floating-point system convenient for audio applications, in that the danger of arithmetic overflow is greatly reduced or eliminated. Floating-point systems have clear advantages to the user (e.g., not having to worry about numerical overflows and samples out of range). On the other hand, fixed-point (integer) systems are cheaper and easier to design and debug than their floating-point counterparts.

The term MIPS (millions of instructions per second) is often used to describe the performance of a microprocessor. Specifications of floating-point performance state how many floating-point operations (typically multiply/adds) a microprocessor performs per second. This is measured in *MFLOPS* or *GFLOPS*—millions or billions of floating-point operations per second, respectively. As we see later, the gap between the manufacturer's theoretical MIPS or MFLOP specification and the practical performance of a microprocessor is often large.

Wavetable Size

In synthesizers and samplers, the question of wavetable memory size is an important topic. In a sampler, the total wavetable size corresponds to the total duration of the sounds the sampler can store. More wavetable memory (or sample memory) means more or longer sounds can be stored. The duration of a sound played on a sampler can be extended indefinitely by means of *looping,* which cycles repeatedly through a fixed-length wavetable (see chapter 3).

Since digital oscillators read through one or more wavetables to generate sound, the fidelity of the original waveform in the wavetable largely determines the amount of noise generated by the oscillator. In general, larger wavetables, which use more samples to represent the waveform, are more accurate and pure than are small wavetables. This is because large wavetables capture the bends and curves of a waveform at a finer grain of resolution.

For example, a simple digital oscillator reading 16-bit values out of a 256-entry wavetable produces a worst-case signal-to-noise ratio of about 43 dB—poor. Increasing the table length to 1024 entries improves the accuracy to about 55 dB, which is still not high fidelity.

Dramatic improvements in signal-to-noise ratio and distortion can be achieved by using more sophisticated interpolating oscillator circuits. These circuits expand the effective wavetable size by computing intermediate values between the samples stored in the wavetable. (See chapter 3.)

Frequency Resolution and Tuning

Frequency resolution in a synthesizer means how finely frequencies can be specified over the audio range. Musically this translates into tuning accuracy for pitches and partials. Specifically, the frequency resolution of a system is the smallest difference between any two frequencies it can generate. For example, if the frequencies 440 and 441 Hz can be generated but not 440.5 Hz, then the frequency resolution is 1 Hz.

The number of different frequencies that can be generated by a synthesizer is directly related to the size of the *frequency select word* (FSW) or *phase increment accumulator*. This is a special word in a synthesizer that specifies the frequency to generate. A 10-bit FSW provides the musician with 2^{10} or 1024 frequency choices. This might seem like plenty (after all, the piano has only 88 keys), but actually it is inadequate for most musical applications. Why is more precision necessary? Because the frequencies chosen by the FSW are all equidistant. If these frequencies are spread out over the range of human hearing, say, 20 Hz to 20 KHz, (a bandwidth of 19,980 Hz) the frequency resolution of the system is

$$19,980 \text{ Hz}/1000 = 19.98 \text{ Hz}.$$

This is adequate to differentiate pitches and partials in the highest register, say, above 10 KHz. But the ear's sensitivity to frequency resolution is more acute in the middle and lower registers, so 19.98 Hz is a coarse resolution for these regions (figure 20.12). In the lowest register, 20 to 40 Hz, a 19.98 Hz interval spans nearly an entire octave!

Increasing the size of the frequency select word from 10 to 16 bits (as in some synthesis chips) is still not enough. Sixteen-bit (3.4 Hz) frequency resolution produces noticeable steps in the lower register when approximating a scale in equal temperament. Musicians want to be able to synthesize any musical scale, spectral component, or frequency change (e.g., glissando, portamento, pitch bend) accurately. Indeed, accurate frequency generation is one of the main advantages of digital synthesis over mechanical-acoustical instruments.

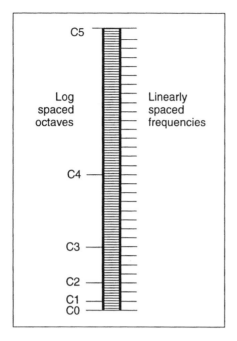

Figure 20.12 Frequency resolution scales. Linear frequency select resolution provides good resolution in the higher registers but poor resolution in the lower registers. Here a linear scale is shown on the right side. Notice that there is one step between C0 and C1 as compared with 16 steps between C4 and C5.

Microtonal compositions explore tunings other than common equal-temperament and require a high degree of frequency resolution in order to be accurately realized (Carlos 1986; Barlow 1986; Polansky 1986; Kirck 1986). This means that a synthesizer should have a resolution finer than 1 Hz throughout the audio bandwidth for accurate reproduction of musical scales and temperaments. This necessitates a FSW in the range of 18 to 24 bits (see Alles and Di Giugno 1977; Moore 1977; Snell 1977b).

Snell (1977) argues that a 21-bit FSW is the minimum phase increment adequate to generate a smooth-sounding glissando or pitch bend. Going further, a 24-bit FSW allows the specification of 2^{24} or 16,777,216 different frequencies, providing a frequency resolution of around 0.001 Hz (a thousandth of a Hz), which exceeds the frequency resolution of the human ear. This level of frequency resolution is not difficult with current technology. Inexpensive digital oscillator circuits offer 32 bits of frequency resolution. Unfortunately, some musical instrument manufacturers continue to introduce synthesizer products with limitations on tuning. At a minimum, it should be possible to reprogram the frequency of all MIDI pitches to within 1 cent (1/100th of a semitone).

Computational Demands of Digital Synthesis

So far we have talked about the basic hardware requirements of high fidelity digital sound processing. Besides meeting audio specifications, a DSP must also be fast enough to realize all the computations needed by synthesis and signal-processing algorithms. In general, synthesis and signal processing make stringent demands on a computing system. The burden of high-speed numerical computations ("number crunching") is especially intensive. At a sampling rate of 50 KHz, the DSP must be able to complete all calculations for a sample within 1/50,000th of a second, or 20 msec, per audio channel. Within this sample period the DSP is performing a multitude of tasks by means of *time-division multiplexing*. The following sections discuss the technique of time-division multiplexing and examine the various factors that go into measuring the performance of a DSP engine.

Time-division Multiplexing

Time-division multiplexing (TDM) is a fundamental concept in the operation of DSP systems. TDM is used extensively in digital synthesizers in order to realize multivoice synthesis. Within a DSP, time is divided into a series of short cycles within the space of a single sample period. On each of these short cycles, the DSP can realize one algorithm, such as an oscillator or a filter algorithm. The benefit of this is that one DSP can realize many oscillators or a mixture of oscillators and other signal-processing algorithms—all within the space of a single sample period. This stands in contrast to analog synthesizers that require one hardware circuit per oscillator or filter.

A TDM device lets the designer trade off the number of DSP functions realized against the sampling rate (and therefore, the audio bandwidth). For example, an early digital synthesizer called the 4B (Alles and DiGiugno 1977) could realize either 64 oscillators at a 16 KHz sampling rate or 32 oscillators at a 32 KHz sampling rate. Today's DSP chips are more powerful than the 4B, but the principle of TDM still applies.

DSP Performance Factors

A good way to measure the performance of a DSP system for music is to determine how many musical oscillators it can realize in real time, that is, to test its suitability for additive synthesis. (Additive synthesis is explained in

Table 20.1 Per-sample requirements of additive synthesis for different synthesis tasks using a monophonic sinusoidal oscillator with piecewise linear amplitude and frequency envelopes.

Synthesis task	Adds	Multiplies	Memory accesses
Interpolating oscillator	3	2	6
One additive synthesis instrument (24 partials)	96	48	240
Additive synthesis chamber orchestra (16 voices)	1536	768	3840
Additive synthesis full ochestra (128 voices)	12288	6144	30720

Source: Moore and Loy (1982).

chapter 4.) This is not exactly the same as determining the number of sine waves that a system can generate. A musical oscillator must be able to look up any waveform (not just a preset sine table), and it must have separate envelopes for frequency and amplitude control (Strawn 1988).

As the estimates in table 20.1 show, if we realize every additive voice by means of an instrument with 24 sine waves (one for each of 24 partials), we consume computational resources quickly. Keep in mind that table 20.1 indicates the amount of computation required to compute a single sample. The cost of the "full orchestra" is especially daunting. If we assume a sampling rate of 48 KHz and stereo sound, we need a system capable of multiplying $6144 \times 48000 \times 2$ channels, or over 498 million multiplications and almost 3 billion memory accesses—all for one second of sound.

Data Memory and Program Memory

Multiplication speed is an important factor in DSP architecture, but it is only one of the criteria that determine a DSP's power in musical performance. The amount of memory can also be a limiting factor. DSPs need memory for two reasons: (1) to store signals, either sampled or synthesized, and (2) to store DSP programs. Most DSPs have at least two separate types of memories: a *data memory* devoted to signal data such as audio waveforms, envelopes, filter parameters, etc., and a *program memory* devoted to programs. When either memory is too small for a given task, the DSP has to make references to external memories, which dramatically slows down the DSP's processing speed.

I/O Bandwidth

Another important factor in the performance of a DSP is its *input/output (I/O) bandwidth*—the rate at which sample data and instructions are shuttled in and out of the DSP. I/O bandwidth has two aspects that are related to the two types of information stored in DSP memories: (1) waveforms and parameters (data), and (2) program instructions. First, a DSP must be capable of high-speed data I/O for sample processing. If a DSP is mixing eight channels of digital audio at a 48 KHz sampling rate, for example, it must be capable of transferring a minimum of $8 \times 48,000$ samples or 768,000 bytes per second (6 Mbits/second) through its sample data I/O channels.

The second aspect of internal communication speed is the rate at which one can update the DSP's program memory from the host (i.e., the user's) computer. If the DSP is being controlled from an automated mixing program, the mixing program is sending thousands of new values to the DSP every second. If the mixing engineer selects a new routing path or signal treatment by pressing a button, it should take effect instantly. Ideally it should be possible to load a new program into the DSP's program memory in the space of one sample period. (See the section on the parameter update problem later.)

Architecture of Digital Signal Processors

It is important to never lose sight of the fact that algorithms, no matter how they are presented, always include an inherent bias or even explicit reference to a particular class of architectures. (John Allen 1985)

Now that we have discussed the basic requirements that DSP systems must meet, we can examine their internal architecture. By architecture we refer to the organization of the major circuit blocks and the set of instructions that the circuits execute.

Fixed- versus Variable-function DSP Architectures

We can divide musical DSP architectures into two basic categories: *fixed-function* and *variable-function*. Fixed-function (or *application-specific*) DSPs are made up of components dedicated to specific functions such as oscillators, filters, and envelope generators (figure 20.13). In this sense, fixed-function systems are similar to the analog synthesizers of the 1960s and 1970s (Moore 1985a; Moorer 1977; Jansen 1991), but with the important caveat that their modules cannot be arbitrarily repatched.

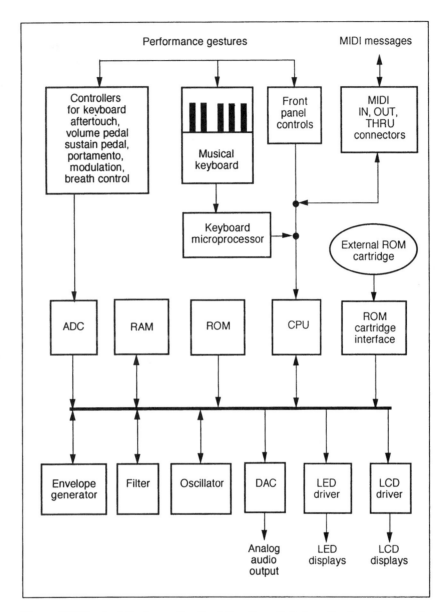

Figure 20.13 Architecture of a fixed-function digital synthesizer. Each unit performs a preset function. The interconnection between the units is set at the factory by the manufacturer.

Many commercial audio products are based on the fixed-function concept. For example, a frequency modulation synthesizer can be manufactured inexpensively with a fixed-function IC designed for FM. Such a design also simplifies the software. A fixed-function organization is best used in closed, well-understood applications where there is no need to extend the functionality of the system in the future.

By contrast, a variable-function DSP contains a more flexible collection of *functional units*. The functional units consist of multiple memories and primitive processors. Each primitive processor performs a specific computation such as compute an address, multiply/add, perform a table lookup, count clock ticks, handle I/O, etc. The functional units intercommunicate via multiple internal buses. Table 20.2 shows a list of typical functional units and describes their use.

By interconnecting the functional units we can realize a great variety of algorithms, in contrast to fixed-function designs. Interconnecting the functional units in software is often called *patching* the DSP, by analogy to the patch cords connecting the modules of analog synthesizers. The sequence of instructions written by a programmer selects which functional units to use in a computation and the order in which they are used. Such a program interconnects the functional units and routes data through the DSP according to this interconnection. Thus a single variable-function DSP can play many roles, including an oscillator, delay, filter, envelope generator, pitch detector, spectrum analyzer, and reverberator.

Variable-function DSPs are sometimes called "general-purpose" DSPs in the literature, but this term is perhaps idealistic and in any case leads to confusion with general-purpose microprocessors, described in the next section.

As compared to fixed-function DSPs, variable-function DSPs offer more programmability, and hence more musical flexibility. Variable-function DSPs are now common in audio signal processing. Hence, in the rest of this chapter, when we refer to a DSP, we mean a variable-function DSP.

Differences between General-purpose Microprocessors and DSPs

As we saw in figure 20.6, a computer music system is managed by a host computer. The host is the computer that musicians interact with (personal computer or workstation), and it typically contains a *general-purpose microprocessor* (GPM). A GPM usually manipulates stored data, while a DSP is optimized to process external signals or to generate signals in a real-time application. The specific architectural features that differentiate a DSP from a GPM include the following:

Table 20.2   Functional units and explanations of their operation

Program Control Unit (PCU)

The PCU performs instruction fetch, instruction decoding, and handles external interrupt signals. When it receives an interrupt signal, it determines the priority of the interrupt, and, if necessary, *traps* (i.e., passes control to) an interrupt service routine that preempts regular program execution. When the interrupt service routine is completed, the PCU resumes regular program execution.

Arithmetic Logic Unit (ALU)

ALUs perform logical and arithmetic operations (such as add, subtract, complement), typically on integer words. The PCU tells the ALU which operation to perform. The ALU's control output indicates errors and other conditions as they occur (e.g., whether the result is zero, whether there was an arithmetic overflow).

Address Generation Unit (AGU)

An AGU is a kind of ALU for addressing. DSP instructions typically support a variety of addressing modes, and the AGU is called upon to load address registers and generate the proper pointers for *index addressing* (to access wavetable and envelope array elements), *modulo addresses* (for oscillator wavetable lookup and delay lines), and *bit-reversal addressing* used in the computation of the fast Fourier transform (see appendix A)

Floating-point Unit

In a microprocessor that handles floating-point data, this is the "engine" of digital signal processing. It performs arithmetic operations on floating-point numbers at high speed. The FPU is usually a separate unit from the ALU in order to allow operation in the parallel with the ALU.

Registers

Fast memory cells used as "scratchpads" for intermediate calculations; usually built into the ALU, AGU, and FPU.

Random-access Memory (RAM)

Memory cells that store binary information that can be written into or read from. Each datum resides at a particular location or address in memory. A read operation asks: "What is the value stored at memory address *X*?" A write operation inscribes a value at the specified address. RAMs differ in their size and speed of writing or reading (*cycle time*). Most RAMs allow one operation at a time—either a read or a write. A *dual-ported RAM* allows two operations at once. RAMs can be used as high-speed "scratchpad" memories or for bulk storage of waveforms (oscillator wavetables, sample memories, delay lines, etc.). Sometimes memories are dedicated to specific functions. For example, a *program memory* stores instructions only, and a *data memory* stores data only. Such a separation allows both memories to be accessed in parallel, thus increasing speed.

Read-only Memory (ROM and EPROM)

Memory units that store data but that cannot be written into by the user. Fixed programs and data can be "burned" into the chip at the factory through a relatively

Table 20.2 (cont.)

expensive process that pays off if the chip is mass-produced. Electrically programmable read-only memories (EPROMs) offer more flexibility since they can be erased and rewritten to using a high-voltage programming device attached to a host computer.

Shifters and Rotators

Moves a binary word one or more places to the right or left. This category includes both parallel and serial devices. A shifter (or *barrel shifter*) shifts a word to the left or right by some number of bits. Rotators shift the word, but the bits that are shifted off one end of the word are inserted back into the other end of the word. Shifters are necessary in floating-point multiplications, fractional addressing, and other applications where digital words are "packed" and "unpacked" in pieces at a time. For example, if a sample is a 16-bit quantity and the DSP has a 32-bit word length, the shifter can shift two samples to their appropriate place in the word, allowing two samples to be stored in one word. Usually built into the ALU, AGU, or FPU.

Multiplexers and Demultiplexers

A multiplexer selects one of its many inputs to send to its output. A demultiplexer distributes a single input to many outputs. These are found in bus controllers and I/O processors.

Counters

Increments a digital value with each clock tick or trigger it receives from another source. When a stored value called the *counter limit* is reached, it emits a signal. Counters are often used as timers in real-time applications, by setting the counter limit to a number of clock ticks.

Comparators

Compares two values. The comparator produces a digital signal that is true when the input value matches a stored value, and false otherwise. Comparators are used in detecting the endpoint of ramps in oscillator phasor tables and envelopes, and in other signal-processing applications. Usually found in ALUs and counters.

DACs and ADCs

A DAC transforms digital number streams into analog voltages. When these voltages are filtered (made smooth) and amplified, they can be sent to speakers to produce sound. ADCs perform the opposite task. They take a smoothly varying analog voltage (such as from a microphone) and convert it into a digital bit stream so that this data can be manipulated by the DSP or host computer.

1. DSPs are optimized for fast multiply/accumulate execution speed (many times faster than typical GPMs); also, the DSP specializes in numerical processing. It has no instructions for character or string processing, for example, but it has special instructions that are useful in DSP operations.

2. The DSP has multiple, special-purpose memories (as opposed to a single general-purpose memory) that can be accessed concurrently: program memories, data memories, sine table read-only memories, high-speed cache memories, memories that can transfer many bits in parallel.

3. The DSP has multiple I/O ports and more than one *direct-memory access* (DMA) *controller;* a DMA controller can transfer blocks of data from the host to the DSP without interrupting ongoing computations.

4. The DSP has multiple functional units that operate in parallel instead of a single *central processing unit* (typical of a GPM).

5. The DSP has multiple high-speed busses that can operate in parallel for shuttling instructions and data to and from functional units and external devices.

6. The DSP has provisions for high-speed interconnection with other DSPs of the same type in a symmetric multiprocessing configuration.

7. A DSP can handle interrupts (external events) very quickly, by assuming that they are parameter updates coming from an input port; that is, unlike a GPM, a DSP may not take the time to save the entire state of the processor before it fields the interrupt.

Figure 20.14 compares a GPM architecture with a DSP architecture. The GPM (figure 20.14a) is a virtual memory monoprocessor with a single random-access memory. The DSP (figure 20.14b) has multiple memories, multiple buses, and a synchronous interface to other DSPs for multiprocessor operation.

RISC Microprocessors for DSP

GPMs based on fast RISC technology compete in the marketplace with DSP chips. RISC refers either to *reduced instruction set computer* or *reduced instruction cycle computer*. RISC processors entered the market in the early 1980s, as an alternative to the *complex instruction set computers* (CISC) then available. In theory, RISC microprocessors execute a small set of simple instructions of the form: load datum into register, perform simple operation, store datum in memory.

Microprocessor operations are driven by a *system clock* running in the MHz range. For a given microprocessor architecture, the faster the system

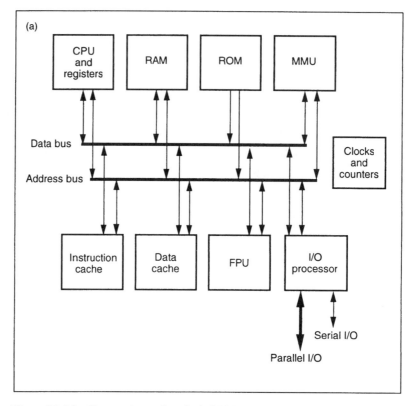

Figure 20.14 Comparison of typical GPM and DSP architectures. These diagrams are simplified and do not show control lines and other details. (*a*) GPM. The CPU is the central processing unit—the main computational engine of the GPM. The registers are a form of high-speed local memory, used for intermediate calculations by the CPU. RAM and ROM are memories; the MMU is a memory management unit that handles references to virtual memory. The data and instruction caches are high-speed memories that contain "prefetched" data and instructions that are likely to be accessed in the future. The FPU is a floating-point processor, and the I/O processor handles communication with external devices. The clock and its internal counters are connected to all units via control lines that are not shown. (*b*) DSP. Notice the multiple memory and multiple bus structure. The functional units can operate in parallel. This is a generalized interconnection diagram; in practice most DSPs link specific functional units to specific buses. The *program control unit* (PCU) performs instruction fetch and decode and intercepts interrupts from the outside world. The ALU/AGU is an *arithmetic logic unit* and *address generation unit* that executes integer and logical instructions and calculates addresses. The sine table ROM is provided for oscillator table lookup. The X RAM and Y RAM are memories that operate concurrently. The I/O interface connects the DSP to a host computer, peripherals, and other DSPs. As in the GPM, the clock and counters connect to the other functional units via dedicated control lines not shown.

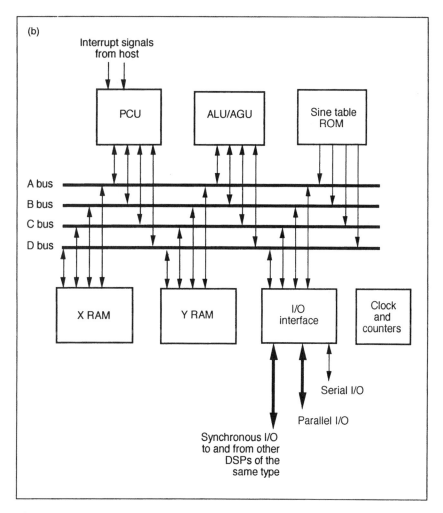

Figure 20.14 (cont.)

clock, the faster the instruction execution. (It is difficult to compare the performance of two microprocessors with different architectures solely on the basis of their respective clock speeds, however.) The key to RISC performance is that they execute a simple instruction on nearly every tick of the system clock, in contrast to CISCs that often take several ticks to finish executing a complex instruction.

Other important features of RISC architectures are a large number of high-speed registers and large on-chip or closely coupled *cache memories*. A *data cache* contains all the data that are near the address of the most recently accessed data in memory, on the theory that it is likely that the next instruction will try to access these data, rather than data somewhere else in memory. An *instruction cache* fetches in a large number of instructions at a time, so that the microprocessor does not have to perform an external memory access on every instruction cycle.

RISC GPMs may have advantages such as good compilers and development environments, cache memories, sophisticated memory management units, and support for *fractional addressing* (described in the next section). A desire for these advantages led to the adoption of a RISC architecture in the IRCAM Musical Workstation board (Lindemann et al. 1991).

Balanced against the advantages of RISC architectures are a number of optimizations built into DSP chips such as speed in (1) data movement between processors, (2) input/output, (3) context-switching from one task to another, and (4) interrupt response—all important factors in real-time musical performance (Agnello 1991). Many other practical concerns enter into comparisons between architectures, so it would be fruitless to make a pronouncement here as to which approach is "best" in all circumstances.

Fractional Addressing

As mentioned, hardware support for fractional addressing is desirable in signal-processing applications, particularly in algorithms based on wavetable lookup such as oscillators and delay lines. (See chapter 1 for an explanation of wavetable lookup.) A microprocessor with fractional addressing can keep an accurate value for the phase index used in table-lookup algorithms since it maintains both an integer part and a fractional part of the wavetable address. If the precise location of the next sample is supposed to be address 510.7, for example, a system without fractional addressing will simply round this to 510, throwing away the fractional part. For a single sample, such a distortion may not be disastrous, but for computing the address of the next sample the fractional part is still needed. That is, keeping the fractional part is more accurate than a purely integer addressing scheme since the integer part includes the accumulation from the fractional part. An interpolating oscillator algorithm (see chapter 3) can use the fractional part to compute where to interpolate between two integer wavetable-lookup points.

Operation of a DSP

A DSP is driven by a program that is loaded into its *program memory* (or *instruction memory*) by a host computer. Once the program is loaded, the host computer gives the DSP the signal to start. The DSP repeatedly executes the program. The execution of the entire program results in the computation of one sample of sound (figure 20.15). Depending on the ap-

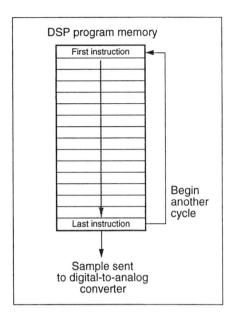

Figure 20.15 The DSP cycles continuously through a program in its program memory. Each iteration of the program produces a sample.

plication, the sample can either be sent to a DAC to make sound, or to a storage device.

At the appropriate time, the host computer stops the sample computation, either by sending a signal to halt, or by the loading of a new signal-processing program into the DSP's instruction memory. Thus interaction between the host computer and the DSP is usually in the form of a master-slave relationship. The host computer loads the DSP's program memory, starts it computing, periodically feeds it updated values, and halts it.

Example of DSP Architecture

A specific example of DSP architecture is the Digital Music Systems DMX-1000 (abbreviated to DMX)—a commercially available DSP (Wallraff 1979a) sold in the 1980s. The technology used to implement the DMX-1000 is obsolete (a large circuit board populated with dozens of transistor-transistor logic chips sapping over 300 watts of power). However, the DMX possesses a simple design that makes it attractive for the purpose of teaching DSP architecture.

Figure 20.16 shows the internal organization of the DMX. Like virtually all DSPs, the DMX is controlled by a host computer. The host loads a synthesis program into the DMX program memory, along with data (waveforms, variables, synthesis parameters) into the data memory. Up to 256

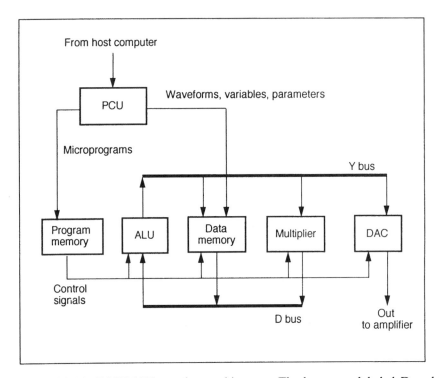

Figure 20.16 DMX-1000 two-bus architecture. The buses are labeled D and Y. The host transfers programs and data to the *program control unit* (PCU), which sends data to the data memory and instructions to the program memory. The ALU and multiplier are the main computation engines; they write their results either to the data memory, internal registers (not shown), or the DAC.

32-bit microcode instruction words can be stored in the DMX program memory. This is a very small program memory. In practice, 256 DMX instructions are just enough to implement about four moderately complex instruments, using oscillators, filters, and associated envelopes. By comparison, today's single-chip DSPs can access much larger internal and external program memories.

Once the microprogram is loaded, the DMX runs through a series of sample cycles. Each instruction in the program memory is executed in sequence; the penultimate instruction sends the sample value to the DAC over the DMX's Y bus. When a HALT instruction is encountered, the sample cycle is over.

The DMX then gives the host computer a chance to update the program memory or data memory. During this interval, the host might want to change a parameter used in the sample computation, for example, the amplitude of the signal. The sequence is repeated as many times as needed to produce a desired number of samples.

The Question of Branching

Conditional branching instructions (i.e., **if-then-goto-else** or **if-then-jump-else** statements) are basic to every general-purpose microprocessor. In DSPs that are optimized for repetitive instruction loops, the question of how to implement branching has been a major issue. In some early DSPs, no conditional branching instructions were allowed. This is because a program without branches always takes the same amount of time to run, ensuring that the stream of audio samples are evenly spaced in time. Program branches to inequal-sized routines can interrupt the synchrony of the sample computation cycle, causing delays that affect the sample stream and other real-time processes.

From a programming standpoint, however, a lack of branching is a severe disadvantage in implementing many signal-processing algorithms. Systems such as the Lucasfilm Audio Signal Processor (also called the ASP or SoundDroid) provided *partial branching* by allowing conditional execution of instructions (Moorer 1982). Conditional instructions check the status of a bit in a *condition code register* to determine whether or not to perform an operation, for example, "If the result of the previous operation was positive, clear register 0." This does not affect the flow of control. Many DSP chips use this method.

Another issue in branching is how to handle ongoing computations in pipelined functional units. (Pipelining is discussed in the next section.) DSPs offer a variety of strategies for handling this issue, from flushing the pipeline (discontinuing the operations in progress), to delaying the branch until the pipeline is empty.

To allow time for program jumps, a classic technique is providing *buffer memories* before the DACs and after the ADCs. Buffer memories queue up samples for subsequent conversion; this allows the DSP to take a break from processing a sample stream and gives it time to execute different-length routines. The principle of buffering was demonstrated in the earliest computer sound synthesis system (David, Mathews, and McDonald 1959). However, when the buffer size is large, this can lead to perceivable delays between gestural inputs (e.g., moving a potentiometer or flicking a switch) and the resulting sound.

Parallelism and Pipelining within a Single DSP

High speed can be achieved within a single DSP through the use of internal *parallelism* and *pipelining*. Parallelism usually refers to the simultaneous operation of several functional units, for example, an add, a multiply, and several table lookups at the same time.

Pipelining is concurrent operation within a single functional unit. A multiplication, for example, may require several steps that take several instruction cycles. In a nonpipelined machine, the hardware for the early steps is idle while a later step computes the end result. In a pipelined machine, all stages of the hardware are kept as busy as possible at all times by working on several multiplications at once. This increases the *throughput* (the amount of data processed per unit of time) of the machine.

Figure 20.17 compares a nonpipelined with a pipelined multiplier. The nonpipelined multiplier (figure 20.17a) wastes three clock cycles in computing a single result. In a pipelined multiplier (figure 20.17b), the multiplication of A and B starts on clock cycle 1, followed by the multiplication of C and D on cycle 2, the multiplication of E and F on cycle 3, and the multiplication of G and H on clock cycle 4. The result of A and B is available on cycle 4. The total time through the multiplier may be 80 ns, but the peak throughput rate is a multiplication every 20 ns (50 million multiplies per second).

Peak rates can only be achieved by keeping the pipeline full. Here is the well-known pitfall of pipelined architectures, since various factors may intervene to prevent a constantly full pipeline. Many signal-processing algorithms, for example, require several memory accesses (or wavetable lookups) before a multiply can take place, so they are difficult to adapt to a pipelined machine. Real-time interrupts at regular intervals also obviate the advantages of pipelining. When an interrupt occurs, the pipeline must be flushed, and all computations in an intermediate state of calculation must be restarted.

The Parameter Update Problem

Consider a DSP that is performing the functions of an automated audio mixing console. Attached to the DSP is a console with hundreds of buttons, knobs, and sliders. When a control is changed, either from memory or by a new gesture of the sound engineer, this value must be conveyed to the DSP. This is a *parameter update*. One problem that DSP system designers face is figuring out how to update the DSP in a manner that is precisely synchronized in time—the *parameter update problem*. For example, filter coefficients and delay lines need to be updated at a particular sample period in order to achieve the proper effect. In a synthesizer, a new note needs pitch, amplitude, and other parameters depending on the synthesis algorithm selected. These parameters may include the initial values of several envelopes—for pitch, amplitude, modulation, etc. As the note plays we need to convey the rest of the envelope data at regular intervals. But what if the

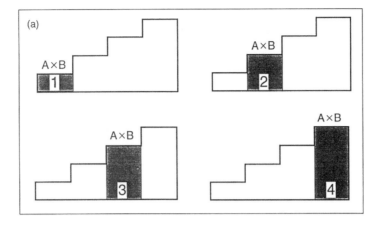

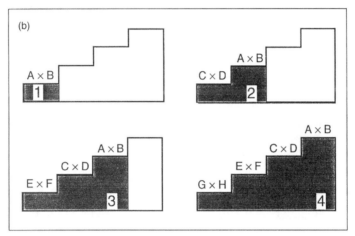

Figure 20.17 Comparison of nonpipelined versus pipelined multipliers. (*a*) In a nonpipelined system, a four-cycle operation performs a single multiply. (*b*) In a pipelined system, several parts of a computation can go on simultaneously, increasing the throughput of the system.

musician twists a filter knob on the front panel while the note plays, or depresses the volume pedal? These data must also be transmitted to the synthesizer immediately.

The creative nature of musical performance makes it difficult to predict the data rates that will be required to control a DSP. We cannot look only at the average flow of data between the host and the DSP. In music, parameter changes are not spread out in a random, uniform time pattern. Rather, there are moments of articulation in which many changes occur simultaneously, such as the beginning of a note, a chord, a tutti crescendo, or a change in instrumentation. This makes it necessary to consider the *burst rate* of the system—the frequency of events that occur all at once (Kahrs

1981; Kaplan 1981; Moorer 1981a, 1982). The job of the system designer is to figure out how to handle these bursts of parameter data.

Especially taxing on the host computer is the generation of envelopes for frequencies, amplitudes, modulations, and other parameters. A variety of solutions to the parameter update problem have been devised. This section discusses two such methods.

Method 1: Provide an Update Period

The most basic update mechanism is to provide a brief *update period* at the beginning of the DSP's sample computation cycle. This allows new information to be incorporated into the next sample's calculation. The updates can take the form of new synthesis commands, changes to existing parameter values, or new waveforms to be loaded in the DSP's data memory. The host computer accomplishes the updates by a limited number of write operations to the DSP's data memory, where synthesis and processing parameters are stored.

A problem with this approach is that the duration of the update period is fixed. Only a certain number of updates can take effect on any one cycle. This means that burst-rate parameter updates must be spread over a number of samples. This works if the gradual updating process is not stretched out over so many samples that it becomes audible. If the number of update commands exceeds the rate at which the DSP can accept them, a backlog of update commands can accumulate, leading to sluggish and erratic musical response.

The Systems Concepts digital synthesizer (Samson 1980, 1985) introduced the notion of an *update queue,* a *time-ordered* or *time-stamped* list of updates supported by special hardware. This concept was incorporated into other DSPs, notably the Lucasfilm ASP/SoundDroid developed in the early 1980s (Moorer 1982, 1985). During the update period, updates at the beginning of the queue are read from the queue and executed at machine speed (one per cycle) until a time-stamped update is encountered (i.e., one with a tag indicating that it is to be performed at a specific time in the near future). At this point the update period ends. In the ASP/SoundDroid, there was adequate time to process thousands of updates or even reconfigure the entire system.

Method 2: Provide a DSP Controller

Another common solution to the real-time update dilemma is a tightly linked *DSP controller* between the host and the DSP (figure 20.18). The

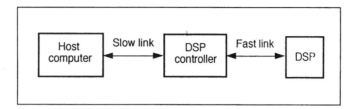

Figure 20.18 One solution to the parameter update problem is a DSP controller between a host computer and a DSP.

controller reduces the need for continual, interrupt-driven communication between the host and the DSP. In particular, the host is relieved of such demanding tasks as fielding interrupts every time the DSP requests a new parameter value (Buxton et al. 1978b; Moorer 1982; Asta et al. 1980). A DSP controller is also used when real-time input devices such as music keyboards, sliders, and switches are attached to the DSP system. The controller mixes the commands from diverse sources into a *command stream* (Kahrs 1981) that is fed to the DSP. The command stream is a mixture of time-stamped updates, for example,

```
AT TIME 0, LOAD AND INITIALIZE INST 1
AT TIME 2.4 SEC, INST 1: PLAY NOTE C(4) FOR 1 SEC
AT TIME 3.4 SEC, DEALLOCATE INST 1
```

along with immediate commands coming from keyboards, footpedals, and sliders, such as

```
INCREASE AMPLITUDE OF CHANNEL 1 BY 20 UNITS
```

The absence of a time stamp indicates that it is to be performed immediately. An alternative arrangement is to keep the immediate commands in a separate list. In this case, the DSP controller always disposes of the immediate command list before handling the time-stamped list. Another approach is to implement a linked list regime in hardware, which inserts immediate commands at the head of the list. (See chapter 2 for a discussion of priority queues and linked lists.)

MIDI Black Boxes

In studios designed around the Musical Instrument Digital Interface (MIDI), many of the functions of the DSP controller have been given over to "black boxes"—smart interfaces and MIDI message processors that stand between the host computer and a studio full of MIDI and

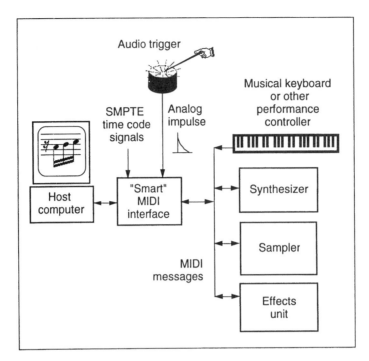

Figure 20.19 MIDI black box. In many studios, the main "real-time parameter processor" is one or more smart MIDI interfaces that handle analog trigger signals and SMPTE timecode as well as processing MIDI message data. These boxes handle message routing, merging of several MIDI streams, message "filtering," and rescaling of messages.

SMPTE devices (figure 20.19). (See chapter 21 for more on MIDI and SMPTE.) Such a device receives messages coming from the host computer and from MIDI and SMPTE devices. As MIDI messages pass through the device it can reroute them or merge them with other message streams, or rescale or filter messages before passing them on. Inside a black box is a microprocessor that interprets the MIDI messages, along with a sizable buffer memory that allows message bursts to be sent to it without overwhelming it. The incoming commands pile up in the black box's memory until the microprocessor is ready to deal with them. Since the rate of incoming commands is limited by the speed of the MIDI line, the effects of a burst of incoming commands can be worked out by the designer of the black box beforehand.

Discussion of the Parameter Update Problem

A generalized solution to the parameter update problem for all DSPs is difficult to imagine. A particular solution depends on the machine architecture, the I/O interfaces, the type of input devices, and the mix of available editing modes. It is always helpful to buffer all I/O. With a buffer memory after the ADCs and before the DACs the DSP has more time for updates before it must generate or process another sample. But as mentioned previously, large buffers can lead to audible delays between real-time gestures and the resulting sound.

All hardware systems have limitations, such as the number of voices they can generate, and the speed at which they can be updated with new information. Every commercial DSP is constrained to meet certain costs, so designers must figure out ways to avoid overwhelming the DSP with new information. One way is to shield the DSP from the user by providing *presets*—settings associated with buttons and knobs that are well within the limits of the DSP device. Even with presets, incoming data sometimes have to be thrown away to avoid overwhelming the system. Kaplan (1981) and Moorer (1981a) discuss several strategies for dealing with this problem.

Programming and Microprogramming a DSP

Now that we have examined the architectural considerations of a DSP, let us look at the software that drives it. DSP software spans the gamut from interactive applications that generate DSP code automatically (Hebel 1989), to object-oriented visual programming environments (Scaletti and Hebel 1991), to programming languages enriched by DSP functions, to low-level microprogram development tools.

A DSP can also run a *real-time operating system* (OS) (Viara 1991). Without an OS, the DSP runs one program at a time. An OS running on the DSP adds the possibility of multitasking (running more than one program at a time), with intertask communications and synchronization. It also provides a means to implement a discipline of event-driven, priority based scheduling of tasks.

Microprograms

At the lowest level DSPs are driven by *microprograms* (the generic term is *microcode*). Microprograms are instructions that route data by controlling the internal switching within a digital circuit. In order to understand microcode and microprogramming, it is necessary to have a basic idea of the operation of the machine at the hardware level. Thus we provide a simple example. In order to execute a simple addition instruction (add two integers) inside a DSP, several operations must take place:

1. The operands are fetched from the data memory over a bus into the arithmetic-logic unit (ALU).

2. The ALU is told to perform an addition.

3. The result is sent out on a data bus and stored back in a register or in data memory; simultaneously, the ALU sets *status bits* that indicate whether or not an error occurred.

In some DSPs, each instruction is implemented as a separate hardware circuit designed to send appropriate control signals to the different parts of the processor in order to execute the instruction. This is called a *hardwired* system.

A microprogrammed DSP is more flexible than a completely hardwired one. In a microprogrammed system, the control information for each instruction is stored in a *microprogram memory* (also called a *microstore, control memory,* or *program memory*) that holds *microinstructions*. To execute an instruction, a microprogrammed machine decodes the instruction to be executed and fetches the appropriate microprogram from the microstore. The microprogram for that instruction sends the control signals to the various parts of the processor.

Microprogramming changes the logical interconnection between the functional units on the bus, altering their sources and destinations. The physical interconnection remains constant, but the addresses to which a functional unit sends data and the address from which it receives data are changed. For example, a multiplier might take its two arguments from two of several sources: locations in a wavetable memory, from the output of an arithmetic-logic-unit (ALU), or from an ADC.

The microprogram may also determine the nature of the operation to be performed. For example, the microprogram control inputs of an arithmetic-logic-unit tell it whether to add, subtract, or perform other logic operations.

Horizontal Microcoding

In a *horizontally microcoded* system (as most microcoded systems are) the instruction word is divided into several *fields*. Each field controls an aspect of the processing. Figure 20.20 shows the horizontal microinstruction layout for the Digital Music Systems DMX-1000 described earlier. Each field in the word tells the DMX-1000 to perform an operation. For example, in one instruction, the machine can test whether the current microinstruction should be executed, access two registers, perform an operation in the arithmetic-logic-unit (ALU), load five pipeline registers from an internal

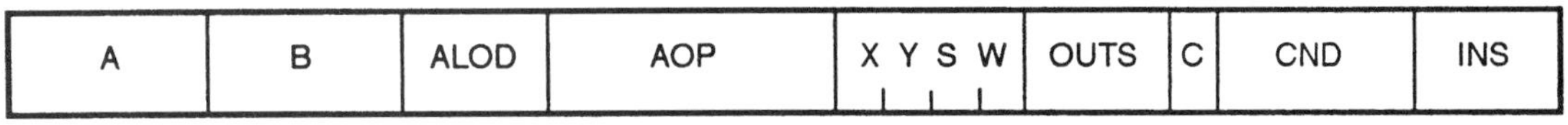

A	B	ALOD	AOP	X Y S W	OUTS	C	CND	INS

Figure 20.20 Fields of a DMX-1000 microcode word. The A and B fields select the two source registers that the ALU uses as operands for the instruction. The ALOD field tells the ALU what to do internally with the result of the operation. For example, ALOD might indicate the register into which the result should should be stored. AOP indicates the type of operation (add, subtract, increment, move, clear, etc.). X, Y, S, and W select memory and multiplier input registers. Putting a 1 in any of these fields causes the corresponding register to be loaded. OUTS serves a function similar to the X, Y, S, and W fields. C is the carry flag of the ALU. CND is a conditional field, specifying conditions under which the microinstruction is to be executed. INS selects one of the source registers onto the ALU input bus of the DMX. (Note: The names of several fields shown here are slightly different from those in the DMX-1000 manual.)

bus (one of these registers is connected to a DAC), and send an operand to another internal bus.

Horizontal microprograms are inherently difficult to write, since each microinstruction controls a number of operations in parallel (Abbott 1985). The programmer has to break up an algorithm into several concurrent streams of computation and then synchronize these streams at appropriate times.

Advantages and Disadvantages of Microprogramming

For the system designer, a main advantage of microprogramming over hardwired circuits is flexibility. The development of complex microprograms is usually faster than the development of similarly complex hardware. This is because algorithms can be tested without long hardware fabrication delays, and bugs can be corrected simply by adding or subtracting code to the existing microprograms. The flexibility of microcode allows special instructions to be added after the basic design of the system is complete. Furthermore, microprograms can be stored in RAMs or various forms of inexpensive ROM.

Another advantage of microprograms versus hardwired circuits is that in a hardwired circuit the complexity of the algorithm to be implemented is limited by the technology used to create the chip. A microprogrammed system, in contrast, lets one increase the algorithm complexity by simply adding more instructions (and increasing the size of the microstore, if necessary).

For the user of a microprogrammed DSP system, the main benefit is the performance of microcoded algorithms over the same algorithms implemented on a general-purpose computer. Horizontal microcode is intrinsically parallel and so offers several times the performance of the same algorithm coded on a serial computer.

Nonetheless, not every digital processor uses microprogramming. Hardwired logic can be much faster than a given microprogrammed implementation of the same instruction set. The hardwired implementation of an algorithm on a chip, for example, will nearly always be faster than a partially hardwired and partially microcoded version of the same logical system.

VLSI and DSP

VLSI (*very-large-scale integration*) circuits combine hundreds of thousands of transistors into a tiny package (Mead and Conway 1980). Using VLSI technology, one chip can perform functions that formerly required many circuit boards full of chips. Since the mid-1980s, it has been possible to compress all the major functions needed for stereo audio DSP into a single integrated circuit.

Besides variable-function DSP chips, demand for digital audio products has prompted manufacturers to apply VLSI technology to specialized audio applications. Audio recorders, video cameras, and CD players use PCM (pulse-code modulation) encoders, decoders, and error-correction chips, filter chips, and high-quality, low-cost DACs and ADCs in monolithic form (Doi 1984; Hirota et al. 1983; van de Plassche and Dijkmans 1984). Many synthesizers and samplers employ proprietary chips for synthesis and signal processing. To cite an example, Yamaha manufactures chips for frequency modulation synthesis (see chapter 6). These chips are used in Yamaha synthesizers and have also been licensed to other manufacturers for use in their products.

Benefits of VLSI

The benefits of a VLSI implementation are as follows:

- Compactness—the DSP can be embedded within a small musical instrument

- Low power—compared to a large circuit board, a chip consumes much less power and can sometimes be powered by batteries

- Low cost—since much of the cost of a circuit is tied to packaging, such factors as cabling, circuit board space, wirewrapping, sockets, connectors, and cabinets are greatly reduced in a VLSI implementation

- High speed—many chips operate faster than their board-level predecessors, partly because the distance between the components is dramatically diminished

The next two sections discuss the benefits of compactness and low power consumption in more detail.

The Trend to Miniaturization: Background

A continuing trend is the compression of functions that formerly occupied an entire circuit board into a single chip (Kahrs 1981). The first "high-density" semiconductor memory was the 1 Kbit dynamic random-access memory introduced by Honeywell and Intel in 1970 (Asai 1986). This made it possible to build digital audio delay lines for the first time. Still, the first digital audio delay units cost thousands of dollars due to the high cost of memory.

Multiplication is central to DSP, yet until the late 1970s there was no standard multiplication circuitry, meaning that for each DSP device it was necessary to design a custom multiplier circuit constructed out of 50 or more chips (Snell 1977a). This made applications such as spectrum analysis using fast Fourier transform processors very expensive (see chapter 13). Prototype digital synthesizers were physically large and consumed a great deal of electrical power. For example, the Bell Laboratories "Portable Digital Synthesizer" installed at the Oberlin Conservatory was fabricated out of some 1400 separate integrated circuits, weighed over 300 pounds (136 kg), and consumed several hundred watts of power (Alles 1977a).

The introduction of 16-bit fixed-point multiplication on a single chip, in the form of parts like the TRW MPY 16 (1977), had a major impact on the design of DSPs. By the late 1970s the state-of-the-art in digital music hardware was the Alles oscillator card (Alles 1980). This 32-oscillator card served as the engine of the Crumar Synergy synthesizer (Kaplan 1981) used by composer Wendy Carlos for her virtuoso electronic realization *Digital Moonscapes* (figure 20.21). The Alles card employed 110 separate chips on a large circuit board and needed a cooling fan to dissipate the heat it generated.

One of the most powerful synthesizers of the 1980s, the 4X (Asta et al. 1980; Boulez and Gerszo 1988), filled eight rack-mounted circuit boards with hundreds of chips (figure 20.22). The 4X was made available to only

Figure 20.21   Crumar Synergy synthesizer from around 1982. Sitting on top is a Kaypro II computer used to program the instrument.

a few composers, since it was controlled by custom software written for each piece that used it. It also required a small battalion of engineers to program, operate, and maintain it.

Single-chip DSPs were introduced in 1980 by AT&T and NEC, but they had severe limitations and so were not useful for music. The Texas Instruments TMS32010 chip, introduced in 1981, was probably the first DSP to be built into audio applications. But the real breakthrough for digital audio came five years later in the form of the Motorola DSP56001, which provided relatively high-quality (24-bit fixed-point) audio processing for low cost (Motorola 1986). The chip was incorporated into dozens of digital audio products. More recent single-chip DSPs offer higher speed, 32-bit or 64-bit floating-point operation, and larger memories than their ancestors.

For many years the power of microprocessors has advanced by over 40 percent per year, though this progress is sometimes blurred by shifting trends in microprocessor architecture (Smith 1991a). We can expect this trend to continue for some time, along with a corresponding decline in the cost of memory. Even as the physical limits of electronic semiconductor technology are broached (e.g., circuit paths smaller than 0.2 microns), it is likely that the long-term acceleration in computing power will continue.

Low Power Consumption: Background

In general, the tendency of integrated circuits is toward lower power consumption. Power consumption of ICs becomes a practical factor when the heat generated by the circuits requires special cooling, such as noisy fans.

Early DSP systems consumed a great deal of electrical power. For example, a single 1 Kbit memory chip fabricated from emitter-coupled logic

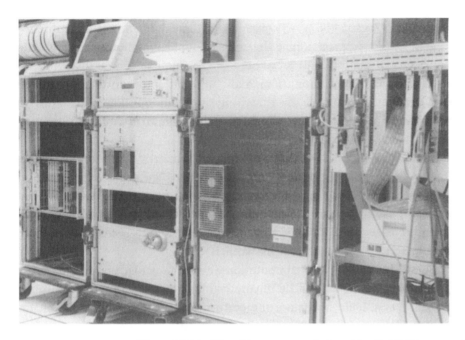

Figure 20.22   The 4X processor, designed by G. Di Giugno and associates. (Photograph by Curtis Roads.)

technology (ECL) used in early DSP systems consumed 0.75 watt (Hasting 1978). Since 800 such chips were needed to create a 100 Kbyte RAM, the power consumption and cooling requirements for large ECL memories were serious. The TRW MPY 16 multiplier chip introduced in 1977 consumed a full 10 watts while completing up to 5 million 16-bit fixed-point multiplies per second. The heat emitted by the chip usually required that any box into which it was built be equipped with cooling fans. As noted earlier, a system built around the TRW multiplier, the Digital Music Systems DMX-1000, consumed 300 watts (Wallraff 1979a). By comparison, in 1990 the Motorola DSP96001 chip, fabricated using low-power *complementary metal-oxide-semiconductor* (CMOS) technology, could execute up to 60 million 32-bit floating-point multiplies per second in a package that consumed less than half a watt.

Array Processors

An *array processor* (AP) is a special kind of parallel multiprocessor DSP architecture. APs are designed for scientific applications such as image processing, but they have also been adapted for musical applications (Eckel,

Rodet, and Potard 1987). APs perform arithmetic operations on entire *arrays* or *blocks* of data at a time. In a musical application these arrays of data can be waveform tables or envelopes. For example, a standard AP operation is array multiplication. In an audio application one array might represent a musical signal while the other is its amplitude envelope. When the AP multiplies one array by the other the result is an array of audio samples scaled by the envelope.

The advantage of APs is that they can perform array operations at speeds far beyond regular computers and serial DSPs. The high performance of APs are a direct result of a specialized architecture. AP architecture makes extensive use of the parallelism and pipelining techniques discussed earlier. Memory references, floating-point arithmetic, address calculations, and high-bandwidth I/O can occur in parallel.

For all but the simplest computations, however, actual computation rates greater than 40 percent of the theoretical maximum are rare (Karplus and Cohen 1981). This is because the performance of an AP depends on the precise nature of the problem at hand and the efficiency of the program written to solve it. In order to achieve high efficiency, the algorithm must exemplify an intrinsic parallelism that is suited to the degree of parallelism implemented in the AP. Most APs are designed around the repetitive execution of a fixed, numerically intensive, array oriented algorithm such as the fast Fourier transform (FFT) (Moore 1978a, 1978b, 1990; Oppenheim 1978; Rabiner and Gold 1975; Gordon and Strawn 1985). (See chapter 13 and appendix A for an explanation of the FFT and its applications to music.)

For digital audio applications, a *block-oriented* software architecture (i.e., one that computes an array of samples at a time) is better suited for implementation on an AP than is a program that computes one sample at a time. For example, Music V and its descendants compute a block of samples at a time. This stands in contrast to Music IV and its descendants, which work on a single sample and then start the synthesis process again for the next sample. (See chapter 17 for a comparison between block-oriented and sample-oriented languages.)

Operation of an Array Processor

APs run under the supervision of a host computer. The host interacts with the user and feeds data to the AP. Working in parallel with the host computer, the AP handles numerically intensive tasks. The host-resident program sends commands and data to the AP and receives results from it. Intercommunication between the host computer and the AP must be fast;

otherwise the numerical engine of the AP wastes cycles. If the host computer's operating system overhead is high and the communication channel is slow, the inefficient data flow can greatly restrict the AP's performance.

The best performance is achieved when the communication between the host and the AP is minimal. Rather than being controlled by software running on the host computer, the AP is driven by a microprogram loaded into its program memory. In this mode the AP acts like a variable-function DSP, except that instead of performing all computations for one sample and then proceeding to the next sample, the AP performs a computation on an array of data, generating an array of samples output at the end.

A *direct memory access* (DMA) channel in the AP fetches data from either the host computer main memory or from a disk memory. A DMA channel can access other devices on the bus without having to interrupt the host processor. This means that update parameters and wavetables can be loaded at high speed without a burden on the host machine.

Multiprocessor Architectures

No single chip will ever attain the speed needed for the most complex real-time musical signal processing; this level of performance can only be achieved by linking many chips into a *multiprocessor* configuration, where each chip functions as a *processing element* (PE) in a larger system.

Fixed-function versus General Processing Elements

In designing a multiprocessor system, a main question is whether to assign each PE to a fixed, specialized task or whether to allocate tasks to PEs on a more dynamic basis through software. This question reprises the fixed-function versus variable-function architecture debate at the level of individual processors, discussed earlier.

As an example of the fixed-task approach, Kahrs (1981) suggested that each PE in a multiprocessor be customized to emulate a popular DSP algorithm, such as filtering or waveshaping. By interconnecting the PEs in a rectangular array, complete signal-processing networks could be realized. The drawback of a specialized PE approach such as this is that the communication links between specialized PEs must themselves be somewhat specialized; this adds yet another later of complexity to the hardware and software. Identical processors allow identical communications links, which simplifies the debugging and programming.

Hegg (1983) demonstrated the advantages of a regular parallel organization with a dynamic task allocation scheme for music. He defined a language called Music 320 (similar to Music V of Max Mathews) to program the system. The Music 320 compiler partitioned synthesis algorithms into a set of discrete subtasks. Each subtask was assigned to a functionally identical PE, in this case a Texas Instruments TMS320 chip. The PEs were arranged in a balanced tree configuration with interprocessor communication occurring at every sample period (see also Kahrs 1986).

The main benefit of a dynamic task allocation scheme is generality. New signal-processing algorithms can be incorporated easily into such a system (Cavaliere, Di Giugno, and Guarino 1992). A liability of a dynamic task allocation scheme is that it is difficult to design a compiler that efficiently partitions and schedules a complicated signal-processing algorithm among more than a few PEs in an optimal way. This means it will be necessary to live with suboptimal performance of computationally dense algorithms.

Many other multiprocessing paradigms exist, although a survey of all their possiblities is beyond the scope of this book. Two paradigms deserve at least a brief look, since they have been studied as possible DSP designs for music. These are *dataflow* and the class of *connectionist* architectures.

Data Flow

Data flow is a *data-driven* model of parallel computation (Dennis 1980). The basic philosophy of data flow systems is that whenever a processor has the data it needs to begin computing, it should begin that part of the computation, regardless of its original place in the logical sequence of a larger program. Hence the data flow concept is intrinsically suited to a multiprocessor architecture (Gaudiot 1987). The main problem with data flow is developing compilers that can automatically map an arbitrary algorithm into a data flow graph suitable to the underlying machine architecture. See Stanek (1979) and Cesari (1981) for applications of data flow to sound synthesis.

Connectionist Architectures

Another route to high-speed multiprocessing operation is the use of *connectionist* architectures (Leiserson 1983; Cavaliere 1991; Wawryznek 1989). A connectionist system is a synchronous network of identical parallel PEs. The PEs are connected to a switching matrix that passes data from one PE to another. The configuration of this switching matrix changes according to the algorithm being executed.

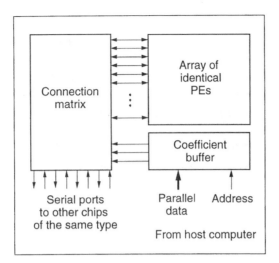

Figure 20.23 Experimental multiprocessor DSP architecture designed by Wawryznek (1989). An array of 64 processing elements (PEs) are interconnected by a switcher called the *connection matrix*. A double-buffered interface handles incoming coefficient updates from a host computer.

The regular structure of connectionist systems makes them especially adaptable to VLSI implementations and matrix computations. Arrays of PEs are well suited to matrix-vector multiplication, convolution, discrete Fourier transforms, linear difference equations, and finite-impulse-response filters—all used throughout digital signal processing (see part III of this book).

A quasi-connectionist approach has been proposed for music synthesis by Wawrzynek (1989) and Wold (1987). Their designs were an attempt to implement efficiently a machine architecture for *physical modeling synthesis*. This type of synthesis models the physics of sound production in an acoustic instrument (see chapter 7). Using a PE designed to solve linear difference equations of the type used in physical modeling, Wawrzynek implemented several interconnection schemes to model different types of instruments. The PE array was implemented as a *bit-serial system,* that is, data are passed into each PE one bit at a time, and output is generated one bit at a time.

Figure 20.23 shows the tripartite global organization of an experimental 64-PE VLSI chip designed by Wawryznek. The first part is an array of identical PEs responsible for arithmetic and delay operations. The second part is a buffer for holding coefficients supplied by the host computer. The buffer is actually a double buffer, meaning it can receive new coefficients from the host while it is transmitting coefficients to the PEs. These coefficients, along with the outputs of other processing elements, form the operands for the processing elements. The third part is a reconfigurable connection matrix that serves all the chip's communication needs. It connects PEs to each other, to the output of the coefficient update buffer, and to I/O connectors on the chip. The exact patterns of interconnection are determined by setting switches in the matrix prior to the computation. Throughout a computation, these switches remain constant. The topology of interconnection can be changed between computations. Interconnections between PEs are not completely general (i.e., any PE to any other PE or any number of other PEs). Rather, to save chip space they are in a kind of tree structure (see Wawryznek 1989 for details).

In pure connectionist architectures the interconnection among processors is generalized by means of an interconnection topology such as a cube, butterfly, or ring (Cavaliere 1991). This general topology allows a program to interconnect any number of PEs to each other. Connectionist architectures are suited for problems in which thousands of PEs can work in parallel on parts of a task. These include simulations of room acoustics, cellular automata simulations, and database search operations.

Conclusion

The 1980s dream of a digital audio workstation, consisting of a personal computer accelerated by a high-speed DSP subsystem, is now a commonplace phenomenon. Many low-cost systems combine sound synthesis with capabilities for audio recording, editing, mixing, and special effects such as echo and reverberation. Over the same period, the young field of DSP hardware design has progressed from the construction of expensive one-of-a-kind filters and oscillators to the variable-function DSP chips of today. High-performance floating-point multiprocessor DSP systems, formerly an exotic laboratory technology, are now available as inexpensive plug-in cards for home computers.

Raw execution speed, as quoted from a manufacturer's sales literature, is a misleading measure of the effectiveness of a DSP in a practical music application. The actual performance of a signal-processing system may be a small percentage of the manufacturer's quoted specification. The musical flexibility and performance of a DSP are determined largely by three factors: the architecture, the speed of its communications channels, and the efficiency of the controlling software. Other factors to be considered in evaluating a DSP include its expense, precision, ease of programming, reliability, and standardization.

Fundamentally, the technology of DSP design must evolve, if for no other reason than to follow the evolution of music itself. Powerful musical techniques have been "waiting in the wings" of research laboratories for some time, poised for the moment when enough numerical processing power is available to permit low-cost real-time implementations. Changes are also being pushed by advances in other technologies, such as memory design. Larger RAMs and higher-capacity storage media point toward increasing emphasis on the manipulation of stored (sampled) sound. This pushes the design of music systems in the direction of querying, editing, mixing, and processing large music databases.

While the pace of integrated circuit development appears relentless, a realistic attitude is prudent. Every season a new batch of chips with impressive performance improvements appears, seemingly rendering last year's technology obsolete. When they are first available, however, new chips are usually expensive. Then it takes months to design a packaged product around a new chip and put it into production. To create a robust software environment that makes good use of the chip in a musically sophisticated way can take years more. Thus the cycle of obsolescence is slower than the cycle of development. Certain combinations of "vintage" hardware and software may continue to serve a musically useful purpose long after they have been rendered technically "obsolete"—as traditional instrument performers would no doubt agree!

21 *MIDI*

MIDI Control Data versus Sound

Background: The MIDI 1.0 Specification

Musical Possibilities of MIDI

MIDI Hardware

> **MIDI Ports**
> *Daisy Chaining and MIDI Patchbays*
> **MIDI Computer Interfaces**
> *Serial Interface*
> *Parallel Interface*
> *Multiport Interface*

MIDI Driver Programs

MIDI Channels

> **More than Sixteen Channels**

MIDI Messages

> **MIDI's Representation of Pitch**
> **Status and Data Bytes**

Channel Messages
System Messages
Running Status

MIDI Modes

Mode 1 "Omni"
Mode 2
Mode 3 "Poly"
Mode 4 "Multi"
General MIDI Mode

Continuous Control via MIDI

Control Change Messages
Defined Controllers
Registered and Unregistered Parameters

Standard MIDI Files

Standard MIDI File Format

Transferring Audio Data

Sample Dump Standard

MIDI Timing

MIDI Clock Messages
MIDI Timecode
Cue Lists

MIDI Machine Control and MIDI Show Control

MIDI Accessories

Limitations of MIDI

Bandwidth Limitations
Microprocessor Delays
Interconnection Limitations
Music Representation Limitations

Speeding up MIDI Communications

Writing MIDI Music Software

Overview of MIDI Programs
MIDI Programming Languages

MIDI Contacts

Conclusion

The Musical Instrument Digital Interface or MIDI protocol has been variously described as an interconnection scheme between instruments and computers, a set of guidelines for transferring data from one instrument to another, and a language for transmitting musical scores between computers and synthesizers. All these definitions capture an aspect of MIDI.

MIDI was designed for real-time control of music devices. The MIDI specification stipulates a hardware interconnection scheme and a method for data communications (IMA 1983; Loy 1985c; Moog 1986). It also specifies a grammar for encoding musical performance information. MIDI information is packaged into small *messages* sent from one device to another. For example, a message can specify the start and stop time of a musical note, its pitch, and its initial amplitude. Another type of message, transmitted at regular intervals, conveys ticks of a master clock, making it possible to synchronize several MIDI instruments to a sequencer that emits these messages.

Every MIDI device contains a microprocessor that interprets and generates MIDI data. Not every MIDI setup needs a separate computer, although there are many advantages to including one.

This chapter describes the nature of MIDI in some detail. The information here should be more than sufficient for most musical users. It is not, however, meant to replace the official MIDI specification and the various addenda and supplements that are added to it from time to time. These are essential documents for anyone developing MIDI hardware or software. See the section on MIDI contacts at the end of this chapter for information on ordering copies of official MIDI documents. Rothstein (1992) and Yavelow (1992) are both good sources for practical advice on setting up a MIDI system.

MIDI Control Data versus Sound

Stepping back, we are reminded that there is nothing specific to music about MIDI. That is, it is not music that MIDI communicates. Rather, MIDI is a means of transmitting information about key presses, knob turnings, and joystick manipulations. What these transducers are controlling is almost secondary. (William Buxton 1986)

MIDI messages are comparable to the player piano rolls of yore, in that they (usually) represent control data as opposed to sound waveforms. This control data includes messages like "start a note event now," "select a new patch now," or "change a parameter now." A sequence of MIDI note messages define a melody, while other sound parameters (primarily the choice of instrument and any pitch bend associated with the notes) are conveyed via separate types of messages. Although most MIDI applications communicate only control data, it is also possible to transfer sampled audio waveforms via MIDI under certain conditions. (See the section on transferring audio data later.)

Sound timbre is not explicitly encoded as a MIDI message. The choice of synthesis technique, envelopes, and signal-processing effects are all left to the receiving device. This means that the same message sent to two different synthesizers or samplers can cause vastly dissimilar sounds. The General MIDI mode, added to the MIDI specification in 1990, provides a set of 128 preset timbre names. This adds a degree of timbre uniformity, primarily to commercial music applications, for a tiny subset of musical timbre space. Even so, a given timbre name (e.g., "Piano [Bright Acoustic]") will not sound exactly the same on devices made by different companies. This is because each company records its own samples, and the internal architecture and audio specifications of various synthesizers differ.

Background: The MIDI 1.0 Specification

Computer control of synthesizers began years before MIDI was conceived. These *hybrid systems* combined digital control of analog synthesizers. As figure 21.1 shows, the computer produced a stream of *control functions* (primarily amplitude and pitch envelopes) that were routed to a DAC channel by a *demultiplexer*. (A demultiplexer divides a high-speed digital stream into several slower streams.) The DAC converted the digital control functions into voltages fed to the control inputs of the synthesizer modules (like oscillators, filters, and amplifiers). Most hybrid systems can also instantaneously *repatch* (interconnect) the modules of the synthesizer into new sound-processing voices or instruments.

Pioneering hybrid synthesizers were the GROOVE system developed at Bell Telephone Laboratories in the early 1970s (Mathews and Moore 1970) and Edward Kobrin's marvelous HYBRID systems (Kobrin 1977), developed initially at the University of Illinois and later at the University of California, San Diego. In both cases, all interface hardware was custom-built, and the software protocols were specific to each system.

By the late 1970s, it became possible to use inexpensive microprocessors to control synthesizers. Microprocessor-controlled hybrid and digital synthesizers were marketed, but they were all incompatible with each other. That is, music and software developed on one system could not be transferred to another. No standard way existed to synchronize the performance of one instrument with another.

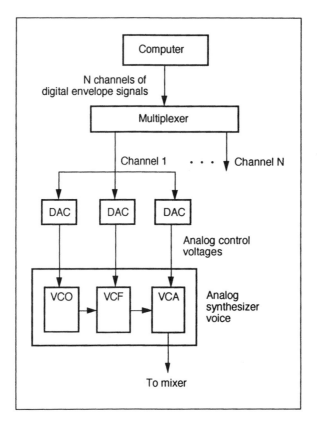

Figure 21.1 Hybrid control scheme. The computer generates digital envelopes that are routed via a multiplexer to several channels of DACs. The analog signals emitted by the DACs feed the control voltage inputs of the analog synthesizer modules. Here the audio output of a voltage-controlled oscillator (VCO) feeds into a voltage-controlled filter (VCF), which feeds into a voltage-controlled amplifier (VCA). A mixer combines the N synthesizer voices into a composite signal.

This state of affairs prompted the creation of the MIDI protocol. The beginnings of MIDI date back to informal contacts between several American and Japanese synthesizer manufacturers in 1981, notably Sequential Circuits, Oberheim, and Roland Corporation. These led to broader communications between more companies in 1982 and the drafting of a preliminary specification for a digital music interface in 1983 by David Smith of the Sequential Circuits company. The first draft involved much collaboration between Smith and several companies, notably Roland and Oberheim (D. Smith 1984).

The first MIDI instruments were introduced into the market in early 1983. In August of that year, the version 1.0 MIDI specification was published by a consortium of Japanese and American synthesizer manufacturers. The specification has been amended numerous times since. (To obtain the latest version of the specification, contact the International MIDI Association listed in the section on MIDI contacts at the end of the chapter.) Hybrid synthesizers, by the way, are still manufactured. In those built since 1983 the control protocol is MIDI.

Musical Possibilities of MIDI

A variety of musical possibilities emerge out of a system wired for MIDI:

1. MIDI separates the input device (for example, a musical keyboard) from the sound generator (synthesizer or sampler). Thus MIDI eliminates the need to have a keyboard attached to every synthesizer. A single keyboard can play many synthesizers.

2. The separation of control from synthesis means that any input device (breath controller, hornlike instrument, drum pad, guitar, etc.) can control a synthesizer. This has led to a wave of innovation in designing input devices (see chapter 14). Even a microphone can become a MIDI input device if a *pitch-to-MIDI converter* is attached to it. (This device tracks the pitch of the sound fed into the microphone and generates MIDI note messages corresponding to the pitches it detects.)

3. Software for interactive performance, algorithmic composition, score editing, patch editing, and sequencing can be run on the computer with the results transmitted to the synthesizer. In the opposite direction, scores, performances, voice tunings, or samples can be created on the synthesizer and transferred to the computer for editing or storage.

4. MIDI makes "generic" (device-independent) music software easier to develop. Generic music software runs on a personal computer and drives synthesizers manufactured by different companies. An example of generic software is a sequencer that allows a musician to record a polyphonic composition one line at a time. The composition can be orchestrated in different ways using a group of synthesizers or a single *multitimbral* synthesizer. (A multitimbral synthesizer can play several different voices or timbres simultaneously.) Generic music education software teaches fundamental concepts of music, regardless of the type of synthesizer or sampler used to illustrate these concepts.

5. MIDI makes "targeted" music software (i.e., software for a specific device) easier to develop. Targeted music software includes *patch editor/ librarian* programs that essentially replace the front panel of a synthesizer, sampler, or effects processor. By pushing graphical buttons and

adjusting the knobs on the screen image with a mouse, one can control the synthesizer as if one were manipulating its physical controls.

6. MIDI codes can be reinterpreted by devices other than synthesizers, such as signal-processing effects boxes (reverberators, etc.). This offers the possibility of real-time control of effects, such as changing the delay or reverberation time. MIDI can synchronize synthesizers with other media such as lighting systems. MIDI can also be linked with other synchronization protocols (such as SMPTE timecode) to coordinate music with video and graphics. Another specialized application of MIDI is the control of audio mixers. See chapter 9 for a discussion of console automation via MIDI.

7. Through MIDI, score, sequencer, and sample data can be exchanged between devices made by different manufacturers.

MIDI Hardware

MIDI hardware implements a simple protocol for the transmission and receipt of electronic signals. Before explaining the hardware, it is important to know the basic form of MIDI signals. MIDI *messages* transmitted between devices are sent in *serial binary form,* that is, as a series of pulses (bits) sent one at a time. Transmission occurs *asynchronously,* that is, whenever one device decides to send a message. This is usually when an event happens (for example, a musician presses a key on a musical keyboard).

The standard rate of transmission is 31,250 bits per second. This figure was derived by dividing the common clock frequency of 1.0 MHz by 32.

The hardware that handles these signals includes *MIDI ports* and *MIDI computer interfaces,* the subjects of the next two sections.

MIDI Ports

A MIDI port on a device receives and transmits the messages. The basic port consists of three connectors: IN, OUT, and THRU. These connectors are usually five-pin DIN jacks. (DIN is the acronym of the German standards organization that designed the connectors.) The wiring of the jacks is specific to the MIDI standard; ordinary audio DIN cables are not designed to work in a MIDI system. In particular, the MIDI protocol wires two pins on the receiving (MIDI IN) port, and a third pin is connected to ground in the MIDI OUT port (figure 21.2). This allows the cable to shield without

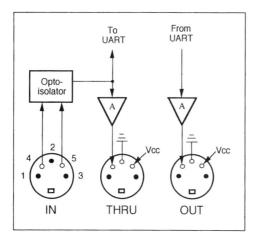

Figure 21.2 A basic MIDI port. The IN connector shows the standard pin numbering. The optoisolator connected to the IN port consists of a light-emitting diode with its light output directed at a photocell, both enclosed in an opaque container. The MIDI signal pulses the light on and off, which switches the photocell on and off. The triangle labeled A is a buffer amplifier that boosts the signal before it is sent on to the next device. *Vcc* indicates a current source. The UART is explained in the text.

grounding problems over a span of up to 15 meters. Notice in figure 21.2 that pins 1 and 3 are never used.

The connectors are optically isolated (i.e., converted into optical signals at the endpoints) to prevent hum and interference from other electrical signals. Ultimately the signals are routed to a *universal asynchronous receiver/ transmitter* (UART) chip.

The UART chip is the workhorse of the MIDI port. It assembles or *frames* the incoming bits into 10-bit packets, collecting the bits one at a time. The first bit always has a value of zero; the last bit has a value of 1. These are the *start* and *stop bits,* respectively, which initiate and terminate a transmission. The UART discards the start and stop bits, leaving the contents: an 8-bit byte (figure 21.3). The UART passes the byte to the microprocessor within the MIDI device (synthesizer, sampler, effects unit, etc.) for decoding. Decoding the byte and acting on its contents takes a certain period of time; this delay depends on the speed of the microprocessor within the receiving MIDI device and is independent of MIDI transmission speed. (Marans 1991 is a study of the delays created by popular synthesizers. Russ 1993 studies the delays caused by computers and sequencers. See the section on microprocessor delays later.) To transmit MIDI data to another device, the UART issues a start bit (0) along with each word, followed by the stop bit (1) when that word's transmission is complete.

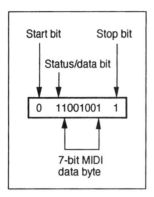

Figure 21.3 Anatomy of a MIDI message. The status/data bit indicates whether this message is a command or an argument to a command.

Electrically, MIDI is a *current loop,* which means it relies on a switching on and off of current, rather than voltage, to represent the logic levels. The "on" current is 5 milliamps, and this (counterintuively) represents a binary value of 0. The "off" current represents a binary value of 1.

Daisy Chaining and MIDI Patchbays

The MIDI THRU port routes incoming data to another MIDI device with minimal processing. The signal at the THRU output is a replica of the signal fed to the IN socket. That is, a THRU port "reamplifies" the signal and passes it to the IN port of the next connected device. Daisy chaining does not mean bypassing intermediate devices. Each device in the chain interprets the incoming messages; depending on the messages, each device may or may not respond to them.

In this way, MIDI devices can be *daisy chained* into a series of devices (figure 21.4a). Note that the daisy chain is a one-way (THRU-to-IN) connection. A reversal of the data path requires repatching the system (figure 21.4b).

Although a link via a MIDI THRU connector is theoretically "electrically transparent," in practice transmission losses (digital waveform distortions) occur after more than two links. In effect, the optoisolator smears the edges of the MIDI pulses (Penfold 1991). Smearing may lead to so-called "frame errors" in daisy chained MIDI transmissions (figure 21.5), meaning that messages are garbled. The effect on the sound is random, depending on the type of messages being confused: missing or stuck notes, inappropriate messages, etc.

To solve these problems and to make repatching easier, it is wise to use a central *MIDI patch bay* to handle the interconnection of a group of devices

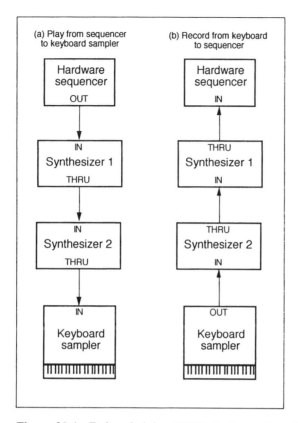

Figure 21.4 Daisy chaining MIDI devices with a MIDI THRU connector. (*a*) Playback from a hardware sequencer to two synthesizers and a sampler. (*b*) To reverse the chain, that is, to record from the keyboard sampler into the sequencer, requires repatching the chain. No additional MIDI data are contributed by the two intermediate synthesizers, although they may sound as the keyboard performer plays.

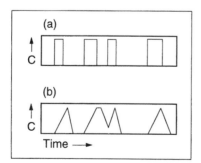

Figure 21.5 Smearing of MIDI pulses. The plots show current (C) versus time. (*a*) Original series of MIDI pulses. (*b*) Same signal after passing through several THRU connections.

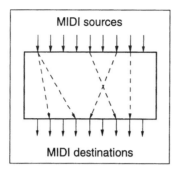

Figure 21.6 MIDI patch bay, with eight possible sources and eight possible destinations. One source can be mapped to all eight destinations. The dashed lines indicate the current "patch" or signal routing between devices. The data being transmitted are MIDI data, not audio signals.

(figure 21.6). That is, the patch bay routes each MIDI input signal to one or more of its outputs. Each of the other MIDI devices connects directly to the patch bay. (See the section on MIDI accessories.) Note that a MIDI patch bay is not the same as an audio patch bay, as discussed in chapter 22. They serve a similar function—simplifying the interconnection of a number of devices—but for different types of signals (MIDI messages versus audio signals).

MIDI Computer Interfaces

Some computers do not have a built-in MIDI port. In this case it is necessary to connect a MIDI computer interface to the computer. The MIDI computer interface transmits messages from the computer through its MIDI OUT port; it converts incoming messages from its MIDI IN port into the protocol required by the computer. Three basic types of interfaces are extant: serial, parallel, and multiline.

Serial Interface

A serial interface transmits and receives data to and from the computer one bit at a time, like the MIDI protocol intself. A serial interface connects to the *serial input/output port* of the computer (figure 21.7a). A MIDI computer interface attached to a serial port is a simple device consisting of a UART with clock-generation circuitry, an output stage, and an optically isolated input stage.

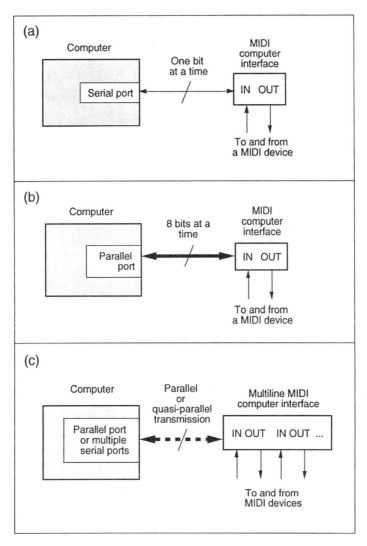

Figure 21.7 MIDI computer interfaces. (*a*) Simple serial interface for 16 channels. (*b*) Parallel interface for 16 channels. (*c*) Multiline interface providing several 16-channel lines.

Parallel Interface

Another type of interface attaches to the *parallel port* of the computer, which typically transmits eight bits at a time (figure 21.7b). The parallel port can operate many times faster than MIDI, meaning that the computer can transmit and receive MIDI data quickly, leaving it free for other tasks. Some of the work of transmitting and receiving MIDI data can be offloaded to the parallel MIDI interface. Note that even though the parallel interconnection with the computer is fast, the basic MIDI rate of MIDI sent to other devices does not change. This means that the parallel interface must buffer data sent to it by the computer before it can be transmitted serially to the rest of the devices on the MIDI chain.

Multiport Interface

A *multiport MIDI interface* connects the computer to several independent MIDI lines (figure 21.7.c). Each line can be thought of as a separate 16-channel MIDI network. Certain sequencers work with multiport interfaces, letting users circumvent the limit on the number of channels fixed by the MIDI protocol. (See the section on channels later.) For multiple-device MIDI installations, a multiport interface may simplify many issues of routing and control.

MIDI Driver Programs

Every synthesizer or digital signal processor (DSP) with a MIDI port contains a microprocessor. One of the jobs of the microprocessor is to decode the messages being sent to it from the UART and invoke the appropriate response. The microprocessor must also translate human gestures sensed on its input devices into the appropriate sequence of MIDI messages to be routed through its output port. The program that handles this MIDI input and output function is called the *MIDI driver*. In effect, the driver "owns" the input/output port; all MIDI communications must be routed through it.

A computer running MIDI software also needs a MIDI driver program. In the past, programs like sequencers contained their own MIDI drivers. This was fine for stand-alone programs in a one-program-at-a-time operating system. But with multitasking operating systems, which can run several programs at the same time, a MIDI driver program has been made a part of the operating system of some computers. By making it a part of the operating system, the MIDI driver becomes a shared resource that can be used by several programs operating in parallel. In this case, the MIDI driver handles the contention between the different programs for the use of the input/output port.

MIDI Channels

The MIDI protocol lets a device send messages over one to sixteen different *channels* to reach different devices, or different logical data streams on one device. (In a multitimbral synthesizer, these different data streams usually correspond to separate timbres or patches.) MIDI channels are not separate physical connections, as they are on a multichannel tape recorder. Rather, a MIDI channel is like an electronic address label that identifies a packet of digital information, specifying its ultimate destination. For example, one channel might contain control messages for altering a certain parameter on a specific device.

All sixteen channels can be routed over one physical MIDI cable. Each receiving device is set up beforehand to listen to one or more channels.

Each MIDI channel corresponds to a distinct stream of data. In the simplest case, each channel carries data for a particular part in a polyphonic score. For example, one channel might carry information for a snare drum part for a drum machine, while another channel plays a legato synthesizer voice. A multitimbral synthesizer that can play several voices with different timbres at once accepts several channels of MIDI data—one for each timbre. Hence, one way to orchestrate a composition is to assign different musical parts to the various MIDI channels (figure 21.8). The orchestration can be modified by changing the part-to-channel assignments.

More than Sixteen Channels

It is possible to address more than sixteen MIDI channels from one computer, provided that the system is configured to support multiple MIDI lines. Many newer computers, interfaces, and software support two separate sixteen-channel MIDI lines as a standard. Older computers require another MIDI interface to be attached to the computer. The additional interface provides another sixteen channels addressed through the alternate port (with its own cabling). In order for this scheme to work, the MIDI software must also be able to interact with more than one port. Multiport interfaces and compatible software can increase the number of available channels into the hundreds. These schemes work by implementing an extension to MIDI's channel addressing scheme using nonstandard messages.

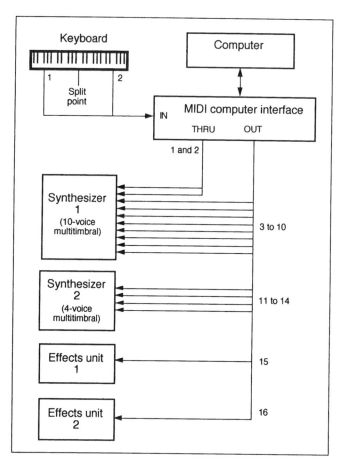

Figure 21.8 A logical (not physical) view of the MIDI channel mechanism. The keyboard output is split into two channels of information, 1 and 2. In order to record a keyboard performance these two channels are routed to the computer, which runs a sequencer program. In order to hear the performance, channels 1 and 2 are routed via the MIDI computer interface to Synthesizer 1. The computer is controlling two synthesizers and one effects unit and is taking in data from a clavier. A total of twelve MIDI channels can be used at once in this configuration. Synthesizer 1 is a ten-voice multitimbral synthesizer, while Synthesizer 2 has four voices, and the effects units respond to one channel each.

MIDI's *mode* mechanism, which specifies how a device interprets channel-specific data, is another way to increase the routing flexibility. Because MIDI's modes can be confusing at first, we postpone their explanation until after we explain more about MIDI messages.

MIDI Messages

The MIDI specification describes a language of messages sent from device to device. Expressions in the MIDI language are sequences of bits that can be parsed into 10-bit *words*. One or more words comprise a MIDI *message*. For the purpose of this discussion, we assume that the start and stop bits tacked onto each word have been stripped off, leaving a series of 8-bit bytes.

The messages that any given MIDI devices responds to are printed in its *MIDI implementation chart, a* document published by the manufacturer.

Table 21.1 enumerates the set of MIDI messages. In order to understand table 21.1, it is helpful to know about the syntax and semantics of the MIDI protocol—the grammar of MIDI, as it were. This grammar includes the distinction between status and data bytes and the different categories of MIDI messages. Before explaining all this, however, let us take a moment to understand an important detail in the MIDI specification: its representation of pitch.

MIDI's Representation of Pitch

The first message documented in table 21.1 is the note-on message—MIDI's way of signaling the start of a sonic event. A note-on message contains a 7-bit field corresponding to a pitch value. Since $2^7 = 128$, this means that the MIDI pitch range extends over 128 pitches. The MIDI specification mandates that these pitches be equal-tempered, although they can be "bent" out of equal temperament by means of the pitch bend message (the sixth message documented in table 21.1). A problem with the pitch bend message is that it is a global operation that applies to all notes assigned to a given channel. This makes it difficult to bend a single note in a chord (as is done on a pedal steel guitar, for example) without resorting to a rigged workaround involving multiple channels.

The usual MIDI pitch range begins in the infrasonic octave with key numbers 0 to 12. This octave spans MIDI C0 or 8.17 Hz up to MIDI C1 or 16.35 Hz. Key 60 represents MIDI C5 or 261.63 Hz (MIDI middle C). In many music theory texts, middle C (261.63 Hz) is usually considered to be C4; thus the MIDI name for octaves is nonstandard. In any case, not all

Table 21.1   Types of MIDI messages

Channel Voice—Addressed to a specific MIDI channel

Note-on

If you play a note on the keyboard, the synthesizer sounds the note and also sends a three-byte message through the MIDI OUT port. If we were to translate a message into English words, it might read like so:

Note event: On

Channel: 1

Key number: 60 (middle C)

Velocity: 116 (fortissimo)

Note: the term "velocity" refers to the way that a MIDI keyboard detects how hard keys are played. If you press hard and fast on a keyboard, the time it takes for the key to travel from its position of rest to its low position is very short, meaning that it moved at high velocity. A soft key depression travels at slow velocity. Thus a high velocity associated with a note usually means "loud," while a low velocity means "soft." But a MIDI device can interpret the velocity value in whatever way it wants, mapping it into control of "brightness" for example, or filter bandwidth. A keyboard that measures velocity of key depressions is said to be *velocity-sensitive*. See chapter 14 for more on the characteristics of keyboards.

Note-off

When the note is released, the keyboard sends another three-byte message:

Note event: Off

Channel: 1

Pitch: 60 (middle C)

Velocity: 40 (piano or soft)

In lieu of a note-off message, some synthesizers transmit a note-on with a velocity of 0.

Polyphonic Key Pressure (aftertouch)

This three-byte message transmits the finger pressure detected by the keyboard and indicates (1) channel, (2) key number of the note, and (3) key pressure.

Channel Pressure (multiple key aftertouch)

This conveys the "average" pressure applied to the keyboard from all notes being pressed down. The message contains two bytes: channel and channel pressure (0-127, with 127 as maximum pressure).

Control Change

Informs a receiving device that the position of a specific wheel, lever, potentiometer, pedal or another *continuous controller* is changing. This is accomplished by sending a new three-byte message every time the controller changes. After the status byte, the first data byte indicates the controller number and the second data byte indicates the value. Controllers 32 to 63 are defined as "least significant byte for values 0 to

Table 21.1 (cont.)

31." This means that these controllers can be logically coupled to controllers 0 to 31. That is, we take the data byte for controller 0 as the most significant byte (coarse resolution) and the data byte for controller 32 as the least significant byte (fine resolution), yielding 14 bits of resolution. The full 14-bit resolution is used for registered and non-registered parameter numbers. (See the section on parameter numbers.)

Pitch Bend

This controller uses two data bytes, for 14 bits of resolution or 16,384 pitch divisions . One byte indicates coarse range and the other indicates fine range. The range of pitch bend is set on the affected synthesizer or sampler. A pitch bend wheel that is slowly turned may generate thousands of pitch bend messages. The amount of pitch change corresponding to a particular value for pitch bend is left up the manufacturer of a given synthesizer.

Program Change

Program change messages contain a channel select byte and a program select byte. These cause the receiving device to switch its voice or patch to the designated program number. For example, a program change might tell a sampler on channel 4 to switch from a pianolike sound to an organlike sound. These change messages tell effects units to switch from, say, a reverberation program to an chorus effect program.

Bank Select

The message switches a system to the specified patch bank (up to 16,384 patch banks). This is useful for devices that support more than 128 patches, voices, or programs, because the usual Program Change message only allows 128 values.

Channel Mode—Conveys the mode of a message. (See table 21.2).

Local/Remote Keyboard Control

Breaks the connection between the keyboard and the sound generator of a synthesizer. In Remote or Local Off mode, an instrument with sound generating capabilities transmits note messages out its MIDI OUT port, but not to its internal synthesizer. The internal synthesizer can be controlled remotely via externally-generated messages coming in to the MIDI IN port of the instrument.

All Notes Off

An emergency message that shuts off all notes.

Reset All Controllers

Returns all controllers to their optimum initial status. For example, such a message would cause a vibrato wheel to be reset to 0 (no vibrato).

ModeSelect

Selects the MIDI mode; see table 21.2.

Table 21.1 (cont.)

System Common—Sent to all units and all channels; these messages were designed to set sequencers to the proper piece and measure for playback.

Song Position Pointer

Addresses a sequence in terms of a 14-bit quantity representing the number of MIDI clock ticks that have occurred since the beginning of the song. (6 MIDI clocks—1 beat.)

Song Select

Selects one of 128 song files in a sequencer library.

Tune Request

Initiates routines within an analog synthesizer to tune the oscillators.

End System Exclusive

Terminates a System Exclusive message (see below).

Quarter Frame

Used by instruments that transmit or réceive MIDI Time Code (MTC). Each of the eight message variations acts as a timing pulse for the system and defines a unique location in SMPTE timecode. Eight quarter-frame messages completely define the SMPTE time (two each for hours, minutes, seconds, and frames).

System Real Time—Clock messages and start and stop commands. These are usually used by sequencers and drum machines to control other MIDI devices. Channel information is not transmitted.

MIDI Clock

Used as a timing pulse by MIDI sequencers and drum machines. Transmitted 24 times per quarter note.

Start

Generated when a play or start button of a sequencer or drum machine is pushed. When received by a sequencer or drum machine, the sequence or pattern plays from the beginning.

Stop

Generated when the stop button on a sequencer or drum machine is pressed. Halts any sequencer or drum machine receiving it.

Continue

Generated when the continue button is pushed on a sequencer or drum machine. The device receiving it will play from the point where the last stop command was received.

Active Sensing

Originally design to prevent "stuck" notes that could occur if the MIDI connection were temporaily interrupted between the receipt of a Note-on and a Note-off

Table 21.1 (cont.)

message. Active sensing works by sending a message when there is no activity on the MIDI line. If the Active Sensing message ceases and there is no other activity on the line, then the slave turns off its sound generators to prevent "stuck" notes. Currently, active sensing is not often used.

System Reset

When a device receives this message, it returns to its default settings (those that are active when it powers up).

System Exclusive—Provided so a manufacturer can send device-specific data; used to communicate sound parameters and to dump programs into a synthesizer or effects unit.

System Exclusive

This message is a "catch all," since it transmits any manufacturer's data that is not covered by other messages. The status byte indicates a System Exclusive ("sysex" in slang) message. Next comes the manufacturer's number (0-127), and following this are a set of data bytes, such as the contents of a synthesizer's memory with all its parameter settings. After the data has been sent the process ends with a one-byte End of System Exclusive message or a Reset message.

System Exclusive is widely used to transmit *bulk patch data*—parameter settings obtained by patch editing. For example, all of the editing information for the Yamaha DX7 synthesizer can be completely contained within its 4096-byte bulk patch data (158 parameters for each voice or patch stored in 128 bytes; some parameters take a bit, others take a byte; 32 patches per bank.)

Sample data in MIDI Sample Dump Standard format is also transmitted via System Exclusive messages, as are MIDI Time Code Set-Up cues and the ten-byte MIDI Time Code Full Frame messages.

Another pair of messages are Device Inquiry and Device ID. Device Inquiry means "who are you?" The transmitting device seeks the manufacturer's ID, the instrument ID, and the software revision level of the receiving device. Using the Device ID message, a device transmits the requested identification data.

System Exclusive also transmits basic notation information, such as time signature changes and measure (bar) markers associated with MIDI clock ticks, as well as master volume and balance settings.

manufacturers confirm to the pitch-naming scheme of MIDI. Some companies call key 60 C3, C4, or C5. The highest key, 127, represents MIDI G10 or 12,543.89 Hz.

Most synthesizers let musicians alter the key to-pitch mapping. In the simplest case, the synthesizer has a "global tuning" control that lets one shift the range by some logarithmic constant. For example, one could tune the synthesizer so that MIDI A5 (concert pitch) corresponded to 438 Hz or 442 Hz instead of 440 Hz. Or one could tune the entire system up an octave so that MIDI's C4 corresponded to the usual C4.

In some synthesizers one can change the pitch mapping on a per-key basis, so that instead of responding in equal temperament, the synthesizer responds in a different scale. Unfortunately, some synthesizers limit the retuning to a one-octave span. That is, one can retune the twelve pitches of one octave only; the synthesizer simply repeats that tuning across all octaves in its pitch range. This makes it impossible to implement microtonal scales that include more than twelve notes per octave or that extend beyond an octave.

Applying this basic knowledge of MIDI's numerical representation of pitches, we are ready to look at the grammar of MIDI messages.

Status and Data Bytes

The stream of MIDI data divides into two types of bytes: *status* bytes and *data* bytes (figure 21.9). A status byte begins with a 1 and identifies a particular function, such as note-on, note-off, pitch wheel change, and so on. A data byte begins with a 0 and provides the value associated with the status byte, such as the particular key and channel of a note-on message, how much the pitch wheel has changed, and so on. For example, a note-on event message consists of three bytes (10010000 01000000 00010010). The first byte is the status. The first four bits (four bits are sometimes referred to as a *nibble*) of the status byte specify the function (in this case, note-on), while the last four bits specify the MIDI channel (0000 = channel 1).

Data bytes begin with a 0, leaving the remaining seven bits to carry the actual value of the data. This allows $2^7 = 128$ different values, from 0 to 127, to be expressed in a single data byte. In a note-on message, for example, the first data byte expresses a key number (usually corresponding to pitch). Here the key value is 64, which corresponds to a frequency of 330 Hz. The remaining byte expresses the key *velocity* (the speed at which a key was pressed, usually interpreted as the amplitude of the note). (See the explanation of velocity in the description of the note-on message in table 21.1.)

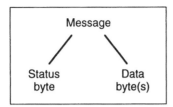

Figure 21.9   MIDI messages can be segmented into status bytes and data bytes.

Channel Messages

MIDI messages fall into two categories: *channel messages* and *system messages*. Channel messages target a specific channel. They are acted upon if the channel number associated with the message correponds to an active channel of the receiving device. In contrast, system messages are received by all MIDI devices, regardless of the channel to which they are assigned.

Channel Voice messages are the most common MIDI messages since they deal with note data. The note-on message, mentioned earlier, is a Channel Voice message. It transmits the timing and pitch of notes played, and their amplitude. Other Channel Voice messages communicate gestures such as manipulations of the pitch bend and modulation wheels and volume pedal.

As an example of the MIDI representation of note data, figure 21.10 depicts a fragment of music notation and its transcription into MIDI message codes.

Another category of Channel Voice message concerns so-called *programs*. Generally, a program change message transmits an integer to a MIDI device that tells it what function to perform. In a MIDI synthesizer, a program change message selects a particular sound synthesis method, like "Patch 37: Bells." In a signal processor, it selects an audio effect, like "Patch 37: Reverberation." The important point here is that a program change message sends only an integer; it is up to the receiving device to interpret this integer.

System Messages

System Common messages convey information such as "song selection" or the number of messages elapsed since a sequence started playing.

System Real Time messages synchronize drum machines, sequencers, and other rhythm-oriented devices. They include clock messages (emitted at regular intervals) and start and stop commands for drum machines.

System Exclusive messages are reserved by each manufacturer for use with their products. By agreement, each manufacturer must publish an ex-

(b)

Delta Time	Status (hex)	Num (hex)	Vel (hex)	Interpretation	Musical Description
0	90	34	35	Note On, channel 1, note=52, vel=53	E, octave 3, medium loud
120		34	00	(Running Status) note=52, vel=0	release E3 after 16th note
0		37	26	(Running Status) note=55, vel=38	G3, medium soft
60		37	00	(Running Status) note=55, vel=0	release G3 after 32nd note
0		3B	28	(Running Status) note=59, vel=40	B3, start crescendo
60		3B	00	(Running Status) note=59, vel=0	release B3 after 32nd note
0		40	2B	(Running Status) note=64, vel=43	E4, continue crescendo
60		40	00	(Running Status) note=64, vel=0	release E4 after 32nd note
0		43	2D	(Running Status) note=67, vel=45	G4, continue crescendo
60		43	00	(Running Status) note=67, vel=0	release G4 after 32nd note
0		47	2F	(Running Status) note=71, vel=47	B4, continue crescendo
60		47	00	(Running Status) note=71, vel=0	release B4 after 32nd note
0		4C	32	(Running Status) note=76, vel=50	E5, continue crescendo
60		4C	00	(Running Status) note=76, vel=0	release E5 after 32nd note
0		4F	3A	(Running Status) note=79, vel=58	G5, medium loud with metrical accent
360		4F	00	(Running Status) note=79, vel=0	release G5 after dotted 8th note
0		4F	2A	(Running Status) note=79, vel=42	G5, softer
120		4F	00	(Running Status) note=79, vel=0	release G5 after 16th note
0		4F	42	(Running Status) note=79, vel=66	chord: G5, medium loud with accent
0		48	37	(Running Status) note=72, vel=55	C5, medium loud
0		45	37	(Running Status) note=69, vel=55	A4, medium loud
0		3C	37	(Running Status) note=60, vel=55	C4, medium loud
0		39	37	(Running Status) note=57, vel=55	A3, medium loud
0		34	37	(Running Status) note=52, vel=55	E3, medium loud
480		4F	00	(Running Status) note=79, vel=0	release G5 after quarter note
0		4E	23	(Running Status) note=78, vel=35	F#5, medium soft
480		4E	00	(Running Status) note=78, vel=0	chord: release F#5 after quarter note
0		48	00	(Running Status) note=72, vel=0	release C5 (after half note)
0		45	00	(Running Status) note=69, vel=0	release A4 (after half note)
0		3C	00	(Running Status) note=60, vel=0	release C4 (after half note)
0		39	00	(Running Status) note=57, vel=0	release A3 (after half note)
0		34	00	(Running Status) note=52, vel=0	release E3 (after half note)

planation of what its System Exclusive codes do. A typical use of System Exclusive codes is to transmit patches and other instrument-specific parameters. Some master keyboards can be programmed to send System Exclusive messages to any synthesizer.

Running Status

The distinction between status bytes and data bytes makes possible a programming trick called *running status*. Running status trims MIDI data flow by cutting three-byte controller and note messages down to two bytes—a major speedup for controller and note messages. A musical implication of this is that chords sound more precise, since the individual notes (sent one after the other) are received in a shorter time period. Notice the use of running status in figure 21.10b.

The process works as follows. Once a status byte has been received, the instrument maintains that command status until a different status byte is received. This means that a musician can play a burst of notes with one note-on status byte followed by pairs of data bytes (representing the note number and the velocity, respectively) for each note in a melody. A new status byte is sent only if a new type of command is required. Using this trick, some software shuts off notes with note-on messages having a velocity of zero, rather than sending more status bytes in the form of note-off messages.

MIDI Modes

MIDI's system of modes is one of its more confusing aspects. Each device that sends and receives MIDI data interprets channel data according to the mode in which it is operating. The five defined modes are as follows:

Mode 1. Omni-on polyphonic (or "Omni" mode)

Mode 2. Omni-on mono

Figure 21.10 Score fragment and corresponding MIDI messages. (*a*) J. S. Bach: *Toccata* from *Partita VI, Clavierübung,* part I, first measure. (*b*) Standard MIDI file with a resolution of 480 ticks per quarter note. *Delta time* means number of ticks since preceding event. Hex means hexadecimal coding. That is, each four-bit nibble is indicated by a number or letter 0, 1, 2, . . . 9, A, B, . . . F corresponding to a value from 0 to 15.

Mode 3. Omni-off polyphonic (or "Poly" mode)

Mode 4. Omni-off ("Multi" mode)

General MIDI

Most devices let one set the mode by pressing a sequence of buttons or by sending it a mode select message via MIDI. Table 21.2 summarizes the features of the various modes. The following sections explain each mode in more detail.

Mode 1 "Omni"

Omni-on polyphonic (mode 1) obviates the MIDI channel mechanism. In this mode, an instrument receives messages sent on all channels. Mode 1 is probably best used for testing. Sending messages in Omni mode is a quick way to test the physical interconnection between two MIDI devices without taking the trouble of assigning specific communication channels.

Mode 2

Mode 2 means that an instrument receives notes on all channels without distinguishing between them, playing, however, only one note at a time. Mode 2 is now vestigal, serving little purpose, and is rarely implemented on modern synthesizers.

Mode 3 "Poly"

In a sequencing or multiple instrument environment, a preferred mode is Poly (Mode 3). This tells each instrument to listen to one channel of information. Within that channel, the slave (receiver) responds to as many different notes as it can. It is up to the user to specify the particular MIDI channel (1–16) on each of the MIDI devices. This can usually be done by pressing a button on a device or selecting a channel number from a software menu. For example, a *monotimbral* instrument like the original Yamaha DX7, which can only play one timbre at a time, might be assigned to receive messages on a single MIDI channel, so one might set it to Poly mode.

Mode 4 "Multi"

Mode 4 supports multitimbral instruments that can play back more than one timbre or patch at a time. Each patch receives data from a different MIDI channel. Usually all available voices in the instrument are placed on

Table 21.2 MIDI modes

Number Mode Explanation of function

1. Omni-on Poly

"Omni" mode. A device receives on all channels, but messages are sent from the device on one channel only. The device can respond polyphonically. Used for testing.

2. Omni-on Mono

A device receives on all channels and assigns data to voices monophonically. Designed for monophonic synthesizers or polyphonic synthesizers operating in unison. Sounds one note at a time. Not implemented on many synthesizers.

3. Omni-off Poly

"Poly" mode. Voice messages are recognized from the basic channel and are assigned to all voices polyphonically. Different devices can be set to respond to different channels, so each device can act as a part in a multipart score. This is the most flexible mode, since individual channels can be turned on and off.

4. Omni-off

"Multi" mode. A multitimbral device can respond on more than one but not necessarily all channels. Data can be received on as many channels as a unit has voices. In the original MIDI specification, the receiver responded monophonically on each channel. Mode 4 is now polyphonic in every channel and is called Multi mode. Mode 4 is often used for MIDI guitars, since each string can send data on a different channel.

5. General MIDI

Devices respond according to a standard mapping between channels, patches, and types of sounds. Provided that the music remains within the limits of the General MIDI standard, this mode greatly improves the transportability of sequencer files created in different places. The first ten channels are preassigned, with channel 4 for melody, channel 8 for harmony, and channel 10 for the percussion part. In addition, all 128 patches are preassigned to specific sound types. For example, in General MIDI mode (GMM), patch 1 always signifies an acoustic grand piano sound, patch 25 is always a nylon-string acoustic guitar sound, and so on.

consecutive MIDI channels, with the lowest one being the *base channel*. For example, an eight-voice instrument set on base channel 4 would have one voice assigned on each of channels 4, 5, 6, 7, 8, 9, 10, and 11. A main use for Multi mode is MIDI guitars. Each of the six strings is set to a MIDI channel, and a voice on the receiving synthesizer is assigned to a guitar string timbre. Another application of Multi mode is pitch bend on individual notes in a polyphonic texture. Multi mode is useful for more than just synthesizers: one application is MIDI-controlled mixers, where each audio channel on the mixer is assigned to its own MIDI channel. Multi mode was originally defined to be monophonic and was called "Mono" mode, but manufacturers extended it to respond polyphonically on each channel.

General MIDI Mode

The design of General MIDI mode (GMM) (introduced in 1990) was inspired by the mass market of a "preset" approach to MIDI configuration. Rather than forcing users to configure their own MIDI network, General MIDI provides a standard setup. That is, devices equipped for GMM respond to MIDI messages according to a standard mapping between channels, patches, and sound categories. Thus, GMM offers a device-independent way to integrate music and sound into multimedia applications.

GMM preassigns the first ten channels, with channel 4 for melody, channel 8 for harmony, and channel 10 for the percussion part. In addition, all 128 patches are preassigned to specific sound categories, mostly based on traditional instruments or "classic" synthesizer sounds. For example, patch 3 is "Piano (Electric Grand)," patch 19 is "Organ (Rock)," patch 57 is "Trumpet," and so on. To obtain a detailed specification of GMM, see the list of MIDI contacts later.

General MIDI in itself is simply a naming scheme and cannot guarantee that two different devices playing, for example, "Honky tonk piano," will sound identical. The goal of GMM is similarity—not equivalence—in timbre. From a commercial standpoint, GMM makes it possible to distribute musical arrangements that sound roughly the same on whatever instrument they are played, yet still allow for MIDI-based interaction and transformation.

Continuous Control via MIDI

Some aspects of performed music change in a discrete, on/off way, like the keys on a keyboard or the pushbuttons on the front of an effects processor.

Other aspects change in a continuous way over time, for example, the overall amplitude of an instrument controlled by a footpedal, or the amount of vibrato on a synthesizer with a modulation wheel. MIDI input devices usually have both *discrete controllers* (e.g., switches or keys) and *continuous controllers* (e.g., levers, wheels, potentiometers, pedals).

The changes generated by discrete controllers result in individual messages like note-on, note-off, and program change. See chapter 14 for more on the process of tracking keyboards and other discrete controllers. For continuous changes, MIDI has three constructs: (1) control change messages, (2) a list of *defined controller numbers,* and (3) a list of *registered parameters.*

Control Change Messages

Control change messages tell a receiving device that the position of a continuous controller is changing. The input device transmits a new three-byte message every time a continuous controller changes—as fast as it can when the controller is constantly varying. A point to be aware of is that the stream of messages from a continuous controller can consume a great deal of MIDI's available transmission capacity (figure 21.11). Thus sometimes this information is allocated to a separate MIDI channel or, in multiport, multiline MIDI systems, its own MIDI line.

Defined Controllers

Defined controllers and registered parameters simplify MIDI communications by assigning standard functions to controllers found on most MIDI devices. For example, when using a defined controller such as a footpedal, any MIDI instrument that receives a message from that footpedal responds with a change in its amplitude parameter. Sometimes these preset correspondences can be reprogrammed by the user, either from the controller (making it emit another controller number) or on the receiving device (making it interpret a controller number in a different way). For example, some companies make "universal" controllers with a number of faders and buttons that can be programmed to emit whatever controller number the user chooses.

Some of MIDI's preset controller numbers are vibrato (1), left-right pan (10), volume (7), and damper (sustain) pedal (64). Since the defined controllers change from time to time, see the latest version of the MIDI specification for the current list.

```
Channel 1        Note on at pitch 60 and velocity 107
Channel 1        Pitchbend change 13569
Channel 1        Pitchbend change 10837
Channel 1        Pitchbend change  8737
Channel 1        Pitchbend change  5418
Channel 1        Pitchbend change  3905
Channel 1        Pitchbend change  2393
Channel 1        Pitchbend change   376
Channel 1        Pitchbend change     0
Channel 1        Pitchbend change  1595
Channel 1        Pitchbend change  4410
Channel 1        Pitchbend change  6427
Channel 1        Pitchbend change  7939
Channel 1        Pitchbend change  9535
Channel 1        Pitchbend change 11130
Channel 1        Pitchbend change 13358
Channel 1        Pitchbend change 15375
Channel 1        Pitchbend change 16384
Channel 1        Note off at pitch 60 and velocity 64
```

Figure 21.11 Continuous controller messages generate a stream of messages. This figure shows the pitch bend messages generated by a one-semitone pitch bend lasting one second.

Registered and Unregistered Parameters

MIDI's regime provides for *registered* and *nonregistered parameter numbers* (RPNs and NRPNs). RPNs are reserved numbers assigned to predefined voice parameters. RPNs are defined by the MIDI manufacturer committees to correspond to functions common to all instruments, just like standard controllers are defined. Typical RPNs include pitch bend sensitivity, fine-tuning, and coarse tuning. NRPNs are defined by each manufacturer and are specific to a device.

Messages with parameter numbers "call up" a voice parameter on a synthesizer that can then be edited via MIDI. Calling up a parameter is like selecting it from the front panel of the device. For example, if the fine-tuning parameter is called, it responds to changes sent via MIDI from another instrument's data slider (controller number 6). This lets musicians edit a synthesizer voice remotely from another MIDI instrument or from a computer.

Standard MIDI Files

Although the original MIDI specification standardized the language of musical control, it did not describe the file format of these data. For a number of years after the introduction of MIDI, various MIDI application programs used mutually incompatible file formats. This meant that MIDI data created with one program could not be read by another. To remedy this situation, the MIDI community adopted a 1988 extension to the MIDI specification called *Standard MIDI Files* (SMF). David Oppenheim of Opcode Systems carried out the original design work. The main use of SMF is the exchange of sequence data created on different programs.

SMF fits with the philosophy that various programs may be best for different tasks. For example, a music- and video-editing system can use one sequencer that works well in a timecode-synchronized environment. Another sequence-reading program may be best for printing music notation, while another offers algorithmic composition routines that can modify the sequence data. Although the internal representation of MIDI data is usually still unique to each program (for reasons of efficiency), most programs can convert this internal format into SMF format for exchange of MIDI data.

SMF can also serve as a common format for program intercommunication in a multitasking operating system running more than one music application. Long-distance communication of MIDI data is also aided by SMF, since musicians running different software can nevertheless exchange sequence data. (See the section on telecommunications in chapter 22.)

Standard MIDI File Format

The essential difference between SMF and other forms of bulk MIDI data, such as System Exclusive data dumps, is that the data stored in SMF are *time-stamped*. This means that every MIDI message has an associated time or position in the file, specified in *clock ticks* as a binary number between 8 and 32 bits (that is, up to 4 billion clock ticks). This number represents the time difference between the current event and the previous event. The time-stamping tells the program reading the data when the MIDI message is to be executed.

SMF files include a *header* and a variable number of tracks. The header indicates one of three types of files:

Type 0: A *single track* of MIDI information with possibly several channels of MIDI note data

Type 1: A *multitrack* MIDI file used for sequencer data

Type 2: Data for *multisequence* or *pattern-based programs* for storing a number of independent sequences or patterns in a single MIDI file. This is similar to a collection of Type 0 sequences in a single file and is not supported by all sequencers

Tempo changes or *tempo maps* are embedded within the single track of the Type 0 format (see the discussion of meta-events in the next paragraph). Type 1 files contain several simultaneous tracks that have the same instantaneous tempo and time signature. The tempo map must be stored in the first track of the file, and it stores the tempo for all subsequent tracks. Type 2 files are also called *drum machine format*. They allow for any number of independent tracks, each with their own time signature and tempo that can change over time.

In addition to note data, most MIDI sequencers also generate what SMF calls meta-events. These include specifications for tempo, time signature, key signature, sequence and track names, lyrics, cue points, score markers (rehearsal points), timing resolution, copyright notices, and sequencer-specific information. As a practical matter, not all sequencers support all meta-events.

Like the rest of the MIDI specification, the MIDI file format is biased toward metered, equal-tempered songs, where each track is played by a single instrumental voice or patch. All the data dumped into SMF are absolute; relative pitch and time specifications are not supported, and there are no conditional structures for the representation of alternative processes in interactive performance (Spiegel 1989).

The bit layouts of the SMF format are of interest to MIDI software developers. Contact the International MIDI Association for a copy of the Standard MIDI Files specification. (See the section on MIDI contacts later for the address of the IMA and other organizations.) Oostrum (1993) describes a program that translates SMF files into a humanly readable format.

Transferring Audio Data

MIDI was originally designed for the transfer of control messages between devices. With the rise of sampling technology in the mid-1980s, however, it became evident that a need existed for transferring digital audio samples as well. For example, a musician might want to transfer samples from a sampler to a computer for editing, then return the edited sound to the sampler.

Sample Dump Standard

The Sample Dump Standard (SDS), created in 1985, is a protocol for transferring sound sample files between devices via a serial MIDI cable. The format allows for 8-to 28-bit linear samples encoded at a wide range of sampling rates (up to 1 GHz!). The maximum length of a sample file, however, is 2,097,151 samples or about 42 seconds at a 48 KHz sampling rate.

Two types of SDS transfer protocols have been defined: *closed loop* and *open loop*. The closed loop protocol sends "handshaking" messages in between sample packets, where a packet is 120 bytes (40 16-bit samples). These handshaking messages confirm the transfer and thus ensure data integrity. The closed loop protocol requires a two-way connection between the sender and receiver; that is, each device should be connected to the MIDI IN of the other device. A typical closed loop transmission includes the following steps:

1. Transmit header, wait for reply

2. Send a packet

3. Transmit checksum, wait for reply

4. If this packet is the last packet number, stop, otherwise go to step 2

The open loop method omits the formalities of handshaking. Instead, the sender inserts pauses between data bytes that slow the transfer. In either the closed or open loop case, transmission is slow. A 10-second 16-bit monaural sound file at a standard sampling rate of 44.1 KHz takes over four minutes to transmit via MIDI closed loop.

Due to the slowness of MIDI serial transmission, sampler manufacturers have bypassed MIDI, implementing parallel interfaces for transfer of samples between certain devices. These efforts led to a new protocol called SCSI Musical Data Interchange (SMDI), introduced in 1991, following a design by Peavey Electronics (Isaacson 1993). Samplers equipped for SMDI can transfer samples at high speed to and from any SCSI device, including computers, disks, and other samplers. See chapter 22 for an explanation of SCSI.

MIDI Timing

Most MIDI-controlled devices (synthesizers, effects units, etc.) operate in the ever-present "now." They do not know what time it is; rather they react to devices such as sequencers and drum machines that are time-conscious. MIDI provides two ways to count time: via MIDI Clock messages, or via MIDI Timecode. The next sections describe these techniques.

MIDI Clock Messages

MIDI Clock signals are one-byte System Common messages sent by a master timekeeper (such as a sequencer) every time it advances in time by a twenty-fourth of a quarter note. Since the MIDI clock system measures time according to musical beats, the rate of timing messages depends on the tempo of the music. Clock messages sent at 60 beats per minute occur half as often as messages sent at 120 beats per minute. Specifically, the rate of messages is 16 to 100 per second for tempos from 40 to 250 beats per minute.

The MIDI clock method allows for a simple form of *autolocate* control based on a song position pointer message. (Tape recorders with an autolocate control go to preset positions at the touch of a button.) A song position pointer message says, in effect, "Go to a point that is *n* sixteenth notes from the start of the song, so we can restart from there."

MIDI Timecode

Film and video studios count time in another way. They reference events by *absolute time* signals (measured in hours, minutes, seconds, and frames) written by a *SMPTE timecode generator*. (See chapter 22 for more on SMPTE timecode.) Since matching sound effects to video and film is a common need, MIDI Timecode (MTC) was introduced in 1987 as a way of converting SMPTE timecode into MIDI messages. MTC generates absolute time signals that synchronize SMPTE devices such as video and audio tape recorders with MIDI devices. Correlating two absolute times is much easier than trying to figure out which sixteenth note in which measure at what tempo corresponds to a given absolute time.

MTC was not meant for multiple tape recorder synchronization. This type of synchronization requires accuracy down to several microseconds. With its 1–2 ms resolution, MTC is best suited for applications such as triggering sound playback from musical workstations and samplers (figure 21.12). This operates as follows. In a workstation, a soundfile manager reads incoming MTC locations and plays a sound upon receipt of a specific location from an external device. To trigger playback from a sampler, the timecode is interpreted by a sequencer program that sends a specific note-on message when it sees the appropriate timecode address. MTC can also trigger *cue events* (see the section on cue lists later).

A drawback of MTC over the old clock method is that it requires more of MIDI's bandwidth. MTC is transmitted via the full frame and quarter frame messages (see table 21.1). A full frame message takes ten bytes and includes a channel number along with the absolute time. The main purpose of this message is to cause a device to advance or return to a stipulated position. A full frame message is too large to send every new SMPTE frame.

In normal operation a transmitter sends two-byte quarter frame messages at a constant rate of 120 messages per second. Each message acts as a kind of timing pulse, but also transmits a 4-bit "nibble" defining a digit of a specific field of the current SMPTE timecode location. It takes eight messages to transmit a complete SMPTE timecode location. Due to the time-critical nature of these messages, MTC should be routed via a dedicated MIDI cable. If not, the timing is subject to "jitter," since timing data may be shoved aside to make room for other commands.

Cue Lists

In addition to absolute time-triggering, MTC has provisions for defining lists of *time-stamped* commands. Time-stamping tells the receiving device to execute a command at a specific time. In order to handle these messages, which are called *cues,* the receiving device must have a *cue list memory* and built-in scheduling software. Typical commands that a musician might want to cue include: start recording, stop recording, start sequence playback, stop sequence playback, or switch to a new reverberation effect. Parameter settings can also be sent along with the time cue.

Using cue list editor software (similar to a sequencer program), we can program a computer to tell every device in the MIDI chain when to perform a specific action. In MIDI parlance, cue list commands are called set-up messages and are classified as a type of System Exclusive message (see table 21.1).

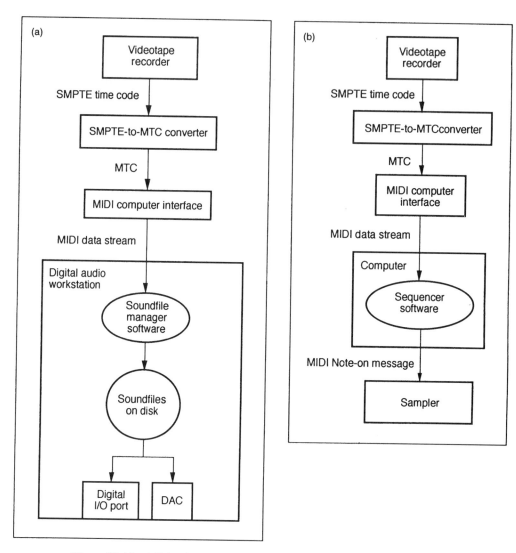

Figure 21.12   MIDI timecode triggering. (*a*) A videotape triggering sound file playback from a digital audio workstation. (*b*) A videotape triggering sound file playback from a sampler.

MIDI Machine Control and MIDI Show Control

MTC is useful for triggering sound effects and audio processing at specific times, but some situations have different requirements. MIDI Machine Control (MMC) is a 1992 extension to the MIDI protocol. MMC controls tape recorders, videocassette recorders (VCRs), and hard disk recorders via MIDI. The goal is to allow commands such as autolocate, select track, mute track, fast forward, rewind, pause, eject, loop, record, cut, copy, and paste to be carried out from a central control panel—on the screen of a MIDI sequencer or from the front panel of a music workstation. These commands can apply either to sequencer tracks stored in software or to audio tracks on connected recorders. Thus a musician does not have to switch between different user interfaces to control several machines linked by MMC.

MMC commands can be sent via the ESbus, a professional standard for remote control, or via System Exclusive messages. MMC is not a replacement for external synchronizer devices, such as those that directly control the operation of video and audio recorders. Instead, MMC communicates with the synchronizer to obtain indirect control of the recorder. In any case, the controlled machine can also send back information to the master MIDI device, such as its identity, various errors, and its current status (play mode, record mode, etc.).

A related extension to MIDI is MIDI Show Control (MSC). MSC was created for control of lighting systems and theatrical productions in general. Instead of counting time in measure numbers or SMPTE timecodes, theatrical productions represent time in terms of *scenes* and *cues* that can happen at variable times, depending on the pace of the performance. MSC is like a random-access step-time sequencer that plays back both individual events and choreographed lighting sequences at the push of a button. For details on MMC and MSC, contact the International MIDI Association.

MIDI Accessories

MIDI accessories or "black boxes" are essential components in a professional MIDI studio. They serve a variety of functions, primarily having to do with device interconnection and data routing within a MIDI setup. Table 21.3 lists MIDI accessories and briefly describes their functions. Figure 21.13 depicts three of the most common functions, an A/B switcher, a merger, and a THRU box.

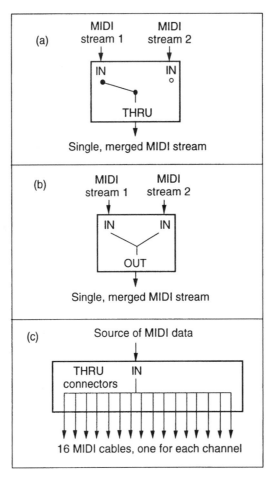

Figure 21.13 MIDI accessories. (*a*) A/B switcher selects between one of two input streams. (*b*) Merger combines two MIDI input streams into one stream. (*c*) MIDI THRU box, splitter, or patch bay distributes one input to several outputs.

Another useful accessory is software, not hardware. A MIDI data analysis program can be a valuable diagnostic tool (figure 21.14). Such a program lets users examine the MIDI data flow; switchable filters let them see only the type of message they are looking for.

Limitations of MIDI

The MIDI specification is a popular and inexpensive protocol, but it was not designed to solve all problems of intercommunication and representation in music. Anyone who works with MIDI should be aware of its shortcomings as well as its capabilities. These limitations can be grouped into

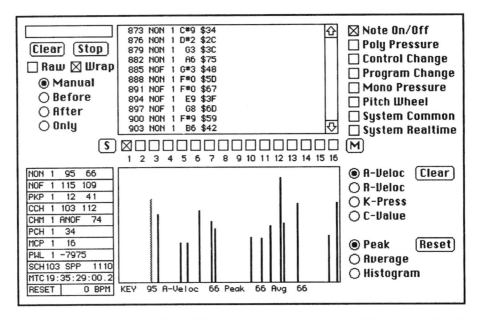

Figure 21.14 Screen of a MIDI data analysis program, Midiscope, by Ralph Muha of Kurzweil Music Systems. Notice the setting of the filter buttons at the top right, where only the Note On/Off item is checked. This means that only note-on and note-off messages are selected for viewing. The note messages appear in the Trace Buffer display at the top center. The first column is an index corresponding to the number of bytes received. The next column shows the note messages, symbolically encoded as NON (note-on) and NOF (not-off), followed by the incoming channel number (1 in all cases). Following the channel is the pitch of the note, again symbollically encoded with the pitch-class (e.g., C#) and the octave (9). The final column displays the release or attack velocity, encoded in hexidecimal format. The histogram display at the bottom shows note velocities. The numerical data in the bottom right lists various details about the most recent message received.

three categories: bandwidth limitations, network routing limitations, and music representation limitations. For further reading on this subject see Loy (1985c) and Moore (1988). See De Poli, Piccialli, and Roads (1991), Pope (1991a), and Todd and Loy (1991) for articles on alternative music representations.

Bandwidth Limitations

The amount of control data that can be transmitted over a MIDI cable is limited to 31,250 bits per second (3125 10-bit words). It takes 320 msec to transmit one word, or 960 msec for a three-word message. With sixteen channels in use, the message rate per channel is held to about 50 to 150 messages per second, depending on the size of the message and the speed of

Table 21.3   MIDI Accessories

A/B switcher

Selects between two MIDI sources to some number of THRU connections (figure 21.13a). The main purpose is to control signal routing with a pushbutton, eliminating manual cable repatching.

Merger

Merges more than one IN stream of MIDI data into a single stream (figure 21.13b). One of the IN signal's clock messages are filtered out. This is necessary to prevent the merger of conflicting clock messages. The merger can also make possible such configurations as the recording of a jam session from two sources, or patch editing from both a software program and a physical instrument controller. A merger causes a small delay, and when there is too much data to merge they may filter the data.

Patch bay

Interconnects *N* inputs with *M* outputs by means of push-button controls. Eliminates delays and distortion caused by daisy-chaining. Some of these can be programmed to alter the data passing through them as well.

Filter

Deletes certain types of messages from the MIDI stream.

Note separator or Mapper

Converts note messages coming from a non-split (single channel) keyboard into "split" messages distributed over several MIDI channels. Can also be used to "remap" Program Change messages so that they correspond to specific effects units and sound generators.

Arpeggiator

Arpeggiates (embellishes), transposes, doubles, inverts the pitch or velocity of a note-on message

THRU box or Splitter

Routes a single input channel to multiple THRU connections (figure 21.13c), thus avoiding the problems of daisy-chaining (delays and signal degradation). Can also be realized with a MIDI patchbay.

MIDI analysis program

Displays the state of a MIDI connection and indicates the messages being transmitted. Can be used as a test program for devices to show the range of outputs they generate, which controller numbers are being used, etc.

SMPTE-to-MIDI TimeCode Converter

Converts SMPTE timecode to MIDI Time Code.

---

the receiving device. This is not fast enough to support certain performance situations.

MIDI's data rate limits the number of voices, their pitch and amplitude fluctuations, and ultimately the complexity of the musical texture. The protocol was designed to record the keyboard performances of one to four human keyboard players without much continuous controller manipulation.

The bandwidth of MIDI can be overwhelmed by a single virtuoso if heavy use is made of continuous controllers such as pitch bend and vibrato wheels, footpedals, and breath controllers (Abbott 1984a; Moore 1988). This is because continuous controllers send out a continual stream of messages for as long as they are activated. As Moore (1988) explains, even a simple effect such as transmitting pitch bend messages to create a 10 Hz vibrato in a single voice consumes nearly the entire bandwidth of MIDI! Some sequencers provide an option to "thin" continuous controller data (i.e., delete a percentage of the messages), but this turns a smooth control function into a jagged stepped function.

Data clogging (referred to as "MIDI choke") can also occur in playback of a moderately complex score. Gaps and timing errors (manifesting as jerkiness or sluggishness) may be evident. Although in theory MIDI permits sixteen voices per cable, individual voices of a chord do not sound at the same time. This is caused by the serial nature of MIDI messages (every note-on message takes about 1 ms to transmit). Since the ear is very sensitive to the transients of note attacks, a time-smeared MIDI chord may sound "flabby" and is heard as an arpeggio in the worst case (i.e., a sixteen-note chord sent over all sixteen channels). Apologists for MIDI have suggested that note onset delays add "life" to certain musical scores. But the introduction of such delays should be a controllable musical parameter that depends on musical context rather than an arbitrary technical limitation.

Microprocessor Delays

One aspect of delay in MIDI systems is not directly related to MIDI, per se. Many devices introduce a delay of their own caused by the slowness of their internal microprocessor. For example, tests show that the response of a single oscillator to a note-on message in Omni mode may take as long as 7 ms in some synthesizers (Marans 1991). Eight "simultaneous" note-on messages sent to a multitimbral synthesizer (one oscillator per timbre) in Multi mode may take as long as 21 ms to be decoded. (Ideally it should take 8 ms, the time it takes for MIDI to transmit the eight note-on messages.) The delays increase dramatically when more oscillators per voice are used, as they often are. Such delays are a fact of life in MIDI setups.

Interconnection Limitations

The MIDI interface specifies that each direction of communication requires a separate cable. This unidirectional bias results in a web of cables. Another factor adding to the cable mess is that more and more multichannel devices have multiple MIDI ports in an effort to work around the bandwidth problems inherent in a single cable. Daisy chaining, which was designed to cut down on the number of MIDI cables, has strict practical limitations due to pulse-smearing in MIDI THRU connections.

These aspects of MIDI's design make a MIDI patch bay and other accessory boxes a necessity in a professional studio. Part of the original argument for MIDI in 1983 as against a more sophisticated network approach was its low cost. And the manufacturing cost is very low for the MIDI hardware within a single device. But present-day MIDI systems require so many cables and accessory boxes that the price of interconnecting a studio is no longer a trivial expense. Meanwhile, high-speed network technology has become much cheaper.

Music Representation Limitations

A fundamental constraint of the MIDI specification is the concept of music embodied in its design. It was conceived to capture a musical dialect that is strongly biased toward popular songs (metered, in equal temperament) as played on a musical keyboard. Digital synthesis and processing can take music far beyond this dialect, but not easily via MIDI.

Part of the problem is MIDI's lack of representation of timbre. Even basic aspects of timbre, such as the overall amplitude envelope of a note, have no standard representation. More generally, MIDI has no explicit control over the parameter envelopes used by the device that creates or plays back the MIDI note messages. This is one of the reasons for the "canned" quality of many MIDI compositions in which every note has the exact same timbre and envelope.

MIDI note messages are a device-independent score representation. This makes generic music software easier to develop, but it also means that any MIDI note list is incomplete—with no instructions as to orchestration. The same message sent to two different devices may produce a completely different sound. One device may emit a thud of a bass drum, while another emits a high-pitched squeal from a simulated guitar. The channel mechanism, which is MIDI's method of separating individual lines of polyphony, says nothing about what instruments are assigned to those channels. The General MIDI mode (table 21.2) has an arbitrary channel-to-instrument map, but this was designed for home entertainment and not for professional musicians. Even if General MIDI could guarantee identical timbres between devices (and it cannot), it would still represent only a tiny fraction of the timbres possible in computer music.

MIDI's concept of pitch is weak. It was originally designed for equal-tempered pitches. It is possible to "bend" (detune) a pitch, but the MIDI Pitch Bend message is a global operation applying to all notes on a channel. This inherent limitation sabotages the musical flexibility of MIDI devices. One of the justifications for computer music is the ability to go beyond the pitch, timing, and timbral limitations of traditional instruments. Answering these limitations, proposals to change MIDI's representation of pitch have circulated among the MIDI community (Scholz 1991).

Speeding up MIDI Communications

In simple MIDI setups and within certain limits of musical style and performance, the MIDI protocol is transparent. In applications such as patch editing, for example, the bandwidth of MIDI is not usually a major issue. But beyond these cases, the bandwidth limitations of MIDI must be confronted. For professional musicians, it is important to try to work with the standard while maximizing its performance.

The main strategy to circumvent the speed limitations of MIDI is to *multiplex* the data stream. To multiplex means to divide the data stream into several paths that operate simultaneously. This division can be done in at least five ways.

1. *Send each channel of MIDI messages via a separate MIDI cable.* This strategy is aided by devices with multiple OUT ports and accessory devices with multiple THRU connectors such as MIDI THRU boxes and patch bays (see figure 21.13c).

2. *Use a multiport MIDI computer interface to operate several discrete 16-channel MIDI lines in parallel.* Today's computers can handle many times the bandwidth of a single MIDI line. Taking advantage of this, several companies offer multiport MIDI interfaces that support several independent MIDI lines. These products work with software that supports multiple-line addressing.

3. *Synchronize several MIDI systems running in parallel by means of SMPTE timecode and SMPTE-to-MTC conversion.* (See chapter 22 for more on SMPTE timecode.)

4. *Use the bandwidth of fiber optic cables to transmit many serial data streams concurrently* (as in the the MidiTap system developed by the Lone Wolf company). The serial data streams adhere to standard protocols such as MIDI, AES/EBU digital audio, SMPTE timecode, and other digital data formats.

5. *Integrate MIDI communications within a high-speed local-area-network (LAN) or a multimedia communications protocol.* When MIDI was introduced in 1983, a LAN interface board for a small computer cost several thousand dollars. In recent years, the price and availability of LAN circuits has declined dramatically, and they are now standard in many computers. Some LAN circuits cost no more than a MIDI computer interface, yet run several hundred times faster.

In a LAN-to-MIDI scheme, a master computer communicates at high speed over the LAN to the MIDI controllers (figure 21.15). Each MIDI controller, in turn, communicates with a synthesizer via a dedicated MIDI link. A problem with certain LAN protocols is that the transmission rate may be dependent on the amount of traffic on the LAN, that is, how many devices are trying to transmit at the same time. "Collisions" between several messages can delay communications.

Experts also make use of special optimizations built into specific MIDI devices when these are available. An example might be a synthesizer that has a global control scheme for loudness that affects all channels even when a message is sent on just one channel.

Writing MIDI Music Software

MIDI software falls into two broad categories: (1) the internal software running on the microprocessor within every MIDI device, (2) music applications running on a computer that is connected to other MIDI devices. The first category consists of an operating system written by the manufacturer of a synthesizer or a real-time signal processor. The details of this program are dependent on the specific hardware employed, so we will not discuss it further here. The rest of this section looks at music applications that musicians are more likely to tackle. Common MIDI applications fall into seven main categories, summarized in table 21.4. Chapter 15 discusses several types of MIDI performance programs, including sequencers.

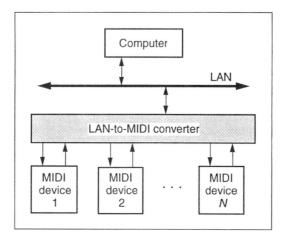

Figure 21.15   Local-area-network/MIDI scheme. A master computer communicates with a set of MIDI devices over a LAN by means of a LAN-to-MIDI converter device.

Overview of MIDI Programs

The organization of most MIDI programs is illustrated in figure 21.16. Graphical and textual interaction is handled by an *event-driven* "front-end" module. By event-driven we mean an interface that presents a number of options to the user at all times. When the user makes a selection, this generates a software event that must be decoded and acted upon. The selection can include the choice of a menu item, the push of a graphical button, or the movement of a graphical slider. Input to the program can also come via the MIDI interface, from an input device such as a musical keyboard (see chapter 14).

MIDI data are grouped into bytes by the MIDI interface and passed to the *MIDI device driver*. This is the code that manages the MIDI input and output ports on the computer. All programs that wish to transmit or receive MIDI data must communicate with the device driver. Some applications provide their own device driver, while others applications leave it to the computer's operating system to provide this set of services. To the programmer, the device driver provides a number of services, such as enabling the MIDI interface, creating input and output buffers, getting a byte from the buffer, sending a byte to the buffer, getting a message, sending a message, filtering data from the input buffer, and clearing the buffers.

The MIDI-specific parts of the program consist of three modules: input, processing, and output. The input stage handles incoming MIDI data by grouping the bit stream into messages. It hands off the decoded messages to

Table 21.4   MIDI application programs and the types of messages they handle

Sequencers

Record, edit, and playback most types of messages, but especially Channel Voice messages concerning note events. Some sequencers handle synchronization chores via MIDI Time Code (MTC) messages.

Patch editors/librarians

Receive and transmit System Exclusive messages from a MIDI device's program and data memories. The data can be edited on the computer screen and new MIDI System Exclusive messages are transfered back to the MIDI device to alter its patch or voicing.

Score editors and notation printers

Maintain an internal data structure that relates a graphic representation to a sequence of MIDI messages, in particular note messages.

Algorithmic composition programs

Generate MIDI sequence data (primarily Channel Voice messages), sometimes starting from note data received via an input device such as a clavier.

Interactive performance software

Receive, modify, and transmit MIDI sequence data in interaction with a human performer.

Sample editors and mixers-

Receive data in the MIDI Sample Dump (MSD) format or a proprietary format, allow the user to edit it, and transmit either MSD or a proprietary format back to the sampler. Some systems allow sample playback in synchrony with specific frames of SMPTE time code that has been translated into MIDI Time Code messages.

Music education programs

Receive and transmit MIDI sequence data; interactive practice and drill with the student, keep track of student progress.

the processing stage for decoding and action. The processing stage interprets the parsed messages. The processing could be, for example, a MIDI sequencer that stores the data in one of its tracks. The output stage takes data from the processor stage and sends it to other MIDI devices, as in a "play" operation of a sequencer or algorithmic composition program.

MIDI Programming Languages

MIDI applications can be written in any language. But the programmer who uses a language with extensions and function libraries that support a MIDI device driver has a head start. Special versions of the languages

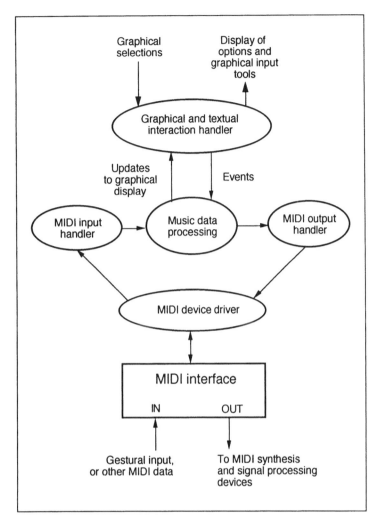

Figure 21.16 Overview of a MIDI program. See the text for a description.

Lisp, C, Forth, Basic, Logo, and Pascal provide a range of MIDI services through routines that access a MIDI device driver (De Furia and Scacciaferro 1988; Conger 1988, 1989; Boynton, et al. 1986; Rahn 1990; Greenberg 1988).

At a higher level, languages like HMSL (Polansky, Rosenboom, and Burk 1987; Polansky et al. 1988), Formula (Andersen and Kuivila 1986), MoxC (Dannenberg 1986), and the CMU MIDI Toolkit (Dannenberg 1986; *Computer Music Journal* 1994) assist with event scheduling and provide timing routines, among other features. A myriad of algorithmic composition languages can generate score files that are compatible with MIDI, for playback by a sequencer. See chapter 17 for more on these languages.

Various interactive toolkits or "visual programming languages" also support MIDI. Each icon represents a procedure that can manipulate a MIDI data stream. The Max program, for example, offers an abstraction facility whereby a network of icons and cables can be compressed into a single, high-level icon (Puckette and Zicarelli 1990; see chapter 15 for more on Max).

MIDI Contacts

Several organizations guide the development of MIDI and distribute documentation and other information. The International MIDI Association (IMA) is a contact for users of MIDI systems and software. Their address is: International MIDI Association, 5316 West 57th Street, Los Angeles, California 90056. Extensions to the MIDI protocol are guided through the MIDI Manufacturers Association (MMA), which can also be reached through the IMA. For information on the SMPTE timecode standard, contact the Society of Motion Picture and Television Engineers, 595 West Hartsdale Avenue, White Plains, New York 10607.

Conclusion

The simple design and inexpensive hardware requirements of MIDI have led to its universal acceptance in the world of commercial music. MIDI has proven beneficial in many musical applications, from education to music production for television and film, and it has opened up an entirely new world of interactive performance possibilities. A diverse electronic music industry has grown up as a side effect of MIDI's success. The presence of a standard interface to synthesizers has led to a proliferation of new musical input devices—the physical instruments manipulated by performers.

MIDI is a dynamic specification. Since it was first proposed in 1983 it has undergone continuous amendment. Extensions to the original MIDI standard have made possible sample transfer (via the Sample Dump Standard), synchronization with SMPTE devices (via MIDI Timecode), interchange of MIDI files (via the Standard MIDI File definition), standardized parameter control, and a preset configuration. But there has always been an awareness of fundamental limitations in MIDI. At some point the amendments will stop, and a new standard will emerge.

22   *System Interconnections*

AC Power Lines

Analog Audio Cables

> **Connectors**
> **Balanced versus Unbalanced**
> **Cable Distance**

Patch Bays

> **Analog Patch Bays**
> **Hybrid Patch Bays**
> **Digital Patch Bays**

Serial Electronic Lines

MIDI Cables

Digital Audio Links

> **Transmission Formats versus File Formats**

Fiber-optic Cables

Synchronization Links

        MIDI Synchronization Links
        Command Synchronization
        Clock Synchronization
        MIDI Time Code Synchronization
        Cue List Synchronization
        SMPTE Synchronization Links
        Digital Audio Synchronization Links

Parallel Ports and Buses

        Asynchronous versus Synchronous Buses
        Interrupt Signals

Direct Memory Access Controllers and Shared Memories

Networks

Telecommunications

Conclusion

Every music system owner faces the issue of device interconnection. New equipment bristles with connectors of all sorts and sizes. Compatibility between devices is incomplete, leading to the purchase of special hardware interfaces and conversion software. Familiarity with device interconnection schemes is a practical necessity. This chapter introduces these concepts and their implications in a music system. To some extent, the chapter builds on chapter 20, which explains the communications paths of *digital signal processors* (DSPs) inside synthesizers, samplers, mixers, and effects boxes. Chapter 21 explains the MIDI specification and is a recommended prerequisite to the section on MIDI in this chapter.

We first look at the basic properties of AC power lines and analog audio cables. Then we survey the various types of digital communication channels:

Serial lines (including the MIDI protocol)

Digital audio links

Synchronization links

Parallel ports and buses

Direct memory access controllers and shared memories

Networks and telecommunications

AC Power Lines

One of the major troublespots in an audio system can be the *alternating current* (AC) power system. Diagnosing and solving power-line and grounding problems is an acquired skill. Fortunately for the studio owner, it is usually addressed only when setting up the studio. These problems are an ongoing issue for the touring musician. In this section we describe some of the most common AC power problems and present measures to alleviate them.

As a general rule, it is helpful to put all audio and computer equipment on an AC power line that is separate from electrical equipment such as light dimmers, air conditioners, and refrigerators. This helps avoid *glitches* (transient peaks) in the line voltage caused by high-power switches in these devices. The dedicated line should have a ground signal coming from the cleanest possible source. The ground signal is an electrical reference point for "no electrical charge." If it is contaminated by electrical noise of any kind this enters into all devices connected to the ground signal and may leak into audio signals. In professional studios the ground cable is often connected to a metal pipe pounded into the earth, which is considered to be electrically neutral.

A major source of audio interference is power-line-related signals leaching into audio signals. AC power lines can induce noise into analog audio cables, so it is preferable to separate the two. In the best case, one can use steel conduits to separate these cables or at least not run the power and audio cables side by side for large distances. Another problem results from the voltage differences that exist between different equipment chassis. These differences can stem from stray magnetic fields, inconsistent grounding, power supply leakage, or radio frequency interference, among other things. One way to address the problem is to connect all equipment in a star configuration to a central AC power line with a central ground, rather than "daisy chaining" AC power and ground through several devices. (Daisy chaining means interconnecting devices serially from one device to the next, and so on.)

When interference in device *A* is caused by magnetic leakage from an internal power transformer in device *B,* moving *A* to a different location, even a meter away, may help. If not, it may be necessary to add extra shielding (copper or steel) within or around the offending device.

A *power-line conditioner* addresses two other sources of noise: radio frequency (RF) interference and electrical spikes. The symptoms of RF interference are an increase in high-frequency noise and the presence of audible program material (talking or music) leaking into another signal. As mentioned, glitches or spikes can emanate from switches in air conditioners, refrigerators, light dimmers, and from electrostatic discharges in the atmosphere (lightning). Hence, power line conditioners are recommended even in small studios, especially those without a separate electrical service for the studio. Power line conditioners typically contain high-frequency filters that eliminate RF interference and surge suppressors that attenuate spikes. A fuse-equipped power-line conditioner is also a cheap insurance policy against the failure of circuit breakers in a building's electrical system, which, as we can attest from experience, does occur.

Another, more expensive device called a *power regulator* goes beyond line filtering to maintain the AC voltage within narrow limits. This is useful because the voltage level emanating from a wall socket can vary a great deal, causing anomalous behavior in electrical equipment. Voltage drops are especially a problem on days when power use is heavy, such as hot summer days.

Analog Audio Cables

Even an "all-digital" studio benefits from clean analog signals when it is time to record through an analog-to-digital converter or to listen through an analog amplifier and loudspeakers. Inattention to analog interconnections can lead to crosstalk (one channel's signal leaking into another), hum, buzz, clicks, RF interference, and generally "colored" sound quality. After a period of emotional debate during the 1980s, it is now well established—through listening trials and scientific cable analysis—that high-quality cables and interconnections are essential to the transmission of transparent analog signals (Greenspun and Klotz 1988; Newell 1991; F. Davis 1991). This fact alone does not resolve all choice of cable selection, since there are competing hypotheses as to which type of cable is "best." Theory and experience indicate that the choice of cable, like every other audio component, involves tradeoffs, and that certain types of cable work best with particular types of audio components. (See F. Davis 1991 for a scientific comparison of several cables.)

Connectors

The dominant types of cable connectors used in audio studios are the standard *phono* (or RCA) connectors used in consumer audio products, quarter-inch *phone* connectors (first used by the telephone company) used on instruments like electric guitars and guitar amplifiers but also on synthesizers, the *TT* or *bantam* miniature phone-type connectors used in patch bays, and the three-pin and five-pin *XLR* connectors used in professional devices. A standard connection protocol for XLR connectors was finally defined in 1992, after decades of conflicting practices (Audio Engineering Society 1992c).

Balanced versus Unbalanced

Analog interconnections can be either *balanced* or *unbalanced*. In a balanced line, two insulated wires carry the signal voltage, but one of the wires carries a 180-degree phase-inverted version (inverted by the transmitting amplifier) (figure 22.1). Neither of the two signal lines is tied to ground. A *shield* for deflecting outside signals is connected to ground and wraps around both signal wires. The circuit to which the cable attaches at both ends passes *differential signals,* meaning that there must be a difference in voltage between the two conductors for current to flow. Since one signal is

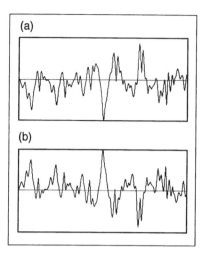

Figure 22.1   View of signals in alternate wires of a balanced cable. (*a*) Original signal. (*b*) Phase-inverted signal.

180 degrees out of phase, there is always a voltage difference between the two signals. Hence the audio signal will always pass through the differential input stage. Such a circuit exhibits the property of *common mode rejection,* which is the key to the noise immunity of balanced lines. If outside interferences leak through the shield they inevitably contaminate both conductors. Hence this "common mode" signal is rejected by the input circuit.

In an unbalanced line, one bundle of wires carries the signal, surrounded by a shield that is grounded. The main problem with an unbalanced line is that it is susceptible to induced noises and signal losses. These potential problems may be insignificant for short cable runs (e.g., less than two meters). But over long lengths of cable the sources of contamination add up. In general, balanced lines are preferable because they reject induced noise and voltage differences caused by inconsistently grounded equipment.

For optimal quality, audio equipment should have high-impedance (~ 10 KOhm) balanced inputs and low-impedance (~ 60 Ohm) balanced outputs. If the equipment does not meet these requirements, as is the case with most consumer audio products, for example, one can purchase interface boxes that provide unbalanced-to-balanced conversion. These boxes also convert between the different voltage levels expected by consumer and professional equipment.

Cable Distance

Distance affects the bandwidth of analog cables. Experiments show that amplifier-to-loudspeaker cable distances greater than three meters begin to degrade audio quality (Newell 1991). For very long cable runs, the capacitance in the cable acts as a lowpass filter, attenuating high frequencies. F. Davis (1991), however, showed that for shorter cable distances (less than three meters) capacitance is irrelevant to audio quality (i.e., high-frequency loss is negligible). At distances less than three meters, the most important property in cables is low inductance for maintaining a constant voltage level across all frequencies and loads. Multistrand and ribbon cables in which each wire is separately insulated exhibit this property.

In a concert situation, it is sometimes possible to substitute a radio transmitter-receiver system in place of an audio cable. This is frequently done in live performance and television broadcasts, where it has the advantage of unencumbering the performer and allowing greater distances between the performer and the equipment. Although convenient, good radio-transmitter systems are much more expensive than cables. In any case they cannot provide the clarity that a high-quality cable delivers.

Patch Bays

Different audio setups require the sound engineer to disconnect the cables of an existing configuration and reconnect them into the desired configuration. When a system reaches a certain level of complexity, this project can be difficult and time-consuming. A *patch bay,* which keeps all the interconnection points in a central location with a standard connection scheme, greatly simplifies this task. The term "patch bay" derives from the *patch cords* used to connect the inputs and outputs of studio devices. We can distinguish three types of patch bays, depending on their technology: analog, hybrid, and digital.

Analog Patch Bays

The traditional analog patch bay is a rack-mountable panel that contains a *jack* (hole) corresponding to the analog input and output of every component or group of wires in the studio. Patch bays can be balanced or unbalanced. A balanced patch bay is recommended due to its common mode rejection characteristics.

In a patch bay, one jack is said to be *normalled* to another if the components connected to the two jacks are connected to each other even when there is no plug inserted in either jack. The purpose of breaking a normalled connection is to reconfigure the interconnection scheme with patch cords.

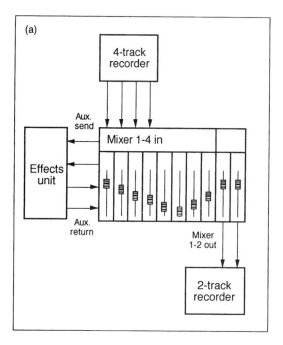
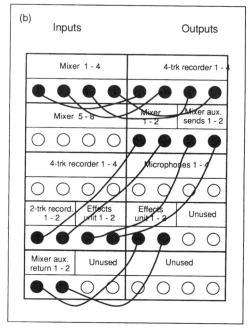

Figure 22.2   Two views of a patch for four-track to two-track remixing with effects. (*a*) Logical device view. (*b*) Patch bay view. The left side of the patch bay is allocated to input jacks, and the right side is allocated to output jacks.

Figure 22.2 shows two views of a patch for remixing a piece on a four-track recorder down to two tracks, with two channels of effects.

A special part of a patch bay is the *mult* (multiplexing) section. A mult is a set of interconnected jacks that send one input to several outputs or vice versa (figure 22.3).

Hybrid Patch Bays

An analog patch bay is a passive system consisting of jacks and interconnection wires; patch cords are plugged and unplugged by hand. A patch bay in which the interconnections are set by electronic switches controlled from a digital source is called a *hybrid patch bay*. It is called hybrid because the audio signals remain in the analog domain, but the control is digital (typically MIDI).

Such a patch bay can distribute a single analog source to *n* destinations, where *n* is set by the manufacturer. In a hybrid patch bay, the incoming analog signals pass through additional circuitry, so it is important that this circuitry be very clean. The main advantage of a digitally controlled patch

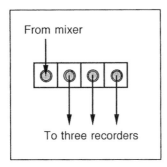

From mixer

To three recorders

Figure 22.3   A four-way mult can take in one input (in this case a channel from a mixer) and send it to four outputs (in this case three different recorders).

bay is that it takes less than a second to repatch the entire system, since patch configurations can be recalled from memory.

Digital Patch Bays

For a one-to-one interconnection, digital audio signals in the AES/EBU balanced format can be patched in a regular (analog) balanced patch bay. A more sophisticated digital patch bay is usually referred to as a *digital audio switching* or *routing matrix*. The core of a digital audio switcher is a *time-domain multiplexer* (TDM) circuit that can route a given input data stream to any number of output addresses (figure 22.4). In a TDM system, each sample period is divided into a number of time slots equal to the number of possible inputs. The inputs load the time slots in a regular sequence, and the outputs read a particular time slot as dictated by the control circuitry. This kind of TDM system requires that all sources are synchronized to the same sample clock and that their sampling rates are all the same. (See the section later on synchronization links.)

Serial Electronic lines

A serial line interface transmits one bit at a time between a host computer and a peripheral device. Most serial lines are electrically compatible with the standard established by the Institute of Electrical and Electronic Engineers (IEEE). The IEEE's RS-232-C is a common serial line standard. (Copies of this standard can be purchased from the Electronic Industries Association, 2001 Eye Street, N.W., Washington, D.C. 20006. See McNamara 1984 for a synopsis of RS-232-C.) Newer standards for serial data transmission called RS-422 and RS-423 are also widely used. Their main advantage is

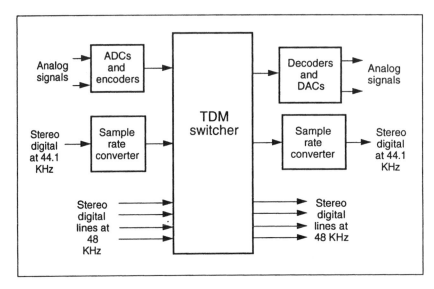

Figure 22.4   Digital patch bay using time-domain multiplexing. The TDM switcher can route an input to many outputs. We assume that before a signal enters the TDM switcher, it must be running at 48 KHz. Analog inputs are converterd to digital, while digital signals that are not at the sampling rate of the TDM must be resampled.

speed. A plain RS-232C line transfers data at rates up to about 20 Kbits per second, while RS-422 allows much higher transmission speeds.

MIDI Cables

This section serves as a brief review of the material in chapter 21, with an emphasis on the physical properties and channel capacity of MIDI cables. The Musical Instrument Digital Interface (MIDI) version 1.0 is a serial line interface protocol designed and supported by musical instrument manufacturers (IMA 1983). MIDI was designed to enable synthesizers, sequencers, computers, and keyboards to be interconnected via a standard interface. This takes the form of cables attached to five-pin DIN connectors that link each MIDI device. (DIN is the acronym of a German standards organization.) The wiring of MIDI connectors is not compatible with regular audio DIN standards.

MIDI transmissions operate at a rate of 31.25 Kbits per second, asynchronous. A MIDI signal consists of a start bit, an 8-bit data byte, and a stop bit in a single transmission word. A MIDI *message* is defined as one or more words, depending on the type of message being sent.

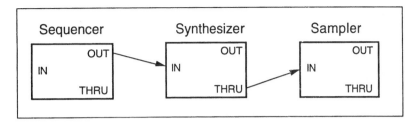

Figure 22.5 MIDI daisy chaining by means of a THRU port on the synthesizer. The synthesizer may respond to messages sent to several MIDI channels while the sampler responds to the same or other channels independently.

A MIDI cable communicates performance control information such as the onset time of key depressions (notes), their velocity (amplitude), and program changes (or patch changes) initiated by the musician. MIDI is not normally used to transmit envelopes or waveforms to a synthesizer. It can transmit monaural sound files to a sampler, but only in non-real time at a very slow rate.

Each MIDI-equipped device contains a MIDI port. This port consists of at least three jacks: IN, OUT, and THRU. The IN jack receives MIDI data. For example, when MIDI note data are sent via a MIDI cable to the IN jack of a synthesizer, the synthesizer plays as if someone were playing its clavier. An OUT jack on a device transmits MIDI messages from it, while a THRU jack allows the MIDI code coming into the IN port to be passed to a third MIDI device more or less transparently. The THRU port makes it possible to interconnect several devices in a *daisy chain* (figure 22.5). Some devices have multiple IN or OUT jacks to accomodate flexible chaining.

A MIDI chain is unidirectional. This means that if we want to be able to both record and play back using a sequencer and a synthesizer, it takes one cable to send data from the synthesizer to the sequencer and another cable to send stored data from the sequencer to the synthesizer.

The physical length of a MIDI cable should not exceed 6.6 meters (20 feet), since transmission losses in the cable start to cause data errors. No more than three devices can be daisy chained due to *pulse smearing* that accumulates as the signal passes along the chain (Cooper 1985; see also chapter 21).

A given MIDI chain or line has 16 *channels* that can address 16 logical devices. These logical devices may be either separate physical devices or just different voices in a multitimbral synthesizer. Many studios run several MIDI lines to obtain more channels. Since each two-way link requires two cables, this can lead to a spaghetti of MIDI cables that is awkward to repatch. Since repatching is often necessary, an essential component of a

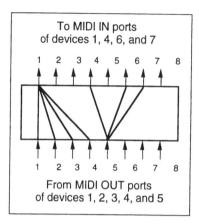

Figure 22.6 MIDI patch bay. This example shows the merging of incoming data (in this case, from devices 1, 2, 3, and 4), and routing it to a single MIDI port. It is also taking data from a single device (device 5) and sending it to the IN port of several other devices (4, 6, and 7 in the figure).

MIDI studio is a *MIDI patch bay*, shown in figure 22.6. Under pushbutton control, a MIDI patch bay routes a given MIDI data stream to one or more devices. Since every device is directly linked to the patch bay, there is no daisy chaining.

The MIDI patch bay routes streams of MIDI data from device to device; the numbered inputs and outputs on the MIDI patch bay correspond to different devices and are not the same as MIDI channels. Other *MIDI accessory boxes* can map data on one channel to another channel, or filter certain data out of the MIDI stream altogether (see chapter 21).

Digital Audio Links

Digital audio links transmit sound samples between computers, tape recorders, and effects units. Since the samples remain in the digital domain, there are no distortions introduced by digital-to-analog or analog-to-digital conversion. If all goes well, the copy sent to the receiving device is a perfect clone of the original.

Various digital audio transmission formats coexist, some public and some proprietary. Table 22.1 summarizes their main features. For more details on digital audio formats in general, see, for example, Pohlmann (1989a) and Lambert (1990).

One important distinction between transmission formats is whether they are *self-clocking*. In a self-clocking format such as IEC 958, clock data are sent along with the audio data. Since the sample rate clocks of any two

Table 22.1   Digital audio transmission formats

EIAJ or PCM-F1

One of the first interconnection schemes, derived from the bus format of the Sony PCM-F1 and 701 digital audio processors. Several companies developed interface units that modified the F1 and 701 to produce electrically isolated versions of the primary input and output bitstreams from the ADCs and DACs of these units.

AES/EBU

Serial two-channel format created by the Audio Engineering Society and the European Broadcast Union; formally known as AES3-1992 or ANSI S4.40-1992 (Finger 1992; Audio Engineering Society 1992a). Uses single *twisted-pair* cable up to 100 meters at a bit rate of 3.072 MHz for 48 KHz audio samples. (Twisted-pair cable consists of two wires that are individually insulated and then twisted together and covered with an insulation jacket. It is inexpensive but may be susceptible to noise interference over long cable runs.) Left and right channels are multiplexed, self-clocking, and self-synchronizing at 32, 44.1, or 48 KHz. Other frequencies are possible. As a self-clocking format, the clock signal is contained within the digital audio stream, which simplifies interconnection since there is no need to synchronize with a master clock, as the SDIF-2 format must. (The AES synchronization clock extension to AES/EBU makes it non-self-clocking in applications that required overall synchronization.) One *frame* is made up of two *subframes* corresponding to the left and right channels. Each subframe is 32 bits, with audio data allotted 24 bits of this, represented in two's complement form. The other 8 bits are for synchronization, error flag, user bit, audio channel status, and subframe parity. The standard format for text and other user data is described by the AES18-1992 standard (Audio Engineering Society 1992b). A block is 192 frames, and a full channel status block is formed from the 192 channel status bits within the block. The channel status block indicates emphasis, sampling frequency, mono/stereo, time of day, and other conditions. The transmission circuit is a differential source. The receiver should be balanced electronic or optical, and the connector can be either XLR or D-type (9-pin). For practical aspects of AES/EBU circuits see Kahrs (1991) and Finger (1992).

IEC 958 and S/PDIF

The International Electrotechnical Commission (IEC), based in Geneva, Switzerland, derives its 958 standard from the AES/EBU format. There are two IEC 958 standards, one "consumer" and one "professional," but it is the former that is usually referred to. IEC 958 is for all practical purposes compatible with the Sony/Philips Digital Interface Format or S/PDIF. IEC-958 is intended for consumer equipment such as compact disc players and DAT (digital audio tape) recorders. Like the AES/EBU interface, IEC 958 is self-clocking. The main differences between the AES/EBU standard and IEC 958 have to do with their handling of channel status and user bits. Also, the transmission format is different depending on the category of the transmitting device (CD player, DAT player, PCM processor, etc.) For example, CD audio subframes are 16 bits in size, while DAT subframes use a 24-bit size. IEC 958 connectors are unbalanced RCA (phono) jacks or fiber optic connectors. An extension to the standard defines the Serial Copy Management System (SCMS) implemented on consumer DAT recorders.

Table 22.1 (cont.)

SDIF-2

SDIF-2 (Sony Digital Interface Format) is a serial interface developed by Sony and is used to interconnect with professional audio products, notably the Sony Compact Disc Mastering System. SDIF-2 is intended for transferring samples at the standard rates of 44.056, 44.1, and 48 KHz. All devices must be synchronized to a master clock. The audio signal is encoded as a 32-bit word, divided into a 20-bit audio sample field, an 8-bit control field, and a 3-bit synchronization field. When 16-bit samples are transmitted, the remaining four bits are packed with zeros. The control field contains flags for emphasis, copy prohibition, and a block flag that indicates the beginning of an SDIF-2 block (256 words). The 3-bit synchronization field is divided into two parts: either a high-to-low pulse (indicating the beginning of a block) or a low-to-high-pulse (indicating a normal sample word). (See Pohlmann 1989a for a detailed diagram of the encoding format.). A 15-pin connector is typical.

AES10 or MADI

MADI (Multichannel Audio Digital Interface) or AES 10 is a multichannel version of the professional AES/EBU protocol. Transmitted serially using standard FDDI (Fiber Distributed Digital Interface) chips, MADI links multichannel digital audio equipment, such as consoles, tape recorders, and digital audio workstations. 100 Mbit/sec data rate. Allows up to 56 channels of 24-bit audio data to be transmitted over a single BNC-terminated 75-ohm coaxial cable for distances up to 50 meters. Two cables are needed for bidirectional communication.

ProDigi

The ProDigi or PD format was developed by Mitsubishi and Otari for their professional digital audio products. Blocks of data are transmitted at the chosen sampling rate. The sample word is 32 bits, but in most cases only the first 16 bits are used. A word clock marks the beginning of every sample, and each channel of audio is transmitted on a separate wire. Two status channels (on separate wires) carry additional information, such as bits indicating the recording state of a multichannel tape recorder.

Yamaha Digital Cascade

A proprietary format for interconnecting certain digital audio products manufactured by Yamaha. A pair of connectors carry two channels of 24-bit samples. A single eight-pin DIN connectorcarries separate word clock and digital audio data. Both the clock and audio data signals are balanced differential signals. Word clock is carried at the sampling frequency and defines the start of a left-channel/right-channel data sequence. 32 bits per channel are transmitted per word cycle. Unused bits are set to zero.

MIDI Sample Dump Format

Developed by sampler manufacturers for the convenience of owners of early samplers with limited sample memory. Since a MIDI connector was the only digital input/output port on these systems, it provided the sole means to import and export digital sample data files. Uses a standard MIDI cable. Transmission is extremely

Table 22.1 (cont.)

slow since the sample data are transmitted one bit at a time. For example, it takes several minutes to transfer via MIDI a 10-second monaural 16-bit sound sampled at 44.1 KHz.

SMDI

SCSI Musical Data Interchange. Introduced in 1991, following a design by Peavey Electronics, and implemented initially on sampling instruments. Devices equipped for SMDI can transfer samples at high speed to and from any SCSI device, including computers, disks, and other samplers (Isaacson 1993). Contact Peavey Electronics Corporation for details.

---

digital audio devices may not be synchronized precisely, a self-clocking system is a simple way of avoiding synchronization difficulties. When a digital audio device must handle more than one stream of digital audio data (as in a digital audio mixer), then a self-clocking scheme becomes more problematic. Some formats permit a separate master clock signal to be sent in parallel on a cable separate from the digital audio data, which solves the problem. These issues are discussed more fully in the section on digital audio synchronization links later.

Transferring audio samples between devices may be as simple as connecting a phono cable between the digital output of one device and the digital input of another device and pressing a "Record" button. But sometimes incompatibilities in transmission formats obstruct a simple solution. Two main types of incompatibilties can occur: *data format differences* and *sampling rate differences*. An example of a data format difference would be a portable DAT recorder that transmits only S/PDIF and a device that receives only AES/EBU format. Another example would be a home DAT recording that was "protected" from copying by the infamous Serial Copy Management System (SCMS) built into DAT recorders. These problems can usually be resolved by special-purpose "problem solver" devices connected between the player and the recorder. Some digital effects processors also perform these format conversions.

Sampling rate differences are more serious and must be resolved by a *sampling rate converter*. This is typically a hardware device placed between a player and a recorder. In order to change the sampling rate of a digital signal, it must be, in effect, resampled. Another strategy is to read the file into a digital audio workstation and perform sample rate conversion in software. In either case, sample rate conversion is not 100 percent clean, since it adds a small amount of noise to the original signal (usually in the range of 1 to 2 dB). (See chapter 4 for more on sample rate conversion.)

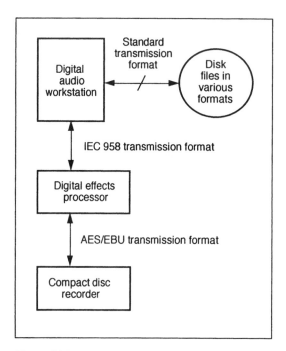

Figure 22.7   Transmission formats versus file formats. The workstation shown at the top writes to its disk using a standard bus transmission format (e.g., SCSI), and the data are stored in a proprietary file format determined by the application that wrote the data. When it is time to send these data to another device, an application on the workstation converts them into a standard transmission format such as the consumer IEC 958. The receiving device may reformat it yet again to the professional AES/EBU format. The data stored on the audio compact disc recorder are stored in a file format specified by the Digital Audio Disc Committee (a manufacturer's organization) according to the so-called Red Book standard (Pohlmann 1989b).

Transmission Formats versus File Formats

Note that the digital audio *transmission formats* listed in table 22.1 are not the same as digital audio *file formats,* which determine how samples are stored within computer files or written onto tape. A file format is not particular to the hardware, but to the application program that writes the data. So a given disk may have files in 50 different file formats corresponding to different types of data and applications (figure 22.7).

At the time a file is transmitted between devices, a microprocessor inside the transmitting device must convert the files it manages into the proper transmission format. For example, the DASH multitrack tape format used by Sony, Studer, and other companies is usually transmitted between machines via the AES10 multitrack transmission format. An audio workstation might store data in a proprietary file format, or allow disk files to be written in a more-or-less standard format like the Apple Interchange File Format (AIFF) (Apple 1989). But at the time of transmission it sends the same data (regardless of file format) via the standard AES/EBU transmission format. In some situations it is necessary to use hardware or software packages to convert between various file and transmission formats.

Fiber-optic Cables

The first optical system for transmitting sound waves was Alexander Graham Bell's Photophone, granted a patent in 1880 (Fagen 1975). Fiber-optic technology driven by *light-emitting diodes* (LEDs) and lasers has only flourished since the late 1970s, however. An optical fiber is a thin (less than 100 μm) flexible medium for transmitting an optical ray.

A typical audio fiber-optic link is driven on one end by an LED source and is detected on the other end by a *positive-intrinsic-negative* (PIN) *photodiode*. Data are transmitted serially—one bit at a time—but at very high rates. A variety of physical connectors are available for fiber-optic links, including common *biconic* and *ST* connectors. The biconic type are inexpensive connectors used in telephone communications. ST connectors are more suitable for multiple-channel audio applications.

Fiber-optic connections have tremendous advantages over traditional electrical copper cables. First, the transmission loss of fiber-optic cables is negligible by comparison. For example, a typical MIDI cable transmitting 31.25 Kbits/second is limited to a distance of 6.6 meters. In contrast, a single thin strand of fiber can transmit thousands of times more data over a range of kilometers without signal losses (Stallings 1988).

High transmission speeds (beyond 1 Gbit/second on a single optical strand) mean that fiber can transmit simultaneously over 500 channels of 20-bit audio sampled at 96 KHz, or a mixture of many channels of digital video and audio.

Fiber-optic cables are immune to electromagnetic sources of interference such as ground loops, crosstalk, and radio frequency interference. Due to their speed, fiber-optical connection systems can run a multitude of serial protocols in parallel through multiplexing. For more on the advantages and disadvantages of fiber-optic applications in audio, see Ajemian and Grundy (1990).

Under the pressure of international telecommunications development, fiber-optic technology continues to evolve. The future of optical transmission media seems clear for all types of data: dozens of channels of digital video and audio, high-resolution still images, SMPTE timecode, computer data, and MIDI communications—simultaneously over vast distances.

Synchronization Links

With all of the devices in today's studios, it is often useful to synchronize the operation of one device with another. Fortunately, multiple-device synchronization, once an expensive luxury, is now commonplace. "Synchronization," however, is a relative term. A delay of 30 ms or more may separate two "synchronized" events in the MIDI world (Moog 1986), while a delay of only a few microseconds may be intolerable in digital audio synchronization. Here we look at three common types of synchronization:

- Synthesizer and effects synchronization—usually handled by MIDI
- Audio and video recorder synchronization—usually handled by SMPTE timecode
- Sample clock synchronization of digital audio processing equipment—usually handled by AES/EBU clock codes

MIDI Synchronization Links

MIDI's first goal was to synchronize the performance of two or more synthesizers. MIDI applications have extended beyond this initial goal, but the core task remains device synchronization. MIDI provides four forms of synchronization, which might be termed (1) *command*, (2) *clock*, (3) *MIDI Time Code* synchronization, and (4) *cue list* synchronization.

Command Synchronization

Real-time command synchronization occurs when messages such as Note-on, Note-off, Controller Change, and Program Change messages are sent over a MIDI channel. At the moment these messages are received by a device they are interpreted into immediate action. The classic case is two synthesizers triggered by a single MIDI keyboard.

Clock Synchronization

MIDI Clock synchronization uses MIDI Clock commands, which are 1-byte timing messages sent between devices every twenty-fourth of a quarter note. Their rate is determined by the tempo of the sequence being played.

When a sequencer sends clock messages to a drum machine, for example, they step forward together, even if the tempo varies a great deal.

MIDI Timecode Synchronization

MIDI Timecode (MTC) synchronization bridges the gap between MIDI and the *absolute time* world of SMPTE timecode. (Later we have more to say about SMPTE timecode.) Absolute time means that the time is counted in terms of hours, minutes, seconds, and frames, as opposed to the measures, beats, and clock ticks of MIDI Clock synchronization. Basically, MTC is a way of encoding SMPTE timecode into MIDI messages. MTC is particularly useful for synchronizing sound effects with video and film. This is because ideo and film already use SMPTE timecode, and the sound effects are not logically tied to musical units such as measures and beats.

Cue List Synchronization

MIDI cue list synchronization is a distributed control scheme. Before a set of events are to occur, a master device sends one or more MIDI Set-Up messages to each device. Each Set-Up message is a *cue*—a time-stamped command that tells the receiving device to perform a certain action at the specified time. Then a clock source sends MIDI Timecode messages to each device in the chain. When a receiving device notices a match between an incoming timecode value and the time of an event in the cue list, it carries out the corresponding action.

SMPTE Synchronization Links

Multiple-device control is often handled by cables that transfer SMPTE (Society for Motion Picture and Television Engineers) timecode among the various devices to be controlled. As explained in chapter 9, two basic varieties of SMPTE timecode exist: *longitudinal timecode* (LTC, recorded horizontally on the side of a tape), and *vertical interval timecode* (VITC, recorded in a frame of a helically scanned videotape). The longitudinal variety can be further subdivided into *24-frame/second* (film), *25-frame/second* (PAL), *30-frame/second* (black-and-white), and *drop-frame* (NTSC). LTC is encoded as an audio tone, whereas VITC is integrated into a video signal.

Each SMPTE number has fields for hours, minutes, seconds, and frames. The SMPTE code "01:58:35:21" means 1 hour, 58 minutes, 35 seconds, and 21 frames. A frame is a portion of a second, typically 1/25th to 1/30th of a second, depending on the particular variant of timecode used. Since the timecode itself does not take up all 80 bits, there is room to encode other information along with the timecode, such as elapsed time, index numbers, or labels. When any event is marked by a SMPTE timecode, that timecode becomes a permanent address for that event. For more details on the format of SMPTE timecode, see Hickman (1984).

Timecode is often transmitted via balanced lines terminating in a three-prong XLR connector. In a typical SMPTE timecode setup, several slave machines follow the timecode movements of a master machine; when the master goes to a particular frame of timecode, the slaves follow. Depending on the system that interprets the timecode, the grain of timing resolution is several milliseconds to several microseconds.

MIDI-controlled devices can be integrated into a SMPTE setup by means of a SMPTE-to-MIDI Time Code converter. As their name indicates, these devices convert SMPTE timecode into MIDI Time Code that can be used to trigger a sequencer or sound file playback system.

Digital Audio Synchronization Links

Synchronization in digital audio systems means something different from the usual timecode type of synchronization. Digital audio synchronization coordinates audio data to the sample frequency to avoid the loss of samples and to ensure the correct operation of signal-processing algorithms.

A number of factors can contribute to synchronization problems, including long cable lengths that introduce delay, clock differences, and clock drifting in various pieces of equipment. Devices may respond differently to clock variations by muting, dropping samples, repeating samples, or causing other errors. This situation becomes acute when a centralized piece of a equipment, such as a digital audio mixer, must handle several streams of incoming digital audio data. If it synchronizes to one stream only, it may be asynchronous with another stream.

Of course, *sample rate converter* boxes are available from various manufacturers, and one of the functions of these devices is to "resynchronize" a source with a wandering sample clock. But using a sample rate converter for this purpose is only a temporary fix and is not a general solution to the problem of interdevice synchronization.

Therefore digital studios can benefit from a studio-wide *master clock* signal that feeds every piece of digital audio equipment (figure 22.8). This includes effects boxes, sample rate converters, recorders, mixers, and computer-based editors. Audio and video equipment can be connected to the same clock, each deriving their respective synchronization clocks from the master clock.

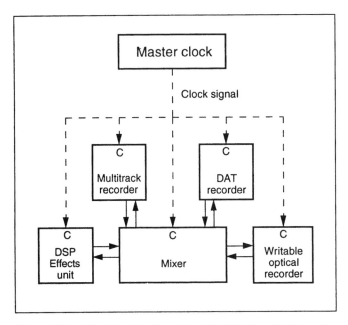

Figure 22.8 Synchronization of an all-digital studio through a master synchronization signal. The inputs marked "C" take in the master synchronization signal, while the other inputs are for digital audio data.

In the scheme recommended by the Audio Engineering Society, each device synchronizes its sample rate clock to that of the master (preferably supplied via a separate input connector), so the phase differences between devices are constant no matter how many are connected. (If the devices were serially interconnected without synchronization the delays would be dependent on the various clocks and the number of devices connected.) In the AES/EBU standard, audio data are transmitted by an interface that allows the sample rate to be recovered along with the audio data. The technical specifications of the synchronization protocol are defined in the AES11-1991 (ANSI S4.44-1991) document (Audio Engineering Society 1991; see also Rumsey 1991).

Parallel Ports and Buses

In contrast to a serial port that sends one bit at a time, a parallel port has several lines and transmits several bits at once. This means that a parallel port usually has a higher bandwidth than a typical serial line. The most common parallel ports send 8 to 64 bits at a time. A typical application for a parallel port is printing, where the packets being transmitted are characters. The speed of a parallel port is dependent on many factors and can range from several hundred Kbytes to many Mbytes per second in a single-user computer. The maximum length of a parallel cable may be less than a serial cable, however.

Within a computer, an internal *bus* is an electronic backbone, transmitting data at high speed between processors, coprocessors, memory cards, DSP cards, video cards, and so on. For a practical discussion of bus interfacing issues in computer music applications see Lowe and Currie (1989).

One type of parallel port extends the internal bus. Examples include the *Small Computer Systems Interface* or SCSI bus extension protocol (ANSI X3.131-1986), and its successor, SCSI-2. Many digital audio products that require high-speed intercommunication with the host computer and peripherals attach logically to the computer's bus. To reduce the number of physical bus lines, *multiplexing* techniques can be applied to use the same lines to transmit both addresses and data on alternative bus cycles.

Since the bus is a shared highway between several devices attached to it, bus systems usually include *arbitration logic* that sorts out requests for use of the bus by the various devices. Each device on the bus has a *priority*. At each bus clock cycle, the bus arbitration logic must give control of the bus to the highest priority device that wants to use it. For example, the host computer must assert control of the bus in order to read from or write to the disk drive.

The controlling device is called the *bus master*, and the other devices are the *bus slaves*. The master selects slaves by placing address information on the bus that each slave compares to its own address. If they match, the master and the slave establish a connection, and the slave becomes a *responder*. Addresses that identify more than one slave are called *broadcast addresses*.

Once the slaves are connected, the master exchanges data with them over the bus. The master breaks the connection with its responders when all of the data have been transferred. The sequence of establishing a connection, transferring data, and breaking a connection is called a *transaction*.

Bus transactions are synchronized by timing information that indicates when address and data are valid. Some buses also let the master transmit control information that indicates what type of transaction it is about to initiate.

Asynchronous versus Synchronous Buses

Buses are either *asynchronous* or *synchronous*. In an asynchronous bus, the master issues a *strobe* timing signal to indicate that subsequent information on the bus lines is valid. The responder returns an acknowledgement timing signal. Receipt of this signal informs the master that the responder received and acted on the information. This strobe-acknowledgement mechanism is called a *handshake*. In a multiplexed bus system, separate handshakes are used for address and data. Asynchronous systems can take full advantage of the speed of the fastest responding devices and yet also adapt to the pace of the slow ones.

In most synchronous bus systems, a central clock generates timing signals that are distributed to all devices on the bus. Changes in the state of the bus lines occur at fixed intervals. The duration of a bus cycle is set by the clock speed, which in some synchronous systems is determined by the slowest device on the bus. Most synchronous buses use a *wait protocol* to avoid this constraint. For example, any responder that cannot process a request at the basic system rate tells the system to wait. When the responder is ready, it cancels the *wait state*, and the bus resumes normal operation.

Interrupt Signals

In many situations, devices attached to a bus require the attention of other devices. They may have to transfer data or signal that they have completed some action. Various schemes have been devised for passing an *interrupt signal* across a bus. The simplest method uses a bus line allocated to interrupt requests. Devices requiring attention transmit an anonymous request over this line, which is monitored by an *interrupt handler routine* (typically part of the operating system). When an interrupt is intercepted by the interrupt handler, it polls all slaves to identify the device that caused the interrupt. This procedure is speeded up if the interrupt-causing device can become the bus master and transmit more voluminous interrupt messages to the required destination. In other systems, polling is not needed because the interrupt signal arrives with the address of the sender attached.

Direct Memory Access Controllers and Shared Memories

A tight coupling between a digital signal processor (DSP) and a host computer can result in more efficient operation than a loosely coupled system. One way to couple a DSP system with a host computer is to put the DSP (usually in the form of a circuit board) on the same bus as the host computer. Since a DSP board can process voluminous quantities of data in a short time, it is important to give it direct access to these data to ensure that

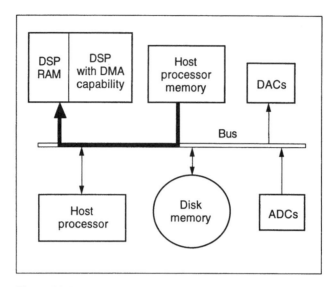

Figure 22.9 DSP interface using a DMA. The DMA channel allows the DSP to grab control of the bus and fetch samples from an ADC, disk, or memory, or write samples to the DAC, disk, or memory without host computer intervention.

its power is not wasted in waiting. This helps to ensure that the DSP and the host computer work in parallel as much as possible.

This section describes two schemes for speeding up the data access of a DSP: *direct memory access* (DMA) and shared memories. The details of how these schemes work (and whether they are available at all) are dependent on the architecture of the computer and DSP and vary from system to system.

A DMA controller attaches to a computer bus and can act as a bus master in order to transfer blocks of data to and from the host computer (figure 22.9). The host computer can finish other calculations while the transfer is going on and is interrupted only at the end of the transfer.

Certain DSPs can act as DMA controllers. The DSP asserts control of the bus in order to move large amounts of sample data to and from its local DSP memory. In some systems the operation of the DMA transfers occurs on unused bus cycles, in between host computer operations. Thus DMA transfers and host processor operations occur in parallel. Once the DSP has the data it needs in its memory, computation in the DSP and the host computer can proceed in parallel.

The most intimate interconnection strategy between a host computer and a DSP is a shared memory scheme. This is achieved by a *dual-ported* memory, implying the existence of two independent pathways into the memory (figure 22.10). Reading from and writing to the memory can be carried out

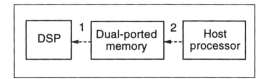

Figure 22.10 Dual-ported memory scheme. Here a DSP is reading from the memory (1) at the same time the host processor is writing into it (2).

simultaneously by two different processors. This eliminates *wait states* in both the host computer and the DSP. Communication between the host and the DSP can be arranged through messages left in a special area of memory. The danger in a dual-ported memory scheme is that two devices will try to read or write to the same location at the same time. Thus, dual-ported memory systems have logic for sorting out conflicting requests.

Networks

An association of interlinked computers is a network. This section introduces the most basic concepts of networks. For more information, see one of the many textbooks on the subject (for example, Stallings 1988). The main purpose of a network is the exchange of data and services between the linked *nodes*, where the nodes can be computers, image scanners, printers, disk drives, or other peripherals. Every device that might be a source or target of transmission on the network—such as a computer or printer—is a node, and every node has an address that is known to the network software. Any kind of digital data can be transmitted via a network, for example, sequence data, audio samples, graphics images, score data, text, or code. Networks permit file transfer, electronic mail, and distributed application programs that run on more than one computer.

The *protocol* of a network is the set of rules governing the exchange of data. That is, the protocol is the logical scheme of message sending and receiving. Modern network protocols have several layers. Table 22.2 shows a typical protocol hierarchy: the seven layers of the International Standards Organization (ISO) Open Systems Interconnection (OSI), a standard for computer networking.

Every node on the network has an address, which can either be a *physical address* (specified by the sender) or a *logical address* (specified by a *network control processor* acting as an *address server*). Most networks use a logical addressing scheme.

Table 22.2   OSI protocol layers

Physical layer

Provides transmission of unstructured bit stream over a physical medium. Deals with the mechanical, electrical, and procedural characteristics to access the physical medium.

Data link layer

Provides reliable transfer of information across the physical medium. Sends blocks of data (frames) with the necessary synchronization, error control, and flow control.

Network layer

Provides upper layers with independence from the data transmission and switching technologies used to connect systems; responsible for establishing, managing, and terminating connections.

Transport layer

Provides reliable, transparent transfer of data between endpoints; also handles error recovery and flow control.

Session layer

Provides the control structure for communication between application programs; establishes, manages, and terminates connections (sessions) between cooperating applications.

Presentation layer

Provides independence to the application programs from differences in data representation (syntax).

Application layer

Provides access to the OSI environment for users.

Two broad classes of networks can be distinguished. *Local area networks* (LANs) (figure 22.11a) interconnect relatively small numbers of computers, usually within a restricted area such as a building or a group of proximate buildings. *Wide area networks* (WANs) (figure 22.11b) span vast geographical spaces, often by means of long-distance telephone lines (including microwave and satellite links). The owner of a LAN is typically an institution with between two to several hundred computers to interconnect. In contrast, ownership of a WAN is distributed between the institution and the various transmission carriers, such as the telephone companies that provide the main transmission channels. The number of interconnected computers in a WAN can be in the thousands. Since LANs are more likely in computer music, the rest of this section focuses on them.

Three components define a LAN: a *protocol*, an *interface*, and a *transmission channel*. The protocol logic controls the LAN, while the interface

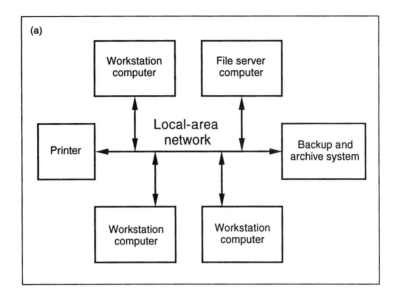

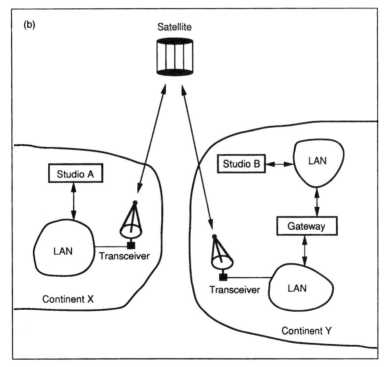

Figure 22.11   LANs versus WANs. (*a*) LAN connecting a small number of nodes. (*b*) An intercontinental WAN connecting two studio computers among thousands of computers via satellite and other long-distance communications media.

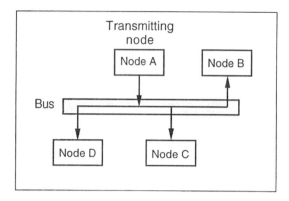

Figure 22.12   Bus topology LAN such as Ethernet. Messages from one node to another are broadcast onto the network. All devices receive the message, which is tagged with a particular address. Only the devices whose addresses match the tag acknowledge receipt. If two nodes transmit a message at the same time, there is a collision, and each sending node waits a random period of time before retransmitting.

translates messages from the software medium of the LAN protocol to the physical medium of the LAN channel. The LAN channel can be a coaxial line like those used in cable television or a fiber optic line. (Coaxial cable is made up of an inner conducting wire surrounded by an outer conductor. Between the inner and outer conductors is an insulating layer, and the entire cable may be shielded to keep out noise.)

Many types of protocols exist for LANs, formalized in the IEEE 802 Local Network Standards Committee recommendations. The most common types of LAN protocols are *carrier sense multiple access with collision detection* (CSMA/CD), as used in the Ethernet standard, and *token ring*, as used in the Fiber Distributed Data Interface (FDDI) standard, a 100 Mbit/second LAN.

The topology of a CSMA/CD network is like that of a bus (figure 22.12). The sender of a packet broadcasts the message to all devices on the network while also "listening" to the network to see if it is busy. If it does not receive an acknowledgement signal from the receiver, then it assumes that another sender also sent a packet at the same time—a state known as a *collision*. If a sender detects a collision, it stops sending the message and briefly sends a collision signal to the rest of the network (Metcalf and Boggs 1976). After transmitting the collision signal, the sender waits a random delay time before transmitting the packet again. A station will attempt to transmit repeatedly in the face of repeated collisions, but after each collision the mean value of the random delay is doubled.

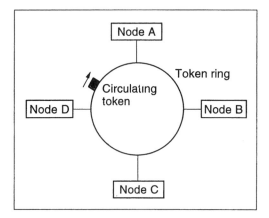

Figure 22.13   Token ring topology LAN. A token circulates around the ring. The token may be empty (no data) or filled with data sent from one node to another.

The topology of a token ring network is a ring. Data circulate around the ring on a series of data links between computers (figure 22.13). A station wishing to transmit waits for a turn and then sends a packet of data. The packet contains source and destination addresses as well as data. As the packet circulates, the destination node copies the data into a local buffer. The packet continues to circulate until it reaches the source node, which serves as a form of acknowledgement. As the number of transmitting nodes increases, token rings show a performance advantage over CSMA/CD schemes because of the increased probability of collisions in the CSMA/CD scheme (Stallings 1988).

The LAN speed standards of the 1980s were between 1 and 20 Mbits/second. Emerging high-speed network standards aim toward 1 Gbit/second as a data rate for the exchange of uncompressed full-motion video, multiple channels of audio, graphical images, and remote control of experiments (presumably including musical performance).

Telecommunications

A relatively inexpensive way to interconnect computer systems is via a *modem* connected on one side to a serial port on the computer and on the other side to a telephone line. "Modem" stands for "modulator/demodulator." A modem converts a digital bitstream into a high-frequency audio signal that can be transmitted via a telephone line (figure 22.14). The destination computer also has needs a modem to convert the audio signal back into a digital bit stream. A modem that can transmit and receive simultane-

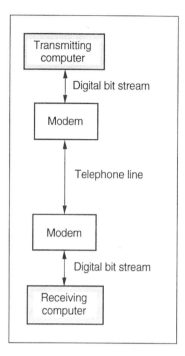

Figure 22.14   A modem converts a digital bit stream into a high-frequency audio signal that can be transmitted over ordinary telephone lines and ultimately to a destination computer with a receiving modem.

ously is called a *full duplex modem*—in effect, full two-way. The rate of transmission varies, depending on hardware and software capabilities, typically between 2400 to 28800 bits/second or more.

Bulletin board systems (BBS) allow musicians with computers to correspond via a central computer that acts as the bulletin board. Each musician has a modem attached to their computer. Sending data to the BBS is called *uploading*, while receiving data from the BBS is called *downloading*. It is possible to upload any type of data via modem to such a BBS, including programs, MIDI sequencer files, or sound files. This helps transcontinental and international collaborations. For example, a composer can transfer, via a network, a sequencer or sound file to a lyricist or studio musician. When the collaborator has added their part, the file is returned to the composer.

A vast range of information and music data is available via telecommunication service providers and via the global Internet.

Conclusion

In the past, analog cables were the primary means of transmitting audio and video information, but digital communications are rapidly becoming

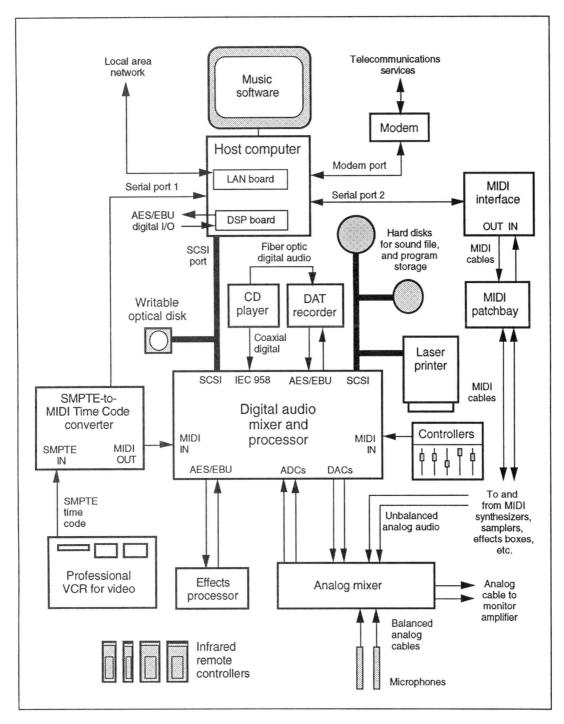

Figure 22.15   The interconnection maze of a small computer music studio based on a single host computer connected to MIDI devices and a digital audio mixer and processor.

dominant. Among digital transmission media, fiber optic technology seems most promising.

As this chapter demonstrates, no single solution exists to all interconnection problems. Despite ongoing standardization efforts, the number of different interconnection protocols continues to expand. This makes it necessary to consider interconnections before purchasing and installing equipment, even in a small studio (figure 22.15). The starting point of designing an interconnection scheme should be a thorough analysis of the desired musical capabilities. Available technology, cost, performance, and even musical style are all factors in designing an interconnection scheme.

Integrated "all-in-one" workstations simplify interconnection problems, but at the expense of flexibility. A modular approach to system design lets the musician select each component according to taste and budget. Upgrading the system becomes a measured, incremental process of replacing one component at a time.

VII   Psychoacoustics

Overview to Part VII

Music touches us according to its inner vibrations, the shape of its gestures, and the texture of its timbres. Sound can literally envelop us, unlocking sensations, emotions, and thoughts as it passes into and through our bodies. Medically speaking, the physiology of human hearing is relatively well understood (Buser and Imbert 1992). But the relationship between acoustics, musical structure, cognition, and emotion is an ongoing study. (See McAdams 1987 for a historical view.) Chapter 23, written by John Gordon, is an introduction to *psychoacoustics*—the scientific study of the relation between sound, perception, and music psychology. Psychoacoustics examines everything from the physiology of the ear to the analysis of musical performance (Deutsch 1982; McAdams 1987).

Going beyond the marks on the printed score page, psychoacoustics elucidates what we actually hear when listening to music. Hence a basic knowledge of psychoacoustics is essential in creating a synthetic world of sound. These concepts may clarify musical thinking and steer us clear of making erroneous presumptions about what our audience can hear. For psychoacoustics also studies the limits of hearing—acuity in perceiving pitch, rhythm, timbre, duration, spatial location, etc., and the limits of musical memory.

Psychoacoustics distinguishes three separate aspects of musical phenomena: the physical properties of acoustic waves, sound as transduced by human hearing mechanisms, and the musical information gleaned by a listener. Sonic waveforms can be measured by scientific instruments in precise and objective terms. We can gauge their amplitude, frequency content, phase relations, and myriad other properties. But physical measurements go only so far. They do not explain which features of music are recognized and which cognitive connotations (logico-rational and emotional) that a piece of music evokes in a human listener.

Hence, psychoacoustics poses fundamental questions about relationships between acoustical laws and human musical cognition. What is the relationship between the physical quantity of sound pressure (amplitude) and perceived loudness? Under what conditions is a frequency perceived as a distinct pitch? What is the relation between spectrum and timbre?

Another branch of psychoacoustics assists audio engineers in developing better audio systems. In this case, the psychoacoustician may ask: How finely can we discriminate between differences induced by the sound system on which a piece of music is reproduced? How do certain data reduction techniques and audio components affect perceived sound quality?

The composer Edgar Varèse characterized music as *organized sound* (Varèse 1971). To the psychoacoustician, this leads to questions about what types of organizations we can hear. How do listeners parse forms spread out over time, such as motives, phrases, and sections? How can they recognize a single musical fragment played at different tempi, and under a variety of transpositions and orchestrations? What are the limits of transformations that preserve the identity of a sound object?

Perhaps the greatest challenge that we can pose for psychoacoustics is to ask it to help us update music theory. Such an update is necessary because musical possibilities have evolved far beyond the bounds of traditional music texts. While aesthetic theories float in a rarified atmosphere, the psychoacoustician can offer empirical evidence that may eventually tether them to firm ground.

23 *Psychoacoustics in Computer Music*

John W. Gordon

Before composers begin to write a piece of music for a particular medium, they usually learn something about that medium. If music is to be written for the violin, say, then the range and tuning of the instrument as well as the bowing and fingering techniques should be known; otherwise, the composer runs the risk of writing something that is impossible to play. But the effort spent to gain this understanding is well rewarded: the greater the command of technical details, the less they interfere with the compositional process, and perhaps the greater the composer's freedom in expressing musical ideas.

If the medium involves traditional instruments, the composer must first communicate the musical ideas to the performers. Then the performers, in expressing these musical ideas, generate the sounds that the listener hears. In other words, the musical gesture is encoded into a sound wave, and the listener, in hearing the sound, interprets it as a musical gesture.

In composing computer music, one often begins with the sound itself. Parameters are manipulated or combined in an attempt to achieve musical effects. However, in many cases there is no way of determining a priori the absolute or relative values for these parameters from traditional musical concepts. One must start over and become acquainted with new building blocks. Previously, it was often sufficient to learn about certain generic properties of a musical instrument. Now the acoustical properties of sound, such as frequency, duration, waveshape, intensity, and spectrum, must be understood. For a further introduction to acoustical concepts, see Backus (1977), Benade (1990), Roederer (1975), and Campbell and Greated (1987).

Since these physical attributes do not, in and of themselves, constitute music, the composer must also learn how the ear perceives them. In other words, the composer needs to know how to construct and balance physical attributes of sound so that the listener will interpret the sound in a way that corresponds (more or less) to the composer's musical concepts. It is logical, then, to turn to the field of *psychophysics* (the study of psychological responses to physical stimuli), or more specifically, its subfield, *psychoacoustics,* to understand better this relationship between sound and music.

The dichotomy between physical events and the mental constructs they induce is a constant theme throughout this chapter. Psychoacoustics knowledge not only promises to give the composer of computer music greater freedom of expression, but may also suggest new musical structures based on perceptual phenomena.

The rest of this chapter examines the basic structures of human hearing and the perception of different aspects of sound: intensity, temporal features, frequency, noise, and timbre. Along the way we discuss phenomena such as fusion and masking effects, and point out their compositional implications. For the student of psychoacoustics, we provide numerous citations to the literature. Several modern books on music psychology deal with psychoacoustic issues in detail; see, for example, Deutsch (1982), Sloboda (1985), Dowling and Harwood (1986), Clynes (1982), McAdams (1987), and Campbell and Greated (1987).

Perception of Intensity

Intensity is related to the energy (or variance of air pressure) in a wave. In a general way, as the intensity (a parameter describing a physical quantity) increases in a sound, we sense an increase in loudness (perceptual attribute). But there is not a simple one-to-one correspondence between intensity and loudness, and loudness is dependent on other physical parameters as well, such as spectrum, duration, and background sounds.

The human ear is capable of hearing an extraordinarily large range of intensities, and its sensitivity to changes in intensity is proportional to the amount of intensity. In other words, the perceptual mechanism for loudness behaves in an exponential way. Thus, in describing sound, it is usually more convenient to take the logarithm of intensity than to use the intensity value directly. Sound intensity is measured in terms of *sound pressure level* (SPL), defined as

$$SPL = 20 \times \log_{10}(P/P_0)$$

where the reference pressure P_0 is 0.00005 (2×10^{-5}) newtons/meter^2, corresponding roughly to the threshold of hearing at 1000 Hz. (A newton is a unit of force such that under its influence a 1 kilogram mass would accelerate at a rate of 1 meter per second per second.) SPL is measured in terms of decibels (dB), the unit of sound intensity (see chapter 1).

Figure 23.1 presents the range of hearing for an average young adult human ear as a plot of intensity in decibels versus frequency. The region shown is the conventional range adapted from Winckel (1967). In certain cases an individual's sensitivity may extend beyond the region shown here. For example, the human body senses low frequencies that are too low for the eardrum to pick up, and recent scientific studies show that the upper limit of sensitivity may extend well beyond 20 KHz (Oohashi et al. 1991).

As figure 23.1 shows, a 1000 Hz sine tone at the threshold of hearing has a pressure P equal to P_0, so its SPL is equal to 0 dB. It takes a sine tone with a pressure roughly one million (10^6) times P_0 to be on the threshold of pain (the top perimeter of the blob in figure 23.1) This tone has an SPL near 120 dB.

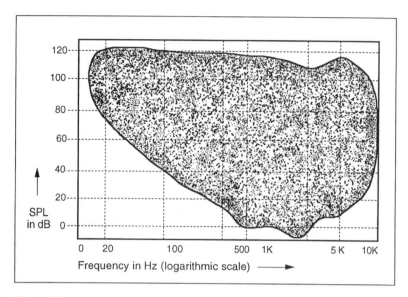

Figure 23.1   The general area of human hearing as a function of frequency and intensity, after data in Winckel (1967).

We mentioned earlier that the ear's sensitivity to changes in intensity is proportional to the intensity's magnitude. This exponential relationship is thus reflected in a nearly constant number of dB. In other words, the absolute intensity difference between 90 and 91 dB SPL (a factor of about 3859) is much greater than between 30 and 31 dB SPL (a factor of about 3.86), but the change in loudness, or perceived intensity difference, is roughly the same in each case. In the middle of the ear's intensity and frequency ranges, the *just noticeable difference* (JND) in intensity varies between a few tenths of a dB and a few dB (Scharf 1978).

The ear is more sensitive to certain frequency regions than to others. The most sensitive region is about 2700–3200 Hz, with sensitivity falling more or less gradually on either side of this region. What this means for the composer is that a sine wave at 3000 Hz with a certain intensity is going to sound much louder than one at either 200 or 8000 Hz with the same intensity.

Along this line, a useful tool is the set of Fletcher-Munson curves, shown in figure 23.2. These are *constant-loudness contours* (called *phon* contours) as functions of frequency. Phons, by definition, correspond to decibels at 1000 Hz. Thus, a sine tone at 1000 Hz with an intensity of 40 dB SPL has a loudness level of 40 phons. If we want to produce a 300-Hz sine tone with the same loudness level as our 1000-Hz, 40-dB tone, we can follow the 40-phon contour from 1000 to 300 Hz, and discover that about 47 dB SPL

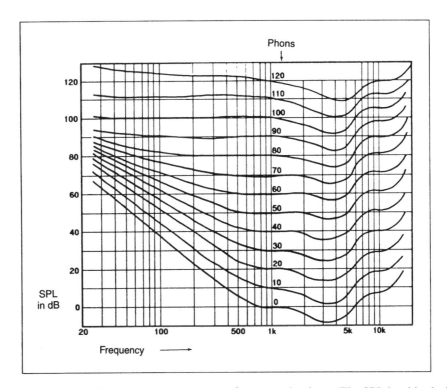

Figure 23.2 Phon contours, or curves of constant loudness. The SPL level in decibels is indicated by the numbers at the left of the figure. The level in phons is indicated above the 1 KHz marker. At 110 dB SPL, 100 Hz, 1 KHz, and 10 KHz would also be perceived as being roughly equal in loudness. At 60 dB, however, 10 KHz and 100 Hz would require a 10 dB boost to be perceived as being equally loud as 1 KHz. (After Fletcher and Munson 1933.)

is needed for the new tone. That is, a 300-Hz sine tone at 47 dB SPL and a 1000-Hz sine tone at 40 dB SPL sound equally loud to the average listener.

Of course, musicians are usually more interested in sounds with complex spectra than in sine waves. The loudness of a complex sound depends to a large extent on its frequency content. In general, each component contributes to the loudness of the sound according to its frequency and intensity per the Fletcher-Munson curves; however, a strict linear relationship does not necessarily apply. (See the discussion on critical bands and masking later.)

Moreover, the ear can be fooled into perceiving a constant loudness as the sound decreases in intensity, provided the sound is also heard as moving away from the listener. On the computer, this effect is enhanced with the addition of artificial reverberation, but it can sometimes occur even without reverberation if the sound is very familiar to the listener (Sheeline 1982).

The threshold of hearing displayed in figure 23.1 is for relatively sustained sine tones. For very short tones, the threshold must be raised. This is because near the threshold the ear seems to integrate energy for tones shorter than about 200 ms. However, at suprathreshold levels, the relationship between loudness and duration is unclear (Scharf 1978).

The Human Ear

Before going on to a discussion of time and frequency perception, it is helpful to include a brief description of how the ear works. Figure 23.3 shows a representation of the ear and its three main subdivisions: the outer ear, middle ear, and inner ear. The outer ear amplifies incoming air vibrations. The middle ear transduces these vibrations into mechanical vibrations. The inner ear performs further processing on these vibrations, filtering and transducing them mechanically, hydrodynamically, and electrochemically, with the result that electrochemical signals are transmitted through nerves to the brain. The outer, middle, and inner ears are collectively classified as the *peripheral auditory system.*

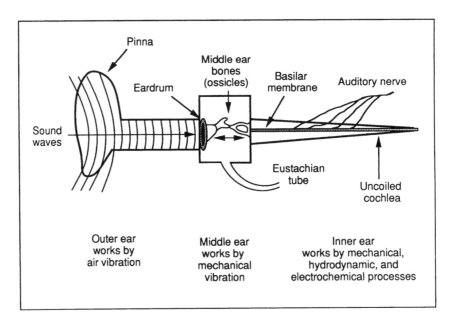

Figure 23.3 Schematic representation of the human peripheral auditory system. The subdivisions into outer, middle, and inner ear are indicated, along with the modes of processing for each. The cochlea is shown uncoiled; normally it is coiled like a snail shell. (After Yost and Nielsen 1977.)

The *cochlea* is the focal point of the inner ear. It contains the *basilar membrane* and *organ of Corti* (not shown in figure 23.3), which together form the complicated mechanisms that transduce vibrations into neural signals or codes. Further auditory processing occurs beyond the cochlea in the brain, using information contained in the neural signals. This central processing is important in that it combines incoming signals from both ears. These mechanisms and processes are all very complex, but it is beyond the scope of this chapter to go into more detail on how the central and peripheral auditory mechanisms operate. For an introductory discussion of these topics, see Yost and Nielsen (1977).

Perception of Temporal Features

Certain mechanisms in the inner ear encode both time and frequency, and supply information to higher-level perceptual processes that sort the information into notes, rhythms, and higher-order musical structures. It appears that the low-level time and frequency mechanisms operate on the incoming waveform in parallel, and that their information is combined by the higher-level processes in determining the nature of the sound. In other words, the peripheral mechanisms cannot be cleanly separated into those that supply only temporal information and those that supply only spectral information. In this section we concentrate primarily on how the temporal mechanisms operate on the incoming sound, and on some of the consequences for computer music. In the next section we examine the frequency mechanisms; then we will see how these combine with the temporal mechanisms in the perception of pitch and timbre.

One kind of mechanism is a *period detector*. It operates on the fine structure of the neurally encoded waveform. The neural pattern is obtained by nerve cells in the organ of Corti firing (individually or in groups) at a rate which corresponds to the wave's period. Individual cells can operate in this manner only up to a certain rate; if the period is too small, they cannot recover and refire quickly enough. However, groups of cells can rotate or stagger their firing, so that they, in effect, follow submultiples of the period. This mechanism as a whole can detect frequencies up to about 4 KHz (Nordmark 1970, 1978).

The inner ear also encodes variations in the envelope of the wave, and there is evidence for mechanisms in the central auditory nervous system that detect amplitude modulation (AM). (See chapter 6 for an explanation of AM in the context of sound synthesis.) This detection is limited to AM frequencies between approximately 75 and 500 Hz. It is also limited by the depth of modulation—that is, there is psychoacoustic evidence that cells fire only if the change in amplitude is significant enough (about 50 to 100 percent modulation). (See Burns and Viemeister 1976 for further details.)

There is also evidence for a mechanism that encodes events. These types of cells fire at the onset or offset of a sound, and different cells operate on different ranges of onset slopes (Kiang and Moxon 1972; Whitfield 1978; Smith and Brachman 1980; Delgutte 1980). When an instrument plays a note, the transients trigger this mechanism, but the steady state portion does not. A model of this event detector has been developed by Gordon (1984) in order to determine the moment of perceptual attack of a musical tone, which may be significantly delayed from its moment of physical onset. This model is useful in synchronizing synthetic or recorded tones of different timbres.

Other cells respond to certain temporal intervals between events. This information may be used in connecting single events into rhythmic streams (i.e., in identifying sequences of events as coming from one or more sources, each with its own rhythm). For more detail on streaming effects, see McAdams and Bregman (1979).

The resolution of rhythm perception is limited by *temporal integration*. Basically this means that if two or more events occur within a certain minimal time frame, the ear "smears" them together into one sensation; in other words, temporal resolution is lost. However, the size of this time frame can vary depending on the duration and kind of events. In some cases, the ear can resolve separate events if the gap between them is only a few milliseconds; in other cases, 20–50 ms (or even more) may be needed for separate resolution. Thus, we cannot speak of a single time frame, or a "time constant" for the ear (Schubert 1979b).

We can see, however, that temporal resolution accounts for some phenomena that may be familiar to musicians. One of these is the distinction between echo (or a sequence of echoes) and reverberation. When a sound reflects off a single surface, we hear both the source and its echo. If other surfaces are present, there are probably several echoes of the source and even more echoes of other echoes. The number of echoes per second is often referred to as the echo density. If this number is larger than 20–30 echoes per second, then individual echoes occur less than 30–50 ms apart; typically the ear no longer hears the echoes as separate events, but fuses them into a sensation of continuous decay, or reverberation (Moorer 1979c; see also chapter 11).

Another phenomenon related to temporal integration is the maximum note rate for a musical phrase (of a single-voiced melody). If notes are played faster than this rate, rather than resolving perceptually into individual tones, they smear together. This has a direct bearing on computer music, inasmuch as tempo is not limited by the dexterity of the performer. Unfortunately, we cannot supply an absolute number for maximum note rate, because again the nature of the sounds is an important factor.

For instance, we would expect to hear both a main note and a preceding grace note (i.e., they would not smear together) if their onsets were only 2–3 ms apart and the grace note were very short. But the longer the grace note, the greater the probability of a smeared percept. Also, the frequency difference between the two notes affects the probability of smearing (Schubert 1979b). If there are many notes in a phrase, there is a general aural buildup, which certainly affects the momentary limits of temporal resolution. In this case, as much as 50 ms may be needed between onsets in order to avoid smearing. (See the discussion on forward and backward masking below.)

Perception of Frequency

When a sine tone excites the ear, a region of the basilar membrane oscillates around its equilibrium position. This region is fairly broad; however, there is a rather sharp point of maximum displacement. The distance of this maximum from the end of the basilar membrane is directly related to the frequency. In other words, frequency is mapped onto a particular place along the membrane. This is the basic low-level mechanism that may allow for the detection of frequency (physical parameter), but it is not the only mechanism that contributes to our sensation of pitch (perceptual attribute). Indeed, we have already seen that there is a temporal mechanism for detecting the period of a waveform, which is the inverse of frequency, and this can contribute to pitch sensation as well.

Even though a young adult ear can detect frequencies within a broad range of approximately 20 Hz to beyond 20 KHz, the perception of pitch is much more narrowly confined. For musical purposes, pitch perception is not accurate, for example, in making octave judgments below 60 Hz or above 5 KHz (Schubert 1979a).

Critical Bands

Since each frequency stimulates a region of the basilar membrane (as opposed to a point), there is a limit to the frequency resolution of the ear. This limit is closely related to an important characteristic of the perceptual mechanism known as the *critical band* (Scharf 1961, 1970). The critical band was first discovered in masking experiments (Fletcher 1940), but it plays a role in many aspects of perception. Let us see how it behaves in certain cases.

If we take two sine waves that are very close to each other in frequency, we find that the total loudness we perceive is less than the sum of the two loudnesses we would hear from the tones played separately. As we separate the tones in frequency, this loudness remains constant up to a point, but then a certain frequency difference is reached where the loudness increases. (At this point, the loudness does approximately equal the sum of the individual loudnesses of the two tones.) This frequency difference corresponds to the critical band. We can think of this as a kind of integration across frequency analogous to the temporal integration we spoke of earlier (Zwicker, Flottorp, and Stevens 1957).

The critical band is presumed to play an important role in most of the sensations of *dissonance* (though the term *roughness* is often preferred in the psychoacoustic literature, due to the connotations associated with the former term derived from traditional music theory). If two sine tones are very close together, they are heard as one tone with a frequency that lies between the two actual frequencies; coupled with this percept is a sensation of beating. As the tones move farther apart, but still remain within a critical band, there is a sensation of roughness. Moving the tones still farther apart enables the ear to discriminate between the two frequencies; but the sensation of roughness continues until the frequency difference between the tones exceeds a critical bandwidth (Roederer, 1975).

Figure 23.4 is a schematic representation (not to scale) of this phenomenon, where one frequency holds fixed while another sweeps through its range. The width of the critical band is dependent on frequency, as can be seen from figure 23.5. Note that the ear can discriminate between two frequencies less than a critical bandwidth apart. Thus, although an integration of loudness occurs across a critical band, this does not imply that there is an integration of frequency over this range.

When many frequencies are present, the auditory system operates on all of them simultaneously, subject to its limits of resolution. If the frequencies are related by the harmonic series, the overall spectrum results in both pitch and timbral effects at a higher perceptual level. However, pitch effects can also arise from inharmonic spectra, including noise. Therefore, before discussing timbre, let us first examine how the auditory system perceives various kinds of noise.

Perception of Noise

Noise can be thought of as a random process. In terms of digital sound, this means that adjacent samples are not related to each other in any meaningful

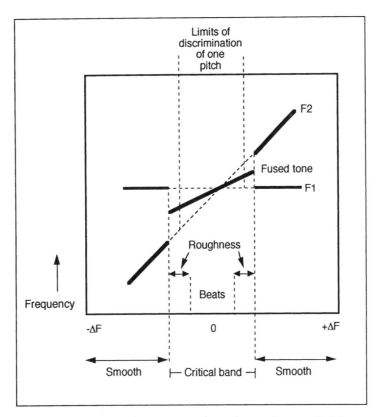

Figure 23.4 Schematic representation of sensations evoked by two simultaneous sine tones *F1* and *F2*, where *F1* is fixed and *F2* sweeps as a function of *F1* + ΔF. The vertical axis is frequency, and the horizontal axis is the width of frequency difference. If the tones are far apart, they sound "smooth" and distinct. As they move together into the critical band, they pass into a region of "rough" fusion. Near the center of fusion the listener hears a beating sound resulting from the interference of the two close frequencies. (After Roederer 1975.)

way. Actually there are degrees of randomness. "Completely" random noise (white noise) has a flat spectrum (i.e., in a long segment of white noise, all frequencies are equally strong on the average). This kind of spectrum is called "white" because it is analogous to all frequencies in the visible spectrum being present in white light. Even though all frequencies are present in white noise, it evokes no sensation of pitch because of the randomness in the waveform. However, there are several ways to "color" noise, and some of these yield at least a vague pitch sensation.

One way is to modulate the amplitude of the noise. Certain studies indicate that if the modulation is within the range of the AM detector, there may be a pitch, corresponding to the modulation frequency, superposed on the sensation of noise. Burns and Viemeister (1976) were even able to play recognizable melodies this way, but the effect was weak.

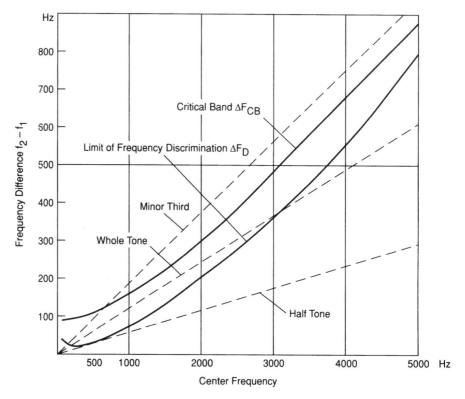

Figure 23.5 Critical bandwidth (ΔF_{CB}) and limit of frequency discrimination (ΔF_D) as a function of the center frequency of a two-tone stimulus (linear scales). The frequency difference corresponding to three musical intervals is shown for comparison. (After Roederer 1975.)

Another way to color noise is to delay the noise for t seconds, and add this to the undelayed noise. This is equivalent to passing the noise through a comb filter (see chapter 10) and is called *comb-filter noise* or *cosine noise,* because the spectral envelope resembles a cosine wave (Bilsen 1977). One can shift the cosine-shaped spectrum higher or lower by altering the phase of the delayed portion with respect to the undelayed portion. Two phase angles have been reported in the literature: 0 degrees (no phase shift), called *cos+ noise*, and 180 degrees (corresponding to subtracting the delayed portion rather than adding it), called *cos− noise.* The resulting pitch sensation from cos+ noise corresponds to a frequency equal to the reciprocal of t (e.g., $t = 2$ ms induces a pitch corresponding to a frequency of 500 Hz). Cos− noise, on the other hand, tends to induce two pitches, one at $1.14/t$ and the other at $0.89/t$. These pitch sensations are strongest at around 500 Hz and are essentially inaudible below 50 Hz or above 2 KHz (Yost and Hill 1978). They also become weaker as the duration of the signal decreases below 200–250 ms (Yost 1980). These pitches could arise either from the detection of frequency (corresponding to place on the basilar membrane), or from the detection of period (time delay), but their existence suggests that pitch determination takes place at a higher than peripheral level.

Passing white noise through a bandpass filter can result in two different pitch judgments, depending on the bandwidth. If the band is narrower than roughly one-fifth of an octave, the resulting pitch corresponds to the band's center frequency; large bandwidths tend to induce pitches corresponding to the edges (low- and high-cutoff frequencies) of the passband (Bilsen 1977). In all these cases, of course, the percept of noise is augmented, and not replaced, by the particular pitch sensations.

We see then that it is possible to make rough predictions as to the pitches that will be perceived in certain kinds of colored noise. This can be useful to the composer of computer music where a transition is needed between noise and spectra with discrete frequency components (harmonic or inharmonic). In other words, one should be able to design noise with some expectations as to how it will be perceived.

Fusion and the Perception of Timbre

Anyone who has written music for the computer (especially if simulation of natural sounds is involved) knows that the steady state spectrum is not the whole of an instrument's identity. The attack and decay portions are also very important cues. Indeed, the spectrum of a natural instrument is constantly changing, and if this temporal activity, or *dynamic spectrum,* is absent (as it sometimes is in electronically produced tones), we perceive the sound as being artificially generated. So, when we speak of timbre, we actually mean something that has more than one dimension. For a more thorough coverage of this topic, including discussions of experiments in timbre perception, see Grey (1975), Plomp (1976), Grey and Gordon (1978), Wessel (1979), and McAdams (1987). A more recent anthology of musical timbre research is available in Barrière (1991).

Here let us consider one of the more salient aspects of timbre: the balance of partials in a harmonic spectrum (i.e., the relationship among the relative strengths of the individual partials). One of the curious things about the perceptual mechanism is that a wave comprising many frequencies can be heard as having one pitch, and that the spectral balance of the harmonics fuses them together into a single sensation of quality, or timbre. Fusion is quite possibly a higher-order phenomenon that results from a combination of spectral and temporal information supplied by the peripheral auditory system. For example, recent studies have suggested that if several partials fall within one critical band, there is more probability of fusion than if they are widely spaced, falling in separate critical bands (Cohen 1980).

Also, if a set of partials is modulated in frequency by a common temporal envelope, they tend to fuse into one timbre. This has been demonstrated by John Chowning (1980; 1989), who synthesized a spectrum to approximate a vowel sung by a soprano. When the harmonics began one after another, there was no percept of a vocal sound, even after all harmonics were present. As soon as a common vibrato was added to all harmonics, however, the sound fused into a convincing sung vowel.

It is much easier to induce a fusion effect if the partials are harmonic; however, inharmonic spectra can fuse if the common temporal envelope is striking enough, such as a sharp attack and exponential decay (Cohen 1980). Indeed, many bell tones have inharmonic spectra with this kind of amplitude envelope.

When many instruments play simultaneously, such as in an orchestra, fusion is an important part of the *source-identification* process—the process that hears a single, complex waveform as a combination of many sounds, each with its own timbre. *Streaming* is another important aspect of this process and is discussed in detail in McAdams and Bregman (1979) and McAdams (1981).

The upper partials of a harmonic spectrum fuse into the perception of a pitch at the fundamental frequency, even if that fundamental component is not present. This is called the *missing-fundamental* phenomenon and gave rise to the so-called periodicity theory of pitch perception (Nordmark 1978). This phenomenon plays an interesting role in opera performance. It has been discovered that professional singers (especially males) develop an extra formant region, called the *singing formant*. This formant is usually between 2500 and 3000 Hz and does not occur in natural speech. The orchestra's greatest intensities occur at frequencies below this and tend to overpower the singer's energy at his fundamental frequency. But with a reinforcement of energy from the singing formant, the listener can hear the upper portion of the singer's spectrum. (The ear is most sensitive to frequencies in this region.) The listener then "tracks" the fundamental pitch from the combination of upper partials, so that the singer can be heard over the background of the orchestra (Sundberg 1972).

Masking Effects

Most music includes more than one sound occurring at or near the same point in time. It is bound to be helpful, therefore, for a composer to under-

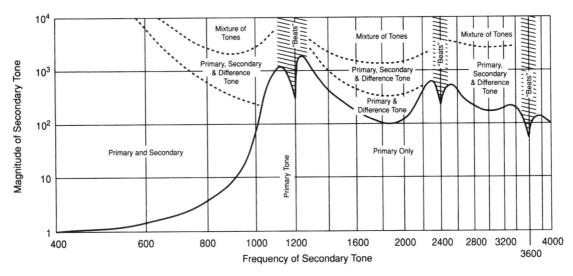

Figure 23.6   The masked threshold, as a function of frequency, of a secondary tone (over a range of frequencies) in the presence of a constant primary tone played at 1200 Hz and 80 dB SPL. The phenomena of beating, aural harmonics, and combination tones are also indicated. (After Wegel and Lane 1924.)

stand how two or more sounds interact with each other in terms of how they are perceived (or even organized) by the human ear. Unfortunately, relatively little research has been done on how sounds are heard in a musical context (although Grey 1978 and McAdams and Bregman 1979 are two good examples). As a step in this direction, however, it is worthwhile to consider some of the work that has been done in masking.

Figure 23.6 presents the results of a classic study by Wegel and Lane (1924). A primary sine tone is played at 1200 Hz and 80 dB SPL. The intensity of a secondary tone is changed to determine its audibility threshold (called the *masked threshold*). The solid curve in figure 23.6 shows the masked threshold for a wide range of frequencies for the secondary tone. One point to realize is that frequencies higher than the primary are masked much more effectively than ones below it. Note also that the presence of beats causes the masked threshold to dip in the vicinity of the primary tone (1200 Hz).

The beating that occurs at 2400 and 3600 Hz indicates the presence of aural harmonics. That is, harmonics of the primary tone that are not present in the incoming sound are being supplied by the nonlinear processing of the ear at this high intensity (80 dB SPL).

When the secondary tone is above 40 dB SPL, another nonlinear effect of the ear takes place: there is a tone at the difference between the primary and secondary. Still higher intensities yield a percept of a mixture of tones at several pitches. When Wegel and Lane presented a 700 Hz tone and a 1200 Hz tone, each at about 95 dB SPL, they claimed nineteen pitches were heard, though they gave no record of their individual loudnesses. In general, the most commonly heard combination tones are the *difference tone* ($|F_2 - F_1|$) and the *cubic difference tone* ($2[F_1 - F_2]$ or $2 \times [F_2 - F_1]$) (Yost and Nielsen 1977). These two were studied in depth by Goldstein (1967). A thorough discussion of combination tones can also be found in Plomp (1976).

Aural harmonics, difference tones, and other combination tones may or may not be desirable for the composer of computer music, but one should be aware of their presence at high intensities. Other experiments in masking have been done, but a detailed discussion of them is beyond the scope of this paper. Masking by a narrow band of noise was explored by Egan and Hake (1950), while Hawkins and Stevens (1950) made a classic study of wideband masking.

Up to now we have been discussing simultaneous masking, but it is also possible for a toneburst or noiseburst to mask a tone that occurs after the burst has been shut off (*forward masking*) or even one that comes before the burst begins (*backward masking*). These and other details about masking are discussed at some length by Zwislocki (1978) and Jeffress (1970).

The reader is invited to examine the paper by Zwicker and Scharf (1965), in which the authors develop a mathematical model to represent how the ear processes any incoming sound. It takes into consideration masking effects, the varying sensitivity of the ear to different frequencies, and phenomena related to the critical band. The model is designed to predict a quantitative value for loudness, but Grey and Gordon (1978) also used it to determine the "balance point" of a musical instrument's spectrum.

Conclusion: Psychoacoustics and Composition

Many composers of computer music have found a knowledge of psychoacoustics greatly enhances their compositional skill. Moreover, there are some who actually gained their inspiration for a composition directly from this knowledge. Jean-Claude Risset (1985a, b) has discussed in some detail his experiences, and David Wessel (1979) has shown how he used the results of a psychoacoustic experiment to help him in composing what Arnold Schoenberg in 1911 called *Klangfarbenmelodie*.

Psychoacoustics can also be exploited to create auditory illusions. Chowning's paper on illusory moving sound sources (Chowning 1971) is a classic example. Risset (1985b) speaks of the many varieties of Shepard tones that move in some direction but never go anywhere! A strong potential for interesting compositional effects is the set of so-called streaming illusions, illustrated by Chowning's vowel example in the discussion above on fusion (more examples are given in McAdams 1981). Indeed, control over streaming and fusion, which are higher-level perceptual phenomena, gives one greater control over texture, density, and other timbral effects, which are higher-level musical concepts. Thus, psychoacoustics promises to be of great benefit to the composer of computer music—not only on the elementary level, but also at the higher levels, where musical structures are built into a compositional whole.

Acknowledgment

The author is very grateful to Stephen McAdams for his contribution to the organization and content of this chapter.

Appendix

Fourier Analysis

with Philip Greenspun

The Short-time Fourier Transform and Phase Vocoder

Windowed DFT Representation
Filter Bank Representation
Inside the Phase Vocoder Filter
Heterodyne Bandpass Filter
Rectangular to Polar Coordinates
Phase Unwrapping

Windowing the Signal

Window Length
Window Shape
Choice of Window
Zero-padding the DFT

The Inverse Discrete Fourier Transform

Overlap-add Resynthesis

Assessment of Overlap-add Resynthesis

Oscillator Bank Resynthesis

Assessment of Oscillator Bank Resynthesis

The Fast Fourier Transform

The Need for a Fast Fourier Transform
The Structure of FFT Algorithms
Radix 2 FFTs
The Butterfly
Data Shuffling and Bit Reversal
Number Theoretic Transforms: Alternatives to the FFT

Conclusion

Fourier analysis is a central tool in musical signal processing. A numerically intensive operation, it was until the mid-1980s confined to scientific laboratories equipped with exotic hardware. Present-day technology brings the agony and the ecstasy of Fourier analysis to the familiar surroundings of the home studio, or with a portable computer to virtually any setting.

Spectrum analysis using Fourier techniques reveals much about the internal structure of sound. But revelation is not merely an end in itself. For the composer, analysis is the starting point for sound transformation. Fourier analysis techniques lead to pitch detection, transformations of timing and pitch, and several forms of cross-synthesis—the mapping of characteristics of one sound to another.

As more musicians use Fourier techniques in their work, there is a broader need to understand its inner mechanisms, its strengths, and its limitations. This appendix presents an introduction to the theory of Fourier analysis and practical aspects of Fourier algorithms. We have kept formulas to a minimum, but in Fourier analysis there is no avoiding mathematical concepts. Therefore, we revert to conventional mathematical notation in this appendix (single-character variables and implicit multiplication).

Chapter 13 surveyed musical applications of sound analysis and is a prerequisite to this appendix. To follow the mathematical descriptions herein, it helps to have a basic understanding of complex numbers and trigonometric functions. To make this appendix as accessible as possible, we include a refresher section that summarizes these concepts. Following this, we present the various incarnations of the Fourier transform, beginning with abstract formulations and descending to practical implementations.

Fourier Analysis: Background

In 1822 the French engineer and aristocrat Jean Baptiste Joseph, Baron de Fourier (1768–1830), finally published a theory that arbitrarily complicated periodic signals could be represented as a sum of many simultaneous simple signals. (A *periodic signal* repeats at regular intervals of time.) He had first presented his ideas in the form of a lecture delivered fifteen years earlier to the French Academy of Sciences. This lecture was severely attacked by established scientists who insisted that such ideas were mathematically impossible (Robinson 1982). The intensity of the controversy is reflected in the fact that the text of Fourier's original lecture was only published for the first time some 165 years later (Grattan-Guiness 1972).

Fourier's theory states that arbitrary periodic waveforms can be deconstructed into combinations of simple sine waves of different amplitudes, frequencies, and phases. Through the middle of the nineteenth century, Fourier analysis was a tedious and error-prone task of manual calculation. Then in the 1870s, the British physicist Lord Kelvin and his brother built the first mechanical harmonic analyzer (Marple 1987). This elaborate gear-and-pulley contraption analyzed hand-traced waveform segments. The analyzer acted as a mechanical integrator, finding the area under the sine and cosine waves for all harmonics of a fundamental period. The Michelson-Stratton harmonic analyzer (1898) was probably the most sophisticated machine of this type. Designed around a spiral spring mechanism, this device could resolve up to 80 harmonics. It could also act as a waveform synthesizer, inverting the analysis mechanically to reconstruct the input signal. (The *inverse Fourier transform* reconstructs a given waveform from its analysis data. See the section on the inverse Fourier transform later.)

In the twentieth century, mathematicians refined and extended the theory of Fourier's method (Wiener 1930). Engineers designed analog filter banks to perform simple types of spectrum analysis. Following the development of stored-program computers in the 1940s, programmers created the first digital implementations of the *Fourier transform* (FT), but these consumed enormous amounts of computer time—a scarce commodity in that era. Finally, in the mid-1960s the voluminous calculations required for Fourier analysis were greatly reduced by a set of algorithms known as the *fast Fourier transform* or FFT, described by James Cooley at Princeton University and John Tukey at Bell Telephone Laboratories (Cooley and Tukey 1965). We present the FFT later in this appendix.

A notable historical discovery in recent years has been the realization that the FT and its fast descendant were originally developed centuries ago. Specifically, the Swiss mathematician Leonard Euler developed a method analogous to Fourier's 1822 theory as early as the 1770s (*Scientific American* 1987), and the German mathematician Karl Friedrich Gauss (1777–1855) developed an algorithm similar to the present-day FFT in 1805. Part of the reason that Gauss's technique remained obscure is that he never published the algorithm. (This was only one of many discoveries Gauss kept to himself. "Gauss seems to have been unwilling to venture publicly into any controversial subject"; Struik 1967.) For more on the history of the FFT see Heideman, Johnson, and Burrus (1984) and Brigham (1974).

Mathematical Representation of Signals

Fourier analysis represents signals as sums of sinusoidal waveforms, each at a different frequency, amplitude, and initial phase. As we will see, this apparently simple concept brings with it several layers of mathematical abstractions. These are the daily diet of physicists and engineers, but may seem arcane to musicians. A fundamental abstraction is the way that sinusoidal signals can be expressed either in terms of trigonometric (circular) functions or in terms of complex numbers, vectors, and exponential functions. An awareness of these representations is essential to the comprehension of Fourier analysis; thus we review them in the next several sections.

Complex Numbers and Rectangular and Polar Coordinates

The real numbers correspond to points on a line. Within this system, there can be no element whose square equals -1. Here we consider a broader class of numbers that includes the real numbers as a subset and also includes an element whose square is -1. These are the *complex numbers*. They cannot be represented as points on a line, but they can be represented as points on a plane. Complex numbers are central to signal processing because they act as a bridge to the circular functions, which are also plotted on a plane. As we see later, one can translate from a complex number representation to a vector representation to a trigonometric representation, using whichever is most appropriate.

A complex number can be plotted as a point (a, b) on a two-dimensional plane (figure A.1). The horizontal dimension is labeled the *real axis,* and the vertical dimension is the *imaginary axis. a* and *b* are the point's *rectangular coordinates*.

Another way to consider a complex number is as a vector, defined by its distance from the origin (zero point) and its direction or angle from the origin. In figure A.1 the distance is labeled *r* and the angle is labeled *θ*. These are the point's *polar coordinates*. Since *r* is a measure of the distance of the point from the origin, it also called the *amplitude, magnitude,* or *modulus*.

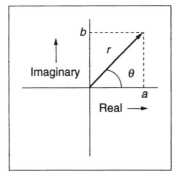

Figure A.1 A complex number plotted as a point (a, b) on a two-dimensional plane. These points define a vector *r*, and the angle they form is labeled *θ*.

In rectangular form, a complex number is written as $a + ib$, where a and b are real numbers and i is the *imaginary unit*, denoting the square root of -1. a and b are called the *real part* and the *imaginary part*, respectively, of a complex number. (See any algebra textbook for rules of algebraic manipulation of complex numbers.) Another term that crops up in Fourier analysis is the *complex conjugate*. This is simply the mirror image of a complex number. That is, the complex conjugate of $a + ib$ is $a - ib$.

Representing Frequency, Amplitude, and Phase

The great plane of complex numbers is a static world. In order to represent musical signals (e.g., frequencies, phases, envelopes), we must introduce a third dimension—the dimension of time. Imagine that the point or vector defined in figure A.1 rotates in a circular motion over time. Now the angle θ varies between 0 and 359.999 ... degrees, rotating through 0 again as time goes by (figure A.2). The circle so inscribed is the *unit circle*, named because its radius is assumed to be equal to "one unit" or 1.0.

The Radian System and Circular Functions

So far we have been describing angles in terms of degrees. The measurement system for angles that is used in higher mathematics is the radian system. Radian measurements define angles in terms of the unit $\pi =$

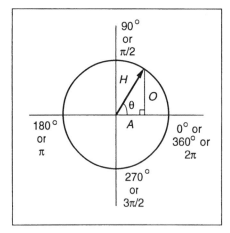

Figure A.2   A vector rotating around a circle. The proportions among the sides of a right triangle inscribed within the circle correspond to sine, cosine, and tangent relations. The angle is θ, the hypotenuse is H, and the two other sides are A and O. See the text for an explanation of how these proportions correspond to sinusoidal functions.

3.1415926536.... Recalling that the circumference of a unit circle is 2π radians, we see the reason for the following definition:

An angle of one revolution around a circle is equal to an angle whose measure is 2π radians.

Thus we can measure any angle inscribed in the circle in terms of radians, that is, factors of π. Converting between degrees and radians is simple: 1 degree = 0.0174532925 ... radians. The advantage of the radian system is its close link to the circular functions, described next.

The sides of the angle in figure A.2 are labeled A for abcissa, O for ordinate, and H for hypotenuse. Trigonometry posits that the proportions among the sides of angles inscribed within a circle correspond to sine, cosine, and tangent relations. Referring to figure A.2, the sine (abbreviated sin), cosine (cos), and tangent (tan) of the angle θ are defined as follows:

$\sin(\theta) = O/H$
$\cos(\theta) = A/H$
$\tan(\theta) = O/A.$

These are the elementary *circular functions*. Notice that $H = 1$ in the case of the unit circle.

Figure A.3 shows the projection of a rotating point along the axis of time extending to the right. We see that it is a regular, periodic function—a sine wave (figure A.3). Each rotation corresponds to one period of the waveform. By means of this correspondence between sinusoidal functions of time and rotations of a point around a circle, we can relate features of sinusoidal

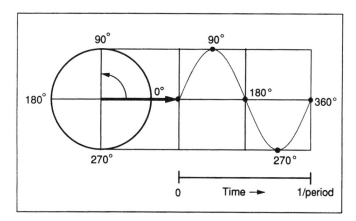

Figure A.3 The projection of a vector rotating in time is a sinusoidal wave. The right part of the diagram shows the projection, starting at 0 and going toward 1/*period*. Each point on the circle maps to a specific phase of a sinusoidal wave.

signals, such as their frequency, phase, and magnitude, to a circular representation. How this is done is the subject of the rest of this section.

Frequency as Radial Velocity

The speed of rotation of the point around a circle can be measured in terms of radians per unit of time—the *radial velocity* (or *angular velocity*). Since there is a direct relationship between the rotation around the circle and sinusoidal functions, we can also characterize the frequency of a plotted sinusoidal function in terms of radians per second:

$$signal(t) = \sin(2\pi ft)$$

where t is the time variable and f is the number of times per second that the point completes a rotation. That is, f is the *frequency* of the signal, measured in cycles per second or hertz (Hz). The sine function repeats itself, so for any frequency f, the time variable can vary from $-\infty$ to $+\infty$ and the sine keeps on cycling from 0 to 1 to 0 to -1 to 0. In the signal-processing literature one often sees the abbreviation ω for $2\pi f$. Since ω is the frequency multiplied by 2π, it is called the *radian frequency*. The two formalisms are interchangeable in the rest of this exposition.

Magnitude as Size of Radius

The magnitude of a sinusoidal function is simply a scale factor r (see figure A.1), as in the following:

$$signal(t) = r\sin(\omega t).$$

Since the sine function varies between $+1$ to -1, so the curve of *signal*(t) also varies from positive to negative and back. In terms of our circular representation, r is the radius of the circle, or equally, the size of the rotating vector. This magnitude r can be calculated from the rectangular coordinates as:

$$r = magnitude = \sqrt{a^2 + b^2}.$$

Phase as Starting Point for Rotation

The *phase offset* of a periodic signal—measured at a specific point on the wave—is its displacement from the beginning of its period. We can measure the phase offset of any sinusoidal function as a displacement from the sine's usual starting point of zero degrees, as in the following equation:

$signal(t) = r\sin(\omega t + \phi)$

Here ϕ is the *phase angle*, an offset expressed in degrees. For example, the phase angle of a cosine wave with respect to a sine is 90 degrees or $\pi/2$ radians.

Looking at the complex plane, one can derive phase from the rectangular coordinates a and b by the following equation:

$\phi = \arctan(b_0/a_0)$

where arctan is the arctangent function and b_0 and a_0 are the position of the rotating point at $t = 0$. Conversions between rectangular and polar coordinates are important in the phase vocoder, as we explain later.

Phase as Sum of Sine and Cosine

The Fourier transform uses one of the most common tricks of engineering mathematics: the representation of a sinusoidal function as a sum of a sine and a cosine at the same frequency but with possibly different amplitudes. That is, single sinusoidal wave of arbitrary phase can be represented as the sum of a cosine and a sine wave, where the amplitudes of the cosine and sine

Table A.1 Phase shifting by adding a sine and a cosine at the same frequency, possibly with sign inversion

Sine	+	Cosine	Phase shift in degrees	Phase shift in terms of π	Phase shift in radians
sin	+	$0\cos$	0	0	0
sin	+	$0.5\cos$	22.5	$\pi/8$	0.3926
sin	+	cos	45	$\pi/4$	0.7853
$0.5\sin$	+	cos	67.5	$3\pi/8$	1.1780
$0\sin$	+	cos	90	$\pi/2$	1.5707
$-0.5\sin$	+	cos	112.5	$5\pi/8$	1.9634
$-\sin$	+	cos	135	$3\pi/8$	2.3561
$-\sin$	+	$0.5\cos$	157.5	$7\pi/8$	2.7488
$-\sin$	+	$0\cos$	180	π	3.1415
$-\sin$	+	$-0.5\cos$	202.5	$9\pi/8$	3.5344
$-\sin$	+	$-\cos$	225	$5\pi/4$	3.9269
$-0.5\sin$	+	$-\cos$	247.5	$11\pi/8$	4.3196
$0\sin$	+	$-\cos$	270	$3\pi/2$	4.7123
$0.5\sin$	+	$-\cos$	292.5	$13\pi/8$	5.1050
sin	+	$-\cos$	315	$7\pi/4$	5.4977
sin	+	$-0.5\cos$	337.5	$15\pi/8$	5.8904
sin	+	$-0\cos$	360	2π	6.2831

depend on the phase of the original sinusoidal waveform. This can be expressed as

$$r\sin(\omega t + \phi) = A\sin(\omega t) + B\cos(\omega t)$$

where A and B are amplitude scaling factors for the sine and cosine respectively. Table A.1 shows how the addition of a sine with a cosine at the same frequency results in a *phase-shifting* operation applied to the sine. It also shows that one can measure the phase shift in terms of either degrees, π, or radians. Figure A.4 plots the first five combinations in table A.1, culminating in a 90-degree phase shift.

The phase ϕ of the sinusoidal signal derives from the coefficients A and B as

$$\phi = \arctan(B/A).$$

This equation should ring a bell. Recall how we defined phase angle offset earlier in terms of rectangular coordinates a and b. Now we come to the point where we can relate the trigonometric functions we have been describing to the universe of complex numbers discussed initially.

Signals as Complex Exponentials

So far we have shown two representations for the frequency and phase of a sinusoid:

1. Sine at a specific radian frequency + a phase offset variable:

    $$\sin(\omega t + \phi)$$

2. Sine + cosine, both at the same radian frequency but with possibly different amplitudes and no phase offset variable:

    $$A\sin(\omega t) + B\cos(\omega t)$$

In both cases, the magnitude is a scaling factor that is multiplied times the total signal.

Now we introduce a third representation that captures the same features of frequency and phase. Here a sinusoid is projected by a *complex exponential function*. This representation is preferred in engineering because it simplifies the algebra of signal manipulation. *Euler's relation,* presented in the next section, makes this representation possible.

A word about notation is in order. Engineers use the symbol j to denote the square root of -1, rather than the mathematician's symbol i. This is because the symbol i is already taken to denote electrical current in the

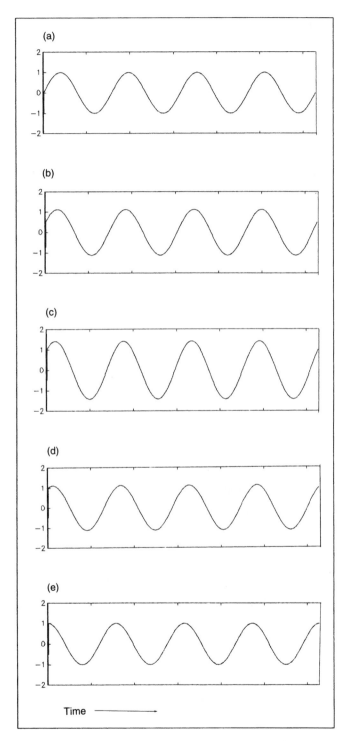

Figure A.4 Plot of the first five combinations of sine plus cosine in table A.1, showing the result as a phase shift applied to the sinusoid. In (*e*), the phase shift reaches 90 degrees: a cosine.

engineering world. To be consistent with the signal processing literature, we use j as the symbol for $\sqrt{-1}$ in the rest of this chapter.

Euler's Relation

The relationship between the circular (sinusoidal) functions, the complex numbers, and the exponential function $e = 2.71728\ldots$ was established in the nineteenth century by the Swiss mathematician Leonard Euler. *Euler's relation* states that the quantity e raised to the power of an imaginary exponent is equivalent to a complex sum of sinusoidal functions. That is,

$$e^{j\theta} = \cos(\theta) + j\sin(\theta).$$

The result of this equation for various values of θ can be plotted as a vector on the complex plane. If this formula seems mysterious, do not worry; simply accept it as the clever sleight of hand that it is! By inverting the algebra one obtains a definition of a cosine wave in terms of complex exponentials:

$$\cos(\theta) = 1/2[e^{j\theta} + e^{-j\theta}).$$

By substituting a time-varying phase ωt for the constant angle θ in the above equation one can represent a sinusoidal wave at a particular frequency. This equation reduces complex exponentials to a real trigonometric function.

Notice that the complex exponential representation represents a pure sinusoid as having a positive frequency component and a negative frequency component, both scaled by half. The negative side of this symmetric "dual spectrum" is simply a "side effect" of the exponential representation. It does appear in the output of the Fourier transform, however.

The essential point is that a representation in terms of complex exponentials is equivalent to a representation in terms of sinusoidal functions. Below we use the complex exponential representation, following engineering convention. This concludes our introduction to the mathematical representation of musical signals. Now we proceed directly to the theory of the Fourier transform.

The Fourier Series and Transform

Fourier analysis takes various forms, depending on whether it is applied to mathematical signals of infinite extent, actual analog signals of limited bandwidth, or a small number of digital samples. The next sections cover each form in turn, beginning with the theoretical FT and proceeding to more practical incarnations, ultimately leading to the fast Fourier transform.

Fourier Series

Fourier showed that a periodic function $x(t)$ of period T can be represented by the Fourier series:

$$x(t) = C_0 + \sum_{n=1}^{\infty} C_n \cos(n\omega_0 t + \theta_n).$$

That is, the function $x(t)$ is a sum of harmonically related sinusoidal functions with the frequency $\omega_n = n\omega_0 = 2\pi/T$. The first sinusoidal component is the *fundamental*; it has the same period as T. The numerical constants C_n and θ_n give the magnitude and phase of each component.

A Fourier series summation is a formula for reconstructing or synthesizing a periodic signal. But it does not tell us how to set the coefficients C_n and θ_n for an arbitrary (possibly aperiodic) input sound. For this we need an analysis method called the Fourier transform.

Fourier Transform

Suppose we wish to analyze the *continuous-time* signal $x(t)$ of infinite extent and bandwidth depicted in figure A.5. Fourier's theory says that $x(t)$ can be

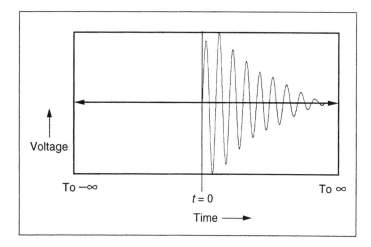

Figure A.5 Plot of voltage versus time for a continuous-time signal $x(t)$ of infinite length.

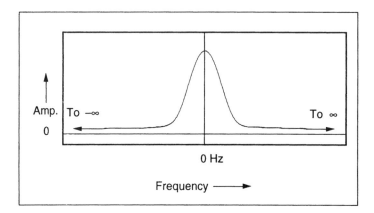

Figure A.6   Fourier transform magnitude $X[j\omega]$ of the input signal $x(t)$ in figure A.5.

accurately reconstructed with an infinite number of pure sinusoidal waves of different amplitudes, frequencies, and initial phases. These waves make up the signal's Fourier transform spectrum. The FT spectrum represents all frequencies from 0 Hz (i.e., a constant unvarying value) to infinity (∞) Hz, with a mirror image in the negative frequencies.

Figure A.6 depicts the magnitude of the Fourier transform of the time-domain signal $x(t)$. We denote this spectrum $X(f)$. By magnitude we mean the absolute value of the amplitude of the frequencies in the spectrum. The capital letter X denotes a Fourier transform, and the f within parentheses indicates that we are now referring to a frequency-domain signal, as opposed to the time-domain signal $x(t)$. Each value of $X(f)$ is a complex number. One can extract the magnitude and phase values from these complex numbers by means of the equations presented earlier.

Figure A.6, which shows just the magnitude, is not a complete picture of the Fourier transform. The curve shows us just the amount of each complex frequency $e^{j\omega t}$ that must be combined to synthesize $x(t)$. It does not show the phase of each of these components. We could also plot the *phase spectrum,* as it is called, but this is less often shown.

Figure A.6 shows that the magnitude of the Fourier transform $X(f)$ is symmetric around 0 Hz. Thus the Fourier representation combines equal amounts of positive and negative frequencies. This is the case for any real-valued input signal, as opposed to a complex-valued signal. As stated earlier, this dual-sided spectrum has no physical significance. (Note that the inverse Fourier transform takes a complex input signal—a spectrum—and generates a real-valued waveform as its output. See the section on the inverse Fourier transform later.)

The formula for the FT or *Fourier integral* is as follows:

$$X(f) = \int_{-\infty}^{\infty} x(t)e^{-j\omega t}\, dt.$$

This says that the FT at any particular frequency f is the integral of the multiplication of the input signal $x(t)$ by the pure tone $e^{-j\omega t}$. Intuitively, we could surmise that this integral will be larger when the input signal is intense and rich in partials.

Spectrum Analysis with Analog Test Instruments

In the first century of Fourier's theorem, the only way to realize a Fourier transform was by hand calculation—a laborious process of hundreds of integrations and summations. Later, mechanical spectrum analyzers helped build the foundations of quantum physics in the early part of the twentieth century. But mechanical analyzers could not handle continuously changing input signals. The development of analog filters in the 1920s and 1930s made it possible to perform a type of Fourier analysis electronically. An analog spectrum analyzer can be constructed as either a *swept filter* or a *filter bank*. The swept filter implements the Fourier transform $X(f)$ with a narrow bandpass filter having a tunable center frequency. To determine the spectrum, the center of the filter sweeps from the lowest to the highest frequency of interest; a printer plots the amplitude of the filter output. This technique is time-consuming and only works for a signal $x(t)$ that is periodic or can be made so by repetition.

If $x(t)$ is not periodic, its Fourier transform $X(f)$ can be determined with a filter bank that contains multiple bandpass filters operating in parallel. An example is the common *one-third-octave analyzer*, so-called because it covers each octave in the audio band with three filters (each one spanning four semitones) (figure A.7). This resolution may be adequate for applications in architectural acoustics (tuning the frequency response of a lecture hall, for example), but a resolution of four semitones is inadequate for most musical purposes. So with conventional analog test instruments, one is forced to accept either the periodicity constraint of the spectrum analyzer or the inaccuracy of the real-time analyzer.

By digitally sampling a signal $x(t)$, we can examine it in greater detail. Figure A.8 shows screen images of a real-time spectrum analyzer running on a computer. The family of digital Fourier transforms analyze discrete sampled signals instead of analog signals. This family is the subject of the rest of this appendix.

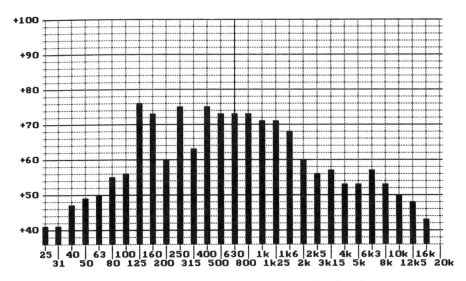

Figure A.7 One-third octave spectrum analyzer covering the almost ten octaves from 25 Hz to 20 Khz with 29 filter channels.

The Discrete-time Fourier Transform

So far we have talked only about signals that are continuous in time. However, digital audio systems cannot handle continuous-time signals; they handle *discrete-time* signals. A discrete-time signal has been sampled. As explained in chapter 1, before a signal is sampled it passes through an *antialiasing filter*. The antialiasing filter attenuates the frequencies in $x(t)$ above half the sampling frequency f_s. This produces a new discrete-time signal $x_f(t)$ whose Fourier transform is shown in figure A.9. Notice that the "tails" beyond 20 KHz and its negative mirror have been cut off. Although it is theoretically impossible to eliminate aliasing completely, because no actual filter can attenuate to zero the "tails" of the Fourier transform $X(f)$, aliasing can be reduced to arbitrarily small amounts with appropriate engineering.

Sampling the filtered signal $x_f(t)$ at a frequency f_s produces the discrete-time signal $x[n]$ shown in figure A.10. Notice the switch from the continuous time index t to the discrete time index n. Also note that we follow the notation convention that where continuous and discrete-time signals co-exist, the discrete-time signals are denoted with square brackets. The *period* between samples is $T = 1/f_s$, so $x[n] = x_f(nT)$.

The *discrete-time Fourier transform* (DTFT) of $x[n]$ can be denoted $X(e^{j\theta})$. Since θ spans both negative and positive angles, this results in another "dual spectrum" representation, although we are interested only in

(a)

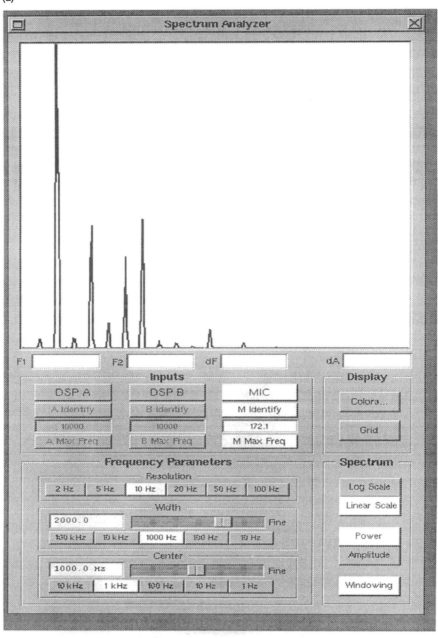

Figure A.8   Real-time spectrum analyzer displays running on a computer. These power spectra display the analysis of a male vocal utterance "Uhh" on a frequency scale from 0 to 2000 Hz. The frequency resolution in both cases is 10 Hz. (*a*) Linear amplitude scale. (*b*) Logarithmic amplitude scale. The outline of this display reveals the formant structure. (Images generated by the Monsterscope program, R. Crandall and C. Lydgate, authors.)

(b)

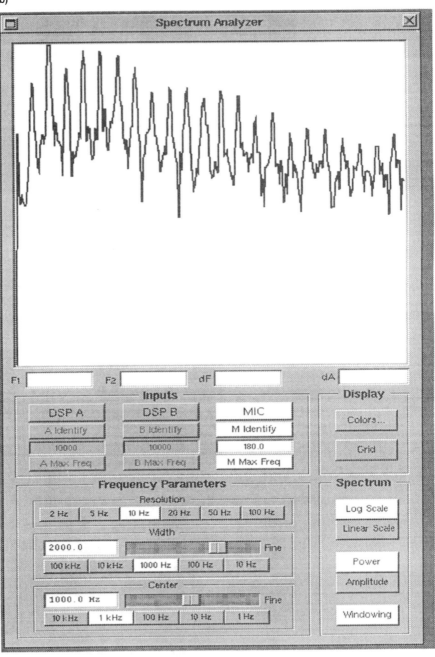

Figure A.8 (cont.)

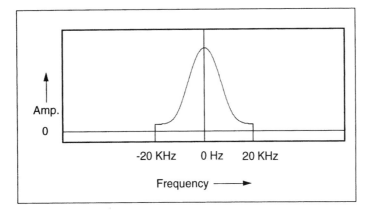

Figure A.9   Antialiased Fourier transform magnitude corresponding to the transform of a finite duration signal $x[n]$.

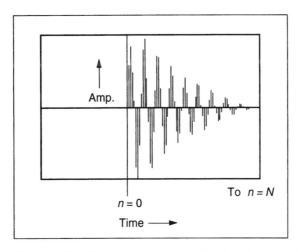

Figure A.10   The continuous-time signal $x(t)$ sampled into a discrete-time (digital) signal $x[n]$.

the positive part. The DTFT reveals the continuous frequency spectrum of $x[n]$. Note that the DTFT is different from the *discrete Fourier transform* (DFT) and the fast Fourier transform (FFT), which are presented later.

The signal $x[n]$ has a value only for discrete integer values of n, but it is composed of an infinite number of samples. Its DTFT, correspondingly, consists of an infinite number of frequencies. As we will see in a moment, however, the vast majority of these frequencies turn out to be the same, since discrete-time complex exponentials that differ in frequency by a multiple of 2π are identical. We can see this "infinite" spectrum in figure A.11 showing the DTFT $X(e^{j\omega})$, which is the Fourier transform of the antialiased signal $x_f(t)$ replicated to infinity at intervals of 2π, corresponding to multi-

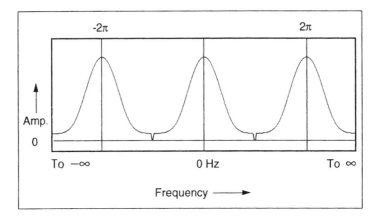

Figure A.11 Plot of the DTFT $X(e^{j\omega})$ of the sampled signal $x[n]$. The DTFT is a continuous-frequency spectrum.

ples of the sampling frequency f_s. This replication is one explanation for the phenomenon of aliasing, since the tails of $X(f)$ may overlap, causing *fold-over* (see chapter 1). If we raise the sampling frequency, there is more space between the peaks and less aliasing; if we lower it, the peaks push closer together and the notches in figure A.11 overlap, a symptom of aliasing.

Since DTFTs repeat themselves according to the equation

$$X(e^{j\theta_0}) = X(e^{j(\theta_0 + 2\pi m)})$$

where m is an arbitrary multiple, in practice we need only consider the values of a DTFT in an interval 2π wide, from $-\pi$ to π. The actual frequency range stays within these bounds, since $x[n]$ is a sampled signal that represents frequencies higher than half the sampling rate as foldover (see chapter 1).

The DTFT $X(e^{j\omega})$ between $-\pi$ and π is, assuming negligible aliasing, an accurate copy of the Fourier transform $X(f)$ of the continuous-time signal $x(n)$ between $-1/2f_s$ and $1/2f_s$. However, $X(e^{j\omega})$ is an infinite spectrum, and a digital computer can only calculate discrete quantities. What we need is an analysis technique that works with discrete spectra as well as discrete signals. This is the *discrete Fourier transform,* discussed next.

The Discrete Fourier Transform

The one kind of signal that has a discrete frequency-domain representation (i.e., isolated spectral lines) is a periodic signal. A periodic signal repeats at every interval T. Such a signal has a Fourier transform containing compo-

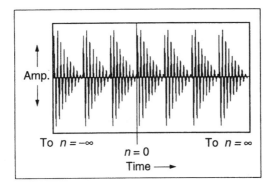

Figure A.12 The sampled signal $\sim x[n]$ consists of replications of $x[n]$ duplicated ad infinitum.

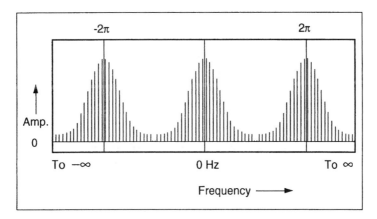

Figure A.13 A plot of the DFT of the sampled signal $\sim x[n]$. The DFT is a discrete-frequency spectrum.

nents at a fundamental frequency $(1/T)$ and its harmonics and is zero everywhere else.

A *periodic signal* in the precise mathematical sense must be defined from $t = -\infty$ to $t = \infty$. Colloquially, one speaks of signals as "periodic" if $x(t) = x(t + T)$ for an amount of time that is long relative to the period T. We can construct this kind of periodic signal by replicating a finite-length signal. Imagine that we infinitely replicate the finite-length signal $x(t)$ backwards and forwards in time. In the discrete-time (sampled) domain, this produces the periodic signal $\sim x[n]$ shown in figure A.12.

The frequency-domain representation of this replicated periodic signal $\sim x[n]$ is shown in figure A.13 and is called its *discrete Fourier transform* (DFT). Note that the DFT of $\sim x[n]$ is composed of samples of the DTFT of $x[n]$. Just as sampling $x(t)$ in the time domain results in replication in the

| Fourier transform (FT)

Continuous in time, continuous in frequency | Discrete-time Fourier transform (DTFT)

Discrete in time, continuous in frequency |
|---|---|
| Fourier series (FS)

Periodic in time, discrete in frequency | Discrete Fourier transform (DFT)

Discrete in time, discrete in frequency |

Figure A.14 The Fourier taxonomy.

frequency domain, replication of $x[n]$ in the time domain results in sampling in the frequency domain.

The DFT provides a sampled look at both the magnitude and phase of the spectrum of $x[n]$, and it is a central tool in musical signal processing. In effect, the DFT sets up a one-to-one correspondence between the number of input samples N and the number of frequencies it resolves.

Figure A.14 locates the place of the DFT in the taxonomy of Fourier transforms.

The Short-time Fourier Transform and Phase Vocoder

The *short-time Fourier transform* (STFT) is the practical cousin of the DFT. Widely used in music systems, the STFT is the core of the *phase vocoder* (PV) (Portnoff 1976, 1978, 1980; Holtzman 1980; Moorer 1978; Dolson 1983, 1986; Gordon and Strawn 1985; Strawn 1985b, 1987a; Serra 1989; Depalle and Poirot 1991; Erbe 1992; Walker and Fitz 1992). Chapter 13 introduced both the STFT and the PV, explaining their overall principles of operation and main parameters. This presentation looks closer, particularly at the insides of the PV analysis filters.

Depending on how one implements the STFT, it can be viewed in two ways: (1) as a series of DFTs of overlapping segments of sound (the *windowed DFT representation*), or (2) as a bank of bandpass filters equally spaced across the frequency domain (the *filter bank representation*). Let us look at each representation in turn.

Windowed DFT Representation

The STFT imposes a sequence of time windows on the input signal. These break the input signal into overlapping segments and shape each segment with a smooth attack and decay. The STFT analyzes each windowed segment separately. Adopting Dolson's (1986) notation, the equation for a DFT of an input signal $x[m]$ multiplied by a time-shifted window $h[n - m]$ is as follows:

$$X[n, k] = \sum_{m=-\infty}^{\infty} \{x[m]h[n - m]\}e^{-j\,(2\pi/N)km}.$$

Thus the output $X[n, k]$ is the Fourier transform of the windowed input at each discrete time n for each discrete frequency bin k. (See chapter 13 for an explanation of frequency bins.) The equation says that m can go from minus to plus infinity; this is a mathematician's way of saying "for an arbitrary-length input signal." For a specific short-time window, the bounds of m are set to the appropriate length. Here k is the index for the frequency bins and N is the number of points in the spectrum. The following relation sets the frequency corresponding to each bin k:

$$f_k = (k/N) \times f_s$$

where f_s is the sampling rate. So for a sampling rate of 44.1 KHz, an analysis window length N of 1024 samples, and a frequency bin $k = 1$, f_k is 43 Hz. The windowed DFT representation is particularly attractive because the transform can be implemented efficiently with the FFT, as discussed later.

An STFT formulation indicating the *hop size* or time advance of each window is:

$$X[l, k] = \sum_{m=0}^{M-1} h[m]x[m + (lH)]e^{-j(2\pi/N)km}$$

where $h[m]$ is the window that selects a block of data from the input signal $x[m]$, l is the *frame index*, and H is the hop size in samples (Serra 1989).

Filter Bank Representation

The filter bank representation is typical of the phase vocoder with its sinusoidal resynthesis stage. The PV filter bank obeys three constraints. First, the frequency response characteristics of all the filters are identical except that each has a passband centered at a different frequency. Second, the center frequencies of the filters are equally spaced from 0 Hz to the Nyquist frequency $f_s/2$. Third, the combined frequency response of the filters is essentially flat across the entire measured spectrum. This last constraint ensures that no frequency region is over- or underemphasized in the analysis.

The individual filters in the PV filter bank are based on the variation of the *heterodyne filtering* technique introduced in chapter 13. The next section explains the operation of the PV filter in more detail.

Inside the Phase Vocoder Filter

The PV filter can be expressed by regrouping the STFT equation as follows:

$$X[k] = \sum_{m=-\infty}^{\infty} \{x[m]e^{-j(2\pi/N)km}\}h[n - m].$$

In this equation, the output of the kth filter results from the multiplication of $x[m]$ by a complex sinusoid at frequency f_k. This shifts the frequency components in the vicinity of the kth frequency down to near 0 Hz and also up near twice f_k. The resulting signal is then convolved with a lowpass filter h. This removes the high frequency components and leaves only those input components originally in the vicinity of the frequency f_k (Dolson 1983, 1986). The effect is that of passing the signal through a bandpass filter centered at each frequency f_k.

The next three sections examine this process in more detail.

Heterodyne Bandpass Filter

Let us look at the graphic representation of the algorithm shown in figure A.15. The left side of stage 1 multiplies the input by a sine wave with an amplitude of 1.0 and a frequency equal to the center frequency of the bandpass filter. The right side does the same with a cosine wave.

What is the effect of this multiplication? If the input signal contains many frequency components, the multiplication of that signal by a constant frequency shifts all the frequency components by both plus and minus the center frequency of the filter. For a single sinusoidal component at 1100 Hz, for example, multiplied by a filter center frequency at 1000 Hz, the result is a split spectrum with a component at 100 Hz and a component at 2100 Hz. (This is equivalent to ring modulation, described in chapter 6.)

Each of the two sides then feeds into a lowpass filter designed to pass only the lower component. In effect, any frequencies that were close to the center frequency pass through the lowpass filter, and any frequencies that were far above or below it are filtered out. The filter is not a pure bandpass filter, because of the frequency shifting or heterodyning involved, but its effect is

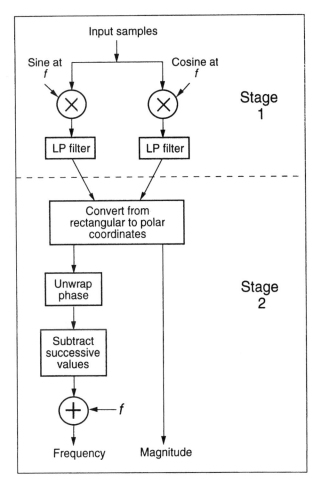

Figure A.15 Phase vocoder bandpass filter in two stages. See the text for an explanation.

that of a bandpass filter. A later stage in the PV compensates for the frequency shifting, so this does not influence the final output.

Rectangular to Polar Coordinates

Stage 2 depicts the conversion from rectangular to polar coordinates. This shows the two parallel paths within the PV filter: one to determine frequency and one to determine magnitude. (Note: these separate paths are not linked to the two paths of Stage 1. That is, both the left and right sides of Stage 1 are used to calculate each side of Stage 2.)

As explained earlier, a sine wave can be represented as a point rotating on a unit circle. If we measure this function in terms of its horizontal and vertical position on the two-dimensional plane on which the circle lies, we are using rectangular coordinates. The next stage of the PV uses an equivalent representation based on polar coordinates. Here the radial velocity (measured in radians per second) around the circle represents the frequency, while the size of the radius represents the amplitude.

In the terminology of Fourier analysis, by changing from rectangular to polar coordinates we are switching from a real and imaginary description to a magnitude and phase description, where "phase" here means angular position in time.

Phase Unwrapping

From a musical standpoint we are interested in working with spectra in terms of time-varying frequencies. Thus the PV filter includes another stage that converts from phase values to frequency values.

Since frequency is the number of rotations of the point around the circle per unit time, we can convert to frequency by measuring the difference in phase values between successive samples and divide by the time interval between them. Hence the *instantaneous frequency* can be defined as the difference between two successive phase values divided by the sample period.

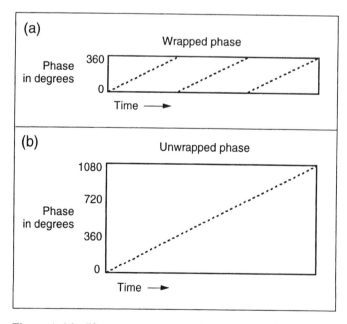

Figure A.16 Phase unwrapping. (*a*) Wrapped phase, cycling from 0 to 360. (*b*) Unwrapped phase, extending linearly over time.

An additional technicality remains, however. The arctan function only returns a value in the range of 0 to 360 degrees. For a constant sine wave the values may read: 45, 90, 135, 180, 225, 270, 315, 0, 45, 90.... Notice that when the sine completes a cycle the phase is 0, and the difference between 0 and 315 is not 45, as it is in the other pairs. Thus the PV filter adds 360 degrees when a full cycle is completed, a process known as *phase unwrapping*, shown in figures A.15 and A.16. The final stage in the PV filter is adding back the original filter center frequency to the instantaneous frequency signal already calculated.

Windowing the Signal

In order for a digital Fourier transform to handle real-world signals, all of which are finite-length, these signals must be *windowed*—multiplied by a brief *window function*—to limit their duration. A window is a mathematical function that is nonzero only over a limited time range. In terms of computer music, a window is nothing more than an envelope tailored to the demands of spectrum analysis.

Window Length

Many types of window functions can be concocted. The first criterion for a window is its length or size, that is, for its duration-limiting property (Hutchins 1986b). As explained in chapter 13, the length of the analysis window has a direct bearing on the frequency resolution of the analysis. For each windowed segment, we can think of the STFT as applying a bank of filters at equally spaced frequency intervals to the windowed input signal. The frequencies are spaced at integer multiples (harmonics) of

$$\frac{sampling\ frequency}{window\ length\ N\ in\ samples}.$$

Thus if the sampling frequency is 50 KHz and the window length is 1000 samples, the analysis frequencies are spaced at intervals 50,000 Hz/1000 = 50 Hz apart, starting at 0 Hz. Artifacts of windowed analysis arise from the fact that the samples analyzed do not always contain an integer number of periods of the frequencies they contain. Chapter 13 discussed the problem of analyzing these frequencies, which are in between the fixed analysis bands.

Window Shape

The second criterion in the choice of a window function is its shape, because this shape affects the spectrum measurement. Recall from chapter 6 that the multiplication of two such signals is a case of *amplitude modulation* (AM), where the input signal serves as the carrier and the window acts as the modulator. The DFT of a windowed signal acts on the product of the signal times the window, that is, $x[n] \times w[n]$. Since multiplication in the time domain results in convolution in the frequency domain (explained in chapter 10), the resulting spectrum is that of $x[n]$ convolved with $w[n]$.

The crudest windowing technique selects a part of an input signal $x[n]$ (say, for $0 \leq n < N$) and sets all other values of $x[n]$ to zero. Such a window is called a *rectangular* or *boxcar* window because it is equivalent to multiplying $x[n]$ by a signal $w[n]$ that looks like a rectangle of length N, starting at 0 with a height of 1 (figure A.17a).

When a single sine wave is fed into an FFT, we would like the the energy to be concentrated exclusively in the main lobe. Unfortunately the process

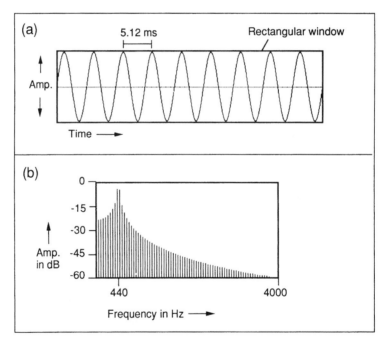

Figure A.17 Effect of a rectangular window on the spectrum reading. (*a*) Rectangular window around eight cycles of a sinusoid at 177 Hz. (*b*) Spectrum of (*a*). Ideally, the spectrum of a sinusoid should be a single line. Instead, a rectangular window indicates sidebands ranging from 22 to 442 Hz.

of windowing distorts the analysis and causes *leakage* or "splatter" (Jaffe 1987b) from the main lobe into the side lobes. Any frequency energy present in the windowed signal splatters across all frequency bins of the output spectrum (Harris 1978). This can clearly be seen in the spectrum of a sine wave windowed by a rectangle. Here the window diffuses the single input frequency component into energy extending across the bandwidth of the analyzer (figure A.17b).

All standard (nonrectangular) windows are symmetric and have spectra whose shapes resemble a mathematical sinc function, that is, $\sin(t)/t$. This shape is characterized by a prominent *main lobe* and a series of *side lobes* on either side of the main lobe. The primary properties of the window are the *width of the main lobe*—defined as the number of frequency bins it spans— and the *highest side lobe level,* which measures how many decibels down the highest side lobe is from the main lobe. The magnitude of the side lobes is dependent on the shape of the window function and is independent of the window's duration.

Figure A.18 depicts a more well-behaved window function, a Gaussian curve. The first side lobe is about 45 dB down from the main lobe.

In addition to the distorting effects of leakage on the spectrum estimate, leakage has a detrimental effect on the detectability of sinusoidal components. In extreme cases, the side lobes of strong frequency components can mask the main lobe of weak frequency components in adjacent bins (figure A.19).

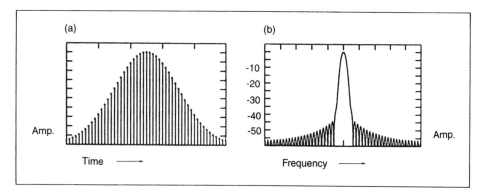

Figure A.18 Window and spectrum. (*a*) Gaussian window. (*b*) Spectrum of window plotted on a dB scale. The first side lobe is about −45 dB from the peak lobe. In any case, it is clear that the window will diffuse the energy of any signal multiplied by it across the bandwidth of the analyzer. One can see a ripple in the spectrum; this is caused by the truncation of the Gaussian window on its left and right sides. (After Marple 1987.)

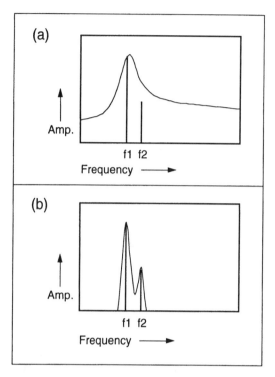

Figure A.19 Spectrum leakage from some windows may obscure the presence of a weaker-frequency component. (*a*) Rectangular window. The existence of the component at *f2* is obscured by leakage. (*b*) A Kaiser window resolves the presence of the component at *f2*.

One indicator of how well a window suppresses leakage is the *peak side lobe level,* relative to the main lobe; another is the *rate of decay* of these levels. A window with a rapid decay is more immune to interferences at frequencies removed from those of interest. Table A.2 lists these characteristics for standard window types.

The convolution of the window spectrum with the signal spectrum means that the most narrow spectral response of the transform is limited to that of the main lobe width of the window transform, independent of the input signal. For a rectangular window, the main lobe width between -3 dB points (therefore the resolution) is approximately the inverse of the observation time. Other windows may be used, but the resolution will always be proportional to the reciprocal of the observation time.

Generally, the price to be paid for a reduction in the side lobes is a broadening of the main lobe width. In other words, reducing the side lobes decreases the resolution of the spectrum estimate. Hence, in selecting an

Table A.2 Side lobe characteristics for standard window types

Window type	Peak sidelobe (in dB)	Sidelobe decay (in dB per octave)
Rectangular	−13	−6
Hamming	−43	−6
Hanning or Hann	−31	−18
Gaussian		
$a = 2.5$	−42	−6
$a = 3.5$	−69	−6
Blackman	−58	−18
Blackman-Harris		
3-term	−71	−6
4-term	−92	−6
Kaiser		
$a = 2$	−40	−6
$a = 3$	−65	−6
$a = 4$	−91	−6

Note: The rectangular window is included as an example of a poor window. In the Gaussian and Blackman-Harris windows, the factor a controls the shape of the window. In general, a larger value for a means more concentration of area at the center of the window, and smaller "tails" at the extremes of the window. Data are from Harris (1978), Nuttall (1981), and Marple (1987).

envelope, one has to choose between distortion (high side lobes, which may smother adjacent peaks) and lack of resolution (too broad a main lobe).

Choice of Window

From a practical standpoint, there is no "universally best" window choice for all sounds and all analysis purposes. For many musical applications involving sound transformation, a smooth bell-shaped curve such as a Kaiser or Gaussian window works reasonably well.

The advanced user of the phase vocoder must decide which aspect of analysis is most important in a specific application. For example, when it is known that the input signal is composed of a distinct number of sine components, then a window with a narrow main lobe is recommended. For noisy signals, where the energy is not centered at individual frequencies, a window with a broad main lobe works best. Since the choice of window affects the plot, spectrum displays for scientific purposes should indicate the type of window used in the analysis.

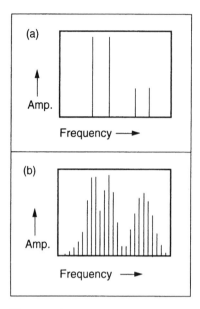

Figure A.20   Zero-padding a window interpolates points in the spectrum. (*a*) Unpadded spectrum. (*b*) Padded spectrum.

Zero-padding the DFT

When the DFT analyzes a short sequence of samples, the spectrum plot consists of a few lines spaced far apart. The leaves an ambiguous visual impression, since it is hard to tell what the spectrum is in between these lines. One trick that is employed in DFT analysis of short sequences is inserting zero-valued samples around $x[n]$ before replicating it. This creates a signal with a larger period and therefore a smaller "fundamental frequency of analysis."

Zero-padding has the effect of interpolating analysis points in between those points that would be obtained with a nonpadded transform (figure A.20). Since this adds sample points to the spectrum, zero-padding is equivalent to oversampling the spectrum. This does not increase the actual frequency resolution since the frequencies between the actual analyzed ones are not being measured. Only analyzing more actual input samples can increase the frequency resolution. But the spectrum points injected by zero-padding can help to visualize certain curves in the spectrum, such as spectrum peaks that are not exact bin frequencies. Zero-padding is also helpful in overlap-add resynthesis when the signal is to be filtered in the frequency domain. Without zero-padding the signal may be *time-aliased* (repeated in time).

The Inverse Discrete Fourier Transform

Following analysis, resynthesis generates a close approximation of the original sampled input signal from its DFT. This operation is called the *inverse discrete Fourier transform* (IDFT) and can be defined by the equation

$$x[n] = 1/N \sum_{k=0}^{N-1} X(k)e^{j(2\pi/N)nk}$$

where $X(k)$ is an analysis frame of N frequencies indexed by bin numbers k. For each analysis frame, this yields a sequence of N samples. In order to reassemble the entire input signal, we must string together all the overlapping IDFTs. This process is called *overlap-add* resynthesis and is the topic of the next section. Following that we describe an alternative approach called *oscillator bank* resynthesis.

Overlap-add Resynthesis

With ideal analysis parameters and infinite precision arithmetic, one can reassemble the original waveform perfectly from a succession of IDFTs by means of *overlap-add* (OA) *resynthesis,* introduced in chapter 13. The basic idea is to perform an inverse FFT for each frame and then sum the overlapping frames. The following procedure describes the analysis/OA-resynthesis process in the phase vocoder.

1. Read M samples of the input signal x into a local buffer memory. M is the frame length, and the time advance or hop size in samples from one frame to the next is H.

2. Multiply the samples in the frame by an analysis window $w[m]$ of length M.

3. Extend the windowed frame on both sizes to obtain a zero-padded frame of length N, where N is a power of two larger than M. N/M is the zero-padding factor.

4. Apply an FFT of length N to the frame to obtain the spectrum. Each frequency channel k of the analysis is referred to as a bin.

5. Convert each frequency bin from rectangular to polar form to obtain the magnitude (absolute value) and phase. (This conversion is explained later.) Differentiate the phase to obtain instantaneous frequency. It is customary to interpolate the amplitude, phase, and frequency trajec-

tories from one hop to the next. The phase is usually discarded at this point, but it can be regenerated as needed as the integral of the instantaneous frequency. (Step 5 is usually referred to as *phase vocoder analysis*.)

6. Apply any desired modifications to the analysis data, including time scaling, pitch transposition, formant modification, etc.

7. Apply an inverse FFT to obtain a time waveform for each frame.

8. If the phase spectrum was edited, apply a resynthesis window to the output of the inverse FFT.

9. Reconstruct the final output by overlapping and adding the output frames.

Assessment of Overlap-add Resynthesis

Overlap-add resynthesis is a rather delicate operation in the sense that modifications made in step 6 can easily affect the quality of the resynthesis process. In particular, if the sum of the overlapping windows does not add up to a constant, then a form of modulation will be heard at the frequency of the hop size. Indeed any additive or multiplicative transformations that disturb the perfect summation criterion cause side effects (Allen and Rabiner 1977). The effects are particularly noticeable in rapidly varying parts of a sound, such as attacks and decays. In general, transformations using OA resynthesis work best for constant or slowly changing sounds.

Oscillator Bank Resynthesis

An alternative to overlap-add resynthesis is *oscillator bank* (OB) resynthesis. A bank of oscillators are driven by a set of amplitude and frequency trajectories derived from the analysis. OB corresponds—on the synthesis side— to the filter bank analysis representation of the STFT presented earlier, and to the *tracking phase vocoder* presented in chapter 13. The main difference between OA resynthesis and OB resynthesis is as follows: rather than summing the overlapping sinusoidal components in each frame, OB constructs continuous frequency "tracks" (time-varying control functions or envelopes) for a bank of sinusoidal oscillators in additive sine wave synthesis.

Assessment of Oscillator Bank Resynthesis

The advantage of sinusoidal resynthesis is that it is more robust and allows more flexible musical transformations. This is because one can directly manipulate frequency and amplitude envelopes without worrying about the perfect overlap constraint of OA resynthesis. OB is not as efficient computationally as OA resynthesis, however, and requires an enormous amount of data—much more than the original sound file. Thus some form of data reduction is usually employed, as discussed in chapter 4. Chapters 4 and 13 also discuss musical applications of OB resynthesis.

The Fast Fourier Transform

This section explains the need for a faster DFT calculation and then presents, in schematic form, the structure of FFT algorithms.

The Need for a Fast Fourier Transform

Until the mid-1960s, the computation of the DFT required an inordinate amount of calculation time. The DFT of N samples ($0 \leq n \leq N - 1$) for N frequencies ($0 \leq k \leq N - 1$) can be written as

$$X[k] = \sum_{n=0}^{N-1} x[n] W_N^{nk}$$

where $k = 0, 1, 2, \ldots, N - 1$, and W_N is the complex exponential:

$$W_N = e^{-j(2\pi/N)}.$$

In other words, a vector of input samples $x[n]$ is multipled by a matrix W_N whose $[n, k]$th element is the constant W_N taken to the power n times k. The N-by-N matrix W is shown below, indexed from 0 to $N - 1$:

$$\begin{bmatrix} W_N^0 & W_N^0 & W_N^0 & W_N^0 \\ W_N^0 & W_N^1 & W_N^2 & W_N^{(N-1)} \\ W_N^0 & W_N^2 & W_N^4 & W_N^{2(N-1)} \\ \vdots & & & \\ W_N^0 & W_N^{(N-1)} & W_N^{2(N-1)} & W_N^{(N-1)(N-1)} \end{bmatrix}$$

Each element in the matrix is called a *twiddle factor*, in the jargon of Fourier analysis (Rabiner et al. 1972). (Other terms for twiddle factor include *phase factor*, or *phase rotation factor*.) The important thing is that these factors are not all unique; there is a great deal of redundancy in W, and this is one of the keys to the efficiency of the FFT. The vector-times-matrix multiplication in the DFT produces a vector result, the elements of which are complex numbers whose components represent the magnitudes and phases of the spectrum $X[k]$.

This matrix or *direct* formulation of the DFT requires about N^2 complex multiplications and additions, plus a smaller number of operations to generate the required powers of W_N^{nk}. Note that each complex multiplication involves four real multiplications:

$$\overset{\text{1}}{} \qquad \overset{\text{2}}{} \qquad \overset{\text{3}}{} \qquad \overset{\text{4}}{}$$
$$(A + jB) \times (C + jD) = ([A \times C] - [B \times D]) + j([A \times D] + [B \times C])$$

When the number of samples being analyzed is small, N^2 complex multiplications are easily handled by modern computers. In musical signal analysis, however, we want analysis at a high sampling rate, using multiple channels, with large overlapping windows—and in real time, of course. In this case, optimization is essential. For example, with a stereo input signal, a windowed DFT every 50th of a second at a sampling rate of 48 KHz and a window overlap factor of 8 soaks up more than 66 million complex multiplications per second. When we toss in the tracking operations in the phase vocoder, real-time interaction, or other simultaneous computations such as spectrum display algorithms, the desirability of a speedup becomes obvious.

Cooley and Tukey (1965) demonstrated a redundancy in the algebraic structure in the computation of the DFT that could be exploited to speed up the process by several orders of magnitude. Rather than requiring the N^2 operations of the DFT, the FFT takes on the order of $N \times \log_2(N)$ operations. Hence for typical audio FFTs of between 64 and 16,000 samples, the FFT is between 10 to 1100 times faster than the DFT. As stated earlier, Cooley and Tukey were not the first to make this discovery, but their paper was widely noticed because by 1965 a number of people were using computers in signal processing.

The Structure of FFT Algorithms

This section gives an overview of the magical FFT, explaining why it is much faster than the directly calculated DFT. Our goal is to impart a basic appreciation of the mechanisms of the FFT without descending into implementation details. Many variations on FFT algorithms exist, and dozens of signal-processing textbooks offer detailed mathematical analyses or complete code listings of FFT programs. (See, for example, Aho and Ullman 1975; Oppenheim and Schafer 1975; Rabiner and Gold 1975; Marple 1987; Nussbaumer 1981; Press et al. 1988; Digital Signal Processing Committee 1980.)

FFT algorithms can be divided into two basic classes: the *decimation in time* or Cooley-Tukey method, and the *decimation in frequency* or Sande-Tukey method (Nussbaumer 1981). The two methods are similar and produce equivalent results. Thus here we present only the decimation-in-time version.

Radix 2 FFTs

A premise underneath all FFTs is that the input sequence is a power of two in length. Hence the literature often refers to the *radix 2 FFT* in order to stress this constraint on the input sequence. In practice, any number of input samples can be turned into a power of two by zero-padding, as explained earlier.

The central idea of the FFT is to divide the original N-point input sequence into two shorter sequences of length $N/2$, the DFTs of which can be combined to give the DFT of the original N-point sequence. One sequence derives from the even-numbered points of the original N, the other from the odd-numbered points. This bifurcation of the stream of input samples, which is the source of the term "decimation-in-time," reduces the number of complex multiplications by half. The bifurcation can be repeated recursively, reducing sequences of length $N/2$ to sequences of length $N/4$, and so on, until one is left with a 2-point DFT. A 2-point DFT is simply the sum and the difference of the two input samples, using no multiplications. Multiplications are needed only when combining the longer-length DFTs with the twiddle factors. Since there are $\log_2(N)$ stages of bifurcation, the number of complex multiplications required to evaluate an N-point DFT is approximately $N/2 \log_2(N)$.

The Butterfly

The core operation of the decimation-in-time is the *butterfly,* shown in figure A.21, in which two inputs A and B combine to yield the two outputs X and Y via the operation:

$$X = A + W_N^{nk} B$$

$$Y = A - W_N^{nk} B$$

Only one multiplication is required per butterfly since the twiddle factor $W_N^{nk} B$ obtained in computing X can be reused in computing Y. Another advantage of the butterfly structure is that only one additional memory location is required to transform an N-point sequence stored in memory. A

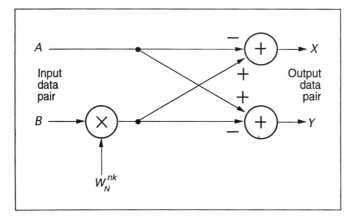

Figure A.21   Schema of the FFT butterfly for a pair of input samples, involving a multiplication, three additions, and a subtraction. W_N^{nk} is the twiddle or phase rotation factor, whose value depends of n, k, and the algorithm's processing step.

program can compute intermediate stages of the FFT and store the results in the same array where the original input data were stored. Such algorithms are called *in-place FFTs*.

Data Shuffling and Bit Reversal

In order for the output sequence $X(k)$ to be in natural order $k = 0, 1, \ldots$ $N - 1$, the input sequence of samples has to be stored in a shuffled order. This order can be derived by the trick of reversing the bits of the binary representation of the index of the input datum, as shown in table A.3. Many digital signal processors provide bit-reversal instructions in hardware for precisely this purpose.

Figure A.22 shows the overall structure of the FFT algorithm. The stages of segmentation and successive power-of-two DFT calculations are carried out by a recursive algorithm. (See chapter 2 for an explanation of recursion.) This recursion means that the code for the FFT can be condensed into a very compact program. For example, Rabiner and Gold (1975) give an algorithm that requires just 32 lines of code in the Fortran language.

Number Theoretic Transforms: Alternatives to the FFT

Alternative methods exist for computing the DFT using *number theoretic transforms* that are even faster than the FFT. The difficulty with these methods is that they apply only in specialized cases, when the parameters of the analysis fit constraints imposed by the transform (Rabiner and Gold 1975;

Table A.3 Correspondence between input index and bit-reversed index used to shuffle data in preparation for butterfly operations in the fast Fourier transform

Index	Binary	Bit-reversed	Bit-reversed index
0	000	000	0
1	001	100	4
2	010	010	2
3	011	110	6
4	100	001	1
5	101	101	5
6	110	011	3
7	111	111	7

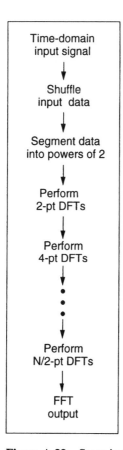

Figure A.22 Steps in the FFT algorithm.

Nussbaumer 1981). Thus in practical applications the FFT is overwhelmingly preferred due to its flexibility.

Conclusion

This chapter has traced a lengthy path to the FFT—a central procedure in sound analysis. Starting from the galaxy of imaginary numbers, and traveling by way of the abstract Fourier transform, the discrete-time Fourier transform, the discrete Fourier transform, the short-time Fourier transform, and the inverse discrete Fourier transform, we arrived at a compact FFT algorithm, the core of so many musical tools: spectrum analyzers and resynthesizers, frequency-domain pitch detectors, spectrum-based filters, and convolvers.

In its infancy, digital Fourier analysis required the special care and feeding of a laboratory environment in order to function. In recent years, robust, real-time Fourier techniques have come of age, graduating to the demands of the concert stage. Exploring the musical potential of real-time Fourier techniques has only just begun.

Alles, H. 1977a. "A portable digital sound synthesis system." *Computer Music Journal* 1(4): 5–6. Revised version in C. Roads and J. Strawn, eds.1985. *Foundations of Computer Music*. Cambridge, Massachusetts: The MIT Press. pp. 244–249.

Alles, H. 1977b. "A 256-channel performer-input device." *Computer Music Journal* 1(4): 14–15. Revised and updated version in C. Roads and J. Strawn, eds. 1985. *Foundations of Computer Music*. Cambridge, Massachusetts: The MIT Press. pp. 257–260.

Alles, H. 1980. "Music synthesis using real-time digital techniques." *Proceedings of the IEEE* 68(4): 436–449.

Alles, H., and G. Di Giugno. 1977. "The 4B: a one-card 64-channel digital synthesizer." *Computer Music Journal* 1(4): 7–9. Revised and updated version in C. Roads and J. Strawn, eds. 1985. *Foundations of Computer Music*. Cambridge, Massachusetts: The MIT Press. pp. 250–256.

Allouis, J.-F. 1979. "The use of high-speed microprocessors for sound synthesis." *Computer Music Journal* 3(1): 14–16. Reprinted in C. Roads and J. Strawn, eds. 1985. *Foundations of Computer Music*. Cambridge, Massachusetts: The MIT Press. pp. 281–288.

Allouis, J.-F., and J.-Y. Bernier. 1982. "The SYTER project: sound processor design and software overview." In J. Strawn and T. Blum, eds. *Proceedings of the 1982 International Computer Music Conference*. San Francisco: International Computer Music Association. pp. 232–240.

Alonso, S. 1973. "A computer terminal for music instruction." *Proceedings of the Acoustical Society of America*. p. 73.

Alonso, S., J. Appleton, and C. Jones. 1977. "A computer music system for every university: the Dartmouth College example." *Creative Computing* 3(2): 57–59.

Ames, C. 1982. "Protocol: motivation, design, and production of a composition for solo piano." *Interface* 11: 213–238.

Ames, C. 1983. "Stylistic automata in *Gradient*." *Computer Music Journal* 7(4): 45–56.

Ames, C. 1985. "The ASHTON score transcription utility." *Interface* 14: 1–19.

Ames, C. 1987a. "Automated composition in retrospect: 1956–1986." *Leonardo* 20(2): 169–186.

Ames, C. 1987b. "Tutorial on automated composition." In J. Beauchamp, ed. *Proceedings of the 1987 International Computer Music Conference*. San Francisco: International Computer Music Association. pp. 1–8.

Ames, C. 1989a. "The Markov process as a compositional model: a survey and tutorial." *Leonardo* 22(2): 175–188.

Ames, C. 1989b. "Introduction to COMPOSE." Unpublished manuscript.

Ames, C. 1990. "Statistics and compositional balance." *Perspectives of New Music* 28(1): 80–111.

Ames, C. 1992. "Cybernetic Composer: an overview." In M. Balaban, K. Ebcioglu, and O. Laske, eds. *Understanding Music with AI*. Cambridge, Massachusetts and Menlo Park, California: The MIT Press and AAAI Press. pp. 186–205.

Amuedo, J. 1984. "Estimation of musical pitch when F[0] is large." Presented at the 1984 International Computer Music Conference, Paris.

Amuedo, J. 1985. "Periodicity estimation by hypothesis-directed search." *Proceedings of the IEEE International Conference on Acoustics, Speech, and Signal Processing*. New York: IEEE. pp. 395–398.

Andersen, K. 1978. "A digital sound synthesizer keyboard." *Computer Music Journal* 2(3): 16–23.

Anderson, D. and R. Kuivila. 1986. "Accurately timed generation of discrete musical events." *Computer Music Journal* 10(3): 49–56.

Anderson, D., and R. Kuivila. 1989. "Continuous abstractions for discrete event languages." *Computer Music Journal* 13(3): 11–23.

Anderson, D., and R. Kuivila. 1991. "Formula: a programming language for expressive computer music." *IEEE Computer* 24(7): 12–21.

Anderson, T. 1990. "E-SCAPE: an extendible sonic composition and performance environment." In S. Arnold and G. Hair, eds. *Proceedings of the 1990 International Computer Music Conference*. San Francisco: International Computer Music Association. pp. 212–215.

Angus, J., and T. Faulkner. 1990. "Practical 20 bit." *Studio Sound* 32(4): 38–45.

Apel, W. 1972. *Harvard Dictionary of Music*. Cambridge, Massachusetts: Harvard University Press.

Apple. 1989. "Audio Interchange File Format. Version 1.3." Cupertino: Apple Computer.

Arfib, D. 1979. "Digital synthesis of complex spectra by means of multiplication of non-linear distorted sine waves." *Journal of the Audio Engineering Society* 27(10): 757–779.

Arfib, D. 1991. "Analysis, transformation, and resynthesis of musical sounds with the help of a time-frequency representation." In G. De Poli, A. Piccialli, and C. Roads, eds. *Representations of Musical Signals*. Cambridge, Massachusetts: The MIT Press. pp. 87–118.

Armani, F., L. Bizzarri, E. Favreau, and A. Paladin 1992. "MARS—DSP environment and applications." In A. Strange, ed. *Proceedings of the 1992 International Computer Music Conference*. San Francisco: International Computer Music Association. pp. 344–347.

Asai, A. 1986. "Semiconductor memory trends." *Proceedings of the IEEE* 74(12): 1623–1633.

Ashton, A. 1971. "Electronics, music, and computers." Ph.D. dissertation. Salt Lake City: University of Utah Computer Science Department.

Asta, V., A. Chauveau, G. Di Giugno, and J. Kott. 1980. "The 4X: a real-time digital synthesis system." *Automazione e Strumentazione* 28(2): 119–133.

Atal, B., and S. Hanauer. 1971. "Speech analysis and synthesis by linear prediction of the speech wave." *Journal of the Acoustical Society of America* 50(2): 637–655.

Atal, B., and J. Remde. 1982. "A new model of LPC excitation for producing natural sounding speech at low bit rates. "*Proceedings of the 1982 IEEE Conference on Speech and Acoustics*. New York: IEEE.

Audio Engineering Society. 1991. "AES11-1991 AES recomended practice for digital audio engineering—synchronization of digital audio equipment in studio operations." *Journal of the Audio Engineering Society* 39(3): 156–162

Audio Engineering Society. 1992a. "AES recommended practice for digital audio engineering—serial transmission format for two-channel linearly represented digital audio data." *Journal of the Audio Engineering Society* 40(3): 148–163.

Audio Engineering Society. 1992b. "AES recommended practice for digital audio engineering—format for the user data channel of the AES digital audio interface." *Journal of the Audio Engineering Society* 40(3): 167–183.

Audio Engineering Society. 1992c. "AES standard for professional audio equipment—application of connectors, part 1, XLR-type polarity and gender." *Journal of the Audio Engineering Society* 40(1/2): 50–51.

Austin, L. 1992. "An interview with John Cage and Lejaren Hiller." *Computer Music Journal* 16(4): 15–29. Revised version of Hiller and Cage 1968.

Babbitt, M. 1960. "Twelve-tone invariants as compositional determinants." *Musical Quarterly* 46: 246–259. Reprinted in P. Lang, ed. 1962. *Problems in Modern Music*. New York: Norton. pp. 108–121.

Babbitt, M. 1961. "Set structure as a compositional determinant." *Journal of Music Theory*. 5(2): 72–94. Reprinted in B. Boretz and E. Cone, eds. 1972. *Perspectives on Contemporary Music Theory*. New York: Norton. pp. 129–147.

Babbitt, M. 1964. "An introduction to the RCA synthesizer." *Journal of Music Theory* 8(2): 251.

Babbitt, M. 1965. "The use of computers in musicological research." *Perspectives of New Music* 3(2): 74–82.

Backhaus, J. 1932. "Über die Bedeutung der Ausgleichsvorgäng in der Akustik." *Zeitschrift für technische Physik* 13(1): 31–46.

Backus, John. 1977. *The Acoustical Foundations of Music*. Second edition. New York: Norton.

Backus, J. 1978. "Can programming be liberated from the von Neumann style? A functional style and its algebra of programs." *Communications of the Association for Computing Machinery* 21(8): 613–641.

Baffioni, C., F. Guerra, and L. T. Lalli. 1984. "The theory of stochastic processes and dynamic systems as a basis for models of musical structures." In M. Baroni and L. Callegari, eds. *Musical Grammars and Computer Analysis*. Florence: L. Olschki. pp. 317–324.

Baggi, D. 1991. "Neurswing: an intelligent workbench for an investigation of swing in jazz." *IEEE Computer* 24(7): 60–64.

Baisnée, P.-F. 1985. *Chant Manual*. Paris: IRCAM.

Baisnée, P.-F., J.-B. Barrière, M.-A. Dalbavie, J. Duthen, M. Lindberg, Y. Potard, and K. Saariaho. 1988. "Esquisse: a compositional environment." In C. Lischka and J. Fritsch. *Proceedings of the 1988 International Computer Music Conference*. San Francisco: International Computer Music Association, and Cologne: Feedback Papers. pp. 108–118.

Baker, R. 1963. "MUSICOMP: MUsic Simulator-Interpreter for COMpositional Procedures for the IBM 7090 electronic digital computer." Technical Report 9. Urbana: University of Illinois Experimental Music Studio.

Balaban, M., K. Ebcioglu, and O. Laske, eds. 1992. *Understanding Music with AI*. Cambridge, Massachusetts and Menlo Park, California: The MIT Press and AAAI Press.

Bamberger, J. 1979. "LOGO music project: experiments in musical perception and design."A. I. Memo 523. Cambridge, Massachusetts: M.I.T. Artificial Intelligence Laboratory.

Banger, C., and B. Pennycook. 1983. "GCOMP: graphics control of mixing and processing." *Computer Music Journal* 7(4): 33–39.

Barbaud, P. 1966. *Initiation—la musique algorithmique*. Paris: Dunod.

Barbaud, P. 1968. *La musique, discipline scientifique*. Paris: Dunod.

Barlow, C. 1980. "Bus journey to parametron." *Feedback Papers* 21–23.

Barlow, C. 1986. "Two essays on theory." *Computer Music Journal* 11(1): 44–60.

Barlow, C. 1989. Personal communication about the MIDIDESK environment.

Baroni, M., R. Brunetti, L. Callegari, and C. Jacobini. 1984. "A grammar for melody: relationships between melody and harmony." In M. Baroni and L. Callegari, eds. *Musical Grammars and Computer Analysis*. Florence: L. Olschki. pp. 201–218.

Barr, A. P. Cohen, and E. Feigenbaum, eds. 1981. *The Handbook of Artificial Intelligence*. Volumes 1, 2, and 3. Los Altos: William Kaufmann.

Barrière, J.-B., ed. 1991. *Le timbre, métaphore pour la composition*. Paris: IRCAM and Cristian Bourgeois.

Barrière, J.-B., F. Iovino, and M. Laurson. 1991. "A new CHANT synthesizer in C and its control environment in Patchwork. "In B. Alphonce and B. Pennycook, eds. *Proceedings of the 1991 International Computer Music Conference*. San Francisco: International Computer Music Association. pp. 11–14.

Barrière, J.-B., Y. Potard, and P. F. Baisnée. 1985. "Models of continuity between synthesis and processing for the elaboration and control of timbre structure." In B. Truax, ed. *Proceedings of the 1985 International Computer Music Conference*. San Francisco: International Computer Music Association. pp. 193–198.

Bartlett, M. 1979. "A microcomputer-controlled synthesis system for live performance." *Computer Music Journal* 3(1): 25–37. Revised and updated version in C. Roads and J. Strawn, eds. 1985. *Foundations of Computer Music*. Cambridge, Massachusetts: The MIT Press. pp. 539–550.

Baruzzi, G., P. Grossi, and M. Milani. 1975. "Musical studies: summary of activity from 1969–1975." Technical report 102. Pisa: Consiglio Nazionale delle Ricerche (CNUCE).

Bass, S., and T. Goeddel. 1981. "The efficient digital implementation of subtractive music synthesis." *IEEE Micro* 1(3): 24–37.

Bastiaans, M. 1980. "Gabor's expansion of a signal into Gaussian elementary signals." *Proceedings of the IEEE* 68: 538–539.

Bastiaans, M. 1985. "On the sliding-window representation of signals." *IEEE Transactions on Acoustics, Speech, and Signal Processing* ASSP-33(4): 868–873.

Bate, J. 1990. "The effect of modulator phase on timbres in FM synthesis." *Computer Music Journal* 14(3): 38–45.

Battier, M. 1978. *Musique et informatique: une bibliographie indexée*. Ivry-sur-Seine: Elmeratto.

Battier, M. 1981. "Les tendences recentes des musiques electroacoustiques et l'environment informatique." Doctoral dissertation. Paris: Université de Paris X.

Bayle, F. 1989. "La musique acousmatique ou l'art des sons projetés." Paris: Encyclopedia Universalis.

Bayle, F. 1993. *Musique Acousmatique*. Paris: Institut National de l'Audiovisuel/ Groupe de Recherches Musicales et Buchet/Chastel.

Beauchamp, J. 1966. "Additive synthesis of harmonic musical tones." *Journal of the Audio Engineering Society* 14(4): 332–342.

Beauchamp, J. 1969. "A computer system for time-variant harmonic analysis and synthesis of musical tones." In H. von Foerster and J. Beauchamp, eds. *Music by Computers*. New York: Wiley.

Beauchamp, J. 1975. "Analysis and synthesis of cornet tones using nonlinear inter-harmonic relationships." *Journal of the Audio Engineering Society* 23(10): 718–795.

Beauchamp, J. 1979. "Brass-tone synthesis by spectrum evolution matching with nonlinear functions." *Computer Music Journal* (2): 35–43. Revised and updated version in C. Roads and J. Strawn, eds. 1985. *Foundations of Computer Music*. Cambridge, Massachusetts: The MIT Press. pp. 95–113.

Beauchamp, J. 1981. "Data reduction and resynthesis of connected solo passages using frequency, amplitude, and 'brightness' detection and the nonlinear synthesis technique." In L. Austin and T. Clark, eds. *Proceedings of the 1981 International Computer Music Conference*. San Francisco: International Computer Music Association. pp. 316–323.

Beauchamp, J. 1992a. "Will the real FM equation please stand up?" in Letters section of *Computer Music Journal* 16(4): 6–7.

Beauchamp, J. 1992b. "Introduction to Music 4C (M4C)." Urbana-Champaign: Computer Music Project, School of Music, University of Illinois.

Beauchamp, J. 1993. "Unix workstation software for analysis, graphics, modification, and synthesis of musical sounds." Unpublished manuscript.

Beauchamp, J., and S. Aurenz. 1985. "New computer music facilities at the University of Illinois." In B. Truax, ed. *Proceedings of the 1985 International Computer Music Conference*. San Francisco: International Computer Music Association. pp. 407–414.

Beauchamp, J., D. Code, and K.-P. Chen. 1990. "Notepro 3.0, a music transcription tool for computer music programs." Urbana-Champaign: Computer Music Project, School of Music, University of Illinois.

Beauchamp, J., and A. Horner. 1992. "Extended nonlinear waveshaping analysis/synthesis technique." In A. Strange, ed. *Proceedings of the 1992 International Computer Music Conference*. San Francisco: International Computer Music Association. pp. 2–5.

Beauchamp, J., R. Maher, and R. Brown. 1993. "Detection of musical pitch from recorded solo performances." Unpublished manuscript.

Beekman, I. 1604–1634. *Journal tenu par Isaac Beekman de 1604 à 1634*. Four volumes. C. de Waard, ed. 1953. The Hague.

Begault, D. 1991. "Challenges to successful implementation of 3-D sound." *Journal of the Audio Engineering Society* 39(11): 864–870.

Beigel, M. 1979. "A digital 'phase shifter' for musical applications using the Bell Labs (Alles-Fischer) digital filter module." *Journal of the Audio Engineering Society* 27(9): 673–676.

Bel, B. 1992. "Music structures: interleaving the temporal and hierarchical aspects in music." In M. Balaban, K. Ebcioglu, and O. Laske, eds. *Understanding Music with AI*. Cambridge, Massachusetts and Menlo Park, California: The MIT Press and AAAI Press. pp. 110–139.

Bel, B., and J. Kippen. 1992. "Bol Processor Grammars." In M. Balaban, K. Ebcioglu, and O. Laske, eds. *Understanding Music with AI*. Cambridge, Massachusetts and Menlo Park, California: The MIT Press and AAAI Press. pp. 366–401.

Benade, A. 1960. "The physics of wood winds." Reprinted in C. M. Hutchins, ed. 1978. *The Physics of Music*. San Francisco: Freeman. pp. 34–43.

Benade, A. 1990. *Fundamentals of Musical Acoustics*. New York: Dover Publications.

Ben Daniel, M. 1983. "Automated transcription of music." B. S. thesis. Cambridge, Massachusetts: M.I.T. Department of Electrical Engineering and Computer Science.

Bennett, G. 1981. "Singing synthesis in electronic music." In J. Sundberg, ed. *Research Aspects of Singing*. Publication 33. Stockholm: Royal Swedish Academy of Music. pp. 34–50.

Bennett, G., and X. Rodet. 1989. "Synthesis of the singing voice." In M. Mathews and J. Pierce, eds. *Current Directions in Computer Music Research*. Cambridge, Massachusetts: The MIT Press. pp. 19–44.

Beranek, L. 1949. *Acoustic Measurements*. New York: John Wiley and Sons.

Berg, P. 1975. "ASP—automated synthesis program." Utrecht: Institute of Sonology.

Berg, P. 1978a. "PILE2—a description of the language. "Utrecht: Institute of Sonology.

Berg, P. 1978b. "A user's manual for SSP." Utrecht: Institute of Sonology.

Berg, P. 1979. "PILE—A language for sound synthesis." *Computer Music Journal* 3(1): 30–41. Revised and updated version in C. Roads and J. Strawn, eds. 1985. *Foundations of Computer Music*. Cambridge, Massachusetts: The MIT Press. pp. 160–190.

Berlioz, H. and R. Strauss. 1948. *Treatise on Orchestration*. New York: Edwin Kalmus. pp. 416–417.

Bernardi, A., G.-P. Bugna, and G. De Poli. 1992. "Analysis of musical signals with chaos theory." In A. Piccialli, ed. *Proceedings of the International Workshop on Models and Representations of Musical Signals*. Naples: Université di Napoli Federico II, Dipartmento di Scienze Fisiche.

Bernardini, N. 1986. "Live electronics." In R. Doati and A. Vidolin, eds. *Nuova Atlantide*. Venice: La Biennale di Venezia. pp. 61–77.

Bernardini, N., and P. Otto. 1989. "TRAILS: an interactive system for sound location." In T. Wells and D. Butler, eds. *Proceedings of the 1989 International Computer Music Conference.* San Francisco: International Computer Music Association. pp. 29–33.

Bernstein, A., and E. D. Cooper. 1976. "The piecewise-linear technique of electronic music synthesis." *Journal of the Audio Engineering Society* 24(7/8): 446–454.

Bernstein, L. 1976. *The Unanswered Question.* Cambridge, Massachusetts: Harvard University Press.

Bertini, G., and P. Carosi. 1991. "Light baton: a system for conducting computer music performances." In *Proceedings of the International Workshop on Man-Machine Interaction in Live Performance.* Pisa: Computer Music Department of CNUCE/CNR. pp. 1–8.

Beyls, P. 1988. "Introducing Oscar." In C. Lischka and J. Fritsch, eds. *Proceedings of the 1988 International Computer Music Conference.* San Francisco: International Computer Music Association. pp. 219–230.

Beyls, P. 1989. "The musical universe of cellular automata." In T. Wells and D. Butler, eds. *Proceedings of the 1989 International Computer Music Conference.* San Francisco: International Computer Music Association. pp. 34–41.

Beyls, P. 1991. Personal communication.

Bidlack, R. 1992. "Chaotic systems as simple (but complex) compositional algorithms." *Computer Music Journal* 16(3): 33–47.

Bilmes, J. 1993. "Techniques to foster drum machine expressivity." In S. Ohteru, ed. *Proceedings of the 1993 International Computer Music Conference.* San Francisco: International Computer Music Association. pp. 276–283.

Bilsen, F. A., 1977. "Pitch of noise signals: evidence for a 'central' spectrum." *Journal of the Acoustical Society of America* 61: 150–161.

Bilsen, F., and R. Ritsma. 1969. "Repetition pitch and its implications for hearing theory." *Acustica* 22: 205–213.

Bischoff, J., R. Gold, and J. Horton. 1978. "A microcomputer-based network for live performance." *Computer Music Journal* 2(3): 24–29. Revised and updated version in C. Roads and J. Strawn, eds. 1985. *Foundations of Computer Music.* Cambridge, Massachusetts: The MIT Press.

Black, H. 1953. *Modulation Theory.* New York: Van Nostrand-Reinhold.

Blackham, E. D. 1965. "The physics of the piano." *Scientific American* 235(12). Reprinted in C. Hutchins, eds. 1978. *The Physics of Music.* San Francisco: W. H. Freeman. pp. 24–33.

Blackman, R., and J. Tukey. 1958. *The Measurement of Power Spectra.* New York: Dover.

Blake, W. 1986. *Mechanics of Flow-induced Sound and Vibration.* 2 vols. New York: Academic Press.

Blauert, J. 1983. *Spatial Hearing.* Cambridge, Massachusetts: The MIT Press.

Blesser, B. 1978. "Digitization of audio." *Journal of the Audio Engineering Society* 26(10): 739–771.

Blesser, B., 1983. "Advanced analog-to-digital conversion and filtering: data conversion." In B. Blesser, B. Locanthi, and T. Stockham, eds. *Digital Audio.* New York: Audio Engineering Society. pp. 37–53.

Blesser, B., K. Baeder and R. Zaorski. 1975. "A real-time digital computer for simulating audio systems." *Journal of the Audio Engineering Society* 23(9): 698–707.

Blesser, B., and J. Kates. 1978. "Digital processing in audio signals." In A. V. Oppenheim, ed. *Applications of Digital Signal Processing.* Englewood Cliffs: Prentice-Hall.

Blevis, E., M. Jenkins, and J. Glasgow. 1988. "Motivations, sources, and initial design ideas for CALM: a composition analysis/generation language for music." In *Workshop on Artificial Intelligence and Music, AAAI–88 Conference.* Menlo Park, California: American Association for Artificial Intelligence.

Bloch, G., et al. 1992. "Spatializer: from room acoustics to virtual acoustics." In A. Strange, ed. *Proceedings of the 1992 International Computer Music Conference.* San Francisco: International Computer Music Association. pp. 253–256.

Bloom, P. J. 1977. "Determination of monaural sensitivity changes due to the pinna by use of minimum audible field measurements in the lateral vertical plane." *Journal of the Acoustic Society of America* 61: 1264–1269.

Bloom, P. J. 1985. "High-quality digital audio in the entertainment industry: an overview of achievements and challenges." *IEEE ASSP Magazine* 2(4): 2–25.

Blum, T. 1979. "Review of Herbert Brün: SAWDUST." *Computer Music Journal* 3(1): 6–7.

Blumlein, A. 1933. "Improvements in and relating to sound-transmission, sound-recording, and sound-reproducing systems." British Patent Specification 394,325. Reprinted in Audio Engineering Society. 1986. *Stereophonic Techniques: An Anthology.* New York: Audio Engineering Society.

Boalch, D. 1956. *Makers of the Harpsichord and Clavichord, 1440–1840.* New York: Macmillan.

Bobrow, L., and M. Arbib. 1974. *Discrete Mathematics.* Philadelphia: W. B. Saunders.

Bode, H. 1967. "The multiplier type ring modulator." *Electronic Music Review* 1.

Bode, H. 1984. "History of electronic sound modification." *Journal of the Audio Engineering Society* 32(10): 730–739.

Bode, H., and R. Moog. 1972. "A highly-accurate frequency shifter for professional audio applications." *Journal of the Audio Engineering Society* 20(6): 453.

Bücker, H-D., and A. Mahling. 1988. "What's in a note?" In C. Lischka and J. Fritsch, eds. *Proceedings of the 1988 International Computer Music Conference.* San Francisco: International Computer Music Association. pp. 166–173.

Boie, B., M. Mathews, and A. Schloss. 1989. "The Radio Drum as a synthesizer controller." In T. Wells and D. Butler, eds. *Proceedings of the 1989 International Computer Music Conference.* San Francisco: International Computer Music Association. pp. 42–45.

Bolognesi, T. 1983. "Automatic composition: experiments with self-similar music." *Computer Music Journal* 7(1): 25–36.

Borgonovo, A., and G. Haus. 1984. "Musical sound synthesis by means of two-variable functions: experimental criteria and results." In D. Wessel, ed. *Proceedings of the 1984 International Computer Music Conference.* San Francisco: International Computer Music Association. pp. 35–42.

Borgonovo, A., and G. Haus. 1986. "Sound synthesis by means of two-variable functions: experimental criteria and results." *Computer Music Journal* 10(4): 57–71.

Borin, G., G. De Poli, and A. Sarti. 1992. "Algorithms and structures for synthesis using physical models." *Computer Music Journal* 16(4): 30–42.

Borish, J. 1984. "Electronic simulation of auditorium acoustics." Department of Music Report STAN-M-18. Stanford: Center for Computer Research in Music and Acoustics, Stanford University.

Bork, I. 1992. "Modal analysis of sound fields of musical instruments." Preprint 3243. Presented at the 92nd Convention. New York: Audio Engineering Society.

Borning, A. 1979. "Thinglab—a constraint-oriented simulation laboratory." Technical Report SSL-79-3. Palo Alto: Xerox Palo Alto Research Centers.

Bosi, M. 1990. "An interactive real-time system for the control of sound localization." *Computer Music Journal* 14(4): 59–64.

Boulanger, R. 1990. *Making Music with Csound.* Supplied with the distribution of the Csound program. Cambridge, Massachusetts: M.I.T. Media Laboratory.

Boulez, P., and A. Gerzso. 1988. "Computers in music." *Scientific American* 258(4): 44–50.

Boutillon, X. 1984. "Fonctionement des instruments à cordes libres. Approche mecanique, traitement du signal." Doctoral thesis. Paris: Université de Paris Sud.

Bowcott, P. 1989. "Cellular automata as a means of high level compositional control of granular synthesis." In T. Wells and D. Butler, eds. *Proceedings of the 1989 International Computer Music Conference.* San Francisco. pp. 55–57.

Bowen, B., and W. Brown. 1980. *VLSI Systems Design for Digital Signal Processing*. Reading, Massachusetts: Addison-Wesley.

Bowers, Q. D. 1972. *Encyclopedia of Automatic Musical Instruments*. New York: The Vestal Press.

Boyer, F., and R. Kronland-Martinet. 1989. "Granular resynthesis and transformation of sounds through wavelet transform analysis." In T. Wells and T. Butler, eds. *Proceedings of the 1989 International Computer Music Conference*. San Francisco: International Computer Music Association. pp. 51–54.

Boynton, L., P. Lavoie, Y. Orlarey, C. Rueda, and D. Wessel. 1986. "MIDI-Lisp, a Lisp-based music programming environment for the Macintosh." In P. Berg, ed. *Proceedings of the 1986 International Computer Music Conference*. San Francisco: International Computer Music Association. pp. 183–186.

Brandao, M., and R. Nascimento. 1991. "A geometrical concordance device for sound synthesis." In A. Alphonce and B. Pennycook, eds. *Proceedings of the 1991 International Computer Music Conference*. San Francisco: International Computer Music Association. pp. 412–415.

Bressin, R., G. De Poli, and A. Vidolin. 1992. "Symbolic and sub-symbolic rules system for real-time performance." In A. Strange, ed. *Proceedings of the 1992 International Computer Music Conference*. San Francisco: International Computer Music Association. pp. 211–214.

Bridwell, N. 1979. "Interactive synthesis without obscure diagnostics. "In C. Roads, ed. *Proceedings of the 1978 International Computer Music Conference*. Evanston: Northwestern University Press. pp. 108–118.

Brigham, O. 1974. *The Fast Fourier Transform*. Englewood Cliffs: Prentice Hall.

Brightman, T., and S. Crook. 1982. "Exploring practical speech I/O." *Mini-Micro Systems* May: 291–304.

Brinch Hansen, P., 1977. *The Architecture of Concurrent Programs*. Englewood Cliffs: Prentice-Hall.

Brinkman, A. 1990. *Pascal Programs for Music Research*. Chicago: University of Chicago Press.

Bristow, D. 1986. Personal communication.

Brooks, F., A. Hopkins, P. Newmann, and W. Wright. 1957. "An experiment in musical composition." *Institute of Radio Engineers Transactions on Electronic Computers* EC-6(1): 175–182.

Brown, F. 1977. "The language Scriptu." *Interface* 6: 9–28.

Brown, J., and M. Puckette. 1987. "Musical information from a narrowed autocorrelation function." Cambridge, Massachusetts: M.I.T. Experimental Music Studio.

Brün, H. 1969. "*Infraudibles*." In H. Von Foerster and J. Beauchamp, eds. *Music By Computers*. New York: John Wiley & Sons.

Brün, H. 1977. *Project Sawdust*. La Jolla: Lingua Press.

Buchner, A. 1978. *Mechanical Musical Instruments*. Westport: Greenwood Press.

Burg, J. 1967. "Maximum entropy spectrum analysis." In *Proceedings of the 37th Meeting of the Society of Exploration Geophysicists,* Oklahoma City, 31 October.

Burg, J. 1975. "Maximum entropy spectral analysis." Ph.D dissertation. Stanford: Stanford University Department of Geophysics.

Burns, E. and N. Viemeister. 1976. "Nonspectral pitch." *Journal of the Acoustical Society of America* 60: 863–869.

Buser, P., and M. Imbert. 1992. *Audition*. Cambridge, Massachusetts: The MIT Press.

Buxton, W. 1978. "Design issues in the foundation of a computer-based tool for music composition." Technical Report CSRG-97. Toronto: University of Toronto.

Buxton, W. 1979. "The evolution of the SSSP score editing tools." *Computer Music Journal* 3(4): 14–25. Revised and updated version in C. Roads and J. Strawn, eds. 1985. *Foundations of Computer Music*. Cambridge, Massachusetts: The MIT Press.

Buxton, W. 1986. "The computer as accompanist." In M. Mantei and P. Orbeton, eds. 1986. *Human Factors in Computer Systems—CHI '86 Conference Proceedings*. New York: Association for Computing Machinery. pp. 41–43.

Buxton, W., et al. 1978a. "The use of hierarchy and instance in a data structure for computer music." *Computer Music Journal* 2(4): 10–20. Revised and updated version in C. Roads and J. Strawn, eds. 1985. *Foundations of Computer Music* Cambridge, Massachusetts: The MIT Press. pp. 443–466.

Buxton, W., et al. 1978b. "An introduction to the SSSP digital synthesizer." *Computer Music Journal* 2(4): 28–38. Revised and updated version in C. Roads and J. Strawn, eds. 1985. *Foundations of Computer Music*. Cambridge, Massachusetts: The MIT Press. pp. 206–224.

Buxton, W., S. Patel, W. Reeves, and R. Baecker. 1981. "Scope in interactive score editors." *Computer Music Journal* 5(3). Reprinted in C. Roads, ed. 1989. *The Music Machine*. Cambridge, Massachusetts: The MIT Press. pp. 255–261.

Buxton, W., S. Patel, W. Reeves, and R. Baecker. 1982. "Objed and the design of timbral resources." *Computer Music Journal* 6(2): 32–44. Reprinted in C. Roads, ed. 1989. *The Music Machine*. Cambridge, Massachusetts: The MIT Press. pp. 263–275.

Byrd, D. 1974. "A system for music printing by computer." *Computers and the Humanities* 8(3) 161–172.

Byrd, D. 1977. "An integrated computer music software system." *Computer Music Journal* 1(2): 55–60.

Byrd, D. 1984. "Music notation by computer." Ph. D. diss.Bloomington: Indiana University Department of Computer Science.

Cadoz, C., M. Luciani, and J. Florens. 1984. "Responsive input devices and sound synthesis by simulation of instrumental mechanisms." *Computer Music Journal* 8(3): 60–73.

Cadoz, C., L. Lisowski, and J.-L. Florens. 1990. "A modular feedback keyboard design." *Computer Music Journal* 14(2): 47–51.

Cage, J. 1937. "The future of music: credo." In J. Cage. 1961. *Silence*. Middletown: Wesleyan University Press.

Cage, J. 1961. *Silence*. Middletown: Wesleyan University Press.

Cage, J. 1969. *Notations*. New York: Something Else Press.

Cahill, T. 1897. U. S. Patents 580,035 (1897);1,107,261 (1914); 1,213,803 (1917); 1,295, 691 (1919).(Patents for the Telharmonium.) Washington, D.C.: U.S. Patent Office.

Calvet, O., R. Laurens, and J.-M. Adrien. 1990. "Modal synthesis: compilation of mechanical sub-structures and acoustical sub-systems." In S. Arnold and G. Hair, eds. *Proceedings of the 1990 International Computer Music Conference*. San Francisco: International Computer Music Association. pp. 57–59.

Camilleri, L., F. Carreras, and A. Mayr, eds. 1987. *Pietro Grossi: Musica Senza Musicisti*. Florence: CNUCE/CNR.

Campbell, M., and C. Greated. 1987. *The Musician's Guide to Acoustics*. London: J. M. Dent and Sons.

Camurri, A., C. Canepa, M. Frixione, C. Innocenti, C. Massucco, and R. Zaccaria. 1991. "A high-level system for music composition." In B. Alphonce and B. Pennycook, eds. *Proceedings of the 1991 International Computer Music Conference*. San Francisco: International Computer Music Association. pp. 27–36.

Cann, R. 1978. "Speech analysis/synthesis for electronic vocal music." Ph.D. dissertation. Princeton: Princeton University Department of Music.

Cann, R. 1979–1980. "An analysis/synthesis tutorial." *Computer Music Journal* 3(3): 6–11; 3(4): 9–13;4(1): 36–42. Reprinted in C. Roads and J. Strawn, eds.1985. *Foundations of Computer Music*. Cambridge, Massachusetts: The MIT Press.

Cannon, H., 1982. "Flavors: A non-hierarchical approach to object-oriented programming." Cambridge, Massachusetts: Symbolics.

Cantor, D. 1971. "A computer program that accepts common music notation." *Computers and the Humanities* 6(2): 103–109.

Carlos, W. 1986. "Tuning: at the crossroads." *Computer Music Journal* 11(1): 29–43.

Carson, J. 1922. "Notes on the theory of modulation." *Proceedings of the Institute of Radio Engineers* 10: 57–64.

Carterette, E., and M. Friedman, eds. 1978. *Handbook of Perception, Volume 4, Hearing.* New York: Academic Press.

Castine, P. 1993. "Whatever happened to CMAP for Macintosh? A status report." In S. Ohteru, ed. *Proceedings of the 1993 International Computer Music Conference.* San Francisco: International Computer Music Association. pp. 360–362.

Cauchy, A. 1841. "Memoire sur diverse formules d'analyse." *Comptes Rendus Hebdomaires des Sciences de l'Academie des Sciences Paris* 12: 283–298.

Cavaliere, S. 1991. "New generation architectures for music and sound processing." In G. De Poli, A. Piccialli, and C. Roads, eds. *Representations of Musical Signals.* Cambridge, Massachusetts: The MIT Press. pp. 391–412.

Cavaliere, S., G. Di Giugno, and E. Guarino. 1992. "MARS—the X20 device and the SM1000 board." In A. Strange, ed. *Proceedings of the 1992 International Computer Music Conference.* San Francisco: International Computer Music Association. pp. 348–351.

Cerruti, R., and G. Rodeghiero. 1983. "Comments on 'Musical sound synthesis by forward differences'." *Journal of the Audio Engineering Society* 31(6): 446.

Cesari, C., 1981. "Application of data flow architecture to computer music synthesis." TR-257. Cambridge, Massachusetts: M.I.T. Laboratory for Computer Science.

Chabot, X. 1990. "Gesture interfaces and a software toolkit for performance with electronics." *Computer Music Journal* 14(2): 15–27.

Chabot, X., and L. Beauregard. 1984. "Control of a real-time sound processor by a traditional instrument." Paper presented at the 1984 International Computer Music Conference, Paris.

Chabot, X., R. Dannenberg, and G. Bloch. 1986. "A workstation in live performance: composed improvisation." In P. Berg, ed. *Proceedings of the 1986 International Computer Music Conference.* San Francisco: International Computer Music Association. pp. 57–59.

Chadabe, J. 1967. "New approaches to analog studio design." *Perspectives of New Music* 6(1): 107–113.

Chadabe, J. 1984. "Interactive composing: an overview." *Computer Music Journal* 8(1): 22–27. Reprinted in C. Roads, ed. 1989. *The Music Machine.* Cambridge, Massachusetts: The MIT Press.

Chadabe, J. 1992. "Flying through a musical space: about real-time composition." In J. Paynter, T. Howell, R. Orton, and P. Seymour, eds. *Companion to Contemporary Musical Thought*. London: Routledge. pp. 454–465.

Chadabe, J., and R. Meyers. 1978. "An introduction to the PLAY program." *Computer Music Journal* 2(1): 12–18. Reprinted in C. Roads and J. Strawn, eds. 1985. *Foundations of Computer Music*. Cambridge, Massachusetts: The MIT Press.

Chafe, C. 1985. "Control of bowed string synthesis from a physical model." Unpublished mss.

Chafe, C., and D. Jaffe. 1986. "Source separation and note identification in polyphonic music." In *Proceedings of the International Conference on Acoustics, Speech and Signal Processing, Tokyo*. New York: IEEE.

Chafe, C., B. Mont-Reynaud, and L. Rush. 1982. "Toward an intelligent editor for digital audio: recognition of musical concepts." *Computer Music Journal* 6(1): 30–41. Reprinted in C. Roads, ed. 1989. *The Music Machine*. Cambridge, Massachusetts: The MIT Press.

Chafe, C., D. Jaffe, K. Kashima, B. Mont-Reynaud, and J. Smith. 1985." Techniques for note identification in polyphonic music." In B. Truax, ed. *Proceedings of the 1985 International Computer Music Conference*. San Francisco: International Computer Music Association. pp. 399–405.

Chaitin, G. 1975. "Randomness and mathematical proof." *Scientific American* 232(5): 47–54.

Chamberlin, H., 1985. *Musical Applications of Microprocessors*. Second edition. Rochelle Park, New Jersey: Hayden Books.

Chapuis, A. ed. 1955. *Histoire de la boîte à musique*. Lausanne: Edition Scriptar.

Charbonneau, G. R. 1981. "Timbre and the effects of three types of data reduction." *Computer Music Journal* 5(2): 10–19. Reprinted in C. Roads, ed. 1989. *The Music Machine*. Cambridge, Massachusetts: The MIT Press. pp. 521–530.

Chareyron, J. 1990. "Digital synthesis of self-modifying waveforms by means of linear automata." *Computer Music Journal* 14(4): 25–41.

Chemillier, M. 1992a. "Automata and music." In A. Strange, ed. *Proceedings of the 1992 International Computer Music Conference*. San Francisco: International Computer Music Association. pp. 370–371.

Chemillier, M. 1992b. "Aspects mathématiques des applications en informatique musicale des automates finis." Cahiers du LIUC. Caen: Licence d'informatique, Université de Caen.

Chion, M. 1982. *La musique électroacoustique*. Paris: Les Presses Universitaires de France.

Chion, M., and G. Reibel. 1976. *Les musiques électroacoustiques*. Aix-en-Provence: Edisud.

Chomsky, N. 1957. *Syntactic Structures*. The Hague: Mouton.

Chomsky, N. 1965. *Aspects of the Theory of Syntax*. Cambridge, Massachusetts: The MIT Press.

Chomsky, N., and M. Schuetzenberger. 1963. "Algebraic theory of context-free languages." In Braffort and Hirschberg, eds. *Computer Programming and Formal Systems*. Amsterdam: North-Holland.

Chowning, J. 1971. "The simulation of moving sound sources." *Journal of the Audio Engineering Society* 19: 2–6. Reprinted in *Computer Music Journal* 1(3): 48–52.

Chowning, J. 1973. "The synthesis of complex audio spectra by means of frequency modulation." *Journal of the Audio Engineering Society* 21(7): 526–534. Reprinted in C. Roads and J. Strawn, eds. 1985. *Foundations of Computer Music*. Cambridge, Massachusetts: The MIT Press. pp. 6–29.

Chowning, J. 1975. "Computers, composition, and research." In G. Bennett, ed. 1975. *Erste Woche fuer Elektronische Musik*. Basel: Verlag der Musik-Akademie der Stadt Basel. pp. 38–48.

Chowning, J. 1977. (see Chowning 1971).

Chowning, J. 1980. "Computer synthesis of the singing voice." In J. Sundberg and E. Jansson, eds. 1980. *Sound Generation in Winds, Strings, Computers*. Publication 29. Stockholm: Royal Swedish Academy of Music. pp. 4–13.

Chowning, J. 1987. "FM is a universe of possibilities with a lot of surprises." Yamaha magazine advertisement.

Chowning, J. 1989. "Frequency modulation synthesis of the singing voice." In M. Mathews and J. Pierce, eds. 1989. *Current Directions in Computer Music Research*. Cambridge, Massachusetts: The MIT Press. pp. 57–63.

Chowning, J., and B. Mont-Reynaud. 1986. "Intelligent analysis of composite acoustic signals." Department of Music Report STAN-M-36. Stanford: Stanford University.

Chowning, J., J. Grey, L. Rush, and J. A. Moorer. 1974. "Computer simulation of music instrument tones in reverberant environments." Department of Music Report STAN-M-2. Stanford: Stanford University.

Chowning, J., L. Rush, B. Mont-Reynaud, C. Chafe, W. A, Schloss, J. Smith. 1984. "Intelligent systems for the analysis of digitized acoustic signals." Department of Music Report STAN-M-15. Stanford: Stanford University.

Church, A., 1941. "The calculus of lambda conversion." *Annals of Mathematical Studies* 6. Princeton: Princeton University Press.

Clark, M. 1959. "A new musical instrument." *Gravenser Blätter* 14: 110–123.

Clark, W., 1980. "From electron mobility to logical structure: a view of integrated circuits." *ACM Computing Surveys* 12(3): 325–356.

Clarke, E. 1987. "Levels of structure in the organization of musical time." *Contemporary Music Review* 2(1): 211–238.

Clarke, J. 1990. "An FOF synthesis tutorial." In B. Vercoe. 1990. *Csound: A Manual for the Audio Processing System*. Cambridge, Massachusetts: MIT Media Laboratory.

Clarke, J., and R. Voss. 1978. "1/*f* noise in music: music from 1/*f* noise." *Journal of the Acoustical Society of America* 63(1): 258–263.

Clocksin, W., and C. Mellish. 1987. *Programming in Prolog*. Third edition. New York: Springer-Verlag.

Clough, J. 1970. "TEMPO: a composer's programming language." *Perspectives of New Music* Fall/Winter: 113–125.

Clough, J. 1971. "An interactive system for computer sound generation." *Proceedings of the American Society of University Composers* 6: 22–26.

Clozier, C. 1993. "Le Gmebaphone." Bourges: Groupe de Musique Expérimentale de Bourges.

Clynes, M. ed. 1982. *Music, Mind, and Brain: The Neuropsychology of Music*. New York: Plenum.

Clynes, M., and N. Nettheim. 1982. "The living quality of music." In M. Clynes, ed. *Music, Mind, and Brain: The Neuropsychology of Music*. New York: Plenum. pp. 47–82.

Clynes, M., and J. Walker. 1982. "Neurobiologic functions of rhythm, time, and pulse in music." In M. Clynes, ed. *Music, Mind, and Brain: The Neuropsychology of Music*. New York: Plenum. pp. 47–82.

Coenen, A., and S. Schäfer. 1992. "Computer-controlled player pianos." *Computer Music Journal* 16(4): 104–111.

Cogan, R. 1984. *New Images of Musical Sound*. Cambridge, Massachusetts: Harvard University Press.

Cohen, E. 1980. "The influence of nonharmonic partials on tone perception." Ph.D. diss. Stanford: Stanford University.

Cohen, H. 1984. *Quantifying Music*. Dordrecht: D. Reidel.

Coker, W. 1972. *Music and Meaning*. New York: The Free Press.

Colburn, H., and N. Durlach. 1978. "Models of binaural interaction." In E. Carterette and M. Friedman, eds. *Handbook of Perception, Volume IV*. New York: Academic. pp. 467–518.

Collinge, D. 1980. "The Moxie user's guide." Victoria: University of Victoria School of Music.

Collinge, D., and S. Parkinson. 1988. "The Oculus Ranae." In C. Lischka and J. Fritsch, eds. *Proceedings of the 1988 International Computer Music Conference.* San Francisco: International Computer Music Association, and Cologne: Feedback Papers. pp. 15–19.

Collinge, D., and D. Scheidt. 1988. "Moxie for the Atari ST." In C. Lischka and J. Fritsch, eds. *Proceedings of the 1988 International Computer Music Conference.* San Francisco: International Computer Music Association, and Cologne: Feedback Papers. pp. 231–238.

Collins, M. 1993. "Infinity: DSP sampling tools for Macintosh." *Sound on Sound* 9(1): 44–47.

Collins, N. 1991a. "Low brass: the evolution of trombone propelled electronics." *Leonardo Music Journal* 1(1): 44–44.

Collins, N. 1991b. "Cargo cult instruments." *Contemporary Music Review* 6: 73–84.

Computer Music Journal. 1979. "Dataland's Scan-note system." *Computer Music Journal* 3(1): 60–61. (Product announcement.)

Computer Music Journal. 1980. "Marantz Pianocorder." *Computer Music Journal* 4(1). (Product announcement.)

Computer Music Journal. 1984. "Key Concepts Notebender keyboard." *Computer Music Journal* 8(3): 92. (Product announcement.)

Computer Music Journal. 1989. "The Mandala—a music synthesizer played in a video performance." *Computer Music Journal* 13(1): 9. (News.)

Computer Music Journal. 1990. "Voice recognition: VoiceWaves MIDI for Apple Macintosh Computers." *Computer Music Journal* 14(2): 92. (Product announcement.)

Computer Music Journal. 1991. "Avid/1 Media Composer for Apple Macintosh Computers." *Computer Music Journal* 15(2): 98–99. (Product announcement.)

Computer Music Journal. 1993a. Special issue on music representation and scoring. *Computer Music Journal* 17(3).

Computer Music Journal. 1993b. Special issue on music representation and scoring. *Computer Music Journal* 17(4).

Computer Music Journal. 1994. "CMU MIDI Toolkit for Macintosh, DOS, and Amiga Computers." *Computer Music Journal* 18(2). (Product announcement.)

Coniglio, M. 1992. "Introduction to the Interactor language." In A. Strange, ed. *Proceedings of the 1992 International Computer Music Conference.* San Francisco: International Computer Music Association. pp. 170–173.

Conger, J. 1988. *C Programming for MIDI*. Redwood City: M & T Books.

Conger, J. 1989. *MIDI Sequencing in C*. Redwood City: M & T Books.

Cook, P. 1991a. "Identification of control parameters in an articulatory vocal tract model, with applications to the synthesis of singing." Ph.D dissertation. Stanford: Stanford University Department of Electrical Engineering.

Cook, P. 1991b. "TBone: an interactive waveguide brass instrument synthesis workbench for the NeXT Machine." In B. Alphonce and B. Pennycook, eds. *Proceedings of the 1991 International Computer Music Conference*. San Francisco: International Computer Music Association. pp. 297–299.

Cook, P. 1992. "A meta-wind-instrument physical model, and a meta-controller for real-time performance control." In. A. Strange, ed. *Proceedings of the 1992 International Computer Music Conference*. San Francisco: International Computer Music Association. pp. 273–276.

Cook, P. 1993. "SPASM: a real-time vocal tract physical model controller and Singer: the companion software synthesis system." *Computer Music Journal* 17(1) 30–44.

Cooley, J., and J. Tukey. 1965. "An algorithm for the machine computation of complex Fourier series." *Mathematical Computation* 19: 297–301.

Cooper, J. 1985. "MIDI specs and switching project." *Keyboard* January 57, 78.

Cooper, J. 1989. "MIDI-based automation." *Recording Engineer/Producer* 20(2): 52–54.

Cope, D. 1987. "An expert system for computer-assisted composition." *Computer Music Journal* 11(4): 30–46.

Cope, D. 1989. "The step by step simulation of a Mozart sonata." In *Proceedings of the European Workshop on Artificial Intelligence and Music*. Genoa: Computer Music Laboratory, University of Genoa.

Cope, D. 1990. "Pattern matching as an engine for the computer simulation of musical style." In S. Arnold and G. Hair, eds. *Proceedings of the 1990 International Computer Music Conference*. pp. 288–294.

Correia, E. 1991. "Music notation software." In W. Hewlett and E. Selfridge-Field, eds. *Computing in Musicology*. Menlo Park: Center for Computer Assisted Research in the Humanities. pp. 119–172.

Cotton, R. B. Jr., 1972. "Tempered scale generation from a single frequency source." *Journal of the Audio Engineering Society* 20(5): 376–382

Courtot, F. 1992. "Logical representation and induction for computer assisted composition." In M. Balaban, K. Ebcioglu, and O. Laske, eds. *Understanding Music with AI*. Cambridge, Massachusetts and Menlo Park, California: The MIT Press and AAAI Press. pp. 156–180.

Craven, P. 1993. "Toward the 24-bit DAC: novel noise-shaping topologies incorporating correction for the nonlinearity in a PWM output stage." *Journal of the Audio Engineering Society* 41(5): 291–313.

Crawford, D., and J. Zeef. 1983. "Gregory's Scribe: inexpensive graphics for pre-1600 music notation." *Computer Music Journal* 7(1): 21–24.

Crawford, F. 1968. *Waves.* Berkeley Physics Course Volume 3. New York: McGraw-Hill.

Crochiere, R., and L. Rabiner. 1983. *Multirate digital signal processing.* Prentice-Hall: Englewood Cliffs.

Cutler, C. 1960. "Transmission systems employing quantization." U. S. Patent 2,927,962, filed in 1954.

Dahl, O.-J., and K. Nygaard. 1966. "Simula—an Algol-based simulation language." *Communications of the Association for Computing Machinery* 9(9): 671–678.

Dahl, O.-J., E. Dijkstra, and C. Hoare. 1972. *Structured Programming.* New York: Academic Press.

D'Allessandro, C., and X. Rodet. 1989. "Synthèse et analyse-synthèse par fonctions d'ondes formantiques." *Journal Acoustique* 2: 163–169.

Dal Molin, A. 1975. "The x-y typewriters and their application as music input terminals for the computer." In J. Beauchamp and J. Melby, eds. *Proceedings of the Second Annual Music Computation Conference: Information Processing Systems.* Urbana: Office of Continuing Education. pp. 28–53.

Dal Molin, A. 1978. "A terminal for music manuscript input." *Computers and the Humanities* 12: 287–289.

Daniélou, A. 1958. *Tableau Comparatif des Intervalles Musicaux.* Pondichéry: Institut Français d'Indologie.

Dannenberg, R. 1984. "An on-line algorithm for real-time accompaniment." In D. Wessel, ed. *Proceedings of the 1984 International Computer Music Conference.* San Francisco: International Computer Music Association. pp. 193–198.

Dannenberg, R. 1986. "The CMU MIDI toolkit." In P. Berg, ed. *Proceedings of the 1986 International Computer Music Conference.* San Francisco: International Computer Music Association. pp. 53–56.

Dannenberg, R. 1989a. "The Canon score language." *Computer Music Journal* 13(1): 47–56.

Dannenberg, R. 1989b. "Real-time scheduling and computer accompaniment." In M. V. Mathews and J. R. Pierce, eds. *Current Directions in Computer Music Research.* Cambridge, Massachusetts: The MIT Press. pp. 225–261.

Dannenberg, R., P. McAvinney, and D. Rubine. 1986. "Arctic: functional language for real-time systems." *Computer Music Journal* 10(4): 67–78.

Dannenberg, R., and K. Bookstein. 1991. "Practical aspects of a MIDI conducting system." In B. Alphonce and B. Pennycook, eds. *Proceedings of the 1991 International Computer Music Conference.* San Francisco: International Computer Music Association. pp. 537–540.

Dannenberg, R., and C. Mercer. 1992. "Real-time software synthesis on superscalar architectures." In A. Strange, ed. *Proceedings of the 1992 International Computer Music Conference.* San Francisco: International Computer Music Association. pp. 174–177.

Dannenberg, R., and B. Mont-Reynaud. 1987. "Following an improvisation in real time." In J. Beauchamp, ed. *Proceedings of the 1987 International Computer Music Conference.* San Francisco: International Computer Music Association. pp. 241–247.

Dannenberg, R., and H. Mukaino. 1988. "New techniques for enhanced quality of computer accompaniment." In C. Lischka and J. Fritsch, eds. *Proceedings of the 1988 International Computer Music Conference.* San Francisco: International Computer Music Association. pp. 243–249.

Darter, T. 1979. "Dave Smith." In T. Darter and G. Armbruster, eds. 1984. *The Art of Electronic Music.* New York: Quill/Keyboard. pp. 98–104.

Dashow, J. 1980. "Spectra as chords." *Computer Music Journal* 4(1): 43–52.

Dashow, J. 1987. "Looking into *Sequence Symbols*." *Perspectives of New Music* 25(1 and 2): 108–137.

Dashow, J. 1989. Personal communication.

D'Autilia, R., and F. Guerra. 1991. "Qualitative aspects of signal processing through dynamic neural networks." In. G. De Poli, A. Piccialli, and C. Roads, eds. *Representations of Musical Signals.* Cambridge, Massachusetts: The MIT Press. pp. 447–462.

David, E., M. Mathews, and H. McDonald. 1958. "Description and results of experiments with speech using digital computer simulation." *Proceedings of the 1958 National Electronics Conference.* New York: Institute of Radio Engineers. pp. 766–775.

David, E., M. Mathews, and H. McDonald. 1959. "A high-speed data translator for computer simulation of speech and television devices." In *Proceedings of the Western Joint Computer Conference.* New York: Institute of Radio Engineers. pp. 354–357.

Davis, D. 1988. *Computer Applications in Music: A Bibliography.* Madison: A-R Editions.

Davis, D. 1992. *Computer Applications in Music: A Bibliography. Supplement 1.* Madison: A-R Editions.

Davis, F. 1991. "Effects of cable, loudspeaker, and amplifier interactions." *Journal of the Audio Engineering Society* 39(6): 461–468.

Deer, J., P. Bloom, and D. Preis. 1985. "Perception of phase distortion in allpass filters." *Journal of the Audio Engineering Society* 33(10): 782–786.

De Furia, S., and J. Scacciaferro. 1988. *MIDI Programming for the Macintosh.* Redwood City: M & T Books.

Degazio, B. 1986. "Musical aspects of fractal geometry." In P. Berg, ed. *Proceedings of the 1986 International Computer Music Conference.* San Francisco: International Computer Music Association. pp. 435–442.

Degli Antoni, G., and G. Haus. 1982. "Music and causality." In T. Blum and J. Strawn, eds. *Proceedings of the 1982 International Computer Music Conference.* San Francisco: International Computer Music Association. pp. 279–296.

deKoning, K., and S. Oates. 1991. "Sound Base: phonetic searching in sound archives." In B. Alphonce and B. Pennycook, eds. *Proceedings of the 1991 International Computer Music Conference.* San Francisco: International Computer Music Conference. pp. 433–436.

Delgutte, Bertrand. 1980. "Representation of speech-like sounds in the discharge patterns of auditory-nerve fibers." *Journal of the Acoustical Society of America* 68: 843–857.

Dennis, J., 1978. "Data flow computer architectures." Computational Structures Group. Memo 160. Cambridge, Massachusetts: MIT Laboratory for Computer Science.

Dennis, J. 1980. "Data flow supercomputers." *I.E.E.E. Computer* November: 48–56.

Depalle, P. 1991. "Analyse, modèlisation et synthèse des sons basées sur le modèle source-filtre." Nantes: Université du Maine, Faculté des sciences.

Depalle, P., and G. Poirot. 1991. "Svp: phase vocodeur modulaire à deux canaux d'entrée." Paris: IRCAM.

Department of Defense. 1980. *Reference Manual for the ADA Programming Language.* Washington, D. C.: Department of Defense.

De Poli, G. 1978. "Musica—programme de codage de la musique." *Rapports IRCAM* 7/78. Paris: IRCAM.

De Poli, G. 1983. "A tutorial on digital sound synthesis techniques." *Computer Music Journal* 7(4): 8–26. Reprinted in C. Roads, ed. 1989. *The Music Machine.* Cambridge, Massachusetts: The MIT Press. pp. 429–447.

De Poli, G. 1984. "Frequency-dependent waveshaping." In W. Buxton, ed. 1985. *Proceedings of the 1984 International Computer Music Conference.* San Francisco: International Computer Music Association. pp. 91–101.

De Poli, G. 1992. Personal communication.

De Poli, G., and A. Piccialli. 1988. "Forma d'onda per la sintesi granulare sincronica." In D. Tommassinni, ed. *Atti di VII Colloquio di Informatica Musicale*. Rome: Associazione Musica Verticale. pp. 70–75.

De Poli, G., A. Piccialli, and C. Roads, eds. 1991. *Representations of Musical Signals*. Cambridge, Massachusetts: The MIT Press.

De Poli, G., and A. Vidolin. 1984. "Music 5: manuale operativo." Padua: Centro di Sonologià Computazionale, University of Padua.

Derry, T., and T. Williams. 1960. *A Short History of Technology*. Oxford: Oxford University Press.

Desain, P., and H. Honing. 1988. "LOCO: a composition microworld in Logo." *Computer Music Journal* 12(3): 30–42.

Desain, P., and H. Honing. 1989. "Quantization of musical time: a connectionist approach." *Computer Music Journal* 13(3): 56–66. Reprinted in P. Todd and D. G. Loy, eds. 1991. *Music and Connectionism*. Cambridge, Massachusetts: The MIT Press.

Desain, P., and H. Honing. 1992a. "Time functions best as functions of multiple times." *Computer Music Journal* 16(2): 17–34.

Desain, P., and H. Honing. 1992b. *Music, Mind, and Machine*. Amsterdam: Thesis Publishers.

Desain, P., and H. Honing. 1992c. "The quantization problem: traditional and connectionist approaches." In M. Balaban, K. Ebcioglu, and O. Laske, eds. *Understanding Music with AI*. Cambridge, Massachusetts and Menlo Park, California: The MIT Press and AAAI Press. pp. 448–462.

Deutsch, D. ed. 1982. *The Psychology of Music*. Orlando: Academic Press.

Diener, G. 1989a. "TTrees: a tool for the compositional environment." *Computer Music Journal* 13(2): 77–85.

Diener, G. 1989b. "Nutation: structural organization versus graphic generality in a common music notation package." In T. Wells and D. Butler, eds. *Proceedings of the 1989 International Computer Music Conference*. San Francisco: International Computer Music Association. pp. 86–89.

die Reihe. 1955. "Vol. 1. Elektronische Musik." Vienna: Universal Edition.

Digipress. 1991. "Century Master." Knoxville: Digipress. (Sales literature.)

Digital Signal Processing Committee. 1980. *Programs for Digital Signal Processing*. New York: IEEE Acoustics,Speech, and Signal Processing Society.

Dijkstra, E., 1976. *A Discipline of Programming*. Englewood Cliffs: Prentice-Hall.

Dijkstra, E. W., 1972. "Notes on Structured Programming." In O.-J. Dahl, E.W. Dijkstra, and C.A.R. Hoare, eds. 1972. *Structured Programming*. London: Academic Press. pp. 1–82.

Di Scipio, A. 1990. "Composition by exploration of nonlinear dynamical systems." In S. Arnold and G. Hair, eds. *Proceedings of the 1990 International Computer Music Conference*. San Francisco: International Computer Music Association.

Distasi, R., M. Nappi, and S. Vitulano. 1992. "Automatic generation of MIDI files by optical reading of music scores." In A. Piccialli, eds. *Proceedings of the International Workshop on Models and Representations of Musical Signals*. Naples: Université di Napoli Federico II.

Divilbiss, J. 1964. "The real-time generation of music with a digital computer." *Journal of Music Theory* 8: 99–111.

Dodge, C. 1985. "*In Celebration:* the composition and its realization in synthetic speech." In C. Roads, ed. 1985. *Composers and the Computer*. Madison: A-R Editions.

Dodge, C. 1988. "*Profile:* a musical fractal." *Computer Music Journal* 12(3): 10–14.

Dodge, C. 1989. "On Speech Songs." In M. Mathews and J. Pierce, eds. *Current Directions in Computer Music Research*. Cambridge, Massachusetts: The MIT Press. pp. 9–17.

Dodge, C., and C. Jerse. 1985. *Computer Music*. New York: Schirmer.

Doi, T. 1983. "Recent Progress in Digital Audio Technology."In B. Blesser, B. Locanthi, and T. Stockham, eds. *Digital Audio*. New York: Audio Engineering Society. pp. 23–33.

Doi, T., Y. Tsuchiya, and A. Iga. 1978. "On several standards for converting PCM signals into video signals." *Journal of the Audio Engineering Society* 26(9): 641–649.

Dolson, M. 1983. "A tracking phase vocoder and its use in the analysis of ensemble sounds." Ph.D. dissertation. Pasadena: California Institute of Technology.

Dolson, M. 1985. Recent advances in musique concrète at CARL." In B. Truax, ed. *Proceedings of the 1985 International Computer Music Conference*. San Francisco: International Computer Music Association. pp. 55–60.

Dolson, M. 1986. "The phase vocoder: a tutorial." *Computer Music Journal* 10(4): 14–27.

Dolson, M. 1989a. "Machine tongues XII: neural networks." *Computer Music Journal* 13(3): 28–40.

Dolson, M. 1989b. "Fourier-transform-based timbral manipulations." In M. Mathews and J. R. Pierce, eds. *Current Directions in Computer Music Research*. Cambridge, Massachusetts: The MIT Press. pp. 105–112.

Dolson, M., and R. Boulanger. 1985. New directions in the musical use of resonators." Unpublished manuscript.

Doppler, C. 1842. *Theorie des farbigen Lichtes der Doppelsterne*. Prague.

Douglas, A. 1968. *The Electronic Musical Instrument Manual*. Fifth edition. New York: Pitman. First edition 1947.

Douglas, A. 1973. *Electronic Music Production*. New York: Pitman.

Dowling, W., and J. Harwood. 1986. *Music Cognition*. Orlando: Academic Press.

Downes, P. 1987. "Motion sensing in music and dance performance." In J. Strawn, ed. *Proceedings of the AES 5th International Conference: Music and Digital Technology*. New York: Audio Engineering Society. pp. 165–172.

Drake, A. 1967. *Fundamentals of Applied Probability Theory*. New York: McGraw-Hill.

Droman, D. 1984. *Exploring MIDI*. Studio City: International MIDI Association.

Dudley, H. 1936. "Synthesizing speech." *Bell Laboratories Record*. December: 98–102.

Dudley, H. 1939a. "The vocoder." *Bell Laboratories Record* 17: 122–126.

Dudley, H. 1939b. "Remaking Speech." *Journal of the Acoustical Society of America* 11: 167–177.

Dudley, H. 1955. "Fundamentals of speech synthesis." *Journal of the Audio Engineering Society* 3(4): 170–185.

Dudley, H., and S. A. Watkins. 1939. "A synthetic speaker." *Journal of the Franklin Institute* 227: 739–764.

Duesenberry, J. 1990. "Understanding amplitude modulation." *Electronic Musician* 6(11): 56–65, 124.

Duffy, C. 1982. "Digital recording: the 3M system." *Studio Sound* 24(12): 30–32.

Duisberg, R. 1984. "On the role of affect in artificial intelligence and music." *Perspectives of New Music* 23(1): 6–35.

Dumour, E. 1993. "Interview with Arthur Roberts." *Computer Music Journal* 17(2): 17–23.

Duncan, A., and D. Rossum. 1988. "Fundamentals of pitch-shifting." Preprint 2714 (A-1). Presented at the 85th Convention of the Audio Engineering Society. New York: Audio Engineering Society.

Durlach, N., and H. Colburn. 1978. "Binaural phenomena." In E. Carterette and M. Friedman, eds. *Handbook of Perception, Volume IV*. New York: Academic Press. pp. 365–466.

Dutilleux, H., A. Grossmann, and R. Kronland-Martinet. 1988. "Application of the wavelet transform to the analysis, transformation, and synthesis of musical sounds." Preprint 2727 (A-2). Presented at the 85th Convention of the Audio Engineering Society. New York: Audio Engineering Society.

Dworak, P., and A. Parker. 1977. "Envelope control with an optical keyboard." In C. Roads, ed. 1978. *Proceedings of the 1977 International Computer Music Conference*. San Francisco: International Computer Music Association.

Eaglestone, B., and S. Oates. 1990. "Analytic tools for group additive synthesis." In S. Arnold and G. Hair, eds. *Proceedings of the 1990 International Computer Music Conference*. San Francisco: International Computer Music Association. pp. 66–68.

Eaglestone, B., and A. Verschoor. 1991. "An intelligent music repository." In B. Alphonce and B. Pennycook, eds. *Proceedings of the 1991 International Computer Music Conference*. San Francisco: International Computer Music Association. pp. 437–440.

Eaton, M. 1971. *Bio Music*. Kansas City: ORCUS Research.

Ebcioglu, K. 1980." Computer counterpoint." In H. S. Howe, Jr., 1980. *Proceedings of the 1980 International Computer Music Conference*. San Francisco: International Computer Music Association.

Ebcioglu, K. 1988. "An expert system for harmonizing four-part chorales." *Computer Music Journal* 12(3): 43–51.

Ebcioglu, K. 1992. "An expert system for harmonic analysis of tonal music." In M. Balaban, K. Ebcioglu, and O. Laske, eds. *Understanding Music with AI*. Cambridge, Massachusetts and Menlo Park, California: The MIT Press and AAAI Press. pp. 294–333.

Eckel, G. 1990. "A signal editor for the IRCAM Musical Workstation." In S. Arnold and G. Hair, eds. *Proceedings of the 1990 International Computer Music Conference*. San Francisco: International Computer Music Association. pp. 69–71.

Eckel, G., X. Rodet, and Y, Potard. 1987. "The Sun-Mercury music workstation." In J. Beauchamp, ed. *Proceedings of the 1987 International Computer Music Conference*. San Francisco: International Computer Music Association. pp. 159–165.

Eckert, J. P. 1946. "Continuous variable input and output devices." In M. Campbell-Kelly and M. Williams, eds. 1985. *The Moore School Lectures*. Cambridge, Massachusetts: The MIT Press. pp. 393–423.

Edison, T. 1878. "Improvements in phonograph or speaking machines." U.S. Patent Number 200,521. Washington, D. C.: U. S. Patent Office.Reprinted in O. Read and W. Welch. 1976. *From Tin Foil to Stereo: Evolution of the Phonograph*. Indianapolis: Howard Sams.

Egan, J., and H. Hake. 1950. "On the masking pattern of a simple auditory stimulus." *Journal of the Acoustical Society of America* 22: 622–630.

Ellis, D. 1992. "Timescale modifications and wavelet representations." In A. Strange, ed. *Proceedings of the 1992 International Computer Music Conference*. San Francisco: International Computer Music Association. pp. 6–9.

Emmerson, S. 1986. *The Language of Electroacoustic Music*. New York: Harwood Academic.

Engramelle, M.-D.-J. 1775. *La Tonotechnie*. Reprinted 1993. Paris: Hermann.

Entwistle, J. 1973. "Visual perception and the analysis of music scores." B. S. thesis. Cambridge, Massachusetts: The MIT Department of Humanities.

Erbe, T. 1992. *SoundHack User's Manual*. Oakland: Mills College.

Erickson, R. 1975. "The DARMS project: a status report." *Computers and the Humanities* 7(2): 291–298.

Ernst, D. 1977. *The Evolution of Electronic Music*. New York: Schirmer.

Evangelista, G. 1991. "Wavelet transforms that we can play." In G. De Poli, A. Piccialli, and C. Roads, eds. *Representations of Musical Signals*. Cambridge, Massachusetts: The MIT Press. pp. 119–136.

Evangelista, G. 1992. "Comb and multiplexed wavelet transforms and their applications to signal processing." Unpublished mss.

Factor, R., and S. Katz. 1972. "The digital audio delay line." *db Magazine*. May. p. 18.

Fagen, M., ed. 1975. *A History of Engineering and Science in the Bell System: The Early Years (1875–1925)*. Murray Hill: Bell Telephone Laboratories.

Fairbanks, G., W. Everitt, and R. Jaeger. 1954. "Method for time or frequency compression-expansion of speech." *Institute of Radio Engineers Transactions on Audio* AV-2(1): 7–12.

Fant, C. 1960. *Acoustic Theory of Speech Production*. Mouton: σ'-Gravenhage.

Federkow, G., W. Buxton, and K. Smith. 1978. "A computer-controlled sound distribution system for performance of electroacoustic music." *Computer Music Journal* 2(3): 33–42.

Feiten, B., and T. Ungvary. 1990. "Sound data base using spectral analysis reduction and an additive synthesis model." In S. Arnold and G. Hair, eds. *Proceedings of the 1990 International Computer Music Conference*. San Francisco: International Computer Music Association. pp. 72–74.

Feiten, B., R. Frank, and T. Ungvary 1991. "Organization of sounds with neural nets." In B. Alphonce and B. Pennycook, eds. *Proceedings of the 1991 International Computer Music Conference*. San Francisco: International Computer Music Association. pp. 441–444.

Ferretti, E. 1965. "The computer as a tool for the creative musician." In *Computers for the Humanities*. New Haven: Yale University Press. pp. 107–112.

Ferretti, E. 1966. "Exploration and organization of sound with the computer." *Journal of the Acoustical Society of America* 39(6): 1245.

Ferretti, E. 1975. "Sound synthesis by rule." In J. Beauchamp and J. Melby, eds. *Proceedings of the Second Annual Music Computation Conference.* Urbana: University of Illinois. pp. 1–21.

Finger, R. 1991. "AES3-1992: the revised two-channel digital audio interface." *Journal of the Audio Engineering Society* 40(3): 107–116.

Flanagan, J. L. 1972. *Speech Analysis, Synthesis, and Perception.* New York: Springer-Verlag.

Flanagan, J. L., et al. 1970. "Synthetic voices for computers." *IEEE Spectrum* 7(10): 22–45.

Flanagan, J. L., and R. Golden 1966. "Phase vocoder." *Bell System Technical Journal* 45: 1493–1509.

Fletcher, H. 1940. "Auditory patterns." *Review of Modern Physics* 12: 47–56.

Fletcher, H., and W. Munson, 1933. "Loudness, its definition, measurement, and calculation." *Journal of the Acoustical Society of America* 5: 82–108.

Fletcher, H., E. Blackham, and R. Stratton. 1962. "Quality of piano tones." *Journal of the Acoustical Society of America* 34(6): 749–761.

Fletcher, H., E. Blackham, and D. Christensen. 1963. "Quality of organ tones." *Journal of the Acoustical Society of America* 35(3): 314–325.

Fletcher, N. and T. Rossing. 1991. *The Physics of Musical Instruments.* New York: Springer-Verlag.

Florens, J., and C. Cadoz. 1991. "The physical model: modeling and simulating the instrumental universe." In G. De Poli, A. Piccialli, and C. Roads, eds. *Representations of Musical Signals.* Cambridge, Massachusetts: The MIT Press. pp. 227–268.

Flurry, H. 1989. "An introduction to the Creation Station." *Computer Music Journal* 13(2): 56–70.

Fokker, A. 1975. *New Music with 31 Tones.* Bonn: Verlag für systematische Musikwissenschaft.

Ford, H. 1984. "The Sony CY-24 digital tape splicer." *Studio Sound* 26(1): 70.

Foster, S., W. A. Schloss, and A. J. Rockmore. 1982. "Toward an intelligent editor fordigital audio: signal processing methods." *Computer Music Journal* 6(1): 42–51. Reprinted in C. Roads, ed. 1989. *The Music Machine.* Cambridge, Massachusetts: The MIT Press. pp. 549–558.

Fourré, R., S. Schwarzenbach, and R. Powers. 1990. "20 bit evolution." *Studio Sound* 32(5): 32–36.

Framjee, P. F. 1958. *Text Book of Indian Music.* Hathras: Sakhi Prakashan.

Franssen, N. 1973. "Tempered tone-scale generation from a single oscillator." *Journal of the Audio Engineering Society* 21(6): 457–460.

Freed, A. 1987. "MacMix: recording, mixing, and signal processing on a personal computer." In J. Strawn, ed. 1987. *Music and Digital Technology*. New York: Audio Engineering Society. pp. 158–162.

Freed, A., and M. Goldstein. 1988. "MacMix: professional sound recording, editing, processing, and mixing software for the DYAXIS digital audio system." Menlo Park: Studer Editech.

Freedman, M. D. 1965. "A technique for analysis of musical instrument tones." Ph.D. diss. Urbana: University of Illinois.

Freedman, M. D. 1967. "Analysis of musical instrument tones." *Journal of the Acoustical Society of America* 41: 793–806.

Freeman, J. P. 1984. "The evolution of high-definition television." *SMPTE Journal* 93(5): 492–501.

Freff, C. 1989. "Raymond Scott's Electronium (1965)." *Keyboard* 15(2): 50–56.

Friberg, A. 1991. "Generative rules for music performance: a formal description of a rule system." *Computer Music Journal* 15(2): 56–71.

Friberg, A., L. Frydèn, L. Bodin, and J. Sundberg. 1991. "Performance rules for computer-controlled contemporary keyboard music." *Computer Music Journal* 15(2): 49–55.

Fry, C. 1980. "YAMIL reference manual." Cambridge, Massachusetts: The MIT Experimental Music Studio.

Fry, C. 1982. "Dancing musicians." *Perspectives of New Music* 21(1–2): 585–589.

Fry, C. 1984. "Flavors Band: a language for specifying musical style." *Computer Music Journal* 8(4): 48–58. Reprinted in C. Roads, ed. 1989. *The Music Machine*. Cambridge, Massachusetts: The MIT Press. pp. 295–309.

Fry, C. 1992. "MidiVox Voice-to-MIDI converter." *Computer Music Journal* 16(1): 94–95.

Frykberg, S. 1978. "Composer and computer." Man-Machine Studies Progress Report UC-DSE/13 (1978). Christchurch: Department of Electrical Engineering, University of Canterbury.

Fujinaga, I., B. Alphonce, and B. Pennycook. 1989. "Issues in the design of an optical music recognition system." In T. Wells and D. Butler, eds. *Proceedings of the 1989 International Computer Music Conference*. San Francisco: International Computer Music Association.

Fujinaga, I, B. Alphonce, B. Pennycook, and K. Hogan 1991. "Optical character recognition: a progress report." In B. Alphonce and B. Pennycook, eds. *Proceedings of the 1991 International Computer Music Conference.* San Francisco: International Computer Music Association. pp. 66–73.

Gabor, D. 1946. "Theory of communication." *Journal of the Institute of Electrical Engineers* Part III, 93: 429–457.

Gabor, D. 1947. "Acoustical quanta and the theory of hearing." *Nature* 159(1044): 591–594.

Gabrielsson, A. 1986. "Rhythm in music." In J. Evans and M. Clynes, eds. 1986. *Rhythm in Psychological, Linguistic, and Musical Processes.* Springfield, Illinois: Charles C. Thomas. pp. 131–167.

Galas, T., and X. Rodet. 1990. "An improved cepstral method for deconvolution of source-filter systems with discrete spectra: application to musical signals." In S. Arnold and G. Hair, eds. *Proceedings of the 1990 International Computer Music Conference.* San Francisco: International Computer Music Association. pp. 82–84.

Gardner, M. 1978. "White and brown music, fractal curves, and 1/f fluctuations." *Scientific American* 238(4): 16–31.

Garnett, G. 1987. "Modeling piano sound using waveguide digital filtering techniques." In J. Beauchamp, ed. *Proceedings of the 1987 International Computer Music Conference.* San Francisco: International Computer Music Association. pp. 89–95.

Garnett, G. 1991. "Music, signals, and representations: a survey." In G. De Poli, A. Piccialli, and C. Roads, eds. *Representations of Musical Signals.* Cambridge, Massachusetts: The MIT Press. pp. 325–369.

Garnett, G., and B. Mont-Reynaud. 1988. "Hierarchical waveguide networks." In C. Lischka and J. Fritsch, eds. *Proceedings of the 1988 International Computer Music Conference.* San Francisco: International Computer Music Association. pp. 297–312.

Garton, B. 1989. "The Elthar program." *Perspectives of New Music* 27(1): 6–41.

Garton, B. 1992. "Virtual performance modeling." In A. Strange, ed. *Proceedings of the 1992 International Computer Music Conference.* San Francisco: International Computer Music Association. pp. 219–222.

Gaudiot, J.-L. 1987. "Data-driven multicomputers in digital signal processing." *Proceedings of the IEEE* 75(9): 1220–1234.

Gelb, A., editor. 1974. *Applied Optimal Estimation.* Cambridge, Massachusetts: The MIT Press.

Genovese, V., M. Cocco, M. DeMicheli, and G. Buttazo. 1991. "Infraread-based MIDI event generator." In *Proceedings of the International Workshop on Man-Machine Interaction in Live Performance.* Pisa: Computer Music Department of CNUCE/CNR. pp. 1–8.

George, E., and M. Smith. 1992. "Analysis-by-synthesis/overlap-add sinusoidal modeling applied to the analysis and synthesis of musical tones." *Journal of the Audio Engineering Society* 40(6): 497–516.

Gerrard, G. 1989. "Music 4C—a Macintosh version of Music4BF in C. "Melbourne: Department of Music, University of Melbourne.

Gerzon, M. 1973. "Periphony: with-height sound reproduction." *Journal of the Audio Engineering Society* 21(3).

Gerzon, M. 1990. "Why do equalisers sound different?" *Studio Sound* 32(7): 58–65.

Gerzon, M. 1991. "Super-resolving short-term spectral analyzers." Preprint 3174 (T-5). Presented at the 91st Convention of the Audio Engineering Society. New York: Audio Engineering Society.

Ghent, E. 1967a. "The Coordinome in relation to electronic music." *Electronic Music Review* 1(1): 33–43.

Ghent, E. 1967b. "Programmed signals to performers." *Perspectives of New Music.* Reprinted in B. Boretz and E. Cone, eds. 1976. *Perspectives on Notation and Performance.* New York: W. W. Norton. pp. 134–144.

Ghent, M. 1979. "Further studies in compositional algorithms."In C. Roads, ed. *Proceedings of the 1978 International Computer Music Conference.* Evanston: Northwestern University Press. pp. 108–118.

Gill, S. 1963. "A technique for the composition of music in a computer." *Computer Journal* 6(2): 29–31.

Gillespie, B. 1992. "Dynamical modeling of grand piano action." In A. Strange, ed. *Proceedings of the 1992 International Computer Music Conference.* San Francisco: International Computer Music Association. pp. 77–80.

Gish, W. 1978. "Analysis and synthesis of musical instrument tones." Preprint 1410. Presented at the 61st Convention of the Audio Engineering Society. New York: Audio Engineering Society.

Gish, W. 1992. "Multistage signal analysis." In A. Strange, ed. *Proceedings of the 1992 International Computer Music Conference.* San Francisco: International Computer Music Association. pp. 387–388.

Gjerdingen, R. 1988. "Shape and motion in the microstructure of song." *Music Perception* 6(1): 35–64.

Glaser, E., and D. Ruchkin. 1976. *Principles of Neurobiological Signal Analysis.* Orlando: Academic Press.

Gleick, J. *Chaos.* 1988. London: Cardinal.

Goeddel, T., and S. Bass. 1984. "High-quality synthesis of musical voices in discrete time." *IEEE Transactions on Acoustics, Speech, and Signal Processing* ASSP-32(3): 623–633.

Gogins, M. 1991. "Iterated function systems music." *Computer Music Journal* 15(1): 40–48.

Gold, B. 1962. "A computer program for pitch extraction." *Journal of the Acoustical Society of America* 34: 916.

Goldberg, D. 1989. *Genetic Algorithms in Search, Optimization, and Machine Learning*. Reading, Massachusetts: Addison-Wesley.

Goldberg, A., and D. Robson. 1983a. *Smalltalk-80: The Language and Its Implementation*. Reading, Massachusetts: Addison-Wesley.

Goldberg, A., and D. Robson. 1983b. *Smalltalk-80: The Interactive Programming Environment*. Reading, Massachusetts: Addison-Wesley.

Goldstein, J. 1967. "Auditory nonlinearity." *Journal of the Acoustical Society of America* 41: 676–689.

Goldstein, J. 1973. "An optimum processor theory for the central formation of the pitch of complex tones." *Journal of the Acoustical Society of America* 54(6): 1496–1516.

Gordon, John W. 1984. "Perception of attack transients in musical tones." Department of Music Report Number STAN-M-17. Stanford: Stanford University,

Gordon, J., and J. Grey. 1977. "Perception of spectral modifications on orchestral instrument tones." *Computer Music Journal* 2(1): 24–31.

Gordon, J., and J. Strawn. 1985. "An introduction to the phase vocoder". In J. Strawn, ed. *Digital Audio Signal Processing: An Anthology*. Madison: A-R Editions. pp. 221–270.

Bird, J. 1982. *Percy Grainger*. South Melbourne: Sun Books.

Grattan-Guinness, I. 1972. *Joseph Fourier: 1768–1830*. Cambridge, Massachusetts: The MIT Press.

Greenberg, G. 1987. "Procedural composition." In J. Beauchamp, ed. *Proceedings of the 1987 International Computer Music Conference*. San Francisco: International Computer Music Association. pp. 25–32.

Greenberg, G. 1988. "Composing with performer objects." In C. Lischka and J. Fritsch, eds. *Proceedings of the 1988 International Computer Music Conference*. San Francisco: International Computer Music Association. pp. 142–149.

Greenspun, P. 1984. "Audio analysis I: phase correction for digital systems." *Computer Music Journal* 8(4): 13–19.

Greenspun, P., and L. Klotz. 1988. "Audio analysis VI: testing audio cables." *Computer Music Journal* 12(1): 58–64.

Greiner, R., and D. Melton. 1991. "Observations on the audibility of acoustic polarity." Preprint 3170-(K-4). Presented at the 91st Convention of the Audio

Engineering Society 1991 October 4–8, New York. New York: Audio Engineering Society.

Grey, J. 1975. "An exploration of musical timbre." Report STAN-M-2.Stanford University Department of Music.

Grey, J. 1978. "Timbre discrimination in musical patterns." *Journal of the Acoustical Society of America* 64: 467–472.

Grey, J., and Gordon, John W. 1978. "Perceptual effects of spectral modifications on musical timbres." *Journal of the Acoustical Society of America* 63, 1493–1500.

Griffiths, M., and P. Bloom. 1982. "A flexible digital sound-editing program for minicomputer systems." *Journal of the Audio Engineering Society* 30(3): 127–134.

Grogono, P. 1984. "Brief history of EMS." Unpublished mss.

Grossi, P. 1987. *Musica senza musicisti.* Florence: CNUCE/CNR.

Grossman, G. 1987. "Instruments, cybernetics, and music." In J. Beauchamp, ed. *Proceedings of the 1987 International Computer Music Conference.* San Francisco: International Computer Music Association. pp. 212–219.

Grout, D. 1973. *A Short History of Western Music.* Revised edition. New York: W. W. Norton.

Guttman, N. 1980. Personal communication.

Haflich, S., and M. Burns. 1983. "Following a conductor: the engineering of an input device." Presented at the 1983 International Computer Music Conference, Eastman School of Music, Rochester, New York, October.

Hall, H. 1937. "Sound analysis." *Journal of the Acoustical Society of America* 8: 257–262.

Haller, H. P. 1980. "Live-Elektronik." In *Teilton Schriftenreihe der Heinrich-Strobel-Stiftung des Südwestfunks.* Kassel: Barenreiter-Verlag. pp. 41–46.

Hamel, K. 1987. "Issues in the design of a music notation system." In. J. Beauchamp, ed. *Proceedings of the 1987 International Computer Music Conference.* San Francisco: International Computer Music Association. pp. 325–332.

Hamel, K. 1989. "A design for music editing and printing software based on a notational syntax." *Perspectives of New Music* 27(1): 70–83.

Hamel, K., B. Pennycook, B. Ripley, and E. Blevis. 1987. "Composition Design System: a functional approach to composition. In J. Beauchamp, ed. *Proceedings of the 1987 International Computer Music Conference.* San Francisco: International Computer Music Association. pp. 33–39.

Hamlin, P., with C. Roads. 1985. "Interview with Herbert Brün." In C. Roads, ed. *Composers and the Computer.* Madison: A-R Editions. pp. 1–15.

Hamming, R. W. 1973. *Numerical Methods for Scientists and Engineers*. New York: McGraw-Hill.

Hanert, J. 1944. U. S. Patent 2,498,367. (Proposed system for producing chorus effect.)

Hanert, J. 1945. "Electronic musical apparatus (L-C delay line with variable inductors for post source vibrato processing)." U. S. Patent 2,382,413.

Hanert, J. 1946. U.S. Patent 2,509,923. (Manufactured system for producing chorus effect.)

Hansen, E. 1975. *A Table of Series and Products*. Englewood Cliffs: Prentice-Hall.

Harada, T., A. Sato, S. Hashimoto, and S. Ohteru. 1992. "Real-time control of 3D space by gesture." In A. Strange, ed. *Proceedings of the 1992 International Computer Music Conference*. San Francisco: International Computer Music Association. pp. 85–88.

Harris, F. 1978. "On the use of windows for harmonic analysis with the discrete Fourier transform." *Proceedings of the IEEE* 66(1): 51–83.

Hartman, W. H. 1978. "Flanging and phasers." *Journal of the Audio Engineering Society* 26(6): 439–443.

Harvey, J. 1981. "*Mortuos Plango, Vivos Voco:* a realization at IRCAM." *Computer Music Journal* 5(4): 22–24.

Hastings, C. 1978. "A recipe for homebrew ECL." *Computer Music Journal* 2(1): 48–59. Revised and updated version in C. Roads, and J. Strawn, eds. 1985. *Foundations of Computer Music*. Cambridge, Massachusetts: The MIT Press. pp. 335–362.

Haus, G. 1981. "Strumenti per l'elaborazione musicale: il sistema 4X." *Strumenti Musicali* 18/19: 60–65.

Haus, G. 1983. "EMPS: A system for graphic transcriptionof electronic music scores." *Computer Music Journal* 7(3): 31–36.

Haus, G. 1984. *Elementi di Informatica Musicale*. Milan: Gruppo Editoriale Jackson.

Hauser, M. 1991. "Principles of oversampling A/D conversion." *Journal of the Audio Engineering Society* 39(1–2): 3–21.

Hawkins, T., Jr., and S. Stevens. 1950. "Masking of pure tones and speech by white noise." *Journal of the Acoustical Society of America* 22: 6–13.

Hawthorne, D. 1985. "Droids shoot the works to post electronically." *Millimeter* 13(4): 89–94.

Haynes, S. 1980. "The musician-machine interface in digital sound synthesis." *Computer Music Journal* 4(4): 23–44.

Haynes, S. 1982. "The computer as a sound processor." *Computer Music Journal* 6(1): 7–17.

Hebel, K. 1987. "Javelina: an environment for the development of software for digital signal processing." In J. Beauchamp, ed. *Proceedings of the 1987 International Computer Music Conference.* San Francisco: International Computer Music Association. pp. 104–107.

Hebel, K. 1989. "Javelina: an environment for digital signal processing." *Computer Music Journal* 13(2): 39–47.

Hegg, T. 1983. "Applications of parallel processing hardware to computer music synthesis." B.S., M.S. thesis. Cambridge, Massachusetts: M.I.T. Department of Electrical Engineering and Computer Science.

Heideman, M., D. Johnson, and C. Burrus. 1984. "Gauss and the history of the fast Fourier transform." *IEEE Magazine* October: pp. 14–21.

Helmers, C. 1979. "Interfacing pneumatic player pianos." In C. Morgan, ed. *The Byte Book of Computer Music.* Peterborough: Byte Books. pp. 85–90.

Helmholtz, H. 1863. *On the Sensations of Tone as a Physiological Basis for the Theory of Music.* Reprinted 1954, A. Ellis, trans. New York: Dover.

Helstrom, C. 1966. "An expansion of a signal in Gaussian elementary signals." *IEEE Transactions on Information Theory* IT-12: 81–82.

Henke, W. 1970. "Musical Interactive Tone Synthesis System." Cambridge, Massachusetts: Massachusetts Institute of Technology.

Hermes, D. 1992. "Pitch analysis." In M. Cooke and S. Beet, eds. *Visual Representations of Speech Signals.* New York: John Wiley and Sons.

Hess, W. 1983. *Pitch Determination of Speech Signals: Algorithms and Devices.* Berlin: Springer.

Hewitt, C., 1977. "Viewing control structures as patterns of passing messages." *Artificial Intelligence* 8: 323–363.

Hewlett, W., and E. Selfridge-Field. 1991. *Computing in Musicology.* Menlo Park: Center for Computer Assisted Research in the Humanities. (525 Middlefield Road, Menlo Park, California.)

Hickman, W. 1984. *Time Code Handbook.* Boston: Cipher Digital.

Hiller, L. 1964, "Informationstheorie und Computermusik." *Darmstädter Beiträge zur Neuen Musik* 8. Mainz: Schott.

Hiller, L. 1969. "Some compositional techniques involving the use of computers." In H. Von Foerster and J. Beauchamp, eds. *Music by Computers.* New York: John Wiley and Sons. pp. 71–83.

Hiller, L. 1970. "Music composed with computers—a historical survey." In H. Lincoln, ed. *The Computer and Music.* Ithaca: Cornell University Press. pp. 42–96.

Hiller, L. 1979. "Phrase structure in computer music." In C. Roads, ed. *Proceedings of the 1978 International Computer Music Conference.* Evanston: Northwestern University Press. pp. 192–213.

Hiller, L. 1981. "Composing with computers: a progress report." *Computer Music Journal* 5(4): 7–21. Reprinted in C. Roads, ed. 1989. *The Music Machine.* Cambridge, Massachusetts: The MIT Press. pp. 75–89.

Hiller, L., and R. Baker. 1964. "*Computer Cantata:* a study in compositional method." *Perspectives of New Music* 3: 62–90.

Hiller, L., and R. Baker. 1965. "Automated music printing." *Journal of Music Theory* 9: 129–150.

Hiller, L., and J. Beauchamp. 1967. "Review of completed and proposed research on analysis and synthesis of musical sounds by analog and digital techniques." Technical Report 19. Urbana: University of Illinois Experimental Music Studio.

Hiller, L., and J. Cage. 1968. "HPSCHD: an interview by Larry Austin." *Source* 2(2): 10–19. See also Austin 1992.

Hiller, L., J. Divilbiss, D. Barron, H. Brün, and E. Lin. 1966. "Operator's manual for the CSX-1 Music Machine." Technical Report 12. Urbana: University of Illinois Experimental Music Studio.

Hiller, L., and L. Isaacson. 1959. *Experimental Music.* New York: McGraw-Hill.

Hiller, L., and A. Leal. 1966. "Revised MUSICOMP Manual." Technical Report 13. Urbana: University of Illinois Experimental Music Studio.

Hiller, L., and B. Levy. 1984. "General system theory as applied to music analysis—part 1." In M. Baroni and L. Callegari, eds. *Musical Grammars and Computer Analysis.* Florence: Leo Olschki Editore. pp. 295–316.

Hiller, L., and P. Ruiz. 1971. "Synthesizing sounds by solving the wave equation for vibrating objects." *Journal of the Audio Engineering Society* 19: 463–470, 542–551.

Hillis, D. 1987. *The Connection Machine.* Cambridge, Massachusetts: The MIT Press.

Hirota, Y., et al. 1983. "LSIs for digital signal processing based on a PCM standard format." *Journal of the Audio Engineering Society* 31(7): 523–537.

Hirschman, S. 1991. "Digital waveguide modeling and simulation of reed woodwind instruments." Engineering thesis. Stanford: Stanford University Department of Electrical Engineering.

Hirschman, S., P. Cook, and J. Smith. 1991. "Digital waveguide modelling of reed woodwinds: an interactive development. In B. Alphonce and B. Pennycook, eds.

Proceedings of the 1991 International Computer Music Conference. San Francisco: International Computer Music Association. pp. 300–303.

Holden, A. 1986. *Chaos.* Princeton: Princeton University Press.

Holloway, B. 1993. "LemurEdit: a graphical editing tool for Lemur analyses." Urbana-Champaign: CERL Sound Group, University of Illinois.

Holloway, B., and L. Haken. 1992. "A sinusoidal synthesis algorithm for generating transitions between notes." In A. Strange, ed. *Proceedings of the 1992 International Computer Music Conference.* San Francisco: International Computer Music Association. pp. 14–17.

Holtzman, S. 1980. "Non-uniform time-scale modification of speech." M. Sc. and E.E. thesis. Cambridge, Massachusetts: M.I.T. Department of Electrical Engineering and Computer Science.

Holtzman, S. R. 1977. "A program for key determination." *Interface* 6: 29–56.

Holtzman, S. R. 1979. "An automated synthesis instrument." *Computer Music Journal* 3(3): 53–61.

Holtzman, S. R. 1981. "Using generative grammars for music composition." *Computer Music Journal* 5(1): 51–64.

Holm, F. 1989. "Frequency scheduling—real-time scheduling in multiprocessing systems." In T. Wells and D. Butler, eds. *Proceedings of the 1989 International Computer Music Conference.* San Francisco: International Computer Music Association. pp. 127–130.

Holm, F. 1992. "Understanding FM implementations: a call for common standards." *Computer Music Journal* 16(1): 34–42.

Honing, H. 1991. "Issues in the representation of time and structure in music." In P. Desain and H. Honing. 1992. *Music, Mind, and Machine.* Amsterdam: Thesis Publishers. pp. 127–148.

Hoover, C. 1971. *Music Machines—American Style.* Washington, D.C.: Smithsonian Institute Press.

Horner, A., J. Beauchamp, and L. Haken. 1992. "Wavetable and FM matching synthesis of musical instrument tones." In A. Strange, ed. *Proceedings of the 1992 International Computer Music Conference.* San Francisco: International Computer Music Association. pp. 18–21.

Horner, A., J. Beauchamp, and L. Haken. 1993. "Methods for multiple wavetable synthesis of musical instrument tones." *Journal of the Audio Engineering Society* 41(5): 336–356.

Horiuchi, Y., and H. Tanaka. 1993. "A computer accompaniment system with independence." In S. Ohteru, ed. *Proceedings of the 1993 International Computer Music Conference.* San Francisco: International Computer Music Association. pp. 418–420.

Hou, S. 1969. "Review of modal synthesis techniques and a new approach." *Shock and Vibration Bulletin, US Naval Laboratories Proceedings* 40(4): 25–39.

Howe, H. S., Jr. 1975. *Electronic Music Synthesis.* New York: W. W. Norton.

Hub, The. 1989. *Computer Network Music.* ART 1002. Berkeley: Artifact Recordings. (compact disc)

Hurty, W., and M. Rubenstein. 1964. *Dynamics of Structures.* Englewood Cliffs: Prentice-Hall.

Hush, D. et al. 1986. "An adaptive IIR structure for sinusoidal enhancement, frequency estimation, and detection." *IEEE Transactions on Acoustics, Speech, and Signal Processing* 34(6): 1380–1390.

Hutchins, B. 1973. "Experimental electronic music devices employing Walsh functions." *Journal of the Audio Engineering Society* 21(8): 640–645.

Hutchins, B. 1975. "Application of real-time Hadamard transform network to sound synthesis." *Journal of the Audio Engineering Society* 23: 558–562.

Hutchins, B. 1982–1988. Various tutorials, appplication notes, and code listings published in *Electronotes.* (1 Pheasant Lane, Ithaca, New York 14850 USA.)

Hutchins, B. 1984. "Special issue D: A review of Fourier methods in signal processing and musical engineering." *Electronotes* 15 (155–160): 2.

Hutchins, B. 1986a. "Interpolation, decimation, and prediction of digital signals." *Electronotes* 15(164–167): 3–46.

Hutchins, B. 1986b. "Windows for signal processing." Application Note 292. Ithaca: Electronotes.

Hutchins, B., and W. Ku. 1982. "A simple hardware pitch extractor." *Journal of the Audio Engineering Society* 30(3): 135–139.

Hutchins, B., D. Parola, and L. Ludwig. 1982. "A pitch extraction scheme based on Hilbert transformations." *Electronotes* 14(136).

Hutchins, C. 1978. *The Physics of Music.* San Francisco: W. H. Freeman.

Hybrid Management. 1984. "About the instrument." Garrison: Hybrid Management.

Hyperception. 1992. *Hypersignal.* Computer software. Dallas: Hyperception.

IMA. 1983. "MIDI musical instrument digital interface specification 1.0." Los Angeles: International MIDI Association. (See also various addenda to this document.)

Imberty, M. 1976. "Signification and meaning in music." Monographies de sémiologie et d'analyse musicales III. Montréal: Université de Montréal.

Imberty, M. 1979. *Entendre la musique: sémantique psychologique de la musique.* Paris: Dunod.

INA/GRM. 1993. "GRM Tools." product literature. Paris: Institut National de l'Audio-visuel/Groupe de Recherches Musicales.

Ingebretsen, R., and T. Stockham. 1984. "Random access editing of digital audio." *Journal of the Audio Engineering Society* 32.

Insam, E. 1974. "Walsh functions in waveform synthesis." *Journal of the Audio Engineering Society* 22: 422–425.

Iovino, F. 1993. *Chant-PatchWork Manual.* Paris: IRCAM.

Isaacson, M. 1993. "What is SMDI?" *Electronic Musician* 9(6): 79–82.

Iverson, K., 1962. *A Programming Language.* New York: John Wiley & Sons.

Iwamura, H., H. Hayashi, A. Miyashita, and T. Anazawa. 1973. "Pulse-code-modulation Recording System." *Journal of the Audio Engineering Society* 21(7): 535–541.

Jacobs, D. 1992. "Muscle music: experience using the BodySynth." Abstract of presentation at IRCAM, Paris. August.

Jaffar, J., and J.-L. Lassez. 1987. "Constraint logic programming." *Proceedings of the Fourteenth Association for Computing Machinery Symposium on Principles of Programming Languages.* New York: Association for Computing Machinery. pp. 111–119.

Jaffe, D. 1985. "Ensemble timing in computer music. "*Computer Music Journal* 9(4): 38–48.

Jaffe, D. 1987a. "Spectrum analysis tutorial, part 1: the discrete Fourier transform." *Computer Music Journal* 11(2): 9–24.

Jaffe, D. 1987b. "Spectrum analysis tutorial, part 2: properties and applications of the discrete Fourier transform." *Computer Music Journal* 11(3): 17–35.

Jaffe, D. 1989. "From the classical software synthesis note-list to the NeXT score-file." Redwood City: NeXT Computer, Inc.

Jaffe, D., and J. Smith. 1983. "Extensions of the Karplus-Strong plucked string algorithm." *Computer Music Journal* 7(2): 56–69.

Jaffe, D., and L. Boynton. 1989. "An overview of the sound and music kits for the NeXT computer." *Computer Music Journal* 13(2): 48–55.

Janse, P., and A. Kaizer. 1983. "Time-frequency distributions of loudspeakers: the application of the Wigner distribution." *Journal of the Audio Engineering Society* 31-(4): 198–223.

Janse, P., and A. Kaizer. 1984. "The Wigner distribution: a valuable tool for investigating transient distortion." *Journal of the Audio Engineering Society* 32: 868–882.

Jansen, C. 1991. "Sine Circuitu: 10,000 high-quality sine waves without detours." In B. Alphonce and B. Pennycook, eds. *Proceedings of the 1991 International Computer Music Conference*. San Francisco: International Computer Music Association. pp. 222–225.

Jaslowitz, M., T. D'Silva, and E. Zwaneveld. 1988. "A high-capacity automated digital sound effects storage and retrieval system." Preprint 130–87. Presented at the Society for Motion Picture and Television Engineers (SMPTE) Technical Conference, October 1988. White Plains: SMPTE.

Jeffress, L. 1970. "Masking." In J. Tobias,ed. *Foundations of Modern Auditory Theory*. Orlando: Academic Press: Vol. 1, pp. 85–114.

Jenny, G. 1958. "L'Ondioline." *Toute la Radio*.

Jensen, K., and N. Wirth. 1974. *Pascal User Manual and Report*. Second ed. New York: Springer-Verlag.

Johnson, M. 1991. "Toward an expert system for expressive performance rules." *IEEE Computer* 24(7): 30–34.

Johnson, S., 1984. "VLSI circuit design reaches the level of architectural description." *Electronics* 57(9): 121–128.

Johnson, W., C. McHugh, H. Rice, T. Rhea. 1970. "History of electronic music, part one." *Synthesis* 1.

Jones, K. 1981. "Compositional applications of stochastic processes." *Computer Music Journal* 5(2): 45–61. Reprinted in C. Roads, ed. 1989. *The Music Machine*. Cambridge, Massachusetts: The MIT Press. pp. 381–398.

Jones, M. 1983. "The digital mixing console." *Studio Sound* 25(10): 52–56.

Jones, M. 1983. "Processing systems for the digital audio studio." In B. Blesser, et al. *Digital Audio*. New York: Audio Engineering Society. pp. 221–225.

Jones, D., and T. Parks. 1988. "Generation and combination of grains for music synthesis." *Computer Music Journal* 12(2): 27–34.

Justice, J. 1979. "Analytic signal processing in music computation." *IEEE Transactions on Acoustics, Speech, and Signal Processing* ASSP-27(6): 670–684.

Kaegi, W. 1967. *Was Ist Elektronisches Musik?* Zürich: Orell Füssli Verlag.

Kaegi, W. 1973. "A minimum description of the linguistic sign repertoire (part 1)." *Interface* 2: 141–156.

Kaegi, W. 1974. "A minimum description of the linguistic sign repertoire (part 2)." *Interface* 3: 137–158.

Kaegi, W., and S. Tempelaars. 1978. "VOSIM—a new sound synthesis system." *Journal of the Audio Engineering Society* 26(6): 418–426.

Kahrs, M. 1981. "Notes on very-large-scale-integration and the design of real-time digital sound processors." *Computer Music Journal* 5(2): 20–28. Reprinted in C. Roads, ed. 1989. *The Music Machine*. Cambridge, Massachusetts: The MIT Press. pp. 623–631.

Kahrs, M. 1986. "DSP*—a DSP32-based multiprocessor." In *Final Program and Paper Summaries of the 1986 IEEE ASSP Workshop on Applications of Signal Processing to Audio and Acoustics*. New York: IEEE.

Kahrs, M. 1991. "An AES/EBU circuit compendium or AES/EBU circuits I have known and loved." Preprint 3104. Presented at the 91st Convention of the Audio Engineering Society. New York: Audio Engineering Society.

Kaiser, J. 1963. "Design methods for sampled data filters." *Proceedings of the First Annual Allerton Conference on Circuit Systems Theory*. Reprinted in L. Rabiner and C. Rader, eds. 1972. *Digital Signal Processing*. New York: IEEE Press. pp. 20–34.

Kaplan, S. J. 1981. "Developing a commercial digital sound synthesizer." *Computer Music Journal* 5(3): 62–73. Reprinted in C. Roads, ed. 1989. *The Music Machine*. Cambridge, Massachusetts: The MIT Press. pp. 611–622.

Karjalainen, M., U. Laine, T. Laakso, and V. Välimäki. 1991. "Transmission-line modeling and real-time synthesis of string and window instruments." In B. Alphonce and B. Pennycook, eds. *Proceedings of the 1991 International Computer Music Conference*. San Francisco: International Computer Music Association. pp. 293–296.

Kashino, K., and H. Tanaka. 1993. "A sound source separation system with the ability of automatic tone modeling." In S. Ohteru, ed. *Proceedings of the 1993 International Computer Music Conference*. San Francisco: International Computer Music Association. pp. 248–255.

Karkoschka, E. 1966. *Das Schriftbild der Neuen Musik*. Celle: Moeck.

Karplus, W. and D. Cohen. 1981. "Architectural and software issues in the design and application of peripheral array processors." *IEEE Computer* 14(9): 11–17.

Karplus, K., and A. Strong. 1983. "Digital synthesis of plucked string and drum timbres." *Computer Music Journal* 7(2): 43–55. Reprinted in C. Roads, ed. 1989. *The Music Machine*. Cambridge, Massachusetts: The MIT Press.

Katayose, H., and S. Inokuchi. 1989. "The Kansei music system." *Computer Music Journal* 11(4): 72–77.

Katayose, H., and S. Inokuchi. 1990. "The Kansei Music System '90." In S. Arnold and G. Hair, eds. *Proceedings of the 1990 International Computer Music Conference*. San Francisco: International Computer Music Association. pp. 309–311.

Katayose, H., K. Takami, T. Fukuoka, and S. Inokuchi. 1989. "Music interpreter in the Kansei Music System." In T. Wells and D. Butler, eds. *Proceedings of the 1989 International Computer Music Conference*. San Francisco: International Computer Music Association. pp. 147–150.

Kay, A., 1977. "Microelectronics and the personal computer." *Scientific American* 237(3): 270–244.

Kay, S., and S. Marple. 1981. "Spectrum analysis—a modern perspective." *Proceedings of the Institute of Electrical and Electronics Engineers* 69(11): 1380–1419.

Keane, D., G. Smecca, and K. Wood. 1990. "The MIDI Baton II." In S. Arnold and G. Hair, eds. *Proceedings of the 1990 International Computer Music Conference.* San Francisco: International Computer Music Association. Supplemental pages.

Keefe, D. 1992. "Physical modeling of wind instruments." *Computer Music Journal* 16(4): 57–73.

Keele, D. 1973. "The design and use of a simple pseudorandom pink-noise generator." *Journal of the Audio Engineering Society* 21(1): 33–41.

Keislar, D. 1987. "History and principles of microtonal keyboards." *Computer Music Journal* 11(1): 18–28.

Keller, A. 1981. "Early hi-fi and stereo recording at Bell Laboratories (1931–1932)." *Journal of the Audio Engineering Society* 29(4): 274–280.

Kelly, J., and C. Lochbaum. 1962. "Speech synthesis." *Proceedingsa of the Fourth International Congress on Acoustics.* Paper G42: 1–4.

Kendall, G., and W. Martens. 1984. "Simulating the cues of spatial hearing in natural environments." In D. Wessel, ed. 1984. *Proceedings of the 1984 International Computer Music Conference.* San Francisco: International Computer Music Association. pp. 111–125.

Kendall, G., W. Martens, D. Freed, D. Ludwig, and R. Karstens. 1986. "Spatial processing software at Northwestern Computer Music." In P. Berg, eds. *Proceedings of the 1986 International Computer Music Conference.* San Francisco: International Computer Music Association. pp. 285–292.

Kendall, G., W. Martens, and S. Decker. 1989. "Spatial reverberation: discussion and demonstration." In M. Mathews and J. R. Pierce. 1989. *Current Directions in Computer Music Research.* Cambridge, Massachusetts: The MIT Press. pp. 65–87.

Kernighan, B., and D. Ritchie. 1978. *The C Programming Language.* Englewood Cliffs: Prentice-Hall.

Kiang, N., and E. Moxon. 1972. "Physiological considerations in artificial stimulation of the inner ear." *Annals of Otolology, Rhinology, and Laryngology* 81: 714–730.

Kirchmeyer, H. 1968. "On the historical constitution of a rationalistic music." *die Reihe* 8. English edition. Bryn Mawr: Theodore Presser Company. pp. 11–24.

Kirck, G. 1986. "Computer realization of extended just intonation compositions." *Computer Music Journal* 11(1): 69–75.

Kleczkowski, P. 1989. "Group additive synthesis." *Computer Music Journal* 13(1): 12–20.

Knapp, B. R., and H. Lustad. 1990. "A bioelectric controller for computer music applications." *Computer Music Journal* 14(1): 42–47.

Knowlton, P. 1971. "Interactive communication and display of keyboard music." Ph.D. diss. Salt Lake City: University of Utah Department of Computer Science.

Knowlton, P. 1972. "Capture and display of keyboard music." *Datamation* 5.

Knuth, D., 1973a. Second edition. *The Art of Computer Programming, Vol. 1: Fundamental Algorithms.* Reading, Massachusetts: Addison-Wesley.

Knuth, D., 1973b. *The Art of Computer Programming, Vol. 3: Sorting and Searching.* Reading, Massachusetts: Addison-Wesley.

Knuth, D., 1974. "Structured programming with goto statements." *ACM Computing Surveys* 6: 260–301.

Knuth, D. 1981. Second edition. *The Art of Computer Programming, Vol. 2: Seminumerical Algorithms.* Reading, Massachusetts: Addison-Wesley.

Kobrin, E. 1977. *Computer in performance.* Berlin: DAAD.

Koenig, G. M. 1970a. "Project 1: a programme for musical composition." *Electronic Music Reports* 2: 32–44. (Reprinted 1977, Amsterdam: Swets and Zeitlinger).

Koenig, G. M. 1970b. "Project 2: a programme for musical composition." *Electronic Music Reports* 3: 1–16. (Reprinted 1977, Amsterdam: Swets and Zeitlinger).

Koenig, G. M. 1978a. "Description of the Project 1 programme. "Utrecht: Institute of Sonology.

Koenig, G. M. 1978b. Lecture at the Institute of Sonology, August.

Koenig, G. M. 1979. "Protocol." Sonological Reports Number 4. Utrecht: Institute of Sonology.

Koenig, R. 1882. *Quelques Expériences d'Acoustique.* Paris.

Koenig, R. 1899. Articles in *Annalen der Physik* 69: 626–660, 721–738. Cited in Miller 1916, 1935.

Koenig, W., et al. 1946. "The sound spectrograph." *Journal of the Acoustical Society of America* 18: 19–49.

Kornfeld, W., 1980. "Everything you always wanted to know about MUZACS but were afraid to grovel through the code to find out." Lecture. Cambridge, Massachusetts: M.I.T. Artificial Intelligence Laboratory.

Kornfeld, W., 1982. "Combinatorially implosive algorithms." *Communications of the Association for Computing Machinery* 25(10): 734–738.

Kowalski, M., and A. Glassner. 1982. "The N.Y.I.T. digital sound editor." *Computer Music Journal* 6(1): 66–73.

Kramer, G., R. Moog, and A. Peevers. 1989. "The Hybrid: a music performance system." In T. Wells and D. Butler, eds. *Proceedings of the 1989 International Computer Music Conference.* San Francisco: International Computer Music Association. pp. 155–159.

Krasner, G. 1980. "Machine tongues VIII: the design of a Smalltalk music system." *Computer Music Journal* 4(4): 4–14.

Kronland-Martinet, R. 1988. "The wavelet transform for the analysis, synthesis, and processing of speech and music sounds." *Computer Music Journal* 12(4): 11–20.

Kronland-Martinet, R., and A. Grossmann. 1991. "Application of time-frequency and time-scale methods (wavelet transforms) to the analysis, synthesis and transformation of natural sounds." In G. De Poli, A. Piccialli, and C. Roads, eds. *Representations of Musical Signals.* Cambridge, Massachusetts: The MIT Press. pp. 45–85.

Kuhn, W. 1990. "A real-time pitch recognition algorithm for music applications." *Computer Music Journal* 14(3): 60–71.

Kühnelt, W. 1980. "Elektroakustische Musikinstrumente." In R. Block, L. Dombois, N. Hertling, and B. Volkmann, eds. *Für Augen und Ohren.* Berlin: Akademie der Künst und Berliner Festspiele.

Kunt, M. 1981. *Traitement numérique des signaux.* Paris: Dunod.

Kussmaul, C. 1991. "Applications of the wavelet transform at the level of pitch contour." In B. Alphonce and B. Pennycook, eds. *Proceedings of the 1991 International Computer Music Conference.* San Francisco: International Computer Music Association. pp. 483–486.

Lachartre, N. 1969. "Les musiques artificielles." *Diagrammes du monde* 146: 1–96.

Lagadec, R. 1983. "Digital sampling frequency conversion." In B. Blesser, B. Locanthi, and T. Stockham, eds. *Digital Audio.* New York: Audio Engineering Society. pp. 90–96.

Lagadec, R., and D. Pelloni. 1983. "Signal enhancement via digital signal processing." Preprint 2037 (G-6). Presented at the 74th Convention of the Audiio Engineering Society. New York: Audio Engineering Society.

Lagadec, R., and J. Takayama. 1985. "DASH and the standardization of digital audio." Preprint 2216 (P-I-3). Presented at the 77th Convention of the Audio Engineering Society, 5–8 March, Hamburg. New York: Audio Engineering Society.

Lambert, M., 1990. "Digital audio interfaces." *Journal of the Audio Engineering Society* 38(9): 681–696.

Lane, J. 1990. "Pitch detection using a tunable IIR filter." *Computer Music Journal* 14(3): 46–59.

Langston, P. 1989. "Six techniques for algorithmic composition (extended abstract)." In T. Wells and D. Butler, eds. *Proceedings of the 1989 International Computer Music Conference*. San Francisco: International Computer Music Association. pp. 164–167.

Lansky, P. 1982. "Digital mixing and editing." Princeton: Godfrey Winham Laboratory, Department of Music, Princeton University.

Lansky, P. 1987. "Linear prediction: the hard but interesting way to do things." In J. Strawn, ed. *Proceedings of the AES 5th International Conference: Music and Digital Technology*. New York: Audio Engineering Society.

Lansky, P. 1989. "Compositional applications of linear predictive coding." In M. Mathews and J. Pierce, eds. *Current Directions in Computer Music Research*. Cambridge, Massachusetts: The MIT Press. pp. 5–8.

Lansky, P. 1990a. "Cmix." Princeton: Godfrey Winham Laboratory, Department of Music, Princeton University.

Lansky, P. 1990b. "It's about time: some NeXT perspectives (part two)." *Perspectives of New Music* 28(1): 170–179.

Lansky, P. 1990c. "The architecture and musical logic of Cmix." In S. Arnold and G. Hair, eds. *Proceedings of the 1990 International Computer Music Conference*. San Francisco: International Computer Music Association. pp. 91–94.

Lansky, P. and K. Steiglitz. 1981. "Synthesis of timbral families by warped linear prediction." *Computer Music Journal* 5(3): 45–49. Reprinted in C. Roads, ed. 1989. *The Music Machine*. Cambridge, Massachusetts: The MIT Press.

LaRoche, J. 1989a. "Etude d'une système d'analyse et de synthèse utilisant la methode de Prony: application aux instrument de musique de type percussif." Thèse de doctorat. Paris: Ecole Nationale Supérieure des Télécommunications.

LaRoche, J. 1989b. "A new analysis/synthesis system based on the use of Prony's method. Application to heavily damped percussive sounds." *Proceedings of the International Conference on Acoustics, Speech, and Signal Processing*. New York: Institute of Electrical and Electronics Engineers.

LaRoche, J., and X. Rodet. 1989. "The use of Prony's method for the analysis of musical sounds: applications to percussive sounds." In T. Wells and D. Butler, eds. *Proceedings of the 1989 International Computer Music Conference*. San Francisco: International Computer Music Association. pp. 168–171.

Laske, O. 1975. "Introduction to a generative theory of music." *Sonological Reports* 1(B). Utrecht: Institute of Sonology.

Laske, O. 1979. "Compositional theory in Koenig's Project One and Project Two." *Computer Music Journal* 5(4): 54–65. Reprinted in C. Roads, ed. 1989. *The Music Machine*. Cambridge, Massachusetts: The MIT Press.

Laurson, M., and J. Duthen. 1989. "PatchWork, a graphical language in Pre-Form." In T. Wells and D. Butler, eds. *Proceedings of the 1989 International*

Computer Music Conference. San Francisco: International Computer Music Association. pp. 172–175.

Lawson, J., and M. Mathews. 1977. "Computer program to control a digital real-time sound synthesizer." *Computer Music Journal* 1(4): 16–21.

Layzer, A. 1971. "Some idiosyncratic aspects of computer synthesized sound." *Proceedings of the Sixth ASUC Conference*. New York: American Society of University Composers. pp. 27–39.

LeBrun, M. 1977. "A derivation of the spectrum of FM with a complex modulating wave." *Computer Music Journal* 1(4): 51–52. Reprinted in C. Roads and J. Strawn, eds. 1985. *Foundations of Computer Music*. Cambridge, Massachusetts: The MIT Press. pp. 65–67.

LeBrun, M. 1979. "Digital waveshaping synthesis." *Journal of the Audio Engineering Society* 27(4): 250–266.

Ledbetter, P. 1985a. "Digital tape transfer console." Preprint 2276 (A-3). Presented at the 79th Convention of the Audio Engineering Society, 1985 October 12–16. New York: Audio Engineering Society.

Ledbetter, P. 1985b. "A technical view of a totally digital audio mixing console." Preprint 2277 (D-12). Presented at the 79th Convention of the Audio Engineering Society, 1985 October 12–16. New York: Audio Engineering Society.

Lee, F. 1972. "Time compression and expansion of speech by the sampling method." *Journal of the Audio Engineering Society* 20(9): 738–742.

Lee, M., G. Garnett, and D. Wessel. 1992. "An adaptive conductor follower." In A. Strange, ed. *Proceedings of the 1992 International Computer Music Conference*. San Francisco: International Computer Music Association. pp. 454–455.

Lee, S., et al. 1985. "A multi-touch three-dimensional touch-sensitive tablet." *CHI '85 Proceedings*. New York: Association for Computing Machinery. pp. 21–25.

Leibig, B. 1974. "Documentation on Music V for the Burroughs B6700 computer." La Jolla: Department of Music, University of California, San Diego.

Leichtentritt, H. 1934. "Mechanical music in olden times." *Musical Quarterly* 20: 15–26.

Leiserson, C. 1983. *Area-efficient VLSI Computation*. Cambridge, Massachusetts: The MIT Press.

Lemouton, S. 1993. "CHANT-Macintosh." Unpublished manuscript.

Lent, K., R. Pinkston, and P. Silsbee. 1989. "Accelerando: a real-time general-purpose computer music system." *Computer Music Journal* 13(4): 54–64.

Lentczner, M. 1984. "Eames: a language and environment for computer music." B. A. thesis. Cambridge, Massachusetts: Department of Applied Mathematics, Harvard University.

Lentczner, M. 1985. "SoundKit: a Smalltalk sound manipulator." In B. Truax, ed. *Proceedings of the 1985 International Computer Music Conference.* San Francisco: International Computer Music Association. pp. 141–144.

Leopold, P. 1987. "MIDI by modem: the future is now." In J. Strawn, ed. *The Proceedings of the AES 5th International Conference: Music and Digital Technology.* New York: Audio Engineering Society. pp. 122–126.

Lerdahl, F., and R. Jackendoff. 1983. *A Generative Theory of Tonal Music.* Cambridge, Massachusetts: The MIT Press.

Lesbros, V. 1993. *Phonogramme.* computer program.

Levitt, D., 1981. "A melody description system for jazz improvisation." M.S. Thesis. Cambridge, Massachusetts: Artificial Intelligence Laboratory.

Levitt, D. 1983. "Learning music by imitating." Unpublished mss.

Levitt, D., 1984. "Machine tongues X: constraint languages." *Computer Music Journal* 8(1): 9–21.

Lewis, J. P. 1989. "Algorithms for music composition by neural nets: improved CBR paradigms." In T. Wells and D. Butler, eds. *Proceedings of the 1989 International Computer Music Conference.* San Francisco: International Computer Music Association. pp. 180–183.

Licklider, J. C. R. 1950. "Intelligibility of amplitude-dichotomized time quantized speech waves." *Journal of the Acoustical Society of America* 22: 820–823.

Licklider, J. 1951. "A duplex theory of pitch perception." *Experimentia* 7: 128–133.

Licklider, J. 1959. "Three auditory theories." In S. Koch, ed. *Psychology: A Study of Science, Volume 1.* New York: McGraw-Hill. pp. 41–144.

Lidov, D., and J. Gabura. 1973. "A melody-writing algorithm using a formal language model." *Computers and the Humanities* 4(3–4): 138–148.

Lieberman, H. 1981. "Seeing what your programs are doing." Cambridge, Massachusetts: M.I.T. Artificial Intelligence Laboratory.

Lieberman, H. 1982. "Machine tongues IX: object-oriented programming." *Computer Music Journal* 6(3): 8–21.

Ligeti, G. 1960. "Pierre Boulez: decision and automatism in *Structure Ia*." *die Reihe* 4: 36–62. English edition. Bryn Mawr: Theodore Presser Company. pp. 36–62.

Ligeti, G., and R. Wehinger. 1970. *Artikulation.* Mainz: Schott.

Lindemann, E., F. Dechelle, B. Smith, and M. Starkier. 1991. "The architecture of the IRCAM musical workstation." *Computer Music Journal* 15(3): 41–49.

Link, B. 1992. "A real-time waveguide toolkit." In A. Strange, ed. *Proceedings of the 1992 International Computer Music Conference.* San Francisco: International Computer Music Association. pp. 396–397.

Linster, C. 1992. "On analyzing and representing musical rhythm." In M. Balaban, K. Ebcioglu, and O. Laske, eds. *Understanding Music with AI.* Cambridge, Massachusetts and Menlo Park, California: The MIT Press and AAAI Press. pp. 415–427.

Lipshitz, S., R. Wannamaker, and J. Vanderkooy. 1992. "Quantization and dither: a theoretical survey." *Journal of the Audio Engineering Society* 40(5): 355–375.

Liskov, B., et al. 1979. *CLU Reference Manual.* TR-225. Cambridge, Massachusetts: Laboratory for Computer Science, M. I. T.

Loescher, F. A. 1959. "The active loudspeaker." *Gravesaner Blätter* 14: 7–9.

Loescher, F. A. 1960. "The problem of the secondary electro-acoustical transducers." *Gravensaner Blätter* 18: 53–60.

Lohner, H. 1986. "The UPIC system: a user's report." *Computer Music Journal* 10(4): 42–49. Reprinted 1987 in *Musik-Konzepte* 54/55: 71–82.

Lonergan, W., and P. King. 1961. "Design of the B5000 system." *Datamation* 7(5): 28–32. Reprinted in D. Siewiorek, C. G. Bell, and A. Newell, eds. 1982. *Computer Structures: Principles and Examples.* New York: McGraw-Hill. pp. 129–134.

Longuet-Higgins, H. C. 1976. "The perception of melodies." *Nature* 263: 646–653. Reprinted in H. C. Longuet-Higgens. 1987. *Mental Processes.* Cambridge, Massachusetts: The MIT Press.

Longuet-Higgins, H.-C. 1983. "The rhythmic interpretation of monophonic music." In J. Sundberg, ed. *Proceedings of the Swedish Musical Acoustics Conference.* Stockholm: Royal Institute of Technology. pp. 7–26.

Longuet-Higgins, H. C. 1987. *Mental Processes.* Cambridge, Massachusetts: The MIT Press.

Longuet-Higgins, H. C., and C. S. Lee. 1983. "The rhythmic interpretation of monophonic music." In J. Sundberg, editor. 1983. *Studies in Musical Performance 39.* Stockholm: Royal Swedish Academy of Music. pp. 7–26.

Lorrain, D. 1980. "A panoply of stochastic 'cannons.'" *Computer Music Journal* 4(1): 53–81. Reprinted in C. Roads. 1989. *The Music Machine.* Cambridge, Massachusetts: The MIT Press. pp. 351–379.

Losano, M. 1990. *Storie de Automi.* Turin: Einaudi.

Loughlin, P., L. Atlas, and J. Pitton. 1992. "Advanced time-frequency representations for speech processing." In M. Cooke and S. Beet, eds. *Visual Representations of Speech Signals.* New York: J. Wiley.

Lowe, B., and R. Currie. 1989. "Digidesign's Sound Accelerator: lessons lived and learned." *Computer Music Journal* 13(1): 36–46.

Loy, D. G. 1981. "Notes on the implementation of MUSBOX: a compiler for the Systems Concepts Digital Synthesizer." *Computer Music Journal* 5(1): 34–50. Reprinted in C. Roads, ed. 1989. *The Music Machine*. Cambridge, Massachusetts: The MIT Press.

Loy, D. G., 1982. "A sound file system for UNIX." In T. Blum and J. Strawn, eds. *Proceedings of the 1982 International Computer Music Conference*. San Francisco: International Computer Music Association. pp. 162–171.

Loy, D. G. 1985a. "Sndpth: a program to interactively create/edit sound trajectories." Unpublished.

Loy, D. G. 1985b. "About AUDIUM: a conversation with Stanley Shaff." *Computer Music Journal* 9(2): 41–48.

Loy, D. G. 1985c. "Musicians make a standard: the MIDI phenomenon." *Computer Music Journal* 9(4): 8–26. Reprinted in C. Roads, ed. 1989. *The Music Machine*. Cambridge, Massachusetts: The MIT Press. pp. 181–198.

Loy, D. G. 1986. "Player." Technical memorandum. La Jolla: Center for Music Experiment, University of California, San Diego.

Loy, D. G. 1987. "On the scheduling of multiple parallel processors executing synchronously." In J. Beauchamp, ed. *Proceedings of the 1987 International Computer Music Conference*. San Francisco: International Computer Music Association. pp. 117–124.

Loy, D. G. 1989a. "Composing with computers—a survey of some compositional formalisms and music programming languages." In M. Mathews and J. R. Pierce, eds. *Current Directions in Computer Music Research*. Cambridge, Massachusetts: The MIT Press. pp. 292–396.

Loy, D. G. ed. 1989b. Special issue on neural nets and connectionism 1. *Computer Music Journal* 13(3).

Loy, D. G. ed. 1989c. Special issue on neural nets and connectionism 2. *Computer Music Journal* 13(4).

Loy, D. G., and C. Abbott. 1985. "Programming languages for computer music." *ACM Computing Surveys* 17(2): 235–266.

Luce, D. 1963. "Physical correlates of nonpercussive instrument tones." Sc. D. dissertation. Cambridge, Massachusetts: M.I.T. Department of Physics.

Lundén, P., and T. Ungvary 1991. "MacSonogram: a programme for produce large scale sonograms for musical purposes." In B. Alphonce and B. Pennycook, eds. *Proceedings of the 1991 International Computer Music Conference*. San Francisco: International Computer Music Association. pp. 554–554C.

Lyon, R., and L. Dyer. 1986. "Experiments with a computational model of the cochlea." *Proceedings of the International Conference on Acoustics, Speech, and Signal Processing, Tokyo*. New York: IEEE. pp. 1975–1978.

Lyr, R. 1955. "Une merveille de mécanisme: le Componium de T. N. Winkel." In A. Chapuis, ed. 1955. *Histoire de la boîte à musique*. Lausanne: Edition Scriptar.

Maher, R. 1990. "Evaluation of a method for separating digitized duet signals." *Journal of the Audio Engineering Society* 38(12): 956–979.

Maher, R. 1992. "On the nature of granulation noise in uniform quantization systems." *Journal of the Audio Engineering Society* 40(1/2): 12–20.

Maher, R., and J. Beauchamp. 1990. "An investigation of vocal vibrato for synthesis." *Applied Acoustics* 30: 219–245.

Maillard, B. 1976. "Sur la modulation de fréquence." *Cahiers recherche/musique* 3: 179–204.

Makhoul, J. 1975. "Linear prediction: a tutorial review." *Proceedings of the Institute for Electrical and Electronic Engineers* 63: 561–580.

Mallat, S. 1989. "A theory of multiresolution signal decomposition: the wavelet representation." *IEEE Transactions on Pattern Analysis and Machine Intelligence* 11(7): 674–693.

Malt, M. 1993. *PatchWork Introduction*. Paris: IRCAM.

Mandelbrot, B. 1977. *Fractals: Form, Chance, and Dimension*. San Francisco: W. H. Freeman.

Mandler, G. 1975. *Mind and Emotion*. New York: John Wiley and Sons.

Manning, P. 1987. *Electronic and Computer Music*. Oxford: Oxford University Press.

Manthey, M. 1978. "The Egg: a purely digital real time polyphonic sound synthesizer." *Computer Music Journal* 2(2): 32–37.

Manthey, M. 1979. "Real-time sound synthesis: a software microcosm." Ph.D. dissertation. Buffalo: State University of New York at Buffalo Department of Computer Science.

Marans, M. 1991. "Timing is everything." *Keyboard* 17(12): 94–103.

Marino, G., J.-M. Raczinski, and M.-H. Serra. 1990. "The new UPIC system." In S. Arnold and G. Hair, eds. *Proceedings of the 1990 International Computer Music Conference*. San Francisco: International Computer Music Association. pp. 249–252.

Marino, G., M.-H. Serra, and J.-M. Raczinski. 1992. "The UPIC system, origins and innovations." *Perspectives of New Music*. To appear.

Markel, J. 1972. "Digital inverse filtering—a new tool for formant trajectory tracking." *IEEE Transactions on Audio and Acoustics* Vol. AU-20(5): 367–377.

Markowitz, J. 1989. *Triumphs and Trials of an Organ Builder*. Macungie: Allen Organ Company.

Markel, J., and A. Gray, Jr. 1976. *Linear Prediction of Speech*. New York: Springer.

Marple, S. 1987. *Digital Spectral Analysis*. Englewood Cliffs: Prentice-Hall.

Martirano, S. 1971. "An electronic music instrument which combines the composing process with performance in real time." Progress Report 1. Department of Music. Urbana: University of Illinois.

Massie, D. 1986. "A survey of looping algorithms for sampled data musical instruments." *Final Program of the IEEE Acoustic, Speech, and Signal Processing Workshop on Applications of Signal Processing to Audio and Acoustics.* New York: IEEE.

Massie, D., and V. Stonick. 1992. "The musical intrigue of pole-zero pairs." In A. Strange, ed. *Proceedings of the 1992 International Computer Music Conference.* San Francisco: International Computer Music Association. pp. 22–25.

Mathews, M. 1969. *The Technology of Computer Music.* Cambridge, Massachusetts: The MIT Press.

Mathews, M. 1989. "The conductor program and mechanical baton." In M. Mathews and J. R. Pierce, eds. 1989. *Current Directions in Computer Music Research.* Cambridge, Massachusetts: The MIT Press. pp. 263–282.

Mathews, M., and C. Abbott. 1980. "The sequential drum." *Computer Music Journal* 4(4): 45–59.

Mathews, M., and J. Miller. 1965." Pitch quantizing for computer music." *Journal of the Acoustical Society of America* 38: 913A.

Mathews, M., J. Miller, and E. David, Jr. 1961. "Pitch synchronous analysis of voiced sounds." *Journal of the Audio Engineering Society of America* 33: 179–186.

Mathews, M., and J. Miller. 1963. *Music IV programmer's manual.* Murray Hill: Bell Telephone Laboratories.

Mathews, M., and F. R. Moore. 1970. "GROOVE—a program to compose, store, and edit functions of time." *Communications of the Association for Computing Machinery* 13(12): 715–721.

Mathews, M., and J. R. Pierce, eds. 1989. *Current Directions in Computer Music Research.* Cambridge, Massachusetts: The MIT Press.

Mathews, M., and L. Rosler. 1968. "Graphical language for the scores of computer-generated sounds." *Perspectives of New Music* 6(2): 92–118.

Mathews, M., and L. Rosler. 1969. "Graphical language for the scores of computer-generated sounds." In H. von Foerster and J. Beauchamp, eds. *Music by Computers.* New York: John Wiley and Sons. pp. 84–114.

Matignon, D. 1991. "Etude de l'application des models en variables d'etat à l'analyse/synthèse." Paris: Université de paris Sud.

Matignon, D., P. Depalle, and X. Rodet. 1992. "State-space models for wind-instrument synthesis." In A. Strange, ed. *Proceedings of the 1992 International Computer Music Conference.* San Francisco: International Computer Music Association. p. 142–145.

Matisoo, J., 1980. "The superconducting computer." *Scientific American.* 242(5): 50–65.

Matossian, N. 1987. *Xenakis.* New York: Taplinger.

Matsushima, T., T. Harada, I. Sonomoto, K. Kanamori, A. Uesugi, Y. Nimura, S. Hashimoto, S. Ohteru. 1985. "Automated recognition system for musical score—the visual system of WABOT-2." *Bulletin of Science and Engineering Research Laboratory, Waseda University,* Number 112, pp. 25–52.

Mauchly, J. 1982. "Merging event lists in real time." In *Proceedings of the Second Symposium on Small Computers in the Arts, 15–17 October 1982, Philadelphia.* Los Angleles: IEEE Computer Society. pp. 23–28.

Maxwell, J., and S. Ornstein. 1983. "Mockingbird: a composer's amanuensis." Technical Report CSL-83-2. Palo Alto: Xerox.

May, R. 1976. "Simple mathematical models with very complicated dynamics." *Nature* 261: 459–467.

Mayer, A. 1878. *Sound.* New York: D. Appleton and Co.

McAdams, S. 1981. "Spectral fusion and the creation of auditory images." In M. Clynes, ed. *Music, Mind, and Brain: The Neuropsychology of Music.* New York: Plenum.

McAdams, S. 1987. "Music: a science of mind?" *Contemporary Music Review* 2(1): 1–61.

McAdams, S., and A. Bregman. 1979. "Hearing musical streams." *Computer Music Journal* 3(4): 26–44. Reprinted in C. Roads and J. Strawn, eds. 1985. *Foundations of Computer Music.* Cambridge, Massachusetts: The MIT Press. pp. 658–698.

McAdams, S., S. Gladkoff, and J.-P. Keller. 1984. "AISE: a prototype laboratory for musical research and the development of conceptual tools." In D. Wessel, ed. *Proceedings of the 1984 International Computer Music Conference.* San Francisco: International Computer Music Association. pp. 143–161.

McAulay, R., and T. Quatieri. 1986. "Speech analysis/synthesis based on a sinusoidal representation." *IEEE Transactions on Acoustics, Speech, and Signal Processing* ASSP-34: 744–754.

McCarthy, J., 1960. "Recursive functions of symbolic expressions and their computation by machine." *Communications of the Association for Computing Machinery* 3(4): 184–195.

McLaren, N., and R. Lewis. 1948. "Synthetic sound on film." *Journal of the Society of Motion Pitcture Engineers* 50: 233–247.

McClellan, J., T. Parks, and L. Rabiner. 1973. "A computer program for designing optimal FIR linear phase digital filters." *IEEE Transactions on Audio and Electroacoustics* AU-21: 506–526.

McCormack, W., and R. Sargent. 1981. "Analysis of future event set algorithms for discrete event simulation." *Communications of the Association for Computing Machinery* 24(12): 801–812.

McCulloch, W. 1965. *Embodiments of Mind.* Cambridge, Massachusetts: The MIT Press.

McGee, D. 1990. "George Massenburg considers new development in automation." *Pro Sound News* April. pp. 13, 37.

McGill, J. F. 1985. "Digital recording and reproduction: an introduction." In John Strawn, ed. *Digital Audio Engineering: An Anthology.* Madison: A-R Editions. pp. 1–28.

McIntyre, M., and J. Woodhouse. 1960. "On the fundamentals of bowed string dynamics." *Acustica* 43(2): 93–108.

McIntyre, M., R. Schumacher, and J. Woodhouse. 1983. "On the oscillations of musical instruments." *Journal of the Acoustical Society of America* 74(5): 1325–1345.

McLaren, N. 1948. "Synthetic sound on film." *Journal of the Society of Motion Picture Engineers* March: 233–247.

McLuhan, M. 1964. *Understanding Media.* New York: Signet.

McNabb, M. 1981. "*Dreamsong*: the composition." *Computer Music Journal* 5(4): 36–53. Reprinted in C. Roads, ed. 1989. *The Music Machine.* Cambridge, Massachusetts: The MIT Press.

McNabb, M. 1986. "Computer music: some aesthetic considerations." In S. Emmerson. 1986. *The Language of Electroacoustic Music.* New York: Harwood Academic. pp. 141–154.

McNally, G. 1984. "Dynamic range control of digital audio signals." *Journal of the Audio Engineering Society* 32(5): 316–327.

McNally, G., et al. 1985. "Digital audio editing." Preprint 2214 (B-2). Presented at the 77th Audio Engineering Society Convention, 5–8 March 1985, Hamburg. New York: Audio Engineering Society.

McNamara, J. 1984. *Technical Aspects of Data Communications.* 2nd edition. Bedford, Massachusetts: Digital Equipment Corporation.

Mead, C., and L. Conway. 1980. *Introduction to VLSI Systems.* Reading, Massachusetts: Addison-Wesley.

Meddis, R., M. Hewitt, and T. Schackleton. 1990. "Implementation details of a computation model of the inner hair-cell/auditory-nerve synapse." *Journal of the Acoustical Society of America* 87: 1813–1816.

Mellinger, S. 1991. "Event formation and separation in musical sound." Ph.D. dissertation. Stanford: Center for Computer Research in Music and Acoustics, Department of Music, Stanford University.

Metcalfe, R., and D. Boggs. 1976. "Distributed packet switching for local computer networks." *Communications of the Association for Computing Machinery* 19(2): 395–404.

Metlay, M. 1990. "The musician-machine interface to MIDI." *Computer Music Journal* 14(2): 73–83.

Meyer, L. B. 1956. *Emotion and Meaning in Music*. Chicago: University of Chicago Press.

Meyer, L. B. 1967. *Music, the Arts, and Ideas*. Chicago: University of Chicago Press.

Meyer, J. 1984. "Time correction of anti-aliasing filters used in digital audio systems." *Journal of the Audio Engineering Society* 32(3): 132–137.

Meyer, E., and G. Buchmann. 1931. "Die Klangspektren der Musikinstrumente." *Sitzungsberichte der Preussischen Akademie der Wissenschaften*. Berlin: Verlag der Akademie der Wissenschaften/Walter de Gruyter. pp. 735–778.

Meyer-Eppler, W. 1955. "Statistic and psychologic problems of sound." *die Reihe* 1: 55–61. (English edition. Bryn Mawr: Theodore Presser Company. pp. 55–61.)

Mian, A., and G. Tisato. 1984. "Sound structuring techniques using parameters derived from a voice analysis/synthesis system." In D. Wessel, ed. *Proceedings of the 1984 International Computer Music Conference*. San Francisco: International Computer Music Association.

Michalski, R., J. Carbonell, and T. Mitchell, eds. 1983. *Machine Learning*. Palo Alto: Tioga Publishing.

Millen, D. 1990. "Cellular automata music." In S. Arnold and G. Hair, eds. *Proceedings of the 1990 International Computer Music Conference*. San Francisco: International Computer Music Association. pp. 314–316.

Millen, D. 1992. "Generation of formal patterns for music composition by means of cellular automata." In A. Strange, ed. *Proceedings of the 1992 International Computer Music Conference*. San Francisco: International Computer Music Association. pp. 398–399.

Miller, D. C. 1916. *The Science of Musical Sounds*. New York: MacMillan.

Miller, D. C. 1935. *Anecdotal History of the Science of Sound*. New York: MacMillan.

Miller, B., D. Scarborough, and J. Jones. 1992. "On the perception of meter." In M. Balaban, K. Ebcioglu, and O. Laske, eds. *Understanding Music with AI*. Cambridge, Massachusetts and Menlo Park, California: The MIT Press and AAAI Press. pp. 429–447.

Miller, G., E. Galanter, and K. Pribram. 1960. *Plans and the Structure of Behavior*. New York: Holt.

Miller, H. 1960. *History of Music*. New York: Barnes and Noble.

Miller, J. 1985. "Personal Composer." *Computer Music Journal* 9(4): 27–37. Reprinted in C. Roads, ed. 1989. *The Music Machine*. Cambridge, Massachusetts: MIT Press. pp. 243–253.

Miller, N. 1973. "Filtering of singing voice signal from noise by synthesis." Ph.D. dissertation. Salt Lake City: Department of Electrical Engineering, University of Utah.

Milne, S. 1980. "A digital sound editor." B.S. thesis. Cambridge, Massachusetts: MIT, Department of Electrical Engineering and Computer Science.

Minsky, M., ed. 1965. *Semantic Information Processing*. Cambridge, Massachusetts: The MIT Press.

Minsky, M. 1981. "Music, mind, and meaning." *Computer Music Journal* 5(3): 28–44. Reprinted in C. Roads, ed. 1989. *The Music Machine*. Cambridge, Massachusetts: The MIT Press. pp. 639–658.

Mitsubishi. 1986. "Preliminary specification sheet for X-86." Osaka : The Mitsubishi PCM Section, Communication Equipment Works.

Mitsuhashi, Y. 1980. "Waveshape parameter modulation in producing complex spectra." *Journal of the Audio Engineering Society* 28(12): 879–895.

Mitsuhashi, Y. 1982a. "Musical sound synthesis by forward differences." *Journal of the Audio Engineering Society* 30(1/2): 2–9.

Mitsuhashi, Y. 1982b. "Piecewise interpolation technique for audio signal synthesis." *Journal of the Audio Engineering Society* 30(4): 192–202.

Mitsuhashi, Y. 1982c. "Audio signal synthesis by functions of two variables." *Journal of the Audio Engineering Society* 30(10): 701–706.

Moles, A. 1960. *Les musiques expérimentales*. Zurich: Editions du Cercle de l'Art Contemporain

Moles, A. 1968. *Information Theory and Esthetic Perception*. Urbana: University of Illinois Press.

Molino, J. 1975. "Fait musicale et sémiologies de la musique." *Musique en jeu* 17: 37–62.

Mont-Reynaud, B. 1985a. "The bounded-Q approach to time-varying spectral analysis." Technical Report STAN-M-28. Stanford: Stanford University Department of Music.

Mont-Reynaud, B. 1985b. "Problem-solving strategies in a music transcription system." In *Proceedings of the International Joint Conference on Artificial Intelligence, Los Angeles*. Los Altos: Morgan-Kaufmann. pp. 915–918.

Mont-Reynaud, B., and M. Goldstein. 1985. "On finding rhythmic patterns in musical lines." In B. Truax, ed. *Proceedings of the 1985 International Computer Music Conference*. San Francisco: International Computer Music Association. pp. 391–397.

Moog, R. 1986. "MIDI: Musical Instrument Digital Interface." *Journal of the Audio Engineering Society* 34(5): 394–404.

Moog, R. 1987. "Position and force sensors and their application to keyboards and related performance devices." In J. Strawn, ed. 1987. The Proceedings of the AES 5th International Conference: Music and Digital Technology. New York: Audio Engineering Society. pp. 173–184

Moog, R., and T. Rhea. 1990. "Evolution of the keyboard interface: the Bösendorfer 290 SE recording piano and the Moog multiply-touch-sensitive keyboards." *Computer Music Journal* 14(2): 52–60.

Moore, F. R. 1977. "Table lookup noise for sinusoidal digital oscillators." *Computer Music Journal* 1(2): 26–29. Reprinted in C. Roads and J. Strawn, eds. 1985. *Foundations of Computer Music.* Cambridge, Massachusetts: The MIT Press. pp. 326–334.

Moore, F. R. 1978a. "An introduction to the mathematics of digital signal processing. Part 1: algebra, trigonometry, and the most beautiful formula in mathematics." *Computer Music Journal* 2(1): 38–47. Reprinted in J. Strawn, ed. 1985. *Digital Audio Signal Processing: An Anthology.* Madison: A-R Editions.

Moore, F. R. 1978b. "An introduction to the mathematics of digital signal processing. Part 2: sampling, transforms, and digital filtering." *Computer Music Journal* 2(2): 38–60. Reprinted in J. Strawn, ed. 1985. *Digital Audio Signal Processing: An Anthology.* Madison: A-R Editions.

Moore, F. R. 1982. "The computer audio research laboratory at UCSD." *Computer Music Journal* 6(1): 18–29.

Moore, F. R. 1983. "A general model for spatial processing of sounds." *Computer Music Journal* 7(3): 6–15. Reprinted in C. Roads, ed. 1989. *The Music Machine.* Cambridge, Massachusetts: The MIT Press.

Moore, F. R., 1985. "The FRMBox—a modular digital music synthesizer." In J. Strawn, ed. *Digital Audio Engineering: An Anthology.* Madison: A-R Editions.

Moore, F. R. 1988. "The dysfunctions of MIDI." *Computer Music Journal* 12(1): 19–28.

Moore, F. R. 1990. *Elements of Computer Music.* Englewood Cliffs: Prentice-Hall.

Moore, F. R., and G. Loy. 1982. "Essays about computer music." La Jolla: Center for Music Experiment, University of California, San Diego.

Moorer, J. A. 1972. "Music and computer composition." *Communications of the ACM* 15(2): 104–113.

Moorer, J. A. 1973. "The optimum comb method of pitch period analysis of continuous digitized speech." AIM-207. Stanford: Stanford Artificial Intelligence Laboratory.

Moorer, J. A. 1975. "On the segmentation and analysis of continuous musical sound." STAN-M-3. Stanford: Stanford University Department of Music.

Moorer, J. A. 1976. "The synthesis of complex audio spectra by means of discrete summation formulas." *Journal of the Audio Engineering Society* 24: 717–724.

Moorer, J. A. 1977. "Signal processing aspects of computer music." *Proceeding of the IEEE* 65(8): 1108–1137. Reprinted in *Computer Music Journal* 1(1): 4–37 and in J. Strawn, ed. 1985. *Digital Audio Signal Processing: An Anthology*. Madison: A-R Editions.

Moorer, J. A. 1978. "The use of the phase vocoder in computer music applications." *Journal of the Audio Engineering Society* 26(1/2): 42–45.

Moorer, J. A. 1979a. "The use of linear prediction of speech in computer music applications." *Journal of the Audio Engineering Society* 27(3): 134–140.

Moorer, J. A. 1979b. "The digital coding of high-quality musical sound." *Journal of the Audio Engineering Society* 27(9): 657–666.

Moorer, J. A. 1979c. "About this reverberation business." *Computer Music Journal* 3 (2): 13–28. Reprinted in C. Roads and J. Strawn, eds. 1985. *Foundations of Computer Music*. Cambridge, Massachusetts: The MIT Press. pp. 605–639.

Moorer, J. A. 1981a. "Synthesizers I have known and loved." *Computer Music Journal* 5(1): 4–12. Reprinted in C. Roads, ed. 1989. *The Music Machine*. Cambridge, Massachusetts: The MIT Press.

Moorer, J. A. 1981b. "General spectral transformations for digital filters." *IEEE Transactions on Acoustics, Speech, and Signal Processing* ASSP-29(5): 1092–1094.

Moorer, J. A. 1982. "The Lucasfilm audio signal processor." *Computer Music Journal* 6(2): 22–32. Reprinted in C. Roads, ed. 1989. *The Music Machine*. Cambridge, Massachusetts: The MIT Press.

Moorer, J. A. 1983a. "The manifold joys of conformal mapping: applications to digital filtering in the studio." *Journal of the Audio Engineering Society* 31(11): 826–841.

Moorer, J. A. 1983b. "The audio signal processor: the next step in digital audio." In B. Blesser, B. Locanthi, and T. Stockham, eds. 1983. *Digital Audio*. New York: Audio Engineering Society. pp. 205–215.

Moorer, J. A. 1985. "A flexible method for synchronizing parameter updates for real-time audio signal processors." Internal memo. San Rafael: The Droid Works.

Moorer, J. A., and M. Berger. 1986. "Linear phase bandsplitting: theory and applications." *Journal of the Audio Engineering Society* 34(3): 143–152.

Moorer, J. A., A. Chauveau, C. Abbott, P. Eastty, and J. Lawson. 1979. "The 4C machine." *Computer Music Journal* 3(3): 16–24. Revised and updated version in

C. Roads and J. Strawn, eds. 1985. *Foundations of Computer Music* Cambridge, Massachusetts: The MIT Press. pp. 261–280.

Moorer, J. A., J. Grey, and J. Snell. 1977. "Lexicon of analyzed tones. Part 1: a violin tone." *Computer Music Journal* 1(2): 39–45.

Moorer, J. A., J. Grey, and J. Strawn. 1977. "Lexicon of analyzed tones. Part 2: clarinet and oboe." *Computer Music Journal* 1(3): 12–29.

Moorer, J. A., J. Grey, and J. Strawn. 1978. "Lexicon of analyzed tones. Part 3: trumpet." *Computer Music Journal* 2(2): 23–31.

Morawska-Büngler, M. 1988. *Schwingende Elektronen*. Cologne: P. J. Tonger.

Mori, T., T. Matsushige, Y. Sato, and Y. Sakurai. 1985. "Four-channel digital mixer/equalizer for mastering." Preprint 2292 (D-13). Presented at the 79th Convention of the Audio Engineering Society, 1985 October 12–16. New York: Audio Engineering Society.

Morita, H., S. Hashimoto, and S. Ohteru. 1991. "A computer music system that follows a human conductor." *IEEE Computer* 24(7): 44–53.

Morrill, D. 1977. "Trumpet algorithms for computer composition." *Computer Music Journal* 1(1): 46–52. Reprinted in C. Roads and J. Strawn, eds. 1985. *Foundations of Computer Music*. Cambridge, Massachusetts: The MIT Press. pp. 30–44.

Morrill, D. 1981a. "The dynamic aspects of trumpet phrases." *Rapports IRCAM* 33/81. Paris: IRCAM.

Morrill, D. 1981b. "Loudspeakers and performers: some problems and proposals." *Computer Music Journal* 5(4): 25–29. Reprinted in C. Roads, ed. 1989. *The Music Machine*. Cambridge, Massachusetts: The MIT Press. pp. 95–99.

Morrison, J., and D. Waxman. 1991. *MOSAIC 3.0*. Paris: IRCAM.

Morrison, J., and J.-M. Adrien. 1991. "Control mechanisms in the MOSAIC synthesis program." In B. Alphonce and B. Pennycook, eds. *Proceedings of the 1991 International Computer Music Conference*. San Francisco: International Computer Music Association. pp. 19–22.

Morse, P. 1936. *Vibration and Sound*. Woodbury, New York: American Institute of Physics.

Motorola. 1986. *Digital Signal Processor User's Manual*. Phoenix: Motorola.

Mozart, W. A. 1770. *Musikalische Würfelspiele*, K. 294D. Catalog number 4474. Mainz: Schott.

Müller, G., and R. Giuletti. 1987. "High quality music notation: interactive editing and input by piano keyboard." In J. Beauchamp and S. Tipei, eds. 1987. *Proceedings of the 1987 International Computer Music Conference*. San Francisco: International Computer Music Association. pp. 333–340.

Mumma, G. 1975. "Live-electronic music." In J. Appleton and R. Perera, eds. 1975. *The Development and Practice of Electronic Music*. Englewood Cliffs: Prentice-Hall. pp. 286–335.

Murail, T. 1991. "Spectres et Lutins." In D. Cohen-Levinas, ed. 1991. *L'Itineraire*. Paris: La Revue Musicale.

Musicus, B. 1984. "Optimal frequency-warped short time analysis/synthesis." Unpublished manuscript.

Musicus, B., J. Stautner, and J. Anderson. 1984. "Optimal least squares short time analysis/synthesis." Technical report. Cambridge, Massachusetts: Research Laboratory of Electronics, M.I.T.

Myhill, J. 1979. "Some simplifications and improvements in the stochastic music program." In C. Roads, ed. *Proceedings of the 1978 International Computer Music Conference*. Evanston: Northwestern University Press. pp. 272–317.

Nakajima, H., T. Doi, Y. Tsuchiya, and A. Iga. 1978. "A new PCM system as an adapter of digital audio tape recorders. "Preprint 1352. Presented at the 60th Convention. New York: Audio Engineering Society.

Nakajima, H, T. Doi, J. Fukuda, and A. Iga. 1983 *Digital Audio Technology*. Blue Bell, Pennsylvania: Tab Books.

Nawab, S., T. Quatieri, and J. Lim. 1983. "Signal reconstruction from short-time Fourier transform magnitude." *IEEE Transactions on Acoustics, Speech, and Signal Processing* ASSP-31(4): 986–998.

Needham, J., W. Ling, and K. Girdwood Robinson. 1962. *Science and Civilisation in China. Volume 4: Physics and Physical Technology*. Cambridge: Cambridge University Press.

Negyesy, J., and L. Ray. 1989. "Zivatar: a performance system." In M. V. Mathews and J. R. Pierce, eds. 1989. *Current Directions in Computer Music Research*. Cambridge, Massachusetts: The MIT Press. pp. 283–289.

Nelson, G. 1977. "MPL—A program library for musical data processing." *Creative Computing* March-April.

Nelson, G. 1980. "MPL: Music program library manual." Oberlin: Department of Music, Oberlin College.

Nelson, G. 1989. "Algorithmic approaches to interactive composition." In T. Wells and D. Butler, eds. *Proceedings of the 1989 International Computer Music Conference*. San Francisco: International Computer Music Association. pp. 219–222.

Nelson, G. 1991. "Gary Lee Nelson: a concert of new works for computers, synthesizers, and MIDI Horn." Program notes.

Neve, R. 1992. "Rupert Neve of Amek replies." *Studio Sound* 34(3): 21–22.

Newcomb, S., and C. Goldfarb. 1989. "X3V1.8M/SD-6 Journal of Development, Standard Music Description Language (SMDL), Part One: Objectives and Methodology." San Francisco: International Computer Music Association.

Newell, A., and H. Simon. 1972. *Human Problem Solving*. Englewood Cliffs: Prentice-Hall.

Newell, P. 1991. "Cable and sound delivery." *Studio Sound* 33(7): 48–55.

New England Digital Corporation. 1981. "SCRIPT user guide." White River Junction: New England Digital Corporation.

New England Digital Corporation. 1982a. "MAX language user manual." White River Junction: New England Digital Corporation.

New England Digital Corporation. 1982b. "MAX language reference manual." White River Junction: New England Digital Corporation.

New England Digital Corporation. 1984. "Music printing option for the Synclavier." White River Junction: New England Digital Corporation.

Newmann, W., and R. Sproull. 1980. *Principles of Interactive Computer Graphics*. 2nd Ed. New York: McGraw-Hill.

Nii, H., E. Feigenbaum, J. Anton, and A. Rockmore. 1982. "Signal-to-symbol transformation: HASP/SIAM case study." *AI Magazine* 3(2): 25–35.

Nikias, C., and M. Raghuveer. 1987. "Bispectrum estimation: a digital signal processing framework." *Proceedings of the IEEE* 75(7): 869–891.

Noike, K., N. Takiguchi, T. Nose, Y. Kotani, and H. Nisimura. 1993. In S. Ohteru, ed. *Proceedings of the 1993 International Computer Music Conference*. San Francisco: International Computer Music Association. pp. 363–365.

Noll, A. M. 1967. "Cepstrum pitch determination." *Journal of the Acoustical Society of America* 41(2): 23.

Nordmark, J. O. 1970. "Time and frequency analysis." In J. Tobias, ed. *Foundations of Modern Auditory Theory, Vol. 1*. New York: Academic Press. pp. 57–83.

Nordmark, J. O. 1978. "Frequency and periodicity analysis." In E. Carterette and M. Friedman, eds. *Handbook of Perception, Vol. 4*. New York: Academic Press. pp. 243–282.

Nussbaumer, H. 1981. *Fast Fourier Transform and Convolution Algorithms*. Springer-Verlag: New York.

Nuttall, A. 1981. "Some windows with very good sidelobe behavior." *IEEE Transactions on Acoustics, Speech, and Signal Processing* ASSP-29(1): 84–91.

Nyquist, H. 1928. "Certain topics in telegraph transmission theory." *Transactions of the American Institute of Electrical Engineers* April.

O'Beirne, T. 1968. "Music from paper tape." In J. Reichardt, ed. 1968. *Cybernetic Serendipity*. London: Studio International.

Ohta, H., H. Akita, M. Ohtari, S. Ishicado, and M. Yamane. 1993. "The development of an automatic bagpipe-playing device." In S. Ohteru, eds. *Proceedings of the 1993 International Computer Music Conference*. San Francisco: International Computer Music Association. pp. 430–431.

Olive, J. 1977. "Rule synthesis of speech from dyadic units." *Proceedings of the 1977 IEEE Conference on Acoustics, Speech, and Signal Processing*. New York: IEEE. pp. 568–570.

Olson, H. F. 1967. *Music, Physics, and Engineering*. Second ed. New York: Dover.

Olson, H. F. 1991. *Acoustical Engineering*. Philadelphia: Professional Audio Journals. Reprint of 1957 edition.

Olson, H., and H. Belar. 1955. "Electronic music synthesizer." *Journal of the Acoustical Society of America* 27(5): 595.

Olson, H., and H. Belar. 1961. "Aid to music composition system employing a random probability system." *Journal of the Acoustic Society of America* 33: 1163–1170.

Oohashi, T., E. Nishina, N. Kawai, Y. Fuwamoto, and H. Imai. 1991. "High frequency sound above the audible range affects brain electric activity and sound perception." Preprint 3207 (W-1). Presented at the 91st Convention of the Audio Engineering Society. New York: Audio Engineering Society.

Oohashi, T., E. Nishina, Y. Fuwamoto, and N. Kawai. 1993. "On the mechanism of hypersonic effect." In S. Ohteru, ed. *Proceedings of the 1993 International Computer Music Conference*. San Francisco: International Computer Music Association. pp. 432–434.

Oostrum, P. 1993. "MF2T/T2MF." Utrecht: Department of Computer Science, P. O. Box 80.089, Utrecht University.

Oppenheim, A. V. ed. 1978. *Applications of Digital Signal Processing*. Englewood Cliffs: Prentice-Hall.

Oppenheim, A., and H. Nawab. 1992. *Symbolic and Knowledge-based Signal Processing*. Englewood Cliffs: Prentice-Hall.

Oppenheim, A. V., and R. Schafer. 1975. *Digital Signal Processing*. Englewood Cliffs: Prentice-Hall.

Oppenheim, A., and A. Willsky. 1983. *Signals and Systems*. Englewood Cliffs: Prentice Hall.

Oppenheim, D. 1987. "The P-G-G environment for music composition." In J. Beauchamp, ed. *Proceedings of the 1987 International Computer Music Conference*. San Francisco: International Computer Music Association. pp. 40–48.

Oppenheim, D. 1992. "Compositional tools for adding expression to music in DMIX." In A. Strange, ed. *Proceedings of the 1992 International Computer Music Conference*. San Francisco: International Computer Music Association. pp. 223–226.

Ord-Hume, A. W. J. G. 1973. *Clockwork Music*. New York: Crown Publishers.

Ord-Hume, A. W. J. G. 1984. *Pianola: The History of the Self-playing Piano*. London: George Allen and Unwin.

Orlarey, Y. 1990. "An efficient scheduling algorithm for real-time musical systems." In S. Arnold and G. Hair, eds. *Proceedings of the 1990 International Computer Music Conference*. San Francisco: International International Computer Music Association. pp. 194–198.

Orton, R., A. Hunt, and R. Kirk. 1991. "Graphical control of granular synthesis using cellular automata and the Freehand program." In B. Alphonce and B. Pennycook, eds. *Proceedings of the 1991 International Computer Music Conference*. San Francisco: International Computer Music Association. pp. 416–418.

Otis, A., G. Grossman, and J. Cuomo. 1968. "Four sound-processing programs for the Illiac II computer and D/A converter." Technical Report 14. Urbana: University of Illinois Experimental Music Studio.

Ozzola, V., G. Melzi, and A. Corghi. 1984. "Experiments in stochastic approximation of musical language." In M. Baroni and L. Callegari, eds. *Musical Grammars and Computer Analysis*. Florence: L. Olschki. pp. 325–327.

Paladin, A., and D. Rocchesso. 1992. "Towards a generalized model of one-dimensional musical instruments." In A. Piccialli, ed. *Proceedings of the International Workshop on Models and Representations of Musical Signals*. Naples: Université di Napoli Federico II.

Pape, G. 1992. "Some musical possibilities of the new UPIC system." Massy: Les Ateliers UPIC.

Penfold, R. 1991. *Advanced MIDI User's Guide*. Tonbridge: PC Publishing.

Pennycook, B. 1984. "Computer music interfaces." *ACM Computing Surveys*. 17(2): 267–289.

Pennycook, B. 1991. "The PRAESCIO Series—Composition-driven Interactive Software." *Computer Music Journal* 15(3): 16–26.

Petersen, G., and H. Barney. 1952. "Control methods used in a study of the vowels." *Journal of the Acoustical Society of America* 24: 175–184.

Petersen, T. L. 1975. "Vocal tract modulation of instrumental sounds by digital filtering." In J. Beauchamp and J. Melby, eds. *Proceedings of the Second Annual Music Computation Conference*. Part 1. Urbana: Office of Continuing Education and Public Service in Music, University of Illinois. pp. 33–41.

Petersen, T. L. 1980. "Acoustic signal processing in the context of a perceptual model." Technical Report UTEC-CSc-80-113. Salt Lake City: University of Utah, Department of Computer Science.

Petersen, T. L. 1985. "Spiral synthesis." In J. Strawn, ed. 1985. *Digital Audio Signal Processing: An Anthology*. Madison: A-R Editions. pp. 137–147.

Petersen, T. L., and S. Boll. 1983. "Critical band analysis-synthesis." *IEEE Proceedings on Acoustics, Speech, and Signal Processing* ASSP-31(3): 656–663.

Peterson, G., and H. Barney. 1952. "Conbtrol methods used in a study of the vowels." *Journal of the Acoustical Society of America* 24: 175.

Peterson, G., W. Wang, and E. Silvertsen. 1958. "Segmentation techniques in speech synthesis." *Journal of the Acoustical Society of America* 30: 739–742.

Piccialli, A., S. Cavaliere, I. Ortosecco, and P. Basile. 1992. "Modifications of natural sounds using a pitch synchronous technique." In A. Piccialli, ed. *Proceedings of the International Workshop on Models and Representations of Musical Signals*. Napoli: Université di Napoli Federico II.

Pierce, J. R. 1974. *Almost All About Waves*. Cambridge, Massachusetts: The MIT Press.

Pinkerton, R. 1956. "Information theory and melody." *Scientific American* 194: 77–86.

Piszczalski, M. 1979a. "Spectral surfaces from performed music: part 1." *Computer Music Journal* 3(1): 18–24.

Piszczalski, M. 1979b. "Spectral surfaces from performed music: part 2." *Computer Music Journal* 3(3): 25–27.

Piszczalski, M., and B. Galler. 1977. "Automatic music transcription." *Computer Music Journal* 1(4): 24–31.

Piszczalski, M., et al. 1981. "Performed music: analysis, synthesis, and display by computer." *Journal of the Audio Engineering Society* 21(1/2): 38–46.

Plomp, R. 1976. *Aspects of Tone Sensation*. London: Academic Press.

Pohlmann, K. 1989a. *Principles of Digital Audio*. Indianapolis: Howard Sams.

Pohlmann, K. 1989b. *The Compact Disc: A Handbook of Theory and Use*. Madison: A-R Editions.

Polansky, L. 1986. "Paratactical tuning: an agenda for the use of computers in experimental intonation." *Computer Music Journal* 11(1): 61–68.

Polansky, L., D. Rosenboom, and P. Burk. 1987. "HMSL: overview (Version 3.1) and notes on intelligent instrument design." In J. Beauchamp, ed. *Proceedings of the 1987 International Computer Music Conference*. San Francisco: International Computer Music Association. pp. 220–227.

Polansky, L., P. Burk, R. Marsanyi, D. Hayes, and M. Gass. 1988. *Hierarchical Music Specification Language Reference and User Manual*. Oakland: Mills College Center for Contemporary Music.

Pope, S. 1986a. "The development of an intelligent composer's assistant." In P. Berg, ed. 1986. *Proceedings of the 1986 International Computer Music Conference*. San Francisco: International Computer Music Association. pp. 131–144.

Pope, S. 1986b. "Music notations and the representation of musical structure and knowledge." *Perspectives of New Music* 24(2): 156–189.

Pope, S. 1989. "Modeling musical structures as EventGenerators." In T. Wells and D. Butler, eds. *Proceedings of the 1989 International Computer Music Conference*. San Francisco: International Computer Music Association. pp. 249–252.

Pope, S. 1991a."Introduction to MODE: the musical object development environment." In S. Pope., ed. 1991. *The Well-Tempered Object*. Cambridge, Massachusetts: The MIT Press. pp. 83–106.

Pope, S., ed.1991b. *The Well-tempered Object*. Cambridge, Massachusetts: The MIT Press.

Pope, S. 1993. "Machine tongues XV: three packages for software sound synthesis." *Computer Music Journal* 17(2): 23–54.

Portnoff, M. 1976. "Implementation of the digital phase vocoder using the fast Fourier transform." *IEEE Transactions on Acoustics, Speech and Signal Processing* 24(3): 243–248.

Portnoff, M. 1978. "Time-scale modification of speech based on short-time fourier analysis." Sc. D. diss. Cambridge, Massachusetts: M.I.T. Department of Electrical Engineering and Computer Science.

Portnoff, M. 1980. "Time-frequency representation of digital signals and systems based on short-time Fourier analysis." *IEEE Transactions on Acoustics, Speech, and Signal Processing* ASSP-28: pp 55–69.

Potard, Y., P. F. Baisnée, and J.-B. Barrière. 1986. "Experimenting with models of resonance produced by a new technique for the analysis of impulsive sounds." In P. Berg, ed. *Proceedings of the 1986 International Computer Music Conference*. San Francisco: International Computer Music Association. pp. 269–274.

Potard, Y., P. F. Baisnée, and J.-B. Barrière. 1991. "Méthodologie de synthèse du timbre: l'exemple des modèles de résonance." In J.-B. Barrière, ed. *Le timbre, métaphore pour la composition*. Paris: IRCAM and Cristian Bourgeois. pp. 135–163.

Potter, R. 1946. Article on visible speech. *Bell Laboratories Record* 24(1): 7.

Potter, C., and D. Teaney. 1980. "Sonic transliteration applied to descriptive music notation." In H. S. Howe, Jr., ed. *Proceedings of the 1980 International Computer Music Conference*. San Francisco: International Computer Music Association. pp. 138–144.

Poynting, J., and J. Thomson. 1900. *Sound.* Second ed. London: Charles Griffin.

Preis, D. 1982. "Phase distortion and phase equalization in audio signal processing—a tutorial review." *Journal of the Audio Engineering Society* 30(11): 774–794.

Preis, D., and P. Bloom. 1983. "Perception of phase distortion in anti-alias filters." Preprint 2008 (H-3). Presented at the 74th Convention, October 8–12. New York: Audio Engineering Society.

Preis, D., F. Hlawatsch, P. Bloom, and J. Deer. 1987. "Wigner distribution analysis of filters with perceptible phase distortion." *Journal of the Audio Engineering Society* 35(12): 1004–1012.

Prerau, D. 1970. "Computer pattern recognition of standard engraved music notation." Ph.D. dissertation. Cambridge, Massachusetts: M.I.T. Department of Electrical Engineering.

Prerau, D. 1971. "Computer pattern recognition of printed music." *Proceedings of the Fall Joint Computer Conference.* Montvale, New Jersey: AFIPS Press.

Press, W., B. Flannery, S. Teukolsky, and W. Vetterling. 1988. *Numerical Recipes in C.* Cambridge, England: Cambridge University Press.

Pressing, J. 1988. "Nonlinear maps as generators of musical design." *Computer Music Journal* 12(2): 35–46.

Pressing, J., and P. Lawrence. 1993. "Transcribe: a comprehensive autotranscription program." In S. Ohteru, ed. *Proceedings of the 1993 International Computer Music Conference.* San Francisco: International Computer Music Association. pp. 343–345.

Pressing, J., C. Scallan, and N. Dicker. 1993. "Visualization and predictive modeling of musical signals using embedding techniques." In S. Ohteru, ed. *Proceedings of the 1993 International Computer Music Conference.* San Francisco: International Computer Music Association. pp. 110–113.

Prieberg, F. 1975. *Musica ex machina.* Italian edition. Turin: Giulio Einaudi Editore.

Prony, G. R. B. de, 1795. "Essai expérimentale et analytique, etc." *Paris Journal de l'Ecole Polytechnique* 1(2): 24–76.

Pruslin, D. 1966. "Automatic recognition of sheet music." Sc. D. dissertation. Cambridge, Massachusetts: M.I.T. Department of Electrical Engineering.

Puckette, M. 1985. "A real-time music performance system." Cambridge, Massachusetts: M.I.T. Experimental Music Studio.

Puckette, M. 1988. "The Patcher." In C. Lischka and J. Fritsch. 1988. *Proceedings of the 1988 International Computer Music Conference.* San Francisco: International Computer Music Association, and Cologne: Feedback Papers. pp. 420–429.

Puckette, M. 1991. "Combining event and signal processing in the MAX graphical programming environment." *Computer Music Journal* 15(3): 68–77.

Puckette, M., and C. Lippe. 1992. "Score following in practice." In A. Strange, ed. *Proceedings of the 1992 International Computer Music Conference.* San Francisco: International Computer Music Association. pp. 182–185.

Puckette, M., and D. Zicarelli. 1990. *MAX—An Interactive Graphical Programming Environment.* Menlo Park: Opcode Systems.

Pulfer, J. K. 1971. "Man-machine interaction in creative applications." *International Journal of Man-Machine Studies* 3: 1–11.

Quatieri, T., and R. McAulay. 1986. "Speech transformations based on a sinusoidal model." *IEEE Transactions on Acoustics, Speech, and Signal Processing* ASSP-34: 1449–1464.

Rabiner, L., J. Cooley, H. Helms, L. Jackson, J. Kaiser, C. Rader, R. Schafer, K. Steiglitz, and C. Weinstein. 1972. "Terminology in digital signal processing." *IEEE Transactions on Audio and Electroacoustics* AU-20: 322–337.

Rabiner, L. 1977. "On the use of autocorrelation analysis for pitch detection." *IEEE Transactions on Acoustics, Speech, and Signal Processing* ASSP-25(1)*.

Rabiner, L. 1983. "Digital techniques for changing the sampling rate of a signal." In B. Blesser, B. Locanthi, and T. Stockham, eds. *Digital Audio.* New York: Audio Engineering Society. pp. 79–89.

Rabiner, L. and B. Gold. 1975. *Theory and Applications of Digital Signal Processing.* Englewood Cliffs: Prentice-Hall.

Rabiner, L., M. Cheng, A. Rosenberg, and M. McGonegal. 1976. "A comparative performance study of several pitch detection algorithms." *IEEE Transactions on Acoustics, Speech, and Signal Processing* ASSP-24(5)*.

Rabiner, L., J. Cooley, H. Helms, L. Jackson, J. Kaiser, C. Rader, R. Schafer, K. Steiglitz, and C. Weinstein. 1972. "Terminology in digital signal processing." *IEEE Transactions on Audio and Acoustics* AU-20: 322–337.

Raczinski. J.-M., and G. Marino. 1988. "A real time synthesis unit." In C. Lischka and J. Fritsch, eds. *Proceedings of the 1988 International Computer Music Conference.* San Francisco: International Computer Music Association. pp. 90–100.

Raczinski, J.-M., G. Marino, and M.-H. Serra. 1991. "New UPIC system demonstration." In B. Alphonce and B. Pennycook, eds. *Proceedings of the 1991 International Computer Music Conference.* San Francisco: International Computer Music Association. pp. 567–570.

Rahn, J. 1988. "Computer music: a view from Seattle." *Computer Music Journal* 12(3): 15–29.

Rahn, J. 1990. "The Lisp kernel: a portable software environment for composition." *Computer Music Journal* 14(4): 42–58.

Rayleigh, J. 1894. *The Theory of Sound*. Reprinted 1945. New York: Dover.

Read, G. 1969. *Music Notation*. New York: Crescendo.

Read, O., and W. Welch. 1976. *From Tin Foil to Stereo: Evolution of the Phonograph*. Indianapolis: Howard Sams.

Reeves, A. 1938. "Electric signal system." British Patent 535, 860. U. S. Patent 2, 272, 070 (1942).

Reeves, W. 1983. "Particle systems—a technique for modeling a class of fuzzy objects. "*ACM Transactions on Graphics* 2(2): 359–376.

Reeves, W., et al. 1979. "Ludwig: an example of interactive computer graphics in a score editor." In C. Roads, ed. *Proceedings of the 1978 International Computer Music Conference*. Evanston: Northwestern University Press.

Reich, S. 1974. *Writings About Music*. Halifax and New York: The Presses of the Nova Scotia College of Art and Design and New York University.

Reiser, J., 1976. "SAIL." STAN-CS-76-574. Stanford: Stanford University Department of Computer Science.

Reitman, W. 1960. "Information processing languages and heuristic programming." *Bionics Symposium*. WADD Technical Report 60-600. Dayton. Ohio: Directorate of Advanced Systems Technology, Wright-Patterson Air Force Base.

Reveillon, F. 1994. Personal communication.

Rhea, T. 1972. "The evolution of electronic musical instruments in the United States." Ph.D diss. Nashville: George Peabody College for Teachers.

Rhea, T. 1977. "Electronic Perspectives: photoelectric acoustic-sound instruments." *Contemporary Keyboard* October: 62.

Rhea, T. 1984. "The history of electronic musical instruments." In T. Darter, ed. 1984. *The Art of Electronic Music*. New York: Quill. pp. 1–63.

Rich, E. 1983. *Artificial Intelligence*. New York: McGraw-Hill.

Richards, J., and I. Craven. 1982. "An experimental 'all-digital' studio mixing desk." *Journal of the Audio Engineering Society* 30(3): 117–126.

Risatti, H. 1975. *New Music Vocabulary*. Urbana: University of Illinois Press.

Risberg, J. 1982. "Non-linear estimation of FM synthesis parameters. Unpublished mss.

Risset, J.-C. 1966. "Computer study of trumpet tones." Murray Hill: Bell Telephone Laboratories.

Risset, J.-C. 1969. "Catalog of computer-synthesized sound." Murray Hill: Bell Telephone Laboratories.

Risset, J.-C. 1985a. "Computer music experiments: 1964–." *Computer Music Journal* 9(!): 11–18. Reprinted in C. Roads, ed. 1989. *The Music Machine*. Cambridge, Massachusetts: The MIT Press. pp. 67–74.

Risset, J.-C. 1985b. "Digital techniques and sound structure in music." In C. Roads, ed. *Composers and the Computer*. Madison: A-R Editions. pp. 113–138.

Risset, J.-C. 1991. "Timbre analysis by synthesis: representations, imitations, and variants for musical composition." In G. De Poli, A. Piccialli, and C. Roads, ed. 1991. *Representations of Musical Signals*. Cambridge, Massachusetts: The MIT Press. pp. 7–43.

Risset, J.-C., and M. Mathews. 1969. "Analysis of musical instrument tones." *Physics Today* 22(2): 23–40.

Risset, J.-C., and D. Wessel. 1982. "Exploration of timbre by analysis and synthesis." In D. Deutsch, ed. 1982. *Psychology of Music*. Orlando: Academic Press.

Ristow, J. 1993. "Audiotechnology in Berlin to 1943: optical sound." Preprint 3487 (H2-8). Presented at the 94th Audio Engineering Society Convention 1993 March Berlin. New York: Audio Engineering Society.

Roads, C. 1973. "Analysis of the composition *ST/10* and the computer program Free Stochastic Music by Iannis Xenakis." Unpublished manuscript.

Roads, C. 1976. "A systems approach to composition." Honors thesis. La Jolla: University of California, San Diego.

Roads, C. 1978a. "An interview with Gottfried Michael Koenig." *Computer Music Journal* 2(3): 11–15. Reprinted in C. Roads and J. Strawn, eds. 1985. *Foundations of Computer Music*. Cambridge, Massachusetts: The MIT Press. pp. 568–580.

Roads, C. 1978b. *Composing Grammars*. San Francisco: International Computer Music Association.

Roads, C. 1978c. "Automated granular synthesis of sound." *Computer Music Journal* 2(2): 61–62. Revised and updated version printed as "Granular synthesis of sound" in C. Roads and J. Strawn, eds. 1985. *Foundations of Computer Music*. Cambridge, Massachusetts: The MIT Press. pp. 145–159.

Roads, C., 1979. "Machine tongues VI: Ada—a complex language." *Computer Music Journal* 3(4): 6–8.

Roads, C. 1980. "Interview with Max Mathews." *Computer Music Journal* 4(4): 15–22. Reprinted in C. Roads, ed. 1989. *The Music Machine*. Cambridge, Massachusetts: The MIT Press. pp. 5–12.

Roads, C. 1981a. "An intelligent composer's assistant." Unpublished mss.

Roads, C. 1981b. "A note on music printing by computer." *Computer Music Journal* 5(3): 57–59. Reprinted in C. Roads, ed. 1989. *The Music Machine*. Cambridge, Massachusetts: The MIT Press.

Roads, C. 1982. "A conversation with James A. Moorer." *Computer Music Journal* 6(4): 10–21. Reprinted in C. Roads, ed. 1989. *The Music Machine*. Cambridge, Massachusetts: The MIT Press. pp. 13–24.

Roads, C. 1983. "Interactive orchestration based on score analysis." In J. Strawn and T. Blum, eds. *Proceedings of the 1982 International Computer Music Conference*. San Francisco: International Computer Music Association. pp. 703–717.

Roads, C. 1984. "An overview of music representations." In M. Baroni and L. Callegari, eds. *Musical Grammars and Computer Analysis*. Florence: Olschki. pp. 7–37.

Roads, C., ed. 1985a. *Composers and the Computer*. Madison: A-R Editions.

Roads, C. 1985b. "Improvisation with George Lewis." In C. Roads, editor. *Composers and the Computer*. Madison: A-R Editions. pp. 75–87.

Roads, C. 1985c. "Interview with James Dashow." In C. Roads, editor. *Composers and the Computer*. Madison: A-R Editions. pp. 27–45.

Roads, C. 1985d. "Research in music and artificial intelligence: a survey." *ACM Computing Surveys* 17(2): 163–190. Reprinted as "Richerche sulla musica e l'intelligenza artificiale" in A. Vidolin and R. Doati, eds. 1986. *Nuova Atlantide*. Venice: La Biennale di Venezia. pp. 121–147. Reprinted in the Japanese computer journal *bit* (Tokyo), 1987.

Roads, C. 1985e. "Grammars as representations for music." In C. Roads and J. Strawn, eds. 1985. *Foundations of Computer Music*. Cambridge, Massachusetts: The MIT Press. pp. 403–442.

Roads, C. 1985f. "The realization of nscor." In C. Roads, ed. 1985. *Composers and the Computer*. Madison: A-R Editions. pp. 140–168.

Roads, C. 1985g. "Granular synthesis of sound." In C. Roads and J. Strawn, eds. 1985. *Foundations of Computer Music*. Cambridge, Massachusetts: The MIT Press. pp. 145–159.

Roads, C. 1986a. "Symposium on composition." *Computer Music Journal* 10(1): 40–63.

Roads, C. 1986b. "The Tsukuba musical robot." *Computer Music Journal* 10(2): 39–43.

Roads, C. 1986c. "The second STEIM symposium on interactive composition in live electronic music." *Computer Music Journal* 10(2): 44–50.

Roads, C. 1987. "Experiences with computer-assisted composition." Translated as "Esperienze di composizione assistata da calculatore." In S. Tamburini and M. Bagella, eds. *I Profili del Suono*. Rome: Musica Verticale and Galzeramo. pp. 173–196.

Roads, C., ed. 1989. *The Music Machine*. Cambridge, Massachusetts: The MIT Press.

Roads, C. 1991. "Asynchronous granular synthesis." In G. De Poli, A. Piccialli, and C. Roads, eds. 1991. *Representations of Musical Signals.* Cambridge, Massachusetts: The MIT Press. pp. 143–185.

Roads, C. 1992a. "Composition with machines." In J. Paynter, T. Howell, R. Orton, and P. Seymour, eds. 1992. *Companion to Contemporary Musical Thought.* London: Routledge. pp. 399–425.

Roads, C. 1992b. "Musical applications of advanced signal representations." Presented at the International Workshop on Models and Representations of Musical Signals, October 1992, Capri, Italy.

Roads, C. 1993a. "Musical sound transformation by convolution." In S. Ohteru, ed. *Proceedings of the 1993 International Computer Music Conference.* San Francisco: International Computer Music Association. pp. 102–109.

Roads, C. 1993b. "Organization of *Clang-tint.*" In S. Ohteru, ed. *Proceedings of the 1993 International Computer Music Conference.* San Francisco: International Computer Music Association. pp. 346–348.

Roads, C., ed. 1993c. *IRCAM Max Documentation Set.* Two volumes. Paris: IRCAM.

Roads, C. 1994. "Sound composition with pulsars." Unpublished manuscript.

Roads, C. 1995. *The Computer Music Tutorial.* Cambridge, Massachusetts: The MIT Press.

Roads, C., and J. Strawn, eds. 1985. *Foundations of Computer Music* Cambridge, Massachusetts: The MIT Press.

Rogers, G. 1987. "Console design and MIDI." *Studio Sound* 29(2): 42–44.

Roberts, A. 1966. "An ALL-FORTRAN music generating computer program." *Journal of the Audio Engineering Society* 14: 17–20.

Roberts, A. 1969. "Some new developments in computer-generated music." In H. Von Foerster and J. Beauchamp, eds. 1969. *Music by Computers.* New York: John Wiley and Sons. pp. 63–68.

Roberts, S. 1979. "Polyphony made easy." In C. Morgan, ed. *The Byte Book of Computer Music* Peterborough: Byte Publications. pp. 117–124.

Robinson, E. 1982. "A historical perspective of spectrum estimation." *Proceedings of the Institute of Electrical and Electronics Engineers* 70(9): 885–907.

Robinson, J. A., 1965. "A machine-oriented logic based on the resolution principle." *Journal of the Association for Computing Machinery* 12(1): 23–41.

Rodet, X. 1980. "Time-domain formant-wave-function synthesis." In J. G. Simon, ed. 1980. *Spoken Language Generation and Understanding.* Dordrecht: D. Reidel. Reprinted in *Computer Music Journal* 8(3): 9–14. 1984.

Rodet, X. 1986. Personal communication.

Rodet, X. 1992. "Nonlinear oscillator models of musical instrument excitation." In A. Strange, ed. *Proceedings of the 1992 International Computer Music Conference.* San Francisco: International Computer Music Association. pp. 412–413.

Rodet, X., and G. Bennett. 1980. "Synthese de la voix chantee par ordinateur." In *Conferences des journees d'etudes 1980.* Paris: Festival International du Son. pp. 73–91.

Rodet, X., and P. Cointe. 1984. "FORMES: composition and scheduling of processes." *Computer Music Journal* 8(3)32–50. Reprinted in C. Roads, ed. 1989. *The Music Machine.* Cambridge, Massachusetts: The MIT Press. pp. 405–426.

Rodet, X., and J. Delatre. 1979. "Time-domain speech synthesis by rules using a flexible and fast signal management system." *Proceedings of the IEEE International Conference on Acoustics, Speech, and Signal Processing, Washington, D. C., 2–4 April.* New York: IEEE. pp. 895–898.

Rodet, X., and P. Depalle. 1992. "A new additive synthesis method using inverse Fourier transform and spectral envelopes." In A. Strange, ed. *Proceedings of the 1992 International Computer Music Conference.* San Francisco: International Computer Music Association. pp. 410–411.

Rodet, X., and C. Santamarina. 1975. "Synthèse, sur un miniordinateur, du signal vocale dans la representation amplitude-temps." *Actes des sixiemes journees d'etude su la parole du GALF, Toulouse.* Paris: GALF. pp. 364–371.

Rodet, X., Y. Potard, and J.-B. Barrière. 1984. "The CHANT project: from synthesis of the singing voice to synthesis in general." *Computer Music Journal* 8(3): 15–31. Reprinted in C. Roads, ed. 1989. *The Music Machine.* Cambridge, Massachusetts. : The MIT Press. pp. 449–466.

Rodet, X., P. Depalle, and G. Poirot. 1988. "Diphone sound synthesis based on spectral envelopes and harmonic/noise excitation functions." In C. Lischka and J. Fritsch, eds. *Proceedings of the 1988 International Computer Music Conference.* San Francisco: International Computer Music Association. pp. 313–321.

Rodgers, C. A. P. 1981. "Pinna transformations and sound reproduction." *Journal of the Audio Engineering Society* 29(4): 226–234.

Roeder, J., and K. Hamel. 1989. "A general-purpose object-oriented system for musical graphics." In T. Wells, and D. Butler, eds. *Proceedings of the 1989 International Computer Music Conference.* San Francisco: International Computer Music Association. pp. 260–263.

Roederer, J. 1975. *Introduction to the Physics and Psychophysics of Music.* Second Edition; New York: Springer-Verlag.

Rogers, G. 1987. "Console design and MIDI." *Studio Sound* 29(2): 42–44.

Rolnick, N. 1978. "A composer's notes on the development and implementation of software for a digital synthesizer." *Computer Music Journal* 2(2): 13–22. Reprinted in C. Roads and J. Strawn, eds. 1985. *Foundations of Computer Music*. Cambridge, Massachusetts: The MIT Press.

Rosenboom, D. 1976. *Biofeedback and the Arts: Results of Early Experiments*. Vancouver: Aesthetic Research Centre Publications.

Rosenboom, D. 1990. "The performing brain." *Computer Music Journal* 14(1): 48–66.

Rosenthal, D. 1988. "A model of the process of listening to simple rhythms." In C. Lischka and J. Fritsch. *Proceedings of the 1988 International Computer Music Conference*. San Francisco: International Computer Music Association. pp. 189–197.

Rosenthal, D. 1992. "Emulation of human rhythm perception." *Computer Music Journal* 16(1): 64–76.

Rossum, D. 1992. "Making digital filters sound 'analog.'" In A. Strange, ed. *Proceedings of the 1992 International Computer Music Conference*. San Francisco: International Computer Music Association. pp. 30–33.

Rothgeb, J. 1980. "Simulating musical skills by digital computer." *Computer Music Journal* 4(3): 36–40. Reprinted in C. Roads, ed. 1989. *The Music Machine*. Cambridge, Massachusetts: The MIT Press.

Rothstein, J. 1992. *MIDI: A Comprehensive Introduction*. Madison: A-R Editions.

Rowe, N. 1975. "Machine perception of musical rhythm." B. S. thesis. Cambridge, Massachusetts: M.I.T. Department of Electrical Engineering.

Rowe, R. 1992a. "Machine listening and composing with Cypher." *Computer Music Journal* 16(1): 43–63.

Rowe, R. 1992b. *Interactive Music Systems*. Cambridge, Massachusetts: The MIT Press.

Rozenberg, M. 1979. "Microcomputer-controlled sound processing using Walsh functions." *Computer Music Journal* 3(1): 42–47.

Rozenberg, M. 1982. "Linear sweep synthesis." *Computer Music Journal* 6(3): 65–71.

Rubine, D., and P. McAvinney. 1990. "Programmable finger-tracking instrument controller." *Computer Music Journal* 14(1): 26–41.

Ruiz, P. 1970. "A technique for simulating the vibrations of strings with a digital computer." M. M. thesis. Urbana: University of Illinois School of Music.

Rumelhart, D., and J. McClelland. 1986. *Parallel Distributed Processing*. 2 vols. Cambridge, Massachusetts: The MIT Press.

Rumsey, F. "Digital audio synchronization." *Studio Sound* 33(3): 74–79.

Rush, L., and J. A. Moorer.1977. "Editing, mixing, and processing digitized audio waveforms." Paper presented at the 57th Convention of the Audio Engineering Society, May. Abstract in *Journal of the Audio Engineering Society* 25: 514.

Russ, M. 1993. "MIDI timing delays: software and hardware thrus." *Sound on Sound* 8(3): 94–98.

Russolo, L. 1916. Published 1986. *The Art of Noises*. Barclay Brown, trans. New York: Pendragon.

Ryan, J. 1991. "Some remarks on musical instrument design at STEIM." *Contemporary Music Review* 6(1): 3–17.

Sabine, W. 1922. *Collected Papers on Acoustics*. Reprinted 1964. New York: Dover.

Sakamoto, N., S. Yamaguchi, and A. Kurahashi. 1982. "A professional digital audio mixer." *Journal of the Audio Engineering Society* 30(1/2): 28–33.

Samson, P. 1980. "A general-purpose synthesizer." *Journal of the Audio Engineering Society* 28(3): 106–113.

Samson, P. 1985. "Architectural issues in the design of the Systems Concepts Digital Synthesizer." In J. Strawn, ed. *Digital Audio Engineering: An Anthology*. Madison: A-R Editions.

Sandel, L. 1989. "Graphical compiler for Music V." Padua: Centro di Sonologià Computazionale, University of Padua.

Sandell, G., and W. Martens. 1992. "Prototyping and interpolation of multiple musical timbres using principle components-based analysis." In A. Strange, ed. *Proceedings of the 1992 International Computer Music Conference*. San Francisco: International Computer Music Association. pp. 34–37.

Sandresky, M. 1981. "The golden section in three Byzantine motets of Dufay." *Journal of Music Theory* 25(2).

Saraswat, V. 1992. *Concurrent Constraint Programming Languages*. Cambridge, Massachusetts: The MIT Press.

Sasaki, L., and K. C. Smith. 1980. "A simple data reduction scheme for additive synthesis." *Computer Music Journal* 4(1): 22–24.

Scaletti, C. 1989a. "The Kyma/Platypus computer music workstation." *Computer Music Journal* 13(2): 23–38. Updated version in S. Pope, ed. 1991. *The Well Tempered Object*. Cambridge, Massachusetts: The MIT Press. pp. 119–140.

Scaletti, C. 1989b. "Composing sound objects in KYMA." *Perspectives of New Music* 27(1): 42–69.

Scaletti, C., and K. Hebel. 1991. "An object-based representation for digital audio signals." In G. De Poli, A. Piccialli, and C. Roads, eds. 1991. *Representations of Musical Signals*. Cambridge, Massachusetts: The MIT Press. pp. 371–389.

Schaeffer, P. 1977. *Traité des Objets Musicaux*. Second edition. Paris. Éditions du Seuil.

Schaeffer, P., and A. Moles. 1952. *À la Recherche d'une Musique Concrète*. Paris: Éditions du Seuil.

Schaeffer, P., G. Reibel, and B. Ferreyra. 1967. *Trois microsillons d'exemples sonores de G. Reibel et Beatriz Ferreyra ullustrant le Traité des Objets Sonores et présentés par l'auteur*. Paris: Éditions du Seuil.

Schafer, R., and L. Rabiner. 1970. "System for automatic formant analysis of voiced speech." *Journal of the Acoustical Society of America* 47(2): 634.

Schafer, R., and L. Rabiner 1973a. "A digital signal processing approach to interpolation." *Proceedings of the IEEE* 61(6): 692–702.

Schafer, R., and L. Rabiner. 1973b. "Design and simulation of a speech analysis-synthesis system based on short-time Fourier analysis." *IEEE Transactions on Audio and Electroacoustics* AU-21: 165–174.

Scharf, B. 1961. "Complex sounds and critical bands." *Psychological Bulletin* 58: 205–217.

Scharf, B. 1970. "Critical bands." In J. Tobias, ed. *Foundations of Modern Auditory Theory*. Orlando: Academic Press.

Scharf, B. 1978. "Loudness." In E. Carterette and M. Friedman, eds., *Handbook of Perception, Volume 4*. New York: Academic Press. pp. 187–242.

Scherpenisse, J. 1977. "Digital control in electronic music studios." *Interface* 6: 73–80.

Schillinger, J. 1946. *The Schillinger System of Musical Composition*. New York: Carl Fischer. Reprinted 1978. New York: Da Capo Press.

Schindler, K. 1984. "Dynamic timbre control for real-time digital synthesis." *Computer Music Journal* 8(1): 28–42.

Schmidt, B. 1987. "A natural language system for music." *Computer Music Journal* 11(2): 25–34.

Schönberg, A. 1911. *Harmonlehre*. Vienna. Universal Edition. Trans. 1978 by R. Carter as *Theory of Harmony*. Berkeley: University of California Press.

Scholes, P. 1975. *The Oxford Companion to Music*. London: Oxford University Press.

Scholz, C. 1991. "A proposed extension to the MIDI specification regarding tuning." *Computer Music Journal* 15(1): 49–54.

Schloss, W. 1985. "On the automatic transcription of percussive music—from acoustic signal to high-level analysis." Report STAN-M-27. Stanford: Stanford University Department of Music.

Schottstaedt, W. 1977. "The simulation of natural instrument tones using frequency modulation with a complex modulation wave." *Computer Music Journal* 1(4): 46–50. Reprinted in C. Roads and J. Strawn, eds. 1985. *Foundations of Computer Music* Cambridge, Massachusetts: The MIT Press. pp. 54–64.

Schottstaedt, W. 1983. "Pla—a composer's idea of a language." *Computer Music Journal* 7(1): 11–20. Reprinted in C. Roads, ed. 1989. *The Music Machine*. Cambridge, Massachusetts: The MIT Press. article 26.

Schottstaedt, W. 1989a. "A computer music language." In M. Mathews and J. R. Pierce. *Current Directions in Computer Music Research*. Cambridge, Massachusetts: The MIT Press. pp. 215–224.

Schottstaedt, W. 1989b. "Automatic counterpoint." In M. Mathews and J. R. Pierce. 1989. *Current Directions in Computer Music Research*. Cambridge, Massachusetts: The MIT Press. pp. 225–262.

Schottstaedt, W. 1991. "Common Lisp Music." Stanford: Center for Computer Research in Music and Acoustics, Stanford University.

Schroeder, M. 1961. "Improved quasi-stereophony and colorless artificial reverberation." *Journal of the Acoustical Society of America* 33: 1061.

Schroeder, M. 1962. "Natural sounding artificial reverberation." *Journal of the Audio Engineering Society* 10(3): 219–223.

Schroeder, M. 1966. "Vocoders: analysis and synthesis of speech." *Proceedings of the IEEE* 54: 720–734.

Schroeder, M. 1970. "Digital simulation of sound transmission in reverberant spaces." *Journal of the Acoustical Society of America* 47(2): 424–431.

Schroeder, M., and B.S. Atal. 1962. "Generalized short-time power spectra and autocorrelation functions." *Journal of the Acoustical Society of America* 34: 1679–1683.

Schubert, E. 1979a. "Editor's comments on papers 1 through 5." In E. Schubert, ed. *Psychological Acoustics*. Stroudsburg: Dowden, Hutchinson, and Ross. pp. 8–16.

Schubert, E. 1979b. "Editor's comments on papers 25 through 31." In E. Schubert, ed. *Psychological Acoustics*. Stroudsburg: Dowden, Hutchinson, and Ross. pp. 254–263.

Schuster, A. 1898. "On the investigation of hidden periodicities with application to the supposed 26 day period of meteorological phenomena." *Terrestial Magnetism* 3: 13–41.

Schwanauer, S. 1988. "MUSE: a learning system for tonal composition." Ph.D. diss. New Haven: Yale University.

Schwartz, R., J. Klovstad. J. Makhoul, D. Klatt, and V. Zac. 1979. "Diphone synthesis for phonetic coding." *Proceedings of the IEEE Acoustics, Speech and Signal Processing Conference*. New York: IEEE. pp. 891–894.

Schwede, G. 1983. "An algorithm and architecture for constant-Q spectrum analysis." *Proceedings of the International Conference on Acoustics, Speech, and Signal Processing.* New York: IEEE.

Scientific American. 1987. "Fourier transformation." *Scientific American* 257(1): 27–28.

Secor, G. 1975. "Specifications of the Motorola Scalatron." *Xenharmonikon* 2(2).

Seeger, C. 1951. "An instantaneous music notator." *Journal of the International Folk Music Society* 3: 103–107.

Sekiguchi, K., R. Amemiya, and H. Kubota. 1993. "The development of an automatic drum-playing robot." In S. Ohteru, ed. *Proceedings of the 1993 International Computer Music Conference.* San Francisco: International Computer Music Association. pp. 428–429.

Sekiguchi, K., K. Ishizawa, T. K. Matsudiara, and M. Nakajima. 1983. "A new approach to high-speed digital signal processing based on microprogramming." *Journal of the Audio Engineering Society* 31(7): 517–522.

Selfridge, O., and U. Neisser. 1960. "Pattern recognition by machine." *Scientific American* 203: 60.

Serra, M.-H. 1992. "Stochastic composition and stochastic timbre: GENDY3 by Iannis Xenakis." Paris: Centre d'Etudes de Mathematiques et Automatiques Musicale.

Serra, M.-H., D. Rubine, and R. Dannenberg. 1990. "Analysis and synthesis of tones by spectral interpolation." *Journal of the Audio Engineering Society* 38(3): 111–128.

Serra, X. 1989. "A system for sound analysis/transformation/synthesis based on a deterministic plus stochastic decomposition." Stanford: Center for Computer Research in Music and Acoustics, Department of Music, Stanford University.

Serra, X., and J. Smith. 1990. "Spectral modeling synthesis: a sound analysis/synthesis system based on a deterministic plus stochastic decomposition." *Computer Music Journal* 14(4): 12–24.

Sheeline, C. 1982. "An investigation of the effects of direct and reverberant signal interactions on auditory distance perception. " Stanford: Stanford University Department of Music Report Number STAN-M-13.

Shannon, C. 1948. "A mathematical theory of communication." *Bell System Technical Journal* 27.

Shannon, C., and W. Weaver. 1949. *The Mathematical Theory of Communication.* Urbana: University of Illinois Press.

Shensa, M. 1992. "The discrete wavelet transform: wedding the à trous and Mallat algorithms." *IEEE Transactions on Signal Processing* 40(10): 2464–2482.

Shpak, D. 1992. "Analytic design of biquadratic filter sections for parametric filters." *Journal of the Audio Engineering Society* 40(11): 876–885.

Siebert, W. 1985. *Circuits, Signals, and Systems.* Cambridge, Massachusetts: The MIT Press.

Siewiorek, D., C. G. Bell, and A. Newell. 1982. *Computer Structures: Principles and Examples.* New York: McGraw-Hill.

Silver, A. L. L. 1957. "Equal beating chromatic scale." *Journal of the Acoustical Society of America* 29: 476–481.

Singleton, R. 1967. "A method for computing the fast Fourier transform with auxiliary memory and limited high-speed storage." *IEEE Transactions on Audio and Electroacoustics* AU-15(2): 91–98.

Slaney, M., and R. Lyon. 1991a. *Apple Hearing Demo Reel.* Apple Computer Technical Report 25. Cupertino: Apple Corporate Library.

Slaney, M., and R. Lyon. 1991b. "Visualizing sound with auditory correlograms." Submitted to the *Journal of the Acoustical Society of America.*

Slaney, M., and R. Lyon. 1992. "On the importance of time—a temporal representation of sound." In M. Cooke and S. Beet, eds. 1992. *Visual Representations of Speech Signals.* New York: John Wiley.

Slaney, R., D. Naar, and R. Lyon. 1994. "Auditory model inversion for sound separation." *Proceedings of the ICASSP 94.* New York: IEEE.

Slawson, A. W. 1969. "A speech-oriented synthesizer of computer music." *Journal of Music Theory* 13(1): 94–127.

Slawson, A. W. 1985. *Sound Color.* Berkeley: University of California Press.

Sloboda, J. 1985. *The Musical Mind.* Oxford: The Clarendon Press.

Small, G. 1973. "Rate-feedback binary counters in musical scale generation." *Journal of the Audio Engineering Society* 21(9): 702–705.

Smith, D. 1984. Interviewed in D. Milano. 1984. "Turmoil in MIDI Land." *Keyboard* 10(6).

Smith, J. 1981. "Digital signal processing committee, IEEE ASSP: Programs for digital signal processing." *Computer Music Journal* 5(2): 62–65.

Smith, J. 1982. "Synthesis of bowed strings." In J. Strawn and T. Blum, eds. 1982. *Proceedings of the 1982 International Computer Music Conference.* San Francisco: International Computer Music Association. pp. 308–340.

Smith, J. 1983. "Techniques for digital filter design and system identification with application to the violin." Ph.D. dissertation. Technical Report STAN-M-14. Stanford: Stanford University Department of Music.

Smith, J. 1985a. "Introduction to digital filter theory." In J. Strawn, ed. 1985. *Digital Audio Signal Processing*: *An Anthology*. Madison: A-R Editions.

Smith, J. 1985b. "Fundamentals of digital filter theory." *Computer Music Journal* 9(3): 13–23. Reprinted in C. Roads, ed. 1989. *The Music Machine*. Cambridge, Massachusetts: The MIT Press.

Smith, J. 1985c. "A new approach to reverberation using Ccosed waveguide networks." In B. Truax, ed. *Proceedings of the 1985 International Computer Music Conference*. San Francisco: International Computer Music Association.

Smith, J. 1986. "Efficient simulation of the reed-bore mechanism and bow-string interactions." In P. Berg, ed. 1986. *Proceedings of the 1986 International Computer Music Conference*. San Francisco: International Computer Music Association. pp. 275–279.

Smith, J. 1987a. "Waveguide filter tutorial." In J. Beauchamp, ed. *Proceedings of the 1987 International Computer Music Conference*. San Francisco: International Computer Music Association. pp. 9–16.

Smith, J. 1987b. "Musical applications of digital waveguides." Technical Report STAN-M-39. Stanford: Stanford University Department of Music.

Smith, J. 1991a. "Viewpoints on the history of digital synthesis." In B. Alphonce and B. Pennycook, eds. *Proceedings of the 1991 International Computer Music Conference*. San Francisco: International Computer Music Association. pp. 1–10.

Smith, J. 1991b. "Waveguide simulation of non-cylindrical acoustic tubes." In B. Alphonce and B. Pennycook, eds. *Proceedings of the 1991 International Computer Music Conference*. San Francisco: International Computer Music Conference. pp. 304–307.

Smith, J. 1992. "Physical modeling using digital waveguides." *Computer Music Journal* 16(4): 74–91.

Smith, J. 1993. "Efficient synthesis of stringed musical instruments." In S. Ohteru, ed. *Proceedings of the 1993 International Computer Music Conference*. San Francisco: International Computer Music Conference. pp. 64–71.

Smith, J., and J. B. Angell. 1982. "A constant-gain digital resonator tuned by a single coefficient." *Computer Music Journal* 6(4): 36–40. Reprinted in C. Roads, ed. 1989. *The Music Machine*. Cambridge, Massachusetts: The MIT Press.

Smith, J., and B. Friedlander. 1985. "Adaptive interpolated time-delay estimation." *IEEE Transactions on Aerospace and Electronic Systems* AES-21(2): 180–199.

Smith, L. 1972. "SCORE—a musician's approach to computer music." *Journal of the Audio Engineering Society* 20(1): 7–14.

Smith, L. 1973. "Editing and printing music by computer." *Journal of Music Theory* 9: 129–150.

Smith, R., and M. Brachman. 1980. "Operating range and maximum response of single auditory-nerve fibers." *Brain Research* 184: 499–505.

Smoliar, S. 1967a. "Euterpe: a computer language for the expression of musical ideas." A. I. Memo 129. Cambridge, Massachusetts: Artificial Intelligence Laboratory, Massachusetts Institute of Technology.

Smoliar, S. 1967. "Euterpe-Lisp: A Lisp System with Music Output." A. I. Memo 141. Cambridge, Massachusetts: Massachusetts Institute of Technology.

Smoliar, S. 1969. "Review of Max Mathews' Technology of Computer Music. *Technology Review* Oct./Nov.: 19.

Smoliar, S. 1971. "A Parallel Processing Model of Musical Structures." A. I. Technic Smoliar, S. 1973. "A data structure for an interactive music system." *Interface* 2(2): 127–140.

Smoliar, S., 1980. "A computer aid for schenkerian analysis." *Computer Music Journal* 4(2): 41–59.

Sneider, T. 1979. "Simple approaches to computer music synthesis." In C. Morgan, ed. *The Byte Book of Computer Music*. Peterborough: Byte Publications. pp. 75–79.

Snell, J. 1977a. "High-speed multiplication." *Computer Music Journal* 1(1): 38–45.

Snell, J. 1977b. "Design of a digital oscillator that will generate up to 256 low-distortion sine waves in real time." *Computer Music Journal* 1(2): 4–25. Revised and updated version in C. Roads and J. Strawn, eds. 1985. *Foundations of Computer Music* Cambridge, Massachusetts: The MIT Press.

Snell, J. 1982. "The Lucasfilm real-time console for recording studios and performance of computer music." *Computer Music Journal* 6(3): 33–45.

Snell, J. 1983. "Sensors for playing computer music with expression." In *Proceedings of the 1983 International Computer Music Conference*. San Francisco: International Computer Music Association.

Sony Corporation. 1983. *Digital Audio Processor PCM-701ES*. Tokyo: Sony Corporation.

Sousa, J. P. 1906. "The menace of mechanical music." *Appleton's Magazine* September: pp: 278–284. Reprinted with an introduction by C. Roads in *Computer Music Journal* 17(1): 12–13, 1993.

Soustrop, B. 1991. *The C++ Programming Language*. Englewood Cliffs: Prentice-Hall.

Sowa, J. 1956. "A machine to compose music." Instruction manual for GENIAC. New Haven: Oliver Garfield Co.

Spiegel, L. 1989. Personal communication.

Springer, A. 1955. "Ein akusticher Zeitregler." *Gravesaner Blätter* 1: 32–37.

Stallings, W. 1988. *Data and Computer Communications*. Second edition. New York: Macmillan.

Stanek, J., 1979. "Exploration of concurrent digital sound synthesis on a prototype data-driven machine." M.S. thesis. Salt Lake City: Department of Computer Science, University of Utah.

Stapely, P. 1991. "Flying faders." *Studio Sound* 33(4): 46–51.

Starke, P. 1972. *Abstract Automata*. Amsterdam: North-Holland.

Stautner, J. 1983. "Analysis and synthesis of music using the auditory transform." M. S. thesis. Cambridge, Massachusetts: M.I.T. Department of Electrical Engineering and Computer Science.

Stautner, J., and M. Puckette. 1982. "Designing multi-channel reverberators." *Computer Music Journal* 6(1): 62–65.

Steele, G. 1984. *Common Lisp: The Language*. Burlington: Digital Press.

Stevens, K. and G. Fant. 1953. "An electrical analog of the vocal tract." *Journal of the Acoustical Society of America* 25: 734–742.

Steward, J. 1922. "An electrical analogue of the vocal organs." *Nature* 110: 311–312.

Stickney, K. 1987. "Computer tools for engraving-quality music notation." In J. Strawn, ed. 1987. *Music and Digital Technology*. New York: Audio Engineering Society.

Stockham, T. 1969. "High-speed convolution and convolution with applications to digital filtering." In B. Gold and C. Rader. *Digital Processing of Signals*. New York: McGraw-Hill. pp. 203–232.

Stockham, T. T. Cannon, and R. Ingebretsen. 1975. "Blind deconvolution through digital signal processing." *Proceedings of the IEEE* 63: 267–270.

Stockhausen, K. 1958. "Musik im Raum." Reprinted in K. Stockhausen. 1963. *Texte zur elektronischen und instrumentalen Musik*. Band 1. Cologne: DuMont Schauberg. pp. 152–175.

Stockhausen, K. 1959. "... how time passes ..." *die Reihe* 3: 10–43. English edition. Bryn Mawr: Theodore Presser Company. Reprinted in K. Stockhausen. 1963. *Texte zur elektronischen und instrumentalen Musik*. Band 1. Cologne: DuMont Schauberg.

Stockhausen, K. 1961. "Two lectures." *die Reihe* 5. English edition. Bryn Mawr: Theodore Presser Company. pp. 59–82.

Stockhausen, K. 1963. "Die Einheit der musikalishcen Zeit." In K. Stockhausen. 1963. *Texte zur elektronischen und instrumentalen Musik*. Band 1. Cologne: DuMont Schauberg. pp. 211–221. Reprinted as "The concept of unity in electronic music." E. Barkin, translator, in B. Boretz and E. Cone, eds. 1972. *Perspectives on Contemporary Music Theory*. New York: W. W. Norton. pp. 129–147.

Stockhausen, K. 1964. "Elektronische Studien I und II." In *Texte zu eigenen Werken zur Kunst Anderer*. Cologne: DuMont Schauberg.

Stockhausen, K. 1968. *Kontakte*. Score number UE 13678. London: Universal Edition.

Stockhausen, K. 1971a. "Osaka-Projekt." In *Texte zur Musik 1963–1970*. Cologne: DuMont Schauberg. pp. 153–187.

Stockhausen, K. 1971b. *Texte zur Musik 1963–1970*. Band 3. Cologne: DuMont Schauberg.

Stockhausen, K. 1978. *Texte zur Musik 1970–1977*. Band 4. Cologne: DuMont Schauberg.

Stone, K. 1963. "Problems and methods of notation." *Perspectives of New Music*. Reprinted in B. Boretz and E. Cone, eds. 1976. *Perspectives on Notation and Performance*. New York: W. W. Norton. pp. 9–31.

Stone, K. 1980. *Music Notation in the Twentieth Century*. New York: W. W. Norton.

Strang, G. 1989. 1989. "Wavelets and dilation equations: a brief introduction." *SIAM Review* 31(4): 614–627.

Strange, A. 1983. *Electronic Music: Systems, Techniques, Controls*. Second ed. Dubuque: W. C. Brown.

Strangio, C., 1980. *Digital Electronics: Fundamental Concepts and Applications*. Englewood Cliffs: Prentice-Hall.

Strawn, J. 1980. "Approximation and syntactic analysis of amplitude and frequency functions for digital sound synthesis." *Computer Music Journal* 4(3): 3–24.

Strawn, J. 1985a. "Modelling musical transitions." Ph.D. diss. Stanford: Stanford University Department of Music.

Strawn, J. ed.1985b. *Digital Audio Signal Processing: An Anthology*. Madison: A-R Editions.

Strawn, J. ed. 1985c. *Digital Audio Engineering: An Anthology*. Madison: A-R Editions.

Strawn, J. 1987a. "Analysis and synthesis of musical transitions using the discrete short-time Fourier transform." *Journal of the Audio Engineering Society* 35(1/2): 3–14.

Strawn, J. 1987b. "Editing time-varying spectra." *Journal of the Audio Engineering Society* 35(5): 337–352.

Strawn, J. 1988. "Implementing table lookup oscillators for music with the Motorola DSP56000 family." Preprint 2716 (-6). Presented at the 85th Convention 3–6 November 1988, Los Angeles. New York: Audio Engineering Society.

Strawn, J., et al. 1982. "Report on the 1981 International Computer Music Conference." *Computer Music Journal* 6(2): 11–31.

Streicher, R., and W. Dooley. 1978. "Basic stereo microphone perspectives—a review." *Journal of the Audio Engineering Society* 33(7/8): 548–556. Reprinted in Audio Engineering Society. 1986. *Stereophonic Techniques: An Anthology.* New York: Audio Engineering Society.

Struik, D. 1967. *A Concise History of Mathematics.* New York: Dover.

Sullivan, C. 1990. "Extending the Karplus-Strong plucked-string algorithm to synthesize electric guitar timbres with disortion and feedback." *Computer Music Journal* 14(3): 26–37.

Sundberg, J. 1972. "A perceptual function of the 'singing formant'." Speech Transmission Lab Quarterly Progress and Status Report 1972. Stockholm: K.T.H. pp. 2–3, 61–63.

Sundberg, J., A. Askenfelt, and L. Frydén. 1983. "Musical performance: a synthesis-by-rule approach." *Computer Music Journal* 7(1): 37–43. Reprinted in C. Roads, ed. 1989. *The Music Machine.* Cambridge, Massachusetts: The MIT Press.

Sussman, G., and G. Steele. 1981. "Constraints: a language for expressing almost-hierarchical descriptions." Memo 502A. Cambridge, Massachusetts: M.I.T. Artificial Intelligence Laboratory. Reprinted in *Artificial Intelligence* 14: 1–39.

Sutherland, I. 1963. "Sketchpad: a man-machine graphical communication system." *Proceedings of the AFIPS Spring Joint Computer Conference.* Detroit: pp. 329–346.

Suzuki, H. 1987. "Modal analysis of a hammer-string interaction." *Journal of the Acoustical Society of America* 82(4): 1145–1151.

Szilas, N., and C. Cadoz. 1993. "Physical models that learn." S. Ohteru, ed. *Proceedings of the 1993 International Computer Music Conference.* San Francisco: International Computer Music Conference. pp. 72–75.

Tadokoro, Y., and T. Higishi. 1978. "Discrete Fourier transform computation via the Walsh transform." *IEEE Transactions on Acoustics, Speech and Signal Processing* ASSP-26(3): 236–240.

Talambirus, R. 1985. "Limitations on the dynamic range of digitized audio." In J. Strawn, ed. *Digital Audio Engineering: An Anthology.* Madison: A-R Editions. pp. 29–60.

Tarabella, L., and G. Bertini. 1989. "A digital signal processing system and a graphical editor for synthesis algorithms." In T. Wells and D. Butler, eds. *Proceedings of the 1989 International Computer Music Conference.* San Francisco: International Computer Music Association. pp. 312–315.

Tatar, D. 1987. *A Programmer's Guide to Common Lisp.* Bedford: Digital Press.

Taube, H. 1991. "Common Music: a music composition language in Common Lisp and CLOS." *Computer Music Journal* 15(2): 21–32.

Tempelaars, S. 1976. "The VOSIM oscillator." Presented at the 1976 International Computer Music Conference, M.I.T., Cambridge, Massachusetts, 28–31 October.

Tempelaars, S. 1977. *Sound Signal Processing*. Ruth Koenig, trans. Utrecht: Institute of Sonology.

Tenney, J. 1963. "Sound generation by means of a digital computer." *Journal of Music Theory* 7: 24–70.

Tenney, J. 1965. "The physical correlates of timbre." *Gravesaner Blätter* 26: 103–109.

Tenney, J. 1969. "Computer music experiments: 1961–64." *Electronic Music Reports* 1: 23–60.

Terhardt, E. 1982. "Algorithm for extraction of pitch and pitch salience from complex tonal signals." *Journal of the Acoustical Society of America* 71(3): 679.

Thomas, J. 1991. "Fractals in algorithmic composition with computers." In *Computers and Music Research Conference Handbook*. Belfast: The Queen's University.

Thompson, K., and D. Ritchie. 1974. "The UNIX timesharing system." *Communication of the Association for Computing Machinery* 17(7): 365–375.

Thompson, T. 1990. "Keynote." *Computing Systems* 3(2). (Journal of the USENIX Association).

Tipei, S. 1989. "The computer: a composer's collaborator." *Leonardo* 22(2): 189–196.

Tjepkema, S. 1981. *A Bibliography of Computer Music*. Iowa City: University of Iowa Press.

Tobenfeld, E. 1984. "A general-purpose sequencer for MIDI synthesizers." *Computer Music Journal* 8(4): 43–54.

Tochetti, G. 1984. "Un preprocessore per il compilatore Music 5." Padova: Universita di Padova, Centro di Sonologia Computazionale.

Todd, N. 1993. "Wavelet analysis of rhythm in expressive musical performance." In S. Ohteru, ed. *Proceedings of the 1993 International Computer Music Conference*. San Francisco: International Computer Music Association. pp. 264–267.

Todd, P. 1989. "A connectionist approach to algorithmic composition." *Computer Music Journal* 13(4): 27–43.

Todd, P., and D. G. Loy, eds. 1991. *Music and Connectionism*. Cambridge, Massachusetts: The MIT Press.

Tomisawa, N. 1981. "Tone production method for an electronic music instrument." U. S. Patent 4,249,447.

Tonality Systems. 1993. *Symbolic Composer*. (Documentation and program.) Wakefield, West Yorkshire: Tonality Systems.

Touretzky, D., 1984. *LISP: A Gentle Introduction to Symbolic Computation*. New York: Harper and Row.

Tovar and L. Smith. 1977. "MUS10 manual." Stanford: Center for Computer Research in Music and Acoustics, Stanford University.

Truax, B. 1975. "The computer composition—sound synthesis programs POD4, POD5, and POD6." *Sonological Reports Number 2*. Utrecht: Institute of Sonology.

Truax, B. 1977. "The POD system of interactive composition programs." *Computer Music Journal* 1(3): 30–39.

Truax, B. 1985. "The PODX system: interactive compositional software for the DMX-1000." *Computer Music Journal* 9(1): 29–38.

Truax, B. 1987. "Real-time granulation of sampled sound with the DMX-1000." In J. Beauchamp, ed. *Proceedings of the 1987 International Computer Music Conference*. San Francisco: International Computer Music Association. pp. 138–145.

Truax, B. 1988. "Real-time granular synthesis with a digital signal processing computer." *Computer Music Journal* 12(2): 14–26.

Truax, B. 1990a. "Time-shifting of sampled sound with a real-time granulation technique." In S. Arnold and G. Hair, eds. *Proceedings of the 1990 International Computer Music Conference*. San Francisco: International Computer Music Association. pp. 104–107.

Truax, B. 1990b. "Composing with real-time granular sound." *Perspectives of New Music* 28(2): 120–134.

Tyndall, J. 1875. *Sound*. Third ed. Akron: Werner.

Uman, M. 1984. *Lightning*. New York: Dover.

Usher, A. P. 1954. *A History of Mechanical Inventions*. Cambridge, Massachusetts: Harvard University Press. Reprinted 1988 by Dover Publications, New York.

Vaggione, H. 1984. "The making of *Octuor*." *Computer Music Journal* 8(2): 48–54.

Vail, M. 1993. "The E-mu Emulator." *Keyboard* 19(1): 108–111.

Valentino, R. 1986. "Le altre elettroniche." In R. Doati and A. Vidolin, eds. 1986. *Nuova Atlantide*. Venice: La Biennale di Venezia. pp. 77–101.

van de Plassche, R. 1983. "Dynamic element matching puts trimless converters on chip." *Electronics* 16 June 1983.

van de Plassche, R., and E. Dijkmans. 1983. "A monolithic 16-bit d/a conversion system for digital audio." In B. Blesser, B. Locanthi, and T. Stockham, eds. *Digital Audio*. New York: Audio Engineering Society. pp. 54–60.

van der Pol, B. 1930. "Frequency modulation." *Proceedings of the Institute of Radio Engineers* 18: 1194–1205.

Vanderkooy, J., and S. Lipschitz. 1984. "Resolution below the least significant bit in digital systems with dither." *Journal of the Audio Engineering Society* 32(3): 106–113.

Van Duyne, S., and J. Smith. 1993. "Physical modeling with a 2-D digital waveguide mesh." In S. Ohteru, ed. *Proceedings of the 1993 International Computer Music Conference.* San Francisco: International Computer Music Association. pp. 40–47.

van Rossum, G. 1992. "Audio file formats." Message posted on Internet News. 35 pages.

Varèse, E. 1920. Quotation from G. Charbonnier. 1970. *Entretiens avec Varèse.* Paris: Editions Pierre Belfond.

Varèse, E. 1971. "The liberation of sound." In B. Boretz and E. Cone, eds. 1971. *Perspectives on American Composers.* New York: W. W. Norton. pp. 26–34.

Vercoe, B. 1984. "The synthetic performer in the context of live performance." Presented at the 1984 International Computer Music Conference, Paris.

Vetterli, M. 1992. "Wavelets and filter banks: theory and design." *IEEE Transactions on Signal Processing* 40(9): 2207–2233.

Viara, E. 1991. "CPOS: a real-time operating system for the IRCAM Musical Workstation." *Computer Music Journal* 15(3): 50–57.

Vidolin, A. 1993. Personal communication.

Voelkel, A. 1985. "A cost-effective input processor pitch-detector for electronic violin." In B. Truax, ed. *Proceedings of the 1985 International Computer Music Conference.* San Francisco: International Computer Music Association. pp. 15–18.

Volonnino, B. 1984. "Programmi per la sintisi del suono tramite distortione non lineare dipendente dalla frequenza." Padua: Centro di Sonologià Computazionale, University of Padua.

Von Foerster, H., and J. Beauchamp, eds. 1969. *Music by Computers.* New York: Wiley.

Von Neumann, J. 1951. "The general and logical theory of automata." In E. Newmann, ed. 1951. *The World of Mathematics.* New York: Simon and Schuster. pp. 2070–2098.

Waisvisz, M. 1985. "The Hands, a set of remote MIDI controllers." In B. Truax, ed. *Proceedings of the 1985 International Computer Music Conference.* San Francisco: International Computer Music Association. pp. 313–318.

Walker, B., and K. Fitz. 1992. "Lemur." Champaign: Computer Engineering Research Laboratory (CERL) Sound Group, University of Illinois.

Wallraff, D. 1979a. "The DMX-1000 signal processing computer." *Computer Music Journal* 3(4): 44–49. Revised and updated version in C. Roads and J. Strawn, eds. 1985. *Foundations of Computer Music*. Cambridge, Massachusetts: The MIT Press. pp. 54–60.

Wallraff, D. 1979b. "Nedit—graphical editor for musical scores." In C. Roads, ed. *Proceedings of the 1978 International Computer Music Conference*. Evanston: Northwestern University Press. pp. 410–429.

Walker, B., and K. Fitz. 1992. *Lemur Manual*. Urbana: CERL Sound Group, University of Illinois.

Walsh, J. 1923. "A closed set of orthonormal functions." *American Journal of Mathematics* 45: 5–24.

Ware, F., and W. McAllister. 1982. "C-MOS chip set streamlines floating-point processing." *Electronics* 55: 149–152.

Warfield, G. 1976. "Writings on contemporary music notation: an annotated bibliography." Ann Arbor: Music Library Association.

Warnock, R. 1976. "Longitudinal digital recording of audio." Preprint 1169. New York: Audio Engineering Society.

Wawryznek, J. 1989. "VLSI models for sound synthesis." In M. Mathews and J. R. Pierce, eds. *Current Directions in Computer Music Research*. Cambridge, Massachusetts: The MIT Press. pp. 113–148.

Waschka, R., and A. Kurepa. 1989. "Using fractals in timbre construction: an exploratory study." In T. Wells and D. Butler, eds. *Proceedings of the 1989 International Computer Music Conference*. San Francisco: International Computer Music Association. pp. 332–335.

Waters, R. 1982. "A knowledge-based program editor." *Proceedings of the 7th IJCAI*. Volume II. Los Altos: Morgan-Kaufmann. pp. 920–926.

Waters, S., and T. Ungvary. 1990. "The sonogram: a tool for visual documentation of music structure." In S. Arnold and G. Hair, eds. *Proceedings of the 1990 International Computer Music Conference*. San Francisco: International Computer Music Association. pp. 159–161.

Watkinson, J. 1985. "Splice handling mechanisms in the DASH format." Preprint 2199 (A-2). Presented at the 77th Audio Engineering Society Convention, 5–8 March, Hamburg. New York: Audio Engineering Society.

Wayne, W. C., Jr. 1961. "Audio modulation system (choral tone modulator)." U. S. Patent 3, 004,460.

Wegel, R., and C. Lane. 1924. "The auditory masking of one pure tone by another and its probable relation to the dynamics of the inner ear." *Physics Review* 23: 266–285.

Weidenaar, R. 1991. "The alternators of the Telharmonium, 1906." In B. Alphonce and B. Pennycook, eds. *Proceedings of the 1991 International Computer Music Conference*. San Francisco: International Computer Music Association. pp. 311–314.

Weinreich, G. 1983. "Violin sound synthesis from first principles." *Journal of the Acoustical Society of America* 74: 1S52.

Weiss-Stauffacher, H., with R. Bruhin. 1976. *The Marvelous World of Music Machines*. Tokyo: Kodansha International.

Weitzman, C., 1980. *Distributed Micro/Minicomputer Systems*. Englewood Cliffs: Prentice Hall.

Wells, T. 1981. *The Technique of Electronic Music*. New York: Schirmer.

Wenker, J. 1972. "MUSTRAN II—an extended music translator." *Computers and the Humanities* 7(2).

Wessel, D. 1979. "Timbre space as a musical control structure." *Computer Music Journal* 3 (2): 45–52. Reprinted in C. Roads and J. Strawn, eds. 1985. *Foundations of Computer Music*. Cambridge, Massachusetts: The MIT Press.

Wessel, D. "Improvisation with highly interactive real-time performance systems." In B. Alphonce and B. Pennycook, eds. *Proceedings of the 1991 International Computer Music Conference*. San Francisco: Computer Music Association. pp. 344–347.

Wessel, D. D. Bristow, and Z. Settel. 1987. "Control of phrasing and articulation in synthesis." In J. Beauchamp, ed. *Proceedings of the 1987 International Computer Music Conference*. San Francisco: International Computer Music Association. pp. 108–116.

Wessel, D., R. Felciano, A. Freed, and J. Wawryznek. 1989. "The Center for New Music and Audio Technologies." In T. Wells and D. Butler, eds. *Proceedings of the 1989 International Computer Music Conference*. San Francisco: International Computer Music Association. pp. 336–339.

Whitfield, I. 1978. "The neural code." In E. Carterette and M. Friedman, eds. 1983. *Handbook of Perception, Volume 4*. Orlando: Academic Press. pp. 163–183.

Wiener, N. 1930. "Generalized harmonic analysis." *Acta Mathematica* 55: 117–258.

Wiener, N. 1964. "Spatial-temporal continuity, quantum theory, and music." In M Capek, ed. 1975. *The Concepts of Space and Time*. Boston: D. Reidel.

Wigner, E. 1932. "On the quantum correction for thermodynamic equilibrium." *Physical Review* 40: 749–759.

Wilkinson, S., P. Freeman, P. Gotcher, M. Jeffrey, and C. Johnson. 1989. *Turbosynth User's Manual*. Menlo Park: Digidesign.

Winham, G. 1966. *The Reference Manual for Music 4B*. Princeton: Princeton University Music Department.

Winham, G., and K. Steiglitz. 1970. "Input Generators for digital sound synthesis." *Journal of the Acoustical Society of America* 27(2): 665–666.

Winckel, F. 1967. *Music, Sound, and Sensation*. New York: Dover Publications.

Winograd, T. 1979. "Beyond programming languages." *Communications of the Association for Computing Machinery*

Winograd, T., 1968. "Linguistics and the computer analysis of tonal harmony." *Journal of Music Theory* 12(1): 2–49.

Winograd, T., 1972. *Understanding Natural Language*. New York: Academic Press.

Winograd, T., 1979. "Towards convivial computing." In M. Dertourzos, and J. Moses, eds. *The Computer Age: A Twenty-year View*. Cambridge: The MIT Press. pp. 6–72.

Winsor, P. 1987. *Computer-assisted Music Composition*. Princeton: Petrocelli Books.

Winsor, P. 1991. *Computer Music in C*. Blue Ridge Summit: Tab Books.

Winsor, P. 1990 *Computer Composer's Tookbox*. Blue Ridge Summit: Tab Books.

Winston, P. 1984. *Artificial Intelligence*. Second edition. Reading, Massachusetts: Addison-Wesley.

Winston, P., and B. Horn. 1981. *LISP*. Reading, Massachusetts: Addison-Wesley.

Wirth, N., 1977. "The module: a system structuring facility in high-level languages." Presented at the Course in Programming Methodology, University of California at Santa Cruz.

Wishart, T. 1988. "The composition of Vox-5." *Computer Music Journal* 12(4): 21–27.

Wold, E. 1987. "Nonlinear parameter estimation of acoustic models." Ph.D. dissertation. Report Number UCB/CSD 87/354. Berkeley: Department of Electrical Engineering and Computer Science.

Wolfram, S. 1984. "Computation theory of cellular automata." *Communications in Mathematical Physics* 96: 15–57. Reprinted in S. Wolfram, ed. 1986. *Theory and Applications of Cellular Automata*. Singapore: World Scientific.

Wolfram, S. 1986. *Theory and Applications of Cellular Automata*. Singapore: World Scientific.

Wolman, A., J. Choi, S. Asgharzadeh, and J. Kahana. 1992. "Recognition of handwritten music notation." In A. Strange, ed. *Proceedings of the 1992 International Computer Music Conference*. San Francisco: International Computer Music Association. pp. 125–127.

Wood, A. 1940. *Acoustics*. London: Blackie and Sons.

Wood, P. 1991. "Recollections with John Robinson Pierce. "*Computer Music Journal* 15(4): 17–28.

Woodhouse, J. 1992. "Physical modeling of bowed strings." *Computer Music Journal* 16(4): 43–56.

Woszczyk, W., and F. Toole. 1983. "A subjective comparison of five analog and digital tape recorders." Preprint 2033 (H-8), presented at the 74th Convention, 8–12 October 1983. New York: Audio Engineering Society.

Wulf, W., R. London, and M. Shaw. 1976. "An introduction to the construction and verification of ALPHARD programs." *IEEE Transactions on Software Engineering* SE-2(4): 253–265.

Xenakis, I. 1960. "Elements of stochastic music." *Gravesaner Blätter* 18: 84–105.

Xenakis, I. 1971. *Formalized Music.* Bloomington: Indiana University Press.

Xenakis, I. 1992. *Formalized Music.* Revised edition. New York: Pendragon Press.

Xin Chong. 1987. Personal communication.

Yamaha. 1993. Marketing literature for the VL1 synthesizer. Buena Park: Yamaha.

Yavelow, C. 1992. *Macworld Music and Sound Bible.* San Mateo: IDG Books.

Yeston, M. 1976. *The Stratification of Musical Rhythm.* New Haven: Yale University Press.

Yost, W. 1980. "Temporal properties of pitch and pitch strength of ripple noise." In G. van den Brin and F. Bilsen, eds. *Psychophysical, Physiological and Behavioural Studies in Hearing: Proceedings of the 5th International Symposium on Hearing.* Noordwijkerhout: Delft University Press. pp. 367–373.

Yost, W., and R. Hill. 1978. "Strength of the pitches associated with ripple noise." *Journal of the Acoustical Society of America* 64: 485–492.

Yost, W., D. and Nielsen. 1977. *Fundamentals of hearing.* New York: Holt, Reinhart, and Winston.

Young, G. 1985. *Hugh LeCaine: Pioneer in electronic music instrument design, compositions and demonstrations 1948–1972.* Long-play phonograph recording. Toronto: JWD Music.

Young, G. 1989. *The Sackbut Blues.* Ottawa: National Museum of Science and Technology.

Yunik, M., M. Borys, and G. W. Swift. 1985. "A digital flute." *Computer Music Journal* 9(2): 49–52.

Zaripov, R. 1960. "An algorithmic descriiption of the music composing process." *Doklady Academiia Nauk* SSSR 132: 1283. English translation in *Automation Express* 3: 17.

Zaripov, R. 1969. "Cyberbetics and music." *Perspectives of New Music* 7(2): 115–154. Translation by J. Russell of *Kibernetika i Muzyka* (1963).

Zicarrelli, D. 1987. "M and Jam Factory." *Computer Music Journal* 11(4): 13–29.

Zinoviev, P. 1968. "Two electronic music projects in Britain." In J. Reichardt, ed. *Cybernetic Serendipity*. New York: Praeger. pp. 28–29.

Zola Technologies. 1991. *DSP Designer*. Computer Software. Atlanta: Zola Technologies.

Zwicker, E., Flottorp, G., and Stevens, S. 1957. "Critical band width in loudness summation." *Journal of the Acoustical Society of America* 29: 548–557.

Zwicker, E., and B. Scharf. 1965. "A model of loudness summation." *Psychological Review* 72: 3–26.

Zwicker, E., and U. Zwicker. 1991. "Audio engineering and psychoacoustics: matching signals to the final receiver, the human auditory system." *Journal of the Audio Engineering Society* 39(3): 115–126.

Zwislocki, J. 1978. "Masking: experiments and theoretical aspects of simultaneous, forward, backward, and central masking." In E. Carterette and M. Friedman, eds. *Handbook of Perception*. New York: Academic Press. Vol. 4, pp. 283–336.

Name Index

Subject Index